Introduction to  Marketing

MCDANIEL/LAMB/HAIR   TWELFTH EDITION

Introduction to Marketing

CARL MCDANIEL

Department of Marketing
University of Texas at Arlington

CHARLES W. LAMB

M. J. Neeley School of Business
Texas Christian University

JOSEPH F. HAIR, JR.

Department of Marketing
Kennesaw State University

SOUTH-WESTERN
CENGAGE Learning

Australia • Brazil • Japan • Korea • Mexico • Singapore • Spain • United Kingdom • United States

Introduction to Marketing, 12th International Edition
McDaniel, Lamb, Hair

Vice President of Editorial, Business: Jack W. Calhoun

Publisher: Erin Joyner

Executive Editor: Mike Roche

Developmental Editor: Laura Rush/B-Books

Editorial Assistant: Megan Fischer

Marketing Manager: Gretchen Swann

Sr. Content Project Manager: Tamborah Moore

Media Editor: John Rich

Manufacturing Planner: Ron Montgomery

Sr, Marketing Communications Manager: Jim Overly

Marketing Coordinator: Leigh Smith

Production Service: MPS Limited, a Macmillan Company

Sr. Art Director: Stacy Shirley

Internal Designer: KeDesign, Mason, Ohio

Cover Designer: Patti Hudepohl

Cover Photo Credits:
   B/W Image: Getty Images/Hisham Ibrahim
   Color Image: istockphoto

Rights Acquisitions Specialist, Text: Sam A. Marshall

Rights Acquisitions Specialist, Images: Deanna Ettinger

Text permissions researcher: Katie Huha, PMG

Photo researcher: Terri Miller/eVisuals

Sr. Inventory Analyst: Terina Bradley

Exam*View*® is a registered trademark of eInstruction Corp. Windows is a registered trademark of the Microsoft Corporation used herein under license. Macintosh and Power Macintosh are registered trademarks of Apple Computer, Inc. used herein under license.

© 2013 Cengage Learning. All Rights Reserved.

Library of Congress Control Number: 2011941854

International Edition:

ISBN-13: 978-1-133-27387-5

ISBN-10: 1-133-27387-4

Cengage Learning International Offices

Asia
www.cengageasia.com
tel: (65) 6410 1200

Australia/New Zealand
www.cengage.com.au
tel: (61) 3 9685 4111

Brazil
www.cengage.com.br
tel.: (55) 11 3665 9900

India
www.cengage.co.in
tel: (91) 11 4364 1111

Latin America
www.cengage.com.mx
tel: (52) 55 1500 6000

UK/Europe/Middle East/Africa
www.cengage.co.uk
tel: (44) 0 1264 332 424

Represented in Canada by
Nelson Education, Ltd.
tel: (416) 752 9100 / (800) 668 0671
www.nelson.com

Cengage Learning is a leading provider of customized learning solutions with office locations around the globe, including Singapore, the United Kingdom, Australia, Mexico, Brazil, and Japan. Locate your local office at: **www.cengage.com/global**

For product information: **www.cengage.com/international**
Visit your local office: **www.cengage.com/global**
Visit our corporate website: **www.cengage.com**

Printed in Canada
1 2 3 4 5 6 7 16 15 14 13 12

Brief Contents

© Andrey Bayda/Shutterstock.com

© AP Images/PRNewsFoto/The J.M. Smucker Company

© Dave & Les Jacobs/Cultura/Newscom

© Andresr/Shutterstock.com

© Violetkaipa/Shutterstock.com

© AP Images/The Canadian Press, Pawel Dwulit

© David Morgan/Alamy

Contents

2 Analyzing Marketing Opportunities 183

Product Decisions   357

4 Distribution Decisions   447

5 Promotion and Communication Strategies 577

6 Pricing Decisions 689

7 Technology-Driven Marketing 771

Preface

Importance of the Course

You experience marketing through billboards, television commercials, and even in the cereal aisle at the grocery store. The 12th edition of *Introduction to Marketing*, with its engaging presentation of concepts, will help you recognize how much marketing principles play a role in your day-to-day lives. With coverage of current marketing practices and exciting new features McDaniel, Lamb, and Hair's *Introduction to Marketing* will have you saying, "Now that's marketing!"

New Content

In addition to the dozens of new examples in each chapter, we have added new topical content and revised and updated existing material throughout the book. There is an entirely new chapter devoted to the hot topic of social media and marketing, which delves into how companies are working to integrate the fast-paced technology into existing marketing plans, and the new ideas that surface every day regarding how to use social media. A new box feature, **Marketing Metrics**, introduces actual metrics, the math behind them, and the importance (and influence) of the marketing department in decision making. For more information, see the inside back cover.

TEXT PEDAGOGY REINFORCES LEARNING

Pedagogical features are meant to reinforce learning, but that doesn't mean that they have to be boring. We have created teaching tools within the text itself that will excite interest as well as teach. Not one of our features is casually included: Each has been designed and written to meet a specific learning need, level, or style.

→ **Terms:** Key terms appear in boldface in the text, with definitions in the margins, making it easy for students to check their understanding of terminology. A complete alphabetical list of key terms appears at the end of each chapter as a study checklist, with page citations for easy reference.

→ **Ethics in Marketing boxes:** In the 12th edition we continue our emphasis on ethics by integrating the discussion throughout the book via Ethics exercises and **Ethics in Marketing** boxes. These boxes offer thought-provoking questions focused on ethical decision making. This feature offers examples of how ethics comes into play in many marketing decisions. Are for-profit universities ethical? Is it right for a country to censor Internet providers? How much control can a person or a company have over online privacy? Is it ethical to charge what the market will bear? Students will consider these and many other hotly debated ethical questions. For more information, see the inside back cover.

→ **Global Perspectives boxes:** Thinking globally should be a part of every manager's tactical and strategic planning. In addition to focusing entirely on global marketing in Chapter 5, the book contains global marketing subject matter that is fully integrated through the **Global Perspectives** boxes. The Global Perspectives boxes provide expanded global examples of the marketing issues facing companies on several continents. Each box concludes with thought-provoking questions carefully prepared to stimulate class discussion. For more information, see the inside back cover.

→ **Customer Experience boxes:** At its very best, marketing is about creating an excellent experience for the consumer. *Introduction to Marketing* showcases the importance of customer service through **Customer Experience** boxes. For more information, see the inside back cover.

→ **"Anatomy of" Feature:** The "Anatomy of" graphics illustrate a particular concept, using a full page layout and photography to demonstrate the connection between the elements of a concept. Anatomies help you visualize the connection between marketing concepts and their real-world applications.

→ **Marketing & You surveys:** Your courses must be relevant and interactive. The short Marketing & You surveys at the beginning of each chapter are a fun way to introduce a chapter's topic. Each survey is adapted from material in the *Marketing Scales Handbook,* and quickly demonstrates that everyone has experience with marketing—even if they don't know it! Though Marketing & You is *not* meant to be used in a scientific context, it offers an interesting and fun way to introduce the chapter material.

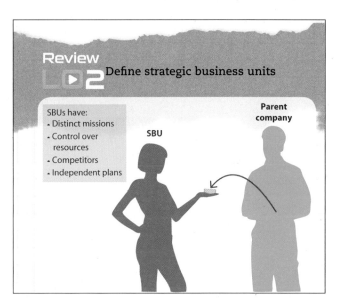

→ **Visual learning outcome summaries:** Everyone doesn't learn the same way; some students can read books and understand the concepts just from their verbal presentation. Other students need to rewrite the material in their own words in order to understand it completely. Still others learn best from diagrams and exhibits. Student focus groups have confirmed this experience, and encouraged the use of the visual Review Learning Outcomes. These boxes are designed to give students a picture of the content to help them recall the major points of the material. These reviews are not meant to repeat every nuance of the chapter content. Rather, they are meant to provide visual cues that prompt the student to recall the salient points in the chapter.

→ **"By the Numbers" feature:** Each chapter concludes with a quick numeric recap of interesting statistics from the chapter. By the Numbers keeps marketing alive for students and acts as an engaging and visual conclusion to the chapter.

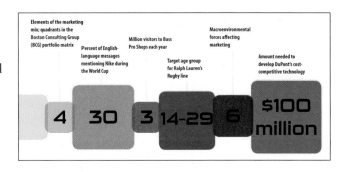

→ **Review and Applications:** The end of each chapter contains a section titled Review and Applications, a summary that distills the main points of the chapter. Chapter summaries are organized around the learning outcomes so that you can quickly check

your understanding of chapter concepts. Discussion questions and activities are under the learning outcome to which they pertain.

→ **Writing questions:** To help improve your writing skills, we have included writing exercises in the review section at the end of each chapter. These exercises are marked with the icon shown here. The writing questions are designed to be brie so that you can accomplish writing assignments in a short time.

→ **Team activities:** The ability to work collaboratively is a key to success in today's business world. End-of-chapter team activities, identified by the icon shown here, give you opportunities to learn to work together by engaging in consensus building and problem solving.

→ **Online activities:** Understanding how to use the Internet for professional (and academic) purposes is critical in today's business environment. End-of-chapter activities accompanied by the icon to the left give you the opportunity to hone your skills in this area.

→ **Application exercise:** These activities are based on winning teaching ideas from the "Best of the Great Ideas in Teaching Marketing" contest held in conjunction with the publication of the eighth edition. Developed by professors across the country, these exercises allow exploration of the principles of marketing in greater detail through engaging and enjoyable activities. For example, you might be assigned to research the complete supply chain for a specified product or create an advertising campaign for a product using the rules from the Hasbro game *Taboo*.

→ **Ethics exercise:** Short ethical dilemmas help students practice doing the right thing. The questions following each scenario prompt students to make an ethical decision and explain the rationale behind it. These exercises demonstrate the limitations to a code of ethics and to reinforce the importance of not simply consulting existing rules of conduct, but also of developing an ethical personality.

→ **Case studies:** All chapters contain a case study with questions that guide you through problems facing real businesses today. These cases focus on a wide variety of companies and products, such as Harmonix, Starbucks, Camelbak, Red Lobster, Terracycle, Dell, Apple, and others.

→ **Company clips:** All chapters contain a summary of the Company Clip video with related viewing and discussion questions. Company Clips segments average 8 minutes in length, which is enough time to cover core marketing issues facing Method, *ReadyMade* magazine, Sephora, Vans, Kodak, and Acid + All.

→ **Marketing miscues:** At the end of each part, you will find new cases that describe good and bad ideas that couldn't make it in the rough-and-tumble marketplace. Often amusing and always interesting, these cases, including Yellow Tail wine's charitable donation faux pas, Microsoft's misstep with *Angry Birds* creators at Rovio, and the controversy behind Four Loko, will help your students avoid the same mistakes made by these well-known companies.

→ **Critical Thinking cases:** In today's dynamic business environment, marketers must be able to quickly evaluate data and craft appropriate response strategies. This edition of *Introduction to Marketing* helps develop critical thinking skills with a more challenging comprehensive case at the end of each of the seven major parts. The seven new Critical Thinking Cases feature issues confronting well-known brands such as Mary Kay Inc., American Airlines, and Lyon College, and ask students to evaluate the situation, identify key issues, and make decisions.

→ **Annotated marketing plan:** The marketing plan appendix at the end of the book includes annotations that tie each part of the plan to the material throughout the book, allowing students to see the correlation between the chapters in the book and the elements of a professional marketing plan for a real company.

All components of our comprehensive support package have been developed to help you prepare lectures and tests as quickly and easily as possible. We provide a wealth of information and activities beyond the text to supplement your lectures, as well as teaching aids in a variety of formats to fit your own teaching style.

Online Resources

The first marketing course is an important foundation course for students who plan on majoring in marketing, and as a foundation course in business administration programs. The discipline builds on the foundation of several fields, borrowing concepts from economics, strategy, psychology, and statistics. At first you may notice that there is not as much assigned homework as you might find in courses such as accounting, statistics, or finance. Do not get into the habit of thinking that you can get by simply by paying attention and cramming before the midterm and final examinations. A disciplined approach to studying, reading the assigned chapters before lectures, and utilizing the online resources that complement this book will help you get the most out of this course and lead to a richer understanding of marketing.

There is a rich collection of study tools that will help you in your marketing course. These resources are available on a number of teaching and learning management systems to best meet you and your instructor's needs. If your instructor required the online component it would be packaged with this textbook at your campus bookstore. If you purchased your book online or obtained it from another source, you can purchase the online resources that accompany this book at CengageBrain: www.cengagebrain.com.

If your instructor did not assign the online resources, you can still purchase access at the same URL. The Marketing CourseMate online resources provide a full complement of study aids and enhancements in a very user friendly interface. A more detailed description of the Marketing CourseMate program is provided on the inside front cover of this book.

Innovative and Valuable Instructor Supplements

ONLINE INSTRUCTOR RESOURCE SITE

Managing your classroom resources is now easier than ever. The Instructor Resource site, login.cengage.com contains all key instructor supplements—Instructor's Manual, Certified Test Bank, PowerPoint with embedded videos, Who Wants to Be a Marketer?, and ExamView testing software.

VIDEO PACKAGE

Available on DVD for in-class viewing, and online for student access outside of the classroom in the CourseMate and CengageNOW Web-based platforms, the video package to accompany the 12th edition of *Introduction to Marketing* continues to showcase the nuts and bolts of marketing at modern companies. The rich Company Clip videos and Integrative Part Videos will help reinforce what your students have learned by showing people who are doing marketing every day—and not according to thematic units.

New to this edition: When viewed online in the Marketing CourseMate, the video cases have assessment questions and simulation exercises embedded within the clips featuring companies with inventive marketing solutions. These questions and simulations will challenge your students' comprehension of key concepts.

A VALUE-ADDED INSTRUCTOR'S MANUAL LIKE NO OTHER

Our Instructor's Manual is the core of our **Integrated Learning System.** For the 12th edition of *Introduction to Marketing,* we have made our popular Instructor's Manual even more valuable for new and experienced instructors alike. Here is a list of the features that will reduce class preparation time:

→ Suggested syllabi for 12- and 16-week terms

→ A pedagogy grid for each chapter briefly outlining:
   (1) all the options the professor has in the chapter, and
   (2) the key points addressed by the features in each chapter (The features included on the grid are the boxed features, Application Exercise, Ethics Exercise, Case Study, and Company Clip.)

→ Three suggested lesson plans for each chapter: a lecture lesson plan, a small-group-work lesson plan, and a video lesson plan

We have retained the proven features such as the chapter outline, lists of support material, additional class activities, and solutions for all Review and Applications, and Case Studies in the book. There are also teaching tips for setting up each of the Application Exercises. Our manual is truly "one-stop shopping" for instructors teaching any size marketing course.

CERTIFIED TEST BANK AND TESTING SOFTWARE

The Test Bank of the 12th edition has been reviewed by a panel of marketing faculty across the country that helped identify questions that may cause problems in their implementation. Faculty reviewers have helped us cull any troublesome questions. You can be sure that, no matter which questions you select for quizzes, tests, and exams, they are of the best quality. The Test Bank is organized around the learning outcomes to help you prepare on a class-by-class basis, and all questions are tagged with relevant AACSB standards to help you monitor trends in student performance necessary for accreditation. The Test Bank is available in Windows software formats (ExamView testing software) on the Instructor's companion Web site. With ExamView, you can choose to prepare tests that cover all learning outcomes or that emphasize only those you feel are most important. This updated Test Bank is one of the most comprehensive on the market, with over 3,500 true/false, multiple-choice, scenario, and essay questions. Our testing database, combined with the ease of ExamView, takes the pain out of exam preparation. The Test Bank is also available on the CengageNOW platforms, which will provide you with the ability to create and administer your own quizzes and also create reports for Assurance of Learning purposes.

MARKETING COURSEMATE AND CENGAGENOW

Preloaded with content and available via an access code when packaged with this text, Marketing CourseMate and CengageNOW pair a range of supplemental content with sophisticated course management functionality. You can assign materials (including online quizzes) and have the results flow automatically to your grade book. Our online teaching and learning solutions are ready to use as soon as you log on—or you can customize its preloaded content by uploading images and other resources, adding Web links, or creating your own practice materials.

OTHER OUTSTANDING SUPPLEMENTS

→ ***Handbook for New Instructors: Getting Started with Great Ideas***
   This helpful supplement was specifically designed for instructors preparing to teach their first course in principles of marketing. We have bolstered our helpful hints on everything from developing a course outline to grading, with winning general teachings from our "Best of the Great Ideas in Teaching Marketing" contest. To give you a complete resource for teaching ideas, we have included all of the winning entries, nearly 100 in all, at the end of the Handbook in the Instructor's Manual. You'll find great teaching ideas for every chapter, plus a wealth of general tips. If you're new, let professors from around the country help you get started teaching principles of marketing!

Innovative and Valuable Student Supplements

Introduction to Marketing provides an excellent vehicle for learning the fundamentals. For students to gain a true understanding of marketing, however, it's best if they can apply the principles they are learning in the classroom. And it's best if they have study aids that address their particular learning style. Our student supplements meet the needs of a variety of learning styles, from visual to auditory, from hands-on to abstract conceptualization.

MARKETING COURSEMATE

There is a rich collection of study tools that will help your students master marketing concepts on a several platforms. The easiest to use for instructors who want to provide students with a range of study tools without tracking their progress in an intensive manner is the Marketing CourseMate supplement to the 12th edition of *Introduction to Marketing*. Here is a summary of the resources that are available in Marketing CourseMate, as well as in the other learning platforms.

Even though Marketing CourseMate requires no setup or administrative requirements for adopting instructors, you can still check on how much students have studied and how well they have performed in practice quizzes through the Engagement Tracker.

CENGAGENOW

Ensure that your students have the understanding of marketing procedures and concepts they need with CengageNOW. This integrated, online course management and learning system combines the best of current technology to save time in planning and managing your course and assignments. With CengageNOW, you can reinforce comprehension with customized student learning paths and efficiently test and automatically grade assignments.

SIMULATIONS

Instructors wishing to integrate a simulation into their course can package access to Music2Go, a leading simulation from Smartsims. In Music2Go, students take over an MP3 player division of a large consumer electronics corporation. The division was created to launch an assault on the MP3 player market and students have the opportunity to formulate their sales, marketing and distribution strategy. The challenge is to build their firm into the leading player in the market. Students will make all the key functional decisions involving price, sales forecasts, advertising, promotion activities, distribution, and research and development, over several periods, just like sales and marketing executives in the real world.

To create the best solution for you and your students, contact your Cengage representative.

MEET THE AUTHORS

CARL MCDANIEL

Carl McDaniel is professor emeritus in service at the University of Texas–Arlington. He currently holds courses for the executive MBA program on the Fort Worth campus and in China. He was the chairman of the marketing department at UTA for 32 years. McDaniel's career spanned more than 40 years, during which he was the recipient of several awards for outstanding teaching. McDaniel has also been a district sales manager for Southwestern Bell Telephone Company and served as a board member of the North Texas Higher Education Authority, a billion-dollar financial institution.

In addition to *Introduction to Marketing*, McDaniel has written and co-authored over 50 textbooks in marketing and business. McDaniel's research has appeared in publications such as the *Journal of Marketing, Journal of Business Research, Journal of the Academy of Marketing Science,* and *California Management Review.*

McDaniel is a member of the American Marketing Association. In addition to his academic experience, McDaniel has business experience as the co-owner of a marketing research firm. McDaniel has also served as senior consultant to the International Trade Centre (ITC), Geneva, Switzerland. The ITC's mission is to help developing nations increase their exports. He has a bachelor's degree from the University of Arkansas and a master's degree and doctorate from Arizona State University.

CHARLES W. LAMB

Charles W. Lamb is the M. J. Neeley Professor of Marketing, M. J. Neeley School of Business, Texas Christian University. He served as chair of the department of marketing from 1982 to 1988 and again from 1997 to 2003. He is currently chair of the Department of Information Systems and Supply Chain Management and is a former president of the Academy of Marketing Science and the Southwestern Marketing Association.

Lamb has authored and co-authored more than a dozen books and anthologies on marketing topics and over 150 articles that have appeared in academic journals and conference proceedings.

In 1997, he was awarded the prestigious Chancellor's Award for Distinguished Research and Creative Activity at TCU. This is the highest honor that the university bestows on its faculty. Other key honors he has received include the M. J. Neeley School of Business Research Award and selection as a Distinguished Fellow of the Academy of Marketing Science and a Fellow of the Southwestern Marketing Association.

Lamb earned an associate's degree from Sinclair Community College, a bachelor's degree from Miami University, an MBA from Wright State University, and a doctorate from Kent State University. He previously served as assistant and associate professor of marketing at Texas A&M University.

JOSEPH F. HAIR

Joseph Hair is Professor of Marketing at Kennesaw State University. He previously held the Alvin C. Copeland Endowed Chair of Franchising and was Director, Entrepreneurship Institute, Louisiana State University. Hair also held the Phil B. Hardin Chair of Marketing at the University of Mississippi. He has taught graduate and undergraduate marketing, sales management, and marketing research courses.

Hair has authored more than 40 books and over 80 articles in scholarly journals. He has also participated in many university committees and has chaired numerous departmental task forces. He serves on the editorial review boards of several journals.

Hair is a member of the Academy of Marketing Science, American Marketing Association, the Society for Marketing Advances, and the Association for Marketing and Healthcare Research. He was selected as the 2011 AMS CUTCO/VECTOR Distinguished Marketing Educator, as the 2007 Innovative Marketer of the Year by the Marketing Management Association, and the 2004 recipient of the Academy of Marketing Science Excellence in Teaching Award.

Hair holds a bachelor's degree in economics, a master's degree in marketing, and a doctorate in marketing, all from the University of Florida. He also serves as a marketing consultant to businesses in a variety of industries, ranging from food and retail, to financial services, health care, electronics, and the U.S. Departments of Agriculture and Interior.

Acknowledgments

This book could not have been written and published without the generous expert assistance of many people. First, we wish to thank Julie Baker and Stacy Landreth Grau, Texas Christian University, and Chad Autry, University of Tennessee, Knoxville, for their contributions to several chapters. We would also like to recognize and thank Vicky Crittenden, Boston College, for contributing the Critical Thinking cases and Marketing Miscues. We must also thank David Ferrell for contributing the Case Studies. Special thanks to Pam Rimer for typing the manuscript.

We also wish to thank each of the following persons for their work on the best supplement package that is available today. Our gratitude goes out to Tom Lewis for revising our comprehensive Test Bank and for writing the quizzes that appear in other parts of the package, Laura Rush for designing the fantastic PowerPoint templates, and David Ferrell for executing the revision beautifully.

Our deepest gratitude goes to the team at Cengage Learning, which has made this text a market leader. Jamie Bryant and Laura Rush, our developmental editors at B-books, are world-class in their abilities and dedication. Tamborah Moore, our production editor, helped make this text a reality. A special thanks goes to Mike Roche, our editor at Cengage, for his suggestions and support.

Finally, we are particularly indebted to our reviewers and to faculty who have contributed to this edition and throughout the years. A special thanks to Randy Stuart, Kennesaw State University, for his keen eye and willingness to suggest revision.

Keith Absher
University of North Alabama

Roshan (Bob) D. Ahuja
Xavier University

Wayne Alexander
Moorhead State University

Jackie Anderson
Davenport University School of Business

Joseph Anderson
Northern Arizona University

Linda Anglin
Mankato State University

Christopher Anicich
California State University, Fullerton

Barry Ashmen
Bucks County Community College

Stephen Baglione
Saint Leo University

Kathleen M. Bailey
Loyola University of New Orleans

Gregory J. Baleja
Alma College

Andrew Banasiewicz
Louisiana State University

Barry L. Bayus
University of North Carolina–Chapel Hill

Fred Beasley
Northern Kentucky University

John L. Beisel
Pittsburgh State University

Christine A. Bell
Albright College

Ken Bell
Ellsworth Community College

Thomas S. Bennett
Gaston Community College

Marcel L. Berard
Community College of Rhode Island

Deirdre Bird
Providence College

Robert J. Blake
Concordia University

David M. Blanchette
Rhode Island College

L. Michelle Bobbitt
Bradley University

James C. Boespflug
Arapahoe Community College

Larry Borgen
Normandale Community College

William H. Brannen
Creighton University

David Brennan
Webster University

Rich Brown
Freed-Hardeman University

William G. Browne
Oregon State University

Pat LeMay Burr
University of Incarnate Word

Richard M. Burr
Trinity University

Victoria Bush
University of Mississippi

Deborah Chiviges Calhoun
College of Notre Dame of Maryland

Joseph E. Cantrell
DeAnza College

Shery Carder
Lake City Community College

G. L. Carr
University of Alaska, Anchorage

Stephen B. Castleberry
University of Minnesota, Duluth

Ed Cerny
University of South Carolina

Meg Clark
Cincinnati State Technical and
Community College

Irvine Clarke III
James Madison University

Barbara Coleman
Augusta College

Robert A. Compton
Valley Forge Military College

Brian I. Connett
California State University,
Northridge

John Alan Davis
Mohave Community College

Debra Decelles
State University of New
York–Brockport

Ronald Decker
University of Wisconsin, Eau Claire

William M. Diamond
State University of New
York–Albany

Gary M. Donnelly
Casper College

John T. Drea
Western Illinois University

Debbie Easterling
University of Maryland–
Eastern Shore

Jacqueline K. Eastman
Valdosta State University

Kevin M. Elliott
Mankato State University

G. Scott Erickson
Ithaca College

Karen A. Evans
Herkimer County Community
College

Theresa B. Flaherty
Old Dominion University

P. J. Forrest
Mississippi College

Raymond Frost
Central Connecticut State
University

John Gardner
State University of New
York–Brockport

S. J. Garner
Eastern Kentucky University

Leonard R. Geiser
Goshen College

Cornelia J. Glenn
Owensboro Community College

James H. Glenn
Owensboro Community College

Lynn R. Godwin
University of St. Thomas

Daniel J. Goebel
University of Southern Mississippi

Jana G. Goodrich
Pennsylvania State University

Darrell Goudge
University of Central Oklahoma

Reginald A. Graham
Eastern Montana College

Gordon T. Gray
Oklahoma City University

Donna H. Green
Wayne State University

Mark Green
Simpson College

Dwayne D. Gremler
University of Idaho

Alice Griswold
Clarke College

Barbara Gross
California State University
at Northridge

Richard A. Halberg
Houghton College

Randall S. Hansen
Stetson University

David M. Hardesty
University of Miami

Martha Hardesty
College of St. Catherine

Dorothy R. Harpool
Wichita State University

Hari S. Hariharan
University of Wisconsin,
Madison

L. Jean Harrison-Walker
University of Houston–Clear
Lake

Michael Hartford
Morehead State University

James W. Harvey
George Mason University

Timothy S. Hatten
Black Hills State University

Paula J. Haynes
University of Tennessee at
Chattanooga

James E. Hazeltine
Northeastern Illinois University

Charlane Bomrad Held
Onondaga Community College

Tom Hickey
State University of New
York–Oswego

Patricia M. Hopkins
California State Polytechnic

Mark B. Houston
University of Missouri

Kristen B. Hovsepian
Ashland University

Amy R. Hubbert
University of Nebraska at Omaha

R. Vish Iyer
University of Northern Colorado

Anita Jackson
Central Connecticut State
University

Anupam Jaju
George Mason University

Bruce H. Johnson
Gustavus Adolphus College

Russell W. Jones
University of Central Oklahoma

Mathew Joseph
University of South Alabama

Vaughn Judd
Auburn University–Montgomery

Jacqueline J. Kacen
University Illinois

Ira S. Kalb
University of Southern California

William J. Kehoe
University of Virginia

J. Steven Kelly
DePaul University

Philip R. Kemp
DePaul University

Raymond F. Keyes
Boston College

Sylvia Keyes
Bridgewater State College

G. Dean Kortge
Central Michigan University

John R. Kuzma
Minnesota State University,
Mankato

Bernard P. Lake
Kirkwood Community
College

Thomas J. Lang
University of Miami

J. Ford Laumer, Jr.
Auburn University

Kenneth R. Lawrence
New Jersey Institute of Technology

Richard M. Lei
Northern Arizona University

Ron Lennon
Barry University

Judith J. Leonard
Eastern Kentucky University

J. Gordon Long
Georgia College

Sandra L. Lueder
Sacred Heart University

Michael Luthy
Bellarmine College

James L. Macke
Cincinnati State Technical and
Community College

Charles S. Madden
Baylor University

Deanna R. D. Mader
Marshall University

Fred H. Mader
Marshall University

Larry Maes
Davenport University

Shirine Mafi
Otterbein College

Jack K. Mandel
Nassau Community College

Karl Mann
Tennessee Tech University

Phylis M. Mansfield
Pennsylvania State University–Erie/
Behrend

Cathy L. Martin
Northeast Louisiana University

Gregory S. Martin
University of West Florida

Irving Mason
Herkimer County Community
College

Lee H. McCain
Seminole Community College

Michael McCall
Ithaca College

Nancy Ryan McClure
University of Central Oklahoma

Kim McKeage
University of Maine

Bronna McNeely
Midwestern State University

Sanjay S. Mehta
Sam Houston State University

Taylor W. Meloan
University of Southern California

Ronald E. Michaels
University of Central Florida

Charles E. Michaels, Jr.
University of South Florida

Mark A. Mitchell
Coastal Carolina University

William C. Moncrief
Texas Christian University

Michael C. Murphy
Langston University

Elwin Myers
Texas A&M University

Suzanne Altobello Nasco
Southern Illinois University

Murugappan Natesan
University of Alberta

N. Chinna Natesan
Southwest Texas State University

Roy E. Nicely
Valdosta State College

Carolyn Y. Nicholson
Stetson University

Chuck Nielson
Louisiana State University

Robert O'Keefe
DePaul University

Patrick A. Okonkwo
Central Michigan University

Brian Olson
Johnson County Community College

Anil M. Pandya
Northeastern Illinois University

Michael M. Pearson
Loyola University, New Orleans

John Perrachione
Truman State University

Monica Perry
California State University, Fullerton

Constantine G. Petrides
Borough of Manhattan Community College

Julie M. Pharr
Tennessee Technological University

Chris Pullig
University of Virginia

William Rech
Bucks County Community College

Allan C. Reddy
Valdosta State University

Joseph Reihing
State University of New York–Nassau

Jamie M. Ressler
Palm Beach Atlantic University

Sandra Robertson
Thomas Nelson Community College

John Ronchetto
University of San Diego

Dick Rose
University of Phoenix (deceased)

Al Rosenbloom
Dominican University

Barbara-Jean Ross
Louisiana State University

Lawrence Ross
Florida Southern College

Anthony Rossi
State University of New York–Brockport

Carl Saxby
University of Southern Indiana

Jan Napoleon Saykiewicz
Duquesne University

Deborah Reed Scarfino
William Jewel College

Jeffrey Schmidt
University of Illinois

Peter A. Schneider
Seton Hall University

James A. Seaman
Nyack College

Trina Sego
Boise State University

Donald R. Self
Auburn University–Montgomery

Matthew D. Shank
Northern Kentucky University

John Shapiro
Northeastern State University

David L. Sherrell
University of Memphis

Peggy O. Shields
University of Southern Indiana

Mandeep Singh
Western Illinois University

Lois J. Smith
University of Wisconsin–Whitewater

Mark T. Spence
Southern Connecticut State College

James V. Spiers
Arizona State University

Thomas Stevenson
University of North Carolina–Charlotte

Karen L. Stewart
Richard Stockton College

James E. Stoddard
University of New Hampshire

Judy Strauss
University of Nevada, Reno

Randy Stuart
Kennesaw State University

Robin Stuart
Marketing Consultant

Susan Sunderline
State University of New York–Brockport

Albert J. Taylor
Austin Peay State University

Janice E. Taylor
Miami University of Ohio

Ronald D. Taylor
Mississippi State University

James L. Thomas
Jacksonville State University

Kay Blythe Tracy
Gettysburg College

Gregory P. Turner
College of Charleston

Richard Turshen
Pace University

Sandra T. Vernon
Fayetteville Technical Community College

Franck Vingeron
California State University at Northridge

Charles R. Vitaska
Metro State College, Denver

James Ward
Arizona State University

Beth A. Walker
Arizona State University

Jim Wenthe
Georgia College and State University

Stacia Wert-Gray
University of Central Oklahoma

Janice K. Williams
University of Central Oklahoma

Laura A. Williams
San Diego State University

Elizabeth J. Wilson
Boston College

Robert D. Winsor
Loyola Marymount University

Leon Winer
Pace University

Arch G. Woodside
Boston College

Barbara Ross-Wooldridge
University of Tampa

Linda Berns Wright
Mississippi State University

William R. Wynd
Eastern Washington University

Merv H. Yeagle
University of Maryland

To Michelle and Mimi Olson
—Carl McDaniel

To my daughters, Christine Stock, Jennifer McPhaul, and Kara Baker,
and to the memory of Frank Mathew Baker.
—Charles W. Lamb

To my newest joy in life, my grandsons Joseph F. Hair, IV (Joss) and Declan
—Joseph F. Hair, Jr.

Introduction to Marketing

1 The World of Marketing

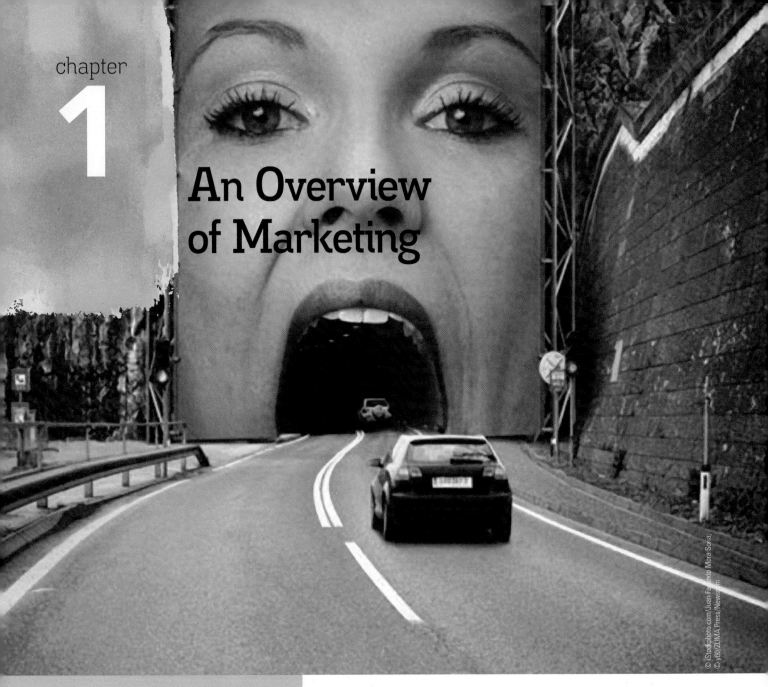

An Overview of Marketing

Learning Outcomes

1 Define the term *marketing*

2 Describe four marketing management philosophies

3 Discuss the differences between sales and market orientations

4 Describe several reasons for studying marketing

LO1

What Is Marketing?

What does the term *marketing* mean to you? Many people think it means the same as personal selling. Others think marketing is the same as advertising. Still others believe marketing has something to do with making products available in stores, arranging displays, and maintaining inventories of products for future sales. Actually, marketing includes all of these activities and more.

Marketing has two facets. First, it is a philosophy, an attitude, a perspective, or a management orientation that stresses customer satisfaction. Second, marketing is activities and processes used to implement this philosophy.

The American Marketing Association's definition of marketing focuses on the second facet. **Marketing** is the activity, set of institutions, and processes for creating, communicating, delivering, and exchanging offerings that have value for customers, clients, partners, and society at large.[1]

Marketing involves more than just activities performed by a group of people in a defined area or department. In the often-quoted words of David Packard, cofounder of HP, "Marketing is too important to be left only to the marketing department." Marketing entails processes that focus on delivering value and benefits to customers, not just selling goods, services, and/or ideas. It uses communication, distribution, and pricing strategies to provide customers and other stakeholders with the goods, services, ideas, values, and benefits they desire when and where they want them. It involves building long-term, mutually rewarding relationships when these relationships benefit all parties concerned. Marketing also entails an understanding that organizations have many connected stakeholder "partners," including employees, suppliers, stockholders, distributors, and society at large.

Research shows that companies that reward employees with incentives and recognition on a consistent basis perform best.[2] Gary Kelly, CEO of Southwest Airlines, maintains, "Our people are our single greatest strength and most enduring competitive advantage."[3] SAS, a business and analytics software solutions company, was voted *Fortune*'s Best Company to Work For in 2010. Employees at SAS enjoy perks such as a gym, on-site day care, massage therapists, classes focusing on health-related issues, and the ability for employees to set their own schedules. CEO Jim Goodnight says, "My chief assets drive out the gate every night. My job is to make sure they come back."[4]

One desired outcome of marketing is an **exchange**: people giving up something to receive something they would rather have. Normally, we think of money as the medium of exchange. We give up money to get the goods and services we want. Exchange does not require money, however. Two (or more) people may barter or trade such items as baseball cards or oil paintings.

> # Marke-ting
> involves more than just activities performed by the marketing department.

marketing
The activity, set of institutions, and processes for creating, communicating, delivering, and exchanging offerings that have value for customers, clients, partners, and society at large.

exchange
People giving up something to receive something they would rather have.

marketing&you.

Please note your opinion on each of the following questions.

Think about where you buy cosmetics or personal care products. Using the following scale, enter the number that indicates how likely you are to:

NOT LIKELY AT ALL 1 2 3 4 5 6 EXTREMELY LIKELY

_____ **Say positive things about the company to other people.**

_____ **Recommend the company to someone who seeks your advice.**

_____ **Encourage friends and relatives to do business with the company.**

_____ **Consider the company your first choice to buy cosmetics or personal care products.**

_____ **Do more business with the company in the next few years.**

Now, total your score. Read the chapter to find out what your score means at the end.

Source: Scale #920, *Marketing Scales Handbook*, G. Bruner, K. James, H. Hensel, eds., Vol. III. © by American Marketing Association. Reprinted with permission.

An exchange can take place only if the following five conditions exist:

1. There must be at least two parties.

2. Each party has something that might be of value to the other party.

3. Each party is capable of communication and delivery.

4. Each party is free to accept or reject the exchange offer.

5. Each party believes it is appropriate or desirable to deal with the other party.[5]

Exchange will not necessarily take place even if all these conditions exist. They are, however, necessary for exchange to be possible. For example, you may place an advertisement in your local newspaper stating that your used automobile is for sale at a certain price. Several people may call you to ask about the car, some may test-drive it, and one or more may even make you an offer. All five conditions are necessary for an exchange to exist. But unless you reach an agreement with a buyer and actually sell the car, an exchange will not take place. Notice that marketing can occur even if an exchange does not occur. In the example just discussed, you would have engaged in marketing by advertising in the local newspaper even if no one bought your used automobile.

LO2

Marketing Management Philosophies

Four competing philosophies strongly influence an organization's marketing processes. These philosophies are commonly referred to as production, sales, market, and societal marketing orientations.

PRODUCTION ORIENTATION

A **production orientation** is a philosophy that focuses on the internal capabilities of the firm rather than on the desires and needs of the marketplace. A production orientation means that management assesses its resources and asks these questions: "What can we do best?" "What can our engineers design?" "What is easy to produce, given our equipment?" In the case of a service organization, managers ask, "What services are most convenient for the firm to offer?" and "Where do our talents lie?" Some have referred to this orientation as a *Field of Dreams* orientation, from the movie's well-known line, "If we build it, they will come." The furniture industry is infamous for its disregard of customers and for its slow cycle times. This has always been a production-oriented industry.

There is nothing wrong with assessing a firm's capabilities; in fact, such assessments are major considerations in strategic marketing planning (see Chapter 2). A production orientation falls short because it does not consider whether the goods and services that the firm produces most efficiently also meet the needs of the marketplace. Sometimes what a firm can best produce is exactly what the market wants. For example, the research and development department of 3M's commercial tape division developed and patented the adhesive component of Post-it® Notes a

production orientation
A philosophy that focuses on the internal capabilities of the firm rather than on the desires and needs of the marketplace.

year before a commercial application was identified. In other situations, as when competition is weak or demand exceeds supply, a production-oriented firm can survive and even prosper. More often, however, firms that succeed in competitive markets have a clear understanding that they must first determine what customers want and then produce it, rather than focusing on what company management thinks should be produced and hoping that product is something customers want.

SALES ORIENTATION

A **sales orientation** is based on the ideas that people will buy more goods and services if aggressive sales techniques are used and that high sales result in high profits. Not only are sales to the final buyer emphasized, but intermediaries are also encouraged to push manufacturers' products more aggressively. To sales-oriented firms, marketing means selling products or services and collecting money in exchange.

The fundamental problem with a sales orientation, as with a production orientation, is a lack of understanding of the needs and wants of the marketplace. Sales-oriented companies often find that, despite the quality of their sales force, they cannot convince people to buy goods or services that are neither wanted nor needed.

Some sales-oriented firms simply fail to understand what is important to their customers. Many of the dot-com businesses that came into existence in the late 1990s are no longer around because they focused on the technology rather than the customer.

MARKET ORIENTATION

The **marketing concept** is a simple and intuitively appealing philosophy that articulates a market orientation. It states that the social and economic justification for an organization's existence is the satisfaction of customer wants and needs while meeting organizational objectives. It is based on an understanding that a sale does not depend on an aggressive sales force, but rather on a customer's decision to purchase a product. What a business thinks it produces is not of primary importance to its success. Instead, what customers think they are buying—the perceived value—defines a business. The marketing concept includes the following:

1. Focusing on customer wants and needs so that the organization can distinguish its product(s) from competitors' offerings

2. Integrating all the organization's activities, including production, to satisfy customer wants

3. Achieving long-term goals for the organization by satisfying customer wants and needs legally and responsibly

The recipe for success is to consistently deliver a unique experience that your competitors cannot match and that satisfies the intentions and preferences of your target buyers.[6] This requires a thorough understanding of your customers, distinctive capabilities that enable your company to execute plans on the basis of this customer understanding, and delivering the desired experience using and integrating all of the resources of the firm.[7]

Firms that adopt and implement the marketing concept are said to be market oriented. Achieving a **market orientation** involves obtaining information about customers, competitors, and markets; examining the information from a total business perspective; determining how to deliver superior customer value; and implementing actions to provide value to customers.

sales orientation
The idea that people will buy more goods and services if aggressive sales techniques are used and that high sales result in high profits.

marketing concept
The idea that the social and economic justification for an organization's existence is the satisfaction of customer wants and needs while meeting organizational objectives.

market orientation
A philosophy that assumes that a sale does not depend on an aggressive sales force but rather on a customer's decision to purchase a product. It is synonymous with the marketing concept.

As an example of how customers come first, L.L. Bean reveals its market orientation through its high-quality service and its focus on continuous improvement in customer satisfaction. Since 1912 the company has guaranteed 100 percent satisfaction or your money back.

© Carl D. Walsh/Aurora Photos

Some firms are known for delivering superior customer value and satisfaction. The sixth annual National Retail Federation/American Express Customer Service Survey listed Zappos.com, Amazon.com, L.L. Bean, Overstock.com, and Lands' End as the top five U.S. retailers for customer service.[8] *Businessweek* listed L.L. Bean, USAA, Apple, Four Season Hotels and Resorts, and Publix Super Markets as its best-in-class Customer Service Champs.[9]

Understanding your competitive arena and competitors' strengths and weaknesses is a critical component of a market orientation. This includes assessing what existing or potential competitors might be intending to do tomorrow and what they are doing today. Western Union failed to define its competitive arena as telecommunications, concentrating instead on telegraph services, and was eventually outflanked by fax technology. Had Western Union been a market-oriented company, its management might have better understood the changes taking place, seen the competitive threat, and developed strategies to counter the threat.

SOCIETAL MARKETING ORIENTATION

The societal marketing orientation extends the marketing concept by acknowledging that some products that customers want may not really be in their best interests or the best interests of society as a whole. This philosophy states that an organization exists not only to satisfy customer wants and needs and to meet organizational objectives, but also to preserve or enhance individuals' and society's long-term best interests. Marketing products and containers that are less toxic than normal, are more durable, contain reusable materials, or are made of recyclable materials is consistent with a societal marketing orientation. The American Marketing Association's definition of marketing recognizes the importance of a societal marketing orientation by including "society at large" as one of the constituencies for which marketing seeks to provide value.

Although the societal marketing concept has been discussed for over 30 years, it did not receive widespread support until the early 2000s. Concerns such as climate change, the depleting ozone layer, fuel shortages, pollution, and health concerns have caused consumers and legislators to be more aware of the need for companies and consumers to adopt measures that conserve resources and cause less damage to the environment.

Studies reporting consumers' attitudes toward, and intentions to buy, environmentally friendly products show widely varying results. P&G has found that consumers want to buy environmentally friendly products, but not if they cost more or don't meet their needs.[10] On the other hand, market-research firm Packaged Facts found that sales of products promoted as environmentally friendly held up well

societal marketing orientation
The idea that an organization exists not only to satisfy customer wants and needs and to meet organizational objectives, but also to preserve or enhance individuals' and society's long-term best interests.

during the recession, despite their premium prices. From 2004 to 2009, sales of "ethical" household products nearly tripled, reaching an estimated $1.6 billion in 2009.[11]

Some people believe that many consumers want to "go green" but don't know where to start.[12] One study found that although half of its respondents thought a company's environmental record was important, only 7 percent could name an environmentally friendly product they had purchased.[13]

Many marketers have made substantial commitments to either produce products using more environmentally friendly processes or making more environmentally friendly products. Coca-Cola has committed to spending $44 million to build the world's largest plastic-bottle-to-bottle recycling plant.[14] Best Buy responded to the environmental concerns raised by its customers and workers by offering free recycling of large and small gadgets. This initiative fits well with the company's overall focus of helping customers get better use of out of technology, whether they are buying, installing, fixing, or disposing of their hardware.[15] Seventh Generation, a company that produces and markets biodegradable and/or natural cleaning and personal care products, saw sales increase by 20 percent from 2008 to 2009. Seventh Generation co-founder Jeffrey Hollender says, "At Seventh Generation, we're trying to create something better, which I call CR 2.0—a new brand of ethical and sustainable corporate behavior that stretches into all corners of our company to intentionally impact each system and guide every decision."[16]

What will the future bring? The current trends indicate that more customers are becoming concerned about the environment each year, more customers are trying to buy environmentally friendly products and support more environmentally friendly companies, and more companies are joining the movement by developing processes and products that do less damage to the environment than in the past. A 2009 Cone Consumer Environmental Survey found that 35 percent of Americans continue to have high expectations for companies to produce and sell environmentally friendly products and services.[17] Adopting a societal marketing orientation and clearly communicating this decision and the actions that support it helps firms differentiate themselves from competitors and strengthens their positioning. The example discussed in the Global Perspectives box in this chapter shows that a societal marketing orientation is part of a global movement to show responsibility for society at large.

Burt's Bees emphasizes its commitment to guiding consumers to better-for-you products as well as its overall societal marketing orientation—its "commitment to the Greater Good."

Kikkoman—Using Soy to Spice Up the Global Community

Kikkoman Corporation, based in Japan, is the world's largest producer of naturally brewed soy sauce, as well as a major international provider of food and beverage products. Kikkoman has factories and distribution centers in a number of countries, including the U.S. and The Netherlands. The company is expanding rapidly in Europe, with estimates of double-digit growth in the next decade.

In order to create global brand awareness and to help customers realize that the company supports sustainable practices, Kikkoman introduced a new program called "Global Vision 2020." Global Vision 2020 has three components:

1. To make its soy sauce a global seasoning

2. To support a healthy lifestyle

3. To be meaningful to global society

Throughout its existence, Kikkoman has been committed to social responsibility as a part of doing business. In fact, in 2001, it was the first Japanese company to sign the United Nations Global Compact (UNGC). The objectives of the UNGC were to resolve global issues through responsible corporate action. Signing the UNGC fit in with what is a cornerstone of Kikkoman's social responsibility programs: to have a mutually beneficial relationship with the communities in which they have plants.

In Wisconsin, the Kikkoman Foods Foundation has made numerous grants to the University of Wisconsin for student scholarships, medical research, and administrative support. The organization has established the need to reduce energy use in the Wisconsin plant. The goals were to improve energy efficiency, reduce maintenance costs, improve overall quality, and improve facility appearance. After installing more energy-efficient lamps in the plant, there was a 45-percent reduction in the plant's energy load, and an anticipated yearly savings of over $97,000. In addition, Kikkoman was able to achieve its overall corporate goal of reducing its impact on the environment. One year after the upgrade, Kikkoman saved almost 8,200 pounds of sulfur dioxide (the main contributor to acid rain) and nearly 2.3 million pounds of carbon dioxide (a contributor to climate change) from being released into the environment.

As Kikkoman continues to expand globally, the UNGC can help to minimize effects of globalization. The company has a willingness to balance growth and a commitment to corporate social responsibility. Kikkoman believes that as they continue to grow internationally, their relationship with the global community grows deeper and their social responsibility greater.[18]

What lessons can other international companies learn from Kikkoman? Explain why corporate social responsibility is so important to companies that serve customers around the world.

© iStockphoto.com/Juan Facundo Mora Soria

Review
LO2
Describe four marketing management philosophies

Orientation	Focus
Production	What can we make or do best?
Sales	How can we sell more aggressively?
Market	What do customers want and need?
Societal	What do customers want and need, and how can we benefit society?

© Cengage Learning 2013

LO3
Differences Between Sales and Market Orientations

The differences between sales and market orientations are substantial. The two orientations can be compared in terms of five characteristics: the organization's focus, the firm's business, those to whom the product is directed, the firm's primary goal, and the tools used to achieve those goals.

THE ORGANIZATION'S FOCUS

Personnel in sales-oriented firms tend to be "inward looking," focusing on selling what the organization makes rather than making what the market wants. Many of the historic sources of competitive advantage—technology, innovation, economies of scale—allowed companies to focus their efforts internally and prosper. Today, many successful firms derive their competitive advantage from an external, market-oriented focus. A market orientation has helped companies such as the Royal Bank of Canada and Southwest Airlines outperform their competitors. These companies put customers at the center of their business in ways most companies do poorly or not at all.

A sales orientation has led to the demise of many firms including Streamline.com, Digital Entertainment Network, and Urban Box Office. As one technology industry analyst put it, "No one has ever gone to a Web site because they heard there was great Java running."[19]

Customer Value   The relationship between benefits and the sacrifice necessary to obtain those benefits is called **customer value**. Customer value is not simply a matter of high quality. A high-quality product that is available only at a high price will not be perceived as a good value, nor will bare-bones service or low-quality goods selling for a low price. Instead, customers value goods and services that are of the quality they expect and that are sold at prices they are willing to pay. Value can be used to sell a Mercedes-Benz as well as a Tyson frozen chicken dinner.

The automobile industry illustrates of the importance of creating customer value. To penetrate the fiercely competitive luxury automobile market, Lexus adopted a customer-driven approach with particular emphasis on service. Lexus stresses product quality with a standard of zero defects in manufacturing. The service quality goal is to treat each customer as one would treat a guest in one's home, to pursue the perfect person-to-person relationship, and to strive to improve continually. This pursuit has enabled Lexus to establish a clear, high-quality image and capture a significant share of the luxury car market.

Marketers interested in customer value:

→ **Offer products that perform:** This is the bare minimum requirement. People expect the goods and services they purchase to perform as promised.

→ **Earn trust:** A stable base of loyal customers enhances a firm's ability to grow and prosper. About 80 percent of Starbucks' revenues come from customers who visit the store an average of 18 times per month.[20]

→ **Avoid unrealistic pricing:** E-marketers are leveraging Internet technology to redefine how prices are set and negotiated. With lower costs, e-marketers can often offer lower prices than their brick-and-mortar counterparts. The enormous popularity of auction sites such as eBay and Amazon.com and the customer-bid model used by Priceline.com illustrates that online customers are interested in bargain prices. Many customers are not willing to pay a premium for the convenience of examining the merchandise and taking it home with them. Others will gladly pay a premium for an experience that is not only functionally rewarding, but emotionally rewarding as well. The superior coffee drinking experience is one reason why people pay $4 and up for a cup of coffee at Starbucks.

→ **Give the buyer facts:** Today's sophisticated consumer wants informative advertising and knowledgeable salespeople. It is becoming very difficult for business marketers to differentiate themselves from competitors. Rather than trying to sell products, salespeople need to find out what the customer needs, which is

customer value
The relationship between benefits and the sacrifice necessary to obtain those benefits.

Old Cardinals Logo

New Cardinals Logo

© AP Images/Arizona Cardinals

usually a combination of products, services, and thought leadership.[21] In other words, salespeople need to start with the needs of the customer and work toward the solution.

→ *Offer organization-wide commitment in service and after-sales support:* The Arizona Cardinals realized that their competitors were not only other NFL teams, but every organization that competes for the customers' entertainment dollars. The team hired Disney Institute, the professional development unit of the Walt Disney Company that helps other companies learn how to adopt Disney best practices and transform how they approach business. The Cardinals wanted Disney Institute to show them how to keep everyone in the organization focused on great customer service.[22]

→ *Co-creation:* Some companies and products allow customers to help create their own experience. For example, TiVo allows people to watch chosen TV shows on their own schedules.

Customer Satisfaction The customer's evaluation of a good or service in terms of whether that good or service has met the customer's needs and expectations is called **customer satisfaction**. Failure to meet needs and expectations results in dissatisfaction with the good or service. Some companies, in their passion to drive down costs, have damaged their relationships with customers. Firms that have a reputation for delivering high levels of customer satisfaction do things differently from their competitors. Top management is obsessed with customer satisfaction, and employees throughout the organization understand the link between their job and satisfied customers. The culture of the organization is to focus on delighting customers rather than on selling products. Singapore Airlines is one of the most admired companies in the world, and occupied the Number 1 spot in the airline industry in 2010. Choon Seng, the CEO, credits the company's success to not compromising on what matters—even during reduced demand because of the global financial crisis. Singapore Airlines did not reduce spending on safety and security, nor on staff training and skills development.[23]

Nordstrom department store is famous for its customer service. The company's impeccable reputation comes not from its executives or its marketing team, but from the customers themselves. The retail giant is willing to take risks, do unusual and often expensive favors for shoppers, and reportedly even accept returns on items not purchased there. Still, they keep improving. For example, the company has installed a database enabling salespeople to assist customers by locating items in inventory somewhere in the chain. Rather than send customers to a particular store, customers can purchase the items online.

Building Relationships Attracting new customers to a business is only the beginning. The best companies view new-customer attraction as the launching point for developing and enhancing a long-term relationship. Companies can expand market share in three ways: attracting new customers, increasing business with existing customers, and retaining current customers. Building relationships with existing customers directly addresses two of the three possibilities and indirectly addresses the other.

The Customer Experience box in this chapter provides more information about providing customers with rewarding experiences that lead to long-term relationships.

Relationship marketing is a strategy that focuses on keeping and improving relationships with current customers. It assumes that many consumers and business customers prefer to have an ongoing relationship with one organization than

customer satisfaction
Customers' evaluation of a good or service in terms of whether it has met their needs and expectations.

relationship marketing
A strategy that focuses on keeping and improving relationships with current customers.

customer experience

The Essence of Marketing

After stripping away all of the functions, plans, and strategies of marketing, you might ask the simple question, "What is this all about?" The answer is the customer experience. Think about it—whether you buy something a second or third time or become loyal to a brand depends on the experience that you had while purchasing and consuming the product or service. Most products need to be sold to a customer more than once in order for the company to start making money. Coca-Cola, for example, would have real problems if people bought just one can of Coke and then never purchased a Coke again.

A theme that you will find running throughout this text is the critical importance of providing a good customer experience. In most chapters you will find a box titled "Customer Experience" that links the chapter material to the customer experience. Quality is the key driver that makes the customer experience a good one. When we speak of quality we aren't simply referring to product quality or service quality. We are talking about having the highest quality personnel operations, financial operations, sales activities, and anything else with which the organization is involved. GE is the pioneer of a concept called "Six Sigma." A company that adheres to Six Sigma will have only 3.4 defects per one million opportunities

to experience failure! By virtually guaranteeing that purchasers will never receive a defective product, a company begins with a solid foundation for a good customer experience.

A good customer experience can lead to customer satisfaction, which, in turn, can lead to loyalty. Customers are satisfied when their needs and expectations are met. Customers are loyal when they buy again due to rational and emotional ties to the product or service. While satisfaction is necessary for loyalty, true loyalty stems from more than a satisfying single purchase.

You would think that all companies would strive to create a great customer experience. However, a recent study showed that this is not the case. A study of executives conducted nationwide found that 80 percent strongly agree that customer strategies are more important to a company's success than ever before, but many companies fail to design and deliver those strategies and, as such, lose customer commitment and loyalty.[24]

Why do you think that some companies don't have policies to maximize the customer experience? Why isn't there a perfect one-to-one relationship between satisfaction and loyalty? That is, if you are satisfied, why might you not be loyal?

to switch continually among providers in their search for value. USAA is a good example of a company focused on building long-term relationships with customers. In 2007, a *BusinessWeek*/J.D. Powers and Associates survey ranked USAA as the top provider of customer service among U.S. firms.[25] Customer retention was a core value of the company long before customer loyalty became a popular business concept. USAA believes so strongly in the importance of customer retention that managers' and executives' bonuses are based, in part, on this dimension.

Most successful relationship marketing strategies depend on customer-oriented personnel, effective training programs, employees with authority to make decisions and solve problems, and teamwork.

Customer-Oriented Personnel For an organization to be focused on building relationships with customers, employees' attitudes and actions must be customer-oriented. An employee may be the only contact a particular customer has with the firm. In that customer's eyes, the employee is the firm. Any person, department, or division that is not customer-oriented weakens the positive image of the entire organization. For example, a potential customer who is greeted discourteously may well assume that the employee's attitude represents the whole firm.

Customer-oriented personnel comes from an organizational culture that supports its people. American Express goes by the theory that "happy employees make

Jeff Bezos of Amazon.com has developed a successful relationship marketing strategy using technology. Amazon.com's e-commerce tools "personalize" the shopping experience for each registered customer. If the customer is logged in, the Web site displays a greeting with the customer's name and offers suggestions based on the customer's previous purchases and searches.

© Dan Lamont/Corbis

happy customers." In giving its global customer-service division a makeover, it asked employees what they wanted, and then delivered. For example, employees received better pay, flexible schedules, and more career development. It also changed from the practice of keeping calls short and transaction-oriented to engaging customers in longer conversations. The results of the changes have improved service margins by 10 percent.[26] Some companies, such as Coca-Cola, Delta Air Lines, Hershey Company, Kellogg, Nautilus, and Sears, have appointed chief customer officers (CCOs). These customer advocates provide an executive voice for customers and report directly to the CEO. Their responsibilities include ensuring that the company maintains a customer-centric culture and that all company employees remain focused on delivering customer value.

The Role of Training Leading marketers recognize the role of employee training in customer service and relationship building. Sales staff at The Container Store receive over 240 hours of training and generous benefits compared to an industry average of eight hours training and modest benefits.[27]

Empowerment In addition to training, many market-oriented firms are giving employees more authority to solve customer problems on the spot. The term used to describe this delegation of authority is **empowerment**. Employees develop ownership attitudes when they are treated like part-owners of the business and are expected to act the part. Empowered employees manage themselves, are more likely to work hard, account for their own performance and the company's, and take prudent risks to build a stronger business and sustain the company's success. FedEx customer service representatives are trained and empowered to resolve customer problems. Although the average FedEx transaction costs only $16, the customer service representatives are empowered to spend up to $100 to resolve a customer problem.

Employees at Ritz-Carlton hotels are encouraged to take whatever steps they feel are necessary to ensure that guests enjoy their visits. Any employee can spend up to $2,000—without seeking permission from management—to solve a problem for guests. One Ritz-Carlton chef in Bali had special eggs and milk imported from Singapore and personally delivered by plane so that he could cook for a young guest with food allergies.[28]

Empowerment gives customers the feeling that their concerns are being addressed and gives employees the feeling that their expertise matters. The result is greater satisfaction for both customers and employees.

Teamwork Many organizations that are frequently noted for delivering superior customer value and providing high levels of customer satisfaction, such as Southwest Airlines and Walt Disney World, assign employees to teams and teach them team-building skills. **Teamwork** entails collaborative efforts of people to accomplish

empowerment
Delegation of authority to solve customers' problems quickly—usually by the first person that the customer notifies regarding a problem.

teamwork
Collaborative efforts of people to accomplish common objectives.

common objectives. Job performance, company performance, product value, and customer satisfaction all improve when people in the same department or work group begin supporting and assisting each other and emphasize cooperation instead of competition. Performance is also enhanced when cross-functional teams align their jobs with customer needs. For example, if a team of telecommunications service representatives is working to improve interaction with customers, back-office people such as computer technicians or training personnel can become part of the team with the ultimate goal of delivering superior customer value and satisfaction.

THE FIRM'S BUSINESS

A sales-oriented firm defines its business (or mission) in terms of goods and services. A market-oriented firm defines its business in terms of the benefits its customers seek. People who spend their money, time, and energy expect to receive benefits, not just goods and services. This distinction has enormous implications. As a senior executive of Coca-Cola noted, Coke is in the hydration business.[29]

Because of the limited way it defines its business, a sales-oriented firm often misses opportunities to serve customers whose wants can be met through a wide range of product offerings instead of specific products. For example, in 1989, 220-year-old Britannica had estimated revenues of $650 million and a worldwide sales force of 7,500. Just five years later, after three consecutive years of losses, the sales force had collapsed to as few as 280 representatives. How did this respected company sink so low? Britannica managers saw that competitors were beginning to use CD-ROMs to store huge masses of information, but chose to ignore the new computer technology, as well as an offer to team up with Microsoft.

It's not hard to see why parents would rather give their children an encyclopedia on a compact disc instead of a printed one. The CD-ROM versions were either given away or sold by other publishers for under $400. A full 32-volume set of *Encyclopaedia Britannica* weighs about 120 pounds, costs a minimum of $1,500, and takes up four and one-half feet of shelf space. If Britannica had defined its business as providing information instead of publishing books, it might not have suffered such a precipitous fall.

Adopting a "better late than never" philosophy, Britannica has made its complete 32-volume set available free on the Internet. The company no longer sells door-to-door and hopes to return to profitability by selling advertising on its Web site.

Answering the question "What is this firm's business?" in terms of the benefits customers seek, instead of goods and services, offers at least three important advantages:

→ It ensures that the firm keeps focusing on customers and avoids becoming preoccupied with goods, services, or the organization's internal needs.

→ It encourages innovation and creativity by reminding people that there are many ways to satisfy customer wants.

→ It stimulates an awareness of changes in customer desires and preferences so that product offerings are more likely to remain relevant.

Having a market orientation and focusing on customer wants do not mean that customers will always receive everything they want. It is not possible, for example, to profitably manufacture and market automobile tires that will last for 100,000 miles for $25. Furthermore, customers' preferences must be mediated by sound professional judgment as to how to deliver the benefits they seek. As Henry Ford once said, "If I had listened to the marketplace, I would have built a faster, cheaper horse."[30] Consumers have a limited set of experiences. They are unlikely to request anything beyond those experiences because they are not aware of benefits they may gain from other potential offerings. For example, before the Internet, many people thought that shopping for some products was boring and time consuming, but could not express their need for electronic shopping.

THOSE TO WHOM THE PRODUCT IS DIRECTED

A sales-oriented organization targets its products at "everybody" or "the average customer." A market-oriented organization aims at specific groups of people. The fallacy of developing products directed at the average user is that relatively few average users actually exist. Typically, populations are characterized by diversity. An average is simply a midpoint in some set of characteristics. Because most potential customers are not "average," they are not likely to be attracted to an average product marketed to the average customer. Consider the market for shampoo as one simple example. There are shampoos for oily hair, dry hair, and dandruff. Some shampoos remove the gray or color hair. Special shampoos are marketed for infants and elderly people. There is even shampoo for people with average or normal hair (whatever that is), but this is a fairly small portion of the total market for shampoo.

A market-oriented organization recognizes that different customer groups want different features or benefits. It may therefore need to develop different goods, services, and promotional appeals. A market-oriented organization carefully analyzes the market and divides it into groups of people who are fairly similar in terms of selected characteristics. Then the organization develops marketing programs that will bring about mutually satisfying exchanges with one or more of those groups.

Paying attention to the customer isn't exactly a new concept. Back in the 1920s, General Motors began designing cars for every lifestyle and pocketbook. This was a breakthrough for an industry that had been largely driven by production needs ever since Henry Ford promised any color as long as it was black. Chapter 8 thoroughly explores the topic of analyzing markets and selecting those that appear to be most promising to the firm.

Most potential customers are not "average" and are not likely to be attracted to an "average" product marketed to an "average" customer. Shampoo ads like this one are aimed at the customer with a special hair care need, such as dandruff control or split ends.

Image courtesy of The Advertising Archives

THE FIRM'S PRIMARY GOAL

A sales-oriented organization seeks to achieve profitability through sales volume and tries to convince potential customers to buy, even if the seller knows that the customer and product are mismatched. Sales-oriented organizations place a higher premium on making a sale than on developing a long-term relationship with a customer. In contrast, the ultimate goal of most market-oriented organizations is to make a profit by creating customer value, providing customer satisfaction, and building long-term relationships with customers. The exception is nonprofit organizations that exist to achieve goals other than profits. Nonprofit organizations can and should adopt a market orientation. Nonprofit organization marketing is explored further in Chapter 12.

TOOLS THE ORGANIZATION USES TO ACHIEVE ITS GOALS

Sales-oriented organizations seek to generate sales volume through intensive promotional activities, mainly personal selling and advertising. In contrast, market-oriented organizations recognize that promotion decisions are only one of four basic marketing mix decisions that have to be made: product decisions, place (or distribution) decisions, promotion decisions, and pricing decisions. A market-oriented organization recognizes that each of these four components is important. Furthermore, market-oriented organizations recognize that marketing is not just a responsibility of the marketing department. Interfunctional coordination means that skills and resources throughout the organization are needed to create, communicate, and deliver superior customer service and value.

A WORD OF CAUTION

This comparison of sales and market orientations is not meant to belittle the role of promotion, especially personal selling, in the marketing mix. Promotion is the means by which organizations communicate with present and prospective customers about the merits and characteristics of their organization and products. Effective promotion is an essential part of effective marketing. Salespeople who work for market-oriented organizations are generally perceived by their customers to be problem solvers and important links to supply sources and new products. Chapter 18 examines the nature of personal selling in more detail.

Review

LO3 Discuss the differences between sales and market orientations

	What is the organization's focus?	What business are you in?	To whom is the product directed?	What is your primary goal?	How do you seek to achieve your goal?
Sales Orientation	Inward, on the organization's needs	Selling goods and services	Everybody	Profit through maximum sales volume	Primarily through intensive promotion
Market Orientation	Outward, on the wants and preferences of customers	Satisfying customer wants and needs and delivering superior value	Specific groups of people	Profit through customer satisfaction	Through coordinated marketing and interfunctional activities

© Cengage Learning 2013

© iStockphoto.com/Juan Facundo Mora Soria

LO 4
Why Study Marketing?

Now that you understand the meaning of the term *marketing*, why it is important to adopt a marketing orientation, and how organizations implement this philosophy, you may be asking, "What's in it for me?" or "Why should I study marketing?" These are important questions, whether you are majoring in a business field other than marketing (such as accounting, finance, or management information systems) or a non-business field (such as journalism, economics, or agriculture). There are several important reasons to study marketing: It plays an important role in society, is important to business, offers outstanding career opportunities, and affects your life every day.

MARKETING PLAYS AN IMPORTANT ROLE IN SOCIETY

The total population of the United States exceeds 310 million people.[31] Think about how many transactions are needed each day to feed, clothe, and shelter a population of this size. The number is huge. And yet it all works quite well, partly because the well-developed U.S. economic system efficiently distributes the output of farms and factories. A typical U.S. family, for example, consumes 2.5 tons of food a year. Marketing makes food available when we want it, in desired quantities, at accessible locations, and in sanitary and convenient packages and forms (such as instant and frozen foods).

MARKETING IS IMPORTANT TO BUSINESS

The fundamental objectives of most businesses are survival, profits, and growth. Marketing contributes directly to achieving these objectives. Marketing includes the following activities, which are vital to business organizations: assessing the wants and satisfactions of present and potential customers, designing and managing product offerings, determining prices and pricing policies, developing distribution strategies, and communicating with present and potential customers.

All businesspeople, regardless of specialization or area of responsibility, need to be familiar with the terminology and fundamentals of accounting, finance, management, and marketing. People in all business areas need to be able to communicate with specialists in other areas. Furthermore, marketing is not just a job done by people in a marketing department. Marketing is a part of the job of everyone in the organization. Therefore, a basic understanding of marketing is important to all businesspeople.

MARKETING OFFERS OUTSTANDING CAREER OPPORTUNITIES

Between a fourth and a third of the entire civilian workforce in the United States performs marketing activities. Marketing offers great career opportunities in areas such as professional selling, marketing research, advertising, retail buying, distribution management, product management, product development, and wholesaling. Marketing career opportunities also exist in a variety of non-business organizations, including hospitals, museums, universities, the armed forces, and various government and social service agencies.

As the global marketplace becomes more challenging, companies all over the world and of all sizes have to become better marketers. For a comprehensive look at career opportunities in marketing and a variety of other useful information about careers, read the Career Appendix at the end of your textbook.

MARKETING AFFECTS YOUR LIFE EVERY DAY

Marketing plays a major role in your everyday life. You participate in the marketing process as a consumer of goods and services. About half of every dollar you spend pays for marketing costs, such as marketing research, product development, packaging, transportation, storage, advertising, and sales expenses. By developing a better understanding of marketing, you will become a better-informed consumer. You will better understand the buying process and be able to negotiate more effectively with sellers. Moreover, you will be better prepared to demand satisfaction when the goods and services you buy do not meet the standards promised by the manufacturer or the marketer.

Review LO 4 Describe several reasons for studying marketing

Why Study Marketing?

Important to society

Important to business

Good career opportunities

+

Marketing affects you every day!

The position in the airline industry held by Singapore Airlines

1

Number of competing marketing philosophies (or orientations) that influence an organization's marketing processes

4

Number of training hours/year for The Container Store sales staff

240

Number of sales staff training hours/year retail industry average

8

The dollar cost of the average FedEx transaction

16

The dollar amount FedEx customer service reps are empowered to spend to resolve a customer problem

100

Tons of food a typical U.S. family consumes each year

2.5

Review and Applications

Define the term *marketing*. Marketing is the activity, set of institutions, and processes for creating, communicating, delivering, and exchanging offerings that have value for customers, clients, partners, and society at large.

LO 1

1.1 What is the AMA? What does it do? How do its services benefit marketers? For more information on the AMA go to www.marketingpower.com.

online

Describe four marketing management philosophies. The role of marketing and the character of marketing activities within an organization are strongly influenced by its philosophy and orientation. A production-oriented organization focuses on the internal capabilities of the firm rather than on the desires and needs of the marketplace. A sales orientation is based on the beliefs that people will buy more products if aggressive sales techniques are used and that high sales volumes produce high profits. A market-oriented organization focuses on satisfying customer wants and needs while meeting organizational objectives.

LO 2

A societal marketing orientation goes beyond a market orientation to include the preservation or enhancement of individuals' and society's long-term best interests.

writing

2.1 Your company president has decided to restructure the firm to make it more market oriented. She is going to announce the changes at an upcoming meeting. She has asked you to prepare a short speech outlining the general reasons for the new company orientation.

2.2 Donald E. Petersen, former chairman of the board of Ford Motor Company, remarked, "If we aren't customer driven, our cars won't be either." Explain how this statement reflects the marketing concept.

2.3 Give an example of a company that might be successfully following a production orientation. Why might a firm in this industry be successful following such an orientation?

LO3 **Discuss the differences between sales and market orientations.** First, sales-oriented firms focus on their own needs; market-oriented firms focus on customers' needs and preferences. Second, sales-oriented companies consider themselves to be deliverers of goods and services, whereas market-oriented companies view themselves as satisfiers of customers. Third, sales-oriented firms direct their products to everyone; market-oriented firms aim at specific segments of the population. Fourth, although the primary goal of both types of firms is profit, sales-oriented businesses pursue maximum sales volume through intensive promotion, whereas market-oriented businesses pursue customer satisfaction through coordinated activities.

3.1 A friend of yours agrees with the adage "People don't know what they want—they only want what they know." Write your friend a letter expressing the extent to which you think marketers shape consumer wants.

writing

3.2 Your local supermarket's slogan is "It's your store." However, when you asked one of the stock people to help you find a bag of chips, he told you it was not his job and that you should look a little harder. On your way out, you noticed a sign with an address for complaints. Draft a letter explaining why the supermarket's slogan will never be credible unless the employees carry it out.

online

3.3 How does Philip Morris handle the sensitive issues associated with marketing tobacco? What kind of information does its Web site at www.philipmorrisusa.com provide about smoking and its negative effects on health? How do you think Philip Morris is able to justify such marketing tactics? After checking around the site, do you think that approach makes the company more or less trustworthy?

LO4 **Describe several reasons for studying marketing.** First, marketing affects the allocation of goods and services that influence a nation's economy and standard of living. Second, an understanding of marketing is crucial to understanding most businesses. Third, career opportunities in marketing are diverse, profitable, and expected to increase significantly during the coming decade. Fourth, understanding marketing makes consumers more informed.

writing

4.1 Write a letter to a friend or family member explaining why you think that a course in marketing will help you in your career in some field other than marketing.

Key Terms

customer satisfaction 10
customer value 9
empowerment 12
exchange 3

marketing 3
marketing concept 5
market orientation 5
production orientation 4

relationship marketing 10
sales orientation 5
societal marketing orientation 6
teamwork 12

Exercises

ETHICS EXERCISE

ethics

In today's business environment, ethics are extremely important. In recent years, there have been numerous scandals and trials that stem from a lack of ethical judgment. For this reason, we include an ethical exercise in every chapter. A brief scenario will present you with a situation in which the right thing to do may or may not be crystal clear, and you will need to decide the ethical way out of the dilemma.

Rani Pharmaceuticals is the maker of several popular drugs used to treat high blood pressure and arthritis. Over time, the company has developed a positive relationship with many of the patients who use its medications through a quarterly newsletter that offers all the latest information on new medical research findings and general health and fitness articles. The company has just been acquired by a group of investors who also own Soothing Waters Hot Tubs and Spas. The marketing director for Soothing Waters would like to use Rani's mailing list for a direct-mail promotion.

Questions

1. What should Rani Pharmaceuticals do?

2. Do you think it is ethical to use customer information across multiple divisions of the same company? Explain.

3. To which marketing management philosophy do you think the marketing director for Soothing Waters subscribes? Explain.

MARKETING PLAN EXERCISE

You can use many of the basic concepts of marketing introduced in this book to get the career you want by marketing yourself to a prospective employer. This exercise and the Career Appendix found online can help you plan that particular marketing campaign. Build a marketing plan for yourself in a one-page document or table with these elements:

1. *What is your mission?* Are you looking for part-time or temporary experience to enhance your résumé, a career stepping stone, or a full-time, long-term career choice? (This mission will help you set the stage for the rest of your plan.)

2. *What are your strengths and weaknesses?* Make an honest self-assessment, because these issues often come up during job interviews. What about opportunities and threats in the marketplace? Who are your competitors? Do you have a competitive advantage? List any special leadership skills, international travel, computer experience, team projects, communications efforts, and other attributes. (Any competitive advantages you possess should be noted in the cover letter of your résumé and in your job interview.)

3. *What are your objectives?* Do you need to find a job within the next 30 days, or are you more flexible? Are there specific job activities that you would like to perform? (These job activities could be stated in the objectives portion of your résumé. Be sure the objectives are very specific: general objectives are of little use to you or an employer.)

4. *What is your target market?* Are you looking only for jobs with big, established organizations or small entrepreneurial firms? Are you looking at companies in a particular industry? Do you have any geographic preferences? When you figure out your target, compile a list of firms that meet your requirements and describe them. (The more you know about your target-market potential employers, the more prepared you will be in an interview.)

5. *How can you best present yourself?* You are the product. Think of your own packaging with regard to dress, appearance, mannerisms, and speech.

6. *Are you willing to travel or relocate?* Or do you need an employer close to home? How will you travel to the employer? Is telecommuting an option?

7. *How will you promote yourself?* A carefully constructed cover letter, résumé, business card, and personal Web site can all help communicate your skills to a potential employer.

8. *What is a fair price for you?* Think carefully about pricing issues, including salary, commission, bonuses, overtime, flexible time, insurance, and other benefits. What is a normal price for a company of that size in that industry to offer?

9. And finally, *how will you implement your plan?* That is, what is your plan for applying to companies? How will you contact them for potential interviews? How will you prepare your wardrobe and work on your interviewing skills? When job offers come in, how will you evaluate them? If job offers don't come in, can you find out why and control for these aspects?

The Career Appendix (online at the website for this book) introduces various aspects of a career in marketing, such as types of marketing jobs, pay scales, preparation for interviewing, and what to expect the first year on the job.

APPLICATION EXERCISE

Understanding the differences among the various marketing management philosophies is the starting point for understanding the fundamentals of marketing.[32] From reading the chapter, you may be convinced that the market orientation is the most appealing philosophy and the one best suited to creating a competitive advantage. Not all companies, however, use the market orientation. And even companies that follow it may not execute well in all areas.

Activities

1. Visit your local grocery store and go through the cereal, snack-food, and dental hygiene aisles. Go up and down each aisle slowly, noticing how many different products are available and how they are organized on the shelves.

2. Count the varieties in each product category. For example, how many different kinds of cereal are on the shelves? How many different sizes? Do the same for snack food and toothpaste.

3. Now try to find a type of product in the grocery store that does not exhibit such variety. There may not be many. Why do you think there are enough kinds of cereals to fill an entire aisle (and then some), but only a few different types of, say, peanut butter? Can this difference be explained in terms of marketing management philosophy (peanut butter manufacturers do not follow the marketing concept) or by something else entirely?

writing

4. Have you ever wanted to see a particular kind of cereal or snack food on the shelf? Think of product varietals (like grapefruit-flavored toothpaste or peanut butter-covered popcorn) that you have never seen on the shelf but would be interested in trying if someone would make it. Write a letter or send an e-mail to an appropriate company, suggesting that it add your concept to its current product line.

CASE STUDY: Harmonix

EMBRACE YOUR INNER ROCK STAR

Little more than three years ago you had probably never heard of Harmonix. In 2005 the videogame design studio released Guitar Hero, which subsequently became the fastest videogame in history to top $1 billion in North American sales. The game concept focuses around a plastic guitar-shaped controller. Players press colored buttons along the guitar neck to match a series of dots that scroll down the TV in time with music from a famous rock tune, such as the Ramones'"I Wanna Be Sedated" and Deep Purple's "Smoke on the Water." Players score points based on their accuracy. In November 2007, Harmonix released Rock Band, adding drums, vocals, and bass guitar options to the game. Rock Band has sold over 3.5 million units with a $169 price tag (most videogames retail at $50–60). In 2006 Harmonix's founders sold the company to Viacom for $175 million, maintaining their operational autonomy while providing them greater budgets for product development and licensing music for their games. Harmonix's success, however, did not come overnight.

The company was originally founded by Alex Rigopulos and Eran Egozy in 1995, focused around some demo software they had created in grad school and a company vision of providing a way for people without much musical training or talent to experience the joy of playing and creating music. The founders believed that if people had the opportunity to create their own music, they would jump at the chance. Their software, which they eventually dubbed The Axe, provided basic music composition tutorials and allowed participants to use a joystick to improvise solos along to popular music tracks. They attempted to market their creation through an interface with Japanese karaoke machines, a demo package deal with Intel, and even in an exhibition at Disney's Epcot. And while the software always proved technically impressive, people generally expressed little initial interest in trying it out, or else it just didn't seem like they were having much fun.

In 2000, Rigopulos and Egozy hit on a concept that would engage consumers, and Harmonix became a videogame company. Where The Axe software provided an improvisation program with no set goal, most videogames were designed with a purpose and offered competition, which helped engage, direct, and motivate players. At the time, the market for music-based games had not fully developed, but especially in Japan, rhythm-based games, in which players would tap different combinations of buttons in time with a beat or a tune, were becoming increasingly more popular. Harmonix created two games, Frequency and Amplitude, in which players hit buttons along with a beat, unlocking tracks for different layers of instruments in a song. Neither of the games proved especially successful, however, as both were very complex and the expense of generating initial interest proved too high for their publisher, Sony, to continue funding them.

Harmonix finally found some measure of success in its 2004 release of Karaoki Revolution, in which players would use a microphone or headset peripheral to score points singing along to pop songs. In a way, it allowed gamers to play the role and be a part of the music. In 2005, when Red Octane, a company that had found success making peripheral videogame controllers, contacted Harmonix about creating Guitar Hero, their philosophy for attracting gamers was based off a similar concept.

Guitar Hero put players in the role of the lead guitarist in a rock band, climbing its way to stardom. The game soundtrack, filled with remixes of classic American rock 'n' roll hits, would appeal to a broader musical audience and the guitar controller put the iconic instrument of American rock 'n' roll directly in the player's hands. The game was released in November of that year, and when retailers set up in-store demo kiosks, game sales went through the roof.

After the success of the first game, even real rock stars began to pick it up, demonstrating its broad appeal. Music labels started to jump on the bandwagon, allowing the licensing of actual songs rather than just composition rights. Rock Band 2, which came out in September 2008, includes songs by AC/DC and Bob Dylan. Gamers can also download additional songs, like The Who's greatest hits, onto their Xbox 360s and Playstation 3s at $1.99 per song, only a dollar more than purchasing a song from Apple's iTunes music store. Licenses for Rock Band have even been secured for songs by the Beatles, which have yet to be licensed to iTunes or other electronic media stores. As the market for music videogames has matured, sales are now expanding beyond the traditional gamers to first-time gamers and even families. The Rock Band franchise has sold over 5 million units since its release in 2007, and with the release of Rock Band 2, the hits just keep on coming.[33]

Questions

1. What marketing management philosophy did Harmonix use at first and how did their philosophy change?

2. As a firm, how do you think Harmonix would describe its business?

3. To whom was Harmonix's product directed and how did they create a product that would appeal to that audience?

COMPANY CLIPS: Method—Live Clean

© NKP MEDIA, INC./Cengage

Method, the innovative branding concept in household cleaning, was conceived by roommates Eric Ryan and Adam Lowry during their drive to a ski lodge. Eric had been thinking of ways to introduce design to the home care industry (i.e., cleaning products) and began talking about his vision to Adam. A chemical engineer from Stanford University with a degree in environmental science, Adam was the perfect sounding board. He soon realized that he could use his expertise to create naturally derived, biodegradable formulas for the beautiful products Eric had in mind.

Questions

1. Is Method best described as having a market orientation or a societal marketing orientation?

2. How does Method implement the marketing concept?

marketing&you: Results.

The higher your score, the more likely you are to do business with the company you thought of and recommend it to others. That is, you have a commitment to the organization and are likely a loyal customer. As you read in this chapter, building relationships is a central part of the market orientation!

Notes

1. American Marketing Association Web site, "Definition of Marketing," www.marketingpower.com/AboutAMA/Pages/DefinitionofMarketing.aspx (Accessed January 14, 2011).
2. George Anderson, "Satisfied Workers Generate Greater Returns," *RetailWire*, January 15, 2008, www.retailwire.com/discussions/sngl_discussion.cfm/12685.
3. Southwest Airlines Web site, "About Southwest," www.southwest.com/html/about-southwest/index.html (Accessed January 14, 2010).
4. David A. Kaplan, "The Best Company to Work For," *Fortune,* February 8, 2010, 57–64.
5. Philip Kotler and Kevin Lane Keller, *A Framework for Marketing Management*, 4th ed. (Upper Saddle River, NJ: Prentice-Hall, 2008), 3.
6. Woody Driggs, "Serving Up Customer Delight," *Customer Relationship Management*, April 2008, 14.
7. *Ibid*.
8. Kathy Grannis, "Zappos.com Tops in Customer Service, According to NRF Foundation/American Express Survey," National Retail Federation, January 11, 2011, www.nrf.com/modules.php?name=News&op=viewlive&sp_id=1067.
9. Jena McGregor, "Customer Service Champs 2010," *Bloomberg Businessweek*, February 18, 2010, http://images.businessweek.com/ss/10/02/0218_customer_service_champs/1.htm.
10. Tom Ryan, "Eco-Conscious Meets Cost-Conscious at P&G," *RetailWire,* March 22, 2010, www.retailwire.com/discussions/sngl_discussion.cfm/14373.
11. Ellen Byron and Suzanne Vranica, "'Green' Products to Get a Push," *Wall Street Journal,* January 11, 2010, B5.
12. Elena Malykhina, "Purex Detergent Joins the 'Green' Movement," *Brandweek*, April 22, 2008, www.brandweek.com/bw/esearch/article_display.jsp?vnu_content_id=1003792174 (Accessed June 7, 2011).
13. Becky Ebenkamp, "Study: 'Green' Products Leave Consumers Puzzled," *Adweek*, July 15, 2008, www.adweek.com/news/advertising-branding/study-green-products-leave-consumers-puzzled-104302 (Accessed July 15, 2008).
14. Marc Gunther, "Coca-Cola's Green Crusader," *Fortune*, April 28, 2008, 150.
15. Marc Gunther, "Best Buy Wants Your Junk," *Fortune,* December 7, 2009, 96–99.
16. Jeffrey Hollender, Seventh Generation Corporate Web Site, www.7genreport.com (Accessed June 6, 2011).
17. Yana Polikarpov, "Consumers Still Have Green Expectations," *Adweek*, February 24, 2009, www.adweek.com/news/advertising-branding/consumers-still-have-green-expectations-105327.
18. "A Seasoned Strategy," *Fortune*, July 20, 2009, 57; Osram Sylvania, "Business Lighting Solutions," www.sylvania.com/BusinessProducts/LightingForBusiness (Accessed August 9, 2010); Kikkoman Corporate Web site, "Global Vision 2020," www.kikkoman.com/corporateprofile/globalvision/index.shtml (Accessed January 14, 2011).
19. Nora Isaacs, "Crash & Burn," *Upside 13* (2001): 187. ProQuest Online, www.lib.duke.edu (Accessed March 4 , 2002).
20. Jeneanne Rae, "Ruthless Focus on the Customer," *BusinessWeek*, July 28, 2006, www.businessweek.com/innovate/content/jul2006/id20060724_426480.htm.
21. A. G. Lafley and Rom Charan, "The Consumer Is Boss," *Fortune*, March 17, 2008, 121–126.
22. "The Art of Customer Service," *Fortune*, March 22, 2010, 74.
23. Anna Bernasek, "The World's Most Admired Companies," *Fortune*, March 22, 2010, 121–126.
24. "Many Companies Not Working to Earn Loyalty," *Quirks Marketing Research Review*, October 2008, 80.
25. McGregor, "The 2009 List of the Customer Service Champs."
26. Christopher Tkaczyk, "American Express," *Fortune*, August 16, 2010, 14.
27. "A Career at the Container Store," The Container Store Corporate Web site, http://www.containerstore.com/careers/index.html (Accessed August 6, 2010).
28. Julie Barker, "Power to the People: Reducing Turnover with Empowerment," February 8, 2008, www.incentivemag.com/News/Industry/Articles/Power-to-the-People–Reducing-Turnover-With-Empowerment.
29. Samuel Fromartz, "Good Enough to Eat," *Fast Company*, September 1 2008, www.fastcompany.com/magazine/128/good-enough-to-eat.html.
30. Lafley and Charan, "The Consumer Is Boss," 122.
31. U.S. Census Bureau, "U.S. & World Population Clocks," www.census.gov/main/www/popclock.html (Accessed January 14, 2011).
32. The application exercises throughout the book are based on the winning entries in the "Best of the Great Ideas in Teaching Marketing" contest held in conjunction with the publication of the Eighth Edition of *Marketing*. Ideas came from marketing professors all across the country who teach many different sizes and types of marketing courses. Information on ways to implement these great ideas in the classroom can be found in the Instructor Manual that accompanies this text.
33. Don Steinberg, "Just Play," *Inc. Magazine,* October 2008, 124–134; Ethan Smith, Yutari Iwatani Kane, Sam Schechner, "Beatles Tunes Join Rock Band Game", *The Wall Street Journal,* October 30, 2008. Available at http://online.wsj.com/article/SB122531701276881747.html (accessed January 5, 2009); Dan Gallagher, "Is 'Guitar Hero' Hitting Its Peak?" Market Watch, December 12, 2008. Available at http://www.marketwatch.com/news/story/guitar-hero-rock-band-games/story.aspx?guid=%7B5CC35A95%2DB667%2D4E97%2DACB7%2D3BA37BACA0FC%7D&dist=TQP_Mod_mktwN (accessed January 5, 2009).

chapter

2 Strategic Planning for Competitive Advantage

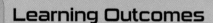

Learning Outcomes

1 Understand the importance of strategic planning

2 Define the term strategic business unit (SBU)

3 Identify strategic alternatives and know a basic outline for a marketing plan

4 Develop an appropriate business mission statement

5 Describe the components of a situation analysis

6 Identify sources of competitive advantage

7 Explain the criteria for stating good marketing objectives

8 Discuss target market strategies

9 Describe the elements of the marketing mix

10 Explain why implementation, evaluation, and control of the marketing plan are necessary

11 Identify several techniques that help make strategic planning effective

LO1
The Nature of Strategic Planning

Strategic planning is the managerial process of creating and maintaining a fit between the organization's objectives and resources and the evolving market opportunities. The goal of strategic planning is long-run profitability and growth. Thus, strategic decisions require long-term commitments of resources.

A strategic error can threaten a firm's survival. On the other hand, a good strategic plan can help protect and grow the firm's resources. For instance, if the March of Dimes had decided to focus on fighting polio, the organization would no longer exist because polio is largely viewed as a conquered disease. The March of Dimes survived by making the strategic decision to switch to fighting birth defects.

Strategic marketing management addresses two questions: What is the organization's main activity at a particular time? How will it reach its goals? Here are some examples of strategic decisions:

→ PepsiCo's decision to grow its portfolio of "healthy fare" business from $10 billion to $30 billion over the next decade: To reach this goal, the company has hired physicians and PhD's who have researched diabetes and heart disease to help in developing healthier snack food options.[1]

> The **goal** of strategic planning is long-run profitability and growth.

strategic planning
The managerial process of creating and maintaining a fit between the organization's objectives and resources and evolving market opportunities.

marketing&you.

What do you think about planning?

Enter your answers on the lines provided. *Describes my style*

NOT AT ALL ⟨ 1 2 3 4 5 6 7 ⟩ PERFECTLY

_____ I start my work without spending too much time on planning.*

_____ I list the steps necessary for completing a task before starting it.

_____ I think about strategies I will fall back on if problems arise.

_____ Because so many aspects of my work are unpredictable, planning is not useful.*

_____ I keep good records of the projects I'm working on.

_____ I set personal goals for myself.

_____ Each week I make a plan for what I need to do.

_____ I do not waste time thinking about what I should do.*

_____ I am careful to work on the highest-priority tasks first.

_____ Planning is a waste of time.*

_____ Planning is an excuse for not working.*

_____ I don't need to develop a strategy for completing my assignments.*

Now, total your score, reversing your score for items with asterisks. That is, if you put a 2, put a 6, and vice versa. Read the chapter, and see what your score means at the end.

Review
LO 1

Understand the importance of strategic planning

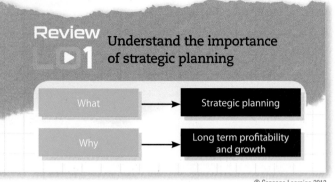

© Cengage Learning 2013

Review
LO 2

Define strategic business units

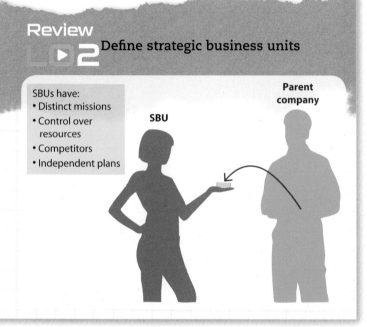

SBUs have:
- Distinct missions
- Control over resources
- Competitors
- Independent plans

SBU

Parent company

© Cengage Learning 2013

→ A Starbucks location in Seattle called "Olive Way" is experimenting with adding wine selections from the Pacific Northwest and beer from local brewers. In addition, an expanded menu will offer savory foods that go well with coffee, wine, and beer.[2]

→ McDonald's is attempting to keep pace with shifting consumer preferences by offering more chicken, beverage, and breakfast items to its menu.[3]

→ SC Johnson's introduction of Shout Color Catcher, a laundry sheet for the washer that collects loose dyes and prevents clothes from bleeding color onto other laundry items.

All these decisions have affected or will affect each organization's long-run course, its allocation of resources, and ultimately its financial success. In contrast, an operating decision, such as changing the package design for Post's cornflakes or altering the sweetness of a Kraft salad dressing, probably won't have a big impact on the long-run profitability of the company.

LO 2
Strategic Business Units

Large companies may manage a number of very different businesses, called **strategic business units (SBUs)**. Each SBU has its own rate of return on investment, growth potential, and associated risks, and requires its own strategies and funding. When properly created, an SBU has the following characteristics:

→ A distinct mission and a specific target market

→ Control over its resources

→ Its own competitors

→ A single business or a collection of related businesses

→ Plans independent of the other SBUs in the total organization

In theory, an SBU should have its own resources for handling basic business functions: accounting, engineering, manufacturing, and marketing. In practice, however, because of company tradition, management philosophy, and production and distribution economies, SBUs sometimes share manufacturing facilities, distribution channels, and even top managers.

LO 3
Strategic Alternatives

strategic business unit (SBU)
A subgroup of a single business or a collection of related businesses within the larger organization.

There are several tools available that a company, or SBU, can use to manage the strategic direction of its portfolio of businesses. Three of the most commonly used tools are Ansoff's Strategy Opportunity matrix, the Boston Consulting Group model, and the General Electric model. Selecting which strategic alternative to pursue depends on the overall company philosophy and culture. The choice also depends on the tool used to make the decision. Companies generally have one of two philosophies about when they expect profits. They either pursue profits right away or first seek to increase market share and then pursue profits. In the long run, market share and profitability are compatible goals. Many companies have long followed this credo: Build market share, and profits will surely follow. Michelin, the tire producer, consistently sacrifices short-term profits to achieve market share. On the other hand, IBM stresses profitability and stock valuation over market share, quality, and customer service. As you can see, the same strategic alternative may be viewed entirely differently by different firms.

ANSOFF'S OPPORTUNITY MATRIX

One method for developing strategic alternatives is Ansoff's Strategic Opportunity matrix (see Exhibit 2.1), which matches products with markets. Firms can explore these four options:

→ **Market penetration:** A firm using the market penetration alternative would try to increase market share among existing customers. Kraft Foods introduced an advertising campaign to try and get consumers of its Philadelphia brand cream cheese to think about using it on more than just bagels for breakfast. For example, one ad shows a female accountant eating a cracker topped with Philadelphia cream cheese during the afternoon to refuel her day.[4] Customer databases, discussed in Chapters 9 and 21, can help managers implement this strategy.

→ **Market development:** Market development means attracting new customers to existing products. Ideally, new uses for old products stimulate additional sales among existing customers while also bringing in new buyers. McDonald's, for example, has opened restaurants in Russia, China, and Italy and is eagerly expanding into Eastern European countries. Best Buy has opened stand-alone mobile phone stores in malls in order to attract the mall shopper.[5] In the nonprofit area, the growing emphasis on continuing education and executive development by colleges and universities is a market development strategy.

→ **Product development:** A product development strategy entails the creation of new products for present markets. McDonald's introduced yogurt parfaits, entrée salads, and fruit to offer their current customers more healthy options. Managers following the product development strategy can rely on their extensive knowledge of the target audience. They usually have a good feel for what customers like and dislike about current products and what existing needs are not being met. In addition, managers can rely on established distribution channels.

→ **Diversification:** Diversification is a strategy of increasing sales by introducing new products into new markets. For example, Ralph Lauren developed a new

market penetration
A marketing strategy that tries to increase market share among existing customers.

market development
A marketing strategy that entails attracting new customers to existing products.

product development
A marketing strategy that entails the creation of new products for current customers.

diversification
A strategy of increasing sales by introducing new products into new markets.

Exhibit 2.1 Ansoff's Strategic Opportunity Matrix

	Present Product	New Product
Present Market	**Market penetration:** McDonald's sells more Happy Meals with Disney movie promotions.	**Product development:** McDonald's introduces premium salads and McWater.
New Market	**Market development:** McDonald's opens restaurants in China.	**Diversification:** McDonald's introduces line of children's clothing.

This ad for Daisy cottage cheese shows five different ways to use the product. Daisy is hoping to increase market share among existing customers by encouraging its use as an ingredient in various meals.

brand of clothing called Rugby to appeal to young people from 14 to 29. Sony practiced a diversification strategy when it acquired Columbia Pictures; although motion pictures are not a new product in the marketplace, they were a new product for Sony. Coca-Cola manufactures and markets water-treatment and water-conditioning equipment, which has been a very challenging task for the traditional soft drink company. A diversification strategy can be risky when a firm is entering unfamiliar markets. On the other hand, it can be very profitable when a firm is entering markets with little or no competition.

THE BOSTON CONSULTING GROUP MODEL

Management must find a balance among the SBUs that yields the overall organization's desired growth and profits with an acceptable level of risk. Some SBUs generate large amounts of cash, and others need cash to foster growth. The challenge is to balance the organization's portfolio of SBUs for the best long-term performance.

To determine the future cash contributions and cash requirements expected for each SBU, managers can use the Boston Consulting Group (BCG) portfolio model. The BCG **portfolio model** classifies each SBU by its current or forecast growth and market share. The underlying assumption is that market share and profitability are strongly linked. The measure of market share used in the portfolio approach is *relative market share*, the ratio between the company's share and the share of the largest competitor. For example, if firm A has a 50 percent share and the competitor has 5 percent, the ratio is 10 to 1. If firm A has a 10 percent market share and the largest competitor has 20 percent, the ratio is 0.5 to 1.

Exhibit 2.2 is a hypothetical portfolio matrix for a large computer manufacturer. The size of the circle in each cell of the matrix represents dollar sales of the SBU relative to dollar sales of the company's other SBUs.

The following categories are used in the matrix:

→ **Stars:** A **star** is a market leader and growing fast. For example, computer manufacturers have identified notebook and handheld models as stars. Star SBUs usually have large profits but need a lot of cash to finance rapid growth. The best marketing tactic is to protect existing market share by reinvesting earnings in product improvement, better distribution, more promotion, and production efficiency. Management must strive to capture most of the new users as they enter the market.

→ **Cash cows:** A **cash cow** is an SBU that usually generates more cash than it needs to maintain its market share. It is in a low-growth market, but the product has a dominant market share. Personal computers and laptops are categorized as cash cows in Exhibit 2.2. The basic strategy for a cash cow is to maintain market dominance by being the price leader and making

portfolio model
A tool for allocating resources among products or strategic business units on the basis of relative market share and market growth rate.

star
In the portfolio matrix, a business unit that is a fast-growing market leader.

cash cow
In the portfolio matrix, a business unit that usually generates more cash than it needs to maintain its market share.

technological improvements in the product. Managers should resist pressure to extend the basic line unless they can dramatically increase demand. Instead, they should allocate excess cash to the product categories where growth prospects are the greatest. For instance, the Clorox Company owns Kingsford Charcoal; the Glad brand of products; Fresh Step, Scoop Away, and other pet litters; Brita water filtration systems; and K.C. Masterpiece barbecue sauce, among others. Traditionally, the company's cash cow has been Clorox bleach, which owns the lion's share of a low-growth market. The Clorox Company has been highly successful in stretching the Clorox line to include scented chlorine bleach as well as Clorox 2, chlorine-free bleach for colored clothing. Another example is Heinz, which has two cash cows: ketchup and Weight Watchers frozen dinners.

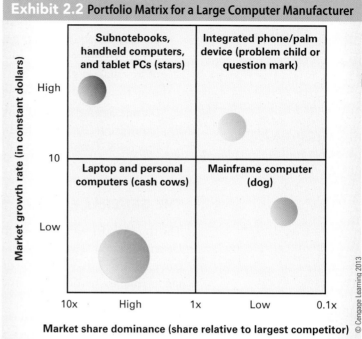

Exhibit 2.2 Portfolio Matrix for a Large Computer Manufacturer

Market growth rate (in constant dollars)

High — Subnotebooks, handheld computers, and tablet PCs (stars) | Integrated phone/palm device (problem child or question mark)

10

Low — Laptop and personal computers (cash cows) | Mainframe computer (dog)

Market share dominance (share relative to largest competitor)

10x High 1x Low 0.1x

Note: The size of the circle represents the dollar sales relative to sales of other SBUs on the matrix—for example, 10x means sales are ten times greater than those of the next largest competitor.

→ **Problem children:** A problem child, also called a question mark, shows rapid growth but poor profit margins. It has a low market share in a high-growth industry. Problem children need a great deal of cash. Without cash support, they eventually become dogs. The strategy options are to invest heavily to gain better market share, acquire competitors to get the necessary market share, or drop the SBU. Sometimes a firm can reposition the products of the SBU to move them into the star category. Zima, a beer alternative targeted at Generation X, was a problem child for Adolph Coors Company. The company ultimately withdrew its heavy marketing investment in Zima and positioned it as a niche product.

→ **Dogs:** A dog has low growth potential and a small market share. Most dogs eventually leave the marketplace. In the computer manufacturer example, the mainframe computer has become a dog. Other examples include Warner-Lambert's Reef mouthwash and Campbell's Red Kettle soups. Frito-Lay has produced several dogs, including Stuffers cheese-filled snacks, Rumbles granola nuggets, and Toppels cheese-topped crackers—a trio irreverently known as Stumbles, Tumbles, and Twofers. The strategy options for dogs are to harvest or divest.

After classifying the company's SBUs in the matrix, the next step is to allocate future resources for each. The four basic strategies are to:

→ **Build:** If an organization has an SBU that it believes has the potential to be a star (probably a problem child at present), building would be an appropriate goal. The organization may decide to give up short-term profits and use its financial resources to achieve this goal. Procter & Gamble built Pringles from a money loser into a record profit maker.

→ **Hold:** If an SBU is a very successful cash cow, a key goal would surely be to hold or preserve market share so that the organization can take advantage of the very positive cash flow. Bisquick has been a prosperous cash cow for General Mills for over two decades.

problem child (question mark)
In the portfolio matrix, a business unit that shows rapid growth but poor profit margins.

dog
In the portfolio matrix, a business unit that has low growth potential and a small market share.

© Cengage Learning 2013

→ **Harvest:** This strategy is appropriate for all SBUs except those classified as stars. The basic goal is to increase the short-term cash return without too much concern for the long-run impact. It is especially worthwhile when more cash is needed from a cash cow with long-run prospects that are unfavorable because of low market growth rate. For instance, Unilever has been harvesting Lifebuoy soap for a number of years with little promotional backing.

→ **Divest:** Getting rid of SBUs with low shares of low-growth markets is often appropriate. Problem children and dogs are most suitable for this strategy. Procter & Gamble dropped Cincaprin, a coated aspirin, because of its low growth potential.

THE GENERAL ELECTRIC MODEL

The third model for selecting strategic alternatives was originally developed by General Electric. The dimensions used in this model—market attractiveness and company strength—are richer and more complex than those used in the BCG model, but are harder to quantify.

Exhibit 2.3 presents the GE model. The horizontal axis, Business Position, refers to how well positioned the organization is to take advantage of market opportunities. Does the firm have the technology it needs to effectively penetrate the market? Are its financial resources adequate? Can manufacturing costs be held below those of the competition? Can the firm cope with change? The vertical axis measures the attractiveness of a market, which is expressed both quantitatively and qualitatively. Some attributes of an attractive market are high profitability, rapid growth, a lack of government regulation, consumer insensitivity to a price increase, a lack of competition and availability of technology. The grid is divided into three overall attractiveness zones for each dimension: high, medium, and low.

Those SBUs (or markets) that have low overall attractiveness (indicated by the red cells in Exhibit 2.3) should be avoided if the organization is not already serving them. If the firm is in these markets, it should either harvest or divest those SBUs. The organization should selectively maintain markets with medium attractiveness (indicated by the yellow cells in Exhibit 2.3). If attractiveness begins to slip, then the organization should withdraw from the market.

Conditions that are highly attractive—an attractive market plus a strong business position, the green cells in Exhibit 2.3—are the best candidates for investment. For instance, STC Craft, an imprint of Abrams Books, saw that there was a market for young, stylish crafters, and now publishes beautiful craft books that bring old skills, such as knitting and quilting, to a modern, funky consumer.

THE MARKETING PLAN

Based on the company's or SBU's overall strategy, marketing managers can create a marketing plan for individual products, brands, lines or customer groups. **Planning** is the process of anticipating future events and determining strategies to achieve organizational objectives in the future. **Marketing planning** involves designing activities relating to marketing objectives and the changing

Exhibit 2.3 General Electric Model

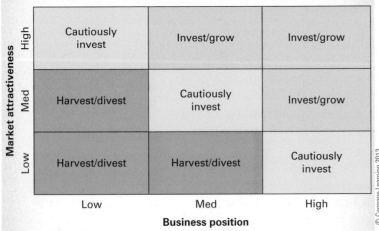

	Low	Med	High
High	Cautiously invest	Invest/grow	Invest/grow
Med	Harvest/divest	Cautiously invest	Invest/grow
Low	Harvest/divest	Harvest/divest	Cautiously invest

Market attractiveness (vertical) / Business position (horizontal)

© Cengage Learning 2013

marketing environment. Marketing planning is the basis for all marketing strategies and decisions. Issues such as product lines, distribution channels, marketing communications, and pricing are all delineated in the **marketing plan**. The marketing plan is a written document that acts as a guidebook of marketing activities for the marketing manager.

© iStockphoto.com/Juan Facundo Mora Soria

marketing plan
A written document that acts as a guidebook of marketing activities for the marketing manager.

Why Write a Marketing Plan? By specifying objectives and defining the actions required to attain them, you can provide the basis by which actual and expected performance can be compared in a marketing plan. Marketing can be one of the most expensive and complicated business activities, but it is also one of the most important. The written marketing plan provides clearly stated activities that help employees and managers understand and work toward common goals.

Writing a marketing plan allows you to examine the marketing environment in conjunction with the inner workings of the business. Once the marketing plan is written, it serves as a reference point for the success of future activities. Finally, the marketing plan allows the marketing manager to enter the marketplace with an awareness of possibilities and problems.

Marketing Plan Elements Marketing plans can be presented in many different ways. Most businesses need a written marketing plan because a marketing plan is large and can be complex. Details about tasks and activity assignments may be lost if communicated orally. Regardless of the way a marketing plan is presented, some elements are common to all marketing plans. These include defining the business mission, performing a situation analysis, defining objectives, delineating a target market, and establishing components of the marketing mix. Exhibit 2.4 shows these elements, which are also described further below. Other elements that may be included in a plan are budgets, implementation timetables, required marketing research efforts, or elements of advanced strategic planning. A marketing planning outline and an example of a marketing plan appear at the end of this book.

Writing the Marketing Plan The creation and implementation of a complete marketing plan will allow the organization to achieve marketing objectives and succeed. However, the marketing plan is only as good as the information it contains and the effort, creativity, and thought that go into its creation. Having a good marketing information system and a wealth of competitive intelligence (covered in Chapter 9) is critical to a thorough and accurate situation analysis. The role of managerial intuition is also important in the creation and selection of marketing strategies. Managers must weigh any information against its accuracy and their own judgment when making a marketing decision.

Note that the overall structure of the marketing plan (Exhibit 2.4) should not be viewed as a series of sequential planning steps. Many of the marketing plan elements are decided on simultaneously and in conjunction with one another. Further, every marketing plan has a different content,

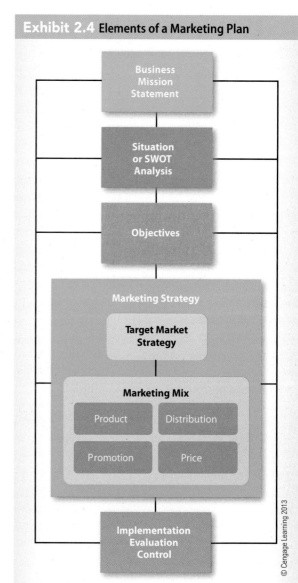

Exhibit 2.4 Elements of a Marketing Plan

Business Mission Statement

Situation or SWOT Analysis

Objectives

Marketing Strategy

Target Market Strategy

Marketing Mix

Product   Distribution

Promotion   Price

Implementation Evaluation Control

© Cengage Learning 2013

Market development = ↑ Customers
Market penetration = ↑ Share
Product development = ↑ Products
Diversification = ↑ New Products + ↑ New Markets

© Cengage Learning 2013

depending on the organization, its mission, objectives, targets, and marketing mix components. The example of a marketing plan in the chapter appendix should not be regarded as the only correct format for a marketing plan. Many organizations have their own distinctive format or terminology for creating a marketing plan. Every marketing plan should be unique to the firm for which it was created. Remember, however, that although the format and order of presentation should be flexible, the same types of questions and topic areas should be covered in any marketing plan. As you can see by the extent of the marketing planning outline and the example of the E-motion Software marketing plan in the appendix, creating a complete marketing plan is not a simple or quick effort.

LO4
Defining the Business Mission

The foundation of any marketing plan is the firm's **mission statement**, which answers the question, "What business are we in?" The way a firm defines its business mission profoundly affects the firm's long-run resource allocation, profitability, and survival. The mission statement is based on a careful analysis of benefits sought by current and potential customers and an analysis of existing and anticipated environmental conditions. The firm's mission statement establishes boundaries for all subsequent decisions, objectives, and strategies. The Southwest Airlines mission statement is shown in Exhibit 2.5.

A mission statement should focus on the market or markets the organization is attempting to serve rather than on the good or service offered. Otherwise, a new technology may quickly make the good or service obsolete and the mission statement irrelevant to company functions. Business mission statements that are stated too narrowly suffer from **marketing myopia**—defining a business in terms of goods and services rather than in terms of the benefits customers seek. In this context, *myopia* means narrow, short-term thinking. For example, Frito-Lay defines its mission as being in the snack-food business rather than in the corn chip business. The mission of sports teams is not just to play games but to serve the interests of the fans.

Alternatively, business missions may be stated too broadly. "To provide products of superior quality and value that improve the lives of the world's consumers" is probably too broad a mission statement for any firm except Procter & Gamble. Care must be taken when stating what business a firm is in. For example, the mission of Ben & Jerry's centers on three important aspects of its ice cream business: (1) Product: "To make, distribute, and sell the finest quality all natural ice cream and euphoric concoctions with a continued commitment to incorporating wholesome, natural ingredients and promoting business practices that respect the earth and the environment"; (2) Economic: "To operate the company on a sustainable financial basis of profitable growth, increasing value for our stakeholders, and expanding

mission statement

A statement of the firm's business based on a careful analysis of benefits sought by present and potential customers and an analysis of existing and anticipated environmental conditions.

marketing myopia

Defining a business in terms of goods and services rather than in terms of the benefits that customers seek.

Exhibit 2.5 Southwest Airlines Mission Statement

The mission of Southwest Airlines is dedication to the highest quality of Customer Service delivered with a sense of warmth, friendliness, individual pride, and Company Spirit.

To Our Employees

We are committed to provide our Employees a stable work environment with equal opportunity for learning and personal growth. Creativity and innovation are encouraged for improving the effectiveness of Southwest Airlines. Above all, Employees will be provided the same concern, respect, and caring attitude within the organization that they are expected to share externally with every Southwest Customer.

Source: http://www.southwestairlines.com/about_swa/mission

opportunities for development and career growth for our employees"; and (3) Social: "To operate the company in a way that actively recognizes the central role that business plays in society by initiating innovative ways to improve the quality of life locally, nationally, and internationally."[6] By correctly stating the business mission in terms of the benefits that customers seek, the foundation for the marketing plan is set. Many companies are focusing on designing more appropriate mission statements because these statements are frequently displayed on the company's Web sites.

LO5
Conducting a Situation Analysis

Marketers must understand the current and potential environment that the product or service will be marketed in. A situation analysis is sometimes referred to as a **SWOT analysis**; that is, the firm should identify its internal strengths (S) and weaknesses (W) and also examine external opportunities (O) and threats (T).

When examining internal strengths and weaknesses, the marketing manager should focus on organizational resources such as production costs, marketing skills, financial resources, company or brand image, employee capabilities, and available technology. For example, a potential weakness for AirTran Airways is the age of its airplane fleet, which could project an image of danger or low quality. Other weaknesses include high labor turnover rates and limited flights. A potential strength is the airline's low operating costs, which translate into lower prices for consumers. Another issue to consider in this section of the marketing plan is the historical background of the firm—its sales and profit history.

When examining external opportunities and threats, marketing managers must analyze aspects of the marketing environment. This process is called **environmental scanning**—the collection and interpretation of information about forces, events, and relationships in the external environment that may affect the future of the organization or the implementation of the marketing plan. Environmental scanning helps identify market opportunities and threats and provides guidelines for the design of marketing strategy. The six most often studied macroenvironmental forces are social, demographic, economic, technological, political and legal, and competitive. These forces are examined in detail in Chapter 4. Rising gas prices and a weakening dollar have created a complex, but possibly advantageous, environment for McDonald's. While increased gas costs may discourage some consumers from visiting its drive-through windows, the fast food giant hopes that its widespread availability, its inexpensive prices, and its new gourmet-style coffee offerings will attract consumers trying to save money by downgrading from Starbucks and other pricy venues. McDonald's marketers are even taking advantage of gas price increases by running commercials in which teenagers decide not to fill their empty gas tank and buy $1 double cheeseburgers to fill their stomachs instead.[7]

Review
LO4 Develop an appropriate business mission statement

Q: What business are we in?

A: Business mission statement

Too narrow → marketing myopia

Too broad → no direction

Just right → focus on markets served and benefits customers seek

© Cengage Learning 2013

SWOT analysis
Identifying internal strengths (S) and weaknesses (W) and also examining external opportunities (O) and threats (T).

environmental scanning
Collection and interpretation of information about forces, events, and relationships in the external environment that may affect the future of the organization or the implementation of the marketing plan.

Review
LO5 Describe the components of
a situation analysis

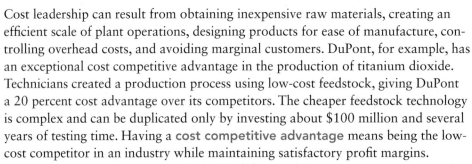

LO6
Competitive Advantage

Performing a SWOT analysis allows firms to identify their competitive advantage. A **competitive advantage** is a set of unique features of a company and its products that are perceived by the target market as significant and superior to the competition. It is the factor or factors that cause customers to patronize a firm and not the competition. There are three types of competitive advantages: cost, product/service differentiation, and niche strategies.

COST COMPETITIVE ADVANTAGE

Cost leadership can result from obtaining inexpensive raw materials, creating an efficient scale of plant operations, designing products for ease of manufacture, controlling overhead costs, and avoiding marginal customers. DuPont, for example, has an exceptional cost competitive advantage in the production of titanium dioxide. Technicians created a production process using low-cost feedstock, giving DuPont a 20 percent cost advantage over its competitors. The cheaper feedstock technology is complex and can be duplicated only by investing about $100 million and several years of testing time. Having a **cost competitive advantage** means being the low-cost competitor in an industry while maintaining satisfactory profit margins.

A cost competitive advantage enables a firm to deliver superior customer value. Walmart, the world's leading low-cost general merchandise store, offers good value to customers because it focuses on providing a large selection of merchandise at low prices and good customer service. Walmart is able to keep its prices down because it has strong buying power in its relationships with suppliers.

Costs can be reduced in a variety of ways.

→ *Experience curves:* Experience curves tell us that costs decline at a predictable rate as experience with a product increases. The experience curve effect encompasses a broad range of manufacturing, marketing, and administrative costs. Experience curves reflect learning by doing, technological advances, and economies of scale. Firms such as Boeing use historical experience curves as a basis for predicting and setting prices. Experience curves allow management to forecast costs and set prices based on anticipated costs as opposed to current costs.

→ *Efficient labor:* Labor costs can be an important component of total costs in low-skill, labor-intensive industries such as product assembly and apparel manufacturing. Many U.S. manufacturers such as Nike, Levi Strauss, and Liz Claiborne have "gone offshore" to achieve cheaper manufacturing costs. Many American companies are also outsourcing activities such as data entry and other labor-intensive jobs.

→ *No-frills goods and services:* Marketers can lower costs by removing frills and options from a product or service. Southwest Airlines, for example, offers low fares but no seat assignments or meals. Low costs give Southwest Airlines a higher load factor and greater economies of scale, which, in turn, mean lower prices for consumers.

competitive advantage
The set of unique features of a company and its products that is perceived by the target market as significant and superior to the competition.

cost competitive advantage
Being the low-cost competitor in an industry while maintaining satisfactory profit margins.

experience curves
The curves represent data on a chart that show costs declining at a predictable rate as experience with a product increases.

→ **Government subsidies:** Governments may provide grants and interest-free loans to target industries. Such government assistance enabled Japanese semiconductor manufacturers to become global leaders.

→ **Product design:** Cutting-edge design technology can help offset high labor costs. BMW is a world leader in designing cars for ease of manufacture and assembly. Reverse engineering—the process of disassembling a product piece by piece to learn its components and obtain clues as to the manufacturing process—can also mean savings. Reverse engineering a low-cost competitor's product can save research and design costs. Japanese engineers have reverse engineered many products, such as computer chips coming out of Silicon Valley.

→ **Reengineering:** Reengineering entails fundamental rethinking and redesign of business processes to achieve dramatic improvements in critical measures of performance. It often involves reorganizing from functional departments such as sales, engineering, and production to cross-disciplinary teams.

→ **Production innovations:** Production innovations such as new technology and simplified production techniques help lower the average cost of production. Technologies such as computer-aided design and computer-aided manufacturing (CAD/CAM) and increasingly sophisticated robots help companies like Boeing, Ford, and General Electric reduce their manufacturing costs.

→ **New methods of service delivery:** Medical expenses have been substantially lowered by the use of outpatient surgery and walk-in clinics. Airlines, such as Delta, are lowering reservation and ticketing costs by encouraging passengers to use the Internet to book flights and by providing self-check-in kiosks at the airport.

PRODUCT/SERVICE DIFFERENTIATION COMPETITIVE ADVANTAGE

Because cost competitive advantages are subject to continual erosion, product/service differentiation tends to provide a longer lasting competitive advantage. The durability of this strategy tends to make it more attractive to many top managers. A **product/service differentiation competitive advantage** exists when a firm provides something unique that is valuable to buyers beyond simply offering a low price. Examples include brand names (Lexus), a strong dealer network (Caterpillar for construction work), product reliability (Maytag appliances), image (Neiman Marcus in retailing), or service (FedEx). A great example of a company that has a strong product/service competitive advantage is Nike. Nike's advantage is built around one simple idea—product innovation. The company's goal is to think of something that nobody has thought of before or improve something that already exists. Nike Air, ACG, Nike Swift, and Nike Shox are examples of innovative shoes introduced by Nike.[8] Another example is PetSmart. Not only does PetSmart offer numerous products for all types of pets, it also offers services such as PetsHotel, grooming, and training.

NICHE COMPETITIVE ADVANTAGE

A **niche competitive advantage** seeks to target and effectively serve a single segment of the market (see Chapter 8). For small companies with limited resources that potentially face giant competitors, niche targeting may be the only viable option. A market segment that has good growth potential but is not crucial to the success of major competitors is a good candidate for developing a niche strategy.

product/service differentiation competitive advantage
The provision of something that is unique and valuable to buyers beyond simply offering a lower price than the competition's.

niche competitive advantage
The advantage achieved when a firm seeks to target and effectively serve a small segment of the market.

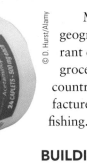

Many companies using a niche strategy serve only a limited geographic market. Buddy Freddy's is a very successful restaurant chain, but is found only in Florida. Migros is the dominant grocery chain in Switzerland. It has no stores outside that small country. Another example is the Orvis Company, which manufactures and sells everything that anyone might ever need for fly-fishing. Orvis is a very successful niche marketer.

BUILDING SUSTAINABLE COMPETITIVE ADVANTAGE

The key to having a competitive advantage is the ability to sustain that advantage. A **sustainable competitive advantage** is one that cannot be copied by the competition. Nike, discussed earlier, is a good example of a company that has a sustainable competitive advantage. Others include Rolex (high-quality watches), Nordstrom department stores (service), and Southwest Airlines (low price). In contrast, when Datril was introduced into the pain-reliever market, it was touted as being exactly like Tylenol, only cheaper. Tylenol responded by lowering its price, thus destroying Datril's competitive advantage and ability to remain on the market. In this case, low price was not a sustainable competitive advantage. Without a competitive advantage, target customers don't perceive any reason to patronize an organization instead of its competitors.

The notion of competitive advantage means that a successful firm will stake out a position unique in some manner from its rivals. Imitation of competitors indicates a lack of competitive advantage and almost ensures mediocre performance. Moreover, competitors rarely stand still, so it is not surprising that imitation causes managers to feel trapped in a seemingly endless game of catch-up. They are regularly surprised by the new accomplishments of their rivals.

Companies need to build their own competitive advantages rather than copy a competitor. The sources of tomorrow's competitive advantages are the skills and assets of the organization. Assets include patents, copyrights, locations, equipment, and technology that are superior to those of the competition. Skills are functions such as customer service that the firm performs better than its competitors. Netflix, for example, created and remains dominant in the market for renting movies by mail. Marketing managers should continually focus the firm's skills and assets on sustaining and creating competitive advantages.

Remember, a sustainable competitive advantage is a function of the speed with which competitors can imitate a leading company's strategy and plans. Imitation requires a competitor to identify the leader's competitive advantage, determine how it is achieved, and then learn how to duplicate it.

Review
LO6 — Identify sources of competitive advantage

To create sustainable competitive advantage, don't copy someone else, build your own:

Sources of Competitive Advantage
- Cost $
- Product/Service Differentiation A vs. B vs. C
- Niche Strategies

© Cengage Learning 2013

LO7
Setting Marketing Plan Objectives

Before the details of a marketing plan can be developed, objectives for the plan must be stated. Without objectives, there is no basis for measuring the success of marketing plan activities.

sustainable competitive advantage
An advantage that cannot be copied by the competition.

A **marketing objective** is a statement of what is to be accomplished through marketing activities. To be useful, stated objectives should meet several criteria:

→ **Realistic:** Managers should develop objectives that have a chance of being met. For example, it may be unrealistic for start-up firms or new products to command dominant market share, given other competitors in the marketplace.

→ **Measurable:** Managers need to be able to quantitatively measure whether or not an objective has been met. For example, it would be difficult to determine success for an objective that states "To increase sales of cat food." If the company sells 1 percent more cat food, does that mean the objective was met? Instead, a specific number should be stated: "To increase sales of Purina brand cat food from $300 million to $345 million."

→ **Time-specific:** By what time should the objective be met? "To increase sales of Purina brand cat food between January 1, 2011 and December 31, 2012."

→ **Compared to a benchmark:** If the objective is to increase sales by 15 percent, it is important to know the baseline against which the objective will be measured. Will it be current sales? Last year's sales? For example, "To increase sales of Purina brand cat food by 15 percent over 2010 sales of $300 million."

Objectives must also be consistent with and indicate the priorities of the organization. Specifically, objectives flow from the business mission statement to the rest of the marketing plan. Exhibit 2.6 shows some well-stated and some poorly stated objectives. Notice how well they do or do not meet the aforementioned criteria.

Carefully specified objectives serve several functions. First, they communicate marketing management philosophies and provide direction for lower-level marketing managers so that marketing efforts are integrated and pointed in a consistent direction. Objectives also serve as motivators by creating something for employees to strive for. When objectives are attainable and challenging, they motivate those charged with achieving the objectives. Additionally, the process of writing specific objectives forces executives to clarify their thinking. Finally, objectives form a basis for control; the effectiveness of a plan can be gauged in light of the stated objectives.

marketing objective
A statement of what is to be accomplished through marketing activities.

Exhibit 2.6 Examples of Marketing Objectives

Poorly Stated Objectives	Well-Stated Objectives
Our objective is to maximize profits.	Our objective is to achieve a 10 percent return on investment from January 1, 2009 until December 31, 2009, with a payback on new investments of no longer than December 31, 2013.
Our objective is to better serve customers.	Our objective is to obtain customer satisfaction ratings of 90 percent on the 2009 annual customer satisfaction survey, and to retain 85 percent of our 2009 customers as repeat purchasers in 2010.
Our objective is to be the best that we can be.	Our objective is to increase market share from 30 percent in 2009 to 40 percent in 2010 by increasing promotional expenditures by 14 percent over 2009 levels from January 1, 2010 to December 31, 2010.

© Cengage Learning 2013

Review
LO7

Explain the criteria for stating good marketing objectives

Realistic, measurable, and time-specific objectives consistent with the firm's objectives:

1. Communicate marketing management philosophy

2. Provide management direction

3. Motivate employees

4. Force executives to think clearly

5. Allow for better evaluation of results

© Cengage Learning 2013

LO8
Describing the Target Market

Marketing strategy involves the activities of selecting and describing one or more target markets and developing and maintaining a marketing mix that will produce mutually satisfying exchanges with target markets.

TARGET MARKET STRATEGY

A market segment is a group of individuals or organizations that share one or more characteristics. They therefore may have relatively similar product needs. For example, parents of newborn babies need products such as formula, diapers, and special foods. The target market strategy identifies the market segment or segments on which to focus. This process begins with a **market opportunity analysis (MOA)**—the description and estimation of the size and sales potential of market segments that are of interest to the firm and the assessment of key competitors in these market segments. After the firm describes the market segments, it may target one or more of them. There are three general strategies for selecting target markets. Target market(s) can be selected by appealing to the entire market with one marketing mix, concentrating on one segment, or appealing to multiple market segments using multiple marketing mixes. The characteristics, advantages, and disadvantages of each strategic option are examined in Chapter 8. Target markets could be smokers who are concerned about white teeth (the target of Crest Whitestrips), people concerned about sugar and calories in their soft drinks (Diet Pepsi), or college students needing inexpensive about-town transportation (Yamaha Razz scooter).

Any market segment that is targeted must be fully described. Demographics, psychographics, and buyer behavior should be assessed. Buyer behavior is covered in Chapters 6 and 7. If segments are differentiated by ethnicity, cultural aspects of the marketing mix should be examined. If the target market is international, it is especially important to describe differences in culture, economic and technological development, and political structure that may affect the marketing plan. Global marketing is covered in more detail in Chapter 5.

marketing strategy
The activities of selecting and describing one or more target markets and developing and maintaining a marketing mix that will produce mutually satisfying exchanges with target markets.

market opportunity analysis (MOA)
The description and estimation of the size and sales potential of market segments that are of interest to the firm and the assessment of key competitors in these market segments.

Review
LO8

Discuss target market strategies

Target Market Options

Entire Market   Multiple Markets   Single Market

© Cengage Learning 2013

LO9
The Marketing Mix

The term **marketing mix** refers to a unique blend of product, place (distribution), promotion, and pricing strategies (often referred to as the **four Ps**) designed to produce mutually satisfying exchanges with a target market. The marketing manager can control each component of the marketing mix, but the strategies for all four components must be blended to achieve optimal results. Any marketing mix is only as good as its weakest component. For example, the first pump toothpastes were distributed over cosmetic counters and failed. Not until pump toothpastes were distributed the same way as tube toothpastes did the products succeed. The best promotion and the lowest price cannot save a poor product. Similarly, excellent products with poor placing, pricing, or promotion will likely fail.

Successful marketing mixes have been carefully designed to satisfy target markets. At first glance, McDonald's and Wendy's may appear to have roughly identical marketing mixes because they are both in the fast-food hamburger business. However, McDonald's has been most successful at targeting parents with young children for lunchtime meals, whereas Wendy's targets the adult crowd for lunches and dinner. McDonald's has playgrounds, Ronald McDonald the clown, and children's Happy Meals. Wendy's has salad bars, carpeted restaurants, and no playgrounds.

Variations in marketing mixes do not occur by chance. Astute marketing managers devise marketing strategies to gain advantages over competitors and best serve the needs and wants of a particular target market segment. By manipulating elements of the marketing mix, marketing managers can fine-tune the customer offering and achieve competitive success.

PRODUCT STRATEGIES

Typically, the marketing mix starts with the product "P." The heart of the marketing mix, the starting point, is the product offering and product strategy. It is hard to design a place strategy, decide on a promotion campaign, or set a price without knowing the product to be marketed.

The product includes not only the physical unit but also its package, warranty, after-sale service, brand name, company image, value, and many other factors. A Godiva chocolate has many product elements: the chocolate itself, a fancy gold wrapper, a customer satisfaction guarantee, and the prestige of the Godiva brand name. We buy things not only for what they do (benefits) but also for what they mean to us (status, quality, or reputation).

Products can be tangible goods such as computers, ideas like those offered by a consultant, or services such as medical care. Products should also offer customer value. Product decisions are covered in Chapters 10 and 11, and services marketing is detailed in Chapter 12.

PLACE (DISTRIBUTION) STRATEGIES

Place, or distribution, strategies are concerned with making products available when and where customers want them. Would you rather buy a kiwi fruit at the 24-hour grocery store within walking distance or fly to Australia to pick your own? A part of this place "P" is physical distribution, which involves all the business activities concerned with storing and transporting raw materials or finished products. The goal is to make sure products arrive in usable condition at designated places when needed. Place strategies are covered in Chapters 13 through 15.

To counter Wendy's attempt to corner a more adult market, McDonald's started to offer healthy salads with Dasani water to target health conscious women on their lunch breaks and healthy moms at the restaurant with their kids.

© HANDOUT/KRT/Newscom

marketing mix
A unique blend of product, place, promotion, and pricing strategies designed to produce mutually satisfying exchanges with a target market.

four Ps
Product, place, promotion, and price, which together make up the marketing mix.

Ambush Marketing

For many highly publicized events, a company will pay to have its brand become the exclusive sponsor of particular portions of the event. This exclusivity theoretically eliminates competitors. Ambush marketing occurs when a company that does not pay a fee to sponsor an event (i.e., is not an official sponsor) runs an advertising or other promotional campaign that links the company in consumers' minds to the event.

During the 2010 FIFA World Cup match in South Africa, several companies engaged in ambush marketing. For example, 36 women were thrown out of the stadium when they were seen wearing short orange dresses made by Dutch brewery Bavaria. Budweiser had paid to be the exclusive beer sponsor at this event. Likewise, Adidas was an official sponsor for FIFA, manufacturing all the game balls and many of the teams' jerseys and cleats. However, research showed that Nike was the most talked-about company in relation to the World Cup. Adidas was second at 14.4 percent. Nike created a high-energy ad featuring prominent soccer players along with stars such as Homer Simpson and Kobe Bryant depicting how the players' futures would change based on their successes or failures during the World Cup games. At the time, the ad had been viewed on YouTube more than 14 million times, and generated buzz around the Internet. Discussions appeared on blogs, message boards, through comments under the videos, and other social media sites such as Facebook. Social media makes ambush marketing easier because it has the power to reach millions of people in a short time.

Event organizers such as FIFA spend significant time and money trying to stop ambush marketing because they make billions of dollars from sponsors paying for exclusive, official sponsor status. If the sponsorship is not exclusive because of ambush marketing, the value of being an official sponsor decreases, losing money for the event organizers. The organizers of the 2012 Olympics in London have already taken the precaution of booking almost all the city's billboard space during the games. Even more protection comes from the London Olympic Games and Paralympic Games Act of 2006. The act created the London Olympic Association Right (LOAR), which gives the games' organizers the power to grant licenses to authorized sponsors to use the symbols, words, and logos of the event. The act also bans any advertisement or merchandise with the combination of words and symbols that could create an unauthorized association with the games.[9]

Do you think ambush marketing is an ethical business practice? How do you feel about exclusive sponsors? Defend your position.

© iStockphoto.com/Juan Facundo Mora Soria

PROMOTION STRATEGIES

Promotion includes advertising, public relations, sales promotion, and personal selling. Promotion's role in the marketing mix is to bring about mutually satisfying exchanges with target markets by informing, educating, persuading, and reminding them of the benefits of an organization or a product. A good promotion strategy, like using the Dilbert character in a national promotion strategy for Office Depot, can dramatically increase sales. Each element of the promotion "P" is coordinated and managed with the others to create a promotional blend or mix. These integrated marketing communications activities are described in Chapters 16 through 18. Technology-driven aspects of promotional marketing are covered in Chapter 21. The social media aspect of promotion is covered extensively in Chapter 22.

PRICING STRATEGIES

Price is what a buyer must give up to obtain a product. It is often the most flexible of the four marketing mix elements—the quickest element to change. Marketers can raise or lower prices more frequently and easily than they can change other marketing mix variables. Price is an important competitive weapon and is very important to the organization because price multiplied by the number of units sold equals total revenue for the firm. Pricing decisions are covered in Chapters 20 and 21.

MARKETING METRICS — Profit Scenario Analysis

The Problem

Maybelline sells 3,000 tubes of mascara per month at $8 per tube. Management would like to increase demand, but wants to determine the most profitable way to increase demand. Management turns to the marketing team to determine the best way to increase demand and increase profitability. The core decisions in marketing determine the product, promotion, placement, and price required to attract and serve the customer. Although many of these decisions are primarily focused on increasing demand, they will also influence production and overhead costs—which all affect the profitability of the firm. How can the marketing team determine which actions will help management increase demand and profitability?

To forecast the effect of a marketing decision on profits, marketers can undertake a profit scenario analysis. In a profit scenario analysis, marketers will compare the current performance to the performance they expect to achieve by changing one of the marketing mix variables. Profit scenario analysis requires calculating the difference between revenue and costs under different assumptions to determine the effect on profit. The basic formula is

$$\text{Profit} = \text{Revenue} - \text{Cost}$$

To determine the revenue, we calculate the product of the number of units sold and the price per unit:

$$\text{Revenue} = (\text{Number of units sold}) \times \text{Price}$$

Costs are the amount of money the firm spends over a given period, presumably to earn the revenue generated. We will consider two types of costs: fixed and variable. Fixed costs are costs that are constant regardless of the number of units sold. Fixed cost items include

property, equipment, and management salaries. Variable costs are costs that increase with the number of units sold. Variable cost items include raw materials and sometimes labor. We can determine variable costs on a per unit basis:

$$\text{Costs} = (\text{Number of units sold}) \times \text{Variable Cost} + \text{Fixed Cost}$$

Inputting these formulas into the basic profit equation gives us a working formula with which to calculate profit:

$$\text{Profit} = (\text{Number of units sold}) \times (\text{Price} - \text{Variable Cost}) - \text{Fixed Cost}$$

Using this profit equation, marketers can conduct a scenario analysis that compares the current mascara demand against the demand it hopes to achieve by changing one of the marketing mix variables, in this case by reducing the price of a tube of mascara.

The Metric

With the current sales of mascara at 3,000 tubes per month at $8 per tube, the marketers can determine current profit. The current variable cost is $3 and the current fixed cost is $12,000. Under these conditions, the profits earned by the firm are:

$$\text{Current Profit} = (3,000 \text{ tubes}) \times (\$8 - \$3) - \$12,000$$
$$\text{Current Profit} = (3,000) \times (\$5) - 12,000$$
$$\text{Current Profit} = 15,000 - 12,000$$
$$\text{Current Profit} = \$3,000$$

The marketing team wants to see how reducing the price affects profits, so they decide to reduce the price of one tube of mascara by 10 percent, making each tube cost $7.20. Marketing research suggest that this price reduction will increase demand by 15 percent, meaning they would

sell 3,450 tubes of mascara a month. The variable and fixed costs remain the same. The anticipated profit is then:

$$\text{Anticipated Profit} = (3,450 \text{ units}) \times (\$7.20 - \$3) - \$12,000$$
$$\text{Anticipated Profit} = (3,450) \times (4.20) - 12,000$$
$$\text{Anticipated Profit} = 14,490 - 12,000$$
$$\text{Anticipated Profit} = \$2,490$$

By comparing the anticipated profits to the current profits, we find that profits are expected to decrease by $510 during the period of the price promotion. That is a 17 percent decrease in profit:

$$\text{Change in Profit} = \text{Anticipated Profit} - \text{Current Profit}$$
$$\text{Change in Profit} = \$2,490 - \$3,000$$
$$\text{Change in Profit} = -\$510$$

$$\text{Percentage Change in Profits}$$
$$= \frac{\text{Change in Profits}}{\text{Current Profit}} = \frac{-\$510}{\$3,000} = -17\%$$

Management Action

Based on the calculations above, the marketers see that reducing the price of mascara for a promotion does not increase profitability. Because profits are anticipated to decrease, the marketing manager should argue against a price reduction.

Marketers regularly conduct a profit scenario analysis with a number of different assumptions and the results will vary according to the conditions facing the firm. Every time a price is reduced or increased, promotions are reduced or increased, products are enhanced are degraded, and distribution is altered, the marketer is influencing demand, and therefore both the ability of the firm to serve customer needs and make a profit.

LO▶10
Following Up on the Marketing Plan

IMPLEMENTATION

Implementation is the process that turns a marketing plan into action assignments and ensures that these assignments are executed in a way that accomplishes the plan's objectives. Implementation activities may involve detailed job assignments, activity descriptions, timelines, budgets, and lots of communication. Implementation requires delegating authority and responsibility, determining a time frame for completing tasks, and allocating resources. Sometimes a strategic plan also requires task force management. A *task force* is a tightly organized unit under the direction of a manager who, usually, has broad authority. A task force is established to accomplish a single goal or mission and thus works against a deadline. Toyota created a task force to build and market its luxury car, the Lexus. AT&T assigned a task force to develop marketing plans that would protect its long-distance market from MCI and Sprint.

Implementing a plan has another dimension: gaining acceptance. New plans mean change, and change creates resistance. One reason people resist change is that they fear they will lose something. For example, when new-product research is taken away from marketing research and given to a new-product department, the director of marketing research will naturally resist this loss of part of his or her domain. Misunderstanding and lack of trust also create opposition to change, but effective communication through open discussion and teamwork can be one way of overcoming resistance to change.

implementation

The process that turns a marketing plan into action assignments and ensures that these assignments are executed in a way that accomplishes the plan's objectives.

A strategic plan cannot be set in stone. As changes occur in the external environment, managers will be pressed to adjust the strategic plan. The key to organizational survival is willingness to examine the changing environment and to adopt appropriate new goals and behaviors. Yet they must not simply be willing to change; they must know how to change.

Although implementation is essentially "doing what you said you were going to do," many organizations repeatedly experience failures in strategy implementation. Brilliant

Best coverage worldwide.

at&t

▼.ıllı More phones that work in more than 200 countries, like Costa Rica.   att.com/global

© AP Images/ PRNewsFoto/AT&T Inc.

marketing plans are doomed to fail if they are not properly implemented. These detailed communications may or may not be part of the written marketing plan. If they are not part of the plan, they should be specified elsewhere as soon as the plan has been communicated. Strong, forward thinking leadership can overcome resistance to change, even in large, highly integrated companies where change seems highly unlikely.

EVALUATION AND CONTROL

After a marketing plan is implemented, it should be evaluated. Evaluation entails gauging the extent to which marketing objectives have been achieved during the specified time period. Four common reasons for failing to achieve a marketing objective are unrealistic marketing objectives, inappropriate marketing strategies in the plan, poor implementation, and changes in the environment after the objective was specified and the strategy was implemented.

Once a plan is chosen and implemented, its effectiveness must be monitored. Control provides the mechanisms for evaluating marketing results in light of the plan's objectives and for correcting actions that do not help the organization reach those objectives within budget guidelines. Firms need to establish formal and informal control programs to make the entire operation more efficient.

The flowchart in Exhibit 2.7 traces the steps of a basic control system. The process starts while planning is taking place. After the managers set goals, they must develop standards to measure performance. When standards have been set, the managers can then put the plan into action. Next, managers measure performance to make sure standards have been met. If they have been, actions continue. Otherwise, the managers study deviations from standards to determine whether they fall within acceptable boundaries. If the deviations are not significant, actions continue with minor changes. When the deviations are major, the plan is halted. To revise the plan or perhaps scrap it, the managers analyze cause-and-effect relationships.

Assume that Jane French, the sales manager of Joy Manufacturing, a producer of heavy industrial equipment, decides that key accounts (customers with over $500,000 sales potential per year) are not getting the attention they deserve from the sales force. Her goal is to increase the calls made to key accounts. She decides that instead of demanding a key account quota from the sales force, she will use positive motivation. She develops a new commission scheme that provides a 2-percent-of-net-sales bonus on key account sales, or $1,500—whichever is greater. She then sends a letter to each salesperson with a list of key accounts in the territory. The standard she sets is a minimum average increase in calls on key accounts of 25 percent per month over the same

evaluation
Gauging the extent to which the marketing objectives have been achieved during the specified time period.

control
Provides the mechanisms for evaluating marketing results in light of the plan's objectives and for correcting actions that do not help the organization reach those objectives within budget guidelines.

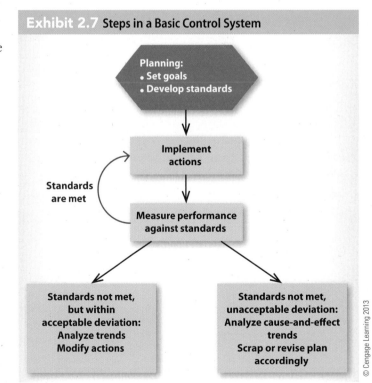

Exhibit 2.7 Steps in a Basic Control System

© Cengage Learning 2013

period a year ago. By studying summary data from individual call-record sheets, she will measure performance.

During the first six months after the new system is installed, calls on key accounts increase on average by 31 percent, and key account sales rise 43 percent over the same period a year ago. The plan is conforming to French's standards. During the seventh month, however, the percentage increase slips to 26 percent and then falls to 22 percent. The deviation from the standard is such that she doesn't consider it a major problem, so she doesn't immediately implement any changes. However, the general downward trend is disturbing, so she asks the eight regional managers to discuss it with the sales force and report back within a week. All reports reflect the same situation. Key accounts are now being visited so often (an average of three times per month) that many sales calls are unproductive. The sales force then begins to call on other accounts and prospects that have a higher sales potential.

After studying the reports, French is satisfied that the key accounts are getting enough attention and that diverting time to other accounts might be more productive. She keeps the key account plan in force to provide incentives to call on key accounts but lowers the standard to an average increase of 15 percent over the previous year. In this example, the general goals were being met, but the control system required a refinement in the standards.

The Marketing Audit Perhaps the broadest control device available to marketing managers is the **marketing audit**—a thorough, systematic, periodic evaluation of the objectives, strategies, structure, and performance of the marketing organization. A marketing audit helps management allocate marketing resources efficiently. It has four characteristics:

marketing audit
A thorough, systematic, periodic evaluation of the objectives, strategies, structure, and performance of the marketing organization.

→ **Comprehensive:** The marketing audit covers all the major marketing issues facing an organization and not just trouble spots.

→ **Systematic:** The marketing audit takes place in an orderly sequence and covers the organization's marketing environment, internal marketing system, and specific marketing activities. The diagnosis is followed by an action plan with both short-run and long-run proposals for improving overall marketing effectiveness.

→ **Independent:** The marketing audit is normally conducted by an inside or outside party who is independent enough to have top management's confidence and to be objective.

→ **Periodic:** The marketing audit should be carried out on a regular schedule instead of only in a crisis. Whether it seems successful or is in deep trouble, any organization can benefit greatly from such an audit.

Although the main purpose of the marketing audit is to develop a full profile of the organization's marketing effort and to provide a basis for developing and revising the marketing plan, it is also an excellent way to improve communication and raise the level of marketing

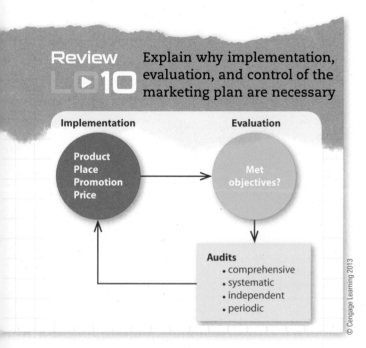

Review
LO 10
Explain why implementation, evaluation, and control of the marketing plan are necessary

Implementation

Product
Place
Promotion
Price

Evaluation

Met objectives?

Audits
- comprehensive
- systematic
- independent
- periodic

© Cengage Learning 2013

consciousness within the organization. It is a useful vehicle for selling the philosophy and techniques of strategic marketing to other members of the organization.

Postaudit Tasks After the audit has been completed, three tasks remain. First, the audit should profile existing weaknesses and inhibiting factors, as well as the firm's strengths and the new opportunities available to it. Recommendations have to be judged and prioritized so that those with the potential to contribute most to improved marketing performance can be implemented first. The usefulness of the data also depends on the auditor's skill in interpreting and presenting the data so decision makers can quickly grasp the major points.

The second task is to ensure that the role of the audit has been clearly communicated. It is unlikely that the suggestions will require radical change in the way the firm operates. The audit's main role is to address the question "Where are we now?" and to suggest ways to improve what the firm already does.

The final postaudit task is to make someone accountable for implementing recommendations. All too often, reports are presented, applauded, and filed away to gather dust. The person made accountable should be someone who is committed to the project and who has the managerial power to make things happen.

LO 11
Effective Strategic Planning

Effective strategic planning requires continual attention, creativity, and management commitment. Strategic planning should not be an annual exercise in which managers go through the motions and forget about strategic planning until the next year. It should be an ongoing process because the environment is continually changing and the firm's resources and capabilities are continually evolving.

Sound strategic planning is based on creativity. Managers should challenge assumptions about the firm and the environment and establish new strategies. For example, major oil companies developed the concept of the gasoline service station in an age when cars needed frequent and rather elaborate servicing. These major companies held on to the full-service approach, but independents were quick to respond to new realities and moved to lower-cost self-service and convenience-store operations. The major companies took several decades to catch up.

Perhaps the most critical element in successful strategic planning is top management's support and participation. For example, Michael Anthony, the former CEO of Brookstone, Inc., and the Brookstone buying team earned hundreds of thousands of frequent flyer miles searching the world for manufacturers and inventors of unique products that can be carried in its retail stores, catalogs, and Internet site. Anthony co-developed some of these products and was also active in remodeling efforts for Brookstone's 250 permanent and seasonal stores.

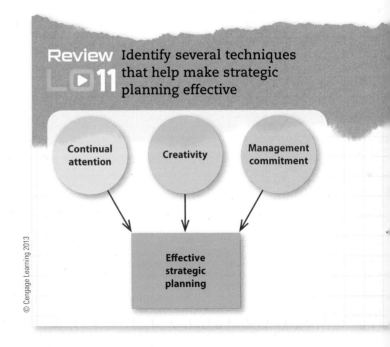

Review LO 11 Identify several techniques that help make strategic planning effective

© iStockphoto.com/Juan Facundo Mora Soria

© Cengage Learning 2013

Elements of the marketing mix; quadrants in the Boston Consulting Group (BCG) portfolio matrix

Percent of English-language messages mentioning Nike during the World Cup

Million visitors to Bass Pro Shops each year

Target age group for Ralph Lauren's Rugby line

Macroenvironmental forces affecting marketing

Amount needed to develop DuPont's cost-competitive technology

4   30   3   14-29   6 $100 million

Review and Applications

LO1 Understand the importance of strategic planning. Strategic planning is the basis for all marketing strategies and decisions. The goal of strategic planning is long-term profitability and growth.

online

1.1 How are Coke and Pepsi using their Web sites, **www.coca-cola.com** and **www.pepsi. com**, to promote their newest product offerings? Do you see hints of any future strategies the companies might implement? If so, where?

LO2 Define strategic business units. Large companies may manage a number of very different businesses, called strategic business units (SBUs). Each SBU has its own rate of return on investment, growth potential, and associated risks, and requires its own strategies and funding.

2.1 Research a large company, such as Coca-Cola, Nike, or Procter & Gamble to find out what its SBUs are.

LO3 Identify strategic alternatives and know a basic outline for a marketing plan. The strategic opportunity matrix can be used to help management develop strategic alternatives. The four options are market penetration, product development, market development, and diversification. In selecting a strategic alternative, managers may use a portfolio matrix, which classifies strategic business units as stars, cash cows, problem children, or dogs, depending on their present or projected growth and market share. Another option is to use the GE Model, which classifies SBUs based on market attractiveness and business position.

The marketing plan is a written document that acts as a guidebook of marketing activities for the marketing manager. A marketing plan provides the basis by which actual and expected performance can be compared.

Although there is no set formula or a single correct outline, a marketing plan should include basic elements such as stating the business mission, setting objectives, performing a situation analysis of internal and external environmental forces, selecting target market(s), delineating a marketing mix (product, place, promotion, and price), and establishing ways to implement, evaluate, and control the plan.

3.1 Your cousin wants to start his own business, but he has decided not to write a marketing plan because he thinks that preparing one would take too long. He says he doesn't need a formal proposal because he has already received funding from your uncle. Explain why it is important for him to write a plan anyway.

3.2 After graduation, you decide to take a position as the marketing manager for a small snack-food manufacturer. The company, Shur Snak, is growing, and this is the first time that the company has ever employed a marketing manager. Consequently, there is no marketing plan in place for you to follow. Outline a basic marketing plan for your boss to give her an idea of the direction you want to take the company.

writing

Develop an appropriate business mission statement. The mission statement is based on a careful analysis of benefits sought by current and potential customers and an analysis of existing and anticipated environmental conditions. The firm's mission statement establishes boundaries for all subsequent decisions, objectives, and strategies. A mission statement should focus on the market or markets the organization is attempting to serve rather than on the good or service offered.

LO**4**

4.1 Thinking back to question 3.2, write a business mission statement for Shur Snak. What elements should you include? Evaluate the mission statement you wrote against some of those you can find online.

writing

Describe the components of a situation analysis. In the situation (or SWOT) analysis, the firm should identify its internal strengths (S) and weaknesses (W) and also examine external opportunities (O) and threats (T). When examining external opportunities and threats, marketing managers must analyze aspects of the marketing environment in a process called environmental scanning. The six most often studied macroenvironmental forces are social, demographic, economic, technological, political and legal, and competitive.

LO**5**

5.1 Competition in the private courier sector is fierce. UPS and FedEx dominate, but other companies, such as DHL and even the United States Postal Service (USPS), still have a decent chunk of the express package delivery market. Perform a mini-situation analysis on one of the companies listed below by stating one strength, one weakness, one opportunity, and one threat. You may want to consult the following Web sites as you build your grid:

writing

UPS	**www.ups.com**	DHL	**www.dhl-usa.com**
FedEx	**www.fedex.com**	USPS	**www.usps.com**

Identify sources of competitive advantage. A competitive advantage is a set of unique features of a company and its products that are perceived by the target market as significant and superior to the competition. There are three types of competitive advantages: cost, product/service differentiation, and niche strategies. Sources of cost competitive advantages include experience curves, efficient labor, no-frills goods and services, government subsidies, product design, reengineering, product innovations, and new methods of service delivery. A product/service differentiation competitive advantage exists when a firm provides something unique that is valuable to buyers beyond just low price. Niche competitive advantages come from targeting unique segments with

LO**6**

specific needs and wants. The goal of all these sources of competitive advantage is to be sustainable.

6.1 Break into small groups and discuss examples (at least two per person) of the last few products you have purchased. What specific strategies were used to achieve competitive advantage? Is that competitive advantage sustainable against the competitors?

LO 7 **Explain the criteria for stating good marketing objectives.** Objectives should be realistic, measurable, and time specific. Objectives must also be consistent and indicate the priorities of the organization.

7.1 Building on the Shur Snak example, imagine that your boss has stated that the marketing objective of the company is to do the best job of satisfying the needs and wants of the customer. Explain that although this objective is admirable, it does not meet the criteria for good objectives. What are these criteria? What is a specific example of a better objective for Shur Snak?

LO 8 **Discuss target market strategies.** The target market strategy identifies which market segment or segments to focus on. This process begins with a MOA, which describes and estimates the size and sales potential of market segments that are of interest to the firm. In addition, an assessment of key competitors in these market segments is performed. After the market segments are described, one or more may be targeted by the firm. The three strategies for selecting target markets are appealing to the entire market with one marketing mix, concentrating on one segment, or appealing to multiple market segments by using multiple marketing mixes.

8.1 You are given the task of deciding the marketing strategy for a transportation company. How do the marketing mix elements change when the target market is (a) low-income workers without personal transportation, (b) corporate international business travelers, or (c) companies with urgent documents or perishable materials to be delivered to customers?

LO 9 **Describe the elements of the marketing mix.** The marketing mix (or four Ps) is a blend of product, place, promotion, and pricing strategies designed to produce mutually satisfying exchanges with a target market. The starting point of the marketing mix is the product offering. Products can be tangible goods, ideas, or services. Place (distribution) strategies are concerned with making products available when and where customers want them. Promotion includes advertising, public relations, sales promotion, and personal selling. Price is what a buyer must give up to obtain a product and is often the easiest to change of the four marketing mix elements.

9.1 Choose three or four other students and make up a team. Create a marketing plan to increase enrollment in your school. Describe the four marketing mix elements that make up the plan.

LO 10 **Explain why implementation, evaluation, and control of the marketing plan are necessary.** Before a marketing plan can work, it must be implemented; that is, people must perform the actions in the plan. The plan should also be evaluated to see if it has achieved its objectives. Poor implementation can be a major factor in a plan's failure. Control provides the mechanisms for evaluating marketing results in light of the plan's objectives and for correcting actions that do not help the organization reach those objectives within budget guidelines. One of the major control tools is the marketing audit, which has four major components: it is comprehensive, systematic, independent, and periodic. After the marketing audit, it is important to perform postaudit tasks, which are to profile strengths and weaknesses, clarify the role of the audit, and assign someone to be responsible for implementing the results of the audit.

10.1 Have your school enrollment marketing plan team (from question 9.1) develop a plan to implement, evaluate, and control the marketing strategy.

Identify several techniques that help make strategic planning effective. First, management must realize that strategic planning is an ongoing process and not a once-a-year exercise. Second, good strategic planning involves a high level of creativity. The last requirement is top management's support and cooperation.

11.1 What techniques can make your school enrollment marketing plan more effective?

Key Terms

cash cow *28*	market opportunity analysis (MOA) *38*	planning *30*
competitive advantage *34*	market penetration *27*	portfolio model *28*
control *43*	marketing audit *44*	problem child (question mark) *29*
cost competitive advantage *34*	marketing mix *39*	product development *27*
diversification *27*	marketing myopia *32*	product/service differentiation competitive advantage *35*
dog *29*	marketing objective *37*	star *28*
environmental scanning *33*	marketing plan *31*	strategic business unit (SBU) *26*
evaluation *43*	marketing planning *30*	strategic planning *25*
experience curves *34*	marketing strategy *38*	sustainable competitive advantage *36*
four Ps *39*	mission statement *32*	
implementation *42*	niche competitive advantage *35*	SWOT analysis *33*
market development *27*		

Exercises

ETHICS EXERCISE

Abercrombie & Fitch, a retail clothing chain based in New Albany, Ohio, launched a line of thong underwear for preteen girls. Words like "eye candy" and "wink wink" were printed on the front of the skimpy underwear that some argued would fit girls aged 5 to 10. Abercrombie is known for its provocative ads and sexually oriented catalogs. Supporters of the strategy claim that producing thong-style underwear for 10- to 16-year-olds is a good move; critics think that the line is tasteless and that marketing it to young girls is contemptuous.

Questions

1. Is marketing adult-styled undergarments to a younger audience unethical? Why or why not?

2. Would Abercrombie have been in the spotlight had the sexy words been omitted from the product? Explain your answer.

MARKETING PLAN EXERCISE

Throughout the rest of this book, these end-of-chapter marketing plan exercises will help you build a strategic marketing plan for a company of your choosing. The company you choose should be one that interests you, such as the manufacturer of your favorite product, a local business where you would like to work, or even a business you would like to start yourself to satisfy an unmet need or want. Once you've completed the marketing plan exercise for each chapter in Part 1 of this textbook, you can complete the Part 1 Marketing Planning Worksheet by logging in to the companion Web site at **www.cengagebrain.com**. Use the following exercises to guide you through the first part of your strategic marketing plan:

Questions

1. Describe your chosen company. How long has it been in business, or when will it start business? Who are the key players? Is the company small or large? Does it offer a good or service?

2. Write the mission statement of your company, keeping in mind the benefits offered to customers rather than the product or service sold. If you are starting the online arm of a traditional store, should you make any changes to the company's overall mission statement?

3. List at least three specific, measurable objectives for your company. Be sure these objectives relate to the mission statement and include a time frame.

4. Begin a SWOT analysis by determining the primary strength of your company by asking, "What is the key differential or competitive advantage of my firm?" What are other keys to the potential success of your company? What other strengths can your firm capitalize on?

5. Continue the SWOT analysis by taking an honest look at the weaknesses of your firm. How can you overcome them?

APPLICATION EXERCISE

As you now know from reading the chapter, an important part of the strategy-making process involves scanning the environment for changes that affect your marketing efforts. This exercise is designed to introduce you to the business press and to help you make the connection between the concepts you learn in the classroom and real-world marketing activities.

Activities

1. Find a current article of substance in the business press (*The Wall Street Journal, The Financial Times, Fortune, Businessweek, Inc.,* etc.) that discusses topics you have covered in this course. Although this is only Chapter 2, you will be surprised by the amount of terminology you have already learned. If you are having trouble finding an article, read through the table of contents at the beginning of the book to familiarize yourself with the names of concepts that will be presented later in the course. Read your article carefully, making notes about relevant content.

writing

2. Write a one-paragraph summary of the key points in your article; then write a list of the terms or concepts critical to understanding the article. Provide definitions of those terms. If you are unfamiliar with a term or concept that is central to the article, do some research in your textbook or see your professor during office hours. Relate these key points to the concepts in your text by citing page numbers.

3. Explain the environments that are relevant to the situation presented in the article. (Chapter 4 contains a full list of environmental factors.)

CASE STUDY: Disney

THE HAPPIEST BRAND ON EARTH

In 2006, Disney's Pixar released the hit movie *Cars*, which grossed $462 million worldwide. Since then, *Cars* merchandise has generated over $2 billion in sales each year. Pixar has since created a series of *Cars* shorts to be aired on the Disney Channel with a subsequent DVD release. A *Cars* sequel was released in 2011 along with an online virtual gaming world on its Web site to help build hype. In 2012, Disney's California Adventure theme park will open its 12-acre Cars Land attraction.

At Disney, the brand is the name of the game, and the cross-platform success of the *Cars* franchise is by no means an exception to the rule. Disney also has the Jonas Brothers, *Hannah Montana*, *High School Musical*, the Disney Princesses, *Pirates of the Caribbean*, and the list goes on and on. The man behind the magic is Disney's CEO, Bob Iger, who has lead a dramatic revitalization of the Disney brand since succeeding longtime head Michael Eisner in 2005. When he first took the post, his strategy shifted Disney's focus to its stable of "franchises." These franchises are distributed across Disney's multiple company platforms and divisions, such as Disney's various television broadcasts platforms (the Disney Channel, ABC, ESPN), its consumer products business, theme parks, Disney's Hollywood Records music label, and Disney's publishing arm in Hyperion, just to name a few.

Iger's franchise strategy has been supported by the other major move he made upon first becoming CEO. On his first day on the job, Iger told the board that revitalizing Disney's animation business was a top priority, which would be improved through the purchase of Pixar. As part of Iger's franchise strategy the deal made perfect sense, as many of Disney's latest TV shows, theme park rides, and merchandise was based of Pixar characters.

Finding a new market to push the Disney franchise into became a priority as well. With the Walt Disney Company experiencing flat growth, it was becoming evident that Disney had missed some opportunities for broader success due to a narrowing of its target market, which was at the time largely associated with younger children.

Iger's first move was to broaden Disney's viewership by moving the Disney Channel from premium to basic cable and launching local versions in key global markets. Then, Disney began pushing franchises to capture the rapidly growing tween market. Putting its support behind the Disney channel's *High School Musical, Hannah Montana*, and the Jonas Brothers (who were emerging out of Disney's music label), Disney quickly generated a series of franchise juggernauts in the tween-girl market.

Though Disney's focus has remained on family-friendly fair, Iger has shown a new willingness to look to even broader markets, if it fits with the Disney brand. Disney's *Pirates of the Caribbean*, the first Disney film with a PG-13 rating, played a major role in re-focusing the brand, being based off the classic theme park ride, and it also helped expand the Disney appeal older kids and even adults. The *Pirates* and *Cars* franchises also provided preliminary steps for Disney's latest endeavors to crack the tween boy market, age 6–14, one traditionally difficult for media companies to sustainably capture. Their efforts focus around the new Disney XD channel, with a broad range of offerings, such as potential new franchises like the science fiction action-adventure show "Aaron Stone" and showcases of new musical talent. Disney will also be able to leverage ESPN to create original sports-based programming. The recent acquisition of Marvell Entertainment also provided Disney with a broad stable of material to create content for that platform. The channel is accompanied by a Disney XD Web site, which will promote the channel's programs, as well as offer games and original videos, social networking, and online community opportunities.

As it continues to expand and provide new franchise offerings, Disney looks to have relatively strong momentum. The success of its cross-platform franchise strategy has certainly helped it weather the economic downturn, as the effects of the recession continue to recede. Disney plans to continue that strategy with the release of many film franchise sequels, including new *Cars*, *Pirates*, and *Monsters Inc.* films. As Apple CEO and Pixar stakeholder Steve Jobs comments, "Family is a renewable resource," and right now, Disney is making the most of it.[10]

Questions

1. Do a brief market opportunity analysis for Disney, identifying the major markets that Disney has expanded into.
2. How does Disney's cross-platform franchising help create sustainable competitive advantage?
3. Describe the marketing mix for one of Disney's franchises.
4. Describe the major components of Bob Iger's strategic plan.

COMPANY CLIPS: Method—Healthy Home

© NKP MEDIA, INC./Cengage

Cash-strapped start-up companies generally do not spend a great deal of time and money on planning. Founders are so busy with the rudiments of business—finding customers and creating, manufacturing, and delivering the product—that they may even forget important things, such as invoicing. Eric Ryan reinforces this notion in the opening of the second Method video segment. Nonetheless, strategic planning is an important part of successful marketing. Listen closely to the segment, which introduces Method's then CEO, Alastair Dorward, and gauge for yourself how much planning you think this innovative start-up did before launching its brand.

Questions

1. Based on what you heard in the video, does Method have a marketing plan?
2. Explain the elements that make up Method's competitive advantage. Is it sustainable?
3. What are the elements in Method's marketing mix?
4. What are Method's target market strategies and how does it use them in its operations?

marketing&you: Results.

© iStockphoto.com/ziggymaj

The higher your score, the greater importance you place on planning. You also develop plans more often and devote more energy to the planning process. High scores also indicate a motivation to work "smart" and efficiently. If your score was low, you are less inclined to spend energy planning and, as a result, may have lower performance.

Notes

1. Nanette Byrnes, "Pepsi Brings in the Health Police," *Bloomberg Businessweek*, January 25, 2010, www.businessweek.com/magazine/content/10_04/b4164050511214.htm.

2. Ashley M. Heher, "Starbucks Shop Tries Wine, 'Coffee Theater,'" *Seattle Times*, June 24, 2010, http://seattletimes.nwsource.com/html/localnews/2012202243_apusstarbucksideapercolator. html?syndication=rss.

3. Janet Adamy, "McDonald's to Expand, Posting Strong Results," *Wall Street Journal*, January 27, 2009, B1.

4. Elaine Wong, "Kraft Goes beyond the Bagel," *Brandweek*, April 3, 2009, www.brandweek.com/bw/content_display/news-and-features/packaged-goods/e3id4d9d8e33174af5aa6460621107d2c8a.

5. Maria Halkias, "Best Buy Goes Mobile with Dallas-Fort Worth Mall Stores," August 17, 2009, www.dallasnews.com.

6. Ben & Jerry's Mission, accessed December 1, 2008, www.benjerry.com/activism/mission-statement. Reprinted with permission.

7. Mark Gongloff, "Golden Arches Offer Shelter in Storm," *Wall Street Journal*, July 23, 2008, C1; Suzanne Vranica, "Marketers Find Ways to Exploit Gas Prices," *Wall Street Journal*, July 7, 2008, B5.

8. Nike Web site, www.nike.com/nikeos/p/nike/en_US/?sitesrc=usns (Accessed January 18, 2011).

9. Joe Daly, "Dutch Brewery Sends in Blondes for World Cup Ambush Stunt," July 23, 2010, www.huffingtonpost.com/2010/06/17/world-cup-ambush-marketin_n_615872.html; Tom Ryan, "Ambush Marketing Hits the World Cup," June 18, 2010, www.retailwire.com/discussions/sngl_discussion.cfm/14571; Ben Klayman, "Ambush Marketing Gives Nike Leg Up for World Cup," June 11, 2010, www.reuters.com/article/idUSTRE65A5AO20100611.

10. Richard Siklos, "Bob Iger Rocks Disney," *Fortune*, January 19, 2009, 80–86; Peter Sanders, "Disney Focuses on Boys," *Wall Street Journal*, January 8, 2009, http://online.wsj.com/article/SB123137513996262627.html; Ethan Smith, "'Alice' Boosts Disney; Theme Parks Disappoint," *Wall Street Journal*, May 12, 2010, http://online.wsj.com/article/SB10001424052748704250104575238640019592022.html.

© iStockphoto.com/Juan Facundo Mora Soria;
© Noel Hendrickson/Digital Vision/Getty Images

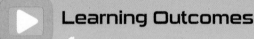
Learning Outcomes

1 Explain the determinants of a civil society

2 Explain the concept of ethical behavior

3 Describe ethical behavior in business

4 Discuss corporate social responsibility

5 Describe the arguments for and against social responsibility

6 Explain cause-related marketing

William Swanson, chairman and CEO of Raytheon, wrote a book entitled *Swanson's Unwritten Rules of Management*. It was later discovered the book contained passages that exactly mirrored a 1944 book by an engineering professor. David Edmondson, former CEO of RadioShack, claimed to have degrees in theology and psychology, but completed only two semesters of course work. Dennis Workman, Chief Technical Officer at Trimble Navigation, a maker of global positioning systems, was listed in SEC filings as having a master's degree in electrical engineering from MIT. Not so, says the University. Other firms where executives have recently overstated their credentials include: Herbalife, Usana Health Sciences, Tetra Tech, Kroll Inc., and Helix Energy Solutions Group.[1]

The activities of these top managers were clearly wrong, going against what is socially accepted as good behavior. For several thousand years religious teaching and secular ethics have sought to encourage socially beneficial behavior. The literature of virtually every religious tradition, as well as Eastern and Western philosophy, are full of examples, rules, and guidance regarding what constitutes right and wrong.

LO1
Determinants of a Civil Society[2]

Have you ever stopped and thought about the social glue that binds society together? That is, what factors are in place that keep people and organizations from running amok and doing harm, and what factors create order in a society like ours? There are social controls in place in order to address those questions, and more. The six modes of social control are listed below:

1. *Ethics:* The first is ethical rules and guidelines along with customs and traditions that provide principles of right action.

2. *Laws:* Often rules and guidelines are codified into law. Laws created by governments are then enforced by governmental authority. Thus, the dictum, "Thou shall not steal," is part of formal law throughout the land. Law, however, is not a perfect mechanism for ensuring good corporate and employee behavior. This is because laws often address the lowest common denominator of socially acceptable behavior. In other words, just because something is not illegal doesn't mean that it is right. For example, an individual goes to Barnes & Noble every day and spends the afternoon reading books and magazines in the store.

> " Defining ethics is like trying to "**nail Jell-O** to the wall." "

marketing&you.

Using the following scale, enter the numbers that reflect your opinions.

COMPLETELY DISAGREE 1 2 3 4 5 6 7 8 9 COMPLETELY AGREE

_____ The ethics and social responsibility of a firm are essential to its long-term profitability.

_____ Business ethics and social responsibility are critical to the survival of a business enterprise.

_____ The overall effectiveness of a business can be determined to a great extent by the degree to which it is ethical and socially responsible.

_____ Good ethics is often good business.

_____ Business has a social responsibility beyond making a profit.

_____ Corporate planning and goal-setting sessions should include discussions of ethics and social responsibility.

_____ Social responsibility and profitability can be compatible.

Now, total your score. Find out what it means after you read the chapter.

The store has big comfortable chairs and the clerks never bother him or ask him to leave. He even takes his own lunch if he plans to spend the day there. He does this at least 20 days per month. The bookstore allows this practice and it is not against the law. It is, however, not ethical. If everyone who bought books followed this individual's behavior, Barnes & Noble would soon be bankrupt!

3. *Formal and Informal Groups:* Businesses, professional organizations (such as the American Marketing Association), clubs (e.g., Shriners or Ducks Unlimited), and professional associations (e.g., American Medical Association) all have codes of conduct. These codes prescribe acceptable and desired behaviors of their members.

4. *Self-Regulation:* Self-regulation involves the voluntary acceptance of standards established by nongovernmental entities such as the American Association of Advertising Agencies (AAAA) or the National Association of Manufacturers. The AAAA has a self-regulation arm that deals with deceptive advertising. Other associations have regulations relating to child labor, environmental issues, conservation, and a host of other issues.

5. *The Media:* In an open, democratic society, the media play a key role in informing the public about actions of individuals and organizations. These stories sometimes praise, such as the media coverage of Intel's investment of $100 million annually in education in 50 countries. Or, they shine the spotlight on unscrupulous behavior, such as the Enron and WorldCom scandals. Business firms dislike negative publicity, which can lead to lost sales, damage to corporate reputations, government actions, and legal liability. Conversely, favorable publicity stimulates sales and builds the firm's reputation.

An example of investigative reporting comes from *Smart Money* magazine. When millions of Americans have problems with a product or service, they often call the Better Business Bureau (BBB). *Smart Money* raises the question, "Is the BBB too cozy with the firms it monitors?" For example, a woman in Shreveport, Louisiana, had a problem with Cingular (now AT&T) regarding her cell phone. The BBB has an online complaint form, which is about ten pages long, that the Shreveport resident carefully filled out. What she didn't know was that the BBB had been asking for extra information from unhappy cell phone customers and giving or selling the data to some of the firms themselves.[3] Cingular, in fact, paid the BBB $50,000 for its customer-driven intelligence.

Gap ignites the season of giving with the help of folks like Ryan Kwanten and Lauren Bush. Gap invites shoppers to indulge in the season's most wanted styles while giving back. On Facebook, "Like" Gap's video vignettes of the influential cast opening up about their personal causes. Here, True Blood's Ryan Kwanten appears in support of City of Hope. By "Liking" his cause, users trigger a $1 donation and get a special treat: a 30 percent discount on one regularly priced item.

Rick Weirick, product development officer of the BBB's national council, said that the fee was just to defray costs.[4]

6. *An Active Civil Society:* An informed and engaged society can help shape and mold individual and corporate behavior. The last state in the union to get a Walmart store was Vermont. Citizen campaigns against the big-box retailer were deciding factors in management's decision to avoid the state. In another example, when the state of Arizona passed an immigration law that many felt was discriminatory, a grass roots campaign sprang up to "boycott Arizona."

All six factors above individually and in combination are critical to achieving a socially coherent, vibrant, civilized society. These six factors (the social glue) are more important today than ever before due to the increasing complexity of the global economy and the melding of customs and traditions within societies.

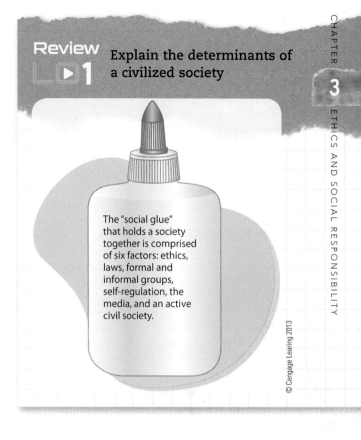

Review LO1 Explain the determinants of a civilized society

The "social glue" that holds a society together is comprised of six factors: ethics, laws, formal and informal groups, self-regulation, the media, and an active civil society.

© Cengage Learning 2013

LO2
The Concept of Ethical Behavior

It has been said that ethics is something everyone likes to talk about but nobody knows exactly what it is. Others have noted that defining ethics is like trying to "nail Jell-O to the wall." You begin to think that you've got it, but that's when it starts slipping between your fingers.

Ethics refers to the moral principles or values that generally govern the conduct of an individual or a group. Ethics also can be viewed as the standard of behavior by which conduct is judged. As noted above, standards that are legal may not always be ethical, and vice versa. Laws are the values and standards enforceable by the courts. Ethics, then, consists of personal moral principles. For example, there is no legal statute that makes it a crime for someone to "cut in line." But if someone doesn't want to wait in line and cuts to the front, it often makes others very angry. Similarly, we sneer at drivers who sneak along the side of the road to get around a line of traffic as we sit and wait our turn.

If you have ever resented a line-cutter, then you understand ethics and have applied ethical standards in life. Waiting your turn in line is one of society's expectations. "Waiting your turn" is not an ordinance, a statute, or even a federal regulation. "Waiting your turn" is an age-old principle developed because it was fair to operate according to the first-in-line, first to be served dictum. "Waiting your turn" exists because when large groups wait for the same road, theater tickets, or fast food at noon in a busy downtown area, lines ensure order; waiting your turn is a just way of allocating the limited space and time allotted for the movie tickets, the traffic, or the food. "Waiting your turn" is an expected but unwritten behavior that plays a critical role in an orderly society.[5]

So it is with ethics. Ethics consists of those unwritten rules we have developed for our interactions with each other. These unwritten rules govern us when we are

ethics
The moral principles or values that generally govern the conduct of an individual.

reactivate with twice the power. regenerist

Olay Regenerist transforms tired skin into skin that looks beautifully regenerated. What better way to reactivate your skin. And your life. Without the drastic measures.

Results not equal to medical procedures.

OLAY
love the skin you're in™

Most beauty companies sell products using idealized language, offering to erase lack of sleep or age lines. In this case, the ad implies the same or similar results to facelift surgery when using the product.

Image courtesy of The Advertising Archives

sharing resources or honoring contracts. "Waiting your turn" is a higher standard than the laws that are passed to maintain order. Those laws apply when physical force or threats are used to push to the front of the line. Assault, battery, and threats are forms of criminal conduct for which the offender can be prosecuted. But the law does not apply to the stealth line-cutter who simply sneaks to the front, perhaps using a friend and a conversation as a decoy for edging into the front. No laws are broken, but the notions of fairness and justice are offended by one individual putting himself above others and taking advantage of others' time and position.

When you say to yourself, "That's unjust!" or "That's not fair!" you have just defined ethics for yourself. Ethics is not just about standards of behavior; ethics is about honesty, justice, and fairness. This is true for both personal and business behavior.

Ethical questions range from practical, narrowly defined issues, such as a business person's obligation to be honest with his customers, to broader social and philosophical questions, such as a company's responsibility to preserve the environment and protect employee rights. Many ethical conflicts develop from conflicts between the differing interests of company owners and their workers, customers, and surrounding community. Managers must balance the ideal against the practical—the need to produce a reasonable profit for the company's shareholders with honesty in business practices, and larger environmental and social issues.

ETHICAL THEORIES

People usually base their individual choice of ethical theory on their life experiences. The following are some of the ethical theories that apply to marketing.[6]

Deontology The **deontological theory** states that people should adhere to their obligations and duties when analyzing an ethical dilemma. This means that a person will follow his or her obligations to another individual or society because upholding one's duty is what is considered ethically correct. For instance, a deontologist will always keep his promises to a friend and will follow the law. A person who follows this theory will produce very consistent decisions because they will be based on the individual's set duties. Note that this theory is not necessarily concerned with the welfare of others. Say, for example, a salesperson has decided that it's his ethical duty (and very practical!) to always be on time to meetings with clients. Today he is running late. How is he supposed to drive? Is the deontologist supposed to speed, breaking the law to uphold his duty to society, or is the deontologist supposed to arrive at his meeting late, breaking his duty to be on time? This scenario of conflicting obligations does not lead us to a clear, ethically

deontological ethical theory
A theory that states that people should adhere to their obligations and duties when analyzing an ethical dilemma.

correct resolution, nor does it protect the welfare of others from the deontologist's decision.

Utilitarianism
The **utilitarian ethical theory** is founded on the ability to predict the consequences of an action. To a utilitarian, the choice that yields the greatest benefit to the most people is the choice that is ethically correct. One benefit of this ethical theory is that the utilitarian can compare similar predicted solutions and use a point system to determine which choice is more beneficial for more people. This point system provides a logical and rational argument for each decision and allows a person to use it on a case-by-case context.

There are two types of utilitarianism: act utilitarianism and rule utilitarianism. *Act utilitarianism* adheres exactly to the definition of utilitarianism as described in the above section. In act utilitarianism, a person performs the acts that benefit the most people, regardless of personal feelings or the societal constraints such as laws. *Rule utilitarianism*, however, takes into account the law and is concerned with fairness. A rule utilitarian seeks to benefit the most people but through the fairest and most just means available. Therefore, added benefits of rule utilitarianism are that it values justice and doing good at the same time.

As is true of all ethical theories, however, both act and rule utilitarianism contain numerous flaws. Inherent in both are the flaws associated with predicting the future. Although people can use their life experiences to attempt to predict outcomes, no human being can be certain that his predictions will be true. This uncertainty can lead to unexpected results, making the utilitarian look unethical as time passes because his choice did not benefit the most people as he predicted.

Another assumption that a utilitarian must make is that he has the ability to compare the various types of consequences against each other on a similar scale. However, comparing material gains such as money against intangible gains such as happiness is impossible because their qualities differ so greatly.

Casuist
The **casuist ethical theory** compares a current ethical dilemma with examples of similar ethical dilemmas and their outcomes. This allows one to determine the severity of the situation and to create the best possible solution according to others' experiences. Usually, one will find examples that represent the extremes of the situation so that a compromise can be reached that will hopefully include the wisdom gained from the previous situations.

One drawback to this ethical theory is that there may not be a set of similar examples for a given ethical dilemma. Perhaps that which is controversial and ethically questionable is new and unexpected. Along the same line of thinking, this theory assumes that the results of the current ethical dilemma will be similar to results in the examples. This may not be necessarily true and would greatly hinder the effectiveness of applying this ethical theory.

Moral Relativists[7]
Moral relativists believe in time-and-place ethics, that is, ethical truths depend on the individuals and groups holding them. Arson is not always wrong in their book. If you live in a neighborhood in which drug dealers are operating a crystal meth lab or crack house, committing arson by burning down the meth labs is ethically justified. If you are a parent and your child is starving, stealing a loaf of bread is ethically correct. The proper resolution to ethical dilemmas is based upon weighing the competing factors at the moment and then making

utilitarian ethical theory
A theory that holds that the choice that yields the greatest benefit to the most people is the choice that is ethically correct.

casuist ethical theory
A theory that compares a current ethical dilemma with examples of similar ethical dilemmas and their outcomes.

moral relativists
Persons who believe that ethical truths depend on the individuals and groups holding them.

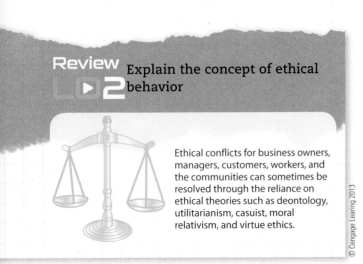

Ethical conflicts for business owners, managers, customers, workers, and the communities can sometimes be resolved through the reliance on ethical theories such as deontology, utilitarianism, casuist, moral relativism, and virtue ethics.

© Cengage Learning 2013

a determination to take the lesser of the evils as the resolution. Moral relativists do not believe in absolute rules. Their beliefs center on the pressure of the moment and whether the pressure justifies the action taken.

Virtue Ethics[8] Aristotle and Plato taught that solving ethical dilemmas requires training—that individuals solve ethical dilemmas when they develop and nurture a set of virtues. A **virtue** is a character trait valued as being good. Aristotle taught the importance of cultivating virtue in his students and then having them solve ethical dilemmas using those virtues once they had become an integral part of their being through their virtue training.

Some modern philosophers have embraced this notion of virtue and have developed lists of what constitutes a virtuous business person. Some common virtues for business people are: self-discipline, friendliness, caring, courage, compassion, trust, responsibility, honesty, determination, enthusiasm, and humility. You may see other lists of virtues that are longer or shorter but here is a good start for core business virtues.

LO 3
Ethical Behavior in Business

Depending upon which, if any, ethical theory a businessperson has accepted and uses in his/her daily conduct, the action taken may vary. For example, faced with bribing a foreign official to get a critically needed contract or shutting down a factory and laying off a thousand workers, a person following a deontology strategy would not pay the bribe. Why? A deontologist always follows the law. However, a moral relativist will probably pay the bribe.

While the boundaries of what is legal and what is not are often fairly clear (e.g., don't run a red light, don't steal money from a bank, and don't kill someone), the boundaries of ethical decision making are predicated on which ethical theory one is following. The law typically relies on juries to determine if an act is legal or illegal. Society determines whether an action is ethical or unethical. Sometimes society decides that a person acted unethically—recall the O. J. Simpson murder trial—but a jury may decide that no illegal act was committed. The jury in Simpson's most recent trial for armed robbery and kidnapping found him guilty (and obviously unethical). In a business-related case, a jury found Richard Scrushy, charged with a $1.4 billion fraud at HealthSouth Corporation, innocent on all counts. However, he was convicted and sentenced to seven years in prison in a separate state government bribery case. In 2009, Scrushy was ordered to pay nearly $2.9 billion to shareholders who sued over a massive accounting fraud that nearly sent HealthSouth into bankruptcy.[9] On the other hand, Bernard Ebbers, former CEO of WorldCom, was found guilty of securities fraud and filing false documents and was sentenced to 25 years in prison.

Morals are the rules people develop as a result of cultural values and norms. Culture is a socializing force that dictates what is right and wrong. Moral standards may also reflect the laws and regulations that affect social and economic behavior. Thus, morals can be considered a foundation of ethical behavior.

Morals are usually characterized as good or bad. "Good" and "bad" have different connotations, including "effective" and "ineffective." A good salesperson

virtue
A character trait valued as being good.

morals
The rules people develop as a result of cultural values and norms.

makes or exceeds the assigned quota. If the salesperson sells a new stereo or television set to a disadvantaged consumer—knowing full well that the person can't keep up the monthly payments—is the salesperson still a good one? What if the sale enables the salesperson to exceed his or her quota?

"Good" and "bad" can also refer to "conforming" and "deviant" behaviors. A doctor who runs large ads offering discounts on open-heart surgery would be considered bad, or unprofessional, in the sense of not conforming to the norms of the medical profession. "Bad" and "good" are also used to express the distinction between criminal and law-abiding behavior. And finally, different religions define "good" and "bad" in markedly different ways. A Muslim who eats pork would be considered bad, as would a fundamentalist Christian who drinks whiskey.

MORALITY AND BUSINESS ETHICS

Today's business ethics actually consist of a subset of major life values learned since birth. The values businesspeople use to make decisions have been acquired through family, educational, and religious institutions.

Ethical values are situation specific and time oriented. Nevertheless, everyone must have an ethical base that applies to conduct in the business world and in personal life. One approach to developing a personal set of ethics is to examine the consequences of a particular act. Who is helped or hurt? How long lasting are the consequences? What actions produce the greatest good for the greatest number of people? A second approach stresses the importance of rules. Rules come in the form of customs, laws, professional standards, and common sense. Consider these examples of rules:

→ Always treat others as you would like to be treated.

→ Copying copyrighted computer software is against the law.

→ It is wrong to lie, bribe, or exploit.

Another approach emphasizes the development of moral character within individuals. Ethical development can be thought of as having three levels:[10]

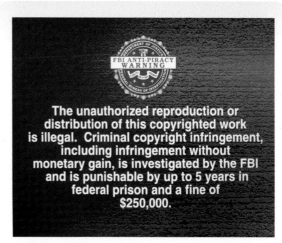

Ethical conduct in the business world and in personal life requires a personal set of ethics and adherence to rules and laws. The copyright notice on CDs and DVDs is often ignored by consumers, even though downloading or distributing copyrighted material for personal use or entertainment without permission from the copyright owner is against the law. Do you break the law or adhere to it?

→ **Preconventional morality**, the most basic level, is childlike. It is calculating, self-centered, and even selfish, based on what will be immediately punished or rewarded. Fortunately, most businesspeople have progressed beyond the self-centered and manipulative actions of preconventional morality.

→ **Conventional morality** moves from an egocentric viewpoint toward the expectations of society. Loyalty and obedience to the organization (or society) become paramount. At the level of conventional morality, a marketing decision maker would be concerned only with whether the proposed action is legal and how it will be viewed by others. This type of morality could be likened to the adage "When in Rome, do as the Romans do."

→ **Postconventional morality** represents the morality of the mature adult. At this level, people are less concerned about how others might see them and more concerned about how they see and judge themselves over the long run. A marketing decision maker who has attained a postconventional level of morality might ask, "Even though it is legal and will increase company profits, is it right

Exhibit 3.1 Unethical Practices Marketing Managers May Have to Deal with

- Entertainment and gift giving
- False or misleading advertising
- Misrepresentation of goods, services, or company capabilities
- Lying to customers in order to get the sale
- Manipulation of data (falsifying or misusing statistics or information)
- Misleading product or service warranties
- Unfair manipulation of customers
- Exploitation of children or disadvantaged groups
- Stereotypical portrayals of women, minority groups, or senior citizens
- Invasion of customer privacy
- Sexually oriented advertising appeals
- Product or service deception
- Unsafe products or services
- Price deception
- Price discrimination
- Unfair or inaccurate statements about competitors
- Smaller amounts of product in the same-size packages

© Cengage Learning 2013

in the long run? Might it do more harm than good in the end?"

ETHICAL DECISION MAKING

How do businesspeople make ethical decisions? There is no cut-and-dried answer. Some of the ethical issues managers face are shown in Exhibit 3.1. Studies show that the following factors tend to influence ethical decision making and judgments:[11]

→ **Extent of ethical problems within the organization:** Marketing professionals who perceive fewer ethical problems in their organizations tend to disapprove more strongly of "unethical" or questionable practices than those who perceive more ethical problems. Apparently, the healthier the ethical environment, the more likely that marketers will take a strong stand against questionable practices.

→ **Top-management actions on ethics:** Top managers can influence the behavior of marketing professionals by encouraging ethical behavior and discouraging unethical behavior. Research found that 13 percent of large-company top executives thought that having strong ethical traits was the most important leadership trait of CEOs.[12] The most important trait to the majority of respondents was the ability to inspire others (37 percent).[13] Other research found three ethics-related actions by managers have the greatest impact on employee ethics. These are: setting a good example, keeping promises and commitments, and supporting others in adhering to ethics standards.[14]

→ **Potential magnitude of the consequences:** The greater the harm done to victims, the more likely that marketing professionals will recognize a problem as unethical.

→ **Social consensus:** The greater the degree of agreement among managerial peers that an action is harmful, the more likely that marketers will recognize a problem as unethical.

→ **Probability of a harmful outcome:** The greater the likelihood that an action will result in a harmful outcome, the more likely that marketers will recognize a problem as unethical.

→ **Length of time between the decision and the onset of consequences:** The shorter the length of time between the action and the onset of negative consequences, the more likely that marketers will perceive a problem as unethical.

→ **Number of people to be affected:** The greater the number of persons affected by a negative outcome, the more likely that marketers will recognize a problem as unethical.

As you can see, many factors determine the nature of an ethical decision. Kellogg Company is the world's largest cereal maker, with sales over $13 billion. In 2010, the Federal Trade Commission said the company overstepped by claiming various types of its Rice Krispies cereals bolstered immunity. As a result, the company has agreed to abide by new restrictions regarding health claims the company made about its Frosted Mini-Wheats cereal. Jon Leibowitz, chairman of the FTC, said, "We expect more from a great American company than making dubious claims—not once but twice—that its cereals improve children's health."[15]

On packages, Kellogg claimed Rice Krispies "now helps support your child's immunity" with "25% daily value of antioxidants and nutrients—vitamins A, B, C and E." The back of boxes stated that Rice Krispies "has been improved to include antioxidants and nutrients that your family needs to help them stay healthy."

The FDA has also warned General Mills over its Cheerios cereal, saying the box's claims about heart benefits contain "serious violations" of federal law. In a warning letter the agency made public, the FDA said statements that Cheerios "is clinically proven to help lower cholesterol" make the cereal a drug under federal law.[16]

ETHICAL GUIDELINES AND TRAINING

Many organizations have become more interested in ethical issues. One sign of this interest is the increase in the number of large companies that appoint ethics officers—from virtually none a few years ago to almost 33 percent of large corporations now. More and more companies are providing ethics resources for their employees. Today over 70 percent of employees in the United States can seek advice on ethics questions via telephone, e-mail, Web, or in person. (See **www.ethics.org** for more information.) In addition, many companies of various sizes have developed a **code of ethics** as a guideline to help marketing managers and other employees make better decisions. Some of the most highly praised codes of ethics are those of Intel, IBM, Starbucks, and Costco.

Creating ethics guidelines has several advantages:

→ The guidelines help employees identify what their firm recognizes as acceptable business practices.

→ A code of ethics can be an effective internal control on behavior, which is more desirable than external controls like government regulation.

→ A written code helps employees avoid confusion when determining whether their decisions are ethical.

→ The process of formulating the code of ethics facilitates discussion among employees about what is right and wrong and ultimately leads to better decisions.

PepsiCo, like virtually all major corporations, has a code of ethics, sometimes referred to as a "code of conduct." PepsiCo has a single code of conduct for Pepsi and all of its subsidiaries around the world. Major topics include: respect for employees, global relations, health and safety, the environment, and a number of other factors. The code, as it applies to consumers, customers, suppliers, and competitors, is shown in Exhibit 3.2.

Businesses, however, must be careful not to make their code of ethics too vague or too detailed. Codes that are too vague give little or no guidance to employees in their day-to-day activities. Codes that are too detailed encourage employees to substitute rules for judgment. For instance, if employees are involved in questionable behavior, they may use the absence of a written rule as a reason to continue behaving that way, even though their conscience may be saying no. The checklist in Exhibit 3.3 is an example of a simple but helpful set of ethical guidelines. Following the checklist

code of ethics
A guideline to help marketing managers and other employees make better decisions.

Exhibit 3.2 Excerpt from PepsiCo's Code of Conduct

Consumers, Customers, Suppliers and Competitors

We are committed to the continuation of free enterprise and the legal and regulatory frameworks that support it. Therefore, we recognize the importance of laws that prohibit restraints of trade, predatory economic activities and unfair, deceptive or unethical business practices.

In all of our business dealings with consumers, customers, supplier and competitors, we will:

- Avoid any unfair or deceptive practice and always present our services and products in an honest and forthright manner.
- Treat all customers and suppliers honestly, fairly and objectively.
- Select suppliers based on merit, and make clear to all suppliers that we expect them to compete fairly and vigorously for our business.
- Compete vigorously and with integrity.
- Never comment on a competitor's product without a good basis for such statements.
- Comply with all competition laws, including those prohibiting agreements or understandings with competitors to fix prices or other sales terms, coordinate bids or divide sales territories, customers or product lines. These types of agreements with competitors are generally illegal in the United States and many other markets where we conduct business.

Source: Pepsico's Code of Conduct. Reprinted with permission.

will not guarantee the "rightness" of a decision, but it will improve the chances that the decision will be ethical. Although many companies have issued policies on ethical behavior, marketing managers must still put the policies into effect. They must address the classic "matter of degree" issue. For example, marketing researchers must often resort to deception to obtain unbiased answers to their research questions. Asking for a few minutes of a respondent's time is dishonest if the researcher knows the interview will last 45 minutes. Not only must management post a code of ethics, but it must also give examples of what is ethical and unethical for each item in the code. Moreover, top management must stress to all employees the importance of adhering to the company's code of ethics. Without a detailed code of ethics and top management's support, creating ethical guidelines becomes an empty exercise.

Ethics Training Ethics training is a good way to help employees put good ethics into practice. Because of the corporate scandals, such as Bernard Madoff's financial trickery costing investors billions, more and more companies are offering ethics training to their employees. Today, about 70 percent of all large employers (over 500 employees) provide ethics training.[17] Simply giving employees a long list of "dos and don'ts" is a start, but doesn't really help navigate the gray areas. What is needed then is a more contextual approach to ethics training.

Lockheed Martin is one firm that has moved to contextual ethics training. Recently, Manny Zulueta met with seven colleagues to watch a DVD. In one

Exhibit 3.3 Ethics Checklist

- Does the decision benefit one person or group but hurt or not benefit other individuals or groups? In other words, is my decision fair to all concerned?
- Would individuals or groups, particularly customers, be upset if they knew about my decision?
- Has important information been overlooked because my decision was made without input from other knowledgeable individuals or groups?
- Does my decision presume that my company is an exception to a common practice in this industry and that I therefore have the authority to break a rule?
- Would my decision offend or upset qualified job applicants?
- Will my decision create conflict between individuals or groups within the company?
- Will I have to pull rank or use coercion to implement my decision?
- Would I prefer to avoid the consequences of my decision?
- Did I avoid truthfully answering any of the above questions by telling myself that the risks of getting caught are low or that I could get away with the potentially unethical behavior?

© Cengage Learning 2013

scene, a worker complained to his manager's boss after the manager yelled at her workers. The manager apologized, but the worker soon felt that the manager was retaliating by giving him lousy assignments, nitpicking his work, and reprimanding him for arriving late. Mr. Zulueta, Lockheed Martin's senior vice president of shared services, then led what he says was a "nuanced" discussion about the ethical issues involved in that scene. Zulueta's colleagues rightly noted that they needed more information—they needed to put the scene in context—to discern whether the manager's actions were retaliatory.[18] Understanding the context of an ethical problem helps employees navigate the gray areas.

Do ethics training programs work? The National Business Ethics survey found that fewer employees said that they had witnessed misconduct on the job; the measure fell from 56 percent in 2007 to 49 percent in 2009. Sixty-three percent said that they had reported misconduct when they had seen it (up from 58 percent). Overall, perceived pressure to commit an ethics violation—to cut corners or worse—was 8 percent.[19] Not only, it seems, are employees becoming more ethical, but they also believe in the value of ethics training programs. Of the workers surveyed, 90 percent said that ethics training is useful or somewhat useful to them.[20] Senior managers were most likely to find ethics training the most valuable.

The Most Ethical Companies Each year, *Ethisphere* magazine (targeted toward top management and focused on ethical leadership) examines over 5,000 companies in 30 separate industries seeking the world's most ethical companies. It then lists the top 100. The magazine uses a rigorous format to identify true ethical leadership. A few of the selected winners are shown in Exhibit 3.4.

Forcing Ethical Standards on Others A company such as Walmart has a huge amount of power over its suppliers. As the world's largest seller of toys, Walmart ordered its suppliers to meet a new set of children's-product safety requirements that goes far beyond existing government regulations. The standards include strict limits for lead and a broad array of other heavy metals and chemicals that have been linked to various medical and developmental problems in children.

The initiative also encourages suppliers to mark children's products with "traceability information," including the factory in which the goods were made. About 80 percent of the toys sold in the United States, including those marketed by U.S.-based toy makers, are manufactured in China.

Walmart's action, and similar moves by rivals such as Target and Toys "R" Us, follow the discovery of high lead levels in children's products, the recall of about 25 million toys in 2007, and toy-related deaths. The Walmart standards are estimated to have increased toy manufacturing costs by 5 to 7 percent.[21]

Walmart also has implemented strict new quality, environmental, and safety standards for its Chinese suppliers. It also has begun requiring specific levels of energy efficiency for its Chinese suppliers. Walmart feels that the standards will help because in some factories up to 20 percent of the goods produced were rejected as not up to quality standards. This resulted in a lot of waste. Walmart hopes to eliminate customer returns due to defective merchandise.[22]

The ultimate question many ask is, "Does being ethical pay?" We explore this issue in the "Customer Experience" box on page 67.

CULTURAL DIFFERENCES IN ETHICS

Studies suggest that ethical beliefs vary only a little from culture to culture. Certain practices, however, such as the use of illegal payments and bribes, are far more acceptable in some places than in others. Some countries have a dual standard

Exhibit 3.4 **Selected Winners of the World's Most Ethical Companies Award**

ACCENTURE

Douglas G. Scrivner, General Counsel, Secretary & Compliance Officer

In Accenture's ethics and compliance program, the company uses six "core values" of stewardship, best people, client value creation, one global network, respect for the individual and integrity.

Douglas Scrivner, General Counsel at Accenture, says that ethics and compliance can't be effective if they're only seen as "bolt-ons," or something that is only done at the end of the day after the "regular work" is complete. "We aim to put ethics and compliance into the way our people work and lead. We seek to leverage existing processes, procedures, structures and functions to ensure the outcomes we are expecting and alignment with the goals of the organization," says Scrivner.

To better understand how the company's ethics and compliance program is being received by employees, Accenture uses employee surveys, risk assessments and results of corporate investigations. Scrivner notes that in a recent survey, over 90 percent of employees feel that Accenture is highly ethical and that the company's commitment to integrity has been communicated to the whole company.

"Those are excellent scores for a company of more than 181,000 people," Scrivner says. "We haven't arrived at the end of our journey (and never will), but I am confident that we continue to move in the right direction and continually reinforce our commitment and our expectations in this area."

CATERPILLAR

Ed Scott, Chief Ethics & Compliance Officer

Ed Scott, Chief Ethics & Compliance Officer at Caterpillar, says that the ethics at Caterpillar start at the top, beginning with CEO Jim Owens. "Our leaders work to ensure that Our Values in Action [Caterpillar's Code of Conduct] are part of everyday life at Caterpillar," says Scott. "They take various opportunities to incorporate Our Values in Action into their communications. In turn, Caterpillar employees are expected to know and live by Our Values in Action."

Scott says that he is most proud of the way that the company's ethics program reaches out to the thousands of Caterpillar employees working in around 50 countries in all regions of the globe. "Over the past few years, we've made significant strides in globalizing our approach," says Scott. "One item in particular is our Annual Assessment and Questionnaire. It is offered in 14 languages and all of our employees are required to complete this. You can imagine that with so many employees, this is a major undertaking.

Scott believes that any company's ethics and compliance program is only as strong as the culture behind it. "You can have the best ethics and compliance program in the world, but if you don't have an ethical culture supported by strong leadership the program will ultimately not succeed," Scott says. "Generations of Caterpillar people built our honorable reputation and ethical culture through their words and deeds."

UNILEVER

Iskah C. Singh, Deputy Global Code & Compliance Officer, Associate General Counsel

Unilever uses a number of approaches to engage its employees in the company ethics and compliance program, according to Iskah Singh, Associate General Counsel for Unilever.

"Our employee training and education program raises awareness and reinforces the values of the Code of Business Principles," says Singh. "Also, employees annually acknowledge understanding and compliance with our Code of Business Principles. In addition to traditional training modules, we have utilized smaller 'Ethical Moments'—3 to 5 minute clips—to raise awareness and strengthen the open ethics and compliance environment."

Singh says that a strong ethics and compliance program provides many benefits: solid leadership; encourages and facilitates open communication; clearly articulates the standards of business conduct; continually reinforces ethics awareness and actively demonstrates that the values are not just words on paper but are lived on a daily basis.

Singh notes that a key differentiator in Unilever's ethics and compliance program is the fact that employees deep within the organization can look to their immediate supervisors as examples of ethical leadership. "It is here that an ethical culture is cultivated and the standards and values of Unilever's Code of Business Principles is given meaning," says Singh.

Source: Selected Winner for the World's Most Ethical Companies Award adapted from *Ethisphere,* June 8, 2010.

concerning illegal payments. For example, German businesspeople typically treat bribes as tax-deductible business expenses. In Russia, bribes and connections in the government are essential for doing business. For instance, bribing a public official is the fastest method for accomplishing bureaucratic tasks such as registering a business. What we call bribery is a natural way of doing business in some other

customer experience

Will Consumers Buy and Pay More for an Ethical Company's Products?

In a perfect world, consumers would pay more for good companies' products than unethical companies' products if the product were relatively homogenous. But does this really happen? To find out, researchers conducted a series of experiments. They showed consumers the same products—coffee and T-shirts—but told one group the items had been made using high ethical standards and another group that low standards had been used. A control group got no information. In all of the tests, consumers were willing to pay a slight premium for the ethically made goods. But they went much further in the other direction: They would buy unethically made products only at a steep discount.[23]

Yet, if the above research is true, then why, for example, does furniture made from rainforest (versus tree farm) wood continue to sell? Why have market forces not eliminated animal testing in the cosmetic industry? A new research study has attempted to discern whether or not consumers are practicing moral hypocrisy. The researchers found that because most retail environments present consumers with a relatively large assortment of products, the buying decision becomes quite complex.

When deciding which product to buy, consumers decide which attributes to *include* as buying possibilities as opposed to which attributes to *exclude*.

For example, a consumer decides to buy a new cell phone, or a device that includes a cell phone. Examining the vast array of choices, the shopper learns that some phones are made with child labor. One approach to selecting a phone is to *exclude* any phones made with child labor. However, the researchers found that, when faced with many choices, consumers typically use an *inclusion* strategy. That is, to simplify decision-making they consider only phones with desired attributes such as value-priced, 4G, performance, and style. Consumers ignore things that they don't want in a phone. Unfortunately, the *exclusion* attribute of "made by child labor" gets lost in the process.[24]

Since *Ethisphere* began its surveys of the world's most ethical (WME) companies in 2002, the WME have significantly outperformed the S&P 500 every year. Does this mean that it pays to be ethical? How can companies get more consumers to consider high ethics of the firm when making product or service choices?

---

cultures. Do these widespread practices suggest that global marketers should adopt a "When in Rome, do as the Romans do" mentality?

Yet another example of cultural differences is the Japanese reluctance to enforce their antitrust laws. Everyday business practices, from retail pricing to business structuring, ignore antitrust regulations against restraint of trade, monopolies, and price discrimination. Not surprisingly, the Japanese are tolerant of scandals involving antitrust violations, favoritism, price fixing, bribery, and other activities considered unethical in the United States.

Concern about U.S. corporations' use of illegal payments and bribes in international business dealings led to passage of the **Foreign Corrupt Practices Act.** This act prohibits U.S. corporations from making illegal payments to public officials of foreign governments to obtain business rights or to enhance their business dealings in those countries. The act has been criticized for putting U.S. businesses at a competitive disadvantage. Many contend that bribery is an unpleasant but necessary part of international business.

ETHICAL DILEMMAS RELATED TO DEVELOPING COUNTRIES

For companies, the benefits of seeking international growth are several. A company that cannot grow further in its domestic market may reap increased sales and economies of scale not only by exporting its product but also by producing it abroad.

Foreign Corrupt Practices Act
A law that prohibits U.S. corporations from making illegal payments to public officials of foreign governments to obtain business rights or to enhance their business dealings in those countries.

A company may also wish to diversify its political and economic risk by spreading its operations across several nations.

Expanding into developing countries offers multinational companies the benefits of low-cost labor and natural resources. But many multinational firms have been criticized for exploiting developing countries. Although the firms' business practices may be legal, many business ethicists argue that they are unethical. The problem is compounded by the intense competition among developing countries for industrial development. Ethical standards are often overlooked by governments hungry for jobs or tax revenues.

In the face of the rising number of smokers in their country, the Malaysian government has banned the advertising of tobacco products. Many firms in the tobacco industry skirt the law by sponsoring sports and entertainment events or by advertising their brands without referring to cigarettes.

Take the tobacco industry, for instance. With tobacco sales decreasing and regulations stiffening in the United States and Western Europe, tobacco companies have come to believe that their future lies elsewhere: in China, Asia, Africa, Eastern Europe, and Russia. Despite the known health risks of their product, the large tobacco companies are pushing their way into markets that typically have few marketing or health-labeling controls. In Hungary, Marlboro cigarettes are sometimes handed out to young fans at pop concerts. In the last ten years, cigarette advertising on Japanese television has soared from 40th to 2nd place in air time and value; it appears even during children's shows.

Interestingly, at a time when smoking is being discouraged in the United States, U.S. trade representatives are talking to developing countries like China and Thailand about lowering their tariffs on foreign cigarettes. Japan, Taiwan, and South Korea have already given in to the threats. Entering these developing countries, the tobacco companies and trade representatives insist, will help U.S. tobacco manufacturers make up for losses in their home market. Worldwide, tobacco causes nearly 5.4 million deaths per year. It is expected to rise to 18 million by 2030.[25] Is it ethical for tobacco executives to promote and export this product?

Environmental issues are another example. As U.S. environmental laws and regulations gain strength, many companies are moving their operations to developing countries, where it is often less expensive to operate. These countries generally enforce minimal or no clean-air and waste-disposal regulations. For example, an increasing number of U.S. companies have located manufacturing plants called *maquiladoras* in Mexico, along the U.S.-Mexican border. Many blame the

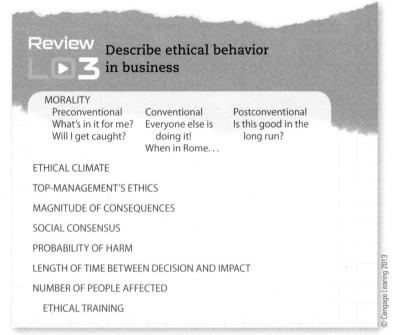

Review
LO3 Describe ethical behavior in business

MORALITY		
Preconventional What's in it for me? Will I get caught?	Conventional Everyone else is doing it! When in Rome…	Postconventional Is this good in the long run?

ETHICAL CLIMATE

TOP-MANAGEMENT'S ETHICS

MAGNITUDE OF CONSEQUENCES

SOCIAL CONSENSUS

PROBABILITY OF HARM

LENGTH OF TIME BETWEEN DECISION AND IMPACT

NUMBER OF PEOPLE AFFECTED

ETHICAL TRAINING

maquiladoras for "not putting back into the border area what they have been taking out," referring to the region's inadequate sewers and water-treatment plants.

Because Mexico has been eager to attract foreign employers, *maquiladoras* pay little in taxes, which would normally go toward improving the country's infrastructure. Cuidad Juárez, a populous and polluted *maquiladora* city bordering El Paso, Texas, generates millions of gallons of sewage a day and has a minimal sewage system.

Corporate Social Responsibility

Corporate social responsibility is a business's concern for society's welfare. This concern is demonstrated by managers who consider both the long-range best interests of the company and the company's relationship to the society within which it operates. A recent addition to social responsibility theory is called **sustainability**. This refers to the idea that socially responsible companies will outperform their peers by focusing on the world's economic, social, and environmental problems and viewing them as opportunities to build profits and help the world at the same time. It is also the notion that companies cannot thrive for long (i.e., lack sustainability) in a world where billions of people are desperately poor and natural resources are being wasted and/or destroyed. Only business organizations have the talent, creativity, and executive ability to do the job.

SUSTAINABILITY

When an organization focuses on sustainability, it is acting with long-term consequences in mind and managing a business such that its processes or overall state can be maintained indefinitely. So a company that believes in sustainability will integrate long-term economic, environmental, and social factors into their business strategies while maintaining their competitiveness and brand reputation. Thus, sustainability requires effective planning for long-run economic growth. This requires focusing on product and service innovation and building customer loyalty. It also means having the highest ethical standards and a meaningful code of conduct. Sustainability also demands managing human resources to maintain workforce capabilities and employee satisfaction.

Sustainability is not simply "green marketing." (This concept is discussed on page 75.) Environmental sustainability is an important component of the sustainability philosophy. An environmentally sustainable process contributes to keeping the environment healthy by using renewable resources and by avoiding actions that depreciate the environment.

Each year Dow Jones evaluates over 5,000 firms around the world for inclusion in its Dow Jones Sustainability Index. The index includes 317 companies that represent leadership in global sustainability. Recent additions to the Index include: Johnson & Johnson, Coca-Cola, and Samsung Electronics; deletions were: Mitsubishi and SABMiller. Several firms were identified as "best in their business sector." A few examples are: Adidas (personal and household goods), BMW (autos), Kingfisher (retail), Nokia (technology), and Unilever (food and beverage).[26]

STAKEHOLDERS AND SOCIAL RESPONSIBILITY

Another aspect of social responsibility is **stakeholder theory**. This says that social responsibility is paying attention to the interest of every affected stakeholder in

corporate social responsibility
Business's concern for society's welfare.

sustainability
The idea that socially responsible companies will outperform their peers by focusing on the world's social problems and viewing them as opportunities to build profits and help the world at the same time.

stakeholder theory
A theory that holds that social responsibility is paying attention to the interest of every affected stakeholder in every aspect of a firm's operation.

Exhibit 3.5 Stakeholders in a Typical Corporation

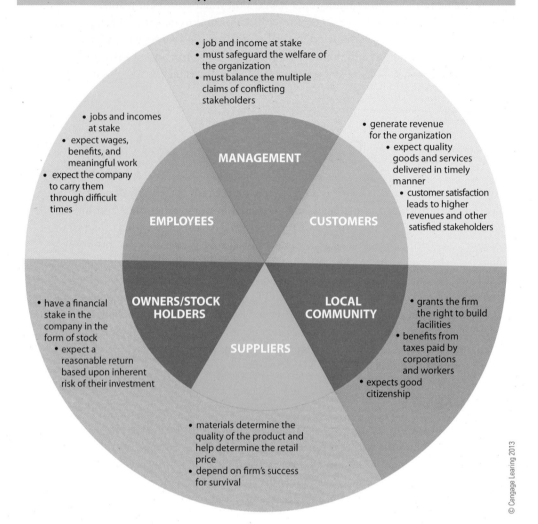

MANAGEMENT
- job and income at stake
- must safeguard the welfare of the organization
- must balance the multiple claims of conflicting stakeholders

EMPLOYEES
- jobs and incomes at stake
- expect wages, benefits, and meaningful work
- expect the company to carry them through difficult times

CUSTOMERS
- generate revenue for the organization
- expect quality goods and services delivered in timely manner
- customer satisfaction leads to higher revenues and other satisfied stakeholders

OWNERS/STOCK HOLDERS
- have a financial stake in the company in the form of stock
- expect a reasonable return based upon inherent risk of their investment

LOCAL COMMUNITY
- grants the firm the right to build facilities
- benefits from taxes paid by corporations and workers
- expects good citizenship

SUPPLIERS
- materials determine the quality of the product and help determine the retail price
- depend on firm's success for survival

every aspect of a firm's operation.[27] The stakeholders in a typical corporation are shown in Exhibit 3.5.

→ **Employees** have their jobs and incomes at stake. If the firm moves or closes, employees often face a severe hardship. In return for their labor, employees expect wages, benefits, and meaningful work. In return for their loyalty, workers expect the company to carry them through difficult times.

→ **Management** plays a special role, as they also have a stake in the corporation. Part of their stake is like that of the employees. On the other hand, management must safeguard the welfare of the organization. Sometimes this means balancing the multiple claims of conflicting stakeholders. For example, stockholders want a higher return on investment and perhaps lower costs by moving factories overseas. This naturally conflicts with employees, the local community, and perhaps suppliers.

→ **Customers** generate the revenue for the organization. In exchange, they expect high-quality goods and services delivered in a timely manner. Customer satisfaction leads to higher revenues and the ability to enhance the satisfaction of other stakeholders.

→ **The local community**, through its government, grants the firm the right to build facilities. In turn, it benefits directly from local taxes paid by the corporation and indirectly by property and sales taxes paid by the workers. The firm is expected to be a good citizen by paying a fair wage, not polluting the environment, and so forth.

→ **Suppliers** are vital to the success of the firm. If a critical part, for example, is not available for an assembly line, then production grinds to a halt. The materials supplied determine the quality of the product produced and create a cost floor, which helps determine the retail price. In turn, the firm is the customer of the supplier and is therefore vital to the success and survival of the supplier. Small firms who sold most of their production to Walmart and were subsequently dropped by Walmart have sometimes gone bankrupt.

→ **Owners** have a financial stake in the form of stock in a corporation. They expect a reasonable return based upon the amount of inherent risk on their investment. Often managers and employees have a portion of their retirement funds in company stock. In the case of Enron's bankruptcy, many workers lost their entire retirement savings.

One theorist suggests that total corporate social responsibility has four components: economic, legal, ethical, and philanthropic. The **pyramid of corporate social responsibility** portrays economic performance as the foundation for the other three responsibilities. At the same time that it pursues profits (economic responsibility), however, a business is expected to obey the law (legal responsibility); to do what is right, just, and fair (ethical responsibilities); and to be a good corporate citizen (philanthropic responsibility). These four components are distinct but together constitute the whole. Still, if the company doesn't make a profit, then the other three responsibilities are moot.

L○5

Arguments Against and for Corporate Social Responsibility

Today very few managers are against social responsibility initiatives. The debate, instead, is the degree and kinds of social responsibility that an organization should pursue.

ARGUMENTS AGAINST CORPORATE SOCIAL RESPONSIBILITY

Skeptics say business should focus on making a profit and leave social and environmental problems to nonprofit organizations (like the World Wildlife Federation or the Sierra Club) and government. The late economist Milton Friedman believed that the free market, not companies, should decide what is best for the world. He asked, "If businesspeople do have a social responsibility other than making maximum profits for stockholders, how are they to know what it is?"[28] Friedman argued that when business executives spend more money than they need to—to purchase

pyramid of corporate social responsibility
A model that suggests corporate social responsibility is composed of economic, legal, ethical, and philanthropic responsibilities and that the firm's economic performance supports the entire structure.

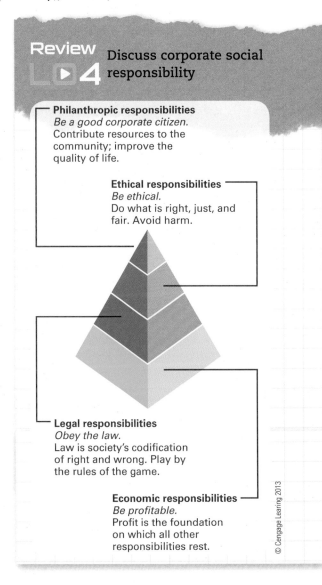

Review
L○4

Discuss corporate social responsibility

Philanthropic responsibilities
Be a good corporate citizen.
Contribute resources to the community; improve the quality of life.

Ethical responsibilities
Be ethical.
Do what is right, just, and fair. Avoid harm.

Legal responsibilities
Obey the law.
Law is society's codification of right and wrong. Play by the rules of the game.

Economic responsibilities
Be profitable.
Profit is the foundation on which all other responsibilities rest.

© Cengage Learing 2013

© iStockphoto.com/Juan Facundo Mora Soria

delivery vehicles with hybrid engines or to pay higher wages in developing countries, or even to donate company funds to charity—they are spending shareholders' money to further their own agendas. It is better to pay dividends and let the shareholders give the money away, if they choose.

Another argument is that businesses are created to produce goods and services, and not to handle welfare activities. They don't have the expertise to make social decisions. And if managers take time and monies to pursue social responsibilities, it will take away from the primary goals of the firm.

A final argument is that being socially responsible might damage the company in the global marketplace. That is, cleaning up the environment, ensuring product safety, and donating money and time for social causes all raise costs. This will be reflected in the final prices of the goods and services a company sells. In countries that don't emphasize social responsibility, a company will have lower costs because it doesn't engage in activities related to social responsibility. If the American company competes with the foreign competitor in the global marketplace, it will be at an economic disadvantage.

ARGUMENTS FOR SOCIAL RESPONSIBILITY

The most basic argument for social responsibility is that it is simply the right thing to do. Some societal problems have been brought about by corporations such as pollution and poverty-level wages; it is the responsibility of business to right these wrongs. Another position is that business has the resources, so business should be given the chance to solve social problems. For example, business can provide a fair work environment, safe products, and informative advertising.

Another, more pragmatic, reason for being socially responsible is that, if business isn't responsible, then government will create new regulations and perhaps levy fines against corporations. Allegheny Ludlum Corporation, a maker of specialty stainless steel, recently agreed to pay a $1.6 million penalty for violating the Clean Air Act. The company agreed to phase out the old mill in 2010 to be followed by construction of a state-of-the-art mill expected to cost $1.5 billion.[29] To the extent that business polices itself with self-disciplined standards and guidelines, government intervention can be avoided.

A final argument for social responsibility is that it can be a profitable undertaking. Smart companies, they say, can prosper and build shareholder value by tackling global problems. For General Electric, selling more wind power and energy-efficient locomotives is a no-brainer. When it comes to philanthropy, supply chain audits designed to keep GE from being linked to sweatshops, or decisions about granting domestic-partner benefits, the business case usually comes down to GE's reputation and its desire to attract and engage great people. Some years back, for example, GE decided not to sell low-end ultrasound machines in China (and to put warning labels on the high-end machines it did sell) because it did not want the machines to be used for gender screening that could lead to abortions. The potential harm to GE's image was too great to take the risk.

But applying that kind of cost-benefit analysis to decisions with moral dimensions is a tricky business. Although GE operates in more than 100 countries, it has decided not to do business in Myanmar because the government there is a notorious violator of human rights and has been spotlighted by human-rights groups—and because the business upside is limited. GE has judged that it has more to lose than gain by being there.

Walmart has experienced its share of criticism for not paying a living wage, putting small independent firms out of business, and using too much energy. However, Walmart has aggressively become proactive toward the environment and hopes to make money by "being green." The firm vows to use 100 percent renewable energy, drastically reduce waste through recycling, and sell "sustainable" products that are more environmentally friendly. Cutting energy use is saving money, and consumers appreciate Walmart's forays into organic cotton products and coffee certified to have earned farm workers a decent wage.

Switching stores to more efficient light bulbs and adding skylights for natural light has trimmed Walmart's electricity bill by 17 percent since 2002. Using less packaging on house-brand toys will save $2.4 million annually in shipping costs. Even Walmart's push to slash America's electricity use—and thus greenhouse gas emissions—by selling 100 million compact fluorescent bulbs a year has a bottom-line benefit. Customers will save $3 billion and the expectation is that these savings will come back in terms of purchases at Walmart.[30]

Arguments for social responsibility include that it is the right thing to do, it is the responsibility of business to right wrongs they have contributed to, and it can be a profitable undertaking. Walmart's push to slash America's electricity use and reduce carbon emissions by selling compact fluorescent bulbs has a bottom-line benefit: Customers will save money and these savings will come back in terms of purchases at Walmart.

GROWTH OF SOCIAL RESPONSIBILITY

Social responsibility of businesses is growing around the world. A recent study of social responsibility, in selected countries, asked the following: "Does your company consider social responsibility factors when making business decisions?" The percentage of firms that said "yes" were: Brazil, 62 percent; Canada, 54 percent; Australia, 52 percent; America, 47 percent; India, 38 percent; China, 35 percent; Mexico, 26 percent.[31] Another survey found that companies around the globe are coming under increasing pressure from governments, advocacy groups, investors, prospective employees, employees, and consumers to make their organizations more socially responsible. In turn, firms are seeing social responsibility as an opportunity. Of the respondents, 87 percent believed that social responsibility can aid in improving operational efficiency and 69 percent felt that it will lead to new revenue opportunities.[32]

The UN Global Compact One way that U.S. firms can do more is to join the UN's Global Compact. The United Nations Global Compact, the world's largest global corporate citizenship initiative, has seen its ranks swell over the past few years. In 2001—the first full year after its launch—just 67 companies joined, agreeing to abide by ten principles covering, among other things, human rights, labor practices, and the environment. The ten principles are shown in Exhibit 3.6. In 2010, there were more than 7,700 participants in 130 countries around the world.[33]

Firms are realizing that corporate social responsibility isn't easy or quick. It doesn't work without long-term strategy and effort, and coordination throughout the enterprise. It doesn't always come cheap, either. And the payoff, both to society and the business itself, isn't always immediate. Businesses say they want to be responsible citizens, but that's often not their only reason for taking action. In a recent survey, the United Nations Global Compact asked members why they had joined. "Networking opportunities" was the second-most-popular reason; "Addressing humanitarian concerns" was third. The first was to "Increase trust in company."[34]

Proactive Social Responsibility Two very different companies that are often lauded for their social responsibility are TOMS Shoes and ice cream company Ben & Jerry's.

Exhibit 3.6 The Principles of the UN Global Compact

Human Rights

- Principle 1: Businesses should support and respect the protection of internationally proclaimed human rights; and
- Principle 2: make sure that they are not complicit in human rights abuses.

Labor Standards

- Principle 3: Businesses should uphold the freedom of association and the effective recognition of the right to collective bargaining;
- Principle 4: the elimination of all forms of forced and compulsory labor;
- Principle 5: the effective abolition of child labor; and
- Principle 6: the elimination of discrimination in respect of employment and occupation.

Environment

- Principle 7: Businesses should support a precautionary approach to environmental challenges;
- Principle 8: undertake initiatives to promote greater environmental responsibility; and
- Principle 9: encourage the development and diffusion of environmentally friendly technologies.

Anti-Corruption

- Principle 10: Businesses should work against corruption in all its forms, including extortion and bribery.

Source: www.unglobalcompact.org/AboutTheGC/TheTenPrinciples/index.html, accessed January 21, 2009

Ben & Jerry's[35]

Ben & Jerry's was founded and built on the concept of sustainability before the term became a business buzzword. The firm's dedication to society and its stakeholders is exemplified by the three components of its mission statement:

→ **Social Mission**—to operate the company in a way that actively recognizes the central role that business plays in society by initiating innovative ways to improve the quality of life locally, nationally, and internationally.

→ **Product Mission**—to make, distribute, and sell the finest-quality all-natural ice cream and euphoric concoctions with a continued commitment to incorporating wholesome, natural ingredients and promoting business practices that respect the Earth and the environment.

→ **Economic Mission**—to operate the company on a sustainable financial basis of profitable growth, increasing value for our stakeholders and expanding opportunities for development and career growth for our employees.

The mission statement also discusses eliminating injustices in the world through their day-to-day business activities. Ben & Jerry's strives to create economic opportunities for people around the globe. The firm recognizes that manufacturing creates waste and they try to minimize their impact on the environment. Making ice cream requires a number of raw ingredients. The firm supports sustainable and safe methods of food production that reduces environmental degradation, maintains the productivity of the land over time, and supports the economic viability of family farms and rural communities.

Ben & Jerry's has created a large number of initiatives and programs to make social responsibility a reality. The Ben & Jerry's Foundation gives over $2 million a year to nonprofit, grassroots organizations working for progressive social change. They buy eggs only from cage-free farms. Working with Yoko Ono, Ben & Jerry's launched "Whirled Peace," named for John Lennon. They then kicked off a search for modern-day peace pioneers on their Web site. Two winners were named and each organization was awarded $10,000.

Recently, Ben & Jerry's announced its commitment to use only fair trade ingredients across its entire global flavor portfolio. From Cherry Garcia to Chocolate Fudge Brownie, all of the flavors in all of the countries where Ben & Jerry's is sold will be converted to Fair Trade Certified ingredients by the end of 2013. Ben & Jerry's was the first ice cream company in the world to use Fair Trade Certified ingredients starting in 2005, and today it's racing ahead as the first ice cream company to make such a significant commitment to fair trade across its global portfolio.

Company co-founder Jerry Greenfield said, "Fair trade is about making sure people get their fair share of the pie. The whole concept of fair trade goes to the heart of our values and sense of right and wrong. Nobody wants to buy something that was made by exploiting somebody else." Ben & Jerry's fair trade commitment means that every needed ingredient available through a Fair Trade Certified source is used. Globally, this involves converting up to 121 different chunks and swirls, working across eleven different ingredients such as cocoa, banana, vanilla and other flavorings, fruits, and nuts. It also means working with fair-trade cooperatives that total a combined membership of over 27,000 farmers.

Ben & Jerry's fun flavors are paired with a commitment to social responsibility that gives the company a highly unique selling point.

TOMS Shoes[36]

In 2006, Blake Mycoskie took off from his online driver's education school business and went to Argentina. There he met a few people involved in a shoe drive for children outside of Buenos Aires. He learned that the children were not allowed to go to school unless they wore shoes. So touched by the experience, Mycoskie grew determined to help more kids on a long-term basis. When he returned to California, his revolutionary business model was created and named simply: TOMS Shoes.

TOMS' premise is simple. With every pair of shoes a customer buys, TOMS will give a pair of shoes to a child in need. One for one. All TOMS Shoes products are made in environmentally friendly factories, in various countries, that pay a fair wage. Since the beginning, TOMS has given away over 600,000 pairs of shoes.

TOMS has started "One Day Without Shoes" to spread awareness about the impact a simple pair of shoes can have on child's life. Once a year, TOMS asks people to go barefoot for the day, or part of the day, to experience a life without shoes firsthand. To date, over 250,000 people have participated in over 1,600 events around the world. Demi Moore walked onto the set of the *Tonight Show with Jay Leno* without shoes.

Blake Mycoskie spends about 25 days a month traveling around the world speaking to companies and universities about his business model. His goal is to inspire the next generation of entrepreneurs to help make the world a better place.

Ben & Jerry's and TOMS Shoes are models of social responsibility with the inspiration coming from their founders. Other, long-established corporations were created before social responsibility was a business mantra. Their success in becoming socially responsible has moved forward at varying paces. Sometimes a nudge is necessary to get a company moving, as the Global Perspectives box explains.

GREEN MARKETING

An outgrowth of the social responsibility movement is green marketing. **Green marketing** is the development and marketing of products designed to minimize negative effects on the physical environment or to improve the environment. A study by

green marketing
The development and marketing of products designed to minimize negative effects on the physical environment or to improve the environment.

Social Media Push Nestlé to Sustainability Action

During the spring of 2010, Greenpeace decided to take on food giant Nestlé over its purchases of palm oil for use in Kit Kat candy bars and other products. Greenpeace created a video on YouTube that linked Kit Kat to destroying the rainforest. Protestors deluged Nestlé's Facebook page and peppered Twitter with claims that Nestlé is contributing to destruction of Indonesia's rain forest, potentially exacerbating global warming and endangering orangutans.

Nestlé said it had already decided to stop dealing with the firm Sinar Mas, which supplied just 1.25 percent of the palm oil Nestlé used in 2009. It says it bought only a tiny fraction of the firm's output, so any impact was negligible, and that it is working toward buying only environmentally sustainable palm oil. Nestlé also issued a statement saying, "We share the deep concern about the serious environmental threat to rain forests and peat fields in Southeast Asia caused by the planting of palm oil plantations."

Greenpeace replied that rain forests play a crucial role in regulating our climate and absorbing CO_2. The companies that produce palm oil are cutting down the lungs of the planet and contributing to making Indonesia the third largest carbon emitter after the United States and China. Deforestation is actually responsible for more carbon emissions than all the cars, trucks, and planes in the world. Sinar Mas is the largest producer of palm oil in Indonesia. Greenpeace calls the firm the "notorious forest destroyer." It also said that the contract cancellations do not go nearly far enough to protect Indonesian rain forests because Nestlé will still be using Sinar Mas palm oil but just getting it from other suppliers.

By May 2010, Nestlé realized it needed to do more to stop the Facebook backlash. It announced that it had partnered with the Forest Trust, a nonprofit group that helps businesses develop practices to harvest forests sustainably. The partnership is designed to reduce the social and environmental impacts of Nestlé's corporate supply chain by severing ties to companies that contribute to deforestation. The first issue addressed was its use of palm oil—Nestlé significantly reduced its use of palm oil in 2011. Greenpeace considers this a major victory.[37]

Can you think of other instances where social media may be used to encourage social responsibility? Why do you think that it took a social media campaign before Nestlé took action to push rain forest sustainability?

PricewaterhouseCoopers states that in 25 years the Earth will run out of raw materials, assuming the top 500 global companies grow at 4 to 5 percent annually.[38]

To make the sale, the green marketer may even use a traditional non-green benefit. For example, General Electric energy-efficient CFL floodlights are good for the environment. The promotion theme is "Long life for hard to reach places." GE is selling convenience because the floodlight doesn't need replacing as often.[39]

Some green products have practical consumer benefits that are readily apparent to consumers. A few examples are: energy-efficient washing machines and other appliances (cut electric bills), heat-reflective windows (cut air conditioning costs), and organic foods (no pesticides poisoning the food or planet). Each Dole organic banana has a sticker with a number. If you enter that number at **www.doleorganic.com,** a Google Earth application will show you the exact place where the fruit was grown.[40]

One company that has done an excellent job of going green is Waste Management, which disposes waste for 22 million customers. The company produces more renewable energy each year than the entire North American solar industry. Its Wheelabrator division combusts waste to create electricity. Waste Management has also had 33 working landfills certified as wildlife habitat preserves. The firm hopes to have 100 certified by the Wildlife Habitat Council before 2020.[41]

This ad demonstrates how Bourjois shows its dedication to organic products, using natural imagery and displaying organic certifications.

Other examples of green marketing abound. Walmart is building stores with baseboards and molding made of plastic left over from diaper manufacturing. ABInBev (parent company of Budweiser, among others) claims to recycle 99.8 percent of everything it uses at its Houston brewery.[42] By 2012, Philips, the electronics giant, aims to generate 30 percent of its total revenues off of green products.[43]

Recent surveys find that both consumers and many firms are still not motivated by the green movement. One survey of 1,500 consumers found that although 75 percent said that buying energy-efficient products is important to them, fewer than half have bought a green electronic product. Of that 1,500, 35 percent said they are unwilling to pay any premium for green products.[44] On the business side, a separate survey of 270 corporate communications professionals found that 43 percent expect to increase their marketing of their sustainability programs. However, only 36 percent said that their businesses embraced recycling and only 20 percent were actively pursuing more efficient electric energy usage.[45]

Review LO5 Describe the arguments for and against social responsibility

FOR	AGAINST
On the one hand:	**On the other hand:**
• it's the right thing to do • government will create new regulations and levy fines if firms aren't socially responsible • it can enhance a company's profitability	• the job of the corporation is to maximize profits for stockholders • businesses are better suited to produce goods and services and not to be involved in welfare services • if global competitors don't have to be socially responsible, they will have lower costs and can compete more effectively in the global marketplace

© Christoph Weihs/Shutterstock.com

LO6
Cause-Related Marketing

A sometimes controversial subset of social responsibility is **cause-related marketing**. Sometimes referred to as simply "cause marketing," it is the cooperative efforts of a "for-profit" firm and a "nonprofit organization" for mutual benefit. Cause-related marketing is sometimes used as any marketing effort for social or other charitable causes. Cause marketing differs from corporate giving (philanthropy) as the latter generally involves a specific donation that is tax deductible, while cause marketing is a marketing relationship not based on a straight donation.

Cause-related marketing is very popular and is estimated to generate about $7 billion a year in revenue. It creates good public relations for the firm and will often stimulate sales of the brand. Yet, the huge growth of cause-related marketing can lead to a case of consumer cause fatigue. It seems that every major firm supports a cause. Researchers have found that businesses need to guard against being perceived as "cause exploitative." Using a cause simply to sell more of a product can hurt both the cause and the company.[46]

Examples of cause-related marketing are abundant. Arby's asked customers for a $1 donation to help Big Brothers Big Sisters. In turn, the customer received a coupon for a dollar. Red, an organization to help fight AIDS, has partnered with the Gap, Emporio Armani, American Express, Apple, and Nike to provide AIDS education and medicine. At Christmas, Macy's made a $1 donation to the

Gap's (Product) RED clothing line is an example of cause-related marketing. It is discussed in more detail in this chapter's Case Study.

Image courtesy of The Advertising Archives

cause-related marketing
The cooperative marketing efforts between a "for-profit" firm and a "nonprofit organization."

© iStockphoto.com/Juan Facundo Mora Soria

Make-A-Wish Foundation when a letter was dropped off to Santa Claus. Whirlpool donated a range and refrigerator to every home built by Habitat for Humanity for a year. Nike and the Lance Armstrong Foundation have sold over $70 million Livestrong bracelets for cancer research.

CAUSE-RELATED MARKETING CONTROVERSY

Few causes have been more saturated with marketing than breast cancer awareness. Consumers can buy everything from food to toilet paper with labels that feature a pink ribbon. This generally signifies that for each product sold money is donated to breast cancer awareness. Yoplait ran a campaign that donated 10 cents to the Canadian Breast Cancer Foundation every time a consumer mailed back one of its yogurt carton lids. Aside from the fact that someone would have to eat three cartons of yogurt a day for more than three months just to raise $20, and that consumers spent more on postage than they raised with each lid, Yoplait left it to the fine print to state it was capping donations at $80,000—keeping the rest as profit.[47]

The Susan G. Komen Breast Cancer Foundation is on the receiving end of much cause-related marketing. Among its key partners are Frito-Lay, Ford, General Mills, and American Airlines. The Foundation recently put out an information piece entitled, "Five Questions to Ask before Participating in a Cause-Related Marketing Program." The questions are:

1. Is this company committed? Read the product packaging and promotional materials or display and visit the company Web site to make sure the company is credible and committed to the cause.

2. How is the program structured? Transparency is key. Is the company clearly stating how the money is raised and how much will be going to charity? For example, if it's a donation per purchase, ask how much of purchase price goes to charity—is it two percent or 10 percent—or some other amount? If there is a minimum contribution guaranteed by the company, what is the amount? Is there a maximum donation that will be made by the company?

3. Who does the program benefit? Does it support a well-managed, reputable nonprofit or fund? Again, the Komen Foundation recommends that consumers read Web sites. The Komen Foundation makes it very clear on its site who they are, how they structure programs, and how the monies are used. The Better Business Bureau's Wise Giving Alliance is one resource for information on nonprofit organizations.

4. How will the organization that benefits use my money? It should be abundantly clear where the monies go. What organization will they support? Will the dollars generated go to research, education, community programs, or all of the above? The Komen Foundation is very specific about their programs, activities, and grants awarded to support their mission to eradicate breast cancer as a life-threatening disease. Visit **ww5.komen.org** to view the Komen Foundation's most recent annual report.

5. Is the program meaningful to me? Is the program supporting a cause you believe in or have been touched by? Based on the details of the program and the potential

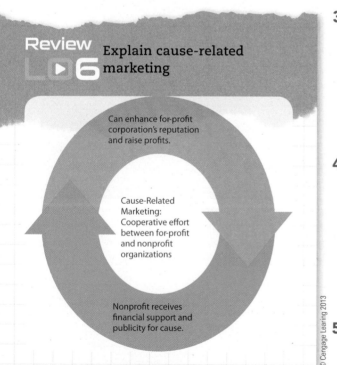

Review LO 6 Explain cause-related marketing

Can enhance for-profit corporation's reputation and raise profits.

Cause-Related Marketing: Cooperative effort between for-profit and nonprofit organizations

Nonprofit receives financial support and publicity for cause.

© Cengage Learing 2013

for dollars to be raised, does the program make sense to you? Selecting the right program is a personal choice based on your interests, your passions, and a cause that is important to you.[48]

Recently, the Komen Foundation found itself embroiled in controversy over its alliance with KFC. The goal was to raise $8.5 million through 50-cent-per-bucket donations. Soon, however, bloggers were attacking the partnership. Nancy Schwartz, a prominent blogger, notes, "How can funding breast cancer research with fried chicken sales make good sense? Especially when fried foods are known to contribute to obesity and other health problems and obesity increases the risks of breast cancer."[49] Margo Lucero, Komen director of global corporate relations, replied that the program's contributions in terms of consumer awareness and funding of Komen's mission made it the right thing to do.[50]

modes of social control

6

Amount Cingular paid the BBB for customer-driven intelligence

$50,000

Percent of large employers offer ethics training

70

Percent of surveyed employees who found ethics training useful

90

Years former WorldCom CEO sentenced to serve in prison for securities fraud

25

Percent Walmart trimmed off electricity bill by switching to efficient light bulbs and adding skylights

17

Countries participating in the United Nations Global Compact

130

Review and Applications

Explain the determinants of a civil society. The "social glue" that holds a society together is composed of six factors. They are: ethics, laws, formal and informal groups, self-regulation, the media, and an active civil society. All of these are necessary for a coherent, vibrant, and civil society. These six factors are more important in countries than ever before because of the increasing complexity of the global economy and the melding of customs and traditions within societies.

LO1

1.1 Explain how each of the six factors contributes to a civil society.

1.2 Why is a free and uncontrolled media important in a country?

1.3 Can customs and laws sometimes conflict, especially when a society experiences an influx of immigrants?

Explain the concept of ethical behavior. Ethics are the moral principles or values that generally govern the conduct of an individual or a group. Ethics can also be viewed as the standard of behavior by which conduct is judged. Ethical conflicts sometimes arise between businesses, customers, workers, and the surrounding community. Conflicts can sometimes be

LO2

resolved through the reliance on ethical theories. Ethical theories that are applicable to marketing include: deontology, utilitarianism, casuist, moral relativism, and virtue ethics.

2.1 It is sometimes said that ethics hold a person to higher standards than laws. Explain.

2.2 Moral relativists are basically time and place ethicists. Explain what this means.

2.3 Explain the differences between utilitarianism, casuist, and deontology theories.

LO3 **Describe ethical behavior in business.** The law typically relies on juries to determine whether an act is legal or illegal. Society determines whether an action is ethical or unethical. Morals are the rules that people develop as a result of cultural values and norms. More and more companies are using ethics training to help put good ethics into practice. Ethical beliefs vary a little from culture to culture. However, some ethical practices vary significantly from one culture to the next.

3.1 Explain the difference between ethics and morals and describe the relationship between the two.

3.2 What are the differences between preconventional morality, conventional morality, and postconventional morality? Give an example of each.

3.3 Give several examples of how ethical practices can vary from one culture to the next.

LO4 **Discuss corporate social responsibility.** Responsibility in business refers to a firm's concern for the way its decisions affect society. A second theory says that the corporation should always pay attention to the interests of its stakeholders. These are: management, customers, the local community, owners/stockholders, suppliers, and employees. Social responsibility has four components: economic, legal, ethical, and philanthropic. These are intertwined, yet the most fundamental is earning a profit. If a firm does not earn a profit, the other three responsibilities are moot. Most businesspeople believe they should do more than pursue profits. Although a company must consider its economic needs first, it must also operate within the law, do what is ethical and fair, and be a good corporate citizen. The concept of sustainability is that socially responsible companies will outperform their peers by focusing on the world's social problems and viewing them as an opportunity to earn profits and help the world at the same time.

4.1 Describe at least three situations in which you would not purchase the products of a firm even though it is very socially responsible.

4.2 A firm's only responsibility to society is to earn a fair profit. Comment.

4.3 Is sustainability a viable concept for America's businesses?

4.4 Illustrate how there can be conflicts between the needs and desires of various stakeholders.

LO5 **Describe the arguments for and against social responsibility.** Today, virtually all managers endorse social responsibility of corporations. It is, instead, a matter of what types of responsibility and the degree of responsibility. The arguments against social responsibility are: The job of the corporation is to maximize profits for stockholders; businesses are better suited to produce goods and services and not to be involved in welfare services; and if global competitors aren't socially responsible it could hurt the domestic competitor. The arguments for social responsibility are: It's the right thing to do; government will create new regulations and levy fines if firms aren't socially responsible; and social responsibility can enhance a company's profitability.

5.1 Explain the relationship between the global economy and social responsibility.

5.2 Defend the proposition that the only responsibility of the firm is to make money for the stockholders.

5.3 Explain how a firm can earn additional profits by being socially responsible.

Explain cause-related marketing. Cause-related marketing is the cooperative effort between a for-profit firm and a nonprofit organization. It is different from philanthropy, which is a specific, tax-deductible donation. Cause-related marketing is very popular because it can enhance the reputation of the corporation and also make additional profit for the company. Sometimes companies have abused cause-related marketing and received much greater benefits than the nonprofit that has supposedly been helped. These cases are a small minority.

LO6

6.1 Why are more firms jumping on the cause-related marketing bandwagon?

6.2 Explain the controversy surrounding some cause-related marketing.

6.3 What are some questions that consumers should consider before participating in a cause-related campaign?

Key Terms

casuist ethical theory *59*	**ethics** *57*	**pyramid of corporate social**
cause-related marketing *77*	**Foreign Corrupt Practices**	**responsibility** *71*
code of ethics *63*	**Act** *67*	**stakeholder theory** *69*
corporate social	**green marketing** *75*	**sustainability** *69*
responsibility *69*	**moral relativists** *59*	**utilitarian ethical theory** *59*
deontological ethical	**morals** *60*	**virtue** *60*
theory *58*		

Exercises

ETHICS EXERCISE

ethics

Jane Barksdale has designed a line of clothing targeted toward Hispanic Americans. The items are sold only by catalog and on the Internet. She thinks that she can increase sales by claiming in ads that the firm is owned by a Hispanic American and all the employees are Hispanic Americans. She is not Hispanic American nor are most of the employees. She needs a high level of sales to pay her bank loan and remain in business.

Questions

1. Should Jane claim that she is Hispanic American? Explain your response.

2. Does the Federal Trade Commission address this issue? Go to **www.ftc.gov** and search for guidelines for small business advertising or e-commerce. What does Jane risk in making false claims in her ads?

MARKETING PLAN EXERCISE

These end-of-chapter marketing plan exercises are designed to help you use what you learned in the chapter to build a strategic marketing plan for a company of your choosing. Once you've completed the marketing plan exercise for each chapter in Part 1 of this textbook, you can complete the Part 1 Marketing Planning Worksheet by logging on to the companion Web site at www.cengagebrain.com.

In the first part of this exercise (in Chapter 2) you described your chosen company, wrote its mission statement, and set its marketing objectives. Use the following exercises to guide you through the next part of your strategic marketing plan:

1. Identify any ethical issues that could affect your chosen firm. What steps should be taken to handle these issues?

2. How should your company integrate corporate social responsibility into its marketing plan?

3. In addition to suggestions for philanthropic responsibilities, write up a brief code of ethics for your firm. To see other codes of ethics, browse the Illinois Institute of Technology's extensive database of codes at http://ethics.iit.edu/index1.php/Programs/Codes of Ethics.

 online

APPLICATION EXERCISE

Many companies today are concerned with social responsibility. They pursue philanthropic activities and/or strive to be ethical. Your goal for this assignment is to evaluate how firms are being socially responsible. Limit your answers to one page and provide a printout of the Web site you visited.

Activities

1. Choose a company and find that company's Web site. On the site, look for information that tells you about the firm's efforts to be socially responsible. Look for news releases, company information, information about community programs, and so on. Look in your textbook and your notes to help you define what might be considered socially responsible activities. Describe what you find and explain why you think the company is involved with the activities you describe.

2. Do the activities described on the Web site seem consistent with the company's products? Why or why not? (For example, a shoe company may sponsor a race that raises money to help prevent a disease. People who participate in the race may use that company's running shoes and therefore the race would be consistent with the company's products.)

3. Evaluate how effective you think the information you find is in terms of how it is presented, what impact it might have, and whether or not it will help to sell the company's products. Be sure to support any claims you make.

4. Does the information you collected during this activity improve your evaluation of the company? Would it influence your decision to buy the company's product? Why or why not?

CASE STUDY: (Product) Red

CAN A T-SHIRT SAVE THE WORLD?[51]

© Susan Van Etten

When Oprah and Bono walked down Chicago's Magnificent Mile together in the fall of 2006, it was the shopping trip seen around the world. The famous duo attracted mobs of fans and extensive media coverage as they promoted a revolutionary new cause-marketing event called (Product) RED. Bono urged people to buy RED products, explaining that a portion of the proceeds would go to The Global Fund to fight HIV/AIDS in Africa. Oprah, wearing an "INSPI(RED)" Gap T-shirt on her talk show that day, proclaimed, "I am wearing the most important T-shirt I've ever worn in my life!"

Other companies that licensed the RED brand and created products for the charity included Apple, which sold a limited edition iPod Nano, and Motorola, which introduced a red Motorazr phone. Emporio Armani designed a special RED capsule collection for London Fashion Week, and Converse designed a line of RED shoes to be sold at Gap stores.

Oprah's shopping spree with Bono drew a reported an incredible one billion media impressions worldwide. (Product) RED set up its own Web site, **www.joinred.com,** and took over Myspace.com for the day to launch a page that now boasts over 600,000 friends. RSS (Really Simple Syndication) funneled news about RED to mobile phones and blog sites, and it quickly became a hot topic of discussion on message boards across the Internet.

(Product) RED was the brainchild of Bono and Bobby Shriver, who designed it as a commercial initiative that could change the way causes are marketed in the future. "They didn't want a one-time event," says Julia Cordua, VP of marketing. "They want five to ten years of ongoing donations."

Gap initially offered to give 100 percent of its profits to the cause, but Bono and Shriver refused to accept more than 50 percent. Shriver insists that they want companies to make money off the campaign, explaining, "We want people buying houses in the Hamptons based on this because if that happens, this thing is sustainable." As a result, Gap treats RED like a business, spending millions on marketing it. Within months of its launch, they saw sales of an estimated $71 million in revenue and donated about $2.5 million to The Global Fund.

According to the (Product) RED Web site, "Each company that becomes (RED) places its logo in this embrace and is then elevated to the power of red." You can be embraced by the RED, it suggests, by purchasing a Gap T-shirt or African-print Converse shoes. "What better way to become a good-looking Samaritan?!"

Some critics, such as Charles Kernaghan, director of the National Labor Committee for Worker and Human Rights, aren't buying it, though. "The thought of using consumer dollars made off the backs of workers held in sweatshops to help fund Bono's causes is really hypocritical—that's not the way to go," he says, referring to Gap's reputation for using factories that violate labor laws.

Since 2004 Gap has been working to combat this type of criticism by releasing social responsibility reports on Gap factories in over 50 countries. Despite their efforts, however, nearly half of the factories still failed inspection as recently as 2005. When questioned, a Gap spokesperson responded by stating that Bono himself had inspected the African factory where RED products were being made, and it was "sparkling."

Some bloggers remain skeptical of the fundraiser, however, declaring it "khaki colonialism." Michael Medved argued that it would be better to forget the overpriced T-shirts and send money directly to The Global Fund. But whether you agree with the way (Product) RED does business or not, the campaign is hard to ignore. David Hessekiel of the Cause Marketing Forum proclaimed it "the launch of the year." Stacy Palmer of *The Chronicle of Philanthropy*, wrote, "These are iconic brands that appeal to younger consumers who are very interested in buying cause-related products. (Product) RED borrows on ideas that have been used a lot, but its scale makes it different. People are getting bombarded by RED."

(Product) RED president Tamsin Smith reported on the campaign's blog that much of the merchandise was sold out within hours of the launch. Oprah's INSPI(RED) T-shirt went on to become the best-selling item in the Gap's 35-year history. Long-term success, however, depends on how well the participating brands continue to market new products. They'll have to find ways to keep socially conscious consumers interested in RED now that most of them have been there, done that, and (literally) bought the T-shirt.

Questions

1. Discuss the four components of corporate social responsibility and how they relate to a charitable campaign such as (Product) RED. How does participation in a cause-marketing event contribute to a company's social responsibility? What role does sustainability play?

2. Do you think a partnership with (Product) RED can improve Gap's image? Is it a sign that they are making a commitment to corporate social responsibility or do you agree with critics who say their involvement is an attempt to spit-shine the company's image while continuing to do business as usual?

3. Describe the various types of technology that have contributed to the media coverage, marketing efforts, and public discussion of the RED campaign.

4. A year after (Product) RED's launch, *Ad Age* reported that although $100 million had been spent on marketing the campaign, only about $25 million had gone to the charity itself. Industry observers speculated that this could trigger a backlash against the campaign. Do you believe the criticism is justified? Do you think the campaign could lose supporters as a result?

COMPANY CLIPS: Method—People Against Dirty

Method's first "lab" was the kitchen of founders Eric Ryan and Adam Lowry, two friends whose goal was to evolve the household cleaner from a toxic object that hid under the sink to an all-natural, biodegradable, and stylish countertop accessory. This video segment shows Method through yet another lens, that of corporate social responsibility and sustainability. Chemical engineer Adam Lowry outlines the chemical aspects of traditional cleaning products and describes how Method's products are better for the environment. As you watch the video, keep in mind the various marketing orientations you learned in Chapter 1.

© NKP Media / Cengage

Questions

1. Does Method have a societal marketing orientation, or is it just a market-oriented company that integrates a number of environmental practices into its operations? Explain.

2. How is Method practicing sustainability?

3. Discuss the changing social factors that have made it possible for Method to be so successful.

Notes

1. "Report to the Principal, Big Shot," *BusinessWeek*, July 30, 2007, 9; Keith Winstein, "Inflated Credentials Surface in Executive Suite," *Wall Street Journal*, November 13, 2008, B1–B6.
2. Adapted from Edwin M. Epstein, "The Good Company: Rhetoric or Reality? Corporate Social Responsibility and Business Ethics Redux," *American Business Law Journal*, July 1, 2007, 207.
3. Neil Parmer, "Taking Care of Business," *SmartMoney*, October 2008, 77–82.
4. *Ibid.*
5. Marianne M. Jennings, *Business Ethics, 6th Ed.* (Mason, Ohio: Thomson Higher Education), 2009, 5–6.
6. "Ethical Theories," from Catherine Rainbow, "Descriptions of Ethical Theories and Principles,"as viewed on www.bio.davidson.edu/people/Kabernd/Indep/carainbow.htm. Reprinted with permission.
7. Jennings, 7.
8. *Ibid.*
9. Associated Press, "Scrushy Ordered to Pay Investors $2.9 Billion," *MSNBC*, June 18, 2009, www.msnbc.msn.com/id/31427676/ns/business-us_business/.
10. "Levels of ethical development," based on Edward Stevens, *Business Ethics* (New York: Paulist Press, 1979). Reprinted with permission of The Paulist Press.
11. Anusorn Singhapakdi, Skott Vitell, and Kenneth Kraft, "Moral Intensity and Ethical Decision-Making of Marketing Professionals," *Journal of Business Research* 36, March 1996, 245–255; Ishmael Akaah and Edward Riordan, "Judgments of Marketing Professionals about Ethical Issues in Marketing Research: A Replication and Extension," *Journal of Marketing Research*, February 1989, 112–120. See also Shelby Hunt, Lawrence Chonko, and James Wilcox, "Ethical Problems of Marketing Researchers," *Journal of Marketing Research*, August 1984, 309–324; Kenneth Andrews, "Ethics in

marketing&you: Results.

© iStockphoto.com/ziggymaj

The higher your score, the more important you think ethics and socially responsible behavior are to achieving corporate objectives. A high score also suggests that you are an ethical idealist, or someone who sees right and wrong as absolute, rather than an ethical relativist, or someone who sees right and wrong as situation dependent.

Practice," *Harvard Business Review,* September/October 1989, 99–104; Thomas Dunfee, Craig Smith, and William T. Ross, Jr., "Social Contracts and Marketing Ethics," *Journal of Marketing,* July 1999, 14–32; Jan Handleman and Stephen Arnold, "The Role of Marketing Actions with a Social Dimension: Appeals to the Institutional Environment," *Journal of Marketing*, July 1999, 33–48; David Turnipseed, "Are Good Soldiers Good? Exploring the Link Between Organizational Citizenship Behavior and Personal Ethics," *Journal of Business Research,* January 2002, 1–16; Tim Barnett and Sean Valentine, "Issue Contingencies and Marketers' Recognition of Ethical Issues, Ethical Judgments and Behavioral Intentions," *Journal of Business Research*, April 2004, 338–346.

12. "The Stat," *BusinessWeek,* September 12, 2005, 16.

13. *Ibid.*

14. "Actions Contributing Most to Ethical Behavior and Compliance Identified," *Workspan,* February 1, 2007, 1.

15. Susan Carey, "Snap, Crackle, Slap: FTC Forbids Rice Krispies Claim," *Wall Street Journal*, June 4, 2010, B1–12.

16. *Ibid.*

17. Terry Mann, "Ethics Training for the Workplace," *eHow.com*, February 6, 2010, http://www.ehow.com/facts_5957733_ethics-training-workplace.html.

18. Erin White, "'What Would You Do?' Ethics Courses Get Context," *Wall Street Journal*, June 12, 2006, B3.

19. *2009 National Business Ethics Survey* (Arlington, Virginia: Ethics Resource Center) 2009, 9–12.

20. "Survey Says: Ethics Training Works," *All Business,* November 1, 2005, www.allbusiness.com/services/educational-services/4284114-1.html.

21. Joseph Pereira and Steve Stecklow, "Walmart Raises Bar on Toy-Safety Standards," *Wall Street Journal,* May 14, 2008, B1–B2.

22. Ann Zimmerman and Mei Fong, "Walmart Suppliers Face Energy, Other Mandates," *Wall Street Journal*, October 22, 2008, B1, B4.

23. Remi Trudel and June Cotte, "Does Being Ethical Pay?" *Wall Street Journal*, May 12, 2008, R4.

24. Julie Irwin and Rebecca Walker Naylor, *Journal of Marketing Research*, April 2009, 234–246.

25. Smoking and Tobacco Use, "Fast Facts," Centers for Disease Control and Prevention Web site, January 21, 2011, www.cdc.gov/tobacco/data_statistics/fact_sheets/fast_facts/index.htm.

26. "SAM, Dow Jones Indexes and STOXX, Ltd. Announce Results of Dow Jones Sustainability Review," SAM Media Release, September 3, 2009; also see Marni Evans, "What Is Sustainability," June, 7, 2010, www.sustainability.about.com/od/Sustainability/a/What-Is-Sustainability.htm.

27. This section is partially adapted from Jennings, *Business Ethics*, 72–75.

28. Milton Friedman, "The Social Responsibility of Business Is to Increase Its Profits," *New York Times*, September 1962, 126.

29. Tom Yerace, "Ludlum to Pay $1.6M Pollution Penalty," *Valley News Dispatch*, May 18, 2010, www.pittsburghlive.com/x/valleynewsdispatch/s_681695.html.

30. *Walmart Global Sustainability Report: 2010 Progress Update*, 2010.

31. "Globally, Companies Are Giving Back," *HR Magazine*, June 1, 2007, 30.

32. "IBM Global Survey Shows Information Gap in 'Green,'" IBM Web site, June 1, 2009, www-03.ibm.com/press/us/en/pressrelease/27622.wss.

33. "UN Global Compact Participants," United Nations Global Compact Web site, June 30, 2009, www.unglobalcompact.org/ParticipantsAndStakeholders/index.html.

34. "Secretary-General Opens Global Compact Leaders Summit as Business, Government, Civil Society Leaders Rally for Corporate Citizenship," UNESCAP Press Release, July 5, 2007, Press Release No. L/38/2007.

35. "Ben & Jerry's Mission," Ben & Jerry's Web site, January 21, 2011, www.benjerry.com/activism/mission-statement. Reprinted with permission.

36. "One for One Movement," TOMS Shoes Web site, January 21, 2011, www.toms.com/our-movement.

37. "Nestlé Doesn't Deserve a Break," www.greenpeace.org, March 23, 2010, www.greenpeace.org/international/en/news/features/Nestle-needs-to-give-rainforest; Jeremy Hance, "Nestlé Caves to Activists Pressure on Palm Oil," May 17, 2010, http://news.mongabay.com/2010/0517-hance_nestle.html; "Update on Deforestation and Palm Oil," Nestle Media Center Web site, February 2, 2011, www.nestle.com/Media/Statements/Pages/Update-on-deforestation-and-palm-oil.aspx; Emily Steel, "Nestlé Takes a Beating on Social-Media Sites," *Wall Street Journal*, March 9, 2010, B5; Sarah Hills, "FBD: Nestlé Switches Palm Oil Supplier in Sustainability Drive," *Food Biz Daily*, March 18, 2010, http://foodbizdaily.com/articles/97020-nestle-switches-palm-oil-supplier-in-sustainability-drive.aspx.

38. Gordon Wyner, "Sustainability Perspectives," *Marketing Management*, Summer 2010, 45.

39. David Giannetto, "It's Not Easy Being Green," *US Business Review* (July–August 2008), 14–15.

40. "Easy but Green, Rider," *Marketing Magazine*, July 14, 2008, 29.

41. "Sustainability: Think Green Every Day," Waste Management Web site, January 21, 2011, www.wm.com/sustainability/index.jsp.

42. Wyner, "Sustainability Perspectives," 46–47.

43. "2009 World's Most Ethical Companies," *Ethisphere,* http://ethisphere.com/wme2009 (Accessed June 7, 2011).

44. "Consumers Doubt Green Efforts," *Marketing Management*, July/August 2009, 5.

45. "Sustainability Marketing Has Legs," *Marketing Management*, July/August 2009, 4.

46. Xueming Luo and C.B. Battacharya, "The Debate over Doing Good: Corporate Social Performance, Strategic Marketing Levers, and Firm-Idiosyncratic Risk," *Journal of Marketing*, November 2009, 198–213.

47. Craig and Marc Kielburger, "Cause-Tied Marketing Not Perfect," *Toronto Star*, July 16, 2007, AA02.

48. Emily Callahan, "Susan G. Komen Breast Cancer Foundation Creates Five Questions to Ask Before Participating in a Cause-Related Marketing Program," *PR Newswire*, September 28, 2005; also see: Michael Barone, Andrew Norman, and Anthony Miyazakij, "Consumer Response to Retailer Use of Cause-Related Marketing: Is More Better?" *Journal of Retailing*, December 2007, 437–445.

49. Nancy Schwartz, "Busted Nonprofit Brand: Anatomy of a Corporate Sponsorship Meltdown (Case Study)," *Getting Attention*, April 28, 2010, http://gettingattention.org/articles/74/branding/nonprofit-brand-mistake-komen-kfc.html.

50. David Hessekiel, "Cause Marketing Today," *Cause Marketing Forum*, May, 2010, http://archive.constantcontact.com/fs068/1011017910039/archive/1103331223400.html.

51. Laura Heller, "Think Pink. Shop RED," *Retailing Today*, November 20, 2006; Betsy Spethmann, "The RED Brigade," *Prism Business Media*, January 1, 2007, http://chiefmarketer.com/advertising/RED_brigade_01122007; Geoffrey Gray, "Achtung, Bono! Activists See Red: Alliance with Gap Upsets Anti-Sweatshop Types," *New York*, October 30, 2006, http://nymag.com/news/intelligencer/23175/; Soo Youn, "Owner of Gap Releases Details of Operations at Textile Factories Worldwide," *Daily News*, May 13, 2004; www.joinred.com; www.theglobalfund.org; www.myspace.com/joinred.

The Marketing Environment

Learning Outcomes

1 Discuss the external environment of marketing, and explain how it affects a firm

2 Describe the social factors that affect marketing

3 Explain the importance to marketing managers of current demographic trends

4 Explain the importance to marketing managers of growing ethnic markets

5 Identify consumer and marketer reactions to the state of the economy

6 Identify the impact of technology on a firm

7 Discuss the political and legal environment of marketing

8 Explain the basics of foreign and domestic competition

LO1
The External Marketing Environment

If there is one constant in the external environment (outside the firm) where firms work and compete, it is that things are constantly changing. If the organization doesn't understand or fails to react to the changing world around it, it will soon be a follower rather than a leader. In the worst case scenario, the firm disappears from the marketplace. In 2010, America's oldest auto brand, Oldsmobile, was closed by General Motors. It had already dropped Pontiac and Saturn earlier. Over time, consumers' desires changed, competitors became more savvy, and demographics evolved. Yet GM was slow to react. The company filed for bankruptcy in 2009 and emerged as a slimmed-down, more flexible and marketing attuned competitor.

Perhaps the most important decisions a marketing manager must make relate to the creation of the marketing mix. Recall from Chapters 1 and 2 that a marketing mix is the unique combination of product, place (distribution), promotion, and price strategies. The marketing mix is, of course, under the firm's control and is designed to appeal to a specific group of potential buyers. A **target market** is a defined group that managers feel is most likely to buy a firm's product.

Managers must alter the marketing mix because of changes in the environment in which consumers live, work, and make purchasing decisions. Also, as markets mature, some new consumers become part of the target market; others drop out. Those who remain may have different tastes, needs, incomes, lifestyles, and buying habits than the original target consumers. Mattel's Barbie was the top selling fashion doll for almost 50 years. Yet she fell victim to changing tastes and competition, most notably from Bratz, a line of edgier, more ethnically diverse dolls. Barbie's

> **"**
> **Managers cannot control elements in the external environment** that continually **mold and reshape** the target market.
> **"**

target market
A defined group most likely to buy a firm's product.

marketing&you.

Using the following scale, enter the numbers that reflect your opinions.

STRONGLY DISAGREE ⟨ 1 2 3 4 5 6 7 ⟩ STRONGLY AGREE

_____ I need more hours in the day to get my work done.

_____ I don't have to overextend myself to find the time to get my work done.

_____ I feel like I'm always "fighting fires."

_____ I seldom have to take shortcuts to get my work done on time.

_____ I never have enough time to think ahead.

_____ I feel like I have a lot of time on my hands.

_____ I feel like no matter how hard I work, I'll never get caught up.

Total your score. Read the chapter and find out what your score means at the end.

Source: Scale #119, *Marketing Scales Handbook*, G. Bruner, K. James, H. Hensel, eds., Vol. III. © by American Marketing Association.

market share in 2000 was over 80 percent. It is now is less than 50 percent.[1] Mattel has launched a major marketing effort to regain market share.

Although managers can control the marketing mix, they cannot control elements in the external environment that continually mold and reshape the target market. Review Learning Outcome 1 shows the controllable and uncontrollable variables that affect the target market, whether it consists of consumers or business purchasers. The uncontrollable elements in the center of the diagram continually evolve and create changes in the target market. In contrast, managers can shape and reshape the marketing mix, depicted on the left side of the diagram, to influence the target market. That is, managers react to changes in the external environment and attempt to create a more effective marketing mix.

UNDERSTANDING THE EXTERNAL ENVIRONMENT

Unless marketing managers understand the external environment, the firm cannot intelligently plan for the future. Thus, many organizations assemble a team of specialists to continually collect and evaluate environmental information, a process called *environmental scanning*. The goal in gathering the environmental data is to identify future market opportunities and threats.

Does environmental scanning really make a difference? The Aberdeen Group is a Boston-based research firm. It found that firms who used feedback from the external environment to create and modify their marketing mix had an average 26 percent increase in return on their marketing investment over the previous year.[2] Companies that used environmental scanning less efficiently had only a 4 percent return. Those firms that didn't use scanning at all tended to be laggards in the marketplace. These figures show that using environmental scanning to understand the ever-changing marketplace and then adapting the marketing mix accordingly is critical to long-term success of the organization.

Philips Electronics is a firm that is proactive in trying to keep a step ahead of the latest environmental trends. The firm's new strategic plan focuses on "sense and simplicity."

Philips Electronics is a firm that is proactive in trying to keep a step ahead of the latest environmental trends. The firm's new strategic plan focuses on "sense and simplicity." The idea is to give consumers what they want in the way of electronic products in the health, lifestyle, and technology areas. Because Philips is dominated by engineers, it decided that if it was really going to create products that are simple to use and consumer-oriented, it needed help. The company created a four-person advisory group of opinion leaders from around the globe. The group consists of Sara Berman, a British fashion designer; Dr. Peggy Fritzsche, a California radiology professor; Gary Chang, a leading Chinese architect; and John Maeda, an MIT graphic designer. They meet several days each month in places like Paris, Rome, or New York to help Philips understand how the environment of business is changing. Their goal is to help Philips create intuitive, easy-to-use products that meet specific needs. Andrea Ragnetti, chief marketing officer for Philips, explains that it took the firm quite a while to adopt the marketing concept. He notes, "In the past we just developed the technology and hoped someone would buy it. Now we are starting from the point of discovering what exactly consumers want a product to do."[3]

Philips Electronics does a good job of understanding the ever-changing external environment. Some of the key areas that firms should monitor in the external environment are:

→ **Understanding current customers.** That is, how they buy, where they buy, what they buy, and when they buy. Research showed shoppers spent an average of 22 minutes in a Walmart, but suggested that the wide product variety was curtailing the number of items they put in their shopping baskets. The company decided to add variety and shelf space in the fastest-growing categories and to trim variety and space in slower ones. It has since increased the number and variety of flat-panel television sets it sells, and finds its share of sales has increased. Space devoted to shaving cream, trash bags, and diapers increased while shelf space for toilet paper and mouthwash dropped.[4]

→ *Understanding what drives consumer decisions.* Successful firms know why customers buy. One study showed that grocery shoppers patronize 3.6 stores regularly. Why? Because distinct stores filled distinct roles in a consumer's shopping portfolio. They went to Costco for bulk items; Trader Joe's (a local chain) to find interesting and unique items; and Walmart for one-stop shopping for a variety of basic goods. The local chain was losing business to niche stores to buy high margin items such as meat, seafood, and produce. Intelligence data showed that the local chain could recapture about half of these consumers by stocking more variety in organic, international foods, and signature products.[5]

→ *Identify the most valuable customers and understand their needs.* Often, 20 percent of a firm's customers produce 80 percent of the firm's revenue. An organization must understand what drives that loyalty and then take steps to ensure that those drivers are maintained and enhanced.

→ *Understand the competition.* Successful firms know their competitors and attempt to forecast those competitors' future moves. Competitors offer both threats to a firm's market share and profitability but also may offer opportunities to a firm to capture competitors' business. During the economic downturn of 2007–2009, T.J. Maxx, the off-price retailer, noted that competitors were taking 60 to 90 days to pay their vendors. T.J. Maxx had the cash and decided to pay within 30 days. This caused the big name fashion brands to flock to the retailer. Now, TJX, which owns T.J. Maxx, Marshalls, and HomeGoods, has a better assortment of well-known brands to sell in its stores. For the first time, T.J. Maxx is selling items such as True Religion jeans for $99 (regularly $160) and Bottega Veneta sweaters for $149 (normally $750). Sales, market share, and profit are up for TJX.[6]

ENVIRONMENTAL MANAGEMENT

No one business is large or powerful enough to create major change in the external environment. Thus, marketing managers are basically adapters rather than agents of change. For example, despite the huge size of firms like General Electric, Walmart, Apple, and Caterpillar, they don't control social change, demographics, or other factors in the external environment.

However, just because a firm cannot fully control the external environment, this doesn't mean that it is helpless. Sometimes a firm can influence external events. For example, extensive lobbying by FedEx has enabled it to acquire virtually all of the Japanese routes that it has sought. Japan had originally opposed new cargo routes for FedEx. The favorable decision was based on months of lobbying by FedEx at the White House, at several agencies, and in Congress for help in overcoming Japanese resistance. When a company implements strategies that attempt to shape the external environment within which it operates, it is engaging in **environmental management**.

The factors within the external environment that are important to marketing managers can be classified as social, demographic, economic, technological, political and legal, and competitive.

environmental management
When a company implements strategies that attempt to shape the external environment within which it operates.

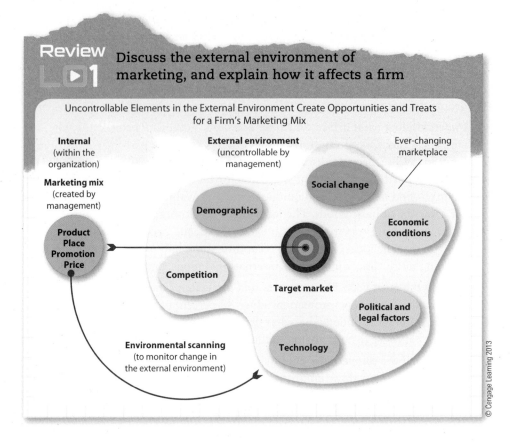

Uncontrollable Elements in the External Environment Create Opportunities and Treats for a Firm's Marketing Mix

LO2
Social Factors

Social change is perhaps the most difficult external variable for marketing managers to forecast, influence, or integrate into marketing plans. Social factors include our attitudes, values, and lifestyles. Social factors influence the products people buy, the prices paid for products, the effectiveness of specific promotions, and how, where, and when people expect to purchase products.

AMERICAN VALUES

A *value* is a strongly held and enduring belief. During the United States' first 200 years, four basic values strongly influenced attitudes and lifestyles:

→ **Self-sufficiency:** Every person should stand on his or her own two feet.

→ **Upward mobility:** Success would come to anyone who got an education, worked hard, and played by the rules.

→ **Work ethic:** Hard work, dedication to family, and frugality were moral and right.

→ **Conformity:** No one should expect to be treated differently from everybody else.

These core values still hold for a majority of Americans today. A person's values are key determinants of what is important and not important, what actions to take or not to take, and how one behaves in social situations.

People typically form values through interaction with family, friends, and other influencers such as teachers, religious leaders, and politicians. The changing environment can also play a key role in shaping one's values. For example, people born

In this ad, Baby Phat targets upwardly mobile customers by showing a wealthy woman in luxurious surroundings. It also suggests that owning the product offers upward mobility and a reward for hard work.

during the 1980s and 1990s tend to be more comfortable with technology and its importance in the home than persons born in the 1960s.

Values influence our buying habits. Today's consumers are demanding, inquisitive, and discriminating. No longer willing to tolerate products that break down, they are insisting on high-quality goods that save time, energy, and often calories. U.S. consumers rank the characteristics of product quality as (1) reliability, (2) durability, (3) easy maintenance, (4) ease of use, (5) a trusted brand name, and (6) a low price. Shoppers are also concerned about nutrition and want to know what's in their food, and many have environmental concerns.

Long before the tragic oil disaster in the Gulf of Mexico, Americans had become more environmentally oriented. Consumers also want a healthy, less complicated lifestyle that focuses on meaningful things in life. That which is phony is out. The Natural Marketing Institute offers the following trends to look for over the next ten years:

→ ***Getting off the grid.*** A new spirit of self-reliance drives how consumers prioritize their spending and behave toward what they believe is purposeful, principled, and powerful. Consumers are pursuing ways to become more self-sufficient, including household-generated energy; water conservation and purification; and private gardens.

→ ***Meaningful green.*** The green wave has penetrated the globe and almost every company and product claims at least a small place at the sustainability table.

customer experience

Seeing Real Beauty

Dove conducted a global study that found that the definition of beauty had become limiting and unattainable, as if only thin, young, and blond were beautiful. Only 2 percent of the women around the world considered themselves beautiful. Eighty-one percent of the American women strongly agreed that "the media and advertising set an unrealistic expectation of beauty that most women can't ever achieve." Based upon this research, Dove started a series of communication campaigns to challenge the stereotypes of beauty. Next came a much-talked about ad featuring real women whose appearances were outside the stereotypical norms of beauty. The ads invited viewers to judge the women's looks at www.campaignforrealbeauty.com.

A second advertising campaign featured six more women and this one also drove thousands of women to the Web site to discuss beauty issues. A third campaign the following year focused upon older women. Research showed that 91 percent of women ages 50–64 believed that it is time for society to change its views of women and age. This led to a new promotional campaign featuring women over 50.

The current campaign is focused on how girls today are bombarded with unrealistic and unattainable messages and images of beauty that affect their self-esteem. Through the Dove Self-Esteem Fund, the company is educating girls ages 8–17 with education resources and hands-on activities. The workshops reached five million young people globally in 2010.[8]

Do you think the Dove Campaign for Real Beauty is a good way to build sales and market share? Have you seen promotional campaigns that have actually made you feel worse about yourself? Did the campaign make you want to buy the product? Why or why not?

The challenge lies in achieving meaningful differentiation. Green initiatives must be distinctive, memorable, and measurable to affect environmental, social, and economic dimensions. Look for the meaning of green to move beyond the struggle of statistics (i.e., X percent less packaging, Y percent more energy efficient, etc.).

→ **EcoTechMed.** New economic realities are motivating many to take greater steps toward proactive health care rather than sick care and greater responsibility for their own health and wellness. Technology is enabling fully customized and predictive prevention alternatives, including a blending of alternative and Western medicine.[7]

An indication of one firm that is out in front of the above trends is Unilever, producer of Dove products. The story is told in the Customer Experience box above.

PERSONALITY TRAITS VARY BY REGION[9]

Certain regional stereotypes have existed for a long time and have become clichés: the stressed and hurried New Yorker and the cool, laid-back Californian. New research, based upon 600,000 interviews, has looked at geography and personality. Even after controlling for variables such as race, income, and education levels, a state's dominant personality turns out to be strongly linked to certain outcomes. Amiable states, such as Minnesota, tend to be lower in crime. Dutiful states—an eclectic bunch that includes New Mexico, North Carolina, and Utah—produce a disproportionate share of mathematicians. States that rank high in openness to new ideas are quite creative, as measured by per-capita patent production. But they're also high-crime and a bit aloof. High-anxiety states include not only New York and New Jersey, but also states stressed by poverty, such as West Virginia and

Mississippi. As a group, these states tend to have higher rates of heart disease and lower life expectancy.

The most conscientious states were mostly in America's heartland, but also included Florida, Georgia, and North Carolina. The states highest on "openness" were along the West Coast but also included Maine. "Extraversion" was strongest in the Upper Midwest along with Georgia, Florida, and Maine. The linking of geography and personalities raises intriguing chicken-and-egg type questions. Do states tend to nurture specific personalities because of their histories, cultures, and even climates? Or do Americans, seeking kindred spirits, migrate to the states where they feel at home? Maybe both forces are at work—but in what balance? As of yet, we don't know the answer.

THE GROWTH OF COMPONENT LIFESTYLES

People in the United States today are piecing together **component lifestyles**. A lifestyle is a mode of living; it is the way people decide to live their lives. In other words, they are choosing products and services that meet diverse needs and interests rather than conforming to traditional stereotypes.

In the past, a person's profession—for instance, banker—defined his or her lifestyle. Today, a person can be a banker and also a gourmet, fitness enthusiast, dedicated single parent, and Internet guru. Each of these lifestyles is associated with different goods and services and represents a target audience. For example, marketers offer cooking utensils, wines, and exotic foods to a gourmet through magazines such as *Bon Appétit* and *Gourmet*. The fitness enthusiast buys Adidas equipment, special jogging outfits, and reads *Runner* magazine. Component lifestyles increase the complexity of consumers' buying habits. The banker might own a BMW but change the oil himself or herself. He or she might buy fast food for lunch but French wine for dinner, own sophisticated photographic equipment and a low-priced home stereo, and shop for socks at Kmart or Walmart and suits or dresses at Brooks Brothers. The unique lifestyles of every consumer can require a different marketing mix.

WHAT'S YOUR **ADVANTAGE?**

This ad is targeting active, adventurous people through snowboarding—but it is for a health bar. Atkins is targeting people with component lifestyles by linking one component (winter adventure sports) to another (health food/nutrition).

THE CHANGING ROLE OF FAMILIES AND WORKING WOMEN

Component lifestyles have evolved because consumers can choose from a growing number of goods and services, and most have the money to exercise more options. The growth of dual-income families has resulted in increased purchasing power. Approximately 59 percent of all females between 16 and 65 years old are now in the workforce. Working wives bring in 45 percent of the total family earnings.[10] The phenomenon of working women has probably had a greater effect on marketing than any other social change.

As women's earnings grow, so do their levels of expertise, experience, and authority. Working-age women are not the same group businesses targeted 30 years ago. They expect different things in life—from their jobs, from their spouses, and from the products and services they buy. Home improvement centers, such as Home Depot or Lowe's, know that women shoppers are vital to their success. Yet women feel that these retailers offer an unnecessarily complex shopping process. One study found that women want a stress-free experience and want to feel that Lowe's and Home Depot appreciate their business. Of all the women interviewed,

component lifestyles
The practice of choosing goods and services that meet one's diverse needs and interests rather than conforming to a single, traditional lifestyle.

97 percent said that having one person capable of answering all of their questions was one of the most important services a home improvement retailer could provide.[11]

THERE IS NEVER ENOUGH TIME

Research shows that the large percentage of people who say they never have enough time to do all that they need to do keeps inching up. It is estimated that over 80 percent of the working population is worried about having too little time.[12] With the economic downturn of 2007–2009, many stay-at-home moms are going back to work to help make ends meet. These time-constrained mothers find that they have even fewer high-quality hours to spend with their families.[13]

Over 31 percent of college-educated male workers are regularly working 50 or more hours a week, up from 22 percent in 1980. About 40 percent of American adults get fewer than seven hours of sleep on weekdays, up from 34 percent in 2001. Almost 60 percent of meals are rushed, and 34 percent of lunches are eaten on the run. To manage their scarce time, about 74 percent of working adults engage in multitasking—doing more than one thing at a time.[14] They're talking on their cell phones while rushing to work or school, answering e-mails during conference calls, waking up at 4 A.M., and generally multitasking day and night.

"With Americans now spending a record-breaking 60 percent of their waking hours at work, the days of stopping by your neighbor's front porch in the afternoon to discuss current events over an iced tea are over," said Stephanie Molnar, CEO of WorkPlace Media. "These days, time-starved consumers are more likely to stop by a colleague's cubicle on their way out for an iced coffee than socialize with neighbors back at home, where household chores and family responsibilities take precedence over casual conversation."[15] On an average day (which includes all seven days of the week), 83 percent of women and 66 percent of men spent some time doing household activities, such as housework, cooking, lawn care, or financial and other household management.[16] Recent research has found that:

→ With rising pump prices and busy schedules, consumers are highly likely to consolidate shopping trips, making purchases on their drive to or from work, or during their lunch break. Almost three-fourths of at-work consumers indicate they regularly or occasionally dine out or purchase groceries and beverages during the workday.

→ At-work consumers research products online before purchasing, with almost half of them (47.2 percent) reporting having researched electronics online in the last 90 days during the workday before making a purchase in a store.

→ Word-of-mouth is highly influential on purchases made by at-work consumers, with 95.6 percent indicating they regularly or occasionally give advice to their peers about products and services, and 92.9 percent indicating they also *seek* advice from peers before making purchases.

→ Because the workplace is full of conversation among peers, it presents the perfect environment to create buzz for product introductions and new store openings. While taking a break from work, 67.8 percent of at-work consumers are likely to socialize with co-workers, and 42.2 percent also indicate they communicate with friends and family during the workday.[17]

A New York sociologist calls the next step in our work-life culture "weisure time." He claims that the work-play environments are blurring together. It means that more Americans are using smartphones and other technology to collaborate with business associates while engaged in family or leisure activities.[18] There is less relaxing time to be our so-called "backstage selves" when we are always mingling work and leisure. There is no time to decompress. Also, new research has shown that being constantly tethered to e-mail, BlackBerrys, iPads, and other digital media can take a toll on a person's life and his or her ability to focus. Such immersion in a digital life can cause multitaskers to have more fractured thinking and to shut out irrelevant information—even when they are offline.[19]

LO3
Demographic Factors

Review
LO2 Describe the social factors that affect marketing

Time pressure

Component lifestyles

Changing role of women

Values

Social Factors

© iStockphoto.com/Juan Facundo Mora Soria; © Cengage Learning 2013

Another uncontrollable variable in the external environment—also extremely important to marketing managers—is **demography**, the study of people's vital statistics, such as their age, race and ethnicity, and location. Demographics are significant because people are the basis for any market. Demographic characteristics are strongly related to consumer buyer behavior in the marketplace.

POPULATION

The most basic statistic of all is population because people are directly or indirectly the basis of all markets. The U.S. population is now above 300 million. But it is the 400 million milestone, which the United States will reach in about 30 to 35 years, that has demographers and economists really talking. Those additional 100 million people, many of them immigrants, will replace aging baby boomers in the workforce, fill the Social Security coffers, and, in all likelihood, keep the economy vital and life interesting. But they also will further crowd cities and highways, put new strains on natural resources, end the majority status of whites, and probably widen the gulf between society's haves and have-nots.

With about 86 people per square mile nation-wide now, the United States would seem to have plenty of room for more. Even after the next 100 million people are added, the United States will have one-sixth the density of Germany, whose population is expected to stop growing within a few years. But those averages hide disparities that could prove worrying. Even as it grows, the population is increasingly concentrating in just a dozen or so states, including Colorado, Florida, North Carolina, and Texas. North Dakota is losing population, Ohio is adding a mere 20,000 people a year, and heartland states such as Kansas and Nebraska average fewer than 14 households per square mile.

The economic downturn of 2007–2009 and slow growth thereafter resulted in more people staying put. The housing slump made it harder to sell a home, so homeowners looking to relocate found it more difficult to do so.[20] Those who were able to move tended to downsize and move from the suburbs back to cities. More job openings are available in the cities relative to the suburbs.[21]

More than half the population lives within 50 miles of the coasts. In the next decade, an additional 25 million people—half the total population increase—will join them there. That concentration of population is likely to result in megacities as people head there for jobs. Despite this trend, economists predict that market forces will eventually shift some of the U.S. population back to interior states where housing is cheaper, land is more abundant, social services are less stressed, and labor is cheaper for businesses.

demography
The study of people's vital statistics, such as their age, race and ethnicity, and location.

Looking at these large numbers offers insight to where people live, and can help marketers begin channeling types of products based on where people are living. However, it is important to be able to understand markets on a more descriptive basis. To do so, we turn our attention to age groups, their impact, and the opportunities they present for marketers. These cohorts are categorized as tweens, Generation Y, Generation X, and baby boomers. You will find that each cohort group has its own needs, values, and consumption patterns.

TWEENS

Walmart is targeting the tween cohort with this colorful, fun ad.

They watch cable channels designed just for them, they cruise the Net with ease, they know what they want—and often get it. They are America's tweens (they are not young children anymore, nor are they teens, at ages 8 to 12), a population of more than 20 million. With attitudes, access to information, sophistication well beyond their years, and purchasing power to match, these young consumers spend over $200 billion annually. The direct economic power of most tweens depends on parents and other family adults through allowances and gifts. Although there is much talk about tweens being the purchase decision-maker, it is ultimately the parent in control. Tweens directly spend about $50 billion per year and the remainder is spent by parents and family members for them.[22]

Tweens are all about discovery and the latest viral sensation that is being buzzed about at school. Many don't have cell phones, although this market is growing rapidly. One phone targeted directly at this market is Tic Talk. The phone gives parents control over what phone numbers can be called any time and which ones can be called only during certain hours. Parents can also set times when the phone can ring. The controls allow family members to send reminder messages to the child as well. Games are included to teach math, spelling, science, and social studies for grades 1 through 6.[23] Another cell phone targeted to tweens is the Wherify Wherifone that has a built-in GPS feature enabling parents to track where their children are as long as the child carries the phone.

Tweens' styles don't reflect those of their parents. They want their own look. And parents spend about $230 per tween on back-to-school clothes to give them just that.[24] Many retailers are expanding to target tweens. For example, P.S. by Aeropostale sells boys and girls casual clothes and accessories for the 7-to-12-year-old market. The company claims that it has created a fun, playful, and inviting shopping environment for both the child and parent.[25] Other retailers targeting tweens are J. Crew with its Crewcuts, GapKids, and American Eagle Outfitters with its online-only 77 Kids.

Tweens respond very favorably to being able to have control over, or being able to create, their own experiences. Two companies that do an excellent job of this are Build-A-Bear and American Girl. Targeted to tween girls, American Girl stores sell dolls, accessories, books, and more. Located in major markets, such as New York, Chicago, and Dallas, the stores offer a unique experience for the child. After purchasing one of the dolls (around $80), the child can shop for accessories and visit the dining room or birthday party area. Each area of the store features a specific doll and associated merchandise. A doll named Molly, for example, not only offers the obligatory clothes but also six books about Molly, camping equipment and a tent, and a bedtime set for Molly. Many outfits are also offered in tween sizes so the doll and child will match. Finally, the purchaser can bring the doll to the American Girl store to have the doll's hair washed and set and, if so inclined, get the doll's ears pierced.[26]

Tweens overwhelmingly (92 percent) recognize television commercials for what they are—"just advertising." About three-quarters regard billboards and radio spots as paid advertising, and about half recognize promotional mediums such as product placements on television shows.[27] Because parents often instruct their tweens not to click on anything in a banner or pop-up, many tweens perceive banner ads as something that clutters up the page and that you are supposed to ignore.[28] The Federal Trade Commission's Bureau of Consumer Protection has developed a program to help tweens understand promotion at www.admongo.gov. This site, via a game, encourages youngsters to always ask three questions: (1) Who is responsible for the ad? (2) What is the ad actually saying? and (3) What does the ad want me to do?[29]

What is really important to tweens? Research found the following (in order of importance): being happy, getting along with family, getting good grades, being healthy, the school he or she goes to, and being good with money. Parents of tweens had generally the same rankings, except they were much more likely than their tweens to mention getting lots of sleep and eating right.[30]

TEENS

There are approximately 25 million teens in the United States. They spend roughly 72 hours per week tuned in electronically. This includes TV, Internet, music, video games, cell phones, and text messages. About 93 percent of U.S. teens are on the Internet, 75 percent own a cell phone, and 66 percent say they text. Of the "wired" teens, 73 percent are into social networking, with Facebook being the most popular destination. Over 50 million teens worldwide post their profiles on Facebook. Only 14 percent of American teens blog but about half post comments on blogs. While Twitter is popular with the older crowd, only 8 percent of teens use the microblogger.[31]

The average teen may spend 11.5 hours a week online, but not everything is more appealing to teens in an online format. Given the choice, teens would rather have real friends (91 percent) than online friends (9 percent), date someone from school (87 percent) than someone from the Internet (13 percent), and shop in a store (82 percent) than shop online (18 percent). Even though teens prefer real stores, they do shop online (58 percent). On average, teens who make a purchase online are spending $46 per month, and 26 percent of teens are spending $50 or more. Clothes and music are the two most popular online purchases, followed by books and electronics.[32]

Two keys to effectively market to teens are:

→ **Make the product modern and convenient.** Apple's iPod addressed the timeless teen trend of listening to music. Apple made a device that was easy to use, compact, and held a large library. It was a huge hit with teens. Electronic books, such as the Kindle, have not yet had the same level of success.

→ **Engage teens through promotion that gets them involved.** Teens want to be a part of the action. On YouTube, there are millions of teens posting videos touting their lifestyles, wants, needs, and emotions. It is important to engage teens with interactive contests and voting challenges, and to empower the teen audience with the opportunity to help a company with new ideas, commercials, and brand names. Companies, such as Disney, have set up online communities to get feedback and ideas from teens.[33]

For teens, shopping has become a social sport online or at the mall. More than 62 percent say that they love to shop. They patronize the big box retailers, such as Best Buy, and luxury brands, with little room for retailers in between. Teens love Armani, Gucci, and Coach. They also go to Taco Bell and drink Coke.

A few more interesting facts about teens:

→ The average teen or tween earns about $45.00 per week (63 percent work a minimum of four weeks per year). A substantial portion of their budget (43 percent) is spent on fashion.

→ Teens are multicultural. Four in ten children between 5 and 9 years of age (40 percent) are non-white or Hispanic, as are 38 percent of those teens between 15 and 17 years of age.

→ Music and entertainment are (still) critical to everyday life. Eight in ten teens (80 percent) listen to music during their free time.

→ Entertainment has to be on-demand for teens. More than 90 percent engage in on-demand media consumption.

→ Life revolves around the mall. More than two-thirds of teens go to the mall at least once a week, both to shop and to socialize.

→ It's not all about new media. The average teen reader spends 43 minutes per day reading.[34]

GENERATION Y

Those designated by demographics as **Generation Y**, also called millennials, were born between 1979 and 1994. Initially, Generation Y was a smaller cohort than the baby boomers (discussed below). However, due to immigration and the aging of the boomer generation, Gen Y passed the boomers in total population in 2010, with more than 75 million members. Millennials are currently in two different stages of the life cycle. The youngest members of Gen Y, born in 1994, are still in their late teens and fit the teen cohort group discussed earlier. For example, young Gen Yers enjoy video games. Seventy-one percent claim that they are gamers and 15 percent said that they play video games over ten hours a week.[35] In contrast, the oldest Gen Yers, born in 1979, were 32 years old in 2011. They have started their careers and many have become parents for the first time. First-time parents often experience a dramatic change in lifestyle. Instead of going out to dinner and a movie, they now stay home with the baby, eat takeout, and watch a Netflix movie. Spending patterns also change as new parents spend money on diapers, pediatricians, and baby food. They read *New Parent* and *American Baby* magazines and go to Web sites such as www.babycenter.com or www.parenthood.com. Sourcing these media was the furthest thing from their minds a few years earlier!

Gen Yers already spend over $200 billion annually and over their lifetimes will likely spend about $10 trillion. Many have already started their careers and are making major purchasing decisions such as cars and homes; at the very least, they are buying lots of computers, MP3 players, cell phones, iPads, and sneakers.

Researchers have found Gen Yers to be:

→ **Impatient:** Gen Y has grown up in a world that's always been automated, and they have had access to computers, Kindles, the Internet, BlackBerrys, chat rooms, instant messaging, and the like, for as long as most can remember, so it's no surprise that they expect things to be done *now.*

→ **Family-oriented:** Unlike Gen X before them, Gen Yers had relatively stable childhoods. They also grew up in a very family-focused time when even big

Generation Y
People born between 1979 and 1994.

companies strived to become more family- and kid-friendly. It's the generation that inspired spin-off stores like BabyGap and the makeover of Las Vegas into a family vacation destination.

→ **Inquisitive:** Knowing more than their parents about computers and technology has always been a source of pride for the millennials. It has led to a natural inquisitiveness that many still possess. They want to know why things happen, how things work, and what they can do next.

→ **Opinionated:** From the time they were children, Gen Yers have been encouraged by their parents, teachers, and other authority figures to share their opinions. That's translated to a group that feels their opinions are always needed and welcomed.

→ **Diverse:** This is the most ethnically diverse generation the nation has ever seen, and many don't identify themselves as being only one race. Consequently, they're much more accepting overall of people who are different from themselves.

→ **Time managers:** Their entire lives have been scheduled—from playgroups to soccer camp to Little League. So it's no surprise that they've picked up a knack for planning along the way.

→ **"Street smart":** The term isn't used in the literal sense, but simply means that these young people have seen a lot. With the Internet and 24-hour cable TV news exposing them to recounts of violence, war, and sexuality at a young age, they're not easily shocked. They're much more aware of the world around them than earlier generations were.[36]

→ **Quick shoppers:** Millennials don't like to waste time in the store. They shop less often than other age cohorts but tend to buy more per trip. They favor mass supercenters and mass merchandisers such as Walmart and Target, over more traditional formats as grocery or drug stores. Gen Yers know how to shop and find what they need. They are more likely to use shopping lists and coupons than other cohort groups.[37]

→ **Want fulfillment:** The divorce rate reached a peak in 1981; it declined steadily until 2000. As families stabilized, they shifted focus and began concentrating more on kids. Authority figures ramped up their roles as teachers, coaches, mentors, and friends to their offspring. Kids were encouraged to specialize and find areas where they could truly excel. This striving for fulfillment spilled over into the workplace as millennials entered the job market. Gen Yers realize that if they are going to work hard for a lifetime they should find something that is meaningful to them. They want to make a difference.[38]

→ **Multitaskers:** Millennials have grown up in a digital, social, mobile technologies world. Multitasking has come naturally to this group. It gives Gen Yers feelings of empowerment, control, productivity, and efficiency as they have mastered these technologies. They can socialize with friends, access news, do research, and be entertained at the same time. Millennials are finding that multitasking can have negative

Gen Yers show how much they care about the environment by patronizing stores such as Whole Foods.

consequences as well. It can be chaotic at times leading to stress and can be distracting causing procrastination and reduced attention. Some Gen Yers find media multitasking addictive, that is, the constant desire to "stay in touch" or "be in the know."[39]

Gen Yers care about the environment. They will often seek out "green" products. They also look to brands for information about the environment. In the case of Honest Tea, many applauded the brand's decision to go to plastic after it was explained via its packaging that less fuel is used to ship plastic than the heavier glass bottles. The favorite green brands of Gen Yers are: Whole Foods, Trader Joe's, Honda, and Google.[40]

GENERATION X

Generation X—people born between 1965 and 1978—consists of 40 million consumers. It was the first generation of latchkey children—products of dual-career households or, in roughly half of the cases, of divorced or separated parents. Gen Xers often spent more time without adult support and guidance than any other age cohort. This experience made them independent, resilient, adaptable, cautious, and skeptical.[41] Gen Xers have been bombarded by multiple media since their cradle days; thus, they are savvy and cynical consumers.

Gen Xers, now in their 30s and 40s, are reaching the age where they are planning to send their kids off to college. Seventy-one percent of Gen Xers still have children under the age of 18.[42] Gen Xers tend to be more protective and involved with their kids than were the baby boomer generation. They highly value the importance of education. Sixty-three percent say they began planning for their kids' college education in elementary school or earlier.[43]

Home ownership is an important goal for Gen Xers. The majority of Gen Xers already own their homes. Of those who do not, close to half worry about saving enough money to purchase one. Yet many feel that their own resourcefulness will enable them to one day own a home.[44] Some furniture retailers, such as Williams-Sonoma's Pottery Barn and Crate & Barrel, target Gen Xers who want to mix and match different styles. Ethan Allen is now attracting Gen Xers with its recent TV ads. Williams-Sonoma also appeals to more Gen Xers with West Elm, its newer furniture concept, which offers edgier designs and lower prices than those found at Pottery Barn.

Gen Xers are avid buyers of the latest clothes, technology, and recreational products. Now that they have advanced in the corporate world, they are demanding certain values from the retailers that they patronize. Gen Xers want frankness, client service, reliability, and authenticity. If retailers aren't true to their word, they quickly lose their Gen X customer.[45]

Researchers have found that a male Gen X traveler is more likely than a boomer to pick a hotel with a sports bar. But the pub must be genuine and the workout room cutting edge. To attract this traveler, Holiday Inn Select is adding Sporting News Grill restaurants and Fitness by Nautilus workout centers to its offerings. In-room amenities will include Wolfgang Puck coffee, Moen showerheads, and Garden Botanika bath products.

A study of over 5,000 Gen Xers in 17 countries determined that their favorite brands were: Google (88 percent), Sony (76 percent), Nokia (69 percent), and BMW (66 percent).[46] Why does tailoring the merchandise to particular age groups matter? One reason is that each generation enters a life stage with its own tastes and biases, and tailoring products to what customers value is key to sales.

Generation X
People born between 1965 and 1978.

Marketing to Gen Xers has often been described as difficult. Yet understanding their needs, wants, and attitudes can make the task much easier. Some of the unique aspects of Gen Xers are:

→ Gen Xers have a unique order of trust: themselves, friends, others, media. They listen to themselves first, then turn to their friends for feedback. Gen Xers put value on actual people's opinions rather than what the masses say.

→ Preferring straight talk instead of manipulation. Gen X is turned off by hype. Marketing to them is a very difficult process, but it can be done with the right tools, mindset, and integrity.

→ Key issues set off Generation X and will help in making decisions on what companies, brands, or products they choose to purchase or support. Political, moral, and emotional issues are hot topics for Gen X and should only be used in marketing/advertising very cautiously.

→ Gen X have specific qualities they look for in products—affordability, quality, and last, if it is trendy. Generation X will jump on a great deal for a product before spending money for some expensive trend.

→ Generation X will test the waters out with a new or different brand than they are used to. Their willingness to venture for a new product is unique to their generation. They place importance on affordability and quality.

→ Communication is key. Gen X wants to feel like they are not being grouped. Communicate to them on a personal level to grab their attention. For example, an e-mail message with the recipient's name in the header makes him or her feel more important.[47]

These boots are typical of the youthful, casual Vera Wang's Lavender line, targeted at Gen X and Gen Y.

BABY BOOMERS

In 2010, there were approximately 75 million **baby boomers** (persons born between 1946 and 1964). Today, their ages range from mid-60s to late 40s. With average life expectancy at an all-time high of 77.4 years, more and more Americans over 50 consider middle age a new start on life. Fewer than 20 percent say they expect to stop work altogether as they age. Of those who plan to keep working at least part-time, 67 percent said they'll do so to stay mentally active, and 57 percent said to stay physically active. People now in their 50s may well work longer than any previous generation. Until recently, boomers typically reached their spending peak at age 54. This contrasts with the cohort prior to boomers (sometimes called the **Greatest Generation** because they grew up in the Great Depression, fought in World War II, and rebuilt America after the war), who are more thrifty than boomers. The greatest generation's spending peaked at age 47.[48] The economic downturn of 2007–2009 has resulted in baby boomers' savings and housing values declining very rapidly. As a result, boomers are postponing retirement. It is estimated that boomers lost over $2 trillion in the 2008 stock market meltdown.[49] Only 23 percent of persons over 55 years old have more than $250,000 in savings and investment.[50] As a result, younger boomers have already reached their spending peak prior to age 54, while older boomers have cut back to build their nest eggs. Historically, boomers have been the big spender age group, spending about 47 percent of the national disposable income.[51] Thrifty boomers are pushing their savings rate from 1 percent to 5 percent as they prepare for retirement.[52]

baby boomers
People born between 1946 and 1964.

Greatest Generation
Cohort before the baby boomers who grew up in the Great Depression and fought in World War II.

Spending cuts by boomers have left upscale retailers scrambling. Designer Vera Wang is now targeting Gen X and Gen Y with a casual line called Lavender. Prices have also been cut on the Vera Wang line. Although Mercedes-Benz still views boomers as its primary target market, it has quietly started doing research among 20 to 32 year olds. It calls the research Generation Benz.[53] Nordstrom has started building fewer full-price department stores and has tripled the pace for opening lower-priced Nordstrom Rack stores. Nordstrom believes that boomers still want fashion, but at a discount.[54]

Despite the financial problems that a number of boomers face, in general they are a happy, confident group that looks forward to the future. Other generations see boomers as socially conscious, productive, and having a positive impact upon society.[55] Boomers do not see themselves as old and they want to keep helping society as long as they are able.[56] A recent survey tapped into the boomer mindset. It found that:

→ Boomers state that "old age" officially begins at 80.

→ Boomers feel much younger due to their "mental attitude."

→ They feel 15 years younger than they actually are.

→ More than 50 percent of boomers exercise regularly.

→ A high percentage of boomers feel that they are "in better shape" as they get older.

→ 72 percent of boomers plan to keep working in some capacity after retirement.

→ New hobbies and multiple interests are key to boomer happiness.

→ One-third of boomers have pursued additional educational opportunities.

→ Volunteering is important to boomers.

→ The cost of living and access to health care are more important than warm climate considerations.[57]

→ 47 percent maintain a profile on a social media Web site.

→ The most popular boomer social sites are: Facebook at 74 percent, Twitter at 13 percent, and LinkedIn at 13 percent.[58]

Baby boomers are also heavily involved in word-of-mouth promotion. When fellow boomers ask them for advice on products and services, 89 percent of them deliver it. And they are likely to seek such a recommendation approximately 90 times per year. Moreover, 93 percent of baby boomers trust their friends for information.[59] Nevertheless, marketers spend countless hours trying to create promotional messages that will resonate with boomers. Here are a few examples:

→ **Connecting with boomers' sense of themselves as trailblazers.** At every stage of their lives, boomers have challenged the status quo. Brands that convey a totally new benefit will appeal to boomers' inherent desire to break from the norm. American Express's Ameriprise Financial division expresses it well: "You changed everything that came before you. That was you then . . . that's still you now."

→ **Focusing on their lives, not their ages.** Boomers don't need to be reminded of how old they are getting. Rather than stress their age, Centrum Silver uses advertising to reflect older consumers' passion to continue doing the things they love.

→ **Linking the brand with a major life event.** Bayer Aspirin's "Do More" effort builds an emotional bond by telling the story of someone who "had a heart attack and lived"; that's why the person is committed to Bayer.

→ *Knowing that boomers are jaded students of ads.*
Boomers are idealists, but they grew up with TV ads, and are skeptical of empty promises. The Dove campaign that shows real-looking women instead of models is not just relatable; it preempts boomers' suspicions about exaggerated beauty claims.[60]

Age	Tweens	Teens	Gen Y	Gen X	Baby Boom
	8 to 12 yrs	13 to 19 yrs	1979–1994	1965–1978	1946–1964
	20 million	25 million	75 million+	40 million	75 million

© iStockphoto.com/Juan Facundo Mora Soria; © Cengage Learning 2013

LO4
Growing Ethnic Markets

The minority population of the United States in 2011 reached 110 million. About one in three U.S. residents is a minority. To put this into perspective, there are more minorities here today than there were people in the United States in 1910. In fact, the minority population in the United States is larger than the total population of all but 11 countries.[61] Whites will compose less than half of the U.S. population by 2042. Currently, non-white minorities account for 49 percent of the children born in the United States.[62]

The Asian population will continue to increase because of immigration and higher birthrates, and the non-Hispanic black population will increase mostly because of higher birthrates. In 2050 the share of the black population will have increased by one percentage point to 14 percent; Asians will rise to about 9 percent from 5 percent today.[63] But it is the Hispanic population that is driving minority growth. The total U.S. population is projected to grow to 439 million by 2050, and most of that growth will come from Hispanics. By 2050 about one in three U.S. residents will be Hispanic. While immigration continues to be a driver of the growing Hispanic population, for the past several years most of the growth has come from births.[64]

Four states and the District of Columbia (68 percent) are majority-minority. The states are Hawaii (75 percent), New Mexico (58 percent), California (58 percent), and Texas (53 percent).[65] Counties around Denver, Las Vegas, and Orlando became majority-minorities in 2010.

In 2013, it is estimated that Hispanics will wield $1.4 trillion in purchasing power. In the same year, African Americans will have $1.2 trillion, followed by Asian Americans at $752 billion.[66]

Companies across the United States have recognized that diversity can result in bottom-line benefits. More than ever, diversity is emerging as a priority goal for visionary leaders who embrace the incontestable fact that the United States is becoming a truly multicultural society. Smart marketers increasingly are reaching out and tapping these growing markets. PepsiCo, for example, has been very successful with Gatorade Xtremo targeted to the Hispanic market. It has now been expanded to five flavors.

Rocawear apparel was launched by hip-hop artist "Jay-Z." The company's marketing strategy is designed to show the target customer that the brand is not merely on the pulse but "creates the pulse"—an appeal to a "street savvy," "urban" customer interested in a hip lifestyle brand.

MARKETING TO HISPANIC AMERICANS

The term *Hispanic* encompasses people of many different backgrounds. Nearly 60 percent of Hispanic Americans are of Mexican descent. The next largest group,

Puerto Ricans, make up just under 10 percent of Hispanics. Other groups, including Central Americans, Dominicans, South Americans, and Cubans, each account for less than 5 percent of all Hispanics.

The diversity of the Hispanic population and the language differences create many challenges for those trying to target this market. Hispanics, especially recent immigrants, often prefer products from their native country. Therefore, many retailers along the southern U.S. border import goods from Mexico. In New York City, more than 6,000 *bodegas* (grocery stores) sell such items as plantains, chorizo (pork sausage), and religious candles to Puerto Rican Americans. The *bodegas* also serve as neighborhood social centers. Fresh produce is usually very important to Hispanics because of the tradition of shopping every day at open-air produce markets in their native country.

In general, Hispanics tend to be very brand loyal, but they often are not aware of many mainstream U.S. brands. Instead, many Hispanics are loyal to the brands found in their homeland. If these are not available, Hispanics will choose brands that reflect their native values and culture. This preference for brands from home has helped Mexico's Jarritos become one of the fastest-growing soft drinks in the United States. Yet until recently it was *una marca desapareciendo*—a dying brand. Despite having name recognition in its homeland that rivaled that of Coca-Cola, the 55-year-old soda was losing ground to imported U.S. rivals. So parent company Novamex boldly crossed the border. In the past few years, it has moved onto the competition's turf with marketing that speaks to Mexican Americans' thirst for the good old days. Today, Jarritos's 12 flavors comprise over 50 percent of the Mexican soft drink market in the United States.[67]

Walmart has been the largest retailer in Mexico since 2000. But until recently, it has taken a low-key approach to targeting Hispanics in the United States. Now the world's largest retailer is stepping up efforts to attract America's fastest-growing immigrant group. In 2004, Walmart began printing its monthly ad circulars in English and Spanish. It also launched its own Hispanic magazine, called *Viviendo* (Living), which it distributes free at 1,300 stores heavily shopped by Hispanics. The glossy quarterly magazine features profiles of Latino leaders and celebrities next to ads highlighting Walmart's expanding line of products and services geared toward Hispanics.

State Farm had traditionally been ranked third or fourth by Hispanics when shopping for auto insurance. Research found that Hispanics thought that State Farm was not "in-tune." Some said, "They don't understand me." So State Farm embarked on an out-of-the-box strategy to build a relationship with the Hispanic market. It launched a TV campaign dubbed "Ahi Estoy," meaning "I'm there," to indicate that the company helped Hispanics. One of those ads featured the fictitious band called Los Felinos de la Noche, played by real-life struggling musicians.

Then, State Farm thought, "What if we create a real band?" and Los Felinos de la Noche (the Felines of the Night) was born. Since launching the band in 2008, one-third of the primarily Spanish-speaking consumers who listen to Northern Mexico regional-type music know that the band is sponsored by State Farm. State Farm never outwardly positioned itself as the sponsor of the band with logos or in the band's lyrics. Instead, band members, in interviews, give credit to State Farm for launching their careers.[68]

About 68 percent of U.S. Hispanics have home Internet access and 42 percent shop online.[69] Hispanics who use the Internet are, on average, much younger than the general online population. Of Hispanics who have Internet access, 63 percent use the Web to look for information rather than to play games or hang out in chat rooms, versus 52 percent of the general population.[70] Yet 42 percent had downloaded digital media in the previous 30 days. Music accounted for one-third of the downloads.[71] Kraft Foods has realized that the Internet is a good way to connect with Hispanics. The company launched **www.comidakraft.com**, where Hispanics can share or post their recipes online, through what's called the Recipe Connection. The Recipe Connection page encourages Hispanic consumers to submit a favorite recipe containing at least one Kraft food product, "perhaps one that has been passed down in your family or an original creation from your own kitchen." Many of the recipes later appear in the magazine, *comida y familia,* a Spanish-language recipe index published by Kraft.

Audiences for Spanish-language radio and TV continue to grow while overall ratings for the big four TV networks are flat. Companies such as Proctor & Gamble, Johnson & Johnson, Verizon, and General Mills are raising their Hispanic market promotional budgets. Since General Mills began buying more ads in Spanish-language media, its sales of its Progresso brand and Honey Nut Cheerios have soared.[72] Marketers have found that simply having TV programs in Spanish is not sufficient to attract the target market. It must also be meaningful to their culture. Previously, MTV en Español was just that—traditional MTV in Spanish. The program today is called MTV Tr3s, which is bilingual (subtitles appear in Spanish when English is spoken) and features shows like *Quiero Mis Quinces,* about *quinceañera* (15th birthday) parties, and *Pimpeando,* about car culture.

MARKETING TO AFRICAN AMERICANS

The African American market is youthful and increasingly more affluent. A few recent finding include:

→ African Americans are nearly six years younger than all consumers; 47 percent are between 18 and 49 years old, which is considered the top-spending age demographic by marketers.

→ Black households making $75,000-plus have increased 47 percent in the last five years—1.5 times faster than the general population.

→ If current trends continue, by 2015 more than half of all black Americans will live in the suburbs.

→ Although their population is smaller, there are more African American households in the U.S. than Hispanic households because the latter tend to have larger families.[73]

Several companies owned by African Americans—such as Soft Sheen-Carson and Pro-Line—target the African American market for health

Loreal markets lip-color to African American women using style icon Beyonce.

and beauty aids. Huge corporations such as Revlon, Gillette, and Alberto Culver have either divisions or major product lines for this market as well. Alberto Culver's hair-care line for this segment includes 75 products. In fact, hair-care items are the largest single category in the African American health and beauty aid industry. Maybelline with its "Shades of You" product line has the largest share (28 percent) of the African American health and beauty aid market.

There are few differences between African American and non–African American households when it comes to shopping at grocery, mass merchandisers (J.C. Penney, Sears), and warehouse club stores. A much larger proportion of African American consumers shop at convenience-oriented formats such as drug, dollar, and convenience/gas stores. Nearly half (46 percent) of African American households shop at beauty supply stores—almost three times the rate for non–African American households. Automotive supply stores and electronics stores follow beauty stores as the most popular alternative channels for African American consumers.[74]

African American consumers create a wide range of possibilities for marketers in various industries:

→ **Food and beverage:** 3.9 million black consumers spend $150 or more per week on groceries.

→ **Health and fitness:** 7.6 million African Americans said they exercise regularly at home, which opens up possibilities for marketers of exercise equipment.

→ **Clothing:** African American men and women represent 22 percent and 26 percent of all suit-buyers, respectively.[75]

Black media continue to offer advertisers access to African American consumers, who nevertheless also share many of the mainstream media preferences of other American viewers and readers:

→ Television is an important source of media consumption, with four in ten households containing four or more televisions.

→ Spending on magazines is 6 percent more than the national average.

→ Newspapers are less popular than the average.[76]

The promotional dollars spent on African Americans continue to rise, as does the number of black media choices. BET, the black cable TV network, has over 80 million viewers. The 45-year-old *Essence* magazine reaches one-third of all black females ages 18 to 49. But radio holds a special appeal. African Americans spend considerable time with radio (an astounding 4 hours a day versus 2.8 hours for other groups), and urban audiences have an intensely personal relationship with the medium. ABC Radio Network's Tom Joyner reaches an audience of more than 8 million in 115 markets, and Doug Banks is heard by 1.5 million listeners in 36 markets. Pepsi used radio to raise the level of Mountain Dew awareness and its market share in urban markets. Artists like Busta Rhymes personify the image of Mountain Dew and create the lyrics and the vibe that sells the product.

African Americans are very tech-savvy, with roughly 31 percent of African American discretionary spending dollars ($39 billion) going toward the purchase of computers, cell phones, and electronics—a proportionally higher percentage when compared to non–African Americans. African Americans also spend more weekly time online (18 hours) than watching television (15 hours). Further, 93 percent of African Americans go online traditionally via their PCs, while 76 percent access the Web via their cell phones or digital device. Approximately 60 percent of African Americans have downloaded music, a TV show, movie, or ringtone in the previous month, while 50 percent regularly update and access a social networking account.[77]

The election of President Obama has given hope and motivation to several generations of African Americans. Young people are realizing that hard work and good education can create opportunities once thought not possible. Recent research shows that more African Americans than ever before are achieving the American dream. In 2011, there were 2.8 million African Americans earning more than $75,000 annually.[78] Some of the characteristics of this group are:

→ Affluent African Americans most often read the newspapers *The New York Times* and *The Wall Street Journal*, as well as the magazines *Business Week*, *Newsweek*, *Jet*, and *The Economist*.

→ 50 percent go out for fine dining and more than 25 percent go to clubs/bars at least once a week.

→ More than 20 percent go clothes shopping at least once a week. Men focus their fashion spending on career wear, casual wear, and shoes, while women spend on purses and shoes.

→ 75 percent shop in higher-end, specialty department stores, and 66 percent shop in traditional department stores. Outlets and "last chance" stores also are popular destinations, suggesting that even affluent shoppers look for bargains.

→ More than 10 percent travel on business at least once a week and about one-quarter shop during business travel.

→ More than 70 percent have a passport and have used it on international travel in the past year. About one-third travel internationally at least three times a year and one-tenth travel internationally at least every other month.

→ While more than 60 percent have gym or fitness center memberships and one-third have home gyms, nearly 40 percent wish they were doing more to stay fit.[79]

MARKETING TO ASIAN AMERICANS

Asian Americans, who represent only 4.2 percent of the U.S. population, have the highest average family income of all groups. At $66,500, it exceeds the average U.S. household income by more than $10,000. Of all Asian Americans, 48 percent have at least a bachelor's degree.[80] Approximately 50 percent of the students at six University of California schools are Asian Americans.

Because Asian Americans are younger (average age is 34), better educated, and have higher incomes than average, they are sometimes called a "marketer's dream." Although there is much cultural diversity, and therefore multiple market segments, Asian Americans are concentrated geographically. California, New York, and Texas are home to 52 percent of all Asian Americans.[81]

A number of products have been developed specifically for the Asian American market. For example, Kayla Beverly Hills salon draws Asian American consumers because the firm offers cosmetics formulated for them. Anheuser-Busch's agricultural products division targets the Asian American market with eight varieties of California-grown rice, each with a different label, to cover a range of nationalities and tastes.

Cultural diversity within the Asian American market complicates promotional efforts. Some of the major cultural differences among key groups of Asian Americans are:

→ CHINESE
   Largest Asian American segment
   Four distinct geographic areas in Chinese category: Taiwan, Hong Kong, People's Republic of China, and Southeast Asia

Two major dialects: Mandarin and Cantonese
May be cautious in personal and business dealings
Tend to be price-conscious
Embrace idea of planning for long term
Strong emphasis on family and education

→ FILIPINO

Second largest Asian American segment
High rate of U.S. acculturation due to English competency
Heritage/cultural values that are similar to Hispanic culture
Strong sense of family and community preservation
Highly religious (predominately Roman Catholic)

→ ASIAN INDIAN

Third largest Asian American segment
Speak many different languages and come from a variety of Indian
cultural and religious backgrounds
National heritage, culture, and values very important
Extreme emphasis on education
Highly price-/value-conscious
Very loyal to strong brands
Respond best to advertising in English, with Indian national cultural values
woven in seamlessly

→ VIETNAMESE

Fourth largest Asian American segment
Large number of immigrants were refugees
Quality-conscious and value seekers
Strong political beliefs
Extremely strong tendency for cultural and community preservation
Strong emphasis on family and education

→ KOREAN

Fifth largest Asian American segment
Most homogeneous of top Asian subgroups, with the majority of Korean
Americans coming from similar socioeconomic backgrounds in Korea
Most likely of all Asian American segments to have immigrated as complete
family units
May be more emotional in decision making
Prefer name brands to lower prices
Strong emphasis on family and education

→ JAPANESE

Sixth largest Asian American segment
Highest percentage of U.S.-born individuals of any Asian American segment
(due to waves of immigration dating back to the mid-1800s)
A critical mass of Japanese temporary residents in the United States, to estab-
lish a subculture; includes students, temporary workers and trainees, and expa-
triate business families
Tend to value group consensus over individual opinion
Value name brands over price
Strong emphasis on family and education[82]

Although Asian Americans embrace the values of the larger U.S. population, they also hold on to the cultural values of their particular subgroup. Consider language. Many Asian Americans, particularly Koreans and Chinese, speak their native tongue at home. Filipinos are far less likely to do so. Cultural values are also apparent in the ways different groups make big-ticket purchases. In Japanese American homes, the husband alone makes the decision on such purchases nearly half the time; the wife decides only about 6 percent of the time. In Filipino families, however, wives make these decisions a little more often than their husbands do, although by far the most decisions are made by husbands and wives jointly or with the input of other family members.

Asian Americans like to shop at stores owned and managed by other Asian Americans. Small businesses such as flower shops, grocery stores, and appliance stores are often best equipped to offer the products that Asian Americans want. For example, at first glance the Hannam Chain, a supermarket in Los Angeles's Koreatown, might be any other grocery store. But next to the Kraft American singles and the State Fair corn dogs are jars of whole cabbage kimchi. A snack bar in another part of the store cooks up aromatic mung cakes, and an entire aisle is devoted to dried seafood.

→ 76 percent of Asian Americans versus 67.8 percent of non-Asians are regular users of the Internet.

→ 95 percent of Asian Americans own PCs (as compared to 83 percent of the overall population).

→ Asian Americans (as well as Hispanics) are more likely to be influenced by a blogger recommendation to purchase a product or service than their non-Hispanic white counterparts.

→ 63 percent of Asian Americans visit a social networking site at least two to three times a month.

→ Asian Americans are more likely to engage in multiple Internet activities, on multiple devices, each day (i.e., e-mail, Skype, and instant messaging).

→ Asian Americans are twice as likely to use LinkedIn and Twitter: 14.5 percent of Asian Americans visit LinkedIn and 10.8 percent visit Twitter regularly compared to 7.1 percent and 5.6 percent of non-Hispanic whites.

→ Asian Americans are more likely to bank online compared to non-Asian households, with 75.3 percent banking online compared to 67.4 percent of non-Asians.[83]

A product in high demand in Asian American supermarkets is kimchi, a staple in many Asian diets.

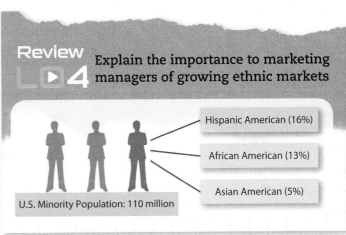

Review LO4 Explain the importance to marketing managers of growing ethnic markets

Hispanic American (16%)

African American (13%)

Asian American (5%)

U.S. Minority Population: 110 million

© Cengage Learning 2013

LO5
Economic Factors

In addition to social and demographic factors, marketing managers must understand and react to the economic environment. The three economic areas of greatest concern to most marketers are consumers' incomes, inflation, and recession.

CONSUMERS' INCOMES

As disposable (or after-tax) incomes rise, more families and individuals can afford the "good life." In recent years, however, U.S. incomes have risen at a rather slow

purchasing power
A comparison of income versus the relative cost of a set standard of goods and services in different geographic areas.

inflation
A measure of the decrease in the value of money, expressed as the percentage reduction in value since the previous year.

pace. After adjustment for inflation, the median household income in the United States in 2010 was $46,326. This means half of all U.S. households earned less and the other half earned more.[84] Two and a half percent of the United States population earns $250,000 a year or more.[85]

Education is the primary determinant of a person's earning potential. For example, only 1 percent of those with only a high school education earn over $100,000 annually. By comparison, 13 percent of college-educated workers earn six figures or more. People with a bachelor's degree take home an average of 38 percent more than those with just a high school diploma. Over a lifetime, an individual with a bachelor's degree will earn twice as much total income as a non-degree holder.[86] Along with "willingness to buy," or "ability to buy," income is a key determinant of target markets. A marketer who knows where the money is knows where the markets are. If you are seeking a new store location for Dollar General, a retail chain that caters to lower-income consumers, you would probably concentrate on the South and Midwest because most households with annual incomes of less than $45,000 are concentrated in these areas.

PURCHASING POWER

Rising incomes don't necessarily mean a higher standard of living. Increased standards of living are a function of purchasing power. **Purchasing power** is measured by comparing income to the relative cost of a set standard of goods and services in different geographic areas, usually referred to as the cost of living. Another way to think of purchasing power is income minus the cost of living (i.e., expenses). In general, a cost of living index takes into account housing, food and groceries, transportation, utilities, health care, and miscellaneous expenses such as clothing, services, and entertainment. The Web site **www.homefair.com**'s salary calculator uses these metrics when it figures that the cost of living in New York City is almost three times the cost of living in Youngstown, Ohio. This means that a worker living in New York must earn nearly $279,500 to have the same standard of living as someone making $100,000 in Youngstown.

When income is high relative to the cost of living, people have more discretionary income. That means they have more money to spend on nonessential items (in other words, on wants rather than needs). This information is important to marketers for obvious reasons. Consumers with high purchasing power can afford to spend more money without jeopardizing their budget for necessities like food, housing, and utilities. They also have the ability to purchase higher-priced necessities, for example, a more expensive car, a home in a more expensive neighborhood, or a designer handbag versus a purse from a discount store.

INFLATION

Inflation is a measure of the decrease in the value of money, generally expressed as the percentage reduction in value since the previous year, which is the rate of inflation. Thus, in simple terms an inflation rate of 5 percent means you will need 5 percent more units of money than you would have needed last year to buy the same basket of products. If inflation is 5 percent, you can expect that, on average, prices have risen by about 5 percent since the previous year. Of course, if pay raises are matching the rate of inflation, then employees will be no worse off in terms of the immediate purchasing power of their salaries.

In times of low inflation, businesses seeking to increase their profit margins can do so only by increasing their efficiency. If they significantly increase prices, no one will purchase their goods or services. The recent "Great Recession" brought inflation rates to almost zero.

In creating marketing strategies to cope with inflation, managers must realize that, regardless of what happens to the seller's cost, the buyer is not going to pay more for a product than the subjective value he or she places on it. No matter how compelling the justification might be for a 10 percent price increase, marketers must always examine its impact on demand. Many marketers try to hold prices level for as long as is practical.

RECESSION

A **recession** is a period of economic activity characterized by negative growth. More precisely, a recession is defined as when the gross domestic product falls for two consecutive quarters. Gross domestic product is the total market value of all final goods and services produced during a period of time. Final goods are the end product of the production process, such as a car. If one counted the value of the engine, brakes, and seats (intermediate goods), plus the value of the car, then that would be double counting. The official beginning of the 2007–2009 recession was December 2007. While the causes of the recession are very complex, it began with the collapse of inflated housing prices. Those high prices led people to take out mortgages they couldn't afford from banks that should have known the money would not be repaid. By 2008, the recession had spread around the globe. A very slow economic recovery began in July 2009.

Economists have argued whether or not this downturn should be called "The Great Recession." Regardless of its name, it was the largest economic downturn since the Great Depression of 1929 to 1939. During the recession, unemployment rose from slightly over 4 percent to over 10 percent.[87] There were very deep cuts in male-heavy sections of the economy such as construction and manufacturing. Because companies automated more tasks or moved whole assembly lines off-shore, many jobs will never be replaced. Instead, new jobs will have to be created in areas such as information technology and service industries.[88] By mid-2010, the unemployment rate was falling, albeit slowly. The reason is that the economy must add a minimum of 100,000 jobs per month just to accommodate new entrants into the workforce.

The declining stock market, growing unemployment, and collapsing home prices took a toll on consumer confidence. Many consumers shifted to store brands that, on average, cost 46 percent less than manufacturers' brands.[89] Kimberly-Clark has noticed a big decline in its potty-training pants as young parents leave their children in diapers longer. Diapers are cheaper than training pants. Procter & Gamble has seen its bargain-priced Gain detergent rise rapidly in sales. More consumers are using coupons than ever before.

Like Gain, some brands that help the consumer save money do very well in a recession. McCormick spices had an uptick in sales as people ate out less and cooked more at home. Similarly, snack foods such as nuts and potato

recession
A period of economic activity characterized by negative growth, which reduces demand for goods and services.

Kool-Aid is a low price alternative to soda or water, a strong selling point in tough economic times.

© iStockphoto.com/Juan Facundo Mora Soria

© Terri Miller/E-Visual Communications, Inc.

chips did well in the down economy. Beer and wine sales tend to hold up quite well during economic downturns, but then consumers don't trade up to higher-price brands. Because people tend to hang on to durable goods longer in a recession, there is a greater demand for repair services, remodeling services, and do-it-yourself products.[90]

Retailers and manufacturers redouble their efforts to cut costs during a recession. They often try to lower prices to attract new customers and hold existing ones, but also often cut costs simply to survive. Burger King sold double cheeseburgers for $1. Procter & Gamble dropped the price of Cheer and repositioned it as a value brand. Applebee's started offering two entrees for $20. Walmart grew market share for its Great Value private-label canned vegetables, breakfast cereals, and bread. ConAgra Foods began advertising its Banquet frozen dinners for the first time in more than a decade, priced at $1.50. Kraft began advertising its low-cost Kool-Aid powdered drink mix on national radio for the first time in 11 years.

Researchers found that during the recession, consumers were sticking very close to shopping lists and doing their best to completely empty their pantries before restocking. Also, consumers were going to fewer stores but selecting stores where they could get the widest array of products at the best value. Many people, for the first time, prepared their lunches to take to work. Kraft came up with a creative solution for budget-strapped consumers. The firm came up with an iPhone app called iFood that promised to save shoppers time and to provide recipes for great meals. When you select your recipe on iFood, you can also choose the store where you want to shop and iFood tells you not only how to get there, but it also tells you the aisles in the store where the items are located. Of course, iFood features Kraft products as key ingredients in the recipes.[91]

Companies must be careful when cutting prices during a recession. Market research has determined that 70 percent of the respondents assume that if the price is lowered on a brand, it must have been overpriced. Further, 62 percent believed that price cuts meant that the product was old, perhaps ready to expire or about to be revamped. In the same survey, 65 percent assumed that leaving prices unchanged was a sign that the brand was popular.[92] To avoid these perceptual problems with price cutting, McDonald's, Chili's, and Applebee's created new value meals that didn't compete with their regular offerings. Some car manufacturers used the same strategy by introducing new, lower-priced models such as the Nissan Cube and the Kia Soul.

Review

LO5 Identify consumer and marketer reactions to the state of the economy

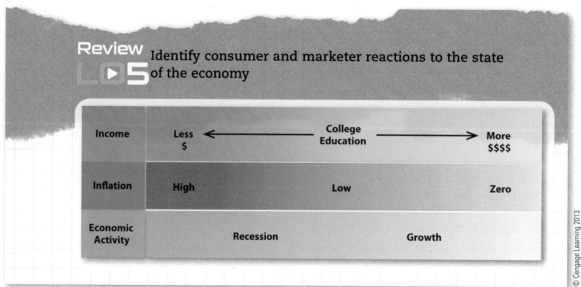

Income	Less $ ←	College Education	→ More $$$$
Inflation	High	Low	Zero
Economic Activity	Recession	Growth	

© Cengage Learning 2013

LO6
Technological Factors

© iStockphoto.com/Juan Facundo Mora Soria

The recent economic downturn and slow recovery has had an impact on research and development (R&D) spending. In order to cut costs and boost short-term profits, many companies, particularly in the auto and drug industries, slashed R&D, product design, and laboratory spending. Other firms have taken a different tact and either increased or held R&D spending steady. Their idea is that they can more effectively compete when the economy improves. Companies such as 3M, Microsoft, Google, Intel, and Cisco Systems have followed this strategy. During the 1999–2002 recession, Apple boosted R&D spending 42 percent despite declining sales. During the same recession, Motorola cut R&D spending 13 percent. Apple's research during that recession created the iPod. Apple, which also increased R&D spending in the latest recession, is a global winner. Motorola is still struggling.[93] Without investment in R&D the United States cannot compete in a knowledge-based global economy.

RESEARCH

The United States, historically, has excelled at both basic and applied research. **Basic research** (or *pure research*) attempts to expand the frontiers of knowledge but is not aimed at a specific, pragmatic problem. Basic research aims to confirm an existing theory or to learn more about a concept or phenomenon. For example, basic research might focus on high-energy physics. **Applied research**, in contrast, attempts to develop new or improved products. The United States has dramatically improved its track record in applied research. For example, the United States leads the world in applying basic research to aircraft design and propulsion systems.

In 2009, non-Americans were granted more U.S. patents than resident inventors.[94] This is partially the result of the United States' companies sending R&D offshore. IBM, for example, has been America's largest generator of new patents for over 15 years. IBM sets up "collaboratories," which match up its researchers with experts from governments, universities. and companies. The company now has "collaboratories" in Saudi Arabia, Switzerland, China, Ireland, Taiwan, and Brazil. If an IBM patent originates in an IBM lab in, say, India, it is counted as a non-U.S. patent.[95] One reason that R&D has moved off-shore is that the United States once had the most generous tax credits for R&D. Now, it ranks 17th among developed countries.

STIMULATING INNOVATION

Companies attempting to innovate often limit their searches to areas that they are already familiar with. This can help lead to incremental progress but rarely leads to a dramatic breakthrough. Companies are now using several approaches to keeping innovation strong. These include:

→ **Build scenarios.** Some firms use teams of writers with diverse perspectives to create complex scenarios of what future markets may look like. The writers try to imagine detailed opportunities and threats for their companies, partners, and collaborators.

→ **Enlist the Web.** A few companies have created Web sites that act as literal marketplaces of ideas. Innocentive.com is a site where people and companies look for help in solving scientific and business challenges. Posters of challenges

basic research
Pure research that aims to confirm an existing theory or to learn more about a concept or phenomenon.

applied research
An attempt to develop new or improved products.

sometimes offer cash rewards for solutions: Amounts have ranged from $5,000 to $1 million.

→ **Talk to early adopters.** Early adopters tend to be innovators themselves. They are risk-takers and look for new things. Sometimes they are working in a specific market and are frustrated by the tools, goods, or services currently available and yearn for something better. Many medical devices, for example, originate from sketches drawn by surgeons, surgical nurses, and other medical staff who feel driven to experiment with new ideas because current products aren't meeting their needs.

→ **Use marketing research.** Find out what customers like and dislike about your products and competitors' products. Find out what would make their lives and jobs easier "if they just had ____." Procter & Gamble's Swiffer came from just a question.

→ **Create an innovative environment.** Let employees know that they have the "freedom to fail." Without risk, there is no innovation. Create intranets so that people can share knowledge and skills within the organization. Most importantly, top management must lead by example, that is, by creating an atmosphere where innovation is encouraged and rewarded. A conservative organizational culture where top management demands, "Prove it first," will never be a leader in innovation.

→ **Cater to entrepreneurs.** Clear policies that reserve blocks of time for scientists or engineers to explore their own ideas have worked well at some companies. At 3M, scientists can spend 15 percent of their time on projects they dream up themselves, and the company has set procedures to take bright ideas forward, including grants and venture funding. Google Inc. takes a similar approach, allowing researchers to devote 20 percent of their schedules to play time, pursuing their own ideas and projects. The company credits this policy with fostering many of its important product innovations, including Gmail, its popular Web-based e-mail service.[96]

An example of how innovation can work is provided by Research in Motion's (RIM) founder Mike Lazaridis, who embedded innovation into the company's culture. He encourages his people to explore big ideas and apparent paradoxes to push beyond what they can prove to be true in order to see what might be true. In the mid-1990s, RIM was a modestly successful pager company. But Lazaridis saw potential in the idea of a portable e-mail device. He began to consider what it might look like, what it could do. He imagined something much smaller than a laptop but easier to type on than a phone. Laptops were already shrinking and bumping up against limitations on how small a QWERTY keyboard could reasonably get. Lazaridis stepped back to consider how a much tinier keyboard could be feasible—and he achieved a leap of logic: What if we typed using only our thumbs? With a prototype and concrete feedback, the BlackBerry was born.[97]

Although developing new technology internally is a key to creating and maintaining a long-term competitive advantage, external technology is also important to managers for two reasons. First, by acquiring the technology, the firm may be able to operate more efficiently or create a better product. Second, a new technology may render your existing products obsolete.

Netflix's innovative distribution model ultimately led to a major loss of market share by Blockbuster. Yet Netflix's CEO realized that sending DVDs by mail was not a sustainable competitive advantage in an Internet world. In 2007, the firm began letting subscribers stream video to their PCs from the Netflix Web site. Now, over 20 percent of the subscribers use this service. By 2010, a subscriber could use a Wii, Xbox, PS3, or Blu-ray player to stream movies to their PC, Mac, or television.[98]

Restaurant promotion is experimenting with the latest technology to increase sales. Burger King, Quiznos, and Applebee's are using technology that recognizes a person's location and, via an iPhone app, helps them find the nearest restaurant and perhaps get a deal or coupon. Sonic has recently tested geo-fencing, a technology from mobile-ad firm 1020, Inc. in San Francisco. In the test, the technology took a virtual map of Atlanta and drew perimeters around roughly 50 Sonic restaurants in the city. The technology used global positioning system (GPS) data and proximity to cell towers to tell when a customer who had signed up for company communications moved close to one of the marked-off locations on the map. It then sent that customer a text message with either a discount offer or an advertisement to entice the customer to stop in at the restaurant. Sonic is now looking at expanding the program and possibly taking it national.[99]

INNOVATION CARRIES TO THE BOTTOM LINE

Innovation pays off big for creative organizations. One study found that the most innovative firms have an average profit margin growth of 3 percent higher than the typical firm.[100] Other research has found higher stock market returns among firms that spend heavily on research and development.[101] Each year *The Wall Street Journal* pays tribute to the most innovative companies around the globe. The latest winners, in rank order, are: Apple (U.S.), Google (U.S.), Microsoft (U.S.), IBM (U.S.), Toyota Motor (Japan), Amazon.com (U.S.), LG Electronics (South Korea), BYD (China), General Electric (U.S.), and Sony (Japan).[102]

Review
LO 6   Identify the impact of technology on a firm

© Cengage Learning 2013

LO 7
Political and Legal Factors

Business needs government regulation to protect innovators of new technology, the interests of society in general, one business from another, and consumers. In turn, government needs business because the marketplace generates taxes that support public efforts to educate our youth, pave our roads, protect our shores, and so on. The private sector also serves as a counterweight to government. The decentralization of power inherent in a private-enterprise system supplies the limitation on government essential for the survival of a democracy.

Every aspect of the marketing mix is subject to laws and restrictions. It is the duty of marketing managers or their legal assistants to understand these laws and conform to them because failure to comply with regulations can have major consequences for a firm. Sometimes just sensing trends and taking corrective action before a government agency acts can help avoid regulation. The tobacco industry failed to do this. As a result, Joe Camel and the Marlboro Man are fading into the sunset in the United States along with other strategies used to promote tobacco products.

The challenge is not simply to keep the marketing department out of trouble, however, but to help it implement creative new programs to accomplish marketing objectives. It is all too easy for a marketing manager or sometimes a lawyer to say "no" to a marketing innovation that actually entails little risk. For example, an overly cautious lawyer could hold up sales of a desirable new product by warning that the package design could prompt a copyright infringement suit. Thus, it is important to have a thorough understanding of the laws established by the federal government, state governments, and regulatory agencies to govern marketing-related issues.

FEDERAL LEGISLATION

Federal laws that affect marketing fall into several categories. First, the Sherman Act, the Clayton Act, the Federal Trade Commission Act, the Celler-Kefauver Antimerger Act, and the Hart-Scott-Rodino Act were passed to regulate the competitive environment. Second, the Robinson-Patman Act was designed to regulate pricing practices. Third, the Wheeler-Lea Act was created to control false advertising. The Lanham Act protects trademarks. These key pieces of legislation are summarized in Exhibit 4.1. The primary federal laws that protect consumers are shown in Exhibit 4.2. A law recently passed by Congress is the Credit Card Act. Now, a credit card company cannot increase the rate on your existing balance and must tell you 45 days in advance before increasing the rate on new transactions. The new law also places limits on fees and rate increases and requires consistency in payment dates and times.

Exhibit 4.1 Primary U.S. Laws That Affect Marketing

Legislation	Impact on Marketing
Sherman Act of 1890	Makes trusts and conspiracies in restraint of trade illegal; makes monopolies and attempts to monopolize a misdemeanor.
Clayton Act of 1914	Outlaws discrimination in prices to different buyers; prohibits tying contracts (which require the buyer of one product to also buy another item in the line); makes illegal the combining of two or more competing corporations by pooling ownership of stock.
Federal Trade Commission Act of 1914	Created the Federal Trade Commission to deal with antitrust matters; outlaws unfair methods of competition.
Robinson-Patman Act of 1936	Prohibits charging different prices to different buyers of merchandise of like grade and quantity; requires sellers to make any supplementary services or allowances available to all purchasers on a proportionately equal basis.
Wheeler-Lea Amendments to FTC Act of 1938	Broadens the Federal Trade Commission's power to prohibit practices that might injure the public without affecting competition; outlaws false and deceptive advertising.
Lanham Act of 1946	Establishes protection for trademarks.
Celler-Kefauver Antimerger Act of 1950	Strengthens the Clayton Act to prevent corporate acquisitions that reduce competition.
Hart-Scott-Rodino Act of 1976	Requires large companies to notify the government of their intent to merge.
Foreign Corrupt Practices Act of 1977	Prohibits bribery of foreign officials to obtain business.

Exhibit 4.2 Primary U.S. Laws Protecting Consumers

Legislation	Impact on Marketing
Federal Food and Drug Act of 1906	Prohibits adulteration and misbranding of foods and drugs involved in interstate commerce; strengthened by the Food, Drug, and Cosmetic Act (1938) and the Kefauver-Harris Drug Amendment (1962).
Federal Hazardous Substances Act of 1960	Requires warning labels on hazardous household chemicals.
Kefauver-Harris Drug Amendment of 1962	Requires that manufacturers conduct tests to prove drug effectiveness and safety.
Consumer Credit Protection Act of 1968	Requires that lenders fully disclose true interest rates and all other charges to credit customers for loans and installment purchases.
Child Protection and Toy Safety Act of 1969	Prevents marketing of products so dangerous that adequate safety warnings cannot be given.
Public Health Smoking Act of 1970	Prohibits cigarette advertising on TV and radio and revises the health hazard warning on cigarette packages.
Poison Prevention Labeling Act of 1970	Requires safety packaging for products that may be harmful to children.
National Environmental Policy Act of 1970	Established the Environmental Protection Agency to deal with various types of pollution and organizations that create pollution.
Public Health Cigarette Smoking Act of 1971	Prohibits tobacco advertising on radio and television.
Consumer Product Safety Act of 1972	Created the Consumer Product Safety Commission, which has authority to specify safety standards for most products.
Child Protection Act of 1990	Regulates the number of minutes of advertising on children's television.
Children's Online Privacy Protection Act of 1998	Empowers the FTC to set rules regarding how and when marketers must obtain parental permission before asking children marketing research questions.
Aviation Security Act of 2001	Requires airlines to take extra security measures to protect passengers, including the installation of stronger cockpit doors, improved baggage screening, and increased security training for airport personnel.
Homeland Security Act of 2002	Protects consumers against terrorist acts. Created the Department of Homeland Security.
Do Not Call Law of 2003	Protects consumers against unwanted telemarketing calls.
CAN-SPAM Act of 2003	Protects consumers against unwanted e-mail, or spam.
Credit Card Act of 2009	Provides many credit card protections.
Restoring American Financial Stability Act of 2010	Created the Consumer Financial Protection Bureau. Protects the consumer against unfair, abusive and deceptive financial practices.

© Cengage Learning 2013

In a number of developing nations around the globe, bribery is an accepted form of doing business. Without paying a bribe to a government official, the contract will go to another firm that is willing to pay. The paying of bribes is discussed in the Ethics in Marketing box.

In 2010, Congress passed the Restoring American Financial Stability Act that brought sweeping changes to bank and financial market regulations. The legislation created the Consumer Financial Protection Bureau to oversee checking accounts, private student loans, mortgages, and other financial products. The agency deals with unfair, abusive, and deceptive practices. For example, suddenly doubling the interest rate on a credit card might be viewed as unfair. The new agency combined under one roof the consumer-protection functions that were divided under a half-dozen different agencies. The law also permanently raised the Federal Deposit Insurance Corporation's insurance on deposits to $250,000. For the first time, mortgage lenders are required to ensure a borrower can repay a home loan by verifying income, credit history, and job status. The law forbids payments to brokers for steering borrowers to high priced loans.

STATE LAWS

Legislation that affects marketing varies state by state. Oregon, for example, limits utility advertising to 0.5 percent of the company's net income. California has forced industry to improve consumer products and has enacted legislation

ethics in marketing

Making the Sale at All Costs

It is not unusual for an international marketing executive, who knows that his firm offers the best product or service and at a fair price, to be told that a bribe is required by government officials to complete the deal. The executive is fully aware that his company's key (non-American) competitors are not bound by the same laws as his firm. The American executive feels like he is not playing on a level field. He knows without the bribe the contract is lost.

The U.S. Foreign Corrupt Practices Act prohibits bribery of foreign officials and provides rather stiff penalties for firms and individuals that do. However, sometimes American companies, fighting for a contract, pay bribes anyway. In 2010, the U.S. Justice Department began investigating Hewlett-Packard (HP) to determine whether the firm paid $10.9 million for the chance to sell a sophisticated computer system to the Russian prosecutor general's office. Investigators were looking into evidence that HP used a series of shell companies located in places like Britain, Austria, Switzerland, Belize, Latvia, and Lithuania to create a fund that paid the Russian prosecutor's office.

Fines for paying bribes can be huge. Siemens reached an $800 million settlement for allegations of $1.4 billion in bribery payments. BAE Systems, one of Europe's largest arms companies, agreed to pay $400 million for defrauding the United States over the sales of fighter aircraft to Saudi Arabia and Eastern Europe. Similarly, Daimler agreed to pay $185 million for bribes in 200 transactions in at least 200 countries. "It is no exaggeration to describe corruption and bribe paying at Daimler as a standard business practice," said Robert Khuzami, Director of the U.S. Securities and Exchange Commission Division of Enforcement.

If "everyone else is doing it," should American companies be penalized for paying a bribe? Why? In 2010, the United Kingdom passed a very tough anti-bribery law. Failing to prevent a bribery will be a criminal offense. Failure to deal with bribery issues can lead to jail terms of up to ten years for individual directors. Simply having a presence in the United Kingdom, such as a subsidiary, office, or operations means that the firm is subject to the new law. This is true even if the offenses take place in a third world country and are unrelated to UK operations. Is this law fair to American companies? Why or why not? One survey of 100 U.S. global companies found that 60 percent don't have systems in place to prevent bribery.[103] Should American companies be doing more to stop bribery?

to lower the energy consumption of refrigerators, freezers, and air conditioners. Several states, including California and North Carolina, are considering levying a tax on all in-state commercial advertising.

Many states and cities are attempting to fight obesity by regulating fast food chains and other restaurants. California has passed a law banning trans fats in restaurants and bakeries. New York City chain restaurants must now display calorie counts on menus. Boston has now banned trans fats in restaurants. And the list goes on.

REGULATORY AGENCIES

Although some state regulatory bodies actively pursue violators of their marketing statutes, federal regulators generally have the greatest clout. The Consumer Product Safety Commission, the Federal Trade Commission, and the Food and Drug Administration are the three federal agencies most directly and actively involved in marketing affairs. These agencies, plus others, are discussed throughout the book, but a brief introduction is in order at this point.

The sole purpose of the **Consumer Product Safety Commission (CPSC)** is to protect the health and safety of consumers in and around their homes. The CPSC has the power to set mandatory safety standards for almost all products that consumers use (about 15,000 items). The CPSC consists of a five-member committee and about 400 staff members, including technicians, lawyers, and administrative

Consumer Product Safety Commission (CPSC)
A federal agency established to protect the health and safety of consumers in and around their homes.

help. The commission can fine offending firms up to $500,000 and sentence their officers to up to a year in prison. It can also ban dangerous products from the marketplace. The CPSC oversees about 400 recalls per year. The CPSC operates under rules that prohibit staff from publicizing information about product complaints until the manufacturer approves the release. Besides handing over a lot of control to companies, this process routinely delays public disclosure of hazards. In 2008, Congress passed the Consumer Product Safety Improvement Act. The law is aimed primarily at children's products, defined as individuals 12 years old or under. The law addresses items such as cribs, electronics, and video games, school supplies, science kits, toys, and pacifiers. The law requires mandatory testing and labeling and increases fines and jail time for violators.

The **Food and Drug Administration (FDA)**, another powerful agency, is charged with enforcing regulations against selling and distributing adulterated, misbranded, or hazardous food and drug products. In 2010, the Tobacco Control Act was passed. This act gave the FDA authority to regulate tobacco products, with a special emphasis on preventing their use by children and young people and reducing the impact of tobacco on public health. Another recent FDA action is the "Bad Ad" program. It is geared toward health care providers to help them recognize misleading prescription drug promotions and gives them an easy way to report the activity to the FDA.

The **Federal Trade Commission (FTC)** also consists of five members, each holding office for seven years. Over the years, Congress has greatly expanded the powers of the FTC. Its responsibilities have grown so large that the FTC has created several bureaus to better organize its operations. One of the most important is the Bureau of Competition, which promotes and protects competition. The Bureau:

→ reviews mergers and acquisitions, and challenges those that would likely lead to higher prices, fewer choices, or less innovation;

→ seeks out and challenges anticompetitive conduct in the marketplace, including monopolization and agreements between competitors;

→ promotes competition in industries where consumer impact is high, such as health care, real estate, oil and gas, technology, and consumer goods;

→ provides information and holds conferences and workshops for consumers, businesses, and policy makers on competition issues for market analysis.[104]

The FTC's Bureau of Consumer Protection works for the consumer to prevent fraud, deception, and unfair business practices in the marketplace. The Bureau claims that it:

→ enhances consumer confidence by enforcing federal laws that protect consumers

→ empowers consumers with free information to help them exercise their rights and spot and avoid fraud and deception

→ wants to hear from consumers who want to get information or file a complaint about fraud or identity theft[105]

Another important FTC bureau is the Bureau of Economics. It provides economic analysis and support to antitrust and consumer protection investigations. Many consumer protection issues today involve the Internet. In 2010, Twitter settled charges that it failed to protect consumers' personal information. The FTC has also filed complaints against Facebook and forced the company to make changes in its privacy policies. Recently, the FTC put companies on notice that services such as

Food and Drug Administration (FDA)
A federal agency charged with enforcing regulations against selling and distributing adulterated, misbranded, or hazardous food and drug products.

Federal Trade Commission (FTC)
A federal agency empowered to prevent persons or corporations from using unfair methods of competition in commerce.

Hotmail, Facebook, and Yahoo! needed to start using HTTPS, commonly known as Secure Sockets Layer (SSL), which guarantees that consumers can use the Web to transmit sensitive information (for example, financial and medical) with relative confidence that it won't be intercepted or stolen. Google has recently enabled HTTPS for Gmail.

THE BATTLE OVER CONSUMER PRIVACY

The popularity of the Internet for direct marketing, for collecting consumer data, and as a repository for sensitive consumer data has alarmed privacy-minded consumers. So many online users have complained about "spam," the Internet's equivalent of junk mail, that the U.S. Congress passed the CAN-SPAM Act in an attempt to regulate it. The act, which took effect on January 1, 2004, does not totally ban spam, but it does prohibit commercial e-mailers from using a false address and presenting false or misleading information. It also requires commercial e-mailers to provide a way for recipients to "opt out" of receiving further e-mail from the sender. A person opting out cannot be required to pay a fee or provide any other personally identifying information other than an email address.

Another problem is that Web surfers, including children, are routinely asked to divulge personal information in order to access certain screens or purchase goods or services online. Internet users who once felt fairly anonymous when using the Web are now disturbed by the amount of information marketers collect on them and their children as they visit various sites in cyberspace. Now the FTC, with jurisdiction under the Children's Online Privacy Protection Act Rule, requires the Web site operator to post a privacy policy on the home page and a link to the policy on every page where personal information is collected. It requires verifiable parental consent before collecting personal information from children. Finally, it gives parents a choice as to whether the child's personal information will be disclosed to third parties.

An area of growing concern to privacy advocates is called "behavioral targeting," and it is discussed in more detail in Chapters 9 and 22. Behavioral targeting is where a company tracks consumers' online activities, such as the searches they make, the Web sites they visit, and the products they buy. Marketers then use this to present ads based on consumers' likely interests, such as showing ads for diapers to people who have visited Web sites on raising children. Currently, the FTC allows self-regulation by companies that practice behavioral targeting. However, it has warned firms that if they don't inform consumers that they are being behaviorally targeted or misuse the information they collect, then regulation will soon follow.

Identity Theft People are right to be concerned about their personal information. The FTC estimates that about nine million Americans have their identity stolen each year.[106] How do thieves steal an identity? By the following ways:

1. **Dumpster diving.** They rummage through trash looking for bills or other paper with your personal information on it.

2. **Skimming.** They steal credit/debit card numbers by using a special storage device when processing your card.

3. **Phishing.** They pretend to be financial institutions or companies and send spam or pop-up messages to get you to reveal your personal information.

4. **Changing your address.** They divert your billing statements to another location by completing a change-of-address form.

5. **Old-fashioned stealing.** They steal wallets and purses; mail, including bank and credit card statement; pre-approved credit offers; and new checks or tax information. They steal personnel records or bribe employees who have access.

6. **Pretexting.** They use false pretenses to obtain your personal information from financial institutions, telephone companies, and other sources. For example, a pretexter may call, claim he's from a research firm, and ask you for your name, address, birth date, and social security number. When the pretexter has the information he wants, he uses it to call your financial institution. He pretends to be you or someone with authorized access to your account. He might claim that he's forgotten his checkbook and needs information about his account. In this way, the pretexter may be able to obtain other personal information about you such as your bank and credit card account numbers, information in your credit report, and the existence and size of your savings and investment portfolios.[107]

In 1998, Congress passed the Identity Theft and Assumption Deterrence Act. This law prohibits knowingly transferring or using another person's identification with the intent to commit an unlawful activity, such as theft of funds. Guilty parties face up to 15 years in prison.

Governmental Actions Two other laws have been passed to protect consumers from identity theft. They are:

→ **Gramm-Leach-Bliley Act (Financial Services Modernization Act):** This act is aimed at financial companies. It requires those corporations to tell their customers how they use their personal information and to have policies that prevent fraudulent access to it. Partial compliance has been required since 2001.

→ **Health Insurance Portability and Accountability Act:** This law is aimed at the health care industry. It limits disclosure of individuals' medical information and imposes penalties on organizations that violate privacy rules. Compliance has been required for large companies since 2003.

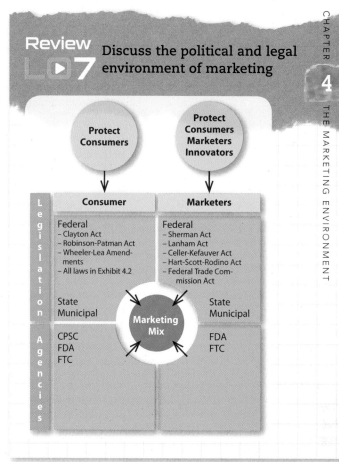

Review LO7 Discuss the political and legal environment of marketing

© Cengage Learning 2013

LO8
Competitive Factors

The competitive environment encompasses the number of competitors a firm must face, the relative size of the competitors, and the degree of interdependence within the industry. Management has little control over the competitive environment confronting a firm.

COMPETITION FOR MARKET SHARE AND PROFITS

As U.S. population growth slows, global competition increases, costs rise, and available resources tighten, firms find that they must work harder to maintain their profits and market share regardless of the form of the competitive market.

Sometimes technology advances can usher in a whole new set of competitors that can change a firm's business model. Barnes & Noble is America's largest book chain. For 40 years, Barnes & Noble has dominated bookstore retailing. In the 1970s it revolutionized publishing by championing discount hardcover best sellers. In the 1990s, it helped pioneer book superstores with selections so vast that they put many independent bookstores out of business.

But the digital revolution sweeping the media world is rewriting the rules of the book industry. Electronic books are still in their infancy, comprising an estimated 5 percent of the market in 2010. But they are quickly accelerating the decline of physical books, forcing retailers, publishers, authors, and agents to reinvent their businesses. By 2013, digital books will account for over 25 percent of unit sales; if one adds in another 25 percent of traditional books purchased online, then half of all units sold will be on the Internet. The competitive advantage Barnes & Noble spent decades amassing—offering an enormous selection of more than 150,000 books under one roof—was already under pressure from online booksellers.

With the recent advent of e-bookstores, Barnes & Noble was facing greater pressure. The bookstore giant has entered the fray with its own e-bookstore and electronic reader called the Nook. While Barnes & Noble claims it will remain focused on its physical bookstores, it is clear the bookseller is hoping to gain market share in the e-reader space. Because of the major players in the e-book game, many question whether book stores will go the way of music stores, which closed en masse once consumers could sample and download music digitally.[108]

American aircraft manufacturer Boeing still faces competition from European company Airbus, even though Airbus recently lost its edge in that $50 billion market. Airbus has been beset with problems, while Boeing's new 787 Dreamliner gave the company a much-needed lift. Marketers tout the Dreamliner's features, which include large windows, mood lighting, electronic shades, wider seats and aisles, and a state-of-the-art climate control system, as providing a unique flying experience. By 2010, Boeing had sold over 866 Dreamliners, whereas the huge Airbus A350 lagged far behind. Both Boeing and Airbus have experienced delivery problems. Boeing's difficulties have been due to parts availability and a machinist strike. Airbus has experienced management and logistics problems.

Review
LO8 Explain the basics of foreign and domestic competition

Highly Competitive Marketplace

Mature Industries

Slow growth/
No growth

Can only increase
market share by
taking it from a competitor.

© Cengage Learning 2013

GLOBAL COMPETITION

Boeing is a very savvy international competitor conducting business throughout the world. Many foreign competitors also consider the United States to be a ripe target market. Thus, a U.S. marketing manager can no longer focus only on domestic competitors. In automobiles, textiles, watches, televisions, steel, and many other areas, foreign competition has been strong. In the past, foreign firms penetrated U.S. markets by concentrating on price, but today the emphasis has switched to product quality. Nestlé, Sony, Rolls-Royce, and Sandoz Pharmaceuticals are noted for high quality, not cheap prices.

For a century, vacuuming has been synonymous with one brand (Hoover), whose iconic status is such that the British and French still refer to "hoovering the carpet." But after launching his bagless cleaners in the United States, English inventor James Dyson's company now makes America's best-selling vacuum. Max Factor cosmetics, owned by Procter & Gamble, had been on American shelves since 1909. The brand was the namesake of Max Factor, the pioneer of Hollywood makeup artists. However, by 2009 the brand's diminished U.S. popularity caused P&G to pull it off the American market. Although domestic and global competition led to the demise of the Max Factor brand in the United States, it still sells $1.2 billion annually. It is a leading brand in both the United Kingdom and Russia.[109]

Global competition is discussed in much more detail in Chapter 5.

components of the external marketing environment

billion spent by tweens in 2010

percent of adult Americans who get less than seven hours of sleep each night

percent of unit sales going to e-books in 2013

maximum fine CPSC can issue for violations

years Barbie was the top selling fashion doll

number of grocery stores shoppers regularly patronize

6   **$50**   **40**   **25**   **$500,000**   **50**   **3.6**

Review and Applications

Discuss the external environment of marketing and explain how it affects a firm. The external marketing environment consists of social, demographic, economic, technological, political and legal, and competitive variables. Marketers generally cannot control the elements of the external environment. Instead, they must understand how the external environment is changing and the impact of that change on the target market. Then marketing managers can create a marketing mix to effectively meet the needs of target customers.

1.1 What is the purpose of environmental scanning? Give an example.

1.2 Form six teams and make each one responsible for one of the uncontrollable elements in the marketing environment. Your boss, the company president, has asked each team to provide one-year and five-year forecasts of the major trends the firm will face. The firm is in the telecommunications equipment industry. It has no plans to become a telecommunications service provider like, for example, Verizon and AT&T. Each team should use the library, the Internet, and other data sources to make its forecasts. Each team member should examine a minimum of one data source. The team members should then pool their data and prepare a recommendation. A spokesperson for each team should present the findings to the class.

team

Describe the social factors that affect marketing. Within the external environment, social factors are perhaps the most difficult for marketers to anticipate. Several major social

© iStockphoto.com/Juan Facundo Mora Soria

trends are currently shaping marketing strategies. First, people of all ages have a broader range of interests, defying traditional consumer profiles. Second, changing gender roles are bringing more women into the workforce and increasing the number of men who shop. Third, an increase in the number of dual-career families and proliferation of mobile devices have created demand for time-saving goods and services.

2.1 Every country has a set of core values and beliefs. These values may vary somewhat from region to region of the nation. Identify five core values for your area of the country. Clip magazine advertisements that reflect these values and bring them to class.

2.2 Give an example of component lifestyles based on someone you know.

LO3 Explain the importance to marketing managers of current demographic trends. Today, several basic demographic patterns are influencing marketing mixes. Because the U.S. population is growing at a slower rate, marketers can no longer rely on profits from generally expanding markets. Marketers are also faced with increasingly experienced consumers among the younger generations such as tweens and teens. And because the population is also growing older, marketers are offering more products that appeal to middle-aged and older consumers.

3.1 Baby boomers in America are aging. Describe how this might affect the marketing mix for the following:

    a. Bally Total Fitness

    b. McDonald's

    c. Whirlpool Corporation

    d. The state of Florida

    e. Target stores

3.2 You have been asked to address a local chamber of commerce on the subject of "Generation Y." Prepare an outline for your talk.

3.3 How should Ford Motor Company market differently to Generation Y, Generation X, and baby boomers?

LO4 Explain the importance to marketing managers of growing ethnic markets. Hispanics are the fastest-growing segment of the population, followed by African Americans. Many companies are now creating departments and product lines to effectively target multicultural market segments. Companies have quickly found that ethnic markets are not homogeneous.

writing

4.1 Go to the library and look up a minority market such as the Hispanic market. Write a memo to your boss that details the many submarkets within this segment.

online

4.2 Using the library and the Internet, find examples of large companies directing marketing mixes to each major ethnic group.

LO5 Identify consumer and marketer reactions to the state of the economy. In recent years, U.S. incomes have risen at a slow pace. At the same time, the financial power of women has increased, and they are making the purchasing decisions for many products in traditionally male-dominated areas. During a time of inflation, marketers generally attempt to maintain level pricing to avoid losing customer brand loyalty. During times of recession, many marketers maintain or reduce prices to counter the effects of decreased demand; they also concentrate on increasing production efficiency and improving customer service.

5.1 Explain how consumers' buying habits may change during a recessionary period.

writing

5.2 Periods of inflation require firms to alter their marketing mix. Suppose a recent economic forecast predicts that inflation will be almost 10 percent during the next 18 months. Your company manufactures hand tools for the home gardener. Write a memo to the company president explaining how the firm may have to alter its marketing mix.

Identify the impact of technology on a firm. Monitoring new technology is essential to keeping up with competitors in today's marketing environment. The United States excels in basic research and, in recent years, has dramatically improved its track record in applied research. Without innovation, U.S. companies can't compete in global markets. Innovation is increasingly becoming a global process.

6.1 Give three examples of how technology has benefited marketers. Also, give several examples of firms that have been hurt because they did not keep up with technological changes.

Discuss the political and legal environment of marketing. All marketing activities are subject to state and federal laws and the rulings of regulatory agencies. Marketers are responsible for remaining aware of and abiding by such regulations. Some key federal laws that affect marketing are the Sherman Act, Clayton Act, Federal Trade Commission Act, Robinson-Patman Act, Wheeler-Lea Act, Lanham Act, Celler-Kefauver Antimerger Act, and Hart-Scott-Rodino Act. Many laws, including privacy laws, have been passed to protect the consumer as well. The Consumer Product Safety Commission, the Federal Trade Commission, and the Food and Drug Administration are the three federal agencies most involved in regulating marketing activities.

7.1 The Federal Trade Commission and other governmental agencies have been both praised and criticized for their regulation of marketing activities. To what degree do you think the government should regulate marketing? Explain your position.

7.2 Can you think of any other areas where consumer protection laws are needed?

7.3 What topics are currently receiving attention in FDA news (www.fdanews.com)? What effect has the attention had on market share?

online

Explain the basics of foreign and domestic competition. The competitive environment encompasses the number of competitors a firm must face, the relative size of the competitors, and the degree of interdependence within the industry. Declining population growth, rising costs, and shortages of resources have heightened domestic competition.

8.1 Explain how the nature of competition is changing in America.

8.2 Might there be times when a company becomes too competitive? If so, what could be the consequences?

Key Terms

Exercises

ETHICS EXERCISE

Gary Caplan has developed a new "energy drink" designed to burn calories while sleeping, which he intends to market to grossly overweight consumers. According the Centers for Disease Control and Prevention, 20 percent of Americans are obese. Gary's mother, a doctor, argues that it's unethical to target the obese—that they are as vulnerable a target market as much as the elderly and children.

Questions

1. Is Gary targeting a "vulnerable" market?
2. Does the AMA Statement of Ethics address this issue? Go to www.marketingpower. com and review the statement. Then write a brief paragraph on what it contains that relates to Gary Caplan's marketing decision.

MARKETING PLAN EXERCISE

These end-of-chapter marketing plan exercises are designed to help you use what you learned in the chapter to build a strategic marketing plan for a company of your choosing. Once you've completed the marketing plan exercise for each chapter in Part 1 of this textbook, you can complete the Part 1 Marketing Planning Worksheet, found on the companion Web site. Log in at www.cengagebrain.com. Now continue building your strategic marketing plan that you started in Chapter 2 by completing the following exercises:

1. Describe how your company will handle privacy concerns.
2. Scan the marketing environment. Identify opportunities and threats to your chosen company in areas such as technology, the economy, the political and legal environment, and competition. Is your competition foreign, domestic, or both? Also identify opportunities and threats based on possible market targets, including social factors, demographic factors, and multicultural issues.
3. Complete your company's SWOT analysis by identifying opportunities and threats in the external marketing environment by performing environmental scanning:

   a. List the demographic, ethnic, and social trends that could impact your firm, by investigating data from the U.S. Census Bureau at www.census.gov.

   b. Determine which economic factors could influence the strategies of your firm by visiting the U.S. Economic and Statistics Administration at www.esa.doc.gov or the Bureau of Economic Analysis at www.bea. gov.

   c. Explore www.lawguru.com and report on at least three political and legal factors that could influence your marketing decisions.

   d. Investigate the Web sites of federal government agencies that regulate your firm and industry and list at least six laws that regulate your business offering.

Agency	Web site
The Federal Trade Commission	www.ftc.gov
The Federal Communications Commission	www.fcc.gov
The Food and Drug Administration	www.fda.gov
The Consumer Product Safety Commission	www.cpsc.gov
The Better Business Bureau	www.bbb.org
The Internal Revenue Service	www.irs.gov

   e. Identify your key competitors. A simple "yellow pages" listing of firms in the same business category can start your search. For online competitors, try www.bizrate.com.

f. Competition often comes from companies that are working on the same exact market as yours. That is especially true on the Internet. After you search for your direct competition, look for and think about what other companies are positioned to execute a similar business strategy for your target market. Determine if there are any players who might be able to develop technology more quickly or reach your target customers more effectively than you.

APPLICATION EXERCISE

Demographic factors play a large role in shaping the external marketing environment. One of those demographic factors is culture. The importance of cultural understanding cannot be overstated, especially in today's global marketplace and our own multicultural country. In general, Americans tend to be ethnocentric; that is, they are quick to prejudge other cultural norms as wrong (or of less significance) because they differ from American practices.

One way to be exposed to another culture is to examine the foods typical of that culture. In this exercise, you will need to work in a team to create a guide to ethnic dining in your city or area. The finished guide will be descriptive in nature; it is not meant to be a rating guide.

Activities

1. Identify ethnic dining categories for inclusion in your guide. Once you have identified categories for your area, make a list of restaurants for each category.

2. You will need to create a data collection form so that the same information is collected from each restaurant. For example, you will want to include the name, address, and phone number for each restaurant. Think of other information that would be helpful.

3. Divide up the restaurant list your team generated in activity 1 so that each team member is responsible for collecting information from a certain number of restaurants. Consider dividing the list geographically so that each team member can visit an assortment of ethnic restaurants. If your budget allows, eat at a few of the restaurants in addition to collecting the information. After you have all the information, meet to review and compare your findings.

4. Was there a meal or type of food that you particularly liked? Disliked? Which type of ethnic restaurant seemed most foreign to you? Why do you think that was?

CASE STUDY: Starbucks

SELLING COFFEE IN THE LAND OF TEA

Starbucks has been doing business in China since 1999 when they opened their first coffee shop in Beijing. Today, hundreds of Starbucks stores sell coffee in the land of tea, including one at the Great Wall. It has become one of the most popular brands among the country's 20-to-40-year-old upwardly mobile Chinese, or "Chuppies," as they're called, but so far China accounts for only about 10 percent of Starbucks' global sales. Nevertheless, Chairman Howard Schultz believes the country will someday be the company's largest market outside North America. "The market response," he says, "has exceeded our expectations."

This may seem surprising when you consider the fact that the majority of China's one billion-plus population are tea drinkers who didn't know what coffee was until Nestlé introduced a powdered version on store shelves in the 1980s. But Starbucks is betting that they can win the new generation over by marketing its signature product as an emblem of modern China's new sophistication.

"Coffee represents the change," says Wang Jinlong, president of Starbucks Greater China. "The disposable income is concentrated on the young people, and this is the place they want to come." Success in China could depend on how well Starbucks markets itself to what Wang calls the "little emperors." China's one-child law has spawned a generation that isn't interested in collective goals, he says. Instead, they embrace the Western belief in individuality that Starbucks embodies.

After surveying Chinese consumers, Starbucks compiled a list of the top reasons they go to cafés. Surprisingly, the number-one reason was "to gather with family and friends," while "to drink coffee" lagged behind at number six. Living spaces are generally small and cramped there, making places to congregate important to the Chinese.

Da Wei Sun, manager of outlets in Beijing, believes that Starbucks found success in China because they took this idea of a place to gather and gave people in the cities a "third space" beyond work and home, making it cool to have a latte and hang out. Starbucks offers more food on the Chinese menu, including duck sandwiches, moon pies, and green-tea cheesecake, than in other countries, and more seating as well. Only 20 percent of North American customers eat and drink inside the store after ordering, but the number is close to 90 percent in China.

China remains a communist country, so a change in its one-party dictatorship could potentially affect business overnight. Schultz says the key to establishing stores there is to first find local partners who understand the changing political and business landscapes. Starbucks initially entered China by authorizing local developers to use their brand and setting up joint ventures with partners.

Industry analyst Pei Liang advised that for long-term success in the country, Starbucks would need to acquire controlling stakes in its joint ventures. This, Pei explained, would strengthen management's control and put them in position to reap more of the profits as the market grew. "Licensing or holding a minority stake is an effective tool when first stepping into a new market because it involves a small investment," says Pei. "But Starbucks, the brand's owner, receives only royalty fees from the licensee."

In late 2006, Starbucks announced that it was buying out its partner in China and taking control of 60 stores. The market had changed after Beijing entered the World Trade Organization in 2001, making it easier for foreign companies to navigate alone. "Buying out one's partner is becoming more common," says industry consultant Kent D. Kedl. "Starbucks probably feels they know better how China works now so they can go it on their own."

Chairman Howard Schultz says that Starbucks will concentrate most of its future expansion efforts in China, and Kedl predicts they will see continued success there: "It's not just a drink in China. It's a destination. It's a place to be seen and a place to show how modern one is." And with China's economy continuing to grow in double digits, the number of Chuppies willing to pay $3.63 for a Mocha Frappuccino Grande is likely to grow, too.[110]

Questions

1. Many of the same environmental factors, such as cultural factors, that operate in the domestic market also exist internationally. Discuss the key cultural factors Starbucks had to consider as it expanded into China.

2. Discuss the key political and legal factors Starbucks had to consider in the Chinese marketplace. What are the risks of entering a country with these factors? What changes have occurred in China's political and legal structure to the advantage of foreign companies?

3. What demographic factors were important for Starbucks to understand in China? What were the demographics they decided to target?

4. What was the initial global-market strategy Starbucks employed to enter China? Discuss the advantages and disadvantages to this early strategy. How has their strategy changed since then and why?

COMPANY CLIPS: Method—Entering a Crowded Market

Companies large and small, new and old are all participants in the market, and as such, are all subject to the forces that act on each entity in the marketplace. The same is true of Method. As you've already seen in the Company Clips from Chapters 2 and 3, Method has been attentive to the customer, analyzed the competition, focused on social change, and identified economic factors that have affected how it does and will do business. Review the Company Clips from Chapters 2 and 3 to hear founders Adam Lowry and Eric Ryan and CEO Alastair Dorward describe several factors in the external environment that have influenced how Method entered the market and the success the company has experienced.

Questions

1. Method's founders and CEO repeatedly reference the role of competition and consumers in their assessments of their external environment. Is there a hierarchy to the environmental factors discussed in this chapter? Explain.

2. Should other companies imitate the emphasis Method gives to certain factors in its external environment? Why or why not?

3. Does Method's assessment of its external environment seem to be lacking anything? What?

Notes

1. "Brand Barbie Gets a Makeover," *Fortune,* July, 20, 2009, 17.
2. "Get in the Loop," *Marketing News,* May 1, 2008, 5.
3. Kerry Capell, "Thinking Simple at Philips," *BusinessWeek,* December 11, 2006, 50.
4. "Retailers Cut Back on Variety, Once the Spice of Marketing," *Wall Street Journal,* June 26, 2009, A1, A12.
5. Calvin Duncan, Constance O'Hare, and John Mathews, "Raising Your Market IQ," *Wall Street Journal,* December 12, 2007, R4.
6. "TJX: Dressed to Kill for the Downturn," *BusinessWeek,* October 27, 2008, 60.
7. This is a partial list of trends projected by the Natural Marketing Institute, "Healthy, Green, Simple—Trends to Watch in the Next Ten Years," *Quirk's Marketing Research Review,* May 2010, 6. Reprinted with permission.
8. Campaign for Real Beauty, "Campaign Feature, Self-Esteem," Dove, www.dove.us/#/cfrb/selfesteem; also see: John Quelch and Katherine Jocz, "Holding Up a Mirror to Marketing," *Marketing Management,* November/December 2008, 17–21.
9. The material on personality and geography is adapted from: Stephanie Simon, "The United States of Mind," *Wall Street Journal,* September 23, 2008, A26.
10. "Older Women Workers, Ages 55 and Older," United States Department of Labor, www.dol.gov/wb/factsheets/qf-olderworkers55.htm.
11. "Women Want Home Improvement Retailers to Boost Service; National Survey Reveals Gaps in Service, Product Knowledge," *PR Newswire,* February 27, 2006.
12. Author's projection based upon J. Walker Smith, "Make Time Worth It," *Marketing Management,* July/August 2005, 56.
13. "Another Casualty Emerges from the Crises: Family Time," *Wall Street Journal,* October 15, 2008, B1.
14. Michael Mandel, "The Real Reasons You're Working So Hard," *BusinessWeek,* October 3, 2005, 60.
15. "Changing Consumer Lifestyles Create New American Neighborhood," *Marketing Matters Newsletter,* www.marketingpower.com, October 27, 2008.

marketing&you: Results.

A high score means you have a strong perception of time limitations for work-related task completion. Research indicates that when you perceive yourself to be working under time pressure your creativity is negatively affected. As you read in Chapter 4, time is an important social factor in the external environment that affects marketing. Understanding your own perceptions and reaction to time constraints will be helpful in planning to meet the needs of the time-constrained consumer. Your challenge as a busy marketer will be to continue thinking creatively on their behalf.

16. *American Time Use Survey—2007 Results* (Washington: Bureau of Labor Statistics) June 25, 2008.
17. "Changing Consumer Lifestyles Create New American Neighborhood."
18. Thom Patterson, "Welcome to the 'Weisure' Lifestyle," *CNN*, May 11, 2009, http://articles.cnn.com/2009-05-11/living/weisure_1_creative-class-richard-florida-leisure-time.
19. Room for Debate, "First Steps to Digital Detox," *New York Times*, June 7, 2010, http://roomfordebate.blogs.nytimes.com/2010/06/07/first-steps-to-digital-detox.
20. "Fewer Americans Are Relocating Within the U.S.," *Wall Street Journal*, July 10, 2008, A3.
21. Conor Dougherty, "Cities Grow at Suburbs' Expense During Recession," *Wall Street Journal*, July 1, 2009, A5.
22. Alicia de Mesa, "Marketing and Tweens," *BusinessWeek*, October 12, 2005, www.businessweek.com/innovate/content/oct2005/id20051012_606473.htm.
23. Barb Dybwad, "Enfora and Leapfrog Put Out TicTalk Cellphone for Kids," *Engadget*, August 4, 2005, www.engadget.com/2005/08/04/enfora-and-leapfrog-put-out-tictalk-cellphone-for-kids.
24. Shop Girl, "Filling a Niche for Tweens," *Houston Chronicle*, August 23, 2007, 5.
25. Sarah Mahoney, "Aeropostale Takes Teen Concept to Tweens," *Marketing Daily*, March 16, 2009, www.mediapost.com/publications/?fa=Articles.showArticle&art_aid=102222.
26. "American Girl Stores," American Girl Web site, www.americangirl.com/stores/experience_index.php.
27. David Kennedy, "Coming of Age in Consumerdom," *American Demographics*, April 2004, 14.
28. Stan Pugsley, "Digital Marketing and the Tweens," *icrossing*, April 23, 2009, http://greatfinds.icrossing.com/marketing-to-the-digital-natives/ .
29. www.admongo.gov (Accessed January 24, 2011).
30. "Literal Fitness for Kids," *Brandweek*, September 24, 2007, 16.
31. Zachary Wilson, "Pew Survey: Teens Love Facebook, Hate Blogging, and Don't Use Twitter," *Fast Company*, February 3, 2010, www.fastcompany.com/blog/zachary-wilson/and-how/pew-survey-finds-increase-social-media-internet-time-decrese-blogging-te.
32. "Teens Prefer Real Friends to Online Ones," *Quirk's Marketing Research Review*, August 2008, 6.
33. John Zaremba, "Teen Marketing Techniques," *eHow*, April 1, 2010, www.ehow.com/way_6167462_teen-marketing-techniques.html; Brian Theriot, "Teen Marketing Tips," *suite101*, April 22, 2010, www.suite101.com/content/teen-marketing-tips-a228866.
34. "Understanding Tweens and Teens," *Youth Markets Alert*, August 1, 2007, 7; and "EPM Offers Advice for Marketing to Tweens and Teens," *Research Alert*, June 1, 2007, 5.
35. "Square-Eyed Gen Yers," *Brandweek*, July 28, 2008, 8.
36. Karen Akers, "Generation Y: Marketing to the Young and the Restless," *Successful Promotions*, January/February 2005, 33–38.
37. "Boomers and Gen X the Most Spend-Happy; Millennials Buy More per Trip," *Quirk's Marketing Research Review*, May 2010, 10.
38. Lynne Lancaster and David Stillman, "The M Factor," *Delta Sky Magazine*, May 2010, 70–73, 100–105.
39. Andrew Rohm, Fareena Sultan, and Fleura Bardhi, "Multitasking Youth," *Marketing Management*, November/December 2009, 20–25.
40. Kenneth Hein, "Gen Y's Fave: Whole Foods," *Brandweek*, July 28, 2008, 13.
41. *Demographic Profile: America's GENX*, MetLife Mature Market Institute, 2009.
42. PriceWaterhouseCoopers, "Gen X, Y Will Lead Economic Recovery," *Marketing Charts*, April 5, 2010, www.marketingcharts.com/direct/gen-xy-will-lead-economic-recovery-12482.
43. "Gen X More Involved Than Boomers," *USA Today*, April 4, 2007, D5.
44. *MetLife Study of the American Dream*, MetLife, 2009.
45. "Gen Xers and Their Concerns Are Reshaping the Retail Landscape: Be True to Your Word, When Marketing to Them, Researcher Advises," *Montreal Gazette*, June 13, 2007, B1.
46. "Gen X Slackers Get Serious," *Brandweek*, June 30, 2008, 8.
47. Adapted from: Cheryl Sowa, "6 Rules of Marketing to Generation X," December 22, 2009, www.americasbestcompanies.com/blog/6-rules-marketing-generation-x.aspx.
48. David Welch, "The Incredible Shrinking Boomer Economy," *BusinessWeek*, August 3, 2009, 27–30.
49. Joe White, "Boomer Bust," *Wall Street Journal*, October 21, 2008, A13.
50. Kelly Greene, "Baby Boomers Delay Retirement," *Wall Street Journal*, September 22, 2008, A4.
51. Welch, "The Incredible Shrinking Boomer Economy," 27–30.
52. *Ibid.*
53. *Ibid.*; also see "The Aging of the Baby Boom Is Having a Profound Impact on Investing," March 5, 2010, http://fc.standardandpoors.com.
54. *Ibid.*
55. "The Generations Judge One Another," *Quirks Marketing Review*, November, 2008, 80.
56. Mark Dolliver, "Middle Boomers: Not Old Yet," *AdWeek*, April 26, 2010. www.adweek.com.
57. "2010 Del Webb Baby Boomer Survey," Del Webb Web site, April 13, 2010, http://dwboomersurvey.com.
58. Jennifer Van Grove, "Baby Boomers and Seniors Are Flocking to Facebook," *Mashable*, January 28, 2010, http://mashable.com/2010/01/28/baby-boomers-social-media.
59. "Personal Touch," *Marketing Management*, May/June 2007, 4.
60. Robert J. Morais, "It's Time to Connect with Baby Boomers," *Brandweek*, March 6, 2006, 20.
61. "Minority Population Tops 100 Million," *US Fed News*, May 17, 2007.
62. Conor Dougherty, "Whites to Lose Majority Status in U.S. by 2042," *Wall Street Journal*, August 14, 2008, A4; also see Conor Dougherty, "U.S. Nears Racial Milestone," *Wall Street Journal*, June 11, 2010, A3.
63. Dougherty, "Whites to Lose Majority Status in U.S. by 2042."
64. *Ibid.*
65. Sean Callebs, "Whites Become Minority in Kansas," *CNN*, May 22, 2009, http://articles.cnn.com/2009-05-22/living/garden.city.kansas.minorities_1_meatpacking-minority-majority?_s=PM:LIVING.
66. "Growing Numbers, More Opportunity to Spend," *Marketing News*, April 30, 2009, 22–24.
67. "Jarritos Trademark Licensing Program," Goldmarks Web site, www.goldmarks.net/pdf/jarritos_licensing.pdf.
68. "La Musica to Their Ears," *Marketing News*, May 15, 2009, 14–16.
69. "Online Shopping by Minorities Up Sharply," *Quirk's Marketing Research Review*, June 2008, 80.
70. "To Woo Gen Y, Marketers Push Culture, Not Language," *Brandweek*, January 1, 2007, 5.
71. Helen Leggatt, "Internet Use among U.S. Hispanics Continues to Rise," *BizReport*, March 24, 2009, www.bizreport.com/2009/03/report_internet_use_among_us_hispanics_continues_to_rise.html#.

72. "The Payoff from Targeting Hispanics," *BusinessWeek*, April 16, 2009, 76.

73. Todd Wasserman, "Report Shows a Shifting African-American Population," *Brandweek*, January 11, 2009, 6.

74. "African-American TV Usage and Buying Power Highlighted," *Marketing Charts,* October 18, 2007, www.marketingcharts.com/television/african-american-tv-usage-and-buying-power-highlighted-2068.

75. "Affluent African Americans Making Impact on Consumer Economy," *Marketing Charts,* February 11, 2008, www.marketingcharts.com/television/affluent-african-americans-making-impact-on-consumer-economy-3412.

76. *Ibid.*

77. "African-Americans Powerful, Tech Savvy and Diverse," *Quirks Marketing Review*, April 2010, 10.

78. Authors' projections based upon U.S. Census data.

79. "Affluent African Americans Wield $29.8 Billion in Spending Power," *Marketing Charts,* September 12, 2008, www.marketingcharts.com/print/affluent-african-americans-wield-298b-in-spending-power-5970.

80. "The Asian-American Market," *delivermagazine*, September 2008, 8.

81. "Marketing to Asian Americans," *Adweek Media*, May 26, 2008, www.adweek.com.

82. "The Asian-American Market Is a Diverse Group, and There Are Cultural Nuances Particular to Each," *National Jeweler*, September 1, 2006.

83. Christine Huang, "GlobalHue Presents: The New Asian American Market," *GlobalHue*, www.slideshare.net/christinewhuang/asian-american-market-ad-tech-sf.

84. U.S. Census Bureau, "Table 689. Money Income of Households--Percent Distribution by Income Level, Race, and Hispanic Origin, in Constant (2008) Dollars: 1980 to 2008," *Statistical Abstract of the United States: 2011*, 452.

85. *Ibid.*

86. Robert Longley, "Lifetime Earnings Soar with Education," About.com: US Government Info, February 13, 2010, http://usgovinfo.about.com/od/moneymatters/a/edandearnings.htm.

87. David Wessel, "Did Great Recession Live Up to Its Name?" *Wall Street Journal,* April 8, 2010, http://online.wsj.com/article/SB10001424052702303591204575169693166352882.html.

88. Sudeep Reddy, "It Will Be Years Before Lost Jobs Return—and Many Never Will," *Wall Street Journal,* October 5, 2009, http://online.wsj.com/article/SB125470053662262957.html.

89. "At the Supermarket Checkout, Frugality Trumps Brand Loyalty," *Wall Street Journal,* November 6, 2008, D1.

90. "Why Some Brands Cheer a Sour Economy," *Brandweek*, October 13, 2008, 5.

91. Julie Jargon, "Food Firms Cook Up Ways to Combat Rare Sales Slump," *Wall Street Journal,* April 21, 2010, A1, A18.

92. John Graham, "A Recession Education: Lessons Learned from a Challenging Economy," *Marketing Matters*, June 2009.

93. Justin Scheck and Paul Glader, "R&D Spending Holds Steady in Slump," *Wall Street Journal,* April 6, 2009, A1, A10.

94. Michael Arndt, "Ben Franklin, Where Are You?" *Bloomberg Businessweek*, January 4, 2010, 29.

95. Steve Hamm, "A Radical Rethink of R&D," *BusinessWeek*, September 7, 2009, 35–39; also see Steve Hamm, "Big Blues Global Lab," *BusinessWeek*, September 7, 2009, 41–45.

96. Partially adopted from: John Bessant, Kathrin Moslein, and Bettina Von Stamm, "In Search of Innovation," *Wall Street Journal*, June 22, 2009, R4.

97. Roger Martin and Jennifer Riel, "Innovation's Accidental Enemies," *Bloomberg Businessweek*, January 25, 2010, 72.

98. Netflix, www.netflix.com.

99. Diana Ransom, "When the Customer Is in the Neighborhood," *Wall Street Journal*, May 17, 2010, R8.

100. "Creativity Pays. Here's How Much," *BusinessWeek*, April 24, 2006, 45.

101. "Yes, Innovations Do Pay Off, Study Finds," *International Herald Tribune*, August 30–31, 2008, 15.

102. Michael Arndt and Bruce Einhorn, "The 50 Most Innovative Companies 2010," *Bloomberg Businessweek*, April 15, 2010, www.businessweek.com/interactive_reports/innovative_companies_2010.html

103. "The UK Bribery Act 2010: What U.S. Companies Need to Know," *DLA Piper*, June 1, 2010, www.dlapiper.com/the-uk-bribery-act-2010-what-us-companies-need-to-know; "U.S. Businesses Plead Ignorance to New UK Bribery and Corruption Laws," *Eversheds LLP*, March 1, 2010, www.eversheds.com/uk/home/services/fraud_and_financial_crime/corruption_clampdown_report.page?; "SEC Charges Daimler AG with Global Bribery," www.sec.gov/news/press/2010/2010-51.htm, April 1, 2010; "BAE Systems to Appeal U.S. Bribery Ruling," *United Press International*, June 17, 2010, www.upi.com/Business_News/Security-Industry/2010/06/17/BAE-Systems-to-appeal-US-bribery-ruling/UPI-15141276781832/; Erik Sherman, "HP Shows Foreign Bribery Can Bite U.S. Companies at Home," *BNET*, April 15, 2010, www.bnet.com/blog/technology-business/hp-shows-foreign-bribery-can-bite-us-companies-at-home/3415; Erica Ogg, "More Details on HP Bribery Allegations," *CNET News*, April 16, 2010, http://news.cnet.com/8301-31021_3-20002713-260.html.

104. "FTC Bureau of Competition," www.ftc.gov/bc/index.shtml (Accessed January 24, 2011).

105. "FTC Bureau of Consumer Protection," www.ftc.gov/bcp/index.shtml (Accessed January 24, 2011).

106. FTC, "About Identity Theft," www.ftc.gov/bcp/edu/microsites/idtheft/consumers/about-identity-theft.html (Accessed January 24, 2011).

107. FTC, "Pretexting," www.ftc.gov/bsp/edu/microsites/idtheft/consumers/pretexting.html (Accessed January 24, 2011).

108. Michael Edwards, "E-Books, Hardcovers, Online Booksellers and Stores: Why Everybody Can Win," *Fortune,* June 21, 2010, http://tech.fortune.cnn.com/2010/06/21/e-books-hardcovers-online-booksellers-and-stores-why-everybody-can-win; Tim Sheehan, "Rise of E-Books Puts Traditional Booksellers In a Bind," *McClatchy*, June 22, 2010, www.mcclatchydc.com/2010/06/22/96355/rise-of-e-books-leaves-traditional.html; Jeffery A. Trachetenberg, "E-Books Rewrite Book Selling," *Wall Street Journal*, May 21, 2010, A1, A12; Associated Press, "Shift to E-Books to Hurt Bookstores Analysts Say," *Seattle Times*, October 23, 2009, http://seattletimes.nwsource.com/html/localnews/2010125675_apapfnusbooksellerssectorsnap2ndldwritethru.html.

109. Ellen Byron, "Max Factor Kisses America Goodbye," *Wall Street Journal*, June 5, 2009, B1.

110. "Starbucks Targets Growing China Market," *AsiaPulse News*, 6/13/2006; Janet Adamy, "Starbucks' Task China? Winning Over Tea Drinkers," *The Seattle Times*, 11/30/2006; Jeffrey S. Harrison, "Exporting a North American Concept to Asia", *Cornell Hotel & Restaurant Quarterly*, May 2005; Craig Harris, "Starbucks Sees China as Key to Its International Growth," *Seattle Post-Intelligencer*, 10/7/2006; Dexter Roberts, "Starbucks Caffeinates Its China Growth Plan," *Business Week Online*, 10/26/2006.

chapter

5

Developing a Global Vision

 Learning Outcomes

1 Discuss the importance of global marketing

2 Discuss the impact of multinational firms on the world economy

3 Describe the external environment facing global marketers

4 Identify the various ways of entering the global marketplace

5 List the basic elements involved in developing a global marketing mix

6 Discover how the Internet is affecting global marketing

LO1
Rewards of Global Marketing

Today, global revolutions are under way in many areas of our lives such as management, politics, communications, and technology. The word *global* has assumed a new meaning, referring to a boundless mobility and competition in social, business, and intellectual arenas. No longer just an option, **global marketing**—marketing that targets markets throughout the world—has become imperative for business.

U.S. managers must develop a global vision not only to recognize and react to international marketing opportunities, but also to remain competitive at home. Often, a U.S. firm's toughest domestic competition comes from foreign companies. Moreover, a global vision enables a manager to understand that customer and distribution networks operate worldwide, blurring geographic and political barriers and making them increasingly irrelevant to business decisions. In summary, having a **global vision** means recognizing and reacting to international marketing opportunities, using effective global marketing strategies, and being aware of threats from foreign competitors in all markets.

Over the past two decades, global trade has climbed from $200 billion a year to $12.5 trillion in 2009. This was a 12 percent contraction from 2008 sparked by the global economic crises.[1] However, in 2010, as the world began to slowly emerge from the "Great Recession," world trade grew by 9.5 percent.[2]

> ## No longer just an option, global marketing has become imperative for business.

global marketing
Marketing that targets markets throughout the world.

global vision
Recognizing and reacting to international marketing opportunities, using effective global marketing strategies, and being aware of threats from foreign competitors in all markets.

marketing&you.

How would you describe your interest in other cultures? Enter your answers on the lines provided.

STRONGLY DISAGREE ◁ 1 2 3 4 5 6 7 ▷ STRONGLY AGREE

NEITHER DISAGREE NOR AGREE

_____ I would like to have opportunities to meet people from other countries.

_____ I am very interested in trying food from different countries.

_____ We should have a respect for traditions, cultures, and ways of life of other nations.

_____ I would like to learn more about other countries.

_____ I have a strong desire for overseas travel.

_____ I would like to know more about foreign cultures and customs.

_____ I have a strong desire to meet and interact with people from foreign countries.

Now, total your score. Read the chapter, and find out what your score means at the end.

Source: Scale #98, *Marketing Scales Handbook*, G. Bruner, K. James, H. Hensel, eds., Vol. III. © by American Marketing Association.

Despite the slow economy and the perceived difficulty of "going global" for the first time, globalization efforts often benefit many companies and individuals. A good example is the global journey that occurs when Cyril Bath Company, a small aerospace manufacturer in Monroe, North Carolina, just outside Charlotte, exports roughly shaped metal ribs for framing the shells of airplanes to a factory in Italy. The Italian plant machines them into finished metal forms, which it ships to Charleston, South Carolina, where they are used to build sections of fuselage. Those sections are then flown to Boeing factories in the Pacific Northwest for final assembly. After all that, many of the finished planes are sold for export.[3]

Adopting a global vision, like Cyril Bath Company, can be very lucrative for a company. Gillette, for example, gets about two-thirds of its revenue from its international division. H. J. Heinz, the ketchup company, gets over half of its revenue from international sales. Although Cheetos and Ruffles haven't done very well in Japan, the potato chip has been quite successful. PepsiCo's (owner of Frito-Lay) overseas snack business brings in more than $5 billion annually. Caterpillar, one of the world's largest manufacturers of construction and mining equipment, diesel and natural gas engines, and industrial turbines, has sales of over $40 billion annually. Almost $14 billion comes from sales outside the United States.[4]

Another company with a global vision is Pillsbury. The Pillsbury Doughboy is used in India to sell a product that the company had just about abandoned in America: flour. Pillsbury (owned by General Mills) has many higher-margin products such as microwave pizzas in other parts of the world, but it discovered that in this tradition-bound market, it needed to push the basics.

Even so, selling packaged flour in India has been almost revolutionary because most Indian housewives still buy raw wheat in bulk, clean it by hand, store it in huge metal hampers, and, every week, carry some to a neighborhood mill, or *chakki*, where it is ground between two stones.

To help reach those housewives, the Doughboy himself has gotten a makeover. In TV advertising, he presses his palms together and bows in the traditional Indian greeting. He speaks six regional languages.

Despite these many examples of U.S. firms working overseas, global marketing is not a one-way street, whereby only U.S. companies sell their wares and services throughout the world. Foreign competition in the domestic market used to be relatively rare but now is found in almost every industry. In fact, in many industries U.S. businesses have lost significant market share to imported products. In electronics, cameras, automobiles, fine china, tractors, leather goods, and a host of other consumer and industrial products, U.S. companies have struggled at home to maintain their market shares against foreign competitors.

IMPORTANCE OF GLOBAL MARKETING TO THE UNITED STATES

Many countries depend more on international commerce than the United States does. For example, France, Britain, and Germany all derive more than 19 percent of their gross domestic product (GDP) from world trade, compared to about 12 percent for the United States. Nevertheless, the impact of international business on the U.S. economy is still impressive:

→ The United States exports about a fifth of its industrial production.

→ Exports create jobs for over ten million Americans.[5]

→ Exports represent approximately 13 percent of our gross domestic product.[6] **Gross domestic product (GDP)** is the total market value of all final goods and services produced in a country for a given time period (usually a year or quarter of a year). "Final" in the definition refers to a final product that is sold, and not intermediate products used in the assembly of a final product. For example, if the value of a brake (an intermediate good) and a car (final good) were both counted, the brake would be counted twice. Therefore, GDP counts only the final goods and services to get a true value of a country's production.

→ Every U.S. state has realized net employment gains directly attributed to foreign trade.

→ Almost a third of U.S. corporate profits comes from international trade and foreign investment.

→ The United States is the world's leading exporter of farm products, selling more than $60 billion in agricultural exports to foreign countries each year.

→ Chemicals, office machinery and computers, automobiles, aircraft, and electrical and industrial machinery make up almost half of all nonagricultural exports.

→ About half of U.S. merchandise imports are raw materials, capital goods, and industrial products used by U.S. manufacturers to make goods in the United States. America is the world's largest importer.

→ America exports over $1.7 trillion in goods and services each year.[7]

These statistics might seem to imply that practically every business in the United States is selling its wares throughout the world, but nothing could be further from the truth. About 85 percent of all U.S. exports of manufactured goods are shipped by 250 companies; less than 10 percent of all manufacturing businesses, or around 25,000 companies, export their goods on a regular basis. Most small- and medium-sized firms are essentially nonparticipants in global trade and marketing. Only the very large multinational companies have seriously attempted to compete worldwide. Fortunately, more of the smaller companies are now aggressively pursuing international markets.

THE FEAR OF TRADE AND GLOBALIZATION

The protests during meetings of the World Trade Organization, the World Bank, and the International Monetary Fund (three organizations that are discussed later in the chapter) show that many people fear world trade and globalization. What do they fear? Some of the negatives of global trade are as follows:

→ Millions of Americans have lost jobs due to imports, production shifts abroad, or outsourcing of tech jobs. Most find new jobs—that often pay less.

→ Millions of others fear losing their jobs, especially at those companies operating under competitive pressure.

→ Employers often threaten to outsource jobs if workers do not accept pay cuts.

→ Service and white-collar jobs are increasingly vulnerable to operations moving offshore.

Jobs Outsourcing The notion of jobs outsourcing (sending U.S. jobs abroad) has been highly controversial for the past several years. Many executives say that it is about corporate growth, efficiency, productivity, and revenue growth. Most companies see cost savings as a key driver in outsourcing. Detroit has suffered from

gross domestic product (GDP)
The total market value of all final goods and services produced in a country for a given time period.

© Max Earey/Shutterstock.com

many factories in the auto industry being shut down and relocated around the world. For example, Ford's new line of compact sedans and hatchbacks, called the Fiesta, is being built in Mexico.

Despite the attraction of lower costs overseas, there have been changes in China that might reverse the trend of job outsourcing. Wages in China are rising 10 to 15 percent a year and shipping costs have risen dramatically around the globe. The cost of sending a 40-foot shipping container from Shanghai to San Diego has soared 150 percent to $5,500 since 2000. Also, the value of the U.S. dollar has fallen against the Chinese yuan during the same time period. This makes imports into the United States more expensive. All of these factors make the possibility of manufacturing in the United States more attractive than in the past.

The problem is that many American factories and supplier networks withered away during the period of globalization. For example, an American inventor has created a long-lasting, fast-charging battery for notebook computers that could revolutionize the industry. The company, Boston-Power, would like to make the batteries in the Unites States. However, there are no battery factories left! Yet in China there are more than 200 battery manufacturers with plenty of workers and laboratories.[8]

Rising costs in China are eroding the 40–50 percent cost advantage it once had. Yet the migration of manufacturing back to America may be a long and slow process. Many goods, such as toys, small appliances, and clothing, will probably never be produced in huge quantities in America because they are very labor-intensive. While there is no doubt that some manufacturers will return to the states as China's cost advantage slips further, perhaps America's best opportunity is in keeping new technologies from ever leaving the country. It is important for the United States to remain in the forefront of innovation in areas such as nanotechnology, solid-state lighting, and renewable energy. It should be economically feasible to produce the goods resulting from the technology in the United States.

BENEFITS OF GLOBALIZATION

Traditional economic theory says that globalization relies on competition to drive down prices and increase product and service quality. Business goes to the countries that operate most efficiently and/or have the technology to produce what is needed.

Globalization expands economic freedom, spurs competition, and raises the productivity and living standards of people in countries that open themselves to the global marketplace. For less developed countries, globalization also offers access to foreign capital, global export markets, and advanced technology while breaking the monopoly of inefficient and protected domestic producers. Faster growth, in turn, reduces poverty, encourages democratization, and promotes higher labor and environmental standards. Though government officials may face more difficult choices as a result of globalization, their citizens enjoy greater individual freedom. In this sense, globalization acts as a check on governmental power by making it more difficult for governments to abuse the freedom and property of their citizens.

Globalization deserves credit for helping lift many millions out of poverty and for improving standards of living of low-wage families. In developing countries around the world, globalization has created a vibrant middle class that has elevated the standards of living for hundreds of millions of people. That's particularly true in China, where the incomes of low-skilled workers have consistently risen. The poor in countries like Vietnam and elsewhere in Southeast Asia have also benefited greatly since those countries have opened their economies. In many developing countries around the world, life expectancies and health care have improved, as have educational opportunities.[9]

In the next 24 hours, approximately 180,000 people in developing counties will move from the countryside to cities such as Shanghai, São Paulo, and Johannesburg. The same will happen tomorrow and every day thereafter for the next 30 years. This rate of movement is equivalent to creating one New York City every two months, according to the United Nations. The men and women entering these cities will need everything— electricity, water, food, health care, shelter, schools, computers, and, of course, jobs.[10]

Many of these workers have the potential to improve their local environments and aspects of the world. The forces of globalization have pushed these individuals to urban areas to seek a better life. In these urban centers globalization will open the world to the growing cities, allowing international agencies to pump in capital, multinational companies to help supply technology and management, and Western universities to transfer knowledge.[11]

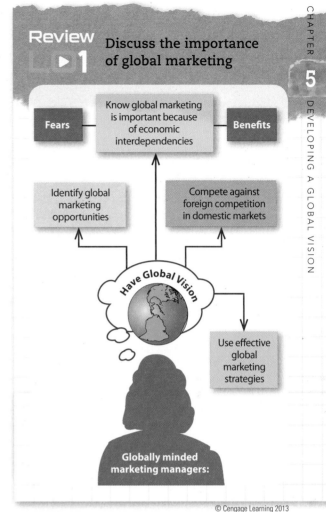

Review

LO 1

Discuss the importance of global marketing

Know global marketing is important because of economic interdependencies

Fears — Benefits

Identify global marketing opportunities

Compete against foreign competition in domestic markets

Have Global Vision

Use effective global marketing strategies

Globally minded marketing managers:

© Cengage Learning 2013

LO 2
Multinational Firms

The United States has a number of large companies that are global marketers. Many of them have been very successful. A company that is heavily engaged in international trade, beyond exporting and importing, is called a **multinational corporation**. Multinational corporations move resources, goods, services, and skills across national boundaries without regard to the country in which the headquarters is located. Many U.S.-based multinationals earn a large percentage of their total revenue abroad. ExxonMobil earns a huge 72 percent of its revenue outside the United States. In contrast, America's largest firm, Walmart, has 24 percent of its sales outside the country. America's largest corporations are shown in Exhibit 5.1.

Are multinationals good for the United States? Although they comprise far less than 1 percent of U.S. companies, they account for about 19 percent of all private jobs, 25 percent of all private wages, 48 percent of total exports of goods, and a remarkable 74 percent of nonpublic R&D spending.[12] For decades, U.S. multinationals have driven an outsized share of U.S. productivity growth, the foundation of

multinational corporation
A company that is heavily engaged in international trade, beyond exporting and importing.

Exhibit 5.1 America's Largest Corporations

Rank	Revenues $Millions
1 Walmart Stores, Bentonville, Arkansas	408,214.0
2 ExxonMobil, Irving, Texas	284,650.0
3 Chevron, San Ramon, California	163,527.0
4 General Electric, Fairfield, Connecticut	156,779.0
5 Bank of America Corp., Charlotte, North Carolina	150,450.0
6 ConocoPhillips, Houston, Texas	139,515.0
7 AT&T, Dallas, Texas	123,018.0
8 Ford Motor, Dearborn, Michigin	118,308.0
9 J.P. Morgan Chase & Co., New York	115,632.0
10 Hewlett-Packard, Palo Alto, California	114,552.0
11 Berkshire Hathaway, Omaha, Nebraska	112,493.0
12 Citigroup, New York	108,785.0
13 Verizon Communications, New York	107,808.0
14 McKesson, San Francisco, California	106,632.0
15 General Motors, Detroit, Michigan	104,589.0
16 American International Group, New York	103,189.0
17 Cardinal Health, Dublin, Ohio	99,612.9
18 CVS Caremark, Woonsocket, Rhode Island	98,729.0
19 Wells Fargo, San Francisco, California	98,636.0
20 International Business Machines, Armonk, New York	95,758.0
21 United Health Group, Minnetonka, Minnesota	87,138.0
22 Procter & Gamble, Cincinnati, Ohio	79,697.0
23 Kroger, Cincinnati, Ohio	76,733.2
24 Amerisourcebergen, Chesterbrook, Pennsylvania	71,789.0
25 COSTCO Wholesale, Issaquah, Washington	71,422.0

Source: Adapted from "Largest U.S. Corporations," *Fortune*, May 3, 2010, F1–2.

rising standards of living for everyone. They are responsible for 41 percent of the increase in private labor productivity since 1990.[13]

Yet multinationals are not without their critics. Despite the common allegations that multinationals simply "export jobs" out of the United States, research shows that expansion abroad by these firms has tended to complement—not substitute—their U.S. operations. More investment and employment abroad have tended to create more American investment and jobs as well. From 1988 to 2007, employment in foreign affiliates rose to 10 million from 4.8 million. During that same period, employment in U.S. parent companies rose to 22 million from 17.7 million.[14] Some multinationals have shifted income to low-tax countries, which has reduced corporate income tax payments in America. The multinationals claim that this was necessary because the United States has a very complicated tax structure with one of the highest corporate income tax rates among industrialized nations.

Multinationals often develop their global business in stages. In the first stage, companies operate in one country and sell into others. Second-stage multinationals set up foreign subsidiaries to handle sales in one country. In the third stage, they operate an entire line of business in another country. The fourth stage has evolved primarily due to the Internet and involves mostly high-tech companies. For these

firms, the executive suite is virtual. Their top executives and core corporate functions are in different countries, wherever the firms can gain a competitive edge through the availability of talent or capital, low costs, or proximity to their most important customers.

A good example of a fourth-stage company is Trend Micro, an Internet anti-virus software company. Its top executives, engineers, and support staff are spread around the world so that they can respond quickly to new virus threats—which can start anywhere and spread like wildfire. The main virus response center is in the Philippines, where 250 ever-vigilant engineers work evening and midnight shifts as needed. Six other labs are scattered from Munich to Tokyo.

Trend Micro's financial headquarters is in Tokyo, where it went public; product development is in Ph.D.-rich Taiwan; and most of its sales are in Silicon Valley—inside the giant American market. When companies fragment this way, they are no longer limited to the strengths, or hobbled by the weaknesses, of their native lands.

Such fourth-stage multinationals are being created around the world. They include Wipro, a tech-services supplier with headquarters in India and Santa Clara, California; and computer-peripherals maker Logitech International, with headquarters in Switzerland and Fremont, California.

A multinational company may have several worldwide headquarters, depending on the location of certain markets or technologies. Britain's APV, a maker of food-processing equipment, has a different headquarters for each of its worldwide businesses. ABB (Asea Brown Boveri) is the European electrical engineering giant based in Zurich, Switzerland, that groups its thousands of products and services into 50 or so business areas. Each is run by a leadership team that crafts global business strategy, sets product development priorities, and decides where to make its products. None of the teams work out of the Zurich headquarters; instead, they are scattered around the world. Leadership for power transformers is based in Germany, electric drives in Finland, and process automation in the United States.

Despite the numerous examples outlined above, the role of multinational corporations in developing nations is a subject of controversy. Multinationals' ability to tap financial, physical, and human resources from all over the world and combine them economically and profitably can be of benefit to any country. Multinationals tend to possess the most up-to-date technology and can transfer it to the countries in which they operate. Critics, however, claim that often the wrong kind of technology is transferred to developing nations. Usually, it is **capital-intensive** (requiring a greater expenditure for equipment than for labor) and thus does not substantially increase employment. A "modern sector" then emerges in the nation, employing a small proportion of the labor force at relatively high productivity and income levels and with increasingly capital-intensive technologies. In addition, multinationals sometimes support reactionary and oppressive regimes if it is in their best interests to do so. Other critics say that the firms take more wealth out of developing nations than they bring in, widening the gap between rich and poor nations. The petroleum industry in particular has been heavily criticized in the past for its actions in some developing countries.

To counter such criticism, more and more multinationals are taking a proactive role in being good global citizens. Sometimes companies are spurred to action by government regulation, and in other cases multinationals are attempting to protect their good brand name.

capital-intensive
Using more capital than labor in the production process.

exchange rate

The price of one country's currency in terms of another country's currency.

CURRENCY FLUCTUATIONS

Multinationals can be helped or hurt by currency fluctuations. The **exchange rate** is the price of one country's currency in terms of another country's currency. If a country's currency appreciates, less of that country's currency is needed to buy another country's currency. If a country's currency depreciates, more of that currency will be needed to buy another country's currency.

How do appreciation and depreciation affect the prices of a country's goods? If, say, the U.S. dollar depreciates relative to the Japanese yen, U.S. residents have to pay more dollars to buy Japanese goods. To illustrate, suppose the dollar price of a yen is $0.012 and that a Toyota is priced at two million yen. At this exchange rate, a U.S. resident pays $24,000 for a Toyota ($0.012 × 2 million yen = $24,000). If the dollar depreciates to $0.018 to one yen, then the U.S. resident will have to pay $36,000 for that same Toyota.

As the dollar depreciates, the prices of Japanese goods rise for U.S. residents, so they buy fewer Japanese goods—thus, U.S. imports decline. At the same time, as the dollar depreciates relative to the yen, the yen appreciates relative to the dollar. This means prices of U.S. goods fall for the Japanese, so they buy more U.S. goods—and U.S. exports rise.

For multinationals selling all over the world, exchange rates can increase or decrease profits. For example, as the dollar declines, the price of the Boeing Dreamliner gets cheaper for airlines outside the United States. Thus, Boeing can perhaps offer a better price than Airbus, its main competitor. If the dollar appreciates, the reverse is true.

The Boeing example assumes that the plane is being exported out of the United States and sold in dollars. Procter & Gamble manufactures and sells Ariel laundry detergent in France. French consumers buy Ariel and pay for it in euros (the currency of France, which is part of the European Union). P&G prefers a weak dollar in order to increase profit from its Ariel sales. For example, in June 2010, the dollar was relatively strong: one euro equaled $1.20. So if you were an American going to France, it would cost you $1.20 to obtain one euro. In 2008, the dollar was very weak against the euro: It would cost you $1.60 to get one euro. The 2008 rate is more profitable for P&G. If P&G France sold 500,000 euros' worth of Ariel and the dollar was strong at $1.20, when P&G France converts the euros to dollars to send to P&G headquarters in Cincinnati, Ohio, they would remit $600,000 (500,000 × $1.20 = $600,000). At the weaker 2008 rate of $1.60, the French subsidiary would remit $800,000 (500,000 × $1.60 = $800,000). This simplified example shows you how currency fluctuations can have a major impact on the profitability of multinationals. You can check out the value of the dollar today versus the euro at www. XE.com/ucc.

GLOBAL MARKETING STANDARDIZATION

Traditionally, marketing-oriented multinational corporations have operated somewhat differently in each country. They use a strategy of providing different product features, packaging, advertising, and so on. However, Ted Levitt, a former Harvard professor, described a trend toward what he referred to as "global marketing," with a slightly different meaning.[15] He contended that communication and technology have made the world smaller so that almost all consumers everywhere want all the things they have heard about, seen, or experienced. Thus, he saw the emergence of global markets for standardized consumer products on a huge scale, as opposed to segmented foreign markets with different products.

In this book, *global marketing* is defined as individuals and organizations using a global vision to effectively market goods and services across national boundaries. To make the distinction, we can refer to Levitt's notion as **global marketing standardization**.

Global marketing standardization presumes that the markets throughout the world are becoming more alike. Firms practicing global marketing standardization produce "globally standardized products" to be sold the same way all over the world. Uniform production should enable companies to lower production and marketing costs and increase profits. Levitt cited Coca-Cola, Colgate-Palmolive, and McDonald's as successful global marketers. His critics point out, however, that the success of these three companies is really based on variation, not on offering the same product everywhere. McDonald's, for example, changes its salad dressings and provides self-serve espresso for French tastes. It sells bulgogi burgers in South Korea and falafel burgers in Egypt. It also offers different products to suit tastes in Germany (where it offers beer) and Japan (where it offers sake). Further, the fact that Coca-Cola and Colgate-Palmolive sell some of their products in more than 160 countries does not signify that they have adopted a high degree of standardization for all their products globally. Only three Coca-Cola brands are standardized, and one of them, Sprite, has a different formulation in Japan. Some Colgate-Palmolive products are marketed in just a few countries. Axion paste dishwashing detergent, for example, was formulated for developing countries, and La Croix Plus detergent was custom made for the French market. Colgate toothpaste is marketed the same way globally, although its advanced Gum Protection Formula is used in only 27 nations.

Companies with separate subsidiaries in other countries can be said to operate using a multidomestic strategy. A **multidomestic strategy** occurs when multinational firms enable individual subsidiaries to compete independently in domestic markets. Simply put, multidomestic strategy is how multinational firms use strategic business units. (See Chapter 2.) The earlier example using P&G France is considered a multidomestic strategy, with P&G France manufacturing and selling its own products according to the French market. The Cincinnati headquarters offers some standardized marketing or products, but overall, P&G France operates independently.

Critics aside, some companies are actively working to move toward global marketing standardization. For example, Alan Mulally, CEO of Ford, claims that his company is moving toward global marketing standardization with its new Focus. The new Focus is Ford's first truly global car—a single vehicle designed and engineered for customers in every region of the world and sold under one name. It is small, fuel-efficient, and packed with technology and safety features that Mr. Mulally believes will appeal to consumers in Europe, Asia, and the Americas. "Why are we doing it this way?" he asked. "Because we believe that customer requirements are going to be more the same around the world than they are different.[16]

Customers in disparate markets were already showing preferences for the same attributes in cars: safety, technology, fuel efficiency, and appearance. The Internet allows car buyers everywhere to examine the specifications of vehicles available in the United States or Europe. This means consumers in developing countries can home in on products in mature markets and demand the more advanced products from those markets.

global marketing standardization
Production of uniform products that can be sold the same way all over the world.

multidomestic strategy
When multinational firms enable individual subsidiaries to compete independently in domestic markets.

© Bettmann/CORBIS

© iStockphoto.com/Juan Facundo Mora Soria

Review LO2 Discuss the impact of multinational firms on the world economy

- Human Resources
- Physical Resources
- Financial Resources

MNC

Growth Revenue Profits

Global Marketing

© Cengage Learning 2013

"Everybody knows everything, and everybody knows what's available," Mr. Mulally said. "You look at the reasons people buy vehicles, and all those requirements are coming together."[17]

LO3
External Environment Facing Global Marketers

A global marketer or a firm considering global marketing must consider the external environment. Many of the same environmental factors that operate in the domestic market also exist internationally. These factors include culture, economic factors, political structure and actions, demographic makeup, and natural resources.

CULTURE

Central to any society is the common set of values shared by its citizens that determines what is socially acceptable. Culture underlies family, the educational system, religion, and the social class system. Networks of social organizations generate overlapping roles and status positions. These values and roles have a tremendous effect on peoples' preferences and thus on marketers' options. A company that does not understand a country's culture is doomed to failure in that country. Cultural blunders lead to misunderstandings and often perceptions of rudeness or even incompetence. For example, when people in India shake hands, they sometimes do so rather limply. This isn't a sign of weakness or disinterest; instead, a soft handshake conveys respect. Avoiding eye contact is also a sign of deference in India.

A U.S. luggage manufacturer found out that culture also affects thinking and perception. The company designed a new Middle East advertising campaign around the image of its luggage being carried on a magic flying carpet. Many of the participants in a marketing research study thought they were seeing advertising for Samsonite *carpets*. Green Giant learned that it could not use its Jolly Green Giant mascot in parts of Asia because wearing a green hat in those cultures signifies that a man has an unfaithful wife. Procter & Gamble research showed that Italians devote 21 hours a week to household chores other than cooking, whereas Americans spend just 4 hours. They wash kitchen and bathroom floors at least four times a week, compared to the U.S. consumer's once-a-week cleansing. Despite those hours and hours of labor, Italians aren't necessarily a perfect market for convenience products. They want products that are tough cleaners, not timesavers. For example, dishwasher makers targeting the Italian market have had to fight the perception that machines don't get dishes as clean as hand washing. When Unilever's Cif brand cleaning spray flopped, company research found that Italian women needed convincing that a spray could be strong enough, especially on kitchen grease. The company spent 18 months reformulating the product, testing its power against grease. It then changed the advertising to focus on cleaning ability rather than convenience. And when the company learned that the women felt they needed different cleaners for different tasks, new varieties were created. Containers were also made 50 percent larger because Italians clean so frequently.

P&G's Swiffer WetJet mop bombed as a cleaner in Italy, but research found that Italian women were using it to polish after mopping. To facilitate how Italian women were using the Swiffer, P&G created a Swiffer with beeswax, which it sells only in Italy. Another variety, the Swiffer Duster, is sold in many countries but is especially popular in Italy, selling five million boxes in its first eight months—twice the company's forecasts. "It was a real shift of mind-set on how to market products like these," said Alessandra Bellini, head of marketing for Unilever's home and personal-care products. "If you present a product as quick and easy, women may feel like a cheat. . . . It took us a while to understand that Italians didn't want that."[18]

Marketers in France have a different cultural challenge. The French have a strong dislike for outdoor advertising. A survey found 58 percent of the French don't care for billboards. As one police chief outside Paris noted, "We have a culture that doesn't like commerce that goes back to the Middle Ages."[19] Because of the prominence of outdoor ads, they are a target for anticapitalist sentiment. On the last Friday of each month Alex Baret, a 31-year-old musician, rides a train to central Paris. When he arrives, he pulls out a can of spray paint and defaces a billboard by spraying the words *Harcèlement Publicitaire*, or in English, "Harassment by Advertising."[20]

Language is another important aspect of culture that can create problems for marketers. Marketers must take care in translating product names, slogans, instructions, and promotional messages so as not to convey the wrong meaning. For example, Mitsubishi Motors had to rename its Pajero model in Spanish-speaking countries because the term describes a sexual activity. Toyota Motors' MR2 model dropped the number 2 in France because the combination sounds like a French swearword. Coca-Cola had difficulty finding a suitable translation for its name into Mandarin. The transliteration of the syllables of Coca-Cola in Chinese characters could have resulted in Chinese people thinking it read "bite the wax tadpole" or other nonsensical phrases.

Each country has its own customs and traditions that determine business practices and influence negotiations with foreign customers. In many countries, personal relationships are more important than financial considerations. For instance, skipping social engagements in Mexico may lead to lost sales. Negotiations in Japan often include long evenings of dining, drinking, and entertaining, and only after a close personal relationship has been formed do business negotiations begin. The Japanese go through a very elaborate ritual when exchanging business cards. An American businesswoman was unaware of this important cultural tradition. She came into a meeting and tossed some of her business cards across the table at a group of stunned Japanese executives. One of them turned his back on her and walked out. The deal never went through.

Making successful sales presentations abroad requires a thorough understanding of the country's culture. Germans, for example, don't like risk and need strong reassurance. A successful presentation to a German client will emphasize three points: the bottom-line benefits of the product or service, that there will be strong service support, and that the product is guaranteed. In southern Europe, it is an insult to show a price list. Without negotiating, you will not close the sale. The English want plenty of documentation for product claims and are less likely to simply accept the word of the sales representative. Scandinavian and Dutch companies are more likely to approach business transactions as Americans do than are companies in any other country.

Never try to do business in Europe in August because you'll find that everyone has gone on vacation. Today, all European countries have laws requiring companies to provide employees with vacations of at least four weeks (the standard in Belgium, Britain, Germany, and Italy, among others) to five weeks (as in Austria, Denmark, France, and Sweden). But most workers get more vacation time because of collective agreements negotiated by unions or other compensation arrangements.

ECONOMIC FACTORS

Economic factors are the second major consideration for marketing managers in the global external environment. An important aspect of this is the level of economic development of various countries. In general, complex and sophisticated industries are found in developed countries, and more basic industries are found in less developed nations. Average family incomes are higher in more developed countries than in the less developed countries. Larger incomes mean greater purchasing power and demand not only for consumer goods and services but also for the machinery and workers required to produce consumer goods.

According to the World Bank, *gross national income (GNI)* per capita average for the world is $10,341.[21] GNI is a country's GDP (defined earlier) together with its income received from other countries (mainly interest and dividends) less similar payments made to other countries. The United States' GNI per capita is $46,790 but it is not the world's highest. That honor goes to Luxembourg at $52,770. Of course, there are many very poor countries: Sierra Leone ($770), Niger ($680), Mozambique ($771), Malawi ($810), Guinea ($970), and Eritrea ($640).[22] GNI per capita is one measure of a country's citizens' ability to buy various goods and services. A marketer, with a global vision, can use this data to aid in measuring market potential in countries around the globe.

Not only is per capita income a consideration when going abroad, but also the cost of doing business in a country as well. Although not the same as the cost of doing business, we can gain insights into expenses by examining the cost of living in various cities. The most expensive cities in the world are Paris, Tokyo, and Oslo. Other cities (with their rank out of 131 cities) are Frankfurt (5), Sydney (12), London (16), Chicago (16), Moscow (45), Beijing (57), Mexico City (84), and Mumbai (131).[23]

THE GLOBAL ECONOMY

A global marketer today must be fully aware of the intertwined nature of the global economy. In the past, the sheer size of the United States economy tended to drive global markets up or down depending upon the health of the U.S. economy. It was said that, "If America sneezes, then the rest of the world catches a cold." This is still true today. The U.S. housing market collapse and speculative financing in 2008 led to a major global recession. It was, in fact, America's deepest decline in economic activity since the Great Depression. As the world slowly pulled itself out of the recession, the possibility of Greece defaulting on its national debt nearly stifled global economic recovery. The Greece crisis was followed by speculation of other debt crises in Spain and Portugal. Moreover, the world now looks to other economies such as China, India, and Brazil to help jump-start economic growth. The lesson for the global marketer is clear: Forecasting global demand and economic growth requires an understanding of what is happening economically in countries around the globe.

ethics in marketing

China Puts the Brakes on Google

In early 2010, Google began haggling with Chinese authorities over censorship of its Web site in China. Google refused to censor its search results, which infuriated the Chinese government. In March 2010, Google announced that it was pulling out of mainland China and moving its operations to Hong Kong. Google's chief legal officer, David Drummond said:

"We have uncovered evidence to suggest that the Gmail accounts of dozens of human rights activists connected with China were being routinely accessed by third parties, most likely via phishing scams or malware placed on their computers. We also made clear that these attacks and the surveillance they uncovered—combined with attempts over the last year to further limit free speech on the web in China including the

persistent blocking of websites such as Facebook, Twitter, YouTube, Google Docs and Blogger—had led us to conclude that we could no longer continue censoring our results on Google.cn."

Moving the Google server to Hong Kong didn't solve Google's problem. The Chinese government immediately began censoring the people on the mainland's access to the Hong Kong site. Government computers either completely disabled searches for objectionable content or blocked links to certain results.[27]

Did Google do the right thing by leaving China? Why? Should other Internet firms, such as Facebook and Twitter, leave also? Why? What about companies like Starbucks or Walmart? Should they leave China as well?

DOING BUSINESS IN CHINA AND INDIA

The two countries of growing interest to many multinationals are India and China because of their huge economic potential. They have some of the highest growth rates in the world and are emerging as megamarkets. Take cell phones. The number of users in China exceeds 780 million, and the estimated figure for India is 401 million—a number that is growing by six million new subscribers a month.[24]

China and India present different but complementary strengths that multinationals can use. China is much stronger than India in mass manufacturing and logistics; in contrast, India is much stronger than China in software and information-technology services.

China and India have the world's two largest populations, two of the world's largest geographical areas, greater linguistic and sociocultural diversity than any other country, and among the highest levels of income disparity in the world—some people are extremely poor whereas others are very rich.

Given this scale and variety, there is no "average Chinese customer" or "average Indian customer." In each country, even the middle of the income pyramid consists of more than 300 million people encompassing significant diversity in incomes, geographic climates, cultural habits, and even language and religious beliefs. Because of this diversity, market success in China and India is rarely possible without finely segmenting the local market in each country and developing a strategy tailored to the needs of the targeted segments.[25]

PepsiCo has plans to invest $2.5 billion in China by 2013, on top of the $1 billion already spent. It is building a dozen new food and beverage plants focusing on the interior of China. The company intends to keep developing products tailored for the Chinese market, such as its Lay's line of cool-cucumber-flavored potato chips and the Cao Ben Le line of drinks based on traditional medicine, such as Yin and Yang, or cooling and warming.[26]

Despite the enthusiasm that PepsiCo and other companies have shown for the Chinese market, there have been some pitfalls for others such as Google, as explained in the Ethics in Marketing Box above.

POLITICAL STRUCTURE AND ACTIONS

Political structure is the third important variable facing global marketers. Government policies run the gamut from no private ownership and minimal individual freedom to little central government and maximum personal freedom. As rights of private property increase, government-owned industries and centralized planning tend to decrease. But a political environment is rarely at one extreme or the other. India, for instance, is a republic with elements of socialism, monopoly capitalism, and competitive capitalism in its political ideology.

A recent World Bank study found that the least amount of business regulation fosters the strongest economies.[28] The least regulated and most efficient economies are concentrated among countries with well-established common-law traditions, including Australia, Canada, New Zealand, the United Kingdom, and the United States. On a par with the best performers are Singapore and Hong Kong; not far behind are Denmark, Norway, and Sweden, which are social democracies that recently streamlined their business regulation.

The World Bank also found that the poorest countries, which need new businesses and entrepreneurship the most, were the most difficult countries in which to start a new business. Heavy regulation and red tape prevent both economic and job growth. The more roadblocks there are, the more opportunities for underpaid government officials to get kickbacks. But there are also other problems. The World Bank report noted that trade unions prevented Peru from reducing mandatory severance payments, while notaries in Croatia have stalled its efforts to simplify procedures to start businesses for years. It takes 153 days to start a business in Mozambique, for example, but 2 days in Canada. Enforcing a contract in Indonesia can cost more than the contract's actual value; doing the same in South Korea costs just 5.4 percent of a contract's value.[29]

AMR Research Inc., a Boston consulting firm, says it surveyed supply-chain managers at big U.S. firms in 2008 about how they would rank the risks they face doing business globally. About 30 percent of them rated "country risk"—geopolitical problems or natural disasters—as their most significant.[30] The managers' worries are not far-fetched, as felt by several energy companies as countries began returning to nationalism. Nationalism is pride in one's country and its sovereignty, and is one part of geopolitical problems. One result of resurging nationalism is that some foreign owned assets become nationalized, or taken over by the government. Countries do this in order to uplift their people and generate income for other social programs. For multinationals, nationalization can mean loss of investment and technology when their business is pushed out or taken over by that country's government. Since oil prices started rising in 2004, Russia, Venezuela, Bolivia, and Ecuador nationalized foreign-owned oil assets in the first big wave of nationalization since the 1970s. After Venezuela's state-owned oil firm doubled its ownership of heavy-oil projects along the Orinoco River in 2007, ConocoPhillips pulled out, taking a $4.5 billion charge.[31] ExxonMobil left as well, and is suing Venezuela for compensation.

LEGAL CONSIDERATIONS

Closely related to and often intertwined with the political environment are legal considerations. In France, nationalistic sentiments led to a law that requires pop music stations to play at least 40 percent of their songs in French (even though French teenagers love American and English rock and roll).

Many legal structures are designed to either encourage or limit trade. Here are some examples:

→ *Tariff: a tax levied on the goods entering a country.* The United States has imposed a 15 percent tariff on Chinese drill pipe. Because a tariff is a tax, it will either reduce the profits of the firms paying the tariff or raise prices to buyers or both. Normally, a tariff raises prices of the imported goods and makes it easier for domestic firms to compete. U.S. shrimpers lobbied for tariffs against foreign pond-raised shrimp, which were enacted. In 2010, Vietnam filed a suit with the World Trade Organization (discussed later in this chapter) challenging the shrimp tariff.

→ *Quota: a limit on the amount of a specific product that can enter a country.* The United States has strict quotas for imported textiles, sugar, and many dairy products. Several U.S. companies have sought quotas as a means of protection from foreign competition. Because quotas restrict available supply of an item, imposing a quota often causes prices to rise. For example, the price of sugar on the world market in March 2010 was 19.8 cents per pound; the U.S. price was 35 cents a pound.[32]

→ *Boycott: the exclusion of all products from certain countries or companies.* Governments use boycotts to exclude companies from countries with which they have a political dispute. Several Arab nations boycotted Coca-Cola because it maintained distributors in Israel.

→ *Exchange control: a law compelling a company earning foreign exchange from its exports to sell it to a control agency, usually a central bank.* A company wishing to buy goods abroad must first obtain foreign currency exchange from the control agency. Generally, exchange controls limit the importation of luxuries. For instance, Avon Products drastically cut back new production lines and products in the Philippines because exchange controls prevented the company from converting pesos to dollars to ship back to the home office. The pesos had to be used in the Philippines. China restricts the amount of foreign currency each Chinese company is allowed to keep from its exports. Therefore, Chinese companies must usually get the government's approval to release funds before they can buy products from foreign companies.

→ *Market grouping (also known as a common trade alliance): occurs when several countries agree to work together to form a common trade area that enhances trade opportunities.* The best-known market grouping is the **European Union (EU)**, which will be discussed in more detail later. The EU, which was known as the European Community before 1994, has been evolving for more than four decades, yet until recently, many trade barriers existed among its member nations.

→ *Trade agreement: an agreement to stimulate international trade.* Not all government efforts are

Mercosur was founded in 1991 to promote free trade and the fluid movement of goods, peoples, and currency in South America. Today Mercosur represents a total population of 270 million people, living in an area larger than the total surface of the European continent.

meant to stifle imports or investment by foreign corporations. The Uruguay Round of trade negotiations is an example of an effort to encourage trade, as was the grant of most favored nation (MFN) status to China. The largest Latin American trade agreement is **Mercosur**, which includes Argentina, Bolivia, Brazil, Chile, Colombia, Ecuador, Paraguay, Peru, Uruguay, and Venezuela. The elimination of most tariffs among the trading partners has resulted in trade revenues of over $20 billion annually. The economic boom created by Mercosur will undoubtedly cause other nations to seek trade agreements on their own or to enter Mercosur.

URUGUAY ROUND, THE FAILED DOHA ROUND, AND BILATERAL AGREEMENTS

The **Uruguay Round** is an agreement that has dramatically lowered trade barriers worldwide. Adopted in 1994, the agreement has been signed by 151 nations. It is the most ambitious global trade agreement ever negotiated. The agreement has reduced tariffs by one-third worldwide—a move that has raised global income by $235 billion annually. Perhaps most notable is the recognition of new global realities. For the first time, an agreement covers services, intellectual property rights, and trade-related investment measures such as exchange controls.

The Uruguay Round made several major changes in world trading practices:

→ *Entertainment, pharmaceuticals, integrated circuits, and software:* The rules protect patents, copyrights, and trademarks for 20 years. Computer programs receive 50 years of protection and semiconductor chips receive 10 years of protection. But many developing nations were given a decade to phase in patent protection for drugs. France, which limits the number of U.S. movies and TV shows that can be shown, refused to liberalize market access for the U.S. entertainment industry.

→ *Financial, legal, and accounting services:* Services came under international trading rules for the first time, creating a vast opportunity for these competitive U.S. industries. Now it is easier for managers and key personnel to be admitted to a country. Licensing standards for professionals, such as doctors, cannot discriminate against foreign applicants. That is, foreign applicants cannot be held to higher standards than domestic practitioners.

→ *Agriculture:* Europe is gradually reducing farm subsidies, opening new opportunities for U.S. farm exports such as wheat and corn. Japan and Korea are beginning to import rice. But U.S. growers of sugar and citrus fruit have had their subsidies trimmed.

→ *Textiles and apparel:* Strict quotas limiting imports from developing countries are being phased out, causing further job losses in the U.S. clothing trade. But retailers and consumers are the big winners, because past quotas have added $15 billion a year to clothing prices.

→ *A new trade organization:* The **World Trade Organization (WTO)** replaced the old **General Agreement on Tariffs and Trade (GATT)**, which was created in 1948. The old GATT contained extensive loopholes that enabled countries to avoid the trade-barrier reduction agreements—a situation similar to obeying the law only if you want to! Today, all WTO members must fully comply with all agreements under the Uruguay Round. The WTO also has an effective dispute settlement procedure with strict time limits to resolve disputes.

The latest round of WTO trade talks began in Doha, Qatar, in 2001. For the most part, the periodic meetings of WTO members under the Doha Round have been very

Mercosur
The largest Latin American trade agreement; includes Argentina, Bolivia, Brazil, Chile, Colombia, Ecuador, Paraguay, Peru, Uruguay, and Venezuela.

Uruguay Round
An agreement to dramatically lower trade barriers worldwide; created the World Trade Organization.

World Trade Organization (WTO)
A trade organization that replaced the old General Agreement on Tariffs and Trade (GATT).

General Agreement on Tariffs and Trade (GATT)
A trade agreement that contained loopholes that enabled countries to avoid trade-barrier reduction agreements.

contentious. After seven years, the Doha Round collapsed in the summer of 2008. One of the goals of the round was for China and India to lower tariffs on industrial goods in exchange for European and American tariff and subsidy cuts on farm products.

In order to lower tariffs, China and India demanded a safeguard clause that would allow them to raise tariffs on key crops such as cotton, sugar, and rice if imports surged. The two sides couldn't agree on where to set the threshold for any import surge that would trigger the clause. The United States wanted to set the trigger at a 40 percent increase in imports, whereas China and India wanted the trigger set at a much lower 10 percent increase.

By 2011, the Doha Round had still not been passed. WTO Director General Pascal Lamy estimated that nearly 80 percent of the issues in the negotiations had been resolved.[33] The slow progress, however, led to suggestions that Round be scrapped. Much of the impasse has come from the United States demanding that major developing countries make better offers to open their farm, manufacturing, and services markets in exchange for U.S. cuts in farm subsidies and other tariffs.

Many countries have moved toward protectionism after the global recession of 2008–2009. This movement discourages new trade agreements, which are designed to encourage international trade. Ecuador, for instance, has hiked tariffs on more than 600 categories of imports. Argentina and 15 other nations asked the WTO if American stimulus and bailout money designed to help pull the country out of the recession was really just industrial subsidies. If so, these countries wanted a right to retaliate.[34] The "Buy American" requirements in the stimulus package locked out foreign competitors, which added fuel to the fire.

The trend toward globalization has resulted in the creation of additional agreements and organizations: the North American Free Trade Agreement, the Central America Free Trade Agreement, the European Union, the World Bank, and the International Monetary Fund.

NORTH AMERICAN FREE TRADE AGREEMENT

At the time it was instituted, the **North American Free Trade Agreement (NAFTA)** created the world's largest free trade zone. Ratified by the U.S. Congress in 1993, the agreement includes Canada, the United States, and Mexico, with a combined population of 441 million and an economy of $17 trillion.

Canada, the largest U.S. trading partner, entered a free trade agreement with the United States in 1988. Thus, many of the new long-run opportunities for U.S. business under NAFTA have been in Mexico, America's third-largest trading partner. Tariffs on Mexican exports to the United States averaged just 4 percent before the treaty was signed, and most goods entered the United States duty-free. Therefore, the main impact of NAFTA was to open the Mexican market to U.S. companies. When the treaty went into effect, tariffs on about half the items traded across the Rio Grande disappeared. The pact removed a web of Mexican licensing requirements, quotas, and tariffs that limited transactions in U.S. goods and services. For instance, the pact allowed U.S. and Canadian financial-services companies to own subsidiaries in Mexico for the first time in 50 years.

In August 2007, the three member countries met in Canada to "tweak" NAFTA, but not make substantial changes. For example, the members agreed to further remove trade barriers on hogs, steel, consumer electronics, and chemicals. They also directed the North American Steel Trade Committee, which represents the three governments, to focus on subsidized steel from China. Most Canadians (73 percent) and Americans (77 percent) feel that NAFTA has played a key role in North American prosperity.[35] The survey was not conducted in Mexico.

North American Free Trade Agreement (NAFTA)
An agreement between Canada, the United States, and Mexico that created the world's largest free trade zone.

The real question is whether NAFTA can continue to deliver rising prosperity in all three countries. America has certainly benefited from cheaper imports and more investment opportunities abroad. Over the years, Mexico has also made huge economic gains due to NAFTA. NAFTA estimates annual trade among the three partners: Trade with Mexico is $394 billion; the United States $920 billion; and Canada is $571 billion. Average inward investment among the partners is: Canada—$240 billion; the United States—$230 billion; and Mexico—$156 billion. In other words, Canada and the U.S. invest, on average, $156 billion in Mexico.[36]

NAFTA has created millions of jobs for all three nations. It is estimated that Canada has gained almost 5 million jobs, the U.S. picked up 25 million jobs, and NAFTA has created nearly 10 million jobs in Mexico.[37]

President Obama wants NAFTA to adopt tougher labor and environmental standards and enforcement. Mexico doesn't guarantee workers' rights to form independent unions or to bargain collectively. Despite the president's wishes, at press time, NAFTA had not been reopened.

CENTRAL AMERICA FREE TRADE AGREEMENT

The newest free trade agreement is the **Central America Free Trade Agreement (CAFTA),** instituted in 2005. Besides the United States, the agreement includes Costa Rica, the Dominican Republic, El Salvador, Guatemala, Honduras, and Nicaragua. U.S. policy prior to CAFTA was to grant these countries relatively open access to American markets for their goods while they protected their own markets with tariffs and other trade barriers. These barriers prevented U.S. access to the markets in these countries for U.S. manufactured goods, agricultural products, professional services, and investments. CAFTA immediately eliminated all tariffs on 80 percent of U.S. manufactured goods, with the remainder phased out over a few years. CAFTA has been an unqualified success. It has created new commercial opportunities for its members, promoted regional stability, and is an impetus for economic development for an important group of U.S. neighbors.

EUROPEAN UNION

The European Union (EU) is one of the world's most important free trade zones and now encompasses most of Europe. More than a free trade zone, it is also a political and economic community. As a free trade zone, it guarantees the freedom of movement of people, goods, services, and capital between member states. It also maintains a common trade policy with outside nations and a regional development policy. The EU represents member nations in the WTO. Recently, the EU also began venturing into foreign policy as well, such as Iran's refining of uranium.

The European Union currently has 27 member states: Austria, Belgium, Bulgaria, Cyprus, the Czech Republic, Denmark, Estonia, Finland, France, Germany, Greece, Hungary, Ireland, Italy, Latvia, Lithuania, Luxembourg, Malta, the Netherlands, Poland, Portugal, Romania, Slovakia, Slovenia, Spain, Sweden, and the United Kingdom (see Exhibit 5.2). There are currently three official candidate countries: Croatia, the Republic of Macedonia, and Turkey. In addition, the western Balkan countries of Albania, Bosnia and Herzegovina, Montenegro, and Serbia are officially recognized as potential candidates.

To join the EU, a country must meet the Copenhagen criteria, defined at the 1993 Copenhagen European Council. These require a stable democracy that respects human rights and the rule of law; a functioning market economy capable of competition within the EU; and the acceptance of the obligations of membership,

Exhibit 5.2 The European Union

EU 27 Member States

Candidate Countries

including EU law. Evaluation of a country's fulfillment of the criteria rests with the European Council.

Governance The government of the EU consists of a number of institutions, primarily the Commission, Council, and Parliament. The European Commission is the EU's executive branch and is responsible for the day-to-day running of the EU. It is currently composed of 27 commissioners, one from each member state. The Council of the European Union (also known as the Council of Ministers) forms part of the EU's legislative branch, the other being the Parliament. It is composed of the national ministers responsible for the specific area of the EU law being addressed. For example, European legislation regarding agriculture would be treated by a Council composed of the national ministers for agriculture. The body's presidency rotates between the member states every six months.

The other half of the legislative branch is the European Parliament, which is the only directly elected institution. The 785 members of the European Parliament are directly elected by European citizens every five years. (The last full election was in June 2009.) Although the elections are in national constituencies, the members are seated in the meeting room according to political groups rather than nationality. The institution has near-equal legislative powers with the Council in community matters and has the power to reject or censure the Commission.

The European Union Commission and the courts have not always been kind to U.S. multinationals. First, the EU court blocked a merger between two U.S.

companies—General Electric and Honeywell. In late 2008, it concluded that Microsoft used its dominance in desktop computer software to muscle into server software and media players. The EU courts said that Microsoft blocked competition and fined the company $1.25 billion.[38] The EU fined Intel $1.45 billion for monopoly abuse. The EU found that Intel was using rebates to large computer manufacturers (Intel's customers) in such a way that they would be penalized if they bought too many chips from Intel's competitor—Advanced Micro Devices. Intel is appealing the fine.[39]

The Importance of the EU to the United States The European Union is one of the largest economies in the world. It has a gross domestic product of about $18 trillion. The unemployment rate is about the same as the United States. Labor productivity is higher in the United States than the European Union.

The EU is also a huge market, with a population of nearly 500 million. The United States and the EU have the largest bilateral trade and investment relationship in world history. Together, they account for more than half of the global economy, while bilateral trade accounts for 7 percent of the world total. U.S. and EU companies have invested an estimated $2 trillion in each other's economies, employing directly and indirectly as many as 14 million workers. Nearly every U.S. state is involved with exporting to, importing from, or working for European firms. California, which has an economy tied closely to Asia, has roughly 1 million workers connected to European investment or trade.[40]

Some economists have called the EU the "United States of Europe." It is an attractive market, with purchasing power almost equal to that of the United States. But the EU will probably never be a United States of Europe. For one thing, even if a united Europe achieves standardized regulations, marketers will not be able to produce a single Europroduct for a generic Euroconsumer. With more than 15 different languages and individual national customs, Europe will always be far more diverse than the United States. Thus, product differences will continue to be necessary. It will be a long time, for instance, before the French begin drinking the instant coffee that Britons enjoy. Preferences for washing machines also differ: British homemakers want front-loaders, and the French want top-loaders; Germans like lots of settings and high spin speeds; Italians like lower speeds. Even European companies that think they understand Euroconsumers often have difficulties producing "the right product." Atag Holdings NV, a diversified Dutch company whose main business is kitchen appliances, was confident it could cater to both the "potato" and "spaghetti" belts— marketers' terms for consumer preferences in northern and southern Europe. But Atag quickly discovered that preferences vary much more than that. For example, on its ovens, burner shape and size, knob and clock placement, temperature range, and colors vary greatly from country to country. Although Atag's kitchenware unit has lifted foreign sales to 25 percent of its total from 4 percent in the mid-1990s, it now believes that its range of designs and speed in delivering them, rather than the magic bullet of a Europroduct, will keep it competitive.

An entirely different type of problem facing global marketers is the possibility of a protectionist movement by the EU against outsiders. For example, European automakers have proposed holding Japanese imports at roughly their current 10 percent market share. The Irish, Danes, and Dutch don't make cars and have unrestricted home markets; they would be unhappy about limited imports of Toyotas and Nissans. But France has a strict quota on Japanese cars to protect Renault and Peugeot. These local carmakers could be hurt if the quota is raised at all.

THE WORLD BANK, THE INTERNATIONAL MONETARY FUND, AND THE G-20

Two international financial organizations are instrumental in fostering global trade. The **World Bank** offers low-interest loans to developing nations. Originally, the purpose of the loans was to help these nations build infrastructure such as roads, power plants, schools, drainage projects, and hospitals. Now the World Bank offers loans to help developing nations relieve their debt burdens. To receive the loans, countries must pledge to lower trade barriers and aid private enterprise. In addition to making loans, the World Bank is a major source of advice and information for developing nations. The United States has granted the organization $60 million to create knowledge databases on nutrition, birth control, software engineering, creation of high-quality products, and basic accounting systems.

One function of the World Bank is to uncover fraud and corruption in projects it finances. It has penalized over 350 companies and individuals by banning them from future World Bank contracts. In 2009, the World Bank reached its first financial settlement with a company. Siemens, the large German engineering company allegedly spent over $1 billion bribing government officials in at least ten different countries. Siemens agreed to pay $100 million to help anticorruption efforts and to not bid on any of the bank's projects for two years.[41]

The **International Monetary Fund (IMF)** was founded in 1945, one year after the creation of the World Bank, to promote trade through financial cooperation and eliminate trade barriers in the process. The IMF makes short-term loans to its 186 member nations that are unable to meet their budgetary expenses. It operates as a lender of last resort for troubled nations. In exchange for these emergency loans, IMF lenders frequently extract significant commitments from the borrowing nations to address the problems that led to the crises. These steps may include curtailing imports or even devaluing the currency. As part of the recent debt problems in Greece, the IMF agreed to loan the country $36 billion.

The **Group of Twenty (G-20)** finance ministers and central bank governors was established in 1999 to bring together industrialized and developing economies to discuss key issues in the global economy. The G-20 is a forum for international economic development that promotes discussion between industrial and emerging-market countries on key issues related to global economic stability. By contributing to the strengthening of the international financial system and providing opportunities for discussion on national policies, international cooperation, and international financial institutions, the G-20 helps to support growth and development across the globe. The members of G-20 are shown in Exhibit 5.3.

The G-20 has reached agreement regarding policies for growth, reducing abuse in the financial system, dealing with financial crises, and combating terrorist financing.[42] In 2009, the G-20 met in Pittsburgh where it adopted President Obama's proposed *Framework for Strong, Sustainable and Balanced Growth*. The document outlined a process to help avoid another financial crisis such as the one started in United States financial markets in 2007. It also provided recommendations for long-term global growth.

The World Bank provides loans to developing countries with the goal of reducing poverty. Their involvement must be to increase trade and promote foreign investment.

The IMF plays a large role in stabilizing global trade and exchange rates.

World Bank
An international bank that offers low-interest loans, advice, and information to developing nations.

International Monetary Fund (IMF)
An international organization that acts as a lender of last resort, providing loans to troubled nations, and also works to promote trade through financial cooperation.

Group of Twenty (G-20)
A forum for international economic development that promotes discussion between industrial and emerging-market countries on key issues related to global economic stability.

Exhibit 5.3 Members of G-20

The G-20 is made up of the finance ministers and central bank governors of 19 countries and the European Union as a whole:

- Argentina
- Australia
- Brazil
- Canada
- China
- France
- Germany
- India
- Indonesia
- Italy

- Japan
- Mexico
- Russia
- Saudi Arabia
- South Africa
- Republic of Korea
- Turkey
- United Kingdom
- United States of America
- EU

The European Union is represented by the rotating Council presidency and the European Central Bank. To ensure global economic forums and that institutions work together, the managing director of the International Monetary Fund (IMF) and the president of the World Bank, plus the chairs of the International Monetary and Financial Committee and Development Committee of the IMF and World Bank, also participate in G-20 meetings on an *ex officio* basis.

Source: www.G20.org.

DEMOGRAPHIC MAKEUP

The three most densely populated nations in the world are China, India, and Indonesia. But that fact alone is not particularly useful to marketers. They also need to know whether the population is mostly urban or rural, because marketers may not have easy access to rural consumers. In Belgium, about 90 percent of the population lives in an urban setting, whereas in Kenya almost 80 percent of the population lives in a rural setting. Belgium is thus the more attractive market. Just as important as population is personal income within a country.

Another key demographic consideration is age. There is a wide gap between the older populations of the industrialized countries and the vast working-age populations of developing countries. This gap has enormous implications for economies, businesses, and the competitiveness of individual countries. It means that while Europe and Japan struggle with pension schemes and the rising cost of health care, countries such as China, Brazil, and Mexico can reap the fruits of what's known as a demographic dividend: falling labor costs, a healthier and more educated population, and the entry of millions of women into the workforce.

The demographic dividend is a gift of falling birthrates, and it causes a temporary bulge in the number of working-age people. Population experts have estimated that one-third of East Asia's economic miracle can be attributed to a beneficial age structure. But the miracle occurred only because the governments had policies in place to educate their people, create jobs, and improve health.

NATURAL RESOURCES

A final factor in the external environment that has become more evident in the past decade is the shortage of natural resources. For example, petroleum shortages have created huge amounts of wealth for oil-producing countries such as Norway, Saudi Arabia, and the United Arab Emirates. Both consumer and industrial markets have blossomed in these countries. Other countries—such as Indonesia, Mexico, and Venezuela—were able to borrow heavily against oil reserves in order to develop more rapidly. On the other hand, industrial countries such as Japan, the United

States, and much of western Europe experienced an enormous transfer of wealth to the petroleum-rich nations. The high price of oil has created inflationary pressures in petroleum-importing nations. It also created major problems for airlines and other petroleum-dependent industries.

Petroleum is not the only natural resource that affects international marketing. Warm climate and lack of water mean that many of Africa's countries will remain importers of foodstuffs. The United States, on the other hand, must rely on Africa for many precious metals. Japan depends heavily on the United States for timber and logs. A Minnesota company manufactures and sells a million pairs of disposable chopsticks to Japan each year. The list could go on, but the point is clear. Vast differences in natural resources create international dependencies, huge shifts of wealth, inflation and recession, export opportunities for countries with abundant resources, and even a stimulus for military intervention.

LO4
Global Marketing by the Individual Firm

A company should consider entering the global marketplace only after its management has a solid grasp of the global environment. Some relevant questions are:

→ "What are our options in selling abroad?"
→ "How difficult is global marketing?" and
→ "What are the potential risks and returns?"

Concrete answers to these questions would probably encourage the many U.S. firms not selling overseas to venture into the international arena. Foreign sales can be an important source of profits.

Companies decide to "go global" for a number of reasons. Perhaps the most important is to earn additional profits. Managers may feel that international sales will result in higher profit margins or more added-on profits. A second stimulus is that a firm may have a unique product or technological advantage not available to other international competitors. Such advantages should result in major business successes abroad. In other situations, management may have exclusive market information about foreign customers, marketplaces, or market situations. While exclusivity can provide an initial motivation for international marketing, managers must realize that competitors can be expected to catch up with the firm's information advantage. Finally, saturated domestic markets, excess capacity, and potential for economies of scale can also be motivators to "go global." Economies of scale mean that average per-unit production costs fall as output is increased.

Review LO3 Describe the external environment facing global marketers

Natural Resources
• dependence
• independence

Cultural
• values
• language
• customs
• traditions

Economic Development

Technological Development

Political Structure
• tariffs
• quotas
• boycotts
• exchange controls
• market groupings
• trade agreements

Demography
• urban vs. rural
• young vs. old
• purchasing power

Global Marketing Mix

© Cengage Learning 2013

Itau is making a mark around the world with first class service, dedication to the environment, and globally recognizable Latin Americans in their advertising.

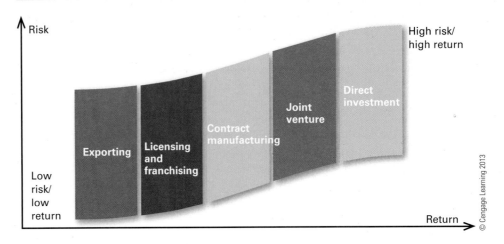

Many firms form multinational partnerships—called strategic alliances—to assist them in penetrating global markets; strategic alliances are examined in Chapter 7. Five other methods of entering the global marketplace are, in order of risk: exporting, licensing and franchising, contract manufacturing, joint venture, and direct investment. (See Exhibit 5.4.)

EXPORTING

When a company decides to enter the global market, exporting is usually the least complicated and least risky alternative. **Exporting** is selling domestically produced products to buyers in another country. A company can sell directly to foreign importers or buyers. Exporting is not limited to huge corporations such as Procter & Gamble or 3M. Indeed, small companies account for 96 percent of all U.S. exporters, but only 30 percent of the export volume.[43] The United States is the world's largest exporter.

The U.S. Commercial Service within the Department of Commerce promotes itself as "Your Global Business Partner." It offers trade specialists in more than a hundred U.S. cities and 150 overseas offices to help beginning exporters, and helps those already engaged in global marketing increase their business. The primary services offered by the U.S. Commercial Service are counseling and advocacy, market research, locating qualified buyers and partners, trade events, and global business consulting. These services are explained in more detail in Exhibit 5.5.

The federal government has created a Web site, **www.export.gov**, that brings together all of the resources across the U.S. government to assist American firms that wish to go global. The site directs you to the U.S. Commercial Service for marketing research and trade leads, the Export-Import Bank for loan information, and the U.S.

exporting
Selling domestically produced products to buyers in another country.

Exhibit 5.5 Assistance Provided by the U.S. Commercial Service to Exporters

COUNSELING AND ADVOCACY

- **Advocacy:** Get a competitive edge with U.S. Commercial Service advocacy. U.S. diplomats and other officials help your company when unanticipated problems arise—resolve payment issues, settle disputes, win contracts, and overcome regulatory hurdles. Support can include government-to-government meetings by U.S. Commercial Service officers and ambassadors with high-level foreign government officials, in addition to direct intervention with international companies.

- **Counseling:** Increase your export sales and enter new international markets with U.S. Commercial Service export counseling. Trade specialists in more than 100 U.S. cities and 80 countries provide in-depth export consulting and customized business solutions. Our trade specialists near you work with our team of experts overseas in getting you the information and advice that you need to succeed.

(Continued)

- **Platinum Key Service:** Get long-term, comprehensive, customized support to achieve your business goals. The Platinum Key Service is solution oriented and custom-tailored to your needs. Identify markets, launch products, develop major project opportunities, resolve market entry questions, and receive assistance on regulatory matters. Our in-country trade specialists will work closely with you to identify needs, provide progress reports, and ensure timely resolution.

MARKET RESEARCH

- **Market Research Library:** Accurate, up-to-date information lets you target the best international markets. Our single comprehensive market research includes overviews on doing business in more than 120 countries and profiles of 110 industry sectors. You can also get updates on new regulations, currency fluctuations, business trends, and government-financed projects. Much of this research is available at no charge.

- **Customized Market Research:** Receive specific intelligence on the export prospects for your product or service in a potential market.

- **Business Facilitation Service:** Get low-cost logistical and administrative support when you're on international business travel. Our Business Facilitation Service offers flexible solutions to let you do business when you're away from home.

FINDING INTERNATIONAL PARTNERS

- **International Partner Search:** Find qualified international buyers, partners, or agents without traveling overseas. U.S. Commercial Service specialists will deliver detailed company information on up to five prescreened international companies that have expressed an interest in your company's products and services.

- **Gold Key Matching Service:** Save time and money by letting the U.S. Commercial Service help you find a buyer, partner, agent, or distributor. The Gold Key Service provides you with one-on-one appointments with prescreened potential agents, distributors, sales representatives, association and government contracts, licensing or joint venture partners, and other strategic business partners in your targeted export market.

- **Commercial News USA:** Promote your products and services to more than 400,000 international buyers in 145 countries. Commercial News USA is a product catalog distributed by U.S. embassies and consulates worldwide and has a proven track record of high response rates and solid sales results.

- **Trade Leads:** View announcements from qualified international companies looking to source U.S. products and services and advertise government tender projects through our trade leads database. All of our trade leads are prescreened by our U.S. embassy or consulate staff overseas and are provided as a free service for U.S. exporters.

- **International Company Profile:** Prevent costly mistakes with quick, low-cost credit checks or due-diligence reports on international companies. Before you do business with a prospective agent, distributor, or partner, the International Company Profile will give you the background information you need to evaluate the company.

TRADE EVENTS AND RELATED SERVICES

- **U.S. Pavilions at Certified Trade Fairs:** Exhibit at U.S. Pavilions certified by the U.S. Commercial Service and increase your chances of finding new business. Certified U.S. Pavilions offer one-on-one business matching, business counseling from trade specialists, and special exhibit services designed to help U.S. exporters maximize returns from trade shows and make more international sales.

- **Trade Fair Certification:** Exhibiting at a trade show abroad can lead to tremendous export opportunities for U.S. companies. This is why the Trade Fair Certification Program was created: to help companies like yours make important exhibiting decisions and free you of many of the concerns you may have about exhibiting outside the United States.

- **International Buyer Program:** Find new international business partners at U.S. trade shows with the International Buyer Program. The IBP recruits more than 125,000 foreign buyers and distributors to 32 top U.S. trade shows per year. U.S. Commercial Service trade specialists arrange meetings for U.S. exporters and international delegates and provide export counseling at the show's International Business Center.

- **Trade Missions:** Meet face-to-face with prescreened international business contacts in promising markets with U.S. Commercial Service trade missions. Trade missions save you time and money by allowing you to maximize contact with qualified distributors, sales representatives, or partners in one to four countries.

- **Virtual Trade Missions:** If your schedule or travel budget limits your ability to travel overseas, consider Virtual Trade Missions. An interactive two-hour videoconference lets you meet virtually. Planning an International Trade Mission? Every year, the U.S. Commercial Service supports dozens of trade missions organized by state economic organizations, elected officials, chambers of commerce, and industry associations through our Certified Trade Mission program.

- **Catalog Events:** Looking for an affordable, low-risk way to promote your products and services in promising markets throughout the world? Increase your company's international sales potential by showcasing your products and services with the International Catalog Exhibition Program.

- **Trade Specialists:** U.S. Commercial Service trade specialists located in international markets will translate your company profile into the local language, display your marketing materials, collect sales leads from interested local buyers, and then assist you as you follow up with the local contacts.

Source: U.S. Commercial Service

buyer for export
An intermediary in the global market that assumes all ownership risks and sells globally for its own account.

export broker
An intermediary who plays the traditional broker's role by bringing buyer and seller together.

export agent
An intermediary who acts like a manufacturer's agent for the exporter. The export agent lives in the foreign market.

licensing
The legal process whereby a licensor agrees to let another firm use its manufacturing process, trademarks, patents, trade secrets, or other proprietary knowledge.

Department of Agriculture for agricultural export assistance. In all, **www.export.gov** brings together 19 federal agencies that offer some form of export assistance. The Export-Import Bank helps in the export of U.S. goods and services. It doesn't compete directly with private banks, but provides export financing that fills gaps in trade financings. The Export-Import Bank assumes credit and country risks that the private sector is unable or unwilling to accept. About 86 percent of the Export-Import Bank's financing is to small businesses.[44] For those interested in international business, a nongovernmental Web site that offers links to hundreds of useful sites is available from the Federation of International Trade Associations (**http://fita.org**).

Instead of selling directly to foreign buyers, a company might decide to sell to intermediaries located in its domestic market. The most common intermediary is the export merchant, also known as a **buyer for export**, which is usually treated as a domestic customer by the domestic manufacturer. The buyer for export assumes all risks and sells internationally for its own account. The domestic firm is involved only to the extent that its products are bought in foreign markets.

A second type of intermediary is the **export broker**, who plays the traditional broker's role by bringing buyer and seller together. The manufacturer still retains title and assumes all the risks. Export brokers operate primarily in agricultural products and raw materials.

Export agents, a third type of intermediary, are foreign sales agents—distributors who live in the foreign country and perform the same functions as domestic manufacturers' agents, helping with international financing, shipping, and so on. The U.S. Department of Commerce has an agent-distributor service that helps about 5,000 U.S. companies a year find an agent or distributor in virtually any country of the world. A second category of agents resides in the manufacturer's country but represents foreign buyers. This type of agent acts as a hired purchasing agent for foreign customers operating in the exporter's home market.

LICENSING AND FRANCHISING

Another effective way for a firm to move into the global arena with relatively little risk is to sell a license to manufacture its product to someone in a foreign country. **Licensing** is the legal process whereby a licensor allows another firm to use its manufacturing process, trademarks, patents, trade secrets, or other proprietary knowledge. The licensee, in turn, pays the licensor a royalty or fee agreed on by both parties.

Because licensing has many advantages, U.S. companies have eagerly embraced the concept, sometimes in unusual ways. Caterpillar, the producer of heavy machinery, has licensed Wolverine World Wide to make "CAT" brand shoes and boots. Europeans have latched onto CAT gear as the new symbol of American outdoor culture. CAT is one of Europe's hottest brands, which translates into almost $1 billion in licensing revenues.

A licensor must make sure it can exercise sufficient control over the licensee's activities to ensure proper quality, pricing, distribution, and so on. Licensing may also create a new competitor in the long run, if the licensee decides to void the license agreement. International law is often ineffective in stopping such actions. Two common ways of maintaining effective control over licensees are shipping one or more critical components from the United States or locally registering patents and trademarks to the U.S. firm, not to the licensee. Garment companies maintain control by delivering only so many labels per day; they also supply their own fabric, collect the scraps, and do accurate unit counts.

Entertainment characters and properties, such as Celine Dion, Antonio Banderas, and SpongeBob SquarePants, account for 24 percent of worldwide retail sales of licensed goods. Total license sales now run over $187 billion annually.[45] Corporate trademark/brand properties and fashion labels each account for 21 percent of the total. The United States and Canada account for a majority of all global licensing sales.

Franchising is a form of licensing that has grown rapidly in recent years. More than 500 U.S. franchisors operate more than 55,000 outlets in foreign countries, bringing in sales of over $12 billion.[46] Over half of the international franchises are for fast-food restaurants and business services. The top global franchises (in order) are: McDonald's, Subway, KFC, Burger King, and 7-Eleven.[47] Franchisors cannot always offer the same product or the same method of distribution in countries around the globe. Domino's Pizza, for example, found that in Japan it had to modify its delivery procedures because addresses there often aren't sequential but instead are determined by a building's age. In Aruba, it soon found that using motorcycles to deliver pizzas was too dangerous because of the island's strong winds, so it used small trucks to solve the problem. In the Philippines, locations of stores at times were chosen by using feng shui, a Chinese art that positions buildings according to spiritual flow. And because many Icelanders stay up all hours, Domino's stores there are open much longer than elsewhere. When the company went into Italy, many Italians found its pizza "too American—the sauce being too bold, the toppings too heavy," a company spokesman recalls.[48]

CONTRACT MANUFACTURING

Firms that do not want to become involved in licensing or to become heavily involved in global marketing may engage in **contract manufacturing**, which is private-label manufacturing by a foreign company. The foreign company produces a certain volume of products to specification, with the domestic firm's brand name on the goods. The domestic company usually handles the marketing. Thus, the domestic firm can broaden its global marketing base without investing in overseas plants and equipment. After establishing a solid base, the domestic firm may switch to a joint venture or direct investment.

Recently, particularly in China, contract manufacturers have been making overruns and selling the excess production directly to either consumers or retailers. New Balance, for example, found that a contract manufacturer was producing extra running shoes and selling them to unauthorized retailers. The retailers were selling the knockoff New Balance shoes for $20, while authorized retailers were trying to sell the same shoe for $60. New Balance changed its relationship with its suppliers. It cut the number of factories it uses in China to six and monitors them more closely. It has also begun using high-tech shoe labels to better spot counterfeits and keep control of its own production. Yet this still didn't solve all of New Balance's problems. One contract manufacturer, Horace Chang, produced a shoe called "the classic," a low-tech shoe without midsole engineering that defines a high performance shoe. Unhappy with Mr. Chang because of "overproduction," New Balance terminated the contract and asked for molds, specifications, signs, labels, packages, wrappers, and ads. They were not returned. He continued to sell in Taiwan, Hong Kong, Italy, and Germany. In addition, Mr. Chang launched a competing brand called "Henkees." A long court battle in China was to no avail. Finally, an American international arbitrator awarded New Balance $9.9 million. To date, the firm hasn't collected a penny. Yet New Balance still uses contract manufacturing in China because the market is too important to pass up. New Balance faced a second problem when a new Chinese competitor launched a brand called New Barlun. New Barlun used packaging, logos, store displays, and advertising brochures that were, by United States standards, audacious copies of New Balance's.[49] New

contract manufacturing
Private-label manufacturing by a foreign company.

New Balance still uses contract manufacturing in China, despite the risk of having proprietary information stolen and used by the workers.

Balance sued for trademark infringement in China and won. New Barlun athletic shoes are no longer produced.

It is estimated that counterfeits, knockoffs, and third-shift merchandise costs manufacturers over $250 billion annually. Also, these practices result in an estimated 750,000 lost jobs.[50] The three terms used to describe brand theft are discussed below:

→ **Counterfeit**—a product that bears a trademark that its maker had no authority to use. The U.S. military has had a rash of problems from counterfeit microchips (tiny electric circuits) being installed in fighter jets, helicopters, and even on long-range radar on board the aircraft carrier USS *Ronald Reagan*. Although no deaths have occurred from the fake chips, numerous malfunctions have occurred. Tiny businesses in rural China heat up circuit boards from old computers and then strip out the chips. They are then sold to firms like Jinlong Electronics that purportedly sells military-quality chips. This means chips that are more durable and can withstand temperature extremes. Instead, the old computer chips are sanded to remove the old markings and restamped "military" with a new date. The Defense Supply Center, a major Pentagon electronics parts buyer, has begun to require suppliers to document that microchips conform to quality standards and can be traced to the manufacturing source.[51]

→ **Knockoff**—a broad term encompassing both counterfeits and items that look like branded products, though they don't actually bear forged trademarks.

→ **Third shift**—an unauthorized product made by an unauthorized or authorized contractor. Thus, a contract manufacturer may use two production shifts to produce authorized products and a third shift to produce goods to be sold through an unauthorized channel. The contract manufacturer gets all of the revenue from production from that third shift.

JOINT VENTURE

Joint ventures are somewhat similar to licensing agreements. In an international **joint venture**, the domestic firm buys part of a foreign company or joins with a foreign company to create a new entity. A joint venture is a quick and relatively inexpensive way to go global and to gain needed expertise. For example, Robert Mondavi Wines entered into a joint venture with Baron Philippe de Rothschild, owner of Bordeaux's First Growth chateau, Mouton-Rothschild. They created a wine in California called Opus One. It was immediately established as the American vanguard of quality and price. Mondavi has entered other joint ventures with the Frescobaldi family in Tuscany and with Errazuriz in Chile.

Joint ventures can be very risky. Many fail; others fall victim to a takeover, in which one partner buys out the other. Sometimes joint venture partners simply can't agree on management strategies and policies. Though joint ventures are very popular in the auto industry, many have not worked out. Joint venture factories—General Motors/Toyota, Suzuki/GM, Mazda/Ford—have not been particular successes. GM has a 50-50 joint venture with the Shanghai Automotive Corporation, owned by the Shanghai city government. The joint venture, founded in 1997, makes Buicks, Cadillacs, and Chevrolets. It has created hundreds of millions of dollars in profit for GM. Now, the Chinese company, using the technology and the money earned from selling joint-venture cars, is becoming a serious competitor to GM; the Chinese Roewe is said to be bigger and more luxurious than the American Buick. The chairman of Shanghai Automotive says, "We now want to build a global Chinese brand."[52]

Similarly, Paris-based Danone is fighting with the Hangzhou Wahaha Group over the terms of its joint-venture. The Wahaha brand of soft drinks, juices, and teas are better known to many in China than Coca-Cola. Wahaha is China's largest soft drink producer. It entered into a joint venture with Danone to speed expansion of the Wahaha brand back in 1996. By 2005, Wahaha controlled many factories outside the joint venture, which Danone claimed was costing it $25 million per month. In 2010, Danone received a cash settlement from the Hangzhou Wahaha Group. In turn, Danone pulled out of the joint venture and relinquished all claims to the name Wahaha.[53]

DIRECT INVESTMENT

Active ownership of a foreign company or of overseas manufacturing or marketing facilities is **direct foreign investment**. Direct foreign investment by U.S. firms is currently about $3,900 billion. Direct investors have either a controlling interest or a large minority interest in the firm. Thus, they have the greatest potential reward and the greatest potential risk. Because of the problems discussed above with contract manufacturing and joint ventures in China, multinationals are going it alone. Today, nearly five times as much foreign direct investment comes into China in the form of stand-alone efforts as comes in for joint ventures.[54]

Walmart is the world's largest global retailer. It serves customers more than 200 million times per week at more than 8,400 retail units under 55 different names in 15 countries. It employs more than two million people, 664,000 of whom are outside the United States. The largest number of stores outside the United States is in Mexico with 1,493. Its latest market entry is in India with just two stores. International sales currently run over $100 billion a year. In one recent quarter, Walmart earned $2.5 billion from the positive impact of currency exchange rate fluctuations.[55]

The company has, on occasion, stumbled in its quest for growth. Walmart had difficulty with local labor laws and discounters undercutting it in Germany. It pulled out after losing $1 billion. Walmart also pulled out of Korea and has struggled in Japan. The company operates 371 stores in Japan under the Seiyu brand

joint venture
When a domestic firm buys part of a foreign company or joins with a foreign company to create a new entity.

direct foreign investment
Active ownership of a foreign company or of overseas manufacturing or marketing facilities.

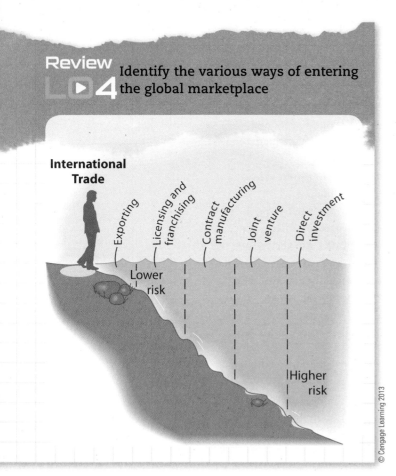

International Trade

Exporting — Licensing and franchising — Contract manufacturing — Joint venture — Direct investment

Lower risk

Higher risk

© Cengage Learning 2013

name. In 2009, Walmart announced a shift in its global focus to emerging markets including Mexico, China, and Brazil. More than half of its global direct investment will be in emerging countries.[56]

A firm may make a direct foreign investment by acquiring an interest in an existing company, such as Walmart did in Japan, or by building new facilities. It might do so because it has trouble transferring some resource to a foreign operation or getting that resource locally. One important resource is personnel, especially managers. If the local labor market is tight, the firm may buy an entire foreign firm and retain all its employees instead of paying higher salaries than competitors. For example, when Walmart decided to enter China, it purchased the general merchandise chain Trust-Mart for about $1 billion.

In most cases, Walmart has built stores from scratch in the global marketplace rather than buying an existing chain. Overcoming the culture of the chain Walmart bought in Germany was too difficult and is part of the reason they pulled out of the market. The difficulty Walmart has experienced with the Seiyu chain it bought in Japan is culturally related.

Cultural differences are not the only obstacle that a firm may face when it invests in other countries. IKEA, the Swedish retailer, has invested over $4 billion in Russia since 2000. The retailer has become such an icon of Russia's boom that today's yuppies are called "the IKEA Generation." Yet when IKEA planned to open a 1.4 million square foot mall in Samara, just outside Moscow, it sat completed but unoccupied for over a year. Local Samara officials said that the mall was "unsafe" but a local construction company could quickly "fix the deficiencies." The corruption was the last straw for IKEA. The firm announced that it was putting on hold all new investment in Russia.[57] A Russian retail consultant said, "Investors need dozens and dozens of approvals from an incredible number of agencies, and that provides for unlimited corruption opportunities."[58]

L▶5
The Global Marketing Mix

To succeed, firms seeking to enter into foreign trade must still adhere to the principles of the marketing mix. Information gathered on foreign markets through research is the basis for the four Ps of global marketing strategy: product, place (distribution), promotion, and price. Marketing managers who understand the advantages and disadvantages of different ways of entering the global market and the effect of the external environment on the firm's marketing mix have a better chance of reaching their goals.

The first step in creating a marketing mix is developing a thorough understanding of the global target market. Often this knowledge can be obtained through the same types of marketing research used in the domestic market. (See Chapter 9.) However, global marketing research is conducted in vastly different environments.

Conducting a survey can be difficult in developing countries, where Internet access (no one "owns" the Internet) is growing but is not always common and mail delivery is slow or sporadic. Drawing samples based on known population parameters is often difficult because of the lack of data. In some cities in South America, Mexico, Africa, and Asia, street maps are unavailable, streets are unidentified, and houses are unnumbered. Moreover, the questions a marketer can ask may differ in other cultures. In some cultures, people tend to be more private than in the United States and will not respond to personal questions on surveys. For instance, in France, questions about one's age and income are considered especially rude.

PRODUCT AND PROMOTION

With the proper information, a good marketing mix can be developed. One important decision is whether to alter the product and the promotion for the global marketplace. Other options are to radically change the product or to moderately adjust either the promotional message or the product to suit local conditions.

ONE PRODUCT, ONE MESSAGE

The strategy of global marketing standardization, which was discussed earlier, means developing a single product for all markets and promoting it the same way all over the world. For instance, Procter & Gamble uses the same product and promotional themes for Head & Shoulders products in China as it does in the United States. The advertising draws attention to a person's dandruff problem, which stands out in a nation of black-haired people. Head & Shoulders is now the best-selling shampoo in China despite costing over 300 percent more than local brands. Buoyed by its success with Head & Shoulders, P&G is using the same product and same promotion strategy with Tide detergent in China. It also used another common promotion tactic that has been successful in the United States. The company spent half a million dollars to reach agreements with local washing machine manufacturers, which now include a free box of Tide with every new washer.

Other multinational firms are also applying uniform branding around the world on products such as Dove, Perrier, L'Oréal, and Hellmann's. Starbucks faced a big obstacle in China. Coffee was traditionally so unpopular in China's tea-drinking culture until recently that many Starbucks didn't brew regular drip coffee until someone ordered it. Starbucks faced a dilemma: Should they change their offerings to have more local appeal, or attempt to change Chinese tastes? Starbucks bet that a new generation of Chinese, with growing spending power and a desire for high status brands would try coffee. Coffee represents change from the old way of doing things. Once people enter a Chinese Starbucks, the education process begins. The chain stacks cream and sugar counters with brochures titled "Coffee Brewing Wisdom" and others that answer questions like "What is espresso?" Workers float through stores passing out small cups of pumpkin-spice latte and other drinks. Good-for-you messages about coffee are sometimes part of the pitch. The process seems to be working. One of your authors recently visited a number of Starbucks in several Chinese cities and observed many young upscale Chinese in every one! China is now Starbucks' fourth-largest global market, following Canada, Japan, and the United Kingdom. Despite recent store closings in the United States, Starbucks plans to add "thousands of stores in China," according to Howard Schultz, CEO of Starbucks.[59]

Global media—especially satellite and cable TV networks such as CNN International, MTV Networks, and British Sky Broadcasting—make it possible to beam advertising to audiences unreachable a few years ago. Parisian 18-year-olds often have more in common with 18-year-olds in New York than with their own parents.

Almost all of MTV's advertisers run unified, English-language campaigns in the nations the firm reaches. The audiences buy the same products, go to the same movies, listen to the same music, and sip the same colas. Global advertising works on that simple premise. Although teens throughout the world prefer movies above all other forms of television programming, they are closely followed by music videos, stand-up comedy, and then sports.

Global marketing standardization can sometimes backfire. Unchanged products may fail simply because of cultural factors. The game *Trivial Pursuit* failed in Japan. It seems that getting the answers wrong can be seen as a loss of face. Any type of war game tends to do very poorly in Germany, even though Germany is by far the world's biggest game-playing nation. A successful game in Germany has plenty of details and thick rulebooks.

Sometimes the desire for absolute standardization must give way to practical considerations and local market dynamics. For example, because of the feminine connotations of the word *diet,* the European version of Diet Coke is Coca-Cola Light. In France, its country of origin, the leading brand of yogurt is called Danone, whereas in the United States, it goes by its Anglicized name, Dannon. Even if the brand name differs by market—as with Lay's potato chips, which are Sabritas in Mexico—a strong visual relationship may be created by uniform application of the brand mark and graphic elements on packaging.

PRODUCT INVENTION

In the context of global marketing, product invention can be taken to mean either creating a new product for a market or drastically changing an existing product. Campbell's Soup invented a watercress and duck gizzard soup that is now selling well in China. It is also considering a cream of snake soup. Frito-Lay's most popular potato chip in Thailand is shrimp flavored. Popular ice cream flavors in Japan include pickled orchid, eel, fish, sea slug, whale meat, soft-shelled turtle, and cedar chips. McDonald's was struggling in Japan until it added a shrimp burger to the menu. Pepsi has found success in Japan with "limited edition" drinks that create buzz on YouTube and other sites. The most successful has been "Ice Cucumber," where bloggers are debating whether it tastes more like melon or cucumber. Another popular "limited edition" drink was a cinnamon-based beverage called "Pepsi Red."[60]

Like Starbucks, Dunkin' Brands has its eye on the Asian market. There are approximately 700 Dunkin' Donuts in South Korea now and they plan to double that in the next decade. The shops are very similar to those found in America, with plush orange and yellow chairs, Wi-Fi Internet access, and plasma-screen televisions. In addition to standard American-style doughnuts, the firm created a number of new items for Korean tastes. Dunkin's offers sweet soybean doughnuts and green tea lattes. Dunkin's Korean menus focus on natural and organic ingredients to appeal to health-conscious consumers. For instance, it sells a 23-grain latte, a warm drink consisting of roasted barley, brown rice, and other grains. The company also sells the drink in powdered form so that customers can make it at home.[61]

Consumers in different countries use products differently. For example, in many countries, clothing is worn much longer between washings than in the United States, so a more durable fabric must be produced and marketed. For Peru, Goodyear developed a tire that contains a higher percentage of natural rubber and has better treads than tires manufactured elsewhere in order to handle the tough Peruvian driving conditions. Rubbermaid has sold millions of open-top wastebaskets in America; Europeans, picky about garbage peeking out of bins, want bins with tight lids that snap into place.

customer experience

Marketing to the Poor Around the Globe

Unexpectedly strong demand for cheap cell phones in recent years revealed the untapped markets in India's villages and slums. Thanks to $20 cell phones and two-cent-a-minute call rates, Indian cell-phone companies are signing up more than five million new subscribers a month—most of them consumers no one would have considered serving in the past.

Other firms saw the demand for cell phones and wanted a piece of the rural Indian action. Only one in five Indian homes has a refrigerator. Examination of the needs of poor rural farm families led to the creation of the "Chotukool" or "Little Cool" in Hindi. The petite fridge looks more like a cooler and sells for under $70. It opens from the top and is about 1.5 feet tall by 2 feet wide. It is tiny because the poor live in small homes and don't buy food in bulk. It has handles to make it portable for the migrant workers who move a lot. It has no compressor to break or make noise. Instead, it runs on a cooling chip and fan similar to those used to cool computers. It can survive power surges and outages common in the country kitchen and even has the option of running on batteries. Although designed with cost in mind, it uses high-end insulation to stay cool for hours without power.

Another company has reinvented the wood-burning stove to make more heat and less smoke and sells for $23. Instead of wood, the stove uses dry pellets made of agricultural waste like corn husks and peanut shells. It is viewed as a life-changing product because the houses are no longer smoky. So far, over 400,000 stoves have been sold.

Many very poor consumers cannot read, write, or use math. Research has shown that while shopping in unfamiliar stores, some low-literacy consumers will choose products at random, buying the first brand they see once they locate a desired product category or aisle. Others simply walk through the store, choosing items that look attractive based on factors such as packaging colors or label illustrations, without regard to whether they even need the product. When shopping in familiar stores, many low-literacy consumers buy only the brands they recognize by appearance or have purchased previously.

One way to help improve the shopping experience for these consumers is to display prices and price reductions graphically—a half-circle to indicate a 50 percent markdown, for example, or a picture of three one-dollar bills to indicate a purchase price of $3. Products priced in whole and half numbers make it easier for low-literacy consumers to calculate the price of, say, two bags of rice. Also, stores might put the ingredients required for the preparation of popular local dishes in the same section of the store. This helps low-literacy consumers who often envision the sequence of activities involved in fixing specific dishes to identify the ingredients and quantities they need to purchase. The same can be done for other domestic tasks.[62]

Why do you think that more multinationals don't target the low-income market? It has been suggested by consultants that "Companies must create new lifestyles among poor consumers to create new markets." What do you think this means?

Marketers have traditionally targeted the middle- to upper-income consumers when they have entered global markets. Some firms are finding profitable opportunities by serving the poor, as the Customer Experience box explains.

PRODUCT ADAPTATION

Another alternative for global marketers is to slightly alter a basic product to meet local conditions. Sometimes it is as simple as changing the package size. In India, Unilever sells single-use sachets of Sunsilk shampoo for 2 to 4 cents. Unilever's Rexona brand deodorant sticks sell for 16 cents and up. They are big hits in India, the Philippines, Bolivia, and Peru—where Unilever has grabbed 60 percent of the deodorant market. A nickel-size Vaseline package and a tube containing enough Close Up toothpaste for 20 brushings sell for about 8 cents each. In Nigeria, Unilever sells 3-inch-square packets of margarine that don't need refrigeration.

Sometimes power sources and/or voltage must be changed on electronic products. It may be necessary, for example, to change the size and shape of the electrical plug. In other cases, the change may be a bit more radical. In India, people often lack reliable access to electricity or can't afford batteries. So, Freeplay Energy Group of London created a radio that is charged by cranking a handle.

One of the world's best at product adaptation is the Korean firm LG Electronics. Kimchi, made from fermented cabbage seasoned with garlic and chili, is served with most meals in Korea, but when it's stored inside a normal refrigerator, its pungent odor taints nearby foods. LG Electronics introduced the kimchi refrigerator, a product specifically designed to address the odor problem. Featuring a dedicated compartment that isolates smelly kimchi from other foods, the fridge became a must-have in Korean homes.

To meet the needs of Indian consumers, LG rolled out refrigerators with larger vegetable- and water-storage compartments, surge-resistant power supplies, and brightly colored finishes that reflect local preferences (red in the south, green in Kashmir). In Iran, LG offers a microwave oven with a preset button for reheating shish kebabs—a favorite dish. Saudi Arabians like LG's Primian refrigerator, which includes a special compartment for storing dates, a Middle Eastern staple that spoils easily. For Saudis and other oil-rich consumers, LG has introduced a gold-plated 71-inch flat-screen television that sells for $80,000.

Chinese don't like sweet cookies and Kraft's Oreos were not selling well. Not only were Oreos too sweet, the Chinese also thought the package was too expensive at 79 cents. The company developed 20 prototypes of reduced-sugar Oreos and tested them with Chinese consumers before arriving at a formula that tasted right. Kraft also introduced packages containing fewer Oreos for just 29 cents.

Although Oreos were selling better, Kraft was still not satisfied. China's cookie-wafer segment was growing faster than traditional biscuit-like cookies. Kraft decided to remake the Oreo itself. The new Chinese Oreo consisted of four layers of crispy wafer filled with vanilla and chocolate cream, coated in chocolate.

PROMOTION ADAPTATION

Another global marketing strategy is to maintain the same basic product but alter the promotional strategy. Bicycles are mainly pleasure vehicles in the United States. In many parts of the world, however, they are a family's main mode of transportation. Thus, promotion in these countries should stress durability and efficiency. In contrast, U.S. advertising may emphasize escaping and having fun.

Harley-Davidson decided that its American promotion theme, "One steady constant in an increasingly screwed-up world," wouldn't appeal to the Japanese market. The Japanese ads combine American images with traditional Japanese ones: American riders passing a geisha in a rickshaw, Japanese ponies nibbling at a Harley motorcycle. Waiting lists for Harleys in Japan are now six months long.

Lenovo, the PC maker, targets rural Chinese customers with low-cost computers. The machines are built to accommodate unpredictable variation in the power supply voltage and include farm management software. Lenovo promotes the machines as high-status wedding gifts, which, by tradition, should appear as generous as possible. The firm uses slogans such as "Buy a Lenovo PC, Be a Happy Bride."

"They like to give desktop PCs because the boxes are large," says Li Zhong, director of Lenovo's consumer business in the Beijing and Hebei regions. "They deliver the computers to brides' families on trucks, which everyone can see. In these cases the bigger the box, the better."[63]

Nowhere has promotion adaptation been taken so far as Lexus in Japan, where personal selling (part of promotion) has a whole new meaning. In the luxury car market in Japan, BMW and Mercedes-Benz overshadow Lexus. To rectify that, Lexus hired a Japanese etiquette school that specialized in teaching the art of beautifying daily behavior. Now, when a Lexus salesperson opens a car door in a Lexus showroom for a potential customer, he or she points with all five fingers to the handle, right hand followed by left. The salesperson then gracefully opens the door with both hands in the same way Japanese samurais in the 14th century would have opened a sliding screen door.

At Lexus showrooms, sales consultants lean 5 to 10 degrees forward and assume a warrior's "waiting position" when a customer is looking at a car. When serving customers coffee or tea, employees must kneel on the floor with both feet together and both knees on the ground. The coffee cup must never make a noise when it is placed on the table. All salespeople use a mirror to practice the "Lexus Face," a closed-mouth smile said to put customers at ease.[64]

Language barriers, translation problems, and cultural differences have generated numerous headaches for international marketing managers. Consider these examples:

→ A toothpaste claiming to give users white teeth was especially inappropriate in many areas of southeast Asia, where the well-to-do chew betel nuts and black teeth are a sign of higher social status.

→ Procter & Gamble's Japanese advertising for Camay soap nearly devastated the product. In one commercial, a man meeting a woman for the first time immediately compared her skin to that of a fine porcelain doll. Although the ad had worked in other Asian countries, the man came across as rude and disrespectful in Japan.

→ A teenager careening down a store aisle on a grocery cart in a Coca-Cola ad was perceived as too rebellious in Singapore.

PLACE (DISTRIBUTION)

Solving promotional and product problems does not guarantee global marketing success. The product still has to get adequate distribution. For example, Europeans don't play sports as much as Americans do, so they don't visit sporting-goods stores as often. Realizing this, Reebok started selling its shoes in about 800 traditional shoe stores in France. In one year, the company doubled its French sales. Harley-Davidson had to open two company-owned stores in Japan to get distribution for its Harley clothing and clothing accessories.

The Japanese distribution system is considered the most complicated in the world. Imported goods wind their way through layers of agents, wholesalers, and retailers. For example, a bottle of 96 aspirins costs about $20 because the bottle passes through at least six wholesalers, each of whom increases the selling price. As a result, the Japanese

SC Johnson's motorcycle distribution project in Nigeria has a two-fold goal—to increase sales with smaller retailers who serve the base of the pyramid consumers while developing skills and growing incomes for local entrepreneurs.

consumer pays the world's most exorbitant prices. These distribution channels seem to be based on historical and traditional patterns of socially arranged trade-offs, which Japanese officials claim are very hard for the government to change. Today, however, the system seems to be changing because of pressure from Japanese consumers, who are putting more emphasis on low prices in their purchasing decisions. The retailer who can cut distribution costs and therefore the retail price gets the sale. For example, Kojima, a Japanese electronics superstore chain like the U.S. chain Best Buy, had to bypass General Electric's Japanese distribution partner Toshiba to import its merchandise at a good price. Toshiba's distribution system required refrigerators to pass through too many hands before they reached the retailer. Kojima went directly to GE headquarters in the United States and persuaded the company to sell it refrigerators, which were then shipped directly to Kojima. It is now selling GE refrigerators for about $800—half the price of a typical Japanese model.

Innovative distribution systems can create a competitive advantage for savvy companies. Every day, dozens of flights touch down at Kenya's Nairobi Airport, unloading tourists. But when some of those same KLM and Kenya Airlines aircraft take off for the late-night trip home, they're carrying far more than weary travelers returning from African safaris. Their planes are crammed with an average 25 tons apiece of fresh beans, bok choy, okra, and other produce that was harvested and packaged just the day before. It's all bound for eager—and growing—markets in Brussels, London, Paris, and other European cities.

Those flights are integral parts of an innovative supply chain. Vegpro Kenya, one of the nation's top produce exporters, operates seven farms within a two-hour drive of the airport. Every morning, trucks full of just-picked vegetables—30 varieties in all—dash to the airport. There, inside Vegpro's 27,000-square-foot air-conditioned cargo bay, more than 1,000 workers wash and sort the vegetables before they are rushed onto planes, ensuring that there's no break in the "cool chain" before the produce arrives in European stores the next day.

To combat distribution problems, companies are using creative strategies. Colgate-Palmolive has introduced villagers in India to the concept of brushing teeth by rolling into villages with video vans that show half-hour infomercials on the benefits of toothpaste. The company received more than half of its revenue in that nation from rural areas until 2006. The rural market has been virtually invisible, due to a lack of distribution. Unilever's Indian subsidiary, Hindustan Lever, sells its cosmetics, toothpastes, and detergents door-to-door. It now has over a million direct-sales consultants.

In many developing nations, channels of distribution and the physical infrastructure are inadequate. In China, the main modes of transport are truck and train. But in a fragmented trucking industry with few major companies, multinationals have difficulty determining which companies are reliable. A lack of refrigerated trucks has meant that poultry giant Tyson Foods can distribute in only a handful of Chinese cities. In the rail system, theft is a major problem.

Most Indian roads are simple two-lane affairs, maintained badly if at all. Shipping goods by rail costs twice as much on average there as in developed countries, and three times as much as in China. At India's ports, shipments often languish for days waiting for customs clearance and loading berths; goods typically take 6 to 12 weeks to reach the United States, compared with 2 to 3 weeks for goods from China. In order to navigate the small, congested Indian streets, UPS uses 37 minivans in Mumbai's very congested streets. Buildings in Mumbai often lack street numbers, so delivery personnel ask passersby for directions. During seasonal monsoons in July and August, workers at UPS depots shrink-wrap packages in plastic to keep them dry, and UPS rolls out its biggest trucks to navigate flooded streets that might swallow a minivan. On the city's industrial outskirts, India's ubiquitous three-wheeled auto rickshaws swarm like bees into any gaps that open up between lumbering trucks and buses. Vehicles might share a thoroughfare with milk deliverers on bicycles and a street merchant pushing a cartload of bananas.[65]

PRICING

Once marketing managers have determined a global product and promotion strategy, they can select the remainder of the marketing mix. Pricing presents some unique problems in the global sphere. Exporters must not only cover their production costs but also consider transportation costs, insurance, taxes, and tariffs. When deciding on a final price, marketers must also determine what customers are willing to spend on a particular product. Marketers also need to ensure that their foreign buyers will pay the price. Because developing nations lack mass purchasing power, selling to them often poses special pricing problems. Sometimes a product can be simplified in order to lower the price. Tata Motors sells the Nano in India for a bargain price of $2,500. With the Nano, Tata installed only a single windshield wiper, used narrow tires, and didn't include a radio or air conditioning.[66]

The firm must not assume that low-income countries are willing to accept lower quality, however. Although the nomads of the Sahara are very poor, they still buy expensive fabrics to make their clothing. Their survival in harsh conditions and extreme temperatures requires this expense. Additionally, certain expensive luxury items can be sold almost anywhere. L'Oréal was unsuccessful selling cheap shampoo in India, so the company targets the rising class. It now sells a $17 Paris face powder and a $25 Vichy sunscreen. Both products are very popular.

DUMPING

Dumping is the sale of an exported product at a price lower than that charged for the same or a like product in the "home" market of the exporter. This practice is regarded as a form of price discrimination that can potentially harm the importing nation's competing industries. Dumping may occur as a result of exporter business strategies that include (1) trying to increase an overseas market share, (2) temporarily distributing products in overseas markets to offset slack demand in the home market, (3) lowering unit costs by exploiting large-scale production, and (4) attempting to maintain stable prices during periods of exchange rate fluctuations.

Historically, the dumping of goods has presented serious problems in international trade. As a result, dumping has led to significant disagreements among countries and diverse views about its harmfulness. Some trade economists view dumping as harmful only when it involves the use of "predatory" practices that intentionally try to eliminate competition and gain monopoly power in a market. They believe that predatory dumping rarely occurs and that antidumping rules are a protectionist tool whose cost to consumers and import-using industries exceeds the benefits to the industries receiving protection.

In 2009, the U.S. accused Chinese and Indonesia of dumping coated paper, used in high-quality writing and printing, in the United States. To date, the dumping claim has not been resolved by the WTO.

COUNTERTRADE

Global trade does not always involve cash. Countertrade is a fast-growing way to conduct global business. In **countertrade**, all or part of the payment for goods

dumping
The sale of an exported product at a price lower than that charged for the same or a like product in the "home" market of the exporter.

countertrade
A form of trade in which all or part of the payment for goods or services is in the form of other goods or services.

List the basic elements involved in developing a global marketing mix

Global Marketing Mix		
PRODUCT + PROMOTION	PLACE (Distribution)	PRICE
One Product, One Message	Channel Choice	Dumping
Product Invention	Channel Structure	Countertrade
Product Adaptation	Country Infrastructure	Exchange Rates
Message Adaptation		Purchasing Power

© Cengage Learning 2013

or services is in the form of other goods or services. Countertrade is thus a form of barter (swapping goods for goods), an age-old practice whose origins have been traced back to cave dwellers. The U.S. Department of Commerce says that roughly 30 percent of all global trade is countertrade. In fact, both India and China have made billion-dollar government purchasing lists, with most of the goods to be paid for by countertrade. Recently, the Malaysian government bought 20 diesel-powered locomotives and paid for them with palm oil.

One common type of countertrade is straight barter. For example, PepsiCo sends Pepsi syrup to Russian bottling plants and in payment gets Stolichnaya vodka, which is then marketed in the West. Another form of countertrade is the compensation agreement. Typically, a company provides technology and equipment for a plant in a developing nation and agrees to take full or partial payment in goods produced by that plant. For example, General Tire Company supplied equipment and know-how for a Romanian truck tire plant. In turn, General Tire sold the tires it received from the plant in the United States under the Victoria brand name. Pierre Cardin gives technical advice to China in exchange for silk and cashmere. In these cases, both sides benefit even though they don't use cash.

LO 6
The Impact of the Internet

Discover how the Internet is affecting global marketing

© Cengage Learning 2013

In many respects "going global" is easier than it has ever been before. Opening an e-commerce site on the Internet immediately puts a company in the international marketplace. Sophisticated language translation software can make any site accessible to persons around the world. Global shippers such as UPS, FedEx, and DHL help solve international e-commerce distribution complexities.

Nevertheless, the promise of "borderless commerce" and the global "Internet economy" are still being restrained by the old brick-and-mortar rules, regulations, and habits. For example, Lands' End is not allowed to mention its unconditional refund policy on its e-commerce site in Germany because German retailers, which normally do not allow returns after 14 days, sued and won a court ruling blocking mention of it. Credit cards may be the currency of the Internet, but not everyone uses them. Whereas Americans spend an average of $6,500 per year by credit card, Japanese spend less than $2,000. Many Japanese don't even have a credit card. So how do they pay for e-commerce purchases? 7-Eleven Japan, with over 8,000 convenience stores, has come to the rescue. Their Web site, www.7netshopping.jp, lets shoppers buy books and videos on the Internet, then specify to which 7-Eleven the merchandise is to be shipped. The buyer goes to that specific store and pays cash for the e-purchase.

Like the Japanese, Scandinavians are reluctant to use credit cards, and the French have an *horreur* of revealing the private information that Internet retailers often request. French Web sites tend to be decidedly French. For example, FNAC, the largest French video, book, and music retailer, offers a daily "cultural newspaper" at its site. A trendy Web site in France will have a black background, while bright colors and a geometrical layout give a site a German feel. Dutch surfers are keen on video downloads, and Scandinavians seem to have a soft spot for images of nature.

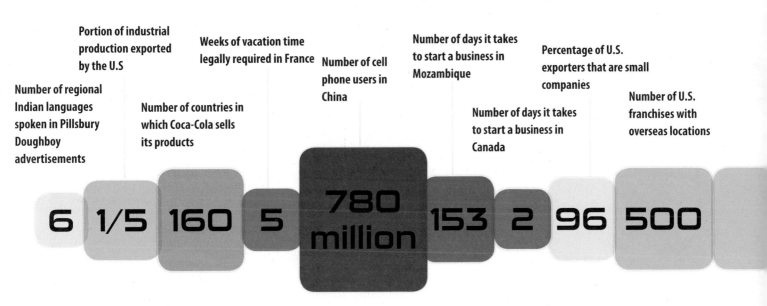

Number of regional Indian languages spoken in Pillsbury Doughboy advertisements — **6**

Portion of industrial production exported by the U.S — **1/5**

Number of countries in which Coca-Cola sells its products — **160**

Weeks of vacation time legally required in France — **5**

Number of cell phone users in China — **780 million**

Number of days it takes to start a business in Mozambique — **153**

Number of days it takes to start a business in Canada — **2**

Percentage of U.S. exporters that are small companies — **96**

Number of U.S. franchises with overseas locations — **500**

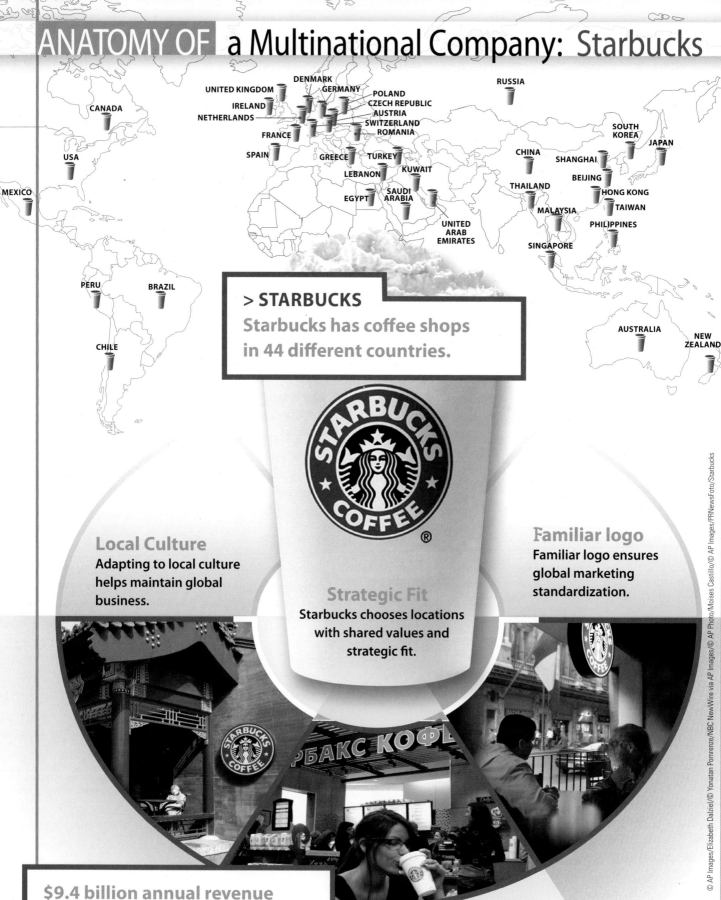

ANATOMY OF a Multinational Company: Starbucks

CANADA

USA

MEXICO

PERU

BRAZIL

CHILE

UNITED KINGDOM
IRELAND
NETHERLANDS
FRANCE
SPAIN
DENMARK
GERMANY
POLAND
CZECH REPUBLIC
AUSTRIA
SWITZERLAND
ROMANIA
GREECE
TURKEY
LEBANON
KUWAIT
EGYPT
SAUDI ARABIA
UNITED ARAB EMIRATES

RUSSIA

CHINA
SHANGHAI
BEIJING
THAILAND
MALAYSIA
SINGAPORE
SOUTH KOREA
JAPAN
HONG KONG
TAIWAN
PHILIPPINES

AUSTRALIA
NEW ZEALAND

> **STARBUCKS**
Starbucks has coffee shops in 44 different countries.

Local Culture
Adapting to local culture helps maintain global business.

Strategic Fit
Starbucks chooses locations with shared values and strategic fit.

Familiar logo
Familiar logo ensures global marketing standardization.

$9.4 billion annual revenue
+15,000 stores
170,000 partners (employees)

Customer Experience
Starbucks maintains control of its customer experience through joint ventures and company-owned operations.

Review and Applications

Discuss the importance of global marketing. Businesspeople who adopt a global vision are better able to identify global marketing opportunities, understand the nature of global networks, create effective global marketing strategies, and compete against foreign competition in domestic markets.

1.1 What is meant by "having a global vision"? Why is it important?

1.2 Isolationists have suggested that America would be much better off economically and politically if we just "built a wall" around the country and didn't deal with outsiders. Do you agree? Why or why not?

1.3 Discuss jobs outsourcing. Is it beneficial to U.S. firms?

Discuss the impact of multinational firms on the world economy. Multinational corporations are international traders that regularly operate across national borders. Because of their vast size and financial, technological, and material resources, multinational corporations have a great influence on the world economy. They have the ability to overcome trade problems, save on labor costs, and tap new technology. However, some countries are beginning to block foreign investment by multinationals.

2.1 Rubbermaid, the U.S. manufacturer of kitchen products and other household items, is considering moving to global marketing standardization. What are the pros and cons of this strategy?

2.2 Do you believe that multinationals are beneficial or harmful to developing nations? Why? What could foreign governments do to make them more beneficial?

Describe the external environment facing global marketers. Global marketers face the same environmental factors as they do domestically: culture, economic, and technological development; political structure and actions; demography; and natural resources. Cultural considerations include societal values, attitudes, and beliefs; language; and customary business practices. A country's economic and technological status depends on its stage of industrial development, which, in turn, affects average family incomes. The political structure is shaped by political ideology and policies such as tariffs, quotas, boycotts, exchange controls, trade agreements, and market groupings. Demographic variables include the size of a population and its age and geographic distribution.

3.1 Many marketers now believe that teenagers in the developed countries are becoming "global consumers." That is, they all want and buy the same goods and services. Do you think this is true? If so, what has caused the phenomenon?

3.2 Renault and Peugeot dominate the French market but have no presence in the U.S. market. Why do you think that this is true?

3.3 Suppose that your state senator has asked you to contribute a brief article to her constituents' newsletter that answers the question, "Will there ever be a United States of Europe?" Write a draft of your article, and include reasons why or why not.

writing

3.4 Divide into six teams. Each team will be responsible for one of the following industries: entertainment; pharmaceuticals; computers and software; financial, legal, or accounting services; agriculture; and textiles and apparel. Interview one or more executives in each of these industries to determine how the WTO, NAFTA, and CAFTA have affected and will affect their organizations. If a local firm cannot be contacted in your industry, use the library and the Internet to prepare your report.

team

3.5 What are the major barriers to international trade? Explain how government policies may be used to either restrict or stimulate global marketing.

LO4 Identify the various ways of entering the global marketplace. Firms use the following strategies to enter global markets, in descending order of risk and profit: direct investment, joint venture, contract manufacturing, licensing and franchising, and exporting.

4.1 Candartel, an upscale manufacturer of lamps and lampshades in America, has decided to "go global." Top management is having trouble deciding how to develop the market. What are some market entry options for the firm?

4.2 Explain how the U.S. Commercial Service can help companies wanting to enter the international market.

4.3 What are some of the advantages and potential disadvantages of entering a joint venture?

4.4 Why is direct investment considered risky?

LO5 List the basic elements involved in developing a global marketing mix. A firm's major consideration is how much it will adjust the four Ps—product, promotion, place (distribution), and price—within each country. One strategy is to use one product and one promotion message worldwide. A second strategy is to create new products for global markets. A third strategy is to keep the product basically the same but alter the promotional message. A fourth strategy is to slightly alter the product to meet local conditions.

5.1 The sale of cigarettes in many developed countries either has peaked or is declining. However, the developing markets represent major growth markets. Should U.S. tobacco companies capitalize on this opportunity?

5.2 Describe at least three situations where an American company might want to keep the product the same but alter the promotion. Also, give three examples where the product must be altered.

5.3 Explain how exchange rates can affect a firm's global sales.

LO6 Discover how the Internet is affecting global marketing. Simply opening a Web site can open the door for international sales. International carriers, like UPS, can help solve logistics problems. Language translation software can help an e-commerce business become multilingual. Yet cultural differences and old-line rules, regulations, and taxes hinder rapid development of e-commerce in many countries.

6.1 Describe how "going global" via the Internet presents opportunities and challenges.

6.2 Give several examples of how culture may hinder "going global" via the Internet.

Key Terms

buyer for export *158*
capital-intensive *139*
Central America Free Trade
   Agreement (CAFTA) *150*
contract manufacturing *159*
countertrade *169*
direct foreign
   investment *161*
dumping *169*
exchange rate *140*
export agent *158*
export broker *158*

exporting *156*
European Union (EU) *147*
General Agreement on Tariffs
   and Trade (GATT) *148*
global marketing *133*
global marketing
   standardization *141*
global vision *133*
gross domestic product *135*
Group of Twenty (G-20) *153*
International Monetary
   Fund (IMF) *153*

joint venture *161*
licensing *158*
Mercosur *148*
multidomestic strategy *141*
multinational
   corporation *137*
North American Free Trade
   Agreement (NAFTA) *149*
Uruguay Round *148*
World Bank *153*
World Trade Organization
   (WTO) *148*

Exercises

ETHICS EXERCISE

ethics

Moore Electronics sells automated lighting for airport runways. The government of an eastern European country has offered Moore a contract to provide equipment for the 15 major airports in the country. The official in charge of awarding the contract, however, is demanding a 5 percent kickback. He told Moore to build this into the contract price so that there would be no cost to Moore. Without the kickback, Moore loses the contract. Such kickbacks are considered a normal way of doing business in this country.

Questions

1. What should Moore do?

2. Review the Foreign Corrupt Practices Act online at **www.usdoj.gov/criminal/fraud/fcpa/**. Write a brief paragraph on what this statute contains that relates to Moore's dilemma. Some American executives think this law causes American corporations to suffer a competitive disadvantage. Do you agree? Why or why not?

MARKETING PLAN EXERCISE

These end-of-chapter marketing plan exercises are designed to help you use what you learned in the chapter to build a strategic marketing plan for a company of your choosing. Once you've completed the marketing plan exercise for each chapter in Part 1 of this textbook, you can complete the Part 1 Marketing Planning Worksheet by logging on to the companion Web site at www.cengagebrain.com. Now continue building your strategic marketing plan that you started in Chapter 2 by completing the following exercises:

1. Assume your company is or will be marketing globally. How should your company enter the global marketplace? How will international issues affect your firm?

2. If you choose an Internet presence, your product or service will be visible to a global community. Assess the international marketplace for your particular offering. A listing of international chambers of commerce is at www.worldchambers.com and the CIA World Factbook is at www.cia.gov/cia/publications/factbook/index.html.

APPLICATION EXERCISE

To be effective as a marketer, it is important to know geography. How will you be able to decide whether to expand into a new territory (domestic or foreign) if you don't know where it is and something about its culture, currency, and economy? If you can't place the European countries on a blank map, or if you can't label the lower 48 states without a list to help you, you're not alone. In one study, students incorrectly located over 50 percent of European countries and over 25 percent of the states in the Unites States. To help you brush up on your geography, we've compiled some tools that you may find useful.

Activities

1. To review domestic geography, go to **www.50states.com/tools/usamap.htm** and print the blank map of the United States. Label the map. For a challenge, add the state capitals to the map.

2. Once you have successfully labeled the U.S. map, you may be ready to try labeling a world map. If so, go to **www.clickandlearn.com** and view the free, printable, blackline maps.

Under the category of The World and Continents, choose the blackline detail map. This shows country outlines, whereas the basic blackline outline map shows only the continents. You will notice that there are also blackline maps for each continent, so if taking on the entire world is too daunting, start with more manageable blocks.

3. To be a global marketer, it is not enough to know where countries are located. You will need to know about the culture, the main exports, the currency, and even the main imports. Select a half-dozen or so countries with which you are unfamiliar, and research basic geographic information about them.

CASE STUDY: NFL International Series

MARKETING AN AMERICAN CLASSIC ACROSS THE POND

In September 2008, *Forbes* dubbed the NFL "the strongest sport in the world." With annual league revenues of roughly $6.5 billion and each of the 32 NFL teams worth $1 billion on average (compared to only four professional soccer teams worldwide worth over $1 billion), the NFL has also proven one of the most lucrative and financially resilient sports leagues worldwide. *Forbes'* August 2008 list of the world's best paid athletes, however, seems to tell a different story.

© Leo Mason/Corbis

Athlete	Nationality	Sport	Estimated Earnings
Tiger Woods	American	Golf	$115 million
David Beckham	British	Soccer	$50 million
Michael Jordan	American	Basketball	$45 million
Phil Mickelson	American	Golf	$45 million
Kimi Raikkonen	Finnish	Auto Racing	$44 million
Kobe Bryant	American	Basketball	$39 million
LeBron James	American	Basketball	$38 million
Ronaldinho	Brazilian	Soccer	$37 million
Valentino Rossi	Italian	Motorcycle Racing	$35 million
Roger Federer	Swiss	Tennis	$35 million

As you'll notice on the chart the names of even the superstars of the NFL, such as LaDainian Tomlinson, Tom Brady, and Peyton Manning, are nowhere to be found.

American football has long been just that: American. Even baseball, a game some might consider more American than football, has gained a substantial following in Japan and Latin America. But considering the amount of athletes' earnings that come from marketing contracts, it's no surprise that the top 10 (and in fact the top 20) are dominated by sports such as golf, soccer, basketball, and tennis, which hold a much more global appeal. For all its success, the vast majority of the NFL's market remains in the United States.

Over the years, numerous attempts have been made to export American football overseas. Its most recent endeavor, NFL Europa, closed down in 2007, without any plans for a replacement. The league originally was designed as a development league, costing team owners about $500,000 per year, which would allow up-and-coming NFL players more field time, and the NFL for some years was able to cite the successes of two-time MVP Kurt Warner and Super Bowl quarterback Jake Delhomme. But Warner and Delhomme played in NFL Europa in 1998 and 1999, and since then the league had produced only journeyman players at best. By its final season, despite some improvements in attendance, the league had shrunk to six teams, five of which played in Germany. NFL Europa had lost money 15 years straight and was largely being used by NFL owners as a place to stash extra players during training camp.

Over the last two years, the NFL has started trying another tack. Rather than promote spin-off leagues, the NFL introduced the new NFL International Series, a program that exports real NFL games overseas. In 2007, the New York Giants and Miami Dolphins played the first NFL game in London's Wembley Stadium to a sellout crowd of over 83,000 fans, followed in 2008 by the New Orleans Saints and San Diego Chargers.

The original game in 2007 proved that offering the real thing to an international audience could generate a lot of excitement, and the game itself provided the Giants a momentum boost in the midst of a run that ended with a Super Bowl victory. In 2008, based on the previous year's success, the NFL made numerous efforts to expand the event in hopes of generating exposure to the London market and reaching out beyond the current fan base. First, in 2007, the teams arrived in London only a couple of days before the match. In 2008, the teams were brought over at the beginning of the week. They held practices throughout the week to which the media was granted access, along with press conferences. At the same time, the Saints' cheerleaders had scheduled various appearances to mingle with the crowds throughout London. The Saints were designated as the home team, and the league promoted them heavily, decorating the stadium with Saints banners. They also hosted a "Taste of New Orleans" festival earlier in the week at the London O2 Arena and a Mardi-Gras-style pregame tailgate party. Perhaps one of the biggest boosts was the agreement the league reached with the BBC to broadcast the game live, which would potentially add an additional 2 million viewers. Previously, NFL games could be viewed only on a British pay channel, which garnered about 120,000 viewers per week.

Though the program is still young, it has produced promising results, and the NFL hopes to continue the International Series over the coming years, possibly playing more than one game overseas, perhaps even having Wembley host a Super Bowl. A 2009 game in London has already been officially scheduled between the New England Patriots and the Tampa Bay Buccaneers. The league has also considered China as a possible venue for a preseason game; however, due to recent economic constraints, these plans have yet to come to fruition.

In the meantime, the NFL has identified education as a key factor in sustaining interest in London (and other potential foreign markets) beyond a one week NFL-fest to a level of understanding where fans tune in every week. After the 2007 game, the league performed surveys among Londoners about what they liked best about the game. One of their top answers was the strategy. Compared to more internationally popular games like soccer, American football is extremely complex, and if viewers don't understand it, it will be difficult for them to appreciate its strategic value. To help with this, the NFL launched an interactive Web site to help present new fans with the basics of American football in laymen's terms. With a cast of fictional characters playing roles in a fictional football organization, led by the hard-nosed Coach Stilo who quizzes viewers on what they're learning as they go, and guest appearances by real NFL football players face-to-face without their helmets, viewers are led through a series of 18 episodes in which they learn the basic terminology, positions, plays, and strategy. The Web site is available in English, Spanish, French, Japanese, and Mandarin. In places like China, the terminology does not translate well, so the league has invented new a nomenclature that better fits with the language. All in all, the NFL believes that a better understanding of the game will make a huge difference in drawing fans in as it continues promoting American football overseas.[67]

Questions

1. Discuss the NFL's current strategy for global market entry. How has this strategy changed and why did the NFL make these changes?

2. Discuss the major environmental challenges that the NFL has encountered and how they have addressed these.

3. Examine each aspect of the global marketing mix for the NFL International Series compared with marketing mix for NFL Europa.

© NKP Media, Inc./Cengage

In the 21st century, start-ups can become global businesses much more quickly than in any time in history. So, while new companies are forging their way domestically, they may also experience an added layer of challenges from trying to enter global markets at the same time. In this final video segment on Method, founder Eric Ryan and CEO Alastair Dorward describe their company's perspective on global expansion and which foreign markets represent good opportunities for Method.

Questions

1. Is Method a multinational company? Explain.

2. Which environmental factors facing all global marketers is Method confronting as it begins to expand into foreign markets?

3. Outline Method's global marketing mix.

4. What is innovative about how Method envisions moving into foreign markets? Would Method's strategy for global expansion work for other companies or industries? Which ones? Explain.

Notes

1. World Trade Organization, "Trade to Expand by 9.5 Percent in 2010 after a Dismal 2009, WTO Reports," International Trade Statistics, March 26, 2010, www.wto.org/english/news_e/pres10_e/pr598_e.htm.
2. *Ibid.*
3. Timothy Aeppel, "Exports Prop Up Local Economies across the U.S.," *Wall Street Journal*, September 11, 2008, A16.
4. "2010 Year in Review," Caterpillar Corporate Web site, www.caterpillar.com/cda/files/2801521/7/CAT-2010AR_pdfversion_English.pdf (Accessed June 13, 2011).
5. *Exports Support American Jobs*, U.S. Department of Commerce: International Trade Administration, October 2008.
6. *Ibid.*
7. *Ibid.*
8. Pete Engardio, "Can the U.S. Bring Jobs Back from China?" *BusinessWeek*, June 30, 2008, 39–43.
9. Bob Davis, John Lyons, and Andrew Batson, "Globalization's Gains Come with a Price," *Wall Street Journal*, May 24, 2007, A1, A12.
10. Jeffrey Garten, "The Dangers of Turning Inward," *Wall Street Journal*, February 28–March 1, 2009, W1.
11. *Ibid.*
12. Martin Neil Baily, Matthew Slaughter, and Laura Tyson, "The Global Jobs Competition Heats Up," *Wall Street Journal*, July 1, 2010, A19.
13. *Ibid.*
14. *Ibid.*
15. Theodore Levitt, "The Globalization of Markets," *Harvard Business Review*, May/June 1983, 92–100.
16. Bill Vlasic, "Ford Chief Bets on One Global Car," *International Herald Tribune*, January 22, 2010, 1, 16.
17. *Ibid.*
18. "Convenience Is a Dirty Word to These Italian Consumers," *Quirk's Marketing Research Review*, October 2006, 6. Reprinted with permission.
19. Max Colchester, "French Protesters Wage War on Billboards," *Wall Street Journal*, September 26, 2008, B5.
20. *Ibid.*
21. The World Bank, "GNI, Atlas Method (Current US$)," http://data.worldbank.org/indicator/NY.GNP.ATLS.CD/countries (Accessed January 26, 2011).
22. *Ibid.*
23. "Trop Cher?" *Economist*, March 10, 2010, www.economist.com/node/15659589.
24. "China Market: Mobile Phone Users Total 786.5 Million in April," C114, May 27, 2010, www.CN-C114.net/577/a511068.html; Raj Paul, "Information Note to the Press (Press Release No. 20/2010)," Telecom Regulatory Authority of India, April 26, 2010, www.trai.gov.in/WriteReadData/trai/upload/PressReleases/732/pr26apr10no20.pdf.
25. Anil K. Gupta and Haiyan Wang, "How to Get China and India Right," *Wall Street Journal*, April 28–29, 2007, R9.
26. Valerie Bauerlein, "Pepsi Battles Coke in China," *Wall Street Journal*, May 22–23, 2010, B6.

marketing&you: Results.

© iStockphoto.com/ziggymaj

This questionnaire measures cultural openness. The higher your score, the more interested you are in learning about other cultures and interacting with people from other countries. People with high cultural openness tend to be less ethnocentric and more open to buying imported products than people with low cultural openness. As you read in Chapter 5, cultural openness is an important aspect of developing a global vision.

27. "China Has Long Dashed Hopes of U.S. Firms," *International Herald Tribune*, January 18, 2010, 17–18; Andrew Browne and Jason Dean, "Business Sours on China," *Wall Street Journal*, March 17, 2010, A1, A14; Bianca Bosker, "Google Shuts Down China Search, Redirects Users to Hong Kong," *Huffington Post,* March 22, 2010, www.huffingtonpost.com/2010/03/22/google-leaves-china-googl_n_508639.html; "A New Approach to China: An Update," *Official Google Blog*, March 22, 2010, http://googleblog.blogspot.com/2010/03/new-approach-to-china-update.html.

28. "Economy Rankings," *Doing Business*, http://www.doingbusiness.org/rankings (Accessed January 26, 2011).

29. *Ibid.*

30. Bob Davis, "Global Ties under Stress as Nations Grab Power," *Wall Street Journal*, April 28, 2008, A1, A16.

31. *Ibid.*

32. Carolyn Cui, "Price Gap Puts Spice in Sugar-Quota Fight," *Wall Street Journal*, March 15, 2010, A1, A4.

33. Doug Palmer and Eric Walsh, "Deal in WTO Doha Round Doubtful in 2010: Kirk," *Reuters*, March 9, 2010, www.reuters.com/article/idUSTRE6283V220100309.

34. Carol Matlack, "The New Protectionism," *BusinessWeek,* June 22, 2009, 16.

35. "Most Canadians, Americans Support NAFTA: Poll," *Xinhua News Agency*, October 1, 2007.

36. "NAFTA at a Glance," North American Free Trade Agreement, www.naftanow.org/facts (Accessed January 26, 2011).

37. *Ibid.*

38. Charles Forelle, "EU Plans Fresh Strike on Microsoft," *Wall Street Journal*, May 30–31, 2009, A1, A6.

39. Charles Forelle and Don Clark "Intel Fine Jolts Tech Sector," *Wall Street Journal*, May 14, 2009, A1–A14.

40. Jonathan Bensky, "World's Biggest Market: European Union Offers Great Opportunities for U.S. Companies, but There Are Also Plenty of Challenges," *Shipping Digest*, July 30, 2007.

41. Vanessa Fuhrmans, "Siemens Settles with World Bank on Bribes," *Wall Street Journal*, July 3–5, 2009, B1.

42. "What Is the G-20," G-20 Web site, www.g20.org/about_what_is_g20.aspx (Accessed June 15, 2010).

43. U.S. Census Bureau, "A Profile of U.S. Exporting Companies, 2007–2008," April 13, 2010, www.census.gov/foreign-trade/Press-Release/edb/2008/text.txt.

44. Maura Policelli, "Pennsylvania Small Business Is First to Benefit from Ex-Im Bank Medium-Term Delegated Authority Program," Export-Import Bank of the United States, March 6, 2009, www.exim.gov/pressrelease.cfm/DD49F2A1-E8E7-A8F2-E1F4AC0 55D14AAA6.

45. "$187 Billion Global Licensing Industry Comes to Life," *Bnet*, June 6, 2008, http://findarticles.com/p/articles/mi_m0EIN/is_2008_June_6/ai_n25489028.

46. International Franchise Association Web site, www.franchise.org (Accessed June 15, 2010).

47. "Announcing 2010's Top 100 Global Franchises," *Franchise Direct*, www.franchisedirect.com/top100globalfranchises/ (Accessed January 24, 2011).

48. "Foreign Flavors," *Wall Street Journal*, September 25, 2006, R8.

49. Roger Parloff, "Not Exactly Counterfeit," *Fortune,* April 26, 2006, http://money.cnn.com/magazines/fortune/fortune_archive/2006/05/01/8375455/index.htm; Jane Baron, "Outsourcing That Leads to Counterfeit Shoe Production," *Article Alley*, October 14, 2009, www.articlealley.com/article_1173315_47.html.

50. "Copying Machines," *AdWeekMedia*, June 29, 2009, 6–9.

51. Brian Grow, Chi-Chu Tschang, Cliff Edwards, and Brian Burnsed, "Dangerous Fakes," *BusinessWeek*, October 13, 2008, 34–44.

52. "GM's China Partner Looms as a New Rival," *Wall Street Journal*, April 20, 2007, A1, A8; "Roewe 350 Production Kicks Off Today. Rowe 350 Running on Android!" *China Car Times*, March 18, 2010, www.chinacartimes.com/2010/03/18/roewe-350-production-kicks-off-today-roewe-350-running-on-android/.

53. "Partners Fight over Wahaha in China," *Wall Street Journal*, July 28, 2008, B1; James Areddy, "Danone Pulls Out of Disputed Chinese Venture," *Wall Street Journal*, October 1, 2009, B1.

54. *Ibid.*

55. "International Data Sheet–May 2010," Walmart Corporate Web site, May 2010, http://walmartstores.com/pressroom/news/9982.aspx.

56. "Investment Will Favor International Markets," *Toronto Star*, October 29, 2008, B2.

57. Jason Bush, "IKEA in Russia: Enough Is Enough," *BusinessWeek*, July 13, 2009, 33.

58. *Ibid.*

59. Mariko Sanchanta, "Starbucks Plans Major China Expansion," *Wall Street Journal*, April 13, 2010, http://online.wsj.com/article/SB10001424052702304604204575181490891231672.html.

60. "Fad Marketing's Balancing Act," *BusinessWeek*, August 6, 2007, 42.

61. Julie Jargon and Sungha Park, "Dunkin' Brands Eyes Asian Expansion," *Wall Street Journal*, June 4, 2009, B6.

62. Erik Simanis, "At the Base of the Pyramid," *Wall Street Journal*, October 26, 2009, R7; Jose Antonio Rosa, Madhubalan Viswanathan, and Julie Ruth, "Emerging Lessons," *Wall Street Journal*, October 20, 2008, R12; "India Engineers a Market: It's Poor," *Wall Street Journal*, October 20, 2009, A1, A18; Don Schultz, "Branding from Emerging Markets," *Marketing Management*, September/October 2008, 10–11.

63. Loretta Chao, "PC Makers Cultivate Buyers in Rural China," *Wall Street Journal*, September 23, 2009, B1.

64. Amy Chozick, "The Samurai Sell: Lexus Dealers Bow to Move Swank Cars," *Wall Street Journal*, July 9, 2007, A1, A12.

65. Bruce Stanley, "UPS Battles Traffic to Gain Ground in India," *Wall Street Journal*, January 25, 2008, B1, B2.

66. Daisuke Wakabayashi, "Panasonic Reaches Wide-and-Low—With Appliances for Emerging Market," *Wall Street Journal*, July 9, 2009, B1–B2.

67. Lacey Rose, "The World's Best-Paid Male Athletes," *Forbes*, August 8, 2008; Tom Van Riper and Kurt Badenhausen, "Top-Earning Female Athletes," *Forbes*, July 22, 2008; Kurt Badenhausen, Michael Ozanian, Christina Settimi, "The Richest Game," *Forbes*, September 11, 2008; Len Pasquarelli, "NFL Europa Failed to Produce Players, Profits," ESPN, June 29, 2007; Mike Carlson, "Saints Put on a Show for 'Home' Crowd at Wembley," NFL.com, October 27, 2008; Lisa Altobelli, "Think Globally: NFL Visits England to Increase Awareness of Football," *Sports Illustrated*, October 24, 2008; Associated Press, "NFL Hoping Rules, Jargon Doesn't Prevent Chinese From Learning Game," ESPN, June 29, 2007; Matthew Futterman, "Football Tries a New Play to Score Overseas," *The Wall Street Journal*, October 9, 2008.

68. Raj Dash, "The Facebook Nestle Mess: When Social Media Goes Anti-Social," *All Facebook,* March 22, 2010, www.allfacebook.com/the-facebook-nestle-mess-when-social-media-goes-anti-social-2010-03; Rick Broida, "Nestlé's Facebook Page: How a Company Can Really Screw Up Social Media," *BNET,* March 19, 2010, www.bnet.com/blog/businesstips/nestles-facebook-page-how-a-company-can-really-screw-up-social-media/6786; "Nestlé and Black Friday," March 23, 2010, www.rgc-media.com/nestle-and-black-friday (Accessed December 31 2010); Emily Steel, "Nestlé Takes a Beating on Social-Media Sites," *Wall Street Journal,* March 29 2010, http://online.wsj.com/article/SB10001424052702304434404575149883850508158.html.

69. "Our Understanding of Sustainability," Telekom/Austria Group, www.telekomaustria.com/verantwortung/understanding_sustainability.php; "The Most Important Figures of Sustainability from Our Markets," Telekom Austria Group, 2009/2010, http://sr2009-10.telekomaustria.com (Accessed November 26 2010).

Marketing Miscue

PART 1: CONCERNS OVER SUSTAINABILITY RESULT IN SOCIAL MEDIA DISASTER FOR NESTLÉ

In March of 2010, Greenpeace began coordinating environmental activists in a protest over Nestlé's alleged purchase of palm oil from an Indonesian company that Greenpeace International claimed was destroying the rain forest in the building of palm plantations. The palm oil was used to make KitKat candy bars. Although Nestlé claimed to have already made the decision to no longer do business with the supplier, while also asserting that the purchase had comprised only 1.25 percent of the company's total palm oil consumption in 2009, the company was a vulnerable target for environmental activists because of its history of questionable practices with respect to child labor and infant formula.

The coordinated efforts of the activists were composed of two major components. Greenpeace staged a protest outside Nestlé's headquarters in Switzerland and a mock KitKat commercial was posted on YouTube. Protesters at the company headquarters wore cutouts of the candy bar but instead of the bar saying "KitKat," it said "Killer." The KitKat commercial parody portrayed an office worker opening the candy bar and munching on a bloody orangutan finger. As YouTube videos go, the Nestlé parody was shared far and wide via social media platforms such as Facebook and Twitter.

Like many companies, Nestlé has a fan page on Facebook to interact with its consumers. The Facebook fan page is a location that enables dialogue about the company's brands. Once the commercial parody hit the social media airwaves, protesters began posting negative comments about the company on Nestlé's Facebook fan page. Nestlé responded with two actions. One, it asked Google's YouTube to remove the commercial parody from the site due to copyright infringement, and YouTube adhered to the request. However, the video had been downloaded and it still spread across the Internet. Two, Nestlé also told Facebook users that the company would delete their comments from the fan page if the "Killer" logo was used. Apparently, angry protesters had begun to replace their profile pictures with the "Killer" logo.

Interestingly, it was Nestlé's response to actions within the social media ecosystem and not the palm oil issue itself that erupted in war for the company. Nestlé's threat to delete comments that included the altered KitKat logo ("Killer") incited the users of the company's fan page. The fan base on Nestlé's Facebook page soared to over 95,000 fans. Unfortunately, the vast majority of these 95,000 were protesters, and Nestlé went on the defensive. The Nestlé online moderator manning the fan page began to respond to individual postings in a derogatory and condescending tone. For example, the moderator is purported to have said something like, " … it's our page, we set the rules. . . . " This just served to fuel the online media firestorm even more, as the exchange quickly hit the Twitter circuit and even more people began to visit the company's Facebook fan page. Many of these visitors likely had no idea about the palm oil issue—they were going to the fan page to see for themselves how Nestlé was engaging with its customers.

Ultimately, Nestlé's rules of engagement for social media became a trending topic on Twitter, which resulted in calls for a boycott of all of Nestlé's products. The trending occurred because such a large number of people were commenting on the same thing about Nestlé. As such, the issue appeared on the trend bar on Twitter's home page. This generated even more negative publicity for the company. Soon, the electronic word of mouth began to spread to the offline world. This rapid spread of negativity led to panic among Nestlé shareholders and share prices began to drop dramatically.

Nestlé had a social media disaster on its hands. Interestingly, that disaster was due to the way Nestlé engaged in interactions on Facebook—not because of the fact that it had purchased palm oil from a non-sustainable company. The negative social media engagement, however, brought the palm oil issue to the forefront of people's minds who might not have otherwise even thought about sustainability concerns related to candy bars. Thus, while the sustainability concern might have lost its luster in a few days and activists would have moved on to the next cause, the social media engagement snowballed and affected the company financially.[68]

Questions

1. How could Nestlé have handled the situation differently? Should the company have simply shut down its Facebook page?

2. Although the KitKat candy bar was at the original heart of the issue, what other products/companies are owned by Nestlé? Could these products be affected by the KitKat social media fiasco?

Critical Thinking Case

TELEKOM AUSTRIA GROUP: SUSTAINABILITY TO INCREASE VALUE

Telekom Austria Group is the largest telecommunications provider in Austria, where it has over two million fixed net lines. The company has close to 20 million mobile subscribers in its eight geographic markets and each market is served by a separately identified subsidiary within the Telekom Austria Group:

→ A1 Telekom Austria

→ Mobiltel in Bulgaria

→ velcom in Belarus

→ Vipnet in Croatia

→ Si.mobil in Slovenia

→ Vip mobile in Republic of Serbia

→ Vip operator in Republic of Macedonia

→ Mobilkom Liechtenstein

© HERWIG PRAMMER/Reuters/Landov

The overarching goal of the company is to be the most innovative and efficient telecommunications provider in the central and eastern European marketplace. Driving the attainment of this goal are four corporate values: innovation, diversity, responsibility, and quality. Through these values, the company aspires to be profitable while satisfying a wide range of stakeholders. These stakeholders include: customers, employees, employee union, shareholders/investors, suppliers, municipalities, neighbors, NGOs, public policy makers, and special interest groups. The company prides itself on its group-wide corporate social responsibility (CSR) efforts that seek to provide benefit to all stakeholders.

Sustainability both Internally and Externally

As an information and communications technologies (ICT) company, Telekom Austria Group seeks to expand and further develop environmentally friendly technologies. One area that the company has a keen interest in is the virtualization of products and services. In the words of the company, think "data traffic instead of road traffic." Examples of such virtualization due to ICT are: music and film downloads instead of the purchase of CDs and DVDs; online tax filing instead of using paper to file via the mail service; video conferencing instead of traveling for meetings; and tele-working instead of making the daily commute to the physical office. Sustainability efforts for ICT at Telekom Austria include: reducing CO_2 emissions, energy efficiency at computer centers, intelligent use of resources by managing capacity according to volume usage, converting to green electricity, using employees as environmental ambassadors, and conserving resources with its motto of "reduce – reuse – recycle." The company's resource conservation efforts flow directly to customers via online billing, a green signature for e-mails so as to encourage reduction of unnecessary printing, mobile phone recycling, toner collection tied to charitable giving (one euro is donated for each toner cartridge collected), and the production of environmentally friendly phones.

ICT Integration into Customer's Lives

ICT is an indispensible aspect of everyday life in the 21st century. At the business-to-consumer (B2C) level, its use appears in everything from social media communications (e.g., Facebook, Twitter, YouTube) to shopping to online banking to online education. From a business-to-business (B2B) perspective, ICT enables everything from product routing via RFID tags to data security. Radio frequency identification (RFID) tags emit radio waves that are decoded by a reading device for the purposes of identification of inventory and tracking. Given the importance of ICT in the lives of all customers, Telekom Austria considers customer service to be a critical success factor for the company. The company's A1 Service Center was the first Austrian service center in the mobile communications industry to be certified according to the new European standard for customer care centers. In 2009, the company launched a new customer service program called "Kundiologie." With the motto of "Meet the Customer," the company attempts to engage its employees in real-time interactions with customers and then channels these insights into the areas of product management and customer service. Thus, the company ties customer satisfaction to its employees in an active manner. As such, employees, particularly those working in customer service departments, receive regular training in customer relationship management and customer service.

Respondents in a 2009 customer satisfaction survey gave employees in the Technical Customer Service department at Telekom Austria scores of "excellent" for their expertise, friendliness, and solutions-oriented attitudes. Additionally, respondents were also highly satisfied with issues related to product installation and waiting times. The importance of customer satisfaction is driven home internally by the fact that a customer satisfaction measure has been incorporated into performance contracts of employees in one division of the company.

Sustainability Audit

The Telekom Austria Group documents its sustainability performance and provides an annual sustainability report to its stakeholders and the general public. The performance measures follow guidelines offered by the Global Reporting Initiative, thus enabling comparisons to generally accepted indicators of international sustainability reporting. To advance sustainability efforts and management, the company recently implemented a group-wide CSR management system. The goal is to integrate all international subsidiaries into the existing sustainability management and reporting system.[69]

Questions

1. How will Telekom Austria's commitment to the triple bottom line (planet, people, profit) provide value to the company's bottom line?

2. Much is discussed about customer service within the context of sustainability at Telekom Austria. Why is customer satisfaction included in the topic of sustainability?

2

Analyzing Marketing Opportunities

6 Consumer Decision Making

YOU JUST ATE 16 PACKS OF SUGAR

All those extra calories can bring on obesity, diabetes and heart disease.

Learning Outcomes

1 Explain why marketing managers should understand consumer behavior

2 Analyze the components of the consumer decision-making process

3 Explain the consumer's postpurchase evaluation process

4 Identify the types of consumer buying decisions and discuss the significance of consumer involvement

5 Identify and understand the cultural factors that affect consumer buying decisions

6 Identify and understand the social factors that affect consumer buying decisions

7 Identify and understand the individual factors that affect consumer buying decisions

8 Identify and understand the psychological factors that affect consumer buying decisions

LO1
The Importance of Understanding Consumer Behavior

Consumers' product and service preferences are constantly changing. Marketing managers must understand these desires in order to create a proper marketing mix for a well-defined market. So it is critical that marketing managers have a thorough knowledge of consumer behavior. **Consumer behavior** describes how consumers make purchase decisions and how they use and dispose of the purchased goods or services. The study of consumer behavior also includes the factors that influence purchase decisions and product use.

Understanding how consumers make purchase decisions can help marketing managers in several ways. For example, if a manager knows through research that gas mileage is the most important attribute for a certain target market, the manufacturer can redesign a car to meet that criterion. If the firm cannot change the

> "
> Surveying buyer **pref-erences** provides marketers information that can be used to tailor products and services.
> "

marketing&you.

What is your buying behavior?

Using the scales below, enter your answers.

VERY OFTEN ‹ 1 2 3 4 5 › NEVER
SOMETIMES

_____ I have felt others would be horrified if they knew of my spending habits.

_____ I've bought things even though I couldn't afford them.

_____ I've written a check when I knew I didn't have enough money in the bank to cover it.

_____ I've bought myself something in order to make myself feel better.

_____ I've felt anxious or nervous on days I didn't go shopping.

_____ I've made only the minimum payments on my credit cards.

STRONGLY AGREE ‹ 1 2 3 4 5 › STRONGLY DISAGREE

_____ If I have any money left at the end of the pay period, I just have to spend it.

_____ Having more money would solve my problems.

_____ I have bought something, arrived home, and didn't know why I had bought it.

Now, total your score. Read the chapter to find out what your score means at the end.

Source: Scale #98, *Marketing Scales Handbook*, G. Bruner, K. James, H. Hensel, eds., Vol. III. © by American Marketing Association.

design in the short run, it can use promotion in an effort to change consumers' decision-making criteria, for example, by promoting style, durability, and cargo capacity.

SHAPING PUBLIC POLICY AND EDUCATING CONSUMERS

Understanding consumer behavior can also help the government make better public decisions and aid in educating consumers against buying and using goods and services that may injure their health or hurting society. Research on childhood obesity has led to public service advertising campaigns targeted toward parents to help them plan healthy diets for their children. This same research has led some states to pass laws regarding the types of meals that can be served at schools. Recent research on the use of tanning beds to get that "healthy glow" has found that it dramatically increases the risk of deadly skin cancers. In light of this research, the U.S. federal government has instituted a 10 percent tax on indoor tanning sessions, which will increase the cost of sessions by approximately $1.70.[1]

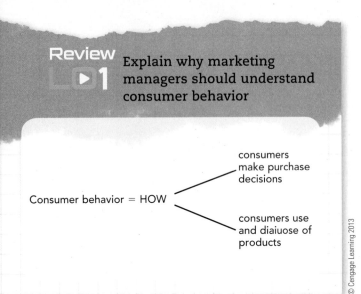
LO2
The Consumer Decision-Making Process

When buying products, particularly new or expensive items, consumers generally follow the **consumer decision-making process** shown in Exhibit 6.1: (1) need recognition, (2) information search, (3) evaluation of alternatives, (4) purchase, and (5) postpurchase behavior. These five steps represent a general process that can be used as a guide for studying how consumers make decisions. It is important to note, though, that consumers' decisions do not always proceed in order through all of these steps. In fact, the consumer may end the process at any time or may not even make a purchase. The section on the types of consumer buying decisions later in the chapter discusses why a consumer's progression through these steps may vary. We begin, however, by examining the basic purchase process in greater detail.

NEED RECOGNITION

The first stage in the consumer decision-making process is need recognition. **Need recognition** occurs when consumers are faced with an imbalance between actual and desired states that arouses and activates the consumer decision-making process. A **want** is the way that a consumer goes about addressing a need. For example, have you ever gotten blisters from an old running shoe? Or maybe you have seen a TV commercial for a new sports car and wanted to buy it. Need recognition is triggered when a consumer is exposed to either an internal or an external **stimulus**. *Internal stimuli* are occurrences you experience, such as hunger or thirst. For example, you may hear your stomach growl and then realize that you are hungry. *External stimuli* are influences from an outside source such as someone's recommendation of a new restaurant, the color of an automobile, the

consumer behavior
Processes a consumer uses to make purchase decisions, as well as to use and dispose of purchased goods or services; also includes factors that influence purchase decisions and product use.

consumer decision-making process
A five-step process used by consumers when buying goods or services.

need recognition
Result of an imbalance between actual and desired states.

want
The way a consumer goes about addressing a need.

stimulus
Any unit of input affecting one or more of the five senses: sight, smell, taste, touch, hearing.

Exhibit 6.1 Consumer Decision-Making Process

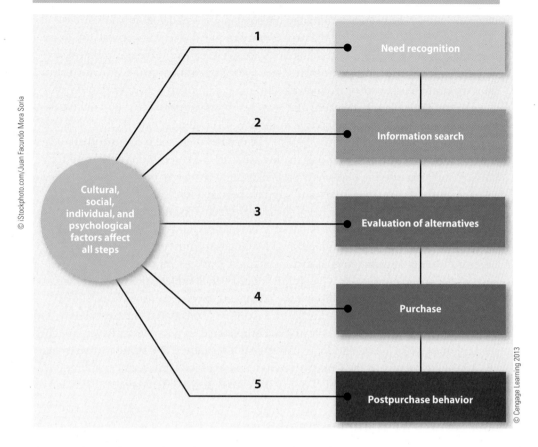

© iStockphoto.com/Juan Facundo Mora Soria

© Cengage Learning 2013

design of a package, a brand name mentioned by a friend, or an advertisement on television or radio.

The imbalance between actual and desired states is sometimes referred to as the "want-got gap." That is, there is a difference between what a customer has and what they would like to have. This gap doesn't always trigger consumer action. The gap must be large enough to drive the consumer to do something. Just because your stomach growls once doesn't mean that you necessarily will stop what you are doing and eat.

A marketing manager's objective is to get consumers to perceive a significant "got-want gap" so that it will drive the consumer to take action. Advertising and sales promotion often provide this stimulus. Surveying buyer preferences provides marketers with information about consumer wants and needs that can be used to tailor products and services. Marketing managers can create wants on the part of the consumer. For example, when college students move in to their own apartment or dorm room, they often need to furnish it and want new furniture rather than hand-me-downs from their parents. A want can be for a specific product, or it can be for a certain attribute or feature of a product. In this example, the college students not only need home furnishings, but also want items that reflect their personal sense of style. Similarly, consumers may want ready-to-eat meals, drive-through dry-cleaning service, and Internet shopping to fill their need for convenience.

Understanding Needs and Wants If marketers don't properly understand the target market's needs, the chances are good that the right good or service may not be produced. An excellent way to understand needs is to view them as job statements or outcome statements.[2] A job is a fundamental goal that consumers are trying to accomplish or a problem they are trying to resolve. Examples include: prevent mildew in a shower, hang a picture, or prepare income taxes. Desired outcome statements help marketers understand what consumers are seeking from a job. A desired outcome might be to minimize the time it takes to file an accurate income tax form that finds all possible legitimate deductions. People then can solve this problem several different ways: do the work themselves using government-provided information, do it themselves using software such as TurboTax, or hire an accountant to do it.

U-Haul understands the needs and wants of its customers. Let's say you live in California and decide to go to college in Florida. U-Haul understands that the job is to get your furniture and stuff to Florida. The desired outcome is to get it there when needed, with the least hassle, and at the lowest cost. U-Haul is a one-stop shop for moving supplies, offering customers prepackaged moving kits that reduce the time it takes to gather the various boxes and supplies required for a move. In addition, an online partnership with eMove helps customers quickly locate a variety of inputs in the form of human helpers such as packers, babysitters, cleaners, and painters.

Marketers selling their products in global markets must carefully observe the needs and wants of consumers in various regions. Unilever hit on an unrecognized need of European consumers when it introduced Persil Tablets, premeasured laundry detergent in tablet form. Though the tablets are more expensive than regular detergents, Unilever found that European consumers considered laundry a chore and wanted the process to be as simple and uncomplicated as possible. Unilever launched the tablets as a less messy and more convenient alternative. The laundry tablets were an immediate success in the United Kingdom and enabled Unilever's Persil brand to beat out rival Procter & Gamble's best-selling Ariel powder detergent.

INFORMATION SEARCH

After recognizing a need or want, consumers search for information about the various alternatives available to satisfy it. For example, as gasoline prices increase, many people search for information on vehicles that use alternatives to gasoline, such as hybrid models. An information search can occur internally, externally, or both. In an **internal information search**, the person recalls information stored in the memory. This stored information stems largely from previous experience with a product. For example, while traveling with your family, you encounter a hotel where you stayed during spring break earlier that year. By searching your memory, you can probably remember whether or not the hotel had clean rooms and friendly service.

In contrast, an **external information search** seeks information in the outside environment. There are two basic types of external information sources: nonmarketing-controlled and marketing-controlled. A **nonmarketing-controlled information source** is not associated with marketers promoting a product. These information sources include personal experiences (trying or observing a new product); personal sources (family, friends, acquaintances, and coworkers who may recommend a product or service); and public sources, such as Underwriters Laboratories, *Consumer Reports*, and other rating organizations that comment on products and services. For example, if you are in the mood to go to the movies, you might search your memory for past experiences at various cinemas when determining which one to go to (personal experience). To choose which movie you will see, you might rely on the recommendation of a friend or family member (personal sources). Alternatively, you could read the critical reviews in the newspaper or online (public sources). Marketers gather information on how these information sources work and use it to attract customers. For example, car manufacturers

internal information search
The process of recalling past information stored in the memory.

external information search
The process of seeking information in the outside environment.

nonmarketing-controlled information source
A product information source that is not associated with advertising or promotion.

MARKETING METRICS — Search Engine Optimization

The Problem

Marketers at VersaceRetailer.com want to increase Web site traffic. To do so, the marketing team is working on search engine optimization, an analytic method which allows companies to determine which keywords and phrases on search engines will return the most profit to the company through customer purchases. Ideally, when a Web user types a keyword or phrase purchased from a search engine by VersaceRetailer.com's marketer in the search box, VersaceRetailer.com will appear in the advertised links at the top of the page.

The advantage of this type of search engine optimization is that it targets customers with an expressed need. These shoppers are far more likely to make a purchase than browsers who aren't shopping for a specific item.

Part of search engine optimization is determining which keyword or keyword phrase to buy for promotion efforts. Each keyword phrase is priced differently on a cost per click (CPC) basis and each delivers a different amount of traffic. Using CPC and other metrics, marketers calculate the market return on investment (MROI) to determine a keyword's effectiveness. VersaceRetailer.com must determine which keyword returns the highest profit to have the most effective search engine optimization.

The Metric

There are five areas VersaceRetailer.com uses to evaluate the effectiveness of individual keywords in search engine optimization: CPC, clicks per purchase, revenue per click, profit per click, and MROI.

The *CPC* is the cost to VersaceRetailer.com to have their Web site appear at the top of search engines such as Yahoo!, Bing, and Google when key words such as "Versace" are searched. In the table below, we see that the CPC for the keyword "Versace" is $0.81, a number that is provided by the search engine on which VersaceRetailer.com would like to advertize.

Clicks per purchase is the number of clicks required to receive one online order. In the case of the keyword "Versace" it is 548. This data can be obtained through market research firms, or by internal purchase information at VersaceRetailer.com.

Revenue per click is determined by knowing how much the average purchase generates in revenue and comparing that number to the clicks per purchase metric:

$$\text{Revenue per Click} = \frac{\text{Average Revenue per Purchase}}{\text{Clicks per purchase}}$$

VersaceRetailer.com's internal purchase information provides the average revenue per purchase. VersaceRetailer.com's average revenue per purchase is $482.25, and the clicks per purchase for the keyword "Versace" is 548, we see:

$$\text{Revenue per Click} = \frac{482.25}{548} = \$0.88$$

The revenue per click for the keyword "Versace" is $0.88.

Profit per click is a key metric to see how much money marketing is making the company. To determine profit per click, multiply the revenue per click by the average profit margin for sales at VersaceRetailer.com and subtract the cost per click from that product:

$$\text{Profit per Click} = (\text{Revenue per Click})(\text{profit margin}) - \text{CPC}$$

VersaceRetailer.com uses a 40 percent margin on its products, which translates to 0.4 in our equation:

$$\text{Profit per Click} = (0.88)(0.4) - 0.81 = -0.46$$

Rather than seeing a profit per click, VersaceRetailer.com is losing $0.46 on each click using the keyword "Versace."

MROI can definitively determine which keyword will return the most profit for the marketer's investment. We calculate the MROI by dividing the profit per click by the cost per click:

$$\text{MROI} = \frac{\text{Profit per Click}}{\text{CPC}}$$

From our previous calculations, we know that the profit per click for the

Keyword	CPC	Clicks per Purchase	Revenue per Click	Profit per Click	MROI
Versace	$0.81	548	$0.88	−$0.46	−57%
Versace Handbag	$1.56	159	$3.02	−$0.35	−23%
Versace Handbag Sale	$0.05	146	$3.29	$1.27	2530%
Discount Handbags	$0.67	133	$3.61	$0.77	115%
Designer Handbags	$0.80	1083	$0.44	−$0.62	−78%

(Continued)

keyword "Versace" is −$0.46 and the CPC is $0.81:

$$MROI = \frac{-0.46}{0.81} = -0.57$$

After converting the resulting number to a percent, we see that the MROI for the keyword "Versace" is −57 percent. A negative MROI indicates that the keyword phrase cost more than it was worth. Keyword phrases associated with a high and positive MROI enable marketers to identify prospective customers with a high purchase intention.

After running several keyword promotions for a month, VersaceRetailer.com collected data regarding the clicks per purchase. The table below illustrates the resulting calculations.

Management Decision

Based on these calculations, the keyword "Versace Handbag Sale" delivers a strong and positive MROI and "Discount Handbags" also has a positive MROI. However, the generic terms "Versace," "Versace Handbags," and "Designer Handbags" each have a negative MROI.

Based on these results, VersaceRetailer .com will stop promoting their Web site using generic terms and focus on specific keyword phrases such as "Versace Handbag Sale" and "Discount Handbags."

A similar approach can be used to measure campaign effectiveness for newspapers, magazines, and broadcast advertising. Each time, the marketer will evaluate the MROI. In this manner, the campaign effectiveness of different communication channels can be compared on an equal basis.

---

know that younger customers are likely to get information from friends and family, so they try to develop enthusiasm for their products via word of mouth.

Living in the digital age has changed the way consumers get nonmarketing-controlled information. It can be from blogs, bulletin boards, activist Web sites, Web forums, and/or consumer opinion sites such as **www.consumerreview.com**, **www.tripadvisor.com**, or **www.epinions.com**. There were 23.7 billion online searches of all types conducted in the United States in April 2010.[3] Nearly 94 percent of U.S. consumers regularly or occasionally research products online before making an offline purchase and nearly half of those consumers then share the information and advice they gleaned online with other consumers, according to Worthington, Ohio–based market research firm BIGresearch.[4]

The latest research has examined how consumers use information picked up on the Internet. For example, in Web forums the information seeker has normally never met the information provider or ever interacted with the person before. Researchers found that an information provider's response speed, the extent to which the provider's previous responses within the forum had been positively evaluated by others, and the breadth of the provider's previous responses across different but related topics affected the information seeker's judgment about the value of the information. So, for example, if other information seekers had found the provider trustworthy, then the current seeker tended to believe the information.[5] Another study found that the more experienced a person is with the Internet, the more likely they are to use and act upon online reviews.[6]

One market where searches for online reviews have greatly increased is the used-car market. Researching cars online is now tied with visiting dealers as the top method for used-car shoppers to locate a vehicle. But it isn't the dealer Web sites receiving the traffic—it's site like CarSoup, Edmunds, Kelly Blue Book, and Auto Tracker. The percentage of used-vehicle buyers who rely on the Internet as a method for getting information about cars and

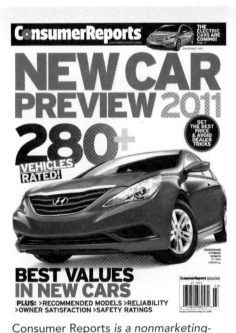

Consumer Reports *is a nonmarketing-controlled information source from which consumers can find objective reviews of products. These* Consumer Reports *magazines are available with a specific focus.*

locating vehicles for sale has increased from 40 percent in 2008 to 68 percent in 2010.[7] This is equal to the percentage of buyers who visit dealer lots as their primary shopping method, according to J.D. Power and Associates. Furthermore, 31 percent of buyers found the vehicle they ultimately purchased on the Internet, compared with 28 percent of buyers who found their vehicle by visiting dealerships.

Among used-vehicle buyers who use the Internet in their shopping process, non-dealer sites are visited during the shopping process much more frequently than dealer Web sites. More than 90 percent of buyers say they visited at least one non-dealer Web site during the shopping process. Slightly more than three-fourths of used-vehicle buyers report visiting a dealer Web site.[8]

A **marketing-controlled information source** is biased toward a specific product because it originates with marketers promoting that product. Marketing-controlled information sources include mass-media advertising (radio, newspaper, television, and magazine advertising), sales promotions (contests, displays, premiums, and so forth), salespeople, product labels and packaging, and the Internet (company blogs, podcasts, search advertising, social media, and Web sites). Many consumers, however, are wary of the information they receive from marketing-controlled sources, believing that most marketing campaigns stress the product's positive attributes and ignore its faults. These sentiments tend to be stronger among better-educated and higher-income consumers. Some marketing-controlled information sources can shift out of marketers' control, however, when there is bad news to report. Toy maker Mattel Inc. made headlines for its recall of toys with lead paint contamination and powerful magnets (which can cause illness or even death in children who ingest them). Newspaper stories across the country, in this instance a nonmarketing-controlled information source, recounted the many toy recalls Mattel has had to make in the past. Mattel then used marketing-controlled information sources to try to combat the negative publicity. Damage control for Mattel took the form of full-page ads in *The New York Times* and *The Wall Street Journal*, and video coverage on Yahoo.com and the Mattel Web site. The ads featured an apology and assurances of future safety of its products from Bob Eckert, Mattel's chairman and CEO. BP started running ads immediately after the Gulf of Mexico rig burned, saying that they were doing everything possible to stop the leak. The BP tag line was "We Will Make This Right."

The extent to which an individual conducts an external search depends on his or her perceived risk, knowledge, prior experience, and level of interest in the good or service. Generally, as the perceived risk of the purchase increases, the consumer enlarges the search and considers more alternative brands. For example, suppose that you want to purchase a surround sound system for your TV. The decision is relatively risky because of the expense and technical nature of the system, so you are motivated to search for information about models, prices, options, compatibility with existing entertainment products, and capabilities. You may decide to compare attributes of many speaker systems because the value of the time expended finding the "right" surround sound system will be less than the cost of buying the wrong system.

A consumer's knowledge about the product or service will also affect the extent of an external information search. A consumer who is knowledgeable and well informed about a potential purchase is less likely to search for additional information. In addition, the more knowledgeable consumers are, the more efficiently they will conduct the search process, thereby requiring less time to search. For example, many consumers know that Southwest Airlines and other discount airlines have much lower fares, so they generally use the discounters and do not even check fares at other airlines.

marketing-controlled information source
A product information source that originates with marketers promoting the product.

evoked set (consideration set)
A group of brands, resulting from an information search, from which a buyer can choose.

The extent of a consumer's external search is also affected by confidence in one's decision-making ability. A confident consumer not only has sufficient stored information about the product, but also feels self-assured about making the right decision. People lacking this confidence will continue an information search even when they know a great deal about the product. Consumers with prior experience in buying a certain product will have less perceived risk than inexperienced consumers. Therefore, they will spend less time searching and limit the number of products that they consider.

A third factor influencing the external information search is product experience. Consumers who have had a positive prior experience with a product are more likely to limit their search to items related to the positive experience. For example, when flying, consumers are likely to choose airlines with which they have had positive experiences, such as consistent on-time arrivals. They will avoid airlines with which they had a negative experience, such as lost luggage.

Finally, the extent of the search is positively related to the amount of interest a consumer has in a product. A consumer who is more interested in a product will spend more time searching for information and alternatives. For example, suppose you are a dedicated runner who reads jogging and fitness magazines and catalogs. In searching for a new pair of running shoes, you may enjoy reading about the new brands available and spend more time and effort than other buyers in deciding on the right shoe.

The consumer's information search should yield a group of brands, sometimes called the buyer's **evoked set (or consideration set)**, which are the consumer's most preferred alternatives. From this set, the buyer will further evaluate the alternatives and make a choice. Consumers do not consider all brands available in a product category, but they do seriously consider a much smaller set. For example, from the many brands of pizza available, consumers are likely to consider only the alternatives that fit their price range, location, take-out/delivery needs, and taste preferences. Having too many choices can, in fact, confuse consumers and cause them to delay the decision to buy or, in some instances, cause them not to buy at all.

EVALUATION OF ALTERNATIVES AND PURCHASE

After getting information and constructing an evoked set of alternative products, the consumer is ready to make a decision. A consumer will use the information stored in memory and obtained from outside sources to develop a set of criteria. Recent research has shown that exposure to certain cues in your everyday environment can affect decision criteria and purchase. For example, when NASA landed the *Pathfinder* spacecraft on Mars, it captured media attention worldwide. The candy maker Mars also noted a rather unusual increase in sales. Although the Mars Bar takes its name from the company's founder and not the planet, consumers apparently responded to news about the planet Mars by purchasing more Mars Bars. In a recent lab experiment, participants who used an orange (green) pen chose more orange (green) products. Thus, conceptual cues or primers (the pen color) influenced product evaluations and purchase likelihood.[9]

The environment, internal information, and external information help consumers evaluate and compare alternatives. One way to begin narrowing the number of choices in the evoked set is to pick a product attribute and then exclude all products in the set that don't have that attribute. For example, assume Jane and Jill, both college sophomores, are looking for their first apartment. They need a two-bedroom apartment, reasonably priced, and located near campus. They want the apartment to have a swimming pool, washer and dryer, and covered parking. Jane and Jill begin their search with all apartments in the area and then systematically eliminate possibilities that lack the features they need. Hence, if there are

50 alternatives in the area, they may reduce their list to just 10 apartments that possess all of the desired attributes.

Another way to narrow the number of choices is to use cutoffs. Cutoffs are either minimum or maximum levels of an attribute that an alternative must pass to be considered. Suppose Jane and Jill set a maximum of $1,000 to spend on combined rent. Then all apartments with rent higher than $1,000 will be eliminated, further reducing the list of apartments from ten to eight. A final way to narrow the choices is to rank the attributes under consideration in order of importance and evaluate the products based on how well each performs on the most important attributes. To reach a final decision on one of the remaining eight apartments, Jane and Jill may decide proximity to campus is the most important attribute. As a result, they will choose to rent the apartment closest to campus.

If new brands are added to an evoked set, the consumer's evaluation of the existing brands in that set changes. As a result, certain brands in the original set may become more desirable. Suppose Jane and Jill find two apartments located an equal distance from campus, one priced at $800 and the other at $750. Faced with this choice, they may decide that the $800 apartment is too expensive given that a comparable apartment is cheaper. If they add a $900 apartment to the list, however, then they may perceive the $800 apartment as more reasonable and decide to rent it.

The purchase decision process described above is a piecemeal process. That is, the evaluation is made by examining alternative advantages and disadvantages along important product attributes. A different way consumers can evaluate a product is according to a categorization process. The evaluation of an alternative depends upon the particular category to which it is assigned. Categories can be very general (motorized forms of transportation), or they can be very specific (Harley-Davidson motorcycles). Typically, these categories are associated with some degree of liking or disliking. To the extent that the product can be assigned membership to a particular category, it will receive an evaluation similar to that attached to the category. If you go to the grocery store and see a new organic food on the shelf, you may evaluate it on your liking and opinions of organic food.

So, when consumers rely on a categorization process, a product's evaluation depends on the particular category to which it is perceived as belonging. Given this, companies need to understand whether consumers are using categories that evoke the desired evaluations. Indeed, how a product is categorized can strongly influence consumer demand. For example, what products come to mind when you think about the "morning beverages" category? To the soft drink industry's dismay, far too few of us include sodas in this category. Several attempts have been made at getting soft drinks on the breakfast table, but with little success.

Brand extensions, in which a well-known and respected brand name from one product category is extended into other product categories, is one way companies employ categorization to their advantage. Brand extensions are a common business practice. Disney

brand extensions
A well-known and respected brand name from one product category is extended into other product categories.

The Huggies line has expanded into sunscreen and baby swimming diapers, among other items for babies.

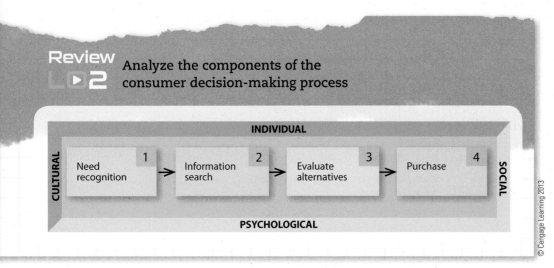

took a name built on cartoon characters and amusement parks and extended it to the cruise line industry. Kimberly-Clark, the maker of Huggies, the best-selling brand of disposable diapers in the United States, has extended the Huggies name to disposable washcloths, liquid soap for babies, Huggies toiletries, sunscreen for babies, baby swimming diapers, and more. Coca-Cola has Coke, Diet Coke, Coke Zero, Cherry Coke, Diet Cherry Coke, Caffeine-Free Coke, and the list goes on.

To Buy or Not to Buy Ultimately, the consumer has to decide whether to buy or not buy. Specifically, consumers must decide:

1. Whether to buy

2. When to buy

3. What to buy (product type and brand)

4. Where to buy (type of retailer, specific retailer, online or in-store)

5. How to pay

When a person is buying an expensive or complex item, it is often a *fully planned purchase* based upon a lot of information. People rarely buy a new home simply on impulse. Often consumers will make a *partially planned purchase* where they know the product category they want to buy (shirts, pants, reading lamp, car floor mats) but wait until they get to the store to choose a specific style or brand. Finally, there is the *unplanned purchase* where people buy on impulse. Research has found that up to 68 percent of the items bought during major shopping trips and 54 percent on smaller shopping trips are unplanned.[10]

LO 3 Postpurchase Behavior

When buying products, consumers expect certain outcomes from the purchase. How well these expectations are met determines whether the consumer is satisfied or dissatisfied with the purchase. For example, if a person bids on a used car stereo from eBay and wins, he may have fairly low expectations regarding performance. If the stereo's performance turns out to be of superior quality, then the person's satisfaction will be high because his expectations were exceeded. Conversely, if the person bid on a new car stereo expecting superior quality and performance, but the stereo broke within one month, he would be very dissatisfied because his expectations were not met. Price often influences the level of expectations for a product or service.

For the marketer, an important element of any postpurchase evaluation is reducing any lingering doubts that the decision was sound. When people recognize inconsistency between their values or opinions and their behavior, they tend to feel an inner tension called **cognitive dissonance**. For example, suppose a person who normally tans in a tanning bed decides to try a new "airbrush" tanning method, called "Hollywood" or "mystic" tanning. Mystic tanning costs $30 to $50, significantly more than artificial tanning cream or a tanning bed. Prior to spending more on the tan, the person may feel inner tension or anxiety, which is a feeling of dissonance. This feeling occurs because she knows the product has some disadvantages, such as being expensive, and some advantages, such as being free of harmful ultraviolet rays. In this case, the disadvantage of higher cost battles the advantage of no harmful UV rays.

Consumers try to reduce dissonance by justifying their decision. They may seek new information that reinforces positive ideas about the purchase, avoid information that contradicts their decision, or revoke the original decision by returning the product. To ensure satisfaction, thereby reducing dissonance, consumers using the "mystic tanning" mentioned above may ask several friends about their experiences, do online research, and talk with the tanning booth representative to obtain additional information about the procedure. In some instances, people deliberately seek contrary information in order to refute it and reduce dissonance. Dissatisfied customers sometimes rely on word of mouth to reduce cognitive dissonance, by letting friends and family know they are displeased.

Marketing managers can help reduce dissonance through effective communication with purchasers. For example, a customer service manager may slip a note inside the package congratulating the buyer on making a wise decision. Postpurchase letters sent by manufacturers and dissonance-reducing statements in instruction booklets may help customers feel at ease with their purchase. Advertising that displays the product's superiority over competing brands or guarantees can also help relieve the possible dissonance of someone who has already bought the product. In the tanning example, the tanning salon may offer a 100 percent money-back guarantee. The **mystictan.com** Web site explains the procedure and even shows endorsements from various celebrities. Because the company offers this additional information and communicates effectively with its customers, its customers are more likely to understand the procedure and the expected results; hence, it is likely that the outcome will meet or exceed their expectations rather than being disappointing.

cognitive dissonance
Inner tension that a consumer experiences after recognizing an inconsistency between behavior and values or opinions.

Review LO3 Explain the consumer's postpurchase evaluation process

Cognitive Dissonance — Product or Service

To Reduce Dissonance

Consumer can
- justify decision
- seek new information
- avoid contradictory information
- return product

Marketer can
- send postpurchase thank you or letter
- display product superiority in ads
- offer guarantees

Satisfied Customer — Product or Service

© Cengage Learning 2013

LO4
Types of Consumer Buying Decisions and Consumer Involvement

All consumer buying decisions generally fall along a continuum of three broad categories: routine response behavior, limited decision making, and extensive decision making. (See Exhibit 6.2.) Goods and services in these three categories can best be described

Exhibit 6.2 Continuum of Consumer Buying Decisions

	Routine	Limited	Extensive
Involvement	low	low to moderate	high
Time	short	short to moderate	long
Cost	low	low to moderate	high
Information Search	internal only	mostly internal	internal and external
Number of Alternatives	one	few	many

© Cengage Learning 2013

in terms of five factors: level of consumer involvement, length of time to make a decision, cost of the good or service, degree of information search, and the number of alternatives considered. The level of consumer involvement is perhaps the most significant determinant in classifying buying decisions. **Involvement** is the amount of time and effort a buyer invests in the search, evaluation, and decision processes of consumer behavior. High involvement signifies personal relevance and importance to the consumer.

Frequently purchased, low-cost goods and services are generally associated with **routine response behavior**. These goods and services can also be called low-involvement products because consumers spend little time on search and decision before making the purchase. Usually, buyers are familiar with several different brands in the product category but stick with one brand. For example, a person may routinely buy Tropicana orange juice. Consumers engaged in routine response behavior normally don't experience need recognition until they are exposed to advertising or see the product displayed on a store shelf. Consumers buy first and evaluate later, whereas the reverse is true for extensive decision making. A consumer who has previously purchased whitening toothpaste and was satisfied with it will probably walk to the toothpaste aisle and select that same brand without spending 20 minutes examining all other alternatives.

Limited decision making typically occurs when a consumer has previous product experience but is unfamiliar with the current brands available. Limited decision making is also associated with lower levels of involvement (although higher than routine decisions) because consumers do expend moderate effort in searching for information or in considering various alternatives. But what happens if the consumer's usual brand of whitening toothpaste is sold out? Assuming that toothpaste is needed, the consumer will be forced to choose another brand. Before making a final decision, the consumer will likely evaluate several other brands based on their active ingredients, their promotional claims, and the consumer's prior experiences.

Consumers practice **extensive decision making** when buying an unfamiliar, expensive product or an infrequently bought item. This process is the most complex type of consumer buying decision and is associated with high involvement on the part of the consumer. This process resembles the model outlined in Exhibit 6.1. These consumers want to make the right decision, so they want to know as much as they can about the product category and available brands. People usually experience the most cognitive dissonance when buying high-involvement products. Buyers use several criteria for evaluating their options and spend much time seeking information. Buying a home or a car, for example, requires extensive decision making.

The type of decision making that consumers use to purchase a product does not necessarily remain constant. For instance, if a routinely purchased product no longer satisfies, consumers may practice limited or extensive decision making to switch to another brand. And people who first use extensive decision making may then use limited or routine decision making for future purchases. For example, when a family gets a new puppy, they will spend a lot of time and energy trying out different toys to determine which one the dog prefers. Once the new owners learn that the dog prefers a bone to a ball, however, the purchase no longer requires extensive evaluation and will become routine.

FACTORS DETERMINING THE LEVEL OF CONSUMER INVOLVEMENT

The level of involvement in the purchase depends on the following factors:

→ *Previous experience:* When consumers have had previous experience with a good or service, the level of involvement typically decreases. After repeated product trials, consumers learn to make quick choices. Because consumers are familiar with the product and know whether it will satisfy their needs, they become less involved in the purchase. For example, a consumer purchasing cereal has many brands to choose from—just think of any grocery store cereal aisle. If the consumer always buys the same brand because it satisfies his hunger, then he has a low level of involvement. When a consumer purchases a high-fiber cereal for the first time, however, it likely will be a more involved purchase.

→ *Interest:* Involvement is directly related to consumer interests, as in cars, music, movies, bicycling, or electronics. Naturally, these areas of interest vary from one individual to another. A person highly involved in bike racing will be very interested in the type of bike she owns and will spend quite a bit of time evaluating different bikes. If a person wants a bike only for recreation, however, he may be fairly uninvolved in the purchase and just look for a bike from the most convenient location. Many consumers are interested in good nutrition when they grocery shop. A recent study found that shoppers interested in nutrition sought out the following ingredients: calcium (77 percent), fiber (72 percent), vitamin C (63 percent), vitamin D (60 percent), antioxidants (60 percent), protein (60 percent), and whole grain (58 percent).[11]

→ *Perceived risk of negative consequences:* As the perceived risk in purchasing a product increases, so does a consumer's level of involvement. The types of risks that concern consumers include financial risk, social risk, and psychological risk.

  → Financial risk is exposure to loss of wealth or purchasing power. Because high risk is associated with high-priced purchases, consumers tend to become extremely involved. Therefore, price and involvement are usually directly related: As price increases, so does the level of involvement. For example, someone who is purchasing a new car for the first time (higher perceived risk) will spend a lot of time and effort making this purchase. Financial risk may carry greater weight today because of the "Great Recession" of 2008–2010. The loss of jobs and potential loss of jobs meant that prices did not necessarily have to be high to have high involvement. One study found that consumers are not only buying less but also want brands to offer "proof of value." The recession has created more "value-driven" buyers who are looking more carefully for deeply discounted goods and services and are critically evaluating bundled items. The global recession also made many consumers think twice, and often delay, purchases of big ticket items such as cars, furniture, and high tech products.[12]

  → Social risks occur when consumers buy products that can affect people's social opinions of them (for example, driving an old, beat-up car or wearing unstylish clothes).

Walmart seeks to provide low financial risk products through its Great Value brand.

→ Psychological risks occur if consumers feel that making the wrong decision might cause some concern or anxiety. For example, some consumers feel guilty about eating foods that are not healthy, such as regular ice cream rather than fat-free frozen yogurt.

→ **Social visibility:** Involvement also increases as the social visibility of a product increases. Products often on social display include clothing (especially designer labels), jewelry, cars, and furniture. All these items make a statement about the purchaser and, therefore, carry a social risk.

NOT ALL INVOLVEMENT IS THE SAME

High involvement means that the consumer cares about a product's category, or a specific good or service. It is relevant, important, and means something to the buyer. Yet high involvement can take a number of different forms. The most important types are discussed below:

→ **Product involvement** means that a product category has high personal relevance. Product enthusiasts are consumers with high involvement in a product category. The fashion industry has a large segment of product enthusiasts. These people are seeking the latest fashion trends and want to wear the latest clothes. Interestingly, the marketing director of one of Europe's great fashion houses told one of your authors that the market for the clothes shown by renowned designers at their runway shows is only 200 persons worldwide. Why? The clothes are extremely expensive, cater to a specific body shape, and require their owner to have a place to wear them. Instead, it is all about buzz and publicity, which leads to custom orders, modified limited editions at lower price points, and, over time, mass merchandising to various larger markets.

→ **Situational involvement** means that the circumstances of a purchase may temporarily transform a low-involvement decision into a high-involvement one. High involvement comes into play when the consumer perceives risk in a specific situation. For example, an individual might routinely buy low-priced brands of liquor and wine. When the boss visits, however, the consumer might make a high-involvement decision and buy more prestigious brands.

→ **Shopping involvement** represents the personal relevance of the process of shopping. Some people simply love shopping whether they buy anything or not. To some, shopping is a grand adventure whether in a mall or on the Internet. These highly involved shoppers are more likely to process information about deals and more likely to react to price reductions and limited offers.[13] They are also more likely to leave slack in their budgets to make unplanned purchases when on a shopping excursion.[14]

→ **Enduring involvement** represents an ongoing interest in some product or activity. The consumer is always searching for opportunities to consume the product or participate in the activity. Enduring involvement typically gives personal gratification to the consumer as they continue to learn about, shop for, and consume these goods and services. Therefore, there is often link among enduring involvement and shopping and product involvement.

→ **Emotional involvement** represents how emotional a consumer gets during some specific consumption activity. Emotional involvement is closely related to enduring involvement because the things that consumers care most about will eventually create high emotional involvement. Sports fans typify consumers with high emotional involvement. Recall the outpouring of emotion at the recent World Cup Soccer Tournament in South Africa.[15]

MARKETING IMPLICATIONS OF INVOLVEMENT

Marketing strategy varies according to the level of involvement associated with the product. For high-involvement product purchases, marketing managers have several responsibilities. First, promotion to the target market should be very informative. A good ad gives consumers the information they need for making the purchase decision, as well as specifying the benefits and unique advantages of owning the product or services. For example, an ad for CitationAir Jet Card, a card that allows an executive to lease a private jet by the hour, features a headline that says "Do The Math." The body of the ad claims that the CitationAir Jet Card is a much better value than competitor Marquis Jet. The CitationAir Jet Card offers hourly rates up to 24 percent lower than Marquis Jet on 355 non-peak days. Citation offers access to a jet every day of the year. The ad concludes by saying, "Get Jet Smart."

For low-involvement product purchases, consumers may not recognize their wants until they are in the store. Therefore, in-store promotion is an important tool when promoting low-involvement products. Marketing managers focus on package design so the product will be eye-catching and easily recognized on the shelf. Examples of products that take this approach are Campbell's soups, Tide detergent, Velveeta cheese, and Heinz ketchup. In-store displays also stimulate sales of low-involvement products. A good display can explain the product's purpose and prompt recognition of a want. Displays of health and beauty aid items in supermarkets have been known to increase sales many times above normal. Coupons, cents-off deals, and two-for-one offers also effectively promote low-involvement items.

Linking a product to a higher-involvement issue is another tactic that marketing managers can use to increase the sales or positive publicity of a low-involvement product. For example, in response to government and consumer concerns about childhood obesity, food manufacturers that advertise to children, such as Kellogg, Hershey, McDonald's, and General Mills, have pledged to devote at least half of their marketing to the promotion of healthy dietary choices and lifestyles. In Kellogg's case, nearly $206 million in advertising dollars is at stake.[16]

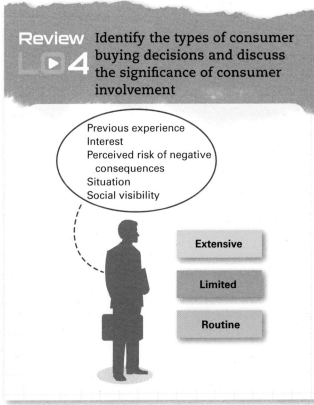

Review LO4 Identify the types of consumer buying decisions and discuss the significance of consumer involvement

Previous experience
Interest
Perceived risk of negative consequences
Situation
Social visibility

Extensive

Limited

Routine

© Cengage Learning 2013

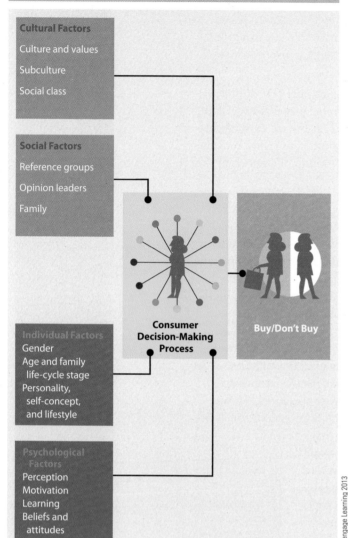

Exhibit 6.3 Factors That Affect the Consumer Decision-Making Process

Cultural Factors

Culture and values

Subculture

Social class

Social Factors

Reference groups

Opinion leaders

Family

Individual Factors

Gender

Age and family
life-cycle stage

Personality,
self-concept,
and lifestyle

Psychological Factors

Perception

Motivation

Learning

Beliefs and
attitudes

Consumer
Decision-Making
Process

Buy/Don't Buy

© Cengage Learning 2013

Factors Influencing Consumer Buying Decisions

The consumer decision-making process does not occur in a vacuum. On the contrary, underlying cultural, social, individual, and psychological factors strongly influence the decision process. These factors have an effect from the time a consumer perceives a stimulus through postpurchase behavior. Cultural factors, which include culture and values, subculture, and social class, exert a broad influence over consumer decision making. Social factors sum up the social interactions between a consumer and influential groups of people, such as reference groups, opinion leaders, and family members. Individual factors, which include gender, age, family life-cycle stage, personality, self-concept, and lifestyle, are unique to each individual and play a major role in the type of products and services consumers want. Psychological factors determine how consumers perceive and interact with their environments and influence the ultimate decisions consumers make. They include perception, motivation, learning, beliefs, and attitudes. Exhibit 6.3 summarizes these influences.

LO5

Cultural Influences on Consumer Buying Decisions

Of all the factors that affect consumer decision making, cultural factors exert the broadest and deepest influence. Marketers must understand the way people's culture and its accompanying values, as well as their subculture and social class, influence their buying behavior.

CULTURE AND VALUES

Culture is the essential character of a society that distinguishes it from other societal groups. The underlying elements of every culture are the values, language, myths, customs, rituals, and laws that shape the behavior of the people, as well as the material artifacts, or products, of that behavior as they are transmitted from one generation to the next. Exhibit 6.4 lists some defining components of American culture.

Culture is pervasive. Cultural values and influences are the ocean in which individuals swim, and yet most are completely unaware that it is there. What people eat, how they dress, what they think and feel, and what language they speak

culture
The set of values, norms, attitudes, and other meaningful symbols that shape human behavior, and the artifacts, or products, of that behavior as they are transmitted from one generation to the next.

Exhibit 6.4 Components of American Culture

Component	Examples
Values	Success through hard work; emphasis on personal freedom
Language	English as the dominant language
Myths	George Washington never told a lie. Abraham Lincoln walked a mile to return a penny.
Customs	Bathing daily; shaking hands when greeting new people; standard gratuity of 15 to 20 percent at restaurants
Rituals	Thanksgiving Day dinner; singing the "Star Spangled Banner" before baseball games; going to religious services on the appropriate day
Laws	Child labor laws; Sherman Antitrust Act guarantees competition
Material artifacts	Diamond engagement rings; cell phones

Source: Adapted from *Consumer Behavior* by William D. Wells and David Prensky.

© iStockphoto.com/Juan Facundo Mora Soria

are all dimensions of culture. It encompasses all the things consumers do without conscious choice because their culture's values, customs, and rituals are ingrained in their daily habits.

Culture is functional. Human interaction creates values and prescribes acceptable behavior for each culture. By establishing common expectations, culture gives order to society. Sometimes these expectations are enacted into laws. For example, drivers in our culture must stop at a red light. Other times these expectations are taken for granted. For example, grocery stores and hospitals are open 24 hours a day, whereas banks are open only during bankers' hours.

Culture is learned. Consumers are not born knowing the values and norms of their society. Instead, they must learn what is acceptable from family and friends. Children learn the values that will govern their behavior from parents, teachers, and peers. As members of our society, they learn to shake hands when they greet someone, to drive on the right-hand side of the road, and to eat pizza and drink Coca-Cola.

Culture is dynamic. It adapts to changing needs and an evolving environment. The rapid growth of technology in today's world has accelerated the rate of cultural change. Television, computers, and hand-held devices have changed entertainment patterns and family communication and have heightened public awareness of political and other news events. Automation has increased the amount of leisure time we have and, in some ways, has changed the traditional work ethic. Cultural norms will continue to evolve because of our need for social patterns that solve problems.

In the United States, rapidly increasing diversity is causing major shifts in culture. For example, the growth of the Hispanic community is influencing American food, music, clothing, and entertainment. Additionally, African American culture has been embraced by the mainstream. Indeed, African American women make up one of the fastest-growing segments of the American population. The projected growth rate of this segment is 8 percent, compared to 4 percent for the total U.S. population. Additionally, one in two married black women is the primary decision maker in buying a house, versus one in four married white women. Traditionally, marketers have not taken advantage of the opportunity to market to African American women. Now, however, many companies are taking note of this rapidly growing segment of the population. For example, Kraft's Honey Bunches of Oats cereal developed an advertising campaign that focused on black women. Research

value

The enduring belief that a specific mode of conduct is personally or socially preferable to another mode of conduct.

showed that African American women do not like to eat cereal when others are around, so the print ad shows a black woman eating a bowl of cereal alone with the caption "Take a breather. This moment is yours. Just you and your bowl of Honey Bunches of Oats."[17]

The most defining element of a culture is its **values**—the enduring beliefs shared by a society that a specific mode of conduct is personally or socially preferable to another mode of conduct. People's value systems have a great effect on their consumer behavior. Consumers with similar value systems tend to react alike to prices and other marketing-related inducements. Values also correspond to consumption patterns. For example, Americans place a high value on convenience. This value has created lucrative markets for products such as breakfast bars, energy bars, and nutrition bars that allow consumers to eat on the go. Values can also influence consumers' TV viewing habits or the magazines they read. For instance, people who strongly object to violence avoid crime shows, and those who oppose pornography do not buy *Hustler*. Core American values—those considered central to the American way of life—have been defined and listed in a variety of ways in a number of research studies. One interesting approach is a list of core American values prepared for foreigners coming to visit the United States. It is entitled "Why Do Americans Act Like That?" and is shown in Exhibit 6.5.

Exhibit 6.5 Why Do Americans Act Like That?

1. Personal Control over the Environment/ Responsibility	Americans do not believe in the power of fate, and they look at people who do as being backward, primitive, or naïve. In the American context, to be "*fatalistic*" is to be superstitious, lazy, or unwilling to take initiative. Everyone should have control over whatever in the environment might potentially affect him or her. The problems of one's life are not seen as having resulted from bad luck as much as having come from one's laziness and unwillingness to take responsibility in pursuing a better life.
2. Change Seen as Natural and Positive	In the American mind, change is seen as indisputably good, leading to development, improvement, progress. Many older, more traditional cultures consider change disruptive and destructive; they value stability, continuity, tradition, and ancient heritage.
3. Time and Its Control	Time is of the utmost importance to most Americans. It is something to be on, kept, filled, saved, used, spent, wasted, lost, gained, planned, given, even killed. Americans are concerned with getting things accomplished on time. Their lives seem controlled by the little machines they wear on their wrists, cutting their discussions off abruptly to make their next appointment on time. This philosophy has helped Americans to be extremely productive, and productivity is highly valued in their country.
4. Equality/Fairness	Americans believe that all people are created equal and that all should have an equal opportunity to succeed. This concept of equality is strange to many places in the world that view status and authority as desirable, even if they happen to be near the bottom of the social order. Because Americans like to treat foreigners "*just like anybody else*," newcomers to the U.S. should realize that no insult or personal indignity is intended if they are treated in a less-than-deferential manner by waiters in restaurants, clerks in stores and hotels, taxi drivers, and other service personnel.
5. Individualism/Independence	Americans view themselves as highly individualistic in their thoughts and actions. They resist being thought of as representatives of any homogeneous group. In the U.S. you will find people freely expressing a variety of opinions anywhere and anytime. Yet, in spite of this independence, almost all Americans end up voting for one of their two major political parties. Individualism leads to **privacy**, which Americans see as desirable. The word *privacy* does not exist in many non-Western languages. If it does, it is likely to have a negative connotation, suggesting loneliness or forced isolation.

(Continued)

6. Self-Help Initiative	Americans take credit for what they accomplish as individuals. They get no credit for having been born into a rich family but pride themselves in having climbed the ladder of success, to whatever level, all by themselves. In an English-language dictionary, there are more than 100 composite words that have the word "*self*" as a prefix: *self*-aware, *self*-confident, *self*-conscious, *self*-contented, *self*-control, *self*-criticism, *self*-deception, *self*-defeating, *self*-denial. The equivalent of these words cannot be found in most other languages. It is an indicator of how highly Americans regard the *self*-made man or woman.
7. Competition	Americans believe that competition brings out the best in any individual and in any system. This value is reflected in the American economic system of free enterprise, and it is applied in the U.S. in all areas—medicine, the arts, education, sports, and so on.
8. Future Orientation	Americans value the culture and the improvements the future will surely bring. Even a happy present goes largely unnoticed because Americans are hopeful that the future will bring even greater happiness. Because Americans believe that humans, not fate, can and should control the environment, they are good at planning short-term projects. This ability has caused Americans to be invited to all corners of the Earth to plan, and often achieve, the miracles that their goal-setting methods can produce.
9. Action/Work Orientation	"*Don't just stand there*," says a typical bit of American advice, "*Do something!*" This expression, though normally used in a crisis situation, in a sense describes most Americans' waking life, where action—any action—is seen as superior to inaction. Americans routinely schedule an extremely active day. Any relaxation must be limited in time and aimed at "recreating" so that they can work harder once their "*recreation*" is over. Such a "*no-nonsense*" attitude toward life has created a class of people known as "workaholics"— people addicted to, and often wholly identified with, their job or profession. The first question people often ask when they meet each other in the U.S. is related to work: "*What do you do?*" "*Where do you work?*" or "*Who (what company) are you with?*"
10. Informality	Americans are even more informal and casual than Western Europeans. For example, American bosses often urge their employees to call them by their first names and feel uncomfortable with the title "*Mr.*" or "*Ms.*" Dress is another area where American informality is most noticeable, perhaps even shocking. For example, one can go to a symphony performance in any large American city and find people dressed in blue jeans. Informality is also apparent in Americans' greetings. The more formal "*How are you?*" has largely been replaced with an informal "*Hi.*" This is as likely to be used with one's superior as with one's best friend.
11. Directness/Openness/Honesty	Many other countries have developed subtle, sometimes highly ritualistic, ways of informing others of unpleasant information. Americans prefer the direct approach. They are likely to be completely honest in delivering their negative evaluations, and consider anything other than the most direct and open approach to be "*dishonest*" and "*insincere.*" Anyone in the U.S. who uses an intermediary to deliver the message will also be considered "*manipulative*" and "*untrustworthy.*" If you come from a country where saving face is important, be assured that Americans are not trying to make you lose face with their directness.
12. Practicality/Efficiency	Americans have a reputation for being realistic, practical, and efficient. The practical consideration is likely to be given highest priority in making any important decision. Americans pride themselves in not being very philosophically or theoretically oriented. If Americans would even admit to having a philosophy, it would probably be that of pragmatism. *Will it make money? What is the bottom line? What can I gain from this activity?* These are the kinds of questions Americans are likely to ask, rather than: *Is it aesthetically pleasing? Will it be enjoyable? Will it advance the cause of knowledge?* This pragmatic orientation has caused Americans to contribute more inventions to the world than any other country in human history. Americans try to avoid being "*too sentimental*" in making their decisions. They judge every situation "*on its own merits.*"
13. Materialism/Acquisitiveness	Foreigners generally consider Americans much more materialistic than Americans are likely to consider themselves. Americans would like to think that their material objects are just the "*natural benefits*" that result from hard work and serious intent—a reward, they think, that all people could enjoy were they as industrious and hard-working as Americans. But by any standard, Americans are materialistic. Because Americans value newness and innovation, they sell or throw away their possessions frequently and replace them with newer ones. A car may be kept for only two or three years, a house for five or six before buying a new one.

Source: "Why Do Americans Act Like That?," from L. Robert Kohls, Director of International Programs at San Francisco University, "Why Do Americans Act Like That?" Reprinted with permission.

Values represent what is most important in people's lives. Therefore, marketers watch carefully for shifts in consumers' values over time. For example, millions of Americans have an interest in spirituality, as evidenced by the soaring sales of books with religious or spiritual themes and the popularity of television shows with similar themes. Similarly, after the September 11 terrorist attacks, when many people were fearful and concerned about self-protection, gun sales soared as did the sale of drugs to cure anthrax. American values toward ecology shifted after the BP oil spill.

James Stengel, global marketing director for Procter & Gamble, had this to say about the changes he's seen in today's consumers: "The biggest thing going on with U.S. consumers is that they want to trust something. They want to be understood, they want to be respected, [and] they want to be listened to. They don't want to be talked to. It's trust in the largest sense of the word. People really do care what's behind the brand, what's behind the business. They care about the values of a brand and the values of a company. We can never forget that. We can never be complacent about that."[18]

UNDERSTANDING CULTURAL DIFFERENCES

As more companies expand their operations globally, the need to understand the cultures of foreign countries becomes more important. A firm has little chance of selling products in a culture it does not understand. Like people, products have cultural values and rules that influence their perception and use. Culture, therefore, must be understood before the behavior of individuals within the cultural context can be understood. Colors, for example, may have different meanings in global markets than they do at home. In China, white is the color of mourning, and brides wear red. In the United States, black is for mourning, and brides wear white.

Language is another important aspect of culture that global marketers must deal with. When translating product names, slogans, and promotional messages into foreign languages, marketers must be careful not to convey the wrong message. General Motors discovered too late that Nova (the name of an economical car) literally means "doesn't go" in Spanish; Coors encouraged its English-speaking customers to "Turn it loose," but the phrase in Spanish means "suffer from diarrhea."

Though marketers expanding into global markets generally adapt their products and business formats to the local culture, some fear that increasing globalization, as well as the proliferation of the Internet, will result in a homogeneous world culture in the future. U.S. companies in particular, they fear, are Americanizing the world by exporting bastions of American culture, such as McDonald's fast-food restaurants, Starbucks coffeehouses, Microsoft software, and American movies and entertainment.

Perhaps the most important aspect of a multinational firm's success in selling in any country is to understand the culture. The Global Perspectives box illustrates one firm's attempt at modifying its products based upon culture.

SUBCULTURE

subculture
A homogeneous group of people who share elements of the overall culture as well as unique elements of their own group.

A culture can be divided into subcultures on the basis of demographic characteristics, geographic regions, national and ethnic background, political beliefs, and religious beliefs. A **subculture** is a homogeneous group of people who share elements of the overall culture as well as cultural elements unique to their own group.

global perspectives

Understanding Taiwanese Behavior Keeps Costco Counting Members

The aisles inside the Taipei, Taiwan, Costco store are stacked floor to ceiling with merchandise. But mixed in with familiar U.S. products such as Tide detergent and Pepperidge Farm cookies are local favorites such as sea cucumber, mahjong sets, and stewed and braised beef noodle soup.

Offering an experience that's authentically American while cultivating local tastes has proved a successful formula for Costco. The Taipei store, located in Taipei's high-tech Neihu district, is the second most profitable, behind a Korean outlet. Though about two-fifths of the chain's merchandise comes from the United States, the U.S. products tend to have a local twist. The Kirkland brand beef steak, for instance, is thinly sliced to satisfy local preferences for hot-pot meat. Fish are sold whole instead of filleted. And in the food court, alongside American frozen yogurt and pepperoni pizza, are such local variations as Peking duck pizza.

One challenge Costco faced in Taipei was convincing consumers to pay a $40 membership fee. This was a new idea in the Taiwan market. Richard Chang, the local manager, said that the store's liberal return policy helped nudge many shoppers to pay the fee. "In Asia, people aren't used to returning [merchandise]," he said. "It was hard for people to understand. We are trying to introduce that. People return half of a watermelon because it's not sweet enough. We say we are happy to do it. We make that return so pleasurable that you are going to tell your family and friends. That's something money can't buy. We consider that part of our advertising."[19]

Why is culture so important to multinational firms? Can you think of a product or service in the global marketplace where culture doesn't matter?

Source: From Andria Cheng, "Costco Cracks Taiwan Market," *Wall Street Journal*, April 2, 2010, B5. Reprinted with permission.

Within subcultures, people's attitudes, values, and purchase decisions are even more similar than they are within the broader culture. Subcultural differences may result in considerable variation within a culture in what, how, when, and where people buy goods and services.

In the United States alone, countless subcultures can be identified. Many are concentrated geographically. People belonging to the Mormon religion, for example, are clustered mainly in Utah; Cajuns are located in the bayou regions of southern Louisiana. Many Hispanics live in states bordering Mexico, whereas the majority of Chinese, Japanese, and Korean Americans are found on the West Coast. Other subcultures are geographically dispersed. Computer hackers, people who are hearing or visually impaired, Harley-Davidson bikers, military families, university professors, and gays may be found throughout the country. Yet they have identifiable attitudes, values, and needs that distinguish them from the larger culture.

Once marketers identify subcultures, they can design special marketing programs to serve their needs. According to the U.S. Census Bureau, the Hispanic population is the largest and fastest-growing subculture, increasing four times as fast as the general population. To tap into this large and growing segment, marketers have been forming partnerships with broadcasters that have an established Latino audience. The Univision Radio network covers approximately 73 percent of the U.S. Hispanic population and has over ten million listeners weekly. State Farm has partnered with Julie Stav, the leading financial expert on the Latino community, to sponsor evening broadcasts of her hugely successful Spanish-language radio show. When Sweden-based furniture manufacturer IKEA found that it wasn't

social class

A group of people in a society who are considered nearly equal in status or community esteem, who regularly socialize among themselves both formally and informally, and who share behavioral norms.

capturing the large Latino demographic in U.S. cities, it started advertising in Spanish. It also launched a series of commercials featuring Latina soap opera stars on Telemundo—the second-largest U.S. Spanish-language broadcaster. IKEA saw immediate results with more Latinos in their stores.[20]

SOCIAL CLASS

The United States, like other societies, has a social class system. A **social class** is a group of people who are considered nearly equal in status or community esteem, who regularly socialize among themselves both formally and informally, and who share behavioral norms.

A number of techniques have been used to measure social class, and a number of criteria have been used to define it. One view of contemporary U.S. status structure is shown in Exhibit 6.6.

As you can see from Exhibit 6.6, the upper and upper middle classes comprise the small segment of affluent and wealthy Americans. In terms of consumer buying patterns, the affluent are more likely to own their own home and purchase new cars and trucks and are less likely to smoke. The very rich flex their financial muscles by spending more on vacation homes, vacations and cruises, and housekeeping and gardening services. The most affluent consumers are more likely to attend art auctions and galleries, dance performances, operas, the theater, museums, concerts, and sporting events. Marketers often pay attention to the superwealthy. For example, the Mercedes-Benz Maybach 62, touted as the "world's most luxurious car," is aimed at this group. Priced at $375,000, the car features electronic doors, reclining seats with footrests, a workstation with media capability, a champagne cooler, and lots more. Similarly, New York-based designer Calvin Stewart sells A.P.O. jeans featuring fully customized denim embellished with diamond, gold, and platinum details—starting at $1,000 a pair.

The majority of Americans today define themselves as middle class, regardless of their actual income or educational attainment. This phenomenon most likely occurs

Exhibit 6.6 U.S. Social Classes

Upper Classes		
Capitalist class	1 percent	People whose investment decisions shape the national economy; income mostly from assets, earned or inherited; university connections
Upper middle class	14 percent	Upper-level managers, professionals, owners of medium-sized businesses; well-to-do, stay-at-home homemakers who decline occupational work by choice; college-educated; family income well above national average
Middle Classes		
Middle class	33 percent	Middle-level white-collar, top-level blue-collar; education past high school typical; income somewhat above national average; loss of manufacturing jobs has reduced the population of this class
Working class	32 percent	Middle-level blue-collar, lower-level white-collar; income below national average; largely working in skilled or semi-skilled service jobs
Lower Classes		
Working poor	11–12 percent	Low-paid service workers and operatives; some high school education; below mainstream in living standard; crime and hunger are daily threats
Underclass	8–9 percent	People who are not regularly employed and who depend primarily on the welfare system for sustenance; little schooling; living standard below poverty line

Source: Adapted from Richard P. Coleman, "The Continuing Significance of Social Class to Marketing," *Journal of Consumer Research*, December 1983, 267; Dennis Gilbert and Joseph A. Kahl, *The American Class Structure: A Synthesis* (Homewood, IL: Dorsey Press, 1982), ch. 11.

because working-class Americans tend to aspire to the middle-class lifestyle while some of those who do achieve affluence may downwardly aspire to respectable middle-class status as a matter of principle. Attaining goals and achieving status and prestige are important to middle-class consumers. People falling into the middle class live in the gap between the haves and the have-nots. They aspire to the lifestyle of the more affluent, but are constrained by the economic realities and cautious attitudes they share with the working class.

A recent poll asked whether the United States is split into "haves" and "have-nots"; 48 percent said it is and 48 percent said it isn't. (The rest declined to choose.) The researchers also asked people to say which class they belong to, if they had to pick. While a large percentage said they're "haves" (45 percent), that's down from the 52 percent who did so in 2001 and down even more from the 59 percent saying so in 1988. The rest said they fit in neither group or refused to pick. More women than men situated themselves among the have-nots (37 percent vs. 30 percent). Even 32 percent of middle-income consumers said that they were have-nots, meaning that they perceived their standard of living as inadequate for their purchasing power.[21]

The working class is a distinct subset of the middle class. Interest in organized labor is one of the most common attributes among the working class. This group often rates job security as the most important reason for taking a job. The working-class person depends heavily on relatives and the community for economic and emotional support. The emphasis on family ties is one sign of the group's intensely local view of the world. They like the local news far more than do middle-class audiences who favor national and world coverage. They are also more likely to vacation closer to home.

Lifestyle distinctions between the social classes are greater than the distinctions within a given class. The most significant difference between the classes occurs between the middle and lower classes, where there is a major shift in lifestyles. Members of the lower class typically have incomes at or below the poverty level. This social class has the highest unemployment rate, and many individuals or families are subsidized through the welfare system. Many are illiterate, with little formal education. Compared to more affluent consumers, lower-class consumers have poorer diets and typically purchase very different types of foods when they shop.

Social class is typically measured as a combination of occupation, income, education, wealth, and other variables. For instance, affluent upper-class consumers are more likely to be salaried executives or self-employed professionals with at least an undergraduate degree. Working-class or middle-class consumers are more likely to

Cartier offers unique jewelry targeted to the wealthy.

be hourly service workers or blue-collar employees with only a high school education. Educational attainment, however, seems to be the most reliable indicator of a person's social and economic status. Those with college degrees or graduate degrees are more likely to fall into the upper classes, while those people with some college experience fall closest to traditional concepts of the middle class.

Marketers are interested in social class for two main reasons. First, social class often indicates which medium to use for advertising. Suppose an insurance company seeks to sell its policies to middle-class families. It might advertise during the local evening news because middle-class families tend to watch more television than other classes do. If the company wants to sell more policies to upscale individuals, it might place a print ad in a business publication such as *The Wall Street Journal*. The Internet, long the domain of more educated and affluent families, has become an increasingly important advertising outlet for advertisers hoping to reach blue-collar workers and homemakers.

Second, knowing what products appeal to which social classes can help marketers determine where to best distribute their products. Affluent Americans, a fifth of the U.S. population, were responsible for nearly half of all new car and truck sales and over half of hotel stays and vacation homes. This same group spent nearly twice as much as less-affluent Americans on restaurant fare, alcohol, sporting events, plays, and club memberships.[22]

For the first time in a long while, however, industry analysts are seeing shares of discount chains faring better than their full-priced and upscale counterparts. These days, analysts say, the big-box and discount retailers' greatest challenge has been courting consumers who fall in the middle-income level. The result is a fiercely competitive retail environment where discount retailers have focused less on their core, low-income consumers, who are most impacted by rising housing and gas costs. Overall, however, shares of discount chains are faring better during the recent "Great Recession" because more affluent customers traded down to obtain more value for their money.

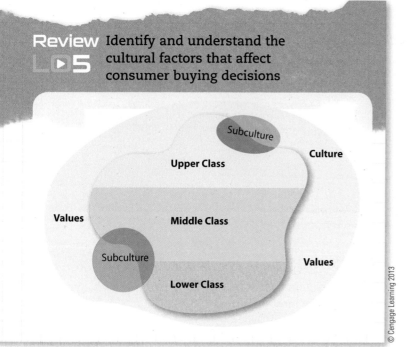

Review LO 5 Identify and understand the cultural factors that affect consumer buying decisions

© Cengage Learning 2013

LO 6
Social Influences on Consumer Buying Decisions

Many consumers seek out the opinions of others to reduce their search and evaluation effort or uncertainty, especially as the perceived risk of the decision increases. Consumers may also seek out others' opinions for guidance on new products or services, products with image-related attributes, or products where attribute information is lacking or uninformative. Specifically, consumers interact socially with reference groups, opinion leaders, and family members to obtain product information and decision approval.

REFERENCE GROUPS

All the formal and informal groups that influence the buying behavior of an individual are that person's **reference groups**. Consumers may use products or brands to identify with or become a member of a group. They learn from observing how members of their reference groups consume, and they use the same criteria to make their own consumer decisions. Reference groups have an impact on how consumers evaluate goods and services, the goods and services they aspire to own, and when and where they buy.

Reference groups can be categorized very broadly as either direct or indirect. (See Exhibit 6.7.) Direct reference groups are face-to-face membership groups that touch people's lives directly. They can be either primary or secondary. **Primary membership groups** include all groups with which people interact regularly in an informal, often face-to-face manner, such as family, friends, and coworkers. Today, they may also communicate by mail, text messages, Facebook, Skype, or other electronic means. In contrast, people associate with **secondary membership groups** less consistently and often more formally. These groups might include clubs, professional groups, Internet communities, and religious groups.

Consumers are also influenced by many indirect, nonmembership reference groups they do not belong to. **Aspirational reference groups** are those a person would like to join. To join an aspirational group, a person must at least conform to the norms of that group. (**Norms** are the values and attitudes deemed acceptable by the group.) Thus, a person who wants to be elected to public office may begin to dress more conservatively, as other politicians do. He or she may go to many of the restaurants and social engagements that city and business leaders attend and try to play a role that is acceptable to voters and other influential people. Similarly, teenagers today may dye their hair and experiment with body piercing and tattoos. Athletes are an aspirational group for several market segments. To appeal to the younger market, Coca-Cola signed basketball star LeBron James to be the spokesperson for its Sprite and

reference group
A group in society that influences an individual's purchasing behavior.

primary membership group
A reference group with which people interact regularly in an informal, face-to-face manner, such as family, friends, or fellow employees.

secondary membership group
A reference group with which people associate less consistently and more formally than a primary membership group, such as a club, professional group, or religious group.

aspirational reference group
A group that someone would like to join.

norm
A value or attitude deemed acceptable by a group.

Exhibit 6.7 Types of Reference Groups

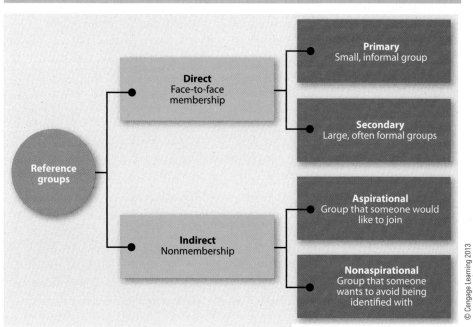

© Cengage Learning 2013

nonaspirational reference group
A group with which an individual does not want to associate.

POWERade brands, and Nike signed a sneaker deal with him reportedly worth $90 million. Coca-Cola and Nike assumed James would encourage consumers to drink Coke brands and buy Nike shoes because they would like to identify with James.

Nonaspirational reference groups, or dissociative groups, influence our behavior when we try to maintain distance from them. A consumer may avoid buying some types of clothing or car, going to certain restaurants or stores, or even buying a home in a certain neighborhood in order to avoid being associated with a particular group.

The activities, values, and goals of reference groups directly influence consumer behavior. For marketers, reference groups have three important implications: (1) they serve as information sources and influence perceptions; (2) they affect an individual's aspiration levels; and (3) their norms either constrain or stimulate consumer behavior. For example, research firms devoted to uncovering what's cool in the teen market have identified a couple of influential groups among today's teens based on their interests in clothes, music, and activities. Tracking these groups reveals how products become cool and how groups influence the adoption of cool products by other groups. A trend or fad often starts with teens who have the most innovative tastes. These teens are on the cutting edge of fashion and music, and they wear their attitude all over their bodies in the form of tattoos, body piercing, studded jewelry, or colored tresses. Certain fads embraced by these "Edgers" will spark an interest in the small group of teens researchers call "Influencers," who project the look other teens covet. Influencers also create their own trends in music and clothing choices. Once a fad is embraced and adopted by Influencers, the look becomes cool and desirable. The remaining groups that comprise the majority of the teen population will not embrace a fad until it gets its seal of approval from the Influencers.

Understanding the effect of reference groups on a product is important for marketers as they track the life cycle of their products. Retailer Abercrombie & Fitch noticed it was beginning to lose its target audience of college students when its stores began attracting large numbers of high school students trying to be more like college students. To solve the problem, A&F created its Hollister store chain specifically for high school students. The retailer also opened a chain called Abercrombie for a target market of boys and girls, ages 7 to 14.

Marketers and researchers can now gauge teen opinions, test new product ideas, and even get help creating marketing buzz by tapping into the ever-expanding online teen communities. For example, Piczo, an online community with a billion page views per month, has a group of influential "insiders" who will advise brands on how to best leverage the site. "Piczo Insiders" exchange opinions and offer feedback on marketing campaigns that are running on the Piczo site. These teens will collaborate online with marketers and are responsive to any research activity or project that they think will improve the Piczo user experience. The Insiders recently contributed real-life stories to "Don't Hide It," a successful new campaign for the National Society for the Prevention of Cruelty to Children (NSPCC).

Research has shown that reference groups are particularly powerful in influencing purchases of fragrances, wine, snack food, candy, clothing, and sodas.[23] People with well-formed networks of somewhat overlapping reference groups and those with strong personal values are less susceptible to reference group influences.[24]

OPINION LEADERS

Reference groups frequently include individuals known as group leaders, or **opinion leaders**—those who influence others. Obviously, it is important for marketing managers to persuade such people to purchase their goods or services. Many products and services that are integral parts of Americans' lives today got their initial boost from opinion leaders. For example, Kindle e-readers and iPads were purchased by opinion leaders well ahead of the general public.

Opinion leaders are often the first to try new products and services out of pure curiosity. They are typically self-indulgent and status-seeking, making them more likely to explore unproven but intriguing products and services.[25] Technology companies have found that teenagers, because of their willingness to experiment, are key opinion leaders for the success of new technologies.

Opinion leadership is often a casual, face-to-face phenomenon and is perhaps inconspicuous, so locating opinion leaders can be a challenge. Thus, marketers often try to create opinion leaders. They may use high school cheerleaders to model new fall fashions or civic leaders to promote insurance, new cars, and other merchandise. On a national level, companies sometimes use movie stars, sports figures, and other celebrities to promote products, hoping they are appropriate opinion leaders. The effectiveness of celebrity endorsements varies, though, depending largely on how credible and attractive the spokesperson is and how familiar people are with him or her. Endorsements are most likely to succeed if a reasonable association between the spokesperson and the product can be established.

Celebrities and sports figures aren't the only people marketers consider opinion leaders, however. Managers at BMW are rethinking who the U.S. opinion leaders are for their brand. Historically, the automaker targeted car enthusiasts. Today, the company is looking at the "idea class," a group composed of roughly 1.5 million architects, professionals, innovators, and entrepreneurs who are more interested in design, authenticity, and independent thinking. Over a seven-year period, BMW has increased U.S. sales but still has less than a 3 percent share of the U.S. market.[26]

Respected organizations such as the American Heart Association and the American Cancer Society may also serve as opinion leaders. Marketers may seek endorsements from them as well as from schools, churches, cities, the military, and fraternal organizations as a form of group opinion leadership. Salespeople often ask to use opinion leaders' names as a means of achieving greater personal influence in a sales presentation.

How Blogs Are Defining Today's Opinion Leaders Increasingly, marketers are looking to Web logs, or blogs, to find opinion leaders. A new blog is created every second of every day according to Technorati, a blog-monitoring site,

Yes. She checks herself out in the mirror.

1 in 5 Americans will develop skin cancer in their lifetime. That's why Jennifer Garner made a promise to herself to examine her skin every month and see her dermatologist for a screening every year.

The Neutrogena Partnership for Skin Health, working with the American Academy of Dermatology (AAD), invites you to join them in their mission to stop skin cancer before it strikes. Empower their cause by wearing broad-spectrum sun protection, covering up and seeking shade between 10:00 am and 4:00 pm. Perform self-examinations regularly and report any changes in existing moles or birthmarks to your doctor. Because with early detection, skin cancer is 99% curable. And that's a statistic we love to share.

Protect yourself starting today.
The AAD and the Neutrogena Partnership for Skin Health encourage you to get a free skin cancer screening in May, June or July. Find one in your area by visiting aad.org or neutrogenaskinhealth.com. Mark the date of your screening on this slip as a healthy reminder.

Neutrogena®
PARTNERSHIP FOR
SKIN HEALTH

The activities, values, and goals of reference groups directly influence consumer behavior. Consumers may use the Neutrogena brand—and participate in skin cancer prevention behavior as she does—because they aspire to be like actress Jennifer Garner.

opinion leader
An individual who influences the opinions of others.

so it's getting harder to separate the true opinion leaders from intermediate Web users who are just looking to share random thoughts or vacation photos with family and friends. As of this printing, Technorati monitors and Nielsen BuzzMetrics boasts coverage of more than 70 million blogs. There are over 126 million blogs worldwide, but that huge number doesn't necessarily mean bloggers get respect or recognition. The fashion industry used to dismiss bloggers as irrelevant and small-time, effectively limiting their access to hot events during semi-annual fashion week shows. Now, however, fashion bloggers have the attention of the fashion establishment because many are claiming bigger followings than traditional media.

One way marketers are identifying true opinion leaders is by looking to teen blogs to identify the social trends that are shaping consumer behavior. During the research phase of development for its teen-targeted RED Blogs service, AOL discovered that over 50 percent of teens do not mind sharing their feelings in public forums. This is especially evident at social networking sites like MySpace and Facebook, where teens and twenty-somethings post extensive personal profiles, photo collections, links to user groups they belong to, and detailed descriptions of their social events.

This is just one of the many reasons marketers are so interested in teens. Raised with MTV, 500-channel cable services, a rapidly maturing Internet, iPhones, and Droids, teens have unprecedented access to the world around them. Furthermore, they are no longer passive observers of the culture their parents have created. They can follow their favorite bands, actors, or athletes via their Web sites and blogs and expect to interact with them instead of just admiring them from afar. With their unprecedented ability to network and communicate with each other, young people rely on each others' opinions more than marketing messages when making purchase decisions. And blogs are becoming a key way that teens communicate their opinions. Consequently, today's marketers are reading teen blogs, developing products that meet the very specific needs that teens express there, and learning unique and creative ways to put key influencers in charge of marketing their brands for them.

Another trend in recent years is sponsored blogs. A **sponsored blog** (or post) is one in which a company pays a blogger to say things (typically positive) about a good or service. More than 80 percent of all bloggers were already writing about goods or services so many firms have used cash to influence what was said.[27] Often bloggers didn't disclose that they were being paid to promote a product. This process is called **shilling**. The growth of shilling led the Federal Communications Commission to require bloggers to disclose sponsored content. For example, Colleen Padilla writes a blog entitled www.classymommy.com, which attracts over 60,000 unique visitors per month.[28] Mrs. Padilla is viewed as an opinion leader by many of her followers. Thus, she receives a lot of free merchandise from firms hoping for some positive comments about their products. Mrs. Padilla acknowledges in each review which products were sent by companies and which items she bought herself. Elsewhere on her site she has her own videos for brands like Healthy Choice that she labels as a sponsored post.

FAMILY

The family is the most important social institution for many consumers, strongly influencing values, attitudes, self-concept—and buying behavior. For example, a family that strongly values good health will have a grocery list distinctly different from that of a family that views every dinner as a gourmet event. Moreover, the family is responsible for the **socialization process**, the passing down of cultural values and norms to children. Children learn by observing their parents' consumption patterns, and so they will tend to shop in a similar pattern.

sponsored blog
A blog in which a company pays a blogger to say things about a good or service.

shilling
When bloggers do not disclose that they were paid to promote a product.

socialization process
How cultural values and norms are passed down to children.

Decision-making roles among family members tend to vary significantly, depending on the type of item purchased. Family members assume a variety of roles in the purchase process. *Initiators* suggest, initiate, or plant the seed for the purchase process. The initiator can be any member of the family. For example, Sister might initiate the product search by asking for a new bicycle as a birthday present. *Influencers* are those members of the family whose opinions are valued. In our example, Mom might function as a price-range watchdog, an influencer whose main role is to veto or approve price ranges. Brother may give his opinion on certain makes of bicycles. The *decision maker* is the family member who actually makes the decision to buy or not to buy. For example, Dad or Mom is likely to choose the final brand and model of bicycle to buy after seeking further information from Sister about cosmetic features such as color, and then imposing additional criteria of his or her own, such as durability and safety. The *purchaser* (probably Dad or Mom) is the one who actually exchanges money for the product. Finally, the *consumer* is the actual user—Sister, in the case of the bicycle.

Marketers should consider family purchase situations along with the distribution of consumer and decision-maker roles among family members. Ordinary marketing views the individual as both decision maker and consumer. Family marketing adds several other possibilities: Sometimes more than one family member or all family members are involved in the decision; sometimes only children are involved in the decision; sometimes more than one consumer is involved; sometimes the decision maker and the consumer are different people. Exhibit 6.8 represents the patterns of family purchasing relationships that are possible.

In most households, when parental joint decisions are being made, spouses consider their partner's needs and perceptions to maintain decision fairness and harmony.[29] This tends to minimize family conflict. Research also shows that in harmonious households the spouse that has "won" a previous decision is less likely to use strong influence in a subsequent decision.[30] This balancing factor is key in maintaining long-term family harmony.

Exhibit 6.8 Relationships among Purchasers and Consumers in the Family

		Purchase Decision Maker		
		Parent(s) Only	Child/Children Only	Some or All Family Members
Consumer	Parent(s)	golf clubs cosmetics wine	Mother's Day card	Christmas gifts minivan
	Child/Children	diapers breakfast cereal	candy small toys	bicycle
	Some Family Members	videos long-distance phone service	children's movies	computers sports events
	All Family Members	clothing life insurance	fast-food restaurant	swim club membership vacations

Source: From Robert Boutilier, FAMILY MARKETING: HOW TO MARKET TO AND THROUGH TODAY'S DIVERSE FAMILIES. Adapted by permission of Robert Boutilier.

Because children influence buying decisions, some companies have begun targeting children's interests for adult purchases.

Children can have great influence over the purchase decisions of their parents. In many families, with both parents working and short on time, children are encouraged to participate. In addition, children in single-parent households become more involved in family decisions at an earlier age. Children are especially influential in decisions about food and eating out. Exactly how much of an influence kids have varies depending on factors such as age, race, socioeconomic status, and region. For example, *Restaurants & Institutions*' New American Diner study shows that children age 5 or younger frequently influence restaurant visits, while children ages 6 to 18 have only occasional influence. Females, Generation Xers, Asian American diners, and Midwesterners are most likely to say children influence which restaurants they visit.[31] Children influence purchase decisions for many more products and services than food. Even though they are usually not the actual purchasers of such items, children often participate in decisions about toys, clothes, vacations, recreation, automobiles, and many other products. And if those children happen to be teenagers? American teens have a total income of $80 billion of their own, and parents spend an additional $110 billion each year on them. Recent data shows that while teens make up only 7 percent of the U.S. population, they actually contribute to 11 percent of U.S. spending.[32] With spending power like that, it is important to know what teens like. Research shows that they like tangible things. One study found that 75 percent would choose a new pair of shoes over 50 new MP3 downloads, and 63 percent would choose a new pair of jeans over tickets to a concert.[33]

Traditionally, children learn about consumption from their parents. In today's technologically overloaded world, that trend is reversing. Teenagers and adult children often contribute information and influence the purchase of parents' technology products.[34] Often they even help with installation and show the parents how to use the product!

Review Identify and understand the social factors that affect consumer buying decisions

Reference Groups	Direct		Indirect	
	Primary	Secondary	Aspirational	Nonaspirational

Opinion Leaders	People you know	Celebrities

Reference Groups	Socialization Process		
	Initiators	Decision Makers	Consumers
	Influencers		Purchasers

© Cengage Learning 2013

LO7

Individual Influences on Consumer Buying Decisions

A person's buying decisions are also influenced by personal characteristics that are unique to each individual, such as gender; age and life-cycle stage; and personality, self-concept, and lifestyle. Individual characteristics are generally stable over the course of one's life. For instance, most people do not change their gender, and the act of changing personality or lifestyle requires a complete reorientation of one's life. In the case of age and life-cycle stage, these changes occur gradually over time.

GENDER

Physiological differences between men and women result in different needs, such as health and beauty products. Just as important are the distinct cultural, social, and economic roles played by men and women and the effects that these have on their decision-making processes. For example, many networks have programming targeted to women, while Spike TV calls itself the "first network for men." Some magazines are geared to men who like to shop. For example, *Details* is an upscale fashion magazine for affluent men in their 20s and 30s; *Complex* is a magazine for younger men whose fashion sense ranges from hip-hop and skateboarding to mainstream style.

Trends in gender marketing are influenced by the changing roles of men and women in society. For example, men used to rely on the women in their lives to shop for them. Today, however, more men are shopping for themselves. The number of men shopping online in the United States is around 60 percent. Men who have begun staying at home with their young children have noticed how few baby items, such as diaper bags, are made with a man's use in mind. One man went so far as to create his own product line, at **dadgear.com.** Whether because of the advent of online shopping or retailers wising up to the way men like to shop, today more men are comfortable shopping for themselves. A study commissioned by *GQ* found that 84 percent of men said they purchase their own clothes.[35]

Men's roles aren't the only ones that are changing. Women around the world are working and earning more, and many industries are attracting new customers by marketing to women. For example, nearly 40 percent, or 50 million, of American Airlines' customers are women. If AA raises that number by 2 percent, it will make another $94 million in revenue each year. Acknowledging that, American has launched an online community resource especially for women travelers at **www.aa.com/women.** Wyndham Hotels and Resorts developed a program called Women on Their Way to enhance the experience of their female guests. American and Wyndham believe that by listening and responding to their female customers' insights, the travel experience for all of their customers will improve. These special programs are also designed to foster female travelers' belief that their business is valued.

The changing roles of women are also forcing companies that have traditionally targeted women to develop new strategies. One reason is because women's decision making tends to be multi-minded and integrative, meaning that they consider and move back and forth among many criteria, as opposed to being single-minded and focused. They tend to view shopping as a learning process, educating themselves on the available options and typically adding criteria as they learn more. It is not unusual for a woman to shift back to an earlier stage of the decision process as she learns something that may cause her even to change categories. For example, a woman may have decided to buy an SUV because her friends all love theirs and she likes the looks of the new models. Once on the showroom floor, however, she may see a new minivan that offers great storage and fuel mileage. Suddenly, she's including minivans in her consideration set and has added two new criteria to the qualifying list.

AGE AND FAMILY LIFE-CYCLE STAGE

The age and family life-cycle stage of a consumer can have a significant impact on consumer behavior. How old a consumer is generally indicates what products he or she may be interested in purchasing. Consumer tastes in food, clothing, cars, furniture, and recreation are often age related.

Related to a person's age is his or her place in the family life cycle. As Chapter 8 explains in more detail, the *family life cycle* is an orderly series of stages through which consumers' attitudes and behavioral tendencies evolve through maturity, experience, and changing income and status. Marketers often define their target markets in terms of family life cycle, such as "young singles," "young married with children," and "middle-aged married without children." For instance, young singles spend more than average on alcoholic beverages, education, and entertainment. New parents typically increase their spending on health care, clothing, housing, and food and decrease their spending on alcohol, education, and transportation. Households with older children spend more on food, entertainment, personal care products, and education, as well as cars and gasoline. After their children leave home, spending by older couples on vehicles, women's clothing, health care, and long-distance calls typically increases. The presence of children in the home is the most significant determinant of the type of vehicle that's driven off the new-car lot. Parents are the ultimate need-driven car consumers, requiring larger cars and trucks to haul their children and all their belongings. It comes as no surprise then that for all households with children, SUVs rank either first or second among new-vehicle purchases, followed by minivans.

Marketers should also be aware of the many nontraditional life-cycle paths that are common today and provide insights into the needs and wants of such consumers as divorced parents, lifelong singles, and childless couples. Three decades ago, married couples with children under the age of 18 accounted for about half of U.S. households. Today, such families make up only 23 percent of all households, while people living alone or with nonfamily members represent more than 30 percent. Furthermore, according to the U.S. Census Bureau, the number of single-mother households grew by 25 percent over the last decade. The shift toward more single-parent households is part of a broader societal change that has put more women on the career track. Although many marketers continue to be wary of targeting nontraditional families, Charles Schwab targeted single mothers in an advertising campaign featuring Sarah Ferguson, the Duchess of York and a divorced mom. The idea was to appeal to single mothers' heightened awareness of the need for financial self-sufficiency.

Life Events Another way to look at the life cycle is to look at major events in one's life over time. Life-changing events can occur at any time. A few examples are: death of a spouse, moving to a different place, birth or adoption of a child, retirement, getting fired, divorce, and marriage. Typically, such events are quite stressful and consumers often take steps to minimize that stress. Many times such life-changing events will mean new consumption patterns.[36] A recently divorced person may try to improve his or her appearance by joining a health club and dieting. A person moving to a different city will need a new dentist, grocery store, auto service center, and doctor, to name a few shops and service providers. Marketers realize that life events often mean a chance to gain a new customer. The Welcome Wagon offers a number of free gifts and services for area newcomers. Lowe's sends out a discount coupon to those moving to a new community. And when you put your home on the market, very quickly you start getting flyers from moving companies promising a great price on moving your household goods.

PERSONALITY, SELF-CONCEPT, AND LIFESTYLE

Each consumer has a unique personality. **Personality** is a broad concept that can be thought of as a way of organizing and grouping how an individual typically reacts to situations. Thus, personality combines psychological makeup and environmental forces. It includes people's underlying dispositions, especially their most dominant characteristics. Although personality is one of the least useful concepts in the study of consumer behavior, some marketers believe that personality influences

personality
A way of organizing and grouping the consistencies of an individual's reactions to situations.

the types and brands of products purchased. For instance, the type of car, clothes, or jewelry a consumer buys may reflect one or more personality traits.

Self-concept, or self-perception, is how consumers perceive themselves. Self-concept includes attitudes, perceptions, beliefs, and self-evaluations. Although self-concept may change, the change is often gradual. Through self-concept, people define their identity, which in turn provides for consistent and coherent behavior.

Self-concept combines the **ideal self-image** (the way an individual would like to be) and the **real self-image** (how an individual actually perceives himself or herself). Generally, we try to raise our real self-image toward our ideal (or at least narrow the gap). Consumers seldom buy products that jeopardize their self-image. For example, someone who sees herself as a trendsetter wouldn't buy clothing that doesn't project a contemporary image.

Human behavior depends largely on self-concept. Because consumers want to protect their identity as individuals, the products they buy, the stores they patronize, and the credit cards they carry support their self-image. No other product quite reflects a person's self-image as much as the car he or she drives. For example, many young consumers do not like family sedans like the Honda Accord or Toyota Camry and say they would buy one for their mom, but not for themselves. Likewise, a cowboy or "cowboy wanna-be" would never drive anything but a pick-up truck. A recent study found that people who were open to other cultures, who channeled lots of energy and effort to accomplish personal goals, and who were open to change, were much more likely to acquire new technology products.[37]

By influencing the degree to which consumers perceive a good or service to be self-relevant, marketers can affect consumers' motivation to learn about, shop for, and buy a certain brand. Marketers also consider self-concept important because it helps explain the relationship between individuals' perceptions of themselves and their consumer behavior.

The extent to which consumers use their current situation to guide their social behavior is known as **self-monitoring**. People who routinely modify their behavior to meet the expectations of others are known as *high self-monitors*. Conversely, people who act primarily on the basis of their internal beliefs and attitudes are known as *low self-monitors*. Put simply, high self-monitors tend to behave like social chameleons, constantly changing and adapting their behaviors to different situations and different people. Low self-monitors march to the beat of their own drums. Research shows that *low* self-monitors have greater attitude-behavior consistency than high self-monitors. Researchers also found that *high* self-monitors show more concern for the self-image they project in social situations. As a result, high self-monitors are more likely to respond to image-based appeals that promise to make them look good, while low self-monitors are more likely to evaluate characteristics, functions, and benefits of a product. Self-monitoring typically involves three somewhat distinct individual differences:

→ Willingness to be the center of attention

→ Concern about the opinions of others

→ Ability and desire to adjust one's behavior to receive positive reactions from others[38]

Personality and self-concept are reflected in lifestyle. A **lifestyle** is a mode of living, as identified by a person's activities, interests, and opinions. Psychographics is the analytical technique used to examine consumer lifestyles and to categorize consumers. Unlike personality characteristics, which are hard to describe and measure, lifestyle characteristics are useful in segmenting and targeting consumers.

self-concept
How consumers perceive themselves in terms of attitudes, perceptions, beliefs, and self-evaluations.

ideal self-image
The way an individual would like to be.

real self-image
The way an individual actually perceives himself or herself.

self-monitoring
The extent to which consumers use their current situation to guide their social behavior.

lifestyle
A mode of living as identified by a person's activities, interests, and opinions.

Lifestyle and psychographic analysis explicitly addresses the way consumers outwardly express their inner selves in their social and cultural environment.

Many companies now use psychographics to better understand their market segments. For many years, marketers selling products to mothers conveniently assumed that all moms were fairly homogeneous and concerned about the same things—the health and well-being of their children—and that they could all be reached with a similar message. But recent lifestyle research has shown that there are traditional, blended, and nontraditional moms, and companies like Procter & Gamble and Pillsbury are using strategies to reach these different types of mothers. Psychographics is also effective with other market segments.

An example of a lifestyle segment are those people who are snackers. Snacking can be part of a healthy diet or it can be loaded with junk food. Thus, there are healthy and unhealthy snackers. Today, 21 percent of all meals are snacks.[39] A few findings on snacks and snackers are:

→ While late-night refrigerator trips are still the most common (38.3 percent), morning snacks are rapidly growing (28.4 percent). Snack foods replaced breakfast more than any other meal. At-home afternoon snacking came in at 29.3 percent, followed by carried snacks (3.8 percent).

→ Fruit is the top food eaten between meals at home and consumption is up from five years ago. Cookies, candy/gum, ice cream, and chips round out the top five most popular snack foods, respectively.

→ Snack-oriented foods are not only eaten between meals, sometimes they serve as side dishes or replace a meal entirely.

→ Most snack foods are purchased more than a day ahead. One in ten snacks is bought within 30 minutes of consumption.

→ Snack consumption is currently most popular among kids ages 6 to 12, but declining among children 2 to 5, adults ages 18 to 34, and those over 55.[40]

Psychographics and lifestyle segmentation are discussed in more detail in Chapter 8.

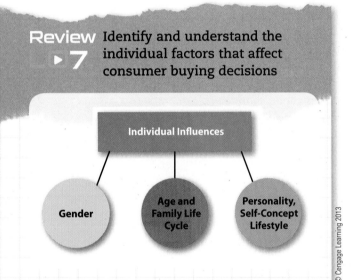

Review
7 Identify and understand the individual factors that affect consumer buying decisions

Individual Influences

Gender

Age and Family Life Cycle

Personality, Self-Concept Lifestyle

© Cengage Learning 2013

LO8

Psychological Influences on Consumer Buying Decisions

An individual's buying decisions are further influenced by psychological factors: perception, motivation, learning, and beliefs and attitudes. These factors are what consumers use to interact with their world. They are the tools consumers use to recognize their feelings, gather and analyze information, formulate thoughts and opinions, and take action. Unlike the other three influences on consumer behavior, psychological influences can be affected by a person's environment because they are applied on specific occasions. For example, you will perceive different stimuli and process these stimuli in different ways depending on whether you are sitting in class concentrating on the instructor, sitting outside of class talking to friends, or sitting in your dorm room watching television.

PERCEPTION

The world is full of stimuli. A stimulus is any unit of input affecting one or more of the five senses: sight, smell, taste, touch, and hearing. The process by which we select, organize, and interpret these stimuli into a meaningful and coherent picture is called **perception**. In essence, perception is how we see the world around us and how we recognize that we need some help in making a purchasing decision.

People cannot perceive every stimulus in their environment. Therefore, they use **selective exposure** to decide which stimuli to notice and which to ignore. A typical consumer is exposed to more than 2,500 advertising messages a day, but notices only between 11 and 20.

The familiarity of an object, contrast, movement, intensity (such as increased volume), and smell are cues that influence perception. Consumers use these cues to identify and define products and brands. The shape of a product's packaging, such as Coca-Cola's signature contour bottle, for instance, can influence perception. Color is another cue, and it plays a key role in consumers' perceptions. Packaged foods manufacturers use color to trigger unconscious associations for grocery shoppers who typically make their shopping decisions in the blink of an eye. When Pepsi departed from its usual blue can for a red can in a marketing campaign for the 2008 Olympics in China, they risked brand confusion with Coke products. One Pepsi drinker in China said "This is so weird. I usually just go for the blue can; it's easy to spot … the red can just doesn't look right." Pepsi officials say they coordinated the can with the color of China's flag to highlight their sponsorship of Team China. Pepsi had used national colors on promotional packages before, such as yellow and green cans to sponsor Brazilian teams.[41]

Ampacet, a world leader in color additives for plastics, reported in 2007 that nature-inspired colors and organic values were becoming more popular as the economy and global focus shifted from the tech-boom to bio- or eco-boom. Ecological consequences and concerns have resulted in marketing initiatives such as "going green." Packaging colors like natural greens, earthy browns, and strong yellows are in, as well as metallics such as steely silver, carbon black, gold, and copper. Color researchers speculate that technological overload has led to resurgence in the appreciation of simplistic luxury. Color names for fabrics and makeup reflect that trend with names such as Grounded, Champagne Chic, and Serene Blue.[42]

Two other concepts closely related to selective exposure are selective distortion and selective retention. **Selective distortion** occurs when consumers change or distort information that conflicts with their feelings or beliefs. For example, suppose a college student buys a SonicBlue Rio MP3 player. After the purchase, if the student gets new information about an alternative brand, such as an Apple iPod, he or she may distort the information to make it more consistent with the prior view that the SonicBlue Rio is just as good as the iPod, if not better. Business travelers who fly often may distort or discount information about airline crashes because they must use air travel constantly in their jobs.

Selective retention is remembering only information that supports personal feelings or beliefs. The consumer forgets all information that may be inconsistent. After reading a pamphlet that contradicts one's political beliefs, for instance, a person may forget many of the points outlined in it. Similarly, consumers may see a news report on suspected illegal practices by their favorite retail store, but soon forget the reason the store was featured on the news.

Which stimuli will be perceived often depends on the individual. People can be exposed to the same stimuli under identical conditions but perceive them very differently. For example, two people viewing a TV commercial may have different

perception
The process by which people select, organize, and interpret stimuli into a meaningful and coherent picture.

selective exposure
The process whereby a consumer notices certain stimuli and ignores others.

selective distortion
A process whereby a consumer changes or distorts information that conflicts with his or her feelings or beliefs.

selective retention
A process whereby a consumer remembers only that information that supports his or her personal beliefs.

© Matthew Cole/Shutterstock.com

interpretations of the advertising message. One person may be thoroughly engrossed by the message and become highly motivated to buy the product. Thirty seconds after the ad ends, the second person may not be able to recall the content of the message or even the product advertised.

Marketing Implications of Perception Marketers must recognize the importance of cues, or signals, in consumers' perception of products. Marketing managers first identify the important attributes, such as price or quality, that the targeted consumers want in a product and then design signals to communicate these attributes. For example, consumers will pay more for candy in expensive-looking foil packages. But shiny labels on wine bottles signify less expensive wines; dull labels indicate more expensive wines. Marketers also often use price as a signal to consumers that the product is of higher quality than competing products. Gibson Guitar Corporation briefly cut prices on many of its guitars to compete with Japanese rivals Yamaha and Ibanez, but found that it sold more guitars when it charged more for them. Consumers perceived that the higher price indicated a better quality instrument.[43]

Of course, brand names send signals to consumers. The brand names of Close-Up toothpaste, DieHard batteries, and Caress moisturizing soap, for example, identify important product qualities. Names chosen for search engines and sites on the Internet, such as Bing, Amazon.com, and Excite, are intended to convey excitement, intensity, and vastness. Companies may even change their names to send a message to consumers. As today's utility companies increasingly enter unregulated markets, many are shaking their stodgy "Power & Light & Electric" names in favor of those that let consumers know they are not just about electricity anymore, such as Reliant Resources, Entergy, and Cinergy.

Consumers also associate quality and reliability with certain brand names. Companies watch their brand identity closely, in large part because a strong link has been established between perceived brand value and customer loyalty. Brand names that consistently enjoy high perceived value from consumers include Kraft, Disney, National Geographic, Mercedes-Benz, and Fisher-Price. Naming a product after a place can also add perceived value by association. Brand names using the words Santa Fe, Dakota, or Texas convey a sense of openness, freedom, and youth, but products named after other locations might conjure up images of pollution and crime.

Marketing managers are also interested in the *threshold level of perception*: the minimum difference in a stimulus that the consumer will notice. This concept is sometimes referred to as the "just-noticeable difference." For example, how much would Apple have to drop the price of its iPad before consumers recognized it as a bargain—$25? $50? or more? One study found that the just-noticeable difference in a stimulus is about a 20 percent change. For example, consumers will likely notice a 20 percent price decrease more quickly than a 15 percent decrease. This marketing principle can be applied to other marketing variables as well, such as package size or loudness of a broadcast advertisement.[44]

Besides changing such stimuli as price, package size, and volume, marketers can change the product or attempt to reposition its image. But marketers must be careful when adding features. How many new services will discounter Target Stores need to add before consumers perceive it as a full-service department store? How many sporty features will General Motors have to add to a basic two-door sedan before consumers start perceiving it as a sports car?

Marketing managers who intend to do business in global markets should be aware of how foreign consumers perceive their products. For instance, in Japan, product labels are often written in English or French, even though they may not translate into anything meaningful. Many Japanese associate foreign words on product labels with the exotic, the expensive, and high quality.

Marketers have often been suspected of sending advertising messages subconsciously to consumers in what is known as *subliminal perception*. The controversy began when a researcher claimed to have increased popcorn and Coca-Cola sales at a movie theater after flashing "Eat popcorn" and "Drink Coca-Cola" on the screen every five seconds for 1/300th of a second, although the audience did not consciously recognize the messages. Almost immediately consumer protection groups became concerned that advertisers were brainwashing consumers, and this practice was pronounced illegal in California and Canada. Although the researcher later admitted to making up the data and scientists have been unable to replicate the study since, consumers are still wary of hidden messages that advertisers may be sending.

MOTIVATION

By studying motivation, marketers can analyze the major forces influencing consumers to buy or not buy products. When you buy a product, you usually do so to fulfill some kind of need. These needs become motives when aroused sufficiently. For instance, suppose this morning you were so hungry before class that you needed to eat something. In response to that need, you stopped at McDonald's for an Egg McMuffin. In other words, you were motivated by hunger to stop at McDonald's. **Motives** are the driving forces that cause a person to take action to satisfy specific needs.

Why are people driven by particular needs at particular times? One popular theory is **Maslow's hierarchy of needs**, shown in Exhibit 6.9, which arranges needs in ascending order of importance: physiological, safety, social, esteem, and self-actualization. As a person fulfills one need, a higher level need becomes more important.

motive
A driving force that causes a person to take action to satisfy specific needs.

Maslow's hierarchy of needs
A method of classifying human needs and motivations into five categories in ascending order of importance: physiological, safety, social, esteem, and self-actualization.

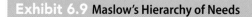

Exhibit 6.9 Maslow's Hierarchy of Needs

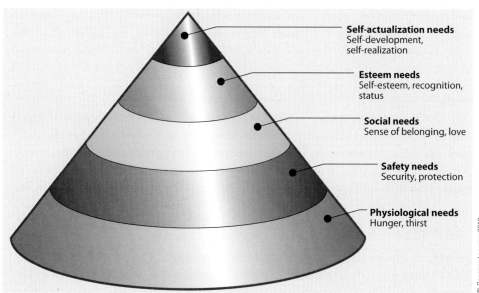

Self-actualization needs
Self-development, self-realization

Esteem needs
Self-esteem, recognition, status

Social needs
Sense of belonging, love

Safety needs
Security, protection

Physiological needs
Hunger, thirst

© Cengage Learning 2013

The most basic human needs are *physiological*—that is, the needs for food, water, and shelter. Because they are essential to survival, these needs must be satisfied first. Ads showing a juicy hamburger or a runner gulping down Gatorade after a marathon are examples of appeals to satisfy the physiological needs of hunger and thirst.

Safety needs include security and freedom from pain and discomfort. Marketers sometimes appeal to consumers' fears and anxieties about safety to sell their products. For example, aware of the aging population's health fears, the retail medical imaging centers Heart Check America and HealthScreen America advertise that they offer consumers a full body scan for early detection of health problems such as coronary disease and cancer. On the other hand, some companies or industries advertise to allay consumer fears. For example, in the wake of the September 11 terrorist attacks, the airline industry found itself having to conduct an image campaign to reassure consumers about the safety of air travel.

After physiological and safety needs have been fulfilled, *social needs*—especially love and a sense of belonging—become the focus. Love includes acceptance by one's peers, as well as sex and romantic love. Marketing managers probably appeal more to this need than to any other. Ads for clothes, cosmetics, and vacation packages suggest that buying the product can bring love. The need to belong is also a favorite of marketers, especially those marketing products to teens.

Love is acceptance without regard to one's contribution. Esteem is acceptance based on one's contribution to the group. *Self-esteem needs* include self-respect and a sense of accomplishment. Esteem needs also include prestige, fame, and recognition of one's accomplishments. Montblanc pens, Mercedes-Benz automobiles, and Neiman Marcus stores all appeal to esteem needs. Most high-end spas and health clubs appeal to consumers' self-esteem needs. Like exclusive country clubs, clubs such as Chicago's East Bank Club are designed to make members feel proud of their commitment to fitness while also giving them a sense of social accomplishment. In fact, the clubs can be so effective that even during an economic recession, patrons will not give up their membership because to do so would be a public admission of financial problems.

Asian consumers, in particular, are strongly motivated by status and appearance. Asians tend to be conscious of their place in a group, institution, or society as a whole. The importance of gaining social recognition turns Asians into some of the most image-conscious consumers in the world. Status-conscious Asians will not hesitate to spend freely on premium brands, such as BMW, Mercedes-Benz, and the best Scotch whiskey and French cognac. Indeed, marketers of luxury products such as Gucci, Louis Vuitton, and Prada find that demand for their products is so strong among image-conscious consumers that their sales are generally unaffected by economic downturns. In some cases, companies have been able to make up for sluggish European and U.S. sales by raising prices and volume in Asia.

The highest human need is *self-actualization*. It refers to finding self-fulfillment and self-expression, reaching the point in life at which "people are what they feel they should be." Maslow felt that very few people ever attain this level. Even so, advertisements may focus on this type of need. For example, American Express ads convey the message that acquiring its card is one of the highest attainments in life.

LEARNING

learning
A process that creates changes in behavior, immediate or expected, through experience and practice.

Almost all consumer behavior results from **learning**, which is the process that creates changes in behavior through experience and practice. It is not possible to observe learning directly, but we can infer when it has occurred by a person's actions.

For example, suppose you see an advertisement for a new and improved cold medicine. If you go to the store that day and buy that remedy, we infer that you have learned something about the cold medicine.

There are two types of learning: experiential and conceptual. *Experiential learning* occurs when an experience changes your behavior. For example, if the new cold medicine does not relieve your symptoms, you may not buy that brand again. *Conceptual learning*, which is not acquired through direct experience, is the second type of learning. Assume, for example, that you are standing at a soft drink machine and notice a new diet flavor with an artificial sweetener. Because someone has told you that diet beverages leave an aftertaste, you choose a different drink. You have learned that you would not like this new diet drink without ever trying it.

Reinforcement and repetition boost learning. Reinforcement can be positive or negative. If you see a vendor selling frozen yogurt (stimulus), buy it (response), and find the yogurt to be quite refreshing (reward), your behavior has been positively reinforced. On the other hand, if you buy a new flavor of yogurt and it does not taste good (negative reinforcement), you will not buy that flavor of yogurt again (response). Without positive or negative reinforcement, a person will not be motivated to repeat the behavior pattern or to avoid it. Thus, if a new brand evokes neutral feelings, some marketing activity, such as a price change or an increase in promotion, may be required to induce further consumption. Learning theory is helpful in reminding marketers that concrete and timely actions are what reinforce desired consumer behavior.

Repetition is a key strategy in promotional campaigns because it can lead to increased learning. Most marketers use repetitive advertising so that consumers will learn what their unique advantage is over the competition. Generally, to heighten learning, advertising messages should be spread out over time rather than clustered together.

A related learning concept useful to marketing managers is stimulus generalization. In theory, **stimulus generalization** occurs when one response is extended to a second stimulus similar to the first. Marketers often use a successful, well-known brand name for a family of products because it gives consumers familiarity with and knowledge about each product in the family. Such brand-name families spur the introduction of new products and facilitate the sale of existing items. Jell-O frozen pudding pops rely on the familiarity of Jell-O gelatin; Clorox bathroom cleaner relies on familiarity with Clorox bleach; and Dove shampoo relies on familiarity with Dove soap. Microsoft entered the video game industry, hoping that the Microsoft brand would guarantee sales for the Xbox. Initial response to the Xbox was strong based on Microsoft's reputation. Since then, Microsoft has worked hard to be successful in an industry dominated by other brand giants Sony and Nintendo.

Another form of stimulus generalization occurs when retailers or wholesalers design their packages to resemble well-known manufacturers' brands. Such imitation often confuses consumers, who buy the imitation thinking it's the original. U.S. manufacturers in foreign markets have sometimes found little, if any, brand protection. BMW recently sued Chinese car manufacturers for creating near-exact replicas of their cars. Cosmetics giant L'Oreal, maker of Gucci and other luxury brands, is threatening legal action against eBay unless the auction site cracks down on sales of counterfeit L'Oreal products on its site. DVD piracy is rampant in China, so much so that special DVD-counterfeit-sniffing dogs have become a common sight in international airports. After the terrorist attacks of September 11 and subsequent stepped-up security regulations, authentication technologies have been used successfully in identifying fake passports, currency, and credit cards. Those same technologies—and others, such as embedded

stimulus generalization
A form of learning that occurs when one response is extended to a second stimulus similar to the first.

stimulus discrimination
A learned ability to differentiate among similar products.

belief
An organized pattern of knowledge that an individual holds as true about his or her world.

attitude
A learned tendency to respond consistently toward a given object.

microchips, holographic symbols, and tamperproof packaging—are now being used in everyday products such as clothing, footwear, computers, cell phones, video games, jewelry, software, pharmaceuticals, and medical devices, making it easier for importers and retailers to spot fakes.

The opposite of stimulus generalization is **stimulus discrimination**, which means learning to differentiate among similar products. Consumers might perceive one product as more rewarding or stimulating. For example, some consumers prefer Coca-Cola and others prefer Pepsi. Many insist they can taste a difference between the two brands.

With some types of products—such as aspirin, gasoline, bleach, and paper towels—marketers rely on promotion to point out brand differences that consumers would otherwise not recognize. This process, called *product differentiation*, is discussed in more detail in Chapter 8. Usually, product differentiation is based on superficial differences. For example, Bayer tells consumers that it's the aspirin "doctors recommend most."

BELIEFS AND ATTITUDES

Beliefs and attitudes are closely linked to values. A **belief** is an organized pattern of knowledge that an individual holds as true about his or her world. A consumer may believe that Sony's Handycam camcorder makes the best home videos, tolerates hard use, and is reasonably priced. These beliefs may be based on knowledge, faith, or hearsay. Consumers tend to develop a set of beliefs about a product's attributes and then, through these beliefs, form a *brand image*—a set of beliefs about a particular brand. In turn, the brand image shapes consumers' attitudes toward the product.

An **attitude** is a learned tendency to respond consistently toward a given object, such as a brand. Attitudes rest on an individual's value system, which represents personal standards of good and bad, right and wrong, and so forth; therefore, attitudes tend to be more enduring and complex than beliefs.

For an example of the nature of attitudes, consider the differing attitudes of consumers around the world toward the practice of purchasing on credit. Americans have long been enthusiastic about charging goods and services and are willing to pay high interest rates for the privilege of postponing payment. To many European consumers, doing what amounts to taking out a loan—even a small one—to pay for anything seems absurd. Germans especially are reluctant to buy on credit. Italy has a sophisticated credit and banking system well suited to handling credit cards, but Italians prefer to carry cash, often huge wads of it. Although most Japanese consumers have credit cards, card purchases amount to less than 1 percent of all consumer transactions. The Japanese have long looked down on credit purchases, but acquire cards to use while traveling abroad.

If a good or service is meeting its profit goals, positive attitudes toward the product merely need to be reinforced. If the brand is not succeeding, however, the marketing manager must strive to change target consumers' attitudes toward it. Changes in attitude tend to grow out of an individual's attempt to reconcile long-held values with a constant stream of new information. This change can be accomplished in three ways: changing beliefs about the brand's attributes, changing the relative importance of these beliefs, and adding new beliefs.

Changing Beliefs about Attributes The first technique is to turn neutral, negative, or incorrect beliefs about product attributes into positive ones. Assume that 24 Hour Fitness does a survey among persons considering joining a health club. They find that most respondents believe that 24 Hour Fitness offers fewer classes and less variety than Shapes, Curves for Women, or Lifestyle Family Fitness. In fact, 24 Hour Fitness offers greater variety and more classes than any other health and fitness center. Thus, target consumers have incorrect beliefs about the service's attributes (number of classes and variety). This means that 24 Hour Fitness must advertise and do other forms of promotion, such as an open house, to correct the misimpressions.

Changing beliefs about a service can be more difficult because service attributes are usually intangible. Convincing consumers to switch hairstylists or lawyers or go to a mall dental clinic can be much more difficult than getting them to change brands of razor blades. Image, which is also largely intangible, significantly determines service patronage.

Usually changing beliefs about a product attribute is easier. For example, GE has created a new light bulb, a compact fluorescent lamp (CFL), that uses one-third the energy of a traditional bulb, lasts nearly ten times longer, and can save up to $30 in energy costs over its lifetime. GE's new campaign urges the use of its new bulb by appealing to Americans' burgeoning ecological awareness, while exhibiting its own "care" for the world's resources. How could the consumer possibly resist when GE has made it so easy to participate? If every American swapped one standard bulb for a CFL, it would collectively prevent burning 30 billion pounds of coal and remove two million cars' worth of greenhouse gas emissions from the atmosphere.[45] Service marketing is explored in detail in Chapter 12.

Changing the Importance of Beliefs The second approach to modifying attitudes is to change the relative importance of beliefs about an attribute. Cole Haan, originally a men's shoe outfitter, used boats and cars in its ads for years to associate the brand with active lifestyles, an important attribute for men. Now that it is selling women's products such as handbags and shoes, some of its ads use models and emphasize how the products look, an important attribute for women. The company hopes the ads will change customers' perceptions and beliefs that it sells only men's products.

Marketers can also emphasize the importance of some beliefs over others. For example, when consumers think of full-sized SUVs, good gas mileage doesn't often come to mind. Now, Cadillac wants to raise the importance of fuel efficiency to buyers of full-size SUVs. The promotion for the Escalade Hybrid says, "Finally, a full-size luxury SUV confident enough to talk about fuel efficiency."

Adding New Beliefs The third approach to transforming attitudes is to add new beliefs. Although changes in consumption patterns often come slowly, cereal marketers are betting that consumers will eventually warm up to the idea of cereal as a snack. A print ad for General Mills Cookie-Crisp cereal features a boy popping the sugary nuggets into his mouth while he does his homework. Koch Industries, the manufacturer of Dixie paper products, is also attempting to add new beliefs about the uses of its paper plates and cups with an advertising campaign aimed at positioning its product as a "home cleanup replacement." Commercials pitch Dixie paper plates as an alternative to washing dishes after everyday meals and not just for picnics.

U.S. companies attempting to market their goods overseas may need to help consumers add new beliefs about a product in general. Coca-Cola and PepsiCo have both found it challenging to sell their diet cola brands to consumers in India partly because diet foods of any kind are a new concept in that country

In a low-fat culture, REAL Butter has been working to add beliefs that real butter (rather than margarine) makes baked goods extra special—perfect for holiday giving.

where malnutrition was widespread not too many years ago. Indians also have deep-rooted attitudes that anything labeled "diet" is meant for a sick person, such as a diabetic. As a general rule, most Indians are not diet-conscious, preferring food prepared in the traditional manner that tastes good. Indians are also suspicious of the artificial sweeteners used in diet colas.

Review
LO8

Identify and understand the psychological factors that affect consumer buying decisions

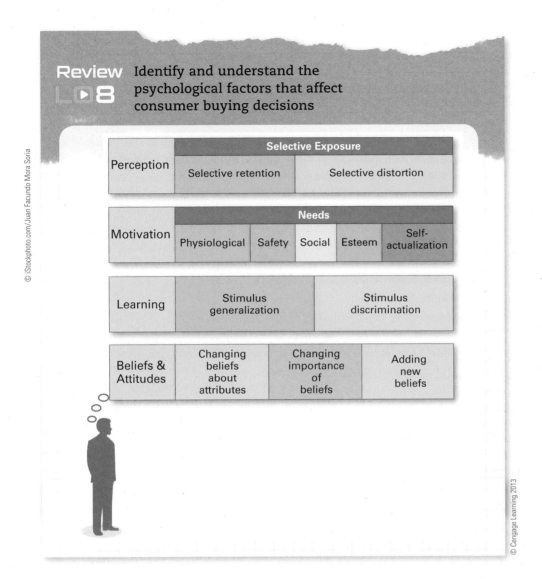

Perception	Selective Exposure	
	Selective retention	Selective distortion

Motivation	Needs				
	Physiological	Safety	Social	Esteem	Self-actualization

Learning	Stimulus generalization	Stimulus discrimination

Beliefs & Attitudes	Changing beliefs about attributes	Changing importance of beliefs	Adding new beliefs

© Cengage Learning 2013

© iStockphoto.com/Juan Facundo Mora Soria

Number of factors determining the three types of consumer buying decisions

Kellogg's cereal advertising budget

Projected growth rate for the U.S. population

Projected growth rate for the population of African American women

Percentage of American Hispanics reached by Univision Radio

Reported worth of Nike's endorsement deal with LeBron James

Number of blogs monitored by Technorati

5 $206 million 4% 8% 73 $90 million 70 million

Review and Applications

LO1 **Explain why marketing managers should understand consumer behavior.** Consumer behavior describes how consumers make purchase decisions and how they use and dispose of the products they buy. An understanding of consumer behavior reduces marketing managers' uncertainty when they are defining a target market and designing a marketing mix.

1.1 The type of decision making a consumer uses for a product does not necessarily remain constant. Why? Support your answer with an example from your own experience.

LO2 **Analyze the components of the consumer decision-making process.** The consumer decision-making process begins with need recognition, when stimuli trigger awareness of an unfulfilled want. If additional information is required to make a purchase decision, the consumer may engage in an internal or external information search. The consumer then evaluates the additional information and establishes purchase guidelines. Finally, a purchase decision is made.

 2.1 Visit Carpoint's Web site at **http://autos.msn.com/.** How does the site assist consumers in the evaluation stage of choosing a new car? Develop your own hypothetical evoked set of three or four car models and present your comparisons. Which vehicle attributes would be most important in your purchase decision?

LO3 **Explain the consumer's postpurchase evaluation process.** Consumer postpurchase evaluation is influenced by prepurchase expectations, the prepurchase information search, and the consumer's general level of self-confidence. Cognitive dissonance is the inner tension that a consumer experiences after recognizing a purchased product's disadvantages. When a purchase creates cognitive dissonance, consumers tend to react by seeking positive reinforcement for the purchase decision, avoiding negative information about the purchase decision, or revoking the purchase decision by returning the product.

writing

3.1 Recall an occasion when you experienced cognitive dissonance about a purchase. In a letter to a friend, describe the event and explain what you did about it.

LO4 **Identify the types of consumer buying decisions and discuss the significance of consumer involvement.** Consumer decision making falls into three broad categories. First, consumers exhibit routine response behavior for frequently purchased, low-cost items that require very little decision effort; routine response behavior is typically characterized by brand loyalty. Second, consumers engage in limited decision making for occasional purchases or for unfamiliar brands in familiar product categories. Third, consumers practice extensive decision making when making unfamiliar, expensive, or infrequent purchases. High-involvement decisions usually include an extensive information search and a thorough evaluation of alternatives. In contrast, low-involvement decisions are characterized by brand loyalty and a lack of personal identification with the product. The main factors affecting the level of consumer involvement are previous experience, interest, perceived risk of negative consequences (financial, social, and psychological), situation, and social visibility.

4.1 Describe the three categories of consumer decision-making behavior. Name typical products for which each type of consumer behavior is used.

4.2 Describe the level of involvement and the involvement factors likely to be associated with buying a new computer. Do you think Apple's Web site at **www.apple.com** simplifies or complicates the process for the average consumer? Explain.

LO5 **Identify and understand the cultural factors that affect consumer buying decisions.** Cultural influences on consumer buying decisions include culture and values, subculture, and social class. Culture is the essential character of a society that distinguishes it from other cultural groups. The underlying elements of every culture are the values, language, myths, customs, rituals, laws, and artifacts, or products, that are transmitted from one generation to the next. The most defining element of a culture is its values—the enduring beliefs shared by a society that a specific mode of conduct is personally or socially preferable to another mode of conduct. A culture can be divided into subcultures on the basis of demographic characteristics, geographic regions, national and ethnic background, political beliefs, and religious beliefs. Subcultures share elements of the overall culture as well as cultural elements unique to their own group. A social class is a group of people who are considered nearly equal in status or community esteem, who regularly socialize among themselves both formally and informally, and who share behavioral norms.

5.1 You are a new marketing manager for a firm that produces a line of athletic shoes to be targeted to the college student subculture. In a memo to your boss, list some product attributes that might appeal to this subculture and the steps in your customers' purchase processes, and recommend some marketing strategies that can influence their decision.

writing

Identify and understand the social factors that affect consumer buying decisions. Social factors include external influences such as reference groups, opinion leaders, and family. Consumers seek out others' opinions for guidance on new products or services and products with image-related attributes or because attribute information is lacking or uninformative. Consumers may use products or brands to identify with or become a member of a reference group. Opinion leaders are members of reference groups who influence others' purchase decisions. Family members also influence purchase decisions; children tend to shop in similar patterns as their parents.

6.1 Family members play many different roles in the buying process: initiator, influencer, decision maker, purchaser, and consumer. Identify the person in your family who might play each of these roles in the purchase of a dinner at Pizza Hut, a summer vacation, Fruit Loops breakfast cereal, an Abercrombie & Fitch sweater, golf clubs, an Internet service provider, and a new car.

Identify and understand the individual factors that affect consumer buying decisions. Individual factors that affect consumer buying decisions include gender; age and family life-cycle stage; and personality, self-concept, and lifestyle. Beyond obvious physiological differences, men and women differ in their social and economic roles, and that affects consumer buying decisions. How old a consumer is generally indicates what products he or she may be interested in purchasing. Marketers often define their target markets in terms of consumers' life-cycle stage, following changes in consumers' attitudes and behavioral tendencies as they mature. Finally, certain products and brands reflect consumers' personality, self-concept, and lifestyle.

7.1 Assume you are involved in the following consumer decision situations: (a) renting a DVD to watch with your roommates, (b) choosing a fast-food restaurant to go to with a new friend, (c) buying a popular music compact disc, and (d) buying jeans to wear to class. List the individual factors that would influence your decision in each situation and explain your responses.

Identify and understand the psychological factors that affect consumer buying decisions. Psychological factors include perception, motivation, learning, values, beliefs, and attitudes. These factors allow consumers to interact with the world around them, recognize their feelings, gather and analyze information, formulate thoughts and opinions, and take action. Perception allows consumers to recognize their consumption problems. Motivation is what drives consumers to take action to satisfy specific consumption needs.

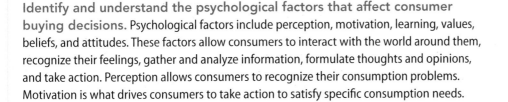

Almost all consumer behavior results from learning, which is the process that creates changes in behavior through experience. Consumers with similar beliefs and attitudes tend to react alike to marketing-related inducements.

8.1 How do beliefs and attitudes influence consumer behavior? How can negative attitudes toward a product be changed? How can marketers alter beliefs about a product? Give some examples of how marketers have changed negative attitudes about a product or added or altered beliefs about a product.

Key Terms

aspirational reference group *209*

attitude *224*

belief *224*

brand extensions *193*

cognitive dissonance *195*

consumer behavior *185*

consumer decision-making process *186*

culture *200*

evoked set (consideration set) *192*

extensive decision making *196*

external information search *188*

ideal self-image *217*

internal information search *188*

involvement *196*

learning *222*

lifestyle *217*

limited decision making *196*

marketing-controlled information source *191*

Maslow's hierarchy of needs *221*

motive *221*

need recognition *186*

nonaspirational reference group *210*

nonmarketing-controlled information source *188*

norm *209*

opinion leader *211*

perception *219*

personality *216*

primary membership group *209*

real self-image *217*

reference group *209*

routine response behavior *196*

secondary membership group *209*

selective distortion *219*

selective exposure *219*

selective retention *219*

self-concept *217*

self-monitoring *217*

shilling *212*

social class *206*

socialization process *212*

sponsored blog *212*

stimulus *186*

stimulus discrimination *224*

stimulus generalization *223*

subculture *204*

value *202*

want *186*

Exercises

ethics

ETHICS EXERCISE

EyeOnU operates a Web filter service for public schools and libraries to protect students from inappropriate material on the Internet. Like the industry as a whole, the company's market share has been stagnant for the past two years. Looking for new sources of revenue, the company is considering selling the data it has collected about student surfing habits to marketers trying to learn more about students' behavior on the Web. The data are anonymous, but privacy advocates are concerned about the precedent of selling information about children to marketers.

Questions

1. What should EyeOnU do? Should it protect the student's data, or should it take the opportunity to create new revenues?

2. Visit the COPPA site dedicated to distributing information about the Children's Online Privacy Protection Act at **www.coppa.org/comply.htm**. Then write a brief paragraph on the responsibilities a Web site operator has to protect children's privacy and safety online and how that relates to EyeOnU's dilemma.

MARKETING PLAN EXERCISE

The next step in preparing a marketing plan for the company you chose in Part 1 is to get a thorough understanding of the marketing opportunities in terms of marketing to customers. Once you've completed the marketing plan exercise for each chapter in Part 2 of this textbook, you can complete the Part 2 Marketing Planning Worksheet by logging on to the companion Web site www.cengagebrain.com. Complete the following exercises:

1. Describe the decision-making process that customers go through when purchasing your company's product or service. What are the critical factors that influence this purchase-behavior process? How will this decision-making affect your e-marketing focus and your market offering? If you have a brick-and-mortar presence, will you encourage any existing customers to shop online? Why or why not?

2. Nonmarketing periodicals can help you understand consumer behavior and apply what you've learned to your marketing plan. Research articles from such publications as the *Journal of Psychology*, *Journal of American Ethnic History*, *Psychology Today*, *Race and Class*, *Working Woman*, *Society*, and others. Select and read three articles that explore different topics (i.e., do not select three articles on psychology). Then, make a list of factors you think could affect consumer purchasing behavior. Include with each factor a way marketers could use this information to their benefit.

APPLICATION EXERCISE

Principles of consumer behavior are evident in many areas of marketing. Perhaps the easiest place to see this critical foundation of marketing activity is in print ads.

Activities

1. Review the main concepts in this chapter and create a checklist that itemizes them. Then, comb through your favorite magazines and newspapers for advertisements that illustrate each concept. To get a wide variety of ads, you will need to look through several magazines. If you don't have many magazines at your disposal, go to the campus library periodical room. Photocopy the ads you select to support this chapter.

2. Because pictures can help reinforce understanding, consider doing this exercise for each chapter in the book. At the end of the semester, you will have a portfolio of ads that illustrate the concepts in the entire book, which can help you study. Simply look through your portfolio and try to recall the concepts at work in each advertisement. This exercise can be a prelude to a longer study session for comprehensive exams.

CASE STUDY: Ethel's Chocolate Lounges

BACK TO THE FUTURE? CHOCOLATE LOUNGES TASTE SWEET SUCCESS

The chocolate house dates back to seventeenth-century London, when members of society's elite would gather in luxurious surroundings to relax and sip hot chocolate. Later, Europeans expanded on that idea and developed solid chocolate treats that sold in upscale boutiques. Lacking the resources and economy of established continentals, bootstrapping American settlers pioneered the development of cheaper chocolate bars for the masses.

Centuries have passed, however, and the American palate has tired of the taste of mass-produced chocolate. The U.S. chocolate industry has experienced growth of less than 3 percent since the turn of the millennium, and the lack of industry innovation has left a bad taste in chocolate purveyors' mouths, too. Enter Ethel's Chocolate Lounges, named in honor of the matriarch of the Mars family, who founded the candy company with her husband Frank in 1911.

Now Ethel Mars's name adorns the signs at the company's latest attempt to breathe fresh life into chocolate. Aware that chocolate sales at upscale retail outlets, like Godiva and Starbucks grew by nearly 20 percent from 2002 to 2004, Mars opened Ethel's Chocolate Lounge in the Lincoln Park neighborhood of Chicago in April 2005. More Ethel's Lounges have opened since then, and the chic chocolate houses are Mars's bet that well-heeled and sweet-toothed consumers will take to premium chocolate the same way that well-to-do coffee lovers flock to Starbucks for high-priced java. Ethel's Lounges are designed to coddle patrons in the lap of luxury, but Mars president John Haugh maintains that what makes Ethel's special is that it offers "approachable gourmet chocolate." In other words, you don't have to be a millionaire to enjoy the sweet taste of the good life.

Prices are not for everyone's wallet, however. Truffles and Tea for Two, which features all 11 of Ethel's truffles served on a silver platter, sells for $15. Chocolates and Cocoa for Two includes two cocoas and 10 pieces of chocolate for $18, and a box of 48 chocolates is $42. Five "Collections" offer over 50 individual chocolates that sell for between $.90 and $1.50.

Supporting Haugh's claim of approachability, though, the menus at Ethel's feature icons and descriptions of the chocolates' contents so that customers won't experience an unwanted surprise. A multitude of hot and cold beverages give visitors more reasons to extend their stays.

But it's not just the chocolate that makes Ethel's such a desirable destination. Advertising describes Ethel's as "a place for chocolate and chitchat." Generously stuffed pink couches with brown accents combine upscale modern and traditional looks to give the stores a hip and classy feel. For those who don't immediately get it, a sign behind the counter reads, "Chocolate is the new black." The stores' appeal is their relaxing ambience and neighborhood vibe—like a modern American coffeehouse, these shops encourage socializing and extended lounging. The effect is carefully planned. Mars's research revealed that even calorie-conscious consumers will splurge for the good stuff as long as a broader social experience comes with it.

Parallels to the Starbucks-led American coffee revival are obvious and inescapable. Confectionary industry insiders note that chocolate cafés are taking hold, and research confirms their belief. Datamonitor, a research firm specializing in trend identification, described chocolate as "the new coffee" on its list of the top ten trends to watch in 2006. The popularity of the Chocolate Bar in New York, billed as a "candy store for grown-ups," and South Bend Chocolate's ten chocolate cafés shows that the trend is for real. Even some Hershey's stores now offer seating for patrons.

Joan Steuer, president of Chocolate Marketing, claims that, for women, enjoying chocolate in a luxurious lounge is like taking a candle-lit bubble bath. She notes, too, that much of the appeal is that the experience is testimony to the person's upward mobility. It's a perfect way to cater to the American desire to have the best that money can buy.[46]

Questions

1. What type of consumer buying decision best describes the choice to indulge at Ethel's?

2. List the factors that might influence a consumer to spend money and time at Ethel's. Which factor do you think will motivate a consumer the most? Why?

3. Review the core American values in Exhibit 6.5. Which value does the Ethel's experience appeal to most? Explain.

COMPANY CLIPS: ReadyMade—Do-It-Yourself

In 2001 when Grace Hawthorne, CEO, and Shoshana Berger, Editor-in-Chief, came up with their idea for *ReadyMade*, there were no other publications with their unique do-it-yourself (DIY) theme. *ReadyMade* was to be a magazine about fun and creative projects for the home. Since its development, the bimonthly magazine has enjoyed a loyal subscriber base and continues to gain readership across the country. All issues include numerous DIY projects, each rated by their level of difficulty, as well as several feature articles exploring the latest in innovation and design. In this video, pay attention to *ReadyMade's* methods as they launched their magazine. Note also how *ReadyMade* uses its knowledge of its consumer base to tailor the product.

Questions

1. While the *ReadyMade* magazine was still in the design stages, very little research was done to determine whether an interested market existed. Did this adversely affect the magazine as it moved forward to publication? Explain.

2. How does the cover of *ReadyMade* magazine reflect the principles of packaging design as influenced by the known behaviors of its consumers?

3. To what extent does *ReadyMade* rely on opinion leaders to promote the magazine? Is this a successful tactic?

marketing&you: Results.

High scores suggest that you tend to shop for value, whereas lower scores indicate compulsive buying, or excessive shopping relative to your disposable income. Lower scores also suggest that you may use excessive shopping to deal with undesirable moods or negative feelings. Even though your mood might improve afterward, beware: The change is temporary, compulsive shopping behavior is very difficult to stop, and you can experience harmful consequences as a result.

Notes

1. "New Tax on Indoor Tanning Goes into Effect," *CBS*, June 30, 2010, www.cbsnews.com/stories/2010/06/30/eveningnews/main6635131.shtml.
2. Lance A. Bettencourt and Anthony W. Ulwich, "The Customer-Centered Innovation Map," *Harvard Business Review*, May 2008, 1–8; also see Anthony W. Ulwich and Lance A. Bettencourt, "Giving Customers a Fair Hearing," *Sloan Management Review*, Spring 2008, 62–68.
3. "By the Numbers," *Next*, May 17, 2010, 24.
4. Elisabeth Sullivan, "Virtually Satisfied," *Marketing News*, October 15, 2008, 26.
5. Allen Weiss, Nicholas Lurie, and Deborah MacInnis, "Listening to Strangers: Whose Responses Are Valuable, How Valuable Are They, and Why?" *Journal of Marketing Research*, August 2008, 450–461.
6. Feng Zhu and Xiaoquan (Michael) Zhang, "Impact of Online Consumer Reviews on Sales: The Moderating Role of Product and Consumer Characteristics," *Journal of Marketing*, March 2010, 133–148.
7. "More Car Shoppers Happy to Peruse a Virtual Lot," *Quirk's Marketing Research Review*, February 2010, 8.
8. *Ibid*.
9. Jonah Berger and Grainne Fitzsimons, "Dogs on the Street, Pumas on Your Feet: How Cues in the Environment Influence Product Evaluation and Choice," *Journal of Marketing Research*, February 2008, 1–14.
10. Jeffrey Inman and Russell Winer, "Impulse Buys," *Wall Street Journal*, April 15, 1999, A1; and David Silvera, Anne Lavack, and Frederic Kropp, "Impulse Buying: The Role of Affect, Social Influence, and Subjective Well-Being," *Journal of Consumer Research*, Vol. 25, Issue 1 (2008) 23–33.
11. "Priorities at the Store," *Adweek Media*, February 9, 2009, 14.
12. "What Post-Recession Behavior Means for Marketers Today," *Marketing News*, September 3, 2009, 34–37.
13. O. T. Howard and R. A. Kerin "Broadening the Scope of Reference Price Advertising Research: A Field Study of Shopping Involvement," *Journal of Marketing*, October 2006, 185–204.
14. Karin Stilley, Jeffrey Inman, and Kirk Wakefield, "Spending on the Fly: Mental Budgets, Promotions, and Spending Behavior," *Journal of Marketing*, May 2010, 34–47; also see Jeffrey Inman, Russell Winer, and Rosellina Ferraro, "The Interplay among Category Characteristics, Customer Characteristics, and Customer Activities on In-Store Decision Making" *Journal of Marketing*, September 2009, 19–29.
15. Types of Involvement from Barry Babin and Eric Harris, *CB²* (Mason: Ohio: South-Western Cengage Learning) 2011, 88–89. Reprinted with permission.
16. Ira Teinowitz, "Kellogg Move Bodes Ill for Ads to Kids," *Advertising Age*, June 18, 2007.
17. Sandra Yin, "Color Blind," *American Demographics*, September 2003, 24, 26.
18. Geoff Calvin, "Selling P&G," *Fortune*, September 17, 2007, 6, 156, 163.
19. Andria Cheng, "Costco Cracks Taiwan Market," *Wall Street Journal*, April 2, 2010, B5.
20. Lorenza Muñoz, "Selling Spanish TV to Ad Buyers," *Los Angeles Times*, May 15, 2007.
21. Harold Meyerson, "Rise of the Have-Nots," *Washington Post*, September 27, 2007, www.washingtonpost.com/wp-dyn/content/article/2007/09/26/AR2007092602069.html.
22. Bradley Johnson, "Mo' Money, Mo' Buyin'," *Advertising Age*, January 15, 2007, 78, 3, 29.
23. Orth Ulrich and Lynn Kahle, "Intrapersonal Variation in Consumer Susceptibility to Normative Influence: Toward a Better Understanding of Brand Choice Decisions," *Journal of Social Psychology*, August 8, 2008, 423–448.
24. *Ibid*.
25. Ronald Clark, James Zboja, and Ronald Goldsmith, "Status Consumption and Role-Relaxed Consumption: A Tale of Two Retail Consumers," *Journal of Retailing and Consumer Services*, January 2007, 45–59.
26. "BMW Aims to Maintain US Market Share in 2009," *Just-auto*, January 12, 2009, www.just-auto.com/news/bmw-aims-to-maintain-us-market-share-in-2009_id97482.aspx.
27. Adam Singer, "Sponsored Posts-Measure the Risk Carefully," *Top Rank*, www.toprankblog.com/2010/04/sponsored-posts (Accessed January 28, 2011).
28. Pradnya Joshi, "Approval by a Blogger May Please a Sponsor," *New York Times*, July 12, 2009.
29. Kevin Zheng Zhou, Nan Zhou and Julie Juan Li, "Harmonizing Conflict in Husband-Wife Purchase Decision-Making: Perceived Fairness and Spousal Influence Dynamics," *Journal of the Academy Marketing Science*, Fall 2008, 378–394; also see Michel Laroche, Zhiyong Yang, Kim Chankon, and Marie-Odile Richard, "How Culture Matters in Children's Purchase Influence: A Multi-Level Investigation," *Journal of the Academy of Marketing Science*, Spring 2007, 113–116.
30. *Ibid*.
31. Derek Gale, "Who's the Boss?" *Restaurants & Institutions*, February 1, 2007, 2, 50, 117.
32. Jeanine Poggi, "Teen Queens: The Age Group's Spending Is on the Rise, Making It a Coveted—Albeit Fickle—Market," *WWD*, June 28, 2007, 85.
33. "Seventeen Survey: Teens Spending and the Recession," *Ypulse*, May 4, 2009, www.ypulse.com/seventeen-survey-teens-spending-and-the-recession.
34. Karen Ekstrom, "Parental Consumer Learning or 'Keeping Up with Their Children'," *Journal of Consumer Behavior*, July/August 2007, 203–217.
35. Nanette Byrnes, "Secrets of the Male Shopper," *BusinessWeek*, September 4, 2006, www.businessweek.com/magazine/content/06_36/b3999001.htm; also see Xin He, Jeffrey Inman, and Vikas Mittal, "Gender Jeopardy in Financial Risk-Taking," *Journal of Marketing Research*, August 2008, 414–424.
36. Anil Mathur, George Moschis, and Euehun Lee, "A Longitudinal Study of the Effects of Life Style Status Changes on Changes in Consumer Preferences," *Journal of the Academy of Marketing Sciences*, Summer 2008, 234–246.
37. Stanford Westjohn, Mark Arnold, Peter Magnusson, Srdan Zdravkovic, and Joyce Xin Zhou, "Technology Readiness and Usage: A Global-Identity Perspective," *Journal of the Academy of Marketing Science*, Fall 2009, 250–265.

38. Frank Kardes, Maria Cronley, and Thomas Cline, *Consumer Behavior* (Mason, Ohio: South-Western Cengage Learning, 2011), 158.

39. "Study: Snacking Has Become the Fourth Meal of the Day," *Brandweek*, September 29, 2008, 8.

40. *Ibid.*

41. Loretta Chao and Betsy McKay, "Pepsi Steps into Coke Realm," *Wall Street Journal*, September 12, 2007.

42. "The Masterbatch Leader," Ampacet Corporate Web site, www.ampacet.com/EN/global/corporate_overview.html (Accessed June 13, 2011).

43. Joshua Rosenbaum, "Guitar Maker Looks for a New Key," *Wall Street Journal*, February 11, 1998, B1, B5.

44. Elizabeth J. Wilson, "Using the Dollar-Metric Scale to Establish the Just Meaningful Difference in Price," in *AMA Educators' Proceedings*, ed. Susan Douglas et al. (Chicago: American Marketing Association, 1987), 107.

45. Press release: "GE Announces Advancement in Incandescent Technology; New High-Efficiency Lamps Targeted for Market by 2010," February 23, 2007; Lloyd Alter, "GE Announces High Efficiency Incandescent Light Bulbs. Why?" *Design & Architecture*, February 24, 2007, www.treehugger.com/files/2007/02/ge_announces_hi.php; and "High Efficiency Light Bulb Market Competition Intensifies Between GE and Home Depot," *American Banking and Marketing News*, May 11, 2010, 1.

46. Amy Chozick and Timothy Martin, "A Place for Cocoa Nuts?" *The Wall Street Journal*, July 15, 2005, B1, B3; www.ethelschocolate.com; "Ethel's Launches First-Ever Approachable, Everyday Gourmet Chocolate and Chocolate Lounges; Opens First Two Stores in Chicago, Expected to Expand to Six by End of Summer," PR Newswire, June 6, 2005; Karen Hawkins, "Chocolate Lounges' Present Themselves as Sweet Alternatives to Coffee Shops, Bars," Associated Press, February 13, 2006; Melinda Murphy, "Trend Report: Chocolate Is Hot," CBS News Online, www.cbsnews.com/stories/2006/02/07/earlyshow/contributors/melindamurphy/main1289922.shtml.

Business Marketing

© iStockphoto.com/Juan Facundo Mora Soria; © Sean Gallup/Getty Images

Learning Outcomes

1 Describe business marketing

2 Describe the role of the Internet in business marketing

3 Discuss the role of relationship marketing and strategic alliances in business marketing

4 Identify the four major categories of business market customers

5 Explain the North American Industry Classification System

6 Explain the major differences between business and consumer markets

7 Describe the seven types of business goods and services

8 Discuss the unique aspects of business buying behavior

LO1
What Is Business Marketing?

Business marketing (also called **industrial marketing**) is the marketing of goods and services to individuals and organizations for purposes other than personal consumption. The sale of a personal computer to your college or university is an example of business marketing. Business products include those that are used to manufacture other products, become part of another product, or aid the normal operations of an organization. The key characteristic distinguishing business products from consumer products is intended use, not physical characteristics. A product that is purchased for personal or family consumption or as a gift is a consumer good. If that same product, such as a personal computer or a cell phone, is bought for use in a business, it is a business product. A survey by *B to B Marketing* revealed that the three primary marketing goals of U.S. business marketers are customer acquisition (62 percent), creating brand awareness (19 percent), and customer retention (12 percent).[1]

The size of the business market in the United States and most other countries substantially exceeds that of the consumer market. In the business market, a single customer can account for a huge volume of purchases. For example, IBM's purchasing department spends more than $40 billion annually on business products. Procter & Gamble, Apple, Merck, Dell, and Kimberly-Clark each spend more than half of their annual revenue on business products.[2]

Some large firms that produce goods such as steel, computer memory chips, or production equipment market exclusively to business customers. Other firms

> "The size of the business market in the **United States** exceeds that of the consumer market."

business marketing (industrial marketing) The marketing of goods and services to individuals and organizations for purposes other than personal consumption.

marketing&you.

Think about the last time you dealt with a salesperson when making a major purchase. Then, using the following scales, indicate your opinions of that salesperson.

Using the scale below, enter your answers.

STRONGLY AGREE ◁ 1 · 2 · 3 · 4 · 5 · 6 · 7 ▷ STRONGLY DISAGREE

_____ **This salesperson was frank in dealing with me.**

_____ **This salesperson did not make false claims.**

_____ **I do not think this salesperson was completely open in dealing with me.***

_____ **This salesperson was concerned only about himself/herself.***

_____ **This salesperson did not seem to be concerned with my needs.***

_____ **I did not trust this salesperson.***

_____ **This salesperson was not trustworthy.***

Now, total your score, reversing your answers for the items followed by an asterisk. That is, if you put a 2, change it to a 6; if you put a 3, change it to a 5, and so forth. Read the chapter and find out what your score means at the end.

Source: Scale #920, *Marketing Scales Handbook*, G. Bruner, K. James, H. Hensel, eds., Vol. III. © by American Marketing Association.

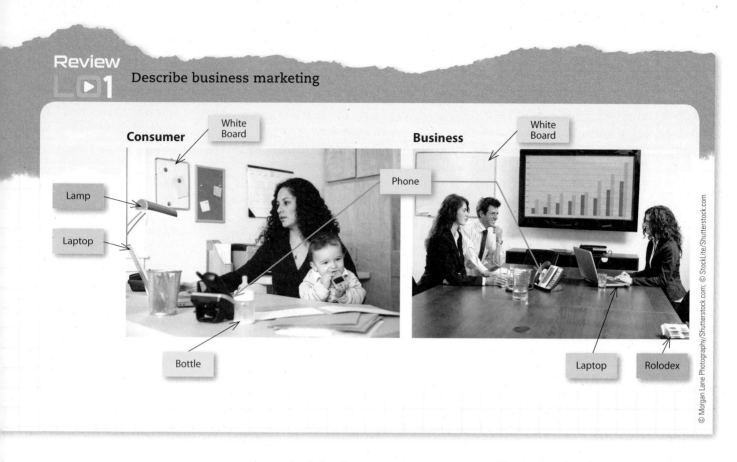

market to both businesses and to consumers. Hewlett-Packard marketed exclusively to business customers in the past, but now markets laser printers and personal computers to consumers. Sony, traditionally a consumer marketer, now sells office automation products to businesses. Both companies have had to make organizational and marketing changes to expand into the new market categories.

LO2
Business Marketing on the Internet

The use of the Internet to facilitate activities between organizations is called **business-to-business electronic commerce** (B-to-B or B2B e-commerce). This method; of conducting business has evolved and grown rapidly throughout its short history. In 1995, the commercial Web sites that did exist were static. Only a few had data-retrieval capabilities. Security of any sort was rare and streaming video did not exist. Today, B2B sites look more like consumer sites with social media and community building applications. Before the Internet, customers had to call Dow Chemical and request a specification sheet for the products they were considering. The information would arrive a few days later by mail. After choosing a product, the customer could then place an order by calling Dow (during business hours, of course). Now, such information is available through MyAccount@Dow, which provides information tailored to the customer's requirements. For example, MyAccount@Dow offers secure internal monitoring of a customer's chemical tank levels. When tanks reach a predetermined level, reordering can be triggered automatically.[3]

business-to-business electronic commerce
The use of the Internet to facilitate the exchange of goods, services, and information between organizations.

Companies selling to business buyers face the same challenges as all marketers including determining who, exactly, the market is and how best to reach them. This is particularly difficult in business marketing because business has rapidly moved online and overseas.[4]

A recent report from Forrester Research, *B2B US Interactive Marketing Forecast 2009–2014*, predicted that interactive spending by B-to-B marketers will reach $4.8 billion by 2014. In 2010, spending was approximately $2.3 billion. Some of the expected increase can be attributed to the recession as companies decide to bypass more expensive offline tactics and opt for more measurable (in most cases) online tactics.[5] Paid search accounts for 70 percent of B-to-B online spending and there have been recent increases in search engine optimization (SEO) and social media as well. Most B-to-B marketers primarily use e-mail marketing, SEO organic, online ads and banners, search keywords, webinars, and viral videos.[6] Many B-to-B brands have a Facebook presence. The use of Twitter and LinkedIn is increasing.[7]

The reviews on social media are mixed. Some B-to-B marketers feel that social media is not as useful to them as it is to business to consumer (B-to-C) marketers.[8] But other experts see a growth in social media use as B-to-B marketers use opportunities to generate high-quality leads. Most of the spending allocation is in creating customer community (32 percent); podcasts (20 percent) and blogs (18 percent) to convey thought leadership; and Twitter (14 percent).[9] It is easy to see that some companies are embracing new tools and applications on their Web sites.

B-to-B marketers are using several tools:

→ **Blogs.** While adoption is slow for some companies, blogs are great ways to highlight expertise. FedEx Corp started its Citizenship Blog, which talks about the company's contributions in community involvement, disaster relief, environmental issues, and work-life balance. This helps its customers feel that they are a good cultural match with FedEx. "We feel this is very powerful medium to get out our stories," said Matt Ceniceros, a FedEx Citizenship Blog editor.[10] Emerson Process Experts, a blog operated by Austin-based Emerson Process Management, is a good example of a company with a narrow focus and specific audience. Chief blogger (and engineer) Jim Cahill blogs to other engineers about topics that are relevant to them, in their own language.[11]

Customers can use FedEx automated shipping, tracking, and invoicing systems to save time and money. Services like these work to solidify customers' loyalty to FedEx.

→ **Social Networking Sites.** Popular social network sites include Facebook and LinkedIn as well as corporate owned online communities. While most B-to-C companies have a Facebook presence, LinkedIn, in particular, has become a popular destination for B-to-B companies for communication as well as a way to search for talent.[12] Constant Contact created an online community called ConnectUp, which allows customers to talk with each other and provide recommendations on not only products but also e-mail marketing campaign strategy in general. Constant Contact argues that this works for them and has gained 30 percent more leads through the community.[13]

→ **Twitter.** Several companies have used the microblogging tool to converse with its customers. They also use it to find out what other people are saying about the company. Technology company EMC uses Twitter to communicate with a variety of constituents including the media, people job hunting, and customers. In fact, EMC employees use Twitter to talk to customers directly.[14]

→ **Video.** With 233 million unique visitors per month, YouTube is one of the most popular Web sites that carries millions of videos online. B-to-B marketers can use YouTube effectively by creating microchannels to boost brand awareness. Google has even released a "how to" guide for B-to-B marketers that contains suggestions on creating content and using YouTube analytics. Video is particularly effective for product demonstrations. Constellation Energy, an energy holding company, has several channels for its various units, such as its solar product line.[15]

→ **Mobile Marketing.** Total marketing spending for mobile reached $561 million in 2010, an increase of 43 percent over 2009 according to Forrester Research. Companies have started experimenting with SMS text messaging, iPhone applications, mobile display advertising, and mobile marketing at trade shows and conferences.[16] PACCAR Inc., a truck manufacturer and parts company, developed a small program using mobile to communicate with its distributor network.[17]

Each year, *BtoB Magazine* identifies ten business marketing Web sites that are particularly good examples of how companies can use the Web to communicate with customers. Exhibit 7.1 identifies the ten great Web sites for 2010. Although the list did not change much from 2009, many of these companies are embracing social networking, mobile connectivity, and integrated campaigns using e-mail, video, and search. Some of these extensions include building out Facebook presence, YouTube channels, blogs, and Twitter presence.[18] Many of these companies have been recognized in past years for effectively communicating with their target markets.[19]

MEASURING ONLINE SUCCESS

Most marketers use some sort of Web analytics (such as Google Analytics or an enterprise system such as Omniture) to determine which activities generate leads and then use that information to make changes to the Web site to be more effective.[20] Metrics include external search traffic, internal search engine analytics, and keyword search results. Three of the most important measurements of online success are recency, frequency, and monetary value. *Recency* relates to the fact that customers who have made a purchase recently are more likely to purchase again in the near future than customers who haven't purchased for a while. *Frequency* data help marketers identify frequent purchasers who are definitely more likely to repeat their purchasing behavior in the future. The *monetary value* of sales is important because big spenders can be the most profitable customers for a business.

NetGenesis has developed a number of equations that can help online marketers better understand their data. For example, combining frequency data with the length of time a visitor spent on the Web site (duration) and the number

Exhibit 7.1 Ten Great Web Sites	
URL	Company
www.accenture.com	Accenture
www.airclic.com	Airclic
www.dropbox.com	Dropbox
www.freightcenter.com	Freight Center
IT.ixda.com	Interactive Design Association
www.istockphoto.com	istockphoto.com
www.macktrucks.com	Mack Trucks
www.sas.com	SAS Institute
www.shawfloors.com	Shaw Industries Group
www.tyco.com	Tyco

Source: "10 Great B-To-B Web Sites," *BtoB Magazine*, online, September 13, 2010. Reprinted with permisssion.

Google AdWords are useful to any business advertising online. In this ad placed by Google, it offers to set businesses at the top of searchers' minds.

of site pages viewed during each visit (total site reach) can provide an analytical measure of a site's **stickiness** factor:

$$\text{Stickiness} = \text{Frequency} \times \text{Duration} \times \text{Site Reach}$$

By measuring the stickiness factor of a Web site before and after a design or function change, the marketer can quickly determine whether visitors embraced the change. By adding purchase information to determine the level of stickiness needed to provide a desired purchase volume, the marketer gains an even more precise understanding of how a site change affected business. An almost endless number of factor combinations can be created to provide a quantitative method for determining buyer behavior online. First, though, the marketer must determine what measures are required and which factors can be combined to arrive at those measurements.[21]

Although 43 percent of marketers are measuring social media on some level, it is still a work in progress for many B-to-B marketers. Most say that social media is there to create awareness and build relationships and community rather than generating leads. "Knowing who the influencers are is far more important and powerful for B-to-B firms than for consumer-facing companies," said Jim Sterne, chairman of the Web Analytics Association and author of *Social Media Metrics: How to Measure Your Marketing Investment*.[22] According to a survey by *BtoB* and the Web Analytics Association, social media measurement was low for mobile (17 percent) and video (14 percent) and high for Web site traffic (88 percent)

stickiness

A measure of a Web site's effectiveness; calculated by multiplying the frequency of visits times the duration of a visit times the number of pages viewed during each visit (site reach).

disintermediation
The elimination of intermediaries such as wholesalers or distributors from a marketing channel.

and e-mail campaigns (76 percent).[23] Awareness, engagement, and conversion are strong metrics to consider for social media. Awareness is the attention that social media attracts, such as the number of followers or fans. Engagement refers to the interactions between the brand and the audience, such as comments, retweets, and searches. Conversions occur when action is taken.[24] Each of these will affect the return on investment.

TRENDS IN B-TO-B INTERNET MARKETING

According to James Soto, president of business marketing agency Industrial Strength Marketing, "the number one thing to keep in mind in terms of trends in B-to-B Internet marketing is the shift of sourcing to the Net." His firm has found that 90 percent of business buyers go to the Internet at some point during the buying process, and over 50 percent start the buying process online.[25]

An Internet marketing technique that hasn't yet lived up to its potential is RSS (Real Simple Syndication) feeds. RSS feeds are used to publish frequently updated materials such as blogs, news headlines, audio, and video in a standard format. Web feeds benefit publishers by letting them syndicate content automatically. They benefit readers who want to subscribe to timely updates or aggregated information from various sources.[26]

A recent survey revealed that seven out of ten business marketers do not consider RSS feeds in their campaigns. However, 71 percent of technology buyers reported using feeds.[27]

W.W. Grainger Inc., a distributor of facility maintenance supplies, provides RSS feeds on its Web site **supplylink.com** to help maintenance professionals identify and solve facility issues such as security, productivity, and energy efficiency. The site features industry articles and resources as well as information on new products that Grainger has recently added.[28]

Over the last decade marketers have become more and more sophisticated in their use of the Internet. Exhibit 7.2 compares three prominent Internet business-marketing strategy initiatives from the late 1990s to five that are currently being pursued. Companies have had to transition from "We have a Web site because our customer does" to having a store that attracts, interests, satisfies, and retains customers. New applications that provide additional information about present and potential customers, increase efficiency, lower costs, increase supply chain efficiency, or enhance customer retention, loyalty, and trust are being developed each year. Chapter 21 on customer relationship management describes several of these applications.

One term in Exhibit 7.2 that may be unfamiliar is **disintermediation**, which means eliminating intermediaries such as wholesalers or distributors from a marketing channel. A prime example of disintermediation is Dell, Inc., which sells directly to business buyers and consumers. Dell is now using Twitter to sell its overstock inventory. Large retailers such as Walmart use a disintermediation strategy to help reduce costs and prices.[29]

A few years ago, many people thought that the Internet would eliminate the need for distributors. Why

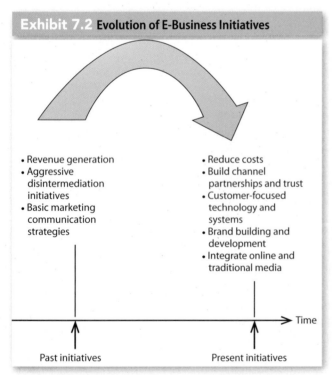

Exhibit 7.2 Evolution of E-Business Initiatives

- Revenue generation
- Aggressive disintermediation initiatives
- Basic marketing communication strategies

- Reduce costs
- Build channel partnerships and trust
- Customer-focused technology and systems
- Brand building and development
- Integrate online and traditional media

Past initiatives

Present initiatives

Time

Source: Andrew J. Rohm and Fareena Sultan, "The Evolution of E-Business," *Marketing Management*, January/February, 2004, p. 35. Used by permission.

would customers pay for distributor markups when they could buy directly from the manufacturers with a few mouse clicks? Yet Internet disintermediation has occurred less frequently than many expected. The reason is that distributors often perform important functions such as providing credit, aggregation of supplies from multiple sources, delivery, and processing returns. Many business customers, especially small firms, depend on knowledgeable distributors for information and advice that are not available to them online. You will notice in Exhibit 7.2 that building channel partnerships and trust has replaced aggressive disintermediation initiatives as a priority for most firms.

Some firms have followed disintermediation with **reintermediation**, the reintroduction of an intermediary between producers and users. They realized that providing direct online purchasing only was similar to having only one store in a city selling a popular brand.[30]

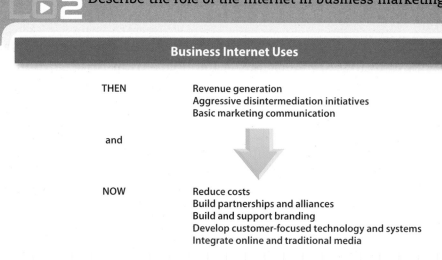

Review
LO2 Describe the role of the Internet in business marketing

Business Internet Uses	
THEN	Revenue generation Aggressive disintermediation initiatives Basic marketing communication
and	
NOW	Reduce costs Build partnerships and alliances Build and support branding Develop customer-focused technology and systems Integrate online and traditional media

© Cengage Learning 2013

LO3
Relationship Marketing and Strategic Alliances

As Chapter 1 explained, relationship marketing is a strategy that entails seeking and establishing ongoing partnerships with customers. Relationship marketing has become an important business marketing strategy as customers have become more demanding and competition has become more intense. Customers want more attention and more advice than ever before. They want to do business with firms that know them and understand their needs. They want to be reassured that their purchase decisions are sound. Basically, they want to know that they are in good hands.[31] Loyal customers are also more profitable than those who are price-sensitive and perceive little or no difference among brands or suppliers. That is why firms such as online printing company Mimeo.com focus on continually improving processes for communicating with customers once they place their first order. To help retain clients, the company has developed an automated system that sends out e-mails or triggers a live contact each time a customer places an order or asks a question.[32] Building long-term relationships with customers offers companies a way to build competitive advantage that is hard for competitors to copy. For example, the FedEx Powership program includes a series of automated shipping, tracking, and invoicing systems that saves customers time and money while solidifying their loyalty to FedEx. This produces a win-win situation.

reintermediation
The reintroduction of an intermediary between producers and users.

STRATEGIC ALLIANCES

A **strategic alliance**, sometimes called a *strategic partnership*, is a cooperative agreement between business firms. Strategic alliances can take the form of licensing or distribution agreements, joint ventures, research and development consortia, and partnerships. They may be between different manufacturers, manufacturers and customers, manufacturers and suppliers, and manufacturers and channel intermediaries.

Business marketers form strategic alliances to strengthen operations and better compete. Hewlett-Packard and Microsoft have formed a strategic alliance designed to more tightly couple their software and hardware products. Goals include helping businesses reduce some of the problems often experienced setting up operating data centers and strengthening HP and Microsoft's competitive position against firms such as Oracle Corp. and IBM.[33]

Sometimes alliance partners are also fierce competitors. For instance, the express delivery service DHL has formed an alliance with rival company UPS. Under the agreement, UPS provides all airlift services for DHL in the United States. According to one DHL executive, "the customer doesn't actually see a difference at all...unless they pay attention to the color of the partner's planes."[34]

Other alliances are formed between companies that operate in completely different industries. Choice Hotels and 1-800-Flowers share call-center employees because doing so is a cheaper alternative than outsourcing. When one company experiences increased demand for its products and services, it can call on its partner's employees rather than add staff or use a temporary agency. At a given time, as many as one hundred call-center agents may be taking orders for the other company. Both companies report higher employee retention and better recruitment.[35]

For an alliance to succeed in the long term, it must be built on commitment and trust. **Relationship commitment** means that a firm believes that an ongoing relationship with some other firm is so important that it warrants maximum efforts at maintaining it indefinitely.[36] A perceived reduction in commitment by one of the parties often leads to a breakdown in the relationship.

Trust exists when one party has confidence in an exchange partner's reliability and integrity.[37] Some alliances fail when participants lack trust in their trading partners. For instance, General Motors, Ford, DaimlerChrysler, Nissan, and Renault SA created an Internet automobile parts exchange, called Covisint, that they hoped would make $300 billion in sales per year. But the auto industry is characterized by mistrust between buyers and sellers. After three years, and hundreds of millions of dollars invested, the exchange was floundering. The investment money was nearly gone and the workforce had been reduced by 35 percent. Automobile industry suppliers did not trust the exchange, which led to its failure.

RELATIONSHIPS IN OTHER CULTURES

Although the terms *relationship marketing* and *strategic alliances* are fairly new, and popularized mostly by American business executives and educators, the concepts have long been familiar in other cultures. Businesses in Mexico, China, Japan, Korea, and much of Europe rely heavily on personal relationships. Chapter 21 explores customer relationship management in detail.

In Japan, for example, exchange between firms is based on personal relationships that are developed through what is called *amae*, or indulgent dependency. *Amae* is the feeling of nurturing concern for, and dependence on, another. Reciprocity and personal relationships contribute to *amae*. Relationships between companies can develop into a **keiretsu**—a network of interlocking corporate affiliates. Within a keiretsu, executives may sit on the boards of their customers or their suppliers. Members of a keiretsu trade with each other whenever possible and often engage in joint product development, finance, and marketing activity. For example, the Toyota Group keiretsu includes 14 core companies and another 170 that receive preferential treatment. Toyota holds an equity position in many of these 170 member firms and is represented on many of their boards of directors.

keiretsu
A network of interlocking corporate affiliates.

Many American firms have found that the best way to compete in Asian countries is to form relationships with Asian firms. For example, General Motors' joint venture with Shanghai Motors produces Buicks, Chevrolets, and Cadillacs. German automaker Volkswagen also has an alliance with Shanghai Motors to produce the Passat.[38]

Some American firms seek out foreign partners to access money and technology. For example, large power companies such as Duke Energy Corp., AES Corp., and Progress Energy Inc. have formed alliances with Chinese energy firms. Duke Energy Corp. has formed alliances with two Chinese firms that focus on solar-power development and methods to capture and store carbon dioxide from coal-burning power plants.[39]

Review
LO3 Discuss the role of relationship marketing and strategic alliances in business marketing

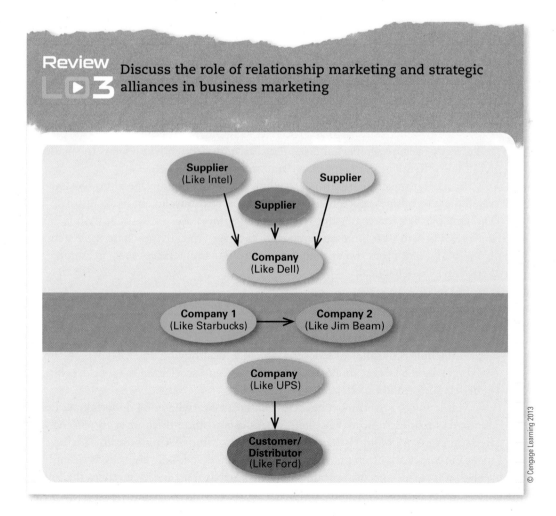

L▶4
Major Categories of Business Customers

The business market consists of four major categories of customers: producers, resellers, governments, and institutions.

PRODUCERS

The producer segment of the business market includes profit-oriented individuals and organizations that use purchased goods and services to produce other products, to incorporate into other products, or to facilitate the daily operations of the organization. Examples of producers include construction, manufacturing, transportation, finance, real estate, and food service firms. In the United States there are over 13 million firms in the producer segment of the business market. Some of these firms are small, and others are among the world's largest businesses.

Producers are often called **original equipment manufacturers (OEMs)**. This term includes all individuals and organizations that buy business goods and incorporate them into the products that they produce for eventual sale to other producers or to consumers. Companies such as General Motors that buy steel, paint, tires, and batteries are said to be OEMs.

RESELLERS

The reseller market includes retail and wholesale businesses that buy finished goods and resell them for a profit. A retailer sells mainly to final consumers; wholesalers sell mostly to retailers and other organizational customers. There are approximately 1.5 million retailers and 500,000 wholesalers operating in the United States. Consumer-product firms such as Procter & Gamble, Kraft Foods, and Coca-Cola sell directly to large retailers and retail chains and through wholesalers to smaller retail units. Retailing is explored in detail in Chapter 15.

Business product distributors are wholesalers that buy business products and resell them to business customers. They often carry thousands of items in stock and employ sales forces to call on business customers. Businesses that wish to buy a gross of pencils or a hundred pounds of fertilizer typically purchase these items from local distributors rather than directly from manufacturers such as Empire Pencil or Dow Chemical.

GOVERNMENTS

A third major segment of the business market is government. Government organizations include thousands of federal, state, and local buying units. They make up what may be the largest single market for goods and services in the world, estimated at $5.5 trillion in 2010.[40]

Marketing to government agencies can be an overwhelming undertaking, but companies that learn how the system works can position themselves to win lucrative contracts and build lasting, rewarding relationships.[41] Contracts for government purchases are often put out for bid. Interested vendors submit bids (usually sealed) to provide specified products during a particular time. Sometimes the lowest bidder is awarded the contract. When the lowest bidder is not awarded the contract, strong evidence must be presented to justify the decision. Grounds for rejecting the lowest bid include lack of experience, inadequate financing, or poor past performance. Bidding allows all potential suppliers a fair chance at winning government contracts and helps ensure that public funds are spent wisely.

Federal Government Name just about any good or service and chances are that someone in the federal government uses it. The U.S. federal government buys goods and services valued at over $600 billion per year, making it the world's largest customer.

Although much of the federal government's buying is centralized, no single federal agency contracts for all the government's requirements, and no single buyer in any agency purchases all that the agency needs. We can view the federal government as a combination of several large companies with overlapping responsibilities and thousands of small independent units.

One popular source of information about government procurement is *Commerce Business Daily*. Until recently, businesses hoping to sell to the federal government found the document unorganized, and it often arrived too late to be useful. The online version (**www.cbd-net.com**) is more timely and lets contractors find leads using keyword searches. Other examples of publications designed to explain how to do business with the federal government include *Doing Business with the General Services Administration, Selling to the Military,* and *Selling to the U.S. Air Force.*

State, County, and City Government Selling to states, counties, and cities can be less frustrating for both small and large vendors than selling to the federal government. Paperwork is typically simpler and more manageable than it is at

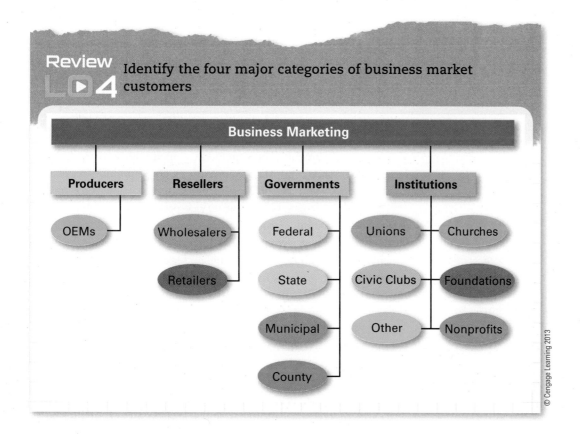

Review
LO4 Identify the four major categories of business market customers

© iStockphoto.com/Juan Facundo Mora Soria

© Cengage Learning 2013

the federal level. On the other hand, vendors must decide which of the over 82,000 government units are likely to buy their wares. State and local buying agencies include school districts, highway departments, government-operated hospitals, and housing agencies.

INSTITUTIONS

The fourth major segment of the business market consists of institutions that seek to achieve goals other than the standard business goals of profit, market share, and return on investment. This segment includes schools, hospitals, colleges and universities, churches, labor unions, fraternal organizations, civic clubs, foundations, and other so-called nonbusiness organizations. Xerox offers educational and medical institutions the same prices as government agencies (the lowest that Xerox offers) and has a separate sales force that calls on these customers.

Exhibit 7.3	NAICS Two-Digit Codes and Corresponding Economic Sectors
NAICS Code	**Economic Sector**
11	Agriculture, forestry, and fishing
21	Mining
22	Utilities
23	Construction
31–33	Manufacturing
43	Wholesale trade
44–45	Retail trade
47–48	Transportation
51	Information
52	Finance and insurance
53	Real estate and rental and leasing
56	Professional and technical services
57	Management and support services
61	Education services
62	Health and social assistance
71	Arts, entertainment, and recreation
72	Food services, drinking places, and accommodations
81	Other services, except public administration
93	Public administration
98	Estates and trusts
99	Nonclassifiable

© Cengage Learning 2013

L◗5

The North American Industry Classification System

The **North American Industry Classification System (NAICS)** is an industry classification system introduced in 1997 to replace the standard industrial classification (SIC) system. NAICS (pronounced *nakes*) is a system for classifying North American business establishments. The system, developed jointly by the United States, Canada, and Mexico, provides a common industry classification system for the North American Free Trade Agreement (NAFTA) partners. Goods- or service-producing firms that use identical or similar production processes are grouped together.

NAICS is an extremely valuable tool for business marketers engaged in analyzing, segmenting, and targeting markets. Each classification group is relatively homogeneous in terms of raw materials required, components used, manufacturing processes employed, and problems faced. The more digits in a code, the more homogeneous the group is. Therefore, if a supplier understands the needs and requirements of a few firms within a classification, requirements can be projected for all firms in that category. The number, size, and geographic dispersion of firms can also be identified. This information can be converted to market potential estimates, market share estimates, and sales forecasts. It can also be

Exhibit 7.4 Examples of NAICS Hierarchy

NAICS Level	Example 1		Example 2	
	NAICS Code	Description	NAICS Code	Description
Sector	31–33	Manufacturing	51	Information
Subsector	334	Computer and electronic product manufacturing	513	Broadcasting and telecommunications
Industry group	3346	Manufacturing and reproduction of magnetic and optical media	5133	Telecommunications
Industry	33461	Manufacturing and reproduction of magnetic and optical media	51332	Wireless telecommunications carriers, except satellite
Industry Subdivision	334611	Reproduction of software	513321	Paging

Source: U.S. Census Bureau, "New Code System In NAICS," http://www.census.gov/epcd/www/naics.html.

used for identifying potential new customers. NAICS codes can help identify firms that may be prospective users of a supplier's goods and services.

Exhibit 7.3 provides an overview of NAICS. Exhibit 7.4 illustrates the six-digit classification system for two of the twenty NAICS economic sectors: manufacturing and information. The hierarchical structure of NAICS allows industry data to be summarized at several levels of detail. To illustrate:

→ The first two digits designate a major economic sector such as agriculture (11) or manufacturing (31–33).

→ The third digit designates an economic subsector such as crop production or apparel manufacturing.

→ The fourth digit designates an industry group, such as grain and oil seed farming or fiber, yarn, and thread mills.

→ The fifth digit designates the NAICS industry, such as wheat farming or broadwoven fabric mills.

→ The sixth digit, when used, identifies subdivisions of NAICS industries that accommodate user needs in individual countries.[42]

For a complete listing of all NAICS codes, see **www.census.gov/epcd/www/naics.html**.

North American Industry Classification System (NAICS)

A detailed numbering system developed by the United States, Canada, and Mexico to classify North American business establishments by their main production processes.

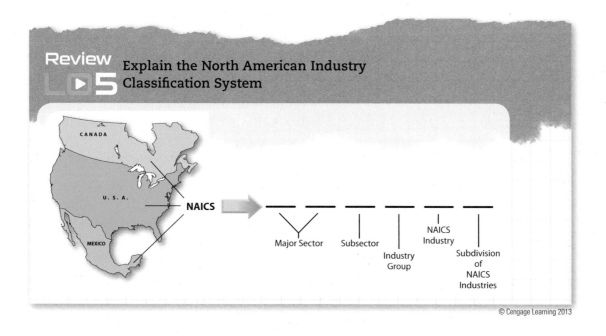

Review
LO 5 Explain the North American Industry Classification System

© Cengage Learning 2013

LO6
Business versus Consumer Markets

The basic philosophy and practice of marketing are the same whether the customer is a business organization or a consumer. Business markets do, however, have characteristics different from consumer markets.

DEMAND

Consumer demand for products is quite different from demand in the business market. Unlike consumer demand, business demand is derived, inelastic, joint, and fluctuating.

Derived Demand The demand for business products is called **derived demand** because organizations buy products to be used in producing their customers' products. For instance, the number of drills or lathes that a manufacturing firm needs is "derived from," or based upon the demand for products that are produced using these machines.

Because demand is derived, business marketers must carefully monitor demand patterns and changing preferences in final consumer markets, even though their customers are not in those markets. Moreover, business marketers must carefully monitor their customers' forecasts, because derived demand is based on expectations of future demand for those customers' products.

Some business marketers not only monitor final consumer demand and customer forecasts, but also try to influence final consumer demand. Aluminum producers use television and magazine advertisements to point out the convenience and recycling opportunities that aluminum offers to consumers who choose to purchase soft drinks in either aluminum or plastic containers.

Inelastic Demand The demand for many business products is inelastic with regard to price. *Inelastic demand* means that an increase or decrease in the price of the product will not significantly affect demand for the product. This will be discussed further in Chapter 19.

The price of a product used in the production of, or as part of, a final product is often a minor portion of the final product's total price. Therefore, demand for the final consumer product is not affected. If the price of automobile paint or spark plugs rises significantly, say, 200 percent in one year, do you think the number of new automobiles sold that year will be affected? Probably not.

Joint Demand Joint demand occurs when two or more items are used together in a final product. For example, a decline in the availability of memory chips will slow production of microcomputers, which will in turn reduce the demand for disk drives. Likewise, the demand for Apple operating systems exists as long as there is demand for Apple computers. Sales of the two products are directly linked.

Fluctuating Demand The demand for business products—particularly new plants and equipment—tends to be less stable than the demand for consumer products. A small increase or decrease in consumer demand can produce a much larger change in demand for the facilities and equipment needed to make the consumer product. Economists refer to this phenomenon as the **multiplier effect** (or **accelerator principle**).

Cummins Engine Company, a producer of heavy-duty diesel engines, uses sophisticated surface grinders to make parts. Suppose Cummins is using 20 surface

derived demand
The demand for business products.

joint demand
The demand for two or more items used together in a final product.

multiplier effect (accelerator principle)
Phenomenon in which a small increase or decrease in consumer demand can produce a much larger change in demand for the facilities and equipment needed to make the consumer product.

grinders. Each machine lasts about ten years. Purchases have been timed so two machines will wear out and be replaced annually. If the demand for engine parts does not change, two grinders will be bought this year. If the demand for parts declines slightly, only 18 grinders may be needed and Cummins won't replace the worn ones. However, suppose that next year demand returns to previous levels plus a little more. To meet the new level of demand, Cummins will need to replace the two machines that wore out in the first year, the two that wore out in the second year, plus one or more additional machines. The multiplier effect works this way in many industries, producing highly fluctuating demand for business products.

PURCHASE VOLUME

Business customers buy in much larger quantities than consumers. Just think how large an order Kellogg typically places for the wheat bran and raisins used to manufacture Raisin Bran. Imagine the number of tires that Nissan buys at one time.

NUMBER OF CUSTOMERS

Business marketers usually have far fewer customers than consumer marketers. The advantage is that it is a lot easier to identify prospective buyers, monitor current customers' needs and levels of satisfaction, and personally attend to existing customers. The main disadvantage is that each customer becomes crucial—especially for those manufacturers that have only one customer. In many cases, this customer is the U.S. government. The success or failure of one bid can make the difference between prosperity and bankruptcy. After five years of development, testing, and politicking, the Pentagon awarded Lockheed Martin a multi-decade contract to build three thousand jet fighter airplanes. Boeing Aircraft Company, the only other bidder on the $200 billion contract, immediately announced plans for substantial layoffs.

LOCATION OF BUYERS

Business customers tend to be much more geographically concentrated than consumers. For instance, more than half the nation's business buyers are located in New York, California, Pennsylvania, Illinois, Ohio, Michigan, and New Jersey. The aircraft and microelectronics industries are concentrated on the West Coast, and many of the firms that supply the automobile manufacturing industry are located in and around Detroit.

DISTRIBUTION STRUCTURE

Many consumer products pass through a distribution system that includes the producer, one or more wholesalers, and a retailer. In business marketing, however, because of many of the characteristics already mentioned, channels of distribution are typically shorter. Direct channels, where manufacturers market directly to users, are much more common. The use of direct channels has increased dramatically in the past decade with the introduction of various Internet buying and selling schemes. One such technique is a business-to-business online exchange, which is an electronic trading floor that provides companies with integrated links to their customers and suppliers. The goal of a B2B online exchange is to simplify business purchasing and make it more efficient. For example, Exostar, the aerospace industry's online exchange, claims more than half of the aerospace industry's firms as its customers and has more than 70,000 registered companies to support those customers.[43] Exchanges such as Exostar facilitate direct channel relationships between producers and their customers.

NATURE OF BUYING

Unlike consumers, business buyers usually approach purchasing rather formally. Businesses use professionally trained purchasing agents or buyers who spend their entire career purchasing a limited number of items. They get to know the items and the sellers well. Some professional purchasers earn the designation of Certified Purchasing Manager (CPM) after participating in a rigorous certification program.

NATURE OF BUYING INFLUENCE

Typically, more people are involved in a single business purchase decision than in a consumer purchase. Experts from fields as varied as quality control, marketing, and finance, as well as professional buyers and users, may be grouped in a buying center (discussed later in this chapter).

TYPE OF NEGOTIATIONS

Consumers are used to negotiating price on automobiles and real estate. In most cases, however, American consumers expect sellers to set the price and other conditions of sale, such as time of delivery and credit terms. In contrast, negotiating is common in business marketing. Buyers and sellers negotiate product specifications, delivery dates, payment terms, and other pricing matters. Sometimes these negotiations occur during many meetings over several months. Final contracts are often very long and detailed.

USE OF RECIPROCITY

Business purchasers often choose to buy from their own customers, a practice known as reciprocity. For example, General Motors buys engines for use in its automobiles and trucks from BorgWarner, which in turn buys many of the automobiles and trucks it needs from GM. This practice is neither unethical nor illegal unless one party coerces the other and the result is unfair competition. Reciprocity is generally considered a reasonable business practice. If all possible suppliers sell a similar product for about the same price, doesn't it make sense to buy from those firms that buy from you?

USE OF LEASING

Consumers normally buy products rather than lease them. But businesses commonly lease expensive equipment such as computers, construction equipment and vehicles, and automobiles. Leasing allows firms to reduce capital outflow, acquire a seller's latest products, receive better services, and gain tax advantages.

The lessor, the firm providing the product, may be either the manufacturer or an independent firm. The benefits to the lessor include greater total revenue from leasing compared to selling and an opportunity to do business with customers who cannot afford to buy.

Review
LO6 Explain the major difference between business and consumer markets

Characteristic	Business Market	Consumer Market
Demand	Organizational	Individual
Purchase volume	Larger	Smaller
Number of customers	Fewer	Many
Location of buyers	Geographically concentrated	Dispersed
Distribution structure	More direct	More indirect
Nature of buying	More professional	More personal
Nature of buying influence	Multiple	Single
Type of negotiations	More complex	Simpler
Use of reciprocity	Yes	No
Use of leasing	Greater	Lesser
Primary promotional method	Personal selling	Advertising

© Cengage Learning 2013

MARKETING METRICS

Business Market Product Launch and Sales Force Size

The Problem

A software company is introducing a new computer system for automating car maintenance scheduling at automotive dealerships. In order to determine who their potential customers are and how to best approach them, the company must understand amount of work qualifying and closing sales leads will require, then use that information to determine how large a salesforce to employ to maximize resources.

The Metric

In order to determine how much work each salesperson will need to do to close a sale, the software company must have a clear understanding of its sales cycle. For the a software company salesperson, a typical sales cycle involves identifying a prospective client company's situation (what does the client use to schedule car maintenance?); determining whether the company perceives a problem with their current situation (Is this client happy with his current car maintenance scheduling system?); establishing the implications for the company if they do not address the problem (What areas of productivity and profitability are affected by the current maintenance scheduling system?); and quantifying the impact of improving the client's current situation (Changing to our new automobile maintenance scheduling program will save you thousands of dollars and improve customer satisfaction).

Conducting all this research and communicating the findings to business customers requires a significant amount of a salesperson's time, and therefore a sufficiently large salesforce. If the salesforce is too small, the firm may not find all its potential customers and may not meet its customers' full needs, therefore losing potential revenue. However, if the salesforce is too large, the firm may be wasting its resources by paying people with nothing to do.

Instead of guessing how many salespeople the software company needs to hire for the new software launch, marketing executives use ratios to determine how many salespeople are needed.

The software company needs to know how many car dealerships there are in the United States. Based on research, the marketing manager knows there are 24,852 new car dealerships in the United States. Based on past experience, a marketing executive expects that 1 out of 200 of these dealerships will purchase a new software product during its first year of sales. Furthermore, the marketing executive knows that a typical salesperson for the software company is responsible for delivering $1.3 million in revenue. If the expected price of the software is $400,000 per sale, the marketing manager can combine these numbers to estimate how many salespeople he or she needs to hire.

First, the marketing manager calculates the expected number of sales in the first year to be roughly 124 by multiplying the number of car dealerships by the number of sales per dealership:

$$24{,}852 \text{ Dealerships} \times \frac{1 \text{ Sale}}{200 \text{ Dealerships}}$$
$$= 124 \text{ Sales}$$

Second, the marketing manager calculates the expected revenue in the first year to be roughly $49.6 million by multiplying the anticipated number of sales by the expected price per software sale:

$$124 \text{ Sales} \times \frac{\$400{,}000}{\text{Sale}} = \$49.6 \text{ million}$$

Finally, the marketing manager calculates the required salesforce by dividing the expected revenue by the expected revenue per salesperson.

$$\$49.6 \text{ million} \div \frac{\$1.3 \text{ million}}{\text{Salesperson}}$$
$$= \frac{\$49.6 \text{ million}}{1} \times \frac{\text{Salesperson}}{\$1.3 \text{ million}}$$
$$= 38 \text{ Salespeople}$$

Management Action

Based on the calculations, a marketing manager would employ 38 salespeople to meet the outlined parameters.

A similar method can be used for projecting revenue and salesforce requirements in a number of industries.

PRIMARY PROMOTIONAL METHOD

Business marketers tend to emphasize personal selling in their promotion efforts, especially for expensive items, custom-designed products, large-volume purchases, and situations requiring negotiations. The sale of many business products requires a great deal of personal contact. Personal selling is discussed in more detail in Chapter 18.

Types of Business Products

Business products generally fall into one of the following seven categories, depending on their use: major equipment, accessory equipment, raw materials, component parts, processed materials, supplies, and business services.

MAJOR EQUIPMENT

Major equipment includes capital goods such as large or expensive machines, mainframe computers, blast furnaces, generators, airplanes, and buildings. (These items are also commonly called **installations**.) Major equipment is depreciated over time rather than charged as an expense in the year it is purchased. In addition, major equipment is often custom-designed for each customer. Personal selling is an important part of the marketing strategy for major equipment because distribution channels are almost always direct from the producer to the business user.

ACCESSORY EQUIPMENT

Accessory equipment is generally less expensive and shorter-lived than major equipment. Examples include portable drills, power tools, microcomputers, and fax machines. Accessory equipment is often charged as an expense in the year it is bought rather than depreciated over its useful life. In contrast to major equipment, accessories are more often standardized and are usually bought by more customers. These customers tend to be widely dispersed. For example, all types of businesses buy microcomputers.

Local industrial distributors (wholesalers) play an important role in the marketing of accessory equipment because business buyers often purchase accessories from them. Regardless of where accessories are bought, advertising is a more vital promotional tool for accessory equipment than for major equipment.

RAW MATERIALS

Raw materials are unprocessed extractive or agricultural products—for example, mineral ore, timber, wheat, corn, fruits, vegetables, and fish. Raw materials become part of finished products. Extensive users, such as steel or lumber mills and food canners, generally buy huge quantities of raw materials. Because there is often a large number of relatively small sellers of raw materials, none can greatly influence price or supply. Thus, the market tends to set the price of raw materials, and individual producers have little pricing flexibility. Promotion is almost always via personal selling, and distribution channels are usually direct from producer to business user.

Lotus knows how to have a meeting in the cloud.

LotusLive™ delivers collaboration and social networking capabilities to a Web-based platform. So you and everyone else on your team can use the "cloud" as an excellent place to get things done.

Smarter software for a Smarter Planet.

lotusknows.com

Many of IBM's products are major purchases and are customized according to a large business' computer and server needs.

Reprint Courtesy of International Business Machines Corporation, © 2011 International Business Machines Corporation

COMPONENT PARTS

Component parts are either finished items ready for assembly or products that need very little processing before becoming part of some other product. Caterpillar diesel engines are component parts used in heavy-duty trucks. Other examples include spark plugs, tires, and electric motors for automobiles. A special feature of component parts is that they can retain their identity after becoming part of the final product. For example, automobile tires are clearly recognizable as part of a car. Moreover, because component parts often wear out, they may need to be replaced several times during the life of the final product. Thus, there are two important markets for many component parts: the original equipment manufacturer (OEM) market and the replacement market.

The availability of component parts is often a key factor in OEMs meeting their production deadlines. For example, Boeing Co. has had to delay final assembly of Boeing 787 Dreamliners by at least 15 months because of slower than expected completion of components prior to their arrival at the final assembly line. In addition to delayed sales and customer disappointment and dissatisfaction, Boeing will have to pay millions of dollars of penalty payments to customers.[44]

Many of the business features listed in the Review for Learning Outcome 6 characterize the OEM market. The difference between unit costs and selling prices in the OEM market is often small, but profits can be substantial because of volume buying.

The replacement market is composed of organizations and individuals buying component parts to replace worn-out parts. Because components often retain their identity in final products, users may choose to replace a component part with the same brand used by the manufacturer—for example, the same brand of automobile tires or battery. The replacement market operates differently from the OEM market, however. Whether replacement buyers are organizations or individuals, they tend to demonstrate the characteristics of consumer markets that were shown in the Review for Learning Outcome 6. Consider, for example, an automobile replacement part. Purchase volume is usually small and there are many customers, geographically dispersed, who typically buy from car dealers or parts stores. Negotiations do not occur, and neither reciprocity nor leasing is usually an issue.

Manufacturers of component parts often direct their advertising toward replacement buyers. Cooper Tire & Rubber, for example, makes and markets component parts—automobile and truck tires—for the replacement market only. General Motors and other car makers compete with independent firms in the market for replacement automobile parts.

PROCESSED MATERIALS

Processed materials are products used directly in manufacturing other products. Unlike raw materials, they have had some processing. Examples include sheet metal, chemicals, specialty steel, lumber, corn syrup, and plastics. Unlike component parts, processed materials do not retain their identity in final products.

Most processed materials are marketed to OEMs or to distributors servicing the OEM market. Processed materials are generally bought according to customer specifications or to some industry standard, as is the case with steel and plywood. Price and service are important factors in choosing a vendor.

SUPPLIES

Supplies are consumable items that do not become part of the final product—for example, lubricants, detergents, paper towels, pencils,

© iStockphoto.com/Juan Facundo Mora Soria

component parts
Either finished items ready for assembly or products that need very little processing before becoming part of some other product.

processed materials
Products used directly in manufacturing other products.

supplies
Consumable items that do not become part of the final product.

Even though the Internet has greatly affected the consumption of many supplies, such as envelopes, paper is still in high demand. In fact, computer technology has increased the demand for paper rather than squelching it.

© AP Images/PR Newsfoto/Boise Paper Solutions

and paper. Supplies are normally standardized items that purchasing agents routinely buy. Supplies typically have relatively short lives and are inexpensive compared to other business goods. Because supplies generally fall into one of three categories—maintenance, repair, or operating supplies—this category is often referred to as MRO items.

Competition in the MRO market is intense. Bic and Paper Mate, for example, battle for business purchases of inexpensive ballpoint pens.

BUSINESS SERVICES

Business services are expense items that do not become part of a final product. Businesses often retain outside providers to perform janitorial, advertising, legal, management consulting, marketing research, maintenance, and other services. Hiring an outside provider makes sense when it costs less than hiring or assigning an employee to perform the task and when an outside provider is needed for particular expertise.

Review
LO7 Describe the seven types of business goods and services

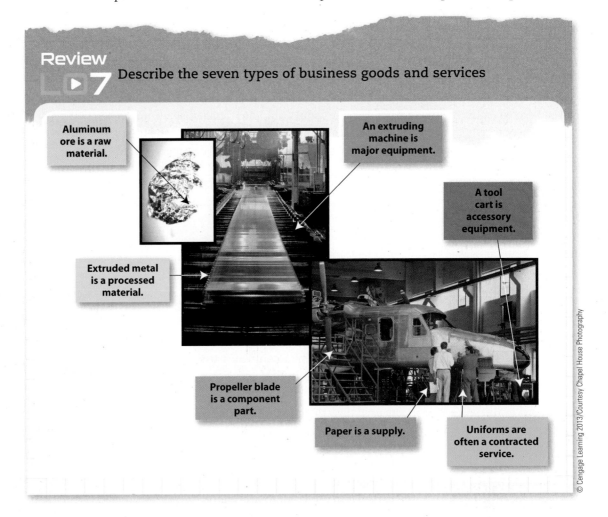

Aluminum ore is a raw material.

An extruding machine is major equipment.

A tool cart is accessory equipment.

Extruded metal is a processed material.

Propeller blade is a component part.

Paper is a supply.

Uniforms are often a contracted service.

© Cengage Learning 2013/Courtesy Chapel House Photography

LO8
Business Buying Behavior

As you probably have already concluded, business buyers behave differently from consumers. Understanding how purchase decisions are made in organizations is a first step in developing a business selling strategy. Business buying behavior has five important aspects: buying centers, evaluative criteria, buying situations, business ethics, and customer service.

BUYING CENTERS

buying center
All those persons in an organization who become involved in the purchase decision.

In many cases, more than one person is involved in a purchase decision. It is not unusual for 10 to 40 people in a company to be involved in an expensive decision.[45] Identifying who these people are and the roles that they play greatly enhances the salesperson's chances for success.[46]

A **buying center** includes all those persons in an organization who become involved in a purchase decision. Membership and influence vary from company to company. For instance, in engineering-dominated firms like Bell Helicopter, the buying center might consist almost entirely of engineers. In marketing-oriented firms like Toyota and IBM, marketing and engineering have almost equal authority. In consumer goods firms like Procter & Gamble, product managers and other marketing decision makers might dominate the buying center. In a small manufacturing company, almost everyone might be a member.

If you are selling capital equipment that is expensive, the finance people are likely involved. If you are selling an everyday lower-priced item, the decision might involve only purchasing agents. Purchases that have an environmental impact might have environmental specialists or engineers in the buying center. Each of these people is likely to have different priorities and biases.[47] The composition of the buying center can change from one purchasing situation to another. Unfortunately, because of the changeable nature of the buying center, its composition does not appear anywhere on an organization chart, but requires sellers to understand the customer's business and be flexible.

Roles in the Buying Center As in family purchasing decisions, several people may play a role in the business purchase process:

→ **Initiator:** the person who first suggests making a purchase.

→ **Influencers/evaluators:** people who influence the buying decision. They often help define specifications and provide information for evaluating options. Technical personnel are especially important as influencers.

→ **Gatekeepers:** group members who regulate the flow of information. Frequently, the purchasing agent views the gatekeeping role as a source of his or her power. A secretary might also act as a gatekeeper by determining which vendors get an appointment with a buyer.

→ **Decider:** the person who has the formal or informal power to choose or approve the selection of the supplier or brand. In complex situations, it is often difficult to determine who makes the final decision.

→ **Purchaser:** the person who actually negotiates the purchase. It could be anyone from the president of the company to the purchasing agent, depending on the importance of the decision.

→ **Users:** members of the organization who will actually use the product. Users often initiate the buying process and help define product specifications.

An example illustrating these basic roles is shown in Exhibit 7.5.

Implications of Buying Centers for the Marketing Manager Successful vendors realize the importance of identifying who is in the decision-making unit, each member's relative influence in the buying decision, and each member's

Exhibit 7.5	Buying-Center Roles for Computer Purchases
Role	**Illustration**
Initiator	Division general manager proposes to replace company's computer network.
Influencers/ evaluators	Corporate controller's office and vice president of information services have an important say in which system and vendor the company will deal with.
Gatekeepers	Corporate departments for purchasing and information services analyze company's needs and recommend likely matches with potential vendors.
Decider	Vice president of administration, with advice from others, selects vendor the company will deal with and system it will buy.
Purchaser	Purchasing agent negotiates terms of sale.
Users	All division employees use the computers.

evaluative criteria. Successful selling strategies often focus on determining the most important buying influences and tailoring sales presentations to the evaluative criteria most important to these buying-center members.

For example, Loctite Corporation, the manufacturer of Super Glue and industrial adhesives and sealants, found that engineers were the most important influencers and deciders in adhesive and sealant purchase decisions. As a result, Loctite focused its marketing efforts on production and maintenance engineers.

Marketers are often frustrated by their inability to directly reach c-level (chief) executives who play important roles in many buying centers. Marketers who want to build executive-level contacts must become involved in the buying process early. This is when 80 percent of executives get involved when major purchase decisions are being made. Executives frequently want to understand current business issues, establish project objectives, and set overall project strategy.[48] Senior executives are typically not involved in the middle phases of the buying process, but often get involved again late in the process to monitor closing the deal. Four characteristics that executives look for in sales representatives are the ability to marshal resources; understanding of the buyer's business goals; responsiveness to requests; and willingness to be held accountable.[49]

Some firms have developed strategies to reach executives throughout the buying process and during non-buying phases of the relationship. For example, FedEx Corp. has initiated a marketing effort called "access," aimed at the c-suite. It includes direct mail, e-mail, and a custom magazine prepared exclusively for c-level executives. It also hosts exclusive leadership events for these senior executives. Other firms, such as Motorola Corp., Intel Corp., SAS, and Xerox Corp., have developed programs utilizing a combination of print, online, and events to reach the elusive c-level audience.[50]

EVALUATIVE CRITERIA

Business buyers evaluate products and suppliers against three important criteria: quality, service, and price—in that order.

Quality In this case, quality refers to technical suitability. A superior tool can do a better job in the production process, and superior packaging can increase dealer and consumer acceptance of a brand. Evaluation of quality also applies to the salesperson and the salesperson's firm. Business buyers want to deal with reputable salespeople and companies that are financially responsible. Quality improvement should be part of every organization's marketing strategy.

Service Almost as much as they want satisfactory products, business buyers want satisfactory service. A purchase offers several opportunities for service. Suppose a vendor is selling heavy equipment. Prepurchase service could include a survey of the buyer's needs. After thorough analysis of the survey findings, the vendor could prepare a report and recommendations in the form of a purchasing proposal. If a purchase results, postpurchase service might consist of installing the equipment and training those who will be using it. Postsale services may also include maintenance and repairs. Another service that business buyers seek is dependability of supply. They must be able to count on delivery of what was ordered when it is scheduled to be delivered. Buyers also welcome services that help them sell their finished products. Services of this sort are especially appropriate when the seller's product is an identifiable part of the buyer's end product.

Price Business buyers want to buy at low prices—at the lowest prices, under most circumstances. However, a buyer who pressures a supplier to cut prices to a point where the supplier loses money on the sale almost forces shortcuts on quality. The buyer also may, in effect, force the supplier to quit selling to him or her. Then a new source of supply will have to be found.

BUYING SITUATIONS

Often business firms, especially manufacturers, must decide whether to make something or buy it from an outside supplier. The decision is essentially one of economics. Can an item of similar quality be bought at a lower price elsewhere? If not, is manufacturing it in-house the best use of limited company resources? For example, Briggs & Stratton Corporation, a major manufacturer of four-cycle engines, might be able to save $150,000 annually on outside purchases by spending $500,000 on the equipment needed to produce gas throttles internally. Yet Briggs & Stratton could also use that $500,000 to upgrade its carburetor assembly line, which would save $225,000 annually. If a firm does decide to buy a product instead of making it, the purchase will be a new buy, a modified rebuy, or a straight rebuy.

New Buy A **new buy** is a situation requiring the purchase of a product for the first time. For example, suppose a manufacturing company needs a better way to page managers while they are working on the shop floor. Currently, each of the several managers has a distinct ring, for example, two short and one long, that sounds over the plant intercom whenever he or she is being paged by anyone in the factory. The company decides to replace its buzzer system of paging with handheld wireless radio technology that will allow managers to communicate immediately with the department initiating the page. This situation represents the greatest opportunity for new vendors. No long-term relationship has been established for this product, specifications may be somewhat fluid, and buyers are generally more open to new vendors.

   If the new item is a raw material or a critical component part, the buyer cannot afford to run out of supply. The seller must be able to convince the buyer that the seller's firm can consistently deliver a high-quality product on time.

Modified Rebuy A **modified rebuy** is normally less critical and less time-consuming than a new buy. In a modified-rebuy situation, the purchaser wants some change in the original good or service. It may be a new color, greater tensile

new buy
A situation requiring the purchase of a product for the first time.

modified rebuy
A situation where the purchaser wants some change in the original good or service.

straight rebuy

A situation in which the purchaser reorders the same goods or services without looking for new information or investigating other suppliers.

strength in a component part, more respondents in a marketing research study, or additional services in a janitorial contract.

Because the two parties are familiar with each other and credibility has been established, buyer and seller can concentrate on the specifics of the modification. But in some cases, modified rebuys are open to outside bidders. The purchaser uses this strategy to ensure that the new terms are competitive. An example would be the manufacturing company buying radios with a vibrating feature for managers who have trouble hearing the ring over the factory noise. The firm might open the bidding to examine the price/quality offerings of several suppliers.

Straight Rebuy A **straight rebuy** is a situation vendors prefer. The purchaser is not looking for new information or other suppliers. An order is placed and the product is provided as in previous orders. Usually, a straight rebuy is routine because the terms of the purchase have been agreed to in earlier negotiations. An example would be the previously cited manufacturing company purchasing additional radios for new managers from the same supplier on a regular basis.

One common instrument used in straight-rebuy situations is the purchasing contract. Purchasing contracts are used with products that are bought often and in high volume. In essence, the purchasing contract makes the buyer's decision making routine and promises the salesperson a sure sale. The advantage to the buyer is a quick, confident decision and to the salesperson, reduced or eliminated competition.

Suppliers must remember not to take straight-rebuy relationships for granted. Retaining existing customers is much easier than attracting new ones.

BUSINESS ETHICS

As we noted in Chapter 3, ethics refers to the moral principles or values that generally govern the conduct of an individual or a group. Ethics can also be viewed as the standard of behavior by which conduct is judged.

Although we have heard a lot about corporate misbehavior in recent years, most people, and most companies, follow ethical practices. To help achieve this, over half of all major corporations offer ethics training to employees. Many companies also have codes of ethics or business conduct that help guide buyers and sellers. The Ethics in Marketing box shows Lockheed Martin's Code of Ethics.

CUSTOMER SERVICE

Business marketers are increasingly recognizing the benefits of developing a formal system to monitor customer opinions and perceptions of the quality of customer service. Companies like McDonald's, L.L. Bean, and Lexus build their strategies not only around products, but also around a few highly developed service skills. These companies understand that keeping current customers satisfied is just as important as attracting new ones, if not more so. These leading-edge firms are obsessed not only with delivering high-quality customer service, but also with measuring satisfaction, loyalty, relationship quality, and other indicators of nonfinancial performance.

Most firms find it necessary to develop measures unique to their own strategy, value propositions, and target market. For example,

Promoting its in-flight customer service, Virgin Airlines' ad promises "If you order it, we will come." That is, you won't have to wait for your meal or drink to be delivered at their convenience, but when you want it.

© Ap Images/PRNewsFoto/Virgin America

ethics in marketing

Code of Ethics at Lockheed Martin

According to Lockheed Martin chairman, president, and chief executive officer Robert J. Stevens, "all of us have a shared responsibility to maintain the highest standard of integrity and ensure that we sustain a place where we are proud to work. If you are faced with an ethical dilemma, you have the responsibility to speak up and seek resolution. We must all be accountable for acting with integrity and upholding the values of the Corporation."[51]

Setting the Standard, the Company's Code of Ethics and Business Conduct, provides guidance on expectations for all employees, contract labor, agents, consultants, members of the Board of Directors, and others when representing or acting for the Corporation.

The Code includes three key components: a culture of integrity, our vision, and our values.

A Culture of Integrity

Lockheed Martin is committed to dealing honestly and fairly with our employees, customers, suppliers, shareholders and the communities in which we live and work. Our success depends on maintaining a culture of integrity.

Our Vision and Our Values

Lockheed Martin holds each director, executive, leader, employee, and agent accountable for upholding Our Vision, Our Values, and Our Code. In so doing, we ensure that Lockheed Martin's business will be conducted consistent with the high ethical standards that we demand from each other, and that others have the right to demand from us.

Our Vision:

Powered by Innovation, Guided by Integrity, We Help Our Customers Achieve Their Most Challenging Goals.

Our Values:

Do What's Right
Respect Others
Perform With Excellence[52]

Discuss the similarities and differences in Lockheed Martin's Code and the American Marketing Association's statement of ethics called its "Ethical Norms and Values for Marketers" at **www.marketingpower.com**.

Anderson Corporation assesses the loyalty of its trade customers by their willingness to continue carrying its windows and doors, recommend its products to colleagues and customers, increase their volume with the company, and put its products in their own homes. Basically, each firm's measures should not only ask "What are your expectations?" and "How are we doing?" but should also reflect what the firm wants its customers to do.

Some customers are more valuable than others. They may have greater value because they spend more, buy higher-margin products, have a well-known name, or have the potential of becoming a bigger customer in the future. Some companies selectively provide different levels of service to customers based on their value to the business. By giving the most valuable customers superior service, a firm is more likely to keep them happy, hopefully increasing retention of these high-value customers and maximizing the total business value they generate over time.

To achieve this goal, the firm must be able to divide customers into two or more groups based on their value. It must also create and apply policies that govern how service will be allocated among groups. Policies might establish which customers' phone calls get "fast tracked" and which customers are directed to use the Web and/or voice self-service, how specific e-mail questions are routed, and who is given access to online chat and who isn't.[53]

Providing different customers with different levels of service is a very sensitive matter. It must be handled very carefully and very discreetly to avoid offending lesser-value, but still important customers.

Review

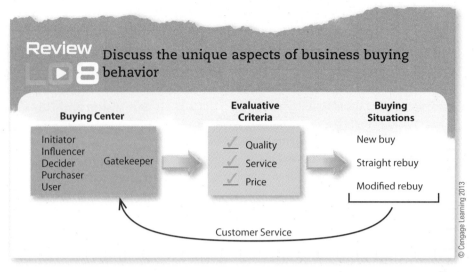

Review LO 8 Discuss the unique aspects of business buying behavior

Buying Center		Evaluative Criteria	Buying Situations
Initiator Influencer Decider Purchaser User	Gatekeeper	✓ Quality ✓ Service ✓ Price	New buy Straight rebuy Modified rebuy

Customer Service

© Cengage Learning 2013

B2B interactive marketing spending in 2010
$2.3 billion

Core companies in the Toyota Group keiretsu
14

Companies that receive preferential treatment from the Toyota Group keiretsu
170

Wholesalers operating in the United States
500,000

Amount government organizations spend each year on goods and services
$5.5 trillion

NAICS economic sectors
20

Size of the contract the Pentagon awarded to Lockheed Martin to build three thousand jet fighter planes
$200 billion

Transactions made each week on Exostar—the online exchange of the aerospace industry
20,000

Review and Applications

LO 1 **Describe business marketing.** Business marketing provides goods and services that are bought for use in business rather than for personal consumption. Intended use, not physical characteristics, distinguishes a business product from a consumer product.

writing

1.1 As the marketing manager for Huggies diapers, made by Kimberly-Clark, you are constantly going head-to-head with Pampers, produced by rival Procter & Gamble. You are considering unlocking the potential of the business market to increase your share of the disposable diaper market, but how? Write an outline of several ways you could transform this quintessentially consumer product into a successful business product as well.

LO 2 **Describe the role of the Internet in business marketing.** The rapid expansion and adoption of the Internet have made business markets more competitive than ever before. The number of business buyers and sellers using the Internet is rapidly increasing. Firms are seeking new and better ways to expand markets and sources of supply, increase sales and decrease costs, and better serve customers. Marketers are becoming more sophisticated in their use of the Internet and are developing quantitative methods that can be used to better measure online success.

2.1 How could you use the Web site **BtoBonline.com** to help define a target market and develop a marketing plan?

online

2.2 Reconsider question 1.1. How could you use the Internet in your business marketing of Huggies diapers?

Discuss the role of relationship marketing and strategic alliances in business marketing. Relationship marketing entails seeking and establishing long-term alliances or partnerships with customers. A strategic alliance is a cooperative agreement between business firms. Firms form alliances to leverage what they do well by partnering with others that have complementary skills.

LO**3**

3.1 Why is relationship or personal selling the best way to promote in business marketing?

Identify the four major categories of business market customers. Producer markets consist of for-profit organizations and individuals that buy products to use in producing other products, as components of other products, or in facilitating business operations. Reseller markets consist of wholesalers and retailers that buy finished products to resell for profit. Government markets include federal, state, county, and city governments that buy goods and services to support their own operations and serve the needs of citizens. Institutional markets consist of very diverse nonbusiness institutions whose main goals do not include profit.

LO**4**

4.1 Understanding businesses is key to business marketing. Publications like *Manufacturing Automation*, *Computer Weekly*, *Power Generation Technology & Markets,* and *Biotech Equipment Update* can give you insights into many business marketing concepts. Research the industrial publications to find an article on a business marketer that interests you. Write a description of the company using as many concepts from the chapter as possible. What major category or categories of business market customers does this firm serve?

writing

4.2 What do you have to do to get a government contract? Check out the Web sites **www.fedbizopps.gov** and **www.governmentbids.com** to find out. Does it seem worth the effort?

online

Explain the North American Industry Classification System. The NAICS provides a way to identify, analyze, segment, and target business and government markets. Organizations can be identified and compared by a numeric code indicating business sector, subsector, industry group, industry, and country industry. NAICS is a valuable tool for analyzing, segmenting, and targeting business markets.

LO**5**

5.1 Pick a product and determine its NAICS code. How easy was it to trace the groups and sectors?

Explain the major differences between business and consumer markets. In business markets, demand is derived, price-inelastic, joint, and fluctuating. Purchase volume is much larger than in consumer markets, customers are fewer in number and more geographically concentrated, and distribution channels are more direct. Buying is approached more formally using professional purchasing agents, more people are involved in the buying process, negotiation is more complex, and reciprocity and leasing are more common. And, finally, selling strategy in business markets normally focuses on personal contact rather than on advertising.

LO**6**

© iStockphoto.com/Juan Facundo Mora Soria

6.1 How might derived demand affect the manufacturing of an automobile?

6.2 Your boss has just asked you, the company purchasing manager, to buy new computers for an entire department. As you have just recently purchased a new home computer, you are well-educated about the various products available. How will your buying process for the company differ from your recent purchase for yourself?

 Describe the seven types of business goods and services. Major equipment includes capital goods, such as heavy machinery. Accessory equipment is typically less expensive and shorter-lived than major equipment. Raw materials are extractive or agricultural products that have not been processed. Component parts are finished or near-finished items to be used as parts of other products. Processed materials are used to manufacture other products. Supplies are consumable and not used as part of a final product. Business services are intangible products that many companies use in their operations.

 7.1 In small groups, brainstorm examples of companies that feature the products in different business categories. (Avoid examples already listed in the chapter.) Compile a list of ten specific business products including at least one in each category. Then match up with another group. Have each group take turns naming a product and have the other group identify its appropriate category. Try to resolve all discrepancies by discussion. Some identified products may appropriately fit into more than one category.

 Discuss the unique aspects of business buying behavior. Business buying behavior is distinguished by five fundamental characteristics. First, buying is normally undertaken by a buying center consisting of many people who range widely in authority level. Second, business buyers typically evaluate alternative products and suppliers based on quality, service, and price—in that order. Third, business buying falls into three general categories: new buys, modified rebuys, and straight rebuys. Fourth, the ethics of business buyers and sellers are often scrutinized. Fifth, customer service before, during, and after the sale plays a big role in business purchase decisions.

 8.1 A colleague of yours has sent you an e-mail message seeking your advice as he attempts to sell a new voice-mail system to a local business. Send him a return e-mail message describing the various people who might influence the customer's buying decision. Be sure to include suggestions for dealing with the needs of each of these individuals.

8.2 Intel Corporation supplies microprocessors to Hewlett-Packard for use in its computers. Describe the buying situation in this relationship, keeping in mind the rapid advance of technology in this industry.

Key Terms

accessory equipment 254
business marketing (industrial marketing) 237
business services 256
business-to-business electronic commerce 238
buying center 257
component parts 255
derived demand 250
disintermediation 242
joint demand 250
keiretsu 245

major equipment (installations) 254
modified rebuy 259
multiplier effect (accelerator principle) 250
new buy 259
North American Industry Classification System (NAICS) 248
original equipment manufacturers (OEMs) 246

processed materials 255
raw materials 254
reciprocity 252
reintermediation 243
relationship commitment 244
stickiness 241
straight rebuy 260
strategic alliance (strategic partnership) 244
supplies 255
trust 244

Exercises

ETHICS EXERCISE

ethics

Cameron Stock, purchasing manager for a sports equipment manufacturer, is responsible for buying $5 million of supplies every year. He has a preferred list of certified suppliers who are awarded a large percentage of his business. Cameron has been offered a paid weekend for two in Las Vegas as a Christmas present from a supplier with whom he has done business for a decade and built a very good relationship.

Questions

1. Would it be legal and ethical for Cameron Stock to accept this gift?
2. How is this addressed in the AMA Statement of Ethics? Go to the AMA Web site at www. marketingpower.com/About_AMA/ and reread the Statement of Ethics. Write a brief paragraph summarizing where the AMA stands on the issue of supplier gifts.

MARKETING PLAN EXERCISE

For continued general assistance in business plans and marketing plans, visit **www. bplans.com** or **www.businessplans.org.** You should also refer to the Marketing Plan Outline–Appendix I in Chapter 2 for additional checklist items. Complete the following exercises to continue the marketing plan you began in Chapter 2:

1. Identify the NAICS code for your chosen company's industry (**www.census.gov/eos/ www/naics/**). Perform a brief industry analysis (from International Trade Administration, U.S. Department of Commerce, at **http://ita.doc.gov/td/industry/otea/**, for example) of your firm's industry, based on the NAICS code.
2. Make a list of consumer markets and business markets for your company's product or business offering. Which is the more important market for your company? Why?
3. How does the buying process differ for consumer markets and business markets for your chosen company's product or business offering?

APPLICATION EXERCISE

Purchasing agents are often offered gifts and gratuities. Increasingly, though, companies are restricting the amount and value of gifts that their purchasing managers can accept from vendors. The idea is that purchasing managers should consider all qualified vendors during a buying decision instead of only those who pass out great event tickets. This exercise asks you to consider whether accepting various types of gifts is ethical.[54]

Activities

1. Review the following list of common types of gifts and favors. Put a check mark next to the items that you think it would be acceptable for a purchasing manager to receive from a vendor.

Advertising souvenirs	Automobiles
Clothing	Dinners
Discounts on personal purchases	Food and liquor
Golf outings	Holiday gifts
Large appliances	Loans of money
Lunches	Small-value appliances
Tickets (sports, theater, amusement parks, etc.)	Trips to vendor plants
Vacation trips	

2. Now look at your list of acceptable gifts through various lenses. Would your list change if the purchasing manager's buying decision involved a low-cost item (say, pens)? Why or why not? What if the decision involved a very expensive purchase (like a major installation)?

3. Form a team and compare your lists. Discuss (or debate) any discrepancies.

CASE STUDY: CamelBak

THEY'VE GOT YOUR 'BAK

© PR Newsfoto/CamelBak Products, LLC

In 1989, Michael Eidson probably never imagined that his homemade, do-it-yourself fix for dehydration during long cycling races would evolve into the world's premier hydration device for outdoor enthusiasts, soldiers, and law enforcement personnel. That is exactly what happened to the CamelBak backpack, however.

The first version, which used medical tubing to flow water from an intravenous drip bag that was insulated by a sock and strapped to the back of his shirt, was born as most inventions are—out of necessity. The special pack made it possible for Eidson to take in fluids while sitting upright without having to sacrifice speed by reaching down for a water bottle during a race. The packs gained fame during the 1991 Gulf War as extreme sports enthusiasts in the U.S. Special Forces carried their personal CamelBaks into combat during Desert Storm. Thereafter, the CamelBak name would be forever associated with extreme performance and the U.S. Armed Forces.

By 1995, Eidsen sold the company for $4 million. Its buyer, Kransco, introduced the first camouflaged models, and the packs continued to gain acclaim. In 1999, two years after buying his first CamelBak pack, cyclist Chuck Hunter left Lockheed Martin to join the upstart company in hopes of growing its military business. He promptly moved the company to the Sonoma Valley, built a research and development center, and leveraged his experience in the defense industry to launch a military-specific line of packs.

Hunter partnered with DuPont to help CamelBak develop the Low Infrared Reflective (LIRR) system. LIRR applies specially developed materials to a pack's compartments, buckles, and straps to shield soldiers from enemy detection systems. As advanced identification and kill technologies are increasingly being deployed on the battlefield, individual protection applications like the LIRR will be the camouflage of tomorrow.

Other CamelBak innovations include the WaterBeast reservoir, a fluid storage system that boasts 30 percent more rigidity than other packs on the market. The WaterBeast has the ability to withstand lengthy field engagements, aided by its silver-ion reservoir and tube linings that eliminate 99.99 percent of all fungus and bacteria in the water delivery system. The WaterBeast reservoir is now a standard feature on all CamelBak packs, as is the company's proprietary drinking nozzle, or bite valve, which must withstand 10,000 compressions to guarantee it will last through 3 years of combat use.

Another CamelBak first is its CBR 4.0 pack system, which is specially designed to perform under chemical or biological weapons attack. The CBR 4.0 took 5 years to develop, and like all CamelBak military and law enforcement products, it was created to meet the specific requests and requirements of the target market. Since its introduction in 2005, the U.S. Special Forces, New York Police Department, U.S. Secret Service, Department of Health and Human Services, and a myriad of HAZMAT, law enforcement, and government agencies from around the world have adopted and deployed the CBR 4.0.

Though CamelBak specializes in offering extreme performance packs for the military, industrial, and professional markets, it also sells a variety of products for hunting, extreme sports, recreational, and "light" law enforcement applications. Having claimed more than 90 percent of the military market for hydration packs, product manager Shawn Cullen likens CamelBak to Kleenex: "Everyone calls a hydration system a CamelBak," he says. Ironically, the company's biggest customer is its biggest competitor. While it continues to use CamelBaks, the U.S. Army is working with a former supplier to develop its own version, most likely in an attempt to reduce costs.

At prices up to $200 for combat-ready systems, one thing CamelBaks aren't is cheap. But then again, neither is CamelBak itself. Its strong product lines, history of innovation, secure strategic relationships, and dominance in government and institutional markets drove its value to over $200 million when investment bank Bear Stearns Company bought the outfit from Kransco in 2003—not bad for a product that started life as an intravenous fluid bag wrapped in a sock.[55]

Questions

1. Discuss how business relationships and strategic partnerships have helped to increase the value of CamelBak's products and the business itself.

2. What type(s) of business market customers does CamelBak sell to?

3. Review the types of demand that most influence business markets. Which ones do you think are most important for CamelBak to consider in its marketing strategy? Why?

4. What type of business product is a CamelBak backpack?

COMPANY CLIPS: *ReadyMade*—Making Business Relationships

Like most periodicals, *ReadyMade* relies on advertisers for much of its revenue. Finding companies interested in advertising in the magazine and cultivating those relationships is an important component of making the company successful. *ReadyMade* must constantly market its product to potential investors through personal contact and solicitation. *ReadyMade* also must develop relationships with distributors and other businesses that will directly or indirectly promote the magazine and help make it successful. As you watch this video, notice the strategies that Darci Andresen describes as she explains the process she goes through as head of Advertising Sales & Special Promotions when seeking new advertisers.

Questions

1. When marketing to potential advertisers, what strategies could *ReadyMade* use to promote itself without having to rely on hard statistics about its readers?

2. What sort of strategic alliances does *ReadyMade* maintain? In what ways are these partnerships beneficial to the magazine?

3. Go to *ReadyMade*'s Web site, **readymademag.com.** What evidence do you see of its business partnerships? How does it use its Web site to market itself to businesses?

1. "2008 Marketing Priorities and Plans," *BtoB,* July 15, 2008, 25.
2. Michael D. Hutt and Thomas W. Speh, *Business Marketing Management: B2B, 10th ed.* (Cincinnati: Thomson, 2010), 4.
3. *Ibid.*
4. Mary E. Morrison, "Industrial Buyers Shopping Online," *BtoB,* October 13, 2008, 19.
5. Sean Callahan, "Interactive Spending Continues to Climb," *BtoB,* March 8, 2010, www.btobonline.com/apps/pbcs.dll/article?AID=/20100308/FREE/303049998/1445/FREE.
6. Ellis Booker, "Social Media Use Soars among B-to-B Marketers," *BtoB,* July 20, 2009, www.btobonline.com/apps/pbcs.dll/article?AID=/20090720/FREE/307159994/1445/FREE.
7. Karen Bannan, "10 Great B-to-B Sites," *BtoB*, September 13, 2010, 13.
8. "B2B Marketers Gain Ground with Social," www.emarketer.tv/Article.aspx?R=1007717, May 27, 2010.
9. "B2B Spending on Social Media to Explode," *eMarketer,* June 1, 2010, www.emarketer.co/Article.aspx?R=1007725.
10. Christopher Hosford, "Socially Challenged: B-to-B Companies Seek New Ways to Push Social Marketing beyond Customer Intelligence to Demand Generation and Sales," *BtoB,* February 8, 2010, www.btobonline.com/apps/pbcs.dll/article?AID=/20100208/FREE/302089965/1445/FREE.
11. Elizabeth Sullivan, "A Long Slog," *Marketing News*, February 28, 2009, 16–18.
12. Paul Gillin, "B-to-B Firmly in Social Media," *BtoB,* April 12, 2010, www.btobonline.com/article/20100412/FREE/304129965/b-to-b-firmly-in-social-media.
13. Josh Bernoff, "Why B-to-B Ought to Love Social Media," *Marketing News*, April 15, 2009.
14. Rich Karpinksi, "B-to-B Followers Flock to Twitter," *BtoB,* April 6, 2009, www.btobonline.com/apps/pbcs.dll/article?AID=/20090406/FREE/304069970/1109/FREE.
15. Karen Bannan, "YouTube for B-to-B: How to Use the Popular Video Site to Expand Your Branding," *BtoB,* May 5, 2010, www.btobonline.com/apps/pbcs.dll/article?AID=/20100503/FREE/305039965/1445/FREE.
16. Sean Callahan, "B-to-B Marketers Cautiously Explore Mobile Marketing," *BtoB,* February 8, 2010, www.btobonline.com/apps/pbcs.dll/article?AID=/20100208/FREE/302089970/1445/FREE.
17. *Ibid.*
18. Karen Bannan, "10 Great B-to-B Sites," *BtoB,* September 13, 2010, www.btobonline.com/apps/pbcs.dll/article?AID=/20090914/FREE/909149997/1151/btobissue.
19. Karen Bannan, "10 Great Web Sites: Overview," *BtoB,* September 15, 2008, 13.
20. Mitch Wagner, "Design by Metrics: Analytics Help Marketers Adapt Their Web Sites to Customer Behavior," *BtoB,* March 8, 2010, www.btobonline.com/apps/pbcs.dll/article?AID=/20100308/FREE/303089985/1007/METRICS.
21. NetGenesis, E-Metrics: Business Metrics for the New Economy, www.spss.com.
22. Ellis Booker, "B-to-B Marketers Apply Analytics to Social Media," *BtoB,* April 12, 2010, www.btobonline.com/apps/pbcs.dll/article?AID=/20100412/FREE/304089975/1445/FREE.
23. *Ibid.*
24. Brian Hook, "Climbing the B2B Social Media Ladder," *E-Commerce Times*, May 27, 2010, www.ecommercetimes.com/rsstory/70081.html?wlc=1296574575.
25. Morrison, "Industrial Buyers Shopping Online."
26. Mike Gate, "RSS Feed—The Definition," *Ezine Articles*, March 26, 2010, http://ezinearticles.com/?RSS-Feed—The-Definition&id=4000731.
27. "B2B Marketers Missing Out on Influencing Buyers Online," *Marketing Matters Newsletter*, Chicago: American Marketing Association, October 28, 2008.
28. "Grainger Introduces SupplyLink Site," *BtoB,* July 24, 2008, www.btobonline.com/apps/pbcs.dll/article?AID=/20080724/FREE/579711465/1078/rss01&rssfeed=rss01.
29. "Disintermediation," www.marketingterms.com/dictionary/disintermediation.
30. "Reintermediation," www.businessdictionary.com/definition/reintermediation.html.
31. Kate Maddox, "Marketers Look to Boost Customer Retention," *BtoB,* May 5, 2008, www.btobonline.com/apps/pbcs.dll/article?AID=/20080505/FREE/491968804/1109/FREE.
32. Elizabeth Sullivan, "B-to-B Marketers, Forget the Spray and Pray Approach," *Marketing News*, May 15, 2009, 11.
33. Nick Wingfield and Justin Scheck, "H-P, Microsoft Partner against Rivals," *Wall Street Journal*, January 15, 2010, http://online.wsj.com/article/SB10001424052748703414504575001171859404254.html.
34. Steven Reinberg, "The Issue: DHL Turns to Rival UPS," *BusinessWeek*, June 11, 2008, www.businessweek.com/managing/content/jun2008/ca20080611_101915.htm.
35. Erin White, "A Cheaper Alternative to Outsourcing: Choice Hotels and 1-800-Flowers Swap Call-Center Employees," *Wall Street Journal*, April 10, 2006, B3.
36. Robert M. Morgan and Shelby D. Hunt, "The Commitment-Trust Theory of Relationship Marketing," *Journal of Marketing*, 58, no. 3 (1994): 23.
37. *Ibid.*
38. Gordon Fairclough, "GM's Chinese Partner Looms as a New Rival," *Wall Street Journal*, April 20, 2007, A1.
39. Rebecca Smith, "U.S. Power Companies Seek Out Chinese Allies," *Wall Street Journal*, November 20, 2009, http://online.wsj.com/article/SB100014240527487045384045745377120288807656.html.

© iStockphoto.com/ziggymaj

marketing&you: Results.

A high score indicates that you found the salesperson to be credible and concerned about your needs. Because you found the salesperson to be open and concerned, you had a higher level of trust in the salesperson than did someone with a lower score. As you read in this chapter, trust is an important element in building strategic alliances and in cultivating business clients.

40. Mary Morrison, "Getting in with Government," *B-to-B*, May 3, 2010, 13.
41. *Ibid.*
42. U.S. Census Bureau, "North American Industry Classification System (NAICS)—United States," January 12, 2009, www.census.gov/epcd/www/naics.html.
43. "Exostar's Global Customer Base," Exostar Web site, www.exostar.com/Exostar_Customers.aspx.
44. J. Lynn Lunsford, "Boeing Delays Dreamliner Delivery Again," *Wall Street Journal*, April 10, 2008, B3.
45. Kate Maddox, "Emerson Rolls Out Global Campaign," *BtoB*, March 3, 2009, www.btobonline.com/apps/pbcs.dll/article?AID=/20090303/FREE/903039986/1078.
46. "Be Sure to Look for Decision-Makers," *BtoB*, October 12, 2009, 12.
47. Marshall Lager, "Listen Up," *Customer Relationship Management*, March 2007, 24–27.
48. Nicholas Read, "How to Sell to the C-Suite," *Forbes*, May 8, 2010, www.forbes.com/2010/05/08/selling-to-the-c-suite-entrepreneurs-sales-management-nicholas-read.html.
49. *Ibid.*
50. Kate Maddox, "Relevant Content Connects with C-suite," *BtoB*, October 13, 2008, 37–38.
51. "Setting the Standard: Code of Ethics and Business Conduct," Lockheed Martin Corporation Web site, www.lockheedmartin.com/data/assets/corporate/documents/ethics/setting-the-standard.pdf (Accessed August 9, 2010).
52. *Ibid.*
53. "Right Channeling: Making Sure Your Best Customers Get Your Best Service," Right Now Technologies, June 3, 2009, http://jobfunctions.bnet.com/abstract.aspx?docid=132740.
54. This application exercise is based on the contribution of Gregory B. Turner (College of Charleston) to *Great Ideas in Teaching Marketing*, a teaching supplement that accompanies Lamb, Hair, and McDaniel's *Marketing*. Professor Turner's entry titled "Student Ethics versus Practitioner Ethics" received an Honorable Mention in the "Best of the Great Ideas in Teaching Marketing" contest held in conjunction with the publication of the eighth edition of *Marketing*.
55. Jonathan Karp, "How Bikers' Water Backpack Became Soldiers' Essential," *The Wall Street Journal*, July 19, 2005, B1, B2; "CamelBak Introduces New Line of Strength/Stealth Technology Responding to Law Enforcement and Military Needs; R&D Innovations Protect Against Infrared Detection, Provide Strongest Hydration Reservoir Available," *PR Newswire*, January 27, 2005; Mark Riedy, "The Birth of CamelBak," *Mountain Bike*, Summer 2004, 104; "CamelBak Announces Chem-Bio Hydration Reservoir for Military, Law Enforcement and First Responders; New Reservoir Is World's Only Hands-Free Hydration System That Withstands Exposure to Chemical and Biological Agents to Provide Safe Drinking Water in All Combat Environments 24/7/365." *PR Newswire*, August 26, 2004.

8

Segmenting and Targeting Markets

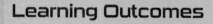

Learning Outcomes

1 Describe the characteristics of markets and market segments

2 Explain the importance of market segmentation

3 Discuss criteria for successful market segmentation

4 Describe the bases commonly used to segment consumer markets

5 Describe the bases for segmenting business markets

6 List the steps involved in segmenting markets

7 Discuss alternative strategies for selecting target markets

8 Explain one-to-one marketing

9 Explain how and why firms implement positioning strategies and how product differentiation plays a role

LO1
Market Segmentation

The term *market* means different things to different people. We are all familiar with the supermarket, stock market, labor market, fish market, and flea market. All these types of markets share several characteristics. First, they are composed of people (consumer markets) or organizations (business markets). Second, these people or organizations have wants and needs that can be satisfied by particular product categories. Third, they have the ability to buy the products they seek. Fourth, they are willing to exchange their resources, usually money or credit, for desired products. In sum, a **market** is (1) people or organizations with (2) needs or wants and with (3) the ability and (4) the willingness to buy. A group of people or an organization that lacks any one of these characteristics is not a market.

Within a market, a **market segment** is a subgroup of people or organizations sharing one or more characteristics that cause them to have similar product needs. At one extreme, we can define every person and every organization in the world as a market segment because each is unique. At the other extreme, we can define the entire consumer market as one large market segment and the business market as another large segment. All people have some similar characteristics and needs, as do all organizations.

From a marketing perspective, market segments can be described as somewhere between the two extremes. The process of dividing a market into meaningful, relatively similar, and identifiable segments or groups is called **market segmentation**. The purpose of market segmentation is to enable the marketer to tailor marketing mixes to meet the needs of one or more specific segments.

> "
> **Market segmentation enables the marketer to meet the needs specific segments.**
> "

market
People or organizations with needs or wants and the ability and willingness to buy.

market segment
A subgroup of people or organizations sharing one or more characteristics that cause them to have similar product needs.

marketing&you.

Please note your opinion on each of the following questions.

Using the following scale, enter your opinion.

STRONGLY AGREE 〈1 2 3 4 5 6〉 STRONGLY DISAGREE

_____ I frequently have problems making ends meet.

_____ My budgeting is always tight.

_____ I often have to spend more money than I have available.

_____ I do not consider myself financially well off.

_____ I am generally on a tight budget.

_____ Meeting an unexpected expense of $1,000 would be a financial hardship.

Source: Scale #646, *Marketing Scales Handbook*, G. Bruner, K. James, H. Hensel, eds., Vol. III. © by American Marketing Association.

Total your score. Now, read the chapter and find out what your score means at the end.

Exhibit 8.1 Concept of Market Segmentation

No market segmentation

Fully segmented market

Market segmentation by
gender: M, F

Market segmentation by
age group: 1, 2, 3

Market segmentation
by gender and age group

Exhibit 8.1 illustrates the concept of market segmentation. Each box represents a market consisting of seven persons. This market might vary as follows: one homogeneous market of seven people; a market consisting of seven individual segments; a market composed of two segments based on gender; a market composed of three age segments; or a market composed of five age and gender market segments. Age and gender and many other bases for segmenting markets are examined later in this chapter.

LO2
The Importance of Market Segmentation

Until the 1960s, few firms practiced market segmentation. When they did, it was more likely a haphazard effort than a formal marketing strategy. Before 1960, for example, the Coca-Cola Company produced only one beverage and aimed it at the entire soft drink market. Today, Coca-Cola offers over a dozen different products to market segments based on diverse consumer preferences for flavors and calorie and caffeine content. Coca-Cola offers traditional soft drinks, energy drinks (such as POWERade), flavored teas, fruit drinks (Fruitopia), and water (Dasani).

Market segmentation plays a key role in the marketing strategy of almost all successful organizations and is a powerful marketing tool for several reasons. Most

market segmentation
The process of dividing a market into meaningful, relatively similar, and identifiable segments or groups.

importantly, nearly all markets include groups of people or organizations with different product needs and preferences. Market segmentation helps marketers define customer needs and wants more precisely. Because market segments differ in size and potential, segmentation helps decision makers to more accurately define marketing objectives and better allocate resources. In turn, performance can be better evaluated when objectives are more precise.

Chico's, a successful women's fashion retailer, thrives by marketing to women aged 35 to 55 who like to wear comfortable, yet stylish, clothing. It sells private-label clothing that comes in just a few nonjudgmental sizes: zero (regular sizes 4–6), one (8–10), two (10–12), and three (14–16). Another example is Best Buy, which identifies the needs of customers depending on their geographic location. For example, the store in Baytown, Texas, caters to Eastern European workers from cargo ships or oil tankers that are temporarily docked at the city's busy port. These workers don't have a lot of time to shop, so the Baytown Best Buy moved the iPods from the back corner of the store to the front, paired them with overseas power converters, and simplified the signage.[1]

LO3
Criteria for Successful Segmentation

Marketers segment markets for three important reasons. First, segmentation enables marketers to identify groups of customers with similar needs and to analyze the characteristics and buying behavior of these groups. Second, segmentation provides marketers with information to help them design marketing mixes specifically matched with the characteristics and desires of one or more segments. Third, segmentation is consistent with the marketing concept of satisfying customer wants and needs while meeting the organization's objectives.

To be useful, a segmentation scheme must produce segments that meet four basic criteria:

→ **Substantiality:** A segment must be large enough to warrant developing and maintaining a special marketing mix. This criterion does not necessarily mean that a segment must have many potential customers. Marketers of custom-designed homes and business buildings,

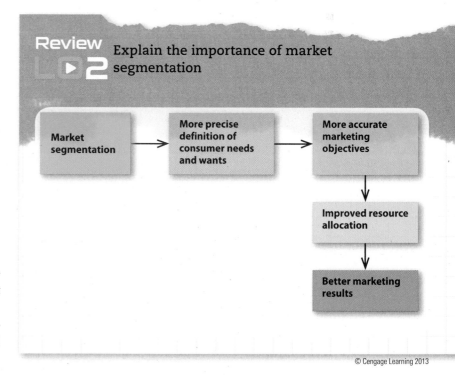

Review LO 1 Describe the characteristics of markets and market segments

Segment

Market

© Cengage Learning 2013

Review LO 2 Explain the importance of market segmentation

Market segmentation → More precise definition of consumer needs and wants → More accurate marketing objectives → Improved resource allocation → Better marketing results

© Cengage Learning 2013

commercial airplanes, and large computer systems typically develop marketing programs tailored to each potential customer's needs. In most cases, however, a market segment needs many potential customers to make commercial sense. In the 1980s, home banking failed because not enough people owned personal computers. Today, a larger number of people own computers, and home banking is a thriving industry.

→ **Identifiability and measurability:** Segments must be identifiable and their size measurable. Data about the population within geographic boundaries, the number of people in various age categories, and other social and demographic characteristics are often easy to get, and they provide fairly concrete measures of segment size. Suppose that a social service agency wants to identify segments by their readiness to participate in a drug and alcohol program or in prenatal care. Unless the agency can measure how many people are willing, indifferent, or unwilling to participate, it will have trouble gauging whether there are enough people to justify setting up the service.

→ **Accessibility:** The firm must be able to reach members of targeted segments with customized marketing mixes. Some market segments are hard to reach—for example, senior citizens (especially those with reading or hearing disabilities), individuals who don't speak English, and the illiterate.

→ **Responsiveness:** As Exhibit 8.1 illustrates, markets can be segmented using any criteria that seem logical. Unless one market segment responds to a marketing mix differently from other segments, however, that segment need not be treated separately. For instance, if all customers are equally price-conscious about a product, there is no need to offer high-, medium-, and low-priced versions to different segments.

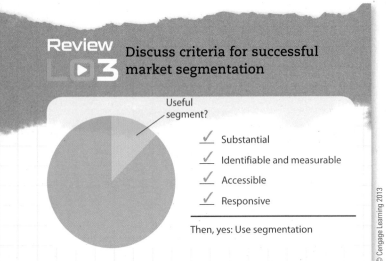

Review LO3 Discuss criteria for successful market segmentation

Useful segment?

✓ Substantial
✓ Identifiable and measurable
✓ Accessible
✓ Responsive

Then, yes: Use segmentation

© Cengage Learning 2013

LO4
Bases for Segmenting Consumer Markets

Marketers use **segmentation bases**, or **variables**, which are characteristics of individuals, groups, or organizations, to divide a total market into segments. The choice of segmentation bases is crucial because an inappropriate segmentation strategy could lead to lost sales and missed profit opportunities. The key is to identify bases that will produce substantial, measurable, and accessible segments that exhibit different response patterns to marketing mixes.

Markets can be segmented using a single variable, such as age group, or several variables, such as age group, gender, and education. Although it is less precise, single-variable segmentation has the advantage of being simpler and easier to use than multiple-variable segmentation. The disadvantages of multiple-variable segmentation are that it is often harder to use than single-variable segmentation; usable secondary data are less likely to be available; and as the number of segmentation bases increases, the size of individual segments decreases. Nevertheless,

segmentation bases (variables)
Characteristics of individuals, groups, or organizations.

the current trend is toward using more rather than fewer variables to segment most markets. Multiple-variable segmentation is clearly more precise than single-variable segmentation.

Consumer goods marketers commonly use one or more of the following characteristics to segment markets: geography, demographics, psychographics, benefits sought, and usage rate.

GEOGRAPHIC SEGMENTATION

Geographic segmentation refers to segmenting markets by region of a country or the world, market size, market density, or climate. Market density means the number of people within a unit of land, such as a census tract. Climate is commonly used for geographic segmentation because of its dramatic impact on residents' needs and purchasing behavior. Snowblowers, water and snow skis, clothing, and air-conditioning and heating systems are products with varying appeal, depending on climate.

Consumer goods companies take a regional approach to marketing for four reasons. First, many firms need to find new ways to generate sales because of sluggish and intensely competitive markets. Second, computerized checkout stations with scanners give retailers an accurate assessment of which brands sell best in their region. Third, many packaged-goods manufacturers are introducing new regional brands intended to appeal to local preferences. Fourth, a more regional approach allows consumer goods companies to react more quickly to competition. For example, Macy's is a department store retailer that uses geographic segmentation. For many years, all Macy's stores carried the same merchandise, regardless of location. Now, the chain's "My Macy's" program tailors each store's merchandise mix to reflect local tastes. For example, the stores in Columbus, Ohio, carry more golf-style clothing than a typical store because of the area's many golf courses.[2] The strategy has paid off for Macy's; total sales between 2009 and 2010 increased by almost 5 percent, in spite of the troubled economy during this time.[3]

DEMOGRAPHIC SEGMENTATION

Marketers often segment markets on the basis of demographic information because it is widely available and often related to consumers' buying and consuming behavior. Some common bases of **demographic segmentation** are age, gender, income, ethnic background, and family life cycle.

Age Segmentation   Marketers use a variety of terms to refer to different age groups. Examples include newborns, infants, young children, tweens, teens and young adults (Generation Y), adults (Generation X), baby boomers, and seniors. Age segmentation can be an important tool, as a brief exploration of the market potential of several age segments illustrates.

Through allowances, earnings, and gifts, children account for, and influence, a great deal of consumption. For example, tweens (roughly 8–12 years old) in the United States spend billions of their own dollars each year on purchases for

Why Quitting May Fail

Stress	67%
Nicotine cravings	56%
Irritability	35%
Social situations too tempting	29%
Weight gain	18%
Lack of support from friends and family	15%

Stress and nicotine cravings were the main reasons why surveyed African-American smokers failed to quit.

DON'T GO COLD TURKEY

While stress is the number one reason why African-American smokers fail at their quit attempt, going cold turkey may also be a significant factor. Quitting cold turkey does not address the nicotine cravings that effect smokers during their quit attempt, yet for 83 percent of African-American smokers surveyed, this is their quitting method of choice. Nicotine replacement therapies such as Nicorette® gum, NicoDerm® CQ® patch and the Commit® lozenge help address these cravings. To make quitting easier, the oral quit aids are available in flavors such as mint, fruit and cherry, and there is a more flexible patch.

Source: GlaxoSmithKline Consumer Healthcare, 2006 African-American Smoking Trend Survey conducted by Kelton Research

A successful segmentation scheme must identify and measure its target customer base. GlaxoSmithKline surveyed the African American smoking population and found that, for the majority, quitting cold turkey wasn't working for them. This data justifies a campaign to promote GlaxoSmithKline's product for gradually quitting smoking to that population.

geographic segmentation
Segmenting markets by region of a country or the world, market size, market density, or climate.

demographic segmentation
Segmenting markets by age, gender, income, ethnic background, and family life cycle.

Baby boomers make up a sizable proportion of affluent households and they want attention and service. They also like to think of themselves as trailblazers, so ads appealing to their adventurous spirit are more effective than ones suggesting aging.

themselves, and also have a considerable influence over major family purchase decisions. They are technology savvy and very social consumers.[4] Tweens desire to be kids, but also want some of the fun of being a teenager. Many retailers, such as Abercrombie Kids, serve this market with clothing that is similar in style to that worn by teenagers and young adults. The members of the Generation Y market, or the Millennial Generation, were born between 1982 and 2003, and make up almost one-third of the U.S. population. This group not only has formidable purchasing power, but it is also more civic-minded than the baby boomers. Seventy-four percent of Millennials say they are more likely to pay attention to a company's overall message if the company has a deep commitment to a cause.[5] The teens in this group are interested in apparel that enhances personalization and self-expression, because they want their look to reflect their personalities and style.[6] College students (also part of the Millennials) all have mobile phones, and use them constantly to communicate and connect. Despite the potential marketing gold-mine such a connected audience presents, a study showed many people in this group were highly negative toward ads on their phones.[7] When Procter & Gamble acquired Herbal Essences, the brand was struggling to compete with other shampoos. So its marketers choose to target Gen Y and Millennial women by redesigning the packaging and adding cute style names like "drama clean." The changes were successful and Herbal Essences sales began growing again.[8]

Generation X is the group that was born after the baby boomers. Members of Generation X, or Xers, tend to be disloyal to brands and skeptical of big business. Many of them make purchasing decisions with thought for and input from their families. Xers desire an experience, not just a product. For example, Starbucks developed a market for expensive coffee by encompassing it in the coffee-drinking experience that appeals to this consumer segment.[9]

People born between 1946 and 1964 are often called "baby boomers." Boomers spend $2.1 trillion a year, and represent half of all spending in the United States. For the next 18 years, one baby boomer will turn 60 every seven seconds. They make up 49 percent of affluent households, and they want attention and service when they shop.[10] This group spends big money on products such as travel, electronics, and automobiles. Baby boomers are not particularly brand loyal, and they are a very diverse group. Some may be the parents of a baby, while others are empty nesters. The Hallmark Channel, owned and operated by Crown Media (owned by Hallmark Cards), targets the baby boom generation because of their wealth and the fact that they are more engaged in TV than are members of other groups.[11] The challenges facing marketers who target boomers are great. Unlike yesterday's generation of 50-plus-year-olds, today's boomers refuse to believe they're aging, so marketers who want to appeal this demographic should appeal to boomers' interests, lifestyles, and values—anything but age. Baby boomers are not as resistant to change as older consumers in the past might have been, and most are comfortable with digital media. According to a study jointly conducted by Nielsen and Hallmark Cards, boomer households account for unexpectedly high percentages of sales of products considered to be mainly purchased by younger consumers. These products include beer, carbonated beverages, and candy.[12]

Consumers in their late 60s and older represent people who are part of the War Generation (ages 67 to 72), the Depression Generation (ages 73 to 82), and the G.I. Generation (age 83 and up). Collectively, they are sometimes called the "Golden Generation" (a term coined by Focalyst, a research and consultancy firm focused on older consumers). Many in this group view retirement not as a passive time, but as an active time they use to explore new knowledge, travel, volunteer, and spend time with family and friends. They are living longer and are healthier than older consumers 20 years ago. However, marketers need to be aware that physical changes in hearing, eyesight, and mobility still occur in this segment. The British grocery store chain Tesco is considering designing a store specifically to meet the needs of older shoppers. Music, non-slip floors, extra-wide aisles, brighter-than-usual lighting, and steps to assist older consumers in reaching high shelves are some the features being examined for inclusion.

Gender Segmentation In the United States, women tend to be the key household decision-makers for many products, making or influencing 80 percent of consumer purchases. They determine 94 percent of home furnishings purchases, 92 percent of vacations, 91 percent of new homes, 68 percent of car purchases, and 51 percent of consumer electronics buys.[13]

Women are buying and playing video games in rapidly increasing numbers. Forty percent of gamers are women and they outnumber under-17 males by nearly two to one in the gaming world. The video game industry has been forced to respond by developing more games with female protagonists and changing its advertising strategy. For example, Ubisoft, a video game company, has doubled its marketing spending on girls and women, and is increasing its investment into researching the female market. Electronic Arts Inc.'s "Littlest Pet Shop" game for girls is one of the company's best-selling games.[14] Other marketers are also recognizing the potential of the female market segment. Hallmark Cards has introduced a new collection called "Girlfriends." The new line of cards and gifts are designed to help women connect in a fun, humorous, and meaningful ways. The cards and gifts address real-life situations that are both celebratory and challenging. The line conveys support, celebrates friendship, strengthens bonds, and reassures the recipient her friends are behind her no matter what.[15]

Brands are also targeted to men; Gillette razors and Rogaine baldness remedy are classic examples. However, several male dominated brands are increasing their efforts to attract women. For example, athletic apparel manufacturers such as Nike and Reebok have typically targeted men and simply mimicked that strategy when marketing women's wear. But these companies are now taking women's unique needs regarding athletics into consideration when they design clothing and shoes for them.

Marketers of products such as clothing, cosmetics, personal-care items, magazines, jewelry, and gifts are beginning to focus more on men. For instance, a clothing store for men called "Lost Boys" offers shoppers free beer and a large flat screen TV in hopes they will enjoy hanging out in the store and shopping a little longer, more like women shop.[16] **CoolStuffForDads.com** targets online shoppers with a wide variety of gifts that men would enjoy.[17] The Boardroom Salon for men offers men a way to pamper themselves without feeling "sissy-fied." Dark wood paneling, hardwood floors, leather chairs, and soft lighting give the Boardroom a masculine, den-like atmosphere. There is a pool table in the middle of the hair-cutting room, and a TV in the waiting area that is tuned to ESPN.[18]

Daily routine.

Many companies are attempting to promote products to men in traditionally female markets.

Income Segmentation Income is a popular demographic variable for segmenting markets because income level influences consumers' wants and determines their buying power. Many markets are segmented by income, including the markets for housing, clothing, automobiles, and food. Wholesale club stores such as Costco and Sam's Club appeal to many income segments. According to a Nielsen study, affluent households (those that earn more than $100,000 annually) are twice as likely to shop warehouse stores compared to households that earn $20,000 or less a year, and the affluent shopper spends an average $46 more than the lower income shopper per trip.[19] High income customers looking for luxury want outstanding customer service. For example, fashion companies use computer technology to customize upscale products that are designed specifically for their wealthy customers' needs.[20] Other companies try to appeal to low income customers. Walmart plans for more of its stores to offer financial services in "Money Centers" to its lower-income customers who do not have banks. These Money Centers will include services such as cashing checks, paying bills, and filling out tax forms.[21]

Ethnic Segmentation In the past, ethnic groups in the United States were expected to conform to a homogenized, Anglo-centric ideal. This was evident both in the marketing of mass-marketed products and in the selective way that films, television, advertisements, and popular music portrayed America's diverse population. Until the 1970s, ethnic foods were rarely sold except in specialty stores. The racial barrier in entertainment lasted nearly as long, except for supporting movie and TV roles—often based on stereotypes dating back to the 19th century.[22] Increasing numbers of ethnic minorities in the United States, along with increased buying power, have changed this. Hispanic Americans, African Americans, and Asian Americans are the three largest ethnic groups in the United States. It is estimated that by 2013, African Americans will account for 42 million, Asian-Americans will account for 16.8 million, and Hispanic Americans will account for 53 million of the U.S. population.[23] Today, companies such as Procter & Gamble, Allstate Insurance, Bank of America, and Reebok have developed multicultural marketing initiatives designed to better understand and serve the wants and preferences of U.S. minority groups. Many consumer goods companies spend 5 to 10 percent of their marketing budgets specifically targeting multicultural consumers; this proportion will likely increase in the future as ethnic groups represent larger and larger percentages of the U.S. population.

Within this segment exists a variety of nationalities (people come from nearly 24 countries), languages, degrees of acculturation, income, and education levels. The Hispanic segment is less likely to have mortgage and credit card debt, and tend to have two or more income earners in the household. They like to buy products and services from brands advertised on TV, and they spend heavily on basics such as packaged goods and wireless phone services.[24] A number of food retailers are making efforts to target Hispanic Americans. For example, 7-Eleven is developing private-label foods that will appeal to this group.[25] Research shows that one-fourth of Hispanic Americans must be served in Spanish if retailers want their business. After their Spanish-speaking customers told Home Depot they prefer shopping in Spanish even if they are bilingual, the company developed a Spanish-language version of its Web site. It is one of only a few retailers offering the online option in Spanish.[26] Similarly,

"Yo quería dientes blancos como artista y el dentista, saludables. Su consejo, cambia a Colgate Total Plus Whitening"

Ahora están blancos y saludables.

Protección completa por 12 horas.

Image courtesy of The Advertising Archives

Amazon introduced the Software en Español Store that offers Spanish-language and bilingual software products.[27]

The African American segment now makes up more than 13 percent of the U.S. population, and will continue to grow. Some characteristics of this group: (1) they are twice as likely to trust black media as they are to trust mainstream media; (2) eight in ten households watch black television at least once a week; and (3) overall, 68 percent of African Americans are online, while over 90 percent of African American teens are online.[28] Companies that have been successful in appealing to groups within this segment include Nissan, Merrill Lynch, and AARP. Nissan found that a sense of inclusion among other ethnic groups was preferable to being singled out, so its ad campaign for the Nissan Altima incorporated people of various ethnic backgrounds. Merrill Lynch & Company sponsors community-based events such as the "Lasting Foundations: The Art of Architecture in Africa" in New York. A membership benefits campaign for AARP recognized that African Americans are not typically close to retirement at age 50. Thus the organization focused on immediate benefits, such as volunteer opportunities, grandparenting programs, and discounts on travel and health care.[29]

Asians in America represent a segment that has higher than average household incomes and education levels than the general population.[30] This group also makes more online purchases a year than African American and Caucasian consumers. More packaged goods companies such as Kraft Foods and Procter & Gamble are showing interest in Asian Americans due to the growth of Asian supermarket chains. The number of Asian media is also growing rapidly. Sovereign Bank in Boston has a branch that is staffed by all Chinese Americans. Their customers are so loyal, they come from around the Northeast to do business there. It's not only that the employees speak Cantonese, but also that they have the cultural sensitivity to know, for example, not to insult their customers by talking to them about saving for a vacation before they do anything else.[31]

Family Life-Cycle Segmentation The demographic factors of gender, age, and income often do not sufficiently explain why consumer buying behavior varies. Frequently, consumption patterns among people of the same age and gender differ because they are in different stages of the family life cycle. The **family life cycle (FLC)** is a series of stages determined by a combination of age, marital status, and the presence or absence of children.

The life-cycle stage consisting of the married-couple household used to be considered the traditional family in the United States. Today, however, married couples make up just about half of households, down from nearly 80 percent in the 1950s. This means that the 86 million single adults in the United States could soon define the new majority. Already, unmarried Americans make up 42 percent of the workforce, 40 percent of home buyers, and one of the most potent consumer groups on record. Exhibit 8.2 illustrates numerous FLC patterns and shows how families' needs, incomes, resources, and expenditures differ at each stage. The horizontal flow shows the traditional family life cycle. The lower part of the exhibit gives some of the characteristics and purchase patterns of families in each stage of the traditional life cycle. The exhibit also acknowledges that many first marriages end in divorce. If young marrieds move into the young divorced stage, their consumption patterns often revert back to those of the young single stage of the cycle. Divorced persons frequently remarry by middle age and reenter the traditional life cycle, as indicated by the "recycled flow" in the exhibit.

Consumers are especially receptive to marketing efforts at certain points in the life cycle. Dating and engaged couples are big spenders. In the two and half years before marriage, many spend over $40,000 on vacations, jewelry, dining, and

family life cycle (FLC)
A series of stages determined by a combination of age, marital status, and the presence or absence of children.

Exhibit 8.2 Family Life Cycle

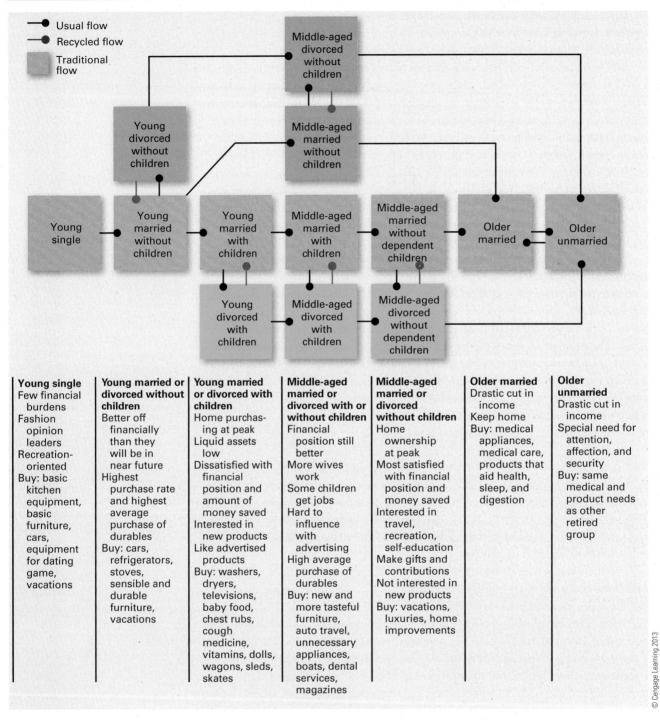

Usual flow
Recycled flow
Traditional flow

Middle-aged divorced without children

Young divorced without children

Middle-aged married without children

Young single

Young married without children

Young married with children

Middle-aged married with children

Middle-aged married without dependent children

Older married

Older unmarried

Young divorced with children

Middle-aged divorced with children

Middle-aged divorced without dependent children

Young single	Young married or divorced without children	Young married or divorced with children	Middle-aged married or divorced with or without children	Middle-aged married or divorced without children	Older married	Older unmarried
Few financial burdens	Better off financially than they will be in near future	Home purchasing at peak	Financial position still better	Home ownership at peak	Drastic cut in income	Drastic cut in income
Fashion opinion leaders	Highest purchase rate and highest average purchase of durables	Liquid assets low	More wives work	Most satisfied with financial position and money saved	Keep home	Special need for attention, affection, and security
Recreation-oriented	Buy: cars, refrigerators, stoves, sensible and durable furniture, vacations	Dissatisfied with financial position and amount of money saved	Some children get jobs	Interested in travel, recreation, self-education	Buy: medical appliances, medical care, products that aid health, sleep, and digestion	Buy: same medical and product needs as other retired group
Buy: basic kitchen equipment, basic furniture, cars, equipment for dating game, vacations		Interested in new products	Hard to influence with advertising	Make gifts and contributions		
		Like advertised products	High average purchase of durables	Not interested in new products		
		Buy: washers, dryers, televisions, baby food, chest rubs, cough medicine, vitamins, dolls, wagons, sleds, skates	Buy: new and more tasteful furniture, auto travel, unnecessary appliances, boats, dental services, magazines	Buy: vacations, luxuries, home improvements		

© Cengage Learning 2013

wedding expenses.[32] For families with teenaged children, some hotels and resorts are trying to develop programs that allow the teens to "ditch the parents." Programs include Wii contests, poker nights, and under-18 hang-out spots with video games and "mocktails."[33]

Another important group is singles. Singles spent $2.2 trillion in 2008, which represented 35 percent of all consumer spending in that year. Most singles are younger than 45 and receptive to advertising, and they spend more time on the Internet. While many marketers ignore this group, Norwegian Cruise Line has gone out of its way to welcome it. Most cruise ships don't have single occupancy rooms, and if a solo patron goes on a cruise, the industry traditionally charges the solo traveler a supplemental fee for staying in the double occupancy room. Norwegian Cruise Line's ship, the Epic, goes against that industry practice by offering 128 single-occupancy rooms with no extra fees.[34]

PSYCHOGRAPHIC SEGMENTATION

Age, gender, income, ethnicity, family life-cycle stage, and other demographic variables are usually helpful in developing segmentation strategies, but often they don't paint the entire picture. Demographics provide the skeleton, but psychographics add meat to the bones. **Psychographic segmentation** is market segmentation on the basis of the following variables:

→ **Personality:** Personality reflects a person's traits, attitudes, and habits. According to a national survey by Roper, almost half of Americans believe their cars match their personalities. For example, SUVs deliver the heady feeling of being independent and above it all. Convertibles epitomize wind-in-the-hair freedom, and off-roaders convey outdoor adventure. About 25 percent of people surveyed say that their cars make them feel powerful.[35]

→ **Motives:** Marketers of baby products and life insurance appeal to consumers' emotional motives—namely, to care for their loved ones. Using appeals to economy, reliability, and dependability, carmakers such as Subaru and Suzuki target customers with rational motives. Mercedes-Benz, Jaguar, and Cadillac appeal to customers with status-related motives.

→ **Lifestyles:** Lifestyle segmentation divides people into groups according to the way they spend their time, the importance of the things around them, their beliefs, and socioeconomic characteristics such as income and education. For example, the companies behind the sport Nordic walking are targeting couch potatoes and other nonathletic types. They hope to make the activity appealing to those for whom regular exercise has been a challenge.[36] Pepsi-Cola is promoting Aquafina Sparkling to consumers who are health conscious by promoting it as a smart choice for hydration that tastes great, is carbonated, yet has low sodium, no sugar, and no calories.[37]

→ **Geodemographics:** **Geodemographic segmentation** clusters potential customers into neighborhood lifestyle categories. It combines geographic, demographic, and lifestyle segmentations. Geodemographic segmentation helps marketers develop marketing programs tailored to prospective buyers who live in small geographic regions, such as neighborhoods, or who have very specific lifestyle and demographic characteristics. H-E-B, a 304-store, Texas-based supermarket chain, specializes in developing its own branded products designed to meet the needs and tastes of specific communities. In the Rio Grande Valley, where summers are hot and many residents don't have air conditioning, H-E-B markets its own brand of rubbing oil that helps cool the skin while adding moisturizers. Along the southern border, the grocer stocks *discos*, large metal disks that Mexican Americans use to cook brisket. In Detroit, Home Depot has stores in some neighborhoods that have charcoal barbecue grills, while others offer gas grills.[38]

Psychographic variables can be used individually to segment markets or be combined with other variables to provide more detailed

psychographic segmentation
Market segmentation on the basis of personality, motives, lifestyles, and geodemographics.

geodemographic segmentation
Segmenting potential customers into neighborhood lifestyle categories.

Adidas "Me, Myself" women's training campaign featuring WNBA MVP Candace Parker. The campaign encourages women with active lifestyles to share training success and struggles with each other.

descriptions of market segments. One combination approach is the Nielsen Claritas lifestyle software program that divides Americans into 66 "clusters," or consumer types, all with catchy names. The clusters combine basic demographic data such as age, ethnicity, and income with lifestyle information, such as magazine and sports preferences, taken from consumer surveys. For example, the "Kids and Cul-de-Sacs" group consists of upscale, married couples with children who live in recently built subdivisions. These families have a median household income of $70,233, tend to own a Honda Odyssey, and are likely to spend large sums of money for child-centered products and services such as video games and Chuck E. Cheese. The "Bohemian Mix" cluster is made up of urbanites under age 35. These young singles, couples, students, and professionals have a median income of $51,100, are early adopters in many product categories, tend to shop at Banana Republic, and are likely to read *Vanity Fair* magazine.[39] The program also predicts to which neighborhoods across the country these clusters are likely to gravitate.

BENEFIT SEGMENTATION

Benefit segmentation is the process of grouping customers into market segments according to the benefits they seek from the product. Most types of market segmentation are based on the assumption that this variable and customers' needs are related. Benefit segmentation is different because it groups potential customers on the basis of their needs or wants rather than some other characteristic, such as age or gender. The snack-food market, for example, can be divided into six benefit segments, as shown in Exhibit 8.3.

Customer profiles can be developed by examining demographic information associated with people seeking certain benefits. This information can be used to match marketing strategies with selected target markets. The many different types of

Exhibit 8.3 Lifestyle Segmentation of the Snack-Food Market

	Nutritional Snackers	Weight Watchers	Guilty Snackers	Party Snackers	Indiscriminate Snackers	Economical Snackers
% of Snackers	23%	145%	9%	15%	18%	20%
Lifestyle Characteristics	Self-assured, controlled	Outdoorsy, influential, adventuresome	Highly anxious, isolated	Sociable	Hedonistic	Self-assured, price-oriented
Benefits Sought	Nutritious, without artificial ingredients, natural	Low in calories, quick energy	Low in calories, good tasting	Good to serve guests, goes well with beverages	Good tasting, satisfies hunger	Low in price, best value
Consumption Level of Snacks	Light	Light	Heavy	Average	Heavy	Average
Type of Snacks Usually Eaten	Fruits, vegetables, cheese	Yogurt, vegetables	Yogurt, cookies, crackers, candy	Nuts, potato chips, crackers, pretzels	Candy, ice cream, cookies, potato chips, pretzels, popcorn	No specific products
Demographics	Better educated, have young children	Young, single	Younger or older, female, lower socioeconomic status	Middle-aged, not urban	Teenager	Have large family, better educated

© Cengage Learning 2013

performance energy bars with various combinations of nutrients are aimed at consumers looking for different benefits. For example, PowerBar is designed for athletes looking for long-lasting fuel, while PowerBar ProteinPlus is aimed at those who want extra protein for replenishing muscles after strength training. LUNA bars are targeted to women who want a bar with soy protein, calcium, and fewer calories; and Clif Bars are for people who want a natural bar with ingredients such as rolled oats, soybeans, and organic soy flour. Dannon introduced its Activia probiotic yogurt as a daily health booster by highlighting its benefits for the digestive tract and immune system.

USAGE-RATE SEGMENTATION

Usage-rate segmentation divides a market by the amount of product bought or consumed. Categories vary with the product, but they are likely to include some combination of the following: former users, potential users, first-time users, light or irregular users, medium users, and heavy users. Segmenting by usage rate enables marketers to focus their efforts on heavy users or to develop multiple marketing mixes aimed at different segments. Because heavy users often account for a sizable portion of all product sales, some marketers focus on the heavy-user segment.

The **80/20 principle** holds that 20 percent of all customers generate 80 percent of the demand. Although the percentages usually are not exact, the general idea often holds true. For example, in the fast-food industry, the heavy user accounts for only one of five fast-food patrons, but makes about 60 percent of all visits to fast-food restaurants. The needs of heavy users differ from the needs of other usage-rate groups. They have intense needs for product and service selection and a variety of types of information, as well as an emotional attachment to the product category. Individuals in this group spend four to fourteen times as much in their favored product category than do light users.[40] Developing customers into heavy users is the goal behind many frequency/loyalty programs such as airline frequent flyer programs. Many supermarkets and other retailers have also designed loyalty programs that reward the heavy-user segment with deals available only to them, such as in-store coupon dispensing systems, loyalty card programs, and special price deals on selected merchandise.

usage-rate segmentation
Dividing a market by the amount of product bought or consumed.

80/20 principle
A principle holding that 20 percent of all customers generate 80 percent of the demand.

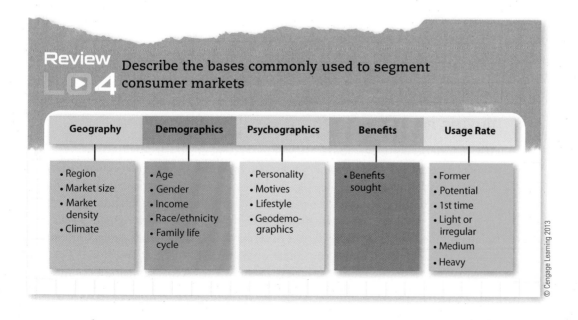

Review
LO4
Describe the bases commonly used to segment consumer markets

Geography	Demographics	Psychographics	Benefits	Usage Rate
• Region • Market size • Market density • Climate	• Age • Gender • Income • Race/ethnicity • Family life cycle	• Personality • Motives • Lifestyle • Geodemographics	• Benefits sought	• Former • Potential • 1st time • Light or irregular • Medium • Heavy

© Cengage Learning 2013

Bases for Segmenting Business Markets

The business market consists of four broad segments: producers, resellers, government, and institutions. (For a detailed discussion of the characteristics of these segments, see Chapter 7.) Whether marketers focus on only one or on all four of these segments, they are likely to find diversity among potential customers. Thus, further market segmentation offers just as many benefits to business marketers as it does to consumer-product marketers.

COMPANY CHARACTERISTICS

Company characteristics, such as geographic location, type of company, company size, and product use, can be important segmentation variables. Some markets tend to be regional because buyers prefer to purchase from local suppliers, and distant suppliers may have difficulty competing in terms of price and service. Therefore, firms that sell to geographically concentrated industries benefit by being close to their markets.

Segmenting by customer type allows business marketers to tailor their marketing mixes to the unique needs of particular types of organizations or industries. Many companies are finding this form of segmentation to be quite effective. For example, Home Depot, one of the largest do-it-yourself retail businesses in the United States, has targeted professional repair and remodeling contractors in addition to consumers. Procter & Gamble is beginning to target business customers by focusing on janitors, fast-food workers, maids, and launderers with products specific to each group's cleaning needs.[41]

Volume of purchase (heavy, moderate, light) is a commonly used basis for business segmentation. Another is the buying organization's size, which may affect its purchasing procedures, the types and quantities of products it needs, and its responses to different marketing mixes. Banks frequently offer different services, lines of credit, and overall attention to commercial customers based on their size.

Many products, especially raw materials such as steel, wood, and petroleum, have diverse applications. How customers use a product may influence the amount they buy, their buying criteria, and their selection of vendors. For example, a producer of springs may have customers that use the product in applications as diverse as making machine tools, bicycles, surgical devices, office equipment, telephones, and missile systems.

BUYING PROCESSES

Many business marketers find it helpful to segment customers and prospective customers on the basis of how they buy. For example, companies can segment some business markets by ranking key purchasing criteria, such as price, quality, technical support, and service. Atlas Corporation has developed a commanding position in the industrial door market by providing customized products in just 4 weeks, which is much faster than the industry average of 12 to 15 weeks. Atlas's primary market is companies with an immediate need for customized doors.

The purchasing strategies of buyers may provide useful segments. Two purchasing profiles that have been identified are satisficers and optimizers. **Satisficers**

satisficers
Business customers who place an order with the first familiar supplier to satisfy product and delivery requirements.

contact familiar suppliers and place the order with the first one to satisfy product and delivery requirements. **Optimizers** consider numerous suppliers (both familiar and unfamiliar), solicit bids, and study all proposals carefully before selecting one.

The personal characteristics of the buyers themselves (their demographic characteristics, decision style, tolerance for risk, confidence level, job responsibilities, etc.) influence their buying behavior and thus offer a viable basis for segmenting some business markets. IBM computer buyers, for example, are sometimes characterized as being more risk averse than buyers of less expensive computers that perform essentially the same functions. In advertising, therefore, IBM stressed its reputation for high quality and reliability.

Review
LO5 Describe the bases for segmenting business markets

© Cengage Learning 2013

LO6
Steps in Segmenting a Market

The purpose of market segmentation, in both consumer and business markets, is to identify marketing opportunities.

1. **Select a market or product category for study:** Define the overall market or product category to be studied. It might be a market in which the firm already competes, a new but related market or product category, or a totally new one. For instance, Anheuser-Busch closely examined the beer market before introducing Michelob Light and Bud Light. Anheuser-Busch also carefully studied the market for salty snacks before introducing the Eagle brand.

2. **Choose a basis or bases for segmenting the market:** This step requires managerial insight, creativity, and market knowledge. There are no scientific procedures for selecting segmentation variables. However, a successful segmentation scheme must produce segments that meet the four basic criteria discussed earlier in this chapter.

3. **Select segmentation descriptors:** After choosing one or more bases, the marketer must select the segmentation descriptors. Descriptors identify the specific segmentation variables to use. For example, if a company selects demographics as a basis of segmentation, it might use age, occupation, and income as descriptors. A company that selects usage segmentation needs to decide whether to go after heavy users, nonusers, or light users.

4. **Profile and analyze segments:** The profile should include the segments' size, expected growth, purchase frequency, current brand usage, brand loyalty, and long-term sales and profit potential. This information can then be used to rank potential market segments by profit opportunity, risk, consistency with organizational mission and objectives, and other factors important to the firm.

5. **Select target markets:** Selecting target markets is not a part of but a natural outcome of the segmentation process. It is a major decision that influences and

optimizers
Business customers who consider numerous suppliers, both familiar and unfamiliar, solicit bids, and study all proposals carefully before selecting one.

often directly determines the firm's marketing mix. This topic is examined in greater detail later in this chapter.

6. ***Design, implement, and maintain appropriate marketing mixes:*** The marketing mix has been described as product, place (distribution), promotion, and pricing strategies intended to bring about mutually satisfying exchange relationships with target markets. Chapters 10 through 20 explore these topics in detail.

Markets are dynamic, so it is important that companies proactively monitor their segmentation strategies over time. Often, once customers or prospects have been assigned to a segment, marketers think their task is done. Once customers are assigned to an age segment, for example, they stay there until they reach the next age bracket or category, which could be ten years in the future. Thus, the segmentation classifications are static, but the customers and prospects are changing. Dynamic segmentation approaches adjust to fit the changes that occur in customers' lives. BCBG uses BCBGeneration to target a younger crowd, and Aéropostale owns P.S., which sells clothing for children ages 7 to 12. However, some segments have too many players, and choosing to enter those kinds of segments can be particularly challenging. High-end denim has so many boutiques and brands that customers have tired of the volume.[42]

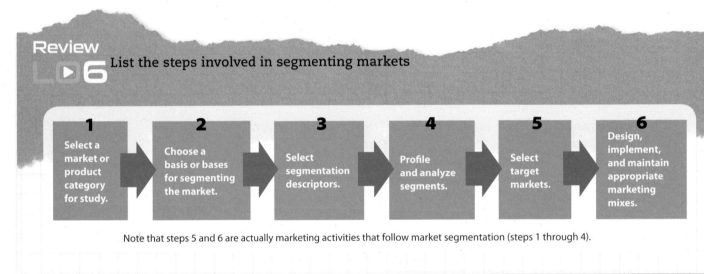

L▶7
Strategies for Selecting Target Markets

target market
A group of people or organizations for which an organization designs, implements, and maintains a marketing mix intended to meet the needs of that group, resulting in mutually satisfying exchanges.

So far this chapter has focused on the market segmentation process, which is only the first step in deciding whom to approach about buying a product. The next task is to choose one or more target markets. A **target market** is a group of people or organizations for which an organization designs, implements, and maintains a marketing mix intended to meet the needs of that group, resulting in mutually satisfying exchanges. Because most markets will include customers with different characteristics, lifestyles, backgrounds, and income levels, it is unlikely that a single marketing mix will attract all segments of the market. Thus,

MARKETING METRICS
Weighted Average Category Incidence Frequency

The Problem

Anne Johnson has a large truck that she would like to turn into a food service truck that would sell 6 inch pizzas during lunch hours. She wants to know the best way to style her truck and pizzas based on the customers who eat the most pizza. In other words, she wants to segment the market. To segment the market, Anne must determine how often people eat pizza.

The Metric

To determine her market segment, Anne uses category incidence. Category incidence is a measure of the frequency that a person purchases from a product category, such as the 6 inch personal pizza category. To uncover who eats the most pizza for lunch, Anne distributes a survey to 307 potential customers, asking if they are male or female and if they eat 6 inch personal pizzas two or more times a week, once a week, twice a month, once a month, twice a year, or once a year or less.

When she receives the survey results, Anne tabulates the information to determine if men or women eat more pizza. To quantify exactly how many pizzas the average male or female eats, Anne uses the weighted average category incidence frequency.

To calculate the weighted average category incidence frequency, Anne first translates the response items into a common scale. In this case, the common scale is how many pizzas are eaten in a year. The response of 1 time a week is interpreted as 52 times a year (1 pizza/week × 52 weeks/year = 52 pizzas/year). The response of 2 times a month is interpreted as 24 times a year (2 pizzas/month × 12 months/year = 24 pizzas/year). The response 2 **or more** times a week is interpreted conservatively, becoming simply 2 times a week. Twice a week becomes 104 times a year on the common scale (2 pizza/week × 52 weeks/year = 104 pizzas/year). Estimated pizza consumption is shown using the scale below.

After calculating pizza consumption, Anne determines the percentage of male and female respondents for each pizza consumption category. To do so, Anne takes the number of respondents by gender and divides by the total number of male or female respondents for all categories:

$$\frac{(\text{Number of men in category})}{(\text{Total number of men})} \times 100$$
$$= \text{Percentage of men in category}$$

For example, the response frequency for the category "2 or more times/week" is 13% (21/159 = .13 × 100 = 13%).

The responses for each category are tabulated below:

By multiplying each category of estimated number of pizzas eaten per year by the percent male or female responses for that category, Anne can see whether, on average, men or women eat more pizza yearly. This is known as calculating a weighted average.

For males, it is 37 pizzas per year:

$$(104 \times .13) + (52 \times .27) + (24 \times .29) + (12 \times .21) + (2 \times .05) + (1 \times .05) = 37 \text{ Pizzas/year}$$

For females it is 25 pizzas per year:

$$(104 \times .04) + (52 \times .22) + (24 \times .20) + (12 \times .36) + (2 \times .05) + (1 \times .05) = 25 \text{ Pizzas/year}$$

The weighted average shows that the average man eats 3 pizzas a month:

$$\frac{37 \text{ pizzas}}{\text{year}} \div \frac{12 \text{ months}}{\text{year}}$$
$$= \frac{37 \text{ pizzas}}{12 \text{ months}} \approx 3 \text{ pizzas/month}$$

The average woman eats two pizzas a month:

$$\frac{25 \text{ pizzas}}{\text{year}} \div \frac{12 \text{ months}}{\text{year}}$$
$$= \frac{25 \text{ pizzas}}{12 \text{ months}} \approx 2 \text{ pizzas/month}$$

Response	Estimated Number of 6 Inch Pizzas Eaten per Year	Number of Male Responses	Number of Female Responses	Percent Male Responses	Percent Female Responses
2 or more times/ week	104	21	6	13%	4%
1/week	52	43	33	27%	22%
2/month	24	46	30	29%	20%
1/month	12	33	53	21%	36%
2/year	2	8	19	5%	13%
1/year	1	8	7	5%	5%
Total Responses		159	148		

(Continued)

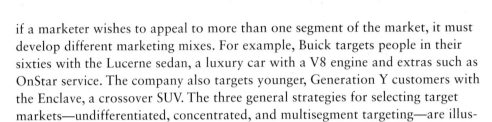
if a marketer wishes to appeal to more than one segment of the market, it must develop different marketing mixes. For example, Buick targets people in their sixties with the Lucerne sedan, a luxury car with a V8 engine and extras such as OnStar service. The company also targets younger, Generation Y customers with the Enclave, a crossover SUV. The three general strategies for selecting target markets—undifferentiated, concentrated, and multisegment targeting—are illustrated in Exhibit 8.4. Exhibit 8.5 illustrates the advantages and disadvantages of each targeting strategy.

UNDIFFERENTIATED TARGETING

A firm using an **undifferentiated targeting strategy** essentially adopts a mass-market philosophy, viewing the market as one big market with no individual segments. The firm uses one marketing mix for the entire market. A firm that adopts an undifferentiated targeting strategy assumes that individual customers have similar needs that can be met with a common marketing mix.

The first firm in an industry sometimes uses an undifferentiated targeting strategy. With no competition, the firm may not need to tailor marketing mixes to the

undifferentiated targeting strategy
A marketing approach that views the market as one big market with no individual segments and thus uses a single marketing mix.

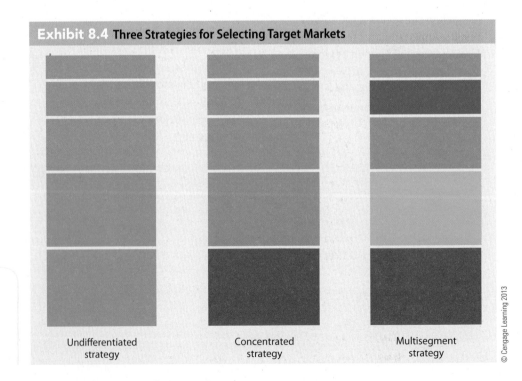

Exhibit 8.4 Three Strategies for Selecting Target Markets

Undifferentiated strategy   Concentrated strategy   Multisegment strategy

© Cengage Learning 2013

Exhibit 8.5 Advantages and Disadvantages of Target Marketing Strategies

Targeting Strategy	Advantages	Disadvantages
Undifferentiated Targeting	• Potential savings on production/ marketing costs • Company more susceptible to competition	• Unimaginative product offerings
Concentrated Targeting	• Concentration of resources • Can better meet the needs of a narrowly defined segment • Allows some small firms to better compete with larger firms • Strong positioning	• Segments too small, or changing • Large competitors may more effectively market to niche segment
Multisegment Targeting	• Greater financial success • Economies of scale in producing/marketing	• High costs • Cannibalization

© Cengage Learning 2013

preferences of market segments. Henry Ford's famous comment about the Model T is a classic example of an undifferentiated targeting strategy: "They can have their car in any color they want, as long as it's black." At one time, Coca-Cola used this strategy with a single product and a single size of its familiar green bottle. Marketers of commodity products, such as flour and sugar, are also likely to use an undifferentiated targeting strategy.

One advantage of undifferentiated marketing is the potential for saving on production and marketing. Because only one item is produced, the firm should be able to achieve economies of mass production. Also, marketing costs may be lower when there is only one product to promote and a single channel of distribution. Too often, however, an undifferentiated strategy emerges by default rather than by design, reflecting a failure to consider the advantages of a segmented approach. The result is often sterile, unimaginative product offerings that have little appeal to anyone.

Another problem associated with undifferentiated targeting is that it makes the company more susceptible to competitive inroads. Hershey lost a big share of the candy market to Mars and other candy companies before it changed to a multisegment targeting strategy. Coca-Cola forfeited its position as the leading seller of cola drinks in supermarkets to Pepsi-Cola in the late 1950s when Pepsi began offering several sizes of containers.

Undifferentiated marketing can succeed in certain situations, though. A small grocery store in a small, isolated town may define all of the people that live in the town as its target market. It may offer one marketing mix and generally satisfy everyone in town. This strategy is not likely to be as effective if there are three or four grocery stores in the town.

CONCENTRATED TARGETING

With a **concentrated targeting strategy**, a firm selects a market **niche** (one segment of a market) for targeting its marketing efforts. Because the firm is appealing to a single segment, it can concentrate on understanding the needs, motives, and satisfactions of that segment's members and on developing and maintaining a highly specialized marketing mix. Some firms find that concentrating resources and

concentrated targeting strategy
A strategy used to select one segment of a market for targeting marketing efforts.

niche
One segment of a market.

meeting the needs of a narrowly defined market segment is more profitable than spreading resources over several different segments.

For example, Starbucks became successful by focusing on consumers who want gourmet coffee products. America Online (AOL) became one of the world's leading Internet providers by targeting Internet newcomers. By making the Internet interface easy to use, AOL was able to attract millions of people who otherwise might not have subscribed to an online service. Watchmakers Patek Philippe, Rolex, and Breguet, which sell watches priced at $200,000 or more, are definitely pursuing a concentrated targeting strategy. AARP pursues a concentrated strategy if you consider people over 50 years old to be a single market segment of the overall population.

Small firms often adopt a concentrated targeting strategy to compete effectively with much larger firms. For example, Enterprise Rent-A-Car rose to number one in the car rental industry by catering to people with cars in the shop. It has now expanded into the airport rental market. Celebrity pots and pans are a growing niche market. They now represent 10 percent of the $2 billion U.S. cookware market—an increase of 7 percent in the past decade.[43] Superdry, the British maker of casual fashion such as T-shirts, and jackets started by targeting young men in their late teens and early twenties. The clothing features good-quality fabrics, vintage designs, and a prominent logo, and is priced lower than rival Abercrombie & Fitch.[44] Some firms, on the other hand, use a concentrated strategy to establish a strong position in a desirable market segment. Porsche, for instance, targets an upscale automobile market through "class appeal, not mass appeal."

Concentrated targeting violates the old adage, "Don't put all your eggs in one basket." If the chosen segment is too small or if it shrinks because of environmental changes, the firm may suffer negative consequences. For instance, OshKosh B'Gosh, Inc., was highly successful selling children's wear in the 1980s. It was so successful, however, that the children's line came to define OshKosh's image to the extent that the company could not sell clothes to anyone else. Attempts at marketing older children's clothing, women's casual clothes, and maternity wear were all abandoned. Recognizing it was in the children's wear business, the company expanded into products such as kids' shoes, children's eyewear, and plush toys.

A concentrated strategy can also be disastrous for a firm that is not successful in its narrowly defined target market. Before Procter & Gamble introduced Head and Shoulders shampoo, several small firms were already selling antidandruff shampoos. Head and Shoulders was introduced with a large promotional campaign, and the new brand captured over half the market immediately. Within a year, several of the firms that had been concentrating on this market segment went out of business.

MULTISEGMENT TARGETING

A firm that chooses to serve two or more well-defined market segments and develops a distinct marketing mix for each has a **multisegment targeting strategy**. Many universities offer full-time (day) MBA programs, professional (evening) programs, and executive (weekend) programs, each targeted at a distinctly different market segment. Many programs are targeting mothers returning to the workplace. Cosmetics companies seek to increase sales and market share by targeting multiple age and ethnic groups. Maybelline and CoverGirl, for example, market different lines to teenage women, young adult women, older women, and African American women. CitiCard offers its Upromise Card to those who want to earn money to save for college, its Platinum Select Card to those who want no annual fee and a competitive interest rate, its Diamond

multisegment targeting strategy
A strategy that chooses two or more well-defined market segments and develops a distinct marketing mix for each.

Preferred Rewards Card to customers who want to earn free rewards like travel and brand-name merchandise, and its Citi AAdvantage Card to those who want to earn American Airlines Advantage frequent flyer miles to redeem for travel. Many credit-card companies even have programs specifically designed for tweens, teens, and college students. Walmart has historically followed a concentrated strategy that targeted lower income segments. Recently, however, the company has segmented its customers into three core groups based on the type of value they seek at the stores. "Brand Aspirationals" are low-income customers who like to buy brand names such as KitchenAid, "Price-Sensitive Affluents" are wealthier shoppers who love deals, and "Value-Price Shoppers" who like low prices and can't afford much more.[46]

Sometimes organizations use different promotional appeals, rather than completely different marketing mixes, as the basis for a multisegment strategy. Beer marketers such as Adolph Coors and Anheuser-Busch advertise and promote special events targeted toward African American, Hispanic American, and Asian American market segments. The beverages and containers, however, do not differ by ethnic market segment.

Gap Inc. takes a different approach. It uses family and individual branding for its alternative format outlets that target different market segments. Banana Republic, Old Navy, and Gap are some of Gap Inc.'s individual brands. The Gap brand operates several family brand stores, including Gap, GapKids, babyGap, gapbody, Gap Outlet and GapMaternity. Multisegment targeting offers many potential benefits to firms, including greater sales volume, higher profits, larger market share, and economies of scale in manufacturing and marketing. Yet it may also involve greater product design, production, promotion, inventory, marketing research, and management costs. Before deciding to use this strategy, firms should compare the benefits and costs of multisegment targeting to those of undifferentiated and concentrated targeting.

Another potential cost of multisegment targeting is **cannibalization**, which occurs when sales of a new product cut into sales of a firm's existing products. In

Brands with a multisegment targeting approach develop marketing mixes for more than one distinct market segment. In this advertisement, Ralph Lauren displays the versatility of its brand by pointing out that it makes clothing for children as well as teenagers and young adults.

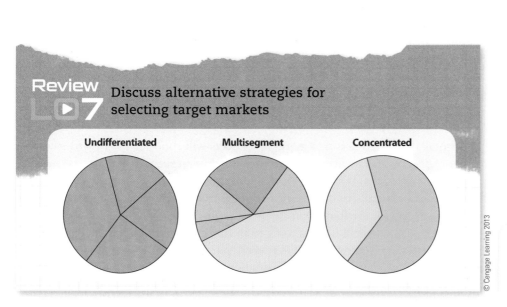

Review LO7 Discuss alternative strategies for selecting target markets

| Undifferentiated | Multisegment | Concentrated |

cannibalization
A situation that occurs when sales of a new product cut into sales of a firm's existing products.

one-to-one marketing
An individualized marketing method that utilizes customer information to build long-term, personalized, and profitable relationships with each customer.

many cases, however, companies prefer to steal sales from their own brands rather than lose sales to a competitor. Also, in today's fast-paced world of Internet business, some companies are willing to cannibalize existing business to build new business.

One-to-One Marketing

Most businesses today use a mass-marketing approach designed to increase *market share* by selling their products to the greatest number of people. For many businesses, however, it is more efficient and profitable to use one-to-one marketing to increase *share of customer*—in other words, to sell more products to each customer. **One-to-one marketing** is an individualized marketing method that utilizes customer information to build long-term, personalized, and profitable relationships with each customer. The goal is to reduce costs through customer retention and increase revenue through customer loyalty. For example, Tesco, the British supermarket chain, sends out a mailing each quarter to 11 million households—but it produces 4 million different versions, tailored to the interests of its diverse customer base.

The difference between one-to-one marketing and the traditional mass-marketing approach can be compared to shooting a rifle and a shotgun. If you have good aim, a rifle is the more efficient weapon to use. A shotgun, on the other hand, increases your odds of hitting the target when it is more difficult to focus. Instead of scattering messages far and wide across the spectrum of mass media (the shotgun approach), one-to-one marketers look for opportunities to communicate with each individual customer (the rifle approach).

Teen retailer Karmaloop developed a system on their Web site that allows customers to preselect by brand or clothing category what types of merchandise they wanted to get e-mail about.[47] Lands' End also engages in one-to-one marketing by custom designing clothing. On Lands' End's Web site, customers provide information by answering a series of questions that takes about 20 minutes. Customer sizing information is saved, and reordering is simple. Customers who customize have been found to be more loyal.

Several factors suggest that personalized communications and product customization will continue to expand as more companies understand why and how their customers make and execute purchase decisions. At least four trends will lead to the continuing growth of one-to-one marketing.

First, the one-size-fits-all marketing is no longer relevant. Consumers want to be treated as the individuals they are, with their own unique sets of needs and wants. By its personalized nature, one-to-one marketing can fulfill this desire.

Second, direct and personal marketing efforts will continue to grow to meet the needs of consumers who no longer have the time to spend shopping and making purchase decisions. With the personal and targeted nature of one-to-one marketing, consumers can spend less time making purchase decisions and more time doing the things that are important.

Third, consumers will be loyal only to those companies and brands that have earned their loyalty and reinforced it at every purchase occasion. One-to-one marketing techniques focus on finding a firm's best customers, rewarding them for their loyalty, and thanking them for their business.

Carl's Jr. and Hardee's Web sites feature a 3D bachelor-pad living room, a live-action video roommate, and a loyalty program that rewards their customers for purchasing food and for interacting with the Web site.

Review
LO8 Explain one-to-one marketing

Traditional Marketing

One-to-One Marketing

Increase market share

Increase share of customer

Market

ABC Company

ABC

ABC ABC

ethics in marketing

Aiming for the Advertising Sweet Spot: Cookies and Online Privacy

Most Americans use the Internet to shop, interact within the social network, and find information, but there is often confusion about what information Web sites gather about users and how that information is used. One way that Web sites gather information is using cookies. Individual sites use cookies to recognize users and their preferences. Data stored ranges from a computer's state (say, Ohio), to information needed for a quick shopping cart purchase. For example, Amazon.com uses cookies to remember username, mailing addresses, credit cards, and shopping history.

Some people feel uneasy about this level of tracking, but most Web sites (including Amazon) promise not to sell personal information and only track information on their site. However, in order to sell advertising space, Web sites will aggregate information about all users to develop an anonymous profile. This allows advertisers to choose ad space based on the market they are targeting. For example, CNET, a technology Web site, will likely show ads for advanced gadgets and not girls' clothing because their advertisers target CNET's visitors—whose interests (technology) are stored because of cookies.

The amount of information you provide a Web site determines how specific a profile it can build. For example, the social networking site Facebook has highly targeted ad sales based on items that consumers have "Liked." While Facebook has come under fire for selling such specific information, the company argues that the user is freely offering information on his or her profile and sharing personal preferences through the "Like" button.

Companies who have presences across many (or most) Web sites have greater access to consumer information. Google is able to track complete user browsing and purchase history. A company called DoubleClick, which most advertisers use to display banner ads, uses cookies that track multiple sites and monitor user activities on any site that displays a DoubleClick banner ad. This level of tracking develops some of the most specific anonymous profiles available, which the company uses to develop and sell products to advertising clients.

As more and more companies move toward highly specific anonymous user profiles, there has been discussion about tying profiles to users' names and addresses. It would be a small step, and companies like Google already have the information—it's just a matter of opting to access and sell it, which Google has resisted doing. But as other companies gain ground using targeted advertising based on hobbies, friends, and personal information, how long before companies begin selling the personal information they gather as a competitive advantage?[48]

Is a company like DoubleClick using information ethically? How about Amazon.com? If you feel differently about the two, why?

Fourth, mass-media approaches will decline in importance as advances in market research and database technology allow marketers to collect detailed information on their customers. New technology offers one-to-one marketers a more cost-effective way to reach customers and enables businesses to personalize their messages. For example, **MyYahoo.com** greets each user by name and offers information in which the user has expressed interest. Similarly, **RedEnvelope.com** helps customers keep track of special occasions and offers personalized gift recommendations. With the help of database technology, one-to-one marketers can track their customers as individuals, even if they number in the millions.

One-to-one marketing is a huge commitment and often requires a 180-degree turnaround for marketers who spent the last half of the 20th century developing and implementing mass-marketing efforts. Although mass marketing will probably continue to be used, especially to create brand awareness or to remind consumers of a product, the advantages of one-to-one marketing cannot be ignored.

There are, however, some concerns about consumer privacy because of the way data is gathered and used to identify specific consumers to target with offers. The Ethics in Marketing box discusses these issues.

LO9
Positioning

The development of any marketing mix depends on **positioning**, a process that influences potential customers' overall perception of a brand, product line, or organization in general. **Position** is the place a product, brand, or group of products occupies in consumers' minds relative to competing offerings. Consumer goods marketers are particularly concerned with positioning. Procter & Gamble, for example, markets 11 different laundry detergents, each with a unique position, as illustrated in Exhibit 8.6.

Positioning assumes that consumers compare products on the basis of important features. Marketing efforts that emphasize irrelevant features are therefore likely to misfire. For example, Crystal Pepsi and a clear version of Coca-Cola's Tab failed because consumers perceived the "clear" positioning as more of a marketing gimmick than a benefit.

Effective positioning requires assessing the positions occupied by competing products, determining the important dimensions underlying these positions, and choosing a position in the market where the organization's marketing efforts will have the greatest impact. Walmart has struggled for years to find a clear fashion positioning strategy. The company has tried to emulate Target by designing trendy outfits and simply selling bulk packages of everyday wear. Most recently, they have decided to focus more on basics such as underwear, socks, T-shirts, and jeans.[49] Consumers associated Radio Shack with private labels, off-brands, and parts for electronic gadgets. To counter this image, the company has launched an ad campaign calling itself "The Shack." Radio Shack hopes that a contemporary nickname will create an awareness that the stores have developed a leadership position in mobility offerings, such as T-Mobile and iPhone.[50] As these examples illustrate, **product differentiation** is a positioning strategy that many firms use to distinguish their products from those of competitors. The distinctions can be either real or perceived. Tandem Computers designed machines with two central processing units and two memories for computer systems that can never afford to be down or lose their databases (for example, an airline reservation system). In this case, Tandem used product differentiation to create a product with very real advantages for the target market. However, many everyday products, such as bleaches, aspirin, unleaded regular gasoline, and some soaps, are differentiated by such trivial means as brand names, packaging, color, smell, or "secret" additives. The marketer attempts to convince consumers that a particular brand is distinctive and that they should demand it over competing brands.

Some firms, instead of using product differentiation, position their products as being similar to competing products or brands. Two examples of this positioning include

positioning
Developing a specific marketing mix to influence potential customers' overall perception of a brand, product line, or organization in general.

position
The place a product, brand, or group of products occupies in consumers' minds relative to competing offerings.

product differentiation
A positioning strategy that some firms use to distinguish their products from those of competitors.

Exhibit 8.6 Positioning of Procter & Gamble Detergents

Brand	Positioning	Market Share
Tide	Tough, powerful cleaning	31.1 percent
Cheer	Tough cleaning and color protection	8.2 percent
Bold	Detergent plus fabric softener	2.9 percent
Gain	Sunshine scent and odor-removing formula	2.6 percent
Era	Stain treatment and stain removal	2.2 percent
Dash	Value brand	1.8 percent
Dreft	Outstanding cleaning for baby clothes, safe for tender skin	1.0 percent
Ivory Snow	Fabric and skin safety on baby clothes and fine washables	0.7 percent
Ariel	Tough cleaner, aimed at Hispanic market	0.1 percent

© Cengage Learning 2013

© iStockphoto.com/Juan Facundo Mora Soria

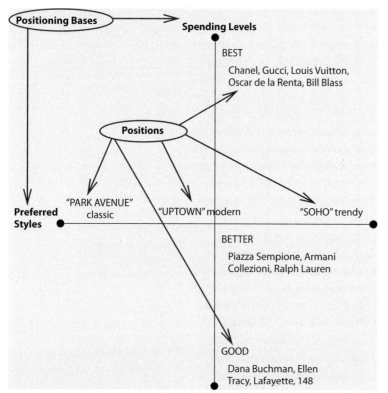

Exhibit 8.7 Perceptual Map and Positioning Strategy for Saks Department Stores

Positioning Bases → Spending Levels

Positions

BEST
Chanel, Gucci, Louis Vuitton, Oscar de la Renta, Bill Blass

Preferred Styles

"PARK AVENUE" classic

"UPTOWN" modern

"SOHO" trendy

BETTER
Piazza Sempione, Armani Collezioni, Ralph Lauren

GOOD
Dana Buchman, Ellen Tracy, Lafayette, 148

Source: Based on Vanessa O'Connell, "Park Avenue Classic or Soho Trendy?" *The Wall Street Journal*, April 20, 2007, B1.

artificial sweeteners advertised as tasting like sugar or margarine tasting like butter.

PERCEPTUAL MAPPING

Perceptual mapping is a means of displaying or graphing, in two or more dimensions, the location of products, brands, or groups of products in customers' minds. For example, Saks Incorporated, the upscale department store chain, stumbled in sales when it tried to attract a younger core customer. To recover, Saks invested in research to determine its core customers in its 54 stores across the country. The perceptual map in Exhibit 8.7 shows how Saks uses customer demographics, such as a matrix that charts the best mix of clothes and accessories, to stock in each store.

POSITIONING BASES

Firms use a variety of bases for positioning, including the following:

→ **Attribute:** A product is associated with an attribute, product feature, or customer benefit. Kleenex has designed a tissue that contains substances to kill germs in an effort to differentiate its product from competing tissues.[51]

→ **Price and quality:** This positioning base might stress high price as a signal of quality or emphasize low price as an indication of value. Neiman Marcus uses the high-price strategy; Walmart has successfully followed the low-price and value strategy. The mass merchandiser Target has developed an interesting position based on price and quality. It is an "upscale discounter," sticking to low prices but offering higher quality and design than most discount chains.

→ **Use or application:** Stressing uses or applications can be an effective means of positioning a product with buyers. Kahlúa Liqueur used advertising to point out 228 ways to consume the product. Snapple introduced a new drink called "Snapple a Day" that is intended for use as a meal replacement.

→ **Product user:** This positioning base focuses on a personality or type of user. Zale Corporation has several jewelry store concepts, each positioned to a different user. The Zales stores cater to middle-of-the-road consumers with traditional styles. Its Gordon's stores appeal to a slightly older clientele with a contemporary look. Guild is positioned for the more affluent 50-plus consumer.

→ **Product class:** The objective here is to position the product as being associated with a particular category of products; for example, positioning a margarine brand with butter. Alternatively, products can be disassociated with a category. Del Monte introduced Fruit Chillers, a shelf-stable sorbet that consumers freeze when they're ready to eat. Fruit Chillers are sold next to single-serve fruit cups, positioned as fruit rather than as a frozen dessert.[52]

→ **Competitor:** Positioning against competitors is part of any positioning strategy. The original Hertz rental car positioning as number two compared to Enterprise exemplifies positioning against specific competitors.

perceptual mapping
A means of displaying or graphing, in two or more dimensions, the location of products, brands, or groups of products in customers' minds.

→ **Emotion:** Positioning using emotion focuses on how the product makes customers feel. A number of companies use this approach. For example, Nike's "Just Do It" campaign didn't tell consumers what "it" was, but most got the emotional message of achievement and courage. Budweiser's advertising featuring talking frogs and lizards emphasized fun. Sears is drawing on the nostalgia of its brand name by remodeling a store outside Atlanta to resemble its stores of the past. The focus is on tapping into Sears' heritage, and its legacy as America's store.[53]

REPOSITIONING

Sometimes products or companies are repositioned in order to sustain growth in slow markets or to correct positioning mistakes. **Repositioning** is changing consumers' perceptions of a brand in relation to competing brands. For example, Procter & Gamble increased its baby-care business in the early 2000s when they changed Pampers' position from being about dryness to being about helping Mom with her baby's development. Post Foods, in an effort to revive its Grape Nuts cereal, repositioned it from a cereal for families and women to a cereal for men. Advertising in *Sports Illustrated* magazine featured men fishing and golfing, with the new slogan "That Takes Grape Nuts."[54] In the retail sector, Walgreens found out from its customers that they viewed the drugstore as a community resource, but the company was not communicating that idea. A new campaign with the slogan "There's a Way" positions the store as a one-stop shopping destination and healthcare provider.[55]

repositioning
Changing consumers' perceptions of a brand in relation to competing brands.

Review
LO 9 Explain how and why firms implement positioning strategies and how product differentiation plays a role

Each car occupies a position in consumers' minds.
Cars can be positioned according to attribute (sporty, conservative, etc.),
to price/quality (affordable, classy, etc.) or other bases.
Cadillac has repositioned itself as a car for younger drivers with edgier ads.

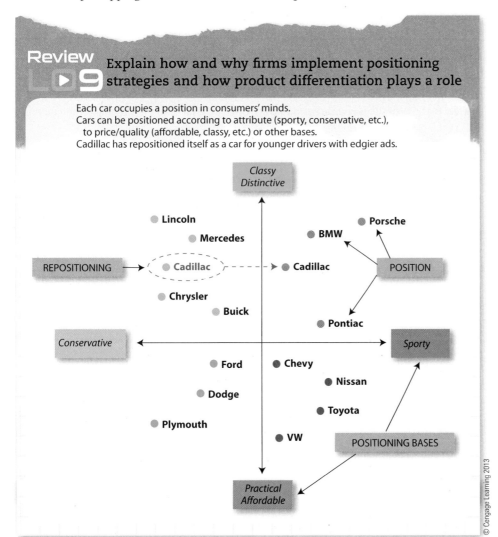

© Cengage Learning 2013

Percentage of Millennials who pay more attention to a company with commitment to a cause	More an affluent shopper spends per shopping trip than lower income shoppers	Spent by baby boomers each year	Percentage of family finances handled by women	Percentage of consumer purchases made or influenced by women	Single adults living in the U.S.	Percentage of people who say cars make them feel powerful	Laundry detergents marketed by Procter & Gamble
74	$46	$2.1 trillion	75	80	86 million	25	11

Review and Applications

LO1 **Describe the characteristics of markets and market segments.** A market is composed of individuals or organizations with the ability and willingness to make purchases to fulfill their needs or wants. A market segment is a group of individuals or organizations with similar product needs as a result of one or more common characteristics.

1.1 Mercedes-Benz is thinking about advertising its cars to college students. Do you think that college students are a viable potential market for Mercedes? Why or why not?

online **1.2** Go to the Web site **www.careermag.com**. How are visitors to the site segmented when seeking relevant job openings? Report your results.

LO2 **Explain the importance of market segmentation.** Before the 1960s, few businesses targeted specific market segments. Today, segmentation is a crucial marketing strategy for nearly all successful organizations. Market segmentation enables marketers to tailor marketing mixes to meet the needs of particular population segments. Segmentation helps marketers identify consumer needs and preferences, areas of declining demand, and new marketing opportunities.

2.1 Describe market segmentation in terms of the historical evolution of marketing.

LO3 **Discuss criteria for successful market segmentation.** Successful market segmentation depends on four basic criteria: (1) a market segment must be substantial and have enough potential customers to be viable; (2) a market segment must be identifiable and measurable; (3) members of a market segment must be accessible to marketing efforts; and (4) a market segment must respond to particular marketing efforts in a way that distinguishes it from other segments.

writing **3.1** As a marketing consultant for a chain of hair salons, you have been asked to evaluate the kids' market as a potential segment for the chain to target. Write a memo to your client discussing your evaluation of the kids' segment in terms of the four criteria for successful market segmentation.

LO4 **Describe the bases commonly used to segment consumer markets.** Five bases are commonly used for segmenting consumer markets. Geographic segmentation is based on region, size, density, and climate characteristics. Demographic segmentation is based on age, gender, income level, ethnicity, and family life-cycle characteristics. Psychographic segmentation includes personality, motives, and lifestyle characteristics. Benefits sought is a type of segmentation that identifies customers according to the benefits they seek in a product. Finally, usage segmentation divides a market by the amount of product purchased or consumed.

4.1 Choose magazine ads for five different consumer products. For each ad, write a description of your perception of the demographic characteristics of the targeted market.

writing

4.2 Investigate how Delta Air Lines (**www.delta.com**) uses its Web site to cater to its market segments.

online

4.3 Is it possible to identify a single market for two distinctly different products? For example, how substantial is the market composed of consumers who use Apple *and* who drive Volkswagens? Can you think of other product combinations that would interest a single market? (Do not use products that are complementary, such as a bike and a bike helmet. Think of products, like the iPod and the car, that are very different.) Complete the following sentences and describe the market for each set of products you pair together.

Consumers of:

Propel fitness water could also be a target market for _____.

Proactiv Solution skin care products could also be a target market for _____.

Alienware computers could also be a target market for _____.

Specialty luggage tags could also be a target market for _____.

Describe the bases for segmenting business markets. Business markets can be segmented on two general bases: First, businesses segment markets based on company characteristics, such as customers' geographic location, type of company, company size, and product use. Second, companies may segment customers based on the buying processes those customers use.

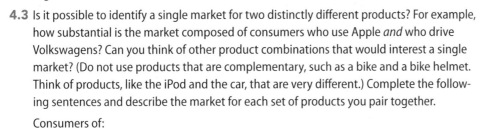
LO5

5.1 Choose five ads from business publications such as *The Wall Street Journal*, *Fortune*, and *BusinessWeek*. For each ad, write a description of how you think the company has segmented its business market.

writing

List the steps involved in segmenting markets. Six steps are involved when segmenting markets: (1) selecting a market or product category for study; (2) choosing a basis or bases for segmenting the market; (3) selecting segmentation descriptors; (4) profiling and evaluating segments; (5) selecting target markets; and (6) designing, implementing, and maintaining appropriate marketing mixes.

LO6

6.1 Write a letter to the president of your bank suggesting ideas for increasing profits and enhancing customer service by improving segmentation and targeting strategies.

writing

Discuss alternative strategies for selecting target markets. Marketers select target markets using three different strategies: undifferentiated targeting, concentrated targeting, and multisegment targeting. An undifferentiated targeting strategy assumes that all members of a market have similar needs that can be met with a single marketing mix. A concentrated targeting strategy focuses all marketing efforts on a single market segment. Multisegment targeting is a strategy that uses two or more marketing mixes to target two or more market segments.

LO7

7.1 Form a team with two or three other students. Create an idea for a new product. Describe the segment (or segments) you are going to target with the product and explain why you chose the targeting strategy you did.

team

7.2 Go to the Web sites of JCPenney, **www.jcpenney.com**, and Target, **www.target.com**. Compare the presentation of women's fashions at the Web sites. What are the major

online

differences? Which site is more designer focused, and which is more brand focused? Which company's approach do you think will appeal more to the "Holy Grail" target market of 25- to 35-year-old women?

 LO8 **Explain one-to-one marketing.** One-to-one marketing is an individualized marketing method that utilizes customer information to build long-term, personalized, and profitable relationships with each customer. Successful one-to-one marketing comes from understanding customers and collaborating with them rather than using them as targets for generic messages. Database technology makes it possible for companies to interact with customers on a personal, one-to-one basis.

writing

8.1 You are the marketing manager for a specialty retailer that sells customized handbags. Write a memo to your boss describing how the company could benefit from one-to-one marketing.

LO9 **Explain how and why firms implement positioning strategies and how product differentiation plays a role.** Positioning is used to influence consumer perceptions of a particular brand, product line, or organization in relation to competitors. The term *position* refers to the place that the offering occupies in consumers' minds. To establish a unique position, many firms use product differentiation, emphasizing the real or perceived differences between competing offerings. Products may be differentiated on the basis of attribute, price and quality, use or application, product user, product class, or competitor.

9.1 Choose a product category (e.g., pickup trucks), and identify at least three different brands and their respective positioning strategies. How is each position communicated to the target audience?

Key Terms

80/20 principle *283*
benefit segmentation *282*
cannibalization *291*
concentrated targeting
    strategy *289*
demographic
    segmentation *275*
family life cycle (FLC) *279*
geodemographic
    segmentation *281*
geographic segmentation *275*
market *271*

market segment *271*
market segmentation *271*
multisegment targeting
    strategy *290*
niche *289*
one-to-one marketing *292*
optimizers *285*
perceptual mapping *296*
position *295*
positioning *295*
product differentiation *295*

psychographic
    segmentation *281*
repositioning *297*
satisficers *284*
segmentation bases
    (variables) *274*
target market *286*
undifferentiated targeting
    strategy *288*
usage-rate segmentation *283*

Exercises

ETHICS EXERCISE

ethics

Tobacco companies are frequently criticized for targeting potential customers below the legal age to purchase and use their products. Critics cite Joe Camel and the Marlboro Man as images meant to make smoking appealing to young people. If tobacco companies are actually following this particular demographic targeting strategy, most would agree that it is unethical if not illegal.

Questions

1. Is marketing tobacco products to younger consumers unethical?

2. Many are beginning to argue that fast-food companies, such as McDonald's and Burger King, are knowingly marketing unhealthy food to consumers. Is it unethical for fast-food companies to market kids' meals to children?

3. What does the AMA Statement of Ethics have to say about marketing unhealthy or harmful products to consumers, particularly children and young adults? Go to the AMA Web site at www.marketingpower.com to review the statement of ethics (**www.marketingpower.com/AboutAMA/Pages/Statement of Ethics.aspx**). Write a brief paragraph summarizing where the AMA stands on this important issue.

MARKETING PLAN EXERCISE

Once you've completed the marketing plan exercise for each chapter in Part 2 of this textbook, you can complete the Part 2 Marketing Planning Worksheet by logging on to the companion Web site at www.cengagebrain.com. Complete the following exercises to continue the marketing plan you began in Chapter 2:

1. To whom does your company market (consumer, industrial, government, not-for-profit, or a combination of targets)? Within each market, are there specific segments or niches that your company can concentrate on? If so, which one(s) would you focus on and why? What are the factors used to create these segments? What are the Internet capabilities in those markets? If you try to encourage those segments to access your product or service via the Internet, will that change which segments are most important to your business? How? What are the factors used to create these segments? Which segments should your company focus on and why?

2. Describe your company's target market segment(s). Use demographics, psychographics, geographics, economic factors, size, growth rates, trends, NAICS codes, and any other appropriate descriptors. What role does the Internet play in your target market's life? How is the target market for your Internet business different from that of a traditional business in your market?

3. Using the list of key competitive advantages you described in Part 1 of your marketing plan, create a series of positioning grids, using two factors each as dimensions. (See grids in LO9 in your textbook for an example.) Then plot the list of key competitors you identified earlier onto these positioning grids. Is your company too close to a key competitor? Are there spaces where the consumer needs and wants are unsatisfied? Consider how the Internet changes what factors are important to your success in your market space. Is technology the most important factor for your firm, or are there other ways for you to differentiate from and beat your competition?

APPLICATION EXERCISE

How tightly do you fit into a particular market segment? Do you think you can be neatly classified? If you think your purchasing habits make you an enigma to marketers, you may need to think again.[56]

Activities

1. To find out what your zip code says about you, follow this link and enter your zip code: www.claritas.com/MyBestSegments/Default.jsp?ID=20. (If the link defaults, search for

"Claritas You Are Where You Live.") The database will generate many cluster descriptions based on your ZIP code. Depending on the functionality of the Web site at the time you access the database, you might need to reenter your ZIP code multiple times if you want to read all the cluster descriptions.

2. Now pick a product category, such as automobiles, athletic shoes, beverages, or health and beauty products. Think about which products in that category would appeal to each of the clusters generated by your ZIP code search. For example, a car that appeals to a cluster titled "Young Bohemians" may not be the car of choice for the cluster "Pools and Patios." If your search generated only one cluster type, you may wish to enter other ZIP codes for your area of town or for your region.

3. Create a perceptual map for the product you chose in step 2. Write a short statement that describes the overall position of each product with an explanation of why you located it where you did on the perceptual map.

CASE STUDY: Coke Zero

DO REAL MEN DRINK DIET COKE?

When a couple of marketing managers for Coca-Cola told attorney Elizabeth Finn Johnson that they wanted to sue their Coke Zero colleagues for "taste infringement," she was baffled. She tried to talk them out of it, but they were determined. They argued that Coca-Cola Classic should be protected from the age discrimination it would suffer with the introduction of a newer, younger soft drink that tasted exactly the same as the original. Frustrated, Finn Johnson held up the Coke can and shouted, "It's not a person! Title VII doesn't cover these things!"

What she didn't know was that the marketing managers were actors. Hidden cameras had been planted around the meeting room to capture the reactions of several unsuspecting attorneys who had been asked to consider the case, including an immigration lawyer who was asked if he could get the Coke Zero marketing head deported back to Canada. The short videos were strategically placed on Web sites such as **www.youtube.com** to promote Coke Zero as the hip, new alternative to Diet Coke for men.

The Coca-Cola Company knows it has to be creative if it's going to sell more soda after sales dropped two years in a row in 2005 and 2006. Morgan Stanley analyst Bill Pecoriello explains, "Consumers are becoming ever more health-conscious, and the image of regular carbonated soft drinks is deteriorating rapidly." In an attempt to appeal to consumers concerned with nutrition, Coke introduced Diet Coke Plus in 2007, a sweeter version of Diet Coke fortified with vitamins and minerals. But what they really needed was a way to reach young male consumers, and Diet Coke Plus, marketed with the tagline "Your Best Friend Just Got Friendlier!" wasn't going to do it.

© Vicki Beaver

A few new products appealed to certain male demographics, such as Coca-Cola Blak, a cola with coffee essence created for older, more sophisticated consumers who are willing to pay more, and Full Throttle Blue Demon, an energy drink with an agave azule flavor (think margaritas) designed to appeal to Hispanic men. However, research showed that there was still a big demographic hole to fill as young men between the ages of 18 and 34 were abandoning the Coca-Cola brand altogether. They didn't want all the calories of regular Coke, but they weren't willing to make the move to Diet Coke, either, which has traditionally been marketed to women who want to lose weight.

Katie Bayne, chief marketing officer for Coca-Cola North America, says that the men who weren't put off by the "feminine stigma" of Diet Coke often rejected it anyway because of its aspartame-sweetened aftertaste. "What we were seeing before Zero launched was that more and more younger people were interested in no-calorie beverages but weren't going to sacrifice taste," Bayne said. "So when they got interested in no-calorie, they were like, 'Forget it, I'm not going to Diet Coke.'"

Testing showed that the name "Coke Zero" would be an effective way to sell a low-calorie cola to men without using the word "diet." And advances in artificial sweeteners made it possible for Coke to finally create a product that tasted more like "the Real Thing." So expectations were high when Coke Zero was introduced in 2005 with a big marketing push, including a commercial that remade the famous 1971 "Hilltop/I'd Like to Teach the World to Sing" ad—this time with rapper G. Love on a rooftop singing that he'd like to teach the world to "chill." Unfortunately, the commercial didn't catch on, and neither did the product it was selling.

Despite disappointing sales in the United States, however, Coke Zero was an immediate hit in Australia, selling more than three times the number of cases expected during its first year on the market. In the United States, the packaging was white and silver, making it difficult for consumers to see the difference between Coke Zero and Diet Coke. In Australia, the bottles and cans were black, making the product stand out on the shelves and look more like the "bloke's Coke" it was intended to be.

The U.S. marketing team took notice and reintroduced Coke Zero with a black and silver label in 2007. Coca-Cola is now investing more money in Coke Zero than any other brand its size, hoping it will someday be a megabrand for the company alongside Coca-Cola Classic and Diet Coke. Chief marketing officer Bayne is enthusiastic about the impact it may have on the company. "We do see this as potentially a bit of a white knight. There's huge opportunity to grow here."[57]

Questions

1. Describe the specific type of consumer that the Coca-Cola Company is targeting with each of the following products: Diet Coke, Coke Zero, Diet Coke Plus, Coca-Cola Blak, and Full Throttle Blue Demon. What types of demographic segmentation is each product's marketing most likely to include?

2. Some industry analysts think soft-drink companies should develop products that will bring new customers into the market rather than just creating variants on the old. They warn that products like Coke Zero will cannibalize lost market share from other soft drink categories instead of increasing the number of consumers overall. Which Coca-Cola products are most likely to lose customers to Coke Zero?

3. Why do you think that the hidden-camera videos used to promote Coke Zero were an effective way to reach its target market? Do you think a similar strategy with a viral marketing campaign on the Internet would appeal to the target market for Diet Coke Plus?

4. Do you think Diet Coke could have been repositioned to change consumers' perceptions of it enough to be considered a drink equally appealing to men? Why or why not?

© NKP Media, INC./Cengage

ReadyMade markets itself as a magazine catering to GenNest, the group of consumers ages 25 to 35 who are just settling down after college.

The young couples that make up this group are buying their first houses and taking on domestic and decorating roles for the first time. They are interested in being stylish, while at the same time maintaining their own unique personalities. But *ReadyMade* appeals to a wider variety of readers than just GenNest. The magazine has subscribers in all age groups, from teens looking to spruce up their rooms to retirees looking for projects to enliven their homes. This diversity offers a unique challenge to *ReadyMade* as it tries to promote itself to advertisers who need to know what sort of people will be reached through advertisements appearing in the publication.

Questions

1. How does *ReadyMade* communicate the demographics of its reader base to advertisers who want to see specific statistics that do not easily represent *ReadyMade*'s target market?

2. What sort of segmentation does *ReadyMade* use when it markets to businesses and investors?

3. What ideas do you have that would help *ReadyMade* reach out to new subscribers without alienating its loyal base?

Notes

1. Jena McGregor, "At Best Buy, Marketing Goes Micro," *BusinessWeek*, May 26, 2008, 52, 53.
2. Tim Feran, "Macy's Trying a Local Approach," *Columbus Dispatch,* September 21, 2009, www.dispatch.com/live/content/business/stories/2009/09/21/MY_MACYS.ART_ART_09-21-09_A8_NQF4DB5.html.
3. Veronica Dagher, "Macy's Tailored Merchandise Pays Off," *Wall Street Journal*, August 12, 2010, B3.
4. Evan Bailyn, "Keeping It Simple: Marketing to Tweens on a Shoestring," *MediaPost*, December 2, 2008, www.mediapost.com/publications/index.cfm?fa=Articles.showArticle&art_aid=95775.
5. Morley Winograd and Michael D. Hais, "The Millennials," *Star Telegram*, October 5, 2008, D1.
6. "JCPenney's 'New Look. New Year. Who Knew!' Back-to-School Campaign Features Cutting Edge, Creative Marketing Aimed at Teens," *Business Wire*, July 14, 2010, http://www.businesswire.com/smp/jcpenney-back-to-school.
7. "College Students Annoyed by Mobile Ads," *emarketer*, July 1, 2010, www.emarketer.tv/Article.aspx?R=1007771.
8. "The Issue: How P&G Brought Back Herbal Essences," *BusinessWeek*, June 17, 2008, www.businessweek.com/managing/content/jun2008/ca20080617_465490.htm.
9. Jessica Sebor, "Y Me," *Customer Relationship Management*, November 2006, 24–35.
10. Toni Whitt, "Boomers Rewrite Rules for Marketing," *Herald-Tribune*, June 25, 2007, www.heraldtribune.com/article/20070625/BUSINESS/706250444.
11. Stuart Elliott, "The Older Audience Is Looking Better Than Ever," *New York Times*, April 20, 2009, www.nytimes.com/2009/04/20/business/20adcol.html.
12. Bernice Hurst, "New Store Considered for Senior Shoppers," *RetailWire*, September 2, 2008, www.retailwire.com/discussions/sngl_discussion.cfm/13203.
13. Tom Ryan, "Women's Purchasing Power Grows," *RetailWire*, February 23, 2009, www.retailwire.com/discussions/sngl_discussion.cfm/13569.

marketing&you: Results.

© iStockphoto.com/ziggymaj

A high score indicates that you operate within budget constraints. Living on a budget doesn't necessarily mean that you change your shopping behavior or your price comparison behavior, however. Low scores relate to financial health and a tendency to be brand loyal. After reading Chapter 8, you can see why income and financial situation can be an important segmentation variable!

14. Yukari Iwatani Kane, "Videogame Firms Make a Play for Women," *Wall Street Journal*, October 21, 2009, http://online.wsj.com/article/SB10001424052748704882404574463652777885432.html.

15. Hallmark Corporate Information, "New Hallmark Card Line Helps Women Celebrate Good Times and Convey Support in Tough Times," *Hallmark,* June 22, 2010, http://corporate.hallmark.com/Current-News/New-Hallmark-Card-Line-Helps-Women-Celebrate-Good-Times-and-Convey-Support-in-Tough-Times.

16. Ray A. Smith, "Belly Up to the Bar and Buy Some Jeans," *Wall Street Journal,* April 2, 2009, http://online.wsj.com/article/SB123862311574879951.html.

17. Jim Hubley, "CoolStuffForDads.com, an Online Store Dedicated to Gifts for Dads, Continues to Add Great Products for Men," September 22, 2008, www.thehawkgroup.com/coolstufffordads_continues_to_add_great_products_for_men.php.

18. Pete Alfano, "Just for Men," *Star Telegram*, February 22, 2009, 5F.

19. Tom Ryan, "Targeting Male Grocery Shoppers," RetailWire, June 4, 2007, www.retailwire.com/discussions/sngl_discussion.cfm/12220.

20. Francine Kizner, "Where the Rich Shop," *Entrepreneur*, February 16, 2007, www.entrepreneur.com.

21. Ian Sherr, "Wal-Mart Plans Expansion of Low-Income Money Services," *Reuters,* March 16, 2010, www.reuters.com/article/2010/03/16/walmart-bank-idUSN1516867520100316.

22. "The New Mainstream: How the Buying Habits of Ethnic Groups Are Creating a New American Identity," November 15, 2005, http://knowledge.wharton.upenn.edu/article.cfm?articleid=1270.

23. Piet Levy, "Growing Numbers, More Opportunity to Spend," *Marketing News*, April 30, 2009.

24. Ronald Grover, "The Payoff from Targeting Hispanics," *BusinessWeek*, April 20, 2009, 76.

25. "7-Eleven Develops Private Label Products for Hispanics," *Supermarket News*, March 19, 2010, http://supermarketnews.com/news/7eleven_private_0319.

26. Ann Zimmerman and Miguel Bustillo, "Home Depot's New Web Site Opens Door to Hispanics," *Wall Street Journal*, November 17, 2008, B1, B9.

27. "Amazon Launches New Software en Español Store as the Software Shopping Destination for Hispanic Consumers," August 12, 2008, www.istockanalyst.com/article/viewiStockNews/articleid/2503227.

28. David Morse, "Brain Trust Query: Do African Americans Require a Targeted Marketing Approach?" *RetailWire*, July 30, 2008, www.retailwire.com/discussions/sngl_discussion.cfm/13128.

29. Deborah L. Vence, "Mix It Up—Segmentation, Unique Events Key to Targeting Blacks," *Marketing News*, October 15, 2006, 19, 22.

30. Andrew Pierce, "Multicultural Markets Demand Multilayered Marketing," *Marketing News*, May 1, 2008, 21.

31. *Ibid.*

32. Alison Damast, "Love Can Hurt—Your Bank Account," *BusinessWeek*, February 7, 2008, www.businessweek.com/lifestyle/content/feb2008/bw2008027_681364.htm.

33. Andrea Petersen, "The Toughest Guest: A Teen," *Wall Street Journal*, July 29, 2010, D1.

34. Andrew Adam Newman, "The Power of One," *Fortune*, April 19, 2010, 15–16.

35. Dianne Hales, "What Your Car Says About You," *Parade*, May 15, 2005, 8.

36. Joseph Pereira, "New Exercise Targets Less-Than-Fit," *Wall Street Journal*, February 1, 2007, B1, B9.

37. Aquafina Sparkling, www.aquafina.com.

38. Ann Zimmerman, "Home Depot Learns to Go Local," *Wall Street Journal*, October 7, 2008, B1.

39. Nielsen Web site, www.nielsen.com/us/en.html

40. George Stalk, Jr., "In Praise of the Heavy Spender," May 21, 2007, theglobeandmail.com/report-on-business/in-praise-of-the-heavy-spender/article/761008.

41. Ellen Byron, "Aiming to Clean Up, P&G Courts Business Customers," *Wall Street Journal*, January 26, 2007, B1, B2.

42. Anne Riley-Katz, "An Age of Specialization: Reworking Retail's Model to Get Smaller, Fresher," *Women's Wear Daily*, July 14, 2010, 8.

43. Juliet Chung, "Cooking Like the Stars?" *Wall Street Journal*, June 20, 2008, http://online.wsj.com/article/SB121390579028789461.html.

44. Julia Werdigier, "Superdry and the Niche That Grew," *New York Times,* May 13, 2010, www.nytimes.com/2010/05/14/business/global/14retail.html.

45. Barry Silverstein, "Trader Joe's: Quirky Mart," February 19, 2007, www.brandchannel.com/features_profile.asp?pr_id=323; Christopher Palmeri, "Trader Joe's Recipe for Success," *BusinessWeek* February 21, 2008, www.businessweek.com/magazine/content/08_09/b4073058455307.htm; "A Unique Grocery Store," December 13, 2008, http://eastontowncenter.com.

46. "Targeting Walmart's Core Customer Segments," April 2, 2008, www.retailwire.com.

47. "How Teen E-Retailer Tripled Revenue by Allowing Consumers to Select What Email Content They Really Want," *Marketing Sherpa*, June 28, 2007, http://www.marketingsherpa.com/consumer-demographic-category.html#.

48. Marshall Brain, "How Internet Cookies Work," *How Stuff Works,* April 26, 2000, http://computer.howstuffworks.com/cookie.htm; Jessica Vascellaro, "Google Agonizes on Privacy as Ad World Vaults Ahead," *Wall Street Journal*, August 10, 2010, A1, 12.

49. Ann Zimmerman, "A Fashion Identity Crisis at Walmart," *Wall Street Journal*, July 29, 2010, B1.

50. Natalie Zmuda, "Rebranding Resuscitates 90-Year-Old Radio Shack," *Advertising Age*, April 12, 2010, http://adage.com/cmostrategy/article?article_id=143203.

51. Ellen Byron, "Can a Re-Engineered Kleenex Cure a Brand's Sniffles?" *Wall Street Journal*, January 22, 2007, B1.

52. Sonia Reyes, "Can Frozen Treats Sell Outside the Freezer Aisle?" *Brandweek*, March 26, 2007, 16.

53. Sandra Jones, "Sears Steps Back in Time to Go Forward," March 12, 2007, http://articles.chicagotribune.com/2007-03-12/business/0703120225_1_great-indoors-sears-holdings-corp-sears-homelife.

54. Suzanne Vranica, "Grape Nuts Takes Aim at Men," *Wall Street Journal*, March 26, 2009, B5.

55. Elaine Wong, "How Walgreens Is Positioning Itself as a One-Stop Shop," *BrandWeek,* September 10, 2009, http://www.adweek.com/news/advertising-branding/how-walgreens-positioning-itself-one-stop-shop-106378.

56. This application exercise is based on the contribution of Kim McKeage (University of Maine) to *Great Ideas in Teaching Marketing*, a teaching supplement that accompanies Lamb, Hair, and McDaniel's *Marketing*. Professor McKeage's entry, titled "Students Practice Making Market/Product Grids on Themselves," received an Honorable Mention in the "Best of the Great Ideas in Teaching Marketing" contest held in conjunction with the publication of the eighth edition of *Marketing*.

57. Case Study: Jerry Adler, "Attack of the Diet Cokes," *Newsweek*, May 14, 2007; "Coke's New 'Coke Zero' Faces Tough Going" *UPI NewsTrack*, June 13, 2005; Duane D. Stanford, "0: That's Zero. As in No Calories," *Atlanta Journal-Constitution*, March 20, 2007; *MMR*, "Coca-Cola Co.," *Bnet*, October 30, 2006, http://findarticles.com/p/articles/mi_hb3235/is_17_23/ai_n29307369; Coke Zero Web site, www.cocacolazero.com/index.jsp.

chapter
9
Decision Support Systems and Marketing Research

Learning Outcomes

1 Explain the concept and purpose of a marketing decision support system

2 Define marketing research and explain its importance to marketing decision making

3 Describe the steps involved in conducting a marketing research project

4 Discuss the profound impact of the Internet on marketing research

5 Discuss the growing importance of scanner-based research

6 Explain the concept of competitive intelligence

LO1
Marketing Decision Support Systems

Accurate and timely information is the lifeblood of marketing decision making. Good information can help an organization maximize sales and efficiently use scarce company resources. To prepare and adjust marketing plans, managers need a system for gathering everyday information about developments in the marketing environment—that is, for gathering **marketing information**. The system most commonly used these days for gathering marketing information is called a *marketing decision support system*.

A marketing **decision support system (DSS)** is an interactive, flexible, computerized information system that enables managers to obtain and manipulate information as they are making decisions. A DSS bypasses the information-processing specialist and gives managers access to useful data from their own desks.

These are the characteristics of a true DSS:

→ **Interactive:** Managers give simple instructions and see immediate results. The process is under their direct control; no computer programmer is needed. Managers don't have to wait for scheduled reports.

→ **Flexible:** A DSS can sort, regroup, total, average, and manipulate the data in various ways. It will shift gears as the user changes topics, matching information to the problem at hand. For example, the CEO can see highly aggregated figures, and the marketing analyst can view very detailed breakouts.

> **Marketing research is the function that links the consumer, customer, and public to the marketer through information.**

marketing information
Everyday information about developments in the marketing environment that managers use to prepare and adjust marketing plans.

decision support system (DSS)
An interactive, flexible, computerized information system that enables managers to obtain and manipulate information as they are making decisions.

marketing&you.

Please note your opinion on each of the following questions.

Using the following scale, enter your opinion.

STRONGLY DISAGREE ‹ 1 2 3 4 5 6 7 › STRONGLY AGREE

During a marketing project, a marketing manager should have formal or informal processes for continuously:

_____ **collecting information from customers.**

_____ **collecting information about competitors' activities.**

_____ **collecting information about relevant publics other than customers and competitors.**

_____ **reexamining the value of information collected in previous studies.**

_____ **collecting information from external experts such as consultants.**

Total your score. Now, read the chapter and find out what your score means at the end.

Source: Scale #66, *Marketing Scales Handbook*, G. Bruner, James, H. Hensel, eds. Vol. III. © by American Marketing Association.

© iStockphoto.com/Juan Facundo Mora Soria

© iStockphoto.com/ziggymaj

→ **Discovery-oriented:** Managers can probe for trends, isolate problems, and ask "what if" questions.

→ **Accessible:** Managers who aren't very skilled with computers and statistics can easily learn how to use a DSS. Novice users should be able to choose a standard, or default, method of using the system. They can bypass optional features so they can work with the basic system right away while gradually learning to apply its advanced features.

As a hypothetical example of how a DSS can be used, consider Renee Smith, vice president and manager of new products for Central Corporation. To evaluate sales of a recently introduced product, Renee can "call up" sales by the week, then by the month, breaking them out at her option by, say, customer segments. As she works at her desktop computer, her inquiries can go in several directions, depending on the decision at hand. If her train of thought raises questions about monthly sales last quarter compared to forecasts, she can use her DSS to analyze problems immediately. Renee might see that her new product's sales were significantly below forecasts. Were her forecasts too optimistic? She compares other products' sales to her forecasts and finds that the targets were very accurate. Was something wrong with the product? Is her sales department getting insufficient leads, or is it not putting leads to good use? Thinking a minute about how to examine that question, she checks ratios of leads converted to sales, product by product. The results disturb her. Only 5 percent of the new product's leads generated orders, compared to the company's 12 percent all-product average. Why? Renee guesses that the sales force is not supporting the new product vigorously enough. Quantitative information from the DSS could perhaps provide more evidence to back that suspicion. But already having enough quantitative knowledge to satisfy herself, the VP acts on her intuition and experience and decides to have a chat with her sales manager.

Perhaps the fastest-growing use of DSSs is for **database marketing**, which is the creation of a large computerized file of customers' and potential customers' profiles and purchase patterns. Data mining is then used to uncover hidden patterns and relationships in the data. It is usually the key tool for successful one-to-one marketing, which relies on very specific information about a market. Huge databases can raise a number of concerns about the safety and use of personal data, as discussed in the Ethics in Marketing box in Chapter 8.

Review
LO1 Explain the concept and purpose of a marketing decision support system

- Interactive
- Flexible
- Discovery-oriented
- Accessible

DSS

Internal and External Marketing Information

database marketing
The creation of a large computerized file of customers' and potential customers' profiles and purchase patterns.

marketing research
The process of planning, collecting, and analyzing data relevant to a marketing decision.

LO2
The Role of Marketing Research

Marketing research is the process of planning, collecting, and analyzing data relevant to a marketing decision. The results of this analysis are then communicated to management. Thus, marketing research is the function that links the consumer, customer, and public to the marketer through information. Marketing research plays a key role in the marketing system. It provides decision makers with data on the effectiveness of the current marketing mix and also with insights for necessary changes. Furthermore, marketing research is a main data source for both management information systems and DSS. In other words, the findings of a marketing research project become data in a DSS.

Each year over $9 billion is spent on marketing research in the United States.[1] That money is used to study products, advertising, prices, packages, names, logos, services, buying habits, taglines, colors, uses, awareness, familiarity, new concepts, traffic patterns, wants, needs, and politics.

Marketing research has three roles: descriptive, diagnostic, and predictive. Its *descriptive* role includes gathering and presenting factual statements. For example, what is the historic sales trend in the industry? What are consumers' attitudes toward a product and its advertising? Its *diagnostic* role includes explaining data. For instance, what was the impact on sales of a change in the design of the package? Its *predictive* function is to address "what if" questions. For example, how can the researcher use the descriptive and diagnostic research to predict the results of a planned marketing decision?

MANAGEMENT USES OF MARKETING RESEARCH

Marketing research can help managers in several ways. It improves the quality of decision making and helps managers trace problems. Most important, sound marketing research helps managers focus on the paramount importance of keeping existing customers, aids them in better understanding the marketplace, and alerts them to marketplace trends.

Marketing research also helps managers gauge the perceived value of their goods and services as well as the level of customer satisfaction. For example, research revealed which brands of plumbing fixtures were traditional to New York City. This helped the Brooklyn Home Depot's store manager Rich Kantor to design his small pilot store to meet the needs of urban communities.

Improving the Quality of Decision Making Managers can sharpen their decision making by using marketing research to explore the desirability of various marketing alternatives. For example, on the heels of the successful launch of its Young & Tender line of bagged spinach, NewStar, a Salinas, California-based produce firm, was wondering what to do for an encore. A line of salad kits featuring spinach in combination with a dressing and/or other ingredients seemed like a natural idea. But rather than introducing a me-too product to the already-crowded salad kit market, the company wanted to add a gourmet twist.

The process began with an idea generation phase, says Christie Hoyer, vice president of product development and evaluation at the National Food Laboratory (NFL). Sessions were conducted with NFL chefs, food technologists, and other culinary arts workers. "We did a number of brainstorming sessions, game-playing, and other, more coordinated exercises. From that we came up with numerous flavor concepts for the salads and the sauté mixes."

The company then began consumer testing. At this stage, Hoyer says, NFL wanted to validate the product concepts and also gauge reactions to them. A four-phase process was conducted with male and female consumers ages 21 to 64 who were their family's primary grocery shopper and were positive toward spinach salad and cooked fresh spinach.

The first phase gathered reactions to the concept of a line of gourmet salad and sauté kits and determined purchase intent for each flavor (based on descriptions

NewStar's Baby Spinach kits come with everything you need for a quick nutritious meal.

© Terri Miller/E-Visual Communications, Inc.

of the flavors, not actual tasting). Next, the respondents tried the product prototypes, which were rotated so that half of the group tried the sautés first, and half tried the salads first.

The third phase was a test of packaging. Respondents were taken to a separate area featuring a mock store display of three packaging concepts and asked to rank their preferences for the different graphics. In the fourth phase, the consumers viewed a large copy of the nutritional information for a salad kit and a sauté kit. "Without specifically asking about it, we were interested in their reaction to things such as fat content," Hoyer says.

Since the salad and sauté mixes were introduced, they have been a hit with retailers and with consumers. Marketing research paved the way![2]

Marketing research has a wide variety of applications. For example, Philips Electronics had gathered information that in 2004, only 18 percent of all men used solely an electric razor. Hoping to increase that number, Philips Electronics, makers of Norelco razors, turned to marketing research to guide the development of a better electric razor. Its target customer was between the ages of 35 and 54, an experienced shaver who is likely to spend more for a premium razor that will last six to seven years. The company interviewed 5,000 men in the U.S., Europe, and China, searching for some undiscovered consumer need that might be met with a dynamite product. Philips found an opportunity in an unlikely place. It learned that one of the most common frustrations of shaving has nothing to do with the face: it's those pesky few flat-lying hairs on the neck under the chin. The men interviewed by the company had to shave over those hairs six or seven times, often irritating their skin and leaving welts or spawning in-grown hairs. Philips decided to develop a razor that closely shaves those neck hairs the first time. To do so, it needed to design an electric razor with much greater maneuverability to navigate the tricky area around the jugular vein. Its research also led the company to a name for the new model: the "Arcitec," a combination of "the arch of the neck" and "technology."[3]

Introducing new products is only one application of market research. Consumer packaging is another. For example, Oscar Meyer marketing researchers had heard plenty from consumers about what they disliked about its bacon packaging: opening a pack of bacon is a messy job—you have to reach into the package; if you only need a few slices, there's no easy way to store the remainder. So marketers used this information from their customers to create a packaging innovation that eliminated the chore of placing the opened package in a plastic bag or wrapping it in plastic or foil to preserve what was left of the bacon. The innovation? Oscar Mayer Center Cut Bacon is sold in a "Stay-Fresh Reclosable Tray." The flip top lid allows easy access to the bacon inside. The top snaps closed, making it readily resealable. The flat tray makes storage simple in the refrigerator.[4]

Tracing Problems When Something Goes Wrong Another way managers use marketing research is to find out why a plan backfired. Was the initial decision incorrect? Did an unforeseen change in the external environment cause the plan to fail? How can the same mistake be avoided in the future?

Keebler introduced Sweet Spots, a shortbread cookie with a huge chocolate drop on it. It has had acceptable sales and is still on the market, but only after the company used marketing research to overcome several problems. Soon after the cookie's introduction, Keebler increased the box size from 10 ounces at $2.29 to 15 ounces at $3.19. Demand immediately fell. Market research showed that at the higher price, Sweet Spots were considered more of a luxury than an everyday item. Keebler lowered the price and went back to the 10-ounce box. Keebler had also tried to target

customer experience

Zappos Otherworldly Customer Service

Las Vegas-based Zappos started in 1999 by selling shoes online, and has since grown to a $1 billion per year retailer. It has expanded into clothing, handbags, sunglasses, and numerous other categories. Early on, Zappos made a deliberate decision to redirect its marketing budget toward delivering exceptional customer service with a great company culture, helping the business to thrive where others have failed. Core customer service policies include:

- encouraging customers to order as many products as they wanted in order to "try them on," then offering free return shipping for a full year.

- listing products on the site only when stock is in the Zappos warehouse (which actually lowered sales by 25 percent at a time when the company was still in the red).

- deciding to run their warehouse operation 24/7 to deliver super-fast turnaround on orders, despite it being an inefficient way to manage fulfillment.

- encouraging customers to call them about nearly everything. Their call center takes 5,000 calls per day, and employees work independent of scripts, quotas, or call time limits. The longest call to date has been four hours. Zappos views the phone experience as a branding device and speaks to virtually every customer at least once.

- deciding to invest in "surprise" (free) upgrades to overnight shipping for most customers. This means that most orders are delivered within 24 hours, despite the Web site indicating it will take two to five business days.

Company culture is important from the start. Zappos conducts two separate interviews—one focusing on the applicant's background and experience, and the second one on cultural fit. Over the years, Zappos has passed on numerous experienced employees for the simple reason that they were wrong for the company culturally. The emphasis on cultural fit extends to the training process, where new employees cycle through work in the Kentucky warehouse and call center, and receive lessons on company history and core values. The first core value is to "Deliver WOW Through Service."

Recently Amazon bought Zappos and the firm is now an Amazon.com subsidiary. Zappos' CEO Tony Hsieh held an all-hands meeting once the deal was announced. He told employees that they would each receive a Kindle and a retention bonus equal to 40 percent of their salary.[8]

How can Zappos use marketing research to further improve customer service? Is it really necessary for Zappos to provide such a high level of service to keep its customers?

two markets with the cookie: kids and upscale adult women. After its research, Keebler found that the package graphics appealed to mothers but not to children.

Focusing on the Paramount Importance of Keeping Existing Customers

An inextricable link exists between customer satisfaction and customer loyalty. Long-term relationships don't just happen but are grounded in the delivery of service and value by the firm. Customer retention pays big dividends for organizations. Powered by repeat sales and referrals, revenues and market share grow. Costs fall because firms spend less money and energy attempting to replace defectors. Steady customers are easy to serve because they understand the modus operandi and make fewer demands on employees' time. Increased customer retention also drives job satisfaction and pride, which lead to higher employee retention. In turn, the knowledge employees acquire as they stay longer increases productivity. A Bain & Co. study estimated that a 5 percent decrease in the customer defection rate can boost profits by 25 to 95 percent.[5] Another study found that the customer retention rate has a major impact on the value of the firm.[6]

Domino's Pizza understands the importance of retaining customers. After research respondents savaged its products, Domino's didn't sit on the results and hide the negative feedback. It accepted the criticism as truth and understood that the pizza could no longer compete: Bland and middle-of-the-road is not sufficient to succeed in today's pizza marketplace.

Domino's latest mea culpa ad campaign features clips from marketing research comments in which, for example, one respondent proclaims that Domino's crust is like cardboard; another comment states it is the worst pizza a customer had ever had; another claimed the pizza to be devoid of flavor; and in another segment the sauce is likened to ketchup—all unappetizing (and potentially brand-damaging) comments if Domino's hadn't responded.

Instead of hiding the fact that its pizza was markedly subpar compared to its adequate scores in service and delivery, Domino's showed America that it is highly in tune with the voice of the customer, aware of its shortcomings, and willing to go to great lengths—and spend millions of dollars—to correct them. It created a new marinara, upgraded its cheese, and added an herb-butter-brush to its pizza crusts.[7]

One company that always goes the extra mile to provide high-quality service and to deliver customer satisfaction is Zappos. Their devotion to customer service is described in the Customer Experience box on the page 311.

UNDERSTANDING THE EVER-CHANGING MARKETPLACE

Marketing research also helps managers understand what is going on in the marketplace and take advantage of opportunities. Historically, marketing research has been practiced for as long as marketing has existed. The early Phoenicians carried out market demand studies as they traded in the various ports of the Mediterranean Sea. Marco Polo's diary indicates he was performing marketing research as he traveled to China. There is even evidence that the Spanish systematically conducted "market surveys" as they explored the New World, and there are examples of marketing research conducted during the Renaissance.

As the price of gasoline hit $4.00 plus per gallon, more and more manufacturers began looking at the hybrid car market. However, before committing hundreds of millions of dollars to producing hybrids, they need a better understanding of the market. Enter marketing research. When consumers were asked whether they would consider a hybrid version of their new vehicle had it been available, roughly seven in ten indicated they would have. In addition to their high likelihood to consider hybrid vehicles, when asked what type of alternative fuel they found most appealing, vehicle buyers most often indicate the hybrid method as their preferred alternative fuel type.

Also, there has been an increased interest in pure electric vehicles. The uptick likely reflects new developments in electric engines and public relations activities surrounding them. When considering purchasing a new vehicle, those who choose hybrids are motivated by a desire to obtain an environmentally friendly vehicle, but even more importantly, to achieve the greatest level of fuel economy. Those who choose hybrids are more likely than owners in general to consider issues such as style, comfort, roominess, and even price to be significantly less important.

However, despite obtaining higher miles per gallon (MPG) and greater satisfaction with it, hybrid owners report their MPG falls far short of their expectations. In fact,

Review LO 2 Define marketing research and explain its importance to marketing decision making

Why marketing research?

☑ Improve quality of decision making

☑ Trace problems

☑ Focus on keeping existing customers

☑ Understand changes in marketplace

hybrid owners are significantly more likely than vehicle purchasers in general to obtain lower-than-expected MPG.[9]

Although the material above is just a tiny piece of a nationwide study of over 100,000 vehicle owners, you can see how the insights from such a study can be extremely valuable to car manufacturers.

LO3
Steps in a Marketing Research Project

Virtually all firms that have adopted the marketing concept engage in some marketing research because it offers decision makers many benefits. Some companies spend millions on marketing research; others, particularly smaller firms, conduct informal, limited-scale research studies. For example, when the Eurasia restaurant, serving Eurasian cuisine, first opened along Chicago's ritzy Michigan Avenue, it drew novelty seekers. But it turned off the important business lunch crowd and sales began to decline. The owner surveyed several hundred businesspeople working within a mile of the restaurant. He found that they were confused by Eurasia's concept and wanted more traditional Asian fare at lower prices. In response, the restaurant altered its concept; it hired a Thai chef, revamped the menu, and cut prices. The dining room was soon full again.

Whether a research project costs $200 or $2 million, the same general process should be followed. The marketing research process is a scientific approach to decision making that maximizes the chance of getting accurate and meaningful results. Exhibit 9.1 traces the steps: (1) identifying and formulating the problem/opportunity, (2) planning the research design and gathering secondary data, (3) specifying the sampling procedures, (4) collecting the primary data, (5) analyzing the data, (6) preparing and presenting the report, and (7) following up.

The research process begins with the recognition of a marketing problem or opportunity. As changes occur in the firm's external environment, marketing managers are faced with the questions, "Should we change the existing marketing mix?" and, if so, "How?" Marketing research may be used to evaluate product, promotion, distribution, or pricing alternatives.

Though famous for its well-known line of household lubricants, San Diego-based WD-40 Co. has repositioned one of its product lines as essential bathroom cleaners—the result of a research process.

Sales of the company's six household product brands (of which X-14 is one) make up a sizable percentage—more than 31 percent—of the overall portfolio. However, rival brands were more popular. Which elements in the company's marketing mix could be adjusted to gain more share of the cleaning products market?

The repositioning of WD-40's X-14 line helped the $287 million company find the brand's niche. "We previously had products that focused on the bathroom, but there wasn't a unified line in its positioning. We had a line of cleaning products that were not meeting their potential in the marketplace," says Heidi Noorany, director of marketing. The marketing research indicated that there was a need for a "bathroom expert" line of products. "We knew we had the positioning and the quality of products within the current line, but we had to communicate it," Noorany adds. That would be translated through the line's

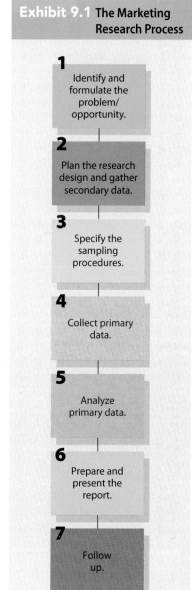

Exhibit 9.1 The Marketing Research Process

1 Identify and formulate the problem/opportunity.

2 Plan the research design and gather secondary data.

3 Specify the sampling procedures.

4 Collect primary data.

5 Analyze primary data.

6 Prepare and present the report.

7 Follow up.

© Cengage Learning 2013

Using marketing research helped the WD-40 Company successfully reposition its X-14 cleaning products in the marketplace. The research also identified opportunities to extend the X-14 brand.

more cohesive packaging design characterized by a variety of reds, greens, and blues, as well as several bottle designs.

Consumer research was also used to measure product effectiveness versus competitors' products, and found that the X-14 Foaming Bathroom Cleaner scored 4.5 on a scale of 1 to 5, and that its Trigger Bathroom Cleaner scored a 91 percent approval rating, placing it higher than four other competing brands. The research also found that consumers engage in two types of cleaning—weekly deep cleanings and quick daily cleanings. "We saw an opportunity for a bathroom expert line of products," says Noorany. Not only did WD-40 learn how to best reposition the X-14 line, but it garnered enough insight from the research process that it could use the data in future product development.[10]

The WD-40 story illustrates an important point about problem/opportunity definition. The **marketing research problem** is information oriented. It involves determining what information is needed and how that information can be obtained efficiently and effectively. The **marketing research objective**, then, is to provide insightful decision-making information. This requires specific pieces of information needed to answer the marketing research problem. Managers must combine this information with their own experience and other information to make a proper decision. WD-40's marketing research problem was to gather information on how consumers clean and how they shop for cleaning products. The marketing research objective was several-fold: identify a better positioning strategy for X-14 and identify opportunities to add new items to the X-14 brand.

Whereas the marketing research problem is information oriented, the **management decision problem** is action oriented. Management problems tend to be much broader in scope and far more general than marketing research problems, which must be narrowly defined and specific if the research effort is to be successful. Sometimes several research studies must be conducted to solve a broad management problem. The management decision problem was: "How do we grow sales of X-14 family brand?" Management then decided to reposition X-14 as The Bathroom Expert—the centerpiece around which its new product line reentered the

marketing research problem

Determining what information is needed and how that information can be obtained efficiently and effectively.

marketing research objective

The specific information needed to solve a marketing research problem; the objective should be to provide insightful decision-making information.

management decision problem

A broad-based problem that uses marketing research in order for managers to take proper actions.

market. Completely redesigned, the line now provides a family look for the set of products rather than a disjointed set of similar products. Yet it also includes two additions: Foaming Bathroom Cleaner and Bathroom Cleaner, which combines oxy and citrus (hydrogen peroxide with citric acid) for general bathroom cleaning. Additionally, several future products are expected to be released soon.[11]

SECONDARY DATA

A valuable tool throughout the research process, but particularly in the problem/opportunity identification stage is **secondary data**—data previously collected for any purpose other than the one at hand. Secondary information originating within the company includes documents such as annual reports, reports to stockholders, product testing results perhaps made available to the news media, and house periodicals composed by the company's personnel for communication to employees, customers, or others. Often this information is incorporated into a company's internal database.

Innumerable outside sources of secondary information also exist, principally coming from government departments and agencies (federal, state, and local) that compile and publish summaries of business data. Trade and industry associations also publish secondary data. Still more data are available in business periodicals and other news media that regularly publish studies and articles on the economy, specific industries, and even individual companies. The unpublished summarized secondary information from these sources corresponds to internal reports, memos, or special-purpose analyses with limited circulation. Economic considerations or priorities in the organization may preclude publication of these summaries. Most of the sources listed above can be found on the Internet.

Secondary data save time and money if they help solve the researcher's problem. Even if the problem is not solved, secondary data have other advantages. They can aid in formulating the problem statement and suggest research methods and other types of data needed for solving the problem. In addition, secondary data can pinpoint the kinds of people to approach and their locations and serve as a basis of comparison for other data. The disadvantages of secondary data come mainly from a mismatch between the researcher's unique problem and the purpose for which the secondary data were originally gathered, which are typically different. For example, a major consumer-products manufacturer wanted to determine the market potential for a fireplace log made of coal rather than compressed wood by-products. The researcher found plenty of secondary data about total wood consumed as fuel, quantities consumed in each state, and types of wood burned. Secondary data were also available about consumer attitudes and purchase patterns of wood by-product fireplace logs. The wealth of secondary data provided the researcher with many insights into the artificial log market. Yet nowhere was there any information that would tell the firm whether consumers would buy artificial logs made of coal.

The quality of secondary data may also pose a problem. Often, secondary data sources do not give detailed information that would enable a researcher to assess their quality or relevance. Whenever possible, a researcher needs to address these important questions: Who gathered the data? Why were the data obtained? What methodology was used? How were classifications (such as heavy users versus light users) developed and defined? When was the information gathered?

The New Age of Secondary Information: The Internet Gathering secondary data, though necessary in almost any research project, has traditionally been a tedious and boring job. The researcher often had to write to government agencies, trade associations, or other secondary data providers and then wait days

secondary data
Data previously collected for any purpose other than the one at hand.

© iStockphoto.com/Juan Facundo Mora Soria

Exhibit 9.2 Popular Secondary Data Sites Used by Marketing Researchers

Organization	URL	Description
American Marketing Association	www.marketingpower.com	Enables users to search all of the AMA's publications by using keywords.
BLS Consumer Expenditure Surveys	www.bls.gov/cex/	Provides information on the buying habits of consumers, including data on their expenditures, income, and credit ratings.
U.S. Census Bureau	www.census.gov	Contains virtually all census data.
U.S. Government	www.fedstats.gov	Source for statistics and reports for more than 100 government agencies. Also links to other sources of relevant information. Highly recommended site but you might have to dig a little.
Nielsen/NetRatings	www.nielsen-netratings.com	Is a source of Internet audience information. Researchers can find data on Internet growth and user patterns.
USADATA	www.usadata.com	Provides access to consumer lifestyle data on a local, regional, and national level.
Opinion Research	www.opinionresearch.com	Offers consulting and research services. The site claims to offer access to the largest private information center for global data in the United States.

© Cengage Learning 2013

or weeks for a reply that might never come. Often, one or more trips to the library were required, and the researcher might find that needed reports were checked out or missing. Now, however, the Internet has eliminated much of the drudgery associated with the collection of secondary data. A few popular sites used by marketing researchers are shown in Exhibit 9.2.

MARKETING RESEARCH AGGREGATORS

The marketing research aggregator industry is a $120 million business that is growing by about 6 percent a year. A **marketing research aggregator** acquires, catalogs, reformats, segments, and resells reports already published by large and small marketing research firms. Even Amazon.com has added a marketing research aggregation area to its high-profile e-commerce site.

The role of aggregator firms is growing because their databases of research reports are getting bigger and more comprehensive—and more useful—as marketing research firms get more comfortable using resellers as a sales channel. Meanwhile, advances in Web technology are making the databases easier to search and deliveries speedier. Research aggregators are also indirectly tapping new markets for traditional research firms. By slicing and repackaging research reports into narrower, more specialized sections for resale to small- and medium-sized clients that often cannot afford to commission their own studies or buy full reports, the aggregators are nurturing a new target market for the information.

Prior to the emergence of research aggregators, a lot of marketing research was available only as premium-priced subscription services. For example, a 17-chapter $2,800 report from Wintergreen Research (based in Lexington, Massachusetts) was recently broken up and sold for $350 per chapter, significantly boosting the overall revenue generated by the report. Other major aggregators are **Mindbranch.com, Aarkstore.com,** and **USADATA.com.**

marketing research aggregator

A company that acquires, catalogs, reformats, segments, and resells reports already published by marketing research firms.

PLANNING THE RESEARCH DESIGN AND GATHERING PRIMARY DATA

Good secondary data can help researchers conduct a thorough situation analysis. With that information, researchers can list their unanswered questions and rank them. Researchers must then decide the exact information required to answer the questions. The research design specifies which research questions must be answered, how and when the data will be gathered, and how the data will be analyzed. Typically, the project budget is finalized after the research design has been approved.

Sometimes research questions can be answered by gathering more secondary data; otherwise, primary data may be needed. Primary data, or information collected for the first time, is used for solving the particular problem under investigation. The main advantage of primary data is that they will answer a specific research question that secondary data cannot answer. For example, suppose Pillsbury has two new recipes for refrigerated dough for sugar cookies. Which one will consumers like better? Secondary data will not help answer this question. Instead, targeted consumers must try each recipe and evaluate the taste, texture, and appearance of each cookie. Moreover, primary data are current, and researchers know the source. Sometimes researchers gather the data themselves rather than assign projects to outside companies. Researchers also specify the methodology of the research. Secrecy can be maintained because the information is proprietary. In contrast, much secondary data is available to all interested parties for relatively small fees or for free.

Gathering primary data is expensive; costs can range from a few thousand dollars for a limited survey to several million for a nationwide study. For instance, a nationwide, 15-minute telephone interview with 1,000 adult males can cost $50,000 for everything, including a data analysis and report. Because primary data gathering in person is so expensive, many firms now use an Internet study instead. Larger companies that conduct many research projects use another cost-saving technique. They *piggyback studies*, or gather data on two different projects using one questionnaire. The drawback is that answering questions about, say, dog food and gourmet coffee may be confusing to respondents. Piggybacking also requires a longer interview (sometimes a half hour or longer), which tires respondents. The quality of the answers typically declines, with people giving curt replies and thinking, "When will this end?" A lengthy interview also makes people less likely to participate in other research surveys.

Nevertheless, the disadvantages of primary data gathering are usually offset by the advantages. It is often the only way of solving a research problem. And with a variety of techniques available for research—including surveys, observations, and experiments—primary research can address almost any marketing question.

Top 5 Reasons for Everyday Headaches

100%

Stress/Tension 73.1
Sinuses/Allergies 51.3
Fatigue/Lack of Sleep 50.5
Dehydration 19.4
Alcohol 17.9

According to a recent survey of headache sufferers, stress and tension came out on top as the main cause of headaches. For those surveyed who have used a headache powder like **Goody's Cool Orange**, 69% of consumers said that headache powders worked fast. Goody's dissolves faster than tablets. Visit www.goodyspowder.com.

Source: Synovate e-Nation Survey, sponsored by Goody's Cool Orange   6/2/08

Companies gather primary data, like the survey results used in this Goody's advertisement, to collect new information directly from consumers. How do you think Goody's used the information it collected?

research design
Specifies which research questions must be answered, how and when the data will be gathered, and how the data will be analyzed.

primary data
Information that is collected for the first time; used for solving the particular problem under investigation.

Exhibit 9.3 Characteristics of Traditional Forms of Survey Research

Characteristic	In-Home Personal Interviews	Mall Intercept Interviews	Central Location Telephone Interviews	Self-Administered and One-Time Mail Surveys	Mail Panel Surveys	Executive Interviews	Focus Groups
Cost	High	Moderate	Moderate	Low	Moderate	High	Low
Time span	Moderate	Moderate	Fast	Slow	Relatively slow	Moderate	Fast
Use of interviewer	Yes	Yes	Yes	No	No	Yes	Yes
Ability to show concepts to respondent	Yes (also taste tests)	Yes (also taste tests)	No	Yes	Yes	Yes	Yes
Management control over interviewer	Low	Moderate	High	N/A	N/A	Moderate	High
General data quality	High	Moderate	High to moderate	Moderate to low	Moderate to low	High	Moderate
Ability to collect large amounts of data	High	Moderate	Moderate to low	Low to moderate	Moderate	Moderate	Moderate
Ability to handle complex questionnaires	High	Moderate	High, if computer-aided	Low	Low	High	N/A

SURVEY RESEARCH

The most popular technique for gathering primary data is **survey research**, in which a researcher interacts with people to obtain facts, opinions, and attitudes. Exhibit 9.3 summarizes the characteristics of traditional forms of survey research.

In-Home Personal Interviews Although in-home personal interviews often provide high-quality information, they tend to be very expensive because of the interviewers' travel time and mileage costs. Therefore, they are rapidly disappearing from the American and European marketing researcher's survey toolbox. They are, however, still popular in many countries around the globe.

Telephone Interviews Compared to the personal interview, the telephone interview costs less, but cost is rapidly increasing due to respondent refusals to participate. Most telephone interviewing is conducted from a specially designed phone room called a **central-location telephone (CLT) facility**. A CLT has many phone lines, individual interviewing stations, headsets, and occasionally monitoring equipment. The research firm typically will interview people nationwide from a single location. The federal "Do Not Call" law does not apply to survey research.

Most CLT facilities offer computer-assisted interviewing. The interviewer reads the questions from a computer screen and enters the respondent's data directly into the computer. The researcher can stop the survey at any point and immediately print out the survey results. Thus, a researcher can get a sense of the project as it unfolds and fine-tune the research design as necessary. An online interviewing system can also save time and money because data entry occurs as the response is recorded rather than as a separate process after the interview. Hallmark Cards found that an interviewer administered a printed questionnaire for its Shoebox greeting

survey research
The most popular technique for gathering primary data, in which a researcher interacts with people to obtain facts, opinions, and attitudes.

central-location telephone (CLT) facility
A specially designed phone room used to conduct telephone interviewing.

cards in 28 minutes. The same questionnaire administered with computer assistance took only 18 minutes.

Approximately 18 percent of homes now have only cell phones—a number that is expected to continue to rise. Federal law forbids automatic dialers for cell phone interviewing so all calls must be dialed manually. This raises interviewing costs but is normally viewed as a necessary expense because cell-phone–only homes have a different demographic makeup from the general population. Cell-phone–only households tend to be younger, have slightly lower incomes, and are more likely to rent than their tethered-telephone peers. Some research firms also reimburse respondents for the cost of the minutes used, which further raises interviewing costs.[12]

Mall Intercept Interviews The **mall intercept interview** is conducted in the common area of a shopping mall or in a market research office within the mall. It is the economy version of the door-to-door interview with personal contact between interviewer and respondent, because the interviewer saves on travel time and mileage costs. To conduct this type of interview, the research firm rents office space in the mall or pays a significant daily fee. One drawback is that it is hard to get a representative sample of the population this way.

However, an interviewer can also probe when necessary—a technique used to clarify a person's response. For example, an interviewer might ask, "What did you like best about the salad dressing you just tried?" The respondent might reply, "Taste." This answer doesn't provide a lot of information, so the interviewer could probe by saying, "Can you tell me a little bit more about taste?" The respondent then elaborates: "Yes, it's not too sweet, it has the right amount of pepper, and I love that hint of garlic."

Mall intercept interviews must be brief. Only the shortest ones are conducted while respondents are standing. Usually, researchers invite respondents to their office for interviews, which are still generally less than 15 minutes long. The researchers often show respondents concepts for new products or a test commercial or have them taste a new food product. The overall quality of mall intercept interviews is about the same as telephone interviews.

Marketing researchers are applying computer technology in mall interviewing. The first technique is **computer-assisted personal interviewing**. The researcher conducts in-person interviews, reads questions to the respondent off a computer screen, and directly keys the respondent's answers into the computer. A second approach is **computer-assisted self-interviewing**. A mall interviewer intercepts and directs willing respondents to nearby computers. Each respondent reads questions off a computer screen and directly keys his or her answers into a computer. The third use of technology is fully automated self-interviewing. Respondents are guided by interviewers or independently approach a centrally located computer station or kiosk, read questions off a screen, and directly key their answers into the station's computer.

Mail Surveys Mail surveys have several benefits: relatively low cost, elimination of interviewers and field supervisors, centralized control, and actual or promised anonymity for respondents (which may draw more candid responses). Some researchers feel that mail questionnaires give the respondent a chance to reply more thoughtfully and to check records, talk to family members, and so forth. A disadvantage is that mail questionnaires usually produce low response rates.

Low response rates pose a problem because certain elements of the population tend to respond more than others. The resulting sample may therefore might not represent the surveyed population. For example, the sample could have too many

mall intercept interview
A survey research method that involves interviewing people in the common areas of shopping malls.

computer-assisted personal interviewing
An interviewing method in which the interviewer reads the questions from a computer screen and enters the respondent's data directly into the computer.

computer-assisted self-interviewing
An interviewing method in which a mall interviewer intercepts and directs willing respondents to nearby computers where the respondent reads questions off a computer screen and directly keys his or her answers into a computer.

© iStockphoto.com/Juan Facundo Mora Soria

retired people and too few working people. In this instance, answers to a question about attitudes toward government programs to aid senior citizens might indicate a much more favorable overall view of the system than is actually the case. Another serious problem with mail surveys is that no one probes respondents to clarify or elaborate on their answers.

Mail panels like those operated by Synovate, Ipsos, and NPD Group offer an alternative to the one-shot mail survey. A mail panel consists of a sample of households recruited to participate by mail for a given period. Panel members often receive gifts in return for their participation. Essentially, the panel is a sample used several times. In contrast to one-time mail surveys, the response rates from mail panels are high. Rates of 70 percent (of those who agree to participate) are not uncommon.

Executive Interviews Marketing researchers use **executive interviews** to conduct the industrial equivalent of door-to-door interviewing. This type of survey involves interviewing professionals and businesspeople, at their offices, concerning products or services. For example, if Oracle wanted information regarding user preferences for different features that might be offered in a new line of CRM software, it would need to interview prospective user-purchasers of the software. It is appropriate to locate and interview these people at their offices.

This type of interviewing is very expensive. First, individuals involved in the purchase decision for the product in question must be identified and located. Sometimes lists can be obtained from various sources, but more frequently screening must be conducted over the telephone or Internet. A particular company is likely to have individuals of the type being sought, but locating those people within a large organization can be expensive and time-consuming. Once a qualified person is located, the next step is to get that person to agree to be interviewed and to set a time for the interview. This is not as hard as it might seem because most professionals seem to enjoy talking about topics related to their work.

Finally, an interviewer must go to the particular place at the appointed time. Long waits are frequently encountered, and cancellations are not uncommon. This type of survey requires the very best interviewers because they are frequently interviewing on topics that they know very little about. Executive interviewing has essentially the same advantages and disadvantages as in-home interviewing.

Focus Groups A **focus group** is a type of personal interviewing. Often recruited by random telephone screening, seven to ten people with certain desired characteristics form a focus group. These qualified consumers are usually offered an incentive (typically $50 to $75) to participate in a group discussion. The meeting place (sometimes resembling a living room, sometimes featuring a conference table) has audio-recording and perhaps video-recording equipment. It also likely has a viewing room with a one-way mirror so that clients (manufacturers or retailers) can watch the session. During the session, a moderator, hired by the research company, leads the group discussion.

Focus groups are much more than question-and-answer interviews. Market researchers draw a distinction between "group dynamics" and "group interviewing." The interaction provided in **group dynamics** is essential to the success of focus-group research; this interaction is the reason for conducting group rather than individual research. One of the essential postulates of group-session usage is the idea that a response from one person might become a stimulus for another, thereby generating an interplay of responses that could yield more information than if the same number of people had contributed independently.

Lewis Stone, former manager of Colgate-Palmolive's research and development division, says the following about focus groups:

"If it weren't for focus groups, Colgate-Palmolive Co. might never know that some women squeeze their bottles of dishwashing soap, others squeeeeeze them, and still others squeeeeeeeeeze out the desired amount. Then there are the ones who use the soap 'neat.' That is, they put the product directly on a sponge or washcloth and wash the dishes under running water until the suds run out. Then they apply more detergent."

Stone was explaining how body language, exhibited during focus groups, provides insights into a product that are not apparent from reading questionnaires on habits and practices. Focus groups represent a most

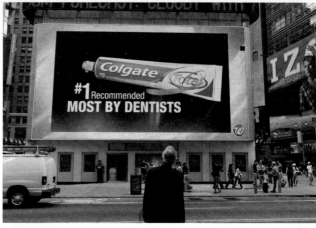

Colgate-Palmolive likely used market research to determine that Colgate Total is recommended most by dentists.

efficient way of learning how one's products are actually used in the home. By drawing out the panelists to describe in detail how they do certain tasks, you can learn a great deal about possible need-gaps that could be filled by new or improved products, and also how a new product might be received. It is estimated that over 600,000 focus groups are conducted around the world each year.[13]

A system created by FocusVision allows client companies and advertising agencies to view live focus groups in over 500 cities worldwide.[14] For example, the private satellite network lets a Taco Bell researcher observing a San Diego focus group control two cameras in the viewing room. The researcher can get a full-group view or a close-up, zoom, or pan the participants. The researcher can also communicate directly with the moderator using an ear receiver. Ogilvy & Mather (a large New York advertising agency whose clients include StarKist Seafood, Seagram's, MasterCard, and Burger King) has installed the system.

Increasingly, focus groups are being conducted online. Online focus groups are examined in detail later in the chapter.

QUESTIONNAIRE DESIGN

All forms of survey research require a questionnaire. Questionnaires ensure that all respondents will be asked the same series of questions. Questionnaires include three basic types of questions: open-ended, closed-ended, and scaled-response. (See Exhibit 9.4.) An **open-ended question** encourages an answer phrased in the respondent's own words. Researchers get a rich array of information based on the respondent's frame of reference. In contrast, a **closed-ended question** asks the respondent to make a selection from a limited list of responses. Traditionally, marketing researchers separate the two-choice question (called *dichotomous*) from the many-item type (often called *multiple choice*). A **scaled-response question** is a closed-ended question designed to measure the intensity of a respondent's answer.

Closed-ended and scaled-response questions are easier to tabulate than open-ended questions because response choices are fixed. On the other hand, unless the researcher designs the closed-ended question very carefully, an important choice could be omitted.

For example, suppose a food study asked this question: "Besides meat, which of the following items do you normally add to a taco that you prepare at home?"

open-ended question
An interview question that encourages an answer phrased in the respondent's own words.

closed-ended question
An interview question that asks the respondent to make a selection from a limited list of responses.

scaled-response question
A closed-ended question designed to measure the intensity of a respondent's answer.

Open-Ended Questions	Closed-Ended Questions	Scaled-Response Question
1. What advantages, if any, do you think ordering from a mail-order catalog offers compared to shopping at a local retail outlet? (*Probe:* What else?)	**Dichotomous** 1. Did you heat the Danish product before serving it? Yes.....................................1 No.......................................2	Now that you have used the rug cleaner, would you say that you . . . (*Circle one.*) Would definitely buy it.............. 1 Would probably buy it 2
2. Why do you have one or more of your rugs or carpets professionally cleaned rather than cleaning them yourself or having someone else in the household clean them?	2. The federal government doesn't care what people like me think. Agree..................................1 Disagree 2	Might or might not buy it .... 3 Probably would not buy it.......... 4 Definitely would not buy it 5
3. What is it about the color of the eye shadow that makes you like it the best?	**Multiple choice** 1. I'd like you to think back to the last footwear of any kind that you bought. I'll read you a list of descriptions and would like for you to tell me which category they fall into. (*Read list and circle proper category.*) Dress and/or formal.....................1 Casual ....2 Canvas/trainer/gym shoes..............3 Specialized athletic shoes ....4 Boots 5	
	2. In the last three months, have you used Noxzema skin cream . . . (*Circle all that apply.*) As a facial wash........................1 For moisturizing the skin ....2 For treating blemishes ....3 For cleansing the skin...................4 For treating dry skin ....5 For softening skin......................6 For sunburn ....7 For making the facial skin smooth 8	

Avocado	1	Olives (black/green)	6
Cheese (Monterey Jack/cheddar)	2	Onions (red/white)	7
Guacamole	3	Peppers (red/green)	8
Lettuce	4	Pimiento	9
Mexican hot sauce	5	Sour cream	0

The list seems complete, doesn't it? However, consider the following responses: "I usually add a green, avocado-tasting hot sauce"; "I cut up a mixture of lettuce and spinach"; "I'm a vegetarian—I don't use meat at all"; or "My taco is filled only with guacamole." How would you code these replies? As you can see, the question needs an "other" category.

A good question must also be clear and concise, and ambiguous language must be avoided. Take, for example, the question "Do you live within ten minutes of here?" The answer depends on the mode of transportation (maybe the person walks), driving speed, perceived time, and other factors. Instead, respondents should see a map with certain areas highlighted and be asked whether they live in one of those areas.

Clarity also implies using reasonable terminology. A questionnaire is not a vocabulary test. Jargon should be avoided, and language should be geared to the target audience. A question such as, "What is the level of efficacy of your preponderant dishwasher powder?" would probably be greeted by a lot of blank stares. It would be much simpler to say "Are you (1) very satisfied, (2) somewhat satisfied, or (3) not satisfied with your current brand of dishwasher powder?"

Stating the survey's purpose at the beginning of the interview also improves clarity. The respondents should understand the study's intentions and the interviewer's expectations. Sometimes, of course, to get an unbiased response, the interviewer must disguise the true purpose of the study. If an interviewer says, "We're conducting an image study for American National Bank" and then proceeds to ask a series of questions about the bank, chances are the responses will be biased. Many times respondents will try to provide answers that they believe are "correct" or that the interviewer wants to hear.

Finally, to ensure clarity, the interviewer should avoid asking two questions in one; for example, "How did you like the taste and texture of the Pepperidge Farm coffee cake?" This should be divided into two questions, one concerning taste and the other texture.

A question should also be unbiased. A question such as "Have you purchased any high-quality Black & Decker tools in the past six months?" biases respondents to think of the topic in a certain way (in this case, to link quality and Black & Decker tools). Questions can also be leading: "Weren't you pleased with the good service you received last night at the Holiday Inn?" (The respondent is all but instructed to say yes.) These examples are quite obvious; unfortunately, bias is usually more subtle. Even an interviewer's clothing or gestures can create bias.

observation research
A research method that relies on four types of observation: people watching people, people watching an activity, machines watching people, and machines watching an activity.

OBSERVATION RESEARCH

In contrast to survey research, **observation research** depends on watching what people do. Specifically, it can be defined as the systematic process of recording the behavioral patterns of people, objects, and occurrences without questioning them. A market researcher using the observation technique witnesses and records information as events occur or compiles evidence from records of past events. Carried a step further, observation might involve watching people or phenomena and might be conducted by human observers or machines. Examples of these various observational situations are shown in Exhibit 9.5.

Two common forms of people-watching-people research are one-way mirror observations and mystery shoppers.

At the Fisher-Price Play Laboratory, children are invited to spend 12 sessions playing with toys. Toy designers watch through one-way mirrors to see how children react to Fisher-Price's and other makers' toys. A one-way mirror allows the researchers to see the participants but they cannot see the researchers. Fisher-Price, for example, had difficulty designing a toy lawn mower that children would play with. A designer, observing behind the mirror, noticed the children's fascination with soap bubbles. He then created a lawn mower that spewed soap bubbles. It sold over a million units in the first year.

Hundreds of children tested toys at a recent Toys "R" Us opening to come up with a list of the season's favorites.

Exhibit 9.5 Observational Situations

Situation	Example
People watching people	Observers stationed in supermarkets watch consumers select frozen Mexican dinners; the purpose is to see how much comparison shopping people do at the point of purchase.
People watching phenomena	Observer stationed at an intersection counts traffic moving in various directions.
Machines watching people	Movie or video cameras record behavior as in the people-watching-people example above.
Machines watching phenomena	Traffic-counting machines monitor traffic flow.

Mystery shoppers are researchers posing as customers who gather observational data about a store (e.g., are the shelves neatly stocked?) and collect data about customer/employee interactions. In the latter case, of course, there is communication between the mystery shopper and the employee. The mystery shopper might ask, "How much is this item?"; "Do you have this in blue?"; or "Can you deliver this by Friday?" The interaction is not an interview, and communication occurs only so that the mystery shopper can observe the actions and comments of the employee. Mystery shopping is, therefore, classified as an observational marketing research method even though communication is often involved.

Mystery shopping can provide a variety of benefits and insights, including:

→ Enabling an organization to monitor compliance with product/service delivery standards and specifications. (Eddie Bauer requires its sales staff to make three attempts to sell "add-ons" to each customer—for example, "Would you like a tie, belt, and sunglasses to go with that shirt?")

→ Enabling marketers to examine the gap between promises made through advertising/sales promotion and actual service delivery.

→ Helping monitor the impact of training and performance improvement initiatives.

→ Identifying differences in the customer experience across different times of day, locations, product/service types, and other potential sources of variation in product/service quality.[15]

Mystery shopping typically has three different levels:

Level 1—The mystery shopper either makes a phone call or shops online. The mystery shopper follows a fixed script or set of instructions and evaluates the level of service. The scenario would involve a live online conversation with a service representative. For example, the mystery shopper claims that she is having a problem with some software that she recently purchased from the firm.

Level 2—The mystery shopper visits an establishment and makes a quick purchase with very little, if any, customer-service employee interaction. For example, buying gasoline at a Shell service station or going to a movie at a Cinemark movie theater. The shopper evaluates the purchase and the image of the facility.

Level 3—The mystery shopper visits a business and has significant interaction with the personnel. Restaurant chains such as McDonald's, Starbucks, Chipotle, T.G.I. Friday's, Sonic, IHOP, and Olive Garden strive for consistent execution of service and quality across their many stores. Results of the mystery shopping research at these chains are tied to employee incentives such as bonuses and rewards. Typical items that are evaluated include: hostess attitude and skills, food quality and presentation, condition of the restaurant (such as clean floors and walls), cleanliness of the restrooms, parking lot condition, interaction with the server (such as the introduction and suggestion selling), and the visibility of and interaction with the management staff.

mystery shoppers
Researchers posing as customers who gather observational data about a store.

Not only does management use mystery shopping as a motivator for employees but also as a coaching tool when results are not meeting standards. Thus, mystery shopping is ultimately a monitor of quality assurance.

ETHNOGRAPHIC RESEARCH

Ethnographic research comes to marketing from the field of anthropology. The technique is becoming increasingly popular in commercial marketing research. **Ethnographic research**, or the study of human behavior in its natural context, involves observation of behavior and physical setting. Ethnographers directly observe the population they are studying. The researcher doesn't have to depend upon the consumer's selective memory of a past experience with a good or service. As "participant observers," ethnographers can use their intimacy with the people they are studying to gain richer, deeper insights into culture and behavior—in short, what makes people do what they do. Ethnographers often question those being observed to gain a fuller understanding of what they are seeing.

Ethnographers can record:

→ what is happening, including what objects are being created or manipulated.

→ where it is happening.

→ the flow of what is happening.

→ the order of what is happening.

→ the time spent on what is happening.

→ who is doing what.

→ what is being communicated verbally and nonverbally.

→ the reactions of the various participants (which are critical).[16]

Marriott hired IDEO, an ethnographic research firm, to rethink the hotel experience for an increasingly important customer: the young, tech-savvy road warrior. "This is all about looking freshly at business travel and how people behave and what they need," explains Michael E. Jannini, Marriott's executive vice president for brand management.[17]

To better understand Marriott's customers, IDEO dispatched a team of seven consultants, including a designer, anthropologist, writer, and architect, on a six-week trip. Covering 12 cities, the group hung out in hotel lobbies, cafes, and bars, and asked guests to graph what they were doing hour by hour. What they learned: Hotels are generally good at serving large parties but not small groups of business travelers. Researchers noted that hotel lobbies tend to be dark and better suited to killing time than conducting casual business. Marriott lacked places where guests could comfortably combine work with pleasure outside their rooms. IDEO consultant and Marriott project manager Dana Cho recalls watching a female business traveler drink wine in the lobby while trying not to spill it on papers spread out on a desk. "There are very few hotel services that address [such] problems," says Cho.[18]

Having studied IDEO's findings, Marriott announced plans to reinvent the lobbies of its Marriott and Renaissance Hotels, creating for each a social zone, with small tables, brighter lights, and wireless Web access, that is better suited to meetings. Another area will allow solo travelers to work or unwind in larger, quiet, semiprivate spaces where they won't have to worry about spilling coffee on their laptops or papers.[19]

Ever wonder what women carry in their purses? As part of one ethnographic study the contents of over one hundred women's purses in Portland, Oregon, and Plano, Texas, were analyzed. The researchers found: financial

ethnographic research
The study of human behavior in its natural context; involves observation of behavior and physical setting.

© iStockphoto.com/Juan Facundo Mora Soria

Ethnographics Reveals How Beleza Natural Thrives by Keeping Close to Its Roots

Caxias is a gritty industrial town of 800,000 just north of Rio de Janeiro. The town's commercial center is home to Beleza Natural, a chain of beauty salons and related hair care products targeted to Brazil's women of color. More than 65 percent of Brazil's population has the wavy-to-kinky hair common to people of African descent. Beleza Natural, which translates as "natural beauty," began to promote its salons and products to its generally low-income target market as salons built just for them. Ethnographers were interested in gaining insights into how to continue to build the brand equity of Beleza Natural and perhaps extend it to other areas.

The research team's experience was not what most beauty salon patrons expect: Beleza Natural's entrance is off a noisy, crowded shopping street in downtown Caxias. The area is a bustling array of small shops featuring stacks of clothes, school supplies, snacks and drinks, consumer electronics, hardware and repair shops, and other personal care establishments. A string of waiting buses belch smoke. The shop is located two blocks from a large *favela*, an informal squatter settlement.

Inside the salon, it is not uncommon to find a queue with over a dozen women waiting at the reception desk. Though Beleza Natural has a strict service philosophy, customers do not find the wait dissatisfying or long. Many of the women think of being in line at Beleza Natural as a display of social status, an opportunity to watch the action, and a chance to make new friends—much like the feelings of trendy young people lining up at the entryways of nightclubs on Los Angeles' Sunset Strip.

The service experience begins with an intake interview that captures critical information about the customer's tastes and hair characteristics in a computer database. This record then tracks the customer's interactions with the brand over time and provides continuous marketing information.

The typical visit to the salon takes about an hour and 20 minutes, during which customers are walked through specialized work areas for shampooing, coloring, cutting, conditioning, and so on. At each location, customers are passed along to personnel who interact with them constantly, offering tips and chatting about things in general. Validation and promoting self-worth are consistent features of the entire experience. Stylists are encouraged to take a friendly and helpful approach, acting as advisors and consultants to women who don't usually have access to professional hair care advice, teaching women about beauty and techniques of personal care.

A full-service treatment costs 90 reais (about $50), which represents approximately 20 percent of the monthly salary of the salon's targeted segments. As a convenience to its customers, Beleza Natural allows them to pay the fee over three installments.

Since treatments are expensive, Beleza Natural encourages customers to bring home the brand between visits with reasonably priced hair care products. Sold exclusively at the salons, the extensive product line helps customers preserve the styles they have achieved inside the store while also keeping the brand alive in their homes on a daily basis.[21]

What insights might the ethnographic researchers obtain that could help Beleza Natural extend the brand to other services? What other types of research could be used to gather brand extension information?

items (checkbooks, credit cards), 99 percent; reward cards and memberships, 98 percent; office supplies (pens, notes), 93 percent; beauty/hair care, 91 percent; identification cards, 91 percent; security and access (keys and remote electronic openers), 86 percent; receipts, 85 percent; cell phones/accessories, 74 percent; insurance, 71 percent; food/gum/candy, 63 percent; medications, 61 percent; coupons, 61 percent; eye care, 61 percent; photos, 59 percent; and trash 51 percent. All other items were carried by less than 50 percent of the participants. This study was used in redesigning purses to make them more functional. Recently, ethnographers have also been researching how people carry their iPads.[20]

Ethnography is a valuable part of the marketing researcher's toolkit almost anywhere in the world, as the Global Perspectives box explains.

Observation Research and Virtual Shopping Advances in computer technology have enabled researchers to simulate an actual retail store environment on a computer screen. Depending on the type of simulation, a shopper can "pick up" a package by touching its image on the monitor and rotate it to examine all sides. Like buying on most online retailers, the shopper touches the shopping cart to add an item to the basket. During the shopping process, the computer unobtrusively records the amount of time the consumer spends shopping in each product category, the time the consumer spends examining each side of a package, the quantity of product the consumer purchases, and the order in which items are purchased.

Computer-simulated environments like this one offer a number of advantages over older research methods. First, unlike focus groups, concept tests, and other laboratory approaches, the virtual store duplicates the distracting clutter of an actual market. Consumers can shop in an environment with a realistic level of complexity and variety. Second, researchers can set up and alter the tests very quickly. Once images of the product are scanned into the computer, the researcher can make changes in the assortment of brands, product packaging, pricing, promotions, and shelf space within minutes. Data collection is also fast and error-free because the information generated by the purchase is automatically tabulated and stored by the computer. Third, production costs are low because displays are created electronically. Once the hardware and software are in place, the cost of a test is largely a function of the number of respondents, who generally are given a small incentive to participate. Fourth, the simulation has a high degree of flexibility. It can be used to test entirely new marketing concepts or to fine-tune existing programs. The simulation also makes it possible to eliminate much of the noise that exists in field experiments.[22]

Kimberly-Clark has refined the virtual shopping experience even more. Located in Appleton, Wisconsin, the firm's virtual testing lab has a woman standing in a room surrounded by three screens showing a store aisle, a retina-tracking device recording her every glance. Asked by a Kimberly-Clark researcher to find a "big box" of Huggies Natural Fit diapers in size three, she pushed forward on a handle like that of a shopping cart, and the video simulated her progress down the aisle. Spotting Huggies' red packages, she turned the handle to the right to face a dizzying array of diapers. After pushing a button to get a kneeling view of the shelves, she reached forward and tapped the screen to put the box she wanted in her virtual cart. Kimberly-Clark hopes these virtual shopping aisles will help it better understand consumer behavior and make the testing of new products faster, more convenient, and more precise.[23]

Kimberly-Clark's lab also features a U-shaped floor-to-ceiling screen that recreates in vivid detail interiors of the big retailers that sell the company's products—a tool that the company will use in presentations to executives in bids to win shelf space. A separate area is reserved for real replicas of store interiors, which can be customized to match the flooring, light fixtures and shelves of retailers such as Target and Walmart.[24]

Kimberly-Clark says its studio allows researchers and designers to get a fast read on new product designs and displays without having to stage real-life tests in the early stages of development. Doing the research in a windowless basement, rather than an actual test market, also avoids tipping off competitors early in the development process. "We're trying to test ideas faster, cheaper, and better," says Ramin Eivaz, a vice president at Kimberly-Clark focusing on strategy. Before, new product testing typically took eight months to two years. Now, that time is cut in half, he says. Projects that test well with the virtual-reality tools will be fast-tracked to real-store trials.[25]

Virtual shopping research is growing rapidly as companies such as Frito-Lay, Goodyear, Procter & Gamble, General Mills, and Coca-Cola realize the benefits from this type of observation research. About 40,000 new consumer package goods are introduced in the United States each year.[26] All are vying for very limited retail shelf space. Any process, such as virtual shopping, that can speed product development time and lower costs is always welcomed by manufacturers.

Large firms such as ConAgra and Frito-Lay do their virtual shopping research in-house. SymphonyIRI, the large Chicago-based research firm, has started offering virtual shopping to smaller consumer goods manufacturers. The SymphonyIRI virtual environment approximates the interior of a Walmart store. SymphonyIRI has a panel of about 60,000 people to virtually shop specific aisles, such as prepared foods, to see what goes in the cart and what doesn't. The price of a virtual shopping simulation starts at about $30,000 and goes up.[27] It is still much cheaper than market testing new products in a real-store environment.

EXPERIMENTS

An **experiment** is a method a researcher can use to gather primary data. The researcher alters one or more variables—price, package design, shelf space, advertising theme, advertising expenditures—while observing the effects of those alterations on another variable (usually sales). Virtual shopping environments lend themselves very well to experiments. The best experiments are those in which all factors are held constant except the ones being manipulated. The researcher can then observe that changes in sales, for example, resulting from changes in the amount of money spent on advertising.

Holding all other factors constant in the external environment is a monumental and costly, if not impossible, task. Such factors as competitors' actions, weather, and economic conditions are beyond the researcher's control. Yet market researchers have ways to account for the ever-changing external environment. Mars, the candy company, was losing sales to other candy companies. Traditional surveys showed that the shrinking candy bar was not perceived as a good value. Mars wondered whether a bigger bar sold at the same price would increase sales enough to offset the higher ingredient costs. The company designed an experiment in which the marketing mix stayed the same in different markets but the size of the candy bar varied. The substantial increase in sales of the bigger bar quickly proved that the additional costs would be more than covered by the additional revenue. Mars increased the bar size—and its market share and profits.

SPECIFYING THE SAMPLING PROCEDURES

Once the researchers decide how they will collect primary data, their next step is to select the sampling procedures they will use. A firm can seldom take a census of all possible users of a new product, nor can they all be interviewed. Therefore, a firm must select a sample of the group to be interviewed. A **sample** is a subset from a larger population.

Several questions must be answered before a sampling plan is chosen. First, the population, or **universe**, of interest must be defined. This is the group from which the sample will be drawn. It should include all the people whose opinions, behavior, preferences, attitudes, and so on are of interest to the marketer. For example, in a study whose purpose is to determine the market for a new canned dog food, the universe might be defined to include all current buyers of canned dog food.

experiment
A method a researcher uses to gather primary data.

sample
A subset from a larger population.

universe
The population from which a sample will be drawn.

Exhibit 9.6 Types of Samples

	Probability Samples
Simple Random Sample	Every member of the population has a known and equal chance of selection.
Stratified Sample	The population is divided into mutually exclusive groups (such as gender or age); then random samples are drawn from each group.
Cluster Sample	The population is divided into mutually exclusive groups (such as geographic areas); then a random sample of clusters is selected. The researcher then collects data from all the elements in the selected clusters or from a probability sample of elements within each selected cluster.
Systematic Sample	A list of the population is obtained—e.g., all persons with a checking account at XYZ Bank—and a *skip interval* is obtained by dividing the sample size by the population size. If the sample size is 100 and the bank has 1,000 customers, then the skip interval is 10. The beginning number is randomly chosen within the skip interval. If the beginning number is 8, then the skip pattern would be 8,18, 28, ...
	Nonprobability Samples
Convenience Sample	The researcher selects the easiest population members from which to obtain information.
Judgment Sample	The researcher's selection criteria are based on personal judgment that the elements (persons) chosen will likely give accurate information.
Quota Sample	The researcher finds a prescribed number of people in several categories—e.g., owners of large dogs versus owners of small dogs. Respondents are not selected on probability sampling criteria.
Snowball Sample	Additional respondents are selected on the basis of referrals from the initial respondents. This method is used when a desired type of respondent is hard to find—e.g., persons who have taken round-the-world cruises in the last three years. This technique employs the old adage "Birds of a feather flock together."

© iStockphoto.com/Juan Facundo Mora Soria

© Cengage Learning 2013

After the universe has been defined, the next question is whether the sample must be representative of the population. If the answer is yes, a probability sample is needed. Otherwise, a nonprobability sample might be considered.

Probability Samples A **probability sample** is a sample in which every element in the population has a known statistical likelihood of being selected. Its most desirable feature is that scientific rules can be used to ensure that the sample represents the population.

One type of probability sample is a **random sample**—a sample arranged in such a way that every element of the population has an equal chance of being selected as part of the sample. For example, suppose a university is interested in getting a cross-section of student opinions on a proposed sports complex to be built using student activity fees. If the university can acquire an up-to-date list of all the enrolled students, it can draw a random sample by using random numbers from a table (found in most statistics books) to select students from the list. Common forms of probability and nonprobability samples are shown in Exhibit 9.6.

Nonprobability Samples Any sample in which little or no attempt is made to get a representative cross-section of the population can be considered a **nonprobability sample**. Therefore the probability of selection of each sampling unit is not known. A common form of a nonprobability sample is the **convenience sample**, which uses respondents who are convenient or readily accessible to the researcher—for instance, employees, friends, or relatives.

Nonprobability samples are acceptable as long as the researcher understands their non-representative nature. Because of their lower cost, nonprobability samples are the basis of much marketing research.

Types of Errors Whenever a sample is used in marketing research, two major types of errors can occur: measurement error and sampling error.

probability sample
A sample in which every element in the population has a known statistical likelihood of being selected.

random sample
A sample arranged in such a way that every element of the population has an equal chance of being selected as part of the sample.

nonprobability sample
Any sample in which little or no attempt is made to get a representative cross-section of the population.

convenience sample
A form of nonprobability sample using respondents who are convenient or readily accessible to the researcher—for example, employees, friends, or relatives.

Glossary (margin)

measurement error
An error that occurs when there is a difference between the information desired by the researcher and the information provided by the measurement process.

sampling error
An error that occurs when a sample somehow does not represent the target population.

frame error
An error that occurs when a sample drawn from a population differs from the target population.

random error
An error that occurs when the selected sample is an imperfect representation of the overall population.

field service firm
A firm that specializes in interviewing respondents on a subcontracted basis.

Main text

Measurement error occurs when there is a difference between the information desired by the researcher and the information provided by the measurement process. For example, people might tell an interviewer that they purchase Coors beer when they do not. Measurement error generally tends to be larger than sampling error.

Sampling error occurs when a sample somehow does not represent the target population. Sampling error can be one of several types. Nonresponse error occurs when the sample actually interviewed differs from the sample drawn. This error happens because the original people selected to be interviewed either refused to cooperate or were inaccessible. For example, people who feel embarrassed about their drinking habits may refuse to talk about them.

Frame error, another type of sampling error, arises if the sample drawn from a population differs from the target population. For instance, suppose a telephone survey is conducted to find out Chicago beer drinkers' attitudes toward Coors. If a Chicago telephone directory is used as the *frame* (the device or list from which the respondents are selected), the survey will contain a frame error. Not all Chicago beer drinkers have a phone and many phone numbers are unlisted. An ideal sample (for example, a sample with no frame error) matches all important characteristics of the target population to be surveyed. Could you find a perfect frame for Chicago beer drinkers?

Random error occurs when the selected sample is an imperfect representation of the overall population. Random error represents how accurately the chosen sample's true average (mean) value reflects the population's true average (mean) value. For example, we might take a random sample of beer drinkers in Chicago and find that 16 percent regularly drink Coors beer. The next day we might repeat the same sampling procedure and discover that 14 percent regularly drink Coors beer. The difference is due to random error.

Error is common to all surveys, yet it is often not reported or is underreported. Typically, the only error mentioned in a written report is sampling error. When errors are ignored, misleading results can end in poor information and, perhaps, bad decisions.

COLLECTING THE DATA

Marketing research field service firms collect most primary data. A **field service firm** specializes in interviewing respondents on a subcontracted basis. Many have offices, often in malls, throughout the country. A typical marketing research study involves data collection in several cities, requiring the marketer to work with a comparable number of field service firms. Besides conducting interviews, field service firms provide focus-group facilities, mall intercept locations, test product storage, and kitchen facilities to prepare test food products.

ANALYZING THE DATA

After collecting the data, the marketing researcher proceeds to the next step in the research process: data analysis. The purpose of this analysis is to interpret and draw conclusions from the mass of collected data. The marketing researcher tries to organize and analyze those data by using one or more techniques common to marketing research: one-way frequency counts, cross-tabulations, and more sophisticated statistical analysis. Of these three techniques, one-way frequency counts are the simplest. One-way frequency tables record the responses to a question. For example, the answers to the question "What brand of microwave popcorn do you buy most often?" would provide a one-way frequency distribution. One-way frequency tables are always done in data analysis, at least as a first step, because they provide the researcher with a general picture of the study's results.

A **cross-tabulation**, or "cross-tab," lets the analyst look at the responses to one question in relation to the responses to one or more other questions. For example, what is the association between gender and the brand of microwave popcorn bought most frequently? Hypothetical answers to this question are shown in Exhibit 9.7.

Although the Orville Redenbacher brand was popular with both males and females, it was more popular with females. Compared with women, men strongly preferred Pops Rite, whereas women were more likely than men to buy Weight Watchers popcorn.

Exhibit 9.7 Hypothetical Cross-Tabulation between Gender and Brand of Microwave Popcorn Purchased Most Frequently

	Purchase by Gender	
Brand	Male	Female
Orville Reddenbacher	31%	48%
T.V. Time	12	6
Pops Rite	38	4
Act II	7	23
Weight Watchers	4	18
Other	8	0

© Cengage Learning 2013

Researchers can use many other more powerful and sophisticated statistical techniques, such as hypothesis testing, measures of association, and regression analysis. A description of these techniques goes beyond the scope of this book, but can be found in any good marketing research textbook. The use of sophisticated statistical techniques depends on the researchers' objectives and the nature of the data gathered.

PREPARING AND PRESENTING THE REPORT

After data analysis has been completed, the researcher must prepare the report and communicate the conclusions and recommendations to management. This is a key step in the process. If the marketing researcher wants managers to carry out the recommendations, he or she must convince them that the results are credible and justified by the data collected.

Researchers are usually required to present both written and oral reports on the project. Today, the written report is no more than a copy of the PowerPoint slides used in the oral presentation. Both reports should be tailored to the audience. They should begin with a clear, concise statement of the research objectives, followed by a complete, but brief and simple, explanation of the research design or methodology employed. A summary of major findings should come next. The conclusion of the report should also present recommendations to management.

Most people who enter marketing will become research users rather than research suppliers. Thus, they must know what to notice in a report. As with many other items we purchase, quality is not always readily apparent. Nor does a high price guarantee superior quality. The basis for measuring the quality of a marketing research report is the research proposal. Did the report meet the objectives established in the proposal? Was the methodology outlined in the proposal followed? Are the conclusions based on logical deductions from the data analysis? Do the recommendations seem prudent, given the conclusions?

FOLLOWING UP

The final step in the marketing research process is to follow up. The researcher should determine why management did or did not carry out the recommendations in the report. Was sufficient decision-making information included? What could have been done to make the report more useful to management? A good rapport between the product manager, or whoever authorized the project, and the market researcher is essential. Often they must work together on many studies throughout the year.

cross-tabulation
A method of analyzing data that lets the analyst look at the responses to one question in relation to the responses to one or more other questions.

© iStockphoto.com/Juan Facundo Mora Soria

Review
LO▶3
Describe the steps involved in conducting
a marketing research project

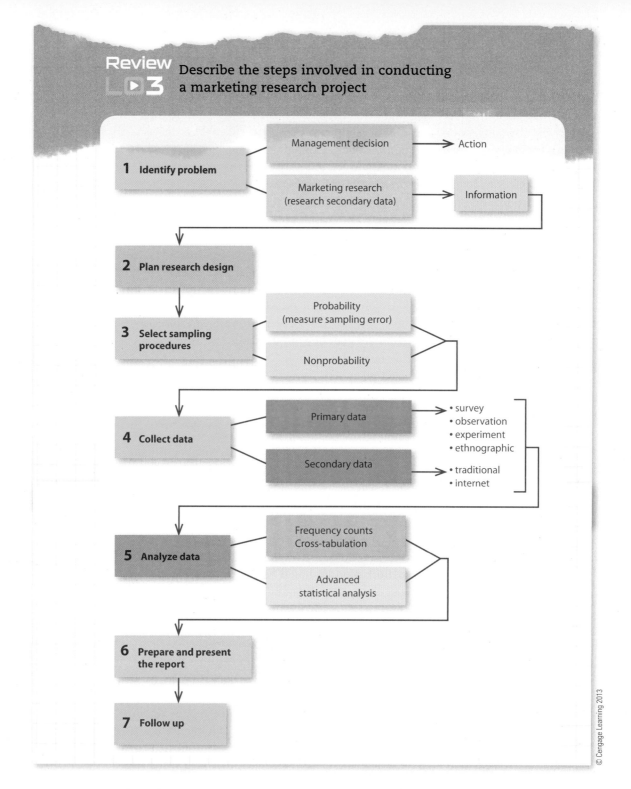

LO▶4

Marketing Research on the Internet

The world's Internet population will be about 1.8 billion users by the time you read this paragraph.[28] That's right—about one-fifth of the world's population is online. In the United States, 71 percent of the population, or 221 million people, are online, spanning every ethnic, socioeconomic, and educational divide. It is no wonder then that most managers accept that online research can, under appropriate conditions, accurately represent U.S. consumers as a whole.[29] Non-adopters of the Internet tend to be older, low-income consumers (aged 65+ and with household income less than $30,000).[30] These consumers are not the target market for many companies' goods and services.

The popularity of online research continues to grow with over 90 percent of America's marketing research companies conducting some form of online research. Today online survey research has replaced computer-assisted telephone interviewing (CATI) as the most popular mode of data collection.[31] Internet data collection is also rated as having the greatest potential for further growth. However, there is no sign that other types of surveys are disappearing—two-thirds of the market research companies are still relying on them.[32]

There are several reasons for the success of Internet marketing research:

→ It allows for better and faster decision making through much more rapid access to business intelligence.

→ It improves the ability to respond quickly to customer needs and market shifts.

→ It makes follow-up studies and tracking research much easier to conduct and more fruitful.

→ It slashes labor- and time-intensive research activities (and associated costs), including mailing, telephone solicitation, data entry, data tabulation, and reporting.

ADVANTAGES OF INTERNET SURVEYS

The huge growth in the popularity of Internet surveys is the result of the many advantages offered by the Internet. The specific advantages of Internet surveys are related to many factors:

→ **Rapid development, real-time reporting:** Internet surveys can be broadcast to thousands of potential respondents simultaneously. Respondents complete surveys simultaneously; then results are tabulated and posted for corporate clients to view as the returns arrive. The result: Survey results can be in a client's hands in significantly less time than would be required for traditional surveys.

→ **Dramatically reduced costs:** The Internet can cut costs by 25 to 40 percent and provide results in half the time it takes to do traditional telephone surveys. Data collection costs account for a large proportion of any traditional market research budget. Telephone surveys are labor-intensive efforts incurring training, telecommunications, and management costs. Electronic methods eliminate these completely. While costs for traditional survey techniques rise proportionally with the number of interviews desired, electronic solicitations can grow in volume with little increase in project costs.

→ **Personalized questions and data:** Internet surveys can be highly personalized for greater relevance to each respondent's own situation, thus speeding the response process. Respondents enjoy a personalized survey because they are asked to answer only pertinent questions, can pause and resume the survey as needed, and can see previous responses and correct inconsistencies.

→ **Improved respondent participation:** Busy respondents may be growing increasingly intolerant of "snail mail" or telephone-based surveys. Internet surveys take half as much time to complete as phone interviews, can be accomplished

Here, a pop-up screen allows marketers to ask customers if they would like to participate in a survey. Customers can opt out, but by specifying the amount of time the survey will take and taking the customer to the survey with a simple click increases the likelihood that customers will participate.

© Nestlé Purina PetCare Company

at the respondent's convenience (after work hours), and are much more stimulating and engaging. Graphics, interactivity, links to incentive sites and real-time summary reports make the interview enjoyable. The result? Much higher response rates.

→ **Contact with the hard-to-reach:** Certain groups—doctors, high-income professionals, top management in Global 2000 firms—are among the most surveyed on the planet and the most difficult to reach. Many of these groups are well represented online. Internet surveys provide convenient anytime/anywhere access that makes it easy for busy professionals to participate.

USES OF THE INTERNET BY MARKETING RESEARCHERS

Marketing researchers are using the Internet to administer surveys, conduct focus groups and observation research, and perform a variety of other types of marketing research.

METHODS OF CONDUCTING ONLINE SURVEYS

There are several basic methods for conducting online surveys: Web survey systems, survey design Web sites, and Web hosting. Each of these methods is briefly discussed.

Web Survey Systems Web survey systems are software systems specifically designed for Web questionnaire construction and delivery. They consist of an integrated questionnaire designer, Web server, database, and data delivery program, designed for use by nonprogrammers. In a typical use, the questionnaire is constructed with an easy-to-use edit feature, using a visual interface, and then automatically transmitted to the Web server system. The Web server distributes the questionnaire and files responses in a database. The user can query the server at any time via the Web for completion statistics, descriptive statistics on responses, and graphical displays of data. Several popular online survey research software packages are SPSS, Inquisite, Sawtooth CiW, Infopoll, SurveyMonkey, and eSurveysPro.

ONLINE PANEL PROVIDERS

Designing a questionnaire is one step in the online survey process; another is procuring a sample to survey. Sometimes do-it-yourself researchers already have a sample or census of those they wish to survey, so sampling is not a problem. For example, members of a country club, persons who just purchased a new Ford, students at a university, or customers at Best Buy. Often, however, researchers don't have a sample available, so they turn to online panel providers. The online panel providers such as Survey Sampling International, Decision Analyst, Greenfield

Online, Common Knowledge, and e-Rewards pre-recruit people who agree to opt in to participate in online market research surveys.

Some online panels are created for specific industries such as construction, medical, or technology, and may have a few thousand panel members, while the large commercial online panels have millions of people who have opted in to participate in online surveys of varying topics. When people join most online panels, they answer an extensive profiling questionnaire that records demographic, lifestyle, and psychographic information, typically with hundreds of dimensions. This profiling information enables the panel provider to record detailed information on every panel member. Using this information, the panel provider can then target research efforts to panel members who meet specific criteria.

For example, a research study may require surveying avid golfers who play golf at least once a week, people who own an HDTV, or people who make decisions regarding information technology and work in companies with over 1,000 employees. Finding people who meet these criteria can be difficult, but online panel providers might be able to more easily identify these people based on their profiling information. By having millions of people pre-recruited and engaged in the research process, online panels help reduce recruitment cost and field time needed to complete a research project. For the really low-incidence groups, many of the larger panel providers, such as e-Rewards or Harris Interactive, are able to develop specialty panels for hard-to-reach audiences, such as small business owners, affluent consumers, and healthcare providers.

ONLINE FOCUS GROUPS

A recent development in qualitative research is the online focus group. Several organizations are currently offering this new means of conducting focus groups. The process is fairly simple.

→ The research firm builds a database of respondents via a screening questionnaire on its Web site.

→ When a client comes to a firm with a need for a particular focus group, the firm goes to its database and identifies individuals who appear to qualify. It sends an e-mail message to these individuals, asking them to log on to a particular site at a particular time scheduled for the group. The firm pays them an incentive for their participation.

→ The firm develops a discussion guide similar to the one used for a conventional focus group.

→ A moderator runs the group by typing in questions online for all to see. The group operates in an environment similar to that of a chat room so that all participants see all questions and all responses.

→ The firm captures the complete text of the focus group and makes it available for review after the group has finished.

The Moderator's Role The basic way the moderator communicates with respondents in an online focus group is "freestyle" or "on the fly." That is, the moderator types in all questions, instructions, and probes into the text-entry area of the chat room in real-time (live, on-the-spot). In a variation on this method, the moderator copies and pastes questions from an electronic version of the guide into the text-entry area. Here, the moderator will toggle back and forth between the document and the chat room. An advantage of the freestyle method is that it forces the moderator to adapt to the group rather than use a series of canned questions.

A disadvantage is that typing everything freestyle (or even copying and pasting from a separate document) takes time.

One way respondents can see stimuli (e.g., a concept statement, a mockup of a print ad, or a short product demonstration on video) is for the moderator to give the respondents a URL. Respondents then copy the URL from the chat stream, open another browser window, paste in the URL, and view it. An advantage of this approach is its simplicity. However, there are several disadvantages. First, if the respondents do not copy the URL correctly, they will not see it. Another disadvantage is that once respondents open another browser, they have "left the room" and the moderator has lost their attention; researchers must hope that respondents will return within the specified amount of time.

More advanced virtual focus group software reserves a frame (section) of the screen for stimuli to be shown. Here, the moderator has control over what is shown in the stimulus area. The advantage of this approach is that the respondent does not have to do any work to see the stimuli.

Using Channel M2 to Conduct Online Focus Groups Channel M2 provides market researchers with user-friendly virtual interview rooms, recruiting, and technical support for conducting virtual qualitative research efficiently and effectively. By using Channel M2, the moderator and client can see and hear every respondent. You can see a demo at **www.channelM2.com**.

To recruit focus groups (from a global panel with access to over 15 million online consumers), Channel M2 uses a blend of e-mail and telephone verification and confirmation. Specifically, e-mails elicit involvement and direct participants to an online qualification questionnaire to ensure that each meets screening criteria. Telephone follow-up confirms that respondents qualify. Participants are sent a Web camera so that both verbal and nonverbal reactions can be recorded. Channel M2 tech support helps participants install the Webcam one to two days prior to the interview. Before participating, respondents must show a photo ID (their driver's license) to their Webcam so that their identity can be verified.

Participants are then provided instructions via e-mail, including a link to the Channel M2 interviewing room and a toll-free teleconference number to call. Upon clicking on the link, participants sign on and see the Channel M2 interview room, complete with live video of the other participants, text chat, screen or slide sharing, and whiteboard. (See Exhibit 9.8.)

Exhibit 9.8 An M2 Online Focus Under Way

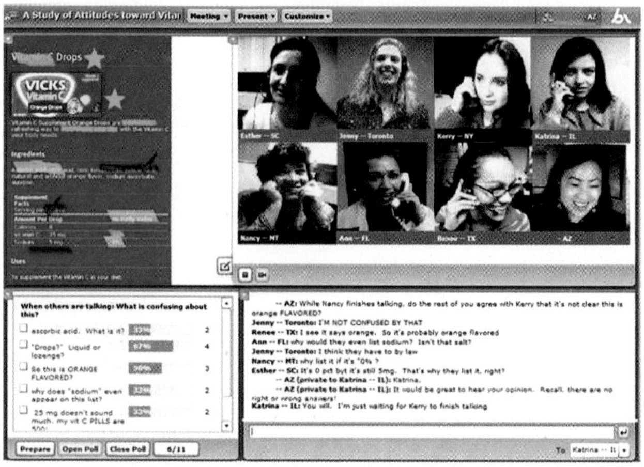

© 2005 CHANNEL M2, LLC

Source: From http://www.ChannelM2.com, accessed January, 2009.

Thus, in a Channel M2 focus group, all the participants can see and hear each other and communicate in a group setting. Once the focus group is under way, questions and answers occur in "real time" in a lively setting. Participants comment spontaneously, both verbally and via text messaging, yet the moderator can provide direction exactly as would be done in a traditional setting.[33]

Advantages of Online Focus Groups Many advantages are claimed for cyber groups. Cyber Dialogue, a marketing research company specializing in cyber groups, lists the following benefits of online focus groups on its Web site:

→ **Speed:** Typically, focus groups can be recruited and conducted, with delivery of results, within five days of client approval.

→ **Cost-effectiveness:** Off-line focus groups incur costs for facility rental, airfare, hotel, and food. None of these costs is incurred with online focus groups.

→ **Broad geographic scope:** In a given focus group, you can speak to people in Boise, Idaho, and Miami, Florida, at the same time.

→ **Accessibility:** Online focus groups give you access to individuals who otherwise might be difficult to recruit (e.g., business travelers, doctors, mothers with infants).

→ **Honesty:** From behind their screen names, respondents are anonymous to other respondents and tend to talk more freely about issues that might create inhibitions in a face-to-face group.

WEB COMMUNITY RESEARCH

A **Web community** is a carefully selected group of consumers who agree to participate in an ongoing dialogue with a particular corporation. A community can be opened or closed by invitation only. All community interaction takes place on a custom-designed Web site. During the life of the community—which may last anywhere from six months to a year or more—community members respond to questions posed by the corporation on a regular basis. These discussions, which typically take the form of qualitative "dialogues," are augmented by the ability of community members to talk to one another about topics that are of interest to them as well.

The popularity and power of Web communities initially came from several key benefits. They:

→ Engage customers in a space where they are most comfortable, allowing clients to interact with them on a deeper level.

→ Uncover "exciters" and "eureka moments," resulting in customer-derived innovations.

→ Establish brand advocates who are emotionally invested in a company's success.

→ Offer real-time results, enabling clients to explore ideas that normal time constraints prohibit.

→ Create a forum where natural dialogue allows customers to initiate topics important to them.[34]

Additionally, Web communities help companies create a customer-focused organization by putting employees into direct contact with consumers from the comfort of their own desks. Because communities provide advantages in speed, flexibility, and 24/7 access to consumers, they enable the organization to be agile in its research decision making and prudent in its spending.

By adding a research focus to the Web community, it becomes a way to:

→ Map the thinking of consumer segments.

→ Brainstorm new ideas.

→ Create and test new products.

→ Observe natural consumer behavior.[35]

Intercontinental Hotels Group learned from its community of loyalty-card members that there was no interest in receiving "tweets" from the hotel chain. So Intercontinental scrapped its plans to use Twitter to communicate with its best customers. Charles Schwab used a community to decide that its checking account should include fee-free ATM use. Del Monte pet products used a MarketTools

Web community
A carefully selected group of consumers who agree to participate in an ongoing dialogue with a particular corporation.

consumer generated media (CGM)
Media that consumers generate and share among themselves.

community to design the shape and ingredients of a doggie snack, Snausages Breakfast Bites. TurboTax's popular bookmarks feature came from member-initiated suggestions in the company's "TurboTax Inner Circle" community.[36]

THE ROLE OF CONSUMER GENERATED MEDIA IN MARKETING RESEARCH

Consumer generated media (CGM) is media that consumers generate themselves and share among themselves. Because it is consumer-based, it is trusted more than traditional forms of advertising and promotion.[37] CGM originates from:

→ Blogs

→ Message boards and forums

→ Public discussions (Usenet newsgroups)

→ Discussions and forums on large e-mail portals (Yahoo!, AOL, MSN)

→ Online opinion/review sites and services

→ Online feedback/complaint sites

→ Shared videos and photos

→ Podcasts

→ Social media (Facebook)

CGM can be influenced but not controlled by marketers. To influence CGM, one must first understand what is being said or shown. Nielsen BuzzMetrics is the leading marketing research firm tracking CGM. The firm uses sophisticated data mining and other technologies to help marketers understand what is being said about their company and brands on the Web. BrandPulse is BuzzMetrics' most popular product. BrandPulse can tell a company about the spread and influence of CGM. How much "buzz" exists? Where is online discussion taking place, and by whom? What issues are most important? Is the tone of discussion negative or positive?

BrandPulse enables clients to listen in on unaided consumer conversations that take place on Internet forums, boards, Usenet newsgroups, and blogs, providing timely understanding of the opinions and trends affecting a company or brand.

A second product, BrandPulse Insight reports, focuses on specific issues and concerns such as:

→ What's the buzz about a certain issue, trend, product, or piece of news?

→ Who's active online, and what are these online consumers saying?

→ Are current trends building or waning?

→ Can any emerging trends be detected early, before they catch fire (or fizzle out prematurely)?

→ What key motivators influence and affect consumer behavior?

→ What are consumer/customer moods and emotions on a particular topic, or about a specific brand?

→ Which online consumers are likely candidates for influencer panels and relationship marketing programs?[38]

A marketer wanting to know about the latest diet trend, technological gadget, automotive perceptions, or health-related concerns can tap into BrandPulse Insights to understand what's being said.

Nielsen BuzzMetrics offers a free service entitled BlogPulse, **www.blogpulse.com,** which is a blog search engine and a trend tracker. You can easily create your own graphs plotting blog buzz by entering a search term. Alternatively, you can check out popular blog trends, follow a story trail between two bloggers, or see profiles of popular bloggers.

BEHAVIORAL TARGETING

Behavioral targeting (BT) began as a simple process by placing cookies on users' browsers to track which Web sites they visited. Researchers could determine pages visited, time at each page, and the number and type of searches made. The objective is to match the Internet user with ads for products and services that they will most likely purchase. Today, the more sophisticated forms of BT combine a consumer's online activity with psychographic and demographic profiles inferred from databases. Thus, the BT firms claim that they use IP addresses and not an individual's actual name and address. Because of the potential effectiveness of BT advertising, its popularity is skyrocketing.

The most exciting growth area of BT is in the area of social networking. The information that a member of MySpace or Facebook shares plus marrying the information with demographic and psychographic databases becomes a very powerful tool for ad placement. Critics have called this form of BT "conversational eavesdropping analysis." Tom Kendall, a Facebook executive, counters by saying that it is simply "user-declared information targeting."[39] This is because much of it is derived from what members provide in their profile such as: gender, age, political views, hobbies, college, and occupation. For example, if a member says that they have a strong interest in kayaking, this is much more useful than knowing that someone using the same computer went to the kayaking site, Kayakonline.com. It could have been a friend using the computer. Both Facebook and MySpace allow marketers to target ads on their sites to consumers based upon profile information.

New BT firms, such as 33Across, think that mapping connections between people, rather than just profile information, is much more valuable. New York-based 33Across tracks how consumers interact with one another—commenting on posts or sharing messages, for instance-across about 20 sites, online networks, and third-party application companies, which build software like games and quizzes for social-networking sites. 33Across says those sites reach a total of 100 million unique U.S. visitors.[40]

EBay, for instance, used online tracking to identify customers who browsed or shopped for products in the clothing, shoes, and accessories section of its site. It then turned to 33Across, which analyzed data from social-networking sites to map out the connections between the customers eBay had identified and other Web surfers, in order to serve up ads at the right time and place.

Companies using behavioral targeting include Allstate, American Express, IBM, and TDAmeritrade to name a few. When Pepsi wanted to make a splash on the Web promoting its new low-calorie vitamin-enhanced water, Aquafina Alive, the company didn't run ads just anywhere on the Internet. It placed ads only on

behavioral targeting (BT)
A form of observation marketing research that uses data mining coupled with identifying Web surfers by their IP addresses.

Review
LO4
Discuss the profound impact of the
Internet on marketing research

sites it knew would be visited by people interested in healthy lifestyles. Pepsi was using behavioral targeting.

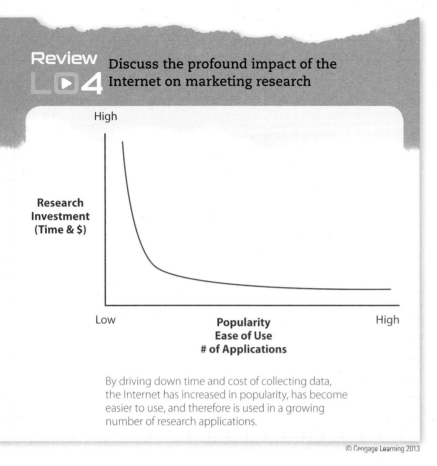

By driving down time and cost of collecting data, the Internet has increased in popularity, has become easier to use, and therefore is used in a growing number of research applications.

© Cengage Learning 2013

LO5
Scanner and Machine-Based Research

Scanner-based research is a system for gathering information from a single group of respondents by continuously monitoring the advertising, promotion, and pricing they are exposed to and the things they buy. The variables measured are advertising campaigns, coupons, displays, and product prices. The result is a huge database of marketing efforts and consumer behavior. Scanner-based research is bringing ever closer the Holy Grail of marketing research: an accurate, objective picture of the direct causal relationship between different kinds of marketing efforts and actual sales.

The two major scanner-based suppliers are SymphonyIRI Group, and the Nielsen Company. Each has about half the market. However, SymphonyIRI is the founder of scanner-based research.

BehaviorScan is a SymphonyIRI testing service that utilizes small markets that allow a high degree of control over test conditions. For example, BehaviorScan can deliver different TV advertisements to selected homes within the same market and then read the impact of the advertising on consumers' actual purchase behavior and attitudes. Different newspaper ads can be sent to selected households either via a print press run or inserts. Direct mail can also be tested using different mailings to selected households. In every BehaviorScan market, a group of at least 3,000 households has been recruited to participate in a panel. When panelists shop, they first present their "Shopper's Hotline" card to be scanned. Next, all purchases are scanned, allowing SymphonyIRI to track electronically each household's purchases, item by item, over time. If a panel member buys items in a nonparticipating retailer, he or she can scan all other purchases at home with a hand-held scanner provided by SymphonyIRI.

SymphonyIRI's most successful product is **InfoScan** Reviews—a scanner-based sales-tracking service for the consumer packaged-goods industry. Retail sales, detailed consumer purchasing information (including measurement of store loyalty and total grocery basket expenditures), and promotional activity by manufacturers and retailers are monitored and evaluated for all bar-coded products. Data

scanner-based research
A system for gathering information from a single group of respondents by continuously monitoring the advertising, promotion, and pricing they are exposed to and the things they buy.

BehaviorScan
A scanner-based research program that tracks the purchases of 3,000 households through store scanners in each research market.

InfoScan
A scanner-based sales-tracking service for the consumer packaged-goods industry.

are collected weekly from more than 70,000 supermarkets, drugstores, and mass merchandisers.

Companies, such as Campbell, have begun studying microscopic changes in skin moisture, heart rate, brain waves, and other biometrics to see how consumers react to things such as package designs and ads. This new approach, called **neuromarketing**, is a fresh attempt to better understand consumer's responses to promotion and purchase motivations.

An **electroencephalograph (EEG)** is a machine that measures electric pulses on the scalp and generates a record of electrical activity in the brain. Although traditional EEG machines are good for detecting arousal, the devices were expensive, bulky, and required the consumer to wear a head cap. EmSense, a marketing research company, has invented a headband device that captures not only brainwaves but also respiration, blinking, head movement, temperature, and changes in heart rate.[41] EmSense has tested over 40,000 people using its headbands.

Galvanic skin response (GSR), also known as *electrodermal response*, is a change in the electric resistance of the skin associated with activation responses. A small electric current of constant intensity is sent into the skin through electrodes attached to the palmar side of the fingers. The changes in voltage observed between the electrodes indicate the level of stimulation. Because the equipment is portable and not expensive, measuring GSR is the most popular way to assess emotional reaction to a stimulus. GSR is used primarily to measure stimulus response to advertisements but is sometimes used in packaging research.

Eye tracking follows and records the movement of the eye as it looks at something. Your eyes blink, they diverge, they fixate, they close—each distinct behavior has a distinct origin, one that the trained researcher can meaningfully interpret. By measuring fluctuations in pupil diameter, researchers can determine precisely when a person is paying attention and when he or she is not.

Eye Tracking, Inc. calls the pupil-based metric the Index of Cognitive Activity (ICA).[42] The firm has used ICA with television advertising to determine which commercials are engaging and which ones tend to be ignored. The advantage of ICA over simply asking a respondent, "Did you like the commercial?" is that it is based upon an involuntary physiological reflex. Thus, consumer bias and desire to give the "right" answer are factored out.

Campbell has begun to use neuromarketing to better understand the condensed-soup market. Researchers interviewed about 40 people at their homes and later in grocery stores. The team also clipped small video cameras to the testers at eye level and had them later watch a recording of themselves shopping for soup. Special vests captured skin-moisture levels, heart rate, depth and pace of breathing, and posture. Sensors tracked eye movements and pupil width.

Researchers found warmth and other positive attributes people associated with Campbell's soup at home evaporated when they faced store shelves. But the array of condensed soups so overwhelmed many participants that they would quickly scan the category and select soups while evidencing little biometric response. The people who spent more time exploring varieties showed more and bigger simultaneous spikes in biometrics—and tended to put more soup cans in their baskets.

The Campbell team figured it could boost sales by triggering more emotional responses in stores and prompting more people to focus on more soups.[43] The neuromarketing research also led to a number of labeling and stocking changes as shown in Exhibit 9.9.

neuromarketing
Studying microscopic changes in skin moisture, heart rate, brain waves, and other biometrics to see how consumers react to things such as package designs and ads.

electroencephalograph (EEG)
A machine that measures electric pluses on the scalp and generates a record of electrical activity in the brain.

galvanic skin response (GSR)
A change in the electric resistance of the skin associated with activation responses.

eye tracking
Following and recording the movement of the eye as it looks at something.

Exhibit 9.9 Campbell's New Soup Labels

New and Improved . . . Labeling!
Campbell Soup used biometrics to analyze consumers' response to their label and changed the packaging to reflect their preferences revealed by the study.

New label

Old shelf label

Source: the company

The different varieties of soup were color-coded to help consumers distinguish them more easily.

Steam was added because people indicated they felt more emotionally engaged if the soup looked warm.

The spoon was removed. People thought it was unnecessary and had little emotional response to it.

The bowl was updated.

Eyetrack studies showed when the logo was placed at the top it drew too much attention and the red background also made all the labels look too similar.

WHEN SHOULD MARKETING RESEARCH BE CONDUCTED?

When managers have several possible solutions to a problem, they should not instinctively call for marketing research. In fact, the first decision to make is whether to conduct marketing research at all.

Some companies have been conducting research in certain markets for many years. Such firms understand the characteristics of target customers and their likes and dislikes about existing products. Under these circumstances, further research would be repetitive and waste money. Procter & Gamble, for example, has extensive knowledge of the coffee market. After it conducted initial taste tests with Folgers Instant Coffee, P&G went into national distribution without further research. Consolidated Foods Kitchen of Sara Lee followed the same strategy with its frozen croissants, as did Quaker Oats with Chewy Granola Bars. This tactic, however, does not always work. P&G marketers thought they understood the pain reliever market thoroughly, so they bypassed market research for Encaprin aspirin in capsules. Because it lacked a distinct competitive advantage over existing products, however, the product failed and was withdrawn from the market.

Managers rarely have such great trust in their judgment that they would refuse more information if it were available and free. But they might have enough confidence that they would be unwilling to pay very much for the information or to wait a long time to receive it. The willingness to acquire additional decision-making information depends on managers' perceptions of its quality, price, and timing. Of course, if perfect information were available—that is, the data conclusively showed which alternative to choose—decision makers would be willing to pay more for it than for information that still left uncertainty. In summary, research should be undertaken only when the expected value of the information is greater than the cost of obtaining it.

Review
LO5 Discuss the growing importance of scanner-based research

BehaviorScan

Panel information from specific groups of people, enables researchers to manipulate variables and see real results

InfoScan

Aggregate consumer information on all bar-coded products

© Cengage Learning 2013

LO6
Competitive Intelligence

Derived from military intelligence, competitive intelligence is an important tool for helping a firm overcome a competitor's advantage. Specifically, competitive intelligence can help identify the advantage and play a major role in determining how it was achieved.

Competitive intelligence (CI) helps managers assess their competitors and their vendors in order to become a more efficient and effective competitor. Intelligence is analyzed information. It becomes decision-making intelligence when it has implications for the organization. For example, one of your firm's primary competitors might have plans to introduce a product with performance standards equal to your own but with a 15 percent cost advantage. The new product will reach the market in eight months. This intelligence has important decision-making and policy consequences for management. Competitive intelligence and environmental scanning (where management gathers data about the external environment—see Chapter 4) combine to create marketing intelligence. Marketing intelligence is then used as input into a marketing decision support system. Nine out of ten large companies have employees dedicated to the CI function. Many firms spend several million dollars a year on the function.

The top corporate CI officer at a multibillion-dollar global technology company claims that competitive intelligence helped his company recover after it began losing market share to a competitor. The rival, after competing directly with the company for years, had figured out its bidding strategy. Instead of competing on price with an off-the-shelf offering, the rival was beginning to offer prospects a customized solution—and it was winning. When the CI officer's company changed to a customized approach, it won hundreds of millions of dollars in new business the following year. At Pergo, Inc., a maker of laminate flooring, CI helped win a major contract. When Pergo told a national retailer what it had learned from a mutual supplier—that the rival would not be able to launch a new product when it said it would—the retailer signed with Pergo instead.

Conferences and professional courses led by rival executives are great places to gather information. A former competitive intelligence chief at telecom-software vendor Telcordia says his firm hit the jackpot when one of its accountants attended a professional course taught by a competitor's CFO. The CFO used his company as the case for the class, revealing all kinds of tantalizing private financial information. Listening in on competitors' presentations to analysts at investment conferences and on conference calls is another good way to get financial data.

Executives, marketers and engineers tend to enjoy talking about what's new or what is coming in the future at their companies. Talking to these people at trade shows or even watching regulatory proceedings can yield fruitful CI. When drug maker Bristol Myers Squibb (BMS) told Congress it needed to increase its harvest of environmentally sensitive yew trees, says a former intelligence executive at SmithKline Beecham, he knew there was a good chance that BMS would soon seek Food and Drug Administration approval for a drug using yew bark.

competitive intelligence (CI)
An intelligence system that helps managers assess their competition and vendors in order to become more efficient and effective competitors.

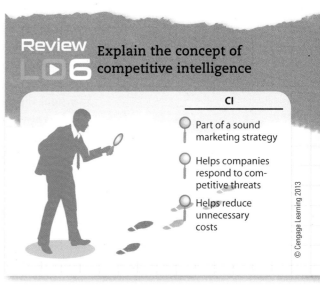

Review
LO6 Explain the concept of competitive intelligence

CI

- Part of a sound marketing strategy
- Helps companies respond to competitive threats
- Helps reduce unnecessary costs

© iStockphoto.com/Juan Facundo Mora Soria

© Cengage Learning 2013

Amount that U.S. marketers spend on research each year

Cost of a 17-chapter report from Wintergreen Research aggregator

Cost of a single chapter

Minutes required to complete a printed questionnaire for Hallmark's Shoebox greeting cards

Minutes required to complete the same questionnaire with computer assistance

Percentage of U.S. research firms conducting marketing research online

Members on the Internet panel Survey Spot

Stores from which InfoScan tracks data

$7 billion **$2, 800** **$ 350** **28** **18** **88** **5 million** **70, 000**

Review and Applications

LO 1 **Explain the concept and purpose of a marketing decision support system.**
A decision support system (DSS) makes data instantly available to marketing managers and allows them to manipulate the data themselves to make marketing decisions. Four characteristics make DSSs especially useful to marketing managers: They are interactive, flexible, discovery oriented, and accessible. That is, they give managers access to information immediately and without outside assistance; they allow users to manipulate data in a variety of ways and to answer "what if" questions; and they are accessible to novice computer users.

→ **Interactive:** Managers give simple instructions and see immediate results. The process is under their direct control; no computer programmer is needed. Managers don't have to wait for scheduled reports.

→ **Flexible:** A DSS can sort, regroup, total, average, and manipulate the data in various ways. It will shift gears as the user changes topics, matching information to the problem at hand. For example, the CEO can see highly aggregated figures, and the marketing analyst can view very detailed breakouts.

→ **Discovery oriented:** Managers can probe for trends, isolate problems, and ask "what if" questions.

→ **Accessible:** Managers who aren't skilled with computers can easily learn how to use a DSS. Novice users should be able to choose a standard, or default, method of using the system. They can bypass optional features so they can work with the basic system right away while gradually learning to apply its advanced features.

1.1 In the absence of company problems, is there any reason to develop a marketing DSS?

1.2 Explain the difference between marketing research and a DSS.

LO 2 **Define marketing research and explain its importance to marketing decision making.** Marketing research is a process of collecting and analyzing data for the purpose of solving specific marketing problems. Marketers use marketing research to explore the profitability of marketing strategies. They can examine why particular strategies failed and analyze characteristics of specific market segments. Managers can use research findings to help keep current customers. Moreover, marketing research allows management to behave proactively, rather than reactively, by identifying newly emerging patterns in society and the economy.

2.1 The task of marketing is to create exchanges. What role might marketing research play in the facilitation of the exchange process?

2.2 Marketing research has traditionally been associated with manufacturers of consumer goods. Today, however, an increasing number of organizations, both profit and nonprofit, are using marketing research. Why do you think this trend exists? Give some examples of specific reasons why organizations might use marketing research.

2.3 Write a reply to the following statement: "I own a restaurant in the downtown area. I see customers every day who I know on a first-name basis. I understand their likes and dislikes. If I put something on the menu and it doesn't sell, I know that they didn't like it. I also read the magazine *Modern Restaurants*, so I know what the trends are in the industry. This is all of the marketing research I need to do."

writing

2.4 Give an example of (a) the descriptive role of marketing research, (b) the diagnostic role, and (c) the predictive function of marketing research.

Describe the steps involved in conducting a marketing research project. The marketing research process involves several basic steps. First, the researcher and the decision maker must agree on a problem statement or set of research objectives. The researcher then creates an overall research design to specify how primary data will be gathered and analyzed. Before collecting data, the researcher decides whether the group to be interviewed will be a probability or nonprobability sample. Field service firms are often hired to carry out data collection. Once data have been collected, the researcher analyzes them using statistical analysis. The researcher then prepares and presents oral and written reports, with conclusions and recommendations, to management. As a final step, the researcher determines whether the recommendations were implemented and what could have been done to make the project more successful.

LO3

3.1 Critique the following methodologies and suggest more appropriate alternatives:

a. A supermarket was interested in determining its image. It dropped a short questionnaire into the grocery bag of each customer before putting in the groceries.

b. To assess the extent of its trade area, a shopping mall stationed interviewers in the parking lot every Monday and Friday evening. Interviewers walked up to people after they had parked their cars and asked them for their ZIP codes.

c. To assess the popularity of a new movie, a major studio invited people to call a 900 number and vote yes, they would see it again, or no, they would not. Each caller was billed a $2 charge.

3.2 You have been charged with determining how to attract more business majors to your school. Write an outline of the steps you would take, including the sampling procedures, to accomplish the task.

writing

3.3 Why are secondary data sometimes preferable to primary data?

3.4 What is a marketing research aggregator? What role do these aggregators play in marketing research?

3.5 Discuss when focus groups should and should not be used.

3.6 Divide the class into teams of eight persons. Each group will conduct a focus group on the quality and number of services that your college is providing to its students. One person from each group should be chosen to act as moderator. Remember, it is the moderator's job to facilitate discussion, not to lead the discussion. These groups should last approximately 45 minutes. If possible, the groups should be videotaped or recorded. Upon completion, each group should write a brief report of its results. Consider offering to meet with the dean of students to share the results of your research.

team

3.7 Why do companies hire mystery shoppers?

3.8 Ethnographic research is a new (and expensive) trend in marketing research. Find an article on ethnographic research. Read and summarize the article. What is your opinion of ethnographic research? Do you think it will be the wave of the future? Explain your reasoning.

Discuss the profound impact of the Internet on marketing research. The Internet has vastly simplified the secondary data search process, placing more sources of information in front of researchers than ever before. Internet survey research is surging in popularity. Internet surveys can be created rapidly and reported in real time. They are also relatively inexpensive and can easily be personalized. Often researchers can use the Internet to contact respondents who are difficult to reach by other means. The Internet can also be used to conduct focus groups, analyze consumer-generated media, engage in behavioral targeting, distribute research proposals and reports, and facilitate collaboration between the client and the research supplier. Clients can access real-time data and analyze the information as the collection process continues.

4.1 Go to **www.strategicbusinessinsights.com/** and take the VALS survey. Report on how marketing researchers are using this information.

4.2 Divide the class into teams. Each team should go to a different opt-in survey site on the Web and participate in an online survey. A spokesperson for each team should report the results to the class.

4.3 What are various ways to obtain respondents for online surveys?

4.4 Describe the advantages and disadvantages of online surveys.

Discuss the growing importance of scanner-based research. A scanner-based research system enables marketers to monitor a market panel's exposure and reaction to such variables as advertising, coupons, store displays, packaging, and price. By analyzing these variables in relation to the panel's subsequent buying behavior, marketers gain useful insight into sales and marketing strategies.

5.1 Why has scanner-based research been seen as "the ultimate answer" for marketing researchers? Do you see any disadvantages of this methodology?

5.2 Detractors claim that scanner-based research is like "driving a car down the road looking only in the rearview mirror." What does this mean? Do you agree?

Explain the concept of competitive intelligence. Competitive intelligence (CI) helps managers assess their competition and their vendors in order to become more efficient and effective competitors. Intelligence is analyzed information, and it becomes decision-making intelligence when it has implications for the organization.

By helping managers assess their competition and vendors, CI leads to fewer surprises. CI allows managers to predict changes in business relationships, guard against threats, forecast a competitor's strategy, and develop a successful marketing plan.

The Internet and databases accessed via the Internet offer excellent sources of CI. Company personnel, particularly sales and service representatives, are usually good sources of CI. Many companies require their salespersons to routinely fill out CI reports. Other external sources of CI include experts, CI consultants, government agencies, UCC filings, suppliers, newspapers and other publications, Yellow Pages, and trade shows.

6.1 Why do you think that CI is so hot in today's environment?

6.2 Prepare a memo to your boss at JetBlue Airlines and outline why the organization needs a CI unit.

6.3 Form a team with three other students. Each team must choose a firm in the PC manufacturing industry and then go to the Web site of the firm and acquire as much CI as possible. Each team will then prepare a five-minute oral presentation on its findings.

Key Terms

behavioral targeting (BT) *339*
BehaviorScan *340*
central-location telephone (CLT) facility *318*
closed-ended question *321*
competitive intelligence (CI) *343*
computer-assisted personal interviewing *319*
computer-assisted self-interviewing *319*
consumer generated media (CGM) *338*
convenience sample *329*
cross-tabulation *331*
database marketing *308*
decision support system (DSS) *307*
electroencephalograph (EEG) *341*
ethnographic research *325*

executive interviews *320*
experiment *328*
eye tracking *341*
field service firm *330*
focus group *320*
frame error *330*
galvanic skin response (GSR) *341*
group dynamics *320*
InfoScan *340*
mall intercept interview *319*
management decision problem *314*
marketing information *307*
marketing research *308*
marketing research aggregator *316*
marketing research objective *314*
marketing research problem *314*

measurement error *330*
mystery shoppers *324*
neuromarketing *341*
nonprobability sample *329*
observation research *323*
open-ended question *321*
primary data *317*
probability sample *329*
random error *330*
random sample *329*
research design *317*
sample *328*
sampling error *330*
scaled-response question *321*
scanner-based research *340*
secondary data *315*
survey research *318*
universe *328*
Web community *337*

Exercises

ETHICS EXERCISE

John Michael Smythe owns a small marketing research firm in Cleveland, Ohio, that employs 75 people. Most employees are the sole breadwinners in their families. John's firm has not fared well for the past two years and is on the verge of bankruptcy. The company recently surveyed over 2,500 people in Ohio about new-car purchase plans for the Ohio Department of Economic Development. Because the study identified many hot prospects for new cars, a car dealer has offered John $8,000 for the names and phone numbers of people saying they are "likely" or "very likely" to buy a new car within the next 12 months. John needs the money to avoid laying off a number of employees.

Questions

1. Should John Smythe sell the names?
2. Does the AMA Statement of Ethics address this issue? Go to www.marketingpower.com/ AboutAMA/Pages/Statement of Ethics.aspx. Then write a brief paragraph on what the AMA Statement of Ethics contains that relates to John Smythe's dilemma.

MARKETING PLAN EXERCISE

For the marketing plan exercise in Chapter 6, you considered the consumer decision-making process as it applies to your marketing plan; in Chapter 7, you analyzed your potential business markets. In Chapter 8, you identified your company's target market and its various segments. Now complete the following exercises to find out more about your competitors and customers through marketing research—a key to any strategic marketing plan. Once completed, you can use your answers to complete the Marketing Plan Worksheet for Part 2, which you can find by logging on to the companion Web site at www.cengagebrain.com.

1. Are there any critical issues that must be explored with primary marketing research before you can implement your marketing plan for your chosen company? These might include items such as customer demand, purchase intentions, customer perceptions of product quality, price perceptions, and reaction to critical promotion. List some critical research questions and decide which form of research you would use.

2. Design a brief Internet customer satisfaction survey that you could place on your company Web site. Use the "Survey Wiz" to help you with your questionnaire at **http://psych.fullerton.edu/mbirnbaum/programs/surveyWiz.HTM**.

3. What type of competitive intelligence will you need to gather in order to monitor your market space? How can analyzing the job offerings, mission or "about us" statement, products and services descriptions, or other general information on your competitors' Web sites help you figure out their strategic direction? What areas of a Web site could you scan to gather competitive information?

APPLICATION EXERCISE

For its study, *Teens and Healthy Eating: Oxymoron or Trend?*, New York–based BuzzBack Market Research focused on snacking. Among its findings: Teens eat an average of three snacks per day; breakfast is the meal they skip most often. Though scads of snacks are stacked on store shelves, when it comes to healthier treats, targeting adolescents is a bit of a teenage wasteland. BuzzBack asked 532 teen respondents to conjure up new foods they'd gobble up. The following are some of their ideas:

→ "Travel fruit. Why can't fruit be in travel bags like chips or cookies? Canned fruit is too messy. Maybe have a dip or something sold with it, too."—Female, age 17

→ "A drink that contains five servings of fruits and vegetables."—Male, age 16, Caucasian

→ "I would invent all natural and fat-free, vitamin-enhanced cookies and chips that had great flavor."—Female, age 16

→ "I would make fruit-based cookies."—Male, age 16, Caucasian

→ "Low-carb trail mix, because trail mix is easy to eat but it has a lot of fat/carbs."—Female, age 15, Caucasian

→ "I would create some sort of microwavable spaghetti."—Male, age 16, Caucasian

→ "Something quick and easy to make that's also cheap. I'll be in college next year, and I'm trying to find things that are affordable, healthier than cafeteria food, and easy to make."—Female, age 17

→ "*Good* vegan mac 'n' cheese."—Female, age 18, Caucasian

→ "A smoothie where you could get all the nutrients you need, that tastes good, helps you stay in shape, and is good for you. Has vitamins A, B_3, B_{12}, C, ginkgo. Packaging would be bright."—Female, age 16, African American

→ "A breakfast shake for teens. Something easy that tastes good, not necessarily for dieters like Slim Fast, etc. Something to balance you off in the morning."—Male, age 18

Activities

1. You are a new-product development specialist at Kraft. What guidance can you get from the BuzzBack study?

2. Choose one of the suggestions from the above list of healthy snack concepts. Imagine that your company is interested in turning the idea into a new product but wants to conduct market research before investing in product development. Design a marketing research plan that will give company managers the information they need before engaging in new-product development of the idea. (Hint: Use steps 1–3 in Exhibit 9.1 as a guide.)

3. Once you have finished your plan, collect the data. Depending on the data-collection methods you have outlined in your plan, you might need to make adjustments so that you can collect actual data to analyze.

4. Analyze the data you collected and create a report for your company either recommending that the company pursue the idea you chose or investigate another.

CASE STUDY: Red Lobster

MARKET RESEARCH REVEALS WHAT'S FRESH TODAY

Remember the Red Lobster commercials featuring lots of fried shrimp bouncing around and lobster claws dripping with butter? They've been replaced by scenes of steaming fresh fish, rice, and vegetables. The old slogan, "For the Seafood Lover in You" has also been canned. Now Red Lobster wants you to "Come See What's Fresh Today." The restaurants themselves will soon look different, too, with a more streamlined, contemporary décor that downplays the traditional nautical themes.

© PRNewsFoto/
Red Lobster

These changes and more are part of an effort to make over the seafood chain after marketing research revealed that the restaurant was considered outdated and unappealing to potential customers. Red Lobster president Kim Lodrup says that in the first stage of the makeover, the chain improved operations so that customers wouldn't have to wait so long for the food to reach their table. The second phase focused on improving the restaurant's image and shifting the focus from low prices to freshness. The third and final challenge will be to increase sales. Lodrup says, "We are positioning Red Lobster to be the best seafood restaurant on the planet."

Lodrup was originally hired as a marketing specialist to revive the sagging brand's image in 2003 when sales were falling and customer satisfaction was at an all-time low. He immediately put the kibosh on promotions like the All-You-Can-Eat Crab Legs Specials that had lost money for the company in the past and emphasized Red Lobster's seafood expertise instead. After sales increased in 2004, he was promoted to president, but he still relies on marketing research to keep his finger on the pulse of customer preferences.

"We find out what they want from idealized dining service and research how to deliver value to guests," Lodrup says. To do that, Red Lobster follows changing consumer habits and pays attention to which dishes patrons prefer. They use phone and Internet surveys to learn about guest attitudes toward the food they've tried and try to determine how well they might respond to new menu items or concept changes before instituting them. The guest-relations department "catalogs the nature of guest contact so we can see if there are changes in trends," Lodrup explains. "Emerging concerns or requests from consumers get captured weekly and recorded for our executives."

More in-depth research measures attitudes and trends that could affect the brand in the future. Before a promotion is launched, featured menu items are chosen through extensive consumer testing. Beginning with a large number of possible dishes, they narrow it down to the one that testers deem most appealing.

After studies indicated that freshness is the single biggest criteria consumers use to judge a seafood restaurant, the chain knew it was vital to get word out that fresh fish is delivered to Red Lobster restaurants six days a week. Interviews with former customers revealed that many still believed that Red Lobster's fish was frozen despite the company's extensive global connections and rapid seafood delivery system.

"It's really important to signal to people food is freshly prepared," says marketing V.P. Salli Setta, who created the Culinary Institute of Tuscany for Olive Garden before being hired by Red Lobster. The company is considering a similar seafood-related school in Maine to add authenticity to Red Lobster's menu. In the meantime, Setta hired a new team of executive chefs to create updated recipes with the herbs that customers said had fresher connotations than the traditional lemon and butter sauces.

They also introduced a separate Fresh Fish Menu that is updated twice a day at the restaurants. Even though fresh fin fish had been on the regular menu for years, it had never really been promoted. Research showed that this could make the restaurant more appealing to their lapsed customers, who tend to be affluent, educated, and over 50. Households with an annual income of more than $70,000 account for half of all food eaten in restaurants and have been shown to be most interested in seafood dining. Reeling these customers back in has become a top priority in the chain's turnaround.

So far the makeover is working. Red Lobster has been reporting same-store sales increases since 2004. Improvements in operations and other cost controls led to the highest operating margin in Red Lobster history and, Lodrup reports, "Every measure of guest satisfaction is at a record level." However, it continues to be a challenge for the chain to change old perceptions of itself. As one surveyed customer put it, "My wife swears by the fish. She just can't get her friends to try it."[44]

Questions

1. Why do you think Red Lobster relies so much on Internet surveys to track customer opinions, preferences, and criticisms? What are the advantages of online questionnaires versus traditional surveys conducted over the phone or through the mail?

2. Go to **www.redlobster.com** and click around. How well do you think the site appeals to the educated, affluent, and over-50 crowd that the chain wants to reel in? What are the primary messages that it communicates about the restaurant, and how effective are they? How does the site attempt to capture information about its customers?

3. Red Lobster's closest competitor in the seafood-dining business is Joe's Crab Shack. Check out their Web site at **www.joescrabshack.com** and compare it to Red Lobster's. How does their marketing approach differ? Do you think they're appealing to the same types of customers? How does the Web site try to get information from its customers?

4. Suppose Red Lobster was wondering how well its new interior design was being received by customers at a redecorated restaurant in Columbus, Ohio, and hired you to create a questionnaire. Write one of each: an open-ended question, a closed-ended question (either dichotomous or multiple choice), and a scaled-response question.

COMPANY CLIPS: *ReadyMade*— Ready Research

Having been in business for five years, *ReadyMade* now has a lot of research on the various characteristics of its readers. Its knowledge of GenNesters, the offspring of baby boomers that engage in DIY home crafts, has made the magazine a leader in identifying and describing that segment. As a new business, *ReadyMade* found that businesses had little interest in marketing to this group. Now that businesses have become more aware of GenNester influence, however, *ReadyMade* is able to fill the need for information. *ReadyMade* has statistics on the ages at which people are marrying and the interests of couples that have just married. Because the magazine is ahead of the curve on gathering information on this segment, *ReadyMade* can help other businesses figure out how to tailor their marketing efforts to fit the needs of GenNesters.

Questions

1. How has *ReadyMade* been able to help Toyota promote its new line of cars? What benefit has *ReadyMade* seen from the partnership?

2. How does *ReadyMade* use new technology to gain information about its consumers?

3. What sorts of long-term decisions is *ReadyMade* making that could be aided by research? What would you recommend?

Notes

1. Jack Honomichl, "Honomichl Top 50," *Marketing News*, June 30, 2009, 14.
2. Joseph Rydholm, "A Natural Extension," *Quirk's Marketing Research Review*, May 2002, 22–23, 69–70.
3. "Case Study: Philips' Norelco," *IN*, June 2007, 18.
4. "Oscar Mayer Prepares a Better Bacon Package," *Brandweek*, June 11, 2007, 11.
5. "Why Some Customers Are More Equal Than Others," *Fortune*, September 19, 1994, 215–224.
6. Sunil Gupta, Donald Lehmann, and Jennifer Ames Stuart, "Valuing Customers," *Journal of Marketing Research*, February 2004, 7–18.
7. "Scathing Research Feedback Guides Domino's Makeover," *Quirks Marketing Research Review*, March 2010, 8.
8. Dave Morgan, "Amazon/Zappos Acquisition: Culture Matters," *OnlineSpin*, July 23, 2009, www.mediapost.com/publications/?fa=Articles. showArticle&art_aid=110395; Matt Mickiewicz, "How Zappos Does Customer Service and Company Culture," *Sitepoint*, March 30, 2009, www.sitepoint. com/how-zappos-does-customer-service-and-company-culture/; Tony Hsieh, "We're Starting a Movement," April 7, 2010, http://blogs.zappos. com/blogs/ceo-and-coo-blog/2010/04/07/were-starting-movement; "100 Best Companies to Work For," *Fortune*, February 8, 2010, 75.
9. Scott Pimley, "Looking to Increase Their Miles per Gallon," *Quirk's Marketing Research Review*, August 2008, 32–38.
10. Michael Fielding, "A Clean Slate," *Marketing News*, May 1, 2007, 9–10.
11. *Ibid.*
12. "Be Mindful of Cellphone Interviews," *Marketing Research*, Summer 2009, 4.
13. Author's projections from: "Second Half of '09 Could Set Research In Motion," *Quirks Marketing Research Review*, July 2009, 80–81.
14. "About Us," FocusVision Web site, www.focusvision.com/home/aboutus.aspx.
15. D. Randall Brandt, "Improve the Customer Service," *Quirk's Marketing Research Review*, January 2006, 68.

marketing&you: Results.

Higher scores indicate that you place greater importance on collecting primary and secondary information when developing marketing campaigns or projects. A lower score means you would be less aggressive in collecting information and might plow ahead regardless of how much information you do (or don't) have. After reading Chapter 9, you can see how involved gathering and analyzing market information can be, but also how critical it is to success.

16. "Watch and Learn," *Marketing News*, February 1, 2006, 60.
17. "The Science of Desire," *BusinessWeek*, June 5, 2006, 104.
18. *Ibid*.
19. *Ibid*.
20. Kelley Styring, "Loose Change, Lotion, and Expired Coupons," *Quirk's Marketing Research Review*, February 2008, 20–26.
21. Hy Mariampolski, Leticia Casotti, and Maribel Suarez, "Creating Beauty at the Base of the Pyramid," *Quirk's Marketing Research Review*, February 2010, 28–31.
22. Raymond R. Burke, "Virtual Shopping: Breakthrough in Marketing Research," *Harvard Business Review*, March/April 1996, 120–131.
23. Ellen Byron, "A Virtual View of the Store Aisle," *Wall Street Journal*, October 3, 2007, B1, B12.
24. *Ibid*.
25. *Ibid*.
26. *Ibid*.
27. "Virtual Shopping, Real Results," *BrandWeek*, April 16, 2009, 14.
28. "Internet Users in the World," Internet World Stats, http://www.internetworldstats.com/stats.htm.
29. Lisa E. Phillips, "US Internet Users," February 2009, *emarketer*, www.emarketer.com/Reports/All/Emarketer_2000561.aspx.
30. Kira Signer and Andy Korman, "One Billion and Growing," *Quirk's Marketing Research Review*, July/August 2006, 62–67.
31. Conversation with Roger Gates, President of DSS Marketing Research, June 2, 2010.
32. *Ibid*.
33. "About ChannelM2," ChannelM2 Web site, http://channelm2.com/AboutChannelM2.html.
34. Gregory S. Heist, "Beyond Brand Building," *Quirk's Marketing Research Review*, July/August 2007, 62–67.
35. *Ibid*.
36. "Research in a Petri Dish: Learning from Communities," *Marketing News*, September 3, 2009, 22.
37. Pete Blackshaw and Mike Nazzarro, "Consumer-Generated Media (CGM) 101: Word-of-Mouth in the Age of the Web-Fortified Consumer," *Nielsen BuzzMetrics*, Spring 2006, 2.
38. *Ibid*.
39. "Behavioral Issues," *Brandweek*, October 20, 2008, 21–25.
40. Emily Steel, "Marketers Watch as Friends Interact Online," *Wall Street Journal*, April 15, 2010, B5; Emily Steel, "Target-Marketing Becomes More Communal," *Wall Street Journal*, November 5, 2009, B10.
41. "Neuromeasurement Designed Specifically for Market Research," Emsense Web site, www.emsense.com/technology.php; "This Is Your Brain on Advertising," *Quirk's Marketing Research Review*, August 2009, 32–38.
42. Mike Bartels, "The Proof Is in the Pupil," *Quirk's Marketing Research Review*, April 2009, 38–42.
43. Ilan Brat, "The Emotional Quotient of Soup Shopping," *Wall Street Journal*, February 17, 2010, B6.
44. "Las Vegas Tourism Agency Announces 1.3 Percent Rise in Visitor Totals for 2003", *Las Vegas Review-Journal*, February 14, 2004; Jennifer Bjorhus, "Las Vegas Tourism Agency Executive Says Research, Marketing are Key to Success", *Las Vegas Review-Journal*, April 6, 2003; Chris Jones, "Las Vegas Tourism Agency Executive Says Research Marketing Are Key to Success," Las Vegas Review-Journal, April 6, 2003; Chris Jones, "Las Vegas Tourism Chief Opposes Ads; Board Members Object to 'Sin City' Phrase'" *Las Vegas Review-Journal*, December 16, 2003; Chris Jones, "Las Vegas Tourism Officials Plan Marketing Blitz to Attract Canadian Tourist", *Travel Weekly*, March 3, 2003; Chris Jones, "New Las Vegas Tourism Ads Target Hispanics with Tradition-Focused Messages", *Las Vegas Review-Journal*, July 17, 2003.

Marketing Miscue

FOUR LOKO TARGETS YOUNG COLLEGE HEDONISTS

Phusion Projects, LLC was founded in 2005 when three friends from Ohio State University had the entrepreneurial idea to start their own company. From this company came the Four Loko product that caused much panic in the fall of 2010. While news reports focus on Four Loko's ingredients—caffeine and alcohol—the real marketing mistake likely came from the market segment that enjoyed the product. That is, Four Loko had quickly become the drink of choice for college students across the United States.

© TRIPPLAAR KRISTOFFER/SIPA/Newscom

THE PRODUCT

Referred to as an alcoholic energy drink, Four Loko comes in a 23.5-ounce can, with alcohol content of 12 percent (comparable to four beers). The Four Loko product, in several fruit-flavored varieties, was displayed on store shelves in brightly colored cans at a retail price of US$2.50 to US$3.00. In addition to the alcohol, the energy drink is packed with caffeine (equivalent to that found in a cup of coffee), taurine, and guarana. What sets Four Loko apart from other energy drinks, however, is wormwood oil. Wormwood oil is the key ingredient in absinthe, a very high-proof spirit believed to cause hallucinations. The hallucinogenic aspect of absinthe, from the thujone in the oil, resulted in its prohibition for years in many countries. However, federal regulators now allow absinthe as long as the thujone has been extracted from the wormwood oil.

Health advocates contend that the caffeine masks the effects of the alcohol that is being consumed when drinking Four Loko. Thus, a person is likely to consume more alcohol than he or she would normally. Four Loko and other caffeinated alcoholic beverages have been referred to as "blackout in a can" and "wide-awake drunk."

THE TARGET MARKET

Today's college student grew up with energy drinks on store shelves. From the high school sports field with Gatorade and Powerade, today's younger generation easily graduated to Red Bull, Monster, Rockstar, and AMP. As such, this twenty-something generation was a primary target market for Four Loko. These energy drink consumers could go away to college and consume their energy drinks in conjunction with alcohol—pre-mixed—and get drunk quickly and cheaply.

THE PANIC

According to health experts, ingesting caffeine with 12 percent alcohol can lead to a heart attack, especially for someone fatigued or with a cardiac condition. The alcoholic energy drink could lead to high blood pressure and arrhythmia. Four Loko gained national attention in the fall of 2010 when nine university freshmen, ranging in age from 17 to 19, were hospitalized with blood-alcohol levels ranging from 0.12 percent to 0.35 percent (a blood-alcohol concentration of 0.30 percent is considered potentially lethal). One of the nine students almost died. All nine had consumed Four Loko in conjunction with drinking vodka, rum, and beer.

RESPONSE

In response to the panic around the safety of Four Loko, law makers in numerous states began lobbying for legislation prohibiting the product and universities across the nation banned the drink from campus. In the state of Washington, an emergency ban was put into effect, with the product pulled from store shelves almost immediately.

In a statement released by Phusion Projects, the company noted that it marketed its products responsibly to those of legal drinking age and shared the concerns of college administrators about underage drinking and abuse of alcoholic beverages. However, the company held strongly to its belief that combining caffeine and alcohol was safe and provided examples such as Irish coffees and rum and cola. Plus, anyone could mix vodka and an energy drink such as Red Bull. In support of Phusion Projects, some commentators expressed concern over the apparent panic surrounding the consumption of alcohol and caffeine and, in particular, Four Loko. It was noted that the publicity surrounding Four Loko was probably one of the best forms of advertising—that is, politicians jumped on the ban-Four-Loko bandwagon, which resulted in a lot of press for a product targeted to hedonistic young people that then prompted more and more young people to sample the product.

Questions

1. Profile the target market for Four Loko.
2. Outline the consumer decision making process for Four Loko.

Critical Thinking Case

MARY KAY INC. TAPS INTO A CHANGING DEMOGRAPHIC

Founded in 1963 by Mary Kay Ash and her son, Richard, Mary Kay Inc. is a company that has long believed in the power of women. Dedicated to making life more beautiful for women, the company was founded on the Golden Rule of "praising people to success" and on the principle of placing faith first, family second, and career third. Before her death in 2001, Mary Kay Ash received numerous awards that exemplified her personal beliefs, which were embedded as the heart and soul of the company.

BEAUTY AND PERSONAL CARE PRODUCTS AND DIRECT SELLING

While the economic situation is such that consumers are scaling back on spending for high-end nonessential items, many beauty and personal care products are considered necessities. At the same time, beauty and personal care products do not have country boundaries—such products are universal. According to one report, beauty and personal care products are a cornerstone of the direct selling industry and, likewise, direct selling is good for the beauty and personal care products industry. By 2009, direct

Courtesy of Mary Kay Inc.

sellers were capturing more than $10 billion in annual sales of beauty and personal care products.

Direct selling is a method of distributing products directly to the consumer via person-to-person selling or party plan selling and away from permanent retail locations. According to the Direct Selling Association, there are an estimated 15.1 million people involved in direct selling in the United States, with more than 66 million people engaged worldwide. Interestingly, more than 80 percent of direct sellers in the United States are women. The predominance of women in the direct selling marketplace has proven especially important for direct sellers like Mary Kay Inc.

MARY KAY INC.

Mary Kay Inc. develops and manufactures beauty and personal care products for both women and men. The company spends millions of dollars and conducts more than 300,000 product tests to ensure that Mary Kay products meet the highest standards of quality, safety, and performance. With products ranging from skin care to makeup to spa and body to fragrances, the company sells its products through its direct sales force of more than two million independent beauty consultants in countries such as: Argentina, Armenia, Australia, Brazil, Canada, China, the Czech Republic, El Salvador, Finland, Germany, Guatemala, Hong Kong, India, Kazakhstan, Korea, Malaysia, Mexico, Moldova, New Zealand, Norway, the Philippines, Poland, Portugal, the Russian Federation, Slovakia, Spain, Sweden, Taiwan, Ukraine, the United Kingdom, the United States, and Uruguay. The company's worldwide wholesale sales topped US$2.5 billion in 2009.

With women as its primary target market, Mary Kay has stayed abreast of changing buyer behavior. For example, the company knows that the younger generation expects to touch and experiment with products, so the company offers products, shades, packaging, and forms that both enable and encourage the potential user to try something new. Although there are geographic differences among preferences (e.g., Asian women focus on skin care, while Latin American and some European women are more interested in color cosmetics and fragrances), the company has found that, worldwide, women are more similar than dissimilar in their preferences.

While the company has been successful product-wise with the younger demographic, Mary Kay Inc. has been particularly astute at tapping into this changing demographic with respect to its independent sales consultants. The average age of the Mary Kay consultant is now 36 years old and the company's fastest growing segment of consultants is in the 24- to 35-year-old age group. Representing the future of the company, Mary Kay Inc. can provide these women with the opportunity to meet any goal they are willing to work toward—whether it is additional income or financial independence.

Yet the company recognizes that other direct selling companies want to harness the power and dynamic of this age group. These young leaders are known for wanting increased flexibility, unlimited earning power, and the freedom to experiment in their work lives. There is a vast market opportunity for Mary Kay Inc. in the millennial generation, and the company wants to take advantage of that opportunity to usher in a new era of direct selling of Mary Kay products.

Questions

1. The younger demographic is important to Mary Kay Inc. both as consumers of the company's products and as its sales force. Since the market is one and the same, can the company utilize one marketing strategy targeting both consumers and sellers? Why or why not?

2. What are particular characteristics about this younger demographic that Mary Kay Inc. will have to tap into in order to capture and maintain the segment's attention?

3

Product Decisions

chapter 10

Product Concepts

 Learning Outcomes

1 Define the term *product*

2 Classify consumer products

3 Define the terms *product item, product line,* and *product mix*

4 Describe marketing uses of branding

5 Describe marketing uses of packaging and labeling

6 Discuss global issues in branding and packaging

7 Describe how and why product warranties are important marketing tools

L▶1
What Is a Product?

The product offering, the heart of an organization's marketing program, is usually the starting point in creating a marketing mix. A marketing manager cannot determine a price, design a promotion strategy, or create a distribution channel until the firm has a product to sell. Moreover, an excellent distribution channel, a persuasive promotion campaign, and a fair price have no value when the product offering is poor or inadequate.

A **product** may be defined as everything, both favorable and unfavorable, that a person receives in an exchange. A product may be a tangible good such as a pair of shoes, a service such as a haircut, an idea such as "don't litter," or any combination of these three. Packaging, style, color, options, and size are some typical product features. Just as important are intangibles such as service, the seller's image, the manufacturer's reputation, and the way consumers believe others will view the product.

To most people, the term *product* means a tangible good. However, services and ideas are also products. (Chapter 12 focuses specifically on the unique aspects of marketing services.) The marketing process identified in Chapter 1 is the same whether the product marketed is a good, a service, an idea, or some combination of these.

> " A marketing manager cannot determine the **marketing** mix until the firm has a product to sell. "

product
Everything, both favorable and unfavorable, that a person receives in an exchange.

marketing&you.

Using the following scale, indicate your opinion on the line before each item.

STRONGLY DISAGREE   ◁ 1 2 3 4 5 6 ▷   STRONGLY AGREE
DISAGREE NEUTRAL AGREE

_____ I usually purchase brand-name products.

_____ Store brands are of poor quality.*

_____ All brands are about the same.*

_____ The well-known national brands are best for me.

_____ The more expensive brands are usually my choices.

_____ The higher the price of a product, the better its quality.

_____ Nice department and specialty stores offer me the best products.

Source: Scale #230, *Marketing Scales Handbook*, G. Bruner, K. James, H. Hensel, eds. Vol. IIII. © by American Marketing Association.

Total your score, reversing your scores for the items followed by an asterisk. That is, if you answered 1, change it to 5 and vice versa. Read the chapter and find out what your score means at the end.

© iStockphoto.com/Juan Facundo Mora Soria

© iStockphoto.com/ziggymaj

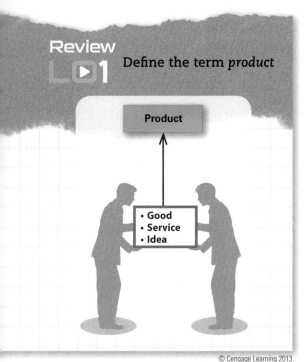
Review

LO1 Define the term *product*

business product

A product used to manufacture other goods or services, to facilitate an organization's operations, or to resell to other customers.

consumer product

A product bought to satisfy an individual's personal wants.

LO2
Types of Consumer Products

Products can be classified as either business (industrial) or consumer products, depending on the buyer's intentions. The key distinction between the two types of products is their intended use. If the intended use is a business purpose, the product is classified as a business or industrial product. As explained in Chapter 7, a **business product** is used to manufacture other goods or services, to facilitate an organization's operations, or to resell to other customers. A **consumer product** is bought to satisfy an individual's personal wants. Sometimes the same item can be classified as either a business or a consumer product, depending on its intended use. Examples include light bulbs, pencils and paper, and computers.

We need to know about product classifications because business and consumer products are marketed differently. They are marketed to different target markets and tend to use different distribution, promotion, and pricing strategies.

Chapter 7 examined seven categories of business products: major equipment, accessory equipment, component parts, processed materials, raw materials, supplies, and services. The current chapter examines an effective way of categorizing consumer products. Although there are several ways to classify them, the most popular approach includes these four types: convenience products, shopping products, specialty products, and unsought products. (See Exhibit 10.1.) This approach classifies products according to how much effort is normally used to shop for them.

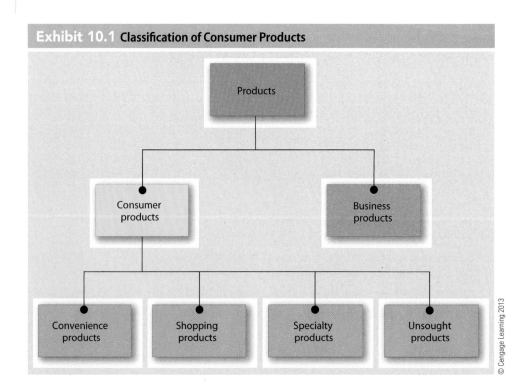

Exhibit 10.1 **Classification of Consumer Products**

© Cengage Learning 2013

CONVENIENCE PRODUCTS

A **convenience product** is a relatively inexpensive item that merits little shopping effort—that is, a consumer is unwilling to shop extensively for such an item. Candy, soft drinks, combs, aspirin, small hardware items, dry cleaning, and car washes fall into the convenience product category.

Consumers buy convenience products regularly, usually without much planning. Nevertheless, consumers do know the brand names of popular convenience products, such as Coca-Cola, Bayer aspirin, and Right Guard deodorant. Convenience products normally require wide distribution in order to sell sufficient quantities to meet profit goals. For example, the gum Dentyne Ice is available everywhere, including Walmart, Walgreens, gas stations, newsstands, and vending machines.

SHOPPING PRODUCTS

A **shopping product** is usually more expensive than a convenience product and is found in fewer stores. Consumers usually buy a shopping product only after comparing several brands or stores on style, practicality, price, and lifestyle compatibility. They are willing to invest some effort into this process to get the desired benefits.

There are two types of shopping products: homogeneous and heterogeneous. Consumers perceive *homogeneous* shopping products as basically similar—for example, washers, dryers, refrigerators, and televisions. With homogeneous shopping products, consumers typically look for the lowest-priced brand that has the desired features. For example, they might compare Kenmore, Whirlpool, and General Electric refrigerators.

In contrast, consumers perceive *heterogeneous* shopping products as essentially different—for example, furniture, clothing, housing, and universities. Consumers often have trouble comparing heterogeneous shopping products because the prices, quality, and features vary so much. The benefit of comparing heterogeneous shopping products is "finding the best product or brand for me"; this decision is often highly individual. For example, it would be difficult to compare a small, private university with a large, public university.

DeBeers uses simple, powerful language to show consumers that for important life decisions (such as marriage), DeBeers provides a quality product that will last a lifetime.

SPECIALTY PRODUCTS

When consumers search extensively for a particular item and are very reluctant to accept substitutes, that item is a **specialty product**. Rolex watches, Rolls Royce automobiles, Bose speakers, Ruth's Chris Steak House, and highly specialized forms of medical care are generally considered specialty products.

Marketers of specialty products often use selective, status-conscious advertising to maintain their product's exclusive image. Distribution is often limited to one or a very few outlets in a geographic area. Brand names and quality of service are often very important.

convenience product
A relatively inexpensive item that merits little shopping effort.

shopping product
A product that requires comparison shopping because it is usually more expensive than a convenience product and is found in fewer stores.

specialty product
A particular item for which consumers search extensively and are very reluctant to accept substitutes.

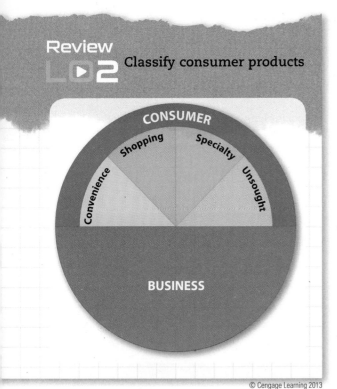
Review

LO 2 Classify consumer products

UNSOUGHT PRODUCTS

A product unknown to the potential buyer or a known product that the buyer does not actively seek is referred to as an **unsought product**. New products fall into this category until advertising and distribution increase consumer awareness of them.

Some goods are always marketed as unsought items, especially needed products we do not like to think about or care to spend money on. Insurance, burial plots, and similar items require aggressive personal selling and highly persuasive advertising. Salespeople actively seek leads to potential buyers. Because consumers usually do not seek out this type of product, the company must go directly to them through a salesperson, direct mail, or direct-response advertising.

LO 3
Product Items, Lines, and Mixes

Rarely does a company sell a single product. More often, it sells a variety of things. A **product item** is a specific version of a product that can be designated as a distinct offering among an organization's products. Campbell's Creamy Chicken soup is an example of a product item (see Exhibit 10.2).

A group of closely related product items is a **product line**. For example, Exhibit 10.2 shows five of the product lines that Campbell's offers, with some examples of the items included in each line. Different container sizes and shapes also distinguish items in a product line. Diet Coke, for example, is available in cans and various plastic containers. Each size or container is a separate product item.

An organization's **product mix** includes all the products it sells. Together, all of Campbell's products—canned soups, microwave soups, gravies, meal kits, and tomato juice—constitute its product mix. Each product item in the product mix

---

unsought product
A product unknown to the potential buyer, or a known product that the buyer does not actively seek.

product item
A specific version of a product that can be designated as a distinct offering among an organization's products.

product line
A group of closely related product items.

product mix
All products that an organization sells.

Exhibit 10.2 Campbell's Product Lines and Product Mix

Depth of the Product Lines	Width of the Product Mix				
	Canned Soups	Microwave Soups	Gravies	Meal Kits	Tomato Juice
	Chicken Noodle	Creamy Tomato	Beef	Chicken Pasta	Regular
	Tomato	Vegetable	Turkey	Stroganoff Pasta	Low Sodium
	Vegetable Beef	Chicken Noodle	Mushroom	Chicken with Rice	Organic
	French Onion	Creamy Chicken	Chicken	Pork Chops with Stuffing	Healthy Request
	More	More	More	More	

Source: Campbell's Web site: http://www.campbellsoup.com, June 10, 2008.

may require a separate marketing strategy. In some cases, however, product lines and even entire product mixes share some marketing strategy components. Nike promotes all of its product items and lines with the theme "Just Do It."

Organizations derive several benefits from organizing related items into product lines, including the following:

→ **Advertising economies:** Product lines provide economies of scale in advertising. Several products can be advertised under the umbrella of the line. Campbell's can talk about its soup being "Mm! Mm! Good!" and promote the entire line.

→ **Package uniformity:** A product line can benefit from package uniformity. All packages in the line might have a common look and still keep their individual identities. Again, Campbell's soup is a good example.

→ **Standardized components:** Product lines allow firms to standardize components, thus reducing manufacturing and inventory costs. For example, many of the components Samsonite uses in its folding tables and chairs are also used in its patio furniture. General Motors uses the same parts on many automobile makes and models.

→ **Efficient sales and distribution:** A product line enables sales personnel for companies like Procter & Gamble to provide a full range of choices to customers. Distributors and retailers are often more inclined to stock the company's products if it offers a full line. Transportation and warehousing costs are likely to be lower for a product line than for a collection of individual items.

→ **Equivalent quality:** Purchasers usually expect and believe that all products in a line are about equal in quality. Consumers expect that all Campbell's soups and all Apple products will be of similar quality.

Product mix width (or breadth) refers to the number of product lines an organization offers. In Exhibit 10.2, for example, the width of Campbell's product mix is five product lines. **Product line depth** is the number of product items in a product line. As shown in Exhibit 10.2, the Tomato Juice product line consists of four product items; the Gravies product line includes more than four product items.

Firms increase the *width* of their product mix to diversify risk. To generate sales and boost profits, firms spread risk across many product lines rather than depend on only one or two. Firms also widen their product mix to capitalize on established reputations. The Oreo cookie brand has been extended to include items such as breakfast cereal, ice cream, Jell-O pudding, and cake mix.

Firms increase the *depth* of their product lines to attract buyers with different preferences, increase sales and profits by further segmenting the market, capitalize on economies of scale in production and marketing, and even out seasonal sales patterns. Coca-Cola and PepsiCo are introducing soft drinks in the United States using the natural, plant-based sweetener Stevia. These companies are targeting consumers looking for healthier sweetener alternatives.[1] As another example, Oreo cookies now come in a variety of flavors, including Double Delight Chocolate Mint'N Creme, Double Stuf Chocolate, and Golden Chocolate Oreos.

ADJUSTMENTS TO PRODUCT ITEMS, LINES, AND MIXES

Over time, firms change product items, lines, and mixes to take advantage of new technical or product developments or to respond to changes in the environment.

product mix width
The number of product lines an organization offers.

product line depth
The number of product items in a product line.

product modification
Changing one or more of a product's characteristics.

planned obsolescence
The practice of modifying products so those that have already been sold become obsolete before they actually need replacement.

They might adjust by modifying products, repositioning products, or extending or contracting product lines.

Product Modification Marketing managers must decide if and when to modify existing products. **Product modification** changes one or more of a product's characteristics:

→ **Quality modification:** change in a product's dependability or durability. Reducing a product's quality can let the manufacturer lower the price and appeal to target markets unable to afford the original product. Conversely, increasing quality can help the firm compete with rival firms. Increasing quality can also result in increased brand loyalty, greater ability to raise prices, or new opportunities for market segmentation. Inexpensive ink-jet printers have improved in quality to the point that they produce photo-quality images. These printers are now competing with camera film. To appeal to a more upscale market, Robert Mondavi Winery introduced a high-end wine called Twin Oaks to prestigious restaurants and hotels. This wine is positioned as a higher-quality wine than the one Mondavi sells in supermarkets.

→ **Functional modification:** change in a product's versatility, effectiveness, convenience, or safety. Tide with Downy combines the functions of cleaning power and fabric softening into one product. Lea & Perrins offers its steak sauce in a value-priced squeeze bottle with a "no mess, stay clean" cap.

→ **Style modification:** aesthetic product change, rather than a quality or functional change. Procter & Gamble developed a line of Febreze fabric freshener called Décor Collection that comes in stylish, clear bottles with botanical or rain-drop designs. Procter & Gamble hopes consumers will showcase the bottles when they're not using them.[2] This product promises its usual function, with a classy package to improve the aesthetics of the brand. Clothing and auto manufacturers also commonly use style modifications to motivate customers to replace products before they are worn out. **Planned obsolescence** is a term commonly used to describe the practice of modifying products so that those that have already been sold become obsolete before they actually need replacement. For example, products such as printers and cell phones become obsolete because technology changes so quickly. Some argue that planned obsolescence is wasteful; some claim it is unethical. Marketers respond that consumers favor style modifications because they like changes in the appearance of goods such as clothing and cars. Marketers also contend that consumers, not manufacturers and marketers, decide when styles are obsolete.

Repositioning Repositioning, as Chapter 8 explained, involves changing consumers' perceptions of a brand. Kool-Aid, the soft drink brand that has stood for fun and refreshment for many years, is adding better-for-you options by introducing new and reformulated products. Kool-Aid is being repositioned as a drink that supports a healthier family lifestyle.[3]

Changing demographics, declining sales, or changes in the social environment often motivate firms to reposition established brands. The clothing retailer Banana Republic started out selling safari-style clothing, but the concept soon became outdated. Gap acquired the chain and repositioned it as a more upscale retailer offering business casual clothing. Because consumers often have a negative perception of healthcare insurance, Cigna has repositioned itself as a health services company rather than a traditional insurer. Its ads focus on the idea that while the current healthcare system isn't perfect, Cigna is doing everything it can to improve it.[4]

Product Line Extensions A **product line extension** occurs when a company's management decides to add products to an existing product line in order to compete more broadly in the industry. Procter & Gamble plans to launch a body wash that is supposed to fight wrinkles as an extension of its Olay line of skin products.[5] Kraft extended a number of its popular Nabisco brands by adding small-portioned packages. Campbell's offers its soups in cans and in microwavable containers and sells its Swanson Broth in "chef" size cartons for serious cooks and 16-ounce packages for simple side dishes.[6]

> **product line extension**
> Adding additional products to an existing product line in order to compete more broadly in the industry.

Product Line Contraction Does the world really need 31 varieties of Head and Shoulders shampoo? Or 52 versions of Crest? Or numerous brands of apparel? When Steve Jobs took over Apple, the company sold over 40 products. He immediately simplified by cutting the product line down to four computers—two desktops and two laptops—that Apple could focus on perfecting. This move helped Apple double its market share.[7] Symptoms of product line overextension include the following:

→ Some products in the line do not contribute to profits because of low sales or because they cannibalize sales of other items in the line.

→ Manufacturing or marketing resources are disproportionately allocated to slow-moving products.

→ Some items in the line are obsolete because of new product entries in the line or new products offered by competitors.

Three major benefits are likely when a firm contracts its overextended product lines. First, resources become concentrated on the most important products. Second, managers no longer waste resources trying to improve the sales and profits of poorly performing products. Third, new product items have a greater chance of being successful because more financial and human resources are available to manage them.

Review
LO3

Define the terms *product item*, *product line*, and *product mix*

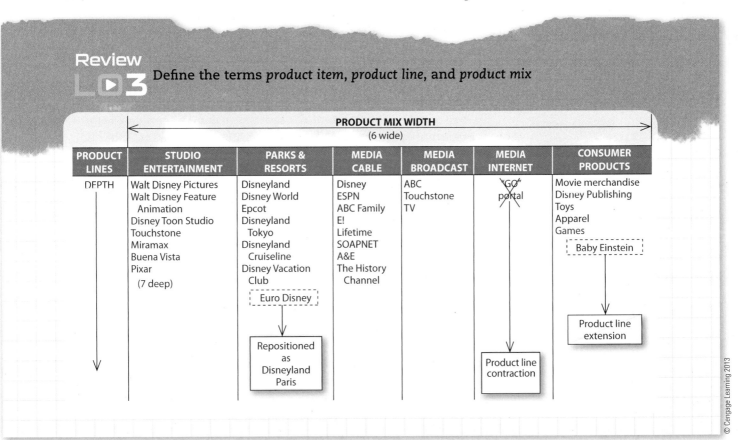

PRODUCT LINES	STUDIO ENTERTAINMENT	PARKS & RESORTS	MEDIA CABLE	MEDIA BROADCAST	MEDIA INTERNET	CONSUMER PRODUCTS
DFPTH	Walt Disney Pictures Walt Disney Feature Animation Disney Toon Studio Touchstone Miramax Buena Vista Pixar (7 deep)	Disneyland Disney World Epcot Disneyland Tokyo Disneyland Cruiseline Disney Vacation Club [Euro Disney] ↓ Repositioned as Disneyland Paris	Disney ESPN ABC Family E! Lifetime SOAPNET A&E The History Channel	ABC Touchstone TV	"GO" portal ✗ ↓ Product line contraction	Movie merchandise Disney Publishing Toys Apparel Games [Baby Einstein] ↓ Product line extension

PRODUCT MIX WIDTH (6 wide)

brand

A name, term, symbol, design, or combination thereof that identifies a seller's products and differentiates them from competitors' products.

brand name

That part of a brand that can be spoken, including letters, words, and numbers.

brand mark

The elements of a brand that cannot be spoken.

brand equity

The value of company and brand names.

global brand

A brand where at least one-third of the product is sold outside its home country or region.

brand loyalty

A consistent preference for one brand over all others.

L▶4
Branding

The success of any business or consumer product depends in part on the target market's ability to distinguish one product from another. Branding is the main tool marketers use to distinguish their products from the competition's.

A **brand** is a name, term, symbol, design, or combination thereof that identifies a seller's products and differentiates them from competitors' products. A **brand name** is that part of a brand that can be spoken, including letters (GM, YMCA), words (Chevrolet), and numbers (WD-40, 7-Eleven). The elements of a brand that cannot be spoken are called the **brand mark**—for example, the well-known Mercedes-Benz and Delta Air Lines symbols.

BENEFITS OF BRANDING

Branding has three main purposes: product identification, repeat sales, and new-product sales. The most important purpose is *product identification*. Branding allows marketers to distinguish their products from all others. Many brand names are familiar to consumers and indicate quality.

The term **brand equity** refers to the value of company and brand names. A brand that has high awareness, perceived quality, and brand loyalty among customers has high brand equity. Starbucks, Volvo, and Dell are companies with high brand equity. A brand with strong brand equity is a valuable asset.

The term **global brand** refers to a brand that obtains at least a third of its earnings from outside its home country, is recognizable outside its home base of customers, and has publicly available marketing and financial data.[8] Exhibit 10.3 lists the top ten global brands. Although it's not on the top of this year's list, Yum! Brands, which owns Pizza Hut, KFC, and Taco Bell, is a good example of a company that has developed strong global brands. Yum! believes that it has to adapt its restaurants to local tastes and different cultural and political climates. In Japan, for instance, KFC sells tempura crispy strips. In northern England, KFC focuses on gravy and potatoes, and in Thailand it offers rice with soy or sweet chili sauce.

The best generator of *repeat sales* is satisfied customers. Branding helps consumers identify products they wish to buy again and avoid those they do not. **Brand loyalty**, a consistent preference for one brand over all others, is quite high in some product categories. Over half the users in product categories such as cigarettes, mayonnaise, toothpaste, coffee, headache remedies, photographic film, bath soap, and ketchup are loyal to one brand. Many students come to college and purchase the same brands they used at home, rather than being "price" buyers. Brand identity is essential to developing brand loyalty.

The third main purpose of branding is to *facilitate new-product sales*. Company and brand names like those listed in Exhibit 10.3 are extremely useful when introducing new products.

The Internet provides firms with a new alternative for generating brand awareness, promoting a desired brand image, stimulating new and repeat brand sales, enhancing brand loyalty, and building brand equity. Nearly all packaged-goods firms have a presence online. Tide.com offers a useful feature called Stain Brain, a collection of Tide's tips on stain removal, and a place where users can post their own tips for removing stains of almost any substance from almost any fabric.

Exhibit 10.3 The Top Ten Global Brands
Global
1. Coca-Cola
2. IBM
3. Microsoft
4. GE
5. Nokia
6. McDonald's
7. Google
8. Toyota
9. Intel
10. Disney

Source: The Top Ten Global Brands from BW Staff, "The 100 Best Global Brands in 2009," *BusinessWeek*, http://images.businessweek.com/ss/09/09/0917_global_brands/index.htm. Reprinted with permission.

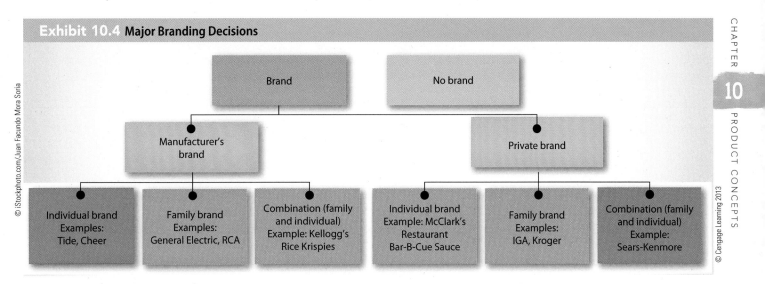

Exhibit 10.4 Major Branding Decisions

```
              Brand                          No brand

     Manufacturer's                    Private brand
         brand

Individual brand   Family brand   Combination (family   Individual brand   Family brand   Combination (family
Examples:          Examples:      and individual)       Example: McClark's  Examples:      and individual)
Tide, Cheer        General Electric, RCA   Example: Kellogg's   Restaurant        IGA, Kroger    Example:
                                   Rice Krispies         Bar-B-Cue Sauce                   Sears-Kenmore
```

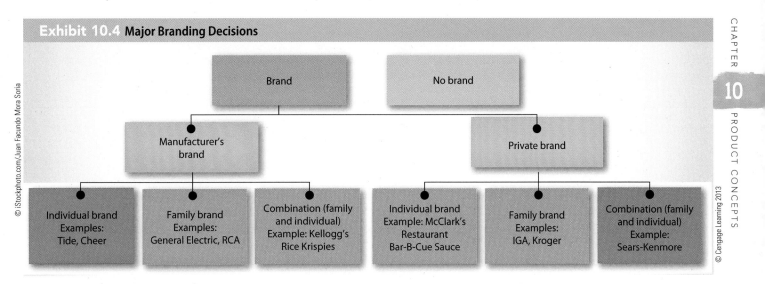

Credit (left margin): © iStockphoto.com/Juan Facundo Mora Soria

(right margin): © Cengage Learning 2013

BRANDING STRATEGIES

Firms face complex branding decisions. As Exhibit 10.4 illustrates, firms might choose to follow a policy of using manufacturers' brands, private (distributor) brands, or both. In either case, they must then decide among a policy of individual branding (different brands for different products), family branding (common names for different products), or a combination of individual branding and family branding.

Manufacturers' Brands versus Private Brands The brand name of a manufacturer—such as Kodak, La-Z-Boy, and Fruit of the Loom—is called a **manufacturer's brand.** Sometimes "national brand" is used as a synonym for "manufacturer's brand." This term is not always accurate, however, because many manufacturers serve only regional markets. Using "manufacturer's brand" more precisely defines the brand's owner.

A **private brand,** also known as a private label or store brand, is a brand name owned by a wholesaler or a retailer. Private brands include Walmart's Ol' Roy dog food, which has surpassed Nestlé's Purina as the world's top-selling dog food, and the George line of apparel, which has knocked Liz Claiborne's clothing out of Walmart. The Nielsen Company reported that unit sales of private label goods increased 8 percent from 2008 to 2010, while brand names have decreased about 4 percent. Furthermore, another recent study showed that 63 percent of consumers plan to buy private labels even after the economy rebounds.[9]

Retailers love consumers' greater acceptance of private brands. Because overhead is low and there are no marketing costs, private-label products bring 10 percent higher margins, on average, than manufacturers' brands. More than that, a trusted store brand can differentiate a chain from its competitors. For example, many shoppers will drive the extra mile to Costco, a wholesale club, to buy the store's Kirkland brands and will also buy other goods while they are there. Costco introduced a Kirkland Signature brand of wines that competes at the premium and super premium price categories.[10] Exhibit 10.5 illustrates key issues that wholesalers and retailers should consider in deciding whether to sell manufacturers' brands or private brands. Many firms offer a combination of both. Instead of marketing private brands as cheaper and inferior to manufacturer's brands, many retailers are creating and promoting their own **captive brands.** These brands carry no evidence of the store's affiliation, are manufactured by a third party, and are sold exclusively at the chains. This strategy allows the retailer to ask a price similar to manufacturer's brands, and they are typically displayed alongside marketed mainstream products. For example, BioInfusion, a line of hair care

manufacturer's brand
The brand name of a manufacturer.

private brand
A brand name owned by a wholesaler or a retailer.

captive brand
A brand that carries no evidence of a retailer's affiliation, is manufactured by a third party, and is sold exclusively at the retailer.

Exhibit 10.5 Comparing Manufacturers' and Private Brands from the Reseller's Perspective

Key Advantages of Carrying Manufacturers' Brands	Key Advantages of Carrying Private Brands
• Heavy advertising to the consumer by manufacturers like Procter & Gamble helps develop strong consumer loyalties.	• A wholesaler or retailer can usually earn higher profits on its own brand. In addition, because the private brand is exclusive, there is less pressure to mark the price down to meet competition.
• Well-known manufacturers' brands, such as Kodak and Fisher-Price, can attract new customers and enhance the dealer's (wholesaler's or retailer's) prestige.	• A manufacturer can decide to drop a brand or a reseller at any time or even to become a direct competitor to its dealers.
• Many manufacturers offer rapid delivery, enabling the dealer to carry less inventory.	• A private brand ties the customer to the wholesaler or retailer. A person who wants a DieHard battery must go to Sears.
• If a dealer happens to sell a manufacturer's brand of poor quality, the customer may simply switch brands and remain loyal to the dealer.	• Wholesalers and retailers have no control over the intensity of distribution of manufacturers' brands. Walmart store managers don't have to worry about competing with other sellers of Sam's American Choice products or Ol' Roy dog food. They know that these brands are sold only in Walmart and Sam's Wholesale Club stores.

This cobranding ad features both Nike and Apple's iPhone, promoting the Nike+iPod software that allows walkers and runners to keep track of the distance and pace of workouts.

Image courtesy of The Advertising Archives

products available only at Walgreens, has grown to become one of the top brands in the entire hair care category.[11]

Individual Brands versus Family Brands Many companies use different brand names for different products, a practice referred to as **individual branding**. Companies use individual brands when their products vary greatly in use or performance. For instance, it would not make sense to use the same brand name for a pair of dress socks and a baseball bat. Procter & Gamble targets different segments of the laundry detergent market with Bold, Cheer, Dash, Dreft, Era, Gain, Ivory Snow, and Tide. Marriott International also targets different market segments with Courtyard by Marriott, Residence Inn, and Fairfield Inn.

In contrast, a company that markets several different products under the same brand name is using a **family brand**. Sony's family brand includes radios, television sets, stereos, and other electronic products. The Heinz brand name is attached to products such as ketchup, mustard, and pickles.

Cobranding Cobranding entails placing two or more brand names on a product or its package. Three common types of cobranding are ingredient branding, cooperative branding, and complementary branding. *Ingredient branding* identifies the brand of a part that makes up the product. Examples of ingredient branding are Intel (a microprocessor) in a personal computer, such as Dell, or a satellite system (OnStar) in an automobile (Cadillac). Barnes & Noble and Hewlett-Packard launched a co-branded HP B&N eBookstore. HP will include a link to the store on its new computers and may preload Barnes & Noble's reading application on some devices in the future. The look of the e-store looks like HP's companywide branding, and the site uses Barnes & Noble's e-commerce platform.[12]

Cooperative branding occurs when two brands receiving equal treatment (in the context of an advertisement) borrow from each other's brand equity. A promotional contest jointly sponsored by Ramada Inns, American Express, and Continental Airlines is an example of cooperative branding. Guests at Ramada who paid with an American

individual branding
Using different brand names for different products.

family brand
Marketing several different products under the same brand name.

cobranding
Placing two or more brand names on a product or its package.

Express card were automatically entered in the contest and were eligible to win more than a hundred getaways for two at any Ramada in the continental United States and round-trip airfare from Continental. Finally, with *complementary branding*, products are advertised or marketed together to suggest usage, such as a spirits brand (Seagram's) and a compatible mixer (7-Up). A partnership between Ann Taylor Loft women's clothing stores and Procter & Gamble will promote the use of Tide Total Care and Downy Total Care to clean clothing and cut down on dry cleaning bills. The store will give free samples and coupons to customers who buy machine washable clothes, and posters and decals placed in the stores will call attention to the product's benefits.[13]

Cobranding is a useful strategy when a combination of brand names enhances the prestige or perceived value of a product, or when it benefits brand owners and users. When Intel launched its Centrino wireless processor, it established cobranding relationships with T-Mobile and hotel chains Marriott International and Westin Hotels & Resorts because there was mutual value in establishing these relationships. T-Mobile was able to set up global "hot spots" to reach Intel's target market of mobile professionals, while the hotel chains enabled Intel to target business professionals.

Cobranding may be used to increase a company's presence in markets where it has little or no market share. For example, Coach was able to build a presence in a whole new category when its leather upholstery with logo was used in Lexus automobiles. European firms have been slower to adopt cobranding than U.S. firms have. One reason is that European customers seem to be more skeptical than U.S. customers about trying new brands. European retailers also typically have less shelf space than their U.S. counterparts and are less willing to give new brands a try.

TRADEMARKS

A **trademark** is the exclusive right to use a brand or part of a brand. Others are prohibited from using the brand without permission. A **service mark** performs the same function for services, such as H&R Block and Weight Watchers. Parts of a brand or other product identification may qualify for trademark protection. Some examples are:

→ Shapes, such as the Jeep front grille and the Coca-Cola bottle

→ Ornamental color or design, such as the decoration on Nike tennis shoes, the black-and-copper color combination of a Duracell battery, Levi's small tag on the left side of the rear pocket of its jeans, or the cutoff black cone on the top of Cross pens

→ Catchy phrases, such as Prudential's "Own a piece of the rock," Mountain Dew's "Do the Dew," and Nike's "Just Do It"

→ Abbreviations, such as Bud or Coke

→ Sounds, such as General Electric's ship's bell clock sound and the MGM lion's roar

trademark
The exclusive right to use a brand or part of a brand.

service mark
A trademark for a service.

Julius Sämann Ltd., which owns the rights to the famous LITTLE TREES air fresheners, and CAR-FRESHNER Corporation, its U.S. licensee, use ads like this one to discourage unauthorized copying of its intellectual property.

It is important to understand that trademark rights come from use rather than registration. A company must have a genuine intention to use a trademark when it files an intent-to-use application with the U.S. Patent and Trademark Office and must actually use the mark within three years of the application being granted. Trademark protection lasts for as long as the mark is being used.

In November 1999, legislation went into effect that explicitly applies trademark law to the online world. This law includes financial penalties for those who violate trademarked products or register an otherwise trademarked term as a domain name.

Companies that fail to protect their trademarks face the possibility that their product names will become generic. A generic product name identifies a product by class or type and cannot be trademarked. Former brand names that were not sufficiently protected by their owners and were subsequently declared to be generic product names by U.S. courts include aspirin, cellophane, linoleum, thermos, kerosene, monopoly, cola, and shredded wheat.

Companies like Rolls Royce, Cross, Xerox, Levi Strauss, Frigidaire, and McDonald's aggressively enforce their trademarks. Rolls Royce, Coca-Cola, and Xerox even run newspaper and magazine ads stating that their names are trademarks and should not be used as descriptive or generic terms. Some ads threaten lawsuits against competitors that violate trademarks.

In order to stem the number of trademark infringements, violations carry steep penalties. Despite the risk of incurring a penalty, infringement lawsuits are still common. One of the major battles is over brand names that closely resemble another brand name. The celebrity chef Wolfgang Puck filed a lawsuit against Wolfgang Zweiner when Zweiner opened Wolfgang's Steakhouse and confused fans began calling to make reservations at what they thought was the new Puck restaurant.[14]

Companies must also contend with fake or unauthorized brands, such as fake Levi's jeans, Microsoft software, Rolex watches, Reebok and Nike footwear, and Louis Vuitton handbags. Hasbro sued the makers of the online game Scrabulous for copyright infringement on its Scrabble game. Scrabulous was an obvious copy of Scrabble, including the rules, game pieces, and board colors.[15]

In Europe, you can sue counterfeiters only if your brand, logo, or trademark is formally registered. Until recently, formal registration was required in each country in which a company sought protection. A company can now register its trademark in all European Union (EU) member countries with one application.

Review

LO 4 Describe marketing uses of branding

Brand name: MGM

Brand mark:

BRANDING

Benefits	Strategies
Brand equity (from product identification)	Generic Brand Trademark — Manufacturer — Individual / Family / Combination — Private
Brand loyalty (from repeat sales)	
Brand recognition (to generate new product sales)	

© Cengage Learning 2013

L▶5
Packaging

Packages have always served a practical function—that is, they hold contents together and protect goods as they move through the distribution channel. Today, however, packaging is also a container for promoting the product and making it easier and safer to use.

PACKAGING FUNCTIONS

The three most important functions of packaging are to contain and protect products, promote products, and facilitate the storage, use, and convenience of products. A fourth function of packaging that is becoming increasingly important is to facilitate recycling and reduce environmental damage.

Containing and Protecting Products The most obvious function of packaging is to contain products that are liquid, granular, or otherwise divisible. Packaging also enables manufacturers, wholesalers, and retailers to market products in specific quantities, such as ounces.

Physical protection is another obvious function of packaging. Most products are handled several times between the time they are manufactured, harvested, or otherwise produced and the time they are consumed or used. Many products are shipped, stored, and inspected several times between production and consumption. Some, like milk, need to be refrigerated. Others, like beer, are sensitive to light. Still others, like medicines and bandages, need to be kept sterile. Packages protect products from breakage, evaporation, spillage, spoilage, light, heat, cold, infestation, and many other conditions.

Promoting Products Packaging does more than identify the brand, list the ingredients, specify features, and give directions. A package differentiates a product from competing products and may associate a new product with a family of other products from the same manufacturer. Welch's repackaged its line of grape juice–based jams, jellies, and juices to unify the line and get more impact on the shelf.

Packages use designs, colors, shapes, and materials to try to influence consumers' perceptions and buying behavior. For example, marketing research shows that health-conscious consumers are likely to think that any food is probably good for them as long as it comes in green packaging. Two top brands of low-fat foods—SnackWell's and Healthy Choice—use green packaging. Procter & Gamble is strategically focusing on package designs in order to attract consumers while they are shopping. Designers spent time researching consumer preferences and behaviors before P&G's new Febreze Home Collection was developed Since introducing the line, P&G gained two share points in the air freshener category.[16] Packaging has a measurable effect on sales. Quaker Oats revised the package for Rice-A-Roni without making any other changes in marketing strategy and experienced a 44 percent increase in sales in one year.

Facilitating Storage, Use, and Convenience Wholesalers and retailers prefer packages that are easy to ship, store, and stock on shelves. They also like packages that protect products, prevent spoilage or breakage, and extend the product's shelf life.

Consumers' requirements for storage, use, and convenience cover many dimensions. Consumers are constantly seeking items that are easy to handle, open, and reclose, although some consumers want packages that are tamperproof or childproof. Research indicates that hard-to-open packages are among consumers' top complaints. Surveys conducted by *Sales & Marketing Management* magazine revealed that consumers dislike—and avoid buying—leaky ice cream boxes, overly heavy or fat vinegar bottles, immovable pry-up lids on glass bottles, key-opener sardine cans, and hard-to-pour cereal boxes. Such packaging innovations as zipper tear strips, hinged lids, tab slots, screw-on tops, and pour spouts were introduced to solve these and other problems. Nestlé improved all its packaging to make it easier for people to rip open its pouches, twist off its caps, and reseal its tubs. Easy openings are especially important for kids and aging baby boomers. The company's package designers spent nine months developing a plastic lid for ice cream that is easier to pull off when the ice cream is frozen and ribbed corners for ice cream cartons that are easier to grip when scooping.[17]

© Terri Miller/E-Visual Communications, Inc.

Some firms use packaging to segment markets. For example, a C&H sugar carton with an easy-to-pour, re-closable top is targeted to consumers who don't do a lot of baking and are willing to pay at least 20 cents more for the package. Different-size packages appeal to heavy, moderate, and light users. Salt is sold in package sizes ranging from single serving to picnic size to giant economy size. Campbell's soup is packaged in single-serving cans aimed at the elderly and singles market segments. Beer and soft drinks are similarly marketed in various package sizes and types. Packaging convenience can increase a product's utility and, therefore, its market share and profits. To appeal to women, Dutch Boy designed a square plastic paint container with a side handle and a spout to replace the traditional wire-handled round metal paint can. The Internet also gives consumers more packaging options. Indeed, the Internet may significantly change the purpose and appearance of packaging. Packaging for some products sold on the Internet will be more under the customer's control and will be customized by consumers to fit their needs. Some designers are already offering to personalize, for a fee, packages such as wine bottle labels.

Facilitating Recycling and Reducing Environmental Damage One of the most important packaging issues today is compatibility with the environment. In a recent study of consumers, a majority said they would give up the following conveniences if it would benefit the environment: packaging designed for easy stacking/storing, packaging that can be used for cooking, and packaging designed for easy transport.[18] Some firms use their packaging to target environmentally concerned market segments. The French winery Boisset Family Estates recently introduced TetraPak cartons of its French Rabbit chardonnay to offer consumers a playful and eco-friendly alternative to glass bottles. When the cartons sold well, other companies followed suit.[19] Dell has plans to cut by 10 percent the amount of materials used in its laptop and desktop packaging worldwide by 2012.[20] Groups such as the Sustainable Packaging Coalition assist companies in creating perpetually recycled packaging so that materials don't ever end up in landfills, damaging the ecosystem.[21]

persuasive labeling
A type of package labeling that focuses on a promotional theme or logo with consumer information being secondary

LABELING

An integral part of any package is its label. Labeling generally takes one of two forms: persuasive or informational. **Persuasive labeling** focuses on a promotional theme or logo, and consumer information is secondary.

ethics in marketing

Not Milk?

Consumers who are lactose-intolerant, or who for other reasons wish to avoid dairy products, often look for non-dairy alternatives to milk that are made from plant-based products. These consumers purchase items such as soy milk, rice milk, and almond milk as substitutes for dairy. The National Milk Producers Federation (NMPF) is not happy about these, and other, beverages labeled "milk" on the shelves. It has petitioned the Food and Drug Administration (FDA) to stop producers of non-dairy food from using terms such as "milk," "cheese," and "ice-cream" on their products. The NMPF calls this kind of labeling a misuse of "traditional dairy terms" and argues that "food labels should clearly and accurately identify the true nature of the food to the consumer."

The NMPF is not arguing that liquid products that come from foods such as grains, seeds, and nuts should not be on the shelves. They are arguing that these products should be labeled "artificial milk" or "imitation milk."

The underlying issue is the importance of accuracy in labeling. NMPF feels that consumers who are interested in purchasing animal-based milk products should be able to understand what they are buying when they read the label. The organization contends that words that falsely connote dairy products risk confusing the consumer.

Accuracy in labeling protects and justifies the trust of consumers, maintains Sherry F. Colb, a legal professional. The NMPF argues that when producers of dairy-free products label their goods with traditional dairy titles, they do so to capitalize on the popularity and nutritional quality that dairy products have. For example, NMPF says that 13 of 15 non-dairy beverages listed in their petition contained less protein than an equal amount of milk.[23]

Why do you think companies use dairy-related words in labeling their alternative foods? Do you agree with the NMPF that the labels are deceptive and should be changed?

Procter & Gamble put real photography on its new Downy fabric softener labels in order to make a more personal connection with consumers. Note that the standard promotional claims—such as "new," "improved," and "super"—are no longer very persuasive. Consumers have been saturated with "newness" and thus discount these claims.

Informational labeling, in contrast, is designed to help consumers make proper product selections and lower their cognitive dissonance after the purchase. Sears attaches a "label of confidence" to all its floor coverings. This label gives product information such as durability, color, features, cleanability, care instructions, and construction standards. Most major furniture manufacturers affix labels to their wares that explain the products' construction features, such as type of frame, number of coils, and fabric characteristics. The Nutritional Labeling and Education Act of 1990 mandated that detailed nutritional information be placed on most food packages and standards for health claims on food packaging. An important outcome of this legislation has been guidelines from the Food and Drug Administration for using terms such as *low fat, light, reduced cholesterol, low sodium, low calorie,* and *fresh*. NuVal LLC is a company that ranks supermarket products on a 1 to 100 scale based on nutritional information presented in on-pack labels. A higher score indicates higher nutritional value. The NuVal score is placed on the shelf label next to the price in stores paying a licensing fee.

informational labeling
A type of package labeling designed to help consumers make proper product selections and lower their cognitive dissonance after the purchase.

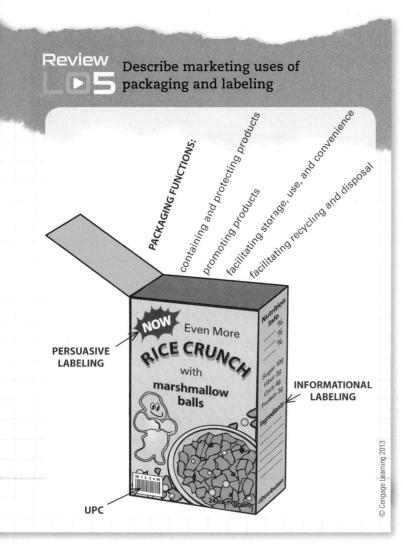

PACKAGING FUNCTIONS:
- containing and protecting products
- promoting products
- facilitating storage, use, and convenience
- facilitating recycling and disposal

PERSUASIVE LABELING

NOW Even More **RICE CRUNCH** with **marshmallow balls**

Nutrition Info %

Sugar 10g
Fiber 2g
Carb 9g
Protein 9g

Ingredients

INFORMATIONAL LABELING

eDistribution

24 oz (grams)

UPC

© Cengage Learning 2013

The scores allow consumers to easily compare the nutritional elements of packaged foods.[22]

UNIVERSAL PRODUCT CODES

The numerical code that appears on most consumer purchased items is called a **universal product code (UPC)**. It appears as a series of thick and thin vertical lines that are read by computerized optical scanners that match codes with brand names, package sizes, and prices. UPCs are often called *bar codes* because of the organization of the lines. UPCs also print information on cash register tapes and help retailers rapidly and accurately prepare records of customer purchases, control inventories, and track sales. The UPC (bar code) system was first introduced in 1974 and has since been adopted for use in single-source research. (See Chapter 9.)

LO6
Global Issues in Branding and Packaging

International marketers must address several concerns regarding branding and packaging.

BRANDING

When planning to enter a foreign market with an existing product, a firm has three options for handling the brand name:

→ **One brand name everywhere:** This strategy is useful when the company markets mainly one product and the brand name does not have negative connotations in any local market. The Coca-Cola Company uses a one-brand-name strategy in 195 countries around the world. The advantages of a one-brand-name strategy are greater identification of the product from market to market and ease of coordinating promotion from market to market.

→ **Adaptations and modifications:** A one-brand-name strategy is not possible when the name cannot be pronounced in the local language, when the brand name is owned by someone else, or when the brand name has a negative or vulgar connotation in the local language. The Iranian detergent "Barf," for example, might encounter some problems in the U.S. market.

→ **Different brand names in different markets:** Local brand names are often used when translation or pronunciation problems occur, when the marketer wants the brand to appear to be a local brand, or when regulations require localization. Gillette's Silkience hair conditioner is called Soyance in France and Sientel in Italy. Coca-Cola's Sprite brand had to be renamed Kin in Korea to satisfy a

universal product code (UPC)
A series of thick and thin vertical lines (bar codes), readable by computerized optical scanners, that represent numbers used to track products.

government prohibition on the unnecessary use of foreign words. Because of the feminine connotations of the word *diet*, the European version of Diet Coke is Coca-Cola Light.

PACKAGING

Three aspects of packaging that are especially important in international marketing are labeling, aesthetics, and climate considerations. The major *labeling* concern is properly translating ingredient, promotional, and instructional information on labels. In Eastern Europe, packages of Ariel detergent are printed in 14 languages, from Latvian to Lithuanian. Care must also be employed in meeting all local labeling requirements. Several years ago, an Italian judge ordered that all bottles of Coca-Cola be removed from retail shelves because the ingredients were not properly labeled. Labeling is also harder in countries like Belgium and Finland, which require it to be bilingual.

Package *aesthetics* may also require some attention. The key is to stay attuned to cultural traits in host countries. For example, colors may have different connotations. Red is associated with witchcraft in some countries, green may be a sign of danger, and white may be symbolic of death. Aesthetics also influence package size. Soft drinks are not sold in six-packs in countries that lack refrigeration. In some countries, products such as detergent may be bought only in small quantities because of a lack of storage space. Other products, like cigarettes, may be bought in small quantities, and even single units, because of the low purchasing power of buyers.

On the other hand, simple visual elements of the brand, such as a symbol or logo, can be a standardizing element across products and countries. For example, in Mexico, Lay's potato chips are known as Sabritas, but the packaging carries the same brand mark and graphic elements as in the United States. Extreme climates and long-distance shipping necessitate sturdier and more durable packages for goods sold overseas. Spillage, spoilage, and breakage are all more important concerns when products are shipped long distances or frequently handled during shipping and storage. Packages may also have to ensure a longer product life if the time between production and consumption lengthens significantly.

warranty
A confirmation of the quality or performance of a good or service.

express warranty
A written guarantee.

implied warranty
An unwritten guarantee that the good or service is fit for the purpose for which it was sold.

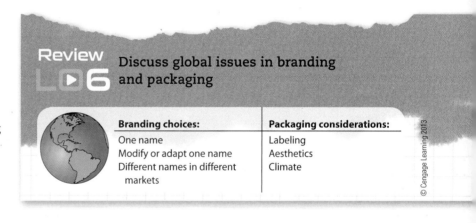

Review
LO6
Discuss global issues in branding and packaging

Branding choices:	Packaging considerations:
One name	Labeling
Modify or adapt one name	Aesthetics
Different names in different markets	Climate

© Cengage Learning 2013

Product Warranties

Just as a package is designed to protect the product, a **warranty** protects the buyer and gives essential information about the product. A warranty confirms the quality or performance of a good or service. An **express warranty** is a written guarantee. Express warranties range from simple statements—such as "100 percent cotton" (a guarantee of quality) and "complete satisfaction guaranteed" (a statement of performance)—to extensive documents written in technical language. In contrast, an **implied warranty** is an unwritten guarantee that the good or service is fit for the purpose for which it was sold. All sales have an implied warranty under the Uniform Commercial Code.

Congress passed the Magnuson-Moss Warranty–Federal Trade Commission Improvement Act in 1975 to help consumers understand warranties and get action from manufacturers and dealers. A manufacturer that promises a full warranty must meet certain minimum standards, including repair "within a reasonable time and without charge" of any defects and replacement of the merchandise or a full refund if the product does not work "after a reasonable number of attempts" at repair. Any warranty that does not live up to this tough prescription must be "conspicuously" promoted as a limited warranty.

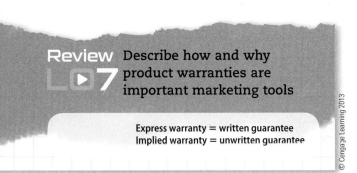

Review LO7 Describe how and why product warranties are important marketing tools

Express warranty = written guarantee
Implied warranty = unwritten guarantee

© Cengage Learning 2013

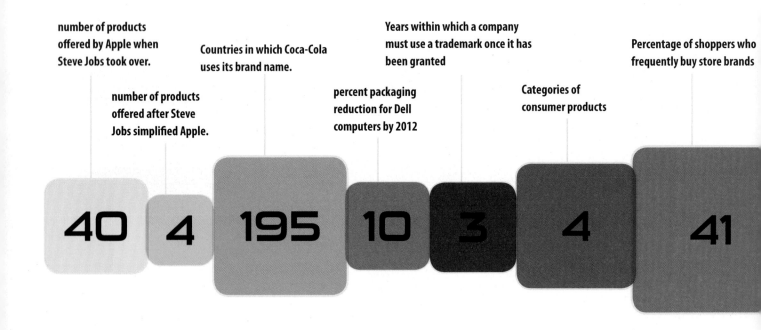

number of products offered by Apple when Steve Jobs took over.

number of products offered after Steve Jobs simplified Apple.

Countries in which Coca-Cola uses its brand name.

percent packaging reduction for Dell computers by 2012

Years within which a company must use a trademark once it has been granted

Categories of consumer products

Percentage of shoppers who frequently buy store brands

40   4   195   10   3   4   41

Mattel updated Barbie's packaging to keep her fresh and familiar.

COURTESY OF CHAPEL HOUSE PHOTOGRAPHY

1 Familiar brand mark

2 Heat- and impact-tested packaging protects Barbie from damage.

3 Die cuts keep Barbie from shifting.

4 Plastic staples facilitate easy removal.

5 Persuasive labeling—"easy for me"—assures parents their kids can open it themselves.

Define the term *product.* A product is anything, desired or not, that a person or organization receives in an exchange. The basic goal of purchasing decisions is to receive the tangible and intangible benefits associated with a product. Tangible aspects include packaging, style, color, size, and features. Intangible qualities include service, the retailer's image, the manufacturer's reputation, and the social status associated with a product. An organization's product offering is the crucial element in any marketing mix.

 1.1 Form a team of four or five members. Have the team determine what the tangible and intangible benefits are for a computer, a tube of toothpaste, a beauty salon, and a dentist.

 Classify consumer products. Consumer products are classified into four categories: convenience products, shopping products, specialty products, and unsought products. Convenience products are relatively inexpensive and require limited shopping effort. Shopping products are of two types: homogeneous and heterogeneous. Because of the similarity of homogeneous products, they are differentiated mainly by price and features. In contrast, heterogeneous products appeal to consumers because of their distinct characteristics. Specialty products possess unique benefits that are highly desirable to certain customers. Finally, unsought products are either new products or products that require aggressive selling because they are generally avoided or overlooked by consumers.

 2.1 Break into groups of four or five. Have the members of the group classify each of the following products into the category (convenience, shopping, specialty, unsought) that they think fits best from their perspective as consumers (i.e., if they were buying the product): Coca-Cola (brand), car stereo, winter coat, pair of shoes, life insurance, blue jeans, fast-food hamburgers, shampoo, canned vegetables, curtains.

2.2 Although major appliances such as washers and dryers are usually considered homogeneous shopping products, the high-efficiency front-loaders that boast many more features than standard machines are gaining in popularity. Do you think high-efficiency technology is enough to make washers and dryers heterogeneous shopping products? Explain.

 Define the terms *product item, product line,* **and** *product mix.* A product item is a specific version of a product that can be designated as a distinct offering among an organization's products. A product line is a group of closely related products offered by an organization. An organization's product mix includes all the products it sells. Product mix width refers to the number of product lines an organization offers. Product line depth is the number of product items in a product line. Firms modify existing products by changing their quality, functional characteristics, or style. Product line extension occurs when a firm adds new products to existing product lines.

 3.1 A local civic organization has asked you to give a luncheon presentation about planned obsolescence. Rather than pursuing a negative approach by talking about how businesses exploit customers through planned obsolescence, you have decided to talk about the benefits of producing products that do not last forever. Prepare a one-page outline of your presentation.

 3.2 Go to Unilever's Web site at **www.unilever.com**. Can Unilever delete anything from its product lines? Visit the company's product category pages on its "Brands" Web page to see the number of existing products and new products planned. Write a proposal for contracting one of Unilever's product lines.

 Describe marketing uses of branding. A brand is a name, term, or symbol that identifies and differentiates a firm's products. Established brands encourage customer loyalty and help new products succeed. Branding strategies require decisions about individual, family, manufacturers', and private brands.

4.1 A local supermarket would like to introduce its own brand of paper goods (e.g., paper towels, facial tissue, etc.) to sell alongside its current inventory. The company has hired you to generate a report outlining the advantages and disadvantages of doing so. Write the report.

4.2 How does Hormel use its Web site (**www.hormel.com**) to promote its store brands? Is the site designed more to promote the company or its brands? Check out the Spam Web site at **www.spam.com**. How do you think Hormel is able to successfully sustain this brand that is often the punch line to a joke?

Describe marketing uses of packaging and labeling. Packaging has four functions: containing and protecting products; promoting products; facilitating product storage, use, and convenience; and facilitating recycling and reducing environmental damage. As a tool for promotion, packaging identifies the brand and its features. It also serves the critical function of differentiating a product from competing products and linking it with related products from the same manufacturer. The label is an integral part of the package, with persuasive and informational functions. In essence, the package is the marketer's last chance to influence buyers before they make a purchase decision.

5.1 Find a product at home that has a distinctive package. Write a paragraph evaluating that package based on the four functions of packaging discussed in the chapter.

Discuss global issues in branding and packaging. In addition to brand piracy, international marketers must address a variety of concerns regarding branding and packaging, including choosing a brand-name policy, translating labels and meeting host-country labeling requirements, making packages aesthetically compatible with host-country cultures, and offering the sizes of packages preferred in host countries.

6.1 List the countries to which Levi Strauss & Co. markets through the Web site **www.levi. com**. How do the product offerings differ between the U.S. and European selections?

Describe how and why product warranties are important marketing tools. Product warranties are important tools because they offer consumers protection and help them gauge product quality.

7.1 Lands' End and L.L. Bean are renowned for their product guarantees. Find and read the exact wording of their guarantees on their Web sites (**www.landsend.com** and **www. llbean.com**). Do you think a company could successfully compete against either without offering the same guarantee?

Key Terms

Exercises

ethics

ETHICS EXERCISE

A product that a potential buyer knows about but is not actively seeking is called an unsought product. Is the marketing of unsought products unethical? Discuss your answer in terms of the AMA Statement of Ethics, found at **www.marketingpower.com**.

MARKETING PLAN EXERCISE

In the first part of your strategic marketing plan, you stated your business mission and objectives, and performed a detailed SWOT analysis. In the second part of the plan you identified and described target market segments and described their buying behaviors and decision-making processes. In addition, you identified sources of competitive intelligence and the need for any further marketing research before the marketing plan could be implemented. The next stages of the strategic planning process involve defining the elements of the marketing mix: (Part 3) product, (Part 4) place, (Part 5) promotion, and (Part 6) pricing strategies.

After reading Chapter 10, you can use the following exercises to guide you through the third part of your strategic marketing plan:

1. How would you classify the offering to your customers? Is it a consumer product? A business-to-business product? A good or a service? How does this classification change the focus of your e-marketing plan? Is your product unique enough to be patented? Check with the U.S. Patent and Trademark Office at **www.uspto.gov.**

2. Place your company's offerings into a product portfolio. Consider the broader impact of marketing a product item within a line or mix. Factors to consider are those such as price, image, complementary products, distribution relationship, and so on. Are there any special product features that selling on the Internet would allow you to add or force you to take away?

3. Does your chosen company have a brand name and brand mark? If not, design both. If so, evaluate the ability of the brand name and mark to communicate effectively to the target market. Is strong branding more or less important in an Internet environment? Why? What makes branding so important?

4. What will your company Internet address be? To check and see what URLs are available, go to www.companyname.com and try some out. Should your URL be the same as your company name? Why or why not? What happens if a customer mistypes your name? Should you register under alternative spellings?

5. Is the product packaged and labeled? How should it be packaged and why? Does the package and label design match other communications tools? How is this an opportunity to communicate with your customers?

6. Evaluate warranties or guarantees offered by your firm, including product return policies. How will customers return products they purchased from the Web site? Design the parameters for warranties and return policies. Should your return policy be stricter online than off-line? Why or why not?

APPLICATION EXERCISE

What is your favorite brand of sandwich cookie? If you're like most Americans, chances are it is Oreo. In fact, Oreos are so popular that many people think Oreo was the original sandwich cookie. But they're wrong. Sunshine first marketed its Hydrox sandwich cookie in 1908. Hydrox thrived until 1912, when Nabisco (now part of Kraft) launched Oreo. With Nabisco's superior distribution and advertising, Hydrox was soon outmatched. By 1998, Hydrox sales totaled $16 million, while Oreo's revenues were at $374 million. Hydrox has been purchased by Keebler (subsequently purchased by Kellogg), whose elves are trying to give the cookie a major facelift. You are part of the Keebler team deciding what to do with the Hydrox brand.

Activities

1. Can you re-create Hydrox through a name change? What kind of brand name could go head-to-head with Oreo? (Most people unfamiliar with Hydrox think it is a cleaning product.) Make a list of three to five possibilities.

2. How can you package your renewed sandwich cookie to make it more attractive on the shelf than Oreo? What about package size? Draft a brief packaging plan for the new Hydrox (or whatever name you chose).

3. Can you modify the original formula to make something new and more competitive? Will a brand extension work here? Why or why not?

CASE STUDY: Terracycle

TURNING WORM POOP INTO A PRODUCT

Environmentally friendly products have never been as hot as they are now, and the number of brands touting their "green" credentials has never been higher, but TerraCycle Plant Food may be the ultimate organic product to hit the market. A college student named Tom Szaky founded TerraCycle in 2003 after buddies from Canada, "where they have more liberal rules about growing certain plants," he says, taught him how to use worm droppings as cheap and eco-friendly fertilizer.

Szaky based his business model on recycling, starting with the trash that TerraCycle turns into compost and feeds to millions of red worms. The worm castings are then liquefied and put into previously used plastic water and soda bottles. Even the company's shipping cartons come from recycled materials.

TerraCycle's organic plant food hit the shelves in 2004 with labels boasting that it "Contains Liquefied Worm Poop!" It didn't take long for the products to take off. By 2006, the company had been named "The Coolest Little Start-Up in America" by *Inc.* magazine and had passed the $1 million mark in sales, growing as much as 300 percent from the previous year. They snagged shelf space in retail giants such as Target, Wal-Mart, and Home Depot.

Founder and president Tom Szaky liked to refer to his company as "the anti-Miracle-Gro." But the industry giant disagreed. It turns out that Scotts Miracle-Gro thought that, if anything, TerraCycle was encroaching too closely on its territory. In March of 2007, Scotts sued Szaky's fledgling company for trademark infringement and for making "false claims" that its organic products are superior to synthetic versions.

Small companies can easily fold under the weight of such a lawsuit. Even if they win, the legal costs can cripple them. So TerraCycle took their case to the Internet with the blog **www.suedbyscotts.com**, hoping to stir public support and raise contributions for its legal fees.

"I knew there was no way I could out-lawyer Scotts," Tom Szaky says. "So as I thought about it, I wondered what core competency our company had that we could exploit. Guerrilla marketing seemed to be the obvious answer." He adds that they hoped to get so much public support for their cause that Scotts would drop their suit.

The blog offered a comparison chart titled "David vs. Goliath" that illustrated the differences between the two companies. A photo of TerraCycle's modest headquarters behind a chain-link fence in New Jersey was in stark contrast to Scotts's grand, pillared entryway in Ohio. The blog listed TerraCycle's CEO's "major perquisite" as "unlimited free worm poop," whereas Scotts's CEO enjoys "personal use of company-owned aircraft."

The blog also countered Scotts's claims that consumers might be confused by its "overly similar yellow and green packaging" by posting photographs of TerraCycle's wacky and unusual bottles in their variety of shapes and sizes beside Miracle-Gro's uniform and professional looking ones. Scotts continued to insist that they change their labels, but TerraCycle's general counsel, Richard Ober Jr., says that changing packaging now would hurt their sales momentum. "There's the loss of customer recognition."

Su Lok, a Scotts spokesperson, argued that the blog was just one of TerraCycle's PR "tactics" and insisted that none of their arguments had merit. "We've spent a lot of time building up brands that consumers trust," she says, "and we are going to protect those brands."

Ira J. Levy, an intellectual property lawyer, warned that Scotts may have more to lose by pursuing TerraCycle than it's worth. "By pursuing a trade dress case," Levy says, "they can allow a small player to promote itself on the national stage. When word gets out that the mega-conglomerate is suing the little guy, you risk having bloggers launching boycotts, and the plaintiff ends up injuring his own business."

Which is precisely what Tom Szaky hoped would happen. The lawsuit wasn't something he would have wanted to fight, he said, but it was a chance to generate buzz. "It's like *The Art of War*," he explained. "You need to have a villain to be up against, and for us, that's Scotts."

Although the fight is over now (in September 2007 TerraCycle reached a settlement with Scotts and has agreed to change its packaging and its advertising claims), in its time, **www.suedbyscotts.com** gained massive media attention, leading major newspapers and magazines to cover the story, and hundreds of bloggers to defend TerraCycle's cause. Online donations actually totaled less than $1,000; however, overall company sales surged 122 percent within weeks of the blog's launch. And TerraCycle's main Web site, which averaged about 1,000 visitors a day, spiked to as high as 13,000.[24]

Questions

1. What type of consumer product is TerraCycle's plant food: convenience, shopping, specialty, or unsought? Why?

2. Go to **www.terracycle.net** and look at the types of products the company sells. Describe their product mix. How wide is it? Which basic product lines does it sell? How long are they?

3. Do you think that product line extension or product line contraction would make more sense for TerraCycle at this stage of the company's growth? Why?

4. How well do TerraCycle's bottles perform the four packaging functions discussed in this chapter? Compare TerraCycle's products to Miracle-Gro's (**www.scotts.com**). Do you think TerraCycle's package design distinguishes their products well enough from those of the industry giant, or are they similar enough to cause customer confusion?

COMPANY CLIPS: Kodak—Reinventing the Brand

Unquestionably, Kodak is one of the most recognized brands in the United States and the world. For over a century, Kodak was known as the company that brought the technology of photography into the everyday, aptly summed up in the tagline, "Celebrate the Moments of Your Life." Grocery stores, convenience stores, and camera stores contained aisles full of little yellow boxes of Kodak film in every possible speed. But after Kodak invented the digital camera, the company was faced with the challenge of leveraging the equity of its brand in a new competitive market—one that didn't include film.

Questions

1. Using Exhibit 10.1 as a guide, create a diagram that organizes the Kodak products mentioned in the video. How are changes in the company's product mix necessitating changes to the way managers market Kodak's offerings?

2. List the attributes of the Kodak brand. What benefits of branding has the company experienced over time? Have there been pitfalls to having a brand with such strong associations?

3. Describe the functions of packaging for a disposable camera.

Notes

1. "Coke, Pepsi to Sell Drinks with Stevia," *Atlantic Journal-Constitution*, December 18, 2008.
2. Ellen Byron, "Consumer Products Getting a Makeover," *Wall Street Journal*, June 2, 2008, http://online.wsj.com/article/SB121236166867236341.html.
3. "Kool-Aid Announces New Products and Better-for-You Brand Direction," *Yahoo! Finance*, May 27, 2008.
4. Mary E. Morrison, "Integrated Campaign Helps Cigna Reposition Brand," *BtoB's Vertical Insight Guide*, 2009, 20.
5. Ellen Byron, "Olay Highlights P&G's Push to Extend Brands," *Wall Street Journal*, January 15, 2010, http://online.wsj.com/article/SB10001424052748703436504574604642148088168.html.
6. Julie Jargon, "Campbell's Chief Looks for Splash of Innovation," *Wall Street Journal*, May 30, 2008, B8.
7. Al Ries, "The Pitfalls of Megabranding," *Advertising Age*, August 4, 2008, www.adage.com/article/al-ries/pitfalls-megabranding/130104.
8. David Kiley and Burt Helm, "The Great Trust Offensive," *BusinessWeek*, September 17, 2009, www.businessweek.com/magazine/content/09_39/b4148038492933.htm.
9. Jenn Abelson, "Seeking Savings, Some Ditch Brand Loyalty," *Boston Globe*, January 29, 2010, www.boston.com/news/local/massachusetts/articles/2010/01/29/shoppers_are_ditching_name_brands_for_store_brands.
10. Brad Broberg, "Costco Buying Power Makes Dent in Private-Label Wine Market," *Puget Sound Business Journal*, April 2, 2007, www.bizjournals.com/seattle/stories/2007/04/02/focus5.html.
11. Elaine Wong, "Retailers Rally behind Their 'Captive Brands,'" *Brandweek*, September 29, 2008, www.brandweek.com/bw/content_display/news-and-features/packaged-goods/e3if624dc1ee34cd1b59869d8b2059df883.
12. "Barnes & Noble and HP Launch a Cobranded e-Book Store," *Internet Retailer*, May 7, 2010, www.internetretailer.com/2010/05/07/barnes-noble-and-hp-launch-cobranded-e-book-store.
13. Douglas Quenqua, "A Way to Save and Still Have Crisp Clothes," *New York Times*, October 9, 2008, www.nytimes.com/2008/10/10/business/media/10adco.html.
14. Jim Edwards, "Brand Defense," *Brandweek*, August 25–September 1, 2008, S1, S2.
15. *Ibid.*
16. "P&G to Build Brands with Packaging and Design Focus," *Store Brands Decisions*, April 13, 2010, www.storebrandsdecisions.com/news/2010/04/13/pandg-to-build-brands-with-packaging-and-design-focus.
17. Deborah Ball, "The Perils of Packaging: Nestlé Aims for Easier Openings," *Wall Street Journal*, November 17, 2005, B1.
18. "Environmentally Responsible Packaging: Convenience vs. Conscience," *RetailWire*, April 30, 2008, www.retailwire.com.
19. Alissa Walker, "Spin the Bottle," *Fast Company*, June 2008, 54.
20. "Dell Expands 'Green' Packaging Initiative," *Austin American Statesman*, December 16, 2008.
21. Ted Mininni, "Packaging That Works for the Planet," *Brandweek*, April 23, 2007.
22. Dan Alaimo, "CPGmatters: Nutritional Labeling Provides CPGs, Retailers with Unique Competitive Edge," *RetailWire*, March 22, 2010, www.retailwire.com/discussions/sngl_discussion.cfm/14384.
23. Sherry F. Colb, "'Not Milk?': Dairy Petitions the FDA to Block Labels Like 'Soy Milk' on Non-Dairy Products," *Findlaw*, May 12, 2010, http://writ.news.findlaw.com/colb/20100512.html; Betsy Friauf, "Not Milk?" *Star-Telegram*, July 24, 2010, D1.
24. Jack Neff, "When the Worm Poop Hits the Fan, Market It," *Advertising Age*, April 23, 2007; Adam Aston, "Now That's Really a Turf War," *BusinessWeek*, April 23, 2007; Angus Loten, "After a Good Fight, David Forced to Settle with Goliath," www.lnc.com, September 24, 2007.

marketing&you: Results.

A higher score on this scale indicates that you are very brand conscious when you shop. You prefer to buy brands that are nationally known rather than private brands or generic brands. Conversely, a lower score suggests that you are not so brand conscious and tend to choose lower-priced, lesser-known brands.

Full HD
3D

chapter
11 Developing and Managing Products

Learning Outcomes

1 Explain the importance of developing new products and describe the six categories of new products

2 Explain the steps in the new-product development process

3 Explain why some products succeed and others fail

4 Discuss global issues in new-product development

5 Explain the diffusion process through which new products are adopted

6 Explain the concept of product life cycles

LO1
The Importance of New Products

New products are important to sustain growth, increase revenues and profits, and replace obsolete items. Research by *Bloomberg Businessweek* and the Boston Consulting Group revealed that the world's 25 most innovative companies have higher average stock returns and higher average revenue growth than companies that were not included in this group.[1] The *Bloomberg Businessweek*–Boston Consulting Group's list of the most innovative companies includes firms such as Apple, Google, Microsoft, and IBM.[2] These firms are known for innovative products. Other firms on the list are known for innovative products, business models, customer experiences, and/or processes.[3]

In this chapter we focus on new products, processes for developing new products, and how new products spread among consumers or business users, locally, nationally, and globally.

Being first on the market has a number of advantages. These include:[4]

→ **Increased sales through longer sales life:** The earlier the product reaches the market, relative to the competition, the longer its life can be.

→ **Increased margins:** The more innovative the product (i.e., the longer it remains unchallenged on the market), the longer consumers will accept a premium purchase price.

→ **Increased product loyalty:** Early adopters are likely to upgrade, customize, or purchase companion products.

> **New products are important to sustain growth, increase revenues and profits, and replace obsolete items.**

marketing&you.

Using the following scale, indicate your opinion on the line before each item.

STRONGLY DISAGREE ‹1 2 3 4 5 6› STRONGLY AGREE

_____ I like introducing new brands and products to my friends.

_____ I like helping people by providing them with information about many kinds of products.

_____ People ask me for information about products, places to shop, or sales.

_____ If someone asked where to get the best buy on several types of products, I could tell him or her where to shop.

_____ My friends think of me as a good source of information when it comes to new products or sales.

_____ I know a lot of different products, stores, and sales, and I like sharing this information.

Total your score. Read the chapter and find out what your score means at the end.

Source: Scale #18, *Marketing Scales Handbook*, G. Bruner, K. James, H. Hensel, eds. Vol. III. © by American Marketing Association.

© iStockphoto.com/Juan Facundo Mora Soria

© iStockphoto.com/zigymai

→ **More resale opportunities:** For components, commodities, or products that other companies can private-label, being first to market can often help ensure sales in other channels.

→ **Greater market responsiveness:** The faster that companies can bring products to market that satisfy new or changing customer needs, the greater the opportunity to capitalize on those products for margin lift and to increase brand recognition.

→ **A sustained leadership position:** Being first is the market position a competitor cannot take away. And repeated firsts establish companies as innovators and leaders in the market.

New technologies allow companies to test new ideas and introduce new products at speeds that were unimaginable just ten years ago. That makes innovation more efficient and less expensive. For example, Procter & Gamble does most of its concept testing in the U.S. online. Google conducts 50 to 200 search experiments at any given time. Even retailers such as Walmart are using sophisticated tracking systems to assess a wide range of data such as customer perceptions and product performance.[5]

One recent study analyzed four different, commonly used innovation strategies. These are: recruiting and cultivating human capital, spending on internal research and development, engaging in strategic alliances, and acquiring technology ventures. The researchers concluded that a company could achieve a higher level of innovation by pursuing any of these options. However, the most effective way to produce innovations over the long run is to hire and cultivate talented people.[6]

CATEGORIES OF NEW PRODUCTS

The term **new product** is somewhat confusing because its meaning varies widely. Actually, the term has several "correct" definitions. A product can be new to the world, to the market, to the producer or seller, or to some combination of these. There are six categories of new products:

→ **New-to-the-world products** (also called **discontinuous innovations**): These products create an entirely new market. New-to-the-world products represent the smallest category of new products. Ten of the most important new-to-the-world products introduced in the past 100 years are:

1. Penicillin

2. Transistor radio

3. Polio vaccine

4. Mosaic (the first graphic Web browser)

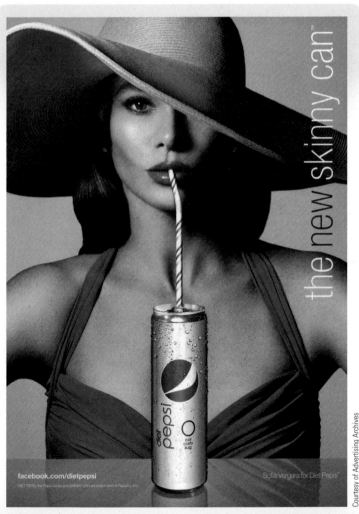

Courtesy of Advertising Archives

Pepsi introduced the new skinny Pepsi can at New York Fashion Week, which classifies as a new product with new packaging.

5. Microprocessor

6. Black-and-white television

7. Plain paper copier

8. Alto personal computer (prototype of today's PCs)

9. Microwave oven

10. Arpanet network (the groundwork for the Internet)

Source: Reprinted from the May 14, 2007, issue of *BusinessWeek* by special permission. Copyright © 2007 by the McGraw-Hill Companies, Inc.

→ ***New product lines:*** These products, which the firm has not previously offered, allow it to enter new or established markets. For example, Disney Consumer Products recently added a new line of fragrances targeting boys 4–11 in Latin communities under the brand names Pirates of the Caribbean and Buzz Lightyear.[7]

→ ***Additions to existing product lines:*** This category includes new products that supplement a firm's established line. The Gillette Company's new razor system called Pro-Glide is an example of a product line extension.

→ ***Improvements or revisions of existing products:*** The "new and improved" product might be significantly or slightly changed. Procter & Gamble's new "Dry Max" technology for Pampers Swaddlers and Cruisers diapers, Ariel and Dash laundry detergents with Actilift to help prevent stains from setting, and a reformulation of Pantene shampoo/conditioner are examples of new and improved products.[8]

→ ***Repositioned products:*** These are existing products targeted at new markets or market segments, or repositioned to change the current market's perception of the product or company. For example, following sales declines for several years, Talbot's decided to reposition from an outlet targeted at middle- and upper-class suburban ladies to a more youthful position. Its research revealed that women 65 years of age and older thought the brand was for "someone older." Talbot's is working on a complete merchandise and image overhaul.[9]

Another company trying to shake off an uncool image and reposition is Radio Shack. The company wants to be known as the place to buy smartphones rather than to find connectors, electronic cables, and batteries.[10]

→ ***Lower-priced products:*** This category refers to products that provide performance similar to competing brands at a lower price. The Hewlett-Packard LaserJet 3100 is a scanner, copier, printer, and fax machine combined. This product is priced lower than many conventional color copiers and much lower than the combined price of the four items purchased separately. Walmart is making headway penetrating the low-price fashion market dominated by Target. Procter & Gamble

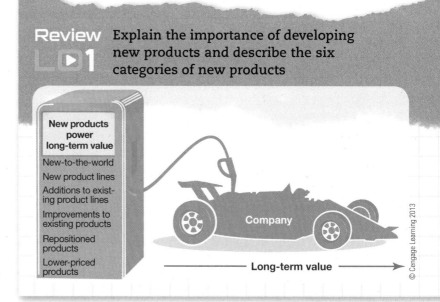

Review LO1 Explain the importance of developing new products and describe the six categories of new products

New products power long-term value

New-to-the-world
New product lines
Additions to existing product lines
Improvements to existing products
Repositioned products
Lower-priced products

Company

Long-term value

has introduced Tide Basic at a price about 20 percent lower than regular Tide. It has also repositioned Cheer as a value brand, reducing the retail price by about 13 percent.[11] The Global Perspectives later in this chapter provides another example of this category of new products.

LO2
The New-Product Development Process

The management consulting firm Booz Allen Hamilton has studied the new-product development process for over 30 years. After analyzing five major studies undertaken during this period, the firm concluded that the companies most likely to succeed in developing and introducing new products are those that take the following actions:

→ Make the long-term commitment needed to support innovation and new-product development.

→ Use a company-specific approach, driven by corporate objectives and strategies, with a well-defined new-product strategy at its core.

→ Capitalize on experience to achieve and maintain competitive advantage.

→ Establish an environment—a management style, organizational structure, and degree of top-management support—conducive to achieving company-specific new-product and corporate objectives.

Most companies follow a formal new-product development process, usually starting with a new-product strategy. Exhibit 11.1 traces the seven-step process, which is discussed in detail in this section. The exhibit is funnel-shaped to highlight the fact that each stage acts as a screen. The purpose is to filter out unworkable ideas.

NEW-PRODUCT STRATEGY

A **new-product strategy** links the new-product development process with the objectives of the marketing department, the business unit, and the corporation. A new-product strategy must be compatible with these objectives, and in turn, all three objectives must be consistent with one another. A new-product strategy is part of the organization's overall marketing strategy. It sharpens the focus and provides general guidelines for generating, screening, and evaluating new-product ideas. The new-product strategy specifies the roles that new products must play in the organization's overall plan and describes the characteristics of products the organization wants to offer and the markets it wants to serve.

The importance of having a well-thought-out new-product strategy is illustrated by a Dun & Bradstreet finding that for each successful new product introduced,

Exhibit 11.1 New-Product Development Process

1. New-product strategy
2. Idea generation
3. Idea screening
4. Business analysis
5. Development
6. Test marketing
7. Commercialization

New product

© Cengage Learning 2013

a company needs between 50 and 60 other new-product ideas somewhere in the new-product development process. Following a slow year in 2009, leading firms such as Procter & Gamble, Kimberly-Clark, Energizer Holdings, and Unilever committed to increasing new product activity in 2010.[13]

IDEA GENERATION

New-product ideas come from many sources, including customers, employees, distributors, competitors, vendors, research and development (R&D), and consultants.

→ **Customers:** The marketing concept suggests that customers' wants and needs should be the springboard for developing new products. Many of today's most innovative and successful marketers are introducing fewer new products, but they are taking steps to ensure that these "chosen few" are truly unique and better and, above all, really do address unmet consumer needs. How do they do that? Many firms rely on "co-creation," inventing new products along with their customers.[14] At **www.MyStarbucksIdea.com**, customers can make suggestions, other customers can vote on and discuss them, and Starbucks can see which ideas gain support.[15] Another approach for generating new product ideas is using what some companies are calling "customer innovation centers." The idea is to provide a forum for meeting with customers and directly involving them in the innovation process. Dr. John Horn, vice president for research and development at a 3M division, says that the goal is to understand what customers are trying to accomplish instead of what they say they need.[16] Customers might be better at designing products than elite teams of product designers.

→ **Employees:** Marketing personnel—advertising and marketing research employees, as well as salespeople—often create new-product ideas because they analyze and are involved in the marketplace. The very successful introduction of Post-it Notes started with an employee's idea. In 1974, the R&D department of 3M's commercial tape division developed and patented the adhesive component of Post-it Notes. However, it was a year before an employee of the commercial tape division, who sang in a church choir, identified a use for the adhesive. He had been using paper clips and slips of paper to mark places in hymn books. But the paper clips damaged his books, and the slips of paper fell out. The solution, as we now all know, was to apply the adhesive to small pieces of paper and sell them in packages.

→ **Distributors:** A well-trained sales force routinely asks distributors about needs that are not being met. Because they are closer to end users, distributors are often more aware of customer needs than are manufacturers. The inspiration for Rubbermaid's litter-free lunch box, named Sidekick, came from a distributor. The distributor suggested that Rubbermaid place some of its plastic containers inside a lunch box and sell the box as an alternative to plastic wrap and paper bags.

→ **Competitors:** No firms rely solely on internally generated ideas for new products. A big part of any organization's marketing intelligence system should be monitoring the performance of competitors' products. One purpose of competitive monitoring is to determine which, if any, of the competitors' products should be

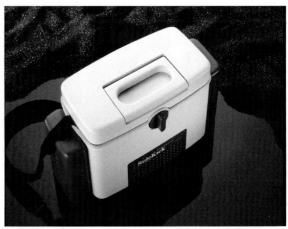

copied. There is plenty of information about competitors on the World Wide Web. For example, AltaVista (**www.altavista.com**) is a powerful index tool that can be used to locate information about products and companies. Fuld & Company's competitive intelligence guide provides links to a variety of market intelligence sites.

→ **Vendors:** 7-Eleven regularly forges partnerships with vendors to create proprietary products such as Candy Gulp (a plastic cup filled with gummies) and Blue Vanilla Laffy Taffy Rope candy developed by Nestlé's Wonka division exclusively for 7-Eleven.

→ **Research and development:** R&D is carried out in four distinct ways. Basic research is scientific research aimed at discovering new technologies. Applied research takes these new technologies and tries to find useful applications for them. **Product development** goes one step further by converting applications into marketable products. *Product modification* makes cosmetic or functional changes in existing products. Many new-product breakthroughs come from R&D activities. Procter & Gamble, the world's largest household goods manufacturer, has 9,000 research and development employees.[17]

Some companies are establishing innovation laboratories to complement or even replace lengthy R&D programs in which scientists spend years coming up with new-product ideas and then pass these ideas along to product developers, then to designers, and finally to marketers. Ideas labs focus on substantially increasing the speed of innovation. Motorola's Razr telephone was developed in an innovation lab called Moto City, located about 50 miles from company headquarters. Most of the development work was done by a team of engineers, designers, and marketers who worked in open spaces and waist-high cubicles. Innovation labs are used by a wide range of organizations including Boeing, Wrigley, Procter & Gamble, and the Mayo Clinic.

→ **Consultants:** Outside consultants are always available to examine a business and recommend product ideas. Examples include the Weston Group, Booz Allen Hamilton, and Management Decisions. Traditionally, consultants determine whether a company has a balanced portfolio of products and, if not, what new-product ideas are needed to offset the imbalance. For instance, an outside consultant conceived Airwick's highly successful Carpet Fresh carpet cleaner.

General Mills' Web site www.openinnovation.generalmills.com includes interactive features that let independent inventors and food scientists know what topics the company is interested in pursuing. If General Mills likes an idea it receives, it might pursue a licensing or joint venture arrangement.[18]

Creativity is the wellspring of new-product ideas, regardless of who comes up with them. A variety of approaches and techniques have been developed to stimulate creative thinking. The two considered most useful for generating new-product ideas are brainstorming and focus-group exercises. The goal of **brainstorming** is to get a group to think of unlimited ways to vary a product or solve a problem. Group members avoid criticism of an idea, no matter how ridiculous it might seem. Objective evaluation is postponed. The sheer quantity of ideas is what matters. As noted in Chapter 9, an objective of focus-group interviews is to stimulate insightful comments through group interaction. Focus groups usually consist of seven to ten people. Sometimes consumer focus groups generate excellent new-product ideas—for example, Cycle dog food, Stick-Up room deodorizers, and DustBuster vacuum cleaners. In the industrial market, machine tools, keyboard designs, aircraft interiors, and backhoe accessories have evolved from focus groups.

IDEA SCREENING

After new ideas have been generated, they pass through the first filter in the product development process. This stage, called **screening**, eliminates ideas that are inconsistent with the organization's new-product strategy or are obviously inappropriate for some other reason. The new-product committee, the new-product department, or some other formally appointed group performs the screening review. At General Motors, only one out of every 20 new car concepts developed will ever become a reality. That's not a bad percentage. In the pharmaceutical business, the percentage is much lower. Most new-product ideas are rejected at the screening stage. Whirlpool has a formalized process to sort through the thousands of new product ideas coming from inside and outside the company. For an idea to be successfully considered for approval to move to the next stage in the process, it must meet three criteria. It must meet a customer need in a fresh way, it must have the breadth to become a platform for related products, and it must increase earnings for the company.[19]

Concept tests are often used at the screening stage to rate concept (or product) alternatives. A **concept test** evaluates a new-product idea, usually before any prototype has been created. Typically, researchers get consumer reactions to descriptions and visual representations of a proposed product.

Concept tests are considered fairly good predictors of success for line extensions. They have also been relatively precise predictors of success for new products that are not copycat items, are not easily classified into existing product categories, and do not require major changes in consumer behavior—such as Betty Crocker Tuna Helper, Cycle dog food, and Libby's Fruit Float. However, concept tests are usually inaccurate in predicting the success of new products that create new consumption patterns and require major changes in consumer behavior—such as microwave ovens, videocassette recorders, computers, and word processors.

BUSINESS ANALYSIS

New-product ideas that survive the initial screening process move to the **business analysis** stage, where preliminary figures for demand, cost, sales, and profitability are calculated. For the first time, costs and revenues are estimated and compared. Depending on the nature of the product and the company, this process can be simple or complex.

The newness of the product, the size of the market, and the nature of the competition all affect the accuracy of revenue projections. In an established market such as soft drinks, industry estimates of total market size are available. Forecasting market share for a new entry is a bigger challenge.

Analyzing overall economic trends and their impact on estimated sales is especially important in product categories that are sensitive to fluctuations in the business cycle. If consumers view the economy as uncertain and risky, they will put off buying durable goods like major home appliances, automobiles, and homes. Likewise, business buyers postpone major equipment purchases if they expect a recession.

These questions are commonly asked during the business analysis stage:

→ What is the likely demand for the product?

→ What impact would the new product probably have on total sales, profits, market share, and return on investment?

screening
The first filter in the product development process, which eliminates ideas that are inconsistent with the organization's new-product strategy or are obviously inappropriate for some other reason.

concept test
A test to evaluate a new-product idea, usually before any prototype has been created.

business analysis
The second stage of the screening process where preliminary figures for demand, cost, sales, and profitability are calculated.

The Problem

Rupert Arles is looking for development opportunities in the mayonnaise market in the United States. He ultimately wants to determine how his mayonnaise brand, Spread-O, is performing in various cities in the United States.

To determine Spread-O's performance, Rupert must calculate the Brand Development Index (BDI). The BDI describes the level of development of market brand sales in comparison to category sales. In other words, Rupert is calculating how sales of Spread-O in specific cities compare to overall Mayonnaise sales in the same city.

The Metric

Through market research, Rupert has discovered that the category sales for Mayonnaise in the United States total $2,350,000. He also found the total mayonnaise sales for Dallas, Los Angeles, and Philadelphia. The company has provided Rupert with the total Spread-O sales for the nation and the same cities.

	Total Mayonnaise Sales	Total Spread-O Sales
	MS	SS
Nationally	$2,350,000,000	$574,281,686
Dallas	$45,167,734	$10,778,510
Philadelphia	$20,896,743	$2,405,602
Los Angeles	$39,378,603	$14,408,430

With this information, Rupert can now begin calculating the BDI. There are three steps: calculate the category sales percentage for all mayonnaise, calculate the brand sales percentage for Spread-O, and use those numbers to find the BDI for Spread-O.

To find the category sales percentage for mayonnaise, Rupert divides the total mayonnaise sales (MS) for one city by the MS for the nation. For Dallas, that means dividing $45,167,734 by $2,350,000,000:

Category Sales Percentage Dallas

$$= \frac{\text{Dallas MS}}{\text{National MS}} = \frac{\$45167734}{\$2350000000}$$
$$= 0.019 \times 100 = 1.9\%$$

Rupert then completes the category sales percentage for Philadelphia ($20,896,743/$2,350,000,000 = 0.89 percent) and Los Angeles ($39,378,603/$2,350,000,000 = 1.68 percent).

The next step is for Rupert to calculate the brand sales percentage for Spread-O. To find the brand sales percentage, Rupert divides the total Spread-O sales (SS) for one city by the SS for the nation. For Dallas, that means dividing $10,778,510 by $574,281,686:

Brand Sales Percentage Dallas

$$= \frac{\text{Dallas SS}}{\text{National SS}}$$
$$= \frac{\$10778510}{\$574281686}$$
$$= 0.018 \times 100 = 1.8\%$$

Rupert completes the brand sales percentage for Philadelphia ($2,405,602/$574,281,686

= 0.42 percent) and Los Angeles ($14,408,430/$574,281,686 = 2.51 percent).

Finally, using the category sales percentage and the brand sales percentage, Rupert can determine the BDI for Spread-O. The BDI is calculated by dividing the brand sales percentage for one city (SS) by the category sales percentage for that same city (MS). For Dallas, that means dividing 1.8 by 1.9 and multiplying by 100 to determine the level of development for Spread-O in Dallas:

$$\text{BDI} = \frac{\text{Dallas SS}}{\text{Dallas MS}} = \frac{1.8}{1.9}$$
$$= 0.95 \times 100 = 95$$

Rupert calculates the BDI for Philadelphia and Los Angeles the same way:

$$\text{BDI} = \frac{\text{Philly SS}}{\text{Philly MS}} = \frac{0.42}{0.89}$$
$$= 0.47 \times 100 = 47$$
$$\text{BDI} = \frac{\text{Los Angeles SS}}{\text{Los Angeles MS}} = \frac{2.51}{1.68}$$
$$= 1.49 \times 100 = 149$$

In Dallas, Spread-O has a BDI of 95, which is a moderately well-developed market from a brand perspective. The BDI for Philadelphia (47) is underdeveloped and the BDI for Los Angeles (149) is very well developed.

	Category Sales Percentage	Brand Sales Percentage	Brand Development Index (BDI)
Dallas	1.92%	1.90%	99
Philadelphia	0.89%	0.42%	47
Los Angeles	1.68%	2.51%	149

(Continued)

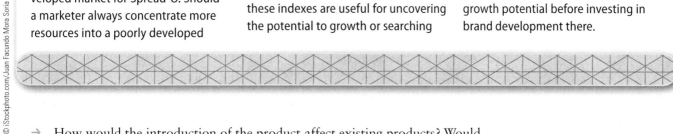

Management Decision

Once Rupert has determined the BDI, he must decide how to use the information that Philadelphia is a poorly developed market for Spread-O. Should a marketer always concentrate more resources into a poorly developed territory? The BDI is insufficient for providing a definitive answer. A poorly developed market might indicate an opportunity for growth, or it might indicate a difference in tastes. As such, these indexes are useful for uncovering the potential to growth or searching for barriers which prevent growth, but do not alone indicate that growth is possible. Rupert will have to do further research to determine whether or not Philadelphia has other indications of growth potential before investing in brand development there.

→ How would the introduction of the product affect existing products? Would the new product cannibalize existing products?

→ Would current customers benefit from the product?

→ Would the product enhance the image of the company's overall product mix?

→ Would the new product affect current employees in any way? Would it lead to hiring more people or reducing the size of the workforce?

→ What new facilities, if any, would be needed?

→ How might competitors respond?

→ What is the risk of failure? Is the company willing to take the risk?

Answering these questions might require studies of markets, competition, costs, and technical capabilities. But at the end of this stage, management should have a good understanding of the product's market potential. This understanding is important as costs increase dramatically once a product idea enters the development stage.

New ideas often face resistance, especially if they are perceived as risky to the company. The ideas that survive the business analysis stage are often ones whose creators blended a careful balance of political and managerial support early in the process.

DEVELOPMENT

In the early stage of **development**, the R&D or engineering department might develop a prototype of the product. During this stage, the firm should start sketching a marketing strategy. The marketing department should decide on the product's packaging, branding, labeling, and so forth. In addition, it should map out preliminary promotion, price, and distribution strategies. The feasibility of manufacturing the product at an acceptable cost should be thoroughly examined.

The development stage can last a long time and be very expensive. Crest toothpaste was in the development stage for 10 years. It took 18 years to develop Minute Rice, 15 years to develop the Polaroid Colorpack camera, 15 years to develop the Xerox copy machine, and 51 years to develop television. Gillette developed three shaving systems over a 27-year period (TracII, Atra, and Sensor) before introducing the Mach3 in 1998, and Fusion in 2006, and Fusion MVP series in 2009.[20]

The development process works best when all the involved areas (R&D, marketing, engineering, production, and even suppliers) work together rather than sequentially, a process called **simultaneous product development**. This approach allows firms to shorten the development process and reduce costs. With

development
The stage in the product development process in which a prototype is developed and a marketing strategy is outlined.

simultaneous product development
A team-oriented approach to new-product development.

In order to increase customer satisfaction, Procter & Gamble began developing a new formula for its Pantene hair care line using extensive scientific research in 2009.

simultaneous product development, all relevant functional areas and outside suppliers participate in all stages of the development process. Rather than proceeding through highly structured stages, the cross-functional team operates in unison. Involving key suppliers early in the process capitalizes on their knowledge and enables them to develop critical component parts.

The Internet is a useful tool for implementing simultaneous product development. On the Internet, multiple partners from a variety of locations can meet regularly to assess new-product ideas, analyze markets and demographics, and review cost information. Ideas judged to be feasible can quickly be converted into new products. Without the Internet it would be impossible to conduct simultaneous product development from different parts of the world.

Global R&D is important for two reasons. First, large companies have become global and are no longer focused only on one market. Global R&D is necessary to connect with customers in different parts of the world. Second, companies want to tap into the world's best talent.

Some firms use online brain trusts to solve technical problems. InnoCentive, Inc., is a network of 80,000 self-selected science problem solvers in 173 countries. Its clients include Boeing, DuPont, and Procter & Gamble. Procter & Gamble has another program called the Connect-and-Develop Model. When the company selects an idea for development, it no longer tries to develop it from the ground up with its own resources and time. Instead, it issues a brief to its network of thinkers, researchers, technology entrepreneurs, and inventors around the world, hoping to generate dialog, suggestions, and solutions. Olay Regenerist Eye Derma Pods, a top-selling skin care item, was developed through Connect-and-Develop.[21]

Innovative firms are also gathering a variety of R&D input from customers online. Google polls millions of Web page creators to determine the most relevant search results. LEGO Group uses the Internet to identify its most enthusiastic customers and to help design and market products. Threadless, a T-shirt company, and Ryz, an athletic shoe manufacturer, ask consumers to vote online for their favorites. The companies use these results to determine the products they sell over the Internet.

Laboratory tests are often conducted on prototype models during the development stage. User safety is an important aspect of laboratory testing, which actually subjects products to much more severe treatment than is expected by end users. The Consumer Product Safety Act of 1972 requires manufacturers to conduct a "reasonable testing program" to ensure that their products conform to established safety standards.

Many products that test well in the laboratory are also tried out in homes or businesses. Examples of product categories well suited for such use tests include human and pet food products, household cleaning products, and industrial chemicals and supplies. These products are all relatively inexpensive, and their performance characteristics are apparent to users. For example, Procter & Gamble tests a variety of personal and home-care products in the community around its Cincinnati, Ohio, headquarters.

TEST MARKETING

After products and marketing programs have been developed, they are usually tested in the marketplace. **Test marketing** is the limited introduction of a product and a marketing program to determine the reactions of potential customers in a market situation. Test marketing allows management to evaluate alternative strategies and to assess how well the various aspects of the marketing mix fit together. Even established products are test marketed to assess new marketing strategies.

The cities chosen as test sites should reflect market conditions in the new product's projected market area. Yet no "magic city" exists that can universally represent market conditions, and a product's success in one city doesn't guarantee that it will be a nationwide hit. When selecting test market cities, researchers should therefore find locations where the demographics and purchasing habits mirror the overall market. The company should also have good distribution in test cities. Moreover, test locations should be isolated from the media. If the TV stations in a particular market reached a very large area outside that market, the advertising used for the test product could pull in many consumers from outside the market. The product might then appear more successful than it really is. Exhibit 11.2 provides a useful checklist of criteria for selecting test markets.

test marketing
The limited introduction of a product and a marketing program to determine the reactions of potential customers in a market situation.

The High Costs of Test Marketing

Test marketing frequently takes one year or longer, and costs can exceed $1 million. Some products remain in test markets even longer. McDonald's spent 12 years developing and testing salads before introducing them. Despite the cost, many firms believe it is a lot better to fail in a test market than in a national introduction.

Because test marketing is so expensive, some companies do not test line extensions of well-known brands. For example, because the Folgers brand is well known, Procter & Gamble faced little risk in distributing its instant decaffeinated version nationally. Consolidated Foods Kitchen of Sara Lee followed the same approach with its frozen croissants. Other products introduced without being test marketed include General Foods' International Coffees, Quaker Oats' Chewy Granola Bars and Granola Dipps, and Pillsbury's Milk Break Bars.

The high cost of test marketing is not just financial. One unavoidable problem is that test marketing exposes the new product and its

Exhibit 11.2 Checklist for Selecting Test Markets

In choosing a test market, many criteria need to be considered, especially the following:

- Similarity to planned distribution outlets
- Relative isolation from other cities
- Availability of cooperative advertising media
- Diversified cross-section of ages, religions, cultural-societal preferences, etc.
- No atypical purchasing habits
- Representative population size
- Typical per capita income
- Good record as a test city, but not overly used
- Not easily "jammed" by competitors
- Stability of year-round sales
- No dominant television station; multiple newspapers, magazines, and radio stations
- Availability of research and audit services
- Availability of retailers that will cooperate
- Freedom from unusual influences, such as one industry's dominance or heavy tourism

© Cengage Learning 2013

marketing mix to competitors before its introduction. Thus, the element of surprise is lost. Competitors can also sabotage or "jam" a testing program by introducing their own sales promotion, pricing, or advertising campaign. The purpose is to hide or distort the normal conditions that the testing firm might expect in the market.

Alternatives to Test Marketing Many firms are looking for cheaper, faster, and safer alternatives to traditional test marketing. Information Resources, Inc., pioneered one alternative in the 1980s: single-source research using supermarket scanner data (discussed in Chapter 9). A typical scanner test costs about $300,000. Another alternative to traditional test marketing is **simulated (laboratory) market testing**. Advertising and other promotional materials for several products, including the test product, are shown to members of the product's target market. These people are then taken to shop at a mock or real store, where their purchases are recorded. Shopper behavior, including repeat purchasing, is monitored to assess the product's likely performance under true market conditions. Research firms offer simulated market tests for $25,000 to $100,000, compared to $1 million or more for full-scale test marketing.

Online Test Marketing Despite these alternatives, most firms still consider test marketing essential for most new products. The high price of failure simply prohibits the widespread introduction of most new products without testing. Many firms are finding that the Internet offers a fast, cost-effective way to conduct test marketing.

Procter & Gamble uses the Internet to assess customer demand for potential new products. Many products that are not available in grocery stores or drugstores can be sampled from P&G's corporate Web site (**www.pg.com**).

Other consumer goods firms that use online test marketing include General Mills and Quaker Oats. Other Web sites have appeared that offer consumers prototype products developed by all sizes of firms.

COMMERCIALIZATION

The final stage in the new-product development process is **commercialization**, the decision to market a product. The decision to commercialize the product sets several tasks in motion: ordering production materials and equipment, starting production, building inventories, shipping the product to field distribution points, training the sales force, announcing the new product to the trade, and advertising to potential customers.

The time from the initial commercialization decision to the product's actual introduction varies. It can range from a few weeks for simple products that use existing equipment to several years for technical products that require custom manufacturing equipment.

The total cost of development and initial introduction can be staggering. Gillette spent $750 million developing the Mach3, and the first-year marketing budget for the new three-bladed razor was $300 million.

For some products, a well-planned Internet campaign can provide new-product information for people

Review LO2 Explain the steps in the new-product development process

New-product strategy
Idea generation
Idea screening
Business analysis
Development
Test marketing
Commercialization

Number of new product ideas

Time

© Cengage Learning 2013

who are looking for the solutions that a particular new product offers. Attempting to reach customers at the point in time when they need a product is much more cost-effective and efficient than communicating with a target market that might eventually have a need for the product.

LO3
Why Some Products Succeed and Others Fail

Despite the amount spent on developing and testing new products, a large proportion of new-product introductions fail. Products fail for a number of reasons. One common reason is that they simply do not offer any discernible benefit compared to existing products. Another commonly cited factor in new-product failures is a poor match between product features and customer desires. For example, there are telephone systems on the market with over 700 different functions, although the average user is happy with just 10 functions. Other reasons for failure include overestimation of market size, incorrect positioning, a price too high or too low, inadequate distribution, poor promotion, or simply an inferior product compared to those of competitors.

In 2009, Procter & Gamble's then CEO A. G. Lafley reported that the new product failure in its industry is 80–85 percent. In contrast, P&G has a failure rate of under 50 percent.[22] Lafley said that P&G has become more successful than other firms in the industry by clarifying and simplifying the innovation process, setting checkpoints with clear measures for each stage of the process from idea generation through commercialization.[23]

Failure can be a matter of degree. Absolute failure occurs when a company cannot recoup its development, marketing, and production costs—the product actually loses money for the company. A relative product failure results when the product returns a profit but fails to achieve sales, profit, or market share goals. Some highly publicized new product failures include the Ford Edsel (1957–1959), Sony Betamax (1975), Webvan.com (1999–2001), and New Coke (1985).[24]

High costs and other risks of developing and testing new products do not stop many companies, such as Rubbermaid, Colgate-Palmolive, Campbell's Soup, 3M, and Procter & Gamble, from aggressively developing and introducing new products.

Dyson vacuums are held in high esteem and are very successful products. The Dyson Ball demonstrates innovative structure, making a chore more efficient and easier.

Review
LO 3
Explain why some products succeed and others fail

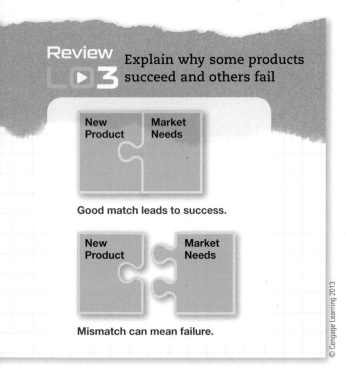

New Product | Market Needs

Good match leads to success.

New Product | Market Needs

Mismatch can mean failure.

© Cengage Learning 2013

The most important factor in successful new-product introduction is a good match between the product and market needs—as the marketing concept would predict. Successful new products deliver a meaningful and perceivable benefit to a sizable number of people or organizations and are different in some meaningful way from their intended substitutes. Firms that routinely experience success in new-product introductions tend to share the following characteristics.[25]

→ A history of carefully listening to customers

→ An obsession with producing the best product possible

→ A vision of what the market will be like in the future

→ Strong leadership

→ A commitment to new-product development

→ A project-based team approach to new-product development

→ Getting every aspect of the product development process right

→ Willingness to fail occasionally

LO 4
Global Issues in New-Product Development

Increasing globalization of markets and of competition provides a reason for multinational firms to consider new-product development from a worldwide perspective. That perspective includes developing countries as well as more established markets.

A firm that starts with a global strategy is better able to develop products that are marketable worldwide. In many multinational corporations, every product is developed for potential worldwide distribution, and unique market requirements are built in whenever possible. Procter & Gamble introduced Pampers Phases into global markets within one month of introducing the product in the United States. P&G's goal was to have the product on the shelf in 90 countries within one year. The objective was to establish brand loyalty among dealers and consumers before foreign competitors could react.

Some global marketers design their products to meet regulations in their major markets and then, if necessary, meet smaller markets' requirements country by country. Nissan develops lead-country car models that, with minor changes, can be sold in most markets. With this approach, Nissan has been able to reduce the number of its basic models from 48 to 18.

Developing countries represent huge automobile markets, but not at prevailing international prices. Renault SA introduced the Dacia Logan, an unassuming econocar with exposed screws, a coarse fabric interior, and a 90-horsepower motor. The Logan sells for about $7,300 in Eastern Europe and the Middle East and $9,000 in Western Europe and has become more successful than predicted. Rivals such as

global perspectives

A $35 iPad: No Way!

It looks like an iPad, only it's one-fourteenth the cost: India has unveiled the prototype of a $35 basic touch-screen tablet that is aimed at students and that it hopes to bring into production in the coming years.

If the government can find a manufacturer, the Linux operating system–based computer would be the latest in a string of "world's cheapest" innovations to hit the market out of India, already home to the $3,000 compact Nano car, the $16 water purifier, and $2,000 open-heart surgery.

The tablet's functions include word processing, Web browsing, and video-conferencing. It has a solar power option, too—important for India's energy-starved rural communities—although it costs extra.

"This is our answer to MIT's $100 computer," Kapil Sibal, human resource development minister, told *The Economic Times* when he unveiled the device.

In 2005, Nicholas Negroponte, co-founder of the Massachusetts Institute of Technology's Media Lab, unveiled a prototype of a $100 laptop for children in the developing world. Unfortunately, the laptop ended up costing about $200, and India rejected it as too expensive. Instead, the country embarked on a multiyear effort to develop an even lower-priced option.

Sibal turned to students and professors at India's elite technical universities to develop the $35 tablet after a "lukewarm" response from the private sector. India plans to subsidize the cost of the tablet for its students, bringing the purchase price down to around $20, but he hopes to eventually get the cost down to $10.

"Depending on the quality of material they are using, certainly it's plausible," said Sarah Rotman Epps, an analyst at Forrester Research. "The question is, is it good enough for students?" Mamta Varma, a ministry spokeswoman, said falling hardware costs and intelligent design make the price plausible. The tablet doesn't have a hard disk but uses a memory card, much like a camera or mobile phone. The tablet design cuts hardware costs, as does the use of open-source software, she said.

Varma said that several global manufacturers, including at least one from Taiwan, have shown interest in making the device but that no manufacturing or distribution deals have been finalized. She declined to name the companies.

Profitability is also a question for the $35 machine.

Epps said government subsidies or dual marketing—where higher-priced sales in the developed world are used to subsidize low-cost sales in markets like India—could persuade a manufacturer to come on board.[29]

What other products can you think of that might be candidates for what has been called "frugal engineering?" Write a memo to a director of marketing research for a U.S. manufacturer proposing and justifying your recommendation.

Toyota Motor Corp. are preparing competitive entries priced under $10,000.[26] India's Tata Motors Ltd launched a new compact car called the Tata Nano that has a sticker price around $3,000.[27]

Some companies could not sell their products at affordable prices and still make an adequate profit in many countries. GE Healthcare engineers figured out a way to develop the MAC 400, a portable electrocardiograph (ECG) machine selling for $1,500 in India. The MAC 400 was based upon technology developed for a U.S. ECG that sold for $5.4 million.[28] The Global Perspectives box in this chapter provides another example of adapting a product designed for developed countries to one for developing countries.

We often hear about how popular American products are in foreign countries. Recently, U.S. companies such as Levi Strauss, Coca-Cola, Nabisco, and Nike have been

Review LO4 Discuss global issues in new-product development

- Single product worldwide
- Modification of products
- Multiple products in multiple countries

finding that products popular in foreign markets can become hits in the United States. For example, Häagen-Dazs' ice cream flavor *dulce de leche*, named after a caramelized milk drink that is popular in Argentina, was originally introduced in Buenos Aires.

In other cases, former alliance partners have become competitors. For years, Shanghai Automotive Industry Corp. has worked with General Motors and Volkswagen to build cars for Chinese consumers. The Chinese automaker now markets its own products in global markets, competing with its partners.

LO5
The Spread of New Products

Managers have a better chance of successfully marketing products if they understand how consumers learn about and adopt products. A person who buys a new product never before tried might ultimately become an **adopter**, a consumer who was happy enough with his or her trial experience with a product to use it again.

DIFFUSION OF INNOVATION

An **innovation** is a product perceived as new by a potential adopter. It really doesn't matter whether the product is "new to the world" or some other category of new product. If it is new to a potential adopter, it is an innovation in this context. **Diffusion** is the process by which the adoption of an innovation spreads.

Five categories of adopters participate in the diffusion process:

→ **Innovators:** the first 2.5 percent of all those who adopt the product. Innovators are almost obsessed with trying new ideas and products. In addition to having higher incomes, they are more worldly and more active outside their community than non-innovators. They rely less on group norms and are more self-confident. Because they are well-educated, they are more likely to get their information from scientific sources and experts. Innovators are characterized as being venturesome.

→ **Early adopters:** the next 13.5 percent to adopt the product. Although early adopters are not the very first, they do adopt early in the product's life cycle. Compared to innovators, they rely much more on group norms and values. They are also more oriented to the local community, in contrast to the innovators' worldly outlook. Early adopters are more likely than innovators to be opinion leaders because of their closer affiliation with groups. Apple Computer spends its entire marketing budget attempting to appeal to early adopters. The attention paid to viral, buzz, or word-of-mouth advertising is on the rise. Marketers focus a lot of attention identifying the group that begins the viral marketing chain—the *influencers*. Part of the challenge is that this group of customers is not distinguished by demographics but by behavior. According to *eMarketer*, influencers come from all age, gender, and income groups, and they do not use media any differently than other users who are considered followers. The

The iPhone is popular, not only for its looks, but also for the fun, useful, and completely new applications (apps) it offers its users—something nearly irresistible to early adopters of tech gadgets.

© QI HENG/Xinhua /Landov

characteristic influencers share is the desire to talk to others about their experiences with goods and services.[30] This type of opinion leadership is also important for professionals. One study examined how prescriptions for a new drug spread from one physician to another. The researchers were actually able to map the word-of-mouth among physicians practicing in a large city.[31] The respect of others is a dominant characteristic of early adopters. Exhibit 11.3 identifies some other characteristics of early adopters.

Exhibit 11.3 Who Are Early Adopters?

- 77 million Americans, 36 million U.S. heads of household
- About 40 percent of Gen Xers (ages 28–41) are early adopters
- 49 percent own an MP3 player
- 70 percent have broadband Internet at home
- Roughly 60 percent are "sick of advertising today"
- 1.5 times more likely than the general population to own a laptop

Source: Daniel B. Honigman, "Who's on First?" *Marketing News*, November 1, 2007, 15. Taken from Forrester Research's "The State of Consumers and Technology: Benchmark 2007" survey, September 2007.

- **Early majority:** the next 34 percent to adopt. The early majority weighs the pros and cons before adopting a new product. They are likely to collect more information and evaluate more brands than early adopters, therefore extending the adoption process. They rely on the group for information but are unlikely to be opinion leaders themselves. Instead, they tend to be opinion leaders' friends and neighbors. *The Wall Street Journal* recently reported that e-readers such as Amazon.com's Kindle and Apple's iPad are just beginning to spread beyond the early adopter stage to the early majority stage.[32]

Marketers know that if our friends buy something, there is a better-than-average chance that we'll buy it too. For example, researchers at Yahoo found that if someone clicked on an online ad, the people on his or her chat buddy list were three or more times more likely to click on it than the average person.[33] The early majority is an important link in the process of diffusing new ideas because they are positioned between earlier and later adopters. A dominant characteristic of the early majority is deliberateness.

- **Late majority:** the next 34 percent to adopt. The late majority adopts a new product because most of their friends have already adopted it. Because they also rely on group norms, their adoption stems from pressure to conform. This group tends to be older and below average in income and education. They depend mainly on word-of-mouth communication rather than on the mass media. The dominant characteristic of the late majority is skepticism.

- **Laggards:** the final 16 percent to adopt. Like innovators, laggards do not rely on group norms, but their independence is rooted in their ties to tradition. Thus, the past heavily influences their decisions. By the time laggards adopt an innovation, it has probably become outmoded and been replaced by something else. For example, they might have bought their first black-and-white TV set after color television was already widely diffused. Laggards have the longest adoption time and the lowest socioeconomic status. They tend to be suspicious of new products and alienated from a rapidly advancing society. The dominant value of laggards is tradition. Marketers typically ignore laggards, who do not seem to be motivated by advertising or personal selling and are virtually impossible to reach online.

New-product ideas come from many sources, including customers, employees, distributors, competitors, vendors, R&D, and consultants.

Note that some product categories, such as black and white televisions, might never have been adopted by 100 percent of the population. The adopter categories refer to all of those who will eventually adopt a product, and not the entire population.

PRODUCT CHARACTERISTICS AND THE RATE OF ADOPTION

Five product characteristics can be used to predict and explain the rate of acceptance and diffusion of a new product:

→ **Complexity:** the degree of difficulty involved in understanding and using a new product. The more complex the product, the slower is its diffusion. For instance, DVD recorders have been around for a few years, but they have been bought mostly by early adopters willing to go to the trouble of linking the gadgets to their PCs or to pay high prices for the first stand-alone machines that connect to a TV.

→ **Compatibility:** the degree to which the new product is consistent with existing values and product knowledge, past experiences, and current needs. Incompatible products diffuse more slowly than compatible products. For example, the introduction of contraceptives is incompatible in countries where religious beliefs discourage the use of birth control techniques.

→ **Relative advantage:** the degree to which a product is perceived as superior to existing substitutes. For example, because it reduces cooking time, the microwave oven has a clear relative advantage over a conventional oven.

→ **Observability:** the degree to which the benefits or other results of using the product can be observed by others and communicated to target customers. For instance, fashion items and automobiles are highly visible and more observable than personal-care items.

→ **"Trialability":** the degree to which a product can be tried on a limited basis. It is much easier to try a new toothpaste or breakfast cereal than a new automobile or microcomputer. Demonstrations in showrooms and test-drives are different from in-home trial use. To stimulate trials, marketers use free-sampling programs, tasting displays, and small package sizes.

Exhibit 11.4 shows the time it took for various audio and video new products to reach sales of 150 million units. Where it took 89 years for the telephone to reach 150 million users, it only took Facebook 5 years to reach 150 million users. The iPad is projected to reach 150 million users in 2015—it was introduced in 2010. Facebook adoptions reached 500 million in 2010.[34]

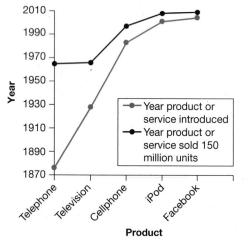

Exhibit 11.4 Diffusion of Technology

Diffusion of Technology adapted from Jessi Hempel, "How Facebook is Taking Over Our Lives," *Fortune*, March 2, 2009.

MARKETING IMPLICATIONS OF THE ADOPTION PROCESS

Two types of communication aid the diffusion process: *word-of-mouth communication* among consumers and communication from marketers to consumers. Word-of-mouth communication within and across groups speeds diffusion. Opinion leaders discuss new products with their followers and with other opinion leaders. Several studies reported in *eMarketer* revealed that word-of-mouth is the method most preferred by college students to learn about new goods and services. This includes advice from family and friends, social networks, blogs, and viral video. Television advertising ranked second followed by free samples.[35]

Marketers must therefore ensure that opinion leaders have the types of information desired in the media that they use. Suppliers of some products, such as professional and healthcare services, rely almost solely on word-of-mouth communication for new business.

The Internet plays an important role in generating word-of-mouth communications. In fact, JWT, a large advertising agency located in New York, estimates that over 85 percent of the country's top 1,000 marketing firms have some form of word-of-mouth communications strategy.[36] These efforts are often referred to as buzz marketing.

Often marketers recruit a core group of opinion leaders to get the buzz going. UPN recruited Alloy.com, a shopping and lifestyle site aimed at teenage girls, to develop a buzz campaign for the TV series *America's Top Model*. After analyzing the chatter on its site, Alloy identified 500 well-connected girls who had expressed interest in the show. Alloy provided the teens with *America's Top Model* party kits and encouraged them to invite an average of four friends over to their homes for gatherings themed around the TV show. According to Alloy, the results were very good.[37]

Business marketers have also developed strategies for obtaining online feedback and ideas from early adopters. Microsoft Corp. has a Most Valuable Professional (MVP) program that has 4,000 participants in 90 countries. MVPs give Microsoft user feedback for almost every new product, from Windows to Xbox. Sony's Web community of about 850 early adopters is called "Sony Frontline."[38]

The second type of communication aiding the diffusion process is communication directly from the marketer to potential adopters. Messages directed toward early adopters should normally use different appeals than messages directed toward the early majority, the late majority, or the laggards. Early adopters are more important than innovators because they make up a larger group, are more socially active, and are usually opinion leaders.

Researchers at DoubleClick found that 39 percent of early adopters reported spending five or more hours online each day, compared to 23 percent of other categories of adopters. Furthermore, 40 percent of early adopters reported using Web sites to learn about products, compared to 31 percent of other categories of adopters. Also, 19 percent of early adopters reported using online advertising as an information source, compared to 8 percent of the other respondents.[39]

As the focus of a promotional campaign shifts from early adopters to the early majority and the late majority, marketers should study the dominant characteristics, buying behavior, and media characteristics of these target

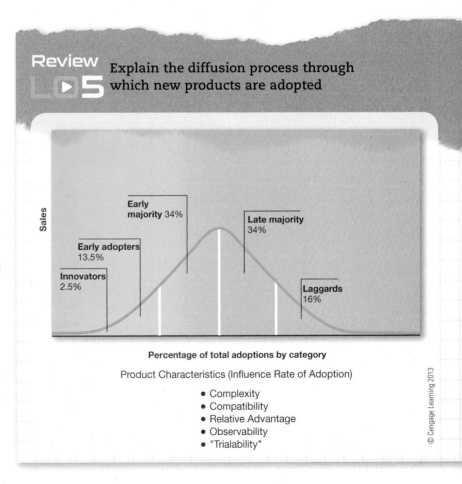

Review LO5 Explain the diffusion process through which new products are adopted

Sales

Innovators 2.5%

Early adopters 13.5%

Early majority 34%

Late majority 34%

Laggards 16%

Percentage of total adoptions by category

Product Characteristics (Influence Rate of Adoption)

- Complexity
- Compatibility
- Relative Advantage
- Observability
- "Trialability"

© Cengage Learning 2013

© iStockphoto.com/Juan Facundo Mora Soria

CHAPTER 11 DEVELOPING AND MANAGING PRODUCTS

403

CHAPTER **11** DEVELOPING AND MANAGING PRODUCTS

product life cycle (PLC)
A biological metaphor that traces the stages of a product's acceptance, from its introduction (birth) to its decline (death).

product category
All brands that satisfy a particular type of need.

markets. Then they should revise messages and a media strategy to fit. The diffusion model helps guide marketers in developing and implementing promotion strategy.

LO6
Product Life Cycles

The **product life cycle (PLC)** is one of the most familiar concepts in marketing. Few other general concepts have been so widely discussed. Although some researchers and consultants have challenged the theoretical basis and managerial value of the PLC, many believe it is a useful marketing management diagnostic tool and a general guide for marketing planning in various "life-cycle" stages.

The product life cycle is a biological metaphor that traces the stages of a product's acceptance, from its introduction (birth) to its decline (death). As Exhibit 11.5 shows, a product progresses through four major stages: introduction, growth, maturity, and decline.

The PLC concept can be used to analyze a brand, a product form, or a product category. The PLC for a product form is usually longer than the PLC for any one brand. The exception would be a brand that was the first and last competitor in a product form market. In that situation, the brand and product form life cycles would be equal in length. Product categories have the longest life cycles. A **product category** includes all brands that satisfy a particular type of need such as shaving products, passenger automobiles, or soft drinks.

The time a product spends in any one stage of the life cycle can vary dramatically. Some products, such as fad items, move through the entire cycle in weeks. Fads are typically characterized by a sudden and unpredictable spike in sales followed by a rather abrupt decline.[40] Examples of fad items are Silly Bandz, Beanie Babies, and Crocs. Others, such as electric clothes washers and dryers, stay in the maturity stage for decades. Exhibit 11.5 illustrates the typical life cycle for a consumer durable good, such as a washer or dryer. In contrast, Exhibit 11.6 illustrates typical life cycles for styles (such as formal, business, or casual clothing), fashions (such as miniskirts or baggy jeans), and fads (such as leopard-print clothing). Changes in a product, its uses, its image, or its positioning can extend that product's life cycle.

As product life cycles continue to decrease, compressing development cycles and accelerating new-product developments are critical. The PLC concept does not tell managers the length of a product's life

Exhibit 11.5 Four Stages of the Product Life Cycle

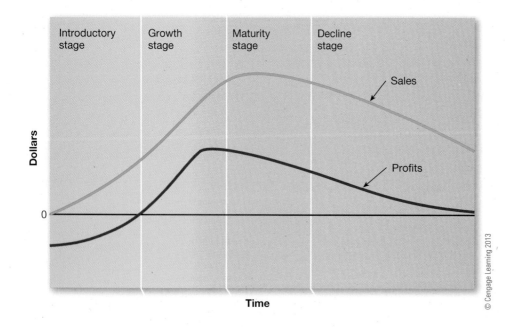

© Cengage Learning 2013

cycle or its duration in any stage. It does not dictate marketing strategy. It is simply a tool to help marketers forecast future events and suggest appropriate strategies. Look at Exhibit 11.7. What conclusions can you draw about the PLCs of Widgets A, B, and C over a five-year period?

INTRODUCTORY STAGE

The **introductory stage** of the product life cycle represents the full-scale launch of a new product into the marketplace. Computer databases for personal use, room-deodorizing air-conditioning filters, and wind-powered home electric generators are all product categories that have recently entered the PLC. A high failure rate, little competition, frequent product modification, and limited distribution typify the introductory stage of the PLC.

Marketing costs in the introductory stage are normally high for several reasons. High dealer margins are often needed to obtain adequate distribution, and incentives are needed to get consumers to try the new product. Advertising expenses are high because of the need to educate consumers about the new product's benefits. Production costs are also often high in this stage, as product and manufacturing flaws are identified and corrected and efforts are undertaken to develop mass-production economies.

As Exhibit 11.5 illustrates, sales normally increase slowly during the introductory stage. Moreover, profits are usually negative because of R&D costs, factory tooling, and high introduction costs. The length of the introductory phase is largely determined by product characteristics, such as the product's advantages over substitute products, the educational effort required to make the product known, and management's commitment of resources to the new item. A short introductory period is usually preferred to help reduce the impact of negative earnings and cash flows. As soon as the product gets off the ground, the financial burden should begin to diminish. Also, a short introduction helps dispel some of the uncertainty as to whether the new product will be successful.

Promotion strategy in the introductory stage focuses on developing product awareness and informing consumers about the product category's potential benefits. At this stage, the communication challenge is to stimulate primary demand—demand for the product in general rather than for a specific brand. Intensive personal selling is often required to gain acceptance for the product among wholesalers and retailers. Promotion of convenience products often requires heavy consumer sampling and couponing. Shopping and specialty products demand educational advertising and personal selling to the final consumer.

GROWTH STAGE

If a product category survives the introductory stage, it advances to the **growth stage** of the life cycle. In this stage, sales typically grow at an increasing rate, many

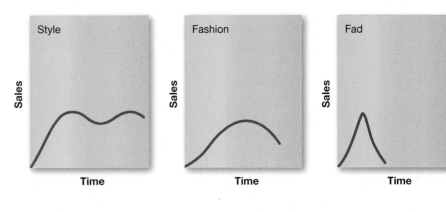

Exhibit 11.6 Product Life Cycles for Styles, Fashions, and Fads

Style — Sales / Time

Fashion — Sales / Time

Fad — Sales / Time

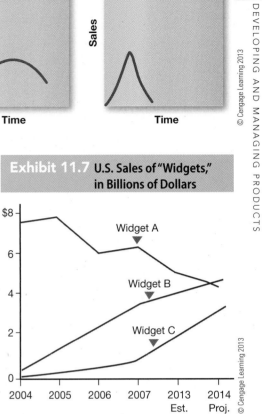

Exhibit 11.7 U.S. Sales of "Widgets," in Billions of Dollars

Widget A
Widget B
Widget C

2004 2005 2006 2007 2013 Est. 2014 Proj.

introductory stage
The first stage of the product life cycle in which the full-scale launch of a new product into the marketplace occurs.

growth stage
The second stage of the product life cycle when sales typically grow at an increasing rate, many competitors enter the market, large companies might start acquiring small pioneering firms, and profits are healthy.

competitors enter the market, and large companies might start to acquire small pioneering firms. Profits rise rapidly in the growth stage, reach their peak, and begin declining as competition intensifies. Emphasis switches from primary demand promotion (for example, promoting smartphones) to aggressive brand advertising and communication of the differences between brands (for example, promoting the iPhone versus the BlackBerry and Palm Pre). Price reductions for earlier models might accompany the introduction of new ones, as when Apple reduced the price of its basic 3G, 8-gigabyte iPhone from $199 to $99.

Distribution becomes a major key to success during the growth stage, as well as in later stages. Manufacturers scramble to sign up dealers and distributors and to build long-term relationships. Without adequate distribution, it is impossible to establish a strong market position. The intense competition among electronic book readers such as the Kindle focuses on distribution as well as price and performance.[41]

MATURITY STAGE

A period during which sales increase at a decreasing rate signals the beginning of the **maturity stage** of the life cycle. New users cannot be added indefinitely and sooner or later the market approaches saturation. Normally, this is the longest stage of the product life cycle. Many major household appliances are in the maturity stage of their life cycles.

For shopping products and many specialty products, annual models begin to appear during the maturity stage. Product lines are lengthened to appeal to additional market segments. Service and repair assume more important roles as manufacturers strive to distinguish their products from others. Product design changes tend to become stylistic (How can the product be made different?) rather than functional. (How can the product be made better?)

As prices and profits continue to fall, marginal competitors start dropping out of the market. Dealer margins also shrink, resulting in less shelf space for mature items, lower dealer inventories, and a general reluctance to promote the product. Thus, promotion to dealers often intensifies during this stage in order to retain loyalty.

Heavy consumer promotion by the manufacturer is also required to maintain market share. Consider these well-known examples of competition in the maturity stage: the "cola war" featuring Coke and Pepsi, the "beer war" featuring Anheuser-Busch's Budweiser brands and Philip Morris's Miller brands, and the "burger wars" pitting leader McDonald's against challengers Burger King and Wendy's.

Another characteristic of the maturity stage is the emergence of "niche marketers" that target narrow, well-defined, underserved segments of a market. Starbucks Coffee targets its gourmet line at the only segment of the coffee market that is growing: new, young, affluent coffee drinkers.

© DANIEL ACKER/Bloomberg via Getty Images

DECLINE STAGE

A long-run drop in sales signals the beginning of the **decline stage**. The rate of decline is governed by how rapidly consumer tastes change or substitute products are adopted. Many convenience products and fad items lose their market overnight, leaving large inventories of unsold items, such as designer jeans. Others die more slowly.

According to a report from the International Federation of the Phonographic Industry, CD sales in the United States fell by 14 percent in 2007. They have fallen 30 percent worldwide in the past three years.[42] It appears that the popularity of iTunes and other digital download options is rapidly making CDs obsolete.

Landline telephone service is another example of a product in the decline stage of the product life cycle. After peaking at about 141 million in 2000, the number of U.S. home phones fell to 78 million by the end of 2008, according to the Federal Communications Commission.[43] People abandoning landlines to go wireless and households replacing landlines with Internet phones have both contributed to this long-term decline.

Some firms have developed successful strategies for marketing products in the decline stage of the product life cycle. They eliminate all nonessential marketing expenses and let sales decline as more and more customers discontinue purchasing the products. Eventually, the product is withdrawn from the market.

Some firms practice what management sage Peter Drucker has called "organized abandonment," which is based upon a periodic audit of all goods and services that a firm markets. One key question is, if we weren't already marketing the product, would we be willing to introduce it now? If the answer is no, the product should be carefully considered as a candidate for elimination from the product mix.

In 2010, Procter & Gamble considered selling some brands that were viewed as extraneous to P&G's focus on health, beauty, and nonfood household staples. Brands such as Duracell batteries, Pringles potato chips, Iams pet food, and Braun small appliances were identified as possible candidates, not because they were in the decline stage of their life cycles but because they were not contributing enough to P&G's growth goals.[44]

decline stage
The fourth stage of the product life cycle, characterized by a long-run drop in sales

IMPLICATIONS FOR MARKETING MANAGEMENT

The product life cycle concept encourages marketing managers to plan so that they can take the initiative instead of reacting to past events. The PLC is especially useful as a predicting or forecasting tool. Because products pass through distinctive stages, it is often possible to estimate a product's location on the curve using historical data. Profits, like sales, tend to follow a predictable path over a product's life cycle.

Exhibit 11.8 shows the relationship between the adopter categories and stages of the PLC. Note that the various categories of adopters first buy products in different stages of the life cycle. Almost all sales in the maturity and decline stages represent repeat purchasing.

Exhibit 11.8 Relationship between the Diffusion Process and the Product Life Cycle

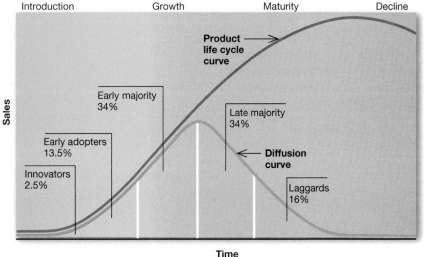

Marketing Mix Strategy	Product Life Cycle Stage			
	Introductory	Growth	Maturity	Decline
Product Strategy	Limited number of models; frequent product modifications	Expanded number of models; frequent product modifications	Large number of models	Elimination of unprofitable models and brands
Distribution Strategy	Distribution usually limited, depending on product; intensive efforts and high margins often needed to attract wholesalers and retailers	Expanded number of dealers; intensive efforts to establish long-term relationships with wholesalers and retailers	Extensive number of dealers; margins declining; intensive efforts to retain distributors and shelf space	Unprofitable outlets phased out
Promotion Strategy	Develop product awareness; stimulate primary demand; use intensive personal selling to distributors; use sampling and couponing for consumers	Stimulate selective demand; advertise brand aggressively	Stimulate selective demand; advertise brand aggressively; promote heavily to retain dealers and customers	Phase out all promotion
Pricing Strategy	Prices are usually high to recover development costs (see Chapter 19)	Prices begin to fall toward end of growth stage as result of competitive pressure	Prices continue to fall	Prices stabilize at relatively low level; small price rises are possible if competition is negligible

Sales

Time

© Cengage Learning 2013

9,000
Research and development employees at Procter & Gamble

18
Years spent developing Minute Rice

80,000
Self-selected science problem solvers using the InnoCentive Inc. online brain trust

$1 million
Cost of full-scale test marketing

$750 million
Amount Gillette spent to develop the Mach3

500
Girls recruited by Alloy.com to generate buzz about the TV show *America's Top Model*

39
Percent of early adopters who reported spending five or more hours online each day

500 million
Number of Facebook adopters in 2010

ANATOMY OF A Product Life Cycle
VCR

VCR sales dropped rapidly in the face of growing DVD competition.

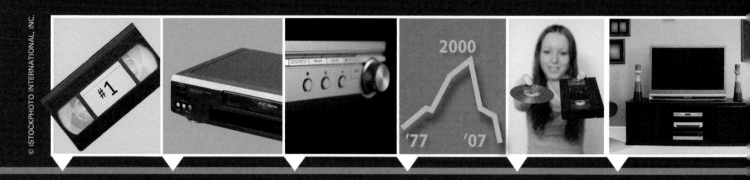

1977
VHS first sold in the U.S.

1992
100 millionth VCR sold

1997
First DVD titles released in the U.S.

2000
VCR sales peak at 23 million units

2001
DVD dollar sales surpass VHS sales

2006
More households own DVD players than VCRs

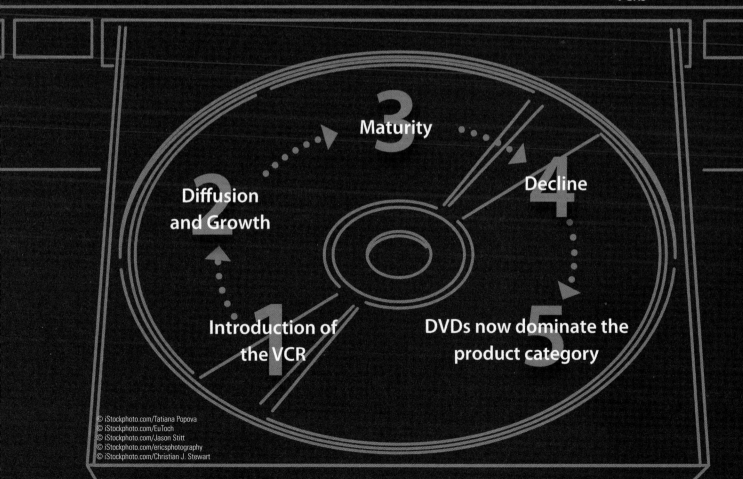

3 Maturity

2 Diffusion and Growth

4 Decline

1 Introduction of the VCR

5 DVDs now dominate the product category

Review and Applications

 1 Explain the importance of developing new products and describe the six categories of new products. New products are important to sustain growth and profits and to replace obsolete items. New products can be classified as new-to-the-world products (discontinuous innovations), new product lines, additions to existing product lines, improvements or revisions of existing products, repositioned products, or lower-priced products. To sustain or increase profits, a firm must innovate.

1.1 How many new products can you identify? Visit the supermarket and make a list of at least 15 items with the word "New" on the label. Include on your list anything that looks like a new product. Next to each item on your list, write the category of new product that best describes the item. Share your results with the class.

1.2 New entertainment products aren't necessarily media products. Form a team of three or four students and brainstorm new nonmedia entertainment products. Try to identify one item for each of the categories of new products discussed in the chapter.

 2 Explain the steps in the new-product development process. First, a firm forms a new-product strategy by outlining the characteristics and roles of future products. Then new-product ideas are generated by customers, employees, distributors, competitors, vendors, and internal R&D personnel. Once a product idea has survived initial screening by an appointed screening group, it undergoes business analysis to determine its potential profitability. If a product concept seems viable, it progresses into the development phase, in which the technical and economic feasibility of the manufacturing process is evaluated. The development phase also includes laboratory and use testing of a product for performance and safety. Following initial testing and refinement, most products are introduced in a test market to evaluate consumer response and marketing strategies. Finally, test market successes are propelled into full commercialization. The commercialization process involves starting up production, building inventories, shipping to distributors, training a sales force, announcing the product to the trade, and advertising to consumers.

2.1 List the advantages of simultaneous product development.

writing

2.2 You are a marketing manager for Nike. Your department has come up with the idea of manufacturing a baseball bat for use in colleges around the nation. Assuming you are in the business analysis stage, write a brief analysis based on the questions in the "Business Analysis" section of the chapter.

2.3 What are the major disadvantages to test marketing, and how might they be avoided?

online

2.4 How could information from customer orders at **www.pizzahut.com** help the company's marketers plan new-product developments?

 3 Explain why some products succeed and others fail. The most important factor in determining the success of a new product is the extent to which the product matches the needs of the market. Good matches are frequently successful. Poor matches are not.

team

3.1 In small groups, brainstorm ideas for a new wet-weather clothing line. What type of product would potential customers want and need? Prepare and deliver a brief presentation to your class.

 4 Discuss global issues in new-product development. A marketer with global vision seeks to develop products that can easily be adapted to suit local needs. The goal is not simply to develop a standard product that can be sold worldwide. Smart global marketers also look for good product ideas worldwide.

4.1 Visit **www.pg.com** and look at the brands it offers around the world. What conclusions can you draw about Procter & Gamble's global new-product development strategy?

online

Explain the diffusion process through which new products are adopted. The diffusion process is the spread of a new product from its producer to ultimate adopters. Adopters in the diffusion process belong to five categories: innovators, early adopters, the early majority, the late majority, and laggards. Product characteristics that affect the rate of adoption include product complexity, compatibility with existing social values, relative advantage over existing substitutes, observability, and "trialability." The diffusion process is facilitated by word-of-mouth communication and communication from marketers to consumers.

5.1 Describe some products whose adoption rates have been affected by complexity, compatibility, relative advantage, observability, and/or "trialability."

5.2 What type of adopter behavior do you typically follow? Explain.

5.3 Review Exhibit 11.4. Analyze each product on the graph according to the characteristics that influence the rate of adoption. For example, what can you conclude from the data about the relative advantage of DVD audio? Write one to two pages explaining your analysis.

writing

Explain the concept of product life cycles. All brands and product categories undergo a life cycle with four stages: introduction, growth, maturity, and decline. The rate at which products move through these stages varies dramatically. Marketing managers use the product life cycle concept as an analytical tool to forecast a product's future and devise effective marketing strategies.

6.1 What is Cheerios doing to compete successfully in the maturity stage? Go to its Web site (**www.cheerios.com**) to find out.

online

Key Terms

adopter *400*
brainstorming *390*
business analysis *391*
commercialization *396*
concept test *391*
decline stage *407*
development *393*
diffusion *400*

growth stage *405*
innovation *400*
introductory stage *405*
maturity stage *406*
new product *386*
new-product strategy *388*
product category *404*
product development *390*

product life cycle (PLC) *404*
screening *391*
simulated (laboratory) market testing *396*
simultaneous product development *393*
test marketing *395*

Exercises

ETHICS EXERCISE

One source of new-product ideas is competitors. Steven Fischer recently joined Frankie and Alex Specialty Products as a brand manager. His new boss told him, "We don't have a budget for new-product development. We just monitor our competitors' new-product introductions and offer knockoffs of any that look like they will be successful."

1. Is this practice ethical?

2. Does the AMA Statement of Ethics address this issue? Go to **www.marketingpower.com** and review the statement. Then write a brief paragraph on what the AMA Statement of Ethics contains that relates to knockoff products.

MARKETING PLAN EXERCISE

Complete the following exercises to continue building your strategic marketing plan for Part 3—Product Decisions. (See Marketing Planning Worksheet, Part 3, on your companion Web site at **www.cengagebrain.com.**) You should also refer to Appendix I of Chapter 2 for additional marketing plan checklist items (Marketing Mix—Product).

1. Place your company's product in the appropriate stage of the product life cycle. What are the implications of being in this stage? Would the PLC be lengthened, shortened, or not affected by selling your product or service online? Would selling your offering on the Internet make it seem earlier on the PLC to your customers? Why?

2. What categories of adopters are likely to buy your company's products? Is the product diffusing slowly or quickly throughout the marketplace? Why? What elements of the diffusion process can you control to make sure your offering diffuses more quickly throughout the adopter categories and marketplace in general? Will positive word-of-mouth be easier or harder to generate online?

APPLICATION EXERCISE

A simple statistical analysis will help you better understand the types of new products. You will be using print advertisements, but you will also be adding information from other sources (TV ads, trips to the store, and the like).[45]

Activities

1. Compile a list of 100 new products. If you are building a portfolio of ads, you can generate part of this list as you collect print advertisements for the topics in this chapter. Consider tabulating television ads for new products that are aired during programs you normally watch. A trip to the grocery store could probably yield your entire list, but then your list would be limited to consumer products.

2. Make a table with six columns labeled as follows: new-to-the-world products, new product line, addition to existing product line, improvement/revision of existing product line, repositioned product, and lower-priced product.

3. Place each of your 100 new products into one of the six categories. Tabulate your results at the bottom of each column. What conclusions can you draw from the distribution of your products? Consider adding your results together with the rest of the class to get a larger and more random sample.

CASE STUDY: Nintendo

A CONSOLE IN EVERY HOME

When Nintendo released its latest video gaming console, the Wii, many industry analysts thought the machine would quickly go by the wayside. At the time (November 2006), the prevailing philosophy was that success in the videogame industry depended on being able to produce the fastest, most powerful machine on the market. Faced with competition from Microsoft's Xbox 360 and Sony's PlayStation 3 (PS3) gaming consoles, both of which fit the bill, Nintendo's strategy of building a console around much simpler and less powerful hardware raised many questions about the Wii's viability.

Fast forward to the end of 2008 and consider the numbers. In November and December of 2008, Nintendo sold 4.1 million Wii consoles, Microsoft sold about 2.2 million Xbox 360, and Sony sold 1.1 million PS3. That's right—Nintendo sold more consoles than both of its major competitors *combined*. In terms of year-over-year growth for that same period, Xbox sales experienced a modest increase, and PS3 sales actually dropped. As for the Wii? During that same period, Wii sales *doubled*. On the software front, the videogame industry as a whole saw software sales increase by 26 percent. With that in mind, consider that the four top-selling games of 2008 were all exclusively for the Wii. The top seller, *Wii Play*, sold more than the combined Xbox and PS3 sales of *Grand Theft Auto 4*. Consider as well that Nintendo's staggering hardware and software sales growth occurred in the middle of a deep recession.

So what exactly has given Nintendo such an edge? Part of it certainly goes back to its hardware design. When designing their next-generation consoles, both Sony and Microsoft invested considerable time and funding into designing entirely new processing systems and several new features to make their machines more versatile. For instance, the PS3 included a Blu-ray player. The hardware for the original PS3 model cost almost $700 per unit, and while Sony has managed to pull its costs on the current model down 35 percent from the previous model, it remains in the red and has yet to make a profit on console sales. Furthermore, after several reductions, the current PS3 model still sells for $399, at least $150 more than its two competitors. Microsoft has not had nearly the same difficulties as Sony in making its console profitable; however, it has recently had to introduce price cuts to its consoles. Nintendo, on the other hand, chose to use a simpler and much less expensive processing system, and has yet to introduce a price reduction on the system.

The Wii's overall game play generally varies from its competitors' as well. While the Xbox 360 and PS3 in many ways appear to be bigger, stronger, faster versions of their predecessors, the Wii—with a much more integrated motion capture system—in many ways has offered gamers something new.

Nintendo isn't looking at just gamers either. Traditionally the core market for video games has been dominated by teen and early-adult male action gamers. With the Wii, Nintendo has been pushing titles that it hopes will have a more casual family-friendly appeal—titles such as *Wii Fit* and *Wii Music*. The top-selling game for 2008—*Wii Play*—includes basic games like pool, ping pong, and target shooting. With offerings like these, the Wii provides relatively inexpensive in-home whole family entertainment.

Nintendo's vision also extends beyond just providing videogame entertainment. For example, the Nintendo DS, a portable gaming system, can also be used as a book reader. By purchasing its book cartridge, users can take advantage of the Nintendo DS's touchscreen to flip a page by swiping a finger (or a stylus) across the screen. Adaptation as an e-reader reflects just one of the ways that Nintendo is looking to make its hardware more versatile. The *Wii Fit* was designed to bring fitness activities into the family room and make it a communal activity. Nintendo, however, hasn't abandoned its core audience. Two of the top-selling games in 2008, *Mario Kart Wii* and *Super Smash Bros. Brawl*, were the latest releases in two longstanding Nintendo game franchises.

When asked about the future direction of Nintendo's software, their chief game designer Shigeru Miyamoto commented that his goal was for the Wii to become "a necessity for every home." Based on the Wii's recent success, it looks like Nintendo is off to a pretty good start.[46]

Questions

1. Imagine that you are charged with designing a successor to the Wii. Briefly describe the new-product strategy you might use.

2. How might the diffusion process differ between the Wii and its competitors?

3. Compare the life cycle of Nintendo's videogame consoles as a whole to a particular console, such as the Wii.

COMPANY CLIPS: Kodak—Reinventing Photography

Designing usable and intriguing products is an integral part of Kodak's marketing process. Paul Porter, director of corporate design and usability, focuses on creating interesting, functional, and intuitive equipment. To make sure the company is on the right track with product development, Kodak marketers interview customers and visit them in their own homes, observing how families use digital photography. The understanding gained from these interactions helps the company create a wide range of products targeted at different market segments.

Questions

1. EasyShare-One didn't sell very well, but Paul Porter claimed this wasn't the purpose of that particular product. What was the purpose of the product?

2. What kind of new product was EasyShare-One?

3. Discuss the product development process at Kodak.

4. Place Kodak's digital cameras in the product life cycle.

Notes

1. Reena Jana, "In Data," *BusinessWeek*, September 22, 2008, 48.
2. "The 50 Most Innovative Companies 2010," *Bloomberg Businessweek*, February 4, 2011, 42–57.
3. *Ibid.*
4. "The Value of New Product Time to Market," *RetailWire*, November 21, 2006, www.retailwirecom (Accessed August 9, 2007).
5. Erik Brynjolfsson and Michael Schrage, "The New Faster Face of Innovation," *Wall Street Journal*, August 17, 2009, R3.
6. Frank T. Rothaermel and Andrew M. Hess, "Finding an Innovation Strategy That Works," *Wall Street Journal*, August 17, 2009, R3.
7. Vanessa L. Facenda, "Oh Boy! Disney Sees Market for Pre-Teen Fragrances," *Brandweek*, July 23, 2007, 5.
8. "Procter and Gamble Plans Product Enhancements," *Business Courier*, February 18, 2010, www.bizjournals.com/cincinnati/stories/2010/02/15/daily45.html.
9. Elizabeth Holmes, "Talbots Politely Shows Granny the Door," *Wall Street Journal*, April 12, 2010, http://online.wsj.com/article/SB10001424052702304703104575174601462751456.html.
10. Miguel Bustillo, "RadioShack, Now the Adapter," *Wall Street Journal*, April 24, 2010, http://online.wsj.com/article/SB10001424052748704464704575208353784825356.html.
11. Ellen Byron, "P&G Plots Course to Turn Lackluster Tide," *Wall Street Journal*, September 11, 2009, B3.
12. Melanie Warner, "P&G's Chemistry Test," *Fast Company*, July/August 2008, 71.

marketing&you: Results.

If your score is high, you are most likely a "market maven." You are aware of new products earlier and talk about a variety of products to your friends. High scores also indicate a greater interest in and attentiveness to the market. Conversely, the lower your score, the less interested you are in the market and new products.

13. "Women's Financial Style," *Adweek Media*, February 16, 2009, 14; Jack Neff, "Package-Good Players Plan New-Product Surge," *Advertising Age*, December 7, 2009, http://adage.com/article/news/brands-package-good-players-plan-product-surge-2010/140906.

14. Jeff Jains, "The Buzz from Starbucks Customers," *BusinessWeek*, April 28, 2008, 42, 44.

15. *Ibid.*

16. "Focus Groups Take on New Format," *RetailWire*, January 25, 2010, www.retailwire.com/discussions/sngl_discussion.cfm/14267.

17. John Karolefski, "CPG Matters: P&G Changes Rules for Product Development," *RetailWire*, February 19, 2008, www.retailwire.com (Accessed August 12, 2009).

18. Chris Newmarker, "General Mills Looks Online for Food Innovations," *Minneapolis/St. Paul Business Journal*, November 4, 2009, www.bizjournals.com/albuquerque/stories/2009/11/02/daily26.html.

19. Andrew Morton, "2006: A Face Odyssey," *Fort Worth Star-Telegram*, February 16, 2006, E1, E8.

20. "NFL Quarterback Matt Ryan Helps Launch Gillette Fusion MVP Razor," *PRNewswire-First Call*, September 28, 2009, www.prweb.com/releases/Gillette_Fusion/MVP_Razor/prweb2956714.htm.

21. Chuck Salter, "The Faces and Voices of the World's Most Innovative Company," *Fast Company*, March 2008, 74–96.

22. Roger O. Crockett, "How P&G Plans to Clean Up," *BusinessWeek*, April 13, 2009, 43, 45.

23. *Ibid.*

24. Betsy Towner, "Biggest Flops," *AARP Bulletin*, November 2009, 43.

25. Jena McGregor, "How Failure Breeds Success," *BusinessWeek*, July 10, 2006, 42–52.

26. Norihiko Shirouzu and Stephen Power, "Unthrilling but Inexpensive, the Logan Boosts Renault in Emerging Markets," *Wall Street Journal*, October 9, 2006, B1.

27. Michael Fielding, "Driving into the Global Market," *Marketing News*, November 1, 2008, 14–17; "Price List," Tata Nano Web site, http://tatanano.inservices.tatamotors.com/tatamotors/index.php?option=com_booking&task=pricelist&Itemid=303 (Accessed July 5, 2011).

28. Jena McGregor, "GE Reinventing Tech for the Emerging World," *BusinessWeek*, April 28, 2008, 68.

29. Erika Kinetz, "iPad? No—IndiaPad," *Fort Worth Star-Telegram*, July 24, 2010, 9B.

30. "Brand Advocates Spread the Word Online," *eMarketer*, March 30, 2010, www.emarketer.tv/Article.aspx?R=1007600.

31. "The Buzz Starts Here: Finding the First Mouth for Word-of-Mouth Marketing," *Knowledge@Wharton*, March 4, 2009, http://knowledge.wharton.upenn.edu/article.cfm?articleid=2170.

32. Geoffrey Fowler and Marie Baca, "The ABCs of E-Reading," *Wall Street Journal*, August 25, 2010, http://online.wsj.com/article/SB10001424052748703846604575448093175758872.html.

33. Stephen Baker, "What's a Friend Worth?" *BusinessWeek*, June 1, 2009, 31–36.

34. Facebook, "Company Timeline," www.facebook.com/press/info.php?timeline (Accessed February 7, 2011).

35. "Colleges Perfect for Word of Mouth," *eMarketer*, August 23, 2007, www.emarketer.com.

36. Todd Wasserman, "Word Games," *Brandweek*, April 14, 2006, 24–28.

37. *Ibid.*

38. Daniel B. Honiaman, "Who's on First?" *Marketing News*, November 1, 2007, 16.

39. "Internet Key to Influencing the Influencers," *Marketing Matters Newsletter*, January 12, 2007.

40. "Surviving Silly Bandz: Prolonging the Shelf Life of Fads," *Knowledge@Wharton*, July 21, 2010, http://knowledge.wharton.upenn.edu/article.cfm?articleid=2551.

41. Geoffrey A. Fowler, "More Makers Jump into E-Reader Fray," *Wall Street Journal*, January 15, 2010, http://online.wsj.com/article/SB10001424052748704854904574644491659206478.html.

42. "Looking for Ways to Replace CD Sales in a Flash," *Retailing Today*, February 11, 2008, www.retailingtoday.com (Accessed August 5, 2009).

43. Arik Hesseldahl, "The Home Phone's Last Gasp," *Bloomberg Businessweek*, July 26–August 1, 2010, 72.

44. Jeffrey McCracken and Ellen Byron, "P&G Considers Booting Some Brands," *Wall Street Journal*, October 29, 2009, B1, B9.

45. This application exercise is based on the contribution of Karen Stewart (Richard Stockton College of New Jersey) to *Great Ideas in Teaching Marketing*, a teaching supplement that accompanies McDaniel, Lamb, and Hair's *Introduction to Marketing*. Professor Stewart's entry titled "New-Product Development" was a winner in the "Best of the Great Ideas in Teaching Marketing" contest held in conjunction with the publication of the eighth edition of *Marketing*.

46. Chris Pereira, "Wii Play is the Best Selling Game of 2008," *1UP.com*, January 15, 2009, **www.1up.com/do/newsStory?cld=3172314** (accessed January 16, 2009); Chris Pereira, "December NPDs: Wii and DS Combine for OVER 5 Million" *1UP.com*, January 15, 2009, **www.1up.com/do/newsStory?cld=3172307** (accessed January 16, 2009); Steve Watts, "NPD Group Suggests Recession is Hurting Games Growth," *1UP.com*, January 15, 2009, **www.1up.com/do/newsStory?cld=3172306** (accessed January 16, 2009); Kathy Shwiff, "New Sony Game Nears Breaking Even," *The Wall Street Journal*, 30 December 2008, **www.wsj.com** (accessed January 16, 2009); Daisuke Wakabayashi, "Hope Fades for PS3 as a Comeback Player," *The Wall Street Journal*, December 29, 2009, **www.wsj.com** (accessed January 16, 2009); Jonathan V. Last, "Playing the Fool," *The Wall Street Journal*, December 30, 2009, **http://online.wsj.com/article/ SB123069467545545011.html** (accessed January 16, 2009); Christopher Lawton and Yukari Iwatani Kane, "Game Makers Push 'Family' Fare," *The Wall Street Journal*, October 29, 2009, **www.wjs.com** (accessed December 8, 2008); Yukari Iwatani Kane, "Nintendo's Wii Music Waits for Fans," *The Wall Street Journal*, December 15, 2008, **http://online. wsj.com/article/ SB122930373918205685.html** (accessed January 16, 2009); Yukari Iwatani Kane, "Interview Excerpts: Shigeru Miyamoto," *The Wall Street Journal*, December 15, 2008, **http://online.wsj.com/article/SB122834417100677251.html** (Accessed January 16, 2009).

chapter

12 Services and Nonprofit Organization Marketing

 Learning Outcomes

1 Discuss the importance of services to the economy

2 Discuss the differences between services and goods

3 Describe the components of service quality and the gap model of service quality

4 Develop marketing mixes for services

5 Discuss relationship marketing in services

6 Explain internal marketing in services

7 Discuss global issues in services marketing

8 Describe nonprofit organization marketing

LO1
The Importance of Services

A **service** is the result of applying human or mechanical efforts to people or objects. Services involve a deed, a performance, or an effort that cannot be physically possessed. Today, the service sector substantially influences the U.S. economy, accounting for 81 percent of both U.S. gross domestic product and U.S. employment.[1] The demand for services is expected to continue. According to the Bureau of Labor Statistics, service occupations will be responsible for nearly all net job growth through the year 2016.[2] Much of this demand results from demographics. An aging population will need nurses, home health care, physical therapists, and social workers. Two-earner families need child-care, housecleaning, and lawn-care services. Also increasing will be the demand for information managers, such as computer engineers and systems analysts. There is also a growing market for service companies worldwide.

The marketing process described in Chapter 1 is the same for all types of products, whether they are goods or services. Many ideas and strategies discussed throughout this book have been illustrated with service examples. In many ways, marketing is marketing, regardless of the product's characteristics. In addition, although a comparison of goods and services marketing can be beneficial, in reality it is hard to distinguish clearly between manufacturing and service firms. Indeed, many manufacturing firms can point to service as a major factor in their success. For example, maintenance and repair services offered by the manufacturer are important to buyers of copy machines. General Electric makes most of its revenues from finance operations rather than from products. Nevertheless, services have some unique characteristics that distinguish them from goods, and marketing strategies need to be adjusted for these characteristics.

> "The service sector substantially influences the **U.S. economy**, accounting for 81 percent of both U.S. GDP and employment."

service
The result of applying human or mechanical efforts to people or objects.

marketing&you.

What do you think about charities?

Using the following scale, enter your answers on the lines provided.

STRONGLY AGREE ‹1 2 3 4 5› STRONGLY DISAGREE

AGREE

_____ The money given to charities goes for good causes.

_____ Much of the money donated to charity is wasted.*

_____ My image of charitable organizations is positive.

_____ Charitable organizations have been quite successful in helping the needy.

_____ Charity organizations perform a useful function for society.

Total your score, reversing your answer for the item followed by an asterisk. That is, if you answered 2, change it to 4, and vice versa. Read the chapter and find out what your score means at the end.

Source: Scale #58, *Marketing Scales Handbook*, G. Bruner, K. James, H. Hensel, eds. Vol. III. © by American Marketing Association.

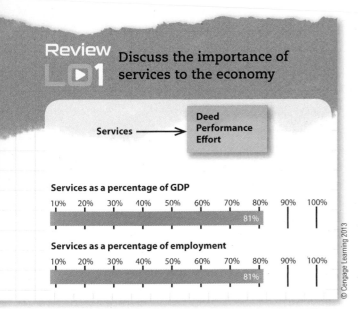

Services ⟶ Deed Performance Effort

Services as a percentage of GDP

10% 20% 30% 40% 50% 60% 70% 80% 90% 100%

81%

Services as a percentage of employment

10% 20% 30% 40% 50% 60% 70% 80% 90% 100%

81%

© Cengage Learning 2013

LO2
How Services Differ from Goods

Services have four unique characteristics that distinguish them from goods. Services are intangible, inseparable, heterogeneous, and perishable.

INTANGIBILITY

The basic difference between services and goods is that services are intangible performances. Because of their **intangibility**, they cannot be touched, seen, tasted, heard, or felt in the same manner that goods can be sensed. Services cannot be stored and are often easy to duplicate.

Evaluating the quality of services before or even after making a purchase is harder than evaluating the quality of goods because, compared to goods, services tend to exhibit fewer search qualities. A **search quality** is a characteristic that can be easily assessed before purchase—for instance, the color of an appliance or automobile. At the same time, services tend to exhibit more experience and credence qualities. An **experience quality** is a characteristic that can be assessed only after use, such as the quality of a meal in a restaurant or the actual experience of a vacation. A **credence quality** is a characteristic that consumers may have difficulty assessing even after purchase because they do not have the necessary knowledge or experience. Medical and consulting services are examples of services that exhibit credence qualities.

These characteristics also make it harder for marketers to communicate the benefits of an intangible service than to communicate the benefits of tangible goods. Thus, marketers often rely on tangible cues to communicate a service's nature and quality. For example, Travelers Insurance Company's use of the umbrella symbol helped make tangible the benefit of protection that insurance provides.

The facilities that customers visit, or from which services are delivered, are a critical tangible part of the total service offering. Messages about the organization are communicated to customers through elements such as the décor, the clutter or neatness of service areas, and the staff's manners and dress. The design of Chinnati's Pizza, a restaurant in Cincinnati, Ohio, reflects this idea. The name represents a combination of Chicago (where the owner is from) and Cincinnati. Because both cities have an industrial past, the designers of the interior chose urban, industrial design elements such as raw steel, dark woods, stained glass, and metal details with exposed riveting.[3]

INSEPARABILITY

Goods are produced, sold, and then consumed. In contrast, services are often sold, produced, and consumed at the same time. In other words, their production and consumption are inseparable activities. This **inseparability** means that, because consumers must be present during the production of services like haircuts or surgery, they are actually involved in the production of the services they buy. That type of consumer involvement is rare in goods manufacturing. Inseparability also means

intangibility
The inability of services to be touched, seen, tasted, heard, or felt in the same manner that goods can be sensed.

search quality
A characteristic that can be easily assessed before purchase.

experience quality
A characteristic that can be assessed only after use.

credence quality
A characteristic that consumers might have difficulty assessing even after purchase because they do not have the necessary knowledge or experience.

inseparability
The inability of the production and consumption of a service to be separated. Consumers must be present during the production.

that customers have an opportunity to provide input into their service experience and outcome. For example, individuals getting a haircut can provide feedback during the process so that their hair looks the way they want it to look.

Simultaneous production and consumption also means that services normally cannot be produced in a centralized location and consumed in decentralized locations, as goods typically are. Services are also inseparable from the perspective of the service provider. Thus, the quality of service that firms are able to deliver depends on the quality of their employees.

The facilities that customers visit or from which services are delivered, such as those in a restaurant, are a critical tangible part of the total service offering. This restaurant exudes luxury with its sumptuous fabrics and dinnerware, as well as intimacy through small tables and a smaller space.

HETEROGENEITY

One great strength of McDonald's is consistency. Whether customers order a Big Mac and french fries in Fort Worth, Tokyo, or Moscow, they know exactly what they are going to get. This is not the case with many service providers. Because services have greater heterogeneity, or variability of inputs and outputs, they tend to be less standardized and uniform than goods. For example, physicians in a group practice or barbers in a barber shop differ from one another in their technical and interpersonal skills. A given physician's or barber's performance might even vary depending on time of day, physical health, or some other factor. Because services tend to be labor-intensive, and production and consumption are inseparable, consistency and quality control can be hard to achieve.

Standardization and training help increase consistency and reliability. Limited-menu restaurants like Pizza Hut and KFC offer customers high consistency from one visit to the next because of standardized preparation procedures. Another way to increase consistency is to mechanize the process. Banks have reduced the inconsistency of teller services by providing automated teller machines (ATMs). Automatic coin receptacles and electronic toll collection systems such as E-ZPass have replaced human collectors on toll roads.

PERISHABILITY

The fourth characteristic of services is their perishability, which means that they cannot be stored, warehoused, or inventoried. An empty hotel room or airplane seat produces no revenue that day. The revenue is lost. Yet service organizations are often forced to turn away full-price customers during peak periods.

One of the most important challenges in many service industries is finding ways to synchronize supply and demand. The philosophy that some revenue is

heterogeneity
The variability of the inputs and outputs of services, which causes services to tend to be less standardized and less uniform than goods.

perishability
The inability of services to be stored, warehoused, or inventoried.

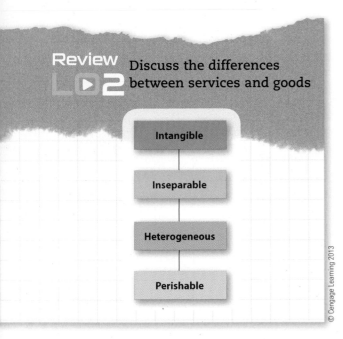

Intangible

Inseparable

Heterogeneous

Perishable

© Cengage Learning 2013

better than none has prompted many hotels to offer deep discounts on weekends and during the off-season and has prompted airlines to adopt similar pricing strategies during off-peak hours. Car rental agencies, movie theaters, and restaurants also use discounts to encourage demand during non-peak periods.

LO3
Service Quality

Because of the four unique characteristics of services, service quality is more difficult to define and measure than is the quality of tangible goods. Business executives rank the improvement of service quality as one of the most critical challenges facing them today. A service quality study done by retail consultants the SALT & Pepper Group revealed that across 73 stores in different industries, average scores were poor.[4] However, well-known companies such as Nordstrom, Southwest Airlines, and Build-A-Bear Workshop consistently provide exceptional customer service. Everything these companies do reflects their commitment to offering customers a quality service experience. Exhibit 12.1 shows the top ten ranked companies that offer outstanding customer service in the United States. How do these companies rise above the rest in delivering superior service quality? Research has shown that customers evaluate service quality by the following five components:[5]

reliability
The ability to perform a service dependably, accurately, and consistently.

responsiveness
The ability to provide prompt service.

assurance
The knowledge and courtesy of employees and their ability to convey trust.

empathy
Caring, individualized attention to customers.

→ **Reliability:** the ability to perform the service dependably, accurately, and consistently. Reliability is performing the service right the first time. An air traveler who gets to the destination on time with his or her luggage intact has experienced reliable service. This component has been found to be the one most important to consumers.

→ **Responsiveness:** the ability to provide prompt service. Examples of responsiveness include calling the customer back quickly, serving lunch quickly to someone who is in a hurry, or mailing a transaction slip immediately. The ultimate in responsiveness is offering service 24 hours a day, 7 days a week. For example, Zappos.com, a successful online shoe company, keeps its warehouse open 24-7 so that customers can order shoes at 11 P.M. and still get next-day delivery.[6]

→ **Assurance:** the knowledge and courtesy of employees and their ability to convey trust. Skilled employees treat customers with respect and make customers feel that they can trust the firm to exemplify assurance.

→ **Empathy:** caring, individualized attention to customers. Firms whose employees recognize customers, call them by name, and learn their customers' specific requirements are providing empathy. At Southwest Airlines, understanding customer needs is a part of the corporate culture. Getting customer feedback and listening to that feedback is a critical aspect of implementing empathy.[7]

→ **Tangibles:** the physical evidence of the service. The tangible parts of a service include the physical facilities, tools, and equipment used to provide the service, such as a doctor's office or an ATM, and the

Exhibit 12.1	The Top Ten Customer Service Elite
1. L.L Bean	
2. USAA	
3. Apple	
4. Four Seasons Hotels and Resorts	
5. Publix Super Markets	
6. Nordstrom	
7. Lexus	
8. The Ritz-Carlton	
9. Barnes & Noble	
10. Ace Hardware	

Source: Jena McGregor, "Customer Service Champs 2010," *Bloomberg Businessweek*, February 18, 2010, www.bloomberg.com/interactive_reports/customer_service_2010.htm.

appearance of personnel. For example, Enterprise Rent-A-Car has strict dress codes for its employees. Female employees have 30 guidelines, including that pants must be creased, skirts must not be shorter than two inches above the knee, and legs must be in stockings. Male employees have to follow 26 dress rules, including dress shirts with coordinated ties and no beards. In fact, "distinctive professional dress" is mentioned in Enterprise's written founding values. Hospitals have found that improving their layouts and looks can translate into better health for their patients.

Overall service quality is measured by combining customers' evaluations for all five components.

tangibles

The physical evidence of a service, including the physical facilities, tools, and equipment used to provide the service.

gap model

A model identifying five gaps that can cause problems in service delivery and influence customer evaluations of service quality.

THE GAP MODEL OF SERVICE QUALITY

A model of service quality called the gap model identifies five gaps that can cause problems in service delivery and influence customer evaluations of service quality.[8] These gaps are illustrated in Exhibit 12.2:

Exhibit 12.2 Gap Model of Service Quality

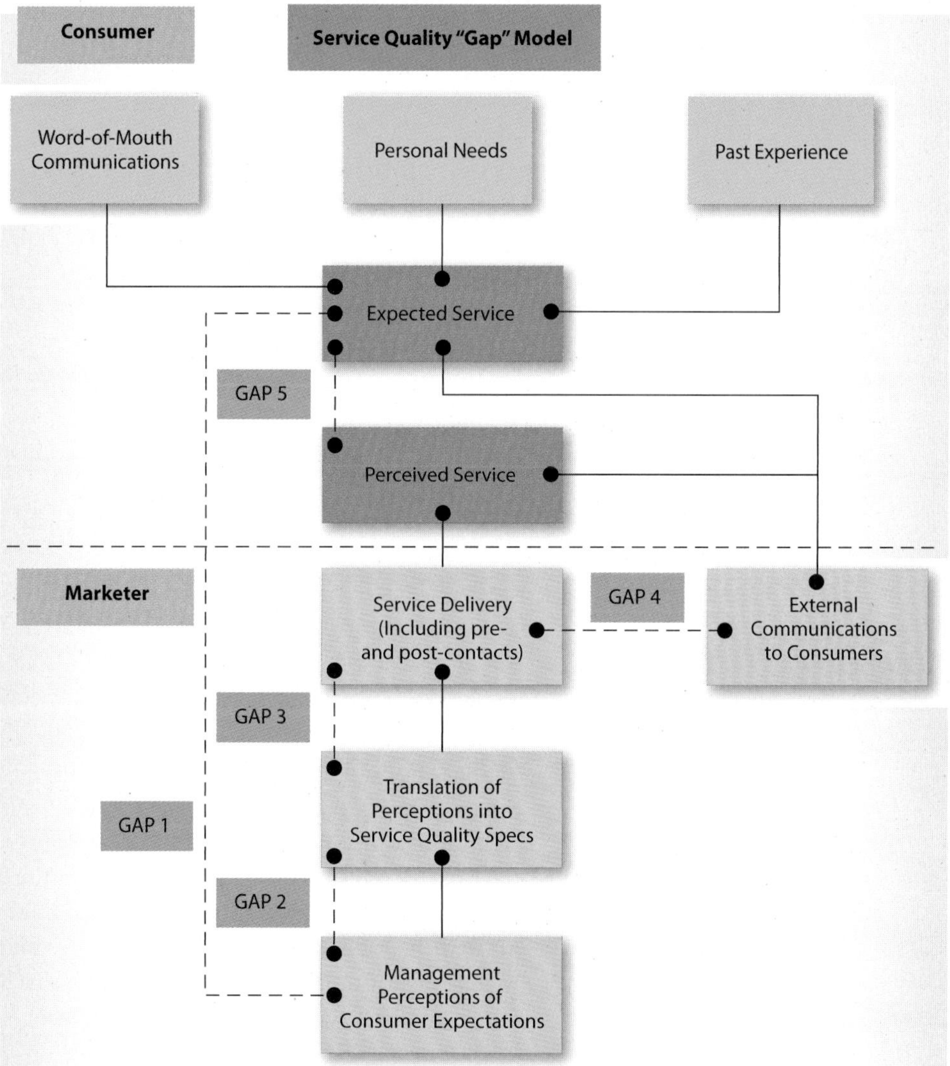

Source: Valarie A. Zeithaml, Mary Jo Bitner, and Dwayne Gremler, *Services Marketing*, 4/e (New York: McGraw-Hill, 2006). Reprinted with permission.

→ **Gap 1:** the gap between what customers want and what management thinks customers want. This gap results from a lack of understanding or a misinterpretation of the customers' needs, wants, or desires. A firm that does little or no customer satisfaction research is likely to experience this gap. An important step in closing gap 1 is to keep in touch with what customers want by doing research on customer needs and customer satisfaction.

→ **Gap 2:** the gap between what management thinks customers want and the quality specifications that management develops to provide the service. Essentially, this gap is the result of management's inability to translate customers' needs into delivery systems within the firm. For example, Kentucky Fried Chicken once rated its managers' success according to "chicken efficiency," or how much chicken they threw away at the end of the night. Customers who came in late at night would either have to wait for chicken to be cooked or settle for chicken several hours old. The "chicken efficiency" measurement did not take customers into account.

→ **Gap 3:** the gap between the service quality specifications and the service that is actually provided. If both gaps 1 and 2 have been closed, then gap 3 is due to the inability of management and employees to do what should be done. Poorly trained or poorly motivated workers can cause this gap. Management needs to ensure that employees have the skills and the proper tools to perform their jobs. Other techniques that help to close gap 3 are training employees so they know what management expects, encouraging teamwork, and hiring employees with the proper attitude. Nick's Pizza & Pub, located in Chicago, has attracted visitors from everywhere who have heard about how the company hires and trains its employees. Among other things, the company interviews candidates twice, and gives them a personality test. Role playing is common. The training program is rigorous and ongoing. In an industry where annual employee turnover is typically 200%, Nick's turnover is just 20%. And customers love the service—on three occasions, waitresses have received tips of $1,000.[9]

→ **Gap 4:** the gap between what the company provides and what the customer is told it provides. This is clearly a communication gap. It may include misleading or deceptive advertising campaigns promising more than the firm can deliver or doing "whatever it takes" to get the business. To close this gap, companies need to create realistic customer expectations through honest, accurate communication about what the firms can provide.

→ **Gap 5:** the gap between the service that customers receive and the service they want. This gap can be positive or negative. For example, if a patient expects to wait 20 minutes in the physician's office before seeing the physician but waits only 10 minutes, the patient's evaluation of service quality will be high. However, a 40-minute wait would result in a lower evaluation. Research has found that customer expectations of service across 35 major industries rose 4.5 percent over the previous year, while the average ability of firms in those industries

Exhibit 12.3 Gaps between Customer Expectations and Service Delivery

	Expectations Index	Delivery Index
Airlines	145	109
Banks	124	108
Car Rental Companies	161	113
Credit Cards	116	114
Hotels	126	109
Insurance Companies	124	106
Parcel Delivery	124	111
Quick Service Restaurants	116	105
Retail	140	111
Wireless Providers	124	106

Source: From 2006 Brand Keys Index as reported in Michael Applebaum, "One Tough Customer," *Brandweek*, March 19, 2007, 19–21.

to keep up with those expectations dropped by 9.2 percent. Consumers generally have low expectations for service from credit card issuers, banks, fast food restaurants, and wireless providers. By contrast, they have high expectations from airlines.[10] Exhibit 12.3 shows the service expectations and actual service delivery scores for 10 industries.

When one or more of these gaps are large, service quality is perceived as low. As the gaps shrink, service quality improves. For instance, Four Seasons has excelled in closing gap 3. Not only does this hotel firm give its employees thorough training, but it also puts potential employees through a comprehensive screening process to match their skills with positions for which they are naturally inclined. USAA, a financial-services organization that serves military families, is great at closing gap 1. It knows what its highly mobile customers who face unique financial challenges need. For example, the company was the first bank to allow iPhone deposits, it texts balances to soldiers on the field, and it heavily discounts customers' car insurance while they are deployed overseas.[11]

Review LO3 Describe the components of service quality and the gap model of service quality

SERVICE

Reliability · Responsiveness · Assurance · Empathy · Tangibles

© Cengage Learning 2013

LO4
Marketing Mixes for Services

Services' unique characteristics—intangibility, inseparability of production and consumption, heterogeneity, and perishability—make marketing more challenging. Elements of the marketing mix (product, place, promotion, and pricing) need to be adjusted to meet the special needs created by these characteristics.

PRODUCT (SERVICE) STRATEGY

A product, as defined in Chapter 10, is everything a person receives in an exchange. In the case of a service organization, the product offering is intangible and consists in large part of a process or a series of processes. Product strategies for service offerings include decisions on the type of process involved, core and supplementary services, standardization or customization of the service product, and the service mix.

Service as a Process Two broad categories of things get processed in service organizations: people and objects. In some cases, the process is physical, or tangible, while in others the process is intangible. Based on these characteristics, service processes can be placed into one of four categories:[12]

→ **People processing** takes place when the service is directed at a customer. Examples are transportation services, hairstyling, health clubs, and dental and health care.

→ **Possession processing** occurs when the service is directed at customers' physical possessions. Examples are lawn care, car repair, dry cleaning, and veterinary services.

Retallack Lodge uses humor in its advertisements to encourage skiers to take advantage of their skiing, snowboarding, and lodge services

→ **Mental stimulus processing** refers to services directed at people's minds. Examples are entertainment, spectator sports events, theater performances, and education.

→ **Information processing** describes services that use technology or brainpower directed at a customer's assets. Examples are insurance, banking, and consulting.

Because customers' experiences and involvement differ for each of these types of services, marketing strategies may also differ. For example, people-processing services require customers to enter the *service factory*, which is a physical location, such as an aircraft, a physician's office, or a hair salon. In contrast, possession-processing services typically do not require the presence of the customer in the service factory; the customer could simply leave the car at the garage for repairs, for example. Marketing strategies for the former would therefore focus more on an attractive, comfortable physical environment and employee training on employee–customer interaction issues than would strategies for the latter.

Core and Supplementary Service Products

The service offering can be viewed as a bundle of activities that includes the **core service**, which is the most basic benefit the customer is buying, and a group of **supplementary services** that support or enhance the core service. Exhibit 12.4 illustrates these concepts for an overnight stay at a luxury hotel. The core service is overnight rental of a bedroom, which involves people processing. The supplementary services, some of which involve information processing, include reservations, check-ins and check-outs, room service, and meals. Starbucks offers a wireless Internet service through agreements with AT&T and T-Mobile that enhances its core offering—the Starbucks' experience of high-quality coffee served in a coffeehouse atmosphere. Starbucks is not trying to become an Internet coffeehouse, but to become the "other place" where people want to be connected to the Internet.

In many service industries, the core service becomes a commodity as competition increases. Thus, firms usually emphasize supplementary services to create a competitive advantage. First-class passengers on Virgin Atlantic's flight from Miami to London enjoy seats that convert into flat beds, a bar and bartender, and a chance for a massage. When passengers land, they can shower in a special lounge and then be taken by limousine to their destinations. On the other hand, some firms are positioning themselves in the marketplace by greatly reducing supplementary services. For example, Microtel Inn is an amenity-free hotel concept known as "fast lodging." These low-cost hotels have one- and two-bedroom accommodations and a swimming pool, but no meeting rooms or other services.

core service
The most basic benefit the consumer is buying.

supplementary services
A group of services that support or enhance the core service.

Customization/Standardization An important issue in developing the service offering is whether to customize or standardize it. Customized services are more flexible and respond to individual customers' needs. They also usually command a higher price. The traditional law firm, which treats each case differently according to the client's situation, offers customized services. Standardized services are more efficient and cost less. Unlike the traditional law firm, for example, Hyatt Legal Services offers low-cost, standardized service "packages" for those with uncomplicated legal needs, such as drawing up a will or mediating an uncontested divorce.

Instead of choosing to either standardize or customize a service, a firm can incorporate elements of both by adopting an emerging strategy called **mass customization**. Mass customization uses technology to deliver customized services on a mass basis, which results in giving each customer whatever she or he asks for.

For example, a feature on Lands' End Web site enables women to define their figures online, receive advice on what swimsuits will flatter their shapes, and mix and match more than 216 combinations of colors and styles. Several airlines design services to cater to travelers' individual needs and preferences. Some serve dinner to passengers when they want to eat it, rather than when the airline wants to serve it. More airlines are offering video-on-demand systems, which let passengers start or stop their movie any time they want.

The Service Mix Most service organizations market more than one service. For example, TruGreen offers lawn care, shrub care, carpet cleaning, and industrial lawn services. Each organization's service mix represents a set of opportunities, risks, and challenges. Each part of the service mix should make a different contribution to achieving the firm's goals. To succeed, each service might also need a different level of financial support.

Designing a service strategy therefore means deciding what new services to introduce to which target market, what existing services to maintain, and what services to eliminate. For example, to increase membership, AAA added financial services, credit cards, and travel perks. Hilton has seven hotel brands that are targeted to different customer segments. For example, the Conrad, in the tower of Hilton's Waldorf Astoria, is one of the fanciest and most expensive Hilton Hotels. The Hampton Inn is a basic, inexpensive hotel, and Embassy Suites are upscale inns that offer a homelike experience, including kitchen facilities.

PLACE (DISTRIBUTION) STRATEGY

Distribution strategies for service organizations must focus on issues such as convenience, number of outlets, direct versus indirect distribution, location, and scheduling. A key factor influencing the selection of a service provider is *convenience*. Therefore, service firms must offer convenience. RediClinic, an in-store medical clinic, has opened numerous clinics in middle-class neighborhoods, and found that convenience is one of its biggest selling points. Consumers can drop into a clinic to have minor health issues addressed instead of waiting days or weeks to see a doctor

Exhibit 12.4 Core and Supplementary Services for a Luxury Hotel

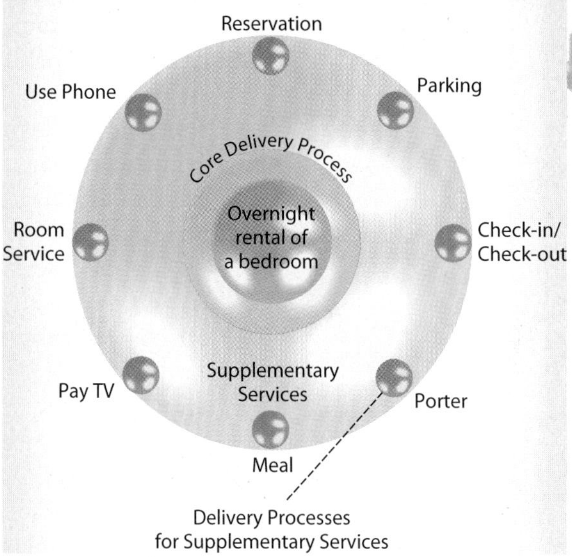

Source: From LOVELOCK, CHRISTOPHER H.; WIRTZ, JOCHEN, "SERVICES MARKETING", 6th ed., © 2007. Reproduced by permission of Pearson Education, Inc., Upper Saddle River, New Jersey.

mass customization
A strategy that uses technology to deliver customized services on a mass basis.

© iStockphoto.com/Juan Facundo Mora Soria

in a scheduled office visit. Restaurants such as Chili's and Macaroni Grill deliver take-out food to customers waiting in their cars. Some doctors even make house calls to elderly and infirm patients.

An important distribution objective for many service firms is the *number of outlets* to use or the number of outlets to open during a certain time. Generally, the intensity of distribution should meet, but not exceed, the target market's needs and preferences. Having too few outlets might inconvenience customers; having too many outlets might boost costs unnecessarily. Intensity of distribution can also depend on the image desired. Having only a few outlets might make the service seem more exclusive or selective.

The next service distribution decision is whether to distribute services to end users *directly* or *indirectly* through other firms. Because of the intangible nature of services, many service firms have to use direct distribution or franchising. Examples include legal, medical, accounting, and personal-care services. The newest form of direct distribution is the Internet. Most of the major airlines use online services to sell tickets directly to consumers, which results in lower distribution costs for the airline companies. Merrill Lynch offers Merrill Lynch Online, an Internet-based service that connects clients with company representatives. Other firms with standardized service packages have developed indirect channels using independent intermediaries. For example, Bank of America offered teller services and loan services to customers in small satellite facilities located in Albertsons Supermarkets in Texas.

The *location* of a service most clearly reveals the relationship between its target market strategy and its distribution strategy. Reportedly, Conrad Hilton claimed that the three most important factors in determining a hotel's success are "location, location, and location."

PROMOTION STRATEGY

Consumers and business users have more trouble evaluating services than goods because services are less tangible. In turn, marketers have more trouble promoting intangible services than tangible goods. Here are four promotion strategies they can try:

→ **Stressing tangible cues:** A tangible cue is a concrete symbol of the service offering. To make their intangible services more tangible, hotels turn down the bedcovers and put mints on the pillows. Insurance companies use symbols such as rocks, blankets, umbrellas, and hands to help make their intangible services appear tangible.

→ **Using personal information sources:** A personal information source is someone consumers are familiar with (such as a celebrity) or someone they know or can relate to personally. Celebrity endorsements are sometimes used to reduce customers' perceived risk in choosing a service. Service firms might also seek to simulate positive word-of-mouth communication among present and prospective customers by using real customers in their ads.

→ **Creating a strong organizational image:** One way to create an image is to manage the evidence, including the physical environment of the service facility, the appearance of the service employees, and the tangible items associated with a service (like stationery, bills, and business cards). For example, McDonald's has created a strong organizational image with its Golden Arches, relatively standardized interiors, and employee uniforms. Another way to create an image is through branding. Disney brands include Disneyland, Disney World, the Disney Channel, and Disney Stores.

"I LIKE TO FLY AT LEAST ONCE A DAY."

People are acquainted with the star, the multi-faceted actor. But John Travolta is also a seasoned pilot with more than 5,000 flight hours under his belt, and is certified on eight different aircraft, including the Boeing 747-400 Jumbo Jet. As a young boy in New Jersey, he already used to dream of flying as he watched planes criss-crossing the sky around the New York airports. Today, John Travolta travels the world at the controls of his own airliner and nurtures a passion for everything that embodies the authentic spirit of aviation. Like BREITLING wrist instruments. Founded in 1884, BREITLING has shared all the finest hours in aeronautical history. Models such as the NAVITIMER have become cult objects for pilots the world over. Where safety is of crucial importance, BREITLING is known as the specialist in reliable and high-performance "wrist instruments" designed and tested for the most demanding professionals. BREITLING chronographs meet the highest standards of sturdiness and functionality, and are equipped with movements that are chronometer-certified by the COSC (Swiss Official Chronometer Testing Institute) – the highest reference in terms of precision and reliability. One simply does not become an aviation supplier by chance.

WWW.BREITLING.COM

**PROFESSION: PILOT
CAREER: ACTOR**

Photographed by Patricia von Ah on the private runway of the Travolta residence in Ocala, Florida.

BREITLING
1884

INSTRUMENTS FOR PROFESSIONALS

Celebrity endorsement can decrease perceived risk in choosing a service. For example, in this ad John Travolta discusses how much he trusts his Breitling watch, which should encourage consumers to trust (and buy) the watch too.

→ ***Engaging in post-purchase communication:*** Post-purchase communication refers to the follow-up activities that a service firm might engage in after a customer transaction. Postcard surveys, telephone calls, brochures, and various other types of follow-up show customers that their feedback matters and their patronage is appreciated.

PRICE STRATEGY

Considerations in pricing a service are similar to the pricing considerations to be discussed in Chapters 19 and 20. However, the unique characteristics of services present two special pricing challenges.

First, in order to price a service, it is important to define the unit of service consumption. For example, should pricing be based on completing a specific service task (cutting a customer's hair), or should it be time based (how long it takes to cut a customer's hair)? Some services include the consumption of goods, such as food and beverages. Restaurants charge customers for food and drink rather than the use of a table and chairs. Some transportation firms charge by distance; others charge a flat rate.

Second, for services that are composed of multiple elements, the issue is whether pricing should be based on a "bundle" of elements or whether each element should be priced separately. A bundled price might be preferable when consumers dislike having to pay "extra" for every part of the service (for example, paying extra for baggage or food on an airplane), and it is simpler for the firm to administer. For instance, many wireless firms offer basic communications packages that include telephone time, Internet access, and text messaging, all for one price. Alternatively, customers might not want to pay for service elements they do not use. Many furniture stores now have "unbundled" delivery charges from the price of the furniture. Customers who wish to can pick up the furniture at the store, saving on the delivery fee.

Marketers should set performance objectives when pricing each service. Three categories of pricing objectives have been suggested:[13]

→ **Revenue-oriented pricing** focuses on maximizing the surplus of income over costs. A limitation of this approach is that determining costs can be difficult for many services.

→ **Operations-oriented pricing** seeks to match supply and demand by varying prices. For example, matching hotel demand to the number of available rooms can be achieved by raising prices at peak times and decreasing them during slow times.

→ **Patronage-oriented pricing** tries to maximize the number of customers using the service. Thus, prices vary with different market segments' ability to pay, and methods of payment (such as credit) are offered that increase the likelihood of a purchase.

A firm might need to use more than one type of pricing objective. In fact, all three objectives probably need to be included to some degree in a pricing strategy, although the importance of each type can vary depending on the type of service provided, the prices that competitors are charging, the differing ability of various customer segments to pay, or the opportunity to negotiate price. For customized services (for example, legal services and construction services), customers might also have the ability to negotiate a price.

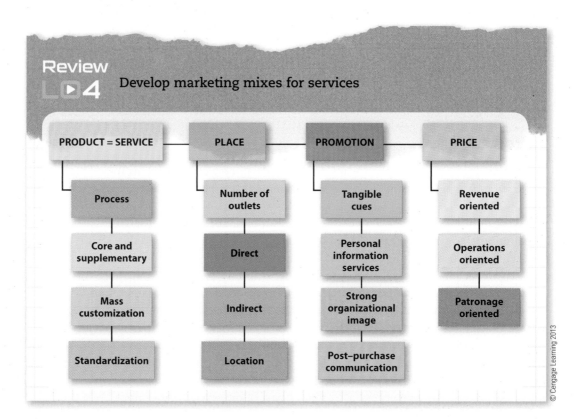

Review LO4 — Develop marketing mixes for services

PRODUCT = SERVICE	PLACE	PROMOTION	PRICE
Process	Number of outlets	Tangible cues	Revenue oriented
Core and supplementary	Direct	Personal information services	Operations oriented
Mass customization	Indirect	Strong organizational image	Patronage oriented
Standardization	Location	Post–purchase communication	

© Cengage Learning 2013

LO5
Relationship Marketing in Services

Many services involve ongoing interaction between the service organization and the customer. Thus, they can benefit from relationship marketing, the strategy described in Chapter 1, as a means of attracting, developing, and retaining customer relationships. The idea is to develop strong loyalty by creating satisfied customers who will buy additional services from the firm and are unlikely to switch to a competitor. Satisfied customers are also likely to engage in positive word-of-mouth communication, thereby helping to bring in new customers.

Many businesses have found that it is more cost-effective to hang on to the customers they have than to focus only on attracting new ones. A bank executive, for example, found that increasing customer retention by 2 percent can have the same effect on profits as reducing costs by 10 percent.

Services that purchasers receive on a continuing basis (for example, cable TV, banking, insurance) can be considered membership services. This type of service naturally lends itself to relationship marketing. When services involve *discrete transactions* (any one-at-a-time sale, such as a movie theater ticket, a meal at a restaurant, or public transportation fare), it can be more difficult to build membership-type relationships with customers. Nevertheless, services involving discrete transactions can be transformed into membership relationships by using marketing tools. For example, the service could be sold in bulk (for example, a theater series subscription or a commuter pass on public transportation). Or a service firm could offer special benefits to customers who choose to register with the firm (for example, loyalty programs for hotels, airlines, and car rental firms). The service firm that has a more formalized relationship with its customers has an advantage because it knows who its customers are and how and when they use the services offered.[14]

It has been suggested that relationship marketing can be practiced at three levels:[15]

→ **Level 1:** The firm uses pricing incentives to encourage customers to continue doing business with it. Examples include the frequent flyer programs offered by many airlines and the free or discounted travel services given to frequent hotel guests. This level of relationship marketing is the least effective in the long term because its price-based advantage is easily imitated by other firms.

→ **Level 2:** This level of relationship marketing also uses pricing incentives but seeks to build social bonds with customers. The firm stays in touch with customers, learns about their needs, and designs services to meet those needs. 1-800-FLOWERS, for example, developed an online Gift Reminder Program. Customers who reach the company via its Web site can register

Review LO5 Discuss relationship marketing in services

3 Creating value-added services not available elsewhere — STRUCTURAL SOCIAL FINANCIAL

2 Designs services to meet customer needs — SOCIAL FINANCIAL

1 Pricing incentives — FINANCIAL

© Cengage Learning 2013

unlimited birthdays, anniversaries, or other special occasions. Five days before each occasion and at their request, 1-800-FLOWERS sends them an e-mail reminder. Level 2 relationship marketing has a higher potential for keeping the firm ahead of the competition than does level 1 relationship marketing.

→ **Level 3:** At this level, the firm again uses financial and social bonds but adds structural bonds to the formula. Structural bonds are developed by offering value-added services that are not readily available from other firms. Hertz's #1 Club Gold program allows members to call and reserve a car, board a courtesy bus at the airport, tell the driver their names, and get dropped off in front of their cars. Hertz also starts up the car and turns on the air conditioning or heat, depending on the temperature. Marketing programs like this one have the strongest potential for sustaining long-term relationships with customers.

Internal Marketing in Service Firms

Services are performances, so the quality of a firm's employees is an important part of building long-term relationships with customers. Employees who like their jobs and are satisfied with the firm they work for are more likely to deliver superior service to customers. In other words, a firm that makes its employees happy has a better chance of keeping its customers coming back. Studies show that replacing an employee costs roughly 1.5 times a year's pay. Also, companies with highly committed employees have been found to post sharply higher shareholder returns. Thus, it is critical that service firms practice **internal marketing**, which means treating employees as customers and developing systems and benefits that satisfy their needs.

Companies have instituted a wide variety of programs designed to satisfy employees. The Container Store offers its employees paid sabbaticals, while Publix Supermarkets provides onsite child care facilities for its employees.[16] Starbucks claims to be in the people business rather than the coffee business and prides itself on its stellar customer service. Its top executives believe that the key to great service is to create an environment of respect and appreciation for all employees. Travelocity keeps its employees engaged in their work by sending them weekly e-mails and hosting a monthly lunch where employees can express their concerns.[17]

These examples illustrate how service firms can invest in their most important resource—their employees. Exhibit 12.5 shows the top ten of *Fortune*'s 100 Best Companies to Work For.

Exhibit 12.5	Top Ten Companies to Work For
1.	SAS
2.	Boston Consulting Group
3.	Wegman's Food Markets
4.	Google
5.	NetApp
6.	Zappos.com
7.	Camden Property Trust
8.	Nugget Market
9.	Recreational Equipment (REI)
10.	DreamWorks Animation SKG

Source: "100 Best Companies to Work for," *Fortune*, February 7, 2011, http://money.cnn.com/magazines/fortune/bestcompanies/2011/full_list/.

L●7
Global Issues in Services Marketing

The international marketing of services is a major part of global business, and the United States has become the world's largest exporter of services. Competition in international services is increasing rapidly, however.

To be successful in the global marketplace, service firms must first determine the nature of their core product. Then the marketing mix elements (additional services, place, promotion, pricing, distribution) should be designed to take into account each country's cultural, technological, and political environment.

Because of their competitive advantages, many U.S. service industries have been able to enter the global marketplace. U.S. banks, for example, have advantages in customer service and collections management. The field of construction and engineering services offers great global potential; U.S. companies have vast experience in this industry, so economies of scale are possible for machinery and materials, human resource management, and project management. The U.S. insurance industry has substantial knowledge about underwriting, risk evaluation, and insurance operations that it can export to other countries. Popular U.S. restaurants have also been successful in other countries. When Taco Bell opened at a large shopping mall in Dubai, customers waited in line as long as four hours to buy food at the chain's first Middle East location.[18]

Review
L●6 Explain internal marketing in services

Management   Employees   Customers

Good service flows from management to customers through employees.

internal marketing
Treating employees as customers and developing systems and benefits that satisfy their needs.

United States is world's largest exporter of services.

© Cengage Learning 2013

LO8 ▶
Nonprofit Organization Marketing

A **nonprofit organization** is an organization that exists to achieve some goal other than the usual business goals of profit, market share, or return on investment. Nonprofit organizations share important characteristics with private-sector service firms. Both market intangible products. Both often require the customer to be present during the production process. Both for-profit and nonprofit services vary greatly from producer to producer and from day to day, even from the same producer. Neither for-profit nor nonprofit services can be stored in the way that tangible goods can be produced, saved, and sold at a later date.

Few people realize that nonprofit organizations account for over 20 percent of the economic activity in the United States. The cost of government (i.e., taxes), the predominant form of nonprofit organization, has become the biggest single item in the American family budget—more than housing, food, or health care. Together, federal, state, and local governments collect tax revenues that amount to more than a third of the U.S. gross domestic product. Moreover, they employ nearly one of every five nonagricultural civilian workers. In addition to government entities, nonprofit organizations include hundreds of thousands of private museums, theaters, schools, and churches.

WHAT IS NONPROFIT ORGANIZATION MARKETING?

Nonprofit organization marketing is the effort by nonprofit organizations to bring about mutually satisfying exchanges with target markets. Although these organizations vary substantially in size and purpose and operate in different environments, most perform the following marketing activities:

→ Identify the customers they wish to serve or attract (although they usually use another term, such as *clients, patients, members,* or *sponsors*).

→ Explicitly or implicitly specify objectives.

→ Develop, manage, and eliminate programs and services.

→ Decide on prices to charge (although they use other terms, such as *fees, donations, tuition, fares, fines,* or *rates*).

→ Schedule events or programs, and determine where they will be held or where services will be offered.

→ Communicate their availability through brochures, signs, public service announcements, or advertisements.

Often, the nonprofit organizations that carry out these functions do not realize they are engaged in marketing.

UNIQUE ASPECTS OF NONPROFIT ORGANIZATION MARKETING STRATEGIES

Like their counterparts in business organizations, nonprofit managers develop marketing strategies to bring about mutually satisfying exchanges with target markets.

nonprofit organization
An organization that exists to achieve some goal other than the usual business goals of profit, market share, or return on investment.

nonprofit organization marketing
The effort by nonprofit organizations to bring about mutually satisfying exchanges with target markets.

However, marketing in nonprofit organizations is unique in many ways—including the setting of marketing objectives, the selection of target markets, and the development of appropriate marketing mixes.

Objectives In the private sector, the profit motive is both an objective for guiding decisions and a criterion for evaluating results. Nonprofit organizations do not seek to make a profit for redistribution to owners or shareholders. Rather, their focus is often on generating enough funds to cover expenses. The Methodist Church does not gauge its success by the amount of money left in offering plates. The Museum of Science and Industry does not base its performance evaluations on the dollar value of tokens put into the turnstile.

Most nonprofit organizations are expected to provide equitable, effective, and efficient services that respond to the wants and preferences of multiple constituencies. These include users, payers, donors, politicians, appointed officials, the media, and the general public. Nonprofit organizations cannot measure their success or failure in strictly financial terms.

The lack of a financial "bottom line" and the existence of multiple, diverse, intangible, and sometimes vague or conflicting objectives make prioritizing objectives, making decisions, and evaluating performance hard for nonprofit managers. They must often use approaches different from the ones commonly used in the private sector. For example, Planned Parenthood has devised a system for basing salary increases on how employees perform in relation to the objectives they set each year.

Target Markets Three issues relating to target markets are unique to nonprofit organizations:

→ **Apathetic or strongly opposed targets:** Private-sector organizations usually give priority to developing those market segments that are most likely to respond to particular offerings. In contrast, nonprofit organizations must often target those who are apathetic about or strongly opposed to receiving their services, such as vaccinations, family-planning guidance, help for problems of drug or alcohol abuse, and psychological counseling.

→ **Pressure to adopt undifferentiated segmentation strategies:** Nonprofit organizations often adopt undifferentiated strategies (see Chapter 8) by default. Sometimes they fail to recognize the advantages of targeting, or an undifferentiated approach might appear to offer economies of scale and low per capita costs. In other instances, nonprofit organizations are pressured or required to serve the maximum number of people by targeting the average user. The problem with developing services targeted at the average user is that there are few "average" users. Therefore, such strategies typically fail to fully satisfy any market segment. The Kansas Department of Tourism discovered that people came to the state for two clear reasons: those who wish to tour and those who want to hunt, fish, and boat. Furthermore, the tourist group consisted of people 60 years old and older who lived in the upper Midwest. The wildlife group consisted of people who were young and lived in the South.[19] This information allowed the state to improve the efficiency and effectiveness of its marketing programs.

→ **Complementary positioning:** The main role of many nonprofit organizations is to provide services, with available resources, to those who are not adequately served by private-sector organizations. As a result, the

State departments of tourism can develop advertisements based on a clear understanding of what the state has to offer and what current tourists enjoy doing there. For example, this advertisement for Nevada shows beautiful ski mountains and the correct pronunciation of the state's name.

For-Profit Universities

Ads for online schools are all over the Internet, in subway cars, and on television. The University of Phoenix, with nearly 500,000 students, is the biggest for-profit college. But some former students said they were duped into paying big bucks and going deeply in debt by slick and misleading recruiters.

A report by the Center for College Affordability and Productivity said enrollment in for-profit universities has reached 1.8 million students. While traditional public and nonprofit universities have grown just 1.6 and 1.4 percent (respectively) each year since 1986, for-profit institutions have seen an 8.4 percent annual growth rate. For-profit universities serve a wide range of student needs, including traditional programs as well as vocational and technical programs. For-profits are especially popular among those students typically underserved by the traditional college model. African-American and Hispanic students are enrolling in for-profit universities at a greater rate than in traditional universities and female enrollment has also greatly increased. Older students who work full-time are attracted to for-profit programs. The most recent target market for these institutions is members of the military.

The for-profit universities offer their programs online. Some of them have easy courses and fast degrees. They entice students to enroll with free textbooks and laptops. Some allow students to transfer courses from other institutions for classes in which they earned grades as low as D. Online schools such as American Military have relocated their headquarters to obtain certification from regional boards with less demanding standards. And when graduates find employment, it's likely to pay less compared to graduates who have a degree from a traditional university. In some cases, students have found that their degrees are not worth much to prospective employers.

Proponents of for-profit universities say the schools serve an important role by providing higher education to students who wouldn't ordinarily get one. For-profit schools have produced millions of success stories, helping students prepare for and find new jobs, advance their careers, and earn higher pay. Graduates find jobs in a wide range of high-demand professions as nurses and health care aides, computer professionals and programmers, chefs and retail managers, solar and wind energy technicians.

Though for-profits get the lion's share of their tuition from financial aid, the default rates on loans for students who attended for-profit schools are alarming. About 50 percent of the students at for-profits drop out, so schools need to keep adding new students, and have to try to recruit just about anyone—those most vulnerable in society.[20] Are for-profit universities a welcome economic alternative, or are they taking advantage of their students? Are their recruiting practices ethical?

nonprofit organization must often complement, rather than compete with, the efforts of others. The positioning task is to identify underserved market segments and to develop marketing programs that match their needs rather than to target the niches that may be most profitable. For example, a university library might see itself as complementing the services of the public library, rather than competing with it.

Product Decisions There are three product-related distinctions between business and nonprofit organizations:

→ **Benefit complexity:** Rather than simple product concepts, such as "Fly the friendly skies" or "We make money the old-fashioned way," nonprofit organizations often market complex behaviors or ideas. Examples include the need to exercise or eat right, not to drink and drive, and not to smoke tobacco. The benefits that a person receives are complex, long term, and intangible, and therefore are more difficult to communicate to consumers. St. Jude Children's

Research Hospital has developed a simple yet compelling way to communicate benefits in its slogan "Finding Cures. Saving Children."

→ **Benefit strength:** The benefit strength of many nonprofit offerings is quite weak or indirect. What are the direct, personal benefits to you of driving 55 miles per hour, donating blood, or asking your neighbors to contribute money to a charity? In contrast, most private-sector service organizations can offer customers direct, personal benefits in an exchange relationship.

→ **Involvement:** Many nonprofit organizations market products that elicit either very low involvement ("Prevent forest fires" or "Don't litter") or very high involvement ("Join the military" or "Stop smoking"). The typical range for private-sector goods is much narrower. Traditional promotional tools might be inadequate to motivate adoption of either low- or high-involvement products.

Place (Distribution) Decisions A nonprofit organization's capacity for distributing its service offerings to potential customer groups when and where they want them is typically a key variable in determining the success of those service offerings. For example, most state land-grant universities offer extension programs throughout their state to reach the general public. Many large universities have one or more satellite campus locations to provide easier access for students in other areas. Some educational institutions also offer classes to students at off-campus locations via interactive video technology.

The extent to which a service depends on fixed facilities has important implications for distribution decisions. Obviously, services such as rail transit and lake fishing can be delivered only at specific points. Many nonprofit services, however, do not depend on special facilities. Counseling, for example, need not take place in agency offices; it might occur wherever counselors and clients can meet. Probation services, outreach youth programs, and educational courses taught on commuter trains are other examples of deliverable services.

Promotion Decisions Many nonprofit organizations are explicitly or implicitly prohibited from advertising, thus limiting their promotion options. Most federal agencies fall into this category. Other nonprofit organizations simply do not have the resources to retain advertising agencies, promotion consultants, or marketing staff. However, nonprofit organizations have a few special promotion resources to call on:

→ **Professional volunteers:** Non-profit organizations often seek out marketing, sales, and advertising professionals to help them develop and implement promotion strategies. In some instances, an advertising agency donates its services in exchange for potential long-term benefits. One advertising agency donated its services to a major symphony because the symphony had a blue-ribbon

PSAs are often aimed at a target market with apathy or opposition to a subject, such as this PSA instructing drivers not to text while driving.

board of directors. Donated services create goodwill, personal contacts, and general awareness of the donor's organization, reputation, and competency.

→ **Sales promotion activities:** Sales promotion activities that make use of existing services or other resources are increasingly being used to draw attention to the offerings of nonprofit organizations. Sometimes nonprofit charities even team up with other companies for promotional activities.

→ **Public service advertising:** A **public service advertisement (PSA)** is an announcement that promotes a program of a federal, state, or local government or of a nonprofit organization. Unlike a commercial advertiser, the sponsor of the PSA does not pay for the time or space. Instead, it is donated by the medium. The Advertising Council has developed PSAs that are some of the most memorable advertisements of all time. For example, Smokey the Bear reminded everyone to be careful not to start forest fires.

→ **Peer-to-peer communications:** Some nonprofit agencies have been successful in offering forums for people to share experiences. For example, the March of Dimes Foundation created an online forum at **www.shareyourstory.org** to gather real life stories that help spread the word about its mission to prevent birth defects, premature birth, and infant mortality. Families can share their experiences in the form of short stories and blogs.

Pricing Decisions Five key characteristics distinguish the pricing decisions of nonprofit organizations from those of the profit sector:

→ **Pricing objectives:** The main pricing objective in the profit sector is revenue or, more specifically, profit maximization, sales maximization, or target return on sales or investment. Many nonprofit organizations must also be concerned about revenue. Often, however, nonprofit organizations seek to either partially or fully defray costs rather than to achieve a profit for distribution to stockholders. Nonprofit organizations also seek to redistribute income—for instance, through taxation and sliding-scale fees. Moreover, they strive to allocate resources fairly among individuals or households or across geographic or political boundaries.

→ **Nonfinancial prices:** In many nonprofit situations, consumers are not charged a monetary price but instead must absorb nonmonetary costs. The importance of those costs is illustrated by the large number of eligible citizens who do not take advantage of so-called free services for the poor. In many public assistance programs, about half the people who are eligible don't participate. Nonmonetary costs consist of the opportunity cost of time, embarrassment costs, and effort costs.

Review
LO8 Describe nonprofit organization marketing

Nonprofit Organization Marketing

PRODUCT
- Benefit complexity
- Benefit strength
- Involvement

PLACE
- Special facilities

TARGET
- Apathetic or strongly opposed
- Undifferentiated segmentation
- Complementary positioning

PROMOTION
- Professional volunteers
- Sales
- Public service advertising

PRICE
- Nonfinancial
- Indirect payment
- Separation between payers and users
- Below-cost pricing

© Cengage Learning 2013

→ **Indirect payment:** Indirect payment through taxes is common to marketers of "free" services, such as libraries, fire protection, and police protection. Indirect payment is not a common practice in the profit sector.

→ **Separation between payers and users:** By design, the services of many charitable organizations are provided for those who are relatively poor and largely paid for by those who are better off financially. Although examples of separation between payers and users can be found in the profit sector (such as insurance claims), the practice is much less prevalent.

→ **Below-cost pricing:** An example of below-cost pricing is university tuition. Virtually all private and public colleges and universities price their services below full cost.

Percentage of U.S. employment influence by the service sector

Swimsuit combinations available on the Lands' End Web site

Percentage of U.S. economic activity generated by nonprofit organizations

Possible gaps in the gap model of service delivery

Time Zappos.com warehouse is processing orders

Age of Kansas tourists

Number of students enrolled in for-profit universities

81 216 20 5 24-7 60+ 1.8 million

Review and Applications

Discuss the importance of services to the economy. The service sector plays a crucial role in the U.S. economy, employing more than 80 percent of the workforce and accounting for a similar percentage of the gross domestic product.

1.1 To keep track of how service employment is affecting the U.S. economy, go to **www.bls.gov/bdm/**. Look at the right sidebar, which gives the latest numbers for business employment dynamics. What trends to you see? Do the numbers support the information from the chapter?

Discuss the differences between services and goods. Services are distinguished by four characteristics. Services are intangible performances in that they lack clearly identifiable physical characteristics, making it difficult for marketers to communicate their specific benefits to potential customers. The production and consumption of services occur simultaneously. Services are heterogeneous because their quality depends on elements such as the service provider, individual consumer, location, and so on. Finally, services are perishable in the sense that they cannot be stored or saved. As a result, synchronizing supply with demand is particularly challenging in the service industry.

2.1 Assume that you are a manager of a bank branch. Write a list of the implications of intangibility for your firm.
writing

2.2 Over 25 years ago, Tim and Nina Zagat began publishing leisure guides containing reviews of restaurants. Today, the renowned *Zagat* guides still contain reviews of restaurants, but they also rate hotels, entertainment, nightlife, movies, shopping, and even music. Go to **www.zagat.com.** In your opinion, are *Zagat* survey guides goods or services? Explain your reasoning.

 3 **Describe the components of service quality and the gap model of service quality.** Service quality has five components: reliability (ability to perform the service dependably, accurately, and consistently), responsiveness (providing prompt service), assurance (knowledge and courtesy of employees and their ability to convey trust), empathy (caring, individualized attention), and tangibles (physical evidence of the service).

The gap model identifies five key discrepancies that can influence customer evaluations of service quality. When the gaps are large, service quality is low. As the gaps shrink, service quality improves. Gap 1 is found between customers' expectations and management's perceptions of those expectations. Gap 2 is found between management's perception of what the customer wants and specifications for service quality. Gap 3 is found between service quality specifications and delivery of the service. Gap 4 is found between service delivery and what the company promises to the customer through external communication. Gap 5 is found between customers' service expectations and their perceptions of service performance.

3.1 Analyze a recent experience that you have had with a service business (for example, hairdresser, movie theater, dentist, restaurant, car repair) in terms of your expectations and perceptions about each of the five components of service quality.

 4 **Develop marketing mixes for services.** "Product" (service) strategy issues include what is being processed (people, possessions, mental stimulus, information), core and supplementary services, customization versus standardization, and the service mix. Distribution decisions involve convenience, number of outlets, direct versus indirect distribution, and scheduling. Stressing tangible cues, using personal sources of information, creating strong organizational images, and engaging in postpurchase communication are effective promotion strategies. Pricing objectives for services can be revenue-oriented, operations-oriented, patronage-oriented, or any combination of the three.

team

4.1 Form a team with at least two other classmates and come up with an idea for a new service. Develop a marketing mix strategy for the new service.

 5 **Discuss relationship marketing in services.** Relationship marketing in services involves attracting, developing, and retaining customer relationships. There are three levels of relationship marketing: level 1 focuses on pricing incentives; level 2 uses pricing incentives and social bonds with customers; and level 3 uses pricing, social bonds, and structural bonds to build long-term relationships.

team

5.1 For the new service developed for question 4.1, have the members of the team discuss how they would implement a relationship marketing strategy.

 6 **Explain internal marketing in services.** Internal marketing means treating employees as customers and developing systems and benefits that satisfy their needs. Employees who like their jobs and are happy with the firm they work for are more likely to deliver good service.

writing

6.1 Choose a service firm with which you do a lot of business. Write a memo to the manager explaining the importance of internal marketing and outlining the factors internal marketing includes.

online

6.2 Return to www.zagat.com and investigate what the site offers. How does *Zagat* propose to help companies with internal services marketing?

 7 **Discuss global issues in services marketing.** The United States has become the world's largest exporter of services. Although competition is keen, the United States has a competitive advantage because of its vast experience in many service industries. To be successful globally, service firms must adjust their marketing mix for the environment of each target country.

7.1 What issues would you have to think about in going global with the new service that you developed in the questions above? How would you change your marketing mix to address those issues?

Describe nonprofit organization marketing. Nonprofit organizations pursue goals other than profit, market share, and return on investment. Nonprofit organization marketing facilitates mutually satisfying exchanges between nonprofit organizations and their target markets. Several unique characteristics distinguish nonbusiness marketing strategy, including: a concern with services and social behaviors rather than manufactured goods and profit; a difficult, undifferentiated, and in some ways marginal target market; a complex product that might have only indirect benefits and elicit very low involvement; distribution that might or might not require special facilities depending on the service provided; a relative lack of resources for promotion; and prices only indirectly related to the exchange between the producer and the consumer of services.

8.1 Form a team with two or three classmates. Using the promotion strategies discussed in the nonprofit section of this chapter, develop a promotion strategy for your college or university.

 team

Key Terms

assurance *420*	intangibility *418*	public service advertisement (PSA) *436*
core service *424*	internal marketing *431*	reliability *420*
credence quality *418*	mass customization *425*	responsiveness *420*
empathy *420*	nonprofit organization *432*	search quality *418*
experience quality *418*	nonprofit organization marketing *432*	service *417*
gap model *421*		supplementary services *424*
heterogeneity *419*	perishability *419*	tangibles *420*
inseparability *418*		

Exercises

ETHICS EXERCISE

 ethics

Web sites such as **www.cancerpage.com** offer cancer patients sophisticated medical data and advice in exchange for personal information that is then sold to advertisers and business partners and used by the Web site to create products to sell back to patients. Some argue that cancer patients visiting these sites are willingly exchanging their personal information for the sites' medical information. Others contend that this kind of exchange is unethical.

Questions

1. Is this practice ethical?

2. Does the AMA Statement of Ethics have anything to say about this issue? Go to **www.marketingpower.com** and review the statement. Then write a brief paragraph on what the AMA Statement of Ethics contains that relates to this situation.

© iStockphoto.com/Juan Facundo Mora Soria

MARKETING PLAN EXERCISE

Continue your strategic marketing plan and complete your Part 3 Marketing Plan Worksheet by logging on to the companion Web site at www.cengagebrain.com and answering the following questions about your chosen company:

1. What service aspects are provided with the product? List specific examples of how you can incorporate all five elements of service quality into your offering. What tactics can you define that would minimize any potential service quality gaps? How is customer service handled? What elements of service quality can your firm focus on? What impact would selling on the Internet have on your customer service operation?

2. With whom should your chosen company practice relationship marketing? E-marketing is particularly vulnerable to breakdowns in client relationships. Which sorts of bonds should be stressed in the relationship marketing strategy? How can your company "touch" its customers differently online from offline? Are there advantages to online customer service? Disadvantages?

APPLICATION EXERCISE

All people know quality when they see it—or do they? Let's take a look at some goods and services and then think about assessing their quality. For this exercise, work in teams of two to three and discuss each item before determining its final placement.[21]

Activities

1. Using the abbreviations in parentheses, place each of the following products and services along the continuum below: a new car (C), designer jeans (J), car oil change (O), dress dry cleaning (D), haircut (H), tax preparation software (T), college education (E).

   100 percent physical good _____ 100 percent service

2. Once you have placed the items along the continuum, consider how easy it is to assess the quality of each item.

   Easy to assess quality _____ Difficult to assess quality

3. What assumptions can you make about the ability to assess the quality of goods compared to services? Is it easier to assess the quality of some goods than others? What about for services?

CASE STUDY: MinuteClinic

SERVING THE SICK WHERE THEY SHOP

© AP Images/Andy King

Susan Lyons woke up on a Saturday morning with all the symptoms of strep throat, but her doctor's office was closed for the weekend. Jeremy Brown struggled to get through his workday because of a sinus infection, but he didn't have time on his lunch break to drive across town to see his family physician. Arun Kumar went to his doctor for a flu shot but was turned away because they had already run out of the vaccine. In the end, all three turned to Minute-Clinic for treatment instead.

MinuteClinic healthcare centers are open seven days a week with later hours than traditional doctors have. They don't require appointments and can provide patients with a diagnosis and prescription within 15–45 minutes, tops. The fact that they are located in convenient retail settings, usually attached to a CVS drugstore where the prescription can be filled in one stop, adds to their growing appeal. "It was such a pleasant experience," Arun Kumar says after paying $30 for a flu shot at MinuteClinic, "that I figured that I would be happy to go back there for minor ailments and avoid the long waits at my doctor's office."

MinuteClinic, which opened its first location in 2000, was the pioneer of in-store clinics and an innovator in what industry analysts call the "retailization of health care." Considering the growing need for cheaper, more accessible health care, it's no surprise that the company is expanding so quickly. CVS acquired MinuteClinic in July 2006 and announced plans to grow from 128 locations to nearly 500 by early 2008.

Staffed by nurse practitioners and physician assistants who specialize in family health care, MinuteClinic provides basic medical services for common ailments such as ear infections and strep throat. Some locations also offer vaccines and physicals. An electronic medical records system streamlines the process for each patient by generating educational materials, invoices, and prescriptions at the end of the visit. Electronic records also make it possible to instantly transfer information to the patients' primary physicians. MinuteClinic prices range from about $50 to $80, making a visit about half as expensive as one to a doctor's office.

MinuteClinic CEO Michael C. Howe says, "MinuteClinic is an example of how creativity and innovation can be brought to our struggling healthcare system to affect change and make basic care more accessible and affordable for today's consumer." The American Medical Association (AMA) has expressed reservations, however. Board member Dr. Rebecca Patchin explains, "The AMA is concerned about patients who would seek care in a freestanding clinic and have a more serious disease that would not be initially diagnosed or diagnosed quickly." Howe insists they are not trying to replace the traditional family physician, however; they simply want to offer a convenient, low-cost alternative for patients with minor illnesses. Patients exhibiting symptoms outside of the clinic's scope of services or showing signs of a chronic condition are referred elsewhere.

MinuteClinic's ability to handle widespread health emergencies within a community was tested when Minnesota was hit with a string of flu-related deaths in 2007. As a record number of residents sought vaccinations, MinuteClinic quickly put a plan in place to address the crisis and meet the unexpected demand. Instead of boosting staff at all facilities in the Minneapolis area, the company chose a hub-and-spoke approach for better inventory control, offering the shots in only eight MinuteClinic locations. They hired supplemental nursing staff for those clinics and administered up to 300 shots a day in each. The lines became so long that they created children's areas to make the wait easier for families, adding televisions, videos, and coloring books to keep little ones entertained and fostering what Donna Haugland of MinuteClinic describes as "a community-building environment."

CEO Howe praised the good work they did during the flu crisis: "It is amazing what practitioners can do in the right environment and given the chance." Patients agree. The response to the clinics has been overwhelmingly positive. A 2006 Harris Interactive poll reported that 92 percent of the people who visited a retail clinic were satisfied with its convenience, 89 percent were satisfied with the quality of care they received, and 80 percent were satisfied with the cost.

Even the AMA is advising traditional physicians to consider changing their practices to better compete with retail clinics by extending office hours, offering same-day appointments, or even doing away with appointments altogether. AMA Board member Patchin admits, "With their quick and easy access and low prices, the store-based clinics are obviously meeting a need."[22]

Questions

1. Describe how MinuteClinic puts the following promotion strategies to work for them: stressing tangible cues, using personal information sources, creating a strong organizational image, and engaging in post-purchase communication. What else could they try?

2. Are MinuteClinic's services customized or standardized for patients? Do they incorporate any elements of mass customization?

3. In what way did MinuteClinic demonstrate reliability and responsiveness during the flu outbreak in Minnesota? How did it impress customers with tangible physical evidence that the clinics cared about them?

4. How important has MinuteClinic's place (distribution) strategy been to the company's success? Which elements does MinuteClinic focus on with its marketing mix? Why?

COMPANY CLIPS: Kodak—Reinventing the Mix

You probably think of Kodak as selling only products. In fact, the company has an entire division, the Graphic Communications Group, dedicated to delivering service solutions to business customers. Mark Webber is vice president of worldwide sales partnerships for Kodak's digital printing solutions group, which provides services to the B-to-B (business-to-business) market. In this video, he explains how Kodak creates both digital and analog printing solutions for a wide variety of clients and how the company is taking advantage of new technology to meet evolving customer demands.

Questions

1. Would you describe Kodak's services as customized or standardized? Why?

2. Describe Kodak's services mix.

3. Outline Kodak's pricing strategy for its services.

Notes

1. Valarie Zeithaml, Mary Jo Bitner, and Dwayne Gremler, *Services Marketing* (New York: McGraw-Hill, 2009).
2. James C. Franklin, "An Overview of BLS Projections to 2016," *Monthly Labor Review*, 130, no. 11 (2007): 3–12.
3. Anne DiNardo, "Chi-nnati's, Cincinnati, Ohio," VMSD, April 26, 2010, http://vmsd.com/content/chi-nnatis-cincinnati-ohio.
4. Alex Palmer, "Report: Retail Customer Service Stinks," http://www.adweek.com/news/advertising-branding/report-retail-customer-service-stinks-106761 (Accessed December 7, 2009).
5. Zeithaml, Bitner, and Gremler, *Services Marketing*.

6. Paula Andruss, "Delivering WOW through Service," *Marketing News*, October 15, 2008, 10.
7. Daniel McCarthy, "CMO Council Explores Customer Experience in Difficult Market," *BtoB*, October 13, 2008, 4.
8. Zeithaml, Bitner, and Gremler, *Services Marketing*.
9. Bo Burlingham, "Lessons From a Blue-Collar Millionaire," *Inc.*, February 2010, 57–63.
10. *Ibid.*
11. Jena McGregor, "USAA's Battle Plan," *Bloomberg Businessweek*, February 18, 2010, www.businessweek.com/magazine/content/10_09/b4168040782858.htm.
12. Much of the material in this section is based on Christopher H. Lovelock and Jochen Wirtz, *Services Marketing*, 6th ed. (Upper Saddle River, NJ: Prentice Hall, 2011).
13. *Ibid.*
14. *Ibid.*
15. Much of the material in this section is based on Leonard L. Berry and A. Parasuraman, *Marketing Services* (New York: Free Press, 1991), 132–150.
16. Barbara Farfan, "100 Best Companies to Work For," *Fortune*, November 14, 2010, http://money.cnn.com/magazines/fortune/bestcompanies/2010/.

marketing&you: Results.

A high score means you have a positive attitude about charitable operations and most likely think that nonprofit organizations fulfill an important role in society. However, a high score does not necessarily mean you give more to charity.

17. Carmine Gallo, "Bringing Passion to Starbucks', Travelocity," *BusinessWeek*, January 2, 2008, www.businessweek.com/smallbiz/content/jan2008/sb2008019_492857.htm.

18. Janet Adamy and Maria Abi-Habib, "Yum Brands Bets on Taco Bell to Win Over Customers Overseas," *Wall Street Journal*, November 19, 2008, B5.

19. Jeff Borden, "Greetings from Kansas," *Marketing News*, May 15, 2008, 13–15.

20. Lanny Davis, "Let's Stick to the Facts on For-Profit Colleges Regulations," *Huffington Post*, October 25, 2010, www.huffingtonpost.com/lanny-davis/lets-stick-to-the-facts-o_b_773305.html; Lindsey Burke, "The Assault on For-Profit Universities," *The Foundry*, August 10, 2010, http://blog.heritage.org/?p=40870; Chris Cuomo, Gerry Wagschal, and Lauren Pente, "ABC News Investigates For-Profit Education: Recruiters at the University of Phoenix," *ABCNews*, August 19, 2010, http://abcnews.go.com/TheLaw/abc-news-investigates-profit-education-recruiters-caught-offering/story?id=12122004; Daniel Golden, "For-Profit Colleges Target the Military," *BusinessWeek*, December 30, 2009, www.businessweek.com/magazine/content/10_02/b4162036095366.htm.

21. This exercise is based on the contribution of Stacia Wert-Gray (University of Central Oklahoma) and Gordon T. Gray (Oklahoma City University) to *Great Ideas in Teaching Marketing*, a teaching supplement that accompanies McDaniel, Lamb, and Hair's *Introduction to Marketing*.

22. Chris Silva, "One-Minute Drill," *Employee Benefit News*, April 15, 2007, http://ebn.benefitnews.com/news/one-minute-drill-black-decker-finds-39958-1.html; Antoinette Alexander, "MinuteClinic Steps Up to Curb Flu Crisis in Twin Cities," *Drug Store News*, March 19, 2007, http://findarticles.com/p/articles/mi_m3374/is_4_29/ai_n27194133/; Pallavi Gogoi, "Drugstore Clinics Are Bursting with Health," *BusinessWeek*, July 18, 2006, www.businessweek.com/investor/content/jul2006/pi20060717_240148.htm; "Most Patients Happy with In-Store Clinics," *Progressive Grocer*, March 30, 2007, www.progressivegrocer.com/top-stories/headlines/health-wellness/id11134/most-patients-happy-with-in-store-clinics-study/; Michelle Andrews, "In-Store Clinics Give Doctors Heartburn," *U.S. News & World Report*, July 20, 2007, http://health.usnews.com/usnews/health/articles/070720/20clinics.htm; Medical Clinic, CVS Web site, www.minuteclinic.com.

23. McAffee Web site, www.mcafee.com; Barry McPherson, "McAfee Response to Current False Positive Issue," April 21, 2010, http://blogs.mcafee.com/enterprise/support/mcafee-response-on-current-false-positive-issue; Larry Barrett, "McAfee Moves on Following Massive Miscue," *eSecurity Planet,* April 27, 2010, www.esecurityplanet.com/news/article.php/3878861/McAfee-Moves-On-Following-Massive-Miscue.htm; Antone Gonsalves, "McAfee Bug Forces Massive PC Cleanup," *InformationWeek*, April 22, 2010, www.informationweek.com/news/software/app_optimization/showArticle.jhtml?articleID=224600157; "McAfee to Compensate Home User for Bad Update," *Technology News*, April 26, 2010, www.the-technology-news.com/2010/04/mcafee-to-compensate-home-users-for-bad-update; Larry Seltzer, "Lessons of the McAfee- False Positive Fiasco," *PCMag*, April 23, 2010, www.pcmag.com/article2/0,2817,2363018,00.asp; Lance Whitney, "McAfee Apologies for Antivirus Update Disaster," *CNet*, April 23, 2010, http://news.cnet.com/8301-1009_3-20003247-83.html.

24. "About Us," Prestige Brands Web site, www.PrestigeBrands.com (Accessed April 20, 2011).

Marketing Miscue

MCAFEE VIRUS PROTECTION UPDATE CRASHES COMPUTERS WORLDWIDE

Headquartered in Santa Clara, California, McAfee was founded is one of the world's largest dedicated security providers. McAfee's customers range from individual home users to large corporations to governments around the world. The company segments its markets into home, small business, mid-sized business, and enterprise. Annual revenue has grown to around $2 billion. The business market is about 60 percent of the company's revenue, with the remainder from the consumer marketplace. Geographically, approximately 60 percent of revenue is derived from the North American marketplace. McAfee's online subscription site, http://home.mcafee.com, provides online software delivery to over two million paid subscribers, making the site one of the largest paid subscription sites on the Internet.

The Botched Update

Oh no… Not the blue screen of death…

While the online software delivery has been a hallmark of McAfee's product design and delivery, it was almost the downfall of the company in early 2010. A faulty anti-virus update file shut down computers worldwide when the update misclassified a fundamental Windows XP system file as a malicious program. McAfee's anti-virus program deleted the "threat." Unfortunately, deleting an essential Windows XP rendered computers useless as many experienced the dreaded "blue screen of death."

The extent of the impact upon McAfee's customer base was never fully disclosed. Media reports and Twitter postings suggested that the affected users numbered in the thousands, while the company suggested that the affected group was less than half of a percent of the company's customers. While the actual number of affected home and business customers might never be known, there were notable shutdowns: a third of the hospitals in Rhode Island had to suspend treatment to non-trauma emergency room patients, state police patrol car computers in Kentucky shut down, and one large U.S. multinational company reported that 50,000 personal computers could only be repaired manually by a technician sitting at each computer.

The Aftermath

McAfee quickly removed the faulty update from its servers and eventually offered an apology, but the major fallout from the update fiasco was the revelation of inadequate quality assurance at McAfee.

According to some reports, McAfee's shoddy quality assurance procedures resulted in the faulty product's release. Critically, the faulty product had not been tested on the version of Windows XP which the product ultimately crashed. With Windows XP in use by a large number of computer users, many questioned why this configuration was left out of the testing processing. Apparently McAfee had recently changed its quality assurance process. In doing so, it allowed the faulty file to get past the test environment and onto the computers of its customers.

Ultimately, the reputation of software security providers such as McAfee hinge on their ability to prevent problems, not cause them. Despite offering to reimburse home and home office users for computer repair costs, McAffee's reputation suffered. Blog comments lambasting the companies quality control processes proliferated. One software consultant noted that 75 percent of his clients had switched away from McAfee prior to the disaster. Unfortunately, the 25 percent that hadn't switched were swamping the consultant's technicians, who were scrambling to fix the software problem in a product they had recommended to their clients. One customer summed up the concerns; a security protection product offering should not be on the list of risky software downloads![23]

1. What is the role of quality assurance in McAfee's product development process?
2. Describe McAfee's customer service recovery process.

Critical Thinking Case

PART 3: PRESTIGE BRANDS, INC.: TRANSFORMING THE BUSINESS

Prestige Brands markets, sells, and distributes over-the-counter healthcare and household cleaning products to retail outlets in the United States, Canada, and certain international markets. In September of 2010, the company's over-the-counter (OTC) healthcare products included:

→ Chloraseptic® Sore Throat Relief
→ Clear Eyes®
→ Cloverine®
→ Compoz®
→ Compound W®
→ Dermoplast®
→ Ezo®
→ Freezone®
→ Kerodex®
→ Little Remedies®
→ Momentum®
→ Mosco®
→ Murine® Earigate®
→ Murine® Ears
→ Murine® Homeopathic

→ Murine® Tears
→ New-Skin® Liquid Bandage
→ New-Skin® Scar Fade
→ Outgro®
→ Oxipor®
→ Percogesic®
→ The Doctor's® Brush Picks®
→ The Doctor's® Night Guard™
→ Wartner®

Household brands included:

→ Chore Boy®
→ Cinch®
→ Comet®
→ Comet® Spray Gel Mildew Stain Remover
→ Spic and Span®

© Terri Miller/E-Visual Communications, Inc.

SHAREHOLDER VALUE CREATION STRATEGY

Shareholder value creation at Prestige Brands follows a three-pronged strategic approach: driving core organic growth, a merger and acquisition effort focusing exclusively on OTC, and strategic portfolio management. To drive organic growth, the company focuses on five key areas: brand positioning, compelling creative concepts, increasing advertising and marketing support, listening to and responding to retail customers, and connecting with consumers as they are end users of the brands. The second prong of the strategy to create shareholder value involves an exclusive OTC merger-and-acquisition focus. The company has three major acquisition criteria. One, the focus is exclusively on the OTC healthcare market. The OTC healthcare market is a growth market with favorable demographic trends and attractive margins. Two, the company seeks to acquire brands that are broadly recognized by consumers, possess scale strength to make them particularly relevant to retailers, and are additive to the core categories within the company. Three, the company looks closely at the financial characteristics of all potential acquisitions: accretive to growth and earnings, a prudent capital structure, and economics driven by the brand's ability to enhance potential shareholder value. The third prong of the corporate strategy is to effectively manage the portfolio of products and brands over time. Specifically, this prong involves periodically reassessing which brands are the best long-term from a portfolio standpoint and then adjusting the portfolio accordingly.

A TRANSFORMATIONAL ACQUISITION: BLACKSMITH BRANDS

With core organic growth and strategic portfolio management in mind, Prestige Brands acquired Blacksmith Brands in the fall of 2010. Blacksmith Brands owned five leading consumer OTC brands:

→ Efferdent® Denture Cleanser

→ Effergrip® Denture Adhesive

→ Luden's® Throat Drops

→ PediaCare® Children's OTC Medicines

→ NasalCrom® Nasal Allergy Spray

This was considered a transformational acquisition for the company, as it was a meaningful step in its long-term strategy of an increasing presence in the OTC healthcare arena and in building a brand portfolio that would enable organic growth. The addition of the well-known Blacksmith brands would strengthen Prestige's platform in its core cough/cold and oral care categories. In particular, Prestige was strengthening its position in key categories with the additions of Efferdent®, PediaCare®, and Luden's®. These three scale brands competed in attractive categories that Prestige Brands knew well, and they offered a clear path for shareholder value creation through increased brand support and line extensions. The acquired brands were well aligned across Prestige's key OTC categories:

OTC Category	Brands
Cough/Cold	Chloraseptic®, Luden's®, PediaCare®, Little Remedies®, NasalCrom®
Oral Care	Efferdent®, Effergrip®, The Doctor's® Night Guard™, Ezo®
Eye & Ear Care	Clear Eyes®, Murine®
Skin & Foot Care	Compound W®, Wartner®, New Skin®, Dermoplast®
Other	Percogesic®, Compoz®

Increased support of the core OTC healthcare franchise after the acquisition of Blacksmith Brands focused on innovative advertising and promotional campaigns and new product launches. The commitment to equity building brand support of the acquired brands was reflected in a national television campaign and digital marketing for PediaCare®; a radio campaign, digital marketing, sampling, and free standing inserts (FSIs) for Luden's®; and bonus packs and FSIs for Efferdent® and Effergrip®.

A MAJOR MILESTONE

Prestige Brand's net revenue for the first nine months of fiscal 2011 grew 8 percent to $240.1 million. As a result of the increased advertising and support behind the core OTC healthcare franchise, the core OTC portfolio significantly outperformed their respective categories for the period. Overall, during the latest quarter, Prestige Brands (with the Blacksmith acquisition) experienced a 26.5 percent gain in consumption of its core OTC sales versus flat category consumption of these categories in aggregate. According to Matthew Mannelly, CEO, "The acquisition of Blacksmith Brands represents a transformative and exciting opportunity for us. Our strategy seems to be working, as evidenced by our growth in revenues and data demonstrating our brands' growth at a rate significantly faster than the overall category growth. And, the Company is strengthened by having a stronger brand portfolio to offer our retail customers."[24]

Questions

1. What role can acquisitions play in building a product portfolio and creating shareholder value?

2. Outline the product line depth, product mix width, and individual product items at Prestige Brands.

4 Distribution Decisions

chapter

13

Marketing Channels

Learning Outcomes

1 Explain what a marketing channel is and why intermediaries are needed

2 Define the types of channel intermediaries and describe their functions and activities

3 Describe the channel structures for consumer and business products and discuss alternative channel arrangements

4 Discuss the issues that influence channel strategy

5 Describe the different channel relationship types and their unique costs and benefits

6 Explain channel leadership, conflict, and partnering

7 Discuss channels and distribution decisions in global markets

8 Identify the special problems and opportunities associated with distribution in service organizations

LO1
Marketing Channels

The term *channel* is derived from the Latin word *canalis*, which means canal. A marketing channel can be viewed as a large canal or pipeline through which products, their ownership, communication, financing and payment, and accompanying risk flow to the consumer. Formally, a **marketing channel** (also called a **channel of distribution**) is a business structure of interdependent organizations that are involved in the process of making a product or service available for use or consumption by end customers or business users. Marketing channels facilitate the physical movement of goods from location to location, thus representing "place" or "distribution" in the marketing mix (product, price, promotion, and place) and encompassing the processes involved in getting the right product to the right place at the right time.

Many different types of organizations participate in marketing channels. **Channel members** (wholesalers, distributors, and retailers, also sometimes referred to as *intermediaries*, *resellers*, and *middlemen*) negotiate with one another, buy and sell products, and facilitate the change of ownership between buyer and seller in the course of moving the product from the manufacturer into the hands of the final consumer. As products move through channels, channel members facilitate the distribution process by providing specialization and division of labor, overcoming discrepancies, and providing contact efficiency.

> "Marketing channels facilitate the **physical** movement of goods from location to location."

marketing channel (channel of distribution)
A set of interdependent organizations that ease the transfer of ownership as products move from producer to business user or consumer.

marketing&you.

Using the following scale, indicate your opinions on the lines before the items.

STRONGLY DISAGREE 1 2 3 4 5 STRONGLY AGREE

_____ I would prefer to be a leader.

_____ I see myself as a good leader.

_____ I will be a success.

_____ People always seem to recognize my authority.

_____ I have a natural talent for influencing people.

_____ I am assertive.

_____ I like to have authority over other people.

_____ I am a born leader.

Source: Scale #119, *Marketing Scales Handbook*, G. Bruner, K. James, H. Hensel, eds., Vol. III. © by American Marketing Association. Used with permission of the American Marketing Association.

Now, total your score. Read the chapter and find out what your score means at the end.

customer experience

Capturing a Bigger Slice of the Pie

The pizza delivery business is very competitive, with both local businesses and national chains competing for a $28.5 billion U.S. consumer market annually. Many of the delivery pizzas ordered in the United States each year are purchased by young adults and teenagers. Papa John's, a 2,700-unit national pizza restaurant chain, believed it could capture more market share if it could find a way to make ordering and delivery easier and more appealing to the technologically savvy members of the younger segment. And if it could do so, it could compete more effectively with larger national companies such as Pizza Hut and Domino's.

To better serve its customers, Papa John's introduced a new marketing and ordering channel designed to attract younger consumers, rolling out a new service so customers could order pizza from a cell phone or PDA via text message. Once customers established their online accounts, they could at any time simply tap in their preferences for one of several favorite pizzas using an abbreviated code. The meal order would be delivered to any of several preprogrammed delivery addresses, and paid for with credit or debit card information already on file in a database, and delivered within a half hour from the closest retail location.

Key additional benefits of customers' willingness to opt into this unique channel arrangement are better overall marketing and customer awareness. By keeping a database of customer purchase behavior, customized promotions flow through the channel to pizza lovers, with great deals offered on favorite crusts, meats, and other toppings according to customer's past preferences. The electronic channel can also be engaged in other ways, such as sending customers digital coupons, providing updates on new menu items, and engaging customers with reminder advertising.

The results of employing this exciting new marketing and delivery channel were impressive, with Papa John's share rising to 6.9 percent of the marketplace despite having far fewer locations than their major competitors. The company also introduced Web site ordering to great success, with 65 million unique visitors in the first year of operations. The company is optimistic that these new channels will allow it to continue to compete strongly with the "big boys" in the world of pizza delivery.[1]

© iStockphoto.com/Juan Facundo Mora Soria

PROVIDING SPECIALIZATION AND DIVISION OF LABOR

According to the concept of *specialization and division of labor*, breaking down a complex task into smaller, simpler ones and allocating them to specialists will create greater efficiency and lower average production costs. Manufacturers achieve economies of scale through the use of efficient equipment capable of producing large quantities of a single product.

Marketing channels can also attain economies of scale through specialization and division of labor by aiding producers who lack the motivation, financing, or expertise to market directly to end users or consumers. In some cases, as with most consumer convenience goods, such as soft drinks, the cost of marketing directly to millions of consumers—taking and shipping individual orders—is prohibitive. For this reason, producers hire channel members, such as wholesalers and retailers, to do what the producers are not equipped to do or what channel members are better prepared to do. Channel members can do some things more efficiently than producers because they have built good relationships with their customers. Therefore, their specialized expertise enhances the overall performance of the channel.

OVERCOMING DISCREPANCIES

Marketing channels also aid in overcoming discrepancies of quantity, assortment, time, and space created by economies of scale in production. For example, assume

channel members
All parties in the marketing channel that negotiate with one another, buy and sell products, and facilitate the change of ownership between buyer and seller in the course of moving the product from the manufacturer into the hands of the final consumer.

that J. M. Smucker can efficiently produce its Hungry Jack instant pancake mix only at a rate of 5,000 units in a typical day. Not even the most ardent pancake fan could consume that amount in a year, much less in a day. The quantity produced to achieve low unit costs has created a **discrepancy of quantity**, which is the difference between the amount of product produced and the amount an end user wants to buy. By storing the product and distributing it in the appropriate amounts, marketing channels overcome quantity discrepancies by making products available in the quantities that customers desire.

Mass production creates not only discrepancies of quantity but also discrepancies of assortment. A **discrepancy of assortment** occurs when a customer does not have all of the items needed to receive full satisfaction from a product. For pancakes to provide maximum satisfaction, several other products are required to complete the assortment. At the very least, most people want a knife, fork, plate, butter, and syrup. Others might add orange juice, coffee, cream, sugar, eggs, and bacon or sausage. Even though J. M. Smucker is a large consumer-products company, it does not come close to providing the optimal assortment to go with its Hungry Jack pancakes. To overcome discrepancies of assortment, marketing channels assemble in one place many of the products necessary to complete a customer's needed assortment.

A **temporal discrepancy** is created when a product is produced, but a customer is not ready to buy it. Marketing channels overcome temporal discrepancies by maintaining inventories in anticipation of demand. For example, manufacturers of seasonal merchandise, such as Christmas or Halloween decorations, are in operation all year even though customer demand is concentrated during certain months of the year.

Furthermore, because mass production requires many potential buyers, markets are usually scattered over large geographic regions, creating a **spatial discrepancy**. Often global, or at least nationwide, markets are needed to absorb the outputs of mass producers. Marketing channels overcome spatial discrepancies by making products available in locations convenient to customers. For example, if Hungry Jack pancake mix is produced in Boise, Idaho, then J. M. Smucker must use an intermediary to distribute the product to other regions of the United States. Consumers elsewhere would be unwilling to drive to Boise to purchase pancake mix. Another example is the distribution of child-friendly malaria drugs in developing countries, specifically Africa, where 200 million people fall ill with the disease each year. The child-friendly malaria drug is mass-produced in Switzerland, resulting in spatial discrepancy due to the size and location of the market. Companies have partnered with nonprofits and governments to distribute the medication through national medical centers and hospitals in Africa. The combined efforts by these groups has made a much needed drug available to people who would often have no access to it.[2]

PROVIDING CONTACT EFFICIENCY

The third need fulfilled by marketing channels is providing contact efficiency. Marketing channels provide contact efficiencies by reducing the number of stores customers must shop in to complete their purchases. Think about how much time you would spend shopping if supermarkets, department stores, and shopping malls did not exist. For example, suppose you had to buy your milk at a dairy and your meat at a stockyard. Imagine buying your

discrepancy of quantity
The difference between the amount of product produced and the amount an end user wants to buy.

discrepancy of assortment
The lack of all the items a customer needs to receive full satisfaction from a product or products.

temporal discrepancy
A situation that occurs when a product is produced but a customer is not ready to buy it.

spatial discrepancy
The difference between the location of a producer and the location of widely scattered markets.

© iStockphoto.com/Juan Facundo Mora Soria

© E. Jane Armstrong/Armstrong Studios/Foodpix/Getty Images

eggs and chicken at a hatchery and your fruits and vegetables at various farms. You would spend a great deal of time, money, and energy just shopping for a few groceries. Channels simplify distribution by cutting the number of transactions required to get products from manufacturers to customers and making an assortment of goods available in one location. In addition, many customers in recent years have begun shopping using a multichannel approach whereby they view products online, in catalogues, and in the brick-and-mortar retail outlet. Savvy retailers are capitalizing on these additional customer contacts by segmenting shoppers according to buying versus simply shopping channels and providing consistent messages to customers regardless of channel choice.

Consider the example illustrated in Exhibit 13.1. Four customers each want to buy a television set. Without a retail intermediary like Best Buy, television manufacturers JVC, Zenith, RCA, Sony, and Toshiba would each have to make four contacts to reach the four buyers who are in the target market, for a total of 20 transactions. However, when Best Buy acts as an intermediary between the producer and customers, each producer has to make only one contact, reducing the number of transactions to nine. Each producer sells to one retailer rather than to four customers. In turn, customers buy from one retailer instead of from five producers.

Contact efficiency is being enhanced even more by information technology. Better information on product availability and pricing increasingly is reducing the need for consumers to actually shop for bargains or view ads in a traditional manner. By making information on products and services easily accessible over the Internet, Google, Yahoo, and similar information assemblers are becoming the starting points for finding and buying products and services. As they examine and organize huge digital warehouses of news, images, traffic and weather reports, and information on automobiles, real estate, and other consumer products, inefficiencies are reduced, as are prices. These developments are revolutionizing marketing channels and benefiting customers because shoppers can find out where the best bargains are and substantially reduce their search time.

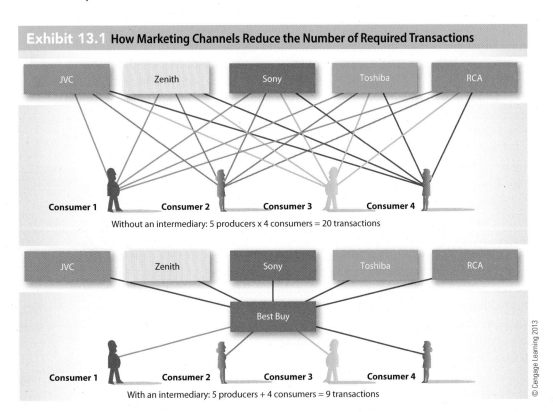

Exhibit 13.1 How Marketing Channels Reduce the Number of Required Transactions

Without an intermediary: 5 producers x 4 consumers = 20 transactions

With an intermediary: 5 producers + 4 consumers = 9 transactions

© Cengage Learning 2013

LO2
Channel Intermediaries and Their Functions

Intermediaries in a channel negotiate with one another, facilitate the change of ownership between buyers and sellers, and physically move products from the manufacturer to the final consumer. The most prominent difference separating intermediaries is whether they take title to the product. *Taking title* means they own the merchandise and control the terms of the sale—for example, price and delivery date. Retailers and merchant wholesalers are examples of intermediaries that take title to products in the marketing channel and resell them. **Retailers** are firms that sell mainly to consumers. Retailers will be discussed in more detail in Chapter 15.

Merchant wholesalers are organizations that facilitate the movement of products and services from the manufacturer to producers, resellers, governments, institutions, and retailers. All merchant wholesalers take title to the goods they sell, and most of them operate one or more warehouses where they receive goods, store them, and later reship them. Customers are mostly small- or medium-sized retailers, but merchant wholesalers also market to manufacturers and institutional clients.

Other intermediaries do not take title to the goods and services they market but do facilitate the exchange of ownership between sellers and buyers. **Agents and brokers** simply facilitate the sale of a product from producer to end user by representing retailers, wholesalers, or manufacturers. Title reflects ownership, and ownership usually implies control. Unlike wholesalers, agents or brokers only facilitate sales and generally have little input into the terms of the sale. They do, however, get a fee or commission based on sales volume. For example, when selling a home, the owner usually hires a real estate agent who then brings potential buyers to see the house. The agent facilitates the sale by bringing the buyer and owner together, but never actually takes ownership of the home.

Variations in channel structures are due in large part to variations in the numbers and types of wholesaling intermediaries. Generally, product characteristics, buyer considerations, and market conditions determine the type of intermediary the manufacturer should use.

→ **Product characteristics** that may require a certain type of wholesaling intermediary include whether the product is standardized or customized, the complexity of the product, and the gross margin of the product. For example, a customized product such as insurance is sold through an insurance agent or broker who may represent one or multiple companies. In contrast, a standardized product such as gum is sold through a merchant wholesaler that takes possession of the gum and reships it to the appropriate retailers.

→ **Buyer considerations** affecting the wholesaler choice include how often the product is purchased and how long the buyer is willing to wait to receive the product. For example, at the beginning of the school term, a student might

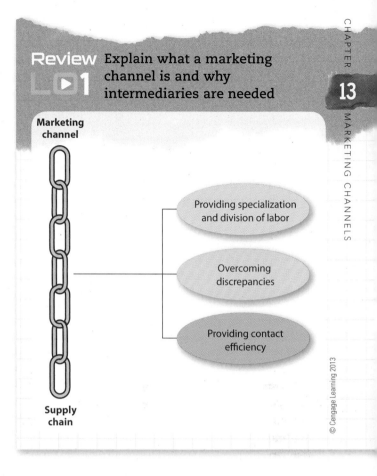

Review LO1 Explain what a marketing channel is and why intermediaries are needed

Marketing channel

Supply chain

- Providing specialization and division of labor
- Overcoming discrepancies
- Providing contact efficiency

© Cengage Learning 2013

retailer
A channel intermediary that sells mainly to consumers.

merchant wholesaler
An institution that buys goods from manufacturers and resells them to businesses, government agencies, and other wholesalers or retailers and that receives and takes title to goods, stores them in its own warehouses, and later ships them.

agents and brokers
Wholesaling intermediaries who do not take title to a product but facilitate its sale from producer to end user by representing retailers, wholesalers, or manufacturers.

be willing to wait a few days for a textbook to get a lower price by ordering online. Thus, this type of product can be distributed directly. But if the student waits to buy the book until the night before an exam and needs the book immediately, it will have to be purchased at the school bookstore.

→ **Market characteristics** determining the wholesaler type include how many buyers are in the market and whether they are concentrated in a general location or are widely dispersed. Gum and textbooks, for example, are produced in one location and consumed in many other locations. Therefore, a merchant wholesaler is needed to distribute the products. In contrast, in a home sale, the buyer and seller are localized in one area, which facilitates the use of an agent/broker relationship.

CHANNEL FUNCTIONS PERFORMED BY INTERMEDIARIES

Retailing and wholesaling intermediaries in marketing channels perform several essential functions that make the flow of goods between producer and buyer possible. The three basic functions that intermediaries perform are summarized in Exhibit 13.2.

Transactional functions involve contacting and communicating with prospective buyers to make them aware of existing products and explain their features, advantages, and benefits. Intermediaries in the channel also provide *logistical* functions. **Logistics** is the efficient and cost-effective forward and reverse flow and storage of goods, services, and related information, into, through, and out of channel member companies. Logistics functions typically include transportation and storage of assets, as well as their sorting, accumulation, consolidation, and/or allocation for the purpose of conforming to customer requirements. For example, grading agricultural products typifies the sorting-out process, while consolidation of many lots of grade A eggs from different sources into one lot illustrates the accumulation process. Supermarkets or other retailers perform the assorting function by assembling thousands of different items that match their customers' desires. Similarly, while large companies typically have direct channels, many small companies depend on wholesalers to promote and distribute their products. For example, small beverage

Exhibit 13.2 Marketing Channel Functions Performed by Intermediaries	
Type of Function	**Description**
Transactional Functions	**Contacting and promoting:** Contacting potential customers, promoting products, and soliciting orders
	Negotiating: Determining how many goods or services to buy and sell, type of transportation to use, when to deliver, and method and timing of payment
	Risk taking: Assuming the risk of owning inventory
Logistical Functions	**Physically distributing:** Transporting and sorting goods to overcome temporal and spatial discrepancies
	Storing: Maintaining inventories and protecting goods
	Sorting: Overcoming discrepancies of quantity and assortment by
	Sorting out: Breaking down a heterogeneous supply into separate homogeneous stocks
	Accumulating: Combining similar stocks into a larger homogeneous supply
	Allocating: Breaking a homogeneous supply into smaller and smaller lots ("breaking bulk")
	Assorting: Combining products into collections or assortments that buyers want available at one place
Facilitating Functions	**Researching:** Gathering information about other channel members and consumers
	Financing: Extending credit and other financial services to facilitate the flow of goods through the channel to the final consumer

© Cengage Learning 2013

manufacturers like Jones Soda, Honest Tea, and Energy Brands depend on wholesalers to distribute their products in a marketplace dominated by large competitors like Coca-Cola and Pepsi. The management of logistics is a key component of supply chain management, which is discussed in greater detail in Chapter 14.

The third basic channel function, *facilitating,* includes research and financing. Research provides information about channel members and consumers by getting answers to key questions: Who are the buyers? Where are they located? Why do they buy? Financing ensures that channel members have the money to keep products moving through the channel to the ultimate consumer.

A single company can provide one, two, or all three functions. Consider Kramer Beverage Company, a Coors beer distributor. As a beer distributor, Kramer provides transactional, logistical, and facilitating channel functions. Sales representatives contact local bars and restaurants to negotiate the terms of the sale, possibly giving the customer a discount for large purchases, and arrange for delivery of the beer. At the same time, Kramer also provides a facilitating function by extending credit to the customer. Kramer merchandising representatives, meanwhile, assist in promoting the beer on a local level by hanging Coors beer signs and posters. Kramer also provides logistical functions by accumulating the many types of Coors beer from the Coors manufacturing plant in Golden, Colorado, and storing them in its refrigerated warehouse. When an order needs to be filled, Kramer then sorts the beer into heterogeneous collections for each particular customer. For example, the local Chili's Grill & Bar might need two kegs of Coors, three kegs of Coors Light, and two cases of Killian's Red in bottles. The beer will then be loaded onto a refrigerated truck and transported to the restaurant. Upon arrival, the Kramer delivery person will transport the kegs and cases of beer into the restaurant's refrigerator and might also restock the coolers behind the bar.

Although individual members can be added to or deleted from a channel, someone must still perform these essential functions. The functions can be performed by producers, end users or consumers, channel intermediaries such as wholesalers and retailers, and sometimes nonmember channel participants. For example, if a manufacturer decides to eliminate its private fleet of trucks, it must still have a way to move the goods to the wholesaler. This task can be accomplished by the wholesaler, which might have its own fleet of trucks, or by a nonmember channel participant, such as an independent trucking firm. Nonmembers also provide many other essential functions that might at one time have been provided by a channel member. For example, research firms can perform the research function; advertising agencies can provide the promotion function; transportation and storage firms the physical distribution function; and banks the financing function.

Review LO2 Define the types of channel intermediaries and describe their functions and activities

CHANNEL INTERMEDIARIES		CHANNEL FUNCTIONS
Retailers		Transactional
Wholesalers	Perform →	Logistical
Agents and Brokers		Facilitating

© Cengage Learning 2013

LO3
Channel Structures

A product can take many routes to reach its final consumer. Marketers search for the most efficient channel from the many alternatives available. Marketing a consumer convenience good such as gum or candy differs from marketing a specialty

A retailer channel is most common when the retailer is large, such as JCPenney, and can buy in large quantities directly from the manufacturer. Large retailers often bypass a wholesaler.

good such as a Mercedes-Benz. The two products require very different distribution channels. Likewise, the appropriate channel for a major equipment supplier like Boeing Company would be unsuitable for an accessory equipment producer like Black & Decker. The next sections discuss the structures of typical marketing channels for consumer and business-to-business products. Alternative channel structures are also discussed.

CHANNELS FOR CONSUMER PRODUCTS

Exhibit 13.3 illustrates the four ways manufacturers can route products to consumers. Producers use the **direct channel** to sell directly to consumers. Direct marketing activities—including telemarketing, mail order and catalog shopping, and forms of electronic retailing such as online shopping and shop-at-home television networks—are a good example of this type of channel structure. For example, home computer users can purchase Dell computers directly over the telephone or from Dell's Web site. There are no intermediaries. Producer-owned stores and factory outlet stores—such as Sherwin-Williams, Polo Ralph Lauren, Oneida, and West Point Pepperell—are other examples of direct channels. Farmers' markets are also direct channels. As the previous examples illustrate, direct channels are utilized by many types of businesses and industries. The most recent company to effectively employ a direct channel is Microsoft. In an effort to compete with Apple Stores, Microsoft is creating their own stores to sell directly to consumers. While the direct channel will allow Microsoft to interact directly with consumers, it also exposes Microsoft to some risks. They will now be responsible for managing the inventory in a direct channel, which could result in damages, theft, and obsolescence—problems they

direct channel
A distribution channel in which producers sell directly to consumers.

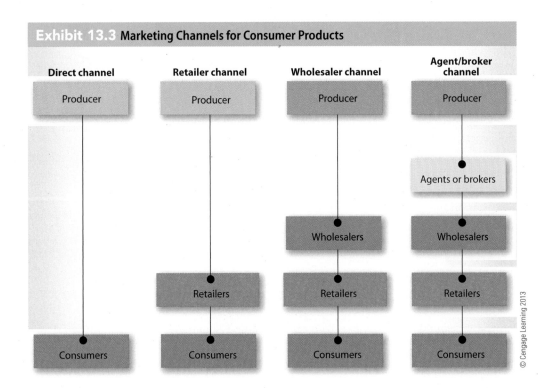

Exhibit 13.3 Marketing Channels for Consumer Products

Direct channel	Retailer channel	Wholesaler channel	Agent/broker channel
Producer	Producer	Producer	Producer
			Agents or brokers
		Wholesalers	Wholesalers
	Retailers	Retailers	Retailers
Consumers	Consumers	Consumers	Consumers

© Cengage Learning 2013

have less experience in handling, that were previously handled by an intermediary.[3] Direct marketing and factory outlets are discussed in more detail in Chapter 15.

At the other end of the spectrum, an *agent/broker channel* involves a fairly complicated process. Agent/broker channels are typically used in markets with many small manufacturers and many retailers that lack the resources to find each other. Agents or brokers bring manufacturers and wholesalers together for negotiations, but they do not take title to merchandise. Ownership passes directly to one or more wholesalers and then to retailers. Finally, retailers sell to the ultimate consumer of the product. For example, a food broker represents buyers and sellers of grocery products. The broker acts on behalf of many different producers and negotiates the sale of their products to wholesalers that specialize in foodstuffs. These wholesalers in turn sell to grocers and convenience stores.

Most consumer products are sold through distribution channels similar to the other two alternatives: the retailer channel and the wholesaler channel. A *retailer channel* is most common when the retailer is large and can buy in large quantities directly from the manufacturer. Walmart, Target, JCPenney, and car dealers are examples of retailers that often bypass a wholesaler. A *wholesaler channel* is commonly used for low-cost items that are frequently purchased, such as candy, cigarettes, and magazines. For example, M&M/Mars sells candies and chocolates to wholesalers in large quantities. The wholesalers then break the large quantities into smaller quantities to satisfy individual retailer orders.

CHANNELS FOR BUSINESS AND INDUSTRIAL PRODUCTS

As Exhibit 13.4 illustrates, five channel structures are common in business and industrial markets. First, direct channels are typical in business and industrial markets. For example, manufacturers buy large quantities of raw materials, major equipment, processed materials, and supplies directly from other manufacturers. Manufacturers that require suppliers to meet detailed technical specifications often prefer direct channels. The direct communication required between Boeing and its

Exhibit 13.4 Channels for Business and Industrial Products

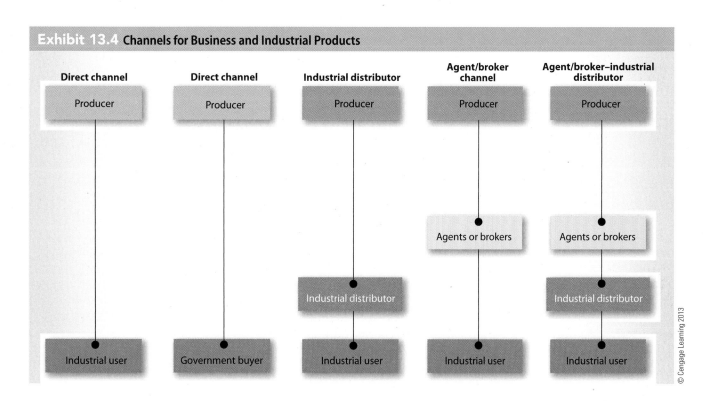

suppliers, for example, along with the tremendous size of the orders, makes anything but a direct channel impractical. The channel from producer to government buyers is also a direct channel. Because much government buying is done through bidding, a direct channel is attractive. Dell, for example, the top seller of desktop computers to federal, state, and local government agencies in the United States, sells the computers through direct channels.

Companies selling standardized items of moderate or low value often rely on *industrial distributors.* In many ways, an industrial distributor is like a supermarket for organizations. Industrial distributors are wholesalers and channel members that buy and take title to products. Moreover, they usually keep inventories of their products and sell and service them. Often small manufacturers cannot afford to employ their own sales force. Instead, they rely on manufacturers' representatives or selling agents to sell to either industrial distributors or users.

Today, though, the traditional industrial distributor is facing many challenges. Manufacturers are getting bigger due to growth, mergers, and consolidation. Through technology, manufacturers and customers have access to information that in the past only the distributor had. Consequently, many manufacturers and customers are bypassing distributors and going direct, often via the Internet. The Internet has enabled virtual distributors to emerge and forced traditional industrial distributors to expand their business model. An example of how the Internet has revolutionized industrial distribution is the P&G e-store, which sells the wide portfolio of P&G household, beauty, and grooming products. The P&G e-store enables consumers to create preferred brand pages and engage in live-chat product consultation, and includes feedback forums for enhancing product presentation and the overall shopping experience. An underlying purpose of the e-store is to learn from consumer insights and create an online shopping experience that is driven by what the customer wants. This is one of the first on-line consumer learning labs created by a manufacturer.[4]

The Internet has also led to the emergence of three other new forms of industrial distribution. Some companies serve as agents that link buyers and sellers and charge a fee. For example, Expedia.com links business travelers to airlines, hotels, and car rental companies. A second form of marketplace has been developed by existing companies looking for a way to drop the intermediary from the channel. For example, the Worldwide Retail Exchange is a marketplace created by 17 major retailers including Target, JCPenney, and Walgreens. Retailers use the exchange to make purchases that in the past would have required telephone, fax, or face-to-face sales calls. Retailers using the exchange estimate they have saved approximately 15 percent in their purchasing costs. Finally, a third type of Internet marketplace is a "private exchange." Private exchanges enable companies to automate their channels while sharing information only with select suppliers. Ace Hardware and Hewlett-Packard, for example, use private exchanges to manage their inventory supplies.

ALTERNATIVE CHANNEL ARRANGEMENTS

Rarely does a producer use just one type of channel to move its product. It usually employs several different or alternative channels, which include multiple channels, nontraditional channels, and strategic channel alliances.

Multiple Channels When a producer selects two (or more) channels to distribute the same product to target markets, this arrangement is called **dual distribution** (or **multiple distribution**). As more people have access to the Internet and embrace online shopping, an increasing number of retailers are using multiple channels of distribution. For example, companies such as Limited Brands, which

dual distribution (multiple distribution)
The use of two (or more) channels to distribute the same product to target markets.

includes The Limited, Express, Victoria's Secret, and Bath and Body Works, sell in-store, online, and through catalogs. Other examples are Sears and Avon. Since Sears purchased Lands' End, a traditional direct business-to-consumer clothing manufacturer, Lands' End products are available in Sears's stores, and Sears credit cards are accepted on the Lands' End Web site. Avon, a direct supplier of health and beauty products for women, offers consumers four alternatives for purchasing products. They can contact a representative in person (the original business model), purchase on the Web, order direct from the company, or pick up products at an Avon Salon & Spa. The buy-online with in-store pickup concept is a strategy that is being employed by many retailers. This technique provides an opportunity to get online consumers into the store for potential add-on purchases through the traditional store-based distribution channel.[5] The Limited, Sears/Lands' End, and Avon are each distributing identical products to existing markets using more than one channel of distribution.

The distribution of identical products through multiple synchronized channels is known as multichannel coordination. Multichannel coordination requires companies to present a cohesive image to consumers regardless of the channel they use, i.e., brick-and-mortar store, catalog, and Internet. It also allows the different channels to share information and provide the delivery options of in-store pickup for Web customers or return and repair an item in store that was purchased online. For example, Best Buy provides several options for their customers and illustrates multichannel coordination. Best Buy allows customers to search online for products and determine if they are stocked at a store in their vicinity. They also allow customers to return products purchased online through the store or the Web site. In addition, repairs of online purchases can be done in the store as well. All of these options are provided with the same image being shown to customers.[6]

Nontraditional Channels Often nontraditional channel arrangements help differentiate a firm's product from the competition. For example, manufacturers might decide to use nontraditional channels such as the Internet, mail-order channels, or infomercials to sell products instead of going through traditional retailer channels. Although nontraditional channels might limit a brand's coverage, they can give a producer serving a niche market a way to gain market access and customer attention without having to establish channel intermediaries. Nontraditional channels can also provide another avenue of sales for larger firms. For example, a London publisher sells short stories through vending machines

An increasing number of retailers use multiple channels of distribution. For example, Sears purchased Lands' End, a traditional direct business-to-consumer clothing manufacturer. Now Lands' End products are available in Sears's stores, and Sears credit cards are accepted on the Lands' End Web site.

in the London Underground. Instead of the traditional book format, the stories are printed like folded maps, making them an easy-to-read alternative for commuters.

Kiosks, long a popular method for ordering and registering for wedding gifts, dispersing cash through ATMs, and facilitating airline check-in, are finding new uses. Ethan Allen furniture stores use kiosks as a product locator tool for consumers and salespeople. Another popular use of kiosks today is the Redbox. The Redbox enables users to check out movies for a 24-hour period for $1.00, and return them to any Redbox kiosk. These kiosks are located at various retail locations including McDonald's, Walgreens, and Kroger. Customers can also go online to reserve movies at Redbox kiosks to ensure that their preferred selection(s) is available when wanted.[7]

Strategic Channel Alliances Companies often form **strategic channel alliances**. Such an alliance enables a company to use another manufacturer's already established channel. Alliances are used most often when the creation of marketing channel relationships might be too expensive and time-consuming. Starbucks, the world's premier coffee marketer, uses strategic alliances both domestically and around the world. When Starbucks wanted to develop ready-to-drink (RTD) coffee beverages for supermarkets and other outlets, it decided not to develop a new channel from scratch. Instead, Starbucks signed an agreement with Pepsi to develop and bottle a Starbucks brand of RTD coffee, a category that had been extremely difficult to develop. The resulting Frappuccino and Doubleshot were so successful when they were launched that they were constantly sold out. Pepsi is still the sole distributor for Starbucks RTD beverages Frappuccino and Doubleshot, and Starbucks has continued access to the thousands of outlets where Pepsi is sold.[8] Similarly, Accenture and Cisco Systems have formed an alliance to work together in the joint development, marketing, and deployment of global network solutions. The combination of Accenture's network consulting services and Cisco's advanced technology will result in cost savings in asset acquisition and service delivery for their customers.[9] Strategic channel alliances are proving to be more successful for growing businesses than mergers and acquisitions. This is especially true in global markets where cultural differences, distance, and other barriers can prove challenging. For example, Heinz has a strategic alliance with Kagome, one of Japan's largest food companies. The companies are working together to find ways to reduce operating costs while expanding both brands' market presence globally.

**Review
LO3** Describe the channel structure for consumer and business products and discuss alternative channel arrangements

CONSUMER CHANNELS	BUSINESS CHANNELS	ALTERNATIVE CHANNELS
• Direct • Retail • Wholesaler • Agent/broker	• Direct • Industrial • Agent/broker • Agent/broker–industrial	• Multiple • Nontraditional • Strategic alliances

© Cengage Learning 2013

LO4
Making Channel Strategy Decisions

Devising a marketing channel strategy requires several critical decisions. Managers must decide what role distribution will play in the overall marketing strategy. In addition, they must be sure that the channel strategy chosen is consistent with product, promotion, and pricing strategies. In making these decisions, marketing managers must determine what factors will influence the choice of channel and what level of distribution intensity will be appropriate.

FACTORS AFFECTING CHANNEL CHOICE

Managers must answer many questions before choosing a marketing channel. The final choice depends on the analysis of several factors, which often interact. These factors can be grouped as market factors, product factors, and producer factors.

Market Factors Among the most important market factors affecting the choice of a distribution channel are target customer considerations. Specifically, managers should answer the following questions: Who are the potential customers? What do they buy? Where do they buy? When do they buy? How do they buy? Additionally, the choice of channel depends on whether the producer is selling to consumers or to industrial customers. Industrial customers' buying habits are very different from those of consumers. Industrial customers tend to buy in larger quantities and require more customer service. For example, Toyota Industrial Equipment manufactures the leading lift truck used to move materials in and out of warehouses and other industrial facilities. Its business customers buy large numbers of trucks at one time and require additional services such as data tracking on how the lift truck is used. In contrast, consumers usually buy in very small quantities and sometimes do not mind if they get little or no service, such as in a discount store like Walmart or Target.

The geographic location and size of the market are also important to channel selection. As a rule, if the target market is concentrated in one or more specific areas, then direct selling through a sales force is appropriate. When markets are more widely dispersed, intermediaries would be less expensive. The size of the market also influences channel choice. Generally, larger markets require more intermediaries. For instance, Procter & Gamble has to reach millions of consumers with its many brands of household goods. It needs many intermediaries, including wholesalers and retailers.

Product Factors Products that are more complex, customized, and expensive tend to benefit from shorter and more direct marketing channels. These types of products sell better through a direct sales force. Examples include pharmaceuticals, scientific instruments, airplanes, and mainframe computer systems. On the other hand, the more standardized a product is, the longer its distribution channel can be and the greater the number of intermediaries that can be involved. For example, with the exception of flavor and shape, the formula for chewing gum is about the same from producer to producer. Chewing gum is also very inexpensive. As a result, the distribution channel for gum tends to involve many wholesalers and retailers.

The product's life cycle is also an important factor in choosing a marketing channel. In fact, the choice of channel might change over the life of the product. For example, when photocopiers were first available, they were typically sold by a direct sales force. Now, however, photocopiers can be found in several places, including warehouse clubs, electronics superstores, and mail order catalogs. As products become more common and less intimidating to potential users, producers tend to look for alternative channels. Gatorade was originally sold to sports teams, gyms, and fitness clubs. As the drink became more popular, mainstream supermarket channels were added, followed by convenience stores and drugstores. Now Gatorade can be found in vending machines and even in some fast-food restaurants.

Another factor is the delicacy of the product. Perishable products such as vegetables and milk have a relatively short life span. Fragile products such as china and crystal require a minimum amount of handling. Therefore, both require fairly short distribution channels. Online retailers such as eBay facilitate the sale of unusual or difficult-to-find products that benefit from a direct channel.

Producer Factors Several factors pertaining to the producer itself are important to the selection of a marketing channel. In general, producers with large financial, managerial, and marketing resources are better able to use more direct channels. These producers have the ability to hire and train their own sales force, warehouse their own goods, and extend credit to their customers. For example, variety store Dollar Tree distributes products through retail locations at low prices. To increase cost-efficiency, Dollar Tree has a coast-to-coast logistics network of nine distribution centers to service its almost 3,000 stores.[10] Smaller or weaker firms, on the other hand, must rely on intermediaries to provide these services for them. Compared to producers with only one or two product lines, producers that sell several products in a related area are able to choose channels that are more direct. Sales expenses then can be spread over more products.

A producer's desire to control pricing, positioning, brand image, and customer support also tends to influence channel selection. For instance, firms that sell products with exclusive brand images, such as designer perfumes and clothing, usually avoid channels in which discount retailers are present. Manufacturers of upscale products, such as Gucci (handbags) and Godiva (chocolates), might sell their wares only in expensive stores in order to maintain an image of exclusivity. Many producers have opted to risk their image, however, and test sales in discount channels. Levi Strauss expanded its distribution to include JCPenney, Sears, and Walmart.

LEVELS OF DISTRIBUTION INTENSITY

Organizations have three options for intensity of distribution: intensive distribution, selective distribution, or exclusive distribution. (See Exhibit 13.5.)

Intensive Distribution Intensive distribution is a form of distribution aimed at maximum market coverage. The manufacturer tries to have the product available in every outlet where potential customers might want to buy it. If buyers are unwilling to search for a product (as is true of convenience goods and operating

Exhibit 13.5 Intensity of Distribution Levels			
Intensity Level	**Distribution Intensity Objective**	**Number of Intermediaries in Each Market**	**Examples**
Intensive	Achieve mass-market selling; popular with health and beauty aids and convenience goods that must be available everywhere	Many	Pepsi, Lay's potato chips, Huggies diapers, Alpo dog food, Crayola crayons
Selective	Work closely with selected intermediaries who meet certain criteria; typically used for shopping goods and some specialty goods	Several	Donna Karan clothing, Hewlett-Packard printers, Burton snowboards, Aveda aromatherapy products
Exclusive	Work with a single intermediary for products that require special resources or positioning; typically used for specialty goods and major industrial equipment	One	BMW cars, Rolex watches

© Cengage Learning 2013

supplies), the product must be very accessible to buyers. A low-value product that is purchased frequently might require a lengthy channel. For example, candy, chips, and other snack foods are found in almost every type of retail store imaginable. These foods typically are sold to retailers in small quantities by food or candy wholesalers. The Wrigley Company could not afford to sell its gum directly to every service station, drugstore, supermarket, and discount store. The cost would be too high. Sysco delivers food and related products to restaurants and other food service companies that prepare meals for customers dining out. It is not economically feasible for restaurants to go to individual vendors for each product. Therefore, Sysco serves as an intermediary by delivering all products necessary to fulfill restaurants' needs.[11]

Most manufacturers pursuing an intensive distribution strategy sell to a large percentage of the wholesalers willing to stock their products. Retailers' willingness (or unwillingness) to handle items tends to control the manufacturer's ability to achieve intensive distribution. For example, a retailer already carrying ten brands of gum may show little enthusiasm for one more brand. Intensive distribution is also susceptible to errors when intermediaries who are shipped products are expected to handle them in a pre-specified manner detailed in buyer-seller agreements. For example, executives at 20th Century Fox were quite alarmed when a planned summer blockbuster, *X-Men Origins: Wolverine*, was released on the Internet a full month before its scheduled wide release. As of now, 20th Century Fox is unclear on where the breakdown within the distribution channel occurred, and is reevaluating its buyer-supplier agreements.[12]

Selective Distribution Selective distribution is achieved by screening dealers and retailers to eliminate all but a few in any single area. Because only a few are chosen, the consumer must seek out the product. For example, when Heelys, Inc. launched Heelys, thick-soled sneakers with a wheel embedded in each heel, the company hired a group of 40 teens to perform exhibitions in targeted malls, skate parks, and college campuses across the country to create demand. Then the company made the decision to avoid large stores such as Target and to distribute the shoes only through selected mall retailers and skate and surf shops in order to position the product as "cool and kind of irreverent." Selective distribution strategies often hinge on a manufacturer's desire to maintain a superior product image so as to be able to charge a premium price. DKNY clothing, for instance, is sold only in select retail outlets, mainly full-price department stores. Likewise, premium pet food brands such as Hill's Pet Nutrition and Nestlé Purina's Pro Plan are distributed chiefly through specialty pet food stores and veterinarians, rather than mass retailers like Walmart, so that a premium price can be charged. Manufacturers sometimes expand selective distribution strategies, believing that doing so will enhance revenues without diminishing their product's image. For example, when Procter & Gamble purchased premium pet food brand Iams, it expanded the brand's selective distribution strategy and began selling Iams food in mass retailer Target. Even though the new strategy created channel conflict with breeders and veterinarians who had supported the product, sales increased.[13] Similarly, Playboy Energy, a new energy drink manufactured and bottled by the media enterprise of the same name, uses selective distribution to position itself as a higher-end option versus more intensively distributed competitor Red Bull.[14] The drink has been introduced in luxurious nightclubs and upscale bars only in Boston, Miami, Las Vegas, and Los Angeles in order to draw the attention of "elite" customers prior to its broader release in grocery and convenience stores in the future.

selective distribution
A form of distribution achieved by screening dealers to eliminate all but a few in any single area.

Recently, a high-tech form of selective distribution has emerged whereby products are pushed through to the membership of exclusive virtual social networks. Scion Speak was developed as a social network Internet portal where Toyota Scion owners could design and share their own unique graffiti-type artwork, which then could be airbrushed onto the body of their cars. Members of the network, which is managed by the cool and quirky marketing firm called StrawberryFrog, have the exclusive rights to the car customization services, as well as to some available custom designs made by a professional artist contracted by the company. This type of service is among the first to leverage the power of social network Web sites as a product distribution medium.[15]

Exclusive Distribution The most restrictive form of market coverage is **exclusive distribution**, which entails only one or a few dealers within a given area. Because buyers might have to search or travel extensively to buy the product, exclusive distribution is usually confined to consumer specialty goods, a few shopping goods, and major industrial equipment. Products such as Rolls-Royce automobiles, Chris-Craft powerboats, and Pettibone tower cranes are distributed under exclusive arrangements. Sometimes exclusive territories are granted by new companies (such as franchisors) to obtain market coverage in a particular area. Limited distribution can also serve to project an exclusive image for the product.

Retailers and wholesalers might be unwilling to commit the time and money necessary to promote and service a product unless the manufacturer guarantees

Actress and recording artist Vanessa Hudgens appears in Candie's spring 2011 multi-media marketing campaign. Candie's brand is sold exclusively at Kohl's, and typically uses big stars to drive customers to Kohl's stores.

them an exclusive territory. This arrangement shields the dealer from direct competition and enables it to be the main beneficiary of the manufacturer's promotion efforts in that geographic area. With exclusive distribution, channels of communication are usually well established because the manufacturer works with a limited number of dealers rather than many accounts.

Exclusive distribution also takes place within a retailer's store rather than a geographic area—for example, when a retailer agrees not to sell a manufacturer's competing brands. Mossimo, traditionally an apparel wholesaler, developed an agreement with Target to design clothing and related items sold exclusively at Target stores. Other exclusive distributors involved in this successful model include Thomas O'Brien domestics, Sonia Kashuk makeup, Isaac Mizrahi domestics and apparel, and Todd Oldham home furnishings for college students.

There may be times when a retailer or manufacturer will seek to change their distribution channel. For example, the music industry had to change distribution channels from CDs and tapes to online music in order to keep up with the changing needs and increased technology sophistication of the customer. The adaption of the music industry coincided with the introduction of the iPod from Apple, which, while offering music companies alternative distribution channels, brought a level of sophistication to audio products and placed pressure on the entertainment industry as a whole to think about different types of distribution.[16]

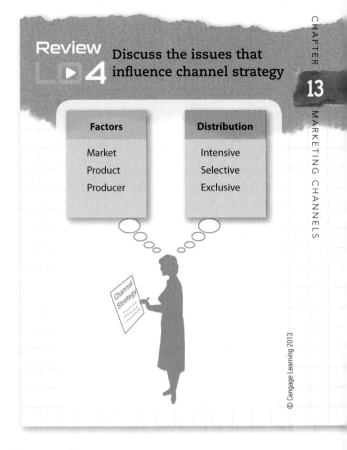

Review LO 4 Discuss the issues that influence channel strategy

Factors	Distribution
Market	Intensive
Product	Selective
Producer	Exclusive

LO 5
Types of Channel Relationships

A marketing channel is more than a set of institutions linked by economic ties. Social relationships play an important role in building unity among channel members. A critical aspect of channel management, therefore, is managing the social relationships among channel members to achieve synergy. Marketing managers should carefully consider the types of relationships they choose to foster between their company and other companies, and in doing so pay close attention to the benefits and hazards associated with each relationship type.

CHANNEL RELATIONSHIP TYPES

Channel members must create and manage multiple relationships with other members in order to create an efficient environment for exchange. Relationships among channel members range from "loose" to "tight," taking the form of a continuum stretching from single transactions to complex interdependent relationships such as partnerships or alliances. The choice of relationship type is important for channel management because each relationship type carries with it different levels of time, financial, and resource investment. Three basic types of relationships, organized by degree of closeness, are commonly considered: arm's-length, integrated relationships, and cooperative.

Arm's-Length Relationships At one end of the relationship continuum are relationships considered by channel members to be temporary or one-time-only. These relationships are often referred to as **"arm's-length"** relationships due to the companies' unwillingness or lack of ability to develop a closer type of relationship. In arm's-length relationships, both parties retain their independence and pursue only their own interests while attempting to benefit from the goods or services provided by the other. This type of relationship is often used when a company has a sudden and/or unique need for a product or service and does not anticipate this need will arise again in the near future. For example, what might happen if Chevrolet were suddenly faced with an unusual situation where Bridgestone, its usual tire producer for the Chevy Tahoe, were unable to provide shipment of tires in reasonable time for a planned production run? One solution might be to engage in a temporary arm's-length relationship with an alternate provider, such as Michelin, that might be able to supply substitute tires on a temporary basis and thus save Chevrolet the costs associated with delaying the production run.

This sort of channel arrangement, however, involves a number of downsides. Because Chevrolet needs the tires on short notice, Michelin might decide to charge a somewhat higher price than usual and, furthermore, because the order placed was a one-time-only order and contained a fixed number of units, it is unlikely that Chevrolet would be able to take advantage of discounts available for customers buying in large quantities. In addition, because the relationship between Chevrolet and Michelin is new, there is no history or friendship to draw on in cases where disagreements or conflicts arise related to the terms of the agreement. In closer relationships, channel members might easily resolve their differences through communication, future promises, or bargaining. But in arm's-length relationships it is sometimes necessary to resolve arm's-length disputes through more formal and costly means such as arbitration or lawsuits. For all of these reasons, companies often find it appealing to develop more concrete, long-term relationships with other channel members.

Another major weakness to arm's-length relationships is opportunism. Opportunistic behavior might occur within arm's-length relationships because there is not a common goal or formal relationship between the two parties. Another factor that might yield opportunism within a relationship is when one company is more dependent on the other. Companies can also behave opportunistically when there is uncertainty within the relationship and the market.

To protect themselves, companies might behave opportunistically at the expense of the arm's-length relationship partner. For example a new supplier to Walmart would have to be concerned with opportunism on the part of the world's largest retailer. Walmart would hold considerable power within any established relationship and does not have historic ties with the new supplier to moderate how their actions might impact the relationship. Therefore, for protection purposes, the new supplier could attempt to charge higher prices and/or find alternate retail channels to ensure their interests were protected.

Integrated Relationships At the opposite end of the relationship continuum from arm's-length relationships is a situation where one company (vertical integration) or several companies acting as one (a supply chain, see Chapter 14) perform all channel functions. These closely bonded types of relationships are collectively referred to as **integrated relationships**. Integrated relationships are characterized by formal arrangements that explicitly define the relationships to the involved channel members. For example, with vertical integration, all of the related channel members are collectively owned by a single legal entity (which could be one of the channel members or a third party), with ownership established through formal legal titles and/or agreements. This sort of relational arrangement has often been employed by McDonald's Corporation, whose subsidiary companies have owned dairy and potato farms, and processing plants that grow and process components of the products served by the chain's fast-food restaurants. A supply chain, which is discussed in greater depth in Chapter 14, consists of several companies acting together in a highly organized and efficient manner, while employing the same or similar techniques as a single vertically integrated company. More recently, Coca-Cola and PepsiCo have both announced and negotiated deals to take over their respective bottling company suppliers. The desire of these two companies is to have more flexibility and control of their products and bottling plants in order to serve customers better.[17]

Based on these descriptions, it seems that integrated relationships would be the preferred relationship type in almost all company-to-company channel settings. However, highly integrated relationships also come with some significant costs and/or hazards. For example, the single-owner model is somewhat risky because a large amount of capital assets must be purchased or leased (requiring a potentially huge initial cash outlay), and the failure of any portion of the business might result in not only the economic loss of that portion, but might also reduce the value of the other business units (or render them totally worthless). Because these trade-offs are sometimes hard to justify, companies often look for a sort of "happy medium" between arm's-length and integrated relationships that enables them to maximize the advantages of both relationship types while limiting their potential risks.

cooperative relationships
A relationship between companies that takes the form of informal partnership with moderate levels of trust and information sharing as needed to further each company's goals.

COOPERATIVE RELATIONSHIPS

Cooperative relationships, which exist between arm's-length and integrated relationships in terms of their connectedness, take many different forms. Cooperative relationships include non-equity agreements such as franchising and licensing, as well as equity-based joint ventures and strategic alliances. (See Chapter 5 for a review.) In general, cooperative relationships are administered using some sort of formal contract. This is in contrast to arm's-length relationships, which are enforced through legal action (or the implied threat thereof), and integrated relationships that rely on informal social enforcement to secure the agreement based on trust, commitment, and loyalty. Cooperative relationships thus tend to be more flexible than integrated relationships, but are also structured with greater detail and depth than arm's-length relationships. They tend to be used when a company wants less ambiguity in the channel relationship than the arm's-length relationship can provide, but without the long-term and/or capital investment required to achieve full integration.

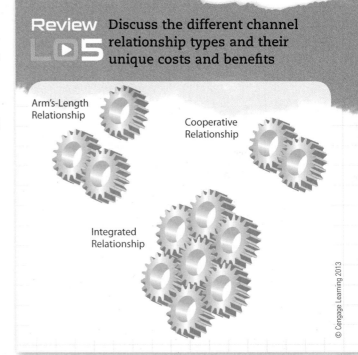

Review LO5 Discuss the different channel relationship types and their unique costs and benefits

Arm's-Length Relationship

Cooperative Relationship

Integrated Relationship

LO6
Managing Channel Relationships

In addition to considering the multiple different types of channel relationships and their costs and benefits, managers must also be aware of the social dimensions that are constantly affecting their relationships. The basic social dimensions of channels are power, control, leadership, conflict, and partnering.

CHANNEL POWER, CONTROL, AND LEADERSHIP

channel power
The capacity of a particular marketing channel member to control or influence the behavior of other channel members.

channel control
A situation that occurs when one marketing channel member intentionally affects another member's behavior.

channel leader (channel captain)
A member of a marketing channel that exercises authority and power over the activities of other channel members.

channel conflict
A clash of goals and methods between distribution channel members.

Channel power is a channel member's ability to control or influence the behavior of other channel members. **Channel control** occurs when one channel member's power affects another member's behavior. To achieve control, a channel member assumes channel leadership and exercises authority and power. This member is termed the **channel leader**, or **channel captain**. In one marketing channel, a manufacturer could be the leader because it controls new-product designs and product availability. In another, a retailer could be the channel leader because it wields power and control over the retail price, inventory levels, and post-sale service.

The exercise of channel power is a routine element of many business activities in which the outcome is often greater control over a company's brands. For example, the Sheraton Hotel chain operates hundreds of hotels across North America and worldwide, most of which are owned by franchisees. As with many franchises, it is in the best interest of the parent company to closely monitor and control operations to prevent the brand name from being devalued. However, when the chain asked its franchisees to invest nearly $4 billion of their own money to make improvements (such as redesigned lobbies and bathrooms) to keep the brand name from weakening, many owners balked and a power struggle ensued. Eventually, the parent company and ownership group came to an agreement detailing the hotel features Sheraton would control, such as lobby design, room layout, and even which coffee brand would be provided in the rooms, and which would be controlled by the owners (including the number of sheets provided on each bed).[18]

CHANNEL CONFLICT

Inequitable channel relationships often lead to **channel conflict**, which is a clash of goals and methods among the members of a distribution channel. In a broad context, conflict might not be bad. Often it arises because staid, traditional channel members refuse to keep pace with the times. Removing an outdated intermediary can result in reduced costs for the entire channel. The Internet has forced many intermediaries to offer services such as merchandise tracking and inventory availability online.

Conflicts among channel members can be due to many different situations and factors. Oftentimes, conflict arises because channel members have conflicting goals. For instance, athletic footwear retailers want to sell as many shoes as possible in order to maximize profits, regardless of whether the shoe is manufactured by Nike, Adidas, or Saucony, but the Nike manufacturer wants a certain sales volume and market share in each market.

Conflict can also arise when channel members fail to fulfill expectations of other channel members—for example, when a franchisee does not follow the rules set down by the franchisor, or when communications channels break down between channel members. As another example, if a manufacturer shortens the period of warranty coverage and fails to inform dealers of this change, conflict can occur when dealers make repairs expecting they will be reimbursed by the manufacturer. Further, ideological differences and different perceptions of reality can also cause conflict among channel members. For instance, retailers might believe "the customer is always right" and offer a very liberal return policy. Wholesalers and manufacturers might feel that people "try to get something for nothing" or don't follow product instructions carefully. Their differing views of allowable returns will undoubtedly conflict with those of retailers.

At other times, conflict arises because stakeholders for one or more organizations in the channel pressure their firm into behaving in ways that are best for their particular firm, but not for the channel as a whole. A marketing channel is generally set up as a network of organizations that work together to deliver the product to customers. When one member of the channel is pressured by its ownership group, customers, or employees to act in ways that channel partners see as too self-serving, then channel conflict is perhaps the inevitable result.

Conflict within a channel can be either horizontal or vertical. **Horizontal conflict** occurs among channel members on the same level, such as two or more different wholesalers or two or more different retailers that handle the same manufacturer's brands. This type of channel conflict is found most often when manufacturers practice dual or multiple distribution strategies. When Apple changed its distribution strategy and began opening its own stores, it angered Apple's traditional retail partners, some of whom ultimately filed lawsuits against the company. The primary allegation was that Apple stores were competing unfairly with them and that Apple favored its own stores when allocating desirable inventory (such as iPods). Horizontal conflict can also occur when some channel members feel that other members on the same level are being treated differently by the manufacturer. For example, the American Booksellers Association, a group representing small independent booksellers, filed a lawsuit against bookstore giant Barnes & Noble claiming it had violated antitrust laws by using its buying power to demand "illegal and secret" discounts from publishers. These deals, the association contended, put independent booksellers at a serious competitive disadvantage.

Many marketers and customers regard horizontal conflict as healthy competition. Much more serious is **vertical conflict**, which occurs between different levels in a marketing channel, most typically between the manufacturer and wholesaler or the manufacturer and retailer. Producer-versus-wholesaler conflict occurs when the producer chooses to bypass the wholesaler and deal directly with the consumer or retailer.

Dual distribution strategies can also cause vertical conflict in the channel. For example, high-end fashion designers traditionally sold their products through luxury retailers such as Neiman Marcus and Saks Fifth Avenue. Interested in increasing sales and gaining additional control over presentation, many designers such as Giorgio Armani, Donna Karan, and Louis Vuitton opened their own boutiques in the same shopping centers anchored by the luxury retailers. As a result, the retailers lost substantial revenues on the designers' items.

Similarly, manufacturers experimenting with selling to customers directly over the Internet create conflict with their traditional retailing intermediaries. For example, by mid-2010, the iTunes Music store had sold about ten billion songs and 200 million videos since its introduction in 2003, most all of which once were sold as traditional cassette tapes, CDs, albums, or DVDs. When television networks, record companies, and artists realized the power of this online model, they became concerned that it was eroding their traditional revenue format. In fact, NBC Universal decided not to renew its contract with Apple for the 2007–2008 television year without changes in the structure of the contract to allow flexible pricing and packaging of shows in order to recoup losses they were experiencing because of this new distribution channel. Apple refused and the 2007–2008 NBC seasons never appeared on iTunes.[19] In another famous case, Hollywood Studios petitioned federal regulators to allow them to release first-run movies over special cable and satellite channels in order to reduce the negative effects of movie piracy. Though the government has not yet ruled whether Hollywood's strategy will be allowed,

horizontal conflict
A channel conflict that occurs among channel members on the same level.

vertical conflict
A channel conflict that occurs between different levels in a marketing channel, most typically between the manufacturer and wholesaler or between the manufacturer and retailer.

procedural justice
Perceptions of fairness within channel interactions based on equal/just treatment by others during business processes that seek to resolve disputes or allocate resources.

distributive justice
Perceptions of fairness within channel interactions based on how resources are actually allocated among competing interests

interactional justice
Perceptions of fairness within channel interactions based on treatment in everyday interactions.

channel partnering (channel cooperation)
The joint effort of all channel members to create a channel that serves customers and creates a competitive advantage.

the measure is being strongly opposed by DVD rental companies currently holding agreements with Hollywood, who would likely experience major sales losses if such first-run movies could be broadcast directly into homes rather than rented from their retail outlets.[20]

Producers and retailers might also disagree over the terms of the sale or other aspects of the business relationship. When Procter & Gamble introduced "everyday low pricing" to its retail channel members, a strategy designed to standardize wholesale prices and eliminate most trade promotions, many retailers retaliated. Some cut the variety of P&G sizes they carried or eliminated marginal brands. Others moved P&G brands from prime shelf space to less visible shelves.

Fundamentally, channel members wish to be treated fairly when dealing with their trading partners during the quest to serve customers. This fairness has come to be known as justice, and takes any of three different forms. **Procedural justice** implies that each firm treats the others equitably according to predefined terms or processes; when two companies within the channel have an agreement, procedural justice reflects the extent to which each is willing to abide by both its written rules and intended spirit. On the other hand, **distributive justice** reflects the extent to which outcomes and rewards shared by both parties are distributed fairly. For example, if one company in the channel feels as though its partner is accruing an unfair share of credit, reputation, or profit as the result of a cooperative action, a "breach" in distributive justice might be perceived. Companies in the channel are also concerned with **interactional justice**—the extent to which each treats the other in socially acceptable or desirable ways, such as showing up on time to meetings, providing clear and useful information, or boosting the other's reputation when the occasion arises. The three forms of justice serve as the basis for all ongoing channel relationships, and managers are wise to ensure that each is attended to in all interactions with customer or suppliers in the channel in order to avoid channel conflict.

In the event that one or more types of justice are breached within a channel relationship, companies may enact conflict response behaviors. In some cases, especially where the degree and frequency of the justice breach are small or rare, the offended company might prefer to do nothing at all, in effect giving the partner a "free pass." However, as conflict increases in frequency or scope due to repeated justice breaches or violations of trust, greater measures must be taken. These include the writing and enforcement of more formalized agreements that can be relied on in case of disputes, economic sanctions such as price increases or less-favorable shipments, and in extreme cases, termination of the relationship.

CHANNEL PARTNERING

Regardless of the locus of power, channel members rely heavily on one another. Even the most powerful manufacturers depend on dealers to sell their products; even the most powerful retailers require the products provided by suppliers. In sharp contrast to the adversarial relationships of the past between buyers and sellers, contemporary management thought emphasizes the development of close working partnerships among channel members. **Channel partnering**, or **channel cooperation**, is the joint effort of all channel members to create a channel that serves customers and creates a competitive advantage. Channel partnering is vital if each member is to gain something from other members. By cooperating, retailers, wholesalers, manufacturers, and suppliers can speed up inventory replenishment, improve customer service, and reduce the total costs of the marketing channel.

Channel alliances and partnerships help managers create the parallel flow of materials and information required to leverage the channel's intellectual material

ethics in marketing

Made in the U.S.A.?

For many years, and for various reasons, companies have found that many customers prefer to purchase goods manufactured in their home nations. In the United States, market-based patriotism is certainly not new, and for many years, several large U.S. retailers promoted themselves based on their "buy American" policy. Often, consumers buy American goods because they like to believe that they are doing their part in stimulating the U.S. economy. In other situations, customers buy domestic goods and services for cost advantages stemming from savings on transportation; if nearly half of the sale price of a good or service is represented by the costs of moving it (or its components) from the location of manufacturing/ supply to the location of consumption, many customers can get a price break by shopping locally. Regardless of the reason, recent customer data indicates that many customers prefer to buy domestic when such a choice is available and the quality is sufficient.

However, as markets have globalized, so have manufacturing processes that provide goods for sale. In some cases, it is becoming difficult to determine where a good was actually made. For example, for many years, Italian clothiers have been importing fabrics and accessories for use in shirts, pants, and jackets from Asian nations such as Malaysia and China, where labor is cheap and skillful textile technicians plentiful. The pieces of the garment would then be cut and final assembly completed in Italy, complete with a "Made in Italy" label sewn into the garment liner. This practice is obviously advantageous for cost reasons, but has begun to raise a question in international clothing markets: when a clothing item has multiple national origins, where is it actually "made" for the purposes of marketing to customers? Customers want to know where their clothing comes from, and the location stated on the tag carries with it connotations of quality and value. Is it ethical to state on a label that a garment manufactured 75 percent in Asia is an Italian item?

Surprisingly, the answer provided by the Italian government in recent years is a resounding "NO." Following a recent legislative debate, the Italian parliament has passed a law that requires clothing manufacturers and other businesses to prove that their products were manufactured entirely or primarily within Italy in order for the "Made in" label to be attached, and if any part of the work was carried out elsewhere, that fact must also be stated on the labeling. This practice is thought to be among the first attempts worldwide to provide customer protection in the form of "truth in origin labeling," and competitors in the Italian fashion industry who were paying the higher costs of local labor greeted the law with much enthusiasm. Still, in most other parts of the world, multi-sourcing issues are not at all addressed with respect to labeling. One U.S. manufacturer in the automotive industry was recently found to have classified one of its products as "American Made" for marketing purposes, even though over 90 percent of the work done to create the product was completed in Asia and Mexico.

What do you think? Do the United States and other nations need "truth in origin" labeling for products, given the globalizing nature of modern marketing channels? Or is this an established and well-accepted business practice that affects European consumers to a much greater degree than Americans?

and marketing resources. The rapid growth in channel partnering is due to new enabling technology and the need to lower costs. A comparison between companies that approach the marketplace unilaterally and those that engage in channel cooperation and form partnerships is detailed in Exhibit 13.6 on the next page.

Collaborating channel partners meet the needs of customers more effectively by ensuring the right products are available at the right time and for a lower cost, thus boosting sales and profits. Forced to become more efficient, many companies are turning formerly adversarial relationships into partnerships. For example, Kraft is the largest coffee purchaser in the world. Kraft partners with coffee bean growers to help build customer demand and develop "sustainable" coffee production (growing coffee in a way that reduces the impact on the environment, providing higher-quality ingredients for manufacturers to meet consumer needs, and increasing value for the farmer).

Exhibit 13.6 Transaction-Based versus Partnership-Based Firms

Intensity Level	Transaction-Based	Partnership-Based
Relationships between Manufacturer and Supplier	• Short-term • Adversarial • Independent • Price more important	• Long-term • Cooperative • Dependent • Value-added services more important
Number of Suppliers	Many	Few
Level of Information Sharing	Minimal	High
Investment Required	Minimal	High

Source: David Frederick Ross, *Competing Through Supply Chain Management: Creating Market-Winning Strategies Through Supply Chain Partnerships* (New York: Chapman & Hall, 1998), p. 61. Reprinted with kind permission from Springer Science and Business Media.

LO7
Channels and Distribution Decisions for Global Markets

With the spread of free-trade agreements and treaties in recent decades, such as the European Union and the North American Free Trade Agreement (NAFTA), global marketing channels and management of the channels have become increasingly important to U.S. companies that export their products or manufacture abroad.

Review
LO6
Explain channel leadership, conflict, and partnering

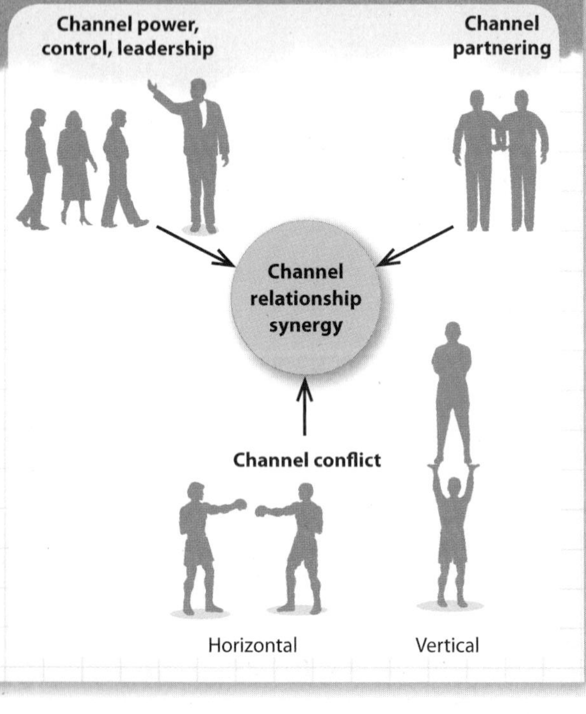

Channel power, control, leadership

Channel partnering

Channel relationship synergy

Channel conflict

Horizontal   Vertical

© Cengage Learning 2013

DEVELOPING GLOBAL MARKETING CHANNELS

Executives should recognize the unique cultural, economic, institutional, and legal aspects of each market before trying to design marketing channels in foreign countries. Manufacturers introducing products in global markets face a tough decision: what type of channel structure to use. Specifically, should the product be marketed directly, mostly by company salespeople, or through independent foreign intermediaries, such as agents and distributors? Using company salespeople generally provides more control and is less risky than using foreign intermediaries. However, setting up a sales force in a foreign country also entails a greater commitment, both financially and organizationally.

Marketers should be aware that channel structures and types abroad may differ from those in the United States. For instance, the more highly developed a nation is economically, the more specialized its channel types. Therefore, a marketer wishing to sell in Germany or Japan will have several channel types to choose from. Conversely, developing countries such as India, Ethiopia, and Venezuela have limited channel types available—there are typically few mail-order channels, vend-ing machines, or specialized retailers and wholesalers—most channels employ tra-ditional small merchant retailers. Some countries also enact economic policies that directly or indirectly regulate channel choices. For example, due to its market size, many companies have an interest in operating in India. India does not explicitly limit foreign retailers from entering its market; however, there are heavy taxes lev-ied on foreign retailers to protect India's domestic businesses. In order to address this issue, many companies such as Mercedes-Benz, Toyota, and General Motors have entered joint ventures with native Indian companies. Through the establish-ment of these joint ventures, foreign companies were able to compete effectively in India's available distribution channels.[21]

Developing effective marketing channels in emerging nations is complicated due to different retail format preferences and differences in the ways locals shop. In many emerging nations, consumers shun large-scale formats popularized in the United States and Western Europe such as supercenter and other big-box retailers, in favor of tiny, independently owned street-side retailers that may be no larger than a closet. These small retailers (known at Procter & Gamble as "high frequency shops") provide small-size packages of goods that are intended to fulfill customer needs for only a day or two. Procter & Gamble estimates that over 620,000 such stores exist in Mexico alone and that 80 percent of emerging nation citizens shop high-frequency stores multiple times per week. New channel strategies are currently being developed by firms like P&G in order to maximize sales and penetration into high frequency shops, including reliance on local sales agents who are paid to ensure that popular products are placed as close as pos-sible to the street and/or cash register. By undertaking this strategy, firms are attempting to minimize the cultural "psychic distance" between the channel mem-ber and the consumer. In other words, they are seeking to adapt to the foreign market environment by changing their United States–based business practices to meet the needs of a Mexican consumer. By embracing the practices that exist in Mexico, the cultural psychic distance is reduced through providing a familiar experience to Mexican customers.[22]

Marketers must also be aware that many countries have "gray" marketing channels in which products are distributed through unauthorized channel in-termediaries. It is estimated that sales of counterfeit luxury items such as Prada handbags and Big Bertha golf clubs have reached almost $2 billion a year. The fakes are harder to detect and hit the market almost instantly. For instance, a fake Christian Dior saddlebag was available just weeks after the original arrived on retailers' shelves. Similarly, Chinese companies are producing so many knock-offs of Yamaha, Honda, and Suzuki motorcycles that the Japanese companies are seeing a drop in sales. What's more, many companies are getting so good at design piracy that they are beginning to launch their own new products.

The Internet has also proved to be a way for pirates to circumvent authorized distribution channels, especially in the case of popular prescription drugs. In recent years, the U.S. Customs Service has seized millions of dollars worth of prescription drugs, most of which were purchased from foreign In-ternet sites. Some were seized because they had not been approved for use in the United States, others because they did not comply with U.S. labeling laws. Most sites offer just a handful of the most popular drugs, such as Viagra. Consumers can get the drugs after obtaining the approval of a doctor, affili-ated with the site, who never sees the patient.

In international contexts, channel governance is also somewhat differ-ent from those found in the United States due to differing cultural dynamics.

The fashion industry works diligently to protect its designers by running ads such as this one to deter people from buying knock-offs in the street.

For example, in China, the concept of *guanxi* means that persons who are socially linked to others are able to "call in favors" whenever a deal is made. This is similar to the notion of an "old boy" network in the United States, whereby members not in the social group are not granted favors at the same rate that group members are. However, Guanxi represents a somewhat stronger force than in the similar U.S. network. In China, favoritism is an expectation that acts more like a social norm that cannot be violated (whereas in the United States, performance differences win out in many situations). Similar network traditions exist in Cuba, Italy, and Spain, among other places. Such arrangements can upset the balance of channel power when a new or foreign company attempts to penetrate the market. The existing network can shun the new entrant, reduce its power by banding together against it, or successfully lobby the government to prevent entry altogether. Due to these social arrangements, multinational companies have to exert more control over their subsidiaries in some nations than in others. Because of political or social network-based favoritism in Brazil, McDonald's exercises tight controls over how franchisees structure supplier deals and write contracts in order to avoid being taken advantage of; in more egalitarian France, franchisees need less protection and therefore the corporation provides more leeway in dealing with channel partners.

Review LO7 Discuss channels and distribution decisions in global markets

- Distribute directly or through foreign partners
- Different channel structures than in domestic markets
- Illegitimate "gray" marketing channels
- Legal and infrastructure differences

© Cengage Learning 2013

LO8

Channels and Distribution Decisions for Services

The fastest growing part of the U.S. economy is the service sector. Although distribution in the service sector is difficult to visualize, the same skills, techniques, and strategies used to manage inventory can also be used to manage service inventory—for instance, hospital beds, bank accounts, or airline seats. The quality of the planning and execution of distribution can have a major impact on costs and customer satisfaction.

One thing that sets service distribution apart from traditional manufacturing distribution is that, in a service environment, production and consumption are simultaneous. In manufacturing, a production setback can often be remedied by using safety stock or a faster mode of transportation. Such substitution is not possible with a service. The benefits of a service are also relatively intangible—meaning, a consumer normally can't see the benefits of a service, such as a doctor's physical exam, but normally can see the benefits provided by a product—for example, cold medicine relieving a stuffy nose.

Because service industries are so customer-oriented, customer service is a priority. To manage customer relationships, many service providers, such as insurance carriers, physicians, hair salons, and financial services, use technology to schedule appointments, manage accounts, and disburse information. Service distribution focuses on four main areas:

→   ***Minimizing wait times:*** Minimizing the amount of time customers wait in line to deposit a check, wait for their food at a restaurant, or wait in a doctor's office for an appointment is a key factor in maintaining the quality of service. People tend to overestimate the amount of time they spend waiting in line, researchers report, and unexplained waiting seems longer than explained waits. To reduce anxiety among waiting customers, some restaurants give patrons pagers that allow them to roam around or go to the bar. Banks sometimes install electronic boards displaying stock quotes or sports scores. Car rental companies reward repeat customers by eliminating their waits altogether. Airports have designed comfortable sitting areas with televisions and children's play areas for those waiting to board planes. Some service companies are using sophisticated technology to further ease their customers' waiting time. For example, many hotels and airlines are using electronic check-in kiosks. Travelers can insert their credit cards to check in upon arrival, receive their room key, get directions, print maps to area restaurants and attractions, and print out their hotel bills.

Car rental services such as Alamo have implemented self-checkout kiosks that allow customers to retrieve reservations and pay for their rental. This eliminates wait time.

→ **Managing service capacity:** For product manufacturers, inventory acts as a buffer, enabling them to provide the product during periods of peak demand without extraordinary efforts. Service firms don't have this luxury. If they don't have the capacity to meet demand, they must either turn down some prospective customers, let service levels slip, or expand capacity. For instance, at tax time a tax preparation firm might have so many customers desiring its services that it has to either turn business away or add temporary offices or preparers. Popular restaurants risk losing business when seating is unavailable or the wait is too long. To manage their capacity, travel Web sites allow users to find last-minute deals to fill up empty airline seats and hotel rooms.

→ **Improving service delivery:** Like manufacturers, service firms are now experimenting with different distribution channels for their services. Choosing the right distribution channel can increase the times that services are available (such as using the Internet to disseminate information and services 24-7) or add to customer convenience (such as pizza delivery, walk-in medical clinics, or a dry cleaner located in a supermarket). The airline industry has found that using the Internet for ticket sales both reduces distribution costs and raises the level of customer service by making it easier for customers to plan their own travel. Cruise lines, on the other hand, have found that travel agents add value by helping customers sort through the abundance of information and complicated options available when booking a cruise. In the real estate industry, realtors are placing kiosks in local malls that enable consumers to directly access listings.

→ **Establishing channel-wide network coherence:** Because services are to some degree intangible, service firms also find it necessary to standardize their service offering quality across different geographic regions in order to maintain brand image. Regardless of where a service is consumed, customers have expectations that must be met in order for the brand to flourish. Having network coherence means that suppliers, service processes, and customer service have quality standards that are maintained regardless of where the service is purchased or consumed. In the passenger airline industry, for example, one major carrier has begun an initiative that tracks on-time arrivals, customer complaint handling, and other similar metrics across its worldwide network of airport terminals. This ensures that customers will be treated fairly and equally regardless of where their departure or destination airport is located, and supports the carrier's brand image as one of high, consistent quality.

The Internet is quickly becoming an alternative channel for delivering services. Consumers can now purchase plane tickets, reserve a hotel room, pay bills, purchase mutual funds, and receive electronic newspapers in cyberspace. Insurance giant Allstate, for instance, now sells auto and home insurance directly to consumers in some states through the Internet in addition to its traditional network of agents. The effort reduces costs so that Allstate can stay competitive with rival insurance companies Progressive and Geico, which already target customers directly. Similarly, several real estate Web sites are making it easier for customers to shop for a new home on the Web. Traditionally, the only way for customers to gain access to realtors' listings was to work through a real estate agent, who would search the listings and then show customers' homes that met their requirements. The new companies offer direct access to the listings, enabling customers to review properties for sale on their own and choose which ones they would like to visit.

Review LO8 Identify the special problems and opportunities associated with distribution in service organizations

Minimizing wait times is a key factor in maintaining service quality.

Managing service capability is critical to successful service distribution.

Improving service delivery makes it easier and more convenient for consumers to use the service.

© Cengage Learning 2013

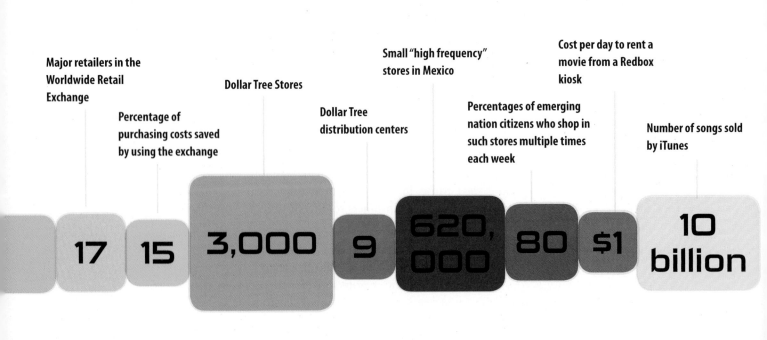

Major retailers in the Worldwide Retail Exchange

Percentage of purchasing costs saved by using the exchange

Dollar Tree Stores

Dollar Tree distribution centers

Small "high frequency" stores in Mexico

Percentages of emerging nation citizens who shop in such stores multiple times each week

Cost per day to rent a movie from a Redbox kiosk

Number of songs sold by iTunes

17   15   3,000   9   620,000   80 $1   10 billion

ANATOMY OF A Marketing Channel

Channel members facilitate the distribution process by providing specialization and division of labor, overcoming discrepancies, and providing contact efficiency.

Producer

Au	Sn	Li
GOLD	TIN	LITHIUM

Materials used to make the components of electronic devices come from around the globe, e.g., South America provides tin (solder), lithium (batteries), and gold (a/v cables).

Customers have the option of buying their computer supplies online through a direct channel with the manufacturer.

Distributor

Dual distribution: Consumers can buy directly from producers or through a retailer.

Wholesaler

Wholesalers may transport and distribute products.

Electronics retailers (such as Best Buy) bridge the gap between companies and consumers.

Retailer

Customer

Review and Applications

LO1 Explain what a marketing channel is and why intermediaries are needed. A marketing channel is a business structure of interdependent organizations that reach from the point of product origin to the consumer with the purpose of physically moving products to their final consumption destination, representing "place" or "distribution" in the marketing mix, and encompassing the processes involved in getting the right product to the right place at the right time. Members of a marketing channel create a continuous and seamless system that performs or supports the marketing channel functions. Channel members provide economies to the distribution process in the form of specialization and division of labor; overcoming discrepancies in quantity, assortment, time, and space; and providing contact efficiency.

1.1 Your family runs a specialty ice cream parlor called Scoops. It manufactures its own ice cream in small batches and sells it only in pint-sized containers. After someone not affiliated with the company sent six pints of its ice cream to a popular talk-show host, she proclaimed on her national TV show that it was the best ice cream she had ever eaten. Immediately after the broadcast, orders came flooding in, overwhelming your small-batch production schedule and your limited distribution system. The company's shipping manager thinks she can handle it, but you disagree. List the reasons why you need to restructure your channel of distribution.

LO2 Define the types of channel intermediaries and describe their functions and activities. The most prominent difference separating intermediaries is whether they take title to the product. Retailers and merchant wholesalers take title, but agents and brokers do not. Retailers are firms that sell mainly to consumers. Merchant wholesalers are organizations that facilitate the movement of products and services from the manufacturer to producers, resellers, governments, institutions, and retailers. Agents and brokers do not take title to the goods and services they market, but they do facilitate the exchange of ownership between sellers and buyers. Channel intermediaries perform three basic types of functions. Transactional functions include contacting and promoting, negotiating, and risk taking. Logistical functions performed by channel members include physical distribution, storing, and sorting functions. Finally, channel members might perform facilitating functions, such as researching and financing.

2.1 What kind of marketing channel functions can be performed over the Internet? Why do you think so?

LO3 Describe the channel structures for consumer and business products and discuss alternative channel arrangements. Marketing channels for consumer and business products vary in degree of complexity. The simplest consumer-product channel involves direct selling from producers to consumers. Businesses might sell directly to business or government buyers. Marketing channels grow more complex as intermediaries become involved. Consumer-product channel intermediaries include agents, brokers, wholesalers, and retailers. Business-product channel intermediaries include agents, brokers, and industrial distributors. Marketers often use alternative channel arrangements to move their products to the consumer. With dual distribution or multiple distribution they choose two or more different channels to distribute the same product. Nontraditional channels help differentiate a firm's product from the competitor's or provide a manufacturer with another avenue for sales. Finally, strategic channel alliances are arrangements that use another manufacturer's already established channel.

3.1 Describe the most likely marketing channel structure for each of these consumer products: candy bars, Tupperware products, nonfiction books, new automobiles, farmers' market produce, and stereo equipment. Now, construct alternative channels for these same products.

3.2 You have been hired to design an alternative marketing channel for a firm specializing in the manufacturing and marketing of novelties for college student organizations. In a memo to the president of the firm, describe how the channel operates.

writing

3.3 Building on question 1.1, determine a new channel structure for Scoops. Write a proposal to present to your key managers.

writing

Discuss the issues that influence channel strategy. When determining marketing channel strategy, the channel manager must determine what market, product, and producer factors will influence the choice of channel. The manager must also determine the appropriate level of distribution intensity. Intensive distribution is distribution aimed at maximum market coverage. Selective distribution is achieved by screening dealers to eliminate all but a few in any single area. The most restrictive form of market coverage is exclusive distribution, which entails only one or a few dealers within a given area.

LO4

4.1 Decide which distribution intensity level—intensive, selective, or exclusive—is used for each of the following products, and explain why: Piaget watches, Land Rover sport-utility vehicles, M&Ms, special edition Barbie dolls, Crest toothpaste.

4.2 Now that you have a basic channel structure for Scoops (from question 3.3), form a team of three to four students and list the market, product, and producer/supplier factors that will affect your final channel structure.

team

Describe the different channel relationship types and their unique costs and benefits. Channel relationships can be plotted on a continuum ranging from arm's-length to integrated, with cooperative relationships somewhere in between. Arm's-length relationships generally consist of unique transactions that are intended to occur once or very infrequently, and are pursued when closer relationships are undesirable or impractical. Although arm's-length relationships are low risk, they also provide few benefits in terms of favorable conditions for the agreement, and disputes are often resolved in court. Integrated relationships, on the opposite end of the spectrum, are very close relationships that are backed by formal agreements and can result in great efficiency and effectiveness. However, given that integrated relationships tend either to involve high levels of expense (in the case of vertical integration) or require enormous amounts of trust in the partner company (as in the case of supply chains), many companies prefer cooperative relationships in some settings. Cooperative relationships are a hybrid form of relationship that is governed by formal contract, are temporary, and are enforced by the agreement itself.

LO5

5.1 Working with another student in the class, decide when it would be most advantageous for large companies like Procter & Gamble, IBM, and/or Ford Motor Company to develop integrated relationships with smaller suppliers. Would the same rules for integrated relationship development also apply to customers? Why or why not?

team

Explain channel leadership, conflict, power, and partnering. Power, control, leadership, conflict, and partnering are the main social dimensions of marketing channel relationships. Channel power refers to the capacity of one channel member to control or influence other channel members. Channel control occurs when one channel member intentionally affects another member's behavior. Channel leadership is the exercise of authority and power. Channel conflict occurs when there is a clash of goals and methods among the members of a distribution channel. Channel conflict can be either horizontal, between channel members at the same level, or vertical, between channel members at different levels of the channel. Channel partnering is the joint effort of all channel members to create an integrated system that serves customers and creates a competitive advantage. Collaborating channel partners meet the needs of consumers more effectively by ensuring that the right products reach shelves at the right time and at a lower cost, boosting sales and profits.

LO6

6.1 Procter & Gamble and Walmart are key partners in a shared channel. P&G is one of Walmart's biggest suppliers, and Walmart provides extremely detailed scanner data about customer purchases of P&G products. Walmart has begun selling its own brand of Sam's Choice laundry detergent in bright orange bottles alongside P&G's Tide, but for a greatly reduced price. What do you think will be the impact of this new product on what has been a stable channel relationship?

 Discuss channels and distribution decisions in global markets. Global marketing channels are becoming more important to U.S. companies seeking growth abroad. Manufacturers introducing products in foreign countries must decide what type of channel structure to use—in particular, whether the product should be marketed through direct channels or through foreign intermediaries. Marketers should be aware that channel structures in foreign markets often are very different from those they are accustomed to in the United States. Global distribution expertise is also emerging as an important skill for channel managers as many countries are removing trade barriers.

 7.1 Go to the World Trade Organization's Web site at **www.wto.org.** What can you learn at the site about how globalization affects channel management and other aspects of business?

 Identify the special problems and opportunities associated with distribution in service organizations. Managers in service industries use the same skills, techniques, and strategies to manage logistics functions as managers in goods-producing industries. The distribution of services focuses on three main areas: minimizing wait times, managing service capacity, and improving service delivery.

 8.1 Assume that you are the marketing manager of a hospital. Write a report indicating the distribution functions that concern you. Discuss the similarities and dissimilarities of distribution for services and for goods.

Key Terms

agents and brokers 453
arm's-length relationships 466
channel conflict 468
channel control 468
channel leader (channel captain) 468
channel members 450
channel partnering (channel cooperation) 470
channel power 468
cooperative relationships 467

direct channel 456
discrepancy of assortment 451
discrepancy of quantity 451
distributive justice 470
dual distribution (multiple distribution) 458
exclusive distribution 464
horizontal conflict 469
integrated relationships 466
intensive distribution 462
interactional justice 470

logistics 454
marketing channel (channel of distribution) 449
merchant wholesaler 453
procedural justice 470
retailer 453
selective distribution 463
spatial discrepancy 451
strategic channel alliance 460
temporal discrepancy 451
vertical conflict 469

Exercises

 ETHICS EXERCISE

Wholesome Snacks, Inc., the maker of a variety of cookies and crackers, has just created a new vitamin-packed cookie. The new cookie has the potential to combat many of the health problems caused by malnutrition in children throughout poverty-stricken areas of the world. To date, however, many of the larger developing markets have resisted opening distribution channels to Wholesome's products. Wholesome realizes that its new cookie could also help open the door for the company to sell its less nutritious products in these markets. Therefore, the company is offering the new cookie at a low cost to government relief programs in exchange for the long-sought distribution channels. The company feels the deal is good for business, but the countries feel it is corporate bullying.

Questions

1. What do you think about Wholesome's idea for opening a new distribution channel?

2. Does the AMA Statement of Ethics address this issue? Go to **www.marketingpower.com** and review the code. Then write a brief paragraph stating what the AMA Statement of Ethics contains that relates to distribution channels in developing nations.

MARKETING PLAN EXERCISE

In Part 1 of your strategic marketing plan, you stated your business mission and objectives and performed a detailed SWOT analysis. In Part 2 of the plan you identified and described target market segments, identified sources of competitive intelligence, and established the need for further marketing research. In Part 3, you began the process of defining the marketing mix, starting with the first component: product. The next stage of the strategic planning process continues defining the elements of the marketing mix, and this section focuses on place, or distribution. Use the following exercises to guide you through the distribution part of your strategic marketing plan:

1. Discuss the implications of dual/multiple distribution. If your chosen company sells through a major department store and its own catalog and then decides to have an online site or open its own store in a factory outlet, what will happen to channel relationships? To the final price offered to consumers? To promotional vehicles? Most e-marketers assume that a direct distribution channel, with no intermediaries, is the most efficient and least costly method for getting product offerings to customers. However, if you decide on a different distribution channel, you will also have to identify warehouses, fulfillment services, transportation firms, packing companies, and many other facilitating agencies. Does your company have the capabilities to handle this, or should your company invest in channel members to take over these tasks and functions?

2. Decide what channel(s) your company should be using. Describe the intermediaries involved and their likely behavior. What are the implications of these channels? Describe the conflict that might arise from having both an e-marketing offering as well as a brick-and-mortar offering. If distribution costs are different, will your company set the same or different prices for end customers?

3. Which distribution intensity level would be best for your company's product? Justify your decision.

APPLICATION EXERCISE

Although it can be easy to understand how distribution channels work just from reading, but you might still not appreciate their broad scope. This exercise will help you see for yourself how complex a single distribution channel is. Then, when you think of the number of products and services available on the market at any one time, you will understand how tremendous the national (and international) distribution network actually is.[23]

Activities

1. Create a list of approximately 20 products that you often purchase for personal use and/or that are present in your home.

2. For each of the products you listed, speculate whether the product was routed through the marketing channel using (a) exclusive, (b) selective, or (c) intensive distribution.

3. Now, for each product/distribution strategy combination, speculate as to the product, market, or producer factors that lead to this distribution strategy.

4. Finally, identify any potential alternative distribution channel options through which you might have purchased this product. Would the alternative channel choice have changed the way (location, timing, price) you purchased this good? Why or why not?

CASE STUDY: Time Warner/Viacom

COUNTDOWN TO A BLACKOUT

© AP Images/PRNewsFoto/Nickelodeon

Why is Dora crying? That was the question readers were faced with when they opened the *New York Times* and *LA Times* on December 31, 2008. Viacom, owner of the Nickelodeon television channel where Dora the Explorer shares the stage with SpongeBob SquarePants and many other favorite children's television stars, purchased full-page advertisements of the cartoon adventurer with a tear streaming down her cheek clutching her frightened looking sidekick, Boots the Monkey. The image was accompanied by this alarming message: Time Warner Cable is taking Dora off the air tonight along with 19 of your favorite channels. Throughout the day, viewers of Viacom channels saw a ticker running across the bottom of their television screens alerting them to the impending blackout, and in the face of Viacom's aggressive media campaign, Time Warner found its call centers swamped by angry customers, many the parents of distraught children, demanding that Time Warner keep the Viacom channels on the air, or else they might look for another cable provider.

Time Warner is the fourth largest cable provider in the United States, with approximately 12.5 million subscribers. Viacom is one of the largest providers of cable TV channel programming, including MTV, VH-1, BET, Spike TV, Nickelodeon, and Comedy Central. Viacom's media campaign came at the climax of a growing dispute between the two companies as the agreement under which Viacom granted Time Warner the rights to broadcast its channels would come to an end at 12:01 a.m. on January 1st. If Time Warner did not come to terms with the programmer, Viacom threatened to pull its channels. To renew the contract, Viacom asked Time Warner to pay an additional $37 million per year for its programming on top of the $300 million it was already paying—roughly a 12 percent rate increase. At the time, Viacom's programming constituted about 7.9 percent of Time Warner's programming costs.

Viacom argued that given the estimated 25 percent of cable viewers who tuned in to Viacom channels over the course of a given day, the amount that Time Warner was paying left Viacom's programming well underpriced in comparison to other channels. Costs for the Disney Channel amount to about 85 cents per subscriber per month, and ESPN costs about $4. In contrast, Viacom's MTV would cost 32 cents and Nickelodeon would cost 45 cents per month. Viacom's rate increase would amount to a monthly cost of about 23 cents per subscriber, a sum they claim is modest in comparison to the likes of ESPN's subscriber costs, especially considering it would cover Viacom's entire package.

Time Warner responded that in the current economic environment, such a rate increase could not be justified. As the company said in response to Viacom's media campaign, the majority of any rate increase would likely have to be absorbed by customers. Furthermore, Time Warner pointed out that in many cases, Viacom was offering the same programming that it was threatening to pull from Time Warner on the Internet for free. Time Warner argued that a rate increase would have Time Warner customers subsidizing Viacom's Internet programming, even going so far during negotiations as to threaten to provide customers a way to connect their laptops to their cable boxes and to stream programs from the Internet onto their TVs.

Fortunately for customers, in the midst of negotiations Viacom agreed to suspend its decision to pull its programming, and the two companies were able to come to terms when their previous contract expired. Traditionally, network programmers hold the upper hand in disputes over programming costs, but in this instance neither Viacom nor Time Warner could afford the fallout of a protracted channel blackout. Viacom's bid for increased subscription fees is not unique; as advertising revenues decreased over the course of the year, many network programmers looked to cable providers for higher fees to fund increasing programming costs. Any sort of blackout, however, would have greatly hurt whatever ad revenue Viacom was already generating. For Time Warner, while increased fees would be unpleasant, a blackout could send increasingly wary cable customers to competitors. In the end, no blackout occurred, and Dora was able to stay on the air.[24]

Questions

1. What is the channel arrangement described between Viacom, Time Warner, and consumers? Who are the intermediaries?

2. What is the channel conflict between Viacom and Time Warner?

3. Obviously the conflict between Viacom and Time Warner has strained their relationship. If you were in charge of one of these companies, what steps would you take to improve their channel relationships?

COMPANY CLIPS: Sephora: Business is Beautiful

© NKP Media, Inc./Cengage

The beauty-retail store Sephora was founded in 1969 in France and since then has become a leader in sales of health-related and beauty-aid products. It opened its first store in the United States in 1998 on Fifth Avenue in New York City and prides itself on being ahead of the market in skin care trends. Its luxurious environment is the selling point for over 250 brands. On its shelves, Sephora maintains a balance of big brand names with lesser known, up-and-coming brands. Sephora also carries its own private brand that it promotes independently in the store. Each sales representative in a Sephora store is trained to best help customers find the products that best fit their skin types and lifestyles. Watch the video to learn what techniques Sephora uses to keep its shelves stocked and customers happy.

Questions

1. Why is important to customers that Sephora keep detailed information about their inventory? What does Sephora do to ensure that their numbers are accurate?

2. How does Sephora manage its marketing channel? What information goes into deciding which suppliers become incorporated?

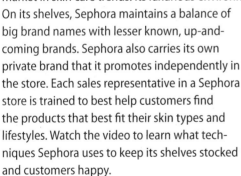

marketing&you:
Results.

A higher score indicates that you like to be a leader and use authority. Studies have linked authority to vanity, so a high score also suggests a high level of vanity. In particular, you have "achievement view vanity," which is strongly linked to authority. That means that you have very high opinions of your accomplishments and think that others consider you successful as well.

Notes

1. Papa John's Web site, www.papajohns.com (Accessed January 2009); Mike Sachoff, "Papa John's Launches Text-Message Ordering," *WebProNews*, November 15, 2007, www.webpronews.com/topnews/2007/11/15/papa-john-s-launches-text-message-ordering; Emily Steel and Suzanne Vranica, "Papa John's Gets Finger Friendlier," *Wall Street Journal*, November 13, 2007, B4; "Papa John's Introduces Text Ordering," *QSR Magazine*, November 16, 2007, www.qsrmagazine.com/news/papa-johns-introduces-text-ordering.

2. Robert Guth, "New Child-Friendly Malaria Drug Presents Distribution Challenge," *Wall Street Journal*, January 27, 2009, http://online.wsj.com/article/SB123301610361717737.html.

3. Nick Wingfield, "Microsoft to Open New Stores, Hires Retail Hand," *Wall Street Journal*, February 13, 2009, B1.

4. Natasha Gural, "P&G to Peddle Products Online," *Forbes*, January 15, 2010, www.forbes.com/2010/01/15/proctor-gamble-psfweb-markets-equities-estore.html.

5. "Making Buy Online/Pick-Up In-Store a Reality," *RetailWire*, February 4, 2009.

6. Iryna Pentina and Ronald Hasty, "Effects of Multichannel Coordination and E-Commerce Outsourcing on Online Retail Performance," *Journal of Marketing Channels* 16, no. 4 (2009): 359–374.

7. Redbox Automated Retail Web site, www.redbox.com (Accessed August 5, 2010).

8. "Pepsi, Supermarkets Teaming Up," *Supermarket News*, October 31, 1994, 31.

9. Cisco Systems, Inc. Web site, www.cisco.com (Accessed January 2006).

10. Dollar Tree, Inc. Web site, www.dollartree.com (Accessed January 2006).

11. Sysco Corporation Web site, www.sysco.com (Accessed January 2006).

12. Scott Mendelson, "X-Men Origins: Wolverine DVD-Quality Bootleg Leaked Online . . . ," *Huffington Post*, April 1, 2009, www.huffingtonpost.com/scott-mendelson/x-men-origins-wolverine-l_b_181745.html.

13. Shelly Branch, "P&G Buys Iams: Will Pet Food Fight Follow?" *Wall Street Journal*, August 12, 1999; George Anderson, "P&G toLaunch Online Learning Lab," *RetailWire*, January 15, 2010, www.retailwire.com/discussion/14248/p-and-g-to-launch-online-learning-lab.

14. Eric Newman, "Red Bull, Meet Black Bunny," *Brandweek*, February 25, 2008, www.adweek.com (Accessed July 22, 2008).

15. Lynnley Browning, "Do-It-Yourself Logos for Proud Scion Owners," *New York Times*, March 24, 2008, www.nytimes.com/2008/03/24/business/media/24adco.html.

16. Filipe Coelho and Chris Easingwood, "An Exploratory Study into the Drivers of Channel Change," *European Journal of Marketing* 42, nos. 9/10 (2009): 1005–1022.

17. Ben Worthen, Cari Tuna, and Justin Scheck, "Companies More Prone to Go 'Vertical,'" *Wall Street Journal*, November 30, 2009, http://online.wsj.com/article/SB125954262100968855.html; Dana Cimilluca, Betsy McCay, and Jeffrey McCraken, "Coke Near Deal for Bottler," *Wall Street Journal*, February 25, 2010, http://online.wsj.com/article/SB100014240527487042400045750858719501463O4.html.

18. Tamara Audi, "Ailing Sheraton Shoots for a Room Upgrade," *Wall Street Journal*, March 25, 2008, A1.

19. Ethan Smith and Nick Wingfield, "More Artists Steer Clear of iTunes," *Wall Street Journal*, August 28, 2008, http://online.wsj.com/article/SB121987440206377643.html; Rex Crum and David B. Wilkerson, "Apple to Stop Selling NBC Shows through iTunes," *MarketWatch*, August 31, 2007, www.marketwatch.com/story/apple-to-pull-nbc-shows-from-itunes-citing-price-dispute.

20. Amy Schatz and Sarah McBride, "Hollywood Studios Seek Control over Deliveries," *Wall Street Journal*, June 12, 2008, B6.

21. Matthias Williams, "India to Levy 10 pct Import Tax on Power Gear," *Reuters*, August 12, 2010, http://in.reuters.com/article/2010/08/12/idINIndia-50795020100812.

22. Ellen Byron, "P&G's Global Target: Shelves of Tiny Stores," *Wall Street Journal*, July 16, 2007, A1; C. Sousa and F. Bradley, "Cultural Distance and Psychic Distance: Two Peas in a Pod?" *Journal of International Marketing* 14, no. 1 (2009): 49–70.

23. This application exercise is based on the contribution of John Beisel (University of Pittsburgh) to *Great Ideas in Teaching Marketing*, a teaching supplement that accompanies McDaniel, Lamb, and Hair's *Introduction to Marketing*. The entry by Professor Beisel was a runner-up in the "Best of the Great Ideas in Teaching Marketing" contest held in conjunction with the publication of the eighth edition of *Marketing*.

24. Meg James, "Viacom, Time Warner Cable Settle Contract Dispute," *LA Times*, January 2, 2009, http://articles.latimes.com/2009/jan/01/business/fi-viacom1; L. Gordon Crovitz, "Consumer Choice Saves 'Dora the Explorer,'" *Wall Street Journal*, January 5, 2009, http://online.wsj.com/article/SB123111692013852693.html; Bill Carter, "Time Warner and Viacom Reach Agreement on Cable Shows," *New York Times*, January 1, 2009; Melissa Block, Robert Siegel, and Meg James, "Dora Roped into Viacom-Time Warner Fee Spat," *All Things Considered*, NPR, December 31, 2009, www.npr.org/templates/story/story.php?storyId=98912395 (Accessed January 15, 2009).

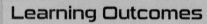

Learning Outcomes

1 Define the terms *supply chain* and *supply chain management*, and discuss the benefits of supply chain management

2 Discuss the concept of supply chain integration and explain why each of the six types of integration is important

3 Identify the eight key processes of excellent supply chain management, and discuss how each of these processes impacts the end customer

4 Discuss the key strategic decisions supply chain managers must make when designing their companies' supply chains

5 Describe the logistical components of the supply chain

6 Explain why supply chain performance measurement is necessary and important

7 Discuss why the supply chains of the present and future will be both environmentally conscious and sustainable, and the implications of these changes

8 Discuss new technology and emerging trends in supply chain management

LO1
Supply Chains and Supply Chain Management

In today's sophisticated marketplace, many companies are focusing on their supply chain and turning to supply chain management for competitive advantages. A company's **supply chain** includes all of the companies involved in all of the upstream and downstream flows of products, services, finances, and information, from initial suppliers (the point of origin) to the ultimate customer (the point of consumption). The goal of **supply chain management** is to coordinate and integrate the activities performed by supply chain members into a collection of seamless end-to-end processes, ultimately giving supply chain managers "total visibility" of the supply chain both inside and outside the firm. The philosophy behind supply chain management is that by visualizing the entire supply chain, managers can maximize strengths and efficiencies at each level of the process to create a highly competitive, customer-driven supply system able to respond immediately to changes in supply and demand. Companies that have a supply chain orientation recognize and embrace this philosophy, and therefore see the implications of managing the flows of products, services, and so on across their direct and indirect suppliers and customers.

> Supply chain **management** is completely customer driven.

supply chain
The connected chain of all of the business entities, both internal and external to the company, that perform or support the logistics function.

marketing&you.

Think about your current (or most recent) job. Enter the number that most closely corresponds with your opinion on the lines provided, using the scale below.

STRONGLY DISAGREE ‹ 1 2 3 4 5 › STRONGLY AGREE

_____ I feel strongly about improving the quality of my organization's services.

_____ I enjoy discussing quality-related issues with people in my organization.

_____ I gain a sense of personal accomplishment in providing high-quality services to my customers.

_____ I am willing to put in a great deal of effort beyond what is normally expected in order to help my organization deliver high-quality services to our customers.

_____ The way I feel about quality is very similar to the way my organization feels about quality.

_____ I really care about the quality of my organization's services.

Now, total your score. Find out what it means after you read the chapter.

Source: Scale #363, *Marketing Scales Handbook,* G. Bruner, K. James, H. Hensel, eds., vol. III. © by American Marketing Association. Used with permission of the American Marketing Association.

An important element of supply chain management is that it is completely customer driven. During the era of mass production (c. 1865–1980), manufacturers produced standardized products that were "pushed" down through the supply channel to the consumer. In contrast, products in today's marketplace are being driven by customers who expect to receive product configurations and services matched to their unique needs. For example, Dell builds computers only according to its customers' precise specifications, such as the amount of RAM memory; type of monitor, with solid state hard drive; and amount of hard disk space. Similarly, car companies offer customers the option to customize even economy-priced cars. For about $20,000, customers can order a Ford Mustang with a V-6 engine, a six-disc CD changer, MP3 player, and eight speakers. The focus is on pulling products into the marketplace and partnering with members of the supply chain to enhance customer value. Customizing an automobile is now possible because of new supply chain relationships between the automobile manufacturers and the after-market auto-parts industry.

This reversal of the flow of demand from a "push" to a "pull" system has resulted in a radical reformulation of market expectations as well as traditional marketing, production, and distribution functions. Through the coordinated partnership of suppliers, manufacturers, wholesalers, and retailers working together along the entire supply chain, supply chain management enables companies to respond with the unique product configuration and mix of services demanded by the customer. Today, supply chain management plays a dual role: first, as a *communicator* of customer demand that extends from the point of sale all the way back to the supplier, and second, as a *physical flow process* that engineers the timely and cost-effective movement of goods through the entire source-to-consumer supply pipeline. Boeing realizes the importance of these supply chain processes as it struggles to get enough engines to assemble the new 787 Dreamliner from its supplier, Rolls-Royce, resulting in another delay for the launch of its widely publicized new luxury airliner.[1] Better communication with Rolls-Royce, combined with better process flow synchronization, could have reduced the stress Boeing executives feel as they scramble to find enough engines to meet the new publicized launch scheduled for third quarter 2011.

Supply chain managers are responsible for making strategic decisions, such as coordinating the sourcing and procurement of raw materials, scheduling production, processing orders, managing inventory, transporting and storing supplies and finished goods, dealing with returns, and coordinating customer service activities. Supply chain managers are also responsible for the management of information that flows through the supply chain. Coordinating the relationships between the company and its external partners, such as vendors, carriers, and third-party companies, is also a critical function of supply chain management. Because supply chain managers play such a major role in both cost control and customer satisfaction, they are more valuable than ever. In fact, demand for supply chain managers has increased substantially in recent years. According to the Council of Supply Chain Management Professionals, the supply chain career field accounts for over 9.5 percent of the U.S. gross domestic product, with thousands of new, high-paying positions becoming available yearly.

In summary, supply chain managers are responsible for directing raw materials and parts to the production department and the finished or semi-finished product through warehouses and eventually to the intermediary or end user. Above all, supply chain management begins and ends with the customer. Instead of forcing a product into the market that may or may not sell quickly, supply chain managers react to actual customer demand. By doing so, they minimize the flow of raw

Exhibit 14.1 A Typical Supply Chain Management Process

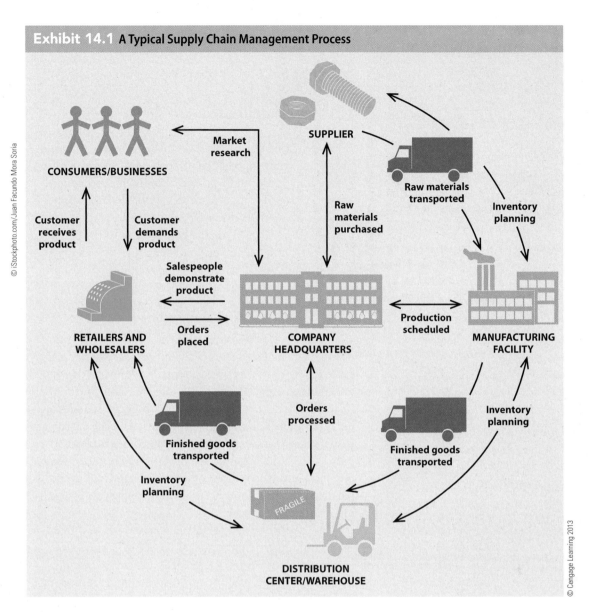

materials, finished product, and packaging materials at every point in the supply chain, resulting in lower costs and increased customer value. Exhibit 14.1 depicts a typical supply chain model that managers attempt to optimize for firm and customer benefit.

BENEFITS OF SUPPLY CHAIN MANAGEMENT

Supply chain management is a key means of differentiation for a firm and a critical component in marketing and corporate strategy. Supply-chain–oriented companies commonly report lower inventory, transportation, warehousing, and packaging costs; greater supply chain flexibility; improved customer service; and higher revenues. Research has shown a clear relationship between supply chain performance and profitability. Specific benefits from effective implementation of supply chain procedures include an almost 20 percent increase in cash flow, a more than 50 percent increase in flexibility of supply chain activities, and a reduction of 5 to 10 percent in supply chain costs, among other potential benefits. For example, to combat the recession Goodyear implemented supply chain management improvements resulting in reductions in inventory of $1 billion in 2009.[2]

Well-managed supply chains . . .

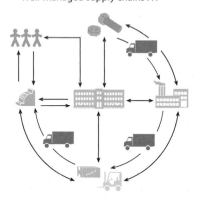

lead to . . .

✓ reduced costs

✓ increased flexibility

✓ improved customer service

✓ greater revenue

© Cengage Learning 2013

LO2
Supply Chain Integration

A key principle of supply chain management is that multiple firms work together to perform tasks as a single, unified system, rather than as several individual companies acting in isolation. Companies in a world-class supply chain combine their resources, capabilities, and innovations so they are used for the best interest of the entire chain as a whole, with the goal being that overall performance of the supply chain will be greater than the sum of its parts. As firms become increasingly supply-chain–oriented, they develop management practices that are consistent with this **systems approach**.

Management practices that reflect a highly coordinated effort between supply chain partners are said to be "integrated." In other words, **supply chain integration** occurs when multiple firms in a supply chain coordinate their activities and processes so that they are seamlessly linked to one another in an effort to satisfy the customer. In a world-class supply chain, the customer might not know where the business activities of one firm or business unit end, and where those of another begin—all of the participating firms and business units appear to be reading from the same script.

In the practice of world-class supply chain management, six types of integration are sought by firms interested in providing top-level service to customers.[3] First, in terms of firm-to-firm social interactions, *relationship integration* provides important benefits. Similarly, for the purposes of operational planning and control, *measurement integration* and *technology and planning integration* have been shown to be important determinants of company and overall supply chain success. When executing daily operations, three other types of integration are worthy of consideration: *material and service supplier integration, internal operations integration,* and *customer integration.* Each of these six types of integration is described in greater detail in the following sections. Firms' success in achieving each of these types of integration is very important. Highly integrated supply chains (those that are successful in achieving many or all of these types of integration) have been shown to be better at satisfying customers, managing costs, delivering high-quality products, enhancing productivity, and utilizing company or business unit assets, all of which translate into greater profitability for the firms and their partners working together in the supply chain.

RELATIONSHIP INTEGRATION

Companies that are integrated with each other are connected in a number of different ways—some very tangible and some less tangible. Tangible connections might include phone lines, storage in common databases, or having common procedures or formal processes. However, some of the most important ways of integrating supply chain partners are more intangible. These linkages

systems approach
A key principle of supply chain management—that multiple firms work together to perform tasks as a single, unified system, rather than as several individual companies acting in isolation.

supply chain integration
When multiple firms in a supply chain coordinate their activities and processes so that they are seamlessly linked to one another in an effort to satisfy the customer.

often take the form of social relationships between the members of coordinating or collaborating companies. **Relationship integration** is the ability of two or more companies to develop social connections that serve to guide their interactions when working together. More specifically, relationship integration is the capability to develop and maintain a shared mental framework across companies that describes how they will depend on one another when working together. This includes the ways in which they will collaborate on activities or projects so the customer gains the maximum amount of total value possible from the supply chain.

When multiple firms in a supply chain have achieved high relationship integration, they have developed certain social characteristics that allow the entire supply chain to perform at a higher level than would be possible for any of the partners operating alone. For example, relationally integrated supply chains typically have high **role specificity**. That is, each firm in the supply chain has clarity in terms of knowing which firm is the leader, which firms are the followers, and which responsibilities are assigned to each firm. Relationally integrated supply chains also tend to be managed by formal or informal social guidelines—a set of rules, policies, and/or procedures that dictate how firms will work together and specify how conflicts among supply chain partners will be resolved. In addition, relationally integrated supply chains tend to be open to information sharing across firm/business unit boundaries, so that everyone involved in the supply chain can clearly see the problems and opportunities that arise while firm-to-firm collaboration is taking place. Finally, the supply chains that have developed the highest degrees of relational integration also tend to practice equitable risk/reward sharing. The firms within such supply chains are openly willing to accept fair amounts of gain and loss when things go better, or significantly worse than expected.

The relationship integration between firms and their employees can lead to companies enacting *interorganizational citizenship behaviors*. Interorganizational citizenship behaviors are positive actions or behaviors that occur between firms that are not part of the formal agreement and are discretionary. For example, a customer might need a spare parts delivery late in the day, outside of the terms of an agreed upon contract. A supplier who is exhibiting interorganizational citizenship would have the delivery dropped off by a manager or employee on their way home, without the charge of an additional delivery.[4]

MEASUREMENT INTEGRATION

At a somewhat more tangible level, firms in integrated supply chains generally come to some consensus as to how each firm in the supply chain,

relationship integration
The ability of two or more companies to develop social connections that serve to guide their interactions when working together.

role specificity
When each firm in a supply chain has clarity in terms of knowing which firm is the leader, which firms are the followers, and which responsibilities are assigned to each firm.

Relationally integrated supply chains have a set of rules, policies, and/or procedures that dictate how firms will work together, and specify how conflicts among supply chain partners will be resolved.

measurement integration
The performance assessment of the supply chain as a whole that also holds each individual firm or business unit accountable for meeting its own goals.

activity-based costing (ABC)
An accounting method used in measurement integration to assess the costs associated with each supply chain activity.

technology and planning integration
The creation and maintenance of information technology systems that connect managers across and through the firms in the supply chain.

and the whole of the supply chain itself, will measure its failures and successes. **Measurement integration** reflects the idea that performance assessments should be transparent and measurable across the borders of different business units and firms, and also assess the performance of the supply chain as a whole while holding each individual firm or business unit accountable for meeting its own goals. Though achieving measurement integration might sound simple, it actually represents a very difficult set of tasks. Supply chain members, though connected, typically come from a variety of industries and play very different roles in the supply chain; standards for performance and measures of performance can vary widely from industry to industry.

Several areas of capability have been identified that are helpful in generating measurement integration across the supply chain. First, managers in all firms and business units must conduct functional assessments—in other words, each department in each business must have its own set of operational success measures, and if possible, similar departments should use the same performance metrics from business to business. Second, the firms in the supply chain should agree on and commit to principles of **activity-based costing (ABC)**. ABC focuses on accounting for costs associated with each enacted activity, regardless of who in the firm or supply chain performs it. Through the use of ABC, costs can be accurately assigned to products, services, departments, or specific customers. Once ABC and functional assessment procedures are in place, all of the firms in the supply chain must then agree to evaluate decisions based on a total cost perspective—the idea that all costs for a decision across the entire supply chain should be considered when making a commitment to a decision or project. Finally, there must be a widely agreed-upon set of supply chain metrics that are to be used as standards, both in terms of operational success (for instance, the number of late shipments in a given time period that are considered to be "acceptable," or the number of damaged cartons that can be shipped without paying a penalty), as well as financial success (for instance, what level of profitability or amount of cash flow should be expected). When supply chains achieve high measurement integration, managers have greater ability to act on information flowing through firms and across the supply chain, and can take better advantage of market opportunities or detect threats before they become problematic.

TECHNOLOGY AND PLANNING INTEGRATION

World-class supply chain management depends on thorough, accurate, and timely information acquisition and usage. If supply chain managers don't know the facts about their business environment, they cannot make good decisions about what to do now or in the future. By achieving **technology and planning integration** across their supply chains, firms can gain the information needed to execute short- and long-term planning, and thereby make better operational decisions. Technology and planning integration refers to the creation and maintenance of information technology systems that connect managers across and through the firms in the supply chain; it requires information hardware and software systems that can exchange information when needed between customers, suppliers, and internal operational areas of each of the supply chain partners.

Several firm-level and supply chain–level capabilities must be developed in order for technology and planning integration to become a reality. First, firms in the supply chain must become experts at information management—there must be seamless information flows related to customers, inventory levels, shipments, and so on, across all relevant supply chain members. Packets of information must be available in real time and accessible whenever and wherever needed in order to enhance the customer's experience. Additionally, supply chain managers within firms and business units should possess strong internal communications capability, meaning that information does not get caught in departmental silos, but rather is spread where needed throughout the company. Similarly, managers must be connected to managers of other firms via some sort of external connectivity, such that they can share and discuss needed information and view it in a timely, responsive, and usable format. By moving toward the development of these types of capabilities, managers have greater access to valuable information when and where they need it and can make important decisions that benefit the firm and the supply chain in time to take advantage of new opportunities or to reduce competitive threats.

MATERIAL AND SERVICE SUPPLIER INTEGRATION

The popularization of demand-based *pull systems* over the past several years has prompted firms to rethink the processes they use when serving customers. To operate pull systems efficiently, it is necessary to acquire materials used in production both cheaply and effectively. As a result, another type of integration—**material and service supplier integration** (sometimes called simply *supplier integration*)—has become a key supply chain focus. Supplier integration, when first considered, sounds simple: Firms should link seamlessly to those outsiders that provide goods and services to them, so that they can streamline work processes and thereby provide smooth, high-quality customer experiences. As with the other types of integration already discussed, however, integrating with suppliers is more complex than it might initially seem.

Firms that have developed high levels of supplier integration typically exhibit significant strategic alignment between themselves and their materials and services providers. This means that both sides have a common vision of the total value creation process and are each willing to share the responsibility for satisfying customer requirements. Because this step is so important, firms must choose their suppliers very carefully, paying close attention to each supplier's strategic goals and operational capabilities. Boeing has realized this while producing the famously delayed Dreamliner aircraft. The delays plaguing Boeing are driven partly by supplier miscommunication and parts shortages. To combat this, Boeing has created the Dreamliner production integration center to create tighter collaboration and coordination with their supplier base.[5] Supplier integration also requires that the supply chain partners interact in ways that minimize waste and redundancy, with such interactions extending upward though the supply chain to the supplier's suppliers, and so on. Finally, for true supplier integration to occur, both firms must have a stake in the outcomes of their interactions. As with relationship integration, risk and reward sharing between the firm and its suppliers should be built into any agreements or contracts so that both firms feel committed to serving the end customer over the long term.

material and service supplier integration
The strategic alignment between a firm and its supply chain materials and services providers that enables the firm to streamline work processes and provide smooth, high-quality customer experiences.

After Volvo Construction Equipment redesigned its supply chain with software that connected all its suppliers to a single order interface, their over-the-counter availability of parts increased from 60 percent to 95 percent.

internal operations integration
Links internally performed work into a seamless process that stretches across departmental and/or functional boundaries, with the goal of satisfying customer requirements.

benchmarks
The standards set by measuring the best, quickest, and most efficient work practices.

customer integration
A competency that enables firms to offer long-lasting, distinctive, value-added offerings to those customers who represent the greatest value to the firm or supply chain.

INTERNAL OPERATIONS INTEGRATION

To provide a seamless and satisfying customer experience, everyone working within the firm must be "on the same page" in terms of daily operations. A fundamental challenge being experienced by most businesses is the need for integrating various departments within the firm, such as marketing, research, sales, and logistics, all of which help in creating and delivering the value-added customer offering. If all of the organizational areas do not work well together, customers might undergo an experience where they receive different answers to the same question depending on whom they call, or they might be delivered a product or service that is not exactly what was ordered or needed. Process excellence within the firm requires that internal operations be fully integrated. **Internal operations integration** is the result of capabilities development toward the goal of linking internally performed work into a seamless process that stretches across departmental and/or functional boundaries, with the goal of satisfying customer requirements.

Five distinct groups of activities are related closely to internal operations integration success. First, the firm must become cross-functionally unified. This means that all activities that are worked on by more than one functional department or area should be viewed as a single activity rather than multiple activities worked on by different groups, and that multi-group synergy should be cultivated where applicable. This task is often (but not necessarily) accomplished through the use of cross-functional work teams, whose membership represents each of the relevant departments where the workflow operates. Next, the firm should seek to standardize operations and work processes across workgroups to reduce uncertainty about the ways and methods through which tasks are completed. Third, once cross-functionality and standardization are established, all work processes should be simplified as much as possible so that the best, quickest, and most efficient practices adopted by any of the departments are adopted (where appropriate) by all departments. Based on these processes, process standards should then be developed that provide internal **benchmarks** for performance. Finally, once common procedures are developed, measured, and evaluated, the overall logistical network of the firm should be reconfigured so that the physical assets owned by the firm can be used in the most efficient order and manner. However, this final step toward internal operations integration should take place only after careful consideration and consultation with work design engineers or other experts, as this step means permanent structural changes to capital assets and can therefore be very costly.

CUSTOMER INTEGRATION

All of the previously discussed forms of integration are critical to the success of the supply chain. However, none may be more important than supply chain firms' integration with end users of the products and services that the supply chain provides. Supply chain success depends on the ability of all of the involved firms and business units to work together and create value for the customer. Furthermore, to be truly successful, the firms in the supply chain must do so at cost levels that allow everyone in the chain to make a profit. The best way to deliver value under profitability constraints is through customer integration. **Customer integration** is a competency that enables firms to offer long-lasting, distinctive, value-added offerings to those customers who represent the greatest value to the firm or supply chain. Customer integration requires that supply chain firms know a lot about both themselves and their potential customer base. Highly customer-integrated firms assess their own capabilities and then match them to customers whose desires they can meet and who offer large enough sales potential for the linkage to be profitable over the long term.

As was the case with several other bases of integration, customer integration implies that a number of drivers be present for overall success. First, firms must understand that not all customers are alike, and they should use market segmentation to discover which of the pool of potential customers would be best satisfied by the core competencies of the supply chain. This segmentation should be based upon both the current needs expressed by the customer, and any potential future needs that have yet to be fully articulated. Once the customer pool is segmented according to the extent to which the supply chain can serve them, firms should select customer groups for whom to provide the highest levels of service. This process is often referred to as **ABC segmentation**—customers are placed into groups A, B, and C according to their overall long-term value to the firm and to the extent to which the firm can serve their desires. Based on ABC segmentation, levels of customer integration are established. For better customers (the A's, for example), high levels of responsiveness, customized offerings, and offering flexibility (in terms of details, finishing, delivery times, etc.) are established. For the next tier of customers, often the B's, standard offerings are made available. At the third tier, usually the C level customers, minimal direct contact is used, with telemarketing or direct mail being the primary method of contact, and little or no extra value services offered. Thus, customer integration provides stronger, more personal and "connected" experiences for the best customers, while minimizing operational flexibility for customers who are determined to be less valuable.

BARRIERS AND FACILITATORS OF INTEGRATION

The previous sections illustrated that integration is important to supply chain success; however, there are barriers and facilitators to integration that can create mixed results. Barriers to integration are practices or processes that make it difficult for integration to occur, such as lack of technology, having only arm's-length relationships, or miscommunication. Continuing with the Boeing Dreamliner example, the supply chain for the Dreamliner is global, it requires the ability to share accurate technical information with suppliers all over the globe, and relationships with these suppliers must be built in order to work toward a common goal. During the early production of the Dreamliner, Boeing was unable to integrate with suppliers at the level that was required to support the Dreamliner. They lacked the technology to monitor and share information and the relationships were not developed enough with global suppliers, resulting in several miscommunications and delays to the final product. To combat these barriers, Boeing began embracing facilitators of integration.

Facilitators of integration are practices or processes that help supply chain companies integrate. Two related and commonly considered facilitators are knowledge management and information sharing. Knowledge management is recognizing the importance of the information that exists within the supply chain and sharing it with supply chain partners in order to improve efficiency and effectiveness. Boeing realized the need to implement facilitators of integration and opened the Dreamliner Production Integration Center. Boeing utilizes video feeds and cameras to interact with suppliers around the clock in order to deal with issues such as product shortages, global weather, and labor issues in real time.[6]

> **ABC segmentation**
> The supply-chain process whereby customers are placed into groups A, B, and C according to their overall long-term value to the firm and to the extent to which the firm can serve their desires.

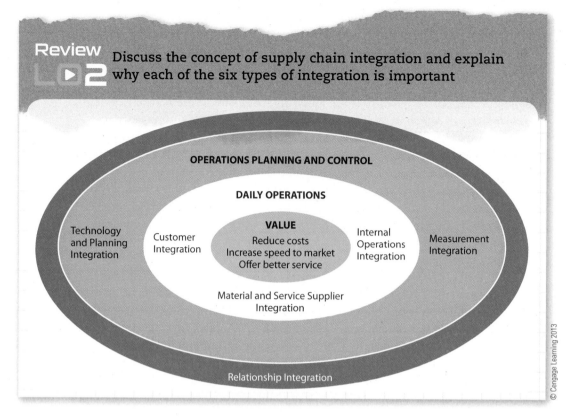

OPERATIONS PLANNING AND CONTROL

DAILY OPERATIONS

VALUE
Reduce costs
Increase speed to market
Offer better service

Technology and Planning Integration

Customer Integration

Internal Operations Integration

Measurement Integration

Material and Service Supplier Integration

Relationship Integration

© Cengage Learning 2013

LO3
The Key Processes of Supply Chain Management

When firms practice good supply chain management, their functional departments or areas, such as marketing, research and development, and production, are integrated both within and across the linked firms. Integration, then, is "how" excellent supply chain management works. The **business processes** on which the linked firms work together represent the "what" of supply chain management—they are the objects of focus on which firms, departments, areas, and people work together when seeking to reduce supply chain costs or generate additional revenues. Business processes are composed of bundles of interconnected activities that stretch across firms in the supply chain; they represent key areas that some or all of the involved firms are constantly working on in order to reduce costs and/or generate revenues for everyone throughout supply chain management.

There are eight critical business processes on which supply chain managers must focus.[7] These are displayed as the horizontal bars in Exhibit 14.2. As can be seen, some processes extend end-to-end in the supply chain; they are touched or affected by all of the supply chain's firms. Others might be the focus of only two to three of the involved companies. Nonetheless, most supply chains operate each of the eight key business processes within some firms and/or business units.

CUSTOMER RELATIONSHIP MANAGEMENT

The **customer relationship management process** (discussed further in Chapter 21) enables companies to prioritize their marketing focus on different

business processes
Bundles of interconnected activities that stretch across firms in the supply chain.

customer relationship management process
The prioritization of a firm's marketing focus on different customer groups according to each group's long-term value to the company or supply chain; designed to identify and build relationships with good customers.

customer groups according to each group's long-term value to the company or supply chain. As noted earlier, some customers are more valuable than others due to their greater purchasing potential or lower cost-to-serve than others. Once higher-value customers are identified, firms should focus on providing customized products and better service to this group than to others. Activities that are included in the customer relationship management process might include customer differentiation and scoring, identification of new opportunities with valued accounts, and developing customized product and service agreements for upper-tier customer groups, among others. Thus, the customer relationship management process includes both segmentation of customers by value and the generation of customer loyalty for the most attractive segments—key activities that are enabled through customer integration. This process provides a set of comprehensive principles for the initiation and maintenance of customer relationships and is often carried out with the assistance of specialized CRM (customer relationship management) computer software.

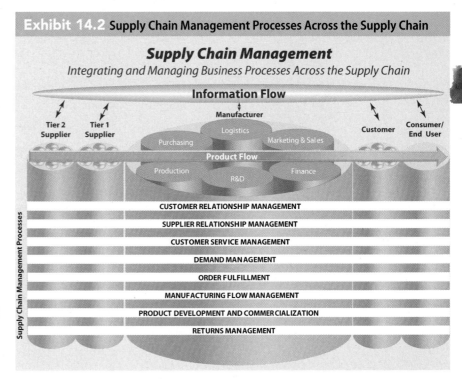

Exhibit 14.2 Supply Chain Management Processes Across the Supply Chain

Source: Douglas M. Lambert, Editor, *Supply Chain Management: Processes, Partnerships, Performance*, Third Edition, Sarasota, FL: Supply Chain Management Institute, 2008, p. 3, adapted from Douglas M. Lambert, Martha C. Cooper, and Janus D. Pagh, "Supply Chain Management Implementation Issues and Research Opportunities," *The International Journal of Logistics Management*, Vol. 9, No. 2, 1998, p. 2. Copyright 2008, Supply Chain Management Institute. For more information see: www.scm-institute.org.

Companies that emphasize the customer relationship management process throughout their supply chains are able to deliver best-in-class customer experiences and generate enormous customer loyalty. For example, at 1-800-Flowers.com, data about customer tastes, preferences, and/or order history is collected at all customer contact points. The company then uses this data to better anticipate customer needs and adapt to new trends in the ways, times, and channels through which customers buy flowers. It also reduces the time required to process orders, evaluate a customer's likelihood of buying a new item based on previous orders, assess customer credit worthiness, and customize promotions so that customers are more likely to respond positively.[8] All of these factors enable 1-800-Flowers.com to invest its resources more efficiently and to make better decisions in response to changes in the flower marketplace.

CUSTOMER SERVICE MANAGEMENT

Whereas the customer relationship management process is designed to identify and build relationships with good customers, the customer service management process is designed to ensure that those customer relationships remain strong. The **customer service management process** presents a multi-company, unified response system to the customer whenever complaints, concerns, questions, or comments are voiced. It includes activities such as taking customer calls or

customer service management process
A multi-company, unified response system to the customer whenever complaints, concerns, questions, or comments are voiced; designed to ensure that customer relationships remain strong.

© iStockphoto.com/Juan Facundo Mora Soria

requests for information, capturing their order amendments or questions, developing response procedures, amending orders, answering questions, aiding in installation, measuring customer satisfaction with the service encounter, and checking warranty status, among many others. When the process is well executed, it can have a strong positive impact on revenues, often as a result of quick positive response to negative customer feedback, and sometimes even in the form of additional sales gained through the additional customer contact. Customers expect service from the moment a product is purchased until it is disposed of, and the customer service management process allows for touch points between the buyer and seller throughout this life cycle.

Customer service management processes are increasingly being enhanced through the use of customer care software applications. For example, customer service agents at companies such as Southwest Airlines, Microsoft, and America Online are able to quickly access customers' purchasing, billing, and ordering records on their computer desktops and can use this information to provide a more pleasant interactive experience when customers call with questions or complaints. Other companies, such as Dell, offer online chat sessions and self-assistance groups on their corporate Web sites so that customers can begin to help themselves prior to (or instead of) making direct contact with the company. Top-level customer service programs also tend to take a very proactive approach to ensuring that customers are satisfied. For example, a person buying a new Lexus automobile can expect to be frequently contacted during their first two years of ownership by associates charged with making sure that the customer's car is meeting their expectations. The associates are empowered to take a wide variety of steps to ensure that customers are satisfied, including offering free service calls, performing customer-location car pickup (including a complimentary loaner car) when adjustments need to be made to automobile settings, and providing free car washes for customers who need unexpected service early in the life of the car.

DEMAND MANAGEMENT

The **demand management process** seeks to align supply and demand throughout the supply chain by anticipating customer requirements at each level and creating demand-related plans of action prior to actual customer purchasing behavior. At the same time, demand management seeks to minimize the costs of serving multiple types of customers who have variable wants and needs. In other words, the demand management process allows companies in the supply chain to satisfy customers in the most efficient and effective ways possible. The activities that enable the demand management process to work include customer data collection, forecasting of future demand, synchronization of supply and demand by comparing production capacity to sales forecasts (known as sales and operations planning), and the development of activities that serve to "smooth out" demand, such as authorizing short-term promotions, changing salesperson incentives, and revising customer credit terms to reduce default rates.

While all of these activities help bring available inventory into alignment with customer desires, accurate forecasting is an extremely critical part of the process. Forecasting allows firms to anticipate the variations that occur with customer demand, such as seasonality and trending. Seasonality refers to peaks in demand surrounding certain times of the year, days of the week, or events. For example, during the summer swimsuits and tanning lotion have peaks in demand due to the season. Trending shows firms whether or not demand is consistently increasing, such as the

demand management process
The alignment of supply and demand throughout the supply chain to anticipate customer requirements at each level and create demand-related plans of action prior to actual customer purchasing behavior.

iPhone, which has seen demand continuously increase since its initial release. Forecasting seeks to identify these variations early, so firms can incorporate them into forecasts and plan ahead for additional or lesser inventory as the situation dictates. Though it is very difficult to predict exactly what items and quantities customers will buy prior to purchase, demand management can ease the pressure on the production process and allow companies to satisfy most of their customers through greater flexibility in manufacturing, marketing, and sales programs. However, much of the uncertainty in demand planning can be mitigated by conducting collaborative planning, forecasting, and replenishment (CPFR) activities with the company's customers and suppliers. One animal food company adopting CPFR reduced its forecasting error by 6 percent, which enabled it to cut prices paid by customers almost 4 percent in under a year's time.[9]

Good demand management can increase both sales and customer satisfaction, and at the same time, it can reduce the overall cost of serving the firm or supply chain's customer base. The positive effects of good demand management can be observed at IKEA. IKEA traditionally focused primarily on manufacturing and merchandising to generate sales—they used a push system, producing what was likely to sell and then selling and promoting what was produced—and managed their base of over 1,600 suppliers manually. When unusually large orders were placed for an item, IKEA's distribution centers were emptied, and when fewer orders than expected came the distribution centers were full of unwanted product. After implementing a demand management program developed for them by logistics solution provider Manugistics, IKEA was able to forecast much more accurately, align production with demand projections, and reduce inventory levels by over 20 percent—money that could be reinvested in distribution systems and new product development and evaluation, among other projects.[10]

ORDER FULFILLMENT

One of the most fundamental processes in supply chain management is the **order fulfillment process**, which involves generating, filling, delivering, and providing on-the-spot service for customer orders. The order fulfillment process is a highly integrated process, often requiring persons from multiple companies and multiple functions to come together and coordinate to create customer satisfaction at a given place and time. The best order fulfillment processes reduce the time between order and customer receipt as much as possible, while ensuring that the customer receives exactly what he/she wanted. The shorter lead times are beneficial in that they allow firms to carry reduced inventory levels and free up cash that can be used on other projects. Activities in the order fulfillment process include working with salespeople to generate and enter orders, order processing and document handling, order filling and delivery, and updating account status following shipment. Overall, the order fulfillment process involves understanding both internal capabilities and external customer needs, and matching these together so the supply chain maximizes profits while minimizing costs and waste.

When the order fulfillment process is managed diligently, the amount of time between order placement and receipt of the customer's payment following

order fulfillment process
A supply chain management process that involves generating, filling, delivering, and providing on-the-spot service for customer orders.

The best order fulfillment processes reduce the time between order and customer receipt as much as possible while ensuring that customers receive exactly what they wanted.

order shipment (known as the **order-to-cash cycle**) is minimized as much as possible. Because many firms do not view order fulfillment as a core competency (versus, for example, product development or marketing), they often outsource this function to a **third party logistics firm (3PL)** that specializes in the order fulfillment process. The 3PL becomes a semi-permanent part of the firm's supply chain assigned to manage one or more specialized functions. When employed for the purposes of order fulfillment, the 3PL is contracted to manage the firm's order fulfillment process from beginning to end, thereby freeing up the firm's time and resources so that they can be expended on core business activities. Many times 3PLs constitute a firm's only interaction with the customer, so they need to represent the needs and interests of the entire firm and supply chain. The development and training of these employees to be empowered and respond to the customer's needs in the best interest of the supply chain is becoming increasingly important.[11]

MANUFACTURING FLOW MANAGEMENT

The **manufacturing flow management process** is concerned with ensuring that firms in the supply chain have the needed resources to manufacture with flexibility and to move products through a multi-stage production process. Firms with flexible manufacturing have the ability to create a wide variety of goods and/or services with minimized costs associated with changing production techniques. The manufacturing flow process includes much more than simple production of goods and services—it means creating flexible agreements with suppliers and shippers so that unexpected demand bursts can be accommodated. Activities in the manufacturing flow process include, but are not limited to: the determination of a supply's route and velocity through manufacturing; materials planning; inventory management and control for both parts and finished goods; and quality management.

The goals of the manufacturing flow management process are centered on leveraging the capabilities held by multiple members of the supply chain to improve overall manufacturing output in terms of quality, delivery speed, and flexibility, all of which tie to profitability. For instance, when GM changed over to flexible manufacturing, managers and shareholders were pleased to discover that switching manufacturing facilities to accommodate different car model lines took only three days, as compared to the six weeks of downtime that was typical prior to the upgrade. GM executives estimate the company is saving over $1.5 billion per year due to more efficient asset utilization. In addition, GM has also added flexible robotics to plants (i.e., robots that can be reprogrammed and thereby adapted for use in more than one production process) at a further savings of $120 million.[12] These types of adjustments to manufacturing flow processes illustrate the enormous potential that fine-tuning the process can have for the firm's bottom line.

SUPPLIER RELATIONSHIP MANAGEMENT

The **supplier relationship management process** is closely related to the manufacturing flow management process and contains several characteristics that parallel the customer relationship management process. The manufacturing flow management process is highly dependent on supplier relationships for flexibility. Furthermore, in a way similar to that found in the customer relationship management process, supplier relationship management provides structural support for developing and maintaining relationships with suppliers. Thus, integrating these two ideas, supplier relationship management supports manufacturing flow by identifying and maintaining relationships with highly valued suppliers. Just as firms benefit from developing close-knit and integrated relationships with customers, close-knit and integrated relationships with suppliers provide a means through which performance advantages can be gained. Basic activities of the supplier relationship management process typically include identifying and selecting suppliers; creating supplier scoring criteria and applying scorecard tools to supplier groups; conducting periodic supplier reviews and visits; and identifying ways suppliers can provide greater service levels at similar costs, among many others.

The management of supplier relationships is a key step toward ensuring that firms' manufacturing resources are available, and thereby the supplier relationship management process has a direct impact on each supply chain member's bottom-line financial performance. In fact, the manufacturing division of Toyota Motor Co. of America takes the supplier relationship management process so seriously that it recently established on-site offices for suppliers when opening a new truck plant. This seemingly drastic move was intended to fully integrate suppliers into the Toyota manufacturing process, including the ability for Toyota to monitor second-tier suppliers, practice on-site quality management, and lower transportation and operating costs.

PRODUCT DEVELOPMENT AND COMMERCIALIZATION

The **product development and commercialization process** (discussed in detail in Chapter 11) includes the group of activities that facilitates the joint development and marketing of new offerings among a group of supply chain partner firms. In many cases, new products and services are not the sole responsibility of a single firm who serves as inventor, engineer, builder, marketer, and sales agent, but rather, they are often the product of a multi-company collaboration with multiple firms and business units playing unique roles in new product development, testing, and launch activities, among others. The capability for developing and introducing new offerings quickly is key for competitive success versus rival firms, and so it is often advantageous to involve many supply chain partners in the effort. Activities that are embedded within the product development and commercialization process commonly include new product idea generation and screening; cross-functional and cross-organization team assembly; product rollout requirement identification; and new offering profitability analysis. The process requires the close cooperation of suppliers and customers who provide input throughout the process and serve as advisors and coproducers for the new offering(s).

RETURNS MANAGEMENT

The final supply chain management process deals with incidents where customers choose to return a product to the retailer or supplier, thus creating a reversed flow of goods within the supply chain. Returns occur for a variety of reasons, including customer dissatisfaction, slow sales or poor quality, asset recapture (i.e., reusable packaging), product recalls, and recycling. The **returns management process** enables firms to manage volumes of returned product efficiently, while minimizing returns-related costs and maximizing the value of the returned assets to the firms in the supply chain. Although this process would seem to be less important than supply chain activities occurring under "normal" circumstances, it is worth considering that though returns average about 6 percent of sales in most cases, they do reach up to 40 percent of sales volume in certain

product development and commercialization process
The group of activities that facilitates the joint development and marketing of new offerings among a group of supply chain partner firms.

returns management process
A process that enables firms to manage volumes of returned product efficiently, while minimizing costs and maximizing the value of the returned assets to the firms in the supply chain.

Response to Customer Unpredictability in the Automotive Industry: Get Lean

In the ultra-competitive U.S. automobile industry, delivering the right car to the customer, in the right color, with the right features, at the right price, and in the shortest amount of time possible, is a critical determinant of customer satisfaction. Automobile makers both foreign and domestic know this, but are faced with a competing goal as well—minimizing inventory costs. Automakers need to sell as many cars as possible, but they also need to be sure to make only as many cars as customers will demand in order to be profitable. Thus, the Big 3 American companies, as well as foreign competitors such as Honda, Toyota, and Mercedes, are turning to lean supply chain management principles in order to get the job done. A lean supply chain is one that has been streamlined to reduce waste and/or other non–value-added activities, minimizing unnecessary inventory, time delays, and production costs.

Automakers have adopted lean supply chain principles as a method for improving customer outcomes. For example, Land Rover is using technologies such as radio-frequency identification (RFID) to track parts and finished automobiles' locations. Using RFID, managers can view the locations of components or finished goods on a virtual color-coded map in real time so the company has constant, complete visibility of inventories and avoids unnecessary ordering of parts and/or manufacturing of models that are already represented within a shipment or geographic area. The company can then reinvest these savings into parts and finished cars that are actually needed at dealerships and/or manufacturing and service facilities.

Executives at Toyota also point out another key benefit of lean supply chain management: Nothing is manufactured until the customer places an order. Then and only then does the company place a replacement unit into production. As one manager at Toyota states, "most production schedules are based on [sales forecasts] . . . production should be based on sold end-customer orders, not forecasts . . . [this allows us to] eliminate just-in-case ordering and the 'noise' in the supply chain." By ordering and manufacturing on a lean, just-in-time basis, everyone in the supply chain holds less unwanted inventory and customers get the car they wanted quickly and at the lowest possible price. In other words, a lean supply chain enables customers to buy exactly what they want, and the automobile company saves money at the same time by making only what they sell. Isn't that what is best for everyone?[13]

industries such as apparel e-retailing. Thus, the activities associated with returns management have the potential to impact the firm's financial position in a major and negative way if mishandled. Activities commonly associated with the returns management process include returns gatekeeping (determination of whether a return is allowed for a product in question), returns routing, deciding on how to dispose of the returned product, and re-crediting or reconciliation of the customer's account.

In addition to the value of managing returns from a pure asset-recovery perspective, many firms are discovering that returns management also creates additional marketing and customer service touch points that can be leveraged for added customer value above and beyond normal sales and promotion-driven encounters. Handling returns gives the company an additional opportunity to please the customer, and customers who have positive experiences with the returns management process can become very confident buyers who are willing to reorder, since they know any problems they encounter with purchases will be quickly and fairly rectified. In addition, the returns management process allows the firm to recognize weaknesses in product design and/or areas for potential improvement through the direct customer feedback that initiates the process.

LO4
Strategic Supply Chain Management Decisions

The establishment of supply chain integration and identification of key business processes make world-class supply chain management possible for businesses. However, to take advantage of these principles, supply chain managers must implement them in practice. Supply chain management strategies guide the implementation of key supply chain management principles. When implementing supply chain management, several strategic questions are relevant and must be answered by managers seeking to gain the benefits of the integrated, process-oriented supply chain. Some of the most important questions are:

→ Based on the markets we compete in, the suppliers available, and the products we sell, what overarching supply chain strategy is most appropriate for my firm or business unit?

→ What does the overall "map" of all of the firm's key supply chain members look like?

These strategic questions are among the most important that supply chain managers will answer as they steer the firm toward operational and financial successes.

Review LO3 Identify the eight key processes of excellent supply chain management and discuss how each of these processes impacts the end customer

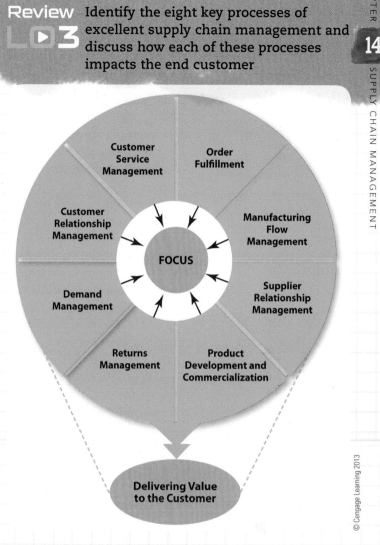

© Cengage Learning 2013

SUPPLY CHAIN STRATEGIES

Because products and marketplaces might differ substantially in their core characteristics from place to place and product to product, supply chain management strategies should be selected according to the situation at hand. In addition, because in many cases supply chains operate on a global scale, with far-away suppliers and customers communicating with, serving, or depending on local firms, companies must take care to adopt supply chain management strategies that strike a balance between the lower costs offered through global supply chain management and the assuredness of top-quality service that more localized solutions may provide.

One of the most interesting issues supply chain managers face in this regard is the mind-set of the firm. Most firms must choose between two strategic philosophies: high responsiveness to customers at any cost, or profitability through waste reduction (and therefore cost reduction) even if it means sometimes disappointing customers. These strategic philosophies are often referred to collectively in what

has come to be known as the "lean" versus "agile" debate. The **lean supply chain
management** strategy embraces removal of waste from the supply chain system
in whatever form it is found. Made famous by Toyota production engineer Taiichi
Ohno, the lean strategy seeks to remove any excesses from the supply chain, including overproduction, product defects, excess inventories, unneeded processing,
movement of people, transport of goods, or employee idling. In lean companies,
these principles are sometimes adhered to even if it means disappointing a small
customer segment that wants more customized services. The implementation of
lean supply chain principles launched Toyota into the upper echelon of automakers
in terms of performance and profitability, and has caused this strategy to become
viewed as a major strategic weapon when properly implemented. Benetton, the
Italian clothing company, has also used lean principles when reviving its brand in
recent years. By narrowing its product lines through the removal of the sportswear
category, outsourcing the production of high-margin accessories to China, building an extensive worldwide distribution network, and breaking up inventory into
smaller, quickly dispatched shipments, the company posted its highest levels of
profitability in several years.

Lean supply chain management does have weaknesses as a competitive strategy. Though "going lean" works well in situations where the advantages generated
by mass manufacturing are present, such as cases where relatively stable and predictable market demand and low variety of customer preferences exist. The lean
strategy does not work as well when customers prefer more customized products
and when demand is more unpredictable. Thus, in contrast to lean supply chain
management, other companies sometimes choose to adopt **agile supply chain
management** strategies. Whereas the lean strategy is mostly concerned with waste
reduction, the agile strategy is concerned primarily with customer responsiveness
and focuses primarily on the ability of the firm to fulfill demand in situations where
consumer wants and needs are less obvious. A key concept for the implementation
of agile SCM is the notion of flexibility. Instead of relying on forecasts that drive
production ahead of demand, agile supply chains adopt a wait-and-see approach

*Porsche manufactures cars using parts from all over the world that arrive just as they are
needed, making a flexible, efficient manufacturing process.*

© Peter Endig/dpa/picture-alliance/Newscom

where commitment to supply chain processes is unknown until the order is placed. They then make products customized to order specifications. With the agile strategy, the customer is always right and is to be served to the utmost even if this means somewhat higher costs.

Although the lean and agile supply chain strategies might at first seem to include opposing perspectives and actions, this is not necessarily always the case. First, the two strategies do, in fact, share a common objective: to fulfill customer requirements at the lowest total cost to the members of the supply chain system. (The difference is at what point the firm determines that cost control becomes more important than customer demands. With the lean strategy, cost control becomes a priority much sooner, and with the agile strategy, customer focus remains the key much longer.) Because of this common goal, some of the elements of each strategy can be combined in a hybrid strategy. The bringing together of principles from each of the main strategic viewpoints has been termed a **Leagile supply chain strategy**. With the Leagile strategy, the best elements of each strategy for the particular product/market combination describing the firm are selected. For example, customers wishing to purchase a Toyota Scion can log onto the company Web site and build their car to a highly customized degree, including the selection of leather versus cloth seats, many different wheel types, and a wide variety of sound and video equipment. However, the base automobile is manufactured and shipped from within Japan using lean principles. The "agile" components selected by the customer are installed later, with the final customization often occurring at the local dealership location. This delay in final production is called **postponement**. Through postponement, the Leagile supply chain management strategy allows the company to take advantage of many of the benefits of lean supply chain management while still providing the agility that makes many customer experiences more desirable.

The big question then is under what conditions should companies use lean, agile, and/or Leagile supply chain management strategies? The answer to this question depends largely on the characteristics of the supply market and customer demand for the product. In situations where aggregate customer demand is predictable, it is generally accepted that lean supply chain management offers the greatest benefits in terms of waste reduction associated with repetitive manufacturing flow and order fulfillment processes. However, when customer demand is less certain, the best supply chain management strategy to choose depends on supply market characteristics. Specifically, when there is an abundance of suppliers, and the supply market as a whole is quick and responsive, an agile strategy is usually best because it maximizes customer responsiveness at the lowest levels of risk. On the other hand, when the supply market is less certain, the firm might be better off implementing a hybrid Leagile strategy, with some generic inventory being held at strategic locations ready for quick customer adaptation and sale. Decisions such as these are often driven by senior management support. The support that senior management provides will affect the decision making process and the credibility of the strategy that is chosen. The lack of support can result in indecision, confusion, and misunderstandings regarding the purpose of the supply chain strategy that is selected.[14] These situations are depicted in Exhibit 14.3.

MAPPING THE SUPPLY CHAIN

In addition to the selection and implementation of an overarching supply chain management strategy, firms must also understand the structure of their supply chain and the many relationships existing between members. In terms of

Leagile supply chain strategy
A supply chain management strategy that combines the best elements of the lean and agile strategies for a particular product/market combination.

postponement
The delay in final production in the Leagile supply chain management strategy that enables the company to take advantage of many of the benefits of lean supply chain management while still providing the agility that improves customer experiences.

Exhibit 14.3 Lean versus Agile Supply Chain Management

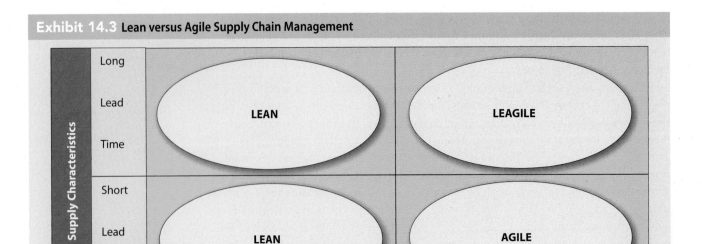

		Predictable	Unpredictable
Supply Characteristics	Long Lead Time	LEAN	LEAGILE
	Short Lead Time	LEAN	AGILE

Demand Characteristics

Source: Martin Christopher, Helen Peck, and Denis Towill, "A Taxonomy for Selecting Global Supply Chain Stategies," *International Journal of Logistics Management,* Vol. 17, No. 2, 2007, 277–287.

their structure, all supply chains can be viewed as groupings of nodes and linkages, with the nodes being firms or business units/functions, and the links being the processes that connect them. A typical supply chain network looks like an uprooted tree lying on its side, as shown in Exhibit 14.4. Viewing this exhibit,

Exhibit 14.4 A Supply Chain Network Map

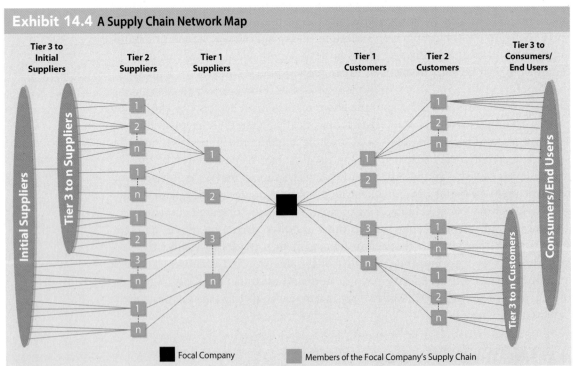

Source: Douglas M. Lambert, Editor, *Supply Chain Management: Processes, Partnerships, Performance,* Third Edition, Sarasota, FL: Supply Chain Management Institute, 2008, p. 6, adapted from Douglas M. Lambert, Martha C. Cooper, and Janus D. Pagh, "Supply Chain Management Implementation Issues and Research Opportunities," *The International Journal of Logistics Management,* Vol. 9, Eight critical processes from *Supply Chain Management: Processes, Partnerships, Performance,* by Douglas M. Lambert (Ed.), 2004, Supply Chain Management Institute: Sarasota, FL. Reprinted with permission. No. 2, 1998, p. 3. Copyright 2008, Supply Chain Management Institute. For more information see: www.scm-institute.org.

global perspectives

Lego Goes to Prague: A Distribution Dream or Supply Chain Nightmare?

Children across the world love to play with the plastic bricks and other modular toys manufactured by Danish toymaker Lego. The colorful pieces can be assembled, taken apart, and reused by children as small as age three, and because of the toys' ability to foster creativity in kids of all ages, they have become a worldwide phenomenon for kids over the past several decades. The Lego brand is particularly popular in modern times in the United States and Western Europe, and demand has been increasing recently in Asia as well, making the company a global player in the ultracompetitive toy marketplace, with products distributed in over 130 countries in 2009.

Despite Lego's popularity, relatively high costs, hard economic times, and the proliferation of many new brands in the toy market combined to place pressure on the company's bottom line in recent years. In 2004, the company began to search out supply chain cost reductions that could potentially relieve some of the financial strain. Following much analysis, the company decided to focus primarily on reducing the costs of distributing toys throughout mainland Europe, where a large portion of its most loyal customers live, and it reduced the number of total distribution center (DC) locations in its European network from 11 to 1, with the single remaining location in Prague, Czech Republic. This was viewed by many of the company's critics as a quite daring maneuver—no major company had ever before (or has since) operated a single European distribution hub from an Eastern European nation, and there was concern about whether Lego would be able to locate enough experienced distribution and logistics workers in the city—though there were many workers there with manufacturing backgrounds, very few were thought to be capable of operating a forklift, driving a large truck, or performing other logistics related tasks.

To set up its radical new distribution, Lego leased over one million square feet of warehouse space in the city and hired a 3PL firm to manage the logistical operations on a daily basis. In order to ease into the new network design, the company launched the new DC and ran parallel operations with the old network still in place. Then it slowly began to shut down the old locations and diverted traffic to the new Prague DC, until the new location was the only remaining hub in Europe. After two years of trials and adjustments and closures, the Prague DC was the sole location serving all locational demand for Europe and Asia.

Almost immediately, the company began to notice some changes that had to be made to the existing network setup it had been using for years. Transportation routes had to be rethought, and the 55 carriers that were being used were trimmed to a more manageable 10 that were known for their ability to handle both continents. Other contingencies also came into play related to local regulations—carriers cannot operate in Germany on bank holidays, for instance. These constraints had to be added to the company's routing plan. Due to the relatively few routes being run, more load consolidation was necessary and shipment schedules had to be adjusted for larger and less frequent drops. And of course, nearly 1,000 employees had to be hired and trained in the fundamentals of logistics and transportation management, over half of which were seasonal workers who handled the high demand that led into each Christmas season.

Following two years of operations, the results from Lego's grand experiment were mixed. Transportation and distribution costs were down significantly, but employee skill levels prevented the company from perhaps saving more money in terms of delivery and training costs, and ground shipments to Western Europe took up to a day more time to accomplish. Do you think the choice to locate the new DC in Prague was a good one? What factors would you say were most important in this decision? If Lego could start over, would it be more efficient to locate in Belgium or the Netherlands, which are more central to the western half of the European continent, based on what they know now? Why or why not?[15]

decisions related to supply chain structure are centered on which nodes should be included in the network and what level or degree of linkage should be used to connect any two nodes. With respect to the first question, firms consider issues such as how long the supply chain for a product should be and what number of suppliers or customers should be included in each level of the network. For example, many firms seek to "optimize" their collection of suppliers (supply base)

Lean firms focus on improving profitability through the removal of waste from the supply chain system.

 Agile firms seek to provide the highest levels of customer responsiveness and service possible, even if the costs of doing so are higher.

 Leagile firms adopt a position somewhere in between, with main components made and shipped using lean principles, but with agility gained later through the postponement of final production.

© Cengage Learning 2013

by including only the certain number of suppliers that can be adequately managed through personal relationships, given that the amount of resources the firm has available to expend on this task is limited. Three dimensions of supply chain network design are commonly considered by supply chain managers: the horizontal structure, the vertical structure, and the horizontal position. The **horizontal structure** is the number of tiers (rows in the supply chain representing the total number of levels through which goods and services must pass from the earliest to end stages of the chain). The **vertical structure** is the number of suppliers or customers included within each individual tier. Given a particular horizontal and vertical structure, the **horizontal position** of the firm can be established. The firm can be at or near the beginning (origin), end (customer), or anywhere between in the supply chain. The horizontal position of the firm is important to establish, as firms that are located near one end of the supply chain often find it very challenging to manage processes that are located closer to the other end.

LO5
The Logistics Function in the Supply Chain

Now that you are familiar with the structure and strategy of supply chain management, it is important to also understand the physical means through which products move through the supply chain. As mentioned earlier, supply chain management coordinates and integrates all of the activities performed by supply chain members into a seamless process. The logistics function of the supply chain is responsible for the movement and delivery of goods and services into, through, and out of each firm in the supply chain network. The logistics function consists of several interrelated and integrated logistical components: (1) sourcing and procurement of raw materials and supplies, (2) production scheduling, (3) order processing, (4) inventory management and control, (5) warehousing and materials handling, and (6) transportation.

A **logistics information system** provides the technological link connecting all of the logistics components of the supply chain. The components of the system include, for example, software for materials acquisition and handling, warehouse-management and enterprise-wide solutions, data storage and integration in data warehouses, mobile communications, electronic data interchange, RFID chips, and the Internet. Working together, the components of the logistics information system are the fundamental enablers of successful supply chain management.

The **supply chain team**, leveraging the capabilities of the logistics information system, orchestrates the movement of goods, services, and information from the source to the consumer. Supply chain teams typically cut across organizational boundaries, embracing all parties who participate in moving the product to market.

horizontal structure
One of three dimensions of supply chain network design; the number of tiers (columns) in the supply chain, representing the total number of levels through which goods and services must pass from the earliest to end stages of the chain.

vertical structure
One of three dimensions of supply chain network design; the number of suppliers or customers included within each individual tier.

horizontal position
One of three dimensions of supply chain network design; the position of a firm, relative to other firms, along the supply chain.

logistics information system
The link that connects all of the logistics components of the supply chain.

supply chain team
An entire group of individuals who orchestrate the movement of goods, services, and information from the source to the consumer.

The best supply chain teams also move beyond the organization to include the external participants in the chain, such as suppliers, transportation carriers, and third-party logistics suppliers. Members of the supply chain communicate, coordinate, and cooperate extensively to make the logistics function as efficiently and effectively as possible.

Today's corporate supply chain logisticians have become so efficient that the U.S. Marine Corps is now consulting with companies such as Walmart, UPS, and Unilever to improve its own supply chain efficiency. The Marine Corps' goal is to reduce the time it takes to deliver supplies to the front lines from one week to 24 hours and lower costs by cutting inventories in half.

SOURCING AND PROCUREMENT

One of the most important links in the supply chain is the one between the manufacturer and the supplier. Purchasing professionals are on the front lines of supply chain management. Purchasing departments plan purchasing strategies, develop specifications, select suppliers, and negotiate price and service levels. Often, goods are procured for use in local manufacturing processes from suppliers halfway around the world. This is especially true for the United States, which is the world's top importer, with nearly $2 trillion worth of purchased merchandise entering the nation annually through its international ports.[16]

The goal of most sourcing and procurement activities is to reduce the costs of raw materials and supplies. Purchasing professionals have traditionally relied on tough negotiations to get the lowest price possible from suppliers of raw materials, supplies, and components. Perhaps the biggest contribution purchasing can make to supply chain management, however, is in the area of vendor relations. Companies can use the purchasing function to strategically manage suppliers in order to reduce the total cost of materials and services. Through enhanced vendor relations, buyers and sellers can develop cooperative relationships that reduce costs and improve efficiency with the aim of lowering prices and enriching profits. By integrating suppliers into their companies' businesses, purchasing managers have become better able to streamline purchasing processes, manage inventory levels, and reduce overall costs of the sourcing and procurement operations.

ORDER PROCESSING

The order is often the catalyst that sets the supply chain in motion, especially in the build-to-order environments of leading computer manufacturers such as Dell. The **order processing system** processes the requirements of the customer and sends the information into the supply chain via the logistics information system. The order goes to the manufacturer's warehouse. If the product is in stock, the order is filled and arrangements are made to ship it. If the product is not in stock, it triggers a replenishment request that finds its way to the factory floor.

The role of proper order processing in providing good service cannot be overemphasized. As an order enters the system, management must monitor two flows: the flow of goods and the flow of information. Often marketers' best-laid plans get entangled in the order processing system. Obviously, good communication among sales representatives, office personnel, and warehouse and shipping personnel is essential to correct order processing. Shipping incorrect merchandise or partially filled orders can create just as much dissatisfaction as stockouts or slow deliveries. The flow of goods and information must be continually monitored so that mistakes can be corrected before an invoice is prepared and the merchandise shipped.

order processing system
A system whereby orders are entered into the supply chain and filled.

Most trading partners that adopt EDI do so for increased efficiencies and cost savings. Sometimes pressures from larger trading partners force smaller trading partners to use EDI. For instance, Walmart will not do business with a supplier that doesn't agree to use its preferred EDI processes.

Order processing is becoming more automated through the use of computer technology known as **electronic data interchange (EDI)**. The basic idea of EDI is to replace the paper documents that usually accompany business transactions, such as purchase orders and invoices, with electronic transmission of the needed information. A typical EDI message includes all the information that would traditionally be included on a paper invoice such as product code, quantity, and transportation details. The information is usually sent via private networks, which are more secure and reliable than the networks used for standard e-mail messages. Most importantly, the information can be read and processed by computers, significantly reducing costs and increasing efficiency. Companies that use EDI can reduce inventory levels, improve cash flow, streamline operations, and increase the speed and accuracy of information transmission. EDI also creates a closer relationship between buyers and sellers.

It should not be surprising that retailers have become major users of EDI. For Walmart, Target, and the like, logistics speed and accuracy are crucial competitive tools in an overcrowded retail environment. Many big retailers are helping their suppliers acquire EDI technology so that they can be linked into the system. EDI works hand in hand with retailers' *efficient consumer response* programs, which are designed to have the right products on the shelf, in the right styles and colors, at the right time, through improved inventory, ordering, and distribution techniques.

INVENTORY MANAGEMENT AND CONTROL

Closely interrelated with the procurement, manufacturing, and ordering processes is the **inventory control system**—a method that develops and maintains an adequate assortment of materials or products to meet a manufacturer's or a customer's demands.

Inventory decisions, for both raw materials and finished goods, have a big impact on supply chain costs and the level of service provided. If too many products are kept in inventory, costs increase—as do risks of obsolescence, theft, and damage. If too few products are kept on hand, then the company risks product shortages and angry customers, and ultimately lost sales. For example, negative sales forecasts for the Christmas buying season in the past few years caused many retailers to cut back on orders because they were afraid of having to discount large end-of-the-year inventories. As a result, many companies, including Panasonic and Lands' End, lost sales due to inventory shortages on popular items. In attempting to match supply and demand, companies can fall victim to the bullwhip effect. The **bullwhip effect** is a distortion that occurs within the supply chain when demand

electronic data interchange (EDI)
Information technology that replaces the paper documents that usually accompany business transactions, such as purchase orders and invoices, with electronic transmission of the needed information to reduce inventory levels, improve cash flow, streamline operations, and increase the speed and accuracy of information transmission.

inventory control system
A method of developing and maintaining an adequate assortment of materials or products to meet a manufacturer's or a customer's demand.

bullwhip effect
A series of observed demand variation events that lead to amplified perceived demand and ordering, leading to a situation where actual supply and demand are misaligned.

and supply are not aligned. For example, P&G reviewed the sales for the Pampers products. There was some variation in retail sales but not much. In contrast, there was huge variability in distributors' orders. The variation in the distributors' orders resulted in large changes in the orders placed to P&G's suppliers. The slight fluctuation in demand at the retail locations created a distortion that resulted in extreme variation in orders to P&G's suppliers. Inventory management attempts to reduce and or eliminate the negative impacts of the bullwhip effect.[17] The goal of inventory management, therefore, is to keep inventory levels as low as possible while maintaining an adequate supply of goods to meet customer demand.

Managing inventory from the supplier to the manufacturer is called **materials requirement planning (MRP)**, or **materials management**. This system also encompasses the sourcing and procurement operations, signaling purchasing when raw materials, supplies, or components will need to be replenished for the production of more goods. The system that manages the finished goods inventory from manufacturer to end user is commonly referred to as **distribution resource planning (DRP)**. Both inventory systems use various inputs, such as sales forecasts, available inventory, outstanding orders, lead times, and mode of transportation to be used, to determine what actions must be taken to replenish goods at all points in the supply chain. Demand in the system is collected at each level in the supply chain, from the retailer back up the chain to the manufacturer. With the use of electronic data interchange, the information can be transmitted much faster to meet the quick-response needs of today's competitive marketplace. Exhibit 14.5 provides an example of inventory replenishment using DRP from the retailer to the manufacturer.

Other inventory management systems that have gained in popularity in recent years, however, use few or no forecasts at all during the scheduling of shipments.

Exhibit 14.5 Inventory Replenishment Example

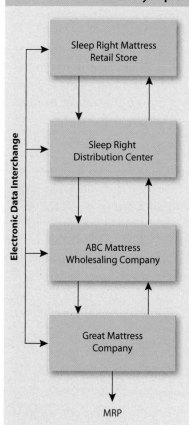

Electronic Data Interchange

Sleep Right Mattress Retail Store

Sleep Right Distribution Center

ABC Mattress Wholesaling Company

Great Mattress Company

MRP

Sleep Right is planning a promotion on the Great Mattress Company's Gentle Rest mattress. Sales forecast is for 50 units to be sold. Sleep Right has 10 open Gentle Rest orders with its distribution center. New mattresses must be delivered in two weeks in time for the promotion.

Sleep Right's Distribution Center is electronically notified of the order of 50 new Gentle Rest mattresses. It currently has 20 Gentle Rest mattresses in inventory and begins putting together the transportation plans to deliver these to the Sleep Right Store. Delivery takes one day. It orders 40 new mattresses from its mattress wholesaler to make up the difference.

ABC Mattress Wholesaling Company is electronically notified of Sleep Right DC's order of 40 new Gentle Rest mattresses. It currently does not have any of these in stock but electronically orders 40 from the Great Mattress Company's factory. Once it receives the new mattresses, it can have them delivered to the Sleep Right DC in two days.

The Great Mattress Company electronically receives ABC's order and forwards it to the factory floor. Production of a new mattress takes 20 minutes. The total order of 40 mattresses can be ready to be shipped to ABC in two days. Delivery takes one day. Raw material supplies for this order are electronically requested from Great Mattress's supply partners, who deliver the needed materials just in time to its stitching machines.

© Cengage Learning 2013

materials requirement planning (MRP) (materials management)
An inventory control system that manages the replenishment of raw materials, supplies, and components from the supplier to the manufacturer.

distribution resource planning (DRP)
An inventory control system that manages the replenishment of goods from the manufacturer to the final consumer.

automatic replenishment program

An inventory management system that triggers shipments only once a good is sold to the customer; the program uses EDI linkage connected with barcode scanners at the point of purchase, so the supplier can view the inventory being held at the next tier of the supply chain in real time.

cross-docking

A tactic where materials or goods are unloaded from an outbound carrier and transferred directly to an inbound carrier with little/no storage taking place in between.

materials-handling system

A method of moving inventory into, within, and out of the warehouse.

Known as **automatic replenishment programs**, these systems trigger shipments only after a product (usually something with a relatively predictable demand pattern) is sold to the customer. Using an EDI linkage connected with barcode scanners at the point of purchase, the supplier can view the inventory being held at the next tier of the supply chain in real time. When inventory at the customer location falls below pre-established safety levels, orders are automatically packed and shipped from the supplier location. Thus, in this type of system the supplier takes responsibility for keeping inventory on the shelves or in the customer's warehouse. This usually results in reduced stockouts and lowers overall inventory levels.

WAREHOUSING AND MATERIALS-HANDLING

Supply chain logisticians oversee the constant flow of raw materials from suppliers to manufacturer and finished goods from the manufacturer to the ultimate consumer. Although build-to-order manufacturing processes can eliminate the need to warehouse many raw materials, manufacturers often keep some safety stock on hand in the event of an emergency, such as a strike at a supplier's plant or a catastrophic event that temporarily stops the flow of raw materials to the production line. Likewise, the final user might not need or want the goods at the same time the manufacturer produces and wants to sell them. Products such as grain and corn are produced seasonally, but customers demand them year-round. Other products, such as Christmas ornaments and turkeys, are produced year-round, but customers do not want them until autumn or winter. Therefore, management must have a storage system to hold these products until they are shipped.

Storage is what helps manufacturers manage supply and demand, or production and consumption. It provides time utility to buyers and sellers, which means that the seller stores the product until the buyer wants or needs it. Even when products are used regularly, not seasonally, many manufacturers store excess products in case the demand surpasses the amount produced at a given time. Storing additional product does have disadvantages, however, including the costs of insurance on the stored product, taxes, obsolescence or spoilage, theft, and warehouse operating costs. Another drawback is opportunity costs—that is, the opportunities lost because money is tied up in stored product instead of being used for something else.

Because businesses are focusing on cutting supply chain costs, the warehousing industry is also changing to better serve its customers. For example, many warehouses are putting greater emphasis on more efficient unloading and reloading layouts and customized services that move merchandise through the warehouse faster, often in the same day. One such process is called cross-docking. **Cross-docking** allows for companies to load and off-load products with minimal warehousing and as previously mentioned often in the same day. Many 3PL firms provide this service so that customers can avoid the expense of operating a warehouse or distribution center. They also are investing in services using sophisticated tracking technology such as materials-handling systems.

A **materials-handling system** moves inventory into, within, and out of the warehouse. Materials-handling includes these functions:

→ Receiving goods into the warehouse or distribution center

→ Identifying, sorting, and labeling the goods

→ Dispatching the goods to a temporary storage area

→ Recalling, selecting, or picking the goods for shipment (might include packaging the product in a protective container for shipping)

The goal of the materials-handling system is to move items quickly with minimal handling. With a manual, non-automated materials-handling system, a product might be handled more than a dozen times. Each time it is handled, the cost and risk of damage increase; each lifting of a product stresses its package. Consequently, most manufacturers today have switched to automated systems. Scanners quickly identify goods entering and leaving a warehouse through bar-coded labels affixed to the packaging. Electronic storage and retrieval systems automatically store and pick goods in the warehouse or distribution center. Automated materials-handling systems decrease product handling, ensure accurate placement of product, and improve the accuracy of order picking and the rates of on-time shipment. In fact, many firms are relying on materials handling systems operated either partially, or in rare cases fully, by robots. For example, at office supply giant Staples, over 150 robots collect materials, process, and pack up to 8,000 orders daily.[18]

At Dell, the OptiPlex system runs the factory. The computer software receives orders, sends requests for parts to suppliers, orders components, organizes assembly of the product, and even arranges for it to be shipped. Thus, instead of hundreds of workers, often fewer than six are working at one time. An order for a few hundred computers can be filled in less than eight hours by using the automated system. With the OptiPlex system, productivity has increased dramatically.

TRANSPORTATION

Transportation typically accounts for 5 to 10 percent of the price of goods. Supply chain logisticians must decide which mode of transportation to use to move products from supplier to producer and from producer to buyer. These decisions are, of course, related to all other logistics decisions. The five major modes of transportation are railroads, motor carriers, pipelines, water transportation, and airways. Supply chain managers generally choose a mode of transportation on the basis of several criteria:

→ **Cost:** The total amount a specific carrier charges to move the product from the point of origin to the destination

→ **Transit time:** The total time a carrier has possession of goods, including the time required for pickup and delivery, handling, and movement between the point of origin and the destination

→ **Reliability:** The consistency with which the carrier delivers goods on time and in acceptable condition

→ **Capability:** The ability of the carrier to provide the appropriate equipment and conditions for moving specific kinds of goods, such as those that must be transported in a controlled environment (for example, under refrigeration)

→ **Accessibility:** A carrier's ability to move goods over a specific route or network

→ **Traceability:** The relative ease with which a shipment can be located and transferred

The mode of transportation used depends on the needs of the shipper, as they relate to these six criteria. Exhibit 14.6 compares

Exhibit 14.6 Criteria for Ranking Transportation Modes

	Highest				Lowest
Relative Cost	Air	Truck	Rail	Pipe	Water
Transit Time	Water	Rail	Pipe	Truck	Air
Reliability	Pipe	Truck	Rail	Air	Water
Capability	Water	Rail	Truck	Air	Pipe
Accessibility	Truck	Rail	Air	Water	Pipe
Traceability	Air	Truck	Rail	Water	Pipe

© Cengage Learning 2013

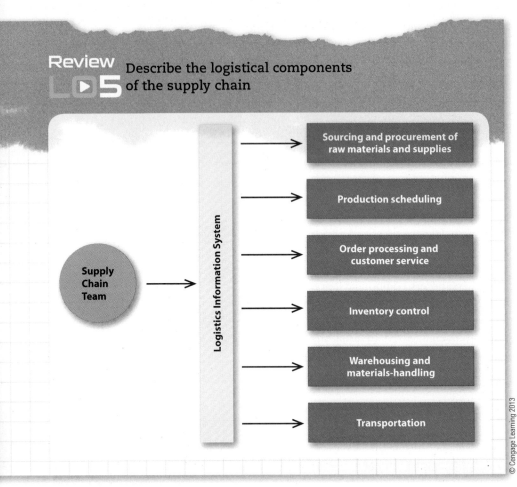

- Supply Chain Team
- Logistics Information System
  - Sourcing and procurement of raw materials and supplies
  - Production scheduling
  - Order processing and customer service
  - Inventory control
  - Warehousing and materials-handling
  - Transportation

© Cengage Learning 2013

the basic modes of transportation on these criteria.

The importance of transportation to modern companies is difficult to overstate. Many industry experts regard on-time delivery and shipment of products as the single most important supply chain management criteria leading to customer satisfaction. This perspective is reflected in companies' investment in transportation management systems—software applications designed to optimize transportation modes' routing, loading, unloading, and other functions. U.S. firms are expected to spend between $500–800 million annually on specialized transportation management software by 2011.[19]

LO6
Supply Chain Performance Measurement

A commonly repeated saying in business is, "That which cannot be measured, cannot be managed." This adage is especially true in the case of supply chain management, where multiple processes, each composed of different types of activities, are operated simultaneously with the goal of enhancing the performance of the business. Firms that are able to develop a well-thought-out system of supply chain measurement procedures are able to constantly monitor their processes, can see where they are doing well in addition to where they are failing, and are best able to gain a competitive advantage through better service and lower costs.

Because supply chains can be very complex and information is not always visible across firms operating in the same supply chain, many of the ways that managers try to measure their success or failure are not always reflective of the chain as a whole; many firms use measures of logistics performance for their own firm (such as on-time delivery rates, order cycle time, or inventory turnover) as proxies for the performance of the whole chain. However, recalling that a primary goal of supply chain management is the optimization of the entire system rather than any single firm within it, many companies are seeking to develop new metrics that will allow them a broader and more comprehensive viewpoint from which to study their supply chain's efficiency and effectiveness. **Metrics** are standard measures that can be used repeatedly to assess performance on a supply chain–related process. Common examples of metrics might include customer satisfaction ratings, orders picked from the warehouse per hour, or the ratio of operating assets to income. From the perspective of the supply chain manager, a good metric is characterized by five qualities:

→ It creates understanding of strategic objectives and tactical plans.

→ It promotes behaviors that are consistent with achieving these objectives.

→ It allows for recording of actual results/outcomes, and therefore the firm can monitor progress toward objectives.

→ It allows companies to compare themselves to competitors (or benchmarks) and customer expectations.

→ It motivates continuous improvement.

For firms using the logistics-proxy approach to supply chain measurement, several measures are often used across four unique categories of performance. The performance categories are customer satisfaction, time, cost, and asset utilization. Customer satisfaction measures often include metrics such as order fulfillment, satisfaction ratings taken from questionnaires, on-time deliveries, number of returned products, or length of delay in executing customer service activities. Time measures often employ metrics such as order-to-receipt time or source-to-make cycle time. Cost measures are often calculated as the total aggregate costs of the supply chain (on an activity basis) for a good or service, from creation through delivery. Asset utilization metrics frequently include days of inventory supply, asset performance ratios, or forecast accuracy, to name a few.

metrics
Standard measures that can be used repeatedly to assess performance on a supply chain-related process.

Balanced Scorecard Approach
A measurement system used to evaluate overall supply chain performance.

THE BALANCED SCORECARD APPROACH

Because supply chain management is concerned with the performance of all firms in the system simultaneously, any performance measurement system used to evaluate a supply chain must address both the chain itself and all of the processes and firms that compose it. One method developed for this purpose is known as the **Balanced Scorecard Approach**. This approach, invented by Robert S. Kaplan and David P. Norton of Harvard Business School, combines multiple different categories of measurements that can be used at all levels of the supply chain. The Balanced Scorecard Approach is shown pictorially in Exhibit 14.7.

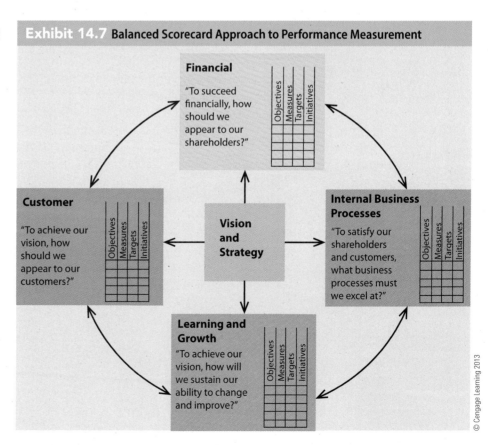

Exhibit 14.7 Balanced Scorecard Approach to Performance Measurement

Financial
"To succeed financially, how should we appear to our shareholders?"
Objectives | Measures | Targets | Initiatives

Customer
"To achieve our vision, how should we appear to our customers?"
Objectives | Measures | Targets | Initiatives

Vision and Strategy

Internal Business Processes
"To satisfy our shareholders and customers, what business processes must we excel at?"
Objectives | Measures | Targets | Initiatives

Learning and Growth
"To achieve our vision, how will we sustain our ability to change and improve?"
Objectives | Measures | Targets | Initiatives

© Cengage Learning 2013

The Balanced Scorecard Approach is an effective method for assessing overall supply chain performance because it implicitly includes the linkage between the supply chain strategy adopted by the firm in conjunction with the processes undertaken to fulfill it. By using the Balanced Scorecard, firms gain different types of feedback related to their supply chain operations, including strategic data for high-level decision makers, diagnostic feedback to guide process improvement, knowledge of trends in important metrics over time, feedback on the effectiveness of the performance measurements themselves, and data that can be used for forecasting future business activities.[20]

At each tier of the supply chain, the Balanced Scorecard addresses four areas of performance that are reflective of supply chain operations: customer-related performance metrics, financial metrics, learning and growth metrics, and of course, business process metrics. Firms take repeated measurements in each of these categories, and then alternate through a system whereby they do things to improve lagging performance in weak areas, check the results following implementation of changes, and act again based on new measurements.

- Financial
- Customer
- **VISION AND STRATEGY**
- Internal Business Processes
- Learning and Growth

© Cengage Learning 2013

LO7
Green and Sustainable Supply Chain Management

green supply chain management
The integration of environmentally conscious thinking into all phases of key supply chain management processes.

In response to the need for companies to both gain cost savings and act as leaders in protecting the natural environment, many are adopting green supply chain management principles as a key part of their supply chain strategy. **Green supply chain management** involves the integration of environmentally conscious thinking into all phases of key supply chain management processes. Such activities include green materials sourcing, the design of products with consideration given to their environmental impact based on packaging, shipment and use, as well as end-of-life management for products including easy recycling and/or clean disposal. By enacting green supply chain management principles, firms hope to simultaneously generate cost savings and protect our natural resources from excess pollution, damage, and/or wastefulness.

A number of relatively simple changes to typical supply chain management processes can achieve significant positive environmental impacts. Trucks can switch to alternative fuels on long routes; drivers can be retrained and routes revised to limit the amount of time

© AP Images/PRNewsFoto/Red Moon Marketing

trucks sit idling; excess materials from manufacturing and staff processes can be recycled, composted, or avoided altogether; and reusable shipping containers and pallets introduced into the supply chain.[21] Other firms "green" their supply chains by buying local goods (thereby reducing carbon pollution to the air from fuel), shipping raw materials to point of use rather than point of manufacture, and creating green procurement guidelines in order to encourage supplier participation in green initiatives. Though these activities might seem costly at first, many firms are recognizing the long-term benefits. Whereas the common assumption among supply chain managers used to be that greening the supply chain would increase costs, many companies are realizing that environmentally conscious supply chain management can increase profits. General Motors, for example, increased profitability by over $12 million annually by switching to reusable containers when receiving shipments from their suppliers.[22]

Closely related to the notion of green supply chain management is the concept of **supply chain sustainability**. If a green supply chain is one that does the minimal possible amount of damage to the physical environment, the sustainable one is that which employs renewable natural resources wherever possible. Generally, sustainable supply chain practices are encouraged by one member of the supply chain and other members follow suit. For example, Walmart's sustainability executives will work with suppliers to determine what types of alternative packaging can be used for a product, or how to use alternative renewable fuels when transporting freight to the retailer, but the actual implementation is left to the supplier. Other firms focus more on creating more efficient and sustainable physical facilities. Many companies are already looking for ways to harness solar, wind, and water power to heat and light buildings and conduct operations. As innovations related to sustainable supply chain management continue to develop, they will undoubtedly change the way business is conducted at all levels of the supply chain in the future. Gaining senior management support for green and sustainable initiatives seems to be the key, and many executives are surprised when they find that being environmentally conscious frequently leads to greater profitability as well.

supply chain sustainability
A sustainable supply chain is one that employs renewable natural resources wherever possible.

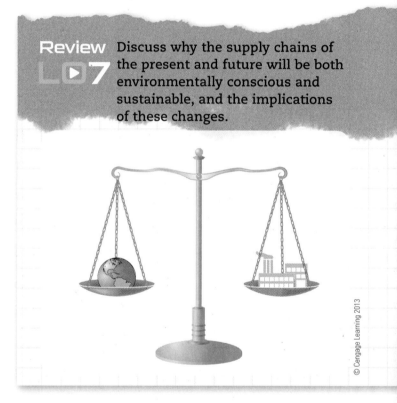

Review LO7 Discuss why the supply chains of the present and future will be both environmentally conscious and sustainable, and the implications of these changes.

© Cengage Learning 2013

LO8
Trends in Supply Chain Management

Several technological advances and business trends are affecting the job of the supply chain manager today. Four of the most important trends are the globalization of supply chain management, advanced computer technology, outsourcing of logistics functions, and electronic distribution.

GLOBAL SUPPLY CHAIN MANAGEMENT

As global trade becomes a more decisive factor in success or failure for firms of all sizes, global supply chain management increases in importance. For example, one supply chain management consultant reported cost savings of 20–40 percent on finished goods imported from China versus their American counterparts.[23] China has offered companies cheap labor alternatives for production, therefore becoming an important part of the supply chain for many. This has resulted in an increase in the global trade with China as well as lengthened the global supply chain. However, due to the dynamic business environment cheaper alternatives are appearing to compete with China such as Bangladesh and Vietnam. China is now feeling pressure to lower its labor costs to compete with these countries.[24]

In addition to savings, another supply chain research team estimated that the output of the global economy will grow at a rate of 3 percent or more until the year 2030, with much of the growth occurring outside the United States, and thereby increasing the U.S. import base.[25] Thus, one of the most critical global supply chain issues for importers of any size is coping with the legalities of trade in other countries. Companies must be aware of the permits, licenses, and registrations they may need to acquire and, depending on the type of product they are importing, the tariffs, quotas, and other regulations that apply in each country. This multitude of different rules is why multinational companies such as Eastman Kodak are so committed to working through the World Trade Organization to develop a global set of rules and to encourage countries to participate. Other goals for these companies include reducing trade barriers, such as tariffs. As these barriers fall, the flow of merchandise across borders is increasing due to more companies sourcing from multiple countries. For instance, a Kodak camera sold in France might have been assembled there, but the camera mechanism probably came from China and the film from the United States.

The presence of different rules hasn't slowed the spread of supply chain globalization, however. In spite of the added costs associated with importing and exporting goods, many companies are looking to other countries for their sourcing and procurement needs. For example, Applica Consumer Products, Inc., a U.S. maker of small appliances, is committed to using technology to improve its relationships with suppliers in Mexico. The company has linked its suppliers directly to sales data from Walmart stores to help manage production and inventory costs. In another case, U.S. soap producers faced with increased prices for a key ingredient due to new government legislation were forced to look for substitutes in Indonesia and Malaysia in order to remain profitable.

Transportation can also be a major issue for companies dealing with global supply chains. Uncertainty regarding shipping usually tops the list of reasons why companies, especially smaller ones, resist international markets. Even companies that have scored overseas successes often are vulnerable to logistical problems. Large companies have the capital to create global logistics systems, but smaller companies often must rely on the services of carriers and freight forwarders to get their products to overseas markets.

In some instances, poor infrastructure makes transportation dangerous and unreliable. And the process of moving goods across the borders of even the most industrialized nations can still be complicated by government regulations. For example, NAFTA was supposed to improve the flow of goods across the continent, but moving goods across the border still requires approvals from dozens of government agencies, broker intervention, and hours spent at border checks. Shipping companies such as Ryder are working to make the process easier. Currently, Ryder operates a cross-border facility in San Antonio to help clients such as General Motors and Xerox with customs and logistics costs. The company also is part of a pilot project to automate border crossings with technology similar to that of an E-ZPass. The new system sends and receives short-range radio signals containing information on the load to tollbooths, weigh stations, and border crossings. If the cargo meets requirements, the truck or train receives a green light to go ahead. Questionable cargo is set aside for further inspection. Transportation industry experts say the system can reduce delivery times by hours.

ADVANCED COMPUTER TECHNOLOGY

Advanced computer technology has boosted the efficiency of logistics dramatically with tools such as automatic identification systems (auto ID) using bar coding and radio-frequency technology, communications technology, and supply chain software systems that help synchronize the flow of goods and information with customer demand. Amazon.com's state-of-the-art distribution centers, for instance, use sophisticated order picking systems that utilize computer terminals to guide workers through the picking and packing process. **Radio-frequency identification (RFID)** technology, which uses radio signals that work with scanned bar codes to identify products, directs Amazon's workers to the exact locations in the warehouse where the product is stored. Warehouse management software examines pick rates, location, and picking and storage patterns, and builds combinations of customer orders for shipping. After installing these supply chain technology tools, Amazon saw a 70 percent improvement in operational efficiency.

Procter & Gamble and many other companies use RFID tags in shipments to Walmart stores. RFID tags are chips attached to a pallet of goods that allow the goods to be tracked from the time they are packed at the manufacturing plant until the consumer purchases them. Benefits include increased revenue for Walmart (because the shelves are always full) and reduced inventory management costs (because overstocking and time spent counting items are minimized). Best Buy is currently planning to use an RFID-enabled payment system to reduce and eventually eliminate checkout lines at the front of the store—customers with a personalized Best Buy RFID shopping card could simply load up their carts and walk out the front door, with their checking or credit card account debited for the price of their merchandise before they even unlock their car.[26] However, RFID has been slower than expected in penetrating the retail sector. While 44 percent of manufacturers have adopted RFID at some level, only about 10 percent of retailers have done so.[27] Though some experts attribute the slowness of retail adoption of RFID to its complexity of implementation, many others suggest that retailers are scared away because of difficulty in determining their return on RFID-related investment.

One of the other major goals of technology is to bring up-to-date information to the supply chain manager's desk. The transportation system has long been referred to as an informational "black hole," where products and materials fall out of sight until they reappear some time later in a plant, store, or warehouse. Now carriers have systems that track freight, monitor the speed and location of carriers, and make routing decisions on the spur of the moment. Roadway Express, named

Amazon.com uses technology to maximize efficiency. Pickers follow a route given by computer guns that is calibrated to exactly fill their cart and follow the most efficient path to get from item to item.

radio-frequency identification (RFID)
An automatic identification method that uses radio signals that work with scanned bar codes to identify products; data is stored in and retrieved from the RFID tag, which is attached to a product.

one of the "Top 100 U.S. Motor Carriers" by Inbound Logistics, handles more than 70,000 shipments a day, many for large retailers such as Walmart, Target, and Home Depot. Information technology systems enable each package to be tracked from the minute it is received at one of Roadway's terminals until it is delivered. Customers can check on the progress of their shipment at any time by logging on to Roadway's Web site and entering the tracking number. Companies needing trucking services can go to the Inbound Logistics Web site and use their Trucking Decision Support Tool to identify motor carriers that can meet their service needs.[28]

Swedish-based communications giant Ericsson, whose operations span the globe, uses specialized supply chain software to gain visibility over the 50,000 outbound shipments it makes a year. As products leave its manufacturing facilities, transportation providers transmit status information at specified intervals to Ericsson's information system, which is accessible to management using a standard Web browser. The company has benefited greatly from the increased visibility of shipments the system has provided. Ericsson's management is now in a position to identify bottlenecks and respond before a crisis occurs, as well as measure the performance of its supply chain at different checkpoints.

There are several different RFID strategies that companies can employ. A company might choose to implement RFID within receiving, putaway, order processing, and/or shipping. These implementation strategies involve the decision between utilizing fixed mounted technology (where a scanner is mounted in a fixed location in a facility and the product passed through or near it) vs. handheld technologies, as well as scanning at the pallet level vs. the case level of inventory. There are pros and cons to each of these decisions. For example, consider the putaway implementation of case-level handheld RFID devices. The putaway process would normally require an employee to search for both products and locations and scan the products individually, but would allow for case level tracking of inventory. On the other hand, pallet-level, fixed-mounted RFID implementation would simplify the employees' tasks and allow tags to withstand harsh conditions; however, mounting the RFID equipment in the appropriate place can be difficult. The type of product and the needs of the operation should be matched in order to drive the appropriate RFID strategy for a particular firm.[29]

OUTSOURCING LOGISTICS FUNCTIONS

External partners are becoming increasingly important in the efficient deployment of supply chain management. Outsourcing, or contract logistics, is a rapidly growing segment of the distribution industry in which a manufacturer or supplier turns over an entire function of the logistics system, such as buying and managing transportation or warehousing, to an independent third party (3PL, as mentioned earlier in the chapter). Many manufacturers are turning to outside partners for their logistics expertise in an effort to focus on the core competencies that they do best. Partners create and manage entire solutions for getting products where they need to be, when they need to be there. Logistics partners offer staff, an infrastructure, and services that reach consumers virtually anywhere in the world. Because a logistics provider is focused, clients receive service in a timely, efficient manner, thereby increasing customers' level of satisfaction and boosting their perception of added value to a company's offerings.

Third-party contract logistics allows companies to cut inventories, locate stock at fewer plants and distribution centers, and still provide the same or increased level of service. The companies then can refocus investment on their core business. Ford Motor Company uses third-party logistics provider UPS Worldwide Logistics

outsourcing (contract logistics)
A manufacturer's or supplier's use of an independent third party to manage an entire function of the logistics system, such as transportation, warehousing, or order processing.

Group to manage the delivery of Ford and Lincoln cars and trucks in the United States, Canada, and Mexico. The alliance between Ford and UPS has substantially reduced the time it takes to move vehicles from Ford's assembly plants to dealers and customers. Moreover, the Web-based system enables Ford and its dealers to track an individual vehicle's location from production through delivery to the final destination. Similarly, in the hospitality industry, procurement services company Avendra enables Fairmont Hotels & Resorts, Hyatt Hotels & Resorts, Intercontinental Hotels Group, Marriott International, and others to enjoy significant savings and value-added supply chain services.[30] Avendra negotiates with suppliers to obtain virtually everything a hotel might need, from food and beverages to golf course maintenance. By relying on Avendra to manage many aspects of the supply chain, the hotels are able to concentrate on their core function—providing hospitality.

Many firms are taking outsourcing one step further by allowing business partners to take over the final assembly of their product or its packaging in an effort to reduce inventory costs, speed up delivery, or better meet customer requirements. Ryder truck lines assembles and packages 22 different combinations of shrink-wrapped boxes that contain the ice trays, drawers, shelves, doors, and other accessories for the various refrigerator models Whirlpool sells. Similarly, outsourcing firm StarTek, Inc. packages and ships products for Microsoft, provides technical support to customers of America Online, and maintains AT&T communication systems.

There are certain interorganizational and company-specific factors that lead companies to outsource. The interorganizational conditions consist of the credibility, trust, and previous success with outsourcing, whereas the company-specific conditions are the level of experience with outsourcing as well as the extent that the company is structured to manage relationships. These two factors combine to influence whether or not a company will choose to outsource and the extent to which outsourcing will occur.[31]

If your supply chain were this simple, any RFID tag would do.

Businesses need strong logistical allies who already have shipping expertise so that they can trust their partners to get the job done. Using the correct tools, such as Avery products, makes the logistics easier.

ELECTRONIC DISTRIBUTION

Electronic distribution is the most recent development in the logistics arena. Broadly defined, **electronic distribution** includes any kind of product or service that can be distributed electronically, whether over traditional forms such as fiber-optic cable or through satellite transmission of electronic signals. For instance, instead of buying and installing software from stores, computer users purchase and download software over the Internet or rent the same software from Internet services that have the program available for use on their servers. For example, Intuit, Inc., allows people to fill out their tax returns on its Web site for a fee rather than

electronic distribution
A distribution technique that includes any kind of product or service that can be distributed electronically, whether over traditional forms such as fiber-optic cable or through satellite transmission of electronic signals.

buying its TurboTax software. Consumers can purchase tickets to sporting events, concerts, and movies over the Internet and print the tickets at home. And music, television shows, and movies have long been delivered to consumers through electronic pipelines. Apple sells millions of songs and TV shows annually through iTunes.

One of the most innovative electronic distribution ventures of late has come from ESPN. The sports broadcaster offers free access on the iPhone to the most comprehensive sports coverage available in a mobile format. Using an iPhone App, ESPN Mobile Web broadcasts a multimedia-rich sports information package unlike anything else, including breaking news and analysis, up-to-the-minute scores, ESPN Fantasy teams, ESPN columnists, the ESPN Podcenter, and more. There's also a special section where users can select to receive news and stats about their favorite players and teams.[32]

SUPPLY CHAIN SECURITY AND RESILIENCE

Firms are expending more effort on securing their supply chains from external threats than at any time in recent memory. Natural disasters, widespread technology failures, political instability, terrorism, disease pandemics, and worker strikes are but a few of the major events that can cause a supply chain to shut down temporarily or for an extended amount of time. The supply chain must be guarded from end to end because it is only as strong as its weakest link, and managers are very concerned with what might happen if their supply chains are breached. Recent research on the topic of food security, for example, shows that many food companies are willing to accept late shipments or pay higher prices if it means that their supplies are able to verify that purchased food supplies have not been tampered with.[33]

Managing supply chain disruptions begins with identifying the risks potentially affecting each node and link in the supply chain network.[34] This is especially true when the supply chain is global, with nodes and links located in or across international boundaries. Global supply chains are particularly at risk because members in far-away places often fail to completely understand the political, legal, and technological culture of the local area. Once risks are identified and assessed, the firm should put controls in place to monitor dangerous or volatile situations, and buy insurance when it appears that things could go wrong in the supply chain. The very best supply chains with respect to security also build contingency plans that are able to address situations quickly in the event of an emergency and get the supply chain back online. In fact, some businesses have completely replicated their systems and facilities in different geographic locations and, in the event of a disaster, can activate these backups within 24 hours. In the event such security measures fail or are not implemented, companies are often left

Review

LO8

Discuss the new and emerging trends in supply chain management

Trends

Many companies are looking globally for their sourcing and procurement needs.

Computer technology increases efficiency.

Third-party logistics allow companies to focus on core business functions.

Electronic distribution of products and services collapses the supply chain.

with a limited set of options, such as reconstituting the supply chain, suspending operations, or, depending on the severity of the breach, exiting the business entirely.

World-class supply chains are being built so they have the ability to "snap back" into action following a disruption. This idea is known as **supply chain resilience**, and it encompasses the ability of a company to get its operations up and running again following disruptions caused by "acts of God" such as tornadoes, earthquakes, or hurricanes, accidents such as nuclear waste leakages or barge crashes, negligence on the part of employees or supply chain partners, or intentional acts such as terrorism or sabotage. Regardless of the cause, the resilient supply chain is generally one where employees in the affected companies have developed a culture of supply chain security awareness, there are continuous communications between partners, employees are empowered to act without guidance in the event of a disruption, and practice for potential scenarios are all key elements.

supply chain resilience
The ability of a supply chain to bounce back from disruptions and continue operations in a timely and effective manner.

© iStockphoto.com/Juan Facundo Mora Soria

Robots processing, collecting, and packing orders at Staples

Percentage of the U.S. gross domestic product generated by supply chain managers

Percent reduction in inventory levels IKEA made with its new logistics management program

Weeks required to make a similar transition with the old system

Money GM saves yearly with the flexible manufacturing system

Percentage of sales returned in apparel e-retailing

Value of purchased goods imported to the U.S.

150 9.5 20 6 $1.5 billion 40 $2 trillion

Review and Applications

Define the terms *supply chain* and *supply chain management*, and discuss the benefits of supply chain management. Supply chain management coordinates and integrates all of the activities performed by supply chain members into a seamless process from the source to the point of consumption. The responsibilities of a supply chain manager include developing channel design strategies, managing the relationships of supply chain members, sourcing and procurement of raw materials, scheduling production, processing orders, managing inventory and storing product, and selecting transportation modes. The supply chain manager is also responsible for managing customer service and the information that flows through the supply chain. The benefits of supply chain management include reduced costs in inventory management, transportation, warehousing, and packaging; improved service through techniques such as time-based delivery and make-to-order; and enhanced revenues, which result from supply chain-related achievements such as higher product availability and more customized products.

1.1 Discuss the benefits of supply chain management. How does implementation of supply chain management result in enhanced customer value?

LO2 **Discuss the concept of supply chain integration and explain why each of the six types of integration is important.** Supply chain integration occurs when multiple firms in a supply chain coordinate their activities and processes so that they are seamlessly linked to one another in the attempt to satisfy customers. The six types of integration are as follows: (1) Relationship integration is the ability of two or more firms to develop tight social connections among their employees, resulting in smoother personal interactions. (2) Measurement integration is the idea that performance assessments should be transparent and similar across all of the supply chain members. (3) Technology and planning integration refers to the creation and maintenance of supply chain technology systems that connect managers throughout the supply chain. (4) Material and service supplier integration reflects a focus on integrating processes and functions with those who provide the company with the things they need in order to execute their core functions. (5) Internal operations integration is the development of capabilities for the firm's internal functional areas to communicate and work together on processes and projects. (6) Customer integration implies that firms evaluate their own capabilities and use them to offer long-lasting, distinctive, value-added offerings in ways that best serve their customers.

2.1 Discuss the concept of supply chain integration. How does it result in better customer-related outcomes?

2.2 What are some of the likely outcomes of a firm's failure to embrace one or more supply chain integration types?

LO3 **Identify the eight key processes of excellent supply chain management and discuss how each of these processes impacts the end customer.** The key processes that leading supply chain companies focus on are (1) customer relationship management, (2) customer service management, (3) order fulfillment, (4) manufacturing flow management, (5) supplier relationship management, (6) product development and commercialization, (7) returns management, and (8) demand management. When firms practice excellent supply chain management, each of these processes is integrated from end to end in the supply chain. These processes are made up of bundles of interconnected activities that supply chain partners are constantly focused on when delivering value to the customer.

3.1 What are the key processes in supply chain management, and who performs them? How does each process lead to increased customer satisfaction?

LO4 **Discuss the key strategic decisions supply chain managers must make when designing their companies' supply chains.** Based on the firm's goals, the markets it competes in, and the availability of supply, firms will adopt a lean, agile, or combination (Leagile) strategy for supply chain management. Lean firms focus on improving profitability through the removal of waste from the supply chain system. Alternatively, agile firms are concerned primarily with customer responsiveness and service, and seek to provide the highest levels of responsiveness possible, even if the costs of doing so are higher. Leagile firms adopt a position somewhere between lean and agile, with main components made and shipped using lean principles, but with agility gained late in the process through the postponement of final production. Firms should also learn to map their supply chains so that they can understand the linkages between firms in the network that are all seeking to achieve the common goal of customer satisfaction.

4.1 When should firms pursue lean, agile, and/or Leagile supply chain strategies?

4.2 What are the expected benefits that can come from supply chain mapping?

LO5 **Describe the logistical components of the supply chain.** The logistics supply chain consists of several interrelated and integrated logistical components: (1) sourcing and procurement of raw materials and supplies, (2) production scheduling, (3) order processing,

(4) inventory control, (5) warehousing and materials-handling, and (6) transportation. The logistics information system is the link connecting all of the logistics components of the supply chain. Information technology connects the various components and partners of the supply chain into an integrated whole. The supply chain team, in concert with the logistics information system, orchestrates the movement of goods, services, and information from the source to the consumer. Supply chain teams typically cut across organizational boundaries, embracing all parties who participate in moving product to market. Procurement deals with the purchase of raw materials, supplies, and components according to production scheduling. Order processing monitors the flow of goods and information (order entry and order handling). Inventory control systems regulate when and how much to buy (order timing and order quantity). Warehousing provides storage of goods until needed by the customer while the materials-handling system moves inventory into, within, and out of the warehouse. Finally, the major modes of transportation are railroads, motor carriers, pipelines, waterways, and airways.

5.1 Assume that you are the supply chain manager for a producer of expensive, high-tech computer components. Identify the most suitable method(s) of transporting your product in terms of cost, transit time, reliability, capability, accessibility, and traceability. Now, assume you are the supply chain manager for a producer of milk. How does this change your choice of transportation?

Explain why supply chain performance measurement is necessary and important. Because supply chains are often very complex, with each firm in the chain seeking to fulfill its own goals, it is sometimes difficult to determine whether the supply chain as a whole is functioning well. Firms in the best supply chains develop and use common metrics to assess whether customers are satisfied and whether operations are completed in a timely fashion, at an acceptable level of cost, and with good asset utilization. Often, this includes the use of the Balanced Scorecard methodology, which ensures not only that will customers be satisfied, but also that the firm will execute its tasks with process efficiency, with financially acceptable returns, and in a way that allows for learning and growth for the company.

6.1 Why is supply chain performance measurement necessary and important?

6.2 How does the Balanced Scorecard Approach help firms within the supply chain to establish and meet common goals?

Discuss why the supply chains of the present and future will be both environmentally conscious and sustainable, and the implications of these changes. Firms are more environmentally conscious with their supply chains because companies feel pressure to gain cost savings and protect the natural environment from excess pollution, damage, and wastefulness. Making small changes in driver habits, fuel, location of materials, and management of resources has positive environmental impact and lead to long-term cost savings for companies. Sustainable supply chains employ renewable resources where possible—in transport, physical facilities, and power supply. Implementing sustainable and green supply chain modifications will change the way business is done, generate profit for the company, and protect our resources for the future.

7.1 Research IBM's recent push to green its supply chain. Write a report discussing the implications for IBM, the electronics industry, and why greening an electronics supply chain has different implications than does greening Pepsi's supply chain.

Discuss new technology and emerging trends in supply chain management. Several emerging trends are changing the job of today's supply chain manager. Technology and automation are bringing up-to-date distribution information to the decision maker's desk. Technology is also linking suppliers, buyers, and carriers for joint decision making, and it has created a new electronic distribution channel. Many companies are saving money and time by outsourcing third-party carriers to handle some or all aspects of the distribution process. Firms are taking major steps toward the goal of securing their supply chains from external threats.

online

8.1 Visit the Web site of Menlo Logistics at **www.menlolog.com.** What logistics functions can this third-party logistics supplier provide? How does its mission fit in with the supply chain management philosophy?

Key Terms

Exercises

ETHICS EXERCISE

For years, labor and environmental groups have criticized and pressured companies whose suppliers pay low wages, run sweatshops, use child labor, or use other similarly illicit labor practices. However, only recently have U.S. companies begun to come under fire for sourcing materials from foreign companies that are contributing to massive pollution problems in their local environments. When it was discovered that the Fuan Textiles plant in southern China, a major fabric supplier for companies such as Nike, Liz Claiborne, and Target, had been dumping large quantities of untreated wastewater into Chinese lakes and rivers, many U.S. companies downstream in the Fuan supply chain were forced to take notice. As Daryl Brown, VP for ethics and compliance at Liz Claiborne, noted, "[T]he environment is the new frontier. We certainly don't want to be associated with a company that's polluting the waters."[35]

Questions

1. Should companies such as Nike, Liz Claiborne, and Target avoid structuring their supply chains so that they include polluters, even if the pollution is occurring somewhere far from the United States?

2. What are the pros and cons associated with using supplies and/or labor sourced from supply chain partners (direct and indirect) based in countries that do not have strict pollution standards?

3. Does the AMA Statement of Ethics address the issue of environmental protection in supply chain management? Go to www.marketingpower.com and review the code. Then write a business memo to the Liz Claiborne president that describes how the AMA Statement of Ethics addresses the dilemma faced by the company.

MARKETING PLAN EXERCISE

As discussed in Chapter 13, Part 4 of the strategic planning process continues defining the elements of the marketing mix, and this section focuses on place (i.e., distribution). The following exercise is designed to continue leading you through the distribution decisions for your strategic marketing plan:

1. What physical distribution facilities will be needed to complete delivery of your chosen company's products and services to the buyer? Where should these facilities be located?

2. How should your company's product be distributed? Justify your selection of transportation mode(s). What other types of channel facilitators will you require for getting your product offering to your customers?

APPLICATION EXERCISE

From your readings, you might feel that you have a general idea as to how supply chain management works. However, in reality, the practice of supply chain management can be very complicated. This exercise will help you to identify the complexities of managing a global supply chain in a real-world setting. By following one of your favorite products as its many components migrate through the supply chain on their long road to your home or office, you might gain additional appreciation for the difficult tasks supply chain managers face daily.

Activities

1. Pick a product with which you are very familiar or that you anticipate being able to research easily. You might want to consult family members, relatives, or even a former or current employer who can give you details of the business.

2. Map the supply chain of your product as far back as is feasible. A simple example is a diamond sold by a local jewelry store, purchased direct from diamond wholesalers in the Netherlands, bought by wholesalers from diamond centers in South Africa, brought out of mines owned by a company in South Africa. Identify as many participants in the channel as possible by company name and location.

3. Identify the mode of transportation used between each stage in the channel.

4. Identify by name and location the component parts of the product, if any. For example, let's expand the diamond example from a single diamond to a diamond necklace. You would need to trace the history of both the metal chain and the diamond back to their origins and forward until the point at which the diamond and chain are combined to form the diamond necklace.

AP Photo/Gautam Singh

CAN THE ICON OF THE LOGISTICS INDUSTRY SUCCEED IN INDIA?

Michael Dell had the idea of selling computer systems directly to customers when he was a student at the University of Texas. In 1985 his new company designed its first computer system and soon began offering next-day, on-site product service. By 1996 Dell was selling computers on the Internet, and by 2000 the company's Web site was pulling in $50 million a day in direct sales.

Today Dell is well established as an icon of the logistics industry. Its lean business model has influenced countless other companies to follow its lead. Dell's 300,000-square-foot Morton L. Topfer Manufacturing Center (known as TMC) in Texas serves as ground zero for the build-to-order (or "just-in-time") manufacturing processes it's famous for. The TMC makes it possible for Dell to assemble hundreds of computers an hour, taking orders as they come in and making them to the customers' specifications. In the computer industry, technological equipment quickly becomes outdated, so Dell wants everything that goes out the door to be fresh off the assembly line—not losing value in a warehouse.

Dell's revolutionary supply chain is characterized by its minimum levels of inventory, a policy of paying suppliers only after the customers have paid Dell, and direct sales. Industry analysts say that these strategies have changed high-tech manufacturing the way Wal-Mart changed retail.

The question for Dell now is how to plan for future growth in emerging global markets such as China and India. Can Dell's business model, which is based on information, efficiency, and speed, work as well in parts of the world where the economic and social contexts are so different from how they are in the United States?

Dell has planned a major capital investment and expansion in its Indian operations, which would employ 20,000 people in a new manufacturing facility similar to TMC. Analysts predict that if Dell is successful in bringing its build-to-order implementation to India, it could spur a movement of manufacturing-focused foreign investment in the country.

A 2005 report by KPMG International concluded that China and India will be the world's two biggest economies by mid-century, and, "although India has underperformed in the last lap of the growth race, there is a strong possibility that India may well move ahead." Dell appears to agree. CEO Kevin Rollins explained: "India currently sells 4 million computers per year and this is projected to rise to 10 million units annually in the next three to five years. Our workforce here is capable and the time is right for the second phase of expansion in contact center activities, research and development and . . . a manufacturing site."

Critics are skeptical that India will be as profitable as Dell hopes, however, citing the country's lack of reliable roads, power, and telecommunications. Although telecommunications have improved with a 53,000-mile fiber-optic network, India maintains only 2,000 miles of highways (the United States has 23 times that). Delivery chains rely almost exclusively on small vehicles with only three wheels that navigate on dirt roads. As for India's power supply, business owners experience nearly 20 significant outages every month (compared to 5 in China). Add to this the hassle of endless red tape required of businesses in India, labor regulations that force businesses to get government permission to lay off workers, and laws that require unanimous worker approval before companies can reorganize, and it becomes clear why critics wonder whether Dell can succeed there.

Dell counters that their computers are lightweight enough to be transported in the three-wheeled trucks that are the backbone of the Indian supply chain. And industry observer Clay Risen adds, "Dell's requirement that suppliers locate warehouses nearby suddenly seems an advantage—after all, the less the supply chain has to deal with the Indian transportation system, the better." Dell can concentrate on the urban middle class with the money to buy computers in major cities like New Delhi, where the country's infrastructure, power, and tele-communications systems are more reliable.

Even with the risks involved with doing business there, Dell has decided that India is too large and full of possibilities to ignore. The industry is watching and waiting to see how the computer giant fares. Dell's success—or failure—could determine whether more manufacturing companies follow its example in the future.[36]

Questions

1. Describe how Dell's manufacturing processes represent a change in chain management from how things were done during the mass-production era. What does it mean that there has been a reversal of the flow of demand from a "push" to a "pull" system?

2. Describe the order processing system. How does it work in a company like Dell? As an order enters the system, what must management monitor? Why is it so important that the order processing system be executed well?

3. Describe the role that a supply chain manager at Dell might play. What would his or her responsibilities be? Why is there such high demand for supply chain managers in companies like Dell today?

4. Describe the benefits that Dell and other companies receive from supply chain management. What benefits do supply-chain–oriented companies commonly report? What has research shown?

COMPANY CLIPS: Sephora—Business Is Beautiful—Part 2

As you saw in the video for Chapter 13, Sephora is a leader in sales of health and beauty-aid products. Its shelves are stocked with a balance of big brand names and lesser known, up-and-coming brands. Sephora also carries and promotes its own private brand. With such an extensive, expanding, and ever-freshened inventory, Sephora must maintain an efficient supply chain—one that handles sourcing and procurement of raw supplies for the Sephora brand, production scheduling, order processing, inventory control, warehousing, materials-handling, and transportation. Review the Company Clip from Chapter 13 to learn what supply-chain techniques Sephora uses to keep its shelves stocked and customers happy.

Questions

1. Why is it important to customers that Sephora keep detailed information about its inventory? What does Sephora do to ensure its numbers are accurate?

2. How does Sephora manage its supply chain? What information goes into deciding which suppliers become incorporated?

marketing&you: Results.

The higher your score, the more you are committed to providing high-quality services to your customers. A high score also suggests that your boss was committed to service quality and empowered you to make decisions, and that you were satisfied with your job. As you learned in this chapter, when everyone working within the company is "on the same page," the company can better provide a seamless and satisfying customer experience.

Notes

1. J. Lynn Lunsford and Paul Glader, "Boeing's Nuts and Bolts Problem," *Wall Street Journal*, June 19, 2007, A8; Massoud Derhally, "Boeing Delay Won't Affect Royal Jordanian Order." *Bloomberg Businessweek,* August 30, 2010, www.businessweek.com/news/2010-08-30/boeing-787-delay-won-t-affect-royal-jordanian-order.html.

2. Goodyear Corporate Newsroom, "New CEO Kramer Confident in Goodyear's Ability to Grow," April 13, 2010, www.goodyear.com/cfmx/web/corporate/media/news/story.cfm?a_id=156.

3. Section on integration from *21st Century Logistics: Making Supply Chain Integration a Reality,* by Donald J. Bowersox, David J. Closs, and Theodore P. Stank, 1999, Council of Logistics Management: Oak Brook, IL. Reprinted with permission.

4. Chad Autry, Laura Skinner, Charles Lamb, "Interorganizational Citizenship Behaviors: An Empirical Study," *Journal of Business Logistics,* 29, No. 1 (2008): 53–74.

5. Daniel Michaels and Peter Sanders, "Dreamliner Production Gets Closer Monitoring," *Wall Street Journal*, October 8, 2009, http://online.wsj.com/article/SB125486824367569007.html.

6. *Ibid.*

7. Much of this and the following sections are based on material adapted from Douglas M. Lambert (ed.), *Supply Chain Management: Processes, Partnerships, Performance* (Supply Chain Management Institute, Sarasota, FL: 2004).

8. Patricia Brown, "Partnering with Your Customers," *Wall Street Journal*, November 20, 2007, D5.

9. Chaman Jain and Mark Covas, "Thinking about Tomorrow," *Wall Street Journal*, July 7, 2008, R10.

10. Dan Scheraga, "Balancing Act at IKEA," *Chain Store Age*, June 2005, 45–47.

11. A. Ellinger, S. Keller, and A. Elmadağ Bas, "The Empowerment of Frontline Service Staff in 3pl Companies," *Journal of Business Logistics,* 31, No. 1 (2010): 79–98.

12. "GM Reaps Huge Savings from Flexible Manufacturing," *Autoparts Report*, January 3, 2003, 1.

13. David Hannon, "Land Rover Leverages RFID for Streamlined Logistics," *Purchasing Magazine*, April 2008, 20; Thomas Craig, "Lean Supply Chain Management," www.webpronews.com, June 18, 2004, www.webpronews.com/lean-supply-chain-management-2004-06; Marcia McLeod, "Treat Them Lean," *Automotive Logistics*, November/December 2005.

14. Dan Gilmore, "What Is Senior Management Support for Supply Chain Projects," *SupplyChainDigest*, July 2, 2009, www.scdigest.com/assets/FirstThoughts/09-07-02.PHP.

15. This text was adapted significantly from James A. Cooke, "Lego's Game Changing Move," *Supply Chain Quarterly*, September 2009, www.supplychainquarterly.com/topics/Logistics/scq200903lego/.

16. Brian Nadel, "Supply and Global Demand," *Fortune*, July 9, 2007, S1–S6.

17. Hau Lee, V. Padmanabhan, and S. Wang, "The Bullwhip Effect in Supply Chains," *Sloan Management Review* 38, No. 3 (1997): 93–102.

18. Evan West, "These Robots Play Fetch," *Fast Company*, July/August 2007, 49–50.

19. Ben Worthen, "Weak Links in the (Supply) Chain," *Wall Street Journal*, June 24, 2008, B5.

20. Balanced Scorecard Institute Web site, www.balancedscorecard.org (Accessed August 2, 2010).

21. Justin Lehrer, "Green Supply Chain: Thinking Outside the (Cardboard) Box," *GreenBiz.com*, September 25, 2008, http://www.usereusables.com/downloads/4.%20GreenBiz_article_Reusables_Lehrer_092508.pdf.

22. Martin Murray, "Introduction to the Green Supply Chain," *About.com*, http://logistics.about.com/od/greensupplychain/a/green_intro.htm (Accessed February 9, 2010).

23. Wharton School, University of Pennsylvania Web site, knowledge.wharton.upenn.edu (Accessed June 2, 2008).

24. Jim Jubak, "China Feels Global-Market Pain," *MSN Money*, August 12, 2010, http://articles.moneycentral.msn.com/Investing/JubaksJournal/global-markets-pain-moves-to-China.aspx.

25. Monica Isbell and Chris Norek, "How Global Trade and Transportation Trends Impact America's Transportation Infrastructure," *CSCMP Explores*, Spring 2008, 3.

26. George Anderson, "Best Buy Focusing RFID Efforts at Front of Store," *RetailWire*, June 6, 2007, www.retailwire.com/discussion/12226/best-buy-focusing-rfid-efforts-at-front-of-store.

27. Faye Brookman, "RFID and Retailers: Will It Ever Be Perfect Together?" *RetailWire,* April 2, 2007, www.retailwire.com/discussion/12086/rfid-and-retailers-will-it-ever-be-perfect-together.

28. Inbound Logistics Web site, www.inboundlogistics.com (Accessed August 2009).

29. Anthony Ross et al., "A Framework for Developing Implementation Strategies for a Radio Frequency Identification (RFID) System in a Distribution Center Environment," *Journal of Business Logistics* 30, No. 1 (2009): 157–183.

30. Onyx Garner, Jr., "Leveraged Procurement," *Outsourcing Center*, June 1, 2005, www.outsourcing-center.com/2005-06-leveraged-procurement-article-37639.html; Avendra Corporate Web site, "Who We Are," www.avendra.com/whoweare/Pages/default.aspx; Michael French, "Ford Motor Company Extends Logistics Contract with UPS," UPS Pressroom, June 30, 2009, www.pressroom.ups.com/Press+Releases/Archive/2009/Q2/ci.Ford+Motor+Company+Extends+Logistics+Contract+with+UPS.print.

31. Adriana Hofer, Michael Knemeyer, and Martin Dresner, "Antecedents and Dimensions of Customer Partnering Behavior in Logistics Outsourcing Relationships," *Journal of Business Logistics* 30, No. 2 (2009): 141–159.

32. "ESPN Mobile Web," iPhone Toolbox Web site, http://iphonetoolbox.com/webapp/espn-mobile-web-iphone-edition (Accessed February 9, 2011).

33. Douglas Voss et al., "The Role of Security in the Food Supplier Selection Decision," *Journal of Business Logistics* 30, No. 1 (2009):127–155.

34. Russ Banham, "Keeping the Links Together," *Wall Street Journal*, June 5, 2007, A17.

35. *Supply Chain Digest* Editorial Staff, "Will Environmental Groups Target Western Companies Over Pollution Issues in Chinese Manufacturing?" *Supply Chain Digest*, September 13, 2007 (Reprinted at www.retailwire.com/discussion/12433/supply-chain-digest-will-environmental-groups-target-western-companies-over-pollution-issues-in-chinese-manufacturing, September 2007).

36. William Hoffman, "Dell Chief Targets Supply-Chain Gaps," *Shipping Digest*, March 12, 2007; Clay Risen, "Dell Takes on India," *World Trade Magazine*, September 2006; David Hannon, "Dell Flies in the Right Direction," *Purchasing*, November 17, 2005.

Learning Outcomes

1 Discuss the importance of retailing in the U.S. economy

2 Explain the dimensions by which retailers can be classified

3 Describe the major types of retail operations

4 Discuss nonstore retailing techniques

5 Define *franchising* and describe its two basic forms

6 List the major tasks involved in developing a retail marketing strategy

7 Describe new developments in retailing

LO1
The Role of Retailing

Retailing—all the activities directly related to the sale of goods and services to the ultimate consumer for personal, nonbusiness use—has enhanced the quality of our daily lives. When we shop for groceries, hairstyling, clothes, books, and many other products and services, we are involved in retailing. The millions of goods and services provided by retailers mirror the needs and styles of U.S. society.

Retailing affects all of us directly or indirectly. The retailing industry is one of the U.S.'s largest employers; over 1.5 million U.S. retailers employ more than 15 million people—about one in five American workers—with expectations that the industry will grow to over 16.5 million by 2018.[1] In addition, retail trade accounts for 10.8 percent of all U.S. employment, and almost 12 percent of all businesses were considered retail in 2009, according to NAICS.[2] At the store level, retailing is still largely a mom-and-pop business. Almost nine out of ten retail companies employ fewer than 20 employees, and, according to the National Retail Federation, over 90 percent of all retailers operate just one store.[3]

The U.S. economy depends heavily on retailing. About two-thirds of U.S. gross domestic product was estimated to come from retail activity in 2010.[4] Although most retailers are quite small, a few giant organizations dominate the industry, most notably Walmart, whose annual U.S. sales alone are greater than the next four U.S. retail giants' sales combined. Who are these giants? Exhibit 15.1 on the next page lists the ten largest U.S. retailers in 2010.

> " Retail **trade** accounts for 10.8 percent of all U.S. employment. "

retailing
All the activities directly related to the sale of goods and services to the ultimate consumer for personal, nonbusiness use.

marketing&you.

How much do you enjoy shopping? Enter your answers on the lines provided.

STRONGLY DISAGREE ‹ 1 · 2 · 3 · 4 · 5 · 6 › STRONGLY AGREE
NEUTRAL

_____ I shop because buying things makes me happy.

_____ Shopping is fun.

_____ I get a real "high" from shopping.

_____ I enjoy talking with salespeople and other shoppers who are interested in the same things I am.

_____ I like having a salesperson bring merchandise out for me to choose from.

_____ I enjoy seeing mall exhibits while shopping.

Total your score and find out what it means after you read the chapter.

EXHIBIT 15.1 Ten Largest U.S. Retailers

2010 Rank	Company	Retailing Format	Revenue (billions $)	Number of Stores
1	Walmart Bentonville, AR	Discount stores, supercenters, and warehouse clubs	304.9	4,304
2	Kroger Cincinnati, OH	Supermarkets	76.7	3,619
3	Target Minneapolis, MN	Discount stores, supercenters	63.4	1,740
4	Walgreen Deerfield, IL	Drugstores	63.3	7,397
5	The Home Depot Atlanta, GA	Home improvement centers	59.1	1,966
6	Costco Issaquah, WA	Warehouse clubs	56.6	406
7	CVS Caremark Woonsocket, RI	Drugstores	55.4	7,025
8	Lowe's Mooresville, NC	Home improvement centers	47.2	1,694
9	Sears Hoffman States, IL	Department stores, automotive centers	44.0	3,519
10	Best Buy Richfield, MN	Electronics specialty stores	37.3	1,192

Source: David Schulz, "The 2010 Top 100 Retailers," *Stores*, July 2010, www.stores.org/2010/Top-100-Retailers.

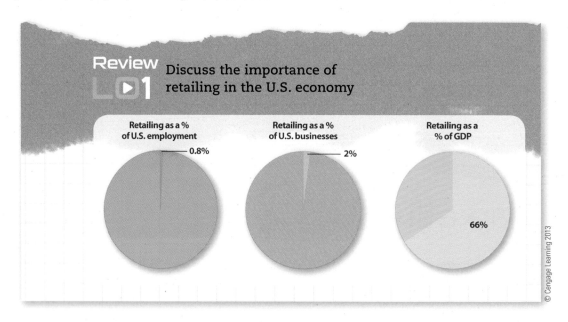

Review LO1 Discuss the importance of retailing in the U.S. economy

Retailing as a % of U.S. employment — 0.8%

Retailing as a % of U.S. businesses — 2%

Retailing as a % of GDP — 66%

© Cengage Learning 2013

LO2
Classification of Retail Operations

A retail establishment can be classified according to its ownership, level of service, product assortment, and price. Specifically, retailers use the latter three variables to position themselves in the competitive marketplace. (As noted in Chapter 7, *positioning* is the strategy used to influence how consumers perceive one product in relation to all competing products.) These three variables can be combined in

Exhibit 15.2 Types of Stores and Their Characteristics

Type of Retailer	Level of Service	Product Assortment	Price	Gross Margin
Department store	Moderately high to high	Broad	Moderate to high	Moderately high
Specialty store	High	Narrow	Moderate to high	High
Supermarket	Low	Broad	Moderate	Low
Convenience store	Low	Medium to narrow	Moderately high	Moderately high
Drugstore	Low to moderate	Medium	Moderate	Low
Full-line discount store	Moderate to low	Medium to broad	Moderately low	Moderately low
Discount specialty store	Moderate to low	Medium to broad	Moderately low to low	Moderately low
Warehouse clubs	Low	Broad	Low to very low	Low
Off-price retailer	Low	Medium to narrow	Low	Low
Restaurant	Low to high	Narrow	Low to high	Low to high

© Cenage Learning 2013

© iStockphoto.com/Juan Facundo Mora Soria

several ways to create distinctly different retail operations. Exhibit 15.2 lists the major types of retail stores discussed in this chapter and classifies them by level of service, product assortment, price, and gross margin.

OWNERSHIP

Retailers can be broadly classified by form of ownership: independent, part of a chain, or franchise outlet. Retailers owned by a single person or partnership and not operated as part of a larger retail institution are **independent retailers**. Around the world, most retailers are independent, operating one or a few stores in their community. Local florists, shoe stores, and ethnic food markets typically fit this classification.

Chain stores are owned and operated as a group by a single organization. Under this form of ownership, many administrative tasks are handled by the home office for the entire chain. The home office also buys most of the merchandise sold in the stores. Gap, Macy's, and Target are examples of chains.

Franchises are owned and operated by individuals but are licensed by a larger supporting organization, such as Subway or Quiznos. The franchising approach combines the advantages of independent ownership with those of the chain store organization. Franchising is discussed in more detail later in the chapter.

LEVEL OF SERVICE

The level of service that retailers provide can be classified along a continuum, from full service to self-service. Some retailers, such as exclusive clothing stores, offer high levels of service. They provide alterations, credit, delivery, consulting, liberal return policies, layaway, gift wrapping, and personal shopping. Discount stores usually offer fewer services. Retailers such as factory outlets and warehouse clubs offer virtually no services.

PRODUCT ASSORTMENT

The third basis for positioning or classifying stores is by the breadth and depth of their product line. Specialty stores—for example, Best Buy, Toys "R" Us, or GameStop—have the most concentrated product assortments, usually carrying single or narrow product lines but in considerable depth. On the other end of the spectrum, full-line discounters typically carry broad assortments of merchandise with limited depth. For example, Target carries automotive supplies,

independent retailers
Retailers owned by a single person or partnership and not operated as part of a larger retail institution.

chain stores
Stores owned and operated as a group by a single organization.

franchise
a business owned or operated by an individual that is licensed by a larger supporting organization.

The Problem

Janine, the owner of a small beauty supply store called ReNewU, wants know roughly how many products she needs to sell each day to recoup ReNewU's fixed monthly costs. To do so, Janine performs a contribution analysis, which shows her how much money each product contributes to her profit, and a break-even volume analysis, which will show her the least amount of units she needs to sell to meet her fixed monthly costs at zero profit. This metric allows Janine to determine the base level of sales needed to simply keep ReNewU running.

The Metric

Janine knows her average product's selling price is $30 per unit. Her supplier also informs Janine that the variable cost per unit in her store is $15. ReNewU also has fixed monthly costs such as rent, utilities, and labor, which add up to $15,000.

First, Janine needs to determine the contribution per unit. This equation lets her know how much money each product contributes to covering her store's fixed costs:

$$\text{Contribution per Unit} = \text{Selling Price per Unit} - \text{Variable Cost per Unit}$$

$$\text{Contribution per Unit} = \$30 - \$15 = \$15$$

Each product Janine sells contributes $15 to covering ReNewU's fixed costs.

With that information, Janine can find out the break-even volume for her store. This equation shows her exactly how many products per month she needs to sell in order to cover all the fixed monthly costs at ReNewU:

$$\text{Break-Even Volume} = \frac{\text{Fixed Costs}}{\text{Contribution per Unit}} = \frac{\$15000}{\$15} = 1,000$$

To cover the fixed monthly costs, Janine needs to sell 1,000 items a month. To determine how many products she needs to sell each day in a month, Janine can simply divide 1,000 by 31 to see that she needs to sell 33 items each day to break even.

Management Decision

Knowing that she needs to sell 1,000 items each month to cover the costs of running ReNewU, Janine can give her sales team and herself the goal of selling a certain number of products during their shifts. If certain days are slower than others, Janine can modify the daily sales goal. The success of her business will depend on many other factors, such as location and how competitive her prices are, but the break-even volume gives her a concrete starting place for daily sales.

---

household cleaning products, clothing, and pet food. Typically, though, it carries only four or five brands of dog food. In contrast, a specialty pet store, such as PetSmart, might carry as many as 20 brands in a large variety of flavors, shapes, and sizes.

Other retailers, such as factory outlet stores, might carry only part of a single line. Nike stores sell only certain items of its own brand. Discount specialty stores such as Home Depot and Rack Room Shoes carry a broad assortment in concentrated product lines, such as building and home supplies or shoes.

PRICE

Price is a fourth way to position retail stores. Traditional department stores and specialty stores typically charge the full "suggested retail price." In contrast, discounters, factory outlets, and off-price retailers use low prices as a major lure for shoppers.

The last column in Exhibit 15.2 shows the typical **gross margin**—how much the retailer makes as a percentage of sales after the cost of goods sold is subtracted. The level of gross margin and the price level generally match. For example, a traditional jewelry store has high prices and high gross margins. A factory outlet has

gross margin
The amount of money the retailer makes as a percentage of sales after the cost of goods sold is subtracted.

low prices and low gross margins. Mark-downs on merchandise during sales and price wars among competitors, in which stores lower prices on certain items in an effort to win customers, cause gross margins to decline. When Walmart entered the grocery business in a small Arkansas community, a fierce price war ensued. By the time the price war was in full swing, the price of a quart of milk had plummeted by more than 50 percent (below the price of a pint) and a loaf of bread sold for only 9 cents—prices at which no retailer could make a profit.

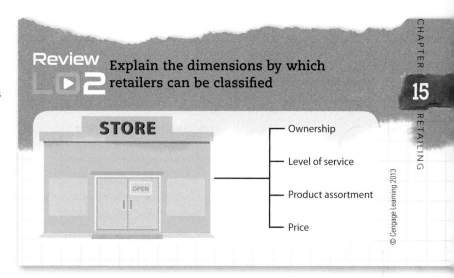

Review LO2 Explain the dimensions by which retailers can be classified

STORE
— Ownership
— Level of service
— Product assortment
— Price

© Cengage Learning 2013

LO3
Major Types of Retail Operations

Traditionally, there have been several distinct types of retail stores, each offering a different product assortment, type of service, and price level, according to its customers' shopping preferences.

In a recent trend, however, retailers are experimenting with alternative formats that make it more difficult to classify them. For instance, supermarkets are expanding their nonfood items and services; discounters are adding groceries; drugstores are becoming more like convenience stores; and department stores are experimenting with smaller stores. Nevertheless, many stores still fall into the basic types.

DEPARTMENT STORES

A **department store** carries a wide variety of shopping and specialty goods, including apparel, cosmetics, housewares, electronics, and sometimes furniture. Purchases are generally made within each department rather than at one central checkout area. Each department is treated as a separate buying center to achieve economies in promotion, buying, service, and control. Each department is usually headed by a **buyer**, a department head who not only selects the merchandise for his or her department, but might also be responsible for promotion and personnel. For a consistent, uniform store image, central management sets broad policies about the types of merchandise carried and price ranges. Central management is also responsible for the overall advertising program, credit policies, store expansion, customer service, and so on.

Large independent department stores are rare today. Most are owned by national chains. Among the largest U.S. department store chains are Macy's (formerly known as Federated Department Stores, Inc.), JCPenney, Sears, Dillard's, and Nordstrom. Dillard's is known for its distribution expertise. Nordstrom offers innovative customer service.

SPECIALTY STORES

Specialty store formats enable retailers to refine their segmentation strategies and tailor their merchandise to specific target markets. A **specialty store** is not only a type of store but also a method of retail operations—namely, specializing in a given

department store
A store housing several departments under one roof.

buyer
A department head who selects the merchandise for his or her department and may also be responsible for promotion and personnel.

specialty store
A retail store specializing in a given type of merchandise.

type of merchandise. Examples include children's clothing, men's clothing, candy, baked goods, gourmet coffee, sporting goods, and pet supplies. A typical specialty store carries a deeper but narrower assortment of specialty merchandise than does a department store. Generally, specialty stores' knowledgeable sales clerks offer more attentive customer service. The format has become very powerful in the apparel market and other areas. In fact, consumers buy more clothing from specialty stores than from any other type of retailer. The Children's Place, Gadzooks, Williams-Sonoma, and Foot Locker are examples of successful chain specialty retailers.

Consumers usually consider price to be secondary in specialty outlets. Instead, the distinctive merchandise, the store's physical appearance, and the caliber of the staff determine its popularity. For example, at 154-year-old London-based Burberry, a luxury fashion retailer known for the trademark golden plaid fabric designs that accentuate its key items, customers pay higher prices versus those found in competitors' shops. But Burberry customers find the prices to be justifiable given the luxurious retail atmosphere and high quality service, and Burberry's sales were up over 20 percent even during the 2009 recession year.[5] Similarly, customers who shop for high-end electronics often find that specialty stores cannot compete on price with big-box stores. Instead, consumer electronics specialty stores compete by offering better-trained sales staff, more expertise, and better customer service than the big-box retailers. For instance, Tweeter, a regional electronics chain in New England, specializes in helping its customers overcome confusion and become comfortable with their purchases. Tweeter's customers can try out the latest technology by accompanying "hyperinformed" salespeople through replica kitchens, dens, and bedrooms loaded with complicated gadgets.[6] In the very best specialty stores, the customer begins to find that store branded products can become indistinguishable facets of the customer's personality or lifestyle. At American Girl Place in Chicago, young children and their parents craft dolls together, and the children then walk with them through a "pretend" cityscape facade including a library, museum, café, and other fantasy locations to create a lifelike companionship experience. In this way, American Girl staffers help children to build not only dolls, but memorable experiences the dolls and customers share together.[7]

SUPERMARKETS

According to the U.S. Department of Agriculture, U.S. consumers spend about 10 percent of their disposable income on food, and roughly half of those expenditures occur in **supermarkets** on food for at-home consumption. Supermarkets are large, departmentalized, self-service retailers that specialize in food and some nonfood items. Following several years of declining sales, many supermarkets have experienced a 2–3 percent upswing in sales since 2007, when economic conditions forced many families to resume eating at home.[8] But demographic and lifestyle changes have also affected the supermarket industry.

One major change has been the increase in dual-income and single-parent families that eat out more or are just too busy to prepare meals at home. According to the U.S. Department of Agriculture, Americans spend about 50 percent of their food money in retail grocery stores, and nearly 50 percent on food away from home. In comparison, Americans spent over three-fourths of their food money in grocery stores in 1950.[9]

As stores seek to meet consumer demand for one-stop shopping, conventional supermarkets are being replaced by bigger *superstores,* which are usually

supermarket
A large, departmentalized, self-service retailer that specializes in food and some nonfood items.

twice the size of supermarkets. Superstores meet the needs of today's customers for convenience, variety, and service. Superstores offer one-stop shopping for many food and nonfood needs, as well as many services—including pharmacies, flower shops, salad bars, in-store bakeries, takeout food sections, sit-down restaurants, health food sections, video rentals, dry-cleaning services, shoe repair, photo processing, and banking. Some even offer family dentistry or optical shops. This tendency to offer a wide variety of nontraditional goods and services under one roof is called **scrambled merchandising**. Safeway supermarkets are a good example of scrambled merchandising. In addition to including a liquor store, floral department, and pharmacy, they also lease space to Starbucks and local banks.

For supercenter operators, food is a customer magnet that sharply increases the store's overall volume, while taking customers away from traditional supermarkets.

Another trend in supermarket diversification is the addition of store-owned gas stations. The gas stations are not only a revenue source for the supermarkets and a convenience for customers, but they also attract customers to the location by offering lower prices than can usually be found at a traditional gas station. Store-owned stations are expected to account for as much as 25 percent of overall gasoline sales in the near future.

To stand out in an increasingly competitive marketplace, many supermarket chains are tailoring marketing strategies to appeal to specific consumer segments. Most notable is the shift toward *loyalty marketing programs* that reward loyal customers carrying frequent shopper cards with discounts or gifts. Once scanned at the checkout, frequent shopper cards help supermarket retailers electronically track shoppers' buying habits. More than half of the customers who shop at the over 600 Piggly Wiggly stores carry the Pig's Favorite loyalty card. Customers use their card each time they shop to get special discounts on items. The supermarket chain was also one of the first grocers to implement biometrics. Instead of carrying a loyalty card, the customer simply places a fingertip on a biometric finger-scan reader at a kiosk positioned near the front of the store. The shopper then receives a printout of personalized offers, which change weekly.[10] Piggly Wiggly also uses consumer purchase data stored in its database to determine customer preferences. If management sees that a customer buys flowers regularly, then it sends that customer a coupon redeemable in its floral department.[11]

DRUGSTORES

Drugstores sell pharmacy-related products and services as their main draw. Consumers are most often attracted to a drugstore by its pharmacy or pharmacist, its convenience, or because it honors their third-party prescription drug plan. Drugstores also carry an extensive selection of over-the-counter (OTC) medications, cosmetics, health and beauty aids, seasonal merchandise, specialty items such as greeting cards and a limited selection of toys, and some non-refrigerated convenience foods. As competition has increased from mass merchandisers and supermarkets with their own pharmacies, as well as from direct-mail prescription services, drugstores have added value-added services such as 24-hour

scrambled merchandising
The tendency to offer a wide variety of nontraditional goods and services under one roof.

drugstore
A retail store that stocks pharmacy-related products and services as its main draw.

operations, drive-through pharmacies, and low-cost health clinics staffed by nurse practitioners.

Demographic trends in the United States look favorable for the drugstore industry. As the baby boom population continues to age, they will spend an increasing percentage of their disposable income on health care and wellness. In fact, the average 60-year-old purchases 15 prescriptions per year, nearly twice as many as the average 30-year-old. Because baby boomers are attentive to their health and keenly sensitive about their looks, the increased traffic at the pharmacy counter in the future should also spur sales in other traditionally strong drugstore merchandise categories, most notably OTC drugs, vitamins, and health and beauty aids.

CONVENIENCE STORES

A **convenience store** can be defined as a miniature supermarket, carrying only a limited line of high-turnover convenience goods. These self-service stores are typically located near residential areas and are open 24 hours, seven days a week. Convenience stores offer exactly what their name implies: convenient location, long hours, and fast service. However, prices are almost always higher at a convenience store than at a supermarket. Thus, the customer pays for the convenience.

When the original convenience stores added self-service gas pumps, full-service gas stations fought back by closing service bays and opening miniature stores of their own, selling convenience items such as cigarettes, sodas, and snacks. Supermarkets and discount stores also wooed customers with one-stop shopping and quick checkout. To combat the gas stations' and supermarkets' competition, convenience store operators have changed their strategy. They have expanded their offerings of nonfood items with video rentals and health and beauty aids and added upscale sandwich and salad lines and more fresh produce. Some convenience stores are even selling Pizza Hut, Subway, and Taco Bell products prepared in the store. For example, Exxon On the Run features Green Mountain Coffee Roasters, Blimpie subs and salads, and an On the Run Café that offers everything from fresh sandwiches and fresh fruits to grilled hamburgers and french fries.[12]

DISCOUNT STORES

A **discount store** is a retailer that competes on the basis of low prices, high turnover, and high volume. Discounters can be classified into four major categories: full-line discount stores, specialty discount stores, warehouse clubs, and off-price discount retailers.

Full-Line Discount Stores Compared to traditional department stores, **full-line discount stores** offer consumers very limited service and carry a much broader assortment of well-known, nationally branded "hard goods," including housewares, toys, automotive parts, hardware, sporting goods, and garden items, as well as clothing, bedding, and linens. Some even carry limited nonperishable food items, such as soft drinks, canned goods, and potato chips. As with department stores, national chains dominate the discounters. Full-line discounters are often called mass merchandisers. **Mass merchandising** is the retailing strategy whereby retailers use moderate to low prices on large quantities of merchandise and lower service to stimulate high turnover of products.

Walmart is the largest full-line discount store in terms of sales. Walmart initially expanded rapidly by locating on the outskirts of small towns and absorbing business for miles around. In recent years, most of its growth has come in larger cities. Today, it has over 8,500 stores on four continents. Much of Walmart's

convenience store
A miniature supermarket that carries only a limited line of high-turnover convenience goods.

discount store
A retailer that competes on the basis of low prices, high turnover, and high volume.

full-line discount stores
A retailer that offers consumers very limited service and carries a broad assortment of well-known, nationally branded "hard goods."

mass merchandising
A retailing strategy using moderate to low prices on large quantities of merchandise and lower service to stimulate high turnover of products.

success has been attributed to its merchandising foresight, cost consciousness, efficient communication and distribution systems, and involved, motivated employees. Walmart is credited with pioneering the retail strategy of "everyday low pricing," a strategy now widely copied by retailers the world over. Besides expanding throughout all 50 states and Puerto Rico, Walmart has expanded globally into Argentina, Brazil, Canada, China, Costa Rica, El Salvador, Guatemala, Honduras, India, Japan, Mexico, Nicaragua, South Korea, and the United Kingdom. Walmart has also become a formidable retailing giant in online shopping, concentrating on toys and electronics. With tie-ins to its stores across the country, Walmart offers online shopping with in-store kiosks linking to the site and the ability to handle returns and exchanges from Internet sales at its physical stores. A key differentiator in Walmart's brand has been its environmentally friendly approach while still offering everyday low prices; the retailer believes it will be supplied by 100 percent renewable energy and create zero net landfill waste in the near future, thus disproving the myth that a large retailer cannot be both environmentally friendly and profitable simultaneously.[13]

Supercenters combine a full line of groceries and general merchandise with a wide range of services, including pharmacy, dry cleaning, portrait studios, photo finishing, hair salons, optical shops, and restaurants—all in one location. For supercenter operators such as Walmart, food is a customer magnet that sharply increases the store's overall volume, while taking customers away from traditional supermarkets. Walmart opened its first supercenter in 1988 and now operates over 2,000 supercenters worldwide. Target was the last major discounter to embrace the supercenter concept. The chain currently has 220 SuperTarget locations and plans to open 200 more over the next ten years.[14]

Supercenters are also threatening to push Europe's traditional small and medium-sized food stores into extinction. Old-fashioned corner stores and family businesses are giving way to larger chains that offer food, drugs, services, and general merchandise all in one place. Today, the largest British food retailer is Tesco, a chain operator that has over 30 percent of the grocery market in the United Kingdom. Tesco is expanding rapidly and now has over 1,800 stores in the UK and more than 2,700 stores globally, including a joint venture with Safeway in the United States.[15]

Some European countries, however, have passed legislation to make it more difficult for supercenters to open. In France, for example, laws ban authorizations for new supercenters over 1,000 square meters (10,800 square feet). Belgium and Portugal have passed similar bans. In Britain and the Netherlands, areas outside towns and cities are off limits to superstores. By imposing planning and building restrictions for large stores, these countries are trying to accommodate environmental concerns, movements to revive city centers, and the worries of small shopkeepers.

An increasingly popular variation of full-line discount stores is *extreme-value retailing*, the most notable examples being Dollar General and Family Dollar. Extreme-value retailers have grown in popularity as major discounters continue to shift toward the supercenter format, broadening their customer base and increasing their offerings of higher-priced goods aimed at higher-income consumers. This has created an opening for extreme-value retailers to entice shoppers from the low-income segment. Low- and fixed-income customers are drawn to extreme-value retailers, whose stores are located within their communities. Extreme-value retailers also build smaller stores (a typical store is about the size of one department in a Walmart superstore) with a narrower selection of merchandise emphasizing day-to-day necessities. Rock-bottom prices are also a key to their success.

supercenter
A retailer that combines a full line of groceries and general merchandize with a wide range of services in one location.

With the average transaction under $10, extreme-value retailers have found low price to be far more critical to building traffic and loyalty than any other retailing format.[16]

Specialty Discount Stores Another discount niche includes the single-line **specialty discount stores**—for example, stores selling sporting goods, electronics, auto parts, office supplies, housewares, or toys. These stores offer a nearly complete selection of single-line merchandise and use self-service, discount prices, high volume, and high turnover to their advantage. Specialty discount stores are often termed **category killers** because they so heavily dominate their narrow merchandise segment. Examples include Toys "R" Us in toys (the first category killer in the market), Best Buy in electronics, Staples and Office Depot in office supplies, Home Depot and Lowe's in home improvement supplies, IKEA in home furnishings, Bed Bath & Beyond in kitchen and bath accessories, and Dick's in sporting goods.

Category killers have emerged in other specialty segments as well, creating retailing empires in highly fragmented mom-and-pop markets. For instance, the home improvement industry, which for years was served by professional builders and small hardware stores, is now dominated by Home Depot and Lowe's. Category-dominant retailers such as these serve their customers by offering a large selection of merchandise, stores that make shopping easy, and low prices every day—which eliminates the need for time-consuming comparison shopping.

Warehouse Membership Clubs **Warehouse membership clubs** sell a limited selection of brand-name appliances, household items, and groceries. These are usually sold in bulk from warehouse outlets on a cash-and-carry basis to members only. Individual members of warehouse clubs are charged low or no membership fees. Currently, the leading stores in this category are Walmart's Sam's Club, Costco, and BJ's Wholesale Club.

Warehouse clubs have had a major impact on supermarkets. With 90,000 square feet or more, warehouse clubs offer 60 to 70 percent general merchandise and health- and beauty-care products, with grocery-related items making up the difference. Warehouse club members tend to be more educated and more affluent and have a larger household than regular supermarket shoppers. These core customers use warehouse clubs to stock up on staples; then they go to specialty outlets or food stores for perishables. Warehouse clubs are also expanding into luxury items. Sam's Club recently had a $347,000 diamond solitaire ring on sale before Christmas and Costco sells Dom Pérignon champagne.

Off-Price Retailers An **off-price retailer** sells at prices 25 percent or more below traditional department store prices because it pays cash for its stock and usually doesn't ask for return privileges. Off-price retailers buy manufacturers' overruns at cost or even less. They also absorb goods from bankrupt stores, irregular merchandise, and unsold end-of-season output. Nevertheless, much off-price retailer merchandise is first-quality, current goods. Because buyers for off-price retailers purchase only what is available or what they can get a good deal on, merchandise styles and brands often change monthly. Today, there are hundreds of off-price retailers, including T.J. Maxx, Ross Stores, Marshalls, HomeGoods, and Tuesday Morning.

Factory outlets are an interesting variation on the off-price concept. A **factory outlet** is an off-price retailer that is owned and operated by a manufacturer. Thus, it carries one line of merchandise—its own. Each season, from 5 to 10 percent of a manufacturer's output does not sell through regular distribution channels because

it consists of closeouts (merchandise being discontinued), factory seconds, and canceled orders. With factory outlets, manufacturers can regulate where their surplus is sold, and they can realize higher profit margins than they would by disposing of the goods through independent wholesalers and retailers. Factory outlet malls are typically located in out-of-the-way rural areas or near vacation destinations. Most are situated 10 to 15 miles from urban or suburban shopping areas so that manufacturers don't alienate their department store accounts by selling the same goods virtually next door at a discount.

Manufacturers reaping the benefits of outlet mall popularity include Gap, J. Crew, and Calvin Klein clothiers; West Point Pepperel textiles; Pottery Barn and Crate & Barrel home products; Oneida silversmiths; and Dansk kitchenwares. Top-drawer department stores have also opened outlet stores to sell hard-to-move merchandise. Dillard's has opened a series of clearance centers to make final attempts to move merchandise that failed to sell in the department store. To move their clearance items, Nordstrom operates Nordstrom Rack, Saks Fifth Avenue has Off Fifth, and Neiman Marcus has Last Call.

RESTAURANTS

Restaurants straddle the line between retailing establishments and service establishments. Restaurants do sell tangible products—food and drink—but they also provide a valuable service for consumers in the form of food preparation and service. As a retailing institution, restaurants deal with many of the same issues as a more traditional retailer, such as personnel, distribution, inventory management, promotion, pricing, and location.

Eating out is an important part of Americans' daily activities and is growing in strength. According to the National Restaurant Association, more than 70 billion meals are eaten in restaurants or cafeterias annually in nearly one million locations. Food eaten away from home accounts for about 49 percent ($2,698 per household) of the annual household food budget. The trend toward eating out has been fueled by the increase in working mothers and dual-income families who have more money to eat out and less time to prepare meals at home. In recent years, the industry has adapted to this increase in family eating out through the introduction of new "midrange" concepts that afford conscientious eaters and their families with options that are positioned as healthier than traditional fast food, but are lower in price than typical full-service restaurant brands. Brands such as Subway and Chipotle have taken advantage of customers who fall into the niche between the two traditional formats. At least in part, this expansion has been responsible for stabilizing sales in the industry during the recent economic downturn. The restaurant industry continues to provide work for more than 10 percent of the American workforce and is expected to provide over 2 million jobs in the next few years, for total employment of 14.7 million people in 2017.[17]

The restaurant industry is one of the most entrepreneurial and competitive in U.S. commerce. Because barriers to entering the restaurant industry are low, the opportunity appeals to many people. The risks, however, are great. Over 50 percent of all new restaurants fail within the first year of operation. Restaurants face competition not only from other restaurants but also from the consumer who can easily choose to cook at home. Competition has fostered innovation and ever-changing menus in most segments of the restaurant industry. Many restaurants are now competing directly with supermarkets by offering takeout and delivery in an effort to capture more of the home meal replacement market.

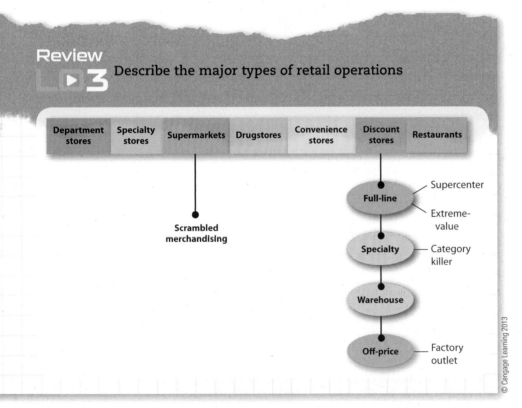

Review

LO3 Describe the major types of retail operations

Department stores | Specialty stores | Supermarkets | Drugstores | Convenience stores | Discount stores | Restaurants

Supermarkets — Scrambled merchandising

Discount stores:
- Full-line — Supercenter, Extreme-value
- Specialty — Category killer
- Warehouse
- Off-price — Factory outlet

© Cengage Learning 2013

LO4
Nonstore Retailing

nonstore retailing
Selling to consumers through other means than by visiting a store.

The retailing formats discussed so far have been in-store methods, in which customers must physically shop at stores. In contrast, **nonstore retailing** is shopping without visiting a store. Because consumers demand convenience, nonstore retailing is currently growing faster than in-store retailing. The major forms of nonstore retailing are automatic vending, direct retailing, direct marketing, and electronic retailing.

AUTOMATIC VENDING

A low-profile yet important form of retailing is **automatic vending**, the use of machines to offer goods for sale—for example, the soft drink, candy, or snack vending machines found in college cafeterias and office buildings. Vending is the most pervasive retail business in the United States, with about six million vending machines selling $40 billion annually. Food and beverages account for about 85 percent of all sales from vending machines. Due to the convenience, consumers are willing to pay higher prices for products from a vending machine than for the same products in traditional retail settings.

Retailers are constantly seeking new opportunities to sell via vending. For example, United Artists Theaters offer moviegoers the option of purchasing hot popcorn, Tombstone pizza, Kraft macaroni-and-cheese, and chicken fingers from a vending machine instead of waiting in line at the concession stand. Many vending machines today also sell nontraditional kinds of merchandise, such as videos, toys, stickers, sports cards, office-type supplies, film, and disposable cameras. A recent legal initiative in Pennsylvania has allowed for the selling of wine through large automated vending kiosks—provided customers are willing to swipe their driver's license through the machine to provide age verification, and blow into an alcohol sensing device to prove they are not intoxicated.[18] And in other signs of the times, shoppers can buy iPod music players, rent DVDs, or even purchase a luxury car through vending machines, all with the swipe of a credit card.[19] Recent estimates suggest that credit card technology is already available in over 11.5 million vending machines of different types, and in fact the cards themselves might soon be unnecessary—customers will be able to make purchases with smartphones or using biometric devices linking retina scan patterns or thumbprints directly to credit accounts at major banks.[20]

DIRECT RETAILING

In **direct retailing**, representatives sell products door-to-door, office-to-office, or at home sales parties. Companies such as Avon, Mary Kay Cosmetics, The Pampered Chef, Usborne Books, and World Book Encyclopedia have used this approach for years. But recently direct retailers' sales have suffered as women have entered the workforce. Working women are not home during the day and have little time to attend selling parties. Although most direct sellers like Avon and Silpada still advocate the party plan method, the realities of the marketplace have forced them to be more creative in reaching their target customer. Direct sales representatives now hold parties in offices, parks, and even parking lots. Others hold informal gatherings where shoppers can drop in at their convenience or offer self-improvement classes. Many direct retailers are also turning to direct mail, telephone, or more traditional retailing venues to find new avenues to their customers and increase sales. Avon, for instance, has begun opening cosmetic kiosk counters, called Avon Beauty Centers, in malls and strip centers. Avon has also launched a new brand—Mark, a beauty "experience" for young women. Similarly, in the health supplements market, Advocare representatives are largely health conscious stay-at-home parents or college students who sell the product as an after-school, part-time job. Prospective representatives and consumers can buy products or register to be a representative in person, online, or over the phone.[21] Direct retailers are also using the Internet as a channel to reach more customers and increase sales. At Avon's site, individual reps have their own home pages that link from Avon's home page so that sales are credited to them.

In response to the decline in U.S. sales, many long-time direct retailers are exploring opportunities in other countries. For example, Mary Kay, Avon, and

automatic vending
Using machines to offer goods for sale.

direct retailing
The selling of products by representatives who work door-to-door, office-to-office, or at home parties.

This man is selling Tupperware directly to customers at their homes. This Tupperware party is also a cooking class.

Amway have started successful operations in China by adapting their business models to China's laws. Mary Kay agents in China do not purchase and resell the products but are paid a sales commission instead. The company also changed its slogan from "God First, Family Second, Career Third," to "Faith First, Family Second, Career Third."

DIRECT MARKETING

According to the Direct Marketing Association, companies spend more than $167 billion annually on direct marketing in the United States and generate about $1.93 trillion in sales, representing over 17 percent of marketing spend among U.S. companies.[22] **Direct marketing**, sometimes called **direct-response marketing**, refers to the techniques used to get consumers to make a purchase from their home, office, or other nonretail setting. These techniques include direct mail, catalogs and mail order, telemarketing, and electronic retailing. Shoppers using these methods are less bound by traditional shopping situations. Time-strapped consumers and those who live in rural or suburban areas are more likely to be direct-response shoppers because they value the convenience and flexibility that direct marketing provides.

Direct Mail Direct mail can be the most efficient or the least efficient retailing method, depending on the quality of the mailing list and the effectiveness of the mailing piece. With direct mail, marketers can precisely target their customers according to demographics, geographics, and even psychographics. Good mailing lists come from an internal database or from list brokers for about $35 to $150 per thousand names.

Direct mailers are becoming more sophisticated in targeting the "right" customers. Using statistical methods to analyze census data, lifestyle and financial information, and past-purchase and credit history, direct mailers can pick out those most likely to buy their products. So, despite increases in postal rates and raw material and logistics costs, U.S. direct mail services were up over 14 percent in 2010, and are expected to surpass $25 billion annually by 2015.[23] We'll explore how direct marketers are using customer relationship management in Chapter 21.

Catalogs and Mail Order Consumers can now buy just about anything through the mail, from the mundane, such as books, music, and polo shirts, to the outlandish, such as the $5 million diamond-and-ruby-studded bra available through the Victoria's Secret catalog. Although women make up the bulk of catalog shoppers, the percentage of male catalog shoppers has recently soared. As changing demographics have shifted more of the shopping responsibility to men, they are viewing shopping via catalog, mail order, and the Internet as more sensible than a trip to the mall.

direct marketing (direct-response marketing)
The techniques used to get consumers to make a purchase from a nonretail setting.

Successful catalogs usually are created and designed for highly segmented markets. For example, Schwan Food Company recently launched Impromptu Gourmet, which offers convenient gourmet and fine dining frozen foods. Certain types of retailers are using mail order successfully. For example, computer manufacturers have discovered that mail order is a lucrative way to sell personal computers to home and small-business users, evidenced by Dell's tremendous success. Dell has used its direct business model to become a $60 billion company and one of the largest PC sellers worldwide. With a global market share of about 13 percent, it sells over $50 million in computers and equipment through its online catalog every day.[24] Moreover, for consumers who live on the edge of environmental technology, new developments in catalog sales go even further. Real Goods Solar, a Colorado-based startup firm, offers a 935 square foot, solar powered house through its new catalog, complete with solar panels, wiring, a one or two bedroom floor plan, and a choice of traditional vinyl or cedar siding.[25]

Telemarketing Telemarketing is the use of the telephone to sell directly to consumers. It consists of outbound sales calls, usually unsolicited, and inbound calls—that is, orders through toll-free 800 numbers or fee-based 900 numbers. The use of telemarketing is not at all insignificant in modern marketing; recent estimates indicate that U.S. companies will spend over $15 billion on inbound and outbound calls by 2015.[26]

Rising postage rates and decreasing long-distance phone rates have made *outbound* telemarketing an attractive direct-marketing technique. Skyrocketing field sales costs have also led marketing managers to use outbound telemarketing. Searching for ways to keep costs under control, marketing managers have learned how to pinpoint prospects quickly, zero in on serious buyers, and keep in close touch with regular customers. Meanwhile, they are reserving expensive, time-consuming, in-person calls for closing sales. So many consumers complained about outbound telemarketing calls, however, that Congress passed legislation establishing a national "do not call" list of consumers who do not want to receive unsolicited telephone calls. In addition, Congress passed laws requiring e-mail marketers to allow recipients to opt out of mass e-mails (spam). The laws also prohibit marketers from camouflaging their identity through false return addresses and misleading subject lines. A problem with the telemarketing law, however, is that it exempts nonprofits, so some companies have set up nonprofit subsidiaries to continue their calling activities. Some industry experts say the lists help them by eliminating non-buyers, but others believe this legislation could have a long-term negative effect on telemarketing sales.

Inbound telemarketing programs, which use 800 and 900 numbers, are mainly used to take orders, generate leads, and provide customer service. Inbound telemarketing has successfully supplemented direct-response TV, radio, and print advertising for more than 25 years.

ELECTRONIC RETAILING

Electronic retailing includes the 24-hour, shop-at-home television networks and online retailing.

SHOP-AT-HOME NETWORKS

The shop-at-home television networks are specialized forms of direct-response marketing. Shows display merchandise, with the retail price, to home viewers. Viewers can phone in their orders directly on a toll-free line and shop with a credit card. The shop-at-home industry has quickly grown into a multibillion-dollar

telemarketing
The use of the telephone to sell directly to consumers.

business with a loyal customer following. Shop-at-home networks have the capability of reaching nearly every home that has a television set.

The best-known shop-at-home networks are the Home Shopping Network and the QVC (Quality, Value, Convenience) Network. Home shopping networks attract a broad audience through diverse programming and product offerings and are now adding new products to appeal to more affluent audiences. For instance, on QVC, cooking programs attract both men and women, fashion programs attract mostly women, and the NFL Team Shop attracts primarily men. Since it began broadcasting, the channel has sold everything from Sony electronics to NutriSystem health products to Gucci items. With annual sales of almost $7.4 billion, QVC ships more than 166 million packages worldwide to over 10 million customers every year. The company owes its success in part to its customer files of more than 20 million people in 40 countries and to the fact that it promotes as many as 1,150 products each week.[27]

Online Retailing For years, shopping at home meant looking through catalogs and then placing an order over the telephone. For many people today, however, it now means turning on a computer, surfing retail Web sites, and selecting and ordering products online with the click of a mouse. **Online retailing**, or *e-tailing*, is a type of shopping available to consumers with access to the Internet. Over 70 percent of Americans have Internet access either at home or at work.

Online retailing has exploded in the last several years as consumers have found this type of shopping convenient and, in many instances, less costly. Consumers are motivated to shop online for several reasons, including convenience, the fun associated with online bidding or haggling, enhanced ability to deal-shop or bargain hunt, and more easily keep up with new trends or fashions, among other factors. However, because online stores provide a different shopping experience for consumers, online retailers must focus on different features that attract customers. Aspects such as safety from identity theft, security in making payments, immediate order confirmation, and timely delivery are critical factors in customers' decisions to patronize online retailers.[28] Many retailers are able to address these factors effectively, and online shopping continues to grow, with online sales accounting for about 8 percent of total retail sales.

As an example of the growing enthusiasm for online retailing, a recent survey indicated that 31 percent of consumers prefer to make their purchases online, versus 27 percent who preferred physical stores.[29] Online retail sales recently topped $160 billion and are projected to reach almost $275 billion, or 9 percent of retail sales, by 2011.[30] Given these levels of success, even high end brands that traditionally rely on high levels of individualized service are getting in on the action. For example, high women's fashion brands Jimmy Choo and Donna Karan have each established a healthy online presence in recent years. Some customers have expressed their preference for buying such brands online, as it provides an opportunity for customers willing to pay full price to enjoy the products without enduring trips to distant retail locations or hassling with snobby salesclerks.

Broadcast and cable television networks are cultivating a new source of income by selling products online that are featured in their TV shows. Delivery Agent, a San Francisco company that calls itself the leader in shopping-enabled entertainment, manages e-commerce for NBC, Bravo, and Martha Stewart Omnimedia, among others. The producers of Bravo's *Project Runway* contracted with Delivery Agent to sell the clothing designed on the reality fashion competition show. After the challenge to create an outfit for My Scene Barbie, the Bravo.com site sold out of the 3,300 dolls wearing the winning design creation.[31]

As the popularity of online retailing grows, it is becoming critical that retailers be online and that their stores, Web sites, and catalogs be closely integrated. Customers expect to find the same brands, products, and prices whether they purchase online, on the phone, or in a store. Therefore, retailers are increasingly using in-store kiosks to help tie the channels together for greater customer service. Retailer and cataloger Williams-Sonoma, for example, has linked its store gift registry to its Web site, allowing brides to see who has bought what in real time. Banana Republic stores in New York and Santa Monica, California, have kiosks so customers can order items that aren't on the shelves. Kiosks are even more popular among retailers that target younger, more environmentally conscious customers. For example, ecoATM e-cycling stations allow consumers in shopping malls to trade in used electronic devices such as smartphones and iPods for cash and credits that can be used to purchase new items at nearby stores. The kiosks visually and electronically scan the used items, establish return prices, and pay the consumer for their device on the spot. The reclaimed items are then sold in secondary markets worldwide, or if their condition dictates, are responsibly recycled to reclaim the basic materials.[32]

Online auctions run by Internet companies such as eBay and Amazon.com have enjoyed phenomenal success in recent years. With more than two million items for sale each day, ranging from antique clocks to car stereos, eBay is the leader in cyberspace auctions. Internet auction services such as eBay run the Web service and collect a listing fee, plus a commission of 1 to 5 percent when a sale is completed. They also host auctions for other companies. For example, eBay and Sotheby's have a joint venture that offers fine art, rare coins, sports collectibles, jewelry, and antiques online. Each item carries a stamp of authenticity from Sotheby's or one of the 2,800 art and antiques dealers worldwide who have signed exclusive agreements with Sotheby's. The joint venture supports eBay's fine arts and antiques division and enables Sotheby's to offer online sales without the overhead expense of managing its own site.[33]

MOBILE RETAILING/M-COMMERCE

M-commerce (mobile e-commerce) involves consumers using wireless mobile devices to connect to the Internet and shop. Essentially, m-commerce goes beyond text message advertisements to enable consumers to purchase goods and services by using wireless mobile devices, such as mobile telephones and handheld computers. For example, both PepsiCo and Coca-Cola have developed smart vending technologies that utilize a "cashless" payment system that accepts credit cards, RFID devices, and even hotel room keys. Offices across the country are installing self-serve coffee machines where office workers can buy freshly brewed single-cup gourmet coffee and conveniently pay with their traditional magnetic stripe credit or debit cards. The company AIR-serv plans to install thousands of cashless transaction terminals in its coin-operated tire inflation and vacuuming machines at gas stations and convenience stores. Cashless services are also available for the vending industry, laundry facilities, parking and toll booths, photo and video kiosks, hotel business centers, and a variety of other commercial markets.[34] M-commerce enjoyed

early success overseas, but has been slower in gaining acceptance and popularity in the United States. For instance, Japan has over 95 million wireless subscribers and there are more than 200 million in the United States. But about $480 million in revenue was generated by about 7 million U.S. m-commerce users compared to Japan's 27 million m-commerce users generating only $10 billion in sales.[35]

M-commerce users adopt the new technology because it saves time and offers more convenience in a greater number of locations. Vending machines have become an important venue for m-commerce. More than 75 million Americans subscribe to mobile Internet providers to search, e-mail, and check weather and sports. Even so, the United States is an immature market compared to Japan and Western Europe.

An emerging alternative format for M-commerce comes through dedicated wireless applications that can be downloaded to a consumer's smartphone or wireless computer device. Retailers such as Barnes & Noble and Tesco, as well as virtual markets such as eBay, have developed a virtual storefront that users can tap on their devices that allows immediate, format-friendly shopping to take place in the palm of the consumer's hand. Customers can order and pay for goods directly from their handsets, using seamless connections between the retailer, package carrier, and financial institutions. In addition, meta-level applications have been developed that search other applications and Web sites quickly in real time to find the best deals within a product category. For example, Kayak's innovative application compares and combines prices and products from hundreds of travel sites simultaneously, and presents users with a single sortable listing of options for any given trip, saving users time and money.[36]

An additional element of rapidly developing M-commerce is the inclusion of social media within the retail buying experience by both traditional and online retailers. Stores such as Whole Foods are using Twitter to keep customers updated on recently added items, shipments of goods that come in, and changing product details. Similarly, Amazon.com has developed a smartphone application that fully interacts with customers' Facebook accounts, placing interesting books (based on the customer's profile) on a virtual bookshelf on their profile page. In this way, friends of customers can instantaneously see what their friends are reading or want to read, and can tap the bookshelf to place an order through the use of another application, ShopIgniter, which both processes payments and gives incentive for future purchases through electronic coupons.[37] The m-commerce category is evolving rapidly—even industry experts do not really know what will happen next.

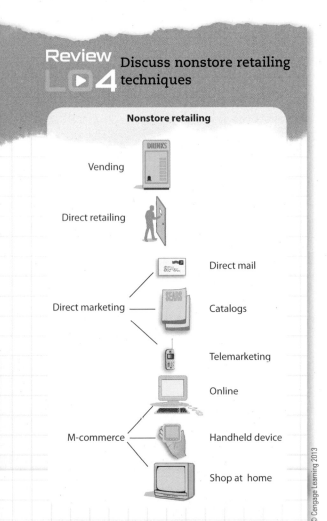

Review
LO4 Discuss nonstore retailing techniques

Nonstore retailing

Vending

Direct retailing

Direct marketing — Direct mail

Catalogs

Telemarketing

Online

M-commerce — Handheld device

Shop at home

---

franchisor
The originator of a trade name, product, methods of operation, and so on, that grants operating rights to another party to sell its product.

franchisee
An individual or business that is granted the right to sell another party's product.

LO5
Franchising

A *franchise* is a continuing relationship in which a franchisor grants to a franchisee the business rights to operate or to sell a product. The **franchisor** originates the trade name, product, methods of operation, and so on. The **franchisee**, in return, pays the franchisor for the right to use its name, product, or business methods.

A franchise agreement between the two parties usually lasts for 10 to 20 years, at which time it can be renewed if both parties are agreeable.

To be granted the rights to a franchise, a franchisee usually pays an initial, one-time franchise fee. The amount of this fee depends solely on the individual franchisor, but it generally ranges from $50,000 to $250,000 or higher. In addition to this initial franchise fee, the franchisee is expected to pay royalty fees, usually in the range of 3 to 7 percent of gross revenues, but occasionally as high as 12 percent or more. The franchisee might also be expected to pay advertising fees, which usually cover the cost of promotional materials and, if the franchise organization is large enough, regional or national advertising. A McDonald's franchise, for example, costs an initial $45,000 franchise fee. The franchisee must make a down payment of 40 percent of the total cost of a new restaurant or 25 percent of the total cost of an existing restaurant plus a monthly fee based on the restaurant's sales performance and base rent. In addition, a new McDonald's franchisee can expect start-up costs for equipment and preopening expenses to range from $506,000 to $1.6 million, for a total investment of up to roughly $1.8 million for a new store.[38] The size of the restaurant facility, area of the country, inventory, selection of kitchen equipment, signage, and style of décor and landscaping affect new restaurant costs. Though the dollar amount will vary depending on the type of franchise, fees such as these are typical for all major franchisors, including Burger King, Jani-King, Athlete's Foot, Sonic, and Subway.

Franchising is not new. General Motors has used this approach since 1898, and Rexall drugstores since 1901. Today, there are over half a million franchised establishments in the United States, with combined sales approaching $1.5 trillion, or about 40 percent of all retail trade. Although franchised restaurants attract most of those dollars, hundreds of retail and service franchises, such as Alphagraphics print shops, Supercuts, and Sylvan Learning Systems, also are thriving. Indeed, there are over 320,000 franchises in 75 industries.[39] Industries expected to see real growth in franchising include home repair, business support services, automotive repairs, hair salons, children's services, and telecommunications. Exhibit 15.3 lists some Web sites that provide information about franchises. Exhibit 15.4 lists some facts about some of the largest and best-known U.S. franchisors.

Two basic forms of franchises are used today: product and trade name franchising and business format franchising. In *product and trade name franchising*, a dealer agrees to sell certain products provided by a manufacturer or a wholesaler. This approach has been used most widely in the auto and truck, soft-drink bottling, tire, and gasoline service industries. For example, a local tire retailer might hold a franchise to sell Michelin tires. Likewise, the Coca-Cola bottler in a particular area is a product and trade name franchisee licensed to bottle and sell Coca-Cola's soft drinks.

Exhibit 15.3 Sources of Franchise Information

Some Web Sites Where People with Franchising-Related Questions Can Find Answers:

- **Federal Trade Commission (http://www.ftc.gov)** Has a host of information consumers looking to buy a franchise might need. Click on the "Franchise & Business Opportunities" link. Contains information on FTC regulation as well as contact information for state regulators.
- **North American Securities Administrators Association (http://www.nasaa.org)** The umbrella group for state securities regulators offers links to find regulators and also has links to other governmental agencies.
- **International Franchise Association (http://www.franchise.org)** Contains information on such topics as buying a franchise and government relations. The site's FAQ section deals with some issues of franchise regulation.
- **American Franchisee Association (http://www.franchisee.org)** Represents franchisees and has information on legal resources, FTC regulations, and state law.
- **American Association of Franchisees & Dealers (http://www.aafd.org)** Offers legal and financial information.

EXHIBIT 15.4 Top U.S. Franchisors

Rank	Franchise	Type of Business	Initial Investment
1	Subway	Submarine sandwiches & salads	$84,300–258,300
2	McDonald's	Hamburgers, chicken, salads	$950,200–1,800,000
3	7-Eleven Inc.	Convenience store	$40,500–775,300
4	Hampton Hotels	Mid-price hotels	$3,716,000–13,148,800
5	Supercuts	Hair salon	$112,600–243,200
6	H&R Block	Tax preparation	$26,427–84,904
7	Dunkin' Donuts	Coffee, doughnuts, baked goods	$537,750–1,765,300
8	Jani-King	Commercial cleaning	$13,200–93,200
9	Servpro	Insurance/disaster restoration	$127,300–174,700
10	ampm	Convenience store and gas stations	$1,835,823–7,615,065
11	Jan-Pro Franchising Int'l Inc.	Commercial cleaning	$3,300–54,300
12	Kumon Math & Reading Centers	Supplemental education	$36,528–145,250
13	Stratus Building Solutions	Commercial cleaning	$3,450–57,750
14	Miracle-Ear Inc.	Hearing instruments	$122,500–570,000
15	Pizza Hut Inc.	Pizza, pasta, wings	$302,000–2,100,000
16	Hardee's	Burgers, chicken, biscuits	$1,182,000–1,583,000
17	Denny's Inc.	Full-service family restaurants	$1,200,000–2,600,000
18	Jazzercise Inc.	Dance fitness classes	$2,980–38,400
19	Matco Tools	Mechanics' tools and service equipment	$79,826–188,556
20	UPS Store/Mailboxes Etc.	Postal, business, and communications services	$150,980–337,950
21	Days Inn	Hotels	$192,300–6,500,000
22	Sonic Drive In Restaurants	Drive-in restaurants	$1,200,000–3,200,000
23	Midas	Auto repair and maintenance	$323,000–418,880
24	KFC Corp.	Chicken	$1,379,900–2,422,000
25	Circle K	Convenience stores	$171,000–1,403,000
26	Papa John's Int'l Inc.	Pizza	$113,823–528,123
27	InterContinental Hotels Group	Hotels	$5,136,370–93,855,035
28	Liberty Tax Service	Income-tax Preparation	$46,000–69,900
29	Instant Tax Service	Retail tax preparation and electronic filing	$39,000–89,000
30	Vanguard Cleaning Systems	Commercial cleaning	$8,200–38,100

Source: "2010 Franchise 500 Rankings," http://www.entrepreneur.com/franchises/rankings/franchise500-115608/2010,-1.html, accessed August 2010.

Business format franchising is an ongoing business relationship between a franchisor and a franchisee. Typically, a franchisor "sells" a franchisee the rights to use the franchisor's format or approach to doing business. This form of franchising has rapidly expanded through retailing, restaurant, food-service, hotel and motel, printing, and real estate franchises. Fast-food restaurants such as McDonald's, Wendy's, and Burger King use this kind of franchising, as do other companies such as Hyatt Corporation and ExxonMobil Corporation. To be eligible to be a Domino's Pizza franchisee, you must have worked in a Domino's pizza store for at least one year. The company believes that after working in an existing location, you will have a better understanding of the company and its values and standards. Then potential franchisees must participate in a series of career development, franchise orientation, presentation skills, and franchise development programs.

Like other retailers, franchisors are seeking new growth abroad. Hundreds of U.S. franchisors have begun international expansion and are actively looking for foreign franchisees to open new locations. KFC serves nearly 12 million customers daily at its more than 15,000 restaurants in over 109 countries and territories around the world, including Australia, China, Indonesia, Japan, and Saudi Arabia. KFC's parent company, Yum! Brands, Inc., the world's largest restaurant system, attributes the franchise's success to its ability to adapt to local cultures and tastes without losing control of quality and brand image.[40] The International Franchise Association includes over 100 franchise organizations in countries from Argentina to Zimbabwe.

Franchisors usually allow franchisees to alter their business format slightly in foreign markets. For example, some McDonald's franchisees in Germany sell beer, and in Japan they offer food items that appeal to Japanese tastes, such as steamed dumplings, curry with rice, and roast pork cutlet burgers with melted cheese. McDonald's franchisees in India serve mutton instead of beef because most Indians are Hindu, a religion whose followers believe cows are a sacred symbol of the source of life. The menu also features rice-based Vegetable Burgers made with peas, carrots, red pepper, beans, and Indian spices as well as Vegetable McNuggets. But, in spite of menu differences, McDonald's foreign franchisees still maintain the company's standards of service and cleanliness.

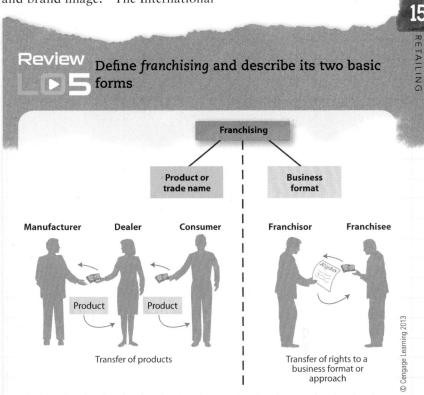

Review LO5 Define *franchising* and describe its two basic forms

LO6
Retail Marketing Strategy

Retailers must develop marketing strategies based on overall goals and strategic plans. Retailing goals might include more traffic, higher sales of a specific item, a more upscale image, or heightened public awareness of the retail operation. The strategies that retailers use to obtain their goals might include a sale, an updated décor, or a new advertisement. The key tasks in strategic retailing are defining and selecting a target market and developing the retailing mix to successfully meet the needs of the chosen target market.

DEFINING A TARGET MARKET

The first and foremost task in developing a retail strategy is to define the target market. This process begins with market segmentation, the topic of Chapter 8. Successful retailing has always been based on knowing the customer. Sometimes retailing chains flounder when management loses sight of the customers the stores should be serving.

Target markets in retailing are often defined by demographics, geographics, and psychographics. For instance, Sportsgirl, a casual fashion e-tailer in Australia, targets young women from their teens to thirties who have a higher-than-average income, read fashion magazines, and favor high-end designers. By understanding who its customers are, the company has been able design a Web site and mobile application that instantaneously sends images of clothing customers are

Exhibit 15.5 **The Retailing Mix**

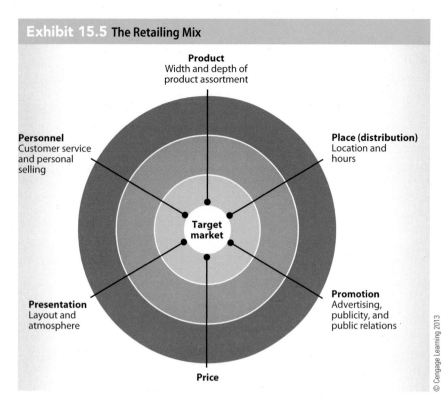

Product
Width and depth of
product assortment

Place (distribution)
Location and
hours

Promotion
Advertising,
publicity, and
public relations

Price

Presentation
Layout and
atmosphere

Personnel
Customer service
and personal
selling

Target
market

© Cengage Learning 2013

considering to their friends' mobile devices for input, opinion, or approval before the customer makes the final purchase.[41] Determining a target market is a prerequisite to creating the retailing mix. For example, Target's merchandising approach for sporting goods is to match its product assortment to the demographics of the local store and region. The amount of space devoted to sporting goods, as well as in-store promotions, also varies according to each store's target market.

CHOOSING THE RETAILING MIX

Retailers combine the elements of the retailing mix to come up with a single retailing method to attract the target market. The **retailing mix** consists of six Ps: the four Ps of the marketing mix (product, place, promotion, and price) plus presentation and personnel. (See Exhibit 15.5.)

The combination of the six Ps projects a store's image, which influences consumers' perceptions. Using these impressions of stores, shoppers position one store against another. A retail marketing manager must make sure that the store's positioning is compatible with the target customers' expectations. As discussed at the beginning of the chapter, retail stores can be positioned on three broad dimensions: service provided by store personnel, product assortment, and price. Management should use everything else—place, presentation, and promotion—to fine-tune the basic positioning of the store.

The Product Offering   The first element in the retailing mix is the **product offering**, also called the *product assortment* or *merchandise mix*. Retailers decide what to sell on the basis of what their target market wants to buy. They can base their decision on market research, past sales, fashion trends, customer requests, and other sources. A recent approach, called data mining, uses complex mathematical models to help retailers make better product mix decisions. Early users of the approach, such as Dillard's, Target, and Walmart, use data mining to determine which products to stock at what price, how to manage markdowns, and how to advertise to draw target customers.

Developing a product offering is essentially a question of the width and depth of the product assortment. *Width* refers to the assortment of products offered; *depth* refers to the number of different brands offered within each assortment. Price, store design, displays, and service are important to consumers in determining where to shop, but the most critical factor is merchandise selection. For example, Target expanded its width by introducing a new line of eco-friendly women's clothing, with the fabrics used made of 100 percent certified organic fiber.[42] This reasoning also holds true for online retailers. Amazon.com, for instance, is building the world's biggest online department store so that shoppers can get whatever they want with one click on their Web browsers. Like

retailing mix
A combination of the six Ps—product, place, promotion, price, presentation, and personnel—to sell goods and services to the ultimate consumer.

product offering
The mix of products offered to the consumer by the retailer; also called the product assortment or merchandise mix.

a traditional department store or mass merchandiser, Amazon offers considerable width in its product assortment with millions of different items, including books, music, toys, videos, tools and hardware, health and beauty aids, electronics, and software. Conversely, online specialty retailers, such as 1-800-Flowers.com, Gloss.com (makeup), and Polo.com (clothing), focus on a single category of merchandise, hoping to attract loyal customers with a larger depth of products at lower prices and better customer service. Many online retailers purposely focus on single product line niches that could never garner enough foot traffic to support a traditional brick-and-mortar store.

After determining what products will satisfy target customers' desires, retailers must find sources of supply and evaluate the products. When the right products are found, the retail buyer negotiates a purchase contract. The buying function can either be performed in-house or be delegated to an outside firm. The goods must then be moved from the seller to the retailer, which means shipping, storing, and stocking the inventory. The trick is to manage the inventory by cutting prices to move slow goods and by keeping adequate supplies of hot-selling items in stock. As in all good systems, the final step is to evaluate the entire process to seek more efficient methods and eliminate problems and bottlenecks.

As margins drop and competition intensifies, retailers are becoming ever more aware of the advantages of *private brands,* or those brands that are designed and developed using the retailer's name. Because the cost of goods typically makes up between 60 and 75 percent of a retailer's expenses, eliminating intermediaries can shave costs. As a result, prices of private-label goods are typically lower than for national brands, giving customers greater value. Private-label branding is not new. For decades, Sears has fashioned its Kenmore, Craftsman, and DieHard brands into household names. Walmart has several successful private-label brands such as White Cloud paper products, Spring Valley nutritional supplements, Sam's American Choice laundry detergent, EverActive alkaline batteries, and EverStart auto batteries. Its Ol' Roy dog food and Sam's American Choice garden fertilizer are now the best-selling brands in their categories.

Promotion Strategy Retail promotion strategy includes advertising, public relations and publicity, and sales promotion. The goal is to help position the store in consumers' minds. Retailers design intriguing ads, stage special events, and develop promotions aimed at their target markets. Today's grand openings are a carefully orchestrated blend of advertising, merchandising, goodwill, and glitter. All the elements of an opening—press coverage, special events, media advertising, and store displays—are carefully planned. For example, when Victoria's Secret opened its megastore in Dallas, the opening featured a $150 gift with a $50 purchase, free makeovers from a Victoria's Secret Fashion Show makeup artist, $10 gift cards that could be redeemed in the store, and an appearance by supermodel Heidi Klum.

Retailers' advertising is carried out mostly at the local level. Local advertising by retailers

Heidi Klum and other Victoria's Secret models celebrate at an opening ceremony for a New York store.

usually provides specific information about their stores, such as location, merchandise, hours, prices, and special sales. In contrast, national retail advertising generally focuses on image. For example, Target has used its "sign of the times" advertising campaign to effectively position itself as the "chic place to buy cheap."

Target's advertising campaign also takes advantage of cooperative advertising, another popular retail advertising practice. Traditionally, marketers would pay retailers to feature their products in store mailers, or a marketer would develop a TV campaign for the product and simply tack on several retailers' names at the end. But Target's advertising makes use of a more collaborative trend by integrating products such as Tide laundry detergent, Tums antacids, or Coca-Cola into the actual campaign. Another common form of cooperative advertising involves promotion of exclusive products. For example, Target hires famous designers to develop reasonably priced product lines available exclusively at Target stores.

Many retailers are forgoing media advertising these days in favor of direct-mail or frequent shopper programs. Direct-mail and catalog programs are luring many retailers, which hope they will prove to be a cost-effective means of increasing brand loyalty and spending by core customers. Nordstrom, for example, mails catalogs featuring brand-name and private-brand clothing, shoes, and accessories to target the shop-at-home crowd. Restaurants and small retailers have successfully used frequent diner or frequent shopper programs for years. For example, customers with a Victoria's Secret Angel credit card are offered monthly specials on store merchandise, including items that generally are not put on sale to the public.

The Proper Location The retailing axiom "location, location, location" has long emphasized the importance of place to the retail mix. The location decision is important first because the retailer is making a large, semipermanent commitment of resources that can reduce its future flexibility. Second, the location will affect the store's future growth and profitability.

Site location begins by choosing a community. Important factors to consider are the area's economic growth potential, the amount of competition, and geography. For instance, retailers such as T.J. Maxx, Walmart, and Target build stores in areas where the population is growing. Often these large retailers will build stores in new communities that are still under development. On the other hand, while population growth is an important consideration for fast-food restaurants, most also look for an area with other fast-food restaurants because being located in clusters helps to draw customers for each restaurant. However, even after careful research the perfect position can be elusive in the face of changing markets. For example, Wendy's found when attempting to enter the competitive breakfast business that its locations weren't positioned on the right side of the road to attract the bulk of commuters looking for breakfast. Finally, for many retailers geography remains the most important factor in choosing a community. For example, Starbucks coffee looks for densely populated urban communities for its stores, Talbots looks for locations near upper-class neighborhoods, and Buckle stores look for locations in small, underserved cities.

After settling on a geographic region or community, retailers must choose a specific site. In addition to growth potential, the important factors are neighborhood socioeconomic characteristics, traffic flows, land costs, zoning regulations, and public transportation. A particular site's visibility, parking, entrance and exit locations, accessibility, and safety and security are also considered. Additionally, a retailer should consider how its store would fit into the surrounding environment. Retail decision makers probably would not locate a Dollar General store next door to a Neiman Marcus department store.

global perspectives

Walmart's New Adventure: Moving into India

Though Walmart is indisputably the most successful retailer in world history, it has not flourished in every worldwide venture it has attempted. The company's initial attempt to establish a presence in Argentina floundered due to slow sales, culminating in 4 percent market share in the second largest South American market. Likewise, when Walmart tried to stake its claim in Mexico, customers reacted very slowly at first because the retailer did not understand how Mexican consumers shop. The company built American-style parking lots outside the store, and sold upscale items such as golf balls inside. Mexican customers arrived in buses, looking for necessities such as food and clothing. A third venture, the opening of several stores in Germany, was an absolute failure. Competitors Aldi and Metro already had strong footholds there; Walmart was unable to shake them, and left the German market entirely after losing over a billion dollars.[43]

Given these problems, it was understandable that the giant retailer's recent attempt to enter India, one of the world's largest and most complex retail marketplaces, was met by both surprise and skepticism by employees, customers, and shareholders alike. Retailer entry into India is different from many other world markets in that foreign businesses are subject to very strict regulations regarding who can sell goods and services directly to the public. Foreign companies might invest only in single-brand stores, and can own only a 51 percent stake in the retailer they support. The laws are designed to protect the thousands of small merchants, known as kirana, that line the streets of most cities and villages across the country.

Walmart was initially flummoxed by the strict Indian regulations, until a relatively new member of its executive team had the bright idea of entering the nation as a supplier to the kirana—that is, as a cash-and-carry wholesaler. Though the company had effectively dabbled in wholesaling through its Sam's Club stores in North America, where corporate as well as individual memberships were welcomed, it had never owned and operated businesses that had as their sole purpose serving as a supplier to other retailers. By setting up as a wholesaler in a small city in northern India, Walmart was able to circumvent the strict regulations that impact foreign retail entrants.

The results thus far have been hard to interpret, but many Walmart stakeholders believe there is reason for optimism. Where many of the kirana had been dealing with over 100 suppliers each, now the shopkeepers could buy most of their wares for public sale at a single Walmart store. Walmart has worked hard to maintain their loyalty, in part by sourcing its produce and meat supplies from local Indian suppliers.[44] Walmart's wholesale locations in India operate with far fewer stock units and much narrower variety than its retail stores in other countries, allowing it to offer much lower prices than other Indian wholesalers and many raw commodity providers. In doing so, it has provided several thousand safe, good-paying jobs to Indian citizens. Still, there are many critics that expect an eventual backlash, as it becomes clearer that Walmart is now putting small Indian suppliers out of business.

What do you think? Was Walmart's venture into the Indian subcontinent a wise maneuver that will ultimately strengthen its worldwide brand? Or is moving into the wholesaling business too much of a risky maneuver? Will operating as a wholesaler damage or augment's the store's worldwide recognition? Why or why not?

Retailers face one final decision about location: whether to have a freestanding unit or become a tenant in a shopping center or mall.

Freestanding Stores An isolated, freestanding location can be used by large retailers such as Walmart or Target and sellers of shopping goods such as furniture and cars because they are "destination" stores. **Destination stores** are stores consumers seek out and purposely plan to visit. An isolated store location might have the advantages of low site cost or rent and no nearby competitors. On the other hand, it might be hard to attract customers to a freestanding location, and no other retailers are around to share costs.

destination stores
Stores that consumers purposely plan to visit.

Freestanding units are increasing in popularity as retailers strive to make their stores more convenient to access, more enticing to shop, and more profitable. Freestanding sites now account for more than half of all retail construction in the United States as more and more retailers are deciding not to locate in pedestrian malls. Perhaps the greatest reason for developing a freestanding site is greater visibility. Retailers often feel they get lost in huge centers and malls, but freestanding units can help stores develop an identity with shoppers. The ability to grow at faster rates through freestanding buildings has also propelled the surge toward stand-alone units. Retailers such as The Sports Authority, Best Buy, and Bed Bath & Beyond choose to be freestanding to achieve their expansion objectives. An aggressive expansion plan might not allow time to wait for shopping centers to be built. Similarly, drugstore chains such as Walgreens and Rite Aid have been aggressively relocating their existing mall and shopping center stores to freestanding sites, especially street corner sites for drive-through accessibility.

Shopping Centers Shopping centers began in the 1950s when the U.S. population started migrating to the suburbs. The first shopping centers were *strip centers,* typically located along busy streets. They usually included a supermarket, a variety store, and perhaps a few specialty stores. Then *community shopping centers* emerged, with one or two small department stores, more specialty stores, a couple of restaurants, and several apparel stores. These community shopping centers provided off-street parking and a broader variety of merchandise.

Regional malls offering a much wider variety of merchandise started appearing in the mid-1970s. Regional malls are either entirely enclosed or roofed to allow shopping in any weather. Most are landscaped with trees, fountains, sculptures, and the like to enhance the shopping environment. They have acres of free parking. The *anchor stores* or *generator stores* (JCPenney, Sears, or major department stores) are usually located at opposite ends of the mall to create heavy foot traffic. Las Vegas's Fashion Show Mall takes the concept to the extreme. The mall has 2 million square feet of retail space and boasts over 250 stores, 8 of which are anchor stores, including Neiman Marcus, Saks Fifth Avenue, Macy's, Bloomingdale Home, and Nordstrom. Mall of America goes even further, with 2.5 million square feet of retail space and over 520 stores.

According to shopping center developers, the newest generation of shopping center is the *lifestyle center.* These new open-air shopping centers are targeted to upper-income shoppers with an aversion for "the mall" and seek to create an atmosphere that is part neighborhood park and part urban shopping center. Lifestyle centers typically combine outdoor shopping areas composed of upscale retailers and restaurants, with plazas, fountains, and pedestrian streets. Newer centers like the Easton Town Center in Columbus, Ohio, and the Legacy Town Center in Plano, Texas, also include luxury apartments and condominiums. Lifestyle centers are appealing to retail developers looking for an alternative to the traditional shopping mall, a concept rapidly losing favor among shoppers. Consumers have also become more pressed for time in recent years and are choosing more convenient stand-alone stores and neighborhood centers instead of malls. And recently, outlet malls are enjoying a sort of resurgence, with many retailers stepping up their outlet offerings in order to capture a greater share of retail dollars. This is true even for upscale retailers such as Neiman Marcus, whose NM Last Call is planning on adding two new locations in the near future.[45] Faced with this trend, mall developers have improved the layout of many malls to make it more convenient for customers to shop. For instance, the RiverTown Crossings center in Grandville, Michigan, clusters competing stores, such as Abercrombie Kids, GapKids, Gymboree, and

Exhibit 15.6	Advantages and Disadvantages of Locating in a Community Shopping Center or Regional Mall	
Advantages	**Disadvantages**
Facilities present a unified image and are designed to attract shoppers	Leases are expensive
Tenants share the expenses of the mall's common area and promotions for the whole mall	Common promotion efforts might not attract customers to a particular store
The shopping environment, anchor stores, and "village square" activities draw customers	Anchor stores dominate the tenants' association
Malls can target different demographic groups, such as upscale or bargain shoppers	Possibility exists of having direct competitors within the same facility
Ample parking is available	Lease restrictions on merchandise carried and hours of operation exist

other kids' clothing stores in one section of the mall to accommodate time-strapped parents. Locating in a community shopping center or regional mall offers several advantages and disadvantages, as shown in Exhibit 15.6.

Retail Prices Another important element in the retailing mix is price. Retailing's ultimate goal is to sell products to consumers, and the right price is critical in ensuring sales. Because retail prices are usually based on the cost of the merchandise, an essential part of pricing is efficient and timely buying.

Price is also a key element in a retail store's positioning strategy. Higher prices often indicate a level of quality and help reinforce the prestigious image of retailers, such as Tiffany, Saks Fifth Avenue, Gucci, Cartier, and Neiman Marcus. On the other hand, discounters and off-price retailers, such as Target and T.J. Maxx, offer good value for the money. There are even stores, such as Dollar Tree, where everything costs one dollar. Dollar Tree's single-price-point strategy is aimed at getting customers to make impulse purchases through what analysts call the "wow factor"—the excitement of discovering that an item costs only a dollar.

A pricing trend among American retailers that seems to be here to stay is *everyday low pricing,* or EDLP. Introduced to the retail industry by Walmart, EDLP offers consumers a low price all the time rather than holding periodic sales on merchandise. Even large retail giants such as Macy's have phased out deep discounts and sales in favor of lower prices every day. Similarly, Gap reduced prices on denim jeans, denim shirts, socks, and other items to protect and broaden the company's share of the casual clothes market. Supermarkets such as Albertsons and Winn-Dixie have also found success in EDLP.

Presentation of the Retail Store The presentation of a retail store helps determine the store's image and positions the retail store in consumers' minds. For instance, a retailer that wants to position itself as an upscale store would use a lavish or sophisticated presentation.

The main element of a store's presentation is its **atmosphere**, the overall impression conveyed by a store's physical layout, décor, and surroundings. The atmosphere might create a relaxed or busy feeling, a sense of luxury or of efficiency, a friendly or cold attitude, a sense of organization or of clutter, or a fun or serious mood. For example, Wolfgang Puck restaurants feature tiles in the shape of a pizza on the floors, walls, and countertops. Urban Outfitters stores, targeted to Generation Y consumers, use raw concrete, original brick, rusted steel, and unfinished wood to convey an urban feel. Likewise, REI sporting-goods stores feature indoor rock-climbing walls, bike test trails, and rain rooms for testing outdoor gear. Apple stores across the world strive for an understated, uncluttered environment with only one or a few units of each item on display and featuring "solution zones" where customers get a hands-on

atmosphere
The overall impression conveyed by a store's physical layout, décor, and surroundings.

Target's partnership with Liberty of London kicked off with a creatively stunning pop-up shop in New York City. The lighting and whimsical displays gave off a romantic, fairy tale atmosphere.

© Andrew H. Walker/Getty Images for Target

guided use of the product before buying, in order to create a sense of simple sophistication that matches its customers' self-concept, and reinforce the idea that each Apple customer receives highly personalized attention.[46]

The layout of retail stores is a key factor in their success. The goal is to use all space in the store effectively, including aisles, fixtures, merchandise displays, and nonselling areas. In addition to making shopping easy and convenient for the customer, an effective layout has a powerful influence on customer traffic patterns and purchasing behavior. For instance, Kohl's unique circular layout encourages customers to pass all of a store's departments to reach the checkout lanes. The stores are smaller than most department stores but have a wide aisle with plenty of room for customers and shopping carts. Each department is limited to five display racks on the main aisle. Displays are spaced widely and are set at varying heights so that customers can see everything in the department, including wall displays, from the main aisle. To further enhance the store's clean crisp presentation, merchandise is displayed from light to dark, which research suggests is most pleasing to the eye. Finally, to encourage last-minute, impulse purchases, Kohl's displays low-cost items at the checkout register. Together with other merchandising strategies, the store layout generates an average of over $300 in sales per square foot (a standard industry measure) in Kohl's over 1,000 stores in 49 states.[47]

Layout also includes where products are placed in the store. Many technologically advanced retailers are using a technique called *market-basket analysis* to analyze the huge amounts of data collected through their point-of-purchase scanning equipment. The analysis looks for products that are commonly purchased together to help retailers place products in the right places. Walmart uses market-basket analysis to determine where in the store to stock products for customer convenience.[48] In a typical Walmart Supercenter, bananas are placed not only in the produce section but also in the cereal aisle. Kleenex tissues are in the paper-goods aisle and also mixed in with the cold medicines. Measuring spoons are in the housewares and also hanging next to Crisco shortening. During October, flashlights are with the Halloween costumes as well as in the hardware aisle.

These are the most influential factors in creating a store's atmosphere:

→ **Employee type and density:** Employee type refers to an employee's general characteristics—for instance, neat, friendly, knowledgeable, or service-oriented. Density is the number of employees per thousand square feet of selling space. A discounter like Kmart has a low employee density that creates a "do-it-yourself," casual atmosphere. In contrast, Neiman Marcus's density is much higher, denoting readiness to serve the customer's every whim. Too many employees and not enough customers, however, can convey an air of desperation and intimidate customers.

→ **Merchandise type and density:** The type of merchandise carried and how it is displayed add to the atmosphere the retailer is trying to create. A prestigious retailer such as Saks or Bloomingdale's carries the best brand names and displays them in a neat, uncluttered arrangement. Discounters and off-price retailers, such as Marshalls and T.J. Maxx, might sell some well-known brands, but many carry seconds or out-of-season goods. Their merchandise is crowded into small spaces and hung on long racks by category—tops, pants, skirts, etc.—to create the impression that "We've got so much stuff, we're practically giving it away."

→ **Fixture type and density:** Fixtures can be elegant (rich woods), trendy (chrome and smoked glass), or consist of old, beat-up tables, as in an antiques store. The fixtures should be consistent with the general atmosphere the store is trying to create. Apple has let its focus on design inform the look of its retail stores. Many Apple stores contain a signature glass staircase designed in part by the late CEO Steve Jobs, and all use large open tables to display company products. Because products are not cluttered on store shelves, it is easier for store visitors to play with them.[49]

→ **Sound:** Sound can be pleasant or unpleasant for a customer. Classical music at a nice Italian restaurant helps create ambience, just as country-and-western music does at a truck stop. Music can also entice customers to stay in the store longer and buy more or eat quickly and leave a table for others. For instance, rapid music tends to make people eat more, chew less, and take bigger bites, whereas slow music prompts people to dine more leisurely and eat less. Retailers can tailor their musical atmosphere to their shoppers' demographics and the merchandise they're selling. Music can control the pace of the store traffic, create an image, and attract or direct the shopper's attention. Starbucks has parlayed its unique in-store music selections into a new business with its Hear Music Cafés and kiosks selling featured Hear Music artists in most Starbucks locations.

→ **Odors:** Smell can either stimulate or detract from sales. The wonderful smell of pastries and breads entices bakery customers. Conversely, customers can be repulsed by bad odors such as cigarette smoke, musty smells, antiseptic odors, and overly powerful room deodorizers. If a grocery store pumps in the smell of baked goods, sales in that department increase threefold. Department stores have pumped in fragrances that are pleasing to their target market, and the response has been favorable. Not surprisingly, retailers are increasingly using fragrance as a key design element, as important as layout, lighting, and background music. Research suggests that people evaluate merchandise more positively, spend more time shopping, and are generally in a better mood when an agreeable odor is present. Retailers use fragrances as an extension of their retail strategy.

→ **Visual factors:** Colors can create a mood or focus attention and therefore are an important factor in atmosphere. Red, yellow, and orange are considered warm colors and are used when a feeling of warmth and closeness is desired. Cool colors like blue, green, and violet are used to open up closed-in places and create an air of elegance and cleanliness. For example, Starbucks uses an eggplant, golden yellow, and dark olive color combination so that customers will feel comfortable yet sophisticated. Some colors are better for display. For instance, diamonds appear most striking against black or dark blue velvet. Lighting can also have an important effect on store atmosphere. Jewelry is best displayed under high-intensity spotlights and cosmetics under more natural lighting. Many retailers have found that natural lighting, either from windows or skylights, can lead to increased sales. Outdoor lighting can also affect consumer patronage. Consumers often are afraid to shop after dark in many areas and prefer strong lighting for safety. The outdoor facade of the store also adds to its ambience and helps create favorable first impressions.

Personnel and Customer Service People are a unique aspect of retailing. Most retail sales involve a customer–salesperson relationship, if only briefly. When customers shop at a grocery store, the cashiers check and bag their groceries. When customers shop at a prestigious clothier, the salesclerks might help select the styles, sizes, and colors. They may also assist in the fitting process, offer alteration services, wrap purchases, and even offer a glass of champagne. Sales personnel provide their customers with the amount of service prescribed in the retail strategy of the store.

Retail salespeople serve another important selling function: They persuade shoppers to buy. They must therefore be able to persuade customers that what they are selling is what the customer needs. Salespeople are trained in two common selling techniques: trading up and suggestion selling. Trading up means persuading customers to buy a higher-priced item than they originally intended to buy. To avoid selling customers something they do not need or want, however, salespeople should take care when practicing trading-up techniques. Suggestion selling, a common practice among most retailers, seeks to broaden customers' original purchases with related items. For example, if you buy a new printer at Office Depot, the sales representative will ask if you would like to purchase paper, a USB cable, and/or extra ink cartridges. Similarly, McDonald's cashiers are trained to ask customers if they would like a hot apple pie with their meal. Suggestion selling by sales or service associates should always help shoppers recognize true needs rather than sell them unwanted merchandise. Recently, this responsibility has been extended to retail managers as well; recent research indicates that retail managers' willingness to exert effort toward sales, sales planning activities, and creating a selling-friendly environment by clarifying sales goals and methods, significantly impacts revenues above and beyond the efforts of the sales staff alone.[50]

Providing great customer service is one of the most challenging elements in the retail mix because customer expectations change. In the past, shoppers wanted personal one-on-one attention. Today, many customers are happy to help themselves as long as they can easily find what they need. To respond to this new perspective, some retailers are adding retail sales technologies that maximize salesperson helpfulness while minimizing intrusion. New handheld devices marketed by Motorola enable sales associates to look up product information on the spot and to communicate with other associates in order to facilitate the quick response needed for customer questions.[51] In addition, customer expectations for service vary considerably. What customers expect in a department store is very different from their expectations for a discount store. Luxury retailers, for whom extreme

© Les and Dave Jacobs Cultura/Newscom

customer service has always been a hallmark, are beginning to add a new level of service personnel to their high-profile locations: the store concierge. Concierges routinely fulfill customer requests that have nothing to do with shopping. Gary Jackson is the concierge for the Dallas store of luxury retailer Barneys New York. He has called a new private club to get a customer on the guest list and has taken another customer's college-age daughter and her out-of-town guests around to Dallas's newest nightspots. When one customer ripped a pair of pants and needed a replacement that matched his suit jacket before an important meeting the next morning, Jackson delivered a selection of pants to the customer's hotel room at 11 P.M. the night before.[52]

Customer service is also critical for online retailers. Online shoppers expect a retailer's Web site to be easy to use, products to be available, and returns to be simple. Therefore, customer-friendly retailers such as Bluefly.com design their sites to give their customers the information they need such as what's new and what's on sale. Other companies, such as Amazon.com and LandsEnd.com, offer product recommendations and personal shoppers. Some retailers that have online, catalog, and traditional brick-and-mortar stores, such as Lands' End, Gap, and Williams-Sonoma, now allow customers to return goods bought through the catalog or online to their traditional store to make returns easier.

Review LO 6 List the major tasks involved in developing a retail marketing strategy

PRODUCT
Width and depth of product assortment

PLACE
Location and hours

PROMOTION
Advertising, publicity, public relations

PRICE

PRESENTATION
Layout and atmosphere

PERSONNEL
Customer service and personal selling

TARGET

LO 7
New Developments in Retailing

In an effort to better serve their customers and attract new ones, retailers are constantly adopting new strategies. Two recent developments are interactivity, both in traditional and online retail formats, and pop-up stores.

INTERACTIVITY

Adding interactivity to the retail environment is one of the most popular strategies in retailing in the past few years. Small retailers as well as national chains are using interactivity in stores to differentiate themselves from the competition. For some time, retailers have used "entertainment" retailing in the form of playing music, showing videos, hosting special events, and sponsoring guest appearances, but the new interactive trend gets customers involved rather than just catching their eye. For example, at the American Girl store in Chicago, customers can purchase a doll made to look like them, take their dolls to the in-store American Girl Café, go to the American Girl Theater, and even have their birthday parties there. Similarly, Build-A-Bear enables customers to make their own stuffed animal by choosing which animal to stuff and then dressing and naming it. You can hold birthday parties there, too.

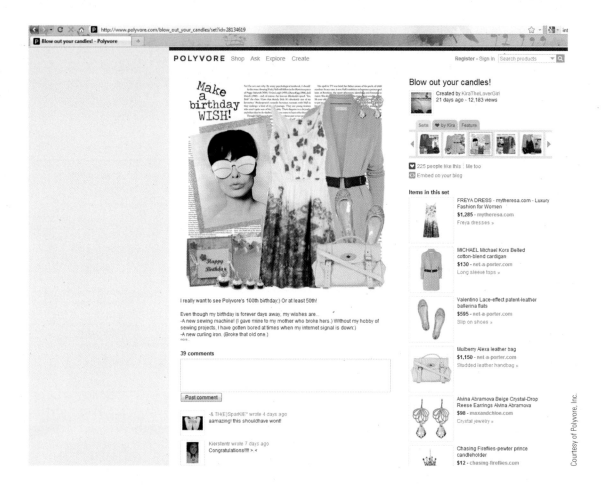

Involvement isn't just for children, either. For Your Entertainment, one of the country's leading specialty retailers of movies, music, and games, regularly invites artists to perform in its stores. Performers might be local favorites or national superstars. FYE even has a MySpace site that features a state-by-state touring schedule and allows local performers to sign up to play at its stores. Fans can request to see a local group perform at an FYE store or ask the stores to stock recordings by their local favorites.[53]

In addition to interactivity being injected into the physical retail environment, many successful electronic retailers are making great strides toward creating an interactive customer experience. However, because the customers in an e-retail environment do not have direct interactions with salespeople and products, the interactivity is mediated through the store's Web site, with multiple images, streaming audio and video, and fully controllable features such as rotating and zooming around items of interest at all angles. The Polyvore Web site empowers fashion conscious customers to become fashion editors, stylists, and models via an active interface that allows them to combine chosen items into an ensemble and create new looks that friends can then view, vote on, and purchase.[54] Similarly, Nordstrom.com gives its Internet shoppers the opportunity to post and share store-related content, upload photos and videos, and solicit fashion advice from "Miss Nordstrom," a virtual fashion expert.[55]

POP-UP SHOPS

pop-up shops
Temporary retail establishments that allow flexible locations without the long-term commitment of a more expensive retail lease.

Companies of all sizes are experimenting with **pop-up shops**. As the name implies, pop-up shops are temporary retail establishments that allow companies flexible locations without the long-term commitment of a more expensive retail lease. Italian coffee maker illy opened a pop-up shop at Time Warner Center in New York for ten days. In addition to selling coffee, the illy shop, created from a shipping container, offered free samples from the company's soon-to-be-released Hyper Espresso System machine.[56] Pop-up shops aren't always sized like kiosks, however. Toys "R" Us opened a 25,000-square-foot temporary store in a former Tower Records building during the Christmas shopping season.[57]

Wired magazine incorporated interactivity in its holiday pop-up shop. Customers could try out over 100 of the latest techie toys and participate in a SoHo scavenger hunt (contestants used a Palm Centro to navigate through the game) for a chance at winning a Nintendo Wii.[58]

Another trend in pop-up retailing is the store-in-a-store model. Companies as diverse as Levenger (whose tagline is "Tools for Serious Readers"), Apple, Kolo (an international photo album company), Procter & Gamble, and more have used the store-in-a-store concept. Levenger has small stores inside two Chicago Macy's locations; Apple has stores in various Best Buy stores in the United States and FNAC stores in France; Kolo opened a 450-square-foot Kolo Boutique inside Kate's Paperie, a famous stationery store in Soho; and Procter & Gamble has dedicated shops for health and beauty inside certain Royal Ahold grocery stores.

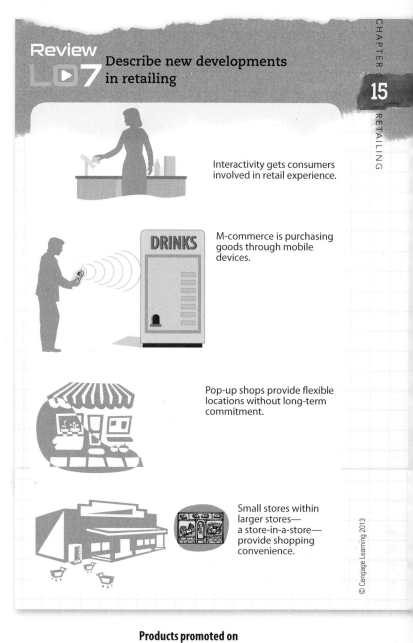

Review LO 7 Describe new developments in retailing

Interactivity gets consumers involved in retail experience.

M-commerce is purchasing goods through mobile devices.

Pop-up shops provide flexible locations without long-term commitment.

Small stores within larger stores— a store-in-a-store— provide shopping convenience.

© Cengage Learning 2013

Percentage of retailers operating just one store
90

Prescriptions purchased by the average 60-year-old each year
15

SuperTarget locations in the U.S.
220

Cost of the diamond solitaire ring offered by Sam's Club at Christmastime
$347,000

Meals Americans eat in restaurants and cafeterias each year
70 billion

Dell's daily online sales of computers and equipment
$50 million

Products promoted on QVC each week
1,150

Percentage of Americans with Internet access at home or work
70

Countries with KFC franchises
109

1 **Discuss the importance of retailing in the U.S. economy.** Retailing plays a vital role in the U.S. economy for two main reasons. First, retail businesses contribute to our high standard of living by providing a vast number and diversity of goods and services. Second, retailing employs a large part of the U.S. working population—over 15 million people.

1.1 To fully appreciate the role retailing plays in the U.S. economy, you might find it helpful to review a selection of press articles related to the retailing industry. Search for articles pertaining to retailing. Read a selection of articles and report your findings to the class.

writing

1.2 Keep a shopping journal that details all the retail establishments you visit in a week, how long you spent in each store, how much money you spent, and the reason for your visit. At the end of the week, review your journal and analyze your relationship to retail. As a class, compile your results to get a picture of shopping habits and consumer behavior.

2 **Explain the dimensions by which retailers can be classified.** Many different kinds of retailers exist. A retail establishment can be classified according to its ownership, level of service, product assortment, and price. On the basis of ownership, retailers can be broadly differentiated as independent retailers, chain stores, or franchise outlets. The level of service retailers provide can be classified along a continuum of high to low. Retailers also classify themselves by the breadth and depth of their product assortments; some retailers have concentrated product assortments, whereas others have extensive product assortments. Last, general price levels also classify a store, from discounters offering low prices to exclusive specialty stores where high prices are the norm. Retailers use these latter three variables to position themselves in the marketplace.

team

2.1 Form a team of three classmates to identify different retail stores in your city where pet supplies are sold. Include nonstore forms of retailing, such as catalogs, the Internet, or the local veterinarian. Team members should divide up and visit all the different retailing outlets for pet supplies. Prepare a report describing the differences in brands and products sold at each of the retailing formats and the differences in store characteristics and service levels. For example, which brands are sold via mass merchandiser, independent specialty store, or other venue? Suggest why different products and brands are distributed through different types of stores.

3 **Describe the major types of retail operations.** The major types of retail stores are department stores, specialty retailers, supermarkets, drugstores, convenience stores, discount stores, and restaurants. Department stores carry a wide assortment of shopping and specialty goods, are organized into relatively independent departments, and offset higher prices by emphasizing customer service and décor. Specialty retailers typically carry a narrower but deeper assortment of merchandise, emphasizing distinctive products and a high level of customer service. Supermarkets are large self-service retailers that offer a wide variety of food products and some nonfood items. Drugstores are retail formats that sell mostly prescription and over-the-counter medications, health and beauty aids, cosmetics, and specialty items. Convenience stores carry a limited line of high-turnover convenience goods. Discount stores offer low-priced general merchandise and consist of four types: full-line discounters, specialty discount retailers, warehouse clubs, and off-price retailers. Finally, restaurants straddle the line between the retailing and services industries; although restaurants sell a product, food and drink, to final consumers, they can also be considered service marketers because they provide consumers with the service of preparing food and sometimes table service.

3.1 Discuss the possible marketing implications of the recent trend toward supercenters, which combine a supermarket and a full-line discount store.

3.2 Explain the function of warehouse clubs. Why are they classified as both wholesalers and retailers?

3.3 Would you be interested in buying luxury items, like expensive jewelry, at a warehouse club? Sam's Club offered a $347,000 diamond solitaire ring during a recent Christmas shopping season. If you could afford such a ring, would you consider buying it at Sam's Club? Why or why not?

Discuss nonstore retailing techniques. Nonstore retailing, which is shopping outside a store setting, has four major categories. Automatic vending uses machines to offer products for sale. In direct retailing, the sales transaction occurs in a home setting, typically through door-to-door sales or party plan selling. Direct marketing refers to the techniques used to get consumers to buy from their homes or places of business. Those techniques include direct mail, catalogs and mail order, telemarketing, and electronic retailing, such as home shopping channels and online retailing. M-commerce goes beyond text message advertisements to enable consumers to purchase goods and services by using wireless mobile devices, such as mobile telephones and handheld computers.

4.1 Go to the Gift Center at the online wine retailer's Web site at **www.wine.com.** How does this site help shoppers select gifts?

4.2 Identify how much the most powerful computer with the fastest modem, most memory, largest monitor, biggest hard drive, and all the available peripherals costs at **www.dell. com.** Then visit a store such as like Best Buy or CompUSA and price a comparable computer. How can you explain any price differences between the two retail operations? Explain any differences in features that you encountered. What conclusions can you draw from your research?

4.3 Most catalog companies also offer online shopping. Visit the Web site of one of your favorite catalogs to see if you can buy online. If so, surf the online catalog for a few minutes. Then compare the two retailing methods (paper and Internet) for prices, products, and so forth. Which do you prefer—the paper catalog or online shopping? Why?

4.4 To what can you attribute the renewed interest in the party format of retailing? Go to the library and research direct sales parties. Write a paragraph describing the target market for these parties and the shifts in the external environment that contribute to their resurgent popularity.

Define *franchising* and describe its two basic forms. Franchising is a continuing relationship in which a franchisor grants to a franchisee the business rights to operate or to sell a product. Modern franchising takes two basic forms. In product and trade name franchising, a dealer agrees to buy or sell certain products or product lines from a particular manufacturer or wholesaler. Business format franchising is an ongoing business relationship in which a franchisee uses a franchisor's name, format, or method of business in return for several types of fees.

5.1 What advantages does franchising provide to franchisors as well as franchisees?

5.2 Curves is the world's largest fitness franchise and was recently the fastest-growing franchise of any kind. What do you need to do to become a Curves franchisee? Visit the Web page **www.curves.com** to find out. Does anything surprise you?

List the major tasks involved in developing a retail marketing strategy. Retail management begins with defining the target market, typically on the basis of demographic, geographic, or psychographic characteristics. After determining the target market, retail managers must develop the six variables of the retailing mix: product, promotion, place, price, presentation, and personnel.

6.1 Identify a successful retail business in your community. What marketing strategies have led to its success?

6.2 How can a company create an atmosphere on its Web site? Visit the pages of some of your favorite retailers to see if they have been able to re-create the store atmosphere on the Internet.

 Describe new developments in retailing. Three major trends are evident in retailing today. First, adding interactivity to the retail environment is one of the most popular strategies in retailing in recent years. Small retailers as well as national chains are using interactivity to involve customers and set themselves apart from the competition. Second, m-commerce (mobile e-commerce) is gaining in popularity. M-commerce enables consumers to purchase goods and services using wireless mobile devices, such as mobile telephones and handheld computers. Pop-up shops give companies flexible locations without the expense of a long-term lease.

7.1 Make a list of stores that actively incorporate some kind of interactivity or entertainment into their retailing strategy. Now, make a list of stores that do not, such as office supply stores. Compare your two lists. Select a company from your second list and draft a strategy to help it become more interactive.

7.2 What kind of retailers or brands do you think would most benefit from a pop-up shop? Why?

Key Terms

atmosphere 559	drugstore 539	pop-up shops 564
automatic vending 545	factory outlet 542	product offering 554
buyer 537	franchisee 550	retailing 533
category killers 542	franchises 535	retailing mix 554
chain stores 535	franchisor 550	scrambled merchandising 539
convenience store 540	full-line discount stores 540	specialty discount store 542
department store 537	gross margin 536	specialty store 537
destination stores 557	independent retailers 535	supercenter 541
direct marketing (direct-response marketing) 546	mass merchandising 540	supermarket 538
	nonstore retailing 544	telemarketing 547
direct retailing 545	off-price retailer 542	warehouse membership
discount store 540	online retailing 548	clubs 542

Exercises

ethics

ETHICS EXERCISE

A–Z Grocery Company is well known for offering high-quality grocery products at the lowest prices in the market. When the company applied for a zoning change to build a new store in a middle-class neighborhood, several members of the city council objected because the company has no stores in low-income neighborhoods, where they argue the low prices are needed most. The company contends that it cannot operate profitably in these neighborhoods because of higher security and operating costs.

Questions

1. Should low-cost retailers be required to locate near low-income customers? Why or why not?

2. Does the AMA Statement of Ethics address this issue? Go to **www.marketingpower.com** and review the code. Then write a brief paragraph on how the AMA Statement of Ethics relates to retailing locations.

MARKETING PLAN EXERCISE

Chapter 15 is the third and final chapter in Part 4, Distribution Decisions. Once you've completed this exercise, you can complete the Marketing Plan Worksheet for Part 4 on your companion Web site at **www.cengagebrain.com.** Distribution is a key component of any business. For the e-business, distribution seems "invisible" to the consumer, because the consumer may not care where your firm is located but wants product delivery quickly and inexpensively. Creating a worldwide distribution system is an additional challenge to the marketer. Use the following exercises to guide you through the retail distribution part of your strategic marketing plan:

1. What types of retail establishments might be used for your firm's product? Are they in locations convenient to the target customers? What is the atmosphere of the facility for each type? How can you get the atmosphere of the brick-and-mortar offering to match the offering of your Web site?

2. If you have developed a service, to what other Web sites might you "distribute" your Internet-based service? How will working with these other Web sites help you reach your target audience? Are there other Web sites from which you might accept distribution deals in order to make your product or service offering stronger? Explain how strategic distribution with other Web sites or services can give you a competitive advantage.

APPLICATION EXERCISE

After reading the chapter, you can see that differences in retailing are the result of strategy. To better understand the relationship between strategic retailing factors and consumer perceptions, you can conduct a simple observation exercise. First, pick a product to shop for, and then identify two stores where you have *never* shopped as places to look for your product. The two stores must be different types of retailers. For example, you can shop for a new HDTV at Best Buy (category killer) and at Sears (department store). Once you have identified what you are looking for and where you're going to look, visit each store and record your observations of specific strategic retailing factors.[59]

Activities

1. Go through each store and make careful observations of the following:

   → *Location:* Where is each store? How congested is the area of town where each store is located? What influence does the neighborhood have on your impression of the store? Would you travel to this store under normal circumstances? Write a detailed paragraph on the location of each store.

   → *Exterior atmosphere:* Is there parking? If so, is it convenient? Is it adequate? Observe other parking issues (cleanliness and size of the lot, size of spaces, well-lit, etc.). What kinds of stores are around the store you are visiting? Do you think being located next to them increases traffic at your store? Are direct competitors nearby? Is the building modern or historic? Is it attractive, clean, and appealing? Is the entrance inviting to shoppers?

> → *Interior atmosphere:* Compare the following attributes at each store: aisle width, lighting, number of customers, noise (background music, loudspeakers, etc.), store layout, signage, accessibility of the cashier, number of products available (depth and width of assortment), ability to inspect the product before purchase, quality of the fixtures (shelves, lights, etc.), availability of salespeople and their knowledge about the product, and willingness of salespeople to help.
>
> → *Product:* Is your product available? If not, is there a satisfactory substitute? What is your perception of the quality of goods offered? Why do you think as you do?
>
> → *Price:* What is the price of the product/brand at this store? Is the price prominently marked? How do the prices at the two stores compare? How does the price compare to your expectations?

2. From which of these two stores would you actually purchase the item? Why, specifically? List the factors that played a role in your decision. Which factor is most important to you? If you would not purchase the item at either store, why not?

3. What are the three most important differences you observed between the stores?

4. Using the results of your research, write a short paper that outlines your observations. Conclude your paper with your answers to questions 2 and 3.

CASE STUDY: Nordstrom

HOW TO SUCCEED BY SELLING JUST ONE SHOE

© AP Images/Elaine Thompson

Upscale retailer Nordstrom has been famous for superior customer service for over 100 years. Robert Spector, coauthor of *The Nordstrom Way*, says his favorite story is of a woman with one leg who jokingly bet a Nordstrom salesperson that he wouldn't sell her just one shoe. He was more than happy to split up the pair, though, to her surprise, and Nordstrom gained a life-long customer in the process. "Who knows how many times she's told that story?" Spector asks. "Do you think that that's worth the price of a shoe? I do." This kind of word-of-mouth publicity means that Nordstrom spends much less on traditional advertising than its competitors do. And the stories told by satisfied customers are much more persuasive than an ad in the Sunday paper.

Patrick McCarthy, who was the first salesperson to generate $1 million, cites an example of a customer who was traveling and accidentally left his plane tickets in the store. An employee who found them paid for a cab to the airport with her own money so that the customer wouldn't miss his plane. This, McCarthy says, is an example of "heroic service," and at Nordstrom they expect nothing less.

Industry observer Lior Arussy calls Nordstrom's business strategy "greed through love." They have perfected the art of focusing on the right customers and giving them undivided attention. A salesperson will often continue the relationship with a customer for years. They may exchange business cards, set future shopping dates, and call customers when new merchandise comes in. "It's a heart experience," says McCarthy, who kept handwritten notes on all 12,000 of his personal customers over the years. "Most companies are head experiences— bean counters are running them. When the heart is running them, it becomes exciting."

Nordstrom is also known for its generous exchange policy. In a familiar story that has been forwarded around the Internet for years, a man claims he was allowed to return snow tires, even though the store never sold auto parts. It may be an urban myth, but it reinforces the company's reputation for putting customers first. Even though the company loses some money on returns, the staff believes it's worth it to keep customers coming back.

Nordstrom has 204 stores in 28 states, with plans to open 24 more by 2012. Erik Nordstrom, the company's president, visits each potential location himself before signing off on it. He says his gut instinct about a location is almost as important as the demographics and statistics they analyze. "Plenty of places look good on paper and we say no."

Even though Nordstrom values the traditions that come with its long history, Nordstrom stores president Erik Nordstrom says that they're not afraid to evolve with the times. "We see the way people shop changing very dramatically," he says. The company analyzed barriers between its sales channels and realized that it was limiting sales opportunities. Customers who purchased Nordstrom merchandise online couldn't return it in the retail stores, for example, and customers who shopped in the stores couldn't always find the same products online. The company now aims for a "seamless" shopping experience across all sales channels, whether mail order, online, or in-store.

The company has also benefited from a new computerized inventory system that gives buyers and salespeople the necessary data to make smarter decisions about what is needed in the stores—and what isn't. Choosing the right handbags to stock, for example, in the right styles, quantities, and colors, enabled them to sell more items at full price, which in turn improved the bottom line.

Erik Nordstrom says that they want a customer's experience to be "aspirational and up-scale, so people feel they are treating themselves." Therefore, he says, the company refuses to hop on the price-promoting bandwagon. "We don't rely on promotions, be it one-day sales, coupons, or 'friends of friends' sales. We think our regular pricing has to have integrity."

In 2006, when many retailers were struggling, Nordstrom thrived, posting $8.6 billion in sales, a 10.8 percent increase from the year before. Nordstrom has also beaten expectations as it has recovered from the recent downturn with the rest of the retail sector, posting an 11 percent sales increase over the year prior in the third quarter of 2010. Erik Nordstrom says, "Retailing is not for everybody. It's a competitive, high-energy business. Every day, you've got to open your doors and sell something." Even if it's just one shoe.[60]

Questions

1. What type of retailer is Nordstrom? Describe the characteristics it shares with other retailers of this type.

2. How would you describe Nordstrom's level of service on the continuum from full service to self-service? Why? Give an example of a store that would be on the opposite end of the continuum and explain their differences.

3. Which of the six components of Nordstrom's retailing mix do you think have been the most important to the company's success? Why?

4. What are the primary challenges Nordstrom faces in the current retail climate? How has the competition changed in recent years, along with consumer expectations?

COMPANY CLIPS: Sephora—Retailing for Success

From the beginning, Sephora has carried quality skincare products. Excellent retailing techniques, however, are the real driving force behinds Sephora's success. The company's open-sale environment allows consumers to try any product, or even take home a free sample, before they buy. A great location in the heart of the New York City retail district makes it easy for Sephora to attract potential buyers. Sephora also invests a lot of time and money into training their sales staff so that when customers enter the store, they gain a total shopping experience in which their every need is met. The salespeople are not paid on commission, so they are free to give honest recommendations of products that would be best for their customers. As you watch the video, notice what other retailing methods Sephora uses to promote sales.

Questions

1. Visit **www.Sephora.com** and browse the online store. How does Sephora use the online environment to promote its products without the advantage of letting customers try before they buy?

2. Sephora is working out the details of a new loyalty program, and they have asked you to give your input and advice. What do you tell them? How should they integrate this new program with the retailing mix they have already adopted?

Notes

1. "Retail Industry Indicators," National Retail Federation, www.nrf.com/modules.php?name=News&op=viewlive&sp_id=933 (Accessed August 10, 2010).
2. "Wholesale and Retail Trade," U.S. Census Web site, www.census.gov/compendia/statab/2011/tables/11s1046.pdf (Accessed August 10, 2010).
3. *Ibid.*
4. 2010 Top 100 Retailers, National Retail Federation/Stores.org Web site, www.stores.org/2010/Top-100-Retailers (Accessed August 12, 2010).
5. Simon Zekaria, "Burberry Has Reasons to Be Bullish," *Wall Street Journal,* July 13, 2010, http://blogs.wsj.com/source/2010/07/13/why-burberry-has-reasons-to-be-bullish.
6. "Tweeter CE Playground Store," *Boston Magazine*, www.bostonmagazine.com/best_of/detail/best_of_boston_2007_electronics (Accessed July 6, 2011).
7. Stefania Borghini et al., "Why Are Themed Brandstores So Powerful? Retail Brand Ideology at American Girl Place," *Journal of Retailing* 85, No. 3 (2009): 363–375.
8. "Supermarket Sales by Department," Food Marketing Institute Web site, www.fmi.org/docs/facts_figs/grocerydept.pdf (Accessed August 21, 2010).
9. *Food CPI, Prices and Expenditures: Food Expenditure Tables*, U.S. Dept. of Agriculture, www.ers.usda.gov/briefing/cpifoodandexpenditures/data (Accessed August 10, 2010).
10. Piggly Wiggly Web site, www.pigglywiggly.com; Michael Garry, "Loyalty Program Cuts Defections," *Supermarket News*, January 22, 2007, http://subscribers.supermarketnews.com/mag/loyalty_program_cuts/index.html.
11. Garry, "Loyalty Program Cuts Defections."
12. On the Run Web site, www.ontherun.com/index.aspx (Accessed February 9, 2010).
13. "Corporate Facts: By the Numbers," Walmart corporate Web site, March 2010, walmartstores.com/download/2230.pdf.
14. "Supercenter Industry," *HHC Publishing*, www.warehouseclubfocus.com (Accessed December 28, 2007).
15. "Our Strategy," Tesco PLC Web site, www.tescoplc.com/about-tesco/our-strategy/.
16. Family Dollar Web site, www.familydollar.com; Dollar General Web site, www.dollargeneral.com.
17. "Restaurant Industry Facts at a Glance," National Restaurant Association, www.restaurant.org/research/facts (Accessed August 12, 2010).
18. Mark Scolforo, "Pennsylvania Grocery Store Wine Kiosks Test Said to Go Well," *Bloomberg Businessweek*, August 20, 2010, www.businessweek.com/ap/financialnews/D9HGQ2Q80.htm.
19. Susan Ladika, "Vending Machines That Take Credit, Debit Cards Catch On," *CreditCards.com*, September 8, 2010, www.creditcards.com/credit-card-news/vending-machines-take-credit-debit-cards-1273.php.
20. Paulina Reso, "Future Vending Machines Will Link Retina Scans to Credit Cards," *New York Daily News*, August 11, 2010, www.nydailynews.com/lifestyle/2010/08/11/2010-08-11_next_generation_of_vending_machines_may_use_thumprint_retinal_scan_to_pay_with_c.html.
21. "Explore," Mark Web site, http://explore.meetmark.com (Accessed May 2, 2011); Advocare Web site, www.advocare.com (Accessed August 10, 2010).
22. DMA: Direct Marketing Association, http://www.the-dma.org/index.php (Accessed May 2, 2011).
23. "Worldwide Spending on Direct Mail Expected to Grow," *Marketing News*, August 24, 2010, www.marketingpower.com/AboutAMA/Pages/AMA Publications/Marketing News/MarketingNews.aspx.

marketing&you:
Results.

© iStockphoto.com/ziggymaj

If your score was on the low side, it means you don't find shopping in stores to be enjoyable. The higher your score, the more likely you are to think shopping is a fun activity. But beware: A high score can also indicate a tendency toward being a compulsive buyer!

24. "PC Maker Good Despite Economic Recession," *Electronic Times* (Accessed August 12, 2010).

25. Catherine Tsai, "Catalog Offers Complete Mail Order Solar Home Kit," *Denver Post*, April 26, 2010, www.denverpost.com/business/ci_14957526.

26. "Telemarketing: A US and Japanese Market Report," www.streetinsider.com, August 10, 2010.

27. QVC Web site, www.qvc.com (Accessed August 12, 2010).

28. Jihyun Kim, Ann Marie Fiore, and Hyun-Hwa Lee, "Influences of Online Store Perception, Shopping Enjoyment, and Shopping Involvement on Customer Patronage Behavior Towards an Online Retailer," *Journal of Retailing*, March 2007, 95–107.

29. eMarketer Web site, www.emarketer.com (Accessed August 12, 2010).

30. Ken Magill, "Great Expectations," *Multichannel Merchant*, December 1, 2007, http://multichannelmerchant.com/crosschannel/great_expectations_5/.

31. Abbey Klaassen, "Buy It from Radio Ads at the Push of a Button," *Advertising Age*, February 21, 2006.

32. Emily Jed, "Coinstar's 'Next Big Idea' Contest Fosters Kiosk Innovation," *Vending Times*, August 26, 2010, www.vendingtimes.com/ME2/dirmod.asp?sid=EB79A487112B48A296B38C81345C8C7F&nm=Vending+Features&type=Publishing&mod=Publications%3A%3AArticle&mid=8F3A7027421841978F18BE895F87F791&tier=4&id=BB13156DA303446E8E352BBDE24EA5F1.

33. Alexander Peers and Nick Wingfield, "Sotheby's, eBay Team Up to Sell Fine Art Online," *Wall Street Journal*, January 31, 2002, B8; Sotheby's: Art Auction House, Private Sales, and Art-Related Financing, www.sothebys.com (Accessed May 2, 2011); eBay Web site, www.ebay.com (Accessed May 2, 2011).

34. "USA Technologies Expands into $4B Office Coffee Industry," USA Technologies Web site, February 18, 2009, http://www.usatech.com/company_info/news/usa_2009_02_18.php.

35. Samantha Murphy, "Getting iReady," *Chain Store Age*, July 30, 2007, www.chainstoreage.com/article/getting-iready.

36. KAYAK Web site, www.kayak.com (Accessed August 12, 2010).

37. ShopIgniter Web site, www.shopigniter.com (Accessed August 12, 2010).

38. McDonald's Corporate Web site, "Purchasing Your Franchise," www.aboutmcdonalds.com/mcd/franchising/us_franchising/purchasing_your_franchise.html (Accessed August 21, 2010).

39. International Franchise Association Web site, www.franchise.org (Accessed December 2007).

40. Kentucky Fried Chicken corporate Web site, www.kfc.com/about (Accessed December 2007).

41. Olga Galacho, "Fashionable Touch for Retail Phone Apps," *Daily Telegraph*, August 9, 2010, www.dailytelegraph.com.au/business/business-owner/fashionable-touch-for-retail-phone-apps/story-e6frez89-1225902938945.

42. Ann Zimmerman, "Target's New Eco-Apparel Line to Debut at Barneys New York," *Wall Street Journal*, January 2008, http://online.wsj.com/article/SB120960471037658107-email.html.

43. Malini Goyal, Indrajit Gupta, and Neelima Mahajan-Bansal, "Wal-Mart Comes to India," *Forbes Asia*, November 16, 2009, www.forbes.com/global/2009/1116/companies-raj-jain-wal-mart-comes-to-india.html.

44. "Carrefour in India: A Wholesale Invasion," *The Economist*, May 22, 2010, www.economist.com/node/16168260.

45. David Moin, "High-End Opportunity for Outlets," *Women's Wear Daily*, April 14, 2008, www.wwd.com/business-news/high-end-opportunity-for-outlets-457792.

46. ifoAppleStore.com blog, "The Stores," www.ifoapplestore.com/the_stores.html (Accessed February 9, 2010).

47. Calmetta Y. Coleman, "Kohl's Retail Racetrack," *Wall Street Journal*, March 13, 2001, B1; Kohl's Web site, www.kohls.com (Accessed August 10, 2010).

48. "Highland Village: A Supercenter with a View," *Retailing Today*, December 10, 2007.

49. Nick Wingfield, "How Apple's Store Strategy Beat the Odds," *Wall Street Journal*, May 17, 2006, B1.

50. Todd J. Arnold et al., "Understanding Retail Managers' Role in the Sales of Products and Services," *Journal of Retailing* 85, No. 2 (2009):129–144.

51. Sara Silver, "Motorola's New Devices Target Retailers," *Wall Street Journal*, January 14, 2008, B4.

52. Ann Zimmerman, "Latest Luxury: The Store Concierge," *Wall Street Journal*, December 20, 2007, B1.

53. F.Y.E. Web site, www.fye.com (Accessed May 2, 2011).

54. Catherine Caines, "Click for Full Ensemble," *Australian*, August 11, 2010, www.theaustralian.com.au/news/executive-lifestyle/click-for-full-ensemble/story-e6frg8k6-1225903672903.

55. Internet Retailer Web site, www.internetretailer.com (Accessed May 2, 2011); Nordstrom, www.nordstrom.com (Accessed August 12, 2010).

56. Leslie Price, "'Tis the Season for Holiday Pop-Up Shops," *Racked NY,* November 14, 2007, http://ny.racked.com/archives/2007/11/14/tis_the_season_for_holiday_pop.php.

57. "New Pop-Up Stores: Wired, illy, Mishka, Toys 'R' Us," *NewYorkology,* November 14, 2007, www.newyorkology.com/archives/2007/11/new_popup_store.php.

58. *Ibid.*

59. This application exercise is based on the contribution of Amy Hubbert (University of Nebraska at Omaha) to *Great Ideas in Teaching Marketing*, a teaching supplement that accompanies McDaniel, Lamb, and Hair's *Introduction to Marketing.* Professor Hubbert's entry titled "Discovery of Strategic Retailing Factors" was a winner in the "Best of the Great Ideas in Teaching Marketing" contest conducted in conjunction with the publication of the eighth edition of *Marketing*.

60. Monica Soto Ouchi, "Sharper Focus Helps Nordstrom," *Seattle Times*, February 27, 2007, http://seattletimes.nwsource.com/html/businesstechnology/2003590861_nordstrom27.html; "Sticking with the Family Formula," *WWD*, May 22, 2006, www.wwd.com/retail-news/sticking-with-the-family-formula-534920?full=true; Dave DeWitte, "Nordstrom Leader Says Retail Business Is Changing," *The Gazette*, October 12, 2006; Monica Soto Ouchi, "Nordstrom Sees a Fashion-Forward Future"; Alexandra DeFelice, "A Century of Customer Love," *CRM Magazine*, June 1, 2005, www.destinationcrm.com/Articles/Editorial/Magazine-Features/A-Century-of-Customer-Love-42958.aspx; Joan E. Solsman, "Nordstrom Net Up Despite Sales Drop at Outlets," *Wall Street Journal*, November 15, 2010, http://online.wsj.com/article/SB10001424052748703326204575616971039595804.html; PRNewswire, "Nordstrom Rack to Open First Kansas City Area Store," *Yahoo! Finance*, January 11, 2011, http://finance.yahoo.com/news/Nordstrom-Rack-to-Open-First-prnews-2843967071.html?x=0&v=1; Nordstrom Web site, "Future Store Openings," http://about.nordstrom.com (Accessed May 2, 2011).

61. Rovio Mobile Web site, http://rovio.com (Accessed May 2, 2011); Jon Mundy, "Interview: Rovio on the Origin of Angry Birds, Being Inspired by Swine Flu, and Why You May Never See an Angry Birds 2," *Pocket Gamer*, October 13, 2010, www.pocketgamer.co.uk/r/Various/Angry+Birds/news.asp?c=24243; Ian Paul, "Angry Birds Maker Is Angry with Microsoft," *PCWorld*, October 11 2010, www.pcworld.com/article/207421/angry_birds_maker_is_angry_with_microsoft.html; Helen Popkin, "Angry Birds Fail to Negotiate Peace Treaty," *Technolog*, November 22, 2010, http://technolog.msnbc.msn.com/_news/2010/11/22/5509508-angry-birds-fail-to-negotiate-peace-treaty.

62. CUTCO Web site, www.cutco.com (Accessed February 28, 2011); Vector Marketing Web site, www.vectormarketing.com (Accessed February 28, 2011).

Marketing Miscue

MICROSOFT IMPLIES DISTRIBUTION OF *ANGRY BIRDS* ON WINDOWS 7 PHONE

Rovio Mobile is a leading independent developer of wireless games. The company has developed games for companies such as Electronic Arts, Nokia, Vivendi, Namco Bandai, and Mr. Goodliving/Real Networks. As a leading provider to platforms such as the iPhone and the Android, the company was not pleased when Microsoft included a screenshot of an *Angry Birds* icon in promotional material on the Windows 7 Phone Web site. According to Rovio, the two companies had not agreed that the Windows 7 Phone would be a distributor of the *Angry Birds* game.

Rovio Mobile and *Angry Birds*

Rovio Mobile started in the early 2000s when three students at the Helsinki University of Technology participated in a mobile game development competition sponsored by Nokia and Hewlett-Packard. The students won the competition with a real-time multiplayer game called *King of the Cabbage World* and started their own company called Relude. The first commercial real-time multiplayer mobile game in the world, *King of the Cabbage World* was later sold to Digital Chocolate and renamed *Mole War*.

After a round of angel investment in 2005, the company changed its name to Rovio Mobile. This was the beginning of the development of numerous successful games that gave the company a reputation for innovative game design. The company's ability to create both two- and three-dimensional games meant that it could offer product for a variety of platforms, including Nokia's N-Gage, Flash, and iPhone.

Angry Birds was released in December 2009 for Apple's iOS platform. The game is a puzzle video game in which players use slingshots to launch birds with the intent of destroying pigs on the playing field. *Angry Birds* can be played on personal computers, gaming consoles, and touchscreen-based smartphones. Since its release, over six million copies of the smartphone game have been purchased from the iTunes Store, making it one of the top-selling paid applications. The Android version of *Angry Birds* was downloaded over two million times in the first weekend of its release, and Rovio is said to receive around $1 million revenue per month from the advertising that appears in the Android version of the game.

The popularity of the *Angry Birds* game is exemplified by the download reports and logged playing time. According to the company, there are more than one million hours of game time logged on the iOS version of the game. Other reports suggest that no other game even comes close to having the following that *Angry Birds* captures in the marketplace. The game's success is attributed to a successful combination of addictive gaming, comical presentation, and low price.

Windows 7 Phone

Launched in 2010 and developed by Microsoft, Windows 7 Phone is a re-branding of Windows Mobile and is targeted to the consumer marketplace instead of the business marketplace. As such, it competes with the Android and the Apple platforms. Nokia is a major partner with Windows 7 Phone. Since the phone was developed by Microsoft, it has access to Outlook, Internet Explorer, and, of course, Xbox Live. With *Angry Birds* holding the top spot for mobile accessed games, it was not surprising that Microsoft wanted to distribute the game on the Windows 7 Phone.

Microsoft, however, apparently jumped the gun on saying that it would be a distributor of *Angry Birds*. Just days before the actual launch of the phone, with an *Angry Birds* icon on the phone's launch site, Rovio said that it had not committed to doing a Windows 7 Phone version of the game and that Microsoft had posted the icon without permission. Interestingly, it was not that Rovio did not plan to do a Windows 7 Phone version of *Angry Birds*—it was that the two companies had not come to such an agreement yet.[61]

Questions

1. Describe the channel of distribution for *Angry Birds*.
2. Who has the channel power in the distribution of online games?

Critical Thinking Case

CUTCO CUTLERY CORPORATION: DIRECT TO CONSUMER FOR OVER 60 YEARS!

CUTCO Corporation, the largest manufacturer and marketer of high-quality kitchen cutlery and accessories in the United States and Canada, celebrated its 60th anniversary in 2009. With the design and manufacture of the highest quality product as its primary objective, over 100 kitchen cutlery products are sold under the CUTCO name. The company also carries a line of cookware, sporting/pocket knives, and garden tools.

© sevenke/Shutterstock.com

The CUTCO corporate family consists of:

→ CUTCO Corporation—parent company

→ CUTCO Cutlery Corporation—manufacturer of CUTCO products since 1949

→ VECTOR Marketing Corporation—exclusive marketer of CUTCO products which are sold direct to consumers

→ CUTCO International, Inc.—marketer of CUTCO products internationally

→ KA-BAR Knives, Inc.—maker of quality sporting knives

→ SCHILLING Forge—manufacturer of precision forgings

All businesses within the corporate family, except for Shilling Forge, are located in Olean, New York (USA) where the company has over 700 manufacturing and administrative employees. Shilling Forge is located in Syracuse, New York. Only a very small percentage of the company's items are manufactured outside the United States and that is only when the company cannot find a partner in the United States that meets stringent quality standards, while simultaneously meeting the pricing needs of the company and its customers. The quality built into a Cutco product at the point of manufacturing is reinforced by the company's direct-to-consumer channel of distribution that enables high quality consumer engagement during the selling process.

The Producer

CUTCO's commitment to quality and innovation is evident throughout every step of the manufacturing process—from the selection of steel to final inspection. The company stands behind each and every product with a FOREVER satisfaction guarantee. The guarantee has four components:

1. FOREVER Performance Guarantee
2. FOREVER Sharpness Guarantee
3. FOREVER Replace Service Agreement for Misuse or Abuse
4. 15-Day Unconditional Money Back Guarantee

CUTCO Cutlery's American-made products and the hard-working craftsmen and women dedicated to creating this high-quality kitchen cutlery were featured on the Travel Channel's "John Ratzenberger's Made in America" program. With its reputation for high quality, accompanied by a FOREVER satisfaction guarantee, CUTCO Cutlery Corporation distributes its products direct to the consumer via its Vector Marketing sales force.

The Consumer

CUTCO Cutlery Corporation has approximately 18 million satisfied consumers in North America. Customer response to CUTCO research directs the development of new products and services, and the sharing of personal stories about special times with family and friends serves as an inspiration to everyone in the company. Thousands of customers have written letters telling the company about the role the company has played in their lives. These customer letters tell how CUTCO has helped them slice and dice fruits and vegetables for weeknight dinners, create weekend party fare, and chop and carve food for holidays, birthdays, and anniversaries. CUTCO cutlery is given as gifts to newly married sons and daughters and is handed down from generation to generation as a family heirloom. The customers praise the quality of CUTCO and offer thanks for the comfort of the ergonomically designed handles and the CUTCO Forever Guarantee.

Producer to Consumer Direct Channel via Vector Marketing Corporation

Unlike many competitive cutlery products, CUTCO cutlery products are not available in mass merchandise or specialty stores. Boasting annual sales of over $200 million, Vector Marketing Corporation is a direct sales firm and the sole distributor of Cutco Cutlery. The independent sales representatives of Vector Marketing Corporation are largely college students from campuses across the nation. According to a company spokesperson, Vector Marketing's sales force is a group of dynamite individuals who represent the company to the consumer in the same high-quality fashion as the CUTCO product. The sales representatives contact potential consumers via referrals, referred to as the "friends of friends" approach. Conversely, consumers can contact the company directly and be connected to a salesperson in the same geographic region.

Divided into six regions (Northeast, Midwest, Eastern, Central, Southwest, and Western), Vector Marketing has over 300 offices across the United States and Canada. Regional headquarters are in Philadelphia (Pennsylvania), Detroit (Michigan), Milwaukee (Wisconsin), Dallas (Texas), Austin (Texas), San Diego (California), and Toronto (Canada). Vector Marketing Corporation belongs to the Direct Selling Association (DSA), whose members are leading companies engaged in direct selling in the United States. All DSA members adhere to a strict code of ethics and promote a high standard of integrity in direct selling.

From production through sales, the CUTCO Corporation takes ownership of its products. Using this direct-to-consumer channel enables the company to guarantee quality from production to consumption.[62]

Questions

1. Why would a company such as CUTCO Cutlery opt for the direct channel instead of the retailer channel for its consumer products?

2. What other companies are similar to CUTCO Cutlery in its approach to direct retailing?

5 Promotion and Communication Strategies

© iStockphoto.com/Juan Facundo Mora Soria; © Violetkaipa/Shutterstock.com

16 Promotional Planning for Competitive Advantage

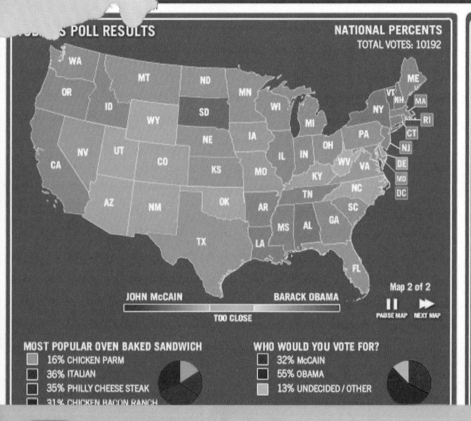

Learning Outcomes

1 Discuss the role of promotion in the marketing mix

2 Describe the communication process

3 Explain the goals of promotion

4 Discuss the elements of the promotional mix

5 Discuss the AIDA concept and its relationship to the promotional mix

6 Discuss the concept of integrated marketing communications

7 Describe the factors that affect the promotional mix

LO1

The Role of Promotion in the Marketing Mix

Few goods or services, no matter how well developed, priced, or distributed, can survive in the marketplace without effective **promotion**—communication by marketers that informs, persuades, and reminds potential buyers of a product in order to influence their opinion or elicit a response.

Promotional strategy is a plan for the optimal use of the promotional mix elements: advertising, public relations, personal selling, sales promotion and social media. As Exhibit 16.1 shows, the marketing manager determines the goals of the company's promotional strategy in light of the firm's overall goals for the marketing mix—product, place (distribution), promotion, and price. Using these overall goals, marketers combine the elements of the promotional mix into a coordinated plan. This promotional plan defines the promotional strategy, which then becomes an integral part of the overall marketing strategy for reaching the target market.

The main function of a marketer's promotional strategy is to convince target customers that the goods and services offered provide a competitive advantage over the competition. A **competitive advantage** is the set of unique features of a company and its products that are perceived by the target market as significant and superior to the competition. Such features can include high product

> **Few goods or services can survive in the marketplace without effective promotion.**

promotion
Communication by marketers that informs, persuades, and reminds potential buyers of a product in order to influence an opinion or elicit a response.

marketing&you.

Using the following scale, enter your opinions on the lines provided.

STRONGLY DISAGREE ◀ 1 · 2 · 3 · 4 · 5 · 6 ▶ STRONGLY AGREE

_____ **People frequently tell me about themselves.**

_____ **I've been told that I'm a good listener.**

_____ **I'm very accepting of others.**

_____ **People trust me with their secrets.**

_____ **I easily get people to "open up."**

_____ **People feel relaxed around me.**

_____ **I enjoy listening to people.**

_____ **I'm sympathetic to people's problems.**

_____ **I encourage people to tell me how they are feeling.**

_____ **I can keep people talking about themselves.**

Total your score, and see what it means after you read the chapter.

Source: Scale #455, *Marketing Scales Handbook*, G. Bruner, K. James, H. Hensel, eds., Vol. III. © by American Marketing Association. Used with permission of the American Marketing Association.

Promotional Strategy

Promotional mix
- Advertising
- Public relations
- Sales promotion
- Personal selling
- Social media

Competitive advantage

Marketer

Consumer

© Cengage Learning 2013

quality, rapid delivery, low prices, excellent service, or a feature not offered by the competition. For example, fast-food restaurant Subway promises fresh sandwiches that are better for you than a hamburger or pizza. Subway effectively communicates its competitive advantage through advertising featuring long-time "spokes-eater" Jared Fogle, who lost weight by eating at Subway every day.[1] Thus, promotion is a vital part of the marketing mix, informing consumers of a product's benefits and thereby positioning the product in the marketplace.

Exhibit 16.1 Role of Promotion in the Marketing Mix

Overall marketing objectives

Marketing mix
- Product
- Place (distribution)
- Promotion
- Price

Promotional mix
- Advertising
- Public relations
- Sales promotion
- Personal selling
- Social media

Target market

© Cengage Learning 2013

promotional strategy

A plan for the optimal use of the elements of promotion: advertising, public relations, personal selling, sales promotion, and social media.

LO2
Marketing Communication

Promotional strategy is closely related to the process of communication. As humans, we assign meaning to feelings, ideas, facts, attitudes, and emotions. **Communication** is the process by which we exchange or share meanings through a common set of symbols. When a company develops a new product, changes an old one, or simply tries to increase sales of an existing good or service, it must communicate its selling message to potential customers. Marketers communicate information about the firm and its products to the target market and various publics through its promotion programs. Domino's Pizza recently had a serious communications problem. After customer complaints about the quality of their product (and a disturbing video posted on YouTube featuring one of its employees doing things to the pizza that went viral), the company decided to do something that no other company had—they promoted the complaints in advertising and social media. Working with ad agency Crispin Porter & Bogusky, Domino's decided to embrace authenticity by announcing that their pizza photos would not have "fancy touch ups" and encouraged consumers to take photos of their pizza and post them to the new Web site. Dubbed the "Pizza Turnaround," the campaign featured the CEO reacting (and apologizing) to consumer complaints about the "crust tasting like cardboard" or the "sauce tasting like ketchup." Domino's changed the recipe and positioned the brand as "real" and "authentic," an old positioning base to be sure, but one that was particularly relevant given consumer mistrust of advertising and corporations in general. And it worked. Sales increased 14 percent from one quarter to the next and research showed the ads were some of the most effective in years.[2] The Marketing Metrics box below explains how using marketing metrics can help determine how give an Arby's restaurant a competitive advantage by choosing the perfect location.

Communication can be divided into two major categories: interpersonal communication and mass communication. **Interpersonal communication** is direct, face-to-face communication between two or more people. When communicating face-to-face, people see the other person's reaction and can respond almost immediately. A salesperson speaking directly with a client is an example of interpersonal marketing communication. **Mass communication** involves communicating a concept or message to large audiences. A great deal of marketing communication is directed to consumers as a whole, usually through a mass medium such as television, newspapers, or the Internet. When a company advertises, it generally does not personally know the people with whom it is trying to communicate. Furthermore, the company often cannot respond immediately to consumers' reactions to its messages (unless they are using social media or other Internet-based marketing tools). Instead, the marketing manager must wait to see whether people are reacting positively or negatively to the mass-communicated promotion. Any clutter from competitors' messages or other distractions in the environment can reduce the effectiveness of the mass-communication effort.

The Obama presidential campaign demonstrated not only knowledge of basic marketing principles, but also an understanding of ground-level tactics on everything from segmentation and database management to analytics, social networking, and online communities.

THE COMMUNICATION PROCESS

Marketers are both senders and receivers of messages. As *senders*, marketers attempt to inform, persuade, and remind the target market to adopt courses of action compatible with the need to promote the purchase of goods and services. As *receivers*, marketers attune themselves to the target market in order to develop the appropriate messages, adapt existing messages, and spot new communication opportunities. In this way, most marketing communication is a two-way, rather than one-way, process. The two-way nature of the communication process is shown in Exhibit 16.2.

The Sender and Encoding The **sender** is the originator of the message in the communication process. In an interpersonal conversation, the sender might be a parent, a friend, or a salesperson. For an advertisement, press release, or social media campaign, the sender is the company or organization itself. For example, the Swedish brand Absolut Vodka launched a marketing campaign using the theme "In an Absolut World." At the outset, the objective of the campaign was to increase Absolut's market share in the crowded and increasingly competitive U.S. vodka market. To appeal to this market, Absolut had to differentiate its message from the "rational benefits" (such as best taste or smooth feel) being claimed by so many of the upstarts in the vodka category. Absolut changed its near-legendary super-premium brand strategy—a print campaign pairing the iconic shape of its bottle with equally iconic art figures—to a campaign that would appeal to the "emotional benefits" of the brand.[4] Thus, Absolut launched a new campaign using the phrase "Absolut World" to promote the message that their vodka was the brand to choose if the customer was intelligent, savvy, and wanted to challenge the status quo by taking on bold and optimistic new world views. The ads assert that Absolut vodka is in a class by itself—indeed, in a world of its own, an "Absolut World." The ad

competitive advantage
One or more unique aspects of an organization that cause target consumers to patronize that firm rather than competitors.

communication
The process by which we exchange or share meaning through a common set of symbols.

interpersonal communication
Direct, face-to-face communication between two or more people.

mass communication
The communication of a concept or message to large audiences.

sender
The originator of the message in the communication process.

MARKETING METRICS

Find a Location for Arby's

The Problem

In 2010, there were more than 300,000 fast food restaurants in the United States (about one for every 1,000 people). That number is much higher than in 1980, where there was one restaurant for every 2,000 people. Recognizing that fast food restaurants are a growing business opportunity, Jacob has decided to open a new restaurant. Upon further research, he has decided to open an Arby's. Opening a new fast food restaurant such as Arby's is a major investment. On average, it costs $1.6 million to buy or lease the land and build an Arby's restaurant. Although these costs are born by the franchisee, Arby's provides support to the franchisee in finding the better locations to enable success. With such an investment on the line, Jacob wants to make the best choice of location for his new Arby's.

The Metric

To determine where to open a store, business owners have to understand their customers. According to Luigi Slvaneschi, a former McDonald's real-estate executive, "Customers are lazybones.... They absolutely will not walk one more step. You literally have to put a store where people are going to smack their face against it."

In 2010, Arby's had 3,600 stores and hoped to add 100 more in 2011. To identify the most optimal locations for the new stores, Arby's sent scouts out to scour neighborhoods and towns for promising sites. In their search, they compared locations against a checklist of key issues. The following site recommendations are those that Jacob will need to use to choose his Arby's location.

1. No stand-alone Arby's stores are to be built within a mile of each other.

2. Seek a surrounding population of 20,000, with at least 3,000 of those hanging around during the day to accommodate daytime traffic.

3. Seek a neighborhood with an average household income of $40,000.

4. Seek sites that are near grocery stores and post offices because most customers must visit these establishments at least once a week. Large shopping malls also do well.

5. Benchmark the location against Wendy's, a competitor that serves the same target market.

6. Ensure customers can make a left-hand turn into the site. Eliminating a left-hand turn into a restaurant can cause a 20- to 30-percent loss in sales.

With this list, Jacob can set up a decision grid to help him determine the relative importance of each criterion when deciding on an Arby's location. Using this grid, each characteristic is ranked against the others. For example, in the first row, Jacob ranked Population and Daytime traffic equally important to the nearest Arby's being more than 1 mile away (0); the nearest Arby's proximity is ranked more important than being near a grocery, mall, or post office (+1); and the nearest Arby's being more than one mile away is less important than the evaluation against Wendy's (−1). After evaluating each criterion, the total weights are summed at the bottom of the grid, allowing Jacob to determine what is absolutely important in his Arby's location.

Management Decision

Based on his evaluations, having an Arby's near a grocery store, post office, or in a mall is Jacob's most important factor in determining a location. Population, daily traffic, and average income are other factors that Jacob ranked highly and will be strong factors in determining a location. He ranked having a left-hand turn into the restaurant the lowest—while this doesn't make it unimportant, if he found a location that met five other criteria, but not a left-hand turn, Jacob might strongly consider that location. More complex metrics will help him determine population density, income, traffic patterns, competitor benchmarking, and distance from same brand stores, which are all key in determining whether a location meets these criteria. Restaurateurs, retailers, and consumer service firms each benefit from using similar decision grids for addressing the challenge of finding a suitable location for distributing and selling their products and services to their target market.

Location Characteristics	A	P	DT	AI	GUM	W	LT
Nearest Arby's + 1 mile (A)		0	0	+1	+1	−1	0
Pop. +20,000 (P)	0		+1	0	0	+1	−1
Daytime traffic +3,000 (DT)	0	−1		−1	0	−1	0
Avg. Income $40,000 (AI)	−1	0	+1		0	0	−1
Near Grocery/USPS/Mall (GUM)	−1	0	0	0		−1	−1
Evaluation against nearest Wendy's (W)	+1	+1	−1	0	+1		−1
Left-hand turn into site (LT)	0	+1	0	+1	+1	+1	
Total Weight	−1	+1	+1	+1	+3	−1	−4

Source: Shirley Leung, "Where's the Beef? A Glutted Market Leaves Food Chains Hungry for Sites; Finding Spots for New Outlets Takes Heaps of Research and an Eye for Details; Hint: Move Next to Wal-Mart," *Wall Street Journal,* October 1, 2003, A1; http://www.arbys.com/about.html.

Exhibit 16.2 Communication Process

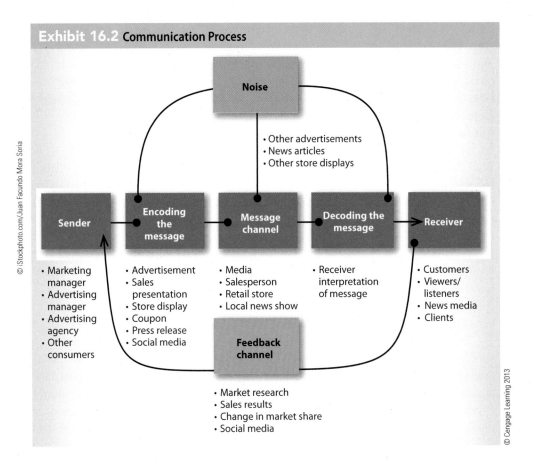

Encoding
the message
• Advertisement
• Sales presentation
• Store display
• Coupon
• Press release
• Social media

Noise
• Other advertisements
• News articles
• Other store displays

Sender
• Marketing manager
• Advertising manager
• Advertising agency
• Other consumers

Message channel
• Media
• Salesperson
• Retail store
• Local news show

Decoding the message
• Receiver interpretation of message

Receiver
• Customers
• Viewers/listeners
• News media
• Clients

Feedback channel
• Market research
• Sales results
• Change in market share
• Social media

© iStockphoto.com/Juan Facundo Mora Soria

© Cengage Learning 2013

campaign also invites Absolut's consumers to visualize a world that appeals to them—even a world that may be idealized or "fantastic."[5]

Encoding is the conversion of the sender's ideas and thoughts into a message, usually in the form of words or signs. A basic principle of encoding is that what matters is not what the source says but what the receiver hears. One way of conveying a message that the receiver will hear properly is to use concrete words and pictures. For example, Absolut's marketers encoded the message by creating a series of life-size outdoor ads, wrapped buildings, and other media that imagined an "Absolut World" where factories emit harmless bubbles instead of smoke, ATMs dispense "free" money, politicians' noses grow if they lie, and people in bars wear buttons labeling their dating status and mindset.[6]

Message Transmission Transmission of a message requires a **channel**—a voice, radio, newspaper, computer, smartphone or other communication medium. A facial expression or gesture can also serve as a channel.

Reception occurs when the message is detected by the receiver and enters his or her frame of reference. In a two-way conversation such as a sales pitch given by a sales representative to a potential client, reception is normally high. Similarly, when the message is a recommendation from a friend, the reception is high as well. In contrast, the desired receivers may or may not detect the message when it is mass communicated because most media are cluttered by **noise**—anything that interferes with, distorts, or slows down the transmission of information. In some media overcrowded with advertisers, such as newspapers and television, the noise level is high and the reception level is low. For example, competing network advertisements, other entertainment option advertisements, or other programming on the network

encoding
The conversion of a sender's ideas and thoughts into a message, usually in the form of words or signs.

channel
A medium of communication—such as a voice, radio, or newspaper—for transmitting a message.

noise
Anything that interferes with, distorts, or slows down the transmission of information.

receiver
The person who decodes a message.

decoding
Interpretation of the language and symbols sent by the source through a channel.

feedback
The receiver's response to a message.

itself might hamper reception of the "Absolut World" advertising campaign message. Transmission can also be hindered by situational factors: physical surroundings such as light, sound, location, and weather; the presence of other people; consumer multitasking, or the temporary moods consumers might bring to the situation. Mass communication may not even reach all the right consumers. Some members of the target audience were likely watching television when Absolut's commercials were shown, but others probably were not.

The Receiver and Decoding Marketers communicate their message through a channel to customers, or **receivers**, who will decode the message. It is important to note that there can be multiple receivers as consumers share their experiences and their recommendations online through social networks and other types of social media. These conversations online are becoming an increasingly influential way to promote products and services. **Decoding** is the interpretation of the language and symbols sent by the source through a channel. Common understanding between two communicators, or a common frame of reference, is required for effective communication. Therefore, marketing managers must ensure a proper match between the message to be conveyed and the target market's attitudes and ideas.

Even though a message has been received, it will not necessarily be properly decoded—or even seen, viewed, or heard—because of selective exposure, distortion, and retention. (Refer to Chapter 6.) Even when people receive a message, they tend to manipulate, alter, and modify it to reflect their own biases, needs, knowledge, and culture. Differences in age, social class, education, culture, and ethnicity can lead to miscommunication, for example. Further, because people don't always listen or read carefully, they can easily misinterpret what is said or written. In fact, researchers have found that consumers misunderstand a large proportion of both printed and televised communications. Bright colors and bold graphics have been shown to increase consumers' comprehension of marketing communication. Even these techniques are not foolproof, however. A classic example of miscommunication occurred when Lever Brothers mailed out samples of its then new dishwashing liquid, Sunlight, which contains real lemon juice. The package clearly stated that Sunlight was a household cleaning product. Nevertheless, many people saw the word *sunlight,* the large picture of lemons, and the phrase "with real lemon juice" and thought the product was lemon juice.

Marketers targeting consumers in foreign countries must also worry about the translation and possible miscommunication of their promotional messages by other cultures. An important issue for global marketers is whether to standardize or customize the message for each global market in which they sell. While Absolut's marketers used the "World" message globally, they tailored the ads to reflect how people in various regions might envision an "Absolut World." For example, a bus shelter on Second Avenue in New York City was wrapped to look like a subway entrance—a dream of many New York commuters.[7] In Germany, consumers were given a firsthand experience of the "Absolut World." For one week, a fleet of Porsche taxis chauffeured passengers quickly—and for free—around Hamburg, Munich, and Berlin. By the end of that week, the taxis had generated over 15 million media contacts through TV, print, and online news coverage.[8]

Feedback In interpersonal communication, the receiver's response to a message is direct **feedback** to the source. Feedback may be verbal, as in saying "I agree," or nonverbal, as in nodding, smiling, frowning, or gesturing.

Because mass communicators such as Absolut are often cut off from direct feedback, they must rely on market research or analysis of viewer responses from indirect feedback. Absolut might use measurements such as the percentage of

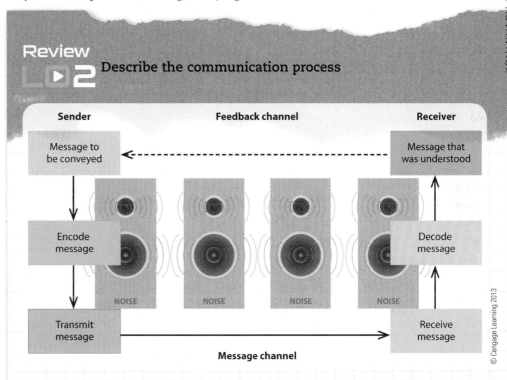

television viewers who recognized, recalled, or stated they were exposed to Absolut's messages. Indirect feedback enables mass communicators to decide whether to continue, modify, or drop a message. Web sites also facilitate feedback. For example, Absolut could capture consumer feedback in e-mail messages, discussion boards, blogs, and other tools from their Web site. Absolut recently introduced a feature on their Web site that allows consumers to submit their Absolut vision and a description of how they would like it to come true. If chosen, Absolut's team will "realize" that vision for the submitter.

Since marketers are spending more money online, they do have the ability to get some feedback. Using analytics, marketers can see how long a consumer stays on their Web site or which pages they view. Moreover, social media enables instant feedback. Many companies, such as JCPenney and Comcast, respond to consumer's posts on Facebook and to complaints posted on Twitter.

Internet and social media have had an impact on the communication model depicted in Exhibit 16.2. That model shows the feedback channel as primarily impersonal and numbers-driven. In the traditional communication process, marketers can see the results of consumer behavior (e.g., a drop in sales), but are only able to explain them using their judgment. Even the information generated by market research is not as natural as that gleaned from bloggers. Social media enables marketers to personalize the feedback channel by opening the door for direct conversation with consumers. However, because there is no control over social media, there is a chance that comments and postings will be negative. Thus, many companies have a crisis communication strategy to deal with negative information. When marketers launch a social media campaign, they create an unfiltered feedback channel.

Review

LO2 Describe the communication process

Sender	Feedback channel	Receiver
Message to be conveyed		Message that was understood
Encode message		Decode message
Transmit message	Message channel	Receive message

NOISE NOISE NOISE NOISE

LO3
The Goals of Promotion

People communicate with one another for many reasons. They seek amusement, ask for help, give assistance or instructions, provide information, and express ideas and thoughts. Promotion, on the other hand, seeks to modify behavior and thoughts in some way. For example, promoters might try to persuade consumers to drink Pepsi rather than Coke, or to eat at Burger King instead of McDonald's. Promotion also strives to reinforce existing behavior—for instance, getting consumers to continue dining at Burger King once they have switched. The source (the seller) hopes to project a favorable image or to motivate purchase of the company's goods and services.

Effective promotion will achieve one or more of three goals: It will *inform* the target audience, *persuade* the target audience, or *remind* the target audience. Often a marketer will try to achieve two or more of these goals at the same time.

INFORMING

Informative promotion seeks to convert an existing need into a want or to stimulate interest in a new product. It is generally more prevalent during the early stages of the product life cycle. People typically will not buy a product or service or support a nonprofit organization until they know its purpose and its benefits to them. Informative messages are important for promoting complex and technical products such as automobiles, computers, and investment services. For example, Philips's original advertisement for the Magnavox flat-screen television showed young, urban consumers trying the flat-screen TV all over the house, including the ceiling. The ad focused on "how to" use the flat-screen TV rather than the Philips Magnavox brand or the technological capabilities.[9] Informative promotion is also important for a "new" brand being introduced into an "old" product class—for example, a new brand of frozen pizza (such as Kashi Frozen Pizza) entering the frozen pizza industry, which is dominated by well-known brands such as Kraft's DiGiorno and Schwan's Grocery Products' Red Baron. Kashi Frozen Pizza cannot establish itself against more mature products unless potential buyers are aware of it, value its benefits, and understand its positioning in the marketplace.

PERSUADING

Persuasive promotion is designed to stimulate a purchase or an action—for example, to eat more Doritos or use Verizon Wireless mobile phone service. Persuasion normally becomes the main promotion goal when the product enters the growth stage of its life cycle. By this time, the target market should have general product awareness and some knowledge of how the product can fulfill their wants. Therefore, the promotional goal switches from informing consumers about the product category to persuading them to buy the company's brand rather than the competitor's. At this time, the promotional message emphasizes the product's real and perceived competitive advantages, often appealing to emotional needs such as love, belonging, self-esteem, and ego satisfaction. For example, the latest advertisement for the Philips Magnavox flat-screen television still features young, urban consumers. But the ad focuses on the product's benefits such as lifestyle enhancements, technological features such as HDTV and Dolby digital surround sound, and the superiority of the brand.[10]

Persuasion can also be an important goal for very competitive mature product categories such as many household items, soft drinks, beer, and banking services. In a marketplace characterized by many competitors, the promotional message often encourages brand switching and aims to convert some buyers into loyal users. For example, to persuade new customers to switch their checking accounts, a bank's marketing manager might offer a year's worth of free checks with no fees.

Critics believe some promotional messages and techniques can be too persuasive, causing consumers to buy products and services they really don't need.

promotional mix
The combination of promotional tools—including advertising, public relations, personal selling, and sales promotion—used to reach the target market and fulfill the organization's overall goals.

REMINDING

Reminder promotion is used to keep the product and brand name in the public's mind. This type of promotion prevails during the maturity stage of the life cycle. It assumes that the target market has already been persuaded of the good's or service's merits. Its purpose is simply to trigger a memory. Crest toothpaste, Tide laundry detergent, Miller beer, and many other consumer products often use reminder promotion. Similarly, Philips Magnavox could advertise just the brand rather than the benefits of the product.

L▶4
The Promotional Mix

As you read earlier, most promotional strategies use several elements or tools—which might include advertising, public relations, sales promotion, personal selling, and social media—to reach a target market. That combination is called the **promotional mix**. The proper promotional mix is the one that management believes will meet the needs of the target market and fulfill the organization's overall goals. The more funds allocated to each promotional element and the more managerial emphasis placed on each technique, the more important that element is thought to be in the overall mix.

ADVERTISING

Almost all companies selling a good or a service use some advertising, whether in the form of a multimillion-dollar campaign or a simple classified ad in a newspaper. *Advertising* is any form of impersonal (one-way) paid communication in which the sponsor or company is identified. One of the primary benefits of advertising is its ability to communicate to a large number of people at one time. Traditional media—such as television, radio, newspapers, magazines, books, direct mail, billboards, and transit cards (advertisements on buses and taxis and at bus stops)—are most commonly used to transmit advertisements to consumers. With the increasing fragmentation of traditional media choices, marketers are using other methods to send their advertisements to consumers, such as Web sites, e-mail, and interactive video kiosks located in department stores and supermarkets. However, as the Internet becomes a more vital component of many companies' promotion and marketing mix, consumers and lawmakers are increasingly concerned about possible violations of consumers' privacy. Read more about this issue in the Ethics in Marketing box about how social networking sites are using all the information that is freely collected.

Review
L▶3 Explain the goals of promotion

- **Informative promotion**
  Increasing the awareness of a new brand, product class, or product attribute
  Explaining how the product works
  Suggesting new uses for a product
  Building a company image

- **Persuasive promotion**
  Encouraging brand switching
  Changing customers' perceptions of product attributes
  Influencing customers to buy now
  Persuading customers to call

- **Reminder promotion**
  Reminding consumers that the product may be needed in the near future
  Reminding consumers where to buy the product
  Maintaining consumer awareness

ethics in marketing

Who's Peeping at Your Facebook? Privacy Concerns and Social Networks

Millions of people have embraced social networking sites such as Facebook (600 million users) and MySpace (50 million users) and increasingly specialized sites such as LinkedIn. Although social networks are easy ways to keep in touch with friends and family, they generate privacy concerns. A study at Carnegie Mellon found that a large portion of the Facebook users the researchers studied generously supplied plenty of personal data and limited privacy settings. Indeed, given the types of information that is regularly displayed on Facebook pages, it is clear that millennials have a different view of privacy than their older counterparts. Does this mean the users were oblivious to several privacy concerns? A simple viewing of personal information can make it easier for stalking and identify theft. More insidiously, Facebook and MySpace allow outside developers to create widgets or apps for the sites. In recent years literally thousands of applications have been created by more than 400,000 developers and more than 95 percent of Facebook users have downloaded at least one application.

No big deal, right? Well, all of those developers are allowed to see your personal information to develop their applications. That's right. Twenty guys you don't know could be looking at your personal information and that of your friends. When a user installs an app, the developer can see everything but contact information. The data is available for only 24 hours, but once that data gets onto a third-party server, there is little Facebook or MySpace can do. Facebook states that developers are not allowed to share data with advertisers but they can use the information to tailor features to users—in essence, they can use it during new product development. Developers interviewed for this case have not ruled out the prospect of using the data for targeted advertising; some think that leveraging this data does make sense for some marketing applications.

Facebook and Microsoft's search engine Bing recently announced a partnership to dissolve the barriers between search and social media as they tighten integration of the two to create Bing Social. People can now use Bing to search Facebook "likes" and content that is posted from a Facebook friend. Bing will rely on Facebook's data to improve results when searching for people and places. Microsoft claims that right now, the tools will not store personally identifiable information. Analysts say that while this is important, it is only one step closer to something larger, more complex, and beneficial than what is currently on the market today. As the pace of technology becomes more rapid, what are the privacy implications for social media integration, search behavior, and consumers?[11]

PUBLIC RELATIONS

Concerned about how they are perceived by their target markets, organizations often spend large sums to build a positive public image. *Public relations* is the marketing function that evaluates public attitudes, identifies areas within the organization the public may be interested in, and executes a program of action to earn public understanding and acceptance. Public relations helps an organization communicate with its customers, suppliers, stockholders, government officials, employees, and the community in which it operates. Marketers use public relations not only to maintain a positive image, but also to educate the public about the company's goals and objectives, introduce new products, and help support the sales effort. Public relations will be covered in more depth in Chapter 17.

PERSONAL SELLING

Personal selling is a purchase situation involving a personal, paid-for communication between two people in an attempt to influence each other. Traditional methods of personal selling include a planned presentation to one or more prospective buyers for the purpose of making a sale. More current notions on personal selling emphasize the relationship that develops between a salesperson and a buyer. Recently, both business-to-business and business-to-consumer selling have focused on building long-term relationships rather than on making a onetime sale.

Personal selling, like other promotional mix elements, increasingly depends on the Internet. Most companies use their Web sites to attract potential buyers seeking information on products and services. While some companies sell products directly to consumers online, many do not. Instead, they rely on the Web site to drive customers to their physical locations where personal selling can close the sale. Whether it takes place face-to-face, over the phone, or online, personal selling attempts to persuade the buyer to accept a point of view or take some action. Personal selling is discussed further in Chapter 18.

SALES PROMOTION

Sales promotion consists of all marketing activities—other than personal selling, advertising, and public relations—that stimulate consumer purchasing and dealer effectiveness. Sales promotion is generally a short-run tool used to stimulate immediate increases in demand. In fact, marketers often use sales promotion to improve the effectiveness of other ingredients in the promotional mix, especially advertising and personal selling. Research shows that sales promotion complements advertising by yielding faster sales responses. Sales promotion can be aimed at end consumers, trade customers, or a company's employees. Sales promotions include free samples, contests, premiums, trade shows, giveaways, and coupons. A major promotional campaign might use several of these sales promotion tools. Sales promotion is discussed in more detail in Chapter 18.

SOCIAL MEDIA

Social media are promotion tools used to facilitate conversations among people online. When used by marketers, these tools facilitate consumer empowerment. For the first time, consumers are able to directly speak to other consumers, the company, and Web communities. Social media include blogs (online journals), microblogs (Twitter), podcasting (online audio shows), vodcasts (online videos and newscasts, especially on YouTube), and social networks such as Facebook and LinkedIn. In the beginning, these tools were used primarily by individuals to express themselves. For example, a lawyer might develop a blog to talk about politics because that is a hobby. Or a college freshman might develop a profile on Facebook to stay in touch with high school friends. Businesses began to see that these tools could be used to engage with consumers as well. The rise of blogging, for example, has created a completely new way for marketers to manage their image, connect with consumers, and generate interest in and desire for their companies' products. Now marketers are using social media as integral aspects of their campaigns and are using it to extend the benefits from their traditional media. Social media is discussed in more detail in Chapter 22.

THE COMMUNICATION PROCESS AND THE PROMOTIONAL MIX

The five elements of the promotional mix differ in their ability to affect the target audience. For instance, promotional mix elements might communicate with the consumer directly or indirectly. The message can flow one way or two ways. Feedback can be fast or slow, a little or a lot. Likewise, the communicator might have varying degrees of control over message delivery, content, and flexibility. Exhibit 16.3 outlines differences among the promotional mix elements with respect to mode of communication, marketer's control over the communication process, amount and speed of feedback, direction of message flow, marketer's

Exhibit 16.3 Characteristics of the Elements in the Promotional Mix

	Advertising	Public Relations	Sales Promotion	Personal Selling	Social Media
Mode of Communication	Indirect and impersonal	Usually indirect and impersonal	Usually indirect and impersonal	Direct and face-to-face	Indirect but instant
Communicator Control over Situation	Low	Moderate to low	Moderate to low	High	Moderate
Amount of Feedback	Little	Little	Little to moderate	Much	Much
Speed of Feedback	Delayed	Delayed	Varies	Immediate	Intermediate
Direction of Message Flow	One-way	One-way	Mostly one-way	Two-way	Two-way, multiple ways
Control over Message Content	Yes	No	Yes	Yes	Varies, generally no
Identification of Sponsor	Yes	No	Yes	Yes	Yes
Speed in Reaching Large Audience	Fast	Usually fast	Fast	Slow	Fast
Message Flexibility	Same message to all audiences	Usually no direct control over message	Same message to varied target audiences	Tailored to prospective buyer	Some of the most targeted opportunities

© Cengage Learning 2013

control over the message, identification of the sender, speed in reaching large audiences, and message flexibility.

Exhibit 16.3 illustrates that most elements of the promotional mix are indirect and impersonal when used to communicate with a target market, providing only one direction of message flow. For example, advertising, public relations, and sales promotion are generally impersonal, one-way means of mass communication. Because they provide little opportunity for direct feedback, it can be more difficult to adapt these promotional elements to changing consumer preferences, individual differences, and personal goals. One exception is how a company uses its Web site, which can provide a forum for some types of feedback.

Personal selling, on the other hand, is personal, two-way communication. The salesperson receives immediate feedback from the consumer and can adjust the message in response. Personal selling, however, is very slow in dispersing the marketer's message to large audiences. Because a salesperson can communicate to only one person or a small group of persons at one time, it is a poor choice if the marketer wants to send a message to many potential buyers. Social media is also considered two-way communication, while not quite as immediate as personal selling. Social media can disperse messages to a wide audience and does allow for engagement and feedback from customers through Twitter, Facebook statuses, and blog posts.

Review

LO4 Discuss the elements of the promotional mix

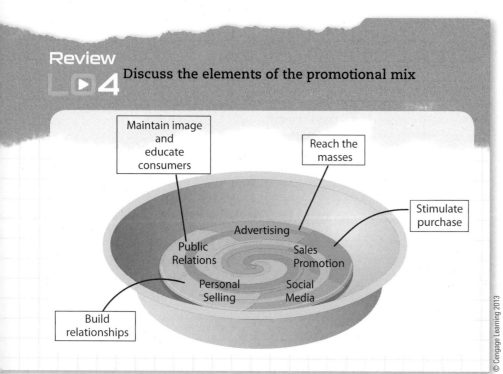

© Cengage Learning 2013

L▶5
Promotional Goals and the AIDA Concept

AIDA concept
A model that outlines the process for achieving promotional goals in terms of stages of consumer involvement with the message; the acronym stands for attention, interest, desire, and action.

The ultimate goal of any promotion is to get someone to buy a good or service or, in the case of nonprofit organizations, to take some action (for instance, donate money or volunteer time). A classic model for reaching promotional goals is called the **AIDA concept**.[12] The acronym stands for *attention, interest, desire,* and *action*— the stages of consumer involvement with a promotional message.

This model proposes that consumers respond to marketing messages in a cognitive (thinking), affective (feeling), and conative (doing) sequence. First, a promotion manager might focus on attracting a person's *attention* by training a salesperson to use a friendly greeting and approach, or by using loud volume, unusual color contrasts, bold headlines, movement, or bright colors in an advertisement. Next, a good sales presentation, demonstration, or advertisement creates *interest* in the product and then, by illustrating how the product's features will satisfy the consumer's needs, arouses *desire*. Finally, a special offer or a strong closing sales pitch might be used to obtain purchase *action*.

The AIDA concept assumes that promotion propels consumers along the following four steps in the purchase-decision process:

1. *Attention:* The advertiser must first gain the attention of the target market. A firm cannot sell something if the market does not know that the good or service exists. When Apple introduced the iPad, it quickly became one of the largest electronics product launches in history. Because the iPad was a revolutionary new tablet computer, Apple had to create awareness and gain attention for it. To do so, it used both traditional media advertising as well as a strategy of contacting influential bloggers and journalists so they would write about the product in newspapers, magazines, and blogs. Because the iPad was a brand extension of the Apple computer, it required less effort than if it had been an entirely new brand. At the same time, because the iPad was an innovative new product line, the promotion had to get customers' attention and create awareness of a new idea from an established company.

2. *Interest:* Simple awareness of a brand seldom leads to a sale. The next step is to create interest in the product. A print ad or TV commercial cannot tell potential customers all the features and benefits of the iPad. Thus, Apple had to arrange iPad demonstrations and target messages to innovators and early adopters to create interest in the new tablet computer. To do this they used not only online videos on YouTube, but personal demonstrations in Apple Stores. They also received extensive media coverage from both online and traditional media outlets.

3. *Desire:* Potential customers for the Apple iPad might like the concept of a portable tablet computer, but perhaps feel it is not necessarily better than a laptop or smartphone. Therefore, Apple had to create brand preference with its iTunes Music Store, apps, multiple functionality, power, light weight, and other features. Specifically, Apple had to convince potential customers that the iPad was the best solution to meet their desire for a combination tablet computer and smartphone.

4. *Action:* Some potential target market customers might have been convinced to buy an iPad but had not yet made the actual purchase. To motivate them to take action, Apple continued advertising to more effectively communicate the features and benefits. And it worked. In less than three months, the iPad sold more than three million units and more than half a million of these sales came during launch week despite the average $429 price tag.[13]

Since the launch, Apple has encouraged developers to create new apps for the iPad. Developers see that rich media could become the standard for display for mobile advertising. Magazines such as *Time* enlisted top marketers like Toyota and Unilever to be a part of its iPad app. More than 15,000 apps are submitted for approval each week as the number of iPad apps grows. These typically fall into the game, media, music, video, utility, and sports categories. Although the iPad has been predicted to kill laptops and e-readers, as well as be the savior of newspapers and magazines, the verdict is still out as to just how revolutionary the product will become. Needless to say, it is off to a great start.

With each product innovation, the cycle of attention, interest, desire, and action began again. But with the familiarity and success of earlier models, the time frame became shorter. Apple sold more than 20 million iPads in the first year and already has more than 35 million iPad app downloads. Moreover, Apple's iTunes Store still sells more music than any other retailer in the United States except for Walmart—and now that inventory includes apps for both iPads and iPhones.[14]

Most buyers involved in high-involvement purchase situations pass through the four stages of the AIDA model on the way to making a purchase. The promoter's task is to determine where on the purchase ladder most of the target consumers are located and design a promotion plan to meet their needs. For instance, if Apple learned from its market research that many potential customers were in the desire stage but had not bought an iPad2 for some reason, then Apple could place advertising on Google, and in video games as well, to target younger individuals who are the primary target market with specific messages to motivate them to take immediate action and buy an iPad2.

The AIDA concept does not explain how all promotions influence purchase decisions. The model suggests that promotional effectiveness can be measured in terms of consumers progressing from one stage to the next. However, the order of stages in the model, as well as whether consumers go through all steps, has been much debated. For example, a purchase can occur without interest or desire, perhaps when a low-involvement product is bought on impulse. Regardless of the order of the stages or

Review LO5 — Discuss the AIDA concept and its relationship to the promotional mix

	Attention	Interest	Desire	Action
Advertising	✓+	✓+	✓	✓−
Public Relations	✓+	✓+	✓+	✓−
Sales Promotion	✓	✓	✓+	✓
Personal Selling	✓	✓+	✓+	✓+
Social Media	✓+	✓+	✓	✓

© Cengage Learning 2013

consumers' progression through these stages, the AIDA concept helps marketers by suggesting which promotional strategy—that is, which plan for using the promotional mix—will be most effective.[15]

LO6
Integrated Marketing Communications

Ideally, marketing communications from each promotional mix element (personal selling, advertising, sales promotion, social media, and public relations) should be integrated—the message reaching the consumer should be the same regardless of whether it is from an advertisement, a salesperson in the field, a magazine article, a Facebook fan page, or a coupon in a newspaper insert.

From the consumer's standpoint, a company's communications are already integrated. Consumers do not think in terms of the five elements of promotion: advertising, sales promotion, public relations, personal selling, and social media. Instead, everything is an "ad." In general, the only people who recognize the distinctions among these elements are the marketers themselves. Unfortunately, many marketers neglect this fact when planning promotional messages and fail to integrate their communication efforts from one element to the next. The most common rift typically occurs between personal selling and the other elements of the promotional mix.

This unintegrated, disjointed approach to promotion has propelled many companies to adopt the concept of **integrated marketing communications (IMC)**. IMC is the careful coordination of all promotional messages—traditional advertising, direct marketing, social media, interactive, public relations, sales promotion, personal selling, event marketing, and other communications—for a product or service to ensure the consistency of messages at every contact point where a company meets the consumer. Following the concept of IMC, marketing managers carefully work out the roles that various promotional elements will play in the marketing mix. Timing of promotional activities is coordinated, and the results of each campaign are carefully monitored to improve future use of the promotional mix tools. Typically, a marketing communications director is appointed who has overall responsibility for integrating the company's marketing communications.

Procter & Gamble's Old Spice was competing in a very mature and competitive market of men's products (like deodorant and body wash). Sales had been declining until ad agency Wieden & Kennedy (of Nike fame) developed a TV spot called "The man your man could smell like" with former football player Isaiah Mustafa. The TV spot aired online during the Superbowl and was quickly viewed by millions of people. Soon it became not only a pop culture

> **integrated marketing communications (IMC)**
> The careful coordination of all promotional messages for a product or a service to ensure the consistency of messages at every contact point at which a company meets the consumer.

INFINITI SPONSORS CIRQUE DU SOLEIL (232/10)
Photos: Camirand Costumes: Dominique Lemieux © 2003, 2006 Cirque du Soleil
For further information please contact Infiniti Communications on +41 21 822 4950/30
© Copyright for editorial use only

Infiniti has announced it has partnered with Cirque du Soleil to become an Official Sponsor and exclusive Automotive Partner.

icon but also a viral blockbuster. The overall campaign included coupons, public relations, coverage on blogs, Facebook, and Twitter as well as print advertising and television advertising. However, what sent this campaign over the top was pure genius. Old Spice solicited questions for the "Old Spice Guy" via Twitter and Facebook and then had Mustafa "answer" the questions by using short video clips online. The Alyssa Milano marriage proposal was probably one of the most successful. The videos have been viewed hundreds of millions of times on YouTube, making the Old Spice YouTube channel one of the most popular channels. The results? Sales were up 107 percent and there are more than one million fans on Facebook, thousands of Twitter followers, higher Web site traffic, and press coverage valued at close to one billion impressions. This campaign leveraged a television spot by extending its life online and by engaging consumers online.[16]

The IMC concept has been growing in popularity for several reasons. First, the proliferation of thousands of media choices beyond traditional television has made promotion a more complicated task. Instead of promoting a product just through mass-media options such as television and magazines, promotional messages today can appear in many varied sources. Furthermore, the mass market has also fragmented—more selectively segmented markets and an increase in niche marketing have replaced the traditional broad market groups that marketers promoted to in years past. For instance, many popular magazines now have Spanish-language editions targeted toward America's growing Hispanic population. Finally, marketers have slashed their advertising spending in favor of promotional techniques that generate immediate sales responses and those whose effects are more easily measured, such as direct marketing. Online advertising has earned a bigger share of the budget as well due to its measurability. Thus, the interest in IMC is largely a reaction to the scrutiny that marketing communications has come under and, particularly, to suggestions that uncoordinated promotional activity leads to a strategy that is wasteful and inefficient.

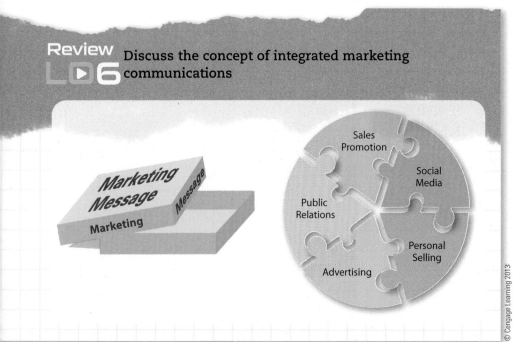

Review
LO6 Discuss the concept of integrated marketing communications

© Cengage Learning 2013

LO7
Factors Affecting the Promotional Mix

Promotional mixes vary a great deal from one product and one industry to the next. Normally, advertising and personal selling are used to promote goods and services, and are supported and supplemented by sales promotion. Public relations helps develop a positive image for the organization and the product line. Social media has been used more for consumer goods, but business-to-business marketers are increasingly using it. However, a firm might choose not to use all five promotional elements in its promotional mix, or to use them in varying degrees. The particular promotional mix chosen by a firm for a product or service depends on several factors: the nature of the product, the stage in the product life cycle, target market characteristics, the type of buying decision, funds available for promotion, and whether a push or a pull strategy will be used.

NATURE OF THE PRODUCT

Characteristics of the product itself can influence the promotional mix. For instance, a product can be classified as either a business product or a consumer product. (Refer to Chapters 7 and 10.) As business products are often custom-tailored to the buyer's exact specifications, they are often not well suited to mass promotion. Therefore, producers of most business goods, such as computer systems or industrial machinery, rely more heavily on personal selling than on advertising. Informative personal selling is common for industrial installations, accessories, and component parts and materials. Advertising, however, still serves a purpose in promoting business goods. Advertisements in trade media can be used to create general buyer awareness and interest. Moreover, advertising can help locate potential customers for the sales force. For example, print media advertising often includes coupons soliciting the potential customer to "fill this out for more detailed information."

In contrast, because consumer products generally are not custom-made, they do not require the selling efforts of a company representative who can tailor them to the user's needs. Thus, consumer goods are promoted mainly through advertising or social media to create brand familiarity. Television and radio advertising, consumer-oriented magazines, and the Internet and other highly targeted media are used extensively to promote consumer goods, especially nondurables. Sales promotion, the brand name, and the product's packaging are about twice as important for consumer goods as for business products. Persuasive personal selling is important at the retail level for shopping goods such as automobiles and appliances.

The costs and risks associated with a product also influence the promotional mix. As a general rule, when the costs or risks of using a product increase, personal selling becomes more important. Items that are a small part of a firm's budget (supply items) or of a consumer's budget (convenience products) do not require a salesperson to close the sale. In fact, inexpensive items cannot support the cost of a salesperson's time and effort unless the potential volume is high. On the other hand, expensive and complex machinery, new buildings, cars, and new homes represent a considerable investment. A salesperson must assure buyers that they are spending their money wisely and not taking an undue financial risk.

Social risk is an issue as well. Many consumer goods are not products of great social importance because they do not reflect social position. People do not experience much social risk in buying a loaf of bread or a candy bar. However, buying some shopping products and many specialty products such as jewelry and clothing does involve a social risk. Many consumers depend on sales personnel for guidance and advice in making the "proper" choice.

STAGES IN THE PRODUCT LIFE CYCLE

The product's stage in its life cycle is a big factor in designing a promotional mix. (See Exhibit 16.4.) During the *introduction stage*, the basic goal of promotion is to inform the target audience that the product is available. Initially, the emphasis

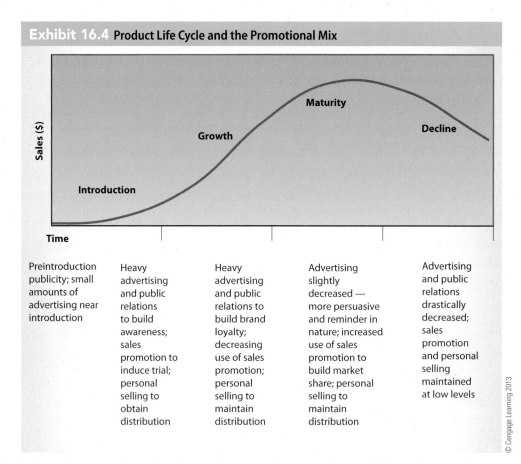

Exhibit 16.4 Product Life Cycle and the Promotional Mix

Introduction		Growth	Maturity	Decline
Preintroduction publicity; small amounts of advertising near introduction	Heavy advertising and public relations to build awareness; sales promotion to induce trial; personal selling to obtain distribution	Heavy advertising and public relations to build brand loyalty; decreasing use of sales promotion; personal selling to maintain distribution	Advertising slightly decreased — more persuasive and reminder in nature; increased use of sales promotion to build market share; personal selling to maintain distribution	Advertising and public relations drastically decreased; sales promotion and personal selling maintained at low levels

is on the general product class—for example, smartphones. The emphasis gradually changes to gaining attention for a particular brand, such as Apple, Nokia, Samsung, Sony Ericsson, or Motorola. Typically, both extensive advertising and public relations inform the target audience of the product class or brand and heighten awareness levels. Sales promotion encourages early trial of the product, and personal selling gets retailers to carry the product.

When the product reaches the *growth stage* of the life cycle, the promotion blend may shift. Often a change is necessary because different types of potential buyers are targeted. Although advertising and public relations continue to be major elements of the promotional mix, sales promotion can be reduced because consumers need fewer incentives to purchase. The promotional strategy is to emphasize the product's differential advantage over the competition. Persuasive promotion is used to build and maintain brand loyalty to support the product during the growth stage. By this stage, personal selling has usually succeeded in getting adequate distribution for the product.

As the product reaches the *maturity stage* of its life cycle, competition becomes much stronger, and thus persuasive and reminder advertising approaches are more strongly emphasized. Sales promotion comes back into focus as product sellers try to increase their market share.

All promotion, especially advertising, is reduced as the product enters the *decline stage*. Nevertheless, personal selling and sales promotion efforts might be maintained, particularly at the retail level.

TARGET MARKET CHARACTERISTICS

A target market characterized by widely scattered potential customers, highly informed buyers, and brand-loyal repeat purchasers generally requires a promotional mix with more advertising and sales promotion and less personal selling. Sometimes, however, personal selling is required even when buyers are well informed and geographically dispersed. Although industrial installations and component parts might be sold to extremely competent people with extensive education and work experience, salespeople must still be present to explain the product and work out the details of the purchase agreement.

Often firms sell goods and services in markets where potential customers are hard to locate. Print advertising can be used to find them. The reader is invited to go online, call, or mail in a reply card for more information. As the online inquiries, calls, or cards are received, salespeople are sent to visit the potential customers.

TYPE OF BUYING DECISION

The promotional mix also depends on the type of buying decision (routine or complex). For example, the most effective promotion for routine consumer decisions, like buying toothpaste or soft drinks, calls attention to the brand or reminds the consumer about the brand. Advertising and, especially, sales promotion are the most productive promotion tools to use for routine decisions.

If the decision is neither routine nor complex, advertising and public relations help establish awareness for the good or service. Suppose a man is looking for a bottle of wine to serve to his dinner guests. As a beer drinker, he is not familiar with wines, yet he has seen advertising for Robert Mondavi wine and has also read an article in a popular magazine about the Robert Mondavi Winery. He might be more likely to buy this brand because he is already aware of it. Indeed, online reviews can be important tools in this type of buying decision.

When does nature surprise you with unexpected flavor?

When you use all natural ingredients from start to finish.

Lay's calls attention to its commitment to natural ingredients as a distinguishing attribute to help customers make a routine buying decision—purchasing Lay's snack food.

In contrast, consumers making complex buying decisions are more extensively involved. They rely on large amounts of information to help them reach a purchase decision. Personal selling is most effective in helping these consumers decide. For example, consumers thinking about buying a car typically research the car online using corporate and third party Web sites. However, few people buy a car without visiting the dealership. They depend on a salesperson to provide the information they need to reach a decision. In addition to online resources, print advertising and brochures can also be used for high-involvement purchase decisions because they often provide a large amount of information to the consumer.

AVAILABLE FUNDS

Money, or the lack of it, might easily be the most important factor in determining the promotional mix. A small, undercapitalized manufacturer might rely heavily on free publicity if its product is unique. If the situation warrants a sales force, a financially strained firm can turn to manufacturers' agents, who work on a commission basis with no advances or expense accounts. Even well-capitalized organizations might not be able to afford the advertising rates of publications such as *Time, Reader's Digest,* and *The Wall Street Journal,* or the cost of running television commercials on *Desperate Housewives, American Idol,* or the Super Bowl. The price of a high-profile advertisement in these media could support several salespeople for an entire year.

When funds are available to permit a mix of promotional elements, a firm will generally try to optimize its return on promotion dollars while minimizing the *cost per contact,* or the cost of reaching one member of the target market. In general, the cost per contact is very high for personal selling, public relations, and sales promotions like sampling and demonstrations. On the other hand, given the number of people national advertising and social media reaches, it has a very low cost per contact.

Usually, there is a trade-off among the funds available, the number of people in the target market, the quality of communication needed, and the relative costs of the promotional elements. A company might have to forgo a full-page, color advertisement in *People* magazine in order to pay for a personal selling effort. Although the magazine ad will reach more people than personal selling, the high cost of the magazine space is a problem. There are plenty of low-cost options available to companies without a huge budget. Many of these include online strategies and public relations efforts, where the company relies on free publicity.

PUSH AND PULL STRATEGIES

The last factor that affects the promotional mix is whether to use a push or a pull promotional strategy. Manufacturers might use aggressive personal selling and trade advertising to convince a wholesaler or a retailer to carry and sell their merchandise. This approach is known as a **push strategy**. (See Exhibit 16.5.) The wholesaler, in turn, must often push the merchandise forward by persuading the retailer to handle the goods. The retailer then uses advertising, displays, and other forms of promotion to convince the consumer to buy the "pushed" products. This concept also applies to services. For example, the Jamaican Tourism Board targets promotions to travel agencies, which, in turn, tell their customers about the benefits of vacationing in Jamaica.

push strategy
A marketing strategy that uses aggressive personal selling and trade advertising to convince a wholesaler or a retailer to carry and sell particular merchandise.

The Jamaican Tourism Board uses a push strategy to encourage people to vacation there.

At the other extreme is a **pull strategy**, which stimulates consumer demand to obtain product distribution. Rather than trying to sell to the wholesaler, the manufacturer using a pull strategy focuses its promotional efforts on end consumers or opinion leaders. For example, Procter & Gamble recently spent $100 million on an advertising campaign to promote a new toothpaste brand. P&G's new Crest Pro-Health claims to deliver everything a consumer could want in one tube—it supposedly protects against gingivitis, plaque, cavities, sensitivity, and stains, and

pull strategy
A marketing strategy that stimulates consumer demand to obtain product distribution.

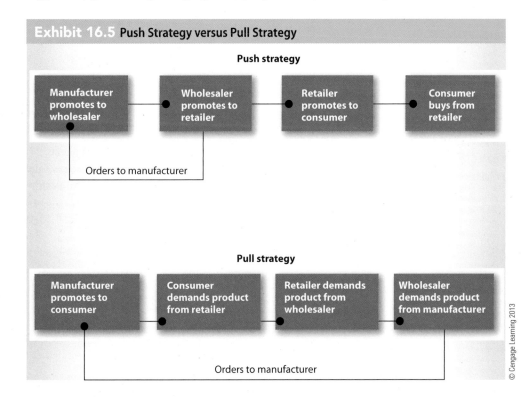

Exhibit 16.5 Push Strategy versus Pull Strategy

it freshens breath. The theme of the campaign, targeted to the information-seeking customer, is "Healthy, beautiful smiles for life."[17] Consumers responded positively to the campaign and began demanding the product from their retailer. The retailer ordered the merchandise from the wholesaler. The wholesaler, confronted with rising demand, then placed an order for the "pulled" merchandise from the manufacturer. Consumer demand pulled the product through the channel of distribution. (See Exhibit 16.5.) Heavy sampling, introductory consumer advertising, cents-off campaigns, and couponing are part of a pull strategy. P&G flooded dental offices with product samples and informational materials in hopes of generating favorable testimonials from users. Similarly, Splenda No Calorie Sweetener offered free samples, recipes, and a coupon to potential consumers who tried Splenda.[18]

Rarely does a company use a pull or a push strategy exclusively. Instead, the mix will emphasize one of these strategies. For example, pharmaceutical companies generally use a push strategy, through personal selling and trade advertising, to promote their drugs and therapies to physicians. Sales presentations and advertisements in medical journals give physicians the detailed information they need to prescribe medication to their patients. Most pharmaceutical companies supplement their push promotional strategy with a pull strategy targeted directly to potential patients through advertisements in consumer magazines and on television.

Review
LO 7 Describe the factors that affect the promotional mix

Promotional Mix
- % Advertising
- % Public Relations
- % Sales Promotion
- % Personal Selling
- % Social Media

Factors:
- Nature of the product
- Product life cycle
- Target market characteristics
- Type of buying decision
- Funds available
- Push or pull strategy

© Cengage Learning 2013

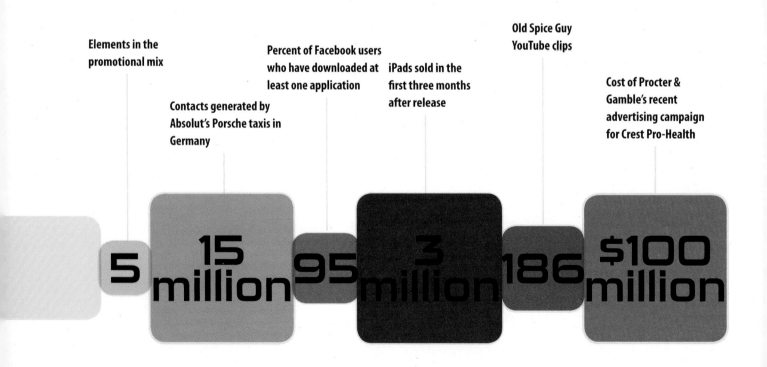

5 Elements in the promotional mix

15 million Contacts generated by Absolut's Porsche taxis in Germany

95 Percent of Facebook users who have downloaded at least one application

3 million iPads sold in the first three months after release

186 Old Spice Guy YouTube clips

$100 million Cost of Procter & Gamble's recent advertising campaign for Crest Pro-Health

ANATOMY OF AN Integrated Marketing Campaign
Indiana Jones movie

Lucasfilm Ltd. used integrated marketing communications to ensure that *Indiana Jones and the Kingdom of the Crystal Skull* was widely and consistently promoted before its release.

NASCAR cars increase publicity.

Hallmark greeting cards and Scholastic books hold kids' interest even after the movie leaves theaters.

Burger King's "Indy Double Whopper" and Mars M&M's tie the movie to summer fun.

Legos and Kellogg's cereal attracts kids.

INDIANA JONES
and the
KINGDOM OF
THE CRYSTAL SKULL

MAY 22

LO1 **Discuss the role of promotion in the marketing mix.** Promotion is communication by marketers that informs, persuades, and reminds potential buyers of a product in order to influence an opinion or elicit a response. Promotional strategy is the plan for using the elements of promotion—advertising, public relations, sales promotion, personal selling, and social media—to meet the firm's overall objectives and marketing goals. Based on these objectives, the elements of the promotional strategy become a coordinated promotion plan. The promotion plan then becomes an integral part of the total marketing strategy for reaching the target market along with product, distribution, and price.

1.1 What is a promotional strategy? Explain the concept of a competitive advantage in relation to promotional strategy.

LO2 **Describe the communication process.** The communication process has several steps. When an individual or organization has a message it wishes to convey to a target audience, it encodes that message using language and symbols familiar to the intended receiver and sends the message through a channel of communication. Noise in the transmission channel distorts the source's intended message. Reception occurs if the message falls within the receiver's frame of reference. The receiver decodes the message and usually provides feedback to the source. Normally, feedback is direct for interpersonal communication and indirect for mass communication.

2.1 Why is understanding the target market a crucial aspect of the communication process?

LO3 **Explain the goals of promotion.** The fundamental goals of promotion are to induce, modify, or reinforce behavior by informing, persuading, and reminding. Informative promotion explains a good's or service's purpose and benefits. Promotion that informs the consumer is typically used to increase demand for a general product category or to introduce a new good or service. Persuasive promotion is designed to stimulate a purchase or an action. Promotion that persuades the consumer to buy is essential during the growth stage of the product life cycle, when competition becomes fierce. Reminder promotion is used to keep the product and brand name in the public's mind. Promotions that remind are generally used during the maturity stage of the product life cycle.

3.1 Why might a marketing manager choose to promote his or her product using persuasion? Give some current examples of persuasive promotion.

team **3.2** Choose a partner from class and go together to interview the owners or managers of several small businesses in your city. Ask them what their promotional objectives are and why. Are they trying to inform, persuade, or remind customers to do business with them? Also determine whether they believe they have an awareness problem or whether they need to persuade customers to come to them instead of to competitors. Ask them to list the characteristics of their primary market, the strengths and weaknesses of their direct competitors, and how they are positioning their store to compete. Prepare a report to present in class summarizing your findings.

LO4 **Discuss the elements of the promotional mix.** The elements of the promotional mix include advertising, public relations, sales promotion, personal selling, and social media. Advertising is a form of impersonal, one-way mass communication paid for by the source. Public relations is the function of promotion concerned with a firm's public image. Sales promotion is typically used to back up other components of the promotional mix by stimulating immediate demand. Personal selling typically involves direct communication, in person or by telephone; the seller tries to initiate a purchase by informing and persuading one or more potential buyers. Finally, social media are promotion tools used to facilitate conversations among people online.

4.1 As the promotional manager for a new line of cosmetics targeted to preteen girls, you have been assigned the task of deciding which promotional mix elements—advertising, public relations, sales promotion, personal selling, and social media—should be used in promoting it. Your budget for promoting the preteen cosmetics line is limited. Write a promotional plan explaining your choice of promotional mix elements given the nature of the product, the stage in the product life cycle, the target market characteristics, the type of buying decision, available funds, and the use of a pull or push strategy.

writing

Discuss the AIDA concept and its relationship to the promotional mix. The AIDA model outlines the four basic stages in the purchase decision-making process, which are initiated and propelled by promotional activities: (1) attention, (2) interest, (3) desire, and (4) action. The components of the promotional mix have varying levels of influence at each stage of the AIDA model. Advertising is a good tool for increasing awareness and knowledge of a good or service. Sales promotion is effective when consumers are at the purchase stage of the decision-making process. Personal selling is most effective in developing customer interest and desire.

LO**5**

5.1 Discuss the AIDA concept. How do these different stages of consumer involvement affect the promotional mix?

5.2 How does a Web site's ease of use affect its ability to create attention, interest, desire, and action? Visit the kitchen and bath pages of Kohler's Web site (**www.us.kohler.com/index. jsp**) and determine how successful the company is at moving consumers through the AIDA process.

online

Discuss the concept of integrated marketing communications. Integrated marketing communications is the careful coordination of all promotional messages for a product or service to ensure the consistency of messages at every contact point where a company meets the consumer—advertising, sales promotion, personal selling, public relations social media, as well as direct marketing, packaging, and other forms of communication. Marketing managers carefully coordinate all promotional activities to ensure that consumers see and hear one message. Integrated marketing communications has received more attention in recent years due to the proliferation of media choices, the fragmentation of mass markets into more segmented niches, and the decrease in advertising spending in favor of promotional techniques that generate an immediate sales response.

LO**6**

6.1 Discuss the importance of integrated marketing communications. Give some current examples of companies that are and are not practicing IMC.

6.2 What do you think is the role of Hallmark's Web site (**www.hallmark.com**) in the company's integrated marketing communications plan? What seems to be the marketing function of the site? Do you think the site is effective?

online

Describe the factors that affect the promotional mix. Promotion managers consider many factors when creating promotional mixes. These factors include the nature of the product, product life-cycle stage, target market characteristics, the type of buying decision involved, availability of funds, and feasibility of push or pull strategies. Because most business products tend to be custom-tailored to the buyer's exact specifications, the marketing manager might choose a promotional mix that relies more heavily on personal selling. On the other hand, consumer products are generally mass produced and lend themselves more to mass promotional efforts such as advertising and sales promotion. As products move through different stages of the product life cycle, marketers will choose to use different promotional elements. For example, advertising is emphasized more in the introductory stage

LO**7**

of the product life cycle than in the decline stage. Characteristics of the target market, such as geographic location of potential buyers and brand loyalty, influence the promotional mix, as does whether the buying decision is complex or routine. The amount of funds a firm has to allocate to promotion may also help determine the promotional mix. Small firms with limited funds might rely more heavily on public relations, whereas larger firms can possibly afford broadcast or print advertising. Last, if a firm uses a push strategy to promote the product or service, the marketing manager might choose to use aggressive advertising and personal selling to wholesalers and retailers. If a pull strategy is chosen, then the manager often relies on aggressive mass promotion, such as advertising and sales promotion, to stimulate consumer demand.

7.1 Explain the difference between a "pull" and a "push" promotional strategy. Under what conditions should each strategy be used?

 7.2 Use Radioguide (**www.radioguide.fm/**) to find a listing of radio Web sites in your area. View several of the stations' sites and compare the promotions featured. What conclusions can you draw about the target market of each station based on the types of promotions they are currently running? Would any of the promotions entice you to tune to a station that you normally don't listen to?

 7.3 Visit **www.teenresearch.com.** What research can this company offer about the size and growth of the teen market, the buying power of teenagers, and their buying habits? Why might these statistics be important to a company targeting teenagers in terms of marketing communications and promotion strategy?

Key Terms

AIDA concept *591*
channel *583*
communication *580*
competitive advantage *579*
decoding *584*
encoding *583*
feedback *584*

integrated marketing
  communications (IMC) *593*
interpersonal
  communication *581*
mass communication *581*
noise *583*
promotion *579*

promotional mix *587*
promotional strategy *579*
pull strategy *599*
push strategy *598*
receiver *584*
sender *581*

Exercises

ETHICS EXERCISE

Integrated Marketing Solutions is a consumer-products marketing services firm. Currently, the firm is handling the launch of a new book for one of its publishing clients. The campaign includes advance review copies for key book reviewers, "Coming Soon" posters for booksellers, an author book-signing tour, and several television interviews. Everything has been produced and scheduled for release next week. Today, Jane Kershaw, the account executive, has learned that although the book received numerous favorable reviews, the review quoted on all of the promotional materials is fabricated.

Questions

1. What should Jane do? Why?

2. What does the AMA Code of Ethics say about accuracy in promotional materials? Go to and review the code. Then, write a brief paragraph describing how the AMA Code of Ethics relates to this issue.

MARKETING PLAN EXERCISE

In Part 4, you began the process of defining the marketing mix, starting with the components of product and distribution. The next stage of the strategic planning process continues defining the elements of the marketing mix, and this section—Part 5—focuses on promotion and communication decisions for the promotion mix, including advertising, public relations, sales promotion, personal selling, and social media. Use the following exercises to guide you through the promotions part of your strategic marketing plan:

1. Define your promotional objectives. What specific results do you hope to accomplish, and which promotional tools will be responsible? How will you use promotions to differentiate yourself from your competition? Remember that promotions cannot be directly tied with sales because there are too many other factors (competition, environment, price, distribution, product, customer service, company reputation, and so on) that affect sales. State specific objectives that can be tied directly to the result of promotional activities—for example, number of people redeeming a coupon, share of audience during a commercial, percent attitude change before and after a telemarketing campaign, or number of people calling a toll-free information hotline. Remember to have offline promotions drive online traffic.

2. Design a promotional message or theme. Does this message inform, remind, persuade, or educate the target market? Make sure this message will work across both traditional and electronic media. How is your promotional message consistent with your branding? Is this message or slogan unique and important enough to be copyrighted? Check with the U.S. Copyright Office at **www.copyright.gov**.

3. Will you be designing and producing all your promotion tools in-house, or do you need to find an agency? What are the advantages of designing promotional tools in-house? Disadvantages? Try to assist in your decision.

APPLICATION EXERCISE 1

Many people are not aware of the rationale behind certain advertising messages. "Why do Infiniti ads show rocks and trees instead of automobiles?" "If car safety is so important, why do automobile ads often show cars skidding on wet, shiny surfaces?" "Target's ads are funky, with all the bright colors and product packaging, but what's the message?"

One way to understand the vagaries of the encoding process is to think of the popular board game *Taboo* by Hasbro. In this game, each team tries to get its members to guess a word without using obvious word clues. For example, to get the team to guess "apple," you may not say words such as *red, fruit, pie, cider,* or *core.* Sometimes advertising is like *Taboo* in that advertisers are not allowed to use certain words or descriptions. For example, pharmaceutical companies are not permitted to make certain claims or to say what a drug treats unless the ad also mentions the potential side effects. Language choices are also limited in advertising. To appreciate this, you can apply the *Taboo* game rules in an advertising format.[19]

Activities

1. Select a product from the list below, and then create a print advertisement or a television storyboard for that product. As part of the exercise, give your product a brand name.

Taboo words, visuals, and concepts are given for each product type. *Taboo* items cannot be present in your work.

Product	Taboo Words, Visuals, and Concepts
Deodorant	Odor, underarm, perspiration, smell, sweat
Pain reliever	Pain, aches, fever, child-proof cap, gel
Soft drinks	Sugar-free, refreshing, thirst, swimwear, any celebrity

2. Now create a second ad or storyboard for your product. This time, however, you must use all the words, visuals, and concepts that are listed in the right column.

Product	Must-Use Words, Visuals, and Concepts
Deodorant	A romantic couple, monster trucks
Pain reliever	A mother and child, oatmeal, homework
Soft drinks	A cup of coffee, cookies, birthday cake, wine

APPLICATION EXERCISE 2

An important concept in promotion is semiotics, or the study of meaning and meaning-producing events. An understanding of semiotics can help you not only to identify objects (denotation) but also to grasp the utility of images and associations (connotation). By manipulating connotations of objects in advertising, you can create, change, or reinforce images for products. Thus, semiotics is a powerful tool for brand management and promotion.[20]

Activities

1. Make a list of ten images and associations that come to mind for each of the following items: baseball, vinyl record album, spoon, rubber band.

2. Look through magazines and see if you can find print advertisements that include each of the items (baseball, vinyl record album, spoon, rubber band) in a supporting role. What seems to be the message of each ad? How does the item help create or reinforce an image for the product being sold in the ad?

3. Think of an everyday object of your own. What are its likely connotations? For example, a dog in a car might signal a family vehicle, but a dog also connotes loyalty, "man's best friend," and dependability. What images and associations are likely with your item? Make a list of as many as you can.

4. Now use your object and list of associations to create an image for another product. Think of the likely connotations your object will have for a certain target market and how such connotations can support a brand image. For example, if your everyday object is a candle, you might choose lingerie for your product, based on a candle's romantic connotations.

CASE STUDY: HBO's Blood Virus

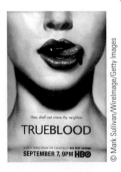

© Mark Sullivan/WireImage/Getty Images

When prominent occult film bloggers and fans began receiving strange letters written in dead languages and mailed in wax-sealed black envelopes, a shockwave of curiosity and excitement rippled through the horror-film fandom. A legion of bloggers and message-board posters set to work translating the letters from languages such as Babylonian and Ugaritic into English, discovering that the missives led them to a mysterious and macabre Web site featuring an image of a seductive lady vampire. The site advertised a beverage called TruBlood—a synthetic blood developed by the Japanese that vampires could drink as an alternative to feeding on humans. As visitors explored the site, they discovered short webisodes for the then-upcoming HBO television series that incorporates the TruBlood beverage into its storyline.

The letters and Web site were developed as part of a viral marketing campaign by HBO and Campfire Media, an independent agency founded by two of the creators of the successful 1999 film *The Blair Witch Project*. Viral marketing is the propagation of brand or product awareness through preexisting social networks, using unconventional media, with the hope that the campaign spreads as a cultural phenomenon. In addition to the letters, Campfire established a fictional blog and MySpace pages written by characters from the show, launched a human-vampire dating service, advertised TruBlood on vending machines, and strategically leaked tidbits of information and multimedia about the show. Campfire employees closely monitored popular horror blogs and message boards in order to gauge and encourage public interest, as well as orchestrate the release of new materials.

The campaign was an incredible, if somewhat subversive success—not only did Campfire generate momentous interest in the show, but a number of individuals actually tried to locate a TruBlood distributor. "We didn't mean to dupe people," said Zach Enterlin, HBO's vice president of advertising and promotions. "We just wanted a campaign that breaks through and resonates a little bit. It's a testament to how true to form the ads are. Some people aren't paying close attention." Viral marketing campaigns are ideal for shows like *True Blood*, whose fans fervently share and discuss ideas within Internet communities. In addition, *True Blood* came with an avid built-in fan base of those already familiar with the story, because the show is adapted from the popular Sookie Stackhouse series of books by Charlaine Harris.

Viral marketing has been a successful part of many advertising campaigns, including *Cloverfield* and *The Dark Knight*. *Cloverfield*, a film in which gargantuan monsters rampage through New York City, is captured on handheld video cameras. It was introduced to viewers through an untitled, unexplained teaser trailer that played before 2007's *Transformers* movie. As speculation mounted, *Cloverfield* marketers unveiled a number of enigmatic Web sites, as well as a tie-in campaign for the fictional Slusho! beverage and a Japanese drilling company, both of which play a part in *Cloverfield*'s mythology.

In May of 2007, 42 Entertainment began a viral campaign for *The Dark Knight*, a sequel to 2005's *Batman Begins*. The campaign focused on the film's antagonists: a Web site titled "I believe in Harvey Dent" was created as an advertisement for district attorney candidate Harvey Dent (played by Aaron Eckhart), as was a site titled "I Believe in Harvey Dent Too," a defiled version of the former that slowly revealed the first image of The Joker (played by Heath Ledger) as visitors sent e-mails through the site. The Joker's catchphrase "Why so serious?" spread virally on the Internet, and was used as the URL of a Web site that sent visitors on a Joker-themed scavenger hunt.

As *True Blood*'s premier drew near, HBO and Campfire turned to less obtuse, if still unorthodox, methods of advertisement. A prequel comic book about an elder vampire and the development of *True Blood* was handed out for free at 2008's San Diego Comic-Con, the largest pop cultural convention in the world. The first episode of *True Blood* was distributed on DVD for free to thousands of moviegoers at the 2008 Toronto International Film Festival, and was made available for rental from Blockbuster Video several days before it aired on television.

True Blood premiered on HBO on September 7, 2008—six months after Campfire's subtle marketing campaign began. According to Nielsen, the first three-quarters of 2008 saw HBO's viewership drop by nearly 23 percent compared to the previous year. However, thanks to interest in new shows such as *True Blood*, HBO saw a 2.4 percent increase in fourth-quarter viewership compared to 2007. Without question, the success of *True Blood* is due in part to the novel marketing developed by Campfire Media.[21]

Questions

1. What is the communication process for viral marketing? Is it different from conventional marketing? How so?

2. What was the initial promotional mix of the *True Blood* campaign, and how might it suggest an observance of IMC?

3. Did *Cloverfield* use a push or pull promotional strategy? What about *The Dark Knight*? Explain.

4. Why did *True Blood* shift its promotional mix as its premier neared? Was this a good or a bad strategy? Explain.

COMPANY CLIPS: Vans—Off the Wall and On Target

© NKP Media, Inc./Cengage

You have undoubtedly heard of Vans. The company has sold footwear, apparel, and extreme sports equipment for over 40 years using the distinct tagline, "Off the Wall." The company's founder wanted to control his own retail channel, so he transformed his manufacturing company into a marketing company. Always carefully protecting its unique brand image, Vans has crafted successful marketing messages and promotions that resonate with the youth culture that represents the company's target market. This video examines the carefully planned strategy that Vans developed to create loyalty in a fickle niche market.

Questions

1. Does Vans use a push or pull strategy to market its apparel? How does Steve feel about the two strategies?

2. What does Steve mean when he refers to tours and events as "planting seeds"?

3. Describe Vans' pyramid strategy. How does it protect the brand?

4. How does Steve's hands-on approach to events and promotion benefit the company?

marketing&you:
Results.

© iStockphoto.com/ziggymaj

Higher scores on this scale indicate that others perceive you to be responsive, warm, and a good listener. A high score also corresponds to a willingness to mentor others. If your score is low, it indicates that you don't actively encourage other people to share information about themselves with you. That doesn't mean you are a poor listener, however. Rather, you prefer not to take the initiative in the interaction.

Notes

1. Stuart Elliot, "Subway's New Campaign," *New York Times*, February 22, 2003; Emily Bryson York, "Subway Can't Stop Jonesing for Jared," February 18, 2008, http://adage.com/article/news/subway-stop-jonesing-jared/125142/.

2. T. L. Stanley, "Domino's Cooks Up New Pizza, TV Spot," *Brandweek*, October 18, 2010, www.adweek.com/news/advertising-branding/dominos-cooks-new-pizza-tv-spot-107900; Todd Wasserman, "As Domino's Gets Real, Its Sales Get Really Good," *Brandweek*, July 11, 2010, www.adweek.com/news/advertising-branding/dominos-gets-real-its-sales-get-really-good-107532; T. L. Stanley, "Marketer of the Year 2010: Russell Weiner, Domino's," *Brandweek*, September 13, 2010, www.adweek.com/news/advertising-branding/russell-weiner-dominos-94427 .

3. Matthew Creamer, "Barack Obama and the Audacity of Marketing," *Advertising Age*, November 10, 2008, http://adage.com/article/news/barack-obama-audacity-marketing/132351; Chris Dannen, "How Obama Won It with the Web," *Fast Company*, November 4, 2008, www.fastcompany.com/articles/2008/11/how-obama-won-it-with-the-web.html; Michael Learmonth, "One-Way Media Lost the Election as Cable, Interactive Dominated," *Advertising Age*, November 10, 2008, http://adage.com/article/mediaworks/media-lost-election-cable-interactive-dominated/132350; Daniel Lyons and Daniel Stone "President 2.0," *Newsweek*, December 1, 2008, www.newsweek.com/2008/11/21/president-2-0.html; Al Ries, "What Marketers Can Learn from Obama's Campaign," *Advertising Age*, November 5, 2008, http://adage.com/article/al-ries/marketers-learn-obama-s-campaign/132237/; Jose Antonio Vargas, "Obama Raised Half a Billion Online," *Washington Post*, November 20, 2008, http://voices.washingtonpost.com/44/2008/11/obama-raised-half-a-billion-on.html.

4. Andrew McMains, "'Absolut World' Debuts," *ADWEEK*, April 27, 2007, www.adweek.com/news/advertising/absolut-world-debuts-88759; Jeremy Mullman, "Breaking with Bottle Fires Up Absolut Sales," *Advertising Age*, February 18, 2008, http://adage.com/article/news/breaking-bottle-fires-absolut-sales/125137/.

5. *Ibid.*

6. "In an Absolut World," www.absolut.com/iaaw.

7. Mullman, "Breaking with Bottle Fires Up Absolut Sales."

8. Stuart Elliott, "In an 'Absolut World,' a Vodka Could Use the Same Ads for More Than 25 Years," *New York Times*, April 27, 2007, www.nytimes.com/2007/04/27/business/media/27adco.html.

9. Koninklijke Philips Electronics Web site, www.philips.com.

10. *Ibid.*

11. Kim Hart, "A Flashy Facebook Page, at a Cost to Privacy," *Washington Post*, June 12, 2008, www.washingtonpost.com/wp-dyn/content/article/2008/06/11/AR2008061103759.html; Nick O'Neill, "10 Privacy Settings Every Facebook User Should Know," All Facebook Web site, February 2, 2009, www.allfacebook.com/facebook-privacy-2009-02; Ralph Gross and Alessandro Acquisti, "Information Revelation and Privacy in Online Social Networks (The Facebook Case)," *ACM Workshop on Privacy in the Electronic Society*, November 7, 2007.

12. The AIDA concept is based on the classic research of E. K. Strong, Jr., as theorized in *The Psychology of Selling and Advertising* (New York: McGraw-Hill, 1925) and "Theories of Selling," *Journal of Applied Psychology* 9 (1925): 75–86.

13. Caroline Waxler, "What You Need to Know About the iPad," *Advertising Age Insights*, August 9, 2010, www.adage.com.

14. Sam Costello, "What Are iPad Sales to Date?", About.com Web site, http://ipod.about.com/od/ipadmodelsandterms/f/ipad-sales-to-date.htm; Bob Keefe, "During the Holiday Quarter, Apple Sold 14 Million iPods, Which Equates to More Than 100 a Minute," *Atlanta Journal Constitution*, January 11, 2006, C-1; Tom Neumayr, "iTunes Now Number Two Music Retailer in the U.S.," February 26, 2008, www.apple.com/pr/library/2008/02/26itunes.html.

15. Thomas E. Barry and Daniel J. Howard, "A Review and Critique of the Hierarchy of Effects in Advertising," *International Journal of Advertising* 9, 1990, 121–135.

16. Jack Neff, "Cracking the Viral Code: Look at Your Ads. Now Look at Old Spice," *Advertising Age*, September 27, 2010, http://adage.com/article/digital/viral-ad-hits-p-g-grooming-biz-point-winning-formula/146090; Jack Neff, "How Much Old Spice Body Wash Has the Old Spice Guy Sold?" *Advertising Age*, July 26, 2010, http://adage.com/article/news/spice-body-wash-spice-guy-sold/145096; Michael Learmonth, "Viral Old Spice 'Responses' Crush Original Ads in Online Views," *Advertising Age*, July 22, 2010, http://adage.com/article/viral-video-charts/viral-spice-responses-crush-original-ads-web-views/145015/; Jessica Shambora, "The Adman Behind Old Spice's New Life," *Fortune*, October 18, 2010, 39.

17. Louise Kramer, "In a Battle of Toothpastes, It's Information vs. Emotion," *New York Times*, January 17, 2007, C6.

18. "Splenda Store," www.splendidlife.com/home.do.

19. This application exercise is based on the contribution of Lyn R. Godwin (University of St. Thomas) to *Great Ideas in Teaching Marketing*, a teaching supplement that accompanies McDaniel, Lamb, and Hair's *Introduction to Marketing*. Professor Godwin's entry titled "Taboo or Not Taboo: That Is the Question" was a runner-up in the "Best of the Great Ideas in Teaching Marketing" contest held in conjunction with the publication of the eighth edition of *Marketing*.

20. This application exercise is based on the contribution of David M. Blanchette (Rhode Island College) to *Great Ideas in Teaching Marketing*, a teaching supplement that accompanies McDaniel, Lamb, and Hair's *Introduction to Marketing*. Professor Blanchette's entry titled "Applying Semiotics in Promotion" was a runner-up in the "Best of the Great Ideas in Teaching Marketing" contest held in conjunction with the publication of the eighth edition of *Marketing*.

21. Sam Schechner, "Winfrey Firm to Produce HBO Shows," *Wall Street Journal*, December 17, 2008; Guy Brighton, "Campfire's True Blood Campaign," *New York Times*; Lynette Rice, "Ad Campaign for HBO's True Blood' Confuses Thirsty Consumers," *Entertainment Weekly*, July 22, 2008, http://insidetv.ew.com/2008/07/22/tru-blood-campa; "Bloodcopy," www.archive.bloodcopy.com; Douglas Quenqua, "The Vampires Are Coming, but Only After Months of Warnings," *New York Times*, July 15, 2008, www.nytimes.com/2008/07/15/business/worldbusiness/15iht-15adco.14494903.html; Jeff Beer, "Campfire Sinks Its Creative Teeth into True Blood," Crain Communications, http://creativity-online.com/news/campfire-sinks-its-creative-teeth-into-true-blood/130134.

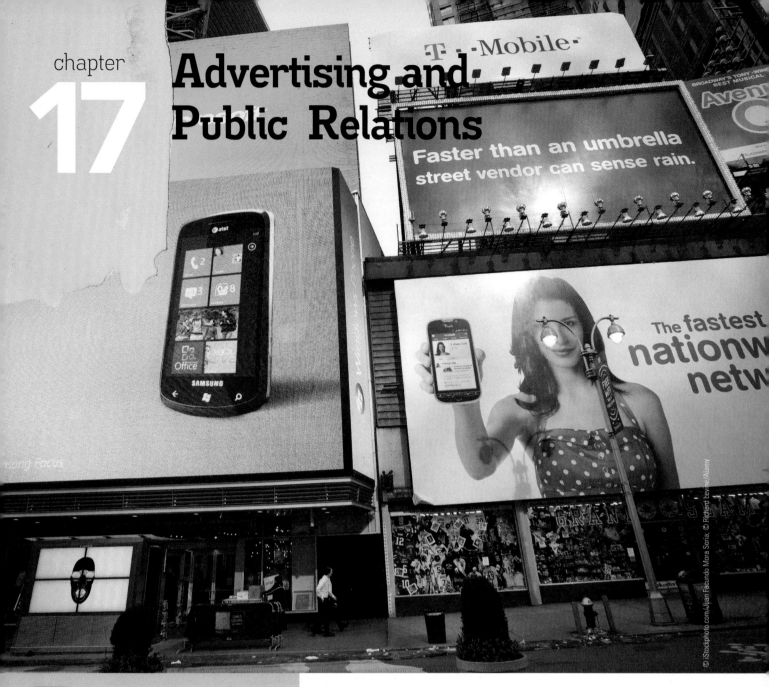

chapter 17
Advertising and Public Relations

Learning Outcomes

1 Discuss the effects of advertising on market share and consumers

2 Identify the major types of advertising

3 Discuss the creative decisions in developing an advertising campaign

4 Describe media evaluation and selection techniques

5 Discuss the role of public relations in the promotional mix

LO1
The Effects of Advertising

Advertising is defined as any form of impersonal, paid communication in which the sponsor or company is identified. It is a popular form of promotion, especially for consumer packaged goods and services. Advertising expenditures typically increase annually but have fallen in recent years. Last year 30 companies spent over $1 billion each, with the top 100 global marketers spending more than $125.3 billion overall on measured media. Among the top brands advertised by these companies were Procter & Gamble ($4.2 billion), Verizon ($3 billion), AT&T ($2.7 billion), General Motors ($2.2 billion), and Pfizer ($2 billion).[1]

Advertising and marketing services agencies and other firms that provide marketing and communications services to marketers employ an estimated 1.4 million people including those working in media advertising, such as newspapers, broadcast and cable TV, radio, magazines, and Internet media companies.[2] This represents a decrease in both areas due to economic conditions and much lower newspaper employment.

The money budgeted for advertising by some firms is staggering. (See Exhibit 17.1.) Procter & Gamble, Verizon, AT&T, General Motors, and Pfizer each spend anywhere from $2 billion to nearly $4 billion annually in the United States on national advertising alone. That's about $8 million a day on national advertising. If local advertising, sales promotion, and public relations are included, this figure rises much higher. Over 100 companies each spend more than $300 million every year on advertising.[3]

Advertising spending varies by industry. For example, book publishers have one of the highest ratios of advertising dollars to sales. They spend roughly 27 cents on advertising for every dollar of book revenue. Similarly, for every

> Advertising is a popular form of **promotion**, especially for consumer packaged goods and services

marketing&you.

What do you think of television advertising?

Using the following scale, enter your answers on the lines provided.

STRONGLY DISAGREE ◁ 1 · 2 · 3 · 4 · 5 ▷ STRONGLY AGREE

NEUTRAL

_____ TV advertising is a good way to learn what products and services are available.

_____ TV advertising results in better products for the public.

_____ In general, TV advertising presents a true picture of the product advertised.

_____ You can trust brands advertised on TV more than brands not advertised on TV.

_____ TV advertising helps raise our standard of living.

_____ TV advertisements help me find products that match my personality and interests.

_____ TV advertising helps me to know which brands have the features I am looking for.

_____ TV advertising gives me a good idea about products by showing the kinds of people who use them.

_____ TV advertising helps me buy the best brand for the price.

_____ I am willing to pay more for a product that is advertised on TV.

Total your score, and find out what it means at the end of the chapter.

Source: Scale #167, *Marketing Scales Handbook*, G. Bruner, K. James, H. Hensel, eds., vol. III. © by American Marketing Association. Used with permission of the American Marketing Association.

Exhibit 17.1 Top Ten Leaders by U.S. Advertising Spending

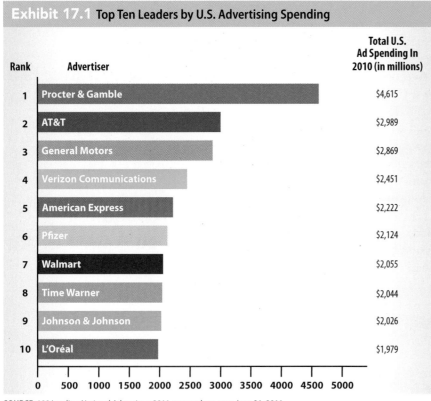

Rank	Advertiser	Total U.S. Ad Spending In 2010 (in millions)
1	Procter & Gamble	$4,615
2	AT&T	$2,989
3	General Motors	$2,869
4	Verizon Communications	$2,451
5	American Express	$2,222
6	Pfizer	$2,124
7	Walmart	$2,055
8	Time Warner	$2,044
9	Johnson & Johnson	$2,026
10	L'Oréal	$1,979

SOURCE: 100 Leading National Advertisers 2011, www.adage.com, June 21, 2011.

dollar of merchandise sold in the game and toy industry, about 12 to 15 cents is spent advertising these products to consumers. Other consumer goods manufacturers that spend heavily on advertising in relation to total sales include sugar and confectionery products manufacturers, leather manufacturers, watch-makers, perfume and cosmetic manufacturers, detergent makers, and wine and liquor companies.[4]

ADVERTISING AND MARKET SHARE

The most successful consumer goods brands, such as Ivory soap and Coca-Cola, were built over many years by heavy advertising and marketing investments. Today's advertising dollars for successful consumer brands are spent on maintaining brand awareness and market share.

New brands with a small market share tend to spend proportionately more for advertising and sales promotion than those with a large market share, typically for two reasons. First, beyond a certain level of spending for advertising and sales promotion, diminishing returns set in. That is, sales and market share improvements slow down and eventually decrease, no matter how much is spent on advertising and sales promotion. This phenomenon is called the **advertising response function**. Understanding the advertising response function helps marketers use budgets wisely. A market leader such as Johnson & Johnson's Neutrogena typically spends proportionately less on advertising than a newcomer, such as Jergens Natural Glow Daily Moisturizer brand. Jergens spends more on its brand to gain attention and increase market share. Neutrogena, on the other hand, spends only as much as is needed to maintain market share—anything more would result in diminishing benefits. Neutrogena has already captured the attention of the majority of its target market. It needs only to remind customers of its product.

The second reason new brands tend to require higher spending for advertising and sales promotion is that a minimum level of exposure is needed to measurably affect purchase habits. If Jergens advertised Natural Glow Daily Moisturizer in only one or two publications and bought only one or two television spots, it certainly would not achieve the exposure needed to penetrate consumers' perceptual defenses, gain attention, and ultimately affect purchase intentions. Instead, Natural Glow Daily Moisturizer was advertised in many different media for a sustained period of time.

THE EFFECTS OF ADVERTISING ON CONSUMERS

Advertising affects consumers' daily lives, informing them about products and services and influencing their attitudes, beliefs, and ultimately their purchases. The average U.S. citizen is exposed to hundreds of advertisements a day from all types of advertising media. In the television medium alone, researchers estimate that

advertising

Impersonal, one-way mass communication about a product or organization that is paid for by a marketer.

advertising response function

A phenomenon in which spending for advertising and sales promotion increases sales or market share up to a certain level but then produces diminishing returns.

the average viewer watches at least six hours of commercial television messages a week. In addition, these TV viewers are exposed to countless print ads and promotional messages seen in other places. Advertising affects the TV programs people watch, the content of the newspapers they read, the politicians they elect, the medicines they take, and the toys their children play with. Consequently, the influence of advertising on the U.S. socioeconomic system has been the subject of extensive debate among economists, marketers, sociologists, psychologists, politicians, consumerists, and many others.

Though advertising cannot change consumers' deeply rooted values and attitudes, it may succeed in transforming a person's negative attitude toward a product into a positive one. For instance, serious or dramatic advertisements are more effective at changing consumers' negative attitudes. Humorous ads, on the other hand, have been shown to be more effective at shaping attitudes when consumers already have a positive image of an advertised brand.[5] However, as much as humor in advertising tends to improve brand recognition, it does not necessarily improve product recall, message credibility, or buying intentions. Consumers who find an ad funny may have good feelings about the product, but their purchasing decisions will not be affected unless they can actually recall the brand. The best results with humorous ads are achieved by making the message relevant to the product. For example, Taco Bell saw a substantial rise in sales after promoting a tiny talking Chihuahua who was crazy about their product, constantly demanding to be fed by saying, "yo quiero Taco Bell." The phrase caught on and got people repeating—and remembering—the company's name across the country. The actual content of the commercial reinforced the company's message in a relevant manner.[6]

Advertising can also affect the way consumers rank a brand's attributes, such as color, taste, smell, and texture. For example, car ads previously emphasized brand attributes such as roominess, speed, and low maintenance. Today, however, car marketers have added safety, versatility, gas mileage, and customization to the list. Safety features such as antilock brakes, power door locks, and front and side air bags are now a standard part of the message in many carmakers' ads. Toyota Scion appeals to consumers' sense of individuality by allowing purchasers to custom-design their cars by selecting features such as the steering wheel color, multi-shade illuminated cup holders, and "sport" pedals.[7] New models, like the Chevy Volt, are touting their new energy sources.

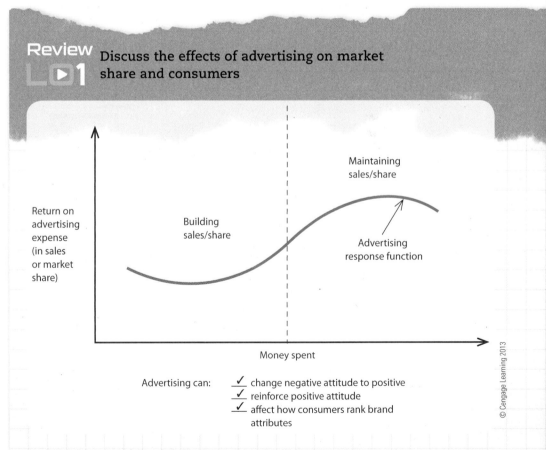

Review LO1 Discuss the effects of advertising on market share and consumers

Return on advertising expense (in sales or market share)

Building sales/share

Maintaining sales/share

Advertising response function

Money spent

Advertising can:
- ✓ change negative attitude to positive
- ✓ reinforce positive attitude
- ✓ affect how consumers rank brand attributes

© Cengage Learning 2013

Pepsi's New Look

How much does a brand logo makeover cost these days? Well more than one million dollars and five months if you are Pepsi-Cola. Pepsi recently revealed its new logo—only the 11th change since 1898, five changes coming in the last 21 years. According to Pepsi's top executives, part of the strategy was to move the brand from the traditional mass marketing and mass distribution era into the current culture of personalization. "By making the logo more dynamic and more alive . . . it is absolutely a huge step in the right direction," said Pepsi VP portfolio brands, Frank Cooper. While the $1 million dollars spent on design could be considered hefty, the real costs come in the other changes—from the trucks, vending machines, stadium signage, point of sale materials, and more. This could easily reach into the hundreds of millions of dollars.

So just what does the new logo signify? According to Pepsi, the new logo has a white band in the middle of the Pepsi circle that represents a series of smiles . . . a smile for Pepsi, a grin for Diet Pepsi, and a laugh for Pepsi Max. Branding experts are mixed: Some think the new look will make the logo less durable and classic while others feel that it is more adventurous and youthful. Indeed, Pepsi has succeeded in the past by targeting the "new generation."

There are also mixed consumer reviews. Some think the new logo looks like the old Diet Pepsi logo with the identical sans-serif typeface and the red and blue Pepsi wave in a diagonal slope. Others feel the new logo looks similar to the campaign for President Barack Obama. Regardless, there is a minimalist feel that has captured the attention of the iPod generation—that idea of simple elegance.

Interestingly, Pepsi's new advertising campaign also comes with a dose of optimism: "every generation refreshes the world." However, arch rival Coca-Cola is also dosing out the optimism with its new advertising

tagline "Open happiness."[8] While both companies have embraced this message at various times, never has this happened simultaneously. So the question is whether this helps or hurts the differentiation of each brand.

LO2
Major Types of Advertising

institutional advertising
A form of advertising designed to enhance a company's image rather than promote a particular product.

product advertising
A form of advertising that touts the benefits of a specific good or service.

The firm's promotional objectives determine the type of advertising it uses. If the goal of the promotion plan is to improve the image of the company or the industry, **institutional advertising** may be used. In contrast, if the advertiser wants to enhance the sales of a specific good or service, **product advertising** is used.

INSTITUTIONAL ADVERTISING

Historically, advertising in the United States has been product oriented. Today, however, companies market multiple products and need a different type of advertising. Institutional advertising, or corporate advertising, promotes the corporation as a whole and is designed to establish, change, or maintain the corporation's identity. It usually does not ask the audience to do anything but maintain a favorable attitude toward the advertiser and its goods and services. For example, when Time Warner dropped AOL from the company's corporate brand name, it hired a branding agency to develop institutional advertising to reposition the brand without the Internet unit and refocus the image on Time Warner as a media giant. In designing the "rebranding," executives did not want a radical change. Rather, they wanted to "freshen" the previous image and maintain its favorable status. The logo itself changed in texture, color, and typeface. In addition to changing the logo on buildings, business cards, and stationery, the company changed its stock ticker symbol to reflect the new image.[9]

A form of institutional advertising called **advocacy advertising** is typically used to safeguard against negative consumer attitudes and to enhance the company's credibility among consumers who already favor its position. Often corporations use advocacy advertising to express their views on controversial issues. At other times, firms' advocacy campaigns react to criticism or blame, some in direct response to criticism by the media. For example, oil and gas companies typically get blamed for high gas prices and high profits. One of the largest in the world, Chevron, recently launched a campaign called "We Agree" (www.chevron.com) to highlight the different areas of energy the company is investing in aside from oil exploration.[10]

Other advocacy campaigns might try to ward off increased regulation, damaging legislation, or an unfavorable outcome in a lawsuit. The tobacco companies have utilized "good citizen campaigns" in the United States and around the world in an effort to create a positive public image for themselves after losing several class-action suits and being accused of targeting children with their marketing campaigns. In an effort to improve its corporate image, Philip Morris has been spending more than $120 million a year promoting its environmental and community development programs, such as building homes for Habitat for Humanity, making donations to food banks, and supporting meal programs for seniors and shelters for battered women.[11]

advocacy advertising
A form of advertising in which an organization expresses its views on controversial issues or responds to media attacks.

Chevron is focusing on how its business practices affect humanity and the environment with its "We Agree" campaign.

PRODUCT ADVERTISING

Unlike institutional advertising, product advertising promotes the benefits of a specific good or service. The product's stage in its life cycle often determines which type of product advertising is used: pioneering advertising, competitive advertising, or comparative advertising.

Pioneering Advertising Pioneering advertising is intended to stimulate primary demand for a new product or product category. Heavily used during the introductory stage of the product life cycle, pioneering advertising offers consumers in-depth information about the benefits of the product class. Pioneering advertising also seeks to create interest. Pharmaceutical companies are the latest big players in pioneering advertising. For instance, one pharma giant, Pfizer, has steadily ramped up consumer advertising of a new drug, Lyrica—first approved by the FDA to treat pain caused by diabetic nerve damage. Then Pfizer found a broader market for Lyrica when it was approved for treatment of the disputed pain condition fibromyalgia. In just six months Pfizer spent $46 million on a new ad campaign for Lyrica as a treatment for fibromyalgia, compared with $33 million the previous year, in spite of the protest by many doctors who do not believe fibromyalgia is a real medical condition. There are no biological tests to diagnose fibromyalgia, and the condition has not been linked to any environmental or biological causes. But worldwide sales of Lyrica reached $1.8 billion in the first year. Analysts predicted sales would rise an additional 30 percent the next year, helped by consumer advertising and the interest from other drug companies who see the potential for a major new market in aggressively pursuing fibromyalgia treatments.[12]

Competitive Advertising Firms use competitive or brand advertising when a product enters the growth phase of the product life cycle and other companies begin to enter the marketplace. Instead of building demand for the product category, the goal of competitive advertising is to influence demand for a specific brand. Often promotion becomes less informative and appeals more to emotions during this phase. Generally, this is where an emphasis on branding begins. Advertisements focus on subtle differences between brands, with the objective of building recall of a brand name and creating a favorable brand attitude. Automobile advertising has long used very competitive messages, drawing distinctions based on factors such as quality, performance, customer satisfaction, and image. Similarly, in an effort to obtain market share from competitors and to build brand awareness in the wireless industry, Nextel Communications signed a ten year title sponsorship agreement with NASCAR. NASCAR executives, interested in building a younger fan base, consider the telecom industry one of the best ways to reach younger consumers because they always have a cell phone "stuck" to their ear.[13]

Comparative Advertising Comparative advertising directly or indirectly compares two or more competing brands on one or more specific attributes. Some advertisers even use comparative advertising against their own brands. Products experiencing slow growth or entering the marketplace against strong competitors are more likely to employ comparative claims in their advertising. For instance, the Mac versus PC ads for Apple have been masterful. The ads create an image of a stodgy PC battling with a hip, cool Mac. The campaign's success has escalated the battle between the two computer icons with each creating new ads aimed at the other. Other recent campaigns include Hoover versus Dyson vacuum cleaners, Miller Lite versus Bud Light, and Pampers versus Huggies. In addition to comparative advertising, some companies have brought back the "taste test." These include Progresso soups versus Campbell's Select Harvest soups and Dunkin' Donuts versus Starbucks, which is even supported by a microsite touting the results of a blind taste test (**www.dunkinbeatstarbucks.com**).[14]

pioneering advertising
A form of advertising designed to stimulate primary demand for a new product or product category.

competitive advertising
A form of advertising designed to influence demand for a specific brand.

comparative advertising
A form of advertising that compares two or more specifically named or shown competing brands on one or more specific attributes.

Before the 1970s, comparative advertising was allowed only if the competing brand was veiled and unidentified. In 1971, however, the Federal Trade Commission (FTC) fostered the growth of comparative advertising by saying that it provided information to the customer and that advertisers were more skillful than the government in communicating this information. Federal rulings prohibit advertisers from falsely describing competitors' products and allow competitors to sue if ads show their products or mention their brand names in an incorrect or false manner.

FTC rules also apply to advertisers making false claims about their own products. For example, the FTC recently filed a false-advertising suit against a company that marketed a weight-loss product which claimed that its users could lose substantial amounts of weight rapidly, including as much as 18 pounds per week and as much as 50 percent of all excess weight in just 14 days, without dieting or exercise. The company also included (false) assurances that clinical studies prove those claims.[15]

The Mac versus PC ads for Apple use comparative advertising by portraying the PC (and everything and everyone associated with it) as "stodgy," and constantly losing to a hip, cool Mac.

Companies must be careful with comparative advertising approaches in other countries as well. Germany, Italy, Belgium, and France, for example, do not permit advertisers to claim that their products are the best or better than competitors' products, both of which are common claims in the United States. In the Netherlands, car manufacturers cannot make claims in their advertising about the fuel consumption or environmental aspects of the car. Similarly, Lands' End ran afoul of a German law prohibiting lifetime guarantee claims, which happen to be one of Lands' End's guiding principles. The law has made it difficult for the direct retailer to sell its products and advertise its lifetime guarantee through the Internet and direct mail in Germany.

In other countries, hard-hitting comparative advertising is not effective because it offends cultural values. For example, Arabic culture generally encourages people not to compete with one another, and the sharing of wealth is common practice. Therefore, comparative advertising is not consistent with social values in

Review LO2 Identify the major types of advertising

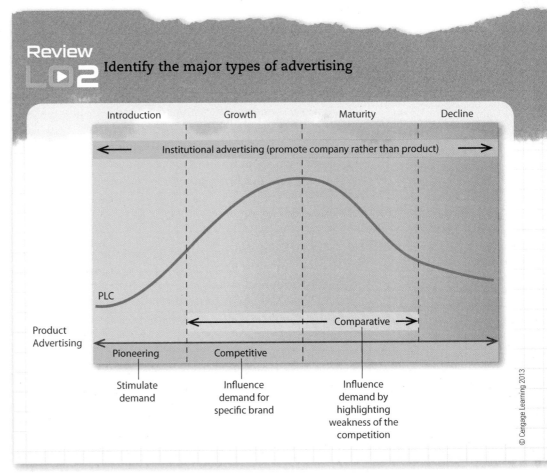

Introduction   Growth   Maturity   Decline

Institutional advertising (promote company rather than product)

PLC

Product Advertising

Pioneering   Competitive   Comparative

Stimulate demand

Influence demand for specific brand

Influence demand by highlighting weakness of the competition

Arabic countries. Japanese advertisers have also been reluctant to use comparative advertising because it is considered confrontational and doesn't promote the respectful treatment of consumers or portray a company in a respectful light. Nevertheless, although the Japanese have traditionally favored soft-sell advertising approaches, consumers are witnessing a trend toward comparative ads.

LO3
Creative Decisions in Advertising

Advertising strategies typically are organized around an advertising campaign. An **advertising campaign** is a series of related advertisements focusing on a common theme, slogan, and set of advertising appeals. It is a specific advertising effort for a particular product that extends for a defined period of time. For example, Hewlett-Packard's celebrity-drenched global ad campaign, "The computer is personal again," helped HP gain the lead in worldwide market share for personal computers, and also imbued a once-faded brand with some cool. The glossy campaign, featuring print, video, and television ads, showcased achievers such as "CEO of Hip-Hop" Jay-Z, "Master of Snowboards" Shaun White, designer Vera Wang, and Brazilian author Paulo Coelho. Each celebrity was shown manipulating images that seemingly revolved around their laptop to show what's on their computer, what they do in their spare time, and why the PC is personal to them. A concurrent online campaign included a virtual motorcycle tour with the Orange County Choppers team, who were also the celebrity stars of HP's Super Bowl ad. That campaign was designed to create demand among 18- to 34-year-olds for the HP Pavilion entertainment notebook and specially designed Orange County Choppers "skins," or computer covers.[16]

Before any creative work can begin on an advertising campaign, it is important to determine what goals or objectives the advertising should achieve. An **advertising objective** identifies the specific communication task a campaign should accomplish for a specified target audience during a specified period. The objectives of a specific advertising campaign often depend on the overall corporate objectives and the product being advertised. For example, McIlhenny Company's Tabasco Hot Sauce launched a print advertising campaign with the objective of educating consumers about how to use the product and the variety of flavors offered. The ads featured product information embedded in the label, which was blown up to cover the entire page. The ad copy for the Garlic Pepper Sauce read: "The only one potent enough to ward off both hypothermia and vampires at once." The original Tabasco Pepper Sauce ad copy read: "It's like love, you always want more no matter how badly you got burned last time." The ad campaign increased sales by over 11 percent in the first four weeks. The print medium was also supported by participation in special events, such as the National Collegiate Tailgate Tour.[17]

The DAGMAR approach (Defining Advertising Goals for Measured Advertising Results) is one method of setting objectives. According to this method, all advertising objectives should precisely define the target audience, the desired percentage change in some specified measure of effectiveness, and the time frame in which that change is to occur. For example, the objectives for an advertising campaign for Coca-Cola's revamped Powerade brand might be to achieve a 15 percent increase in its share of the sports-drink market within eight months.

Once objectives are defined, creative work can begin on the advertising campaign. Advertising campaigns often follow the AIDA model, which was discussed in Chapter 16. Depending on where consumers are in the AIDA process, the creative

advertising campaign
A series of related advertisements focusing on a common theme, slogan, and set of advertising appeals.

advertising objective
A specific communication task that a campaign should accomplish for a specified target audience during a specified period.

development of an advertising campaign might focus on creating attention, arousing interest, stimulating desire, or ultimately leading to the action of buying the product. Specifically, creative decisions include identifying product benefits, developing and evaluating advertising appeals, executing the message, and evaluating the effectiveness of the campaign.

IDENTIFYING PRODUCT BENEFITS

A well-known rule of thumb in the advertising industry is, "Sell the sizzle, not the steak"—that is, in advertising the goal is to sell the benefits of the product, not its attributes. Consumers don't buy attributes, they buy benefits. An attribute is simply a feature of the product such as its easy-open package, special formulation or new lower price. A benefit is what consumers will receive or achieve by using the product such as convenience or ease of use. A benefit should answer the consumer's question, "What's in it for me?" Benefits might be such things as pleasure, improved health, savings, or relief. A quick test to determine whether you are offering attributes or benefits in your advertising is to ask, "So?" Consider this example:

→ **Attribute:** "SoBe Life Water has reformulated five delicious, low-calorie flavors—Blackberry Grape, Pomegranate Cherry, Orange Tangerine, Strawberry Kiwi, and Passionfruit Citrus—each infused with a unique mix of antioxidant vitamins C & E, essential B vitamins and healthy herbal ingredients. . . ." "So . . . ?"

→ **Benefit:** "So . . . SoBe Life Water is not only an enhanced water; it is a lifestyle unto itself . . . providing consumers the healthiest, most fun and refreshing products, delivering the incredibly positive benefits of hydration and unmatched brand experiences."[18]

Eggland's Best lists the attributes of its eggs. The implied benefit is more nutritious eggs, which are better for customers.

Marketing research and intuition are typically used to unearth the perceived benefits of a product and to rank consumers' preferences for these benefits. Coke's rival, PepsiCo, has its own sports drink, Gatorade. Already positioned as *the* thirst-quencher, Gatorade's advertising touts its refueling benefits to serious athletes of mainstream sports. Similarly, Kellogg's ad campaign for its latest cereal, Frosted Flakes Gold, has partnered with ESPN to promote the new frosted flake as a product that provides longer-lasting energy because it's a whole grain cereal. The ads underscore the message of increased, longer-lasting energy by featuring adolescent athletes being cheered on by Tony the Tiger.[19]

DEVELOPING AND EVALUATING ADVERTISING APPEALS

An **advertising appeal** identifies a reason for a person to buy a product. Developing advertising appeals, a challenging task, is typically the responsibility of the creative team (e.g., art directors and copywriters) in the advertising agency. Advertising appeals

advertising appeal
A reason for a person to buy a product.

Exhibit 17.2 Common Advertising Appeals

Profit	Lets consumers know whether the product will save them money, make them money, or keep them from losing money
Health	Appeals to those who are body-conscious or who want to be healthy
Love or Romance	Is used often in selling cosmetics and perfumes
Fear	Can center around social embarrassment, growing old, or losing one's health; because of its power, requires advertiser to exercise care in execution
Admiration	Is the reason that celebrity spokespeople are used so often in advertising
Convenience	Is often used for fast-food restaurants and microwave foods
Fun and Pleasure	Are the key to advertising vacations, beer, amusement parks, and more
Vanity and Egotism	Are used most often for expensive or conspicuous items such as cars and clothing
Environmental Consciousness	Centers around protecting the environment and being considerate of others in the community

© Cengage Learning 2013

typically play off of consumers' emotions, such as fear or love, or address some need or want the consumer has, such as a need for convenience or the desire to save money.

Advertising campaigns can focus on one or more advertising appeals. Often the appeals are quite general, thus allowing the firm to develop a number of subthemes or mini-campaigns using both advertising and sales promotion. Several possible advertising appeals are listed in Exhibit 17.2.

Choosing the best appeal from those developed usually requires market research. Criteria for evaluation include desirability, exclusiveness, and believability. The appeal first must make a positive impression on and be desirable to the target market. It must also be exclusive or unique. Customers must be able to distinguish the advertiser's message from competitors' messages. Most importantly, the appeal should be believable. An appeal that makes extravagant claims not only wastes promotional dollars but also creates ill will for the advertiser.

The advertising appeal selected for the campaign becomes what advertisers call its **unique selling proposition**. The unique selling proposition usually becomes the campaign's slogan. For example, "Red Bull gives you wings" touts Red Bull's benefits including improved concentration and reaction time, better performance, and increased endurance (**www.redbullusa.com**). Similarly, Powerade's advertising campaign aimed at the sports enthusiast carries the slogan "Sport Is What You Make It." This is Powerade's unique selling proposition, implying that you can push yourself to the limit if you are motivated and use Powerade.[20]

Effective slogans often become so ingrained that consumers hearing the slogan immediately conjure up images of the product. For example, many consumers can easily name the companies and products behind these memorable slogans or even hum the jingle that goes along with them: "Have it your way," "Tastes great, less filling," "Ring around the collar," and "Tum te Tum Tum." Advertisers often revive old slogans or jingles in the hope that the nostalgia will create good feelings with consumers. Burger King brought back the King for several years in its advertising, and re-retired it in August 2011. Maytag refreshed its campaign featuring its appliance pitchman by changing the actor who plays him and giving him a helper—the third change since the ads originated in 1967. And Hershey's Kit Kat bar's jingle "Gimme a Break" is so etched in consumers' minds that recently the agency hired a film crew to ask people on the street to sing the jingle for use on the Internet, in future ad campaigns, and in its Kit Kat "Gimme a Break" Café.[21]

unique selling proposition
A desirable, exclusive, and believable advertising appeal selected as the theme for a campaign.

EXECUTING THE MESSAGE

Message execution is the way an advertisement portrays its information. In general, the AIDA plan (see Chapter 16) is a good blueprint for executing an advertising message. Any ad should immediately draw the reader's, viewer's, or listener's attention. The advertiser must then use the message to hold interest, create desire for the good or service, and ultimately motivate action—a purchase.

The style in which the message is executed is one of the most creative elements of an advertisement. Exhibit 17.3 lists some examples of executional styles used by advertisers. Executional styles often dictate what type of media is to be employed to convey the message. For example, scientific executional styles lend themselves well to print advertising where more information can be conveyed. The ad campaign for Restasis, a medication for chronically dry eyes, features print ads with a doctor spokeswoman who happens to also be a user of the product. She talks about the specific problems associated with chronic dry eyes and the benefits of the medication. On the other hand, demonstration and musical styles are more likely found in broadcast advertising. Many "before and after" demonstrations for everything from detergents to weight loss ads play particularly well on television.

Testimonials by athletes are one of the more popular executional styles. LeBron James and Shaquille O'Neal are two of the most successful athlete spokespersons. Read Shaq's own words about the power of marketing and advertising in Exhibit 17.4.

Exhibit 17.3 Ten Common Executional Styles for Advertising	
Slice-of-Life	Depicts people in normal settings, such as at the dinner table or in their car. McDonald's often uses slice-of-life styles showing youngsters munching french fries and Happy Meals on family outings.
Lifestyle	Shows how well the product will fit in with the consumer's lifestyle. As their Volkswagen Jetta moves through the streets of the French Quarter, the Gen X drivers plug in a techno music CD and marvel at how the rhythms of the world mimic the ambient vibe inside their vehicle.
Spokesperson/ Testimonial	Can feature a celebrity, company official, or typical consumer making a testimonial or endorsing a product. Sarah Michelle Gellar, star of *Buffy the Vampire Slayer*, endorses Maybelline cosmetics while country singer Shania Twain introduced Revlon's ColorStay Liquid Lip. Dell, Inc. founder Michael Dell touts his vision of the customer experience via Dell in television ads.
Fantasy	Creates a fantasy for the viewer built around use of the product. Carmakers often use this style to let viewers fantasize about how they would feel speeding around tight corners or down long country roads in their cars.
Humorous	Advertisers often use humor in their ads, such as Snickers' "Not Going Anywhere for a While" campaign featuring hundreds of souls waiting, sometimes impatiently, to get into heaven.
Real/Animated Product Symbols	Creates a character that represents the product in advertisements, such as the Energizer bunny, Starkist's Charlie the Tuna, or General Mills' longtime icon, Betty Crocker, redesigned for the new millennium.
Mood or Image	Builds a mood or image around the product, such as peace, love, or beauty. De Beers ads depicting shadowy silhouettes wearing diamond engagement rings and diamond necklaces portrayed passion and intimacy while extolling that a "diamond is forever."
Demonstration	Shows consumers the expected benefit. Many consumer products use this technique. Laundry-detergent spots are famous for demonstrating how their product will clean clothes whiter and brighter. Fort James Corporation demonstrated in television commercials how its Dixie Rinse & ReUse disposable stoneware product line can stand up to the heat of a blowtorch and survive a cycle in a clothes washer.
Musical	Conveys the message of the advertisement through song. For example, Nike's ads depicting a marathoner's tortured feet, skier Picabo Street's surgery-scarred knee, and a surfer's thigh scarred by a shark attack while strains of Joe Cocker's "You Are So Beautiful" are heard in the background.
Scientific	Uses research or scientific evidence to give a brand superiority over competitors. Pain relievers like Advil, Bayer, and Excedrin use scientific evidence in their ads.

© Cengage Learning 2013

Injecting humor into an advertisement is a popular and effective executional style. Selection of a humorous approach is based on the communications goal. Humorous executional styles are more often used in radio and television advertising than in print or magazine advertising where humor is less easily communicated. Regardless of the advertising medium, however, humor can be tricky to use because not all people find the same things funny and marketers have to be sure the humor won't be misconstrued. For instance, a print and e-mail ad campaign for Timbuk2's limited-edition messenger bags caused an uproar even while the ad's creators protested it was supposed to be funny. The ad featured a photo of a crying girl in a prom dress next to a photo of a tough-looking guy across whom was written: "Here today. Gone tomorrow. Just like that jerk who stole your virginity, these bags are only around for a short time." Timbuk2 finally pulled the ad in response to a storm of negative blog postings and e-mail protests against the ad saying that trying to be funny by using a reference to date rape was offensive.[22]

Used appropriately, humor can be effective in attracting and holding audience attention. The "Real Men of Genius" radio ads are great examples of using humor in radio advertising. For example, Altoids used humor to create and reinforce its quirky yet strong persona. With a significantly lower budget than key competitors, the Altoids campaign helped the product grow from a sleepy brand to the number one mint in America based on flavor.[23]

Executional styles for foreign advertising are often quite different from those we are accustomed to in the United States. Sometimes they are sexually oriented or aesthetically imaginative. For example, Adidas commissioned a German ad company to come up with a "talk-of-the-world, spectacular" outdoor ad to welcome visitors to the FIFA World Cup soccer match. They designed a 65-meter, front-and-back billboard of soccer star Oliver Kahn diving to catch a soccer ball, which stretched across a four-lane highway near the airport in Munich, Germany. Four million cars drove under the installation and it became the global visual that accompanied almost every foreign news coverage of the World Cup event.[24] European advertising avoids the direct-sell approaches common in U.S. ads and instead is more indirect, more symbolic, and, above all, more visual. Nike, known in the United States for "in-your-face" advertising and irreverent slogans such as "Just Do It," discovered that its brash advertising did not appeal to Europeans.

Sometimes a company will modify its executional styles to make its advertising more effective. For decades, Procter & Gamble has advertised shampoo in China by using a demonstrational executional style. Television ads demonstrated how the science of shampoo worked and then showed a woman with nice, shiny hair. Because today's urban Chinese customers are more financially secure, they no longer make solely utilitarian purchases. To reflect that shift, Procter & Gamble has begun incorporating more of an emotional appeal into its advertisements. TV ads show a woman emerging from an animated cocoon as a sophisticated butterfly. A voice-over says, "Head & Shoulders metamorphosis—new life for hair."[25]

Purveyors of fine scooters to the Amusing

"Oh Bugger..."

m‑cro
SKATE SCOOTER
The Original
www.citybug.co.uk
+44 (0)118 973 6222

This ad for a scooter uses quirky humor to sell a fun product.

POST-CAMPAIGN EVALUATION

Evaluating an advertising campaign can be the most demanding task facing advertisers. How do advertisers know whether the campaign led to an increase in sales or market share or elevated awareness of the product? Many advertising campaigns aim to create an image for the good or service instead of asking for action, so their real effect is unknown. So many variables shape the effectiveness of an ad that advertisers often must guess whether their money has been well spent. Despite this gray area, marketers spend a considerable amount of time studying advertising effectiveness and its probable impact on sales, market share, or awareness.

Testing ad effectiveness can be done before and/or after the campaign. Before a campaign is released, marketing managers use pretests to determine the best advertising appeal, layout, and media vehicle. After advertisers implement a campaign, they often conduct tests to measure its effectiveness. Several monitoring techniques can be used to determine whether or not the campaign has met its original goals.

Even if a campaign has been highly successful, advertisers still typically do a post-campaign analysis. They assess how the campaign might have been more efficient and what factors contributed to its success. For example, Hallmark's market researchers wanted to capitalize on aging baby boomers. Research indicated that baby boomers do not want to age, but since that is inevitable, boomers want to see the positive side of aging. Therefore, Hallmark created the "Time of Your Life" series that flattered their egos. The cards were not successful, however, because they were placed in the "over 50" section of the store and baby boomers do not want to shop in that section.[26]

Set advertising objectives DAGMAR

Identify the benefits of product/service

Develop appeal (unique selling proposition)

Execute the message

Evaluate campaign results

Evaluating results helps marketers adjust objectives for future campaigns

© Cengage Learning 2013

LO4
Media Decisions in Advertising

A major decision for advertisers is the choice of **medium**—the channel used to convey a message to a target market. **Media planning**, therefore, is the series of decisions advertisers make regarding the selection and use of media, enabling the marketer to optimally and cost-effectively communicate the message to the target audience. Specifically, advertisers must determine which types of media will best communicate the benefits of their product or service to the target audience and when and for how long the advertisement will run.

Promotional objectives and the appeal and executional style of the advertising strongly affect the selection of media. It is important to understand that both creative and media decisions are made at the same time. Creative work cannot be completed without knowing which medium will be used to convey the message to the target market. For instance, creative planning will likely differ for an ad to be displayed on a Web site versus one placed in a print medium, such as a newspaper or magazine. In many cases, the advertising objectives dictate the medium and the creative approach to be used. For example, if the objective is to demonstrate how fast a product operates, a TV commercial that shows this action might be the best choice.

U.S. advertisers spend about $300 billion on media advertising annually. Almost half of that is spent on media monitored by national reporting services—newspapers, magazines, Internet, radio, television, and outdoor media. The remainder is spent on unmonitored media, such as direct mail, trade exhibits, cooperative advertising, brochures, coupons, catalogs, and special events. Exhibit 17.5 shows advertising spending by media type. About 48 percent of every media dollar goes toward TV ads (cable, syndicated, spot and network), 19 percent to magazines, 2.7 percent to outdoor advertising, and 16.5 percent for newspaper ads.[27] But these traditional mass-market media are declining in usage and more targeted media are growing. Indeed, almost 8 percent of advertising dollars are spent on the Internet.[28]

medium
The channel used to convey a message to a target market.

media planning
The series of decisions advertisers make regarding the selection and use of media, allowing the marketer to optimally and cost-effectively communicate the message to the target audience.

MEDIA TYPES

Advertising media are channels that advertisers use in mass communication. The six major advertising media are newspapers, magazines, radio, television, outdoor media, and the Internet. Exhibit 17.6 summarizes the advantages and disadvantages of these major channels. In recent years, however, alternative media vehicles have emerged that give advertisers innovative ways to reach their target audience and avoid advertising clutter.

Newspapers Newspapers are one of the oldest forms of media. The advantages of newspaper advertising include geographic flexibility and timeliness. Because copywriters can usually prepare newspaper ads quickly and at a reasonable cost, local merchants can reach their target market almost daily. While there has been a decline in circulation as well as the number of newspapers nationally, there are several major newspapers including *The Wall Street Journal, USA Today, New York Times, Los Angeles Times,* and *The Washington Post.* But most newspapers are local. Because newspapers are generally a mass-market medium, however, they might not be the best vehicle for marketers trying to reach a very narrow market. For example, local newspapers are not the best media

Exhibit 17.5 Domestic Advertising Spending by Media Type, in billions

Source: Adapted from "Total U.S. Advertising Spending by Medium," *Advertising Age,* June 21, 2011.

Exhibit 17.6 Advantages and Disadvantages of Major Advertising Media

Medium	Advantages	Disadvantages
Newspapers	Geographic selectivity and flexibility; short-term advertiser commitments; news value and immediacy; year-round readership; high individual market coverage; co-op and local tie-in availability; short lead time	Little demographic selectivity; limited color capabilities; low pass-along rate; often expensive
Magazines	Good reproduction, especially for color; demographic selectivity; regional selectivity; local market selectivity; relatively long advertising life; high pass-along rate	Long-term advertiser commitments; slow audience buildup; limited demonstration capabilities; lack of urgency; long lead time
Radio	Low cost; immediacy of message; can be scheduled on short notice; relatively no seasonal change in audience; highly portable; short-term advertiser commitments; entertainment carryover	No visual treatment; short advertising life of message; high frequency required to generate comprehension and retention; distractions from background sound; commercial clutter
Television	Ability to reach a wide, diverse audience; low cost per thousand; creative opportunities for demonstration; immediacy of messages; entertainment carryover; demographic selectivity with cable stations	Short life of message; some consumer skepticism about claims; high campaign cost; little demographic selectivity with network stations; long-term advertiser commitments; long lead times required for production; commercial clutter
Outdoor Media	Repetition; moderate cost; flexibility; geographic selectivity	Short message; lack of demographic selectivity; high "noise" level distracting audience
Internet	Fastest-growing medium; ability to reach a narrow target audience; relatively short lead time required for creating Web-based advertising; moderate cost; ability to measure ad effectiveness; ability to engage consumers through search engine marketing, social media, display advertising, and mobile marketing	Most ad exposure relies on "click-through" from display ads; measurement for social media needs much improvement; not all consumers have access to the Internet and many consumers are not using social media

© Cengage Learning 2013

vehicles for reaching purchasers of specialty steel products or even tropical fish. These target consumers make up very small, specialized markets. Newspaper advertising also encounters a lot of distractions from competing ads and news stories. Therefore, one company's ad may not be particularly visible.

The main sources of newspaper ad revenue are local retailers, classified ads, and cooperative advertising. In **cooperative advertising**, the manufacturer and the retailer split the costs of advertising the manufacturer's brand. For example, Estée Lauder might split the cost of an advertisement with Macy's department store provided that the ad focuses on Estée Lauder's products. One reason manufacturers use cooperative advertising is the impracticality of listing all their dealers in national advertising. Also, co-op advertising encourages retailers to devote more effort to the manufacturer's lines.

Magazines Magazines are another traditional medium that has been successful. Some of the top magazines according to circulation include *AARP*, *Better Homes and Gardens*, *Reader's Digest*, *National Geographic*, and *Good Housekeeping*. However, compared to the cost of other media, the cost per contact in magazine advertising is usually high. The cost per potential customer can be much lower, however, because magazines are often targeted to specialized audiences and thus reach more potential customers. The types of products most frequently advertised in magazines include automobiles, apparel, computers, and cigarettes.

One of the main advantages of magazine advertising is its market selectivity. Magazines are published for virtually every market segment. For instance, *Lucky* "The Magazine about Shopping and Style" is a leading fashion magazine; *ESPN the Magazine* is a successful sports magazine; *Essence* is targeted toward African American women; *Marketing News* is a trade magazine for the marketing professional; and *The Source* is a niche publication geared to young urbanites with a passion for hip-hop music.

Philips Electronics used an innovative magazine advertising campaign by sponsoring the magazines' contents page. Issues of four Time Warner magazines (*Time*, *Fortune*, *People*, and the now defunct *Business 2.0*) featured the table of contents on the first page rather than several pages later. The inside front cover featured a Philips ad with the following copy: "Philips Electronics is bringing the table of contents to the front of selected Time, Inc. magazines to make things easier for readers." In general, the placement of the contents page varies from magazine to magazine, but it is not uncommon for the contents to appear after numerous advertisements; as many as 24 pages of ads can appear before a magazine's contents page. Philips paid Time, Inc., $5 million to sponsor the contents pages in the four magazines for only one issue each.[29]

Radio Radio has several strengths as an advertising medium: selectivity and audience segmentation, a large out-of-home audience, low unit and production costs, timeliness, and geographic flexibility. Local advertisers are the most frequent users of radio advertising, contributing over 75 percent of all radio ad revenues. Like newspapers, radio also lends itself well to cooperative advertising.

Radio advertising is enjoying a resurgence in popularity. As Americans become more mobile and pressed for time, media such as network television and newspapers have lost viewers and readers, particularly in the youth market. Radio listening, however, has grown in step with population increases mainly because its immediate, portable nature meshes so well with a fast-paced lifestyle. The ability to target specific demographic groups is a major selling point for radio stations, attracting advertisers pursuing narrowly defined audiences that are more likely to respond to certain kinds of ads and products. Radio listeners also tend to listen habitually and at predictable times, especially during "drive time," when commuters form a vast captive audience. Finally, satellite radio (e.g., Sirius XM) has attracted new audiences that are exposed to ads when allowed on that format.

Television Because television is an audiovisual medium, it provides advertisers with many creative opportunities. Television broadcasters include network television, independent stations, cable television, and direct broadcast satellite television. ABC, CBS, NBC, and the Fox Network dominate network television, which reaches a wide and diverse market. Conversely, cable television and direct broadcast satellite systems, such as DirecTV and Dish Network, offer consumers a multitude of channels devoted exclusively to particular audiences—for example, women, children, African Americans, nature lovers, senior citizens, Christians, Hispanics, sports fans, and fitness enthusiasts. Recent niche market entries include CSTV Network (college sports) and the NFL Network—focused exclusively on the sports enthusiast—and the casino and gambling channel. Because of its targeted channels, cable television is often characterized as "narrowcasting" by media buyers.

The ad-skipping functionality offered by TiVo and other digital video recorders has been the most significant recent trend to affect TV advertising.

Advertising time on television can be very expensive, especially for network and popular cable channels. The top-ranked TV programs in recent years are aired on networks ABC, CBS, NBC, and Fox. The biggest draws are Fox's *American Idol* and *House,* ABC's *Dancing with the Stars,* NBC's *The Biggest Loser,* ABC's *Grey's Anatomy,* NBC's *Sunday Night Football* and *The Office,* and CBS's crime series *CSI.*[30] First-run prime-time shows and special events command the highest rates for a typical 30-second spot, with the least expensive ads costing about $200,000 and the more expensive costing $500,000. Recently, cable networks have scored high ratings with original programming such as TNT's *The Closer* that can command high prices due to both their target audiences as well as their ratings. Super Bowl spots are the most expensive—a 30-second spot during the 2011 Super Bowl telecast cost advertisers an average of $3 million.[31] The two dozen or so marketers paying such a premium price include typical big ad spenders such as Procter & Gamble, Anheuser-Busch, and E-Trade. Most marketers consider the Super Bowl the "last bastion" of mass marketing available, with more than 100 million viewers tuning in.[32]

One of the more successful recent television formats to emerge is the **infomercial**, a 30-minute or longer advertisement. Infomercials are an attractive advertising vehicle for many marketers because of the relatively inexpensive airtime and the lower production costs. Advertisers say the infomercial is an ideal way to present complicated information to potential customers, which other advertising vehicles typically don't allow time to do. For example, some products, such as the Snuggie, Sweatin' to the Oldies, Billy Blanks Tae Bo, and P90X Workout DVDs, have all been successful using this format. Now a $200 billion-dollar industry, infomercials are increasingly being used by some mainstream marketers. Once relegated to late-night TV, infomercials are showing up in early evening time slots, such as Fox's *The O'Reilly Factor,* CBS's *60 Minutes,* and CNBC's *Mad Money.* Consumers who

infomercial
A 30-minute or longer advertisement that looks more like a TV talk show than a sales pitch.

might have been skeptical of an ad's veracity on shopping networks are less likely to suspect an ad shown during prime-time television programs. A shorter direct-retail infomercial is more common in daytime programming, running an average of 120 seconds.[33]

Probably the most significant trend to affect television advertising is the rise in popularity of digital video recorders (DVRs) such as TiVo. For every hour of television programming, an average of 15 minutes is dedicated to nonprogram material (ads, public service announcements, and network promotions), so it's hardly surprising that viewers weary of ad breaks have embraced ad-skipping DVR technology as the solution to interruptions during their favorite shows. Marketers of the products featured in those advertisements are not the only ones trying to figure out ways to keep consumers from avoiding them. Networks are also concerned about ad skipping. If consumers are not watching advertisements, then marketers will spend a greater proportion of their advertising budgets on alternative media, and a critical revenue stream for networks will disappear. NBC did run a test to measure the effectiveness of running shorter blocks of advertising. But the company also said that it has no intention of changing its business model relative to advertising sales. Some networks have created small icons in the bottom of the screen to promote their other programs. TiVo then began offering interactive banner ads to advertisers, making those sponsors' names visible as their ads are being fast-forwarded. The full impact of DVR technology on television as an advertising medium has yet to be determined, but research companies such as Nielsen have started to measure the number of people who time shift—that is, record a show and watch at their convenience.[34]

Outdoor Media Outdoor or out-of-home advertising is a flexible, low-cost medium that takes a variety of forms. Examples include billboards, skywriting, giant inflatables, mini-billboards in malls and on bus stop shelters, signs in sports arenas, lighted moving signs in bus terminals and airports, and ads painted on cars, trucks, buses, water towers, manhole covers, drinking glass coasters, and even people, called "living advertising." Students in London "rented" their foreheads for temporary tattoos of brands and then walked around specified areas of the city.[35] The plywood scaffolding that rings downtown construction sites can also carry ads. Manhattan's Times Square, with an estimated 1.5 million daily pedestrians, has been a popular area for outdoor advertising using scaffolding.

Outdoor advertising reaches a broad and diverse market and is, therefore, ideal for promoting convenience products and services as well as directing consumers to local businesses. One of outdoors' main advantages over other media is that its exposure frequency is very high, yet the amount of clutter from competing ads is very low. Outdoor advertising also has the ability to be customized to local marketing needs. For these reasons, local business establishments, such as local services and amusements, retailers, public transportation, and hotels and restaurants, are the leading outdoor advertisers. Outdoor advertising categories on the rise include telecommunications with a heavy emphasis on wireless services, financial services, and packaged goods.

Outdoor advertising is becoming more innovative. New technology is enabling outdoor ads to become interactive and to be more like online ads. For example, Nike commissioned a 23-story interactive, digital billboard in New York's Times Square. People passing the display on the sidewalk could use their cell phones to temporarily control the billboard and design their own shoes.[36] Virgin Atlantic Airways projected ads onto New York's and Chicago's skyscrapers, inviting passersby to access the airline's "Love From Above" campaign rewards.[37]

Unusual outdoor advertising campaigns are not limited to the United States. Adidas Japan created a "living billboard" in the form of a vertical soccer field on the side of a skyscraper. The billboard featured live players and a ball attached by ropes to the side of the building.[38] Virgin Atlantic painted an ad on the grass next to the runway at South Africa's Johannesburg International Airport to greet arriving and departing passengers. A world's first, the ad required 1,000 liters of paint and nine separate permits from different regulatory authorities due to the sensitive nature of the site.[39]

The Internet and Alternative Media Marketing The Internet has dramatically changed the advertising industry. With ad revenues exceeding $26 billion annually, the Internet has become a solid advertising medium. Online advertising continues to grow at double-digit rates—well ahead of other advertising media.[40] In fact, online ad spending is expected to exceed $34 billion annually by 2014 and account for 20 percent of all marketing expenditures.[41] Internet advertising provides an interactive and versatile platform that offers rich data on consumer usage, enabling advertisers to improve their ad targetability and achieve measurable results.[42]

Sprint Nextel Corp., Verizon Communications, General Motors, AT&T, and Ford Motor Company have been among the top 50 advertisers on the Internet in recent years. There are several types of online advertising formats. Search advertising (paid and organic) accounts for the largest expenditure ($11 billion). Popular Internet sites and search engines such as Google and Yahoo! generally sell advertising space to marketers to promote their goods and services. Marketers buy key words that they believe will drive traffic to their Web sites. Internet surfers click on these ads to be linked to more information about the advertised product or service. Of the billions of searches conducted daily, Google has the largest market share, followed by Yahoo! and Microsoft's Bing.[43] Social media, such as Facebook, are also making inroads into search ads. Marketers' primary objective in using search engine ads is to enhance brand awareness. Banner ads and display ads are one of the earliest formats and still quite popular with marketers. The creativity for display advertising has increased and the sizes are standard, allowing for ease of use. Other types of Internet advertising include classified advertising, lead generation, rich media, video sponsorships, and e-mail marketing.

The effectiveness of Internet advertising has been hotly debated, however. Early research on banner ads found response rates as high as 30 percent, but more recent studies indicate much lower response rates. With high-speed broadband spreading rapidly in the United States, advertisers increasingly are switching to other online approaches. For example, marketers are using ads that float, sing, or dance; video commercials similar to traditional TV spots; and ads that pop up in another window, use larger, hard-to-miss shapes, and include both online and offline cross-promotions. These new formats are often large enough for marketers to include their entire message so that users don't have to click through to another site.

Advergaming Another popular Internet advertising format is advergaming. In **advergaming**, companies put ad messages in Web-based or video games (on Playstation or Wii) to advertise or promote a product, service, organization, or issue. Sometimes the entire game amounts to a virtual commercial; other times advertisers sponsor games or buy ad space for product placement in them. Organizations using advergaming include Disney, Viacom's Nickelodeon, and even the U.S. Army.[44] The format encourages users to register for sweepstakes and other promotions and play the game. For example, a company with a heritage of aligning its products with gamers, Pepsi developed a multiplayer online game in which

advergaming
Placing advertising messages in Web-based or video games to advertise or promote a product, service, organization, or issue.

An advergame campaign, such as this *SpongeBob* fan site that Nickelodeon recently launched, taps into the explosive popularity of online connected game play.

players get a chance to choose the next flavor of Mt. Dew. The site, dewmocracy.com, drew 700,000 unique visitors and 200,000 registered users who spent an average of 28 minutes per gaming session. Pepsi's "dewmocracy" advergame campaign taps into the explosive popularity of online connected game play, such as "World of Warcraft" with more than ten million paying subscribers.[45]

Advertainment To cut through the clutter of traditional advertising media, advertisers are creating even more new media vehicles to advertise their products, some ordinary and others quite innovative. Alternative media vehicles can include shopping carts in grocery stores, computer screen savers, apps for smartphones or iPads, DVDs, interactive kiosks in department stores, advertisements run before movies at the cinema, and "advertainments"—"mini movies" that promote a product and are shown via the Internet.[46] For example, BMW shows films by recognized directors that run six to eight minutes and feature the cars in extreme situations.[47] Likewise, Coca-Cola sponsored a 25-minute advertainment program called "Sound Check" that was available only on TiVo. The program featured exclusive interviews, music videos, live shows, behind-the-scenes filming, and recordings by artists such as Ashanti, Sting, and Mary J. Blige.[48]

Indeed, almost anything can become a vehicle for displaying advertising. For instance, supermarkets have begun using "Flooranimation"—ads that are animated with graphics and sounds and installed on supermarket floors. Unanimated floor ads have been in use for some time, and research shows they increase sales 15 to 30 percent. Marketers are hoping that with animation and sound, sales will increase even more.[49] Billboards now include motion graphics and sound, and as an additional advertising media, are an excellent way to communicate with consumers in the evenings in metro markets such as New York City, Chicago, Los Angeles, and San Francisco.[50] Marketers are also looking for more innovative ways to reach captive and often bored commuters. For instance, subway systems now show ads via lighted boxes installed along tunnel walls. As a train passes through the tunnel, the passengers view the illuminated boxes, which create the same kind of illusion as a child's flip book, in which the images appear to move as the pages are flipped rapidly.

Video Game Advertising When trying to reach males aged 18 to 34, video game advertising is emerging as an excellent medium, second only to prime-time *Monday Night Football*. The medium first attracted attention when Massive, Inc., started a video game advertising network and later established a partnership with The Nielsen Company, to provide ad ratings. Massive provides the capability to have ads with full motion and sound inserted into games played on Internet-connected computers. This is a big improvement over previous ads, which had to be inserted when the games were made and therefore quickly became obsolete. When Microsoft later acquired Massive, it claimed it would help the company "deliver dynamic, relevant ads" across its online services including Xbox Live and MSN Games.[51]

Stealth or Guerilla Marketing The term "stealth" might conjure images of undercover operations, possibly even sneakiness. In marketing, however, stealth implies a campaign of outsmarting the competition rather than outspending them. Stealth marketing, also known as guerrilla marketing, or buzz, is usually just any unconventional way of performing marketing promotions on a low budget. Stealth marketing is often designed to leave the target audience unaware they have been marketed to, but that they have simply participated in something fun, or sometimes shocking. Movies such as *The Dark Knight* use this type of marketing quite effectively to build excitement for the opening (as discussed in Chapter 16). For instance, in a recent guerilla campaign to promote the film *The Water Horse: Legend of the Deep*, a 50-foot dragon (think Loch Ness monster) was created by way of hologram projection on the water surface of Tokyo Bay, in Japan. Conjuring a huge monster practically out of thin air created marketing "buzz" online, on the street, and in the media.[52]

MEDIA SELECTION CONSIDERATIONS

An important element in any advertising campaign is the media mix, the combination of media to be used. Media mix decisions are typically based on several factors: cost per contact, cost per click, reach, frequency, target audience considerations, flexibility of the medium, noise level, and the life span of the medium.

Cost per contact is the cost of reaching one member of the target market. Naturally, as the size of the audience increases, so does the total cost. Cost per contact enables an advertiser to compare media vehicles, such as television versus radio or magazine versus newspaper, or even the same media, such as *Newsweek* versus *Time*. This is also referred to as cost per thousand (CPM), which also allows marketers to compare the relative costs of specific media. An advertiser debating whether to spend local advertising dollars for TV spots or radio spots could consider the cost per contact of each. The advertiser might then pick the vehicle with the lowest cost per contact to maximize advertising punch for the money spent. Cost per click is the cost associated with a consumer clicking on a display or banner ad. While there are several variations, this enables the marketer to pay only for "engaged" consumers—those who opted to click on an ad.

Reach is the number of different target consumers exposed to a commercial at least once during a specific period, usually four weeks. Media plans for product introductions and attempts at increasing brand awareness usually emphasize reach. For example, an advertiser might try to reach 70 percent of the target audience during the first three months of the campaign. Reach is related to a medium's ratings, generally referred to in the industry as *gross ratings points*, or GRP. A television program with a higher GRP means that more people are tuning in to the show and the reach is higher. Accordingly, as GRP increases for a particular medium, so does cost per contact.

Because the typical ad is short-lived and because often only a small portion of an ad may be perceived at one time, advertisers repeat their ads so that consumers will remember the message. Frequency is the number of times an individual is exposed to a message during a specific period. Advertisers use average frequency to measure the intensity of a specific medium's coverage. For example, Coca-Cola might want an average exposure frequency of five for its Powerade television ads. That means each of the television viewers who saw the ad saw it an average of five times.

Media selection is also a matter of matching the advertising medium with the product's target market. If marketers are trying to reach teenage females, they might select *Seventeen* magazine. If they are trying to reach consumers over 50 years old, they may choose *Modern Maturity* magazine. A medium's ability to reach

media mix
The combination of media to be used for a promotional campaign.

cost per contact
The cost of reaching one member of the target market.

cost per thousand (CPM)
Allows marketers to compare the relative costs of specific media.

cost per click
The cost associated with a consumer clicking on a display or banner ad.

reach
The number of target consumers exposed to a commercial at least once during a specific period, usually four weeks.

frequency
The number of times an individual is exposed to a given message during a specific period.

a precisely defined market is its **audience selectivity**. Some media vehicles, like general newspapers and network television, appeal to a wide cross section of the population. Others—such as *Brides, Popular Mechanics, Architectural Digest, Lucky,* MTV, ESPN, and Christian radio stations—appeal to very specific groups.

The *flexibility* of a medium can be extremely important to an advertiser. In the past, because of printing timetables, production requirements, and so on, some magazines required final ad copy several months before publication. Therefore, magazine advertising traditionally could not adapt as rapidly to changing market conditions. While this is changing quickly due to computer technology that creates electronic ad images and layouts, the lead time for magazine advertising is still considerably longer. Radio and Internet advertising, on the other hand, provide maximum flexibility. Usually, the advertiser can change a radio ad on the day it is aired, if necessary. Similarly, advertisements on the Internet can be changed in minutes with the click of a few buttons.

Noise level is the level of distraction associated with a medium. For example, to understand a televised promotional message, viewers must watch and listen carefully. But they often watch television with others, who may well provide distractions. Noise can also be created by competing ads, as when a street is lined with billboards or when a television program is cluttered with competing ads. About two-thirds of a newspaper's pages is now filled with advertising. A recent Sunday issue of the *Los Angeles Times* contained over 1,200 ads, not counting the small classifieds. Even more space is dedicated to ads in magazines. For example, 85 percent of the space in the February/March issue of *Brides* magazine is typically devoted to advertisements. In contrast, direct mail is a private medium with a low noise level. Typically, no other advertising media or news stories compete for direct-mail readers' attention.

Noise level, or the level of distraction to the target audience, is high in an ad-jammed city street such as this one.

© Alan Copson/Photographer's Choice/Getty Images

Media have either a short or a long life span. *Life span* means that messages can either quickly fade or persist as tangible copy to be carefully studied. For example, a radio commercial may last less than a minute. Listeners can't replay the commercial unless they have recorded the program. One way advertisers overcome this problem is by repeating radio ads often. In contrast, a magazine has a relatively long life span. A person may read several articles, put the magazine down, and pick it up a week later to continue reading. In addition, magazines often have a high pass-along rate. That is, one person will read the publication and then give it to someone else to read.

Media planners have traditionally relied on the previously mentioned factors in selecting an effective media mix, with reach, frequency, and cost often the overriding criteria. But some experts question the reliance media planners have traditionally placed on reach and frequency. For instance, well-established brands with familiar messages probably need fewer exposures to be effective, while newer brands or brands with unfamiliar messages likely need more exposures to become familiar.

Additionally, media planners have hundreds more media options today than they had when network television reigned. For instance, there are over 1,600 television stations across the country. Similarly, in the Los Angeles market alone there are more than 80 radio stations, with 7 offering an "adult contemporary" format. The number of unique magazine titles has more than doubled over the last decade, with publications now targeting every possible market segment. Satellite television brings hundreds of channels into viewers' homes. The Internet provides media planners with even more targeted choices in which to send their messages. And alternative media choices are popping up in some very unlikely places. *Media fragmentation* is forcing media planners to pay as much attention to where they place their advertising, as to how often the advertisement is repeated. Indeed, experts recommend evaluating reach along with frequency in assessing the effectiveness of advertising. That is, in certain situations it might be important to reach potential consumers through as many media vehicles as possible. When this approach is considered, however, the budget must be large enough to achieve sufficient levels of frequency to have an impact. In evaluating reach versus frequency, therefore, the media planner ultimately must select an approach that is most likely to result in the ad being understood and remembered when a purchase decision is being made.

Advertisers also evaluate the qualitative factors involved in media selection. These qualitative factors include such things as attention to the commercial and the program, involvement, lack of distractions, how well the viewer likes the program, and other audience behaviors that affect the likelihood a commercial message is being seen and, hopefully, absorbed. While advertisers can advertise their product in as many media as possible and repeat the ad as many times as they like, the ad still may not be effective if the audience is not paying attention. Research on audience attentiveness for television, for example, shows that the longer viewers stay tuned to a particular program, the more memorable they find the commercials. Holding power, therefore, can be more important than ratings (the number of people tuning in to any part of the program) when selecting media vehicles, challenging the long-held assumption that the higher the rating of a program, the more effective the advertising run during the program, even though it is more costly. For instance, *Dancing with the Stars,* one of the top-rated shows among 25- to 54-year-olds, costs about $200,000 for a 30-second spot but ranks relatively low for holding power. In contrast, the low-rated *Candid Camera,* which ranks high in holding power, costs only about $55,000 for a 30-second spot.[53]

See the Global Perspectives box to find out how marketers capitalized on one of the biggest sporting events in the world—the 2010 World Cup.

MEDIA SCHEDULING

After choosing the media for the advertising campaign, advertisers must schedule the ads. A **media schedule** designates the medium or media to be used (such as magazines, television, or radio), the specific vehicles (such as *People* magazine, the TV show *CSI,* or Rush Limbaugh's national radio program), and the insertion dates of the advertising.

There are three basic types of media schedules:

→ Products in the latter stages of the product life cycle, which are advertised on a reminder basis, use a **continuous media schedule**. A continuous schedule allows the advertising to run steadily throughout the advertising period. Examples include Ivory soap, Tide detergent, Bounty paper towels, and Charmin toilet tissue, which might have an ad in the newspaper every Sunday and a TV commercial on NBC every Wednesday at 7:30 P.M. over a three-month time period.

→ With a **flighted media schedule,** the advertiser might schedule the ads heavily every other month or every two weeks to achieve a greater impact with an increased frequency and reach at those times. Movie studios might schedule television advertising on Wednesday and Thursday nights, when moviegoers are deciding which films to see that weekend. A variation is the **pulsing media schedule,** which combines continuous scheduling with flighting. Continuous advertising is simply heavier during the best sale periods. A retail department store might advertise on a year-round basis but place more advertising during certain sale periods such as Thanksgiving, Christmas, and back-to-school. For

media schedule
Designation of the media, the specific publications or programs, and the insertion dates of advertising.

continuous media schedule
A media scheduling strategy in which advertising is run steadily throughout the advertising period; used for products in the latter stages of the product life cycle.

flighted media schedule
A media scheduling strategy in which ads are run heavily every other month or every two weeks, to achieve a greater impact with an increased frequency and reach at those times.

pulsing media schedule
A media scheduling strategy that uses continuous scheduling throughout the year coupled with a flighted schedule during the best sales periods.

The Rise of Social Media Celebrity Endorsers

Celebrities have been used to sell products for quite some time. While it is popular in the United States, it is also popular the world over. Companies select celebrities who are famous in the target country—whether it is an athlete (Yao Ming is pretty famous in China and Wayne Rooney is very popular in England) or film star (think of all of the Bollywood film stars). With the rise of social media, particularly YouTube, we also see a rise in a new type of celebrity endorser—one whose fame lives entirely online. They are the social media celebrity endorsers.

Enter the iJustine, Rhett & Link, Smosh, Michelle Phan, and What the Buck.[54] Never heard of them? Well this cadre of stars is raking in six figures ad revenue from Google and commanding up to $20,000 for branded videos aimed to their own home grown audience of thousands—even millions—of viewers. On YouTube. Yes, not on television, but on the hugely popular video sharing site that has made its name as a place to launch new campaigns (for example, Old Spice's spots with Isaiah Mustafa) and movie trailers. Many of these celebs do offbeat skits, such as comic Shane Dawson, who averages more than 1.5 million viewers daily. IJustine has more than 1 million subscribers and develops brand videos that take product placement to new heights for Ezarik and Mattel's Video Girl Barbie. Michelle Phan now works for Lancôme. She films and then shares cosmetic tutorials and is famous for recreating Lady Gaga's Poker Face look. That garnered her more than 14 million views in ten months. Recently GE signed 15 YouTube celebs to make a series of videos for its "Tag Your Green" campaign.

These endorsers are turning everything we know about how celebrity endorsers work on its head. Is attractiveness important? Is trust important? Or are things like authenticity more important in the new age of social media? And what about geographic barriers? With these new celebs, it does not matter where they are from and where the brands are from because it all goes onto the World Wide Web. Marketers have discovered that "web-video celebrities offer trusted voices and an engaged viewership."[55] They have built up their reputations by engaging with their audiences in a whole new way—ways that brands are currently struggling to do. Many of these celebs also offer their audience many ways to engage—they often use Facebook and Twitter as well as YouTube. As the uses for social media continue to multiply, companies are beginning to explore how to capitalize on these unique marketing opportunities.

© iStockphoto.com/Juan Facundo Mora Soria

example, beer might be advertised more heavily during summer months and football season given the higher consumption levels during those times.

→ Certain times of the year call for a **seasonal media schedule**. Products such as Sudafed cold tablets and Coppertone sunscreen lotion, which are used more during certain times of the year, tend to follow a seasonal strategy. Advertising for champagne is concentrated during the weeks of Christmas and New Year's, whereas health clubs like LA Fitness and diet plans like Jenny Craig concentrate their advertising in January to take advantage of New Year's resolutions.

New research comparing continuous media schedules and flighted ones finds that continuous schedules for television advertisements are more effective than flighting in driving sales. The research suggests that it might be more important to get exposure as close as possible to the time someone is going to make a purchase. For example, if a consumer shops on a weekly basis, the best time to reach that person is right before he or she shops. Therefore, the advertiser should maintain a continuous schedule over as long a period of time as possible. Often called *recency planning,* this theory of scheduling is now commonly used for scheduling television advertising for frequently purchased products such as Coca-Cola or Tide detergent. Recency planning's main premise is that advertising works by influencing the brand choice of people who are ready to buy.

seasonal media schedule
A media scheduling strategy that runs advertising only during times of the year when the product is most likely to be used.

Mobile advertising might be one of the most promising tactics for contacting consumers when they are thinking about a specific product. For example, a GPS-enabled mobile phone can get text messages for area restaurants around lunchtime to advertise specials to professionals working in a big city.

LO5
Public Relations

Public relations is the element in the promotional mix that evaluates public attitudes, identifies issues that might elicit public concern, and executes programs to gain public understanding and acceptance. Like advertising and sales promotion, public relations is a vital link in a company's promotional mix. Marketing managers plan solid public relations campaigns that fit into overall marketing plans and focus on targeted audiences. These campaigns strive to maintain a positive image of the corporation in the eyes of the public. Before launching public relations programs, managers evaluate public attitudes and company actions. Then they create programs to capitalize on factors that enhance the firm's image and minimize the factors that could generate a negative image.

In recent years, fast-food companies like McDonald's and soft drink companies like Coca-Cola have been criticized for contributing to childhood obesity, particularly in the United States. In response, the companies have undertaken public relations campaigns to try to minimize the impact on their reputations and ultimately sales. For example, Coca-Cola created the Beverage Institute for Health and Wellness to support nutrition research, education, and outreach. The company also spent $4 million to develop the "Live Positively" Web site (www.livepositively.com), which focuses on people, planet, and products. Specifically, one issue it focuses on is children's fitness in schools across the country. Coke's nutrition communication manager says the campaign will not address childhood obesity or encourage students to drink Coke and that the company's logo will not appear on "Live It" materials. In addition to promoting the campaign, Coke is paying for campaign posters, pedometers, and nutrition education materials and offering prizes to children who meet the program's exercise goal of walking 10,000 steps a day. Such efforts are designed to offset a push by the Center for Science in the Public Interest to persuade the Food and Drug Administration to require labels on sodas warning about obesity, tooth decay, and diabetes.[56]

A public relations program can generate favorable **publicity**—public information about a company, product, service, or issue appearing in the mass media as a new item. Organizations generally do not pay for the publicity and are not identified

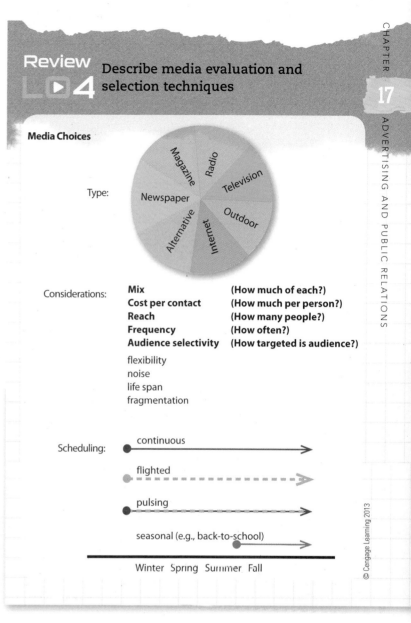

Review LO4 Describe media evaluation and selection techniques

Media Choices

Type: Magazine, Radio, Television, Newspaper, Outdoor, Alternative, Internet

Considerations:
Mix	**(How much of each?)**
Cost per contact	**(How much per person?)**
Reach	**(How many people?)**
Frequency	**(How often?)**
Audience selectivity	**(How targeted is audience?)**

flexibility
noise
life span
fragmentation

Scheduling:
continuous
flighted
pulsing
seasonal (e.g., back-to-school)

Winter Spring Summer Fall

© Cengage Learning 2013

public relations
The marketing function that evaluates public attitudes, identifies areas within the organization the public may be interested in, and executes a program of action to earn public understanding and acceptance.

publicity
Public information about a company, product, service, or issue appearing in the mass media as a news item.

as the source of the information, but they can benefit tremendously from it. For example, the rapid growth of the satellite radio industry is partly due to publicity. Subscribers exceeded 21 million in 2011. Satellite radio's profile received a huge boost from the storm of publicity surrounding the decision by the country's most notorious and popular radio host, "shock jock" Howard Stern, to quit CBS radio and join censor-free Sirius satellite radio. Stern's first satellite broadcast was a major event, with the national media breathlessly reporting on the number of times he swore and looking for acceptable ways to report the more graphic—usually sexual—content of the show. Satellite radio, now called Sirius XM after the merger, benefited from the publicity Stern generated for the whole satellite broadcast medium as well as by signing up both Oprah Winfrey and reclusive music legend Bob Dylan to host shows.[57]

Again, although organizations do not directly pay for publicity, it should not be viewed as free. Preparing news releases, staging special events, and persuading media personnel to broadcast or print publicity messages costs money. Public relations departments perform any or all of the following functions:

→ **Press relations:** Placing positive, newsworthy information in the news media or for influential bloggers to attract attention to a product, a service, or a person associated with the firm or institution

→ **Product publicity:** Publicizing specific products or services through a variety of traditional and online channels

→ **Corporate communication:** Creating internal and external messages to promote a positive image of the firm or institution

→ **Public affairs:** Building and maintaining local, national, or global community relations

→ **Lobbying:** Influencing legislators and government officials to promote or defeat legislation and regulation

→ **Employee and investor relations:** Maintaining positive relationships with employees, shareholders, and others in the financial community

→ **Crisis management:** Responding to unfavorable publicity or a negative event

MAJOR PUBLIC RELATIONS TOOLS

Public relations professionals commonly use several tools, including new-product publicity, product placement, consumer education, sponsorship, and Web sites. Although many of these tools require an active role on the part of the public relations professional, such as writing press releases and engaging in proactive media relations, some techniques create their own publicity.

New-Product Publicity Publicity is instrumental in introducing new products and services. Publicity can help advertisers explain what's different about their new product by prompting free news stories or positive word of mouth about it. During the introductory period, an especially innovative new product often needs more exposure than conventional, paid advertising affords. Public relations professionals write press releases or develop videos in an effort to generate news about their new product. They also jockey for exposure of their product or service at major events, on popular television and news shows, or in the hands of influential people. Consider the publicity Apple generated for the release of the iPad, which included press coverage in traditional media as well as online blogs and forums. That was a small aspect of the entire marketing campaign.

Product Placement Marketers are increasingly using product placement to reinforce brand awareness and create favorable attitudes. **Product placement** is a strategy that involves getting one's product, service, or name to appear in a movie, television show, radio program, magazine, newspaper, video game, video or audio clip, book, or commercial for another product; on the Internet; or at special events. Indeed, a product mention on the Oprah Winfrey show has been linked to increased sales for many products, especially books. Including an actual product such as a can of Pepsi adds a sense of realism to a movie, TV show, video game, book, or similar vehicle that a can simply marked "soda" cannot. Product placements are arranged through barter (trade of product for placement), through paid placements, or at no charge when the product is viewed as enhancing the vehicle where it is placed.

Product placement expenditures amount to about $5 billion annually. Though this amount is small relative to other marketing expenditures, it is growing about 30 percent annually due to increasing audience fragmentation and the spread of ad-skipping technology.[58] More than two-thirds of product placements are in movies and TV shows, but placements in alternative media are growing, particularly on the Internet and in video games. Most product placements are for transportation, clothing, food, beverages, home furnishings, travel, and leisure time activities. Companies such as BMW, Lexus, Coca-Cola, Pepsi, Procter & Gamble, and Hershey have frequently used product placement as a public relations strategy. Digital technology now enables companies to "virtually" place their products in any audio or video production. Virtual placement not only reduces the cost of product placement for new productions, but also enables companies to place products in previously produced programs, such as reruns of television shows and movies.

Companies obtain valuable product exposure, brand reinforcement, and increased sales through product placement, often at a much lower cost than in mass media like television ads. For example, Burger King products were woven into *The Apprentice* when contestants wore Burger King uniforms and flipped burgers as part of a challenge; Ford sponsored the show *24*, with the main character, Jack Bauer, driving a Ford Expedition; and S.C. Johnson placed the ant killer RAID in an episode of the popular HBO series *The Sopranos*. The television show *Seinfeld* had several products prominently displayed in various episodes. When Red Stripe, a Jamaican-brewed beer, appeared in the movie *The Firm*, its U.S. sales increased more than 50 percent in the first month after the movie was released.[59]

Consumer Education Some major firms believe that educated consumers are better, more loyal customers. BMW of North America, for example, sponsored an instructional driving school for teenagers in major cities across the United States. Teens received a special four-hour training session that included driving techniques, accident avoidance skills, and traction aid tricks from a professional driver. Financial planning firms often sponsor free educational seminars on money management, retirement planning, and investing in the hope that the seminar participants will choose the sponsoring organization for their future financial needs. Likewise, computer hardware and software firms, realizing that many consumers are intimidated by new technology and recognizing the strong relationship between learning and purchasing patterns, sponsor computer seminars and free in-store demonstrations.

Sponsorships Sponsorships are increasing both in number and as a proportion of companies' marketing budgets, with spending reaching $17 billion annually in the United States and Canada. Probably the biggest reason for the increasing use of sponsorships is the difficulty of reaching audiences and differentiating a product from competing brands through the mass media. With a **sponsorship**, a company spends money to support an issue, cause, or event that is consistent with corporate objectives, such as improving brand awareness or enhancing corporate image. The biggest category is sports, which accounts for almost 68 percent of spending in sponsorships (valued at $11.6 billion annually). Examples of sports sponsorships include various sponsors of college bowl games, Jose Cuervo Tequila's sponsorship of the Pro Beach Volleyball Tour; Domino's Pizza's sponsorship of Michael Waltrip for NASCAR; Hilton Hotels' sponsorship of the Hilton Family Skating & Gymnastics Spectacular on NBC; Levi Strauss & Co.'s partnership with the San Francisco Giants to sponsor the right field section of the park to be named "Levi's Landing," and Anheuser-Busch's Bud Bowl that featured hip-hop star Snoop Dogg and rock band 3 Doors Down.[60] In addition, multiple companies sponsor the Olympics every two years as well as the World Cup every four years. While sports sponsorships make up the majority, there are several other viable categories as well. Nonsports categories include entertainment tours and attractions (10 percent; $1.7 billion annually) such as the Essence Music Festival sponsored by Bank of America,

© 157/ZUMA Press/Newscom

McDonald's, and Kraft Foods; causes (9 percent; $1.6 billion annually); arts (5 percent; $841 million annually); festivals, fairs, and annual events (5 percent; $787 million annually) such as MSN Music and Milwaukee's Summerfest and Manchester, Tennessee's Bonnaroo Music and Arts Festival; and association and membership organizations (3 percent; $500 million annually).[61]

Although companies have recently been turning to specialized events such as tie-ins with schools, charities, and other community service organizations, the most popular sponsorship events are still those involving sports, music, or the arts.[62]

Marketers sometimes create their own events tied around their products. The state of Hawaii organized its own mall touring event, titled "Experience Aloha: Hawaii on Tour," to promote the islands as a tourist destination. The tour traveled to 22 U.S. cities for weekend mall visits that included hula dancers, chefs cooking Hawaiian cuisine, lei-making demonstrations, and a virtual reality film simulating a helicopter ride over Hawaii's islands. Many other states also sponsor events promoting tourism.

One major type of sponsorship, **cause-related marketing**, involves the association of a for-profit company with a nonprofit organization. The donation to the nonprofit is typically made based on some type of consumer behavior—such as purchasing a product or mailing in a label. Through the sponsorship, the company's product or service is promoted, and money is raised for the nonprofit. In a common type of cause-related sponsorship, a company agrees to donate a percentage of the purchase price of a particular item to a charity, but some arrangements are more complex. In the United States Avon, Yoplait Yogurt, and BMW support the Susan G. Komen for the Cure, and J.P. Morgan Chase & Co. Bank works with St. Jude Children's Research Hospital.[63] Recently, companies are partnering with nonprofit organizations to create new "cause brands." For example, the American Heart Association and several corporations have developed the "Go Red for Women" campaign to increase the awareness of heart disease in women

sponsorship
A public relations strategy in which a company spends money to support an issue, cause, or event that is consistent with corporate objectives, such as improving brand awareness or enhancing corporate image.

cause-related marketing
A type of sponsorship involving the association of a for-profit company and a nonprofit organization; through the sponsorship, the company's product or service is promoted, and money is raised for the nonprofit.

(www.goredforwomen.org).[64] Findings from several studies suggest that some consumers consider a company's reputation when making purchasing decisions and that a company's community involvement boosts employee morale and loyalty.[65]

Internet Web Sites Companies increasingly are using the Internet in their public relations strategies. Company Web sites are used to introduce new products; provide information to the media including social media news releases; promote existing products; obtain consumer feedback; communicate legislative and regulatory information; showcase upcoming events; provide links to related sites including blogs, Facebook, and Twitter; release financial information; interact with customers and potential customers; and perform many more marketing activities. In addition, social media is playing a larger role in how companies interact with customers online, particularly through other sites, like Facebook, Yelp, or Twitter. Indeed, online reviews (good and bad) from opinion leaders and other consumers help marketers sway purchasing decisions in their favor. On its Web site for PlayStation 3 (**www.playstation.com**), Sony has online support, events and promotions, game trailers, and new and updated product releases such as *Killzone 3, Street Fighter IV, F.E.A.R. 3,* and *MLB 11: The Show.* The site also includes message boards where the gaming community posts notes and chats, exchanges tips on games, votes on lifestyle issues like music and videos, and learns about promotional events.[66]

More and more often, companies are also using blogs—both corporate and noncorporate—as a tool to manage their public images. Noncorporate blogs cannot be controlled, but marketers must monitor them to be aware of and respond to negative information and encourage positive content. Walmart has been especially active in cultivating bloggers to get the company's message out. Mona Williams, Walmart's spokeswoman, says, "We reach out to bloggers in the same way we reach out to reporters. A lot of people are looking to bloggers for their news source, and this is a good way to get our message out."[67] The company hired a public relations firm to combat negative publicity. The publicist assigned to the Walmart account, Marshall Manson, contacts bloggers who write pro-Walmart content and asks if he can send them materials to use in their commentaries. Those who agree become champions for the giant retailer.[68]

In addition to "getting the message out," companies are using blogs to create communities of consumers who feel positively about the brand. The hope is that the positive attitude toward the brand will build into strong word-of-mouth marketing. Companies must exercise caution when diving into corporate blogging, however. Coca-Cola launched a blog authored by a fictional character that did little except parrot the company line. Consumers immediately saw the blog for what it was (a transparent public relations platform) and lambasted Coca-Cola for its insincerity.[69]

MANAGING UNFAVORABLE PUBLICITY

Although marketers try to avoid unpleasant situations, crises do happen. In our free-press environment, publicity is not easily controlled, especially in a crisis. **Crisis management** is the coordinated effort to handle the effects of unfavorable publicity, ensuring fast and accurate communication in times of emergency.

A good public relations staff is as important in bad times as in good. Companies must have a communication policy firmly in hand before a disaster occurs, because timing is uncontrollable. For example, McDonald's was caught by the wave of negative publicity that followed the release of *Super Size Me,* a documentary film that chronicled the deterioration of filmmaker Morgan Spurlock's health while he experimented with an all-McDonald's diet. In anticipation of a similar response to the movie version of Eric Schlosser's best seller *Fast Food Nation,* McDonald's contemplated dispatching a "truth squad" and a team of "ambassadors of the brand" to remind

crisis management
A coordinated effort to handle all the effects of unfavorable publicity or of another unexpected unfavorable event.

consumers that the restaurant offers a healthy menu and provides good jobs. The company also modified its menu to include more salads and apple dippers. McDonald's new marketing communication focused on the importance of a balanced lifestyle appears to have offset potential negative publicity resulting from the documentary.[70]

When Walmart became the target of negative publicity regarding its low wages and sparse benefits, publicist Marshall Manson sent a special missive to his network of bloggers. It revealed that unions were hiring homeless and day laborers to protest at nonunion businesses, including Walmart. The unions paid the picketers minimum wage and gave them no benefits. Manson's release was used by numerous bloggers and represented a counterattack in the publicity war over Walmart's employment practices.[71] Crisis communications is playing an even larger role for many marketers than it has in the past, primarily because they don't own the message anymore. When BP was launched into the public eye as a result of the largest oil spill in U.S. history, the company did not do a very good job with transparency. Indeed, it was so slow to use social media to interact with the public that the Twitter hashtag "BPGlobalPR" was already in use by a comedian, who then posted satirical information regarding the oil spill. Interestingly, for a while it had many more followers than any officially sanctioned BP Twitter presence.

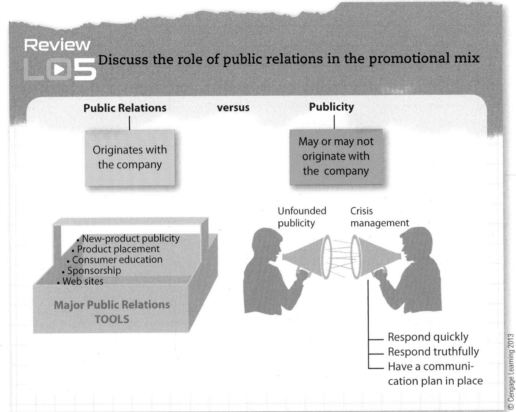

Review
LO5 Discuss the role of public relations in the promotional mix

Public Relations versus **Publicity**

Originates with the company

May or may not originate with the company

- New-product publicity
- Product placement
- Consumer education
- Sponsorship
- Web sites

Major Public Relations TOOLS

Unfounded publicity

Crisis management

— Respond quickly
— Respond truthfully
— Have a communication plan in place

© Cengage Learning 2013

Spending by top 100 global marketers for marketing

People employed in media advertising

Cost of Pfizer's recent advertising campaign for the fibromyalgia medication Lyrica

Daily pedestrians in Manhattan's Times Square

Percentage of the February/March issue of *Brides* magazine devoted to ads

Hours of commercial television messages the average viewer sees each week

Seconds in the average direct-retail daytime infomercial

Percent by which unanimated floor ads increase sales

Television stations in the U.S.

$125.3 billion **1.4 million** **6** **$46 million** **120** **1.5 million** **15-30** **85** **1,600**

1 Media type: Magazine

2 Good color reproduction = Advantage of magazine

3 Advertising appeal = Health, charity

4 Cause-related marketing

5 Long life span: Campaign still running in 2009

6 Product advertising

7 Executional style = Mood

Even

the

lid

is

good

for

you.

Save Lids to Save Lives™

For every pink lid you mail back by December 31, 2003, Yoplait will make a 10-cent donation to the Susan G. Komen Breast Cancer Foundation, up to $1.2 million. Combined with Yoplait's guaranteed donation of $830,000, we can raise $2 million. Yoplait and you – partners in the fight against breast cancer. This September and October, look for Yoplait pink lids at a store near you. www.YoplaitUSA.com.

© 2003 General Mills, Inc.

Yoplait
Original
99% fat free
FRENCH VANILLA

Yoplait
Save Lids to Save Lives

Review and Applications

L◉1 **Discuss the effects of advertising on market share and consumers.**
Advertising helps marketers increase or maintain brand awareness as well as market share. Typically, more is spent to advertise new brands with a small market share than to advertise older brands. Brands with a large market share use advertising mainly to maintain their share of the market. Advertising affects consumers' daily lives as well as their purchases. Although advertising can seldom change strongly held consumer attitudes and values, it may transform a consumer's negative attitude toward a product into a positive one. Additionally, when consumers are highly loyal to a brand, they may buy more of that brand when advertising is increased. Lastly, advertising can also change the importance of a brand's attributes to consumers. By emphasizing different brand attributes, advertisers can change their appeal in response to consumers' changing needs or try to achieve an advantage over competing brands.

1.1 Discuss the reasons why new brands with a smaller market share spend proportionately more on advertising than brands with a larger market share.

 team

1.2 Form a three-person team. Divide the responsibility for getting newspaper advertisements and menus for several local restaurants. While you are at the restaurants to obtain copies of their menus, observe the atmosphere and interview the manager to determine what he or she believes are the primary reasons people choose to dine there. Pool your information and develop a table comparing the restaurants in terms of convenience of location, value for the money, food variety and quality, atmosphere, and so on. Rank the restaurants in terms of their appeal to college students. Explain the basis of your rankings. What other market segment would be attracted to the restaurants and why? Do the newspaper advertisements emphasize the most effective appeal for a particular restaurant? Explain.

L◉2 **Identify the major types of advertising.** Advertising is any form of impersonal, paid communication in which the sponsor or company is identified. The two major types of advertising are institutional advertising and product advertising. Institutional advertising is not product oriented; rather, its purpose is to foster a positive company image among the general public, investment community, customers, and employees. Product advertising is designed mainly to promote goods and services, and it is classified into three main categories: pioneering, competitive, and comparative. A product's place in the product life cycle is a major determinant of the type of advertising used to promote it.

2.1 At what stage in a product's life cycle are pioneering, competitive, and comparative advertising most likely to occur? Give a current example of each type of advertising.

L◉3 **Discuss the creative decisions in developing an advertising campaign.** Before any creative work can begin on an advertising campaign, it is important to determine what goals or objectives the advertising should achieve. The objectives of a specific advertising campaign often depend on the overall corporate objectives and the product being advertised. Once objectives have been defined, creative work can begin on the advertising campaign. Creative decisions include identifying the product's benefits, developing possible advertising appeals, evaluating and selecting the advertising appeals, executing the advertising message, and evaluating the effectiveness of the campaign.

3.1 What is an advertising appeal? Give some examples of advertising appeals you have observed recently in the media.

3.2 Design a full-page magazine advertisement for a new brand of soft drink. The name of the new drink and its package design are at your discretion. On a separate sheet, specify the benefits stressed or appeals made in the advertisement.

writing

Describe media evaluation and selection techniques. Media evaluation and selection make up a crucial step in the advertising campaign process. Major types of advertising media include newspapers, magazines, radio, television, outdoor advertising such as billboards and bus panels, and the Internet. Recent trends in advertising media include video shopping carts, computer screen savers, cinema and DVD advertising, cell phones, and video games. Promotion managers choose the advertising campaign's media mix on the basis of the following variables: cost per contact, reach, frequency, characteristics of the target audience, flexibility of the medium, noise level, and the life span of the medium. After choosing the media mix, a media schedule designates when the advertisement will appear and the specific vehicles it will appear in.

LO4

4.1 What are the advantages of radio advertising? Why is radio expanding as an advertising medium?

4.2 You are the advertising manager of a sailing magazine, and one of your biggest potential advertisers has questioned your rates. Write the firm a letter explaining why you believe your audience selectivity is worth the extra expense for advertisers.

writing

4.3 Identify an appropriate media mix for the following products:

  a. Chewing tobacco
  b. *People* magazine
  c. Weed-Eaters
  d. Foot odor killers
  e. "Drink responsibly" campaigns by beer brewers

4.4 How easy is it to find out about advertising options on the Internet? Go to LookSmart's and Yahoo!'s advertiser pages (**www.looksmart.com/aboutus/**, then click on Newsroom, and **www.yahoo.com/advertising**). What kind of information do they require from you? Send an e-mail message requesting information and compare what you receive.

online

Discuss the role of public relations in the promotional mix. Public relations is a vital part of a firm's promotional mix. A company fosters good publicity to enhance its image and promote its products. Popular public relations tools include new-product publicity, product placements, consumer education, sponsorships, and Internet Web sites. An equally important aspect of public relations is managing unfavorable publicity to minimize damage to a firm's image.

LO5

5.1 How can advertising and publicity work together? Give an example.

5.2 As the new public relations director for a sportswear company, you have been asked to set public relations objectives for a new line of athletic shoes to be introduced to the teen market. Draft a memo outlining the objectives you propose for the shoe's introduction and your reasons for them.

writing

5.3 Review the newspapers in your area for one week. Try to review several and varied newspapers (local, campus, cultural, countercultural, etc.). During this period, cut out all the event advertisements that list sponsors. Once you have your collection, spread them out so you can see them all at once. Identify any patterns or connections between the type of event and its sponsors. Identify companies that sponsor more than one event. What do sponsors tell you about target markets? After analyzing the ads, write a brief paragraph summarizing your discoveries.

Key Terms

Exercises

ETHICS EXERCISE

Creative Advertising Agency has been asked to help its largest client improve its corporate image after a highly publicized product recall. The client requests a television advertisement highlighting the company's generous donation of products to low-income families. The only such donation the company has made, however, is a donation of the recalled products. The account executive fears promoting the donation could cause further consumer backlash, but the client continues to press for the spot.

Questions

1. Should Creative Advertising meet the client's expectations (i.e., create the promotional spot) or risk losing the account? Explain your reasoning.

2. What does the AMA Statement of Ethics say about truth in advertising? Go to **www .marketingpower.com** and review the code. Then write a brief paragraph describing how the AMA Statement of Ethics relates to this issue.

MARKETING PLAN EXERCISE

In Part 5 of your strategic marketing plan you'll continue defining the elements of the marketing mix, focusing on promotion and communication decisions. Use the following exercises to guide you through the advertising and public relations decisions you'll make for your chosen company:

1. Investigate different media placement rates (such as for a school newspaper, local newspaper, national newspaper, local radio station, local TV station, general or specialty interest magazine, local billboard, transit advertising, or the Internet). You can either call local media or consult Standard Rate and Data Services (SRDS). Which media should your firm use? Which media can your firm afford? When should media be used?

2. Are there different advertising concerns for the Internet-only firm than for the firm with an established brick-and-mortar presence? If so, what are they? Design the advertising for each medium selected in question 1. Do all advertising pieces carry a uniform theme and style? Is there sufficient information about benefits offered to consumers? Do customers have an option for obtaining further information?

3. List the public relations activities that your company should do. Be sure to make them consistent with your branding and other promotions. In addition, write a plan for handling bad publicity. Bad publicity travels at light speed over the Internet and is much more of a challenge to an e-marketer. Check out http://urbanlegends.about.com to see how misinformation can travel the Internet and cause public relations nightmares for companies.

APPLICATION EXERCISE 1

You may think that creating advertising is easy. After all, you have a lot of experience with advertising, having been bombarded with advertisements since you were a child. But creating advertising presents real challenges. In this exercise, you will be challenged to create an ad for a new product for animal use that is based on a product used by humans. Some examples include bras for cows, claw polish for tigers, and "Minute Mice" for cats. You can pick any product and any animal, but the combination must make sense.[72]

Activities

1. You have been hired by the purveyor of your chosen product to create a print advertisement. Lay out your ad on a piece of paper that is no smaller than 8.5 by 11 inches and no larger than 11 by 14 inches. Include a headline, illustration, logo, and body copy. Your illustration can be either hand-drawn, clipped from a magazine, or copied from a Web site.

2. Include the copy for your ad directly on the front of the ad unless your copy blocks are too large for you to be legible or neat. If that is the case, then label your copy blocks with letters, put them on the back of your ad, and write the corresponding letter in the appropriate place on the front of the ad.

3. Don't forget to pick your own brand name for the product or service (such as "Minute Mice").

APPLICATION EXERCISE 2

In this age of 24-hour cable news channels, tabloid news shows, and aggressive local and national news reporters intent on exposing corporate wrongdoing, one of the most important skills for a manager to learn is how to deal effectively with the press. Test your ability to deal effectively with the press by putting yourself in the following situation. To make the situation more realistic, read the scenario and then give yourself two minutes to write a response to each question.[73]

Activity

Today, in the nation's capital, a public-interest group held a press conference to release the results of a study that found that the food sold in most Chinese restaurants is high in fat. The group claims that the most popular Chinese dishes, including orange chicken, pork fried rice, and Hunan beef, contain nearly as much fat as the food you get from fast-food chains like McDonald's, Wendy's, and Burger King. (Much of it is fried or is covered with heavy sauces.) Furthermore, the group says that customers who hope to keep their cholesterol and blood pressure low by eating Chinese food are just fooling themselves.

A TV reporter from Channel 5 called you at Szechuan Palace, your Szechuan-style Chinese restaurant, to get your response to this study. When he and the camera crew arrived, he asked you the following questions:

1. "A new study released today claims that food sold in Chinese restaurants is on average nearly as fattening as that sold at fast-food restaurants. How healthy is the food that you serve at Szechuan?"

2. "Get the camera in close here [camera closes in to get the shot] because I want the audience at home to see that you don't provide any information on your menu about calories, calories from fat, or cholesterol. Without this information [camera pulls back to get a picture of you and the reporter], how can your customers know whether the food that you serve is healthy for them?"

3. "These new studies were based on lunches and dinners sampled from Chinese restaurants across the nation. A local company, Huntington Labs, has agreed to test foods from local restaurants so that we can provide accurate information to our viewers. Would you agree to let us sample the main dishes in your restaurant to test the level of calories, calories from fat, and cholesterol? Furthermore, can we take the cameras into your restaurant so that we can get your customers' reactions to these studies?"

CASE STUDY: Burger King

HAVING IT THEIR WAY FOR A CHANGE

© AP Images/PRNewsFoto/Burger King Corporation

So how do you get your name out when you're the number two burger joint in the country? By the turn of the millennium, in the minds of many, Burger King had been relegated to sitting the bench in the fast food industry. And in a way, after having changed owners and being rebranded so many times, it might come as no surprise. Then, in 2003, Burger King hired the advertising agency Crispin Porter & Bogusky, which brought on some major brand changes for the fast food franchise. At the time, Burger King was viewed as a boring brand with very little personality and identity. Crispin Porter & Bogusky quickly took steps to give Burger King a new image, an image that would be fun and that people would want to be associated with. Over the last few years, Burger King's new advertising campaigns have certainly caught people's attention.

Attention, however, is not necessarily a positive thing. The Crispin Porter & Bogusky agency has been known for edgy and controversial advertising and its work for Burger King has been no exception. It certainly gave Burger King a new face. Early promotions included Burger King's "subservient chicken" Web site, where a man in a chicken suit sitting in front of a video camera would respond to commands put in by viewers. BK spun off the subservient chicken theme in 2005 with a faux metal band called Coq Roq to promote its new Chicken Fries. The campaign included commercials featuring the band—a group of six musicians wearing chicken masks—along with a Web site and music videos for four songs singing the praises of subservient chickens and Chicken Fries. If the name of the band itself did not set the tone (never mind the lead singer: Fowl Mouth), the Web site launched with a photo gallery containing pictures of young women with captions like "Groupies love the Coq." The images set off a major controversy, with many viewers claiming the images were demeaning to women and inappropriate for children. The captions quickly came down. The company blamed the captions on malfunctions in Flash and XML programming. The innuendo of Coq Roq was not an anomaly in BK's new advertising messages either; about the same time BK released a series of commercials featuring former Hootie and the Blowfish frontman Darius Rucker singing a rewritten version of the "Have It Your Way" theme song with suggestive lyrics while traveling through a fantasy land of food and provocatively dressed women. Though controversial, Crispin Porter & Bogusky was setting Burger King apart, and sales began to improve.

BK's advertising, however, has not just relied on sex to sell its products. While it has established the 18- to 34-year-old male as a major target demographic, many of BK's more recent advertising campaigns have been simply designed to surprise consumers and shake things up. One of Crispin's early moves was a resurrection of Burger King's stale old mascot: the King. But rather than give him a hip contemporary makeover, they kept the crown, red beard, and kingly apparel topped with a creepy smiling immobile mask. The King has since been featured in many of Burger King's recent campaigns, such as their "Waking Up with the King" feature in which a confused young man wakes up to find the King in bed right next to him. The King then gives him a breakfast sandwich. In 2007, Burger King launched its "Whopper Freakout" hoax campaign, where they pulled the Whopper off the menu at a couple of select Burger King locations and filmed customers' reactions on hidden cameras.

In late 2008, Burger King advertisers stoked further controversy with their "Whopper Virgins" commercials. The campaign focused around taste tests between the Whopper and McDonald's Big Mac similar to Pepsi-Cola's "Pepsi Challenge" against Coca-Cola, but as ever, Burger King added a twist. Their ad firm hired an independent research team to perform the tests among three separate people groups (the Inuit tribes of Greenland, the Hmong in Thailand, and a group of rural farmers in Transylvania) who they identified as having no exposure to either the McDonald's or Burger King brands or marketing (or fast food at all). The taste testers appeared in their traditional garb, and according to the filming by the research team, the majority choose the Whopper. And while the research team and the advertisers at Crispin claimed that the project was undertaken with the utmost care and respect for the people and their cultures, the ads (again) set off a flurry of controversy with accusations that Burger King's campaign was exploitative and culturally degrading.

Whether their advertising crosses the line or not, BK's promotions have certainly been successful. The subservient chicken Web site drew 439 million visitors, the Coq Roq Web site drew substantial traffic as well, and the Chicken Fries proved a success on the BK menu. When Burger King released an Xbox videogame featuring the King, the game sold several million copies. Burger King caught significant attention as well with a new social media stunt, titled "Whopper Sacrifice." The campaign, featuring the tagline "Friendship is strong, but the Whopper is stronger" was run on Facebook, where the company created an application that would send out a message every time the user defriended someone. For every ten people users defriended, BK offered them a coupon for a free Whopper. Shortly after the launch, Facebook banned the application. BK responded by posting the following message on the campaign's Web site: "Facebook has disabled Whopper Sacrifice after your love for the Whopper proved to be stronger than 233,906 friendships."[74]

Questions

1. What do you think of Burger King's advertising tactics? Is it OK to attract new customers while alienating others? Is Burger King's advertising ethical? Explain.

2. How did Burger King manage the negative publicity it received over the content of its Coq Roq Web site?[72]

COMPANY CLIPS: Vans—Off The Wall and On Message

Even though Vans generates $500 million a year in sales, the company uses only a small team to manage the company's advertising and public relations—Stacy and Chris. The Vans PR team (or duo) uses vertical advertising to cater to a core group of consumers. With only a small advertising budget, the team must develop partnerships with its advertisers and use tours and events to spread the Vans culture.

Questions

1. Who does Vans consider to be its core consumers? How does the company reach them with its marketing messages?

2. How does Vans choose causes for its cause-related marketing?

3. What does Vans do to ensure that its print ads fit the publications in which they appear?

4. Describe the role of the Internet in Vans' communication strategy.

Notes

1. "100 Leading National Advertisers: 2009 edition index," *Advertising Age*, June 21, 2010, http://adage.com/article/datacenter-advertising-spending/100-leading-national-advertisers/136308/.
2. "U.S. Advertising Industry Employment," Advertising Age Data Center, www.adage.com.
3. Bradley Johnson, "Global Marketers," Ad Industry Jobs: Advertising Age Data Center, www.adage.com; Bradley Johnson, "New Source: Media Work Force Sinks to 15-Year Low," *Advertising Age*, February 18, 2008, www.adage.com.
4. Bradley Johnson, "Global Marketers."
5. Michael R. Solomon, *Consumer Behavior*, 6th ed. (Upper Saddle River, NJ: Prentice Hall, 2004), 275.
6. Mark Levit, "Humor in Advertising," *Marketing Source*, www.marketingsource.com/articles/view/2190.
7. Scion Web site, www.scion.com.
8. Natalie Zmuda, "What Went into the Updated Pepsi Logo" *Advertising Age*, October 27, 2008, www.adage.com; Natalie Zmuda, "Pepsi, Coke Try to Outdo Each Other with Rays of Sunshine," *Advertising Age*, January 19, 2009, www.adage.com; Jim Edwards, "Pepsi's New $1 Million Logo Looks Like Old Diet Pepsi Logo," *BNET Industries*, October 27, 2008, www.bnet.com/blog/advertising-business/pepsis-new-1-million-logo-looks-like-old-diet-pepsi-logo/110.
9. Saul Hansell, "The Loneliness of Being AOL," *New York Times*, February 11, 2008, C8.
10. Chevron Web site, www.chevron.com.
11. Philip Morris USA Web site, www.philipmorrisusa.com; Altria Group Web site, www.altria.com/en/cms/Home/default.aspx.
12. Alex Berenson, "Drug Approved. Is Disease Real?" *New York Times*, January 14, 2008, A1.
13. Sean Callahan, "Nextel Wins the Race to Sponsor NASCAR," *BtoB*, July 14, 2003; Rich Thomaselli, "Nextel Link Takes Nascar to New Level," *Advertising Age*, October 27, 2003, S-7.
14. Emily Bryson York, "Brand vs. Brand: Attacks Ads on the Rise," *Advertising Age*, October 27, 2008, www.adage.com.
15. Press release, "FTC Sues Sellers of Weight-Loss Pills for False Advertising," February 8, 2008, www.ftc.gov/opa/2008/02/zyladex.shtm.
16. Press release, "HP Gets Personal with Super Bowl Ad, Extends PC Marketing Campaign," February 2, 2007, http://h41131.www4.hp.com/prelive/us/en/press/070202a.html; Neal Leavitt, "HP Goes Wide to Get Personal," *iMedia Connection*, June 2006, www.imediaconnection.com/content/10070.asp.
17. Tabasco advertisement, *Advertising Age*, October 13, 2003, 8.
18. "SoBe Lizards Take Manhattan by Storm: Unleashing SoBe Life Water Thrillicious Movement in Times Square," *PR Newswire*, February 27, 2008.
19. Vanessa L. Facenda, "Kellogg Injects Some New Energy into Frosted Flakes," *Brand Week*, February 4, 2008, www.adweek.com.
20. Powerade Web site, www.us.powerade.com.
21. Laura Q. Hughes and Wendy Davis, "Revival of the Fittest," *Advertising Age*, March 12, 2001, 18–19; Hershey's Chocolate World, www.hersheys.com/chocolateworld.
22. "What the Heck Were These People Thinking?" http://people.tribe.net/jenni/blog/dad552c0-67e1-42b9-887a-a2ac71ded4f1, May 17, 2007.
23. David Gianatasio, "Altoids Honors Facebook's Curiously Strong," *Adweek*, March 28, 2011, www.adweek.com/adfreak/altoids-honors-facebooks-curiously-strong-126896.
24. "Nike Selected as Clio Awards 2007 Advertiser of the Year," Clio Awards press release, May 12, 2007, www.clioawards.com/press/index.cfm?year=2007.
25. Geoffrey A. Fowler, "For P&G in China, It's Wash, Rinse, Don't Repeat," *Wall Street Journal*, April 7, 2006.
26. Pamela Paul, "Sell It to the Psyche," *Time*, September 29, 2003, www.time.com/time/magazine/article/0,9171,1005703,00.html.
27. Press release, "TNS Media Intelligence Forecasts 4.2 Percent Increase in U.S. Advertising Spending for 2008," www.tnsglobal.com/news/news-1DD79A9F88EF4923B9A99CFEF6A1A9CB.aspx.
28. *Ibid.*
29. Brian Steinberg, "Philips and Time Agree to Keep It Simple," *Wall Street Journal*, April 21, 2006, B3.
30. Steven Levingston, "Spots on Traditional TV Still the Biggest Show on Super Bowl Sunday," *Washington Post*, Saturday, January 14, 2006.
31. Aaron Smith, "Super Bowl Ad: Is $3 Million Worth It?" *CNN*, February 3, 2011, http://money.cnn.com/2011/02/03/news/companies/super_bowl_ads/index.htm.
32. Matthew Boyle, "Superbucks," *Fortune*, February 4, 2008.
33. Gergana Koleva, "Don't Buy It," *MarketWatch*, January 24, 2008.
34. Suzanne Vranica, "TV-Ad Test to Show If Less Is More; NBC Universal's Trial Run Will Measure Effectiveness of Fewer Commercials," *Wall Street Journal*, April 5, 2006, B3; Maria Aspan, "TiVo Shifts to Help Companies It Once Threatened," *New York Times*, Dec 10, 2007, www.nytimes.com/2007/12/10/technology/10tivo.html.
35. Erin White, "In-Your-Face Marketing: Ad Agency Rents Foreheads," *Wall Street Journal*, February 11, 2003, B2; Commercial Alert Web site, www.commercialalert.org.
36. Mike Esterl, "Going Outside, Beyond the Billboard," *Wall Street Journal*, July 21, 2005, B3.
37. Press release, "Virgin Atlantic Airways Takes Off with New Marketing Campaign," *PR Newswire*, February 11, 2008, www.prnewswire.com/news-releases/virgin-atlantic-airways-takes-off-with-new-marketing-campaign-56890592.html.
38. Ryan Woo, "Adidas Wows Japan with Vertical Soccer Field," *Wall Street Journal*, September 22, 2003, B1.
39. The Loerie Awards, Virgin Atlantic Airways, www.theloerieawards.co.za/default.aspx?link=archive_winners_single_entry&id=39029.

© iStockphoto.com/ziggymaj

marketing&you: Results.

High scores indicate that you like television advertising. Not only do you like it, you think television ads have informational benefits. Low scores correspond to a more skeptical attitude toward television advertising. If you are skeptical about television ads, are you also skeptical about print ads and other forms of advertising? How much do you tune out (or tune in)?

40. TNS Media Intelligence Forecast, January 7, 2008, www.tnsmi.com/news/01072008.htm#; Internet Advertising Bureau, www.iab.com.

41. Brian Morrissey, "Web Ad Spend to Diversify," *Adweek*, October 11, 2007, www.adweek.com.

42. David Ho, "Advertisers Ditch Pop-Ups for New Tricks," *Atlanta Journal-Constitution*, December 4, 2005, C-3.

43. Mike Shields, "Google Leads Search Party," *Adweek*, February 18, 2008, www.adweek.com.

44. Michael McCarthy, "Disney Plans to Mix Ads, Video Games to Target Kids, Teens," *USA Today*, January 15, 2005, B-1.

45. John Gaudiosi, "Mountain Dew Makes MMO More Than Just a Game," *Advertising Age*, January 28, 2008, 21.

46. Press release, "Microsoft Bringing Ads to Shopping Carts," www.cnn.com/2008/TECH/01/14/microsoft.shoppingcart.ap/index.html (Accessed January 15, 2008).

47. "BMW Films," www.bmwusa.com/Standard/Content/Uniquely/TVAndNewMedia/BMWFilms.aspx.

48. Tobi Elkin, "Coca-Cola's First TiVo Advertisement Airs Today," October 9, 2003, www.adage.com.

49. Jack Neff, "Floors in Stores Start Moving," *Advertising Age*, August 20, 2001, 15.

50. "Who We Are," Alt Terrain, www.altterrain.com/light_projection_advertising.htm (Accessed July 22, 2011); "BroadSign Works with Zoom Media & Marketing Digital Signage Network to Manage Advertainment Screens in Popular Nightlife Venues Nationwide," *Internet Wire*, January 22, 2008, www.broadsign.com/Resources/pdfs/Broadsign-Zoom FINAL 1.22.08.pdf.

51. Christopher Lawton, "Videogame Ads Attempt Next Level," *Wall Street Journal*, July 25, 2005, B6; "Video Game Advertising Gets a Boost," *USA Today*, December 16, 2004, B-1; Derek Sooman, "World's First Video Game Advertising Network," *TechSpot*, October 20, 2004, www.techspot.com/news/16134-worlds-first-video-game-advertising-network.html; Press release, "Microsoft to Acquire In-Game Advertising Pioneer Massive Inc.," May 6, 2006, www.microsoft.com/presspass/press/2006/may06/05-04 MassiveIncPR.mspx.

52. "Sony's Stunning Water and Laser Hologram," *Core 77*, January 30, 2008, www.core77.com/blog/videos/sonys_stunning_water_ and_laser_hologram_8818.asp.

53. Sally Beatty, "Ogilvy's TV-Ad Study Stresses 'Holding Power' Instead of Ratings," *Wall Street Journal*, June 4, 1999, B2; www.ogilvy .com/viewpoint.

54. Brian Morrisey, "Meet the YouTube Stars Brands Love," *AdWeek*, November 7, 2010, www.adweek.com/news/technology/ meet-youtube-stars-brands-love-103733.

55. Irene Slutsky, "Meet YouTube's Most In-Demand Brand Stars," *Advertising Age*, September 13, 2010, http://adage.com/article/ digital/meet-youtube-s-demand-brand-stars/145844/.

56. John Frank, "Coke and Weber Shandwick to Promote Children's Fitness Campaign," *PRWeek*, www.prweekus.com/pages/login .aspx?returl=/coke-and-weber-shandwick-to-promote-childrens-fitness-campaign/article/52712.

57. "Satellite Cured the Radio Star," *Yahoo!*, January 15, 2006, http://news.yahoo.com/s/afp/20060116/ts_alt_afp/afpentertainmen- tusradiosatellite_060115161248; Lorne Manly, "Oprah Signs Three-Year Deal with XM Satellite Radio," *New York Times News Service*, www.signonsandiego.com/uniontrib/20060210/news_1b10oprah.html(Accessed July 22, 2011).

58. Adam Bluestein, "Prime-Time Exposure: How Companies Can Make a Splash in the Big-Money World of TV Product Placement— Without Spending a Dime," *Inc.*, March 2008, 66; "Product Placement," *Source Watch*, www.sourcewatch.org/index.php?title= Product_placement (Accessed May 4, 2011); Kris Oser, "How a Product Placement Strategy Worked for Yahoo," *AdAge.com*, January 31, 2005, http://adage.com; Katherine Neer, "How Product Placement Works," *How Stuff Works*, July 4, 2003, http:// money.howstuffworks.com/product-placement.htm; "Product Placement Spending in Media 2005," March 29, 2005, PQ Media Web site, www.pqmedia.com/product-placement-spending-in-media.html.

59. *Ibid.*

60. Sponsorship Community, IEG Web site, www.sponsorship.com; "Sponsorship," Domino's Web site, www.dominos.com.au/corporate/ inside/sponsorship.aspx; "Media," Hilton Worldwide Web site, www.hiltonworldwide.com/media/index.htm; "Bud Light's Major Sports Sponsorships," "Bud Bowl Makes Return Visit to Tampa Bay to Delight of Gridirom Fans," January 6, 2009, Anheuser-Busch Web site, www.anheuser-busch.com/s/index.php/bud-bowl-makes-return-visit-to-tampa-bay-to-delight-of-gridirom-fans.

61. "Sponsorship Community," IEG Web site, www.sponsorship.com.

62. *Ibid.*

63. "St. Jude Corporate Partners," St. Jude Children's Research Hospital Web site, www.stjude.org/stJude/v/index.jsp?vgnextoid= 56297ff0be118010VgnVCM1000000e2015acRCRD; "Corporate Partners," Susan G. Komen for the Cure Web site, ww5.komen.org/ CorporatePartners.aspx.

64. "Our Partners," American Heart Association Go Red Web site, www.goredforwomen.org/our_partners.aspx.

65. "IEG's Guide to Why Companies Sponsor," St. Jude Children's Research Hospital Web site, www.stjude.org/SJFile/alsac_ieg_guide_ why_companies_sponsor.pdf.

66. PlayStation Web site, www.playstation.com.

67. Ann Zimmerman, "Walmart Enlists Bloggers to Combat Negative News," *Wall Street Journal*, March 7, 2006, D7.

68. *Ibid.*

69. "Blogs Can Offer a Big Advantage to Brands—If They're Honest," *New Age Media*, March 23, 2006, 15.

70. Janet Adamy and Richard Gibson, "McDonald's Isn't Slow to React to 'Fast-Food Nation' This Time," *Wall Street Journal*, April 12, 2006, B3.

71. Zimmerman, "Walmart Enlists Bloggers to Combat Negative News."

72. This application exercise is based on the contribution of S. J. Garner (Eastern Kentucky University) to *Great Ideas in Teaching Marketing*, a teaching supplement that accompanies McDaniel, Lamb, and Hair's *Introduction to Marketing*. Professor Garner's entry titled "Creating Advertising for Illegal Products/Services" was a runner-up in the "Best of the Great Ideas in Teaching Marketing" contest conducted in conjunction with the publication of the eighth edition of *Marketing*.

73. This application exercise is taken from Chuck Williams, *Management*, 3rd ed. (Cincinnati: South-Western, 2005). The idea to include a crisis management exercise in this chapter came from a contribution by Jack K. Mandel (Nassau Community College) to *Great Ideas in Teaching Marketing*, a teaching supplement that accompanies McDaniel, Lamb, and Hair's *Introduction to Marketing*. Professor Mandel's entry titled "Putting Students in the Line of Fire to Learn Crisis Management Techniques" received an honorable mention in the "Best of the Great Ideas in Teaching Marketing" contest held in conjunction with the publication of the eighth edition of *Marketing*.

74. Joe Kovacs, "Fowl-Mouthed Slogans too Hot for Burger King," *WorldNetDaily*, July 28, 2005, www.wnd.com/?pageId=31516; Elaine Walker, "Crispin + Bogusky Revs Up BK's Image," *Miami Herald*, August 1, 2005; Andrew LaVallee, "Burger King Cancels Facebook Ad Campaign," *Wall Street Journal*, January 15, 2009, http://blogs.wsj.com/digits/2009/01/15/burger-king-cancels- facebook-ad-campaign; Brian Grow, "Burger King: Raunch with Those Fries?" ed. Dan Beucke, *BusinessWeek*, August 15, 2005, i3947, 9; Todd Wasserman, "Burger King Doesn't Have It Your Way," *BrandWeek*, January 19, 2009, www.brandweek.com/bw/ content_display/current-issue/e3i4edf08b57868094d4c25f75cbb9-bab13; Suzanne Vranica, "Fresh Palates for Burger King," *Wall Street Journal*, December 4, 2008, http://online.wsj.com/article/SB122834728675077461.html.

Sales Promotion and Personal Selling

Learning Outcomes

1 Define and state the objectives of sales promotion

2 Discuss the most common forms of consumer sales promotion

3 List the most common forms of trade sales promotion

4 Describe personal selling

5 Discuss the key differences between relationship selling and traditional selling

6 List the steps in the selling process

7 Describe the functions of sales management

LO1
Sales Promotion

In addition to using advertising, public relations, and personal selling, marketing managers can use sales promotion to increase the effectiveness of their promotional efforts. **Sales promotion** is marketing communication activities, other than advertising, personal selling, and public relations, in which a short-term incentive motivates consumers or members of the distribution channel to purchase a good or service immediately, either by lowering the price or by adding value.

Advertising offers the consumer a reason to buy. Sales promotion offers an incentive to buy. Both are important, but sales promotion is usually cheaper than advertising and easier to measure. A major national TV advertising campaign often costs over $5 million or more to create, produce, and place. In contrast, promotional campaigns using the Internet or direct marketing methods can cost less than half that amount. It is also very difficult to determine how many people buy a product or service as a result of radio or TV ads. But with sales promotion, marketers know the precise number of coupons redeemed or the number of contest entries.

Sales promotion is usually targeted toward either of two distinctly different markets. **Consumer sales promotion** is targeted to the ultimate consumer market. **Trade sales promotion** is directed to members of the marketing channel, such as wholesalers and retailers. Sales promotion has become an important element in a marketer's integrated marketing communications program. (See Chapter 16.) Sales promotion expenditures have been steadily increasing over the last several years as a result of increased competition, the ever-expanding array of available media choices, consumers

> "Sales promotion **offers** consumers an incentive to buy."

sales promotion
Marketing activities—other than personal selling, advertising, and public relations—that stimulate consumer buying and dealer effectiveness.

consumer sales promotion
Sales promotion activities targeting the ultimate consumer.

marketing&you.

What do you think of coupons? Enter your answers on the lines provided.

STRONGLY DISAGREE 1 2 3 4 5 STRONGLY AGREE

_____ Coupons can save a person a lot of money.

_____ The money I can save by using coupons does not amount to much.*

_____ I believe that people can help their families financially by using coupons.

_____ Overall, I like using coupons.

_____ Personally for me, using coupons for supermarket products is or would be useless.*

_____ Taking everything into account, using coupons for supermarket shopping is wise.

Source: Scale #115, *Marketing Scales Handbook*, G. Bruner, K. James, H. Hensel, eds., Vol. III. © by American Marketing Association.

Now, total your score, reversing your answers for the items followed by an asterisk (for example, if you answered 4, change it to 2). Find out what your score means after you read the chapter.

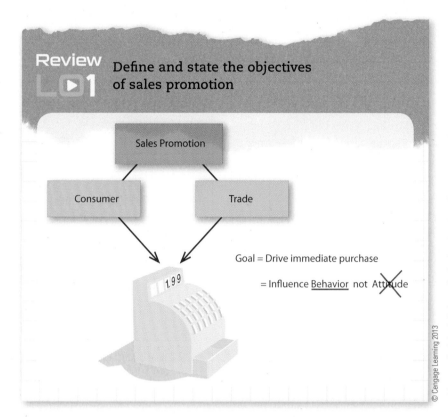

Review
LO1 Define and state the objectives of sales promotion

Sales Promotion

Consumer

Trade

Goal = Drive immediate purchase

= Influence <u>Behavior</u> not Attitude

1.99

© Cengage Learning 2013

and retailers demanding more deals from manufacturers, and the continued reliance on accountable and measurable marketing strategies. In addition, product and service marketers who have traditionally ignored sales promotion activities, such as power companies and restaurants, have discovered the marketing power of sales promotion. In fact, annual expenditures on promotion marketing in the United States now exceed $400 billion. Direct mail is the most widely used promotional medium, accounting for 50 percent of annual promotional expenditures.[1] The next two most widely used media are sampling and in-store promotions. Examples of these include point-of-purchase promotions (17 percent of expenditures), events and sponsorships (14 percent), and promotions via Internet and mobile devices (7 percent).[2]

THE OBJECTIVES OF SALES PROMOTION

Sales promotion usually has more effect on behavior than on attitudes. Immediate purchase is the goal of sales promotion, regardless of the form it takes. Therefore, it seems to make more sense when planning a sales promotion campaign to target customers according to their general behavior. For instance, is the consumer loyal to your product or to your competitor's? Does the consumer switch brands readily in favor of the best deal? Does the consumer buy only the least expensive product, no matter what? Does the consumer buy any products in your category at all?

The objectives of a promotion depend on the general behavior of target consumers. (See Exhibit 18.1.) For example, marketers targeting loyal users of their product

trade sales promotion
Sales promotion activities targeting a channel member, such as a wholesaler or retailer.

Exhibit 18.1 Types of Consumers and Sales Promotion Goals

Type of Buyer	Desired Results	Sales Promotion Examples
Loyal customers People who buy your product most or all of the time	Reinforce behavior, increase consumption, change purchase timing	• Loyalty marketing programs, such as frequent buyer cards or frequent shopper clubs • Bonus packs that give loyal consumers an incentive to stock up or premiums offered in return for proofs of purchase
Competitor's customers People who buy a competitor's product most or all of the time	Break loyalty, persuade to switch to your brand	• Sampling to introduce your product's superior qualities compared to their brand • Sweepstakes, contests, or premiums that create interest in the product
Brand switchers People who buy a variety of products in the category	Persuade to buy your brand more often	• Any promotion that lowers the price of the product, such as coupons, price-off packages, and bonus packs • Trade deals that help make the product more readily available than competing products
Price buyers People who consistently buy the least expensive brand	Appeal with low prices or supply added value that makes price less important	• Coupons, price-off packages, refunds, or trade deals that reduce the price of the brand to match that of the brand that would have been purchased

Source: From *Sales Promotion Essentials*, 2nd ed., by Don E. Schultz, William A. Robinson, and Lisa A. Petrison.

customer experience

How Starbucks Lost (and Then Found) Its Mojo

Often considered a master at branding and one of the most admired companies in the world, the company that taught America about coffee and provided a "third place" to enjoy it began to lose its luster four years ago. At one point, Starbucks was opening a new store every day. It still has more than 15,000 stores in 44 countries and Starbucks represents more than half (2.9 billion servings) of total coffee consumption (4.6 billion servings) according to NPD Group/CREST. But sales of specialty coffee were down in 2008 (the first decline in five years) and many people traded down to other new (and less expensive) competitors, such as Dunkin' Donuts and McDonald's. Some experts cited the recession but Starbucks' slide started long before the economy took a downturn.

The real reason behind Starbucks' trouble was that management began to ignore the customer. While trying to solve some customer complaints, Starbucks degraded the overall customer experience, becoming less passionate about customer relationships and their coffee experiences. For example, when some customers complained about the length of the lines and the pace of the service, Starbucks elected to take out some of the sofas and comfortable chairs that made Starbucks unique. This made space for more people in line, but not much room for people to relax. And in order to speed up the service, Starbucks got rid of the coffee bean grinders and hand-pulled shots, both of which took a lot of time. But once the couches and coffee bean smells were gone, so was much of the Starbucks experience. Soon customers began to realize the price they paid for their lattes was expensive relative to the experience.

When Starbucks' stock prices and sales began to tumble, management attempted to recover. Founder Howard Schultz returned as CEO after eight years away from the role. Starbucks planned to reignite the customer connection, slow store growth, shut down underperforming stores, increase global expansion, and improve the state of the U.S. business. New coffee blends, new products (particularly hot food), and even coupons were introduced.

One thing that Starbucks did well was extend its reach into cyberspace through social media. So much so that in 2009 Starbucks was named the world's most "engaged brand" by Altimeter Group in California and surpassed Coca-Cola in number of Facebook fans. Indeed, Starbucks' deft moves in the social media space have helped its reputation and its sales. Using a crowdsourcing site, MyStarbucksIdea.com, the company encouraged customers to make suggestions, ask questions, and lodge complaints. The site was designed to build relationships with customers rather than exist as simply another marketing channel. Starbucks engaged customers via Twitter, YouTube, and Facebook and, as a result, has managed to improve its consumer perceptions as well as its sales.[3]

do not want to change behavior. Instead, they need to reinforce existing behavior or increase product usage. An effective tool for strengthening brand loyalty is the *frequent buyer program* that rewards consumers for repeat purchases. Other types of promotions are more effective with customers prone to brand switching or with those who are loyal to a competitor's product. A cents-off coupon, free sample, or eye-catching display in a store will often entice shoppers to try a different brand. Consumers who do not use the product may be enticed to try it through the distribution of free samples.

Once marketers understand the dynamics occurring within their product category and have determined the particular consumers and consumer behaviors they want to influence, they can then go about selecting promotional tools to achieve these goals.

LO2
Tools for Consumer Sales Promotion

Marketing managers must decide which consumer sales promotion devices to use in a specific campaign. The methods chosen must match the objectives to ensure success of the overall promotion plan. Popular tools for consumer sales promotion are coupons and rebates, premiums, loyalty marketing programs, contests and sweepstakes, sampling, and point-of-purchase promotion. Consumer sales promotion tools have also been easily transferred to online versions to entice Internet users to visit sites, purchase products, or use services on the Web. Indeed, some of the most exciting things are happening by combining sales promotions and social media. For

example, Groupon.com is a Web site that presents deals to consumers who must then purchase the deal. Once the predetermined number of people commit to purchasing, the deal becomes active. If enough people do not commit to the deal, it never becomes active and no one receives the deal. To date Groupon.com has amassed more than 115 million subscribers and while there are some national deals, it focuses primarily on local deals. The concept is so popular that companies such as Walmart are now adopting the strategy (Walmart calls it Crowdsaver) and offering deals to Facebook friends who then "like" the deals until a certain number is reached and then it is activated. For example, Healthy Choice launched a coupon that increased in value as more people "liked" it on Facebook.[4]

COUPONS AND REBATES

A coupon is a certificate that entitles consumers to an immediate price reduction when the product is purchased. Coupons are a particularly good way to encourage product trial and repurchase. They are also likely to increase the amount of a product bought.

Traditional types of coupon distribution, such as newspapers, direct mail, and magazines, had been declining but began increasing in recent years. Indeed, one result of the recession was the largest increase in coupon usage in 17 years. For example, coupon redemption surged 23 percent to 3.2 billion coupons, with the largest increase among the millennials. Internet coupons experienced the largest surge in redemption rates (to 15.9 percent) despite being a relatively small share of total coupon market share. Electronic dispensed coupons have also seen a surge in redemption rates as well (to 7.9 percent).[5] These trends are the result of intense competition in the consumer packaged goods category and the introduction of over 1,200 new products a year, as well as the economic downturn. Though coupons are often criticized for reaching customers who have no interest in the product or service, or for encouraging repeat purchase by regular users, studies indicate coupons promote new product use and are likely to stimulate purchases. The use of colorful free-standing inserts (FSIs), mostly in Sunday newspapers, continues to grow despite declines in newspaper readership. Indeed, coupon inserts could be propping up Sunday newspaper circulation. FSIs are the most frequent way marketers distribute coupons (88.1 percent) followed by handouts (4.7 percent), direct mail (2.2 percent), magazines (2.1 percent), newspapers (1.2 percent), in/on pack (1.2 percent), and the Internet (0.4 percent). One of

coupon
A certificate that entitles consumers to an immediate price reduction when they buy the product.

the growing areas for coupons is through mobile distribution but they currently do not go through clearinghouses. Other online coupon distribution sites such as www.coolsavings.com and www.valpak.com are emerging as major coupon distribution outlets. Unfortunately, redemption rates for coupons often are 2 percent or lower.[6]

To overcome the low redemption rates for coupons, marketers are using new strategies. Marketers are shortening the time in which coupons can be redeemed or reducing the requirement for multiple purchases. At the same time, some companies have increased the value of the coupons or increased the redemption rate by creating a greater sense of urgency to redeem the coupon. Others are simply de-emphasizing their use of coupons in favor of everyday low pricing, or distributing single, all-purpose coupons that can be redeemed for several brands. More recently, marketers are tying in geo-social location sites (such as Gowalla, Foursquare, or Facebook Places) where customers can "check in" at the retail store and receive a promotional coupon on their mobile phone. For example, a Betsey Johnson outlet in California was one of the first marketers to do this.[7] Similarly, Facebook launched a new feature called Facebook Deals that enables people to search for and redeem deals at businesses when they check in using Facebook Places. Macy's, American Eagle Outfitters, Chipotle Mexican Grill, McDonald's, and JCPenney are among the first to offer Facebook Deals.[8]

In-store coupons have become popular because they are more likely to influence customers' buying decisions. Instant coupons on product packages, coupons distributed from on-shelf coupon-dispensing machines, and electronic coupons issued at the check-out counter are achieving much higher redemption rates. Indeed, instant coupons are redeemed more than 15 times more frequently than traditional newspaper coupons, indicating that consumers are making more in-store purchase decisions.

Starbucks has taken in-store coupons to a new level by installing interactive units on grocery store shelves. Each unit provides consumers with product information related to brewing, coffee education, and a taste matcher. In one test the units resulted in a 200 percent increase in sales. Internet coupons are also gaining in popularity. For example, Kroger has launched "Coupons that you click. Not clip" on Kroger.com. Registered Kroger Plus Shopper card members just log on to the Web site and click on the coupons they want. Coupons are automatically loaded onto the Kroger Plus card and redeemed at checkout when the shopper's Kroger Plus card is scanned.[9]

As marketing tactics grow more sophisticated, coupons are no longer viewed as a stand-alone tactic, but as an integral component of a larger promotional campaign. For example, Papa John's Pizza teamed up with Warner Bros. Home Entertainment and DC Comics to offer an instantly redeemable $3 coupon for online purchases as well as a limited edition "Dark Knight" gift card that could be redeemed for Papa John's products in store or online. Exclusive content and trailers from the movie were made available on the restaurant's Web site. Subway restaurants in Buffalo, New York, developed a campaign to offer consumer alerts and discount coupons via customers' mobile phones. This was a major breakthrough in marketing to the 18- to 34-year-old customer. **Rebates** are similar to coupons in that they offer the purchaser a price reduction; however, because the purchaser must mail in a rebate form and usually some proof of purchase, the reward is not as immediate. Traditionally used by food and cigarette manufacturers, rebates now appear on all types of products, from computers and software to film and cell phones. In the run-up to Super Bowl XL, Pepsi-Cola offered consumers a $10 dollar rebate as an incentive to stock up on the company's soda products and Frito-Lay brand chips in time for the big game.[10]

rebate
A cash refund given for the purchase of a product during a specific period.

Manufacturers prefer rebates for several reasons. Rebates enable manufacturers to offer price cuts directly to consumers. Manufacturers have more control over rebate promotions because they can be rolled out and shut off quickly. Further, because buyers must fill out forms with their names, addresses, and other data, manufacturers use rebate programs to build customer databases. Perhaps the best reason of all to offer rebates is that although rebates are particularly good at enticing purchase, most consumers never bother to redeem them. Studies show only about one-half of customers eligible for rebates actually collect them.[11]

PREMIUMS

A **premium** is an extra item offered to the consumer, usually in exchange for some proof that the promoted product has been purchased. Premiums reinforce the consumer's purchase decision, increase consumption, and persuade nonusers to switch brands. Premiums such as telephones, tote bags, and umbrellas are given away when consumers buy cosmetics, magazines, bank services, rental cars, and so on. Probably the best example of the use of premiums is the McDonald's Happy Meal, which rewards children with a small toy. Cosmetics companies, such as Estée Lauder, are also known to provide a "gift with purchases" where consumers get a bag of small-sized cosmetics with the purchase of a full-priced item. Many companies have been built around furnishing clients with customized premiums. Because of the widespread use of premiums, especially in trade relationships, it is getting harder to capture someone's attention with a premium. Kellogg's decided to use the animated character Shrek in a mix of premium-based promotions to get kids to eat healthy. Three games aimed at healthy lifestyles were created and appeared on 100 million cereal boxes. And for the first time, a bilingual promotional insert was included in Spanish using Puss 'n' Boots, Shrek's Latin sidekick. As a result, 125,000 cereal bowls, 85,000 boogie boards, 43,000 helmet covers, 37,000 talking key chains, and 16,000 soccer balls were redeemed. Kellogg's also saw major sales increases for Rice Krispies (21.5 percent), Froot Loops (16.7 percent), and Corn Pops (5.6 percent).[12]

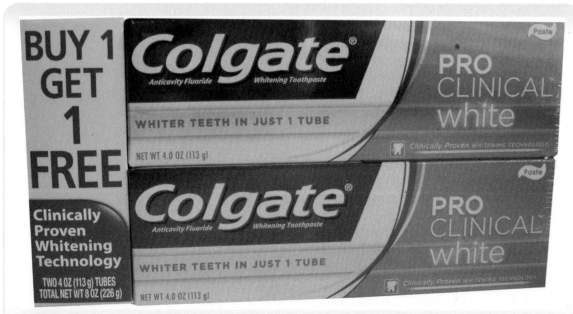

Colgate offers a second tube of toothpaste with the purchase of one, a "buy one, get one free" premium.

Premiums can also include more product for the regular price, such as two-for-the-price-of-one bonus packs or packages that include more of the product. Kellogg's, for instance, added two more pastries and waffles to its Pop-Tarts and Eggo packages without increasing the price in an effort to boost market share lost to private-label brands and new competitors. The promotion was so successful the company decided to keep the additional product in its regular packaging. Another possibility is to attach a premium to the product's package. For example, when research showed that consumers who drink tequila are often trendsetters who entertain at home, 1-800-Tequila launched a holiday promotion that included an instant camera and entertainment guide attached to the bottle.[13]

LOYALTY MARKETING PROGRAMS

Loyalty marketing programs, or **frequent buyer programs**, reward loyal consumers for making multiple purchases. Promotional spending related to loyalty programs has increased almost 4 percent to $2.1 billion. Popularized by the airline industry through frequent flyer programs, loyalty marketing enables companies to strategically invest sales promotion dollars in activities designed to capture greater profits from customers already loyal to the product or company. This is critical, as studies show that consumer loyalty is on the decline. Forrester Research showed the percentage of consumers ranking price as more important than brand rose from 41 to 47 percent over three years. According to research conducted by Gartner, more than 75 percent of consumers have more than one loyalty card that rewards them with redeemable points. Furthermore, there are almost 1.5 billion loyalty program memberships in the United States, with the average household participating in 12 programs.[14]

The objective of loyalty marketing programs is to build long-term, mutually beneficial relationships between a company and its key customers. In the retail sector, programs such as My Coke Rewards and Nike Plus are enabling these brands to learn more about what customers buy and their choice of rewards. Frequent shopper card programs offered by many supermarkets and other retailers have exploded in popularity. Research from Forrester shows that 54 percent of primary grocery shoppers belong to two or more supermarket loyalty programs. Although this speaks to the popularity of loyalty cards, it also shows that customers are pledging "loyalty" to more than one store: 15 percent of primary grocery shoppers are cardholders in at least three programs, and 4 percent participate in four or five programs.[15] Combined with the statistics on the growing importance of price over brands, frequent shopper programs need to offer something more than just discounts to build customer loyalty. One of the more successful recent premium promotions is Starbucks' Duetto Card, which combines a Visa credit card with a reloadable Starbucks card. The card allows members to collect "Duetto Dollars" that can be redeemed for anything they want to purchase at a Starbucks location. Starbucks also sends members quarterly opportunities based on usage, such as product samples and previews. One study reported that over 60 percent of Duetto cardholders said they were more likely to purchase Starbucks products as a result of the program.[16]

Cobranded credit cards are an increasingly popular loyalty marketing tool. Annually more than six billion direct marketing appeals for a cobranded credit card are sent to potential customers in the United States. Gap, Sony, and American Airlines are only a few examples of companies sponsoring cobranded Visa, MasterCard, or American Express cards. Target has a card (Take Charge of Education) that enables consumers to identify the school they would like to give money to (**www.target.com**). In addition, many nonprofit organizations participate in these cobranded affinity

loyalty marketing program
A promotional program designed to build long-term, mutually beneficial relationships between a company and its key customers.

frequent buyer program
A loyalty program in which loyal consumers are rewarded for making multiple purchases of a particular good or service.

programs. Discover Card has a cobranded card with proceeds going to the Children's Miracle Network.

Through loyalty programs, shoppers receive discounts, alerts on new products, and other enticing offers. In exchange, retailers are able to build customer databases that help them better understand customer preferences. Verizon Wireless builds loyalty with its "New Every Two" program. Consumers who have been Verizon customers for two years are eligible for a $100 credit toward a new digital phone.[17]

Companies increasingly are using the Internet to build customer loyalty through e-mail and blogs. Over 80 percent of supermarket chains are using e-mail to register customers for their loyalty programs and to entice them with coupons, flyers, and promotional campaigns.[18] Blogs are becoming a critical component of some companies' loyalty marketing programs. Blogging technology enables marketers to create a community of consumers who feel positively about the company's brand and to build deeper relationships with them. Starwood Hotels launched a corporate blog called TheLobby.com. Although the blog is open to the public, the company is aiming the content specifically at members of the Starwood Preferred Guest loyalty program. Features include postings about special events at specific Starwood properties and how travelers can earn loyalty points through special promotions. The company's goal is to combine advertising with useful information to create a Web destination for its guests—and divert them away from other travel blogs that might contain negative postings about Starwood hotels.[19]

Reader's Digest *is visiting towns around America to offer promotional and financial support. Individuals can support their town, and also enter to win an RV, trip, or cash.*

Courtesy of Reader's Digest

CONTESTS AND SWEEPSTAKES

Contests and sweepstakes are generally designed to create interest in a good or service, often to encourage brand switching. *Contests* are promotions in which participants use some skill or ability to compete for prizes. A consumer contest usually requires entrants to answer questions, complete sentences, or write a paragraph about the product and submit proof of purchase. Winning a *sweepstakes,* on the other hand, depends on chance or luck, and participation is free. Sweepstakes usually draw about ten times more entries than contests do. Marketers spend more than $2 billion annually building games, contests, and sweepstakes. Contests and sweepstakes calling for consumer-generated content remain the favorite. Domino's encouraged consumers to send in their photos of pizzas in their new marketing effort to turn around their image. Dole launched its Sweet Retreat contest using blogs and parfait parties. In order to enter, people have to submit photos of themselves enjoying Dole's parfaits and include a caption about their "indulgent moment." Consumers then vote on the winners who then receive a variety of prizes. Bloggers that focus on moms, health, and wellness were asked to talk about the Dole parfait parties. Last, specific groups such as book clubs, scrapbooking groups, and others were identified in several cities to participate in the parfait parties.[20]

While contests and sweepstakes may draw considerable interest and publicity, generally they are not effective tools for generating long-term sales. To increase their effectiveness, sales promotion managers must make certain the award will appeal to the target market. For example, Home & Garden Television Network's annual "Dream Home Giveaway" sweepstakes awards a fully furnished, custom-built home to one lucky viewer. The promotion is cosponsored by General Motors, which fills the garage with a new sport-utility vehicle, and other home-related companies such as Sherwin-Williams paint, Lumber Liquidators flooring, California Closets, and Jeld-Wen windows and doors. The annual sweepstakes typically draws over four million entries.[21] Offering several smaller prizes to many winners instead of one huge prize to just one person often will increase the effectiveness of the promotion, but there's no denying the attractiveness of a jackpot-type prize.

SAMPLING

Consumers generally perceive a certain amount of risk in trying new products. Many are afraid of trying something they will not like (such as a new food item) or spending too much money and getting little reward. Sampling enables customers to try a product risk-free. Sampling can increase retail sales by more than 40 percent. It is no surprise, therefore, that product sampling is the dominant in-store marketing method when it comes to influencing consumer purchase decisions.[22]

Sampling can be accomplished by directly mailing the sample to the customer, delivering the sample door-to-door, packaging the sample with another product, or demonstrating or sampling the product at a retail store or service outlet. Coca-Cola partnered with Domino's Pizza to sample its Coca-Cola Zero beverage. Every Domino's customer placing an order got a complimentary 20-ounce bottle of Coca-Cola Zero.[23] Kleenex launched its broadest sampling program ever for the new enhanced tissue with lotion product. The campaign put 60 million samples in places consumers would not typically find tissues, such as free-standing dispensers so consumers could try it. Kleenex supported the effort with magazine advertising, a sampling van tour, and a very successful advertising campaign. Similarly, when Masterfoods wanted to increase sales of its Dove "Promises" product line of dark and milk chocolates, it used both print media and sampling. To reach the upscale target market, samples were handed out at high-end hotels, spas, and gourmet cooking shows.[24]

Sampling at special events is a popular, effective, and high-profile distribution method that permits marketers to piggyback onto fun-based consumer activities—including sporting events, college fests, fairs and festivals, beach events, and chili cook-offs. General Mills used 500 "meal assembly kitchens" to provide samples of its Chocolate Turtle Chex Mix where busy moms could prepare ready-to-eat food. Companies such as Tabasco, Juicy Juice, and Lipton Iced Tea are also sampling in these kitchens. Product sampling during tailgating at college and professional football stadiums enables marketers to reach from 10,000 to 100,000 consumers in a single afternoon. H.J. Heinz tests products such as new barbecue sauces and ketchups to get immediate feedback about what consumers like and dislike about the products.[25]

Distributing samples to specific location types where consumers regularly meet for a common objective or interest, such as health clubs, churches, or doctors' offices, is one of the most efficient methods of sampling. What better way to get consumers to try a product than to offer a sample exactly when it is needed most? If someone visits a health club regularly, chances are he or she is a good prospect for a health-food product or vitamin supplement. Health club instructors are also handing out body wash, deodorant, and face cloths to sweating

sampling
A promotional program that allows the consumer the opportunity to try a product or service for free.

point-of-purchase (P-O-P)
A promotional display set up at the retailer's location to build traffic, advertise the product, or induce impulse buying.

participants at the end of class, and, more surprisingly, hot drinks! Dunkin' Donuts used a sampling program in more than 200 health clubs to promote its new Latte Lite drink, a zero-percent fat product that gives health-conscious consumers a lighter alternative.[26] Meanwhile, makers of stain removers and hand cleansers are giving away samples in mall food courts and petting zoos. Likewise, pharmaceutical companies offer free samples of new and expensive drugs as a tactic to entice doctors and consumers to become loyal to a product. Online sampling is gaining momentum as Web communities bring people together with common interests in trying new products, often using blogs to spread the word. Nail polish company OPI used SheSpeaks.com to encourage trials of new lacquer nail polish pens. Consumers had to register and then order one of five color pens and coupons. Consumers also blogged about the new pens and passed along the coupons to friends.[27]

POINT-OF-PURCHASE PROMOTION

Point-of-purchase (P-O-P) promotion includes any promotional display set up at the retailer's location to build traffic, advertise the product, or induce impulse buying. Point-of-purchase promotions include shelf "talkers" (signs attached to store shelves), shelf extenders (attachments that extend shelves so products stand out), ads on grocery carts and bags, end-aisle and floor-stand displays, television monitors at supermarket checkout counters, in-store audio messages, and audiovisual displays. One big advantage of P-O-P promotion is that it offers manufacturers a captive audience in retail stores. Another advantage is between 70 and 80 percent of all retail purchase decisions are made in-store, so P-O-P promotions can be very effective. P-O-P promotions can increase sales by as much as 65 percent. Strategies to increase sales include adding header or riser cards, changing messages on base or case wraps, adding inflatable or mobile displays, and using signs that advertise the brand's sports, movie, or charity tie-in.[28] When Hershey launched its new Swoops, a "chip" version of popular candy bars such as Almond Joy, Reese's, and Hershey Bars, it successfully used in-store displays to stimulate in-store, impulse purchases of the new candy.[29]

ONLINE SALES PROMOTION

Online sales promotions have expanded dramatically in recent years. Marketers are now spending billions of dollars annually on such promotions. Sales promotions

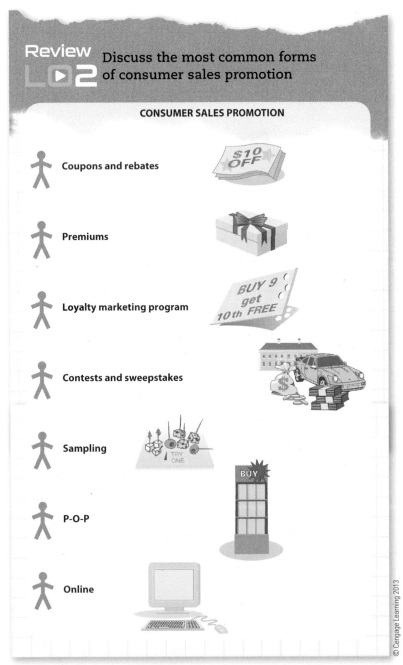

Review LO2 Discuss the most common forms of consumer sales promotion

CONSUMER SALES PROMOTION

- Coupons and rebates
- Premiums
- Loyalty marketing program
- Contests and sweepstakes
- Sampling
- P-O-P
- Online

© Cengage Learning 2013

online have proved effective and cost-efficient, generating response rates three to five times higher than off-line promotions. The most effective types of online sales promotions are free merchandise, sweepstakes, free shipping with purchases, and coupons.

Eager to boost traffic, Internet retailers are busy giving away free services or equipment, such as personal computers and travel, to lure consumers not only to their own Web sites, but to the Internet in general. Another goal is to add potential customers to their databases. For example, Heineken USA, Inc. launched the "Headline Hoax" online promotional campaign in which consumers (hoaxers) trick a friend (victim). The hoax is a fake headline with a photograph that looks as though it is on the front page of a major magazine's Web page such as *Maxim* or *The Sporting News*. The hoaxer can choose from a selection of pictures and headlines. One photo shows two football players attacking one another and the tackler has one hand inside the other's shirt and another hand pulling on his shorts; the headline reads "[Person's Name] is too touchy at touch football game." Once the victim opens this e-mail message, other friends on the hoaxer's list are alerted to the joke. At the start of the campaign, Heineken had only 5,000 e-mail addresses in its database. Within six months, it had collected an additional 95,000 e-mail addresses. The program has been so successful that it has been updated and expanded to the "Heineken Holiday Headline Hoax" and similar programs.[30]

LO3
Tools for Trade Sales Promotion

Whereas consumer promotions *pull* a product through the channel by creating demand, trade promotions *push* a product through the distribution channel. (See Chapter 14.) When selling to members of the distribution channel, manufacturers use many of the same sales promotion tools used in consumer promotions—such as sales contests, premiums, and point-of-purchase displays. Several tools, however, are unique to manufacturers and intermediaries:

→ **Trade allowances:** A **trade allowance** is a price reduction offered by manufacturers to intermediaries such as wholesalers and retailers. The price reduction or rebate is given in exchange for doing something specific, such as allocating space for a new product or buying something during special periods. For example, a local Best Buy outlet could receive a special discount for running its own promotion on Sony Surround Sound Systems.

→ **Push money:** Intermediaries receive **push money** as a bonus for pushing the manufacturer's brand through the distribution channel. Often the push money is directed toward a retailer's salespeople. LinoColor, the leading high-end scanner company, produces a Picture Perfect Rewards catalog filled with merchandise retailers can purchase with points accrued for every LinoColor scanner they sell. The cover of the catalog features a wave runner that was brought to three industry trade shows and given away in a sweepstakes to one of the dealers who had visited all the product displays and passed a quiz. The program resulted in a 26 percent increase in LinoColor sales, and the manufacturer recruited 32 new dealers to carry the product line.[31]

→ **Training:** Sometimes a manufacturer will train an intermediary's personnel if the product is rather complex—as frequently occurs in the computer and telecommunication industries. For example, representatives of a speaker manufacturer such

trade allowance
A price reduction offered by manufacturers to intermediaries, such as wholesalers and retailers.

push money
Money offered to channel intermediaries to encourage them to "push" products—that is, to encourage other members of the channel to sell the products.

© iStockphoto.com/Juan Facundo Mora Soria

as Bang & Olufsen might train salespeople in how to demonstrate the new features of the latest models to consumers. This is particularly helpful when salespeople must explain the features to older consumers who are less technology oriented.

→ **Free merchandise:** Often a manufacturer offers retailers free merchandise in lieu of quantity discounts. For example, a breakfast cereal manufacturer may throw in one case of free cereal for every 20 cases ordered by the retailer. Occasionally, free merchandise is used as payment for trade allowances normally provided through other sales promotions. Instead of giving a retailer a price reduction for buying a certain quantity of merchandise, the manufacturer may throw in extra merchandise for "free" (that is, at a cost that would equal the price reduction).

→ **Store demonstrations:** Manufacturers can also arrange with retailers to perform an in-store demonstration. Food manufacturers often send representatives to grocery stores and supermarkets to let customers sample a product while shopping. Cosmetic companies also send their representatives to department stores to promote their beauty aids by performing facials and makeovers for customers.

→ **Business meetings, conventions, and trade shows:** Trade association meetings, conferences, and conventions are an important aspect of sales promotion and a growing, multibillion-dollar market. At these shows, manufacturers, distributors, and other vendors have the chance to display their goods or describe their services to customers and potential customers. Moreover, the cost of closing leads generated at trade shows is often less than 50 percent of those developed in the field.[32] Trade shows have been uniquely effective in introducing new products; they can establish products in the marketplace more quickly than advertising, direct marketing, or sales calls can. Companies participate in trade shows to attract and identify new prospects, serve current customers, introduce new products, enhance corporate image, test the market response to new products, enhance corporate morale, and gather competitive product information.

Trade promotions are popular among manufacturers for many reasons. Trade sales promotion tools help manufacturers gain new distributors for their products, obtain wholesaler and retailer support for

In a multi-sensory sampling campaign, Stove Top stuffing workers handed out samples to commuters and shoppers in Chicago. The campaign also included heated bus shelters and bus shelter print ads.

© AP Images/PRNewsFoto/Kraft Foods Inc.; Stove Top. Aynsley Floyd

Review
LO3 List the most common forms of trade sales promotion

Training
Business Meetings
Conventions
Push Money
Trade Allowance
Store Demonstrations
Free Merchandise
Trade Shows

Trade Sales Promotion Tools

© Cengage Learning 2013

consumer sales promotions, build or reduce dealer inventories, and improve trade relations. Car manufacturers annually sponsor dozens of auto shows for consumers. Many of the displays feature interactive computer stations where consumers enter vehicle specifications and get a printout of prices and local dealer names. In return, the local car dealers get the names of good prospects. The shows attract millions of consumers, providing dealers with increased store traffic as well as good leads.

LO4
Personal Selling

As mentioned in Chapter 16, **personal selling** is direct communication between a sales representative and one or more prospective buyers in an attempt to influence each other in a purchase situation.

In a sense, all businesspeople are sales people. An individual might become a plant manager, a chemist, an engineer, or a member of any profession and yet still have to sell. During a job search, applicants must "sell" themselves to prospective employers in an interview. Indeed, the proper use of social media has become an important aspect of selling applicants' skills. To reach the top in most organizations, individuals need to sell ideas to peers, superiors, and subordinates. Most important, people must sell themselves and their ideas to just about everyone with whom they have a continuing relationship and to many other people they see only once or twice. Chances are that students majoring in business or marketing will start their professional careers in sales. Even students in non-business majors may pursue a sales career.

Personal selling offers several advantages over other forms of promotion:

→ Personal selling provides a detailed explanation or demonstration of the product. This capability is especially needed for complex or new goods and services.

→ The sales message can be varied according to the motivations and interests of each prospective customer. Moreover, when the prospect has questions or raises objections, the salesperson is there to provide explanations. In contrast, advertising and sales promotion can respond only to the objections the copywriter thinks are important to customers.

→ Personal selling can be directed only to qualified prospects. Other forms of promotion include some unavoidable waste because many people in the audience are not prospective customers.

→ Personal selling costs can be controlled by adjusting the size of the sales force (and resulting expenses) in one-person increments. On the other hand, advertising and sales promotion must often be purchased in fairly large amounts.

→ Perhaps the most important advantage is that personal selling is considerably more effective than other forms of promotion in obtaining a sale and gaining a satisfied customer.

→ Technology now plays an important role in personal selling through the use of social media such as LinkedIn and Facebook, as well as the use of blogs and Twitter to establish expertise within a field.

personal selling
A purchase situation involving a personal, paid-for communication between two people in an attempt to influence each other.

Review
LO4 Describe personal selling

Personal Selling Advantages

✓ Detailed explanation or demonstration

✓ Variable sales message

✓ Directed at qualified prospects

✓ Controllable adjustable selling costs

✓ Effective at obtaining sales and gaining customer satisfaction

© Cengage Learning 2013

Exhibit 18.2 Comparison of Personal Selling and Advertising/Sales Promotion

Personal Selling Is More Important if . . .	Advertising and Sales Promotion Are More Important if . . .
The product has a high value.	The product has a low value.
It is a custom-made product.	It is a standardized product.
There are few customers.	There are many customers.
The product is technically complex.	The product is easy to understand.
Customers are concentrated.	Customers are geographically dispersed.
Examples: insurance policies, custom windows, airplane engines	**Examples:** soap, magazine subscriptions, cotton T-shirts

© Cengage Learning 2013

Personal selling can work better than other forms of promotion given certain customer and product characteristics. Generally speaking, personal selling becomes more important as the number of potential customers decreases, as the complexity of the product increases, and as the value of the product grows. (See Exhibit 18.2.) When there are relatively few potential customers and the value of the good or service is relatively high, the time and travel costs of personally visiting each prospect are justifiable. For highly complex goods, such as business jets, pharmaceutical drugs, or private communication systems, a salesperson is needed to determine the prospective customer's needs, explain the product's basic advantages, and propose the exact features and accessories that will meet the client's needs.

L►5
Relationship Selling

Until recently, marketing theory and practice concerning personal selling focused almost entirely on a planned presentation to prospective customers for the sole purpose of making the sale. In contrast, modern views of personal selling emphasize the relationship that develops between a salesperson and a buyer. **Relationship selling**, or **consultative selling**, is a multistage process that emphasizes personalization and empathy as key ingredients in identifying prospects and developing them as long-term, satisfied customers. The old way was to sell a product, but with relationship selling, the objective is to build long-term branded relationships with consumers/buyers. Thus, the focus is on building mutual trust between the buyer and seller through the delivery of anticipated, long-term, value-added benefits to the buyer.

Relationship or consultative salespeople, therefore, become consultants, partners, and problem solvers for their customers. They strive to build long-term relationships with key accounts by developing trust over time. The emphasis shifts from a one-time sale to a long-term relationship in which the salesperson works with the customer to develop solutions for enhancing the customer's bottom line. Moreover, research has shown that positive customer-salesperson relationships contribute to trust, increased customer loyalty, and the intent to continue the relationship with the salesperson.[33] Thus, relationship selling promotes a win-win situation for both buyer and seller.

The result of relationship selling tends to be loyal customers who purchase from the company time after time. A relationship selling strategy focused on

relationship selling (consultative selling)
A sales practice that involves building, maintaining, and enhancing interactions with customers in order to develop long-term satisfaction through mutually beneficial partnerships.

retaining customers costs a company less than constantly prospecting and selling to new customers. Companies that focus on customer retention through high customer service gain 6 percent market share per year, while companies that offer low customer service lose 2 percent market share per year.[34] In fact, it typically costs businesses six times more to gain a new customer than to retain a current one.[35]

Relationship selling is more typical with selling situations for industrial-type goods, such as heavy machinery or computer systems, and services, such as airlines and insurance, than for consumer goods. For example, FedEx Office has built a long-term business relationship with PeopleSoft. The software maker gives many of its training and educational materials printing jobs to FedEx Office—a deal worth more than $5 million in revenues. FedEx Office forged such a close relationship with the company that their representatives were even invited to sit in on internal planning meetings in PeopleSoft's human resources department at the company's headquarters. Indeed, FedEx Office promotes this partnership idea with businesses touting the benefits of letting them handle most printing needs.

Technology is making inroads into how salespeople can communicate with prospects right from their desks. Webinars (online seminars lasting about an hour) are a popular way to support relationship selling tasks such as lead generation, client support, sales training, and corporate meetings. For example, one division of HP held a webinar that was attended by 1,300 executives in 80 countries. The session generated 60 percent of the division's five-month lead generation goals. Similarly, Polycom, a provider of wireless phone and text messaging systems to Verizon and AT&T, uses webinars to give new-product demonstrations so that channel managers can focus on other tasks. DMReview, a Web-based portal on technology, has found webinars to be so successful that it offers them continuously "on demand" on business intelligence and data mining topics. The webinars are cosponsored by major firms in insurance, banking, health care, and related fields. To maximize the opportunities provided by webcasting, marketers are using technology that effectively delivers content to other audiences using devices such as mobile phones, TiVo-type digital video recorders, and game consoles.[36]

Other tools, such as Skype and GoToMeeting, are enabling people to meet with prospects from around the world without having to leave their offices. This technology substantially reduces expenses related to the sales function. The Salesforce.com Chatter tool enables employees to communicate easily online. Although organizations have been slower to embrace some technologies—especially social media—there is a huge interest in how these technologies can be used to harness contacts, personal social networks, employee recruiting and selection to be more effective.

Exhibit 18.3 lists the key differences between traditional personal selling and relationship or consultative selling. These differences will become more apparent as we explore the personal selling process later in the chapter.

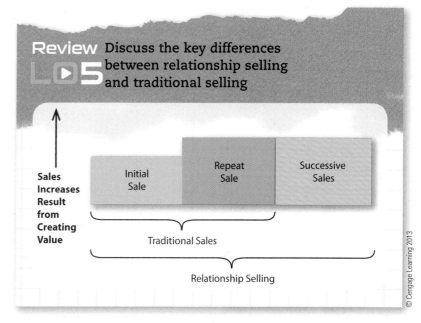

Exhibit 18.3 Key Differences between Traditional Selling and Relationship Selling

Traditional Personal Selling	Relationship or Consultative Selling
Sell products (goods and services)	Sell advice, assistance, and counsel
Focus on closing sales	Focus on improving the customer's bottom line
Limited sales planning	Consider sales planning as top priority
Spend most contact time telling customers about product	Spend most contact time attempting to build a problem-solving environment with the customer
Conduct "product-specific" needs assessment	Conduct discovery in the full scope of the customer's operations
"Lone wolf" approach to the account	Team approach to the account
Proposals and presentations based on pricing and product features	Proposals and presentations based on profit impact and strategic benefits to the customer
Sales follow-up is short term, focused on product delivery	Sales follow-up is long term, focused on long-term relationship enhancement

Source: Robert M. Peterson, Patrick L. Schul, and George H. Lucas, Jr., "Consultative Selling: Walking the Walk in the New Selling Environment," National Conference on Sales Management, *Proceedings*, March 1996.

Steps in the Selling Process

Although personal selling might sound like a relatively simple task, completing a sale actually requires several steps. The **sales process**, or **sales cycle**, is simply the set of steps a salesperson goes through to sell a particular product or service. The sales process or cycle can be unique for each product or service, depending on the features of the product or service, characteristics of customer segments, and internal processes in place within the firm, such as how leads are gathered.

Some sales take only a few minutes, but others can take much longer to complete. Sales of technical products, such as a Boeing or Airbus airplane, and customized goods and services, typically take many months, perhaps even years, to complete. On the other end of the spectrum, sales of less technical products such as copy machines or office supplies are generally more routine and might take only a few days. Whether a salesperson spends a few minutes or a few years on a sale, these are the seven basic steps in the personal selling process:

1. Generating leads

2. Qualifying leads

3. Approaching the customer and probing needs

4. Developing and proposing solutions

5. Handling objections

6. Closing the sale

7. Following up

Like other forms of promotion, these steps of selling follow the AIDA concept discussed in Chapter 16. Once a salesperson has located a prospect with the authority to buy, he or she tries to get the prospect's attention. A thorough needs assessment turned into an effective sales proposal and presentation should generate interest. After developing the customer's initial desire (preferably during the presentation of the sales proposal), the salesperson seeks action in the close by trying to get an agreement to buy. Follow-up after the sale, the final step in the selling process, not only lowers cognitive dissonance (refer to Chapter 6) but also can open

sales process (sales cycle)
The set of steps a salesperson goes through in a particular organization to sell a particular product or service.

up opportunities to discuss future sales. Effective follow-up will also lead to repeat business in which the process might start again at the needs assessment step.

Traditional selling and relationship selling follow the same basic steps. They differ in the relative importance placed on key steps in the process. (See Exhibit 18.4.) Traditional selling efforts are transaction oriented, focusing on generating as many leads as possible, making as many presentations as possible, and closing as many sales as possible. Minimal effort is placed on asking questions to identify customer needs and wants or matching these needs and wants to the benefits of the product or service. In contrast, salespeople practicing relationship selling emphasize an up-front investment in the time and effort needed to uncover each customer's specific needs and wants and match the product or service offering to them as closely as possible. By doing their homework up front, relationship salespeople create the conditions necessary for a relatively straightforward close. Let's look at each step of the selling process individually.

Exhibit 18.4	Relative Amount of Time Spent in Key Steps of the Selling Process	
Key Selling Steps	Traditional Selling	Relationship/ Consultative Selling
Generating leads	High	Low
Qualifying leads	Low	High
Approaching the customer and probing needs	Low	High
Developing and proposing solutions	Low	High
Handling objections	High	Low
Closing the sale	High	Low
Following up	Low	High

© Cengage Learning 2013

GENERATING LEADS

Initial groundwork must precede communication between the potential buyer and the salesperson. **Lead generation**, or **prospecting**, is the identification of the firms and people most likely to buy the seller's offerings. These firms or people become "sales leads" or "prospects."

Sales leads can be obtained in several different ways, most notably through advertising, trade shows and conventions, social media, webinars or direct-mail, and telemarketing programs. One accounting firm used direct mail, telephone, sales visits, and seminars in a four-step process aimed at generating business-to-business leads. The initial step was a direct-mail piece, in the form of an introductory letter from a firm partner. The second piece, sent one month later, was a black and white direct-mail circular with company contact information. The third step was a follow-up call from a firm partner to arrange a meeting. In the last stage, partners contacted prospects that had initially declined appointments and invited them to attend a free tax seminar the following month. Of the 1,100 businesses targeted, 200 prospects set up meetings. Favorable publicity also helps to create leads. Company records of past client purchases are another excellent source of leads. Many sales professionals are also securing valuable leads from their firm's Internet Web site. Sites asking users to register for newsletters or to use interactive media may use that information to generate sales leads.

Another way to gather a lead is through a **referral**—a recommendation from a customer or business associate. The advantages of referrals over other forms of prospecting include highly qualified leads, higher closing rates, larger initial transactions, and shorter sales cycles. Simply put, the salesperson and the company can earn more money in less time when prospecting using referrals. Referrals typically are as much as ten times more productive in generating sales than are cold calls. Unfortunately, although most clients are willing to give referrals, many salespeople do not ask for them. Effective sales training can help to overcome this reluctance to ask for referrals. To increase the number of referrals, some companies even pay or send small gifts to customers or suppliers that provide referrals. Generating referrals is one area that social media and technology can usually make much more efficient.

Networking is using friends, business contacts, coworkers, acquaintances, and fellow members in professional and civic organizations to identify potential clients.

lead generation (prospecting)
Identification of those firms and people most likely to buy the seller's offerings.

referral
A recommendation to a salesperson from a customer or business associate.

networking
A process of finding out about potential clients from friends, business contacts, coworkers, acquaintances, and fellow members in professional and civic organizations.

Indeed, a number of national networking clubs have been started for the sole purpose of generating leads and providing valuable business advice. The networking clubs usually have between 15 and 30 members in noncompeting business categories. During weekly breakfast or lunch meetings, each member is allowed to talk about the company he or she represents for an allotted period of time. Then members exchange lead cards. Research suggests that, on average, chapter members see an increase in business volume of between 16 and 25 percent after they've been with their group for three to six months. Increasingly, sales professionals are also using online networking sites such as Ryze, LinkedIn, and The Ladders to connect with targeted leads and clients around the world 24 hours a day. Some of LinkedIn's 100 million users have reported response rates between 50 and 60 percent, versus 3 percent from direct marketing efforts.[37]

QUALIFYING LEADS

When a prospect shows interest in learning more about a product, the salesperson has the opportunity to follow up, or qualify, the lead. Personally visiting unqualified prospects wastes valuable salesperson time and company resources. Often many leads go unanswered because salespeople are given no indication as to how qualified the leads are in terms of interest and ability to purchase. Unqualified prospects give vague or incomplete answers to a salesperson's specific questions, try to evade questions on budgets, and request changes in standard procedures like prices or terms of sale. In contrast, qualified leads are real prospects that answer questions, value your time, and are realistic about money and when they are prepared to buy. Salespersons given accurate information on qualified leads are more than twice as likely to follow up.[38]

Lead qualification involves determining whether the prospect has three things: a recognized need, willingness to see a salesperson, and buying power. Lead qualification is often handled by a telemarketing group or a sales support person who prequalifies the lead for the salesperson. But companies are increasingly using Web sites to qualify leads. When leads are qualified online, companies want visitors to register, indicate the products and services they are interested in, and provide information on their time frame and resources. Leads from the Internet can then be prioritized (those indicating a short time frame, for instance, given a higher priority) and then transferred to salespeople. Often Web site visitors can be enticed to answer questions with offers of free merchandise or information. Enticing visitors to register also enables companies to customize future electronic interactions—for example, by giving prospects who visit the Web site their choice from a menu of products tailored specifically to their needs.

lead qualification
Determination of a sales prospect's (1) recognized need, (2) buying power, and (3) receptivity and accessibility.

APPROACHING THE CUSTOMER AND PROBING NEEDS

Before approaching customers, the salesperson should learn as much as possible about the prospect's organization and its buyers. This process, called the **preapproach**, describes the "homework" that must be done by the salesperson before contacting the prospect. This can include visiting company Web sites, consulting standard reference sources such as Moody's, Standard & Poor's, or Dun & Bradstreet, or contacting acquaintances or others who might have information about the prospect. Another preapproach task is to determine whether the actual approach should be a personal visit, a phone call, a letter, or some other form of communication.

During the sales approach, the salesperson either talks to the prospect or secures an appointment for a future time in which to probe the prospect further as to his or her needs. Relationship selling theorists suggest that salespeople should begin developing mutual trust with their prospect during the approach. Salespeople should use the approach as a way of introducing themselves and their company and products. They must sell themselves before they can sell the product. Small talk that projects sincerity and some suggestion of friendship is encouraged because it builds rapport with the prospect, but remarks that could be construed as insincere should be avoided.

The salesperson's ultimate goal during the approach is to conduct a **needs assessment** to find out as much as possible about the prospect's situation. This involves interviewing the customer to determine his or her specific needs and wants and the range of options the customer has for satisfying them. The salesperson should be determining how to maximize the fit between what can be offered and what the prospective customer wants. In conducting a needs assessment, consultative salespeople must learn about the product or service, the customers and their needs, the competition, and the industry. Using this information, a customer profile is created.

Creating a *customer profile* during the approach helps salespeople optimize their time and resources. This profile is then used to help develop an intelligent analysis of the prospect's needs in preparation for the next step, developing and proposing solutions. Customer profile information is typically stored and manipulated using sales force automation software packages designed for use on laptop computers. Sales force automation software provides sales reps with a computerized and efficient method of collecting customer information for use during the entire sales process. Further, customer and sales data stored in a computer database can be easily shared among sales team members. The information can also be appended with industry statistics, sales or meeting notes, billing data, and other information that might be pertinent to the prospect or the prospect's company. The more salespeople know about their prospects, the better they can meet their needs.

DEVELOPING AND PROPOSING SOLUTIONS

Once the salesperson has gathered the appropriate information about the client's needs and wants, the next step is to determine whether his or her company's products or services match the needs of the prospective customer. The salesperson then develops a solution, or possibly several solutions, in which the salesperson's product or service solves the client's problems or meets a specific need.

These solutions are typically offered to the client in the form of a sales proposal delivered during a sales presentation. A **sales proposal** is a written document or professional presentation that outlines how the company's product or service will meet or exceed the client's needs. The **sales presentation** is the formal meeting in which the salesperson has the opportunity to present the sales proposal. The presentation should be explicitly tied to the prospect's expressed needs. Further, the prospect should be involved in the presentation by being encouraged to participate in demonstrations or by exposure to computer exercises, slides, video or audio, flip charts, photographs, and the like.

preapproach
A process that describes the "homework" that must be done by a salesperson before he or she contacts a prospect.

needs assessment
A determination of the customer's specific needs and wants, and the range of options the customer has for satisfying them.

sales proposal
A formal written document or professional presentation that outlines how the salesperson's product or service will meet or exceed the prospect's needs.

sales presentation
A formal meeting in which the salesperson presents a sales proposal to a prospective buyer.

Technology has become an important part of presenting solutions for many salespeople. Pen manufacturer BIC uses the Internet to connect with its wholesale and convenience store customers. Before launching BIClink.com, BIC received 80 percent of its order volume by fax. Processing these orders was time-consuming, and the orders often were filled with errors. BIClink.com has eliminated the potential for errors and made it easier and faster to validate purchase order numbers, ship dates, case quantities, and pricing. When customers sign on (through a secure, password-protected system), the welcome screen is personalized with their company's name and the name of their BIC rep. On placing an order, customers receive both a hard copy and e-mail confirmation statement with the salesperson's name and contact information including e-mail, voice mail, phone, and fax numbers. Virtually all of BIC's customers now order online.[39]

Because the salesperson often has only one opportunity to present solutions, the quality of both the sales proposal and presentation can make or break the sale. Salespeople must be able to present the proposal and handle any customer objections confidently and professionally. For a powerful presentation, salespeople must be well prepared, use direct eye contact, ask open-ended questions, be poised, use hand gestures and voice inflection, focus on the customer's needs, incorporate visual elements that impart valuable information, know how to operate the audio/visual or computer equipment being used for the presentation, make sure the equipment works, and practice, practice, practice.[40] Nothing dies faster than a boring presentation. If the salesperson doesn't have a convincing and confident manner, then the prospect will very often forget the information. Prospects take in body language, voice patterns, dress, and body type. Customers are more likely to remember how salespeople present themselves than what they say.

HANDLING OBJECTIONS

Rarely does a prospect say "I'll buy it" right after a presentation. Instead, the prospect often raises objections or asks questions about the proposal and the product. The potential buyer might insist that the price is too high, that he or she does not have enough information to make a decision, or that the good or service will not satisfy the present need. The buyer might also lack confidence in the seller's organization or product.

One of the first lessons every salesperson learns is that objections to the product should not be taken personally as confrontations or insults. Rather, salespeople should view objections as requests for information. A good salesperson considers objections a legitimate part of the purchase decision. To handle objections effectively, the salesperson should anticipate specific objections, such as concerns about price, fully investigate the objection with the customer, be aware of what the competition is offering, and, above all, stay calm. When Dell introduced its direct selling model, salespeople anticipated that customers would worry that they would not receive the same level of service and dedication as they would get from a reseller. As a result, the salespeople included assurances about service and support following the sale in their sales presentations.

Zig Ziglar, a renowned sales trainer, created a popular method for handling objections: "When an objection occurs, always use the fundamentals of FEEL, FELT, FOUND. It gives you an extra cushion of time and allows the prospect to identify with others." For example: "I see how

© Peter Lilja/Getty Images

you FEEL! Others have FELT the same way too until they FOUND. . . ." Imagine a copy machine salesperson pitching his machine to a doctor. The doctor might say, "The copy machine seems to be very expensive." Using the Zig Ziglar method the salesperson would respond, "I see how you *feel*. Other doctors have *felt* the same way until they *found* out how much money they were saving after the first year."[41]

Often salespeople can use objections to close the sale. If the customer tries to pit suppliers against each other to drive down the price, the salesperson should be prepared to point out weaknesses in the competitor's offer and stand by the quality in his or her own proposal.

CLOSING THE SALE

At the end of the presentation, the salesperson should ask the customer how he or she would like to proceed. If the customer exhibits signs that he or she is ready to purchase and all questions have been answered and objections have been met, then the salesperson can try to close the sale. Customers often give signals during or after the presentation that they are ready to buy or are not interested. Examples include changes in facial expressions, gestures, and questions asked. The salesperson should look for these signals and respond appropriately.

Closing requires courage and skill. Naturally, the salesperson wants to avoid rejection, and asking for a sale carries with it the risk of a negative answer. A salesperson should keep an open mind when asking for the sale and be prepared for either a yes or a no. Rarely is a sale closed on the first call. In fact, the typical salesperson makes several hundred sales calls a year, many of which are repeat calls to the same client in an attempt to make a sale. Some salespeople might negotiate with large accounts for several years before closing a sale. As you can see, building a good relationship with the customer is very important. Often, if the salesperson has developed a strong relationship with the customer, only minimal efforts are needed to close a sale.

Negotiation often plays a key role in the closing of the sale. **Negotiation** is the process during which both the salesperson and the prospect offer special concessions in an attempt to arrive at a sales agreement. For example, the salesperson might offer a price cut, free installation, free service, or a trial order. Effective negotiators, however, avoid using price as a negotiation tool because cutting price directly affects a company's profitability. Because companies spend millions on advertising and product development to create value, when salespeople give in to price negotiations too quickly, it decreases the value of the product. Instead, effective salespeople should emphasize value to the customer, rendering price a nonissue. Salespeople should also be prepared to ask for trade-offs and try to avoid giving unilateral concessions. If you're making only a 30 percent margin on a product, and you need at least a 40 percent margin, raise your prices or drop the product. Moreover, if the customer asks for a 5 percent discount, the salesperson should ask for something in return, such as higher volume or more flexibility in delivery schedules.

negotiation
The process during which both the salesperson and the prospect offer special concessions in an attempt to arrive at a sales agreement.

FOLLOWING UP

Unfortunately, many salespeople have the attitude that making the sale is all that's important: Once the sale is made, they can forget about their customers. They are wrong. Salespeople's responsibilities do not end with making the sales and placing

© iStockphoto.com/Juan Facundo Mora Soria

© iStockphoto.com/Dmitriy Shironosov

18

SALES PROMOTION AND PERSONAL SELLING

the orders. One of the most important aspects of their jobs is **follow-up**—the final step in the selling process, in which they must ensure that delivery schedules are met, that the goods or services perform as promised, and that the buyers' employees are properly trained to use the products.

In the traditional sales approach, follow-up with the customer is generally limited to successful product delivery and performance. A basic goal of relationship selling is to motivate customers to come back, again and again, by developing and nurturing long-term relationships. Most businesses depend on repeat sales, and repeat sales depend on thorough and continued follow-up by the salesperson. Finding a new customer is far more expensive than retaining an existing customer. When customers feel abandoned, cognitive dissonance arises and repeat sales decline. Today, this issue is more pertinent than ever because customers are far less loyal to brands and vendors. Buyers are more inclined to look for the best deal, especially in the case of poor after-the-sale follow-up. More and more buyers favor building a relationship with sellers. One Farmers Insurance agent suggests following up on insurance claims with a question to determine the customer's level of satisfaction. For example, he might ask, "Were you happy with the way your claim was handled?" Depending on the response, the agent can either get a referral from the customer or try to fix any problems so that the customer does not choose another agency in the future. This agent also makes telephone and personal follow-up visits after a marriage, death, birth, or birthday in the customer's family. These visits are used as sales opportunities to cross-sell products such as life insurance.[42]

Automated e-mail follow-up marketing—a combination of sales automation and Internet technology—is enhancing customer satisfaction as well as bringing in more business for some marketers. Here's how it works: After the initial contact with a prospect, a software program automatically sends a series of personalized e-mail messages over a period of time. CollegeRecruiter.com is one company taking advantage of this technology. The company posts ads for businesses recruiting recent college graduates on its Web site and has seen phenomenal results from auto-response marketing. Prospects start receiving a series of e-mail messages once they have visited the site and requested advertising rates. The first message goes out immediately. The next two go out in 4 to 11 days. From there, e-mail messages go out monthly. Using the automated follow-up e-mail system has helped CollegeRecruiter.com become the highest traffic career site used by job-hunting students and recent graduates. Its Web site regularly posts more than 100,000 job openings.[43]

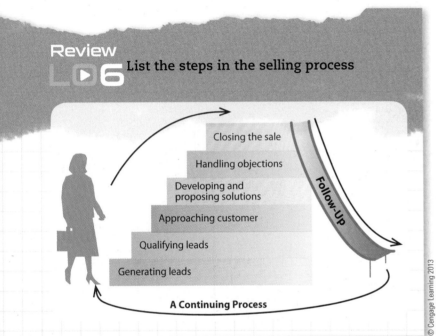

Review

 List the steps in the selling process

Closing the sale

Handling objections

Developing and proposing solutions

Approaching customer

Qualifying leads

Generating leads

Follow-Up

A Continuing Process

© Cengage Learning 2013

follow-up
The final step of the selling process, in which the salesperson ensures that delivery schedules are met, that the goods or services perform as promised, and that the buyers' employees are properly trained to use the products.

L⯈7
Sales Management

There is an old adage in business that nothing happens until a sale is made. Without sales there is no need for accountants, production workers, or even a company president. Sales provide the fuel that keeps the corporate engines humming. Companies such as Cisco Systems, International Paper, Johnson Controls, and several thousand other manufacturers would cease to exist without successful salespeople. Even companies such as Procter & Gamble and Kraft Foods that mainly sell consumer goods and use extensive advertising campaigns still rely on salespeople to move products through the channel of distribution. Thus, sales management is one of marketing's most critical specialties. Effective sales management stems from a highly success-oriented sales force that accomplishes its mission economically and efficiently. Poor sales management can lead to unmet profit objectives or even to the downfall of the corporation.

Just as selling is a personal relationship, so is sales management. Although the sales manager's basic job is to maximize sales at a reasonable cost while also maximizing profits, he or she also has many other important responsibilities and decisions:

1. Defining sales goals and the sales process

2. Determining the sales force structure

3. Recruiting and training the sales force

4. Compensating and motivating the sales force

5. Evaluating the sales force

DEFINING SALES GOALS AND THE SALES PROCESS

Effective sales management begins with a determination of sales goals. Without goals to achieve, salesperson performance would be mediocre at best, and the company would likely fail. Like any marketing objective, sales goals should be stated in clear, precise, and measurable terms and should always specify a time frame for their fulfillment. Overall sales force goals are usually stated in terms of desired dollar sales volume, market share, or profit level. For example, a life insurance company may have a goal to sell $50 million in life insurance policies annually, to attain a 12 percent market share, or to achieve $1 million in profits. Individual salespeople are also assigned goals in the form of quotas. A **quota** is simply a statement of the salesperson's sales goals, usually based on sales volume alone but sometimes including key accounts (those with greatest potential), new accounts, repeat sales, and specific products.

DETERMINING THE SALES FORCE STRUCTURE

Because personal selling is so costly, no sales department can afford to be disorganized. Proper design helps the sales manager organize and delegate sales duties and provide direction for salespeople. Sales departments are most commonly organized by geographic regions, by product line, by marketing function performed (such as account development or account maintenance), by market or industry, or by individual client or account. The sales force for Hewlett-Packard could be organized into sales territories covering New England, the Midwest, the South, and the West Coast or into distinct groups selling different product lines. HP salespeople might also be assigned to a specific industry or market, for example, the telecommunications industry, or to key clients such as AT&T, Virgin Mobile, and Verizon.

Market- or industry-based structures and key account structures are gaining popularity in today's competitive selling environment, especially with the emphasis on relationship selling. Being familiar with one industry or market allows sales reps to become experts in their fields and thereby offer better solutions and service. Further, by organizing the sales force around specific customers, many companies hope to improve customer service, encourage collaboration with other arms of the company, and unite salespeople in customer-focused sales teams.

quota
A statement of the individual salesperson's sales objectives, usually based on sales volume alone but sometimes including key accounts (those with greatest potential), new accounts, repeat sales, and specific products.

RECRUITING AND TRAINING THE SALES FORCE

Sales force recruitment should be based on an accurate, detailed description of the sales task as defined by the sales manager. For example, General Electric recruits over 1,000 students on 100 college campuses across the United States for entry-level, internship, and co-op positions each year. Its Web site provides prospective salespeople with explanations of different career entry paths and video accounts of what it is like to have a career at GE. Aside from the usual characteristics such as level of experience or education, what traits should sales managers look for in applicants? One of the most important traits of top performers is ego strength, or having a strong, healthy self-esteem and the ability to bounce back from rejection. Great salespeople also have a sense of urgency and competitiveness that pushes their sales to completion. Moreover, they have a desire to persuade people and close the sale. Effective salespeople are also assertive; they have the ability to be firm in one-to-one negotiations, to lead the sales process, and to get their point across confidently, without being overbearing or aggressive. They are sociable, willing to take risks, and capable of understanding complex concepts and ideas. Additionally, great salespeople are creative in developing client solutions, and they possess empathy—the ability to place oneself in someone else's shoes. Not surprisingly, virtually all successful salespeople say their sales style is relationship oriented rather than transaction oriented.[44]

After the sales recruit has been hired and given a brief orientation, training begins. A new salesperson generally receives instruction in company policies and practices, selling techniques, product knowledge, industry and customer characteristics, and non-selling duties such as filling out sales and market information reports or using a sales automation computer program. Firms that sell complex products generally offer the most extensive training programs. Once applicants are hired at General Electric, they enter one of the many "rotational" training programs depending on their interest and major. For example, the Sales and Marketing Commercial Leadership Program (CLP) is geared toward developing skills needed for a successful career at GE. The program ranges from one to two years, depending on which GE business area the employee selects, and includes several rotations between business headquarters and the field. On completing the program, the new employees are better prepared to sell GE products because of their high level of product knowledge and on-the-job experience interacting with customers.[45] See the Ethics in Marketing box, which questions whether lobbying is any different from marketing, personal selling, or another form of promotion. Is a lobbyist just another kind of specially trained salesperson or marketer?

COMPENSATING AND MOTIVATING THE SALES FORCE

Compensation planning is one of the sales manager's toughest jobs. Only good planning will ensure that compensation attracts, motivates, and retains good salespeople. Generally, companies and industries with lower levels of compensation suffer higher turnover rates, which increase costs and decrease effectiveness. Therefore, compensation needs to be competitive enough to attract and motivate the best salespeople. Firms sometimes take profit into account when developing their compensation plans. Instead of paying salespeople on overall volume, they pay according to the profitability achieved from selling each product. Still other companies tie a part of the salesperson's total compensation to customer satisfaction assessed through periodic customer surveys.

As the emphasis on relationship selling increases, many sales managers feel that tying a portion of a salesperson's compensation to a client's satisfaction with the salesperson and the company encourages relationship building. To determine this, sales managers can survey clients on a salesperson's ability to create realistic expectations and his or her responsiveness to customer needs. At PeopleSoft, which was

ethics in marketing

Lobbying—Is It Just Good Marketing?

Lobbyist. The very word conjures up images of evil. Lobbyists have been widely criticized, and politicians and the media are among the first to vilify their existence. But just what is lobbying? According to the U.S. Senate, it is the "practice of trying to persuade legislators to propose, pass, or defeat legislation or to change existing laws. A lobbyist may work for a group, organization, or industry and present information on legislative proposals to support his or her client's interest." Sound familiar? Sounds a lot like what marketers do for their companies or on behalf of their clients.

But when examined, lobbying might not be all bad. Rather than impeding democracy, lobbying could be an expression of democracy guaranteed in the Constitution. It is not solely for the wealthy. It allows all special interest groups—large and small—the opportunity to influence policy. Indeed, the middle class and poor have some of the most powerful lobbyists—the AFL-CIO, the AARP, and the Center on Budget and Policy Priorities. Last, lobbyists persuade legislators based on their knowledge and perspective about the situation. In short, it is based on modern marketing: trying to transform a group's narrow interest into something perceived, rightly or wrongly, as serving the broad public interest. Sounds like segmentation, branding, and promotion.

About 16,000 lobbyists are registered by law under the Lobbying Disclosure Act. Additionally, there are scores of local and state lobbyists and public relations firms, advertising managers, technology experts, pollsters, and direct mail experts that could be considered to lobby on behalf of their clients. Lobbyists see their job as persuading lawmakers that voters are on the lobbyist's side—much like persuading a consumer to make a purchase. Using direct mail and telemarketing, issues are created and then sold like toothpaste.

Typically the most powerful tools used by lobbyists are the skills learned from personal selling. For example, leaders of the National Beer Wholesalers Association see a direct connection between lobbying and marketing. They view lobbying for a specific regulation as selling a product and routinely use basic marketing principles such as positioning and differentiation as a foundation. They elect to keep their message simple, repeat it, keep it consistent, and repeat it. They even use personal selling principles to develop and train their members who are meeting with Congress by using a sales kit called "Making the Capitol Hill Sales Call" that includes everything from worksheets to record responses to issues to a follow-up message after completing the sale.[46]

Do you think lobbying is marketing? Do you believe its impact is positive or negative?

once one of the world's largest applications software companies, structure, culture, and strategies were built around customer satisfaction. Sales force compensation was tied to both sales quotas and a satisfaction metric that allows clients to voice their opinions on the service provided.[47]

Although the compensation plan motivates a salesperson to sell, sometimes it is not enough to produce the volume of sales or the profit margin required by sales management. Sales managers, therefore, often offer rewards or incentives, such as recognition at ceremonies, plaques, vacations, merchandise, and pay raises or cash bonuses. For example, Lorry I. Lokey, founder and chairman of the board of Business Wire, has invited employees from one of the company's 26 offices nationwide to join him on a free trip to a predetermined location, usually overseas. To qualify, employees must have celebrated their five-year anniversary with the company.[48] But of course, cash awards are the most popular sales incentive and are used by virtually all companies. Another possibility is to reward salespeople with a Visa gift card, available from Visa in any amount between $25 and $600. The gift card, which functions like a credit card, can be personalized with a message about the salesperson's performance. It can then be reloaded at the employer's discretion. To recognize and further motivate employees, General Electric uses various rewards including stock options, recognition

programs unique to each department, tuition assistance, and product discounts.[49] Rewards may help increase overall sales volume, add new accounts, improve morale and goodwill, move slow items, and bolster slow sales. They can also be used to achieve long-term or short-term objectives, such as unloading overstocked inventory and meeting a monthly or quarterly sales goal. In motivating their sales force, sales managers must be careful not to encourage unethical behavior.

EVALUATING THE SALES FORCE

The final task of sales managers is evaluating the effectiveness and performance of the sales force. To evaluate the sales force, the sales manager needs feedback—that is, regular information from salespeople. Typical performance measures include sales volume, contribution to profit, calls per order, sales or profits per call, or percentage of calls achieving specific goals such as sales of products that the firm is heavily promoting.

Performance information helps the sales manager monitor a salesperson's progress through the sales cycle and pinpoint where breakdowns might be occurring. For example, by learning the number of prospects an individual salesperson has in each step of the sales cycle process and determining where prospects are falling out of the sales cycle, a manager can determine how effective a salesperson might be at lead generation, needs assessment, proposal generation, presenting, closing, and follow-up stages. This information can then tell a manager what sales skills might need to be reassessed or retrained. For example, if a sales manager notices that a sales rep seems to be letting too many prospects slip away after presenting proposals, it might mean he or she needs help with developing proposals, handling objections, or closing sales.

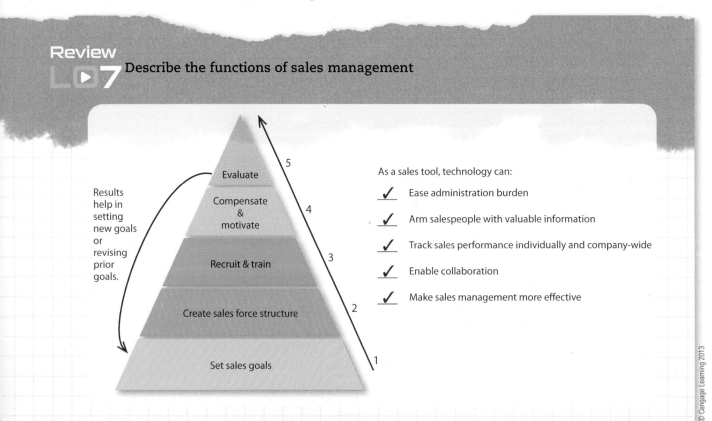

Review
LO 7 Describe the functions of sales management

Results help in setting new goals or revising prior goals.

5 — Evaluate
4 — Compensate & motivate
3 — Recruit & train
2 — Create sales force structure
1 — Set sales goals

As a sales tool, technology can:

✓ Ease administration burden

✓ Arm salespeople with valuable information

✓ Track sales performance individually and company-wide

✓ Enable collaboration

✓ Make sales management more effective

Cost of creating, producing, and placing a national TV advertising campaign

Percentage of online coupons that are redeemed

Health clubs in which Dunkin' Donuts distributed samples of its Latte Lite drink

Percentage of market share lost by companies with low customer service

Billions of coupons redeemed annually

Loyalty program memberships in the U.S.

New products introduced

Percentage of market share gained each by companies with high customer service

Job openings on CollegeRecruiter .com

$5 million   **1,200**   **3.2**   **15.9**   **1.5 billion**   **200**   **6**   **2**   **100,000**

Review and Applications

Define and state the objectives of sales promotion. Sales promotion consists of those marketing communication activities, other than advertising, personal selling, and public relations, in which a short-term incentive motivates consumers or members of the distribution channel to purchase a good or service immediately, either by lowering the price or by adding value. The main objectives of sales promotion are to increase trial purchases, consumer inventories, and repeat purchases. Sales promotion is also used to encourage brand switching and to build brand loyalty. Sales promotion supports advertising activities.

1.1 What is the primary factor that determines sales promotion objectives? Name some different types of sales promotion techniques, and explain the type of customer they are intended to influence.

1.2 You have recently been assigned the task of developing promotional techniques to introduce your company's new product, a Cajun chicken sandwich. Advertising spending is limited, so the introduction will include only some low-budget sales promotion techniques. Write a sales promotion plan that will increase awareness of your new sandwich and allow your customer base to try it risk-free.

writing

Discuss the most common forms of consumer sales promotion. Consumer forms of sales promotion include coupons and rebates, premiums, loyalty marketing programs, contests and sweepstakes, sampling, and point-of-purchase displays. Coupons are certificates entitling consumers to an immediate price reduction when they purchase a product or service. Coupons are a particularly good way to encourage product trial and brand switching. Similar to coupons, rebates provide purchasers with a price reduction, although it is not immediate. To receive a rebate, consumers generally must mail in a rebate form with a proof of purchase. Premiums offer an extra item or incentive to the consumer for buying a product or service. Premiums reinforce the consumer's purchase decision, increase consumption, and persuade nonusers to switch brands. Rewarding loyal customers is the basis of loyalty marketing programs. Loyalty programs are extremely effective at building long-term, mutually beneficial relationships between a company and its key customers. Contests and sweepstakes are generally designed to create interest, often to encourage brand switching. Because consumers perceive risk in trying new products, sampling is an effective method for gaining new customers. Finally, point-of-purchase displays set up at the retailer's location build traffic, advertise the product, and induce impulse buying.

2.1 Discuss how different forms of sales promotion can erode or build brand loyalty. If a company's objective is to enhance customer loyalty to its products, what sales promotion techniques will be most appropriate?

2.2 What forms of consumer sales promotion might induce impulse purchases? What forms of sales promotion are more effective at persuading consumers to switch brands?

2.3 Consider the different consumer sales promotion tools. Give an example of how each type of tool has influenced you to purchase—or purchase more of—a product or service.

2.4 Not everyone thinks supermarket shopper cards are a bargain. Go to **www.nocards.org** and read several pages. Is the information on the site compelling? What do you think of shopper cards? You may want to use the Internet to research shopper cards in more detail before forming an opinion.

2.5 Contests and sweepstakes are very common in the entertainment industry. Radio stations have contests almost weekly (some daily); local television morning shows quiz viewers on trivia; even movies offer sweepstakes in conjunction with film previews and premiere nights. Think of a television or radio program unlikely to have contests or sweepstakes (things like *Cops, The View, Scooby Doo,* or your local classical music radio station, for example). Once you have chosen your program, design a contest or sweepstake to promote the show or the channel on which it airs. List the objectives and describe the rationale behind each part of your promotion.

2.6 How can uPromote.com help you with your sales promotions efforts (visit **www.upromote.com**)? What kind of marketing budget would you need to take advantage of its services? What kind of company would be best served by uPromote.com?

LO3 List the most common forms of trade sales promotion. Manufacturers use many of the same sales promotion tools used in consumer promotions, such as sales contests, premiums, and point-of-purchase displays. In addition, manufacturers and channel intermediaries use several unique promotional strategies: trade allowances, push money, training programs, free merchandise, store demonstrations, and meetings, conventions, and trade shows.

3.1 How does trade sales promotion differ from consumer sales promotion? How is it the same?

3.2 What are the main forms of trade sales promotion? Which type might be most enticing to a grocery store manager? To a buyer for a major electronics chain?

3.3 Form a team of three to five students. As marketing managers, you are in charge of selling Dixie cups. Design a consumer sales promotion plan and trade sales promotion plan for your product. Incorporate at least three different promotion tools into each plan. Share your results with the other teams in the class.

LO4 Describe personal selling. Personal selling is direct communication between a sales representative and one or more prospective buyers in an attempt to influence each other in a purchase situation. Broadly speaking, all businesspeople use personal selling to promote themselves and their ideas. Personal selling offers several advantages over other forms of promotion. Personal selling allows salespeople to thoroughly explain and demonstrate a product. Salespeople have the flexibility to tailor a sales proposal to the needs and preferences of individual customers. Personal selling is more efficient than other forms of promotion because salespeople target qualified prospects and avoid wasting efforts on unlikely buyers. Personal selling affords greater managerial control over promotion costs. Finally, personal selling is the most effective method of closing a sale and producing satisfied customers.

4.1 Discuss the role of personal selling in promoting products. What advantages does personal selling offer over other forms of promotion?

4.2 What are the major advantages of personal selling to the company selling a product? What are the advantages to the person or company buying the product?

Discuss the key differences between relationship selling and traditional selling. Relationship selling is the practice of building, maintaining, and enhancing interactions with customers in order to develop long-term satisfaction through mutually beneficial partnerships. Traditional selling, on the other hand, is transaction focused. That is, the salesperson is most concerned with making onetime sales and moving on to the next prospect. Salespeople practicing relationship selling spend more time understanding a prospect's needs and developing solutions to meet those needs.

5.1 What are the key differences between relationship selling and traditional methods of selling? What types of products or services do you think would be conducive to relationship selling?

5.2 Based on the key differences between traditional and relationship selling, which type of sales approach would you use as a salesperson? Do the different approaches require different personal strengths or attributes?

List the steps in the selling process. The selling process is composed of seven basic steps: (1) generating leads, (2) qualifying leads, (3) approaching the customer and probing needs, (4) developing and proposing solutions, (5) handling objections, (6) closing the sale, and (7) following up.

6.1 You are a new salesperson for a well-known medical software company, and one of your clients is a large group of physicians. You have just arranged an initial meeting with the office manager. Develop a list of questions you might ask at this meeting to uncover the group's specific needs.
writing

6.2 What does sales follow-up entail? Why is it an essential step in the selling process, particularly from the perspective of relationship selling? How does it relate to cognitive dissonance?

6.3 How many ways can zapdata (**www.zapdata.com**) benefit salespeople? Which of its services would be most useful to marketing managers? Other businesspeople?
online

6.4 Consider each step in the selling process. Which steps could be conducted through technology (Internet, webinars, etc.)? Which are most important to handle "face-to-face"?

Describe the functions of sales management. Sales management is a critical area of marketing that performs several important functions. Sales managers set overall company sales goals and define the sales process most effective for achieving those goals. They determine sales force structure based on geographic, product, functional, or customer variables. Managers develop the sales force through recruiting and training. Sales management motivates the sales force through compensation planning, motivational tools, and effective sales leadership. Finally, sales managers evaluate the sales force through salesperson feedback and other methods of determining their performance.

7.1 What kinds of sales management opportunities are available at Amway Global? Use the Web site (**www.amwayglobal.com** to research this company and determine its sales process, sales force structure, and how it recruits and trains its salespeople.
online

7.2 How does each of the sales management functions contribute to a successful, high-performing sales force?

Key Terms

consumer sales promotion *651*	networking *667*	relationship selling
coupon *654*	personal selling *663*	(consultative selling) *664*
follow-up *672*	point-of-purchase (P-O-P) *660*	sales presentation *669*
frequent buyer program *657*	preapproach *669*	sales process (sales cycle) *666*
lead generation	premium *656*	sales promotion *651*
(prospecting) *667*	push money *661*	sales proposal *669*
lead qualification *668*	quota *673*	sampling *659*
loyalty marketing program *657*	rebate *655*	trade allowance *661*
needs assessment *669*	referral *667*	trade sales promotion *651*
negotiation *671*		

Exercises

ethics

ETHICS EXERCISE

Sally Burke works for Hi-Tech Electronics. Her responsibilities include selecting items to advertise in her company's Sunday newspaper FSIs. One hot item is a 50-inch flat-panel plasma TV. The list price is $4,999, but her manager tells her to advertise it at $3,999, because customers can apply for a $1,000 mail-in rebate. The advertised price has attracted many people to buy the TV; however, Sally has heard several complaints from customers who found the rebate process unusually complex and were denied a rebate because the manufacturer claimed they hadn't provided the required information. She would prefer to advertise the "real" list price, knowing that customers are not guaranteed to receive a rebate.

Questions

1. Is it unethical to advertise products at their post-rebate price in order to increase sales? Why or why not? What is another sales promotion method Hi-Tech Electronics could use to persuade customers to buy their plasma TV at the store?

2. Rebate programs are commonly used by electronics manufacturers because the rebates arouse consumers' interest in buying products, yet only half of purchasers ultimately claim their rebates. Is a rebate program itself unethical if the manufacturer knows consumers are unlikely to receive their money?

3. Visit a local electronics store—or Web site—and find a product being sold with a mail-in rebate offer. Are the rebate instructions clear? Would you take the time to complete the process?

MARKETING PLAN EXERCISE

For the next stage of the strategic planning process you'll focus on your chosen company's sales promotion and personal selling decisions. Use the following exercises to guide you through the final elements of Part 5 of your strategic marketing plan:

1. Evaluate or create printed materials for your chosen company (such as data sheets, brochures, stationery, or rate cards). Does the literature sufficiently answer questions? Provide enough information for further contact? Effectively promote product features and customer service? Note a differential or competitive advantage?

2. Think about ways your promotions could turn a first-time customer or deal-hunter into a repeat, loyal customer. Which sales promotion tools should your company use? What

trade shows could your firm attend? Search the Eventline database (**www.eventslisted .com/eventline/**) for trade shows appropriate to your firm. Order media kits and explore the feasibility and costs of attending those trade shows. For a listing of tradeshows, go to **www.exhibitornet.com** and look for the directory of shows, or the Trade Show News Network at **www.tsnn.com**.

3. What other sales promotion tools could your firm use? What are the costs? What is the impact of using these methods on pricing?

4. Will you need a sales force? Identify and justify the best type (internal or external) and structure (product, customer, geographic, etc.) for your firm's sales force. You might find that in e-marketing, a sales force is more of a customer service and customer relations management tool. True selling activities might be limited to selling and buying online media space and links. In many circumstances, forming strategic partnerships and distribution deals have replaced traditional sales in the Internet space. What types of alliances and partnerships will you pursue? Will you work with other online firms, offline firms, or both?

APPLICATION EXERCISE

Have you ever waited forever to get a fast-food hamburger? Have you even been left to languish in a dressing room by a salesperson who left for a coffee break? If so, you already know that sales and customer service are integral parts of marketing. As you work on this chapter, keep a journal of your personal sales and/or customer service experiences with local merchants. Don't ignore the details. Even things such as how crowded a store or restaurant is when you visit might affect your perceptions of the service you received.[50]

Activities

1. Keep your journal for a week, recording all sales and service transactions, if possible, on the day they occur.

2. At the end of the week, examine your journal and pick the most noteworthy entry. Provide the basic information about the transaction: company where it occurred, type of transaction (purchase, return, complaint, etc.), type of good or service involved, and so forth.

3. Once you have outlined the situation, evaluate the experience. Use the information about selling in this chapter as support for your evaluation. For example, did the salesperson seem to treat the situation as an individual, discrete transaction, or did he or she seem interested in building a relationship?

4. Finally, make recommendations as to how the company can improve its sales and/or service. Suggestions should be logical and achievable (meaning you have to consider the cost of implementing your suggestion).

CASE STUDY: Ron Popeil

RON POPEIL WHEELS, DEALS, HAS MASS APPEAL

At age 76, Ron "Ronco" Popeil is an avid inventor, tireless entrepreneur, clever marketer, and master salesman all in one. He just happens to be an American icon, too. The godfather of the infomercial, Popeil even has his famous Veg-O-Matic on display in the Smithsonian Institution as an American cultural artifact. His other famous products include the food dehydrator, the Ronco spray gun, and the Popeil Pocket Fisherman.

As a teenager, Popeil helped his father sell his kitchen gadgets at local Woolworth's and later, in the 1950s, on the Chicago fair circuit. That is probably why his famous shtick, which included such memorable catchphrases as "But wait, there's more," "Priced so low," and "Operators are standing by," always seemed like a blend between sincere eccentric inventor and excitable carnival barker. The combination suited him well and brought him enough financial success that he could afford to take his act to television. In the 1960s, he incorporated Ronco, and its name became synonymous with gadgets like the smokeless ashtray and Mr. Microphone.

Regardless of the product he is selling or the catchy pitch phrases he invents on the fly to sell them, Popeil is always sincere. "The easiest thing to do in the world is to sell a product I believe in," he has said. "If I spent two years creating a product, conceiving it, tinkering with it, I can get up and sell it. Who can sell it better than the guy who invented it?" Len Green, a professor in entrepreneurship at Babson College, says, "Ron is one of a kind. He is different from the rest because he not only invents, he sells. Most entrepreneurs come up with a concept and then give it to others to manufacture or sell. He's his own best salesman."

Though Popeil has suffered his fair share of flops, like spray-on hair and a brief bankruptcy in 1987, he has always managed to bounce back. Returning from bankruptcy, he relaunched the popular food dehydrator in 1990, and eight years later he designed and sold his most successful product ever, the Showtime rotisserie BBQ. Having sold over seven million units for four installments of $39.95 each, the rotisserie alone has grossed over $1 billion in sales. During the taping of the infomercial for that product, the live studio audience was treated to yet another of Popeil's catchphrases that has become part of the fabric of American speech. "Just set it and forget it!" is now used to sell all kinds of non-Popeil products from TVs and digital video recorders to ovens and coffeemakers.

Through the medium of television, Popeil was able to reach tens of millions of people. With an innate ability to invent or improve on everyday household products, his live product demonstrations captured the imaginations and dollars of generations of consumers. In 1976, he was even the subject of what was probably Dan Aykroyd's most famous bit on *Saturday Night Live*. Parodying Popeil, Aykroyd hawked the "Super Bass-O-Matic '76," which was capable of turning a bass or any other "small aquatic creature" into liquid without any "scaling, cutting, or gutting."

Having recently sold Ronco to an investment group for over $55 million and accumulated a personal net worth of over $100 million, Popeil has had the last laugh. He has continued to serve as a product developer, pitchman, and consultant for the new company and already promises an even bigger hit than the Showtime rotisserie. Having identified a market of over 20 million Americans who fry turkeys every year, Popeil says he has a new fryer on the way that will make it possible to safely fry a 20-pound turkey in 70 minutes—indoors. Given that he has created over 150 products and invented personal selling via the mass marketing medium, there is little reason to doubt him.

As Barbara Gross, professor of marketing at California State University, Northridge, states, "His success speaks for itself; probably that has more to do with his personality. He's comfortable and sincere. He comes across like he really believes in it. When you hear him talk, you never feel like he's lying to you."[51]

Questions

1. What does Ron Popeil bring to personal selling that makes him so effective?

2. What trade sales promotion tools does he use? Why does he use sales promotion tools when he is selling direct to consumers?

3. Explain how Popeil's selling tactics allow him to achieve the desired objectives of sales promotions.

4. Do you think it is likely that America will ever see someone like Ron Popeil in the future? Why or why not?

COMPANY CLIPS: Vans—Off the Wall Promotions

Steve Van Doren, son of Vans' founder, is the self-proclaimed "ambassador of fun" at Vans. Because the company doesn't want to discount its products or lower its prices, it has to find other ways to create value for consumers. So, to keep the brand energized, the company is constantly developing promotions that can only be described as fun, an important element for attracting trendsetting customers. The core of Vans' strategy revolves around unique and authentic contests and giveaways. The company relies on word-of-mouth advertising and credible personal selling. In this video segment, Vans marketers explain how they use Web sites, contests, giveaways, and athletic events to attract and keep customers.

Questions

1. How does Vans use giveaways and contests to market its products? Why do these strategies work so well for Vans?

2. How does Vans approach recruiting and training its sales force?

3. How have trade shows changed in recent years? What is Vans' main goal at trade shows today?

Notes

1. Annual Report: Industry Report, October 2008, *PROMO Magazine*, http://promomagazine.com/lp/research/icgroup_promolite/.

2. *Ibid.*

3. Robert Passikoff, "Why Starbucks Has Ground to a Halt," *Brandweek*, November 10, 2008, www.adweek.com; Andy Serwer, "Starbucks Fix: Howard Schultz Spills the Beans on His Plans to Save the Company He Founded," CNNMoney, January 18, 2008, http://money.cnn.com/2008/01/17/news/newsmakers/starbucks.fortune/index.htm?postversion=2008011805; Emily Bryson York, "Consumers Skip Starbucks for Plain Ol' Joe," *Advertising Age*, January 19, 2009, http://adage.com/article/news/consumers-skip-starbucks-coffee-plain-ol-joe/133871; Howard Schultz Transformation Agenda #1, http://news.starbucks.com/article_display. cfm?article_id=76..

4. Kunur Patel, "Suddenly, Everyone Wants to Be Groupon" *Advertising Age*, November 1, 2010, http://adage.com/article/digital/coupons-walmart-groupon/146819/.

5. Jack Neff, "Coupon Clipping Stages a Comeback," *Advertising Age*, November 1, 2010, http://adage.com/article/news/newspaper-print-coupon-clipping-stages-a-comeback/146816/

6. Annual Report: Industry Report October 2008, *PROMO Magazine*.

7. Brian Quinton, "Facebook Goes Places: Implications of New Geo-Social Features," *Promo Magazine,* October 1, 2001, http://chiefmarketer.com/disciplines/online/facebook-geosocial-features-1001/index.html.

8. Patricia Odell, "Macy's, McDonald's, Others Test New Facebook Deals App," *Promo Magazine*, November 9, 2010, http://promomagazine.com/viralmarketing/news/macys-mcdon-alds-facebook-deals-app-1109/index.html.

9. Kroger Web site, "My Kroger," www.kroger.com/mykroger/Pages/default.aspx.

10. Suzanne Vita Palazzo, "Countdown to Kickoff," *Grocery Headquarters*, December 2005, 43.

11. Brian Grow, "The Great Rebate Runaround," *BusinessWeek*, November 23, 2005 www.businessweek.com/bwdaily/dnflash/nov2005/nf20051123_4158_db016.htm.

12. Patricia Odell, "Shrek Premiums Drive Big Sales for Kellogg's," *PROMO Magazine*, November 1, 2008, http://promomaga-zine.com/incentives/1101-kellogg-uses-shrek/index.html.

13. News Briefs, "Skyy Vodka," *Promo Magazine*, October 16, 2003, http://promomagazine.com/news/marketing_news_briefs_52.

14. Annual Report: Industry Report October 2008, *PROMO Magazine*.

15. "Loyalty Programs," Crmtrends Web site, www.crmtrends.com/loyalty.html; Matthew Haeberle, "Loyalty Is Dead: Great Experiences, Not Price, Will Create Loyal Customers," *Chain Store Age*, January 2004, 17.

16. Ben Woolsey, "The New Starbucks Duetto Visa: Wake Up and Smell the Plastic," www.creditcards.com/

marketing&you: Results.

High scores on this poll indicate a preference for using coupons, which could indicate that you are a comparison shopper. If your score was low, you probably don't see any economic benefits to using coupons, and you're likely not a comparison shopper. Instead, you probably prefer to buy what you want regardless of any coupon promotion.

New-Starbucks-Duetto-Visa-Credit-Card.php; "Which Starbuck's Credit Card Should You Get," Ask Mr. Credit Card Web site, www.askmr-creditcard.com/starbucksduettovisa.html.

17. Verizon Wireless Web site, www.verizonwireless.com.

18. "Grocers' Use of E-Mail Growing: Survey," *Promo P&I*, August 17, 2005, http://promomagazine.com/incentives/grocers_survey_081705/.

19. Peter Sanders, "Starwood's Web Log Caters to Loyalty," *Wall Street Journal*, April 12, 2006, B3; Starwood Hotels and Resorts Web site, "Company Overview," www.starwoodhotels.com/corporate/company_info.html.

20. Patricia Odell, "Dole Uses Blogs and Parties to Promote Fruit Parfaits," *PROMO Magazine*, January 1, 2009, http://promomagazine.com/retail/0109-dole-builds-business/index.html

21. "Dream Home Central," HGTV Web site, www.hgtv.com/hgtv-dream-home-2011-giveaway/package/index.html.

22. "Advertising to Life Scientists: Maximizing Ad Effectiveness," *BioInformatics, LLC*, January 1, 2006, www.marketresearch.com/product/display.asp?productid=1278351&g=1, bloggybiz.com/business-news/use-product-samples-to-boost-your-business-in-2008; Tim Parry, "Sampling—Teaching Tools," *PROMO Magazine*, www.promomagazine.com.

23. "Domino's Customers Get Free Coca-Cola Zero," *PROMO Xtra*, December 22, 2005, http://promomagazine.com/sampling/dominos_cocacolazero_122205.

24. Stephanie Thompson, "Dove Targets the Chocoholic," *Advertising Age*, September 15, 2003, 45.

25. Patricia Odell, "Brands Test Sampling at Meal Assembly Kitchens," *PROMO Magazine*, December 1, 2008, http://promomagazine.com/retail/1201-brands-test-sampling/index.html.

26. Patricia Odell, "Sampling Reigns as Key Method to Drive In-Store Sales," *PROMO Magazine*, October 17, 2006, http://promomagazine.com/incentives/sampling_drives_instore_roi_101706/index.html.; "Dunkin' Donuts Targets Health Clubs with Sampling Program," *PROMO Xtra*, December 28, 2005, http://promomagazine.com/sampling/dunkindonuts_sampling_122805/index.html.

27. Annual Report: Industry Report October 2008, *PROMO Magazine*.

28. "Point-of-Purchase: $17 Billion," *PROMO Magazine*, October 29, 2001, 3; "In Praise of Promotion," *PROMO Xtra*, September 1, 2005, http://promomagazine.com/awards/marketing_praise_promotion/index.html.

29. Stephanie Thompson, "Hershey Sets $30M Push," *Advertising Age*, September 15, 2003, 3, 45.

30. Mickey Khan, "Heinekin Hoaxes Are Real Deal for Building E-mail Names," *DM News Online*, October 7, 2003, www.dmnews.com/heineken-hoaxes-are-real-deal-for-building-e-mail-names/article/82152/.

31. Roger O. Crocket, "Penny-Pinchers' Paradise," *BusinessWeek*, January 22, 2001, EB12.

32. "Trade Show Survey Indicates Strong Value," Trade Show Advisor Web site, www.trade-show-advisor.com/trade-show-survey.html.

33. Michael Beverland, "Contextual Influences and the Adoption and Practice of Relationship Selling in a Business-to-Business Setting: An Exploratory Study," *Journal of Personal Selling & Sales Management*, Summer 2001, 207.

34. Richard Morrison, "The Business Process of Customer Retention and Loyalty," *Customer Interaction Solutions*, October 2001, 4.

35. "The Right Questions and Attitudes Can Beef Up Your Sales, Improve Customer Retention," *Selling*, June 2001, 3.

36. Larry Rigs, "Hit 'Em Where They Work," *Direct*, October 15, 2003, http://directmag.com/casehistories/b2b/marketing_hit_em_work/index.html; "Webcast Essentials," supplement to *CRM Magazine*, 2005.

37. Alf Nucifora, "Need Leads? Try a Networking Group," *Business News New Jersey*, November 14, 2000, 22; Catherine Seda, "The Meet Market," *Entrepreneur*, August 2004, 68; Jim Dickie, "Is Social Networking an Overhyped Fad or a Useful Tool?" *Destination CRM*, January 21, 2005, www.destinationcrm.com/Articles/Columns-Departments/Reality-Check/Is-Social-Networking-an-Overhyped-Fad-or-a-Useful-Tool-42799.aspx; Kristina Dell, "What Are Friends For?" *Time*, September 21, 2004.

38. B. Weitz, S. Castleberry, and J. Tanner, *Selling* (Burr Ridge, IL: McGraw-Hill/Irwin, 2007), 196–197.

39. "Welcome to BICLiNK.com 4.0," BIC Consumer Products Web site, www.BIClink.com.

40. *Presentations Magazine*, www.presentations.com.

41. Chanimal Web site forum, http://www.chanimal.com/forums.

42. Troy Korsgaden, "Fine-Tuning Your Agency's Office Systems," *Rough Notes*, www.roughnotes.com/rnmagazine/2000/june00/06p116.htm.

43. College Recruiter Web site, www.collegerecruiter.com.

44. Weitz, Castleberry, and Tanner, *Selling*, 17–22.

45. General Electric Web site, www.ge.com.

46. United States Senate, www.senate.gov/reference/reference_index_subjects/lobbying_vrd.htm; Conor McGrath, "Grass Roots Lobbying: Marketing Politics and Policy 'Beyond the Beltway' Elections on the Horizon: Marketing Politics to the Electorate in the USA and UK," March 15, 2004; Robert J. Samuelson, "Lobbying Is Democracy in Action" *Newsweek*, December 22, 2008, www.newsweek.com/2008/12/12/lobbying-is-democracy-in-action.html.

47. Oracle Web site, www.oracle.com/index.html.

48. "About Us," *Business Wire*, www.businesswire.com/portal/site/home/about.

49. Kathleen Joyce, "In the Cards," *PROMO Magazine*, September 1, 2003, http://promomagazine.com/mag/marketing_cards_3.

50. This application exercise is based on the contribution of John Ronchetto (University of San Diego) to *Great Ideas in Teaching Marketing*, a teaching supplement that accompanies McDaniel, Lamb, and Hair's *Introduction to Marketing*. Professor Ronchetto's entry titled "Sales and Customer Service Experiential Journal and Paper" was a winner in the "Best of the Great Ideas in Teaching Marketing" contest held in conjunction with the publication of the eighth edition of *Marketing*.

51. "Ron Popeil, He of the Pocket Fisherman and Spray-On Hair, Has Perfected His Formula for Success: Invent, Market, and Sell with a Passion," *BusinessWeek*, October 3, 2005; Brent Hopkins, "How Ron Popeil Invented Himself," *Knight-Ridder/Tribune Business News*, August 31, 2005; Matt Myerhoff, "Infomercial King Sells Company, Ronco Goes Public for Expansion," *Los Angeles Business Journal*, July 29, 2005, 1.

52. Amanda Radke, "Yellow Tail Wine Donates $100,000 to HSUS," *Beef*, February 4, 2010, http://blog.beefmagazine.com/beef_daily/2010/02/04/yellow-tail-wine-donates-100000-to-hsus; Humane Society, www.humanesociety.org; The Grain Board, www.thegrainboard.com; Walter Pidgeon to Dill Deutsch, January 27, 2010, www.ussportsmen.org/Document.Doc?id=126 (accessed February 28, 2011); [Yellow Tail], www.yellowtailwine.com; Kay Smith of Animal Agriculture Alliance to Bill Deutsch, February 5, 2010, "Letter in Response to Yellow Tail's HSUS Donation," www.facebook.com/notes/animal-agriculture-alliance/letter-in-response-to-yellow-tails-hsus-donation/288862008417 (accessed 31 January 2011); Susan Crowell, "Yellow Tail Wine Donation to HSUS Incurs Farmers' Wrath," Farm and Dairy, February 9, 2010, www.farmanddairy.com/columns/yellow-tail-wine-donation-to-hsus-incurs-farmers-wrath/14217.html, accessed 31 January 2011; "Jolley: Five Minutes with the Yellow Tail Fiasco," Drovers Cattle Network, February 5, 2010, www.cattlenetwork.com/templates/newsarchive.html?sid=cn&cid=983537.

53. Rob Anderson, "In Lap-Dance Apology, Boston Blazers President Dodges Responsibility," Boston.com, January 19, 2011, www.boston.com/bostonglobe/editorial_opinion/blogs/the_angle/2011/01/boston_blazers.html; Anne-Marie Dorning, "Out of Bounds: Lacrosse Mascot Gets Lap Dance During Game," *ABC News*, January 18 2011, http://abcnews.go.com/US/video-catches-soccer-mascot-lap-dance/story?id=12642649; Todd Feathers, "Blazing Apology," *HuntNewsNU.com*, January 27 2011, p. 5; "Racy Half-Time Show at Boston Blazers Game Featured Mascot Getting Lap Dance," *Fox News*, January 17, 2011, www.myfoxboston.com/dpp/news/local/racy-halftime-show-at-boston-blazers-game-featured-lap-dance-competition-20110116.

Marketing Miscue

YELLOW TAIL'S TAILS-FOR-TAILS CAMPAIGN

Yellow Tail is an Australian wine produced by Casella Wines Pty Ltd. The company entered into bottled wine commercialization around the beginning of 2000 and quickly became a top imported wine into the United States. As such, it is not surprising that the company has targeted cause-related promotional efforts in the United States. However, the company created quite a stir in 2010 when it donated US$100,000 to the Humane Society of the United States (HSUS). At first glance, one might think (as probably did executives at Yellow Tail) that this type of donation would engender strong support and affinity among American consumers. Unfortunately, just the opposite happened!

The Humane Society of the United States

According to the HSUS Web site, the society " . . . is the nation's largest and most effective animal protection organization—backed by 11 million Americans. . . . HSUS seeks a humane and sustainable world for all animals. . . . We are America's mainstream force against cruelty, exploitation and neglect, as well as the most trusted voice extolling the human-animal bond." Based on that mission, one might expect the HSUS to be a critical advocate for animals. Yet the firestorm associated with the Tails-for-Tails campaign highlighted several possible flaws in the interpretation of what HSUS really does. For example, numerous reports point out that HSUS is not an animal shelter group seeking to take care of abandoned pets. Rather, some writers even suggest that the group is an animal rights extremist group opposed to the consumption of meat products and a group that seeks to outlaw progressive and humane agricultural practices. Adding fuel to the fire is the evidence that less than one percent of the HSUS budget actually goes toward the caring of animals. In a comment attributed to the Animal Agriculture Alliance, the American Institute of Philanthropy gave the HSUS a grade of "C-" in its Charity Rating Guide. Supposedly, the vast majority of the HSUS budget goes to fundraising, lobbying, and salaries.

Tails for Tails

On February 4, 2010, a Yellow Tail press release announced a collaboration between the company and the HSUS. In support of the HSUS mission to celebrate animals, the wine company made a donation of US$100,000. The company said that it embraced animals and pointed to the company's logo of a Yellow-footed Rock Wallaby as an example of that affiliation. In addition to point-of-sale visibility for the Tails-for-Tails campaign, Yellow Tail's Facebook page would include a link to the HSUS pet photo contest. Via this online collaboration, consumers would receive information on how to make a donation to the HSUS animal rescue program.

The Uproar

The agriculture community has long felt like it has been a target of the HSUS. It was thought that the HSUS was an organization with a core mission of removing meat, dairy, and eggs from the American diet and, as such, putting farmers and ranchers out of business. Soon after the announcement of the Tails-for-Tails campaign, the U.S. Sportsmen's Alliance sent a letter to the American distributor of Yellow Tail wine. In the letter, it was pointed out that efforts by the HSUS weaken wildlife conservation within the United States while attacking a major economic sector. The Alliance also tweeted about the collaboration between Yellow Tail and the HSUS. The agricultural community picked up on the news and word began to spread throughout the Twitterverse, and a public relations nightmare began for Yellow Tail.

Within days, a "Yellow Fail" Facebook page was created and fans of the page skyrocketed to almost equal that of a Yellow Tail fan page. Bloggers condemned both Yellow Tail and the HSUS. A call to action was made to stop buying Yellow Tail wine. A fifth generation rancher in South Dakota (USA) digitally recorded himself pouring Yellow Tail wine onto the snow while his cattle watched in the background. The recording quickly garnered thousands of views. Another rancher was seen with a bottle of Yellow Tail being used for target practice. People even became fans on Yellow Tail's Facebook page just so they could write negative comments on the company's wall. The agriculture community took a stand against Yellow Tail and the HSUS and used social media to disseminate its concerns.[52]

Questions

1. Yellow Tail engaged in cause-related marketing. Why did the effort misfire?
2. What role did the social media ecosystem play in this public relations nightmare?

Critical Thinking Case

LAP DANCE AT BOSTON BLAZERS LACROSSE GAME: PROMOTIONAL MISTAKE OR CREATIVE GENIUS?

The Boston Blazers is a professional indoor lacrosse team based in Boston, Massachusetts, that began play in 2009. It is one of ten teams in the National Lacrosse League (NLL). Other teams are: Buffalo Bandits, Calgary Roughnecks, Colorado Mammoth, Edmonton Rush, Minnesota Swarm, Philadelphia Wings, Rochester Nighthawks, Toronto Rock, and Washington Stealth.

The Boston Blazers lacrosse team also faces pretty stiff competition in the professional sports arena with teams such as the Boston Celtics (basketball), the Boston Red Sox (baseball), the Boston Bruins (hockey), the New England Patriots (football), and the New England Revolution (soccer).

Professional indoor lacrosse is in its infancy when compared to other professional sporting events and professional sports players. Event-wise, the average number of fans at a NLL game is 10,000 while game attendance at other professional sporting events averages anywhere from 20,000 to 30,000 for basketball, hockey, and baseball to 70,000 for football. Another huge differential is in terms of pricing. For example, in 2011, the Boston Blazers offered four tickets with food and drink (hamburger, fries, soft drink) for US$99.00. That compares to around US$500 for four tickets with food and drink at Fenway Park when attending a Boston Red Sox game. Player-wise, a professional indoor lacrosse player usually holds a "real" job and plays part-time for the NLL, receiving an average salary of $1,000 per game. In contrast, the average 2009 salary of a Major League Baseball player was $3 million.

© iStockphoto.com/4x6

Nationwide Media Attention

Professional sporting events have long focused on halftime entertainment as a critical aspect of overall fan experience. Probably one of the more memorable halftime shows occurred at the Super Bowl XXXVIII in February of 2004 with the oft referenced "wardrobe malfunction" in which Janet Jackson's breast was exposed by Justin Timberlake for about a half a second. On January 15, 2011, however, the Boston Blazers rivaled the Super Bowl incident when the team captured the attention of news outlets across America for its controversial halftime show.

Billed as a promotional event during halftime of the game against the Edmonton Rush, Scorch, the Blazer's mascot, soon became the central figure in what became a YouTube sensation. According to fans, with the rap song "Low" blaring in on the sound system, a red carpet was put down with a chair for Scorch to sit in. Scantily clad dancers then competed to see which one of them could give Scorch the best lap dance. The lap dance event was broadcast on the Jumbotron video display during the performance.

Numerous fans videotaped the performance on their cell phones and posted it to YouTube. However, these videos were soon removed from YouTube citing a copyright claim by the National Lacrosse League. Before their removal from the YouTube site, fans can be heard saying "Oh my God" and young children can be seen sitting in their seats watching the halftime performance. A portion of the performance was captured and aired by a local news channel, with the video remaining on the news Web site. Criticism of the halftime performance used vocabulary such as "raunchy," "scandalous," and "extremely offensive."[53]

The Apology

The day after the game, the president and general manager of the Boston Blazers, Doug Reffue, posted an apology on the team's Facebook page. He said, in part:

> The Boston Blazers halftime act for Saturday's game was clearly not executed according to plan. We are extremely disappointed with elements of the halftime show. We had intended to provide an entertaining and fun halftime environment for our fans and that is not what transpired.

In addition to the posted apology, Reffue offered 2,000 free tickets to the team's next home game. Reffue's apology, however, did not stem the media flare over the halftime performance. While it seemed that Reffue was attributing the performance to an unplanned and unexpected mistake, the detail and clarity of the performance made it obvious to fans that the performance was well-choreographed.

The Outcome

While some might have seen the performance as a mistake that would have an effect on fan patronage, this was not the case. Attendance at the game the night of the lap dance performance was 8,536. Attendance the week after the highly publicized lap dance was 10,422. Plus, the story was the biggest news coverage to ever hit the NLL. While the NLL commissioner noted that the lap dance performance was an error in judgment, he noted the bright side of the story by saying that it was a good thing in the long run if it helped people find out about the NLL and the Blazers.[53]

Questions

1. Do you think the performance was a well-thought-out effort to generate publicity for the Boston Blazers?

2. How did viral marketing affect the Boston Blazers?

6

Pricing Decisions

19 Pricing Concepts

Learning Outcomes

1 Discuss the importance of pricing decisions to the economy and to the individual firm

2 List and explain a variety of pricing objectives

3 Explain the role of demand in price determination

4 Understand the concept of yield management systems

5 Describe cost-oriented pricing strategies

6 Demonstrate how the product life cycle, competition, distribution and promotion strategies, guaranteed price matching, customer demands, the Internet, and perceptions of quality can affect price

© iStockphoto.com/Juan Facundo Moca Soria, © David Muscroft/Age fotostock/Photolibrary

LO1
The Importance of Price

Price means one thing to the consumer and something else to the seller. To the consumer, it is the cost of something. To the seller, price is revenue, the primary source of profits. In the broadest sense, price allocates resources in a free-market economy. With so many ways of looking at price, it's no wonder that marketing managers find the task of setting prices a challenge. Yet over the past two decades managers have learned that meeting the challenge of setting the right price can have a significant impact on the firm's bottom line. Large organizations that successfully manage prices do so by creating a pricing infrastructure within the company. This means defining pricing goals, searching for ways to create greater customer value, assigning authority and responsibility for pricing decisions, and creating tools and systems to continually improve pricing decisions. Obtaining pricing excellence is a very worthwhile activity: a 1-percent improvement in the average price of goods and services leads to an 8.7 percent increase in net profits for the typical Global 1200 company.[1] The Global 1200 are the world's largest 1,200 public companies.

WHAT IS PRICE?

Price is that which is given up in an exchange to acquire a good or service. Price plays two roles in the evaluation of product alternatives: as a measure of sacrifice and as an information cue. To some degree, these are two opposing effects.[2]

> ❝ Meeting the challenge of **setting** the right price can have a significant impact on the firm's bottom line. ❞

price
That which is given up in an exchange to acquire a good or service.

marketing&you.

Using the following scale, enter your opinion of the following items on the lines provided.

STRONGLY DISAGREE ‹ 1 2 3 4 5 6 7 › STRONGLY AGREE

_____ People notice when you buy the most expensive brand of a product.

_____ Buying the most expensive brand of a product makes me feel classy.

_____ I enjoy the prestige of buying a high-priced brand.

_____ It says something to people when you buy the high-priced version of a product.

_____ I have purchased the most expensive brand of a product just because I knew other people would notice.

_____ Even for a relatively inexpensive product, I think that buying a costly brand is impressive.

Total your score, and find out what it means after you read the chapter.

The Sacrifice Effect of Price Price is, again, "that which is given up," which means what is sacrificed to get a good or service. In the United States, the sacrifice is usually money, but can be other things as well. It might also be time lost while waiting to acquire the good or service. Standing in long lines at the airport first to check in and then to get through the security checkpoint procedures is a cost. In fact, these delays are one reason more people are selecting alternative modes of transportation for relatively short trips. Price might also include "lost dignity" for individuals who lose their jobs and must rely on charity to obtain food and clothing.

The Information Effect of Price Consumers do not always choose the lowest-priced product in a category, such as shoes, cars, or wine, even when the products are otherwise similar. One explanation of this, based upon research, is that we infer quality information from price.[3] That is, higher quality equals higher price. The information effect of price can also extend to favorable price perceptions by others because higher prices can convey the prominence and status of the purchaser to other people. Thus, a Swatch and a Rolex both can accurately tell time but convey different meanings. Similarly, a Buick Enclave and the Lexus 450LX are both SUVs, and both can take you from point A to B. However, the two vehicles convey different meanings. We will return to the price–quality relationship later in the chapter.

Value Is Based upon Perceived Satisfaction Consumers are interested in obtaining a "reasonable price." "Reasonable price" really means "perceived reasonable value" at the time of the transaction. One of the authors of this textbook bought a fancy European-designed toaster for about $45. The toaster's wide mouth made it possible to toast a bagel, warm a muffin, and, with a special $15 attachment, make a grilled sandwich. The author felt that a toaster with all these features surely must be worth the total price of $60. But after three months of using the device, toast that burned around the edges and remained cool in the middle lost its appeal. The disappointed buyer put the toaster in the attic. Why didn't he return it to the retailer? The boutique had gone out of business and no other local retailer carried the brand. Also, there was no U.S. service center. Remember, the price paid is based on the satisfaction and value consumers *expect* to receive from a product and not necessarily the satisfaction they actually receive.

Price can relate to anything with perceived value, not just money. When goods and services are exchanged, the trade is called *barter*. For example, if you exchange this book for a chemistry book at the end of the term, you have engaged in barter. The price you paid for the chemistry book was this textbook.

THE IMPORTANCE OF PRICE TO MARKETING MANAGERS

As noted in the chapter introduction, prices are the key to revenues, which in turn are the key to profits for an organization. **Revenue** is the price charged to customers multiplied by the number of units sold. Revenue is what pays for every activity of the

revenue
The price charged to customers multiplied by the number of units sold.

company: production, finance, sales, distribution, and so on. What's left over (if anything) is **profit**. Managers usually strive to charge a price that will earn a fair profit.

To earn a profit, managers must choose a price that is not too high or too low, a price that equals the perceived value to target consumers. If, in consumers' minds, a price is set too high, the perceived value will be less than the cost, and sales opportunities will be lost. Many mainstream purchasers of cars, sporting goods, CDs, tools, wedding gowns, and computers are buying "used or pre-owned" items to get a better deal. Pricing a new product too high gives some shoppers an incentive to go to a "pre-owned" or consignment retailer. Lost sales mean lost revenue. Conversely, if a price is too low, the consumer might perceive it as a great value, but the firm loses revenue it could have earned.

Trying to set the right price is one of the most stressful and pressure-filled tasks of the marketing manager, as trends in the consumer market attest:

→ Confronting a flood of new products, potential buyers carefully evaluate the price of each one against the value of existing products.

→ The increased availability of bargain-priced private and generic brands has put downward pressure on overall prices.

→ Many firms are trying to maintain or regain their market share by cutting prices. For example, IKEA has gained market share in the furniture industry by aggressively cutting prices.

→ The Internet has made comparison shopping easier.

→ The United States was in a recession from late 2007 until late 2009 and was still recovering very slowly in 2011.

In the organizational market, where customers include both governments and businesses, buyers are also becoming more price sensitive and better informed. Computerized information systems enable the organizational buyer to compare price and performance with great ease and accuracy. Improved communication and the increased use of direct marketing and computer-aided selling have also opened up many markets to new competitors. Finally, competition in general is increasing, so some installations, accessories, and component parts are being marketed like indistinguishable commodities.

Review LO1 Discuss the importance of pricing decisions to the economy and to the individual firm

Price × Sales Unit − Revenue
Revenue − Costs = Profit
Profit drives growth, salary increases, and corporate investment.

© Cengage Learning 2013

LO2
Pricing Objectives

To survive in today's highly competitive marketplace, companies need pricing objectives that are specific, attainable, and measurable. Realistic pricing goals then require monitoring to determine the effectiveness of the company's strategy. For convenience, pricing objectives can be divided into three categories: profit oriented, sales oriented, and status quo.

PROFIT-ORIENTED PRICING OBJECTIVES

Profit-oriented objectives include profit maximization, satisfactory profits, and target return on investment. A brief discussion of each of these objectives follows.

profit
Revenue minus expenses.

Profit Maximization Profit maximization means setting prices so that total revenue is as large as possible relative to total costs. (A more theoretically precise definition and explanation of profit maximization appears later in the chapter.) Profit maximization does not always signify unreasonably high prices, however. Both price and profits depend on the type of competitive environment a firm faces, such as whether it is in a monopoly position (being the only seller) or in a much more competitive situation. Also, remember that a firm cannot charge a price higher than the product's perceived value. Many firms do not have the accounting data they need for maximizing profits. It is easy to say that a company should keep producing and selling goods or services as long as revenues exceed costs. Yet it is often hard to set up an accounting system that can accurately determine the point of profit maximization.

Sometimes managers say that their company is trying to maximize profits—in other words, trying to make as much money as possible. Although this goal might sound impressive to stockholders, it is not good enough for planning. The statement "We want to make all the money we can" is vague and lacks focus. It gives management license to do just about anything it wants to do.

In attempting to maximize profits, managers can try to expand revenue by increasing customer satisfaction, or they can attempt to reduce costs by operating more efficiently. A third possibility is to attempt to do both. Research has shown that striving to enhance customer satisfaction leads to greater profitability (and customer satisfaction) than following a cost reduction strategy or attempting to do both.[4] This means that companies should consider allocating more resources to customer service initiatives, loyalty programs, and customer relationship management programs and allocating fewer resources to programs that are designed to improve efficiency and reduce costs. Both types of programs, of course, are critical to the success of the firm.

Satisfactory Profits Satisfactory profits are a reasonable level of profits. Rather than maximizing profits, many organizations strive for profits that are satisfactory to the stockholders and management—in other words, a level of profits consistent with the level of risk an organization faces. In a risky industry, a satisfactory profit might be 35 percent. In a low-risk industry, it might be 7 percent. To maximize profits, a small-business owner might have to keep his or her store open seven days a week. However, the owner might not want to work that hard and might be satisfied with less profit.

Target Return on Investment The most common profit objective is a target **return on investment (ROI)**, sometimes called the firm's *return on total assets*. ROI measures management's overall effectiveness in generating profits with the available assets. The higher the firm's ROI, the better off the firm is. Many companies—including DuPont, Procter & Gamble, Navistar, ExxonMobil, and Union Carbide—use a target ROI as their main pricing goal. In summary, ROI is a percentage that puts a firm's profits into perspective by showing profits relative to investment.

Return on investment is calculated as follows:

$$\text{Return on investment} = \frac{\text{Net profits after taxes}}{\text{Total assets}}$$

Assume that in 2012 Johnson Controls had assets of $4.5 million, net profits of $550,000, and a target ROI of 10 percent. This was the actual ROI:

$$\text{ROI} = \frac{\$550,000}{\$4,500,000}$$

$$= 12.2 \text{ percent}$$

return on investment (ROI)
Net profit after taxes divided by total assets.

As you can see, the ROI for Johnson Controls exceeded its target, which indicates that the company prospered in 2012.

Comparing the 12.2 percent ROI with the industry average provides a more meaningful picture, however. Any ROI needs to be evaluated in terms of the competitive environment, risks in the industry, and economic conditions. Generally speaking, firms seek ROIs in the 10 to 30 percent range. For example, General Electric seeks a 25 percent ROI, whereas Alcoa, Rubbermaid, and most major pharmaceutical companies strive for a 20 percent ROI. In some industries such as the grocery industry, however, a return of under 5 percent is common and acceptable.

A company with a target ROI can predetermine its desired level of profitability. The marketing manager can use the standard, such as 10 percent ROI, to determine whether a particular price and marketing mix are feasible. In addition, however, the manager must weigh the risk of a given strategy even if the return is in the acceptable range.

SALES-ORIENTED PRICING OBJECTIVES

Sales-oriented pricing objectives are based either on market share or on dollar or unit sales. The effective marketing manager should be familiar with these pricing objectives.

Market Share Market share is a company's product sales as a percentage of total sales for that industry. Sales can be reported in dollars or in units of product. It is very important to know whether market share is expressed in revenue or units because the results might be different. Consider four companies competing in an industry with 2,000 total unit sales and total industry revenue of $4 million. (See Exhibit 19.1.) Company A has the largest unit market share at 50 percent, but it has only 25 percent of the revenue market share. In contrast, company D has only a 15 percent unit share but the largest revenue share: 30 percent. Usually, market share is expressed in terms of revenue and not units.

Many companies believe that maintaining or increasing market share is an indicator of the effectiveness of their marketing mix. Larger market shares have indeed often meant higher profits, thanks to greater economies of scale, market power, and ability to compensate top-quality management. Conventional wisdom also says that market share and return on investment are strongly related. For the most part they are; however, many companies with low market share survive and even prosper. To succeed with a low market share, companies need to compete in industries with slow growth and few product changes—for instance, industrial component parts and supplies. Otherwise, they must vie in an industry that makes frequently bought items, such as consumer convenience goods.

The conventional wisdom about market share and profitability isn't always reliable, however. Because of extreme competition in some industries, many market

market share
A company's product sales as a percentage of total sales for that industry.

Exhibit 19.1 Two Ways to Measure Market Share (Units and Revenue)

Company	Units Sold	Unit Price	Total Revenue	Unit Market Share	Revenue Market Share
A	1,000	$1.00	$1,000	50%	25%
B	200	4.00	800	10	20
C	500	2.00	1,000	25	25
D	300	4.00	1,200	15	30
Total	2,000		$4,000		

© Cengage Learning 2013

© AP Images/Kiichiro Sato

share leaders either do not reach their target ROI or actually lose money. Freightliner, a manufacturer of heavy trucks, aggressively fought for market share gains during the past decade. Though Freightliner grew to become the market leader with a 36 percent market share, its profits suffered. It lost hundreds of millions of dollars and slashed 8,000 jobs in an effort to cut costs.[5] The personal computer and food industries have also had this problem. Procter & Gamble switched from market share to ROI objectives after realizing that profits don't automatically follow from a large market share. PepsiCo says its new Pepsi challenge is to be number one in share of industry profit, not in share of sales volume.

Still, the struggle for market share can be all-consuming for some companies. Kroger, the large food chain, is focusing on sales gains and not increasing profits. In 2009, the grocer increased its national market share by 0.5 percent, which translated into $1 billion in new revenue. Kroger Chief Executive David Dillon noted, "We are not opposed to having higher gross profits but fattening profits could cost Kroger shoppers and reduce brand equity."[6] (See Chapter 10.) Kroger expects to benefit from shopper loyalty as the economy improves. Research organizations such as Nielsen and Symphony IRI Group provide excellent market share reports for many different industries. These reports enable companies to track their performance in various product categories over time.

Sales Maximization Rather than strive for market share, sometimes companies try to maximize sales. A firm with the objective of maximizing sales ignores profits, competition, and the marketing environment as long as sales are rising.

If a company is strapped for funds or faces an uncertain future, it might try to generate a maximum amount of cash in the short run. Management's task when using this objective is to calculate which price-quantity relationship generates the greatest cash revenue. Sales maximization can also be effectively used on a temporary basis to sell off excess inventory. It is not uncommon to find Christmas cards, ornaments, and other seasonal items discounted at 50 to 70 percent off retail prices after the holiday season. In addition, management can use sales maximization for year-end sales to clear out old models before introducing the new ones.

Maximization of cash should never be a long-run objective because cash maximization might mean little or no profitability. Without profits, a company cannot survive.

STATUS QUO PRICING OBJECTIVES

Status quo pricing seeks to maintain existing prices or to meet the competition's prices. This third category of pricing objectives has the major advantage of requiring little planning. It is essentially a passive policy.

Often firms competing in an industry that has an established price leader simply meet the competition's prices. These industries typically have fewer price wars than those with direct price competition. In other cases, managers regularly shop competitors' stores to ensure that their prices are comparable. For example, Target's middle managers might visit competing Walmart stores to compare prices and then make adjustments.

status quo pricing
A pricing objective that maintains existing prices or meets the competition's prices.

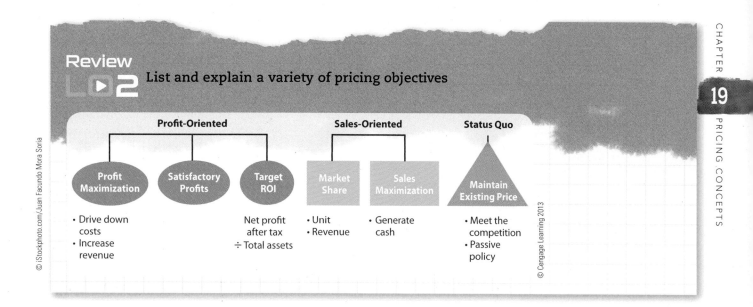

Profit-Oriented

Sales-Oriented

Status Quo

| Profit Maximization | Satisfactory Profits | Target ROI | Market Share | Sales Maximization | Maintain Existing Price |

- Drive down costs
- Increase revenue

Net profit after tax ÷ Total assets

- Unit
- Revenue

- Generate cash

- Meet the competition
- Passive policy

© Cengage Learning 2013

Status quo pricing often leads to suboptimal pricing. This is because the strategy ignores perceived customer value of both the firm's and its competitors' perceived value of the goods and services offered. Status quo pricing also ignores demand and costs. While the policy is simple to implement, it can lead to a pricing disaster.

LO3

The Demand Determinant of Price

After marketing managers establish pricing goals, they must set specific prices to reach those goals. The price they set for each product depends mostly on two factors: the demand for the good or service and the cost to the seller for that good or service. When pricing goals are mainly sales oriented, demand considerations usually dominate. Other factors, such as distribution and promotion strategies, perceived quality, demands of large customers, the Internet, and stage of the product life cycle, can also influence price.

THE NATURE OF DEMAND

Demand is the quantity of a product that will be sold in the market at various prices for a specified period. The quantity of a product that people will buy depends on its price. The higher the price, the fewer goods or services consumers will demand. Conversely, the lower the price, the more goods or services they will demand.

This trend is illustrated in Exhibit 19.2(a), which graphs the demand per week for fruit smoothies at a local retailer at various prices. This graph is called a *demand curve*. The vertical axis of the graph shows different prices of fruit smoothies, measured in dollars per package. The horizontal axis measures the quantity of fruit smoothies that will be demanded per week at each price. For example, at a price of $2.50, 50 smoothies will be sold per week; at $1.00, consumers will demand 120 smoothies—as the demand schedule in Exhibit 19.2(b) shows.

demand
The quantity of a product that will be sold in the market at various prices for a specified period.

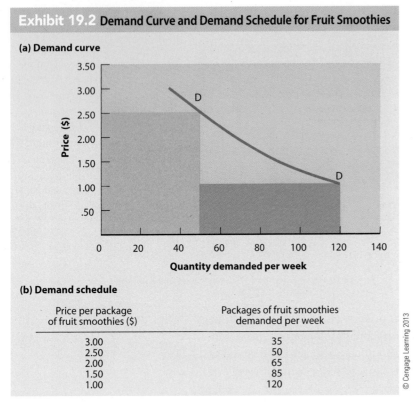

Exhibit 19.2 Demand Curve and Demand Schedule for Fruit Smoothies

(a) Demand curve

Price ($) vs. Quantity demanded per week

(b) Demand schedule

Price per package of fruit smoothies ($)	Packages of fruit smoothies demanded per week
3.00	35
2.50	50
2.00	65
1.50	85
1.00	120

© Cengage Learning 2013

supply

The quantity of a product that will be offered to the market by a supplier at various prices for a specified period.

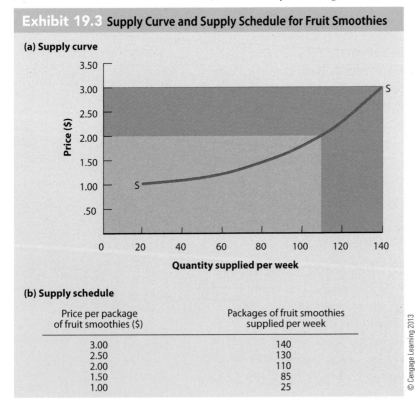

Exhibit 19.3 Supply Curve and Supply Schedule for Fruit Smoothies

(a) Supply curve

Price ($) vs. Quantity supplied per week

(b) Supply schedule

Price per package of fruit smoothies ($)	Packages of fruit smoothies supplied per week
3.00	140
2.50	130
2.00	110
1.50	85
1.00	25

© Cengage Learning 2013

The demand curve in Exhibit 19.2 slopes downward and to the right, which indicates that more fruit smoothies are demanded as the price is lowered. In other words, if smoothie makers put a greater quantity on the market, then their hope of selling all of it will be realized only by selling it at a lower price.

One reason more is sold at lower prices than at higher prices is that lower prices bring in new buyers. This fact might not be so obvious with fruit smoothies, but consider the example of steak. As the price of steak drops lower and lower, some people who have not been eating steak will probably start buying it rather than hamburger. With each reduction in price, existing customers might also buy extra amounts. Similarly, if the price of smoothies falls low enough, some people will buy more than they have bought in the past.

Supply is the quantity of a product that will be offered to the market by a supplier or suppliers at various prices for a specified period. Exhibit 19.3(a) illustrates the resulting supply curve for fruit smoothies. Unlike the falling demand curve, the supply curve for smoothies slopes upward and to the right. At higher prices, smoothie makers will obtain more resources (apples, peaches, strawberries) and make more smoothies. If the price consumers are willing to pay for smoothies increases, producers can afford to buy more ingredients.

Output tends to increase at higher prices because a smoothie shop can sell more smoothies and earn greater profits. The supply schedule in Exhibit 19.3(b) shows that at $2 suppliers are willing to place 110 smoothies on the market, but that they will offer 140 drinks at a price of $3.

HOW DEMAND AND SUPPLY ESTABLISH PRICES

At this point, let's combine the concepts of demand and supply to see how competitive market prices are determined. So far, the premise is that if the price is X, then consumers will purchase Y amount of smoothie. How high or low will prices actually go? How many drinks will be produced? How many will be consumed? The demand curve cannot predict consumption, nor can the supply curve alone forecast production. Instead, we need to look at what happens when supply and demand interact—as shown in Exhibit 19.4.

At a price of $3, the public would demand only 35 smoothies. However, suppliers stand ready to place 140 smoothies on the market at this price (data from the demand and supply schedules). If they do, they would create a surplus of 105 smoothies. How does a merchant eliminate a surplus? It lowers the price.

At a price of $1, 120 smoothies would be demanded, but only 25 would be placed on the market. A shortage of 95 units would be created. If a product is in short supply and consumers want it, how do they entice the seller to part with one unit? They offer more money—that is, pay a higher price.

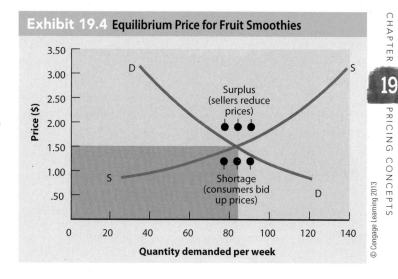

Exhibit 19.4 Equilibrium Price for Fruit Smoothies

Now let's examine a price of $1.50. At this price, 85 smoothies are demanded and 85 are supplied. When demand and supply are equal, a state called **price equilibrium** is achieved. A temporary price below equilibrium—say, $1.00—results in a shortage because at that price the demand for fruit smoothies is greater than the available supply. Shortages put upward pressure on price. As long as demand and supply remain the same, however, temporary price increases or decreases tend to return to equilibrium. At equilibrium, there is no inclination for prices to rise or fall.

An equilibrium price may not be reached all at once. Prices may fluctuate during a trial-and-error period as the market for a good or service moves toward equilibrium. Sooner or later, however, demand and supply will settle into proper balance.

ELASTICITY OF DEMAND

To appreciate demand analysis, you should understand the concept of elasticity. **Elasticity of demand** refers to consumers' responsiveness or sensitivity to changes in price. **Elastic demand** occurs when consumers buy more or less of a product when the price changes. Conversely, **inelastic demand** means that an increase or a decrease in price will not significantly affect demand for the product.

Elasticity over the range of a demand curve can be measured by using this formula:

$$\text{Elasticity (E)} = \frac{\text{Percentage change in quantity demanded of good A}}{\text{Percentage change in price of good A}}$$

If E is greater than 1, demand is elastic.
If E is less than 1, demand is inelastic.
If E is equal to 1, demand is unitary.

Unitary elasticity means that an increase in sales exactly offsets a decrease in prices, so total revenue remains the same.

Elasticity can be measured by observing these changes in total revenue:

If price goes down and revenue goes up, demand is elastic.
If price goes down and revenue goes down, demand is inelastic.
If price goes up and revenue goes up, demand is inelastic.
If price goes up and revenue goes down, demand is elastic.
If price goes up or down and revenue stays the same, elasticity is unitary.

price equilibrium
The price at which demand and supply are equal.

elasticity of demand
Consumers' responsiveness or sensitivity to changes in price.

elastic demand
A situation in which consumer demand is sensitive to changes in price.

inelastic demand
A situation in which an increase or a decrease in price will not significantly affect demand for the product.

unitary elasticity
A situation in which total revenue remains the same when prices change.

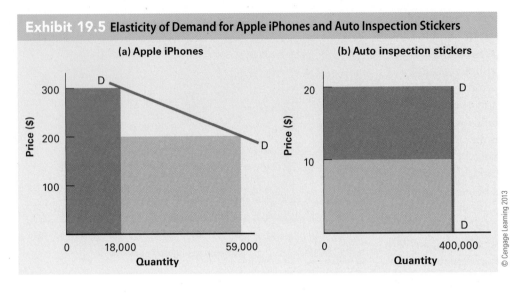

Exhibit 19.5 Elasticity of Demand for Apple iPhones and Auto Inspection Stickers

(a) Apple iPhones

(b) Auto inspection stickers

Exhibit 19.5(a) shows a very elastic demand curve. Decreasing the price of Apple iPads from $300 to $200 increases sales from 18,000 units to 59,000 units. Revenue increases from $5.4 million ($300 × 18,000) to $11.8 million ($200 × 59,000). The price decrease results in a large increase in sales and revenue.

Exhibit 19.5(b) shows a completely inelastic demand curve.

The state of Nevada dropped its used-car vehicle inspection fee from $20 to $10. The state continued to inspect about 400,000 used cars annually. Decreasing the price (inspection fee) 50 percent did not cause people to buy more used cars. Demand is completely inelastic for inspection fees, which are required by law. Thus, it also follows that Nevada could double the original fee to $40 and double the state's inspection revenues. People won't stop buying used cars if the inspection fee increases—within a reasonable range.

Exhibit 19.6 presents the demand curve and demand schedule for three-ounce bottles of Spring Break suntan lotion. Let's follow the demand curve from the highest price to the lowest and examine what happens to elasticity as the price decreases.

Inelastic Demand The initial decrease in the price of Spring Break suntan lotion from $5.00 to $2.25 results in a decrease in total revenue of $969 ($5,075–$4,106). When price and total revenue fall, demand is inelastic. The decrease in price is much greater than the increase in suntan lotion sales (810 bottles). Demand is therefore not very flexible in the price range $5.00 to $2.25.

When demand is inelastic, sellers can raise prices and increase total revenue. Often items that are relatively inexpensive but convenient tend to have inelastic demand.

Elastic Demand In the example of Spring Break suntan lotion, shown in Exhibit 19.6, when the price is dropped from $2.25 to $1.00, total revenue increases by $679 ($4,785–$4,106). An increase in total revenue when price falls indicates that demand is elastic. Let's measure Spring

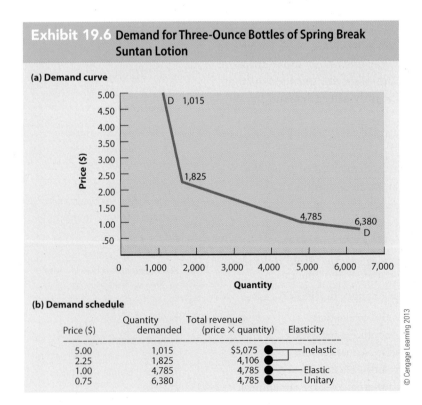

Exhibit 19.6 Demand for Three-Ounce Bottles of Spring Break Suntan Lotion

(a) Demand curve

(b) Demand schedule

Price ($)	Quantity demanded	Total revenue (price × quantity)	Elasticity
5.00	1,015	$5,075	Inelastic
2.25	1,825	4,106	
1.00	4,785	4,785	Elastic
0.75	6,380	4,785	Unitary

© Cengage Learning 2013

Break's elasticity of demand when the price drops from \$2.25 to \$1.00 by applying the formula presented earlier:

$$E = \frac{\text{Change in quantity/(Sum of quantities/2)}}{\text{Change in price/(Sum of prices/2)}}$$

$$= \frac{(4{,}785 - 1{,}825)/[(1{,}825 + 4{,}785)/2]}{(2.25 - 1.00)/[(2.25 + 1.00)/2]}$$

$$= \frac{2{,}960/3{,}305}{1.25/1.63}$$

$$= \frac{.896}{.769}$$

$$= 51.17$$

Because E is greater than 1, demand is elastic.

Factors That Affect Elasticity Several factors affect elasticity of demand, including the following:

→ **Availability of substitutes:** When many substitute products are available, the consumer can easily switch from one product to another, making demand elastic. The same is true in reverse: A person with complete renal failure will pay whatever is charged for a kidney transplant because there is no substitute. Interestingly, Bose stereo equipment is priced 300 to 500 percent higher than other stereo brands, yet consumers are willing to pay the price because they perceive the equipment as being so superior to other brands that there is no acceptable substitute.

→ **Price relative to purchasing power:** If a price is so low that it is an inconsequential part of an individual's budget, demand will be inelastic. For example, if the price of salt doubles, consumers will not stop putting salt and pepper on their eggs because salt is cheap anyway.

→ **Product durability:** Consumers often have the option of repairing durable products rather than replacing them, thus prolonging their useful life. If a person plans to buy a new car and prices suddenly begin to rise, he or she might elect to fix the old car and drive it for another year. In other words, people are sensitive to the price increase, and demand is elastic.

→ **A product's other uses:** The greater the number of different uses for a product, the more elastic demand tends to be. If a product has only one use, as may be true of a new medicine, the quantity purchased probably will not vary as price varies. A person will consume only the prescribed quantity, regardless of price. On the other hand, a product such as steel has many possible applications. As its price falls, steel becomes more economically feasible in a wider variety of applications, thereby making demand relatively elastic.

→ **Rate of inflation:** Recent research has found that when a country's inflation rate (the rate at which the price level is rising) is high, demand becomes more elastic. In other words, rising price levels make consumers more price sensitive. The research also found that during inflationary periods consumers base their timing (when to buy) and quantity decisions on price promotions. This suggests that a brand gains additional sales or market share if the product is effectively promoted or if the marketing manager keeps the brand's price increases low relative to the inflation rate.[7]

Examples of both elastic and inelastic demand abound in everyday life. Recently, fans balked at high prices for concerts. Promoters lost money and some shows, including some by artists Christina Aguilera and Marc Anthony, were canceled. This is price elasticity in action. On the other hand, demand for some tickets

© A3615 Patrick Lux Deutsch Presse Agentur/Newscom

was highly inelastic. The Rolling Stones are still selling out concerts with tickets priced at up to $400. Garden Fresh Restaurant Corporation is a soup and salad buffet restaurant chain with 118 locations in the United States. The chain has not raised prices since 2008. "The concern right now [late 2011] is that we would drive away more people than what we would gain from the price increase," said CEO Michael Mack.[8] In other words, the CEO is saying that he believes demand is elastic—an increase in price will result in lower total revenues.

Elasticity also comes into play in public policy decisions. For example, will raising the price of electricity result in increased conservation of power? Many policy makers feel that demand is highly inelastic. That is, rich people can afford to use as much as they want regardless of price and poor people would still need electricity to live, so raising the price would just make them poorer. Sometimes elasticity can be inferred from naturally occurring experiments. New York City electric rates provide an example. About 1.75 million New York apartments have metered electricity, paying an average of 21 cents per kilowatt hour, among the highest rates in the nation. At the same time, about 250,000 older apartments have unlimited, unmetered electric power included in the rent. Is demand infinite when the good is free? Demand is greater in unmetered apartments. Some people do use electricity very wastefully, for example, running their air conditioners full blast while they are at work so that their cats will be comfortable. Still, demand does not increase without limit. Electric use is only about 30 percent higher in unmetered apartments than metered ones. And yes, charging for electricity does provide an effective incentive for conservation.[9]

The United States Surgeon General's office has recently issued a report summarizing a number of studies that have examined elasticity of demand for cigarettes. While the estimates differ some, the difference of elasticity between adults and youth smokers is significant. For example, one report focused on recent increases in federal taxes on cigarettes and chewing tobacco. It found that a 10 percent rise in cigarette prices resulted in a 7 percent drop in smoking among youth and a 4 percent drop among adults. Demand is more inelastic among adults. Why? Perhaps youths are less addicted than adult long-term smokers. Also, young people generally have less disposable income than adults. The relative inelasticity among adults indicates that raising taxes puts more money in government coffers.[10]

Pricing Power For many companies most pricing power vanished long ago. A lack of pricing power means that when a company tries to raise its prices, it loses sales volume as customers shift to low cost competitors or find a substitute product. Ultimately, many of these companies have had to lower prices again—sometimes dropping them even further than they were before the attempted price increase—in an effort to recapture lost share.

In contrast, pricing power means making a price increase stick. It means that demand is relatively inelastic for the product. How does a firm gain pricing power? One strategy is to produce something radically new, and most importantly, better than the competition. Eric Soule had been waiting 15 months for this moment. The semiconductor engineer was about to launch a new chip, and he needed his pricing approved. In a conference room at Linear Technology Corp., Mr. Soule anxiously explained why his amplifier chip is so advanced that it should sell for $1.68, a third more than its rivals. His bosses' reaction: Charge even more. The chip is 20 times better than the competition, they asserted, and high-end customers will crave it on any terms. Why not boost the $1.68 list price by 10 cents? Mr. Soule was nervous. "I can live with that," he guardedly replied, "but what does that accomplish?"

"It's a dime!" declared Linear's chairman and founder, Robert Swanson. "And those dimes add up."[11] The moral of the story is: If you have pricing power, use it because it doesn't last forever.

Parker Hannifin Corporation, a manufacturer of over 800,000 different parts—from heat resistant seals for jet engines to steel valves for hoist buckets—took a different approach to find pricing power. Initially, no matter how much a product improved, the company ended up charging the same markup it would for a more standard product. And if the company found a way to make a product less expensively, it ultimately cut the product's price as well. Hannifin's President, Donald Washkewicz, knew that there must be a better way. He analyzed the product line searching for items that would offer pricing power. Remember, pricing power is all about perceived value to the customer. Not only must the customer believe that the product will deliver high value, but it also must do so at a price that will cause the customer to buy it. Generally speaking, the greater the perceived value, the greater the pricing power. But pricing power has a ceiling. If the item is priced too high, then the sale is lost. This is illustrated in Hannifin's new strategy outlined in Exhibit 19.7. In core products, without pricing power, prices were actually dropped. Those with the greatest perceived value and having the highest inelasticity of demand received the largest price increase. The new strategy increased revenue by $200 million.[12]

Exhibit 19.7 Parker Hannifin's Strategy to Create Pricing Power

Product Categories	Pricing Strategy Rationale	Price Increase (%)
Core products	Basic commodity in high volume with market competition	−3–5
Partially differentiated products (A)	Some differentiation to core product that meets wider market's needs in competitive market	0–5
Partially differentiated products (B)	Some differentiation to product or niche product with little or no market competition	0–9
System or differentiated products	Custom engineering to customer specifications that improves customer's productivity and profitability; some market competition	0–25
Classic or special products	Custom-designed or unique product with no market competition	>25

Source: Adapted from Timothy Aeppel's *Wall Street Journal* article, "Seeking Perfect Prices, CEO Tears Up the Rules," March 27, 2007, James Sagar's article "Pricing Strategy: Capture More Revenue," Marketing M.O. Consulting, online at **http://www.marketingmo.com**, March 27, 2007, and Parker Hannifin Corporation, online at **http://www.parker.com**, accessed June 30, 2007.

The Problem

A multi-billionaire has decided to venture into the soft-drink market by introducing a new grape soda. As he thinks about how many production facilities to build, how many delivery trucks to buy, and how much raw material the bottling plants will need, he realizes that he will first have to understand how large the market for grape soda is. If there are 310 million Americans, is the relevant market size 310 million? That is, should the fledgling soda bottler expect every single American to purchase his grape soda? Men and women alike? Rich and poor alike? Babies and retirees alike? That would be a ridiculous claim whether we're talking about luxury cars, heavy earth-moving machinery, or, in this case, grape soda. Consequently, he charges his marketing manager to estimate the demand for his product because the demand will inform production strategy, distribution requirements, shelf space, promotional intensity, sales force size, and almost every other dimension of a company.

To estimate demand, marketers collect the relevant facts available, make a few assumptions concerning how the facts are related, and use the assumptions and facts to calculate demand estimates. Many times, the assumptions can be expressed in the form of ratios. Demand estimates generated with ratio expressions of assumptions are often called the "chain ratio method." The chain ratio method is highly flexible and can be used in a number of situations.

The Metric

To calculate the demand estimate for grape soda, the marketer begins with two facts: (1) the market consists of 310 million people; (2) a person in that market buys 50 sodas a month on average.

With these facts, the marketer can now estimate the overall annual demand for all soda using the chain ratio. Expressing the average demand as a ratio and the relationship between months and years as a ratio, we find from the chain ratio method the following facts.

$$\frac{50 \text{ sodas}}{\text{person} - \text{month}} \cdot \frac{12 \text{ months}}{\text{year}}$$
$$\times \ 310 \text{ million people} = \frac{186 \text{ billion sodas}}{\text{year}}$$

The marketer has now determined that the overall market for sodas is 186 billion sodas per year. (To convert millions into billions, recall one million equals 1,000,000 and one billion equals 1,000,000,000.)

The marketer must also determine how much of this overall market grape soda occupies. Suppose the overall market for sodas can be broken down into categories and market shares of colas (54 percent), lemon-lime (12 percent), orange (4 percent), mixers (2 percent), Dr. Pepper (7 percent), and other (23 percent). Furthermore, suppose grape sodas constitute only 10 percent of the "other" category.

Given these expectations, the marketer can continue use the chain ratio method again to estimate demand for his brand of sodas.

(186 billion sodas nationally)/year
$\times$ (23% other sodas)/(all sodas)
$\times$ (10% grape soda)/(all specialty sodas)

After converting percents to decimals (divide each percent by 100), the calculation looks like:

(186,000,000,000)(0.23)(0.1)
= 4,278,000,000

The marketer can therefore estimate sales of grape soda at 4.3 billion units per year.

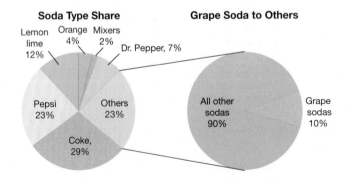

Soda Type Share

Lemon lime 12% · Orange 4% · Mixers 2% · Dr. Pepper, 7% · Pepsi 23% · Others 23% · Coke, 29%

Grape Soda to Others

All other sodas 90% · Grape sodas 10%

(Continued)

Management Decision

Based on the chain ratio above, the marketer determined that grape soda is a large 4.3 billion soda industry. However, the marketer also knows that his company won't take the entire market. By using the chain ratio method, he will also need to look at geographic share (based on the size of the company's distribution) and brand share (determined by market research). By examining several different marketing mixes and doing marketing research, the firm can effectively estimate the demand for the firm's soda.

In general, the more specific marketers can be in identifying their target market, the more accurate their forecast of demand will be. Moreover, by clearly defining the target market, the marketer can better define the product strategy, pricing strategy, placement strategy, and promotion strategy necessary to profitably capture their target market.

Review

LO3 Explain the role of demand in price determination

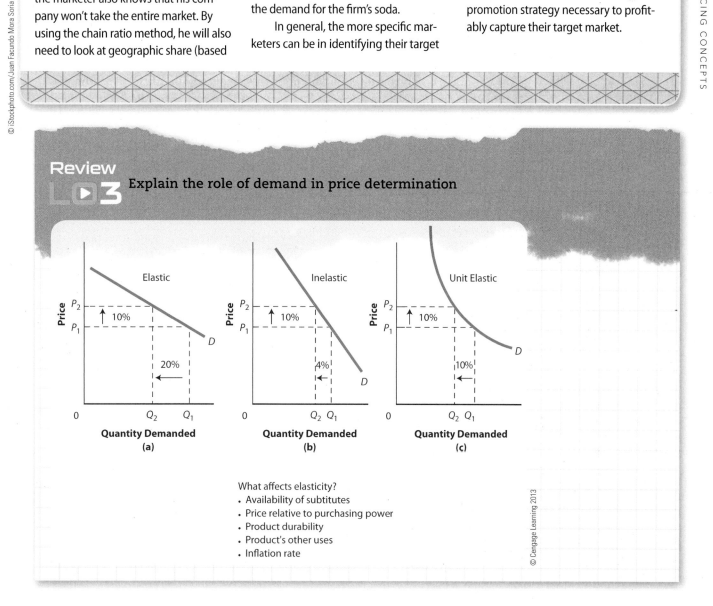

What affects elasticity?
- Availability of subtitutes
- Price relative to purchasing power
- Product durability
- Product's other uses
- Inflation rate

© Cengage Learning 2013

LO4
The Power of Yield Management Systems and Targeting Technology

Another important tool for gaining pricing power is the yield management system, also known as a revenue management system. More and more companies are turning to yield management systems to help fine-tune prices. First

© iStockphoto.com/Juan Facundo Mora Soria

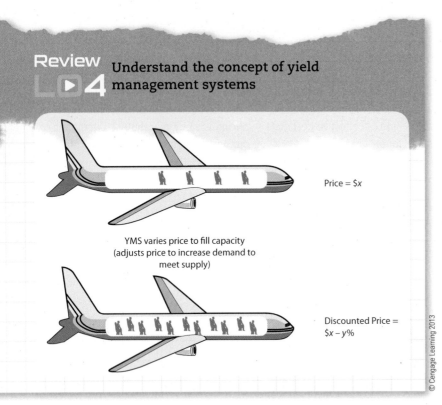

Price = $x

YMS varies price to fill capacity (adjusts price to increase demand to meet supply)

Discounted Price = $x − y%

© Cengage Learning 2013

developed in the airline industry, **yield management systems (YMSs)** use complex mathematical software to profitably fill unused capacity. The software employs techniques such as discounting early purchases, limiting early sales at these discounted prices, and overbooking capacity. One of the key inputs in airlines' yield management systems is what has been the historical pattern of demand for a specific flight. YMSs now are appearing in other services such as lodging, other transportation forms, rental firms, retailers, and even hospitals.

Yield management systems are spreading beyond service industries as their popularity increases. The lessons of airlines and hotels aren't entirely applicable to other industries, however, because plane seats and hotel beds are perishable—if they go empty, the revenue opportunity is lost forever. So it makes sense to slash prices to move toward capacity if it's possible to do so without reducing the prices that other customers pay. Cars and steel aren't so perishable. Still, the capacity to make these goods is perishable. An underused factory or mill is a lost revenue opportunity. So it makes sense to cut prices to use up capacity if it's possible to do so while getting other customers to pay full price. Royal Caribbean Cruises uses its yield management system to adjust hundreds of prices through the course of a day.

LO 5
The Cost Determinant of Price

Sometimes companies minimize or ignore the importance of demand and decide to price their products largely or solely on the basis of costs. Prices determined strictly on the basis of costs might be too high for the target market, thereby reducing or eliminating sales. On the other hand, cost-based prices might be too low, causing the firm to earn a lower return than it should. Nevertheless, costs should generally be part of any price determination, if only as a floor below which a good or service must not be priced in the long run.

The idea of cost might seem simple, but it is actually a multifaceted concept, especially for producers of goods and services. A **variable cost** is a cost that varies with changes in the level of output; an example of a variable cost is the cost of materials. In contrast, a **fixed cost** does not change as output is increased or decreased. Examples include rent and executives' salaries.

To compare the cost of production to the selling price of a product, it is helpful to calculate costs per unit, or average costs. **Average variable cost (AVC)**

---

yield management systems (YMS)
A technique for adjusting prices that uses complex mathematical software to profitably fill unused capacity by discounting early purchases, limiting early sales at these discounted prices, and overbooking capacity.

variable cost
A cost that varies with changes in the level of output.

fixed cost
A cost that does not change as output is increased or decreased.

average variable cost (AVC)
Total variable costs divided by quantity of output.

equals total variable costs divided by quantity of output. **Average total cost (ATC)** equals total costs divided by output. As the graph in Exhibit 19.8(a) shows, AVC and ATC are basically U-shaped curves. In contrast, average fixed cost (AFC) declines continually as output increases because total fixed costs are constant.

Marginal cost (MC) is the change in total costs associated with a one-unit change in output. Exhibit 19.8(b) shows that when output rises from seven to eight units, the change in total cost is from $640 to $750; therefore, marginal cost is $110.

Exhibit 19.8 Hypothetical Set of Cost Curves and a Cost Schedule

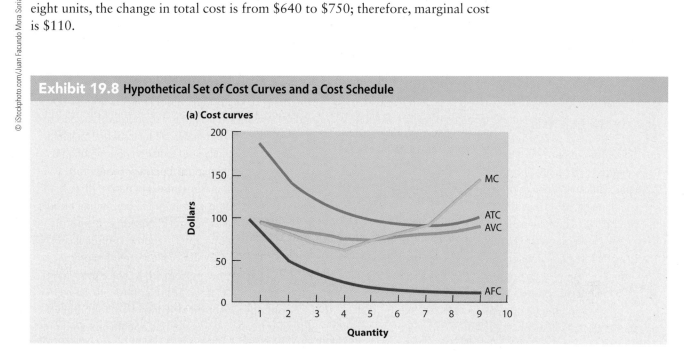

(a) Cost curves

(b) Cost schedule

	Total-cost data, per week			Average-cost data, per week			
(1) Total product (Q)	**(2)** Total fixed cost (TFC)	**(3)** Total variable cost (TVC)	**(4)** Total cost (TC)	**(5)** Average fixed cost (AFC)	**(6)** Average variable cost (AVC)	**(7)** Average total cost (ATC)	**(8)** Marginal cost (MC)
			$TC = TFC + TVC$	$AFC = \dfrac{TFC}{Q}$	$AVC = \dfrac{TVC}{Q}$	$ATC = \dfrac{TC}{Q}$	$MC = \dfrac{\text{change in TC}}{\text{change in Q}}$
0	$100	$ 0	$ 100	—	—	—	—
1	100	90	190	$100.00	$90.00	$190.00	$ 90
2	100	170	270	50.00	85.00	135.00	80
3	100	240	340	33.33	80.00	113.33	70
4	100	300	400	25.00	75.00	100.00	60
5	100	370	470	20.00	74.00	94.00	70
6	100	450	550	16.67	75.00	91.67	80
7	100	540	640	14.29	77.14	91.43	90
8	100	650	750	12.50	81.25	93.75	110
9	100	780	880	11.11	86.67	97.78	130
10	100	930	1,030	10.00	93.00	103.00	150

All the curves illustrated in Exhibit 19.8(a) have definite relationships:

→ AVC plus AFC equals ATC.

→ MC falls for a while and then turns upward, in this case with the fourth unit. At that point diminishing returns set in, meaning that less output is produced for every additional dollar spent on variable input.

→ MC intersects both AVC and ATC at their lowest possible points.

→ When MC is less than AVC or ATC, the incremental cost will continue to pull the averages down. Conversely, when MC is greater than AVC or ATC, it pulls the averages up, and ATC and AVC begin to rise.

→ The minimum point on the ATC curve is the least cost point for a fixed-capacity firm, although it is not necessarily the most profitable point.

Costs can be used to set prices in a variety of ways. For example, markup pricing is relatively simple. Profit maximization pricing and break-even pricing make use of the more complicated concepts of cost.

MARKUP PRICING

Markup pricing, the most popular method used by wholesalers and retailers to establish a selling price, does not directly analyze the costs of production. Instead, markup pricing uses the cost of buying the product from the producer, plus amounts for profit and for expenses not otherwise accounted for. The total determines the selling price.

A retailer, for example, adds a certain percentage to the cost of the merchandise received to arrive at the retail price. An item that costs the retailer $1.80 and is sold for $2.20 carries a markup of 40 cents, which is a markup of 22 percent of the cost ($.40 ÷ $1.80). Retailers tend to discuss markup in terms of its percentage of the retail price—in this example, 18 percent ($.40 ÷ $2.20). The difference between the retailer's cost and the selling price (40 cents) is the gross margin, as Chapter 15 explained.

$$\text{Retail price} = \frac{\text{Cost}}{1 - \text{Desired return on sales}}$$

$$= \frac{\$1.80}{1.00 - .18}$$

$$= \$2.20$$

If the retailer wants a 30 percent return, then:

$$\text{Retail price} = \frac{\$1.80}{1.00 - .30}$$

$$= \$2.57$$

The reason that retailers and others speak of markups on selling price is that many important figures in financial reports, such as gross sales and revenues, are sales figures, not cost figures.

To use markup based on cost or selling price effectively, the marketing manager must calculate an adequate gross margin—the amount added to cost to determine price. The margin must ultimately provide adequate funds to cover selling expenses and profit. Once an appropriate margin has been determined, the markup technique has the major advantage of being easy to employ. Walmart, for example, strives for a gross margin of around 16 percent. Because supermarket chains, such as Safeway and Kroger, have typically had gross margins of 24 percent, they are now finding it extremely difficult to compete with Walmart supermarkets. Walmart is now the nation's largest grocery chain.

Markups are often based on experience. For example, many small retailers mark up merchandise 100 percent over cost. (In other words, they double the cost.) This tactic is called **keystoning**. Some other factors that influence markups are the merchandise's appeal to customers, past response to the markup (an implicit demand consideration), the item's promotional value, the seasonality of the goods, their fashion appeal, the product's traditional selling price, and competition. Most retailers avoid any set markup because of such considerations as promotional value and seasonality.

PROFIT MAXIMIZATION PRICING

Producers tend to use more complicated methods of setting prices than distributors use. One is **profit maximization**, which occurs when marginal revenue equals marginal cost. You learned earlier that marginal cost is the change in total costs associated with a one-unit change in output. Similarly, **marginal revenue (MR)** is the extra revenue associated with selling an extra unit of output. As long as the revenue of the last unit produced and sold is greater than the cost of the last unit produced and sold, the firm should continue manufacturing and selling the product.

Exhibit 19.9 shows the marginal revenues and marginal costs for a hypothetical firm, using the cost data from Exhibit 19.8(b). The profit-maximizing quantity, where MR = MC, is six units. You might say, "If profit is zero, why produce the sixth unit? Why not stop at five?" In fact, you would be right. The firm, however, would not know that the fifth unit would produce zero profits until it determined that profits were no longer increasing. Economists suggest producing up to the point where MR = MC. If marginal revenue is just one penny greater than marginal costs, it will still increase total profits.

Exhibit 19.9 Point of Profit Maximization

Quantity	Marginal Revenue (MR)	Marginal Cost (MC)	Cumulative Total Profit
0	—	—	—
1	$140	$90	$50
2	130	80	100
3	105	70	135
4	95	60	170
5	85	70	185
*6	80	80	185
7	75	90	170
8	60	110	120
9	50	130	40
10	40	150	(70)

*Break-even point

© Cengage Learning 2013

BREAK-EVEN PRICING

Now let's take a closer look at the relationship between sales and cost. **Break-even analysis** determines what sales volume must be reached before the company breaks even (its total costs equal total revenue) and no profits are earned.

The typical break-even model assumes a given fixed cost and a constant average variable cost. Suppose that Universal Sportswear, a hypothetical firm, has fixed costs of $2,000 and that the cost of labor and materials for each unit produced is 50 cents. Assume that it can sell up to 6,000 units of its product at $1 without having to lower its price.

Exhibit 19.10(a) illustrates Universal Sportswear's break-even point. As Exhibit 19.10(b) indicates, Universal Sportswear's total variable costs increase by 50 cents every time a new unit is produced, and total fixed costs remain constant at $2,000 regardless of the level of output. Therefore, for 4,000 units of output, Universal Sportswear has $2,000 in fixed costs and $2,000 in total variable costs (4,000 units × $.50), or $4,000 in total costs.

Revenue is also $4,000 (4,000 units × $1), giving a net profit of zero dollars at the break-even point of 4,000 units. Notice that once the firm gets past the

keystoning
The practice of marking up prices by 100 percent, or doubling the cost.

profit maximization
A method of setting prices that occurs when marginal revenue equals marginal cost.

marginal revenue (MR)
The extra revenue associated with selling an extra unit of output or the change in total revenue with a one-unit change in output.

break-even analysis
A method of determining what sales volume must be reached before total revenue equals total costs.

(a) Break-even point

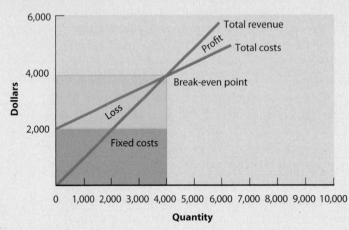

(b) Costs and revenues

Output	Total fixed costs	Average variable costs	Total variable costs	Average total costs	Average revenue (price)	Total revenue	Total costs	Profit or loss
500	$2,000	$0.50	$ 250	$4.50	$1.00	$ 500	$2,250	($1,750)
1,000	2,000	0.50	500	2.50	1.00	1,000	2,500	(1,500)
1,500	2,000	0.50	750	1.83	1.00	1,500	2,750	(1,250)
2,000	2,000	0.50	1,000	1.50	1.00	2,000	3,000	(1,000)
2,500	2,000	0.50	1,250	1.30	1.00	2,500	3,250	(750)
3,000	2,000	0.50	1,500	1.17	1.00	3,000	3,500	(500)
3,500	2,000	0.50	1,750	1.07	1.00	3,500	3,750	(250)
*4,000	2,000	0.50	2,000	1.00	1.00	4,000	4,000	0
4,500	2,000	0.50	2,250	.94	1.00	4,500	4,250	250
5,000	2,000	0.50	2,500	.90	1.00	5,000	4,500	500
5,500	2,000	0.50	2,750	.86	1.00	5,500	4,750	750
6,000	2,000	0.50	3,000	.83	1.00	6,000	5,000	1,000

*Break-even point

break-even point, the gap between total revenue and total costs gets wider and wider because both functions are assumed to be linear.

The formula for calculating break-even quantities is simple:

$$\text{Break-even quantity} = \frac{\text{Total fixed costs}}{\text{Fixed cost contribution}}$$

Fixed cost contribution is the price minus the average variable cost. Therefore, for Universal Sportswear,

$$\text{Break-even quantity} = \frac{\$2,000}{(\$1.00 - \$50)}$$

$$= \frac{\$2,000}{\$.50}$$

$$= 4,000 \text{ units}$$

The advantage of break-even analysis is that it provides a quick estimate of how much the firm must sell to break even and how much profit can be earned if a higher sales volume is obtained. If a firm is operating close to the break-even point, it might want to see what can be done to reduce costs or increase sales. Moreover, in a simple break-even analysis, it is not necessary to compute marginal costs and marginal revenues because price and average cost per unit are assumed to be constant. Also, because accounting data for marginal cost and revenue are frequently unavailable, it is convenient not to have to depend on that information.

Break-even analysis is not without several important limitations. Sometimes it is hard to know whether a cost is fixed or variable. If labor wins a tough guaranteed-employment contract, are the resulting expenses a fixed cost? Are middle-level executives' salaries fixed costs? More important than cost determination is the fact that simple break-even analysis ignores demand. How does Universal Sportswear know it can sell 4,000 units at $1? Could it sell the same 4,000 units at $2 or even $5? Obviously, this information would profoundly affect the firm's pricing decisions.

LO6
Other Determinants of Price

Other factors besides demand and costs can influence price. For example, the stages in the product life cycle, the competition, the product distribution strategy, the promotion strategy, and perceived quality can all affect pricing.

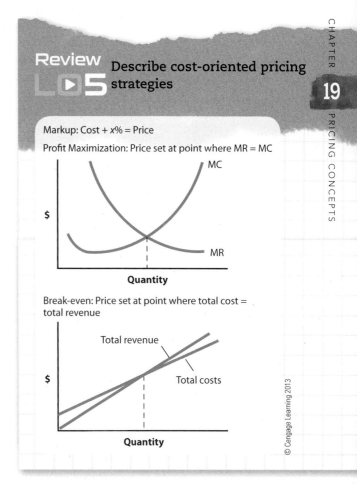

Review LO5 Describe cost-oriented pricing strategies

Markup: Cost + x% = Price

Profit Maximization: Price set at point where MR = MC

Break-even: Price set at point where total cost = total revenue

© Cengage Learning 2013

STAGES IN THE PRODUCT LIFE CYCLE

As a product moves through its life cycle (see Chapter 11), the demand for the product and the competitive conditions tend to change:

→ **Introductory stage:** Management usually sets prices high during the introductory stage. One reason is that it hopes to recover its development costs quickly. In addition, demand originates in the core of the market (the customers whose needs ideally match the product's attributes) and thus is relatively inelastic. On the other hand, if the target market is highly price sensitive, management often finds it better to price the product at the market level or lower. For example, when Kraft Foods brought out Country Time lemonade, it was priced like similar products in the highly competitive beverage market because the market was price sensitive.

→ **Growth stage:** As the product enters the growth stage, prices generally begin to stabilize for several reasons. First, competitors have entered the market, increasing the available supply. Second, the product has begun to appeal to a broader market, often lower-income groups. Finally, economies of scale are lowering costs, and the savings can be passed on to the consumer in the form of lower prices.

→ **Maturity stage:** Maturity usually brings further price decreases as competition increases and inefficient, high-cost firms are eliminated. Distribution channels become a significant cost factor, however, because of the need to offer wide product lines for highly segmented markets, extensive service requirements, and the sheer number of dealers necessary to absorb high-volume production. The manufacturers that remain in the market toward the end of the maturity stage typically offer similar prices. Usually, only the most efficient remain, and they have comparable costs. At this stage, price increases are usually cost initiated, not demand initiated. Nor do price reductions in the late phase of maturity stimulate much demand. Because demand is limited and producers have similar cost structures, the remaining competitors will probably match price reductions.

→ **Decline stage:** The final stage of the life cycle might see further price decreases as the few remaining competitors try to salvage the last vestiges of demand. When only one firm is left in the market, prices begin to stabilize. In fact, prices might eventually rise dramatically if the product survives and moves into the specialty goods category, as horse-drawn carriages and vinyl records have.

THE COMPETITION

Competition varies during the product life cycle, of course, and so at times it strongly affects pricing decisions. Although a firm might not have any competition at first, the high prices it charges could eventually induce another firm to enter the market. A number of Internet auto sellers, such as Autobytel.com, have sprung up in response to the perceived high profit margins earned by car dealers.

On the other hand, intense competition can sometimes lead to price wars. One company recently took action to avoid a calamitous price war by outsmarting its competition. A company (call it Acme) heard that its competitor was trying to steal some business by offering a low price to one of its best customers. Instead of immediately cutting prices, Acme reps visited three of its competitor's best clients and said they figured the client was paying x, the same price that the competitor had quoted to Acme's own customer. Within days, the competitor had retracted its low-price offer to Acme's client. Presumably, the competitor had received calls from three angry clients asking for the same special deal.

Target is using low-price and one-stop shopping advertising in stores to convince shoppers that purchasing at Target is less expensive than purchasing at other discount retailers.

Often, in hotly competitive markets, price wars break out. For Christmas 2009, Walmart launched a price war against Amazon.com. Walmart announced it would sell a number of new, hotly anticipated books for just $10 each on Walmart.com. Hours later, Amazon matched the $10 price. Walmart fired back by dropping its price to $9. Walmart announced that its book pricing was part of a larger strategy to establish Walmart. com as the biggest and cheapest retailer

global perspectives

Carrefour Moves to a Low Price Strategy in Hypermarkets to Fight Discounters

French-based Carrefour operates in 33 countries and is the second largest retailer in the world behind Walmart. Carrefour's hypermarkets sell everything from appliances to clothes and groceries. With smaller households and a worldwide increasing demand for convenience, shoppers are less interested in driving out-of-town to hypermarkets. Clothing chains, such as Zara, and electronics retailers, such as Darty, offer lower prices and better selections. Carrefour's food business is under attack by deep discounters such as Germany's Aldi.

Recently, Lars Olofsson was brought in from Nestlé as new chief executive. His first move was to restore the firm's low price reputation among consumers who have come to see Carrefour as too expensive, especially during the recent recession. Mr. Olofsson has noted, "If I'm the number one preferred retailer . . . I'm most likely to be the most profitable." Also, he believes that a leading market position will give the firm added leverage with suppliers, forcing costs down and profits up.

Mr. Olofsson has decided to reinvent the hypermarket based upon 50,000 customer interviews. The stores will be converted into a new format called "Carrefour Planet." The goal is to delight the customer with an enhanced shopping experience. Emphasis will be on clothing, food,

and electronics with specialists in each area to help the customer. The food section will feature a chef offering many free samples. A new computer system will aid the customer in selecting the right wine. Specialists will show shoppers how to try out the latest electronic gadgets including Apple products. New services will be offered such as baby sitting while the parents shop.

Most importantly, the stores will feature a much greater variety of items with the Carrefour brand. These products will be high quality and priced 15 to 20 percent below manufacturers' brands. Signs will focus on price instead of the old banners which said, "Quality for All." There will be fewer promotions at Carrefour Planet but much bigger sales promotions.

The results of the first pilot stores in France, Belgium, and Spain have been very positive. Consumers have rated the new stores 9.5 out of 10 in terms of quality, service, and comfort. Mr. Olofsson has been particularly pleased that sales in the new Carrefour Planets are up 25 percent.[15]

Do you agree with Mr. Olofsson that the most preferred retailer is likely the most profitable retailer? Carrefour operates in 33 countries, some of which are developing nations. Do you think that the Carrefour Planet model will work in all of these countries? Why or why not?

online.[13] In most cases, consumers are the winners in a price war and the firms are the losers. Price wars make consumers more sensitive to price changes. Also, price wars can negatively impact the price-value image on higher priced retailers,[14] in this case Barnes & Noble.

When companies lose profits and market share over time to lower-priced competitors, it can lead them to rethink their pricing strategy. Such was the case for Carrefour as explained in the Global Perspectives box.

DISTRIBUTION STRATEGY

An effective distribution network can often overcome other minor flaws in the marketing mix.[16] For example, although consumers might perceive a price as being slightly higher than normal, they may buy the product anyway if it is being sold at a convenient retail outlet.

Adequate distribution for a new product can often be attained by offering a larger-than-usual profit margin to distributors. A variation on this strategy is to give dealers a large trade allowance to help offset the costs of promotion and further stimulate demand at the retail level.

Manufacturers have gradually been losing control within the distribution channel to wholesalers and retailers, which often adopt pricing strategies that serve their own purposes. For instance, some distributors are **selling against the brand**: They place well-known brands on the shelves at high prices while offering other brands—typically, their private-label brands, such as Craftsman tools, Kroger canned pears, or Cost Cutter paper towels—at lower prices. Of course, sales of the higher-priced brands decline.

Wholesalers and retailers might also go outside traditional distribution channels to buy gray-market goods. As explained previously, distributors obtain the goods through unauthorized channels for less than they would normally pay, so they can sell the goods with a bigger-than-normal markup or at a reduced price. Imports seem to be particularly susceptible to gray marketing. Porsches, JVC stereos, and Seiko watches are among the brand-name products that have experienced this problem. Although consumers might pay less for gray-market goods, they often find that the manufacturer won't honor the warranty.

Manufacturers can regain some control over price by using an exclusive distribution system, by franchising, or by avoiding doing business with price-cutting discounters. Manufacturers can also package merchandise with the selling price marked on it or place goods on consignment. The best way for manufacturers to control prices, however, is to develop brand loyalty in consumers by delivering quality and value.

THE IMPACT OF THE INTERNET

The Internet, corporate networks, and wireless setups are linking people, machines, and companies around the globe—and connecting sellers and buyers as never before. This link is enabling buyers to quickly and easily compare products and prices, putting them in a better bargaining position. At the same time, the technology allows sellers to collect detailed data about customers' buying habits, preferences, and even spending limits so that the sellers can tailor their products and prices.

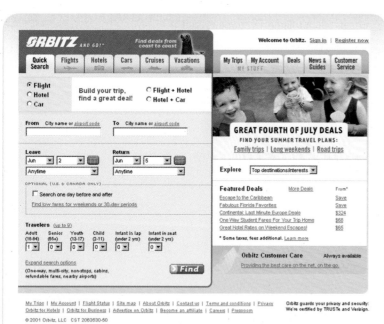

If you want to buy an airline ticket, where do you go? Straight to your preferred airline's Web site? Or do you do some comparison shopping on a site like Orbitz? What other sites offer comparison shopping online? Which kind of products or services does it compare?

Picking a Product to Buy Online
The online shopping process begins with selecting a product. If you want a pet, camera, electronics product, or computer but don't know which brand, try **www. activebuyersguide.com**, which will help you narrow your choice. If you want help with outdoor gear, try **http://outsideonline.com**. Once you select a brand, you can always get a second opinion at **www.consumersearch. com**. This is an expert site that aggregates reviews from many sources such as *Consumer Digest, Consumer Reports*, and *PC World*. For example, a quick click on sleeping bags leads to reviews from *Backpacker* and *Outside* magazines. The problem with expert reviews is that each judgment reflects the views of a few people at most. Many shoppers find **www.consumerreview.com** or **www.epinions.com** helpful. These sites provide user opinions of hundreds of different products. Unfortunately, consumer reviews vary widely in quality. Some are quite terse and others ramble on and on.

Using Shopping Bots A shopping bot is a program that searches the Web for the best price for a particular item that you wish to purchase. *Bot* is short for *robot*. Shopping bots theoretically give pricing power to the consumer. The more information that the shopper has, the more efficient his or her purchase decision will be. When consumers use their money wisely, they can raise their standard of living by approximately one-third. This applies not only to purchasing but to the wise use of credit as well.

There are two general types of shopping bots. The first is the broad-based type that searches a wide range of product categories such as **mySimon.com**, **DealTime. com**, and **PriceGrabber.com**. These sites operate using a Yellow Pages–type of model, in that they list every retailer they can find. The second is the niche-oriented type that searches for only one type of product, such as electronics (**Cnet.com**), books (**BookFinder.com**), or CDs (**CDPriceShop.com**).

Most shopping bots give preferential listings to those e-retailers that pay for the privilege. Typically, the bot lists its merchant partners first, not the retailer that offers the lowest price.

If a bot steers you to really low prices, be careful, as Internet fraud is huge. If you are considering buying from a site that you don't know, check out customer feedback at **www.resellerratings.com** or **http://ratingwonders.com**. Also, if a merchant's site doesn't answer questions about the product, call for details before giving out your credit-card information. Sometimes a really low price is for a reconditioned or refurbished item, or, in the case of clothing and similar items, a "second." Also, ask about in-stock status, pricing breakdowns such as taxes and shipping, and return policies including restocking charges.

In summary, recent research on 1,500 car purchases found that consumers who used the Internet received about a 2 percent lower price. The Internet lowers prices for two distinct reasons: First, the Internet informs consumers. The information that seems to be most valuable to consumers in the auto study was the invoice price of the dealer; it enables them to negotiate a low price at a given dealership. Internet information seems not to help consumers find low-price dealerships. In particular, the Internet does not substitute for searching at multiple dealers, and searching at multiple dealers does not substitute for being better informed.

Second, the incentives provided by online buying services' contracts with dealerships help consumers obtain lower prices through a referral process. Referrals from manufacturer Web sites do not lower prices. Online buying services, such as **Autobytel.com** or **Edmunds.com**, are more effective because unlike manufacturers, they can exert pressure on dealers by directing incremental business to affiliated (and away from unaffiliated) dealerships.[17]

Internet Auctions The Internet auction business is huge. Part of the lure of buying online is that shoppers don't have to go to a flea market or use up a coveted weekend day or worry about the weather. Plus, bidding itself can be fun and exciting. Among the most popular consumer auction sites are the following:

→ ***www.ubid.com:*** Offers a large range of product categories. "My page" consolidates all of the user's activity in one place.

→ ***www.ebay.com:*** The most popular auction site.

→ ***http://bidz.com/:*** Buys closeout deals in very large lots and offers them online in their no-reserve auctions.

Even though consumers are spending billions on Internet auctions, business-to-business (B2B) auctions are likely to be the dominant form in the future. Recently, Whirlpool began holding online auctions. Participants bid on the price of the items that they would supply to Whirlpool, but with a twist: They had to include the date when Whirlpool would have to pay for the items. The company wanted to see which suppliers would offer the longest grace period before requiring payment. Five auctions held over five months helped Whirlpool uncover savings of close to $2 million and more than doubled the grace period.

Whirlpool's success is a sign that the B2B auction world is shifting from haggling over prices to niggling over parameters of the deal. Warranties, delivery dates, transportation methods, customer support, financing options, and quality have all become bargaining chips.

There is also a dark side to Internet auctions, however, especially those where most participants are consumers. Every day crooks lure hundreds of unsuspecting users with auctions that appear legitimate but are really a hollow shell. They hop from user ID to user ID, feeding the system with fake information and stolen credit cards so that the auction site can't tell who they are. In response to a dramatic increase in auction-fraud complaints, the Federal Trade Commission banded together with the National Association of Attorneys General to conduct Operation Bidder Beware, a nationwide crackdown and consumer-education campaign.

Of course, not all bidding sites are based upon auctions. **Priceline.com** lets you name your own price for hotels, flights, cruises, and vacation packages. **Pricewhispers**.com integrates its service directly with participating retailer Web sites to allow shoppers to specify the price that they are willing to pay for an item and an expiration date for their price commitment. Then the retailer will contact the shopper, if and when the bid has been accepted.

PROMOTION STRATEGY

Price is often used as a promotional tool to increase consumer interest. The weekly flyers sent out by grocery stores in the Sunday newspaper, for instance, advertise many products with special low prices. Crested Butte Ski Resort in Colorado tried a unique twist on price promotions. It made the unusual offer of free skiing between Thanksgiving and Christmas. Its only revenues were voluntary contributions from lodging and restaurant owners who benefited from the droves of skiers taking advantage of the promotion. Lodging during the slack period is now booked solid, and on the busiest days 9,000 skiers jam slopes designed for about 6,500. Crested Butte Resort no longer loses money during this time of the year.

Pricing can be a tool for trade promotions as well. For example, Levi's Dockers (casual men's pants) are very popular with white-collar men ages 25 to 45, a growing and lucrative market. Sensing an opportunity, rival pants-maker Bugle Boy began offering similar pants at cheaper wholesale prices, which gave retailers a bigger gross margin than they were getting with Dockers. Levi Strauss had to either lower prices or risk its $400 million annual Dockers sales. Although Levi Strauss intended its cheapest Dockers to retail for $35, it started selling Dockers to retailers for $18 a pair. Retailers could then advertise Dockers at a very attractive retail price of $25.

GUARANTEED PRICE MATCHING AND MONEY BACK GUARANTEES

Closely related to promotion pricing is the price guarantee. In its most basic form, a firm promotes the fact that it will match any competitor's price. Others, such as **Hotwire.com,** claim that they will refund double the difference if you find a lower airfare or hotel price. One of your authors recently booked a hotel on Hotwire. com and subsequently found a lower rate through **Mobissimo.com**. Mobissimo is a Web crawler that searches over 175 sites and then passes you directly to the site that you select. After finding the cheaper rate, Hotwire credited his account for $160—double the difference in prices! On the downside, the same author booked a car on Hotwire for a week for $265. He had to cancel the trip and Hotwire kept his $265 because of its "no cancellation" policy.

Research shows that when a retailer offers a price-matching guarantee, it is signaling to the target market that it is positioned as a low-price dealer. Conversely, a lack of a price-matching guarantee signals a high-service positioning.[18] A second study found different reactions to price matching depending upon whether the consumer was price conscious or not. Non–price conscious consumers perceived a deep refund (to match a competitor's price) as a signal of low prices. Yet for the price conscious consumer, the same deep refund was perceived as the retailer having increased prices.[19] Certainly not a desired outcome for the retailer.

Money back guarantees have been around for over 100 years, ever since Sears and Roebuck proclaimed "Your Satisfaction or Your Money Back." A money back guarantee attracts customers' attention in difficult economic times. Consumers tend to view money back offers as a psychological safety net. People often perceive the item being offered as high quality when there is a money back guarantee. In other words, the seller must be confident in the quality or the guarantee would have never been offered. This, in turn, bolsters consumer confidence in the product. Also, it lowers the perceived risk associated with making the purchase.

Money back guarantees are not limited just to consumer goods. **Forbes.com**, the online version of the Forbes financial magazine, said that if an advertiser would spend a minimum of $1 million over a 90-day period, it would guarantee a certain level of advertising reach and frequency. (See Chapter 17.) If the levels are not attained, the advertiser gets a full refund.[20]

DEMANDS OF LARGE CUSTOMERS

Manufacturers find that their large customers such as Walmart, JCPenney, and other stores often make specific pricing demands that the suppliers must agree to. Department stores are making greater-than-ever demands on their suppliers to cover the heavy discounts and markdowns on their own selling floors. They want suppliers to guarantee their stores' profit margins, and they insist on cash rebates if the guarantee isn't met. They are also exacting fines for violations of ticketing, packing, and shipping rules. Cumulatively, the demands are nearly wiping out profits for all but the very biggest suppliers, according to fashion designers and garment makers.

With gas, grain, and dairy prices rising, you'd think the biggest seller of corn flakes and Cocoa Puffs would be getting hit by rising food costs. But Walmart temporarily rolled back prices on hundreds of food items by as much as 30 percent. How? By pressuring vendors to take costs out of the supply chain. "When our grocery suppliers bring price increases, we don't just accept them," says Pamela Kohn, Walmart's general merchandise manager for perishables.[21] To be sure, Walmart isn't the only retailer working to cut fat from the food chain, but as the largest grocer—Walmart's food and consumables revenue is nearly $100 billion—it has a disproportionate amount of leverage. Here's how the retailer is throwing its weight around.

Shrink the Goods Ever wonder why that cereal box is only two-thirds full? Foodmakers love big boxes because they serve as billboards on store shelves. Walmart has been working to change that by promising suppliers that their shelf space won't shrink even if their boxes do. As a result, some of its vendors have reengineered their packaging. General Mills' Hamburger Helper is now made

Jif uses the fact that it is still 18 ounces as a selling point because other brands have decreased the amount of peanut butter in containers.

© Terri Miller/E-Visual Communications, Inc.

with denser pasta shapes, allowing the same amount of food to fit into a 20 percent smaller box at the same price. The change has saved 890,000 pounds of paper fiber and eliminated 500 trucks from the road, giving General Mills a cushion to absorb some of the rising costs.[22]

Cut Out the Middleman Walmart typically buys its brand-name coffee from a supplier, which buys from a cooperative of growers, which works with a roaster—which means "there are a whole bunch of people muddled in the middle," says Walmart spokeswoman Tara Raddohl.[23] The chain now buys directly from a cooperative of Brazilian coffee farmers for its Sam's Choice brand, cutting three or four steps out of the supply chain.

Go Local Walmart has been going green, but not entirely for the reasons you might think. By sourcing more product locally—it now sells Wisconsin-grown yellow corn in 56 stores in or near Wisconsin—it is able to cut shipping costs.

Throw Out the Producer When all else fails, a large retailer might cut its orders or simply stop doing business with the manufacturer. Unilever demanded that Delhaize, a large Belgian-based grocery chain, carry a broad range of Unilever products. Delhaize told Unilever that it preferred not to stock some of the items because they were unpopular with customers. Unilever threatened to raise prices by an average of 30 percent on the remaining items. Delhaize retaliated by dropping 300 of the 500 Unilever products it normally carried, claiming that they were priced too high.[24]

THE RELATIONSHIP OF PRICE TO QUALITY

As mentioned at the beginning of the chapter, when a purchase decision involves uncertainty, consumers tend to rely on a high price as a predictor of good quality. Reliance on price as an indicator of quality seems to occur for all products, but it reveals itself more strongly for some items than for others.[25] Among the products that benefit from this phenomenon are coffee, stockings, aspirin, salt, floor wax, shampoo, clothing, furniture, perfume, whiskey, and many services. In the absence of other information, people typically assume that prices are higher because the products contain better materials, because they are made more carefully, or, in the case of professional services, because the provider has more expertise. In other words, consumers assume that "You get what you pay for."

Research has found that products that are perceived to be of high quality tend to benefit more from price promotions than products perceived to be of lower quality.[26] However, when perceived high- and lower-quality products are offered in settings where consumers have difficulty making comparisons, then price promotions have an equal effect on sales. Comparisons are more difficult in end-of-aisle displays, feature advertising, and the like.

Knowledgeable merchants take these consumer attitudes into account when devising their pricing strategies. **Prestige pricing** is charging a high price to help promote a high-quality image. A successful prestige pricing strategy requires a retail price that is reasonably consistent with consumers' expectations. No one goes shopping at a Gucci's shop in New York and expects to pay $9.95 for a pair of loafers. In fact, demand would fall drastically at such a low price. Bayer aspirin would probably lose market share over the long run if it lowered its prices. A new mustard packaged in a crockery jar was not successful until its price was doubled.

prestige pricing
Charging a high price to help promote a high-quality image.

Some of the latest research on price–quality relationships has focused on consumer durable goods. The researchers first conducted a study to ascertain the dimensions of quality. These are (1) ease of use; (2) versatility (the ability of a product to perform more functions—for example, special stitch types on sewing machines; or be more flexible—such as continuous temperature controls on microwave ovens); (3) durability; (4) serviceability (ease of obtaining high-quality repairs); (5) performance; and (6) prestige. The researchers found that when consumers focused on prestige and/or durability to assess quality, price was a strong indicator of perceived overall quality. Price was less important as an indicator of quality if the consumer was focusing on one of the other four dimensions of quality.[27]

Other research has found three basic effects associated with the price–quality relationship. These are: prestige, hedonistic, and allocative effects.[28] As noted earlier, the purchase, use, display, and consumption of goods and services that bear high prices can provide a means to gain social status. Therefore, consumers also might perceive price as an indicator of prestige. For example, some consumers purchase an expensive car not because of their quality perceptions per se but because of their perception that the purchase will signal prestige and wealth to others.

High purchase prices may also create feelings of pleasure and excitement associated with consuming higher priced products. This is the hedonistic effect. Hedonistic consumption refers to pursuing emotional responses associated with using a product, such as pleasure, excitement, arousal, good feelings, and fun. Hedonistic consumers prefer high prices as a means of affirming their own self-worth and to satisfy their egos.

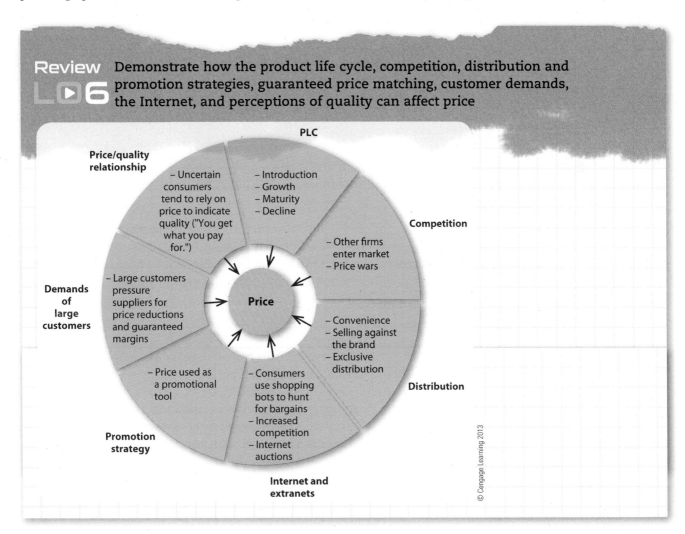

Review LO6 Demonstrate how the product life cycle, competition, distribution and promotion strategies, guaranteed price matching, customer demands, the Internet, and perceptions of quality can affect price

Price

PLC
– Introduction
– Growth
– Maturity
– Decline

Competition
– Other firms enter market
– Price wars

Distribution
– Convenience
– Selling against the brand
– Exclusive distribution

Internet and extranets
– Consumers use shopping bots to hunt for bargains
– Increased competition
– Internet auctions

Promotion strategy
– Price used as a promotional tool

Demands of large customers
– Large customers pressure suppliers for price reductions and guaranteed margins

Price/quality relationship
– Uncertain consumers tend to rely on price to indicate quality ("You get what you pay for.")

© Cengage Learning 2013

The allocative effect refers to the notion that consumers must allocate their budgets across alternative goods and services. The more you spend on one product, the less you have to spend on all others. Consumers sensitive to the allocative effects likely prefer low prices. However, managers must be aware that setting low prices or lowering prices with a discount offer not only attracts buyers but also threatens to lower perceptions of product quality, prestige value, and hedonistic value. This is because of the negative cues associated with lower selling prices.[29]

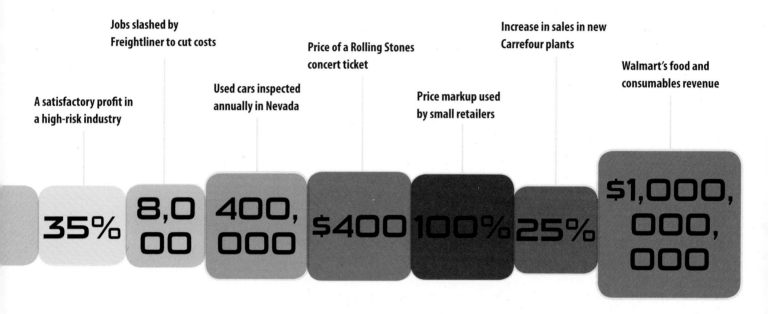

A satisfactory profit in a high-risk industry — **35%**

Jobs slashed by Freightliner to cut costs — **8,000**

Used cars inspected annually in Nevada — **400,000**

Price of a Rolling Stones concert ticket — **$400**

Price markup used by small retailers — **100%**

Increase in sales in new Carrefour plants — **25%**

Walmart's food and consumables revenue — **$1,000,000,000**

Review and Applications

LO1 **Discuss the importance of pricing decisions to the economy and to the individual firm.** Pricing plays an integral role in the U.S. economy by allocating goods and services among consumers, governments, and businesses. Pricing is essential in business because it creates revenue, which is the basis of all business activity. In setting prices, marketing managers strive to find a level high enough to produce a satisfactory profit.

1.1 Why is pricing so important to the marketing manager?

1.2 How does price allocate goods and services?

LO2 **List and explain a variety of pricing objectives.** Establishing realistic and measurable pricing objectives is a critical part of any firm's marketing strategy. Pricing objectives are commonly classified into three categories: profit oriented, sales oriented, and status quo. Profit-oriented pricing is based on profit maximization, a satisfactory level of profit, or a target return on investment. The goal of profit maximization is to generate as much revenue as possible in relation to cost. Often, a more practical approach than profit maximization is setting prices to produce profits that will satisfy management and stockholders. The most common profit-oriented strategy is pricing for a specific return on investment relative to a firm's assets. The second type of pricing objective is sales oriented, and it focuses on either maintaining a percentage share of the market or maximizing dollar or unit sales. The third type of pricing objective aims to maintain the status quo by matching competitors' prices.

2.1 Give an example of each major type of pricing objective.

2.2 Why do many firms not maximize profits?

Explain the role of demand in price determination. Demand is a key determinant of price. When establishing prices, a firm must first determine demand for its product. A typical demand schedule shows an inverse relationship between quantity demanded and price: When price is lowered, sales increase; and when price is increased, the quantity demanded falls. For prestige products, however, there might be a direct relationship between demand and price: The quantity demanded will increase as price increases.

Marketing managers must also consider demand elasticity when setting prices. Elasticity of demand is the degree to which the quantity demanded fluctuates with changes in price. If consumers are sensitive to changes in price, demand is elastic; if they are insensitive to price changes, demand is inelastic. Thus, an increase in price will result in lower sales for an elastic product and little or no loss in sales for an inelastic product. Inelastic demand creates pricing power.

3.1 Explain the role of supply and demand in determining price.

3.2 If a firm can increase its total revenue by raising its price, shouldn't it do so?

3.3 Explain the concepts of elastic and inelastic demand. Why should managers understand these concepts?

Understand the concept of yield management systems. Yield management systems use complex mathematical software to profitably fill unused capacity. The software uses techniques such as discounting early purchases, limiting early sales at these discounted prices, and overbooking capacity. These systems are used in service and retail businesses and are substantially raising revenues. The use of Internet cookies and targeting software enables online retailers to offer different pricing and promotional offers to online buyers based upon their online shopping and browsing habits.

4.1 Why are so many companies adopting yield management systems?

4.2 Explain the relationship between supply and demand and yield management systems.

4.3 Why is targeting technology so effective?

Describe cost-oriented pricing strategies. The other major determinant of price is cost. Marketers use several cost-oriented pricing strategies. To cover their own expenses and obtain a profit, wholesalers and retailers commonly use markup pricing: They tack an extra amount onto the manufacturer's original price. Another pricing technique is to maximize profits by setting price where marginal revenue equals marginal cost. Still another pricing strategy determines how much a firm must sell to break even and uses this amount as a reference point for adjusting price.

5.1 Your firm has based its pricing strictly on cost in the past. As the newly hired marketing manager, you believe this policy should change. Write the president a memo explaining your reasons.

writing

5.2 Why is it important for managers to understand the concept of break-even points? Are there any drawbacks?

Demonstrate how the product life cycle, competition, distribution and promotion strategies, guaranteed price matching, customer demands, the Internet, and perceptions of quality can affect price. The price of a product normally changes as it moves through the life cycle and as demand for the product and competitive conditions change. Management often sets a high price at the introductory stage, and the high price tends to attract competition. The competition usually drives prices down because individual competitors lower prices to gain market share.

Adequate distribution for a new product can sometimes be obtained by offering a larger-than-usual profit margin to wholesalers and retailers. The Internet enables consumers to compare products and prices quickly and efficiently. Price is also used as a promotional tool to attract customers. Special low prices often attract new customers and entice existing customers to buy more. Price matching positions the retailer as a low price vendor. Firms that don't match prices are perceived as offering a higher level of service. Large buyers can extract price concessions from vendors. Such demands can squeeze the profit margins of suppliers.

Perceptions of quality can also influence pricing strategies. A firm trying to project a prestigious image often charges a premium price for a product. Consumers tend to equate high prices with high quality.

 team

6.1 Divide into teams of five. Each team will be assigned a different grocery store from a different chain. (An independent is fine.) Appoint a group leader. The group leaders should meet as a group and pick 15 nationally branded grocery items. Each item should be specifically described as to brand name and size of the package. Each team will then proceed to its assigned store and collect price data on the 15 items. The team should also gather price data on 15 similar store brands and 15 generics, if possible.

Each team should present its results to the class and discuss why there are price variations between stores, national brands, store brands, and generics.

As a next step, go back to your assigned store and share the overall results with the store manager. Bring back the manager's comments and share them with the class.

6.2 How does the stage of a product's life cycle affect price? Give some examples.

online

6.3 Go to Priceline.com. Can you research a ticket's price before purchasing it? What products and services are available for purchasing? How comfortable are you with naming your own price? Relate the supply and demand curves to customer-determined pricing.

Key Terms

average total cost (ATC) *707*
average variable cost (AVC) *706*
break-even analysis *709*
demand *697*
elastic demand *699*
elasticity of demand *699*
fixed cost *706*
inelastic demand *699*
keystoning *709*

marginal cost (MC) *707*
marginal revenue (MR) *709*
market share *695*
markup pricing *708*
prestige pricing *718*
price *691*
price equilibrium *699*
profit *693*
profit maximization *709*

return on investment (ROI) *694*
revenue *692*
selling against the brand *714*
status quo pricing *696*
supply *698*
unitary elasticity *699*
variable cost *706*
yield management systems (YMS) *706*

Exercises

 ethics

ETHICS EXERCISE

Advanced Bio Medics (ABM) has invented a new stem-cell-based drug that will arrest even advanced forms of lung cancer. Development costs were actually quite low because the drug was an accidental discovery by scientists working on a different project. To stop the disease requires a regimen of one pill per week for 20 weeks. There is no substitute offered by competitors. ABM is thinking that it could maximize its profits by charging $10,000 per pill. Of course, many people will die because they can't afford the medicine at this price.

Questions

1. Should ABM maximize its profits?

2. Does the AMA Statement of Ethics address this issue? Go to www.marketingpower.com and review the code. Then write a brief paragraph on what the AMA Statement of Ethics contains that relates to ABM's dilemma.

MARKETING PLAN EXERCISE

In the last part of your strategic marketing plan you began the process of defining the marketing mix, starting with the components of product, distribution, and promotion. The next stage of the strategic planning process—pricing—completes the elements of the marketing mix.

In recent years, pricing has become a special challenge to the marketer because prices can be quickly and easily compared on the Internet. In any case, your goal should be to make pricing competitive and value-driven, as well as cover costs. Other features and benefits of your offering are likely to be more important than price. Use the following exercises to guide you through the pricing part of your strategic marketing plan:

1. List possible pricing objectives for your chosen firm. How might adopting different pricing objectives change the behavior of the firm and its marketing plans?

2. Gather information on tactics you decided on for the first parts of your marketing plan. What costs are associated with those decisions? Will you incur more or fewer costs by selling online? Will your marketing costs increase or decrease? Why? Calculate the break-even point for selling your offering. Can you sell enough to cover your costs?

3. Pricing is an integral component of marketing strategy. Discuss how your firm's pricing can affect or be affected by competition, the economic environment, political regulations, product features, extra customer service, changes in distribution, or changes in promotion.

4. Is demand elastic or inelastic for your company's product or service? Why? What is the demand elasticity for your offering in an off-line world? Whatever the level, it is likely to be *more* elastic online. What tactics can you use to soften or reduce this online price sensitivity?

APPLICATION EXERCISE

Reliance on price as a predictor of quality seems to occur for all products. Does this mean that high-priced products are superior? Well, sometimes. Price can be a good predictor of quality for some products, but for others, price is not always the best way to determine the quality of a product or service before buying it. This exercise (and worksheet) will help you examine the price–quality relationship for a simple product: canned goods.[30]

Activities

1. Take a trip to a local supermarket where you are certain to find multiple brands of canned fruits and vegetables. Pick a single type of vegetable or fruit you like, such as creamed corn or peach halves, and list five or six brands in the following worksheet:

		Price				
(1) Brand	(2) Quality/Rank (y)	(3) Price/Weight	(4) Price per Ounce	(5) Price Rank (x)	(6) d ($y - x$)	(7) d^2
Total						

2. Before going any further, rank the brands according to which you think is the highest quality (1) to the lowest quality (5 or 6, depending on how many brands you find). This ranking will be y.

3. Record the price and the volume of each brand. For example, if a 14-ounce can costs $.89, you would list $.89/14 oz.

4. Translate the price per volume into price per ounce. For example, that 14-ounce can costs $.064 per ounce.

5. Now rank the price per ounce (we'll call it x) from the highest (1) to the lowest (5 or 6, again depending on how many brands you have).

6. We'll now begin calculating the coefficient of correlation between the price and quality rankings. The first step is to subtract x from y. Enter the result, d, in column 6.

7. Now calculate d^2 and enter the value in column 7. Write the sum of all the entries in column 7 in the final row.

8. The formula for calculating a price-quality coefficient r is as follows:

   In the formula, r_s is the coefficient of correlation, 6 is a constant, and n is the number of items ranked.

9. What does the result of your calculation tell you about the correlation between the price and the quality of the canned vegetable or fruit you selected? Now that you know this, will it change your buying habits?

CASE STUDY: Apple iPhone

LIFE IN THE TECHNOLOGY LANE

Before Apple introduced the iPhone, it was hard for most people to imagine that they'd ever pay as much as $599 for a cell phone. But on June 29, 2007, Apple customers stood in line for hours to do just that, eager to be among the first to get their hands on the sleek new device dubbed "the God machine." *Newsweek* columnist Steven Levy described how the proud new owners were "lofting their newly acquired iPhones in the air like they'd won the Stanley Cup." Within the first three days alone, Apple sold 270,000 iPhones at premium prices ($499 for a 4GB model, $599 for 8GB), and CEO Steve Jobs was predicting that they'd cross the 10-million mark by the end of 2008.

Industry analyst Lev Grossman says that Jobs, who had already revolutionized the portable music player market with the iPod, turned his attention to mobile phones because he believed they were "broken." And Jobs likes things that are broken, Grossman says. "It means he can make something that isn't and sell it to you for a premium price." And members of the "Apple Nation" have proven that they are willing to pay.

In a company of 20,000 employees, Apple has only one committee, and its job is to establish prices. In September of 2007, Jobs announced the decision to slash the price of the iPhone, even though it had only been 68 days since its launch. Company research had shown that it was priced too high for holiday shoppers. "If we don't take that chance, we wait a whole other year," Jobs explained. "We're willing to make less money to get more iPhones out there." The same iPhone that had sold for $599 would now cost $399. At the same press conference in San Francisco, Jobs introduced the new iPod nano, the iPod classic, and the iPod touch. The only thing that made headlines, however, was the unexpected iPhone price cut and stories of the consumer outrage that followed.

Elaine Soloway, a longtime Mac user, said, "Apple really infuriated their fans, the people who urge other people to buy Apple products. We are ambassadors for them." Like Soloway, thousands of iPhone early adopters expressed their disappointment.

"This is life in the technology lane," Jobs said in an attempt to defend the company's decision to drop the price so soon. "There is always something better and less expensive on the horizon." Some call it the curse of the early adopter. But usually they get bragging rights for more than two months before the masses can afford to buy the same product they paid a premium for. In an attempt to appease his angry customers, Jobs announced that those who paid the original price would now be eligible for a $100 refund in the form of store credit.

The store credit pleased some but wasn't enough for others. One customer, who bought his iPhone only weeks before the price drop, said the $100 was merely a pay-off for being a sucker. "Steve Jobs actually put a price tag on my suckerdom—$200—and now he's trying to drain off some of that embarrassment."

The price cut didn't just disappoint Apple's core customers. Investors were concerned, as well, suspecting that the iPhone wasn't selling as well as expected. Apple shares immediately fell $1.75 to $135.01 after the announcement. Industry analysts suggest that the price change could indicate that Apple, which has long been immune to the pricing wars among other personal computer companies, may have found the cell phone business more competitive than anticipated. Whatever the reasons, Jobs acknowledged, "We need to do a better job of taking care of our early iPhone customers as we aggressively go after new ones with a lower price."

The Cult of Mac shows no sign of waning in the aftermath of the company's rare misstep, however. Customers love their iPhones, they say, and remain devoted to Apple as the arbiter of cutting-edge technology that is intuitively and beautifully designed. Sure, admits one loyal customer, "It sucks. But if they had told me then they were going to drop the price in a few months, I still would have bought it. I was obsessed."[31]

Questions

1. Apple CEO Steve Jobs alluded to the price a customer may have to pay to own an iPhone when he said that the steep and sudden price change was simply part of "life in the technology lane." What did he mean? Beyond the simple exchange of money, what else might the price of such a product include?

2. Discuss the role that product demand played in pricing the iPhone. How did this demand influence Apple's decision to price it high in the beginning and then lower it two months later?

3. Discuss how the availability of substitutes affects elasticity of demand for Apple products such as the iPhone.

4. How do you think the relationship of price to quality affects how customers perceive Apple products?

© NKP MEDIA, INC./Cengage

As long as people have stomach aches, companies will sell remedies. Acid+All is banking that America will continue its love affair with bad food and has made an interesting move into the antacid market. The tiny pills come packaged in a tin priced at $3.89, which clearly sets the product apart from competitors such as Rolaids, Tums, and others. The gambit of staking out a position as a prestige product is high. Watch the video to see what issues helped forge the $3.89 unit price and if the company has been successful at this price point.

Questions

1. How do the product, place, and promotion elements of Acid+All's marketing mix influence the pricing strategy the company has chosen?

2. Would you expect demand for Acid+All to be elastic? Why or why not?

3. What role do the product life cycle, competition, and perceptions of quality play in Acid+All's suggested retail price?

4. Would you buy Acid+All for the $3.89 retail price? Why or why not?

Notes

1. Walter Baker, Michael Marn, and Craig Zawada, "Building a Better Price Structure," *McKinsey Quarterly*, August 2010, www.mckinseyquarterly.com/Building_a_better_pricing_structure_2652 (Accessed August 13, 2010).
2. Franziska Volckner, "The Dual Role of Price: Decomposing Consumers' Reactions to Price," *Journal of the Academy of Marketing Science*, Fall 2008, 359–377.
3. *Ibid.*
4. Roland Rust, Christine Moorman, and Peter R. Dickson, "Getting Return on Quality: Revenue Expansion, Cost Reduction, or Both?" *Journal of Marketing*, October 2002, 7–24.
5. "DaimlerChrysler's Freightliner Puts New Chief at the Wheel," *Wall Street Journal*, May 29, 2001, B4.
6. Timothy W. Martin, "Kroger: No Fears on Price," *Wall Street Journal*, September 30, 2010, B8.
7. Tammo H. A. Bijmolt, Harald J. vanHeerde, and Rik G. M. Pieters, "New Empirical Generalizations on the Determinants of Price Elasticity," *Journal of Marketing Research*, May 2005, 141–156; Christian Homburg, Wayne Hoyer, and Nicole Koschate, "Customers' Reactions to Price Increases: Do Customer Satisfaction and Perceived Motive Fairness Matter?" *Journal of the Academy of Marketing Science*, Winter 2005, 35–49; Gadi Fibich, Arieh Gavious, and Oded Lowengart, "The Dynamics of Price Elasticity of Demand in the Presence of Reference Price Effects," *Journal of the Academy of Marketing Science*, Winter 2005, 66–78.
8. Dana Mattioli, "Executives Zero in on Pricing," *Wall Street Journal*, September 27, 2010, B7.
9. "A Natural Experiment in Demand Elasticity: Metered vs. Unmetered Electricity," Ed Dolan's Econ Blog, http://dolanecon.blogspot.com/2010/08/natural-experiment-in-demand-elasticity.html, August 17, 2010.
10. "Cigarettes Are Price Inelastic," *Plain Sense Economics*, April 4, 2009, www.plain-sense.com/2009/04/04/cigarettes-are-price-inelastic/ (Accessed on October 3, 2010).
11. "In a Tech Backwater, a Profit Fortress Rises," *Wall Street Journal*, July 10, 2007, A1.
12. Timothy Aeppel, "Seeking Perfect Prices, CEO Tears Up the Rules," *Wall Street Journal*, March 27, 2007, A1, A16.
13. Miguel Bustillo and Jeffrey A. Trachtenberg, "Walmart Strafes Amazon in Book War," *Wall Street Journal*, October 16, 2009, A1, A15.
14. Harald van Heerde, Els Gijsbrechts, and Koen Pauwels, "Winners and Losers in a Major Price War," *Journal of Marketing Research*, October 2008, 499–518.

marketing&you: Results.

© iStockphoto.com/ziggymaj

High scores on this poll relate to a belief that you'll get more enjoyment and make better impressions if you buy high-priced brands. That is, you have a higher prestige sensitivity than someone with a lower score. If your score was low, compare it with your score for the Chapter 18 poll, which was probably high. That's because people with lower prestige sensitivities are more likely to use coupons!

15. "Carrefour: Reinventing the Hypermarket," Cantos Communications Web site, September 16, 2010, http://www.cantos.com/company/Carrefour/project/7048; Christian Passariello "Carrefour's Makeover Plan: Become IKEA of Groceries," *Wall Street Journal*, September 16, 2010, B1–B2; Cecilie Rohwedder, "Carrefour Restores Low-Price Strategy in Hypermarkets to Fight Discounters," *Wall Street Journal*, June 30, 2009, B1–B2; and Scheherazade Daneshkhu, "Carrefour Sets Sights on Key Growth Markets," *Financial Times*, www.ft.com/cms/s/0/258430be-b4cc-11df-b0a6-00144feabdc0.html#axzz1LzTTZ1z6, August 31, 2010.

16. Joseph Cannon and Christian Homburg, "Buyer-Supplier Relationships and Customer Firm Costs," *Journal of Marketing*, January 2001, 29–43.

17. Florian Zettelmeyer, Fiona Scott Morton, and Jorge Silva-Risso, "How the Internet Lowers Prices: Evidence from Matched Survey and Auto Transaction Data," *Journal of Marketing Research*, May 2006, 168–181.

18. Sridhar Moorthy and Xubing Zhang, "Price Matching by Vertically Differentiated Retailers: Theory and Evidence," *Journal of Marketing Research*, May 2006, 156–167.

19. Monika Kukar-Kinney, Rockney Walters, and Scott MacKenzie, "Consumer Responses to Characteristics of Price-Matching Guarantees: The Moderating Role of Price Consciousness," *Journal of Retailing*, April 2007, 211–221.

20. "Guaranteeing Success," *Marketing News*, May 15, 2009, 20.

21. Suzanne Kapner, "Walmart Puts the Squeeze on Food Costs," *Fortune*, June 9, 2008, 16.

22. *Ibid.*

23. *Ibid.*

24. Cecilie Rohwedder, Aaron O. Patrick, and Timothy W. Martin, "Big Grocer Pulls Unilever Items over Pricing," *Wall Street Journal*, February 11, 2009, B1, B5.

25. R. Chandrashekaran, "The Implications of Individual Differences in Reference to Price Utilization for Designing Effective Price Communications," *Journal of Business Research*, August 2001, 85–92.

26. Katherine Lemon and Stephen Nowlis, "Developing Synergies between Promotions and Brands in Different Price-Quality Tiers," *Journal of Marketing Research*, May 2002, 171–185. Also see Valerie Taylor and William Bearden, "The Effects of Price on Brand Extension Evaluations: The Moderating Role of Extension Similarity," *Journal of the Academy of Marketing Science*, Spring 2002, 131–140; and Raj Sethuraman and V. Srinivasan, "The Asymmetric Share Effect: An Empirical Generalization on Cross-Price Effects," *Journal of Marketing Research*, August 2002, 379–386.

27. Merrie Brucks, Valarie Zeithaml, and Gillian Naylor, "Price and Brand Name as Indicators of Quality Dimensions for Consumer Durables," *Journal of the Academy of Marketing Science*, Summer 2000, 359–374; Wilford Amaldoss and Sanjay Jain, "Pricing of Conspicuous Goods: A Competitive Analysis of Social Effects," *Journal of Marketing Research*, February 2005, 30–42; Margaret Campbell, "Says Who?! How the Source of Price Information and Affect Influence Perceived Price (UN)fairness," *Journal of Marketing Research*, May 2007, 261–271.

28. Volckner, "The Dual Role of Price."

29. *Ibid.*

30. This application exercise is based on the contribution of Vaughn C. Judd (Auburn University, Montgomery, AL) to *Great Ideas in Teaching Marketing*, a teaching supplement and accompanies McDaniel, Lamb, and Hair's *Introduction to Marketing*. Professor Judd's entry, titled "Analyzing the Price-Quality Relationship," was a winner in the "Best of the Great Ideas in Teaching Marketing" contest held in conjunction with the publication of the eighth edition of *Marketing*.

31. Steven Levy, "How Apple's iPhone Ate the New iPods," *Newsweek*, September 17, 2007; Chris Nuttall, "Apple Apologizes to Early Buyers of iPhone After New Discounts," *The Financial Times*, September 7, 2007; Eric Benderoff, "Apple Credits iPhone Buyers," *Chicago Tribune*, September 7, 2007; Chris Churchill, "Few Hang-Ups in Wake of iPhone Price Cut," *Times Union*, September 7, 2007; John Markoff, "Apple Cuts iPhone Price Ahead of Holidays," *The New York Times*, September 6, 2007; Lev Grossman, "Apple's New Calling: the iPhone," *Time*, January 9, 2007.

Learning Outcomes

1 Describe the procedure for setting the right price

2 Identify the legal and ethical constraints on pricing decisions

3 Explain how discounts, geographic pricing, and other pricing tactics can be used to fine-tune the base price

4 Discuss product line pricing

5 Describe the role of pricing during periods of inflation and recession

LO1
How to Set a Price on a Product or Service

As Quizno's is demonstrating in the opening photo, and as you saw in chapter 19, setting the right price requires strategy and research. As such, setting the right price on a product is a four-step process (see Exhibit 20.1):

1. Establish pricing goals.

2. Estimate demand, costs, and profits.

3. Choose a price strategy to help determine a base price.

4. Fine-tune the base price with pricing tactics.

The first three steps are discussed next; the fourth step is discussed later in the chapter.

> "The basic, long-term **pricing** framework for a good or service should be a logical extension of the pricing objectives."

ESTABLISH PRICING GOALS

The first step in setting the right price is to establish pricing goals. Recall from Chapter 19 that pricing objectives fall into three categories: profit oriented, sales oriented, and status quo. These goals are derived from the firm's overall

marketing&you.

How price conscious are you?

Enter your answers on the lines provided.

STRONGLY DISAGREE   1 · · 2 · · 3 · · 4 · · 5 · · 6 · · 7   STRONGLY AGREE

_____ I shop a lot for "specials."

_____ I find myself checking the prices in the grocery store even for small items.

_____ I usually watch the advertisements for announcements of sales.

_____ A person can save a lot of money by shopping around for bargains.

_____ I check the prices even for inexpensive items.

_____ I pay attention to sales and specials.

_____ Clothing, furniture, appliances—whatever I buy, I shop around to get the best prices.

_____ I usually purchase the cheapest item.

_____ I usually purchase items on sale only.

Total your score and find out what it means at the end of the chapter.

Source: Scale #29, *Marketing Scales Handbook*, G. Bruner, K. James, H. Hensel, eds., Vol. III. © by American Marketing Association.

© iStockphoto.com/ Juan Facundo Mora Soria

© iStockphoto.com/ziggymaj

Exhibit 20.1 Steps in Setting the Right Price on a Product

Establish pricing goals

Estimate demand, costs, and profits

Choose a price strategy to help determine a base price

Fine-tune the base with pricing tactics

Results lead to the right price

© Cengage Learning 2013

objectives. If, for example, a company's objective is to be the dominant sales leader in an industry, then it will pursue a sales-oriented market share pricing goal. A conservative organization that is attempting to lower risks by being a follower, rather than attempting to be a market leader, might establish a status quo goal. This company is simply trying to preserve its position in the marketplace. Finally, a company committed to maximizing shareholder value will establish aggressive profit-oriented pricing goals.

A good understanding of the marketplace and of the consumer can sometimes tell a manager very quickly whether a goal is realistic. For example, if firm A's objective is a 20 percent target return on investment (ROI), and its product development and implementation costs are $5 million, the market must be rather large or must support the price required to earn a 20 percent ROI. Assume that company B has a pricing objective that all new products must reach at least 15 percent market share within three years after their introduction. A thorough study of the environment might convince the marketing manager that the competition is too strong and the market share goal can't be met.

All pricing objectives have trade-offs that managers must weigh. A profit maximization objective might require a bigger initial investment than the firm can commit or wants to commit. Reaching the desired market share often means sacrificing short-term profit because without careful management, long-term profit goals might not be met. Meeting the competition is the easiest pricing goal to implement. But can managers really afford to ignore demand and costs, the life-cycle stage, and other considerations? When creating pricing objectives, managers must consider these trade-offs in light of the target customer, the environment, and the company's overall objectives.

ESTIMATE DEMAND, COSTS, AND PROFITS

Chapter 19 explained that total revenue is a function of price and quantity demanded and that quantity demanded depends on elasticity. Elasticity is a function of the perceived value to the buyer relative to the price. Some key questions that a manager might consider when conducting marketing research on demand and elasticity are:

→ What price is so low they would question its quality?

→ What is the highest price at which the product would still be a bargain?

→ What is the price at which the product is starting to get expensive?

→ What is the price at which the product becomes too expensive to consider buying?

After establishing pricing goals, managers should estimate total revenue at a variety of prices. Next, they should determine corresponding costs for each price. They are then ready to estimate how much profit, if any, and how much market share can be earned at each possible price. These data become the heart of the developing price policy. Managers can study the options in light of revenues, costs, and profits. In turn, this information can help determine which price can best meet the firm's pricing goals.

CHOOSE A PRICE STRATEGY

The basic, long-term pricing framework for a good or service should be a logical extension of the pricing objectives. The marketing manager's chosen **price strategy** defines the initial price and gives direction for price movements over the product life cycle.

The price strategy sets a competitive price in a specific market segment, based on a well-defined positioning strategy. Changing a price level from premium to super-premium might require a change in the product itself, the target customers served, the promotional strategy, or the distribution channels. Thus, changing a price strategy can require dramatic alterations in the marketing mix. A carmaker cannot successfully compete in the super-premium category if the car looks and drives like an economy car.

A company's freedom in pricing a new product and devising a price strategy depends on the market conditions and the other elements of the marketing mix. If a firm launches a new item resembling several others already on the market, its pricing freedom will be restricted. To succeed, the company will probably have to charge a price close to the average market price. In contrast, a firm that introduces a totally new product with no close substitutes will have considerable pricing freedom.

Most companies do not do a good job of doing research to create a price strategy. A study found that only about 8 percent of the companies surveyed conducted serious pricing research to support the development of an effective pricing strategy. In fact, 88 percent of them did little or no serious pricing research. McKinsey & Co.'s Pricing Benchmark Survey estimated that only about 15 percent of companies do serious pricing research. A Coopers & Lybrand study found that 87 percent of the surveyed companies had changed prices in the previous year. Only 13 percent of the price changes, however, came after a scheduled review of pricing strategy.[1]

These numbers indicate that strategic pricing decisions tend to be made without an understanding of the likely buyer or the competitive response. Further, the research shows that managers often make tactical pricing decisions without reviewing how they fit into the firm's overall pricing or marketing strategy. The data suggest that many companies make pricing decisions and changes without an existing process for managing the pricing activity. As a result, many of them do not have a serious pricing strategy and do not conduct pricing research to develop their strategy.[2]

Companies that do serious planning for creating a price strategy can select from three basic approaches: price skimming, penetration pricing, and status quo pricing. A discussion of each type follows.

Price Skimming Price skimming is sometimes called a "market-plus" approach to pricing because it denotes a high price relative to the prices of competing products. The term **price skimming** is derived from the phrase "skimming the cream off the top." Companies often use this strategy for new products when the product is perceived by the target market as having unique advantages. For example, Caterpillar sets premium prices on its construction equipment to support and capture its high perceived value. Genzyme Corporation introduced Ceredase as the first effective treatment for Gaucher's disease. The pill allows patients to avoid years of painful physical deterioration and lead normal lives. The cost of a year's supply for one patient can exceed $300,000.

Often companies will use skimming initially and then lower prices over time. This is called "sliding down the demand curve." Hardcover book publishers, such as HarperCollins and Random House, lower the price when the books are re-released in paperback. Calloway lowers the price of its old model golf clubs as new models hit the sales floor. Yet some manufacturers such as Porsche and Cuisinart, the maker

price strategy
A basic, long-term pricing framework, which establishes the initial price for a product and the intended direction for price movements over the product life cycle.

price skimming
A pricing policy whereby a firm charges a high introductory price, often coupled with heavy promotion.

© iStockphoto.com/Juan Facundo Mora Soria

of kitchen appliances, maintain skimming prices throughout a product's life cycle. A manager of the factory that produces Chanel purses (retailing for over $2,000 each) told one of your authors that the company takes back unsold inventory and destroys it rather than selling it at a discount. Retailers such as Tiffany and Neiman Marcus maintain skimming policies. Though both retailers occasionally have sales, their basic price strategy is price skimming.

Price skimming works best when the market is willing to buy the product even though it carries an above-average price. If, for example, some purchasing agents feel that Caterpillar equipment is far superior to competitors' products, then Caterpillar can charge premium prices successfully. Firms can also effectively use price skimming when a product is well protected legally, when it represents a technological breakthrough, or when it has in some other way blocked the entry of competitors. Managers might follow a skimming strategy when production cannot be expanded rapidly because of technological difficulties, shortages, or constraints imposed by the skill and time required to produce a product. As long as demand is greater than supply, skimming is an attainable strategy.

A successful skimming strategy enables management to recover its product development or "educational" costs quickly. (Often consumers must be "taught" the advantages of a radically new item, such as Viking's new combination steam/convection oven that lists for $4,440.) Even if the market perceives an introductory price as too high, managers can easily correct the problem by lowering the price. Firms often feel it is better to test the market at a high price and then lower the price if sales are too slow. They are tacitly saying, "If there are any premium-price buyers in the market, let's reach them first and maximize our revenue per unit." Successful skimming strategies are not limited to products. Well-known athletes, entertainers, lawyers, and hairstylists are experts at price skimming. Naturally, a skimming strategy will encourage competitors to enter the market.

Above all, if price skimming is to be successful, customers must perceive a high value for the product or service. Otherwise, failure can come at a high price. Iridium phones are an example of a technology-driven, feature-loaded, high-cost, high-price innovation. The phones were billed as a "use anywhere" mobile phone system. The original developers of the system poured $5 billion into a 66-satellite system. But phones and needed accessories took up so much space that they required a special briefcase. The purchase price for a phone system was $3,000, and airtime fees were $7 per minute. At the same time, cellular phones—with more limited coverage but adequate for many customers—were selling for less than $100 and were much more "user friendly." Though the Iridium system was technologically brilliant, it was clear from its inception that customers would neither pay the high purchase price nor accept the high user fees. Approximately 50,000 customers purchased phone systems, but this was well below the volume required to sustain the business. The original owners sold the system for $25 million.

A variation of skimming can come into play in pricing a product line and is called **anchoring**. An anchor, typically used by luxury retailers, is a high-priced product that might never sell but makes everything else look cheap by comparison. Ralph Lauren was selling a "Ricky" alligator bag for $16,995. This made the "Tiffin" bag seem like a steal at $2,595 to some customers. William-Sonoma once offered a breadmaker for $279. Then it added a $429 model. The costly model was not successful but sales of the cheaper one doubled.[3]

Penetration Pricing Penetration pricing is at the opposite end of the spectrum from skimming. **Penetration pricing** means charging a relatively low price for a

anchoring
Luxury retailers set a very high price on an item, which may never sell at that price, but makes all other offerings of the retailer seem cheap by comparison.

penetration pricing
A pricing policy whereby a firm charges a relatively low price for a product initially as a way to reach the mass market.

product in order to reach the mass market. The low price is designed to capture a large share of a substantial market, resulting in lower production costs. If a marketing manager has made obtaining a large market share the firm's pricing objective, penetration pricing is a logical choice.

Penetration pricing does mean lower profit per unit, however. Therefore, to reach the break-even point, it requires a higher volume of sales than would a skimming policy. If reaching a high volume of sales takes a long time, then the recovery of product development costs will also be slow. As you might expect, penetration pricing tends to discourage competition.

Procter & Gamble examined the electric toothbrush market and noted that most electric brushes cost over $50. The company brought out the Crest SpinBrush that works on batteries and sells for just $5. It is now the nation's best-selling toothbrush, manual or electric, and has helped the Crest brand of products become P&G's 12th billion-dollar brand.

A penetration strategy tends to be effective in a price-sensitive market. Price should decline more rapidly when demand is elastic because the market can be expanded through a lower price. Also, price sensitivity and greater competitive pressure should lead to a lower initial price and a relatively slow decline in the price later or to a stable low price.

Although Walmart is associated with penetration pricing, other chains have done an excellent job of following this strategy as well. Dollar stores, those bare-bones, strip-mall chains that sell staples at cut-rate prices, are now one of the fastest-growing retailers in America. Led by Dollar General, Family Dollar, and Dollar Tree, the sector adds about 1,500 stores per year. Walmart usually opens its huge stores on the edge of town. Dollar chains can put their much smaller stores right in downtown neighborhoods, closer to where people live. Parking is usually a snap, and shoppers can be in and out in less time than it takes to hike across a jumbo Walmart lot. And as their name implies, the dollar stores offer low prices, sometimes even beating Walmart.

Another form of extreme penetration pricing that has dramatically increased sales during the recent economic downturn is salvage or surplus grocers. Salvage grocers sell "close-outs," which include products that manufacturers have discontinued, seasonal items that are outdated, and goods that are near the date when manufacturers expect freshness to wane. Many such grocers also sell products that were damaged in transit but remain edible, such as a dented box of Cheerios. Prices tend to be significantly lower than those at conventional stores and big discounters such as Walmart.[4]

If a firm has a low fixed cost structure and each sale provides a large contribution to those fixed costs, penetration pricing can boost sales and provide large increases in profits—but only if the market size grows or if competitors choose not to respond. Low prices can attract additional buyers to the market. The increased sales can justify production expansion or the adoption of

Dollar General, like most dollar stores, sells staple products at cut-rate prices. Dollar stores are now one of the fastest-growing retailers in America. The chains can put their much smaller stores right in downtown neighborhoods, closer to where people live.

new technologies, both of which can reduce costs. And, if firms have excess capacity, even low-priced business can provide incremental dollars toward fixed costs.

Penetration pricing can also be effective if an experience curve will cause costs per unit to drop significantly. The experience curve proposes that per-unit costs will go down as a firm's production experience increases. On average, for each doubling of production, a firm can expect per-unit costs to decline by roughly 20 percent. Cost declines can be significant in the early stages of production. Manufacturers that fail to take advantage of these effects will find themselves at a competitive cost disadvantage relative to others that are further along the curve.

The big advantage of penetration pricing is that it typically discourages or blocks competition from entering a market. The disadvantage is that penetration means gearing up for mass production to sell a large volume at a low price. What if the volume fails to materialize? The company will face huge losses from building or converting a factory to produce the failed product. Skimming, in contrast, lets a firm "stick its toe in the water" and see if limited demand exists at the high price. If not, the firm can simply lower the price. Skimming lets a company start out with a small production facility and expand it gradually as price falls and demand increases.

Penetration pricing can also prove disastrous for a prestige brand that adopts the strategy in an effort to gain market share and fails. When Omega—once a more prestigious brand than Rolex—was trying to improve the market share of its watches, it adopted a penetration pricing strategy that succeeded in destroying the watches' brand image by flooding the market with lower-priced products. Omega never gained sufficient share on its lower-priced/lower-image competitors to justify destroying its brand image and high-priced position with upscale buyers. Lacoste clothing experienced a similar outcome from a penetration pricing strategy.

Sometimes, multinational firms will follow a skimming strategy in developed countries and a penetration strategy in developing countries. Proctor & Gamble, for example, sees winning over low-income consumers in developing countries as crucial to its long-run growth strategy. The company that sells premium Pampers diapers and Olay moisturizers in developed countries has created the Gillette Guard, which costs 15 rupees, or 34 cents, and uses blades that cost 5 rupees, or 11 cents for the India market. This contrasts to its Fusion Pro Glide sold in the United States that requires manual cartridges that sell for $16.99. In the United States, P&G creates new products, and then sets a price. In developing markets, the company starts with what the consumer can afford and then adjusts features and manufacturing processes to meet the target price. The Gillette Guard features a light-weight handle, preferred by Indian men, and eliminates the lubrication strip and colorful handle designs. P&G hopes that, as the Indian economy grows, it can trade customers up to more expensive products.[5]

Although penetration pricing means a low price, an even better price for buyers is no price . . . yes, free. The notion is discussed in the Customer Experience box.

Status Quo Pricing The third basic price strategy a firm can choose is status quo pricing, also called *meeting the competition* or *going rate pricing*. (See also Chapter 19.) It means charging a price identical to or very close to the competition's price. JCPenney, for example, makes sure it is charging comparable prices by sending representatives to shop at similar retailers.

Although status quo pricing has the advantage of simplicity, its disadvantage is that the strategy might ignore demand or cost or both. If the firm is comparatively small, however, meeting the competition can be the safest route to long-term survival.

! customer experience

You Can Have This for Only $0.00

Everyday, we use services that cost us nothing. That's right—zip, zero. In the online world we use travel sites, Google, Wikipedia, and open source software for free. In some cases, advertisers pay for content such as Google and Facebook and we get it free. In other cases, a few paying customers trade up to premium versions and the rest of us get it for free. Take Tapulous, the creator of Tap Tap Revenge, a popular music game program for iPhones. Like Guitar Hero, notes stream down the screen and you have to hit them on the beat. Millions have tried the free version, and a number of them are paying for versions built around specific bands, such as Weezer and Nine Inch Nails. Similarly, picnik.com lets users crop and adjust photos within their browser window. A premium account ($24.95 per year) offers features including batch photo uploading, advanced editing tools, and no ads.

The free model is also expanding to products. Of course, free samples have been around for years. Go to Costco around noon on Saturday and you will get so many free tastings you won't need to eat lunch. Shops are now opening in Brazil where everything is free. The Free Sample Club, in Sao Paulo, requires an annual registration fee of 50 reals, or about $28. They then can go to the store and choose from 200 different products from over 130 companies. The free samples give manufacturers a way to evaluate tastes and preferences through marketing research. Customers are required to fill out online surveys. Other firms participate in hopes of creating ties and brand preference with a new wave of consumers.[6]

Do you think that free sample stores would be popular in the United States? Why or why not? If you were the president of YouTube or Flicker, what would you do to dramatically increase cash flow?

LO2

The Legality and Ethics of Price Strategy

As we mentioned in Chapter 4, some pricing decisions are subject to government regulation. Before marketing managers establish any price strategy, they should know the laws that limit their decision making. Among the issues that fall into this category are unfair trade practices, price fixing, price discrimination, and predatory pricing.

UNFAIR TRADE PRACTICES

In over half the states, **unfair trade practice acts** put a floor under wholesale and retail prices. Selling below cost in these states is illegal. Wholesalers and retailers must usually take a certain minimum percentage markup

Review LO1 Describe the procedure for setting the right price

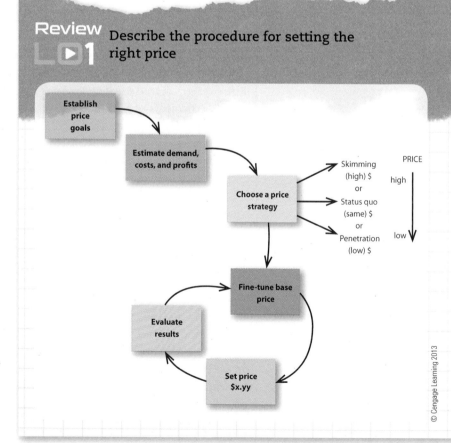

unfair trade practice acts
Laws that prohibit wholesalers and retailers from selling below cost.

price fixing
An agreement between two or more firms on the price they will charge for a product.

resale price maintenance
Retailers must sell a manufacturer's product at or above a specific price.

on their combined merchandise cost and transportation cost. The most common markup figures are 6 percent at the retail level and 2 percent at the wholesale level. If a specific wholesaler or retailer can provide "conclusive proof" that operating costs are lower than the minimum required figure, lower prices may be allowed.

The intent of unfair trade practice acts is to protect small local firms from giants like Walmart and Target, which operate very efficiently on razor-thin profit margins. State enforcement of unfair trade practice laws has generally been lax, however, partly because low prices benefit local consumers.

PRICE FIXING

Price fixing is an agreement between two or more firms on the price they will charge for a product. For instance, two or more executives from competing firms might meet to decide how much to charge for a product or to decide which of them will submit the lowest bid on a certain contract. Such practices are illegal under the Sherman Act and the Federal Trade Commission Act. Offenders have received fines and sometimes prison terms. Price fixing is one area where the law is quite clear, and the Justice Department's enforcement is vigorous.

Chinese manufacturers currently supply more than 85 percent of the vitamin C used in the United States. Just like the oil cartel, they can heavily influence world prices. After an agreement among China's four largest producers, spot prices for vitamin C rose to as high as $9 a kilogram from lows of less than $3. Chinese companies deny breaking U.S. law. The companies are expected to argue they are acting as agents of the Chinese government and therefore aren't subject to American laws against price fixing. The Chinese government stepped in to defend the four companies.[7]

The German car-parts maker Leoni was visited recently by European Commission investigators over alleged price fixing. The FBI visited the United States offices of Japanese parts makers Yazak Group, Denso, and Tokai Rika on the same charges. Lear Corporation of Southfield, Michigan, was also notified that it is part of the investigation. The firms are charged with fixing prices on wiring harnesses that power everything from interior lights to power windows.[8] The case was still pending as this book went to press.

Fresh Del Monte Produce paid $3 million on fixing the price of bananas. In a little over a year, the price of bananas jumped from $5.40 a box to more than $10 a box. Settlements of $2.5 million were also reached with Chiquita Brands and Dole Food.[9] Michelin has recovered excess payments from suppliers of chemicals used to make synthetic rubber. The defendants in the price fixing case were Royal Dutch Shell, Bayer, and Dow Chemical. The European Commission has levied fines of over ten billion euros on companies for price fixing since 2004.[10]

Price-fixing prosecution is not limited to huge, global competitors. In San Diego, two groups of anesthesiologists recently settled federal charges that they conspired to set prices for Sharp Grossmont Hospital.

Most price-fixing cases focus on high prices charged to customers. A reverse form of price fixing occurs when powerful buyers force their suppliers' prices down. Recently, Maine blueberry growers alleged that four big processors conspired to push down the price they would pay for fresh wild berries. A state court jury agreed and awarded millions in damages. In South Carolina, International Paper Company faces a lawsuit alleging that it conspired with its timber buyers to depress softwood prices in several states. In Alabama and Pennsylvania, federal antitrust enforcers targeted insurance companies that imposed contracts forcing down fees charged by doctors and hospitals. The insurers abandoned the practice.

Resale Price Maintenance Resale price maintenance is the practice whereby a manufacturer and its distributors agree that the retailers will sell the producer's product at a certain price (resale price maintenance), at or above a price floor. These rules prevent retailers from competing too fiercely on price and thus driving down profits. Some argue that the manufacturer might do this because it wishes to keep retailers profitable, and thus keep the manufacturer profitable. Others contend that minimum resale price maintenance, for instance, ensures that distributors who invest in promoting the manufacturer's product are able to recoup the additional costs of the promotion in the price they charge consumers. Some manufacturers also defend resale price maintenance by saying it ensures fair returns for all. The primary negative argument is that resale price maintenance results in higher consumer prices because efficient retailers, such as Walmart, Costco, or Best Buy must sell at a higher price than they would normally charge.

For over 100 years, resale price maintenance has been illegal under the Sherman Antitrust Act because it was viewed as *horizontal price fixing* (price fixing at the same level—such as two or more retailers). The Supreme Court said that it was illegal per se, meaning that resale price maintenance was illegal without regard to its impact on the marketplace or consumers. Then, in July 2007, the Supreme Court abandoned the "per se" rule and said that, instead, resale price maintenance agreements should be judged by a "rule of reason" analysis. That is, a balancing of pro-competitive justifications and anti-competitive harms. Critics say that the ruling gives manufacturers the ability to raise prices and this will hurt consumers. It is estimated that it could add $300 billion to consumer costs.[11]

Retailers say an array of manufacturers now require them to abide by minimum-pricing pacts, or risk having their supplies cut off. Jacob Weiss of BabyAge.com, which specializes in maternity and children's gear, says nearly 100 of his 465 suppliers now dictate minimum prices, and nearly a dozen have cut off shipments to him. "If this continues, it's going to put us out of the baby business," he says.[12]

Consumer advocates say they are seeing the impact particularly in baby goods, consumer electronics, home furnishings, and pet food. Recently, Old Mother Hubbard Dog Food Company wrote a letter to Morris Sussex Pet Supply, a New Jersey pet shop that complained about Morris Sussex selling 30-pound bags of its dog-food brand, Wellness Chicken Super5Mix, at 20 cents below the minimum $39.99 price. The director of Old Mother Hubbard said he would stop shipping the brand to the store for as long as six months if price-cutting continued.

The pet-supply shop fought back. It placed a billboard in front of its store urging customers to "Boycott Wellness Pet Food for Price Fixing," and aggressively steered customers to other types of dog food. "Our suppliers can set pricing policies all they want—but it's their loss, not ours," says Nancy Ruiz, the store's manager. Morris Sussex persuaded 85 percent of its Wellness customers to switch to another brand, Ms. Ruiz says. It now sells only a handful of Old Mother Hubbard products.[13]

At least one state is fighting back against the Supreme Court ruling.

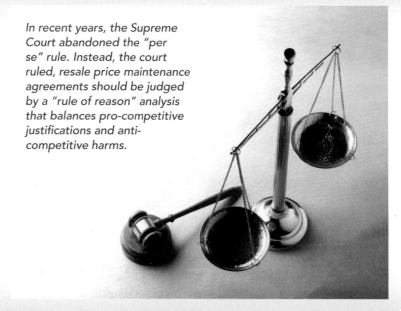

In recent years, the Supreme Court abandoned the "per se" rule. Instead, the court ruled, resale price maintenance agreements should be judged by a "rule of reason" analysis that balances pro-competitive justifications and anti-competitive harms.

Maryland has passed a law that prohibits manufacturers from requiring retailers to charge minimum prices for their goods. Retailers can sue manufacturers that impose resale price maintenance agreements.[14]

PRICE DISCRIMINATION

The Robinson-Patman Act of 1936 prohibits any firm from selling to two or more different buyers, within a reasonably short time, commodities (not services) of like grade and quality at different prices where the result would be to substantially lessen competition. The act also makes it illegal for a seller to offer two buyers different supplementary services and for buyers to use their purchasing power to force sellers into granting discriminatory prices or services.

Six elements are therefore needed for a violation of the Robinson-Patman Act to occur:

→ There must be price discrimination; that is, the seller must charge different prices to different customers for the same product.

→ The transaction must occur in interstate commerce.

→ The seller must discriminate by price among two or more purchasers; that is, the seller must make two or more actual sales within a reasonably short time.

→ The products sold must be commodities or other tangible goods.

→ The products sold must be of like grade and quality, not necessarily identical. If the goods are truly interchangeable and substitutable, then they are of like grade and quality.

→ There must be significant competitive injury.

The Robinson-Patman Act provides three defenses for the seller charged with price discrimination (in each case the burden is on the defendant to prove the defense):

→ **Cost:** A firm can charge different prices to different customers if the prices represent manufacturing or quantity discount savings.

→ **Market conditions:** Price variations are justified if designed to meet fluid product or market conditions. Examples include the deterioration of perishable goods, the obsolescence of seasonal products, a distress sale under court order, and a legitimate going-out-of-business sale.

→ **Competition:** A reduction in price might be necessary to stay even with the competition. Specifically, if a competitor undercuts the price quoted by a seller to a buyer, the law authorizes the seller to lower the price charged to the buyer for the product in question.

PREDATORY PRICING

Predatory pricing is the practice of charging a very low price for a product with the intent of driving competitors out of business or out of a market. Once competitors have been driven out, the firm raises its prices. This practice is illegal under the Sherman Act and the Federal Trade Commission Act. Proving predatory pricing is difficult and expensive, however. The Justice Department must demonstrate that the predator, the destructive company, explicitly tried to ruin a competitor and that the predator's intent was to raise prices to recover its losses once competitors had been driven out of business. The U.S. Supreme Court recently noted, "Predatory pricing is rarely tried and even more rarely successful."[15] The Court also said that lowering prices typically signals legitimate competition.

Predatory bidding is similar to predatory pricing and is held to the same legal standards. In the recent case of *Weyerhaeuser v. Ross-Simmons Hardwood Lumber*

predatory pricing
The practice of charging a very low price for a product with the intent of driving competitors out of business or out of a market.

Company, Ross-Simmons claimed that Weyerhaeuser had driven them out of business. Ross-Simmons had operated a single sawmill in the Pacific Northwest since 1962. The mill purchased alder logs and processed them into finished lumber. Logs can account for up to 75 percent of a mill's cost. Weyerhaeuser entered the Pacific Northwest in 1980 and opened six mills. Ross-Simmons claimed that Weyerhaeuser deliberately overpaid for raw alder logs in order to raise the prices that Ross-Simmons had to pay for logs. By artificially "bidding up" log costs, Weyerhaeuser forced Ross-Simmons into bankruptcy. The Court held in favor of Weyerhaeuser, noting that there are many reasons why the company may have bid up the price of alder logs. It could have been miscalculation, part of a risk strategy, or in response to increased consumer demand for the final product.[16]

Pricing laws have basically been passed to protect the buyer or businesses from unfair or discriminatory practices. Patents are meant to offer incentives to inventors by giving them the exclusive, but time limited right, to recoup their investment and earn a profit from the investment. Again, the basic notion is fairness and protection. But can a product be too crucial for saving lives to merit profits and protection? We explore this complex issue in the Ethics in Marketing Box on the next page.

Review
LO2 ▶ Identify the legal and ethical constraints on pricing decisions

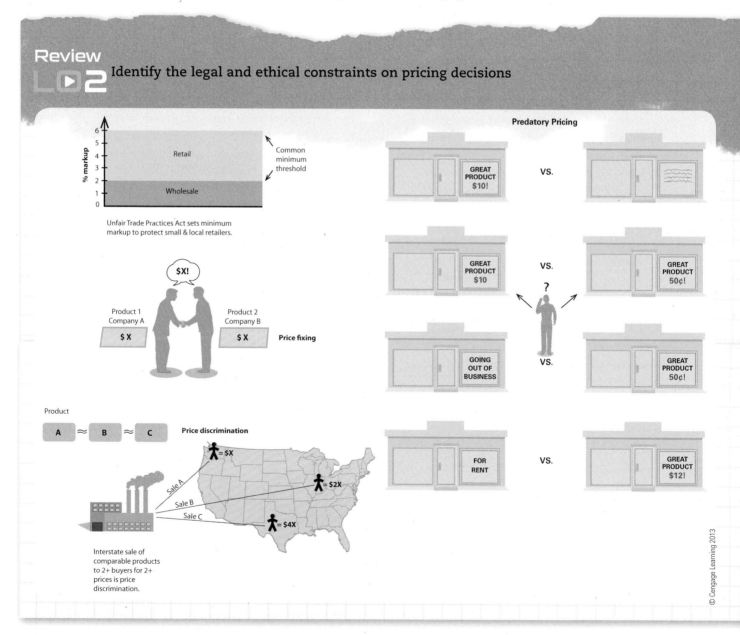

A Product Too Crucial for Profit Protection?

The story begins with a humanitarian French physician who had been looking for some way to solve the starvation problem around the world. One morning while having breakfast, he glanced at a jar of Nutella on the table and he had that eureka moment! His invention is called Plumpy'nut, an edible paste made of peanuts that is loaded with calories and vitamins. The product could be made by poor people, for poor people, to the benefits of patients and farmers. One doctor who decided to take a chance on Plumpy'nut was Mark Manary, a pediatrician and professor, who was working at a hospital in Malawi. His malnutrition ward was crammed full of dozens of children lying on mats. "It was really an incredible burden," Manary recalled. "These kids are deathly ill, you're doing what you can for them, and you think you're on the right track, and then you come in the next morning and four of them have died." Manary emptied out the ward, sending his patients home with Plumpy'nut. Many malnutrition experts were horrified. "It seemed dangerous to them, and it made them afraid," said Manary, who recalled that one eminent figure stood up at a conference and said, "You're killing children." In fact, when the results were analyzed, it was found that 95 percent of the subjects who received Plumpy'nut at home made a full recovery, a rate far better than that achieved with inpatient treatment.

The Malawi test emboldened Doctors Without Borders, which recognized that treating children outside clinical settings would allow a vastly larger response to humanitarian emergencies. It distributed Plumpy'nut to 60,000 children with severe acute malnutrition during a famine in Niger. Ninety percent completely recovered, and only 3 percent died. Within two years, the United Nations endorsed home care with Plumpy'nut as the preferred treatment for severe acute malnutrition. "This is an enormous breakthrough," said Werner Schultink, chief of nutrition for Unicef. "It has created the opportunity to reach many more children with relatively limited resources."

Yet the story does not have a fairy tale ending. The product is produced and patented by a French company called Nutriset. It defends its intellectual property rights for Plumpy'nut to the hilt. The firm has extended its patent to line extensions as well. This means people in developing countries who want to produce the product using local ingredients can't do it. Plumpy'nut costs about $60 per child for a two-month treatment. It is estimated that about 20 million children around the world suffer from acute malnutrition. UNICEF is spending a substantial portion of its budget on Plumpy'nut. The founder of Meds & Foods for Kids, St. Louis pediatrician Patricia Wolff, says "poverty is a business." She complained mightily about Nutriset's market dominance. Shortly thereafter, the nonprofit became a franchisee of Nutriset to provide the fortified nut paste in Haiti.

Two small nonprofit firms have filed a lawsuit challenging the Nutriset patent. One spokesperson said that Plumpy'nut is nothing more than fortified peanut butter. Do you think that the courts should uphold the patent? Why? Should developing nations be allowed to produce the product with local ingredients and not pay a fee to Nutriset? Each foil package of Plumpy'nut contains about 500 calories. One-third of the calories come from sugar so kids love it. Is it a good idea to give packaged sweetened products to kids whose families cannot continue to provide such things once the crisis is over?[17]

LO3
Tactics for Fine-Tuning the Base Price

base price
The general price level at which the company expects to sell the good or service.

After managers understand both the legal and the marketing consequences of price strategies, they should set a **base price**, the general price level at which the company expects to sell the good or service. The general price level is correlated with the pricing policy: above the market (price skimming), at the market (status quo pricing), or below the market (penetration pricing). The final step, then, is to fine-tune the base price.

Fine-tuning techniques are short-run approaches that do not change the general price level. They do, however, result in changes within a general price level. These pricing tactics allow the firm to adjust for competition in certain markets, meet ever-changing government regulations, take advantage of unique demand situations, and meet promotional and positioning goals. Fine-tuning pricing tactics include various sorts of discounts, geographic pricing, and other pricing tactics.

DISCOUNTS, ALLOWANCES, REBATES, AND VALUE-BASED PRICING

A base price can be lowered using discounts and the related tactics of allowances, rebates, low or zero percent financing, and value-based pricing. Managers use the various forms of discounts to encourage customers to do what they would not ordinarily do, such as paying cash rather than using credit, taking delivery out of season, or performing certain functions within a distribution channel.[18] The following are of the most common tactics:

→ **Quantity discounts:** When buyers get a lower price for buying in multiple units or above a specified dollar amount, they are receiving a **quantity discount**. A **cumulative quantity discount** is a deduction from list price that applies to the buyer's total purchases made during a specific period; it is intended to encourage customer loyalty. In contrast, a **noncumulative quantity discount** is a deduction from list price that applies to a single order rather than to the total volume of orders placed during a certain period. It is intended to encourage orders in large quantities.

→ **Cash discounts:** A **cash discount** is a price reduction offered to a consumer, an industrial user, or a marketing intermediary in return for prompt payment of a bill. Prompt payment saves the seller carrying charges and billing expenses and allows the seller to avoid bad debt.

→ **Functional discounts:** When distribution channel intermediaries, such as wholesalers or retailers, perform a service or function for the manufacturer, they must be compensated. This compensation, typically a percentage discount from the base price, is called a **functional discount** (or **trade discount**). Functional discounts vary greatly from channel to channel, depending on the tasks performed by the intermediary.

→ **Seasonal discounts:** A **seasonal discount** is a price reduction for buying merchandise out of season. It shifts the storage function to the purchaser. Seasonal discounts also enable manufacturers to maintain a steady production schedule year-round.

→ **Promotional allowances:** A **promotional allowance** (also known as a **trade allowance**) is a payment to a dealer for promoting the manufacturer's products. It is both a pricing tool and a promotional device. As a pricing tool, a promotional allowance is like a functional discount. If, for example, a retailer runs an ad for a manufacturer's product, the manufacturer might pay half the cost. If a retailer sets up a special display, the manufacturer might include a certain quantity of free goods in the retailer's next order.

→ **Rebates:** A **rebate** is a cash refund given for the purchase of a product during a specific period. The advantage of a rebate over a simple price reduction for stimulating demand is that a rebate is a temporary inducement that can be taken away without altering the basic price structure. A manufacturer that uses

quantity discount
A price reduction offered to buyers buying in multiple units or above a specified dollar amount.

cumulative quantity discount
A deduction from list price that applies to the buyer's total purchases made during a specific period.

noncumulative quantity discount
A deduction from list price that applies to a single order rather than to the total volume of orders placed during a certain period.

cash discount
A price reduction offered to a consumer, an industrial user, or a marketing intermediary in return for prompt payment of a bill.

functional discount (trade discount)
A discount to wholesalers and retailers for performing channel functions.

seasonal discount
A price reduction for buying merchandise out of season.

promotional allowance (trade allowance)
A payment to a dealer for promoting the manufacturer's products.

rebate
A cash refund given for the purchase of a product during a specific period.

a simple price reduction for a short time might meet resistance when trying to restore the price to its original, higher level. Fully 30 percent of all rebates never get redeemed because consumers fail to apply for them or their applications are rejected. A recent study found that 21 percent of those who had applied for a rebate during a recent 12 month period didn't succeed. Some that had applied simply never received anything, and some were turned down by a technicality.[19] Also, complex rules, filing periods of as little as a week, repeated requests for copies of receipts, and long delays in sending out checks discourage consumers from even attempting to retrieve their money.

That translates into more than $2 billion of extra revenue for retailers and their suppliers each year. What rebates do is get consumers to focus on the discounted price of a product, then buy it at full price. "The game is obviously that anything less than 100 percent redemption is free money," says Paula Rosenblum, director of retail research at consulting firm Aberdeen Group, Inc. The quest for consumers who never file for a rebate has resulted in new terminology. Purchases by consumers who never file for their rebates are called *breakage*. Wireless companies that pay 100 percent rebates on some cell phones, for example, rely in part on "breakage" to make money. Rebate checks that are never cashed are called *slippage*. Persons most likely to apply for rebates have household incomes of $100,000 or more, are 35 to 64 years old, and are typically female.[20]

→ **Zero percent financing:** During the late 2000s, new-car sales needed a boost. To get people back into automobile showrooms, manufacturers offered zero-percent financing, which enabled purchasers to borrow money to pay for new cars without incurring an interest charge. The tactic created a huge increase in sales but not without cost to the manufacturers. A five-year interest-free car loan represented a cost of over $3,000 on a typical vehicle sold during the zero-percent promotion. Automakers were still offering such incentives in 2011.

→ **Markdown money:** For decades, department stores have expected clothing companies and other merchandise suppliers to share in their sales risk. Whenever a suit or a sweater doesn't sell at full price, it is marked down. Department stores have required vendors to absorb some of the cost by paying the retailers **markdown money** at the end of each season. It's a perpetual negotiation in which each side moans that the other isn't shouldering enough of the risk. But recently, as department stores struggle for survival against discounters and specialty chains, vendors say certain retailers have been pushing too hard, relying too much on markdowns to move merchandise, and demanding higher rebates than what were originally agreed upon. Critics say markdown allowances, while legal, create an uneven playing field for vendors. Some big, powerful suppliers hold more sway with retailers and might pay lower allowances, creating an unfair advantage over smaller ones, according to some smaller vendors. Markdown money might be onerous for suppliers, but most have no choice but to "comply because they need the business," said Madison Riley, a principal at Kurt Salmon Associates, a consumer products consulting company. "If a vendor can't help a department store improve its profit margins, department stores have plenty of alternatives."[21]

Value-Based Pricing Value-based pricing, also called *value pricing*, is a pricing strategy that has grown out of the quality movement. It has become very popular during the recent recession. Instead of figuring prices based on costs or competitors' prices, it starts with the customer, considers the competition, and then determines the appropriate price. The basic assumption is that the firm is customer

markdown money
Money or discounts provided by vendors to department stores to help cover end-of-season discounts offered by department stores to clients.

value-based pricing
Setting the price at a level that seems to the customer to be a good price compared to the prices of other options.

driven, seeking to understand the attributes customers want in the goods and services they buy and the value of that bundle of attributes to customers. Because very few firms operate in a pure monopoly, however, a marketer using value-based pricing must also determine the value of competitive offerings to customers. Customers determine the value of a product (not just its price) relative to the value of alternatives. In value-based pricing, therefore, the price of the product is set at a level that seems to the customer to be a good price compared with the prices of other options.

Shoppers in competitive markets are seeing prices fall as Walmart pushes rivals to match its value prices. The firm continued to up the ante in 2010 by further reducing prices on over 10,000 items.[22] Recently, a number of regional grocery chains have switched to value pricing. In the past, they offered weekly specials to attract shoppers and then made up the lost profit by keeping nonsale prices substantially higher. Now, stores such as Costco and Walmart have conditioned consumers to expect inexpensive goods every day. Safeway long banked on customers paying higher prices in return for top quality fresh produce and upscale ambience. Even though it has been cutting prices, they were still over 10 percent higher than Kroger's prices. The result has been sales and profitability declines.[23]

Ethan Allen Interiors, the furniture retailer, dropped its six or seven sales events each year and moved to value pricing. Value pricing has also eliminated some production bottlenecks and inefficiencies caused by sales-driven order surges. Despite a move to value pricing, Ethan Allen has had trouble gaining market share. Critics say price cuts haven't gone far enough. Large Chinese manufacturers are producing Ethan Allen–quality products at much lower price points. Although Ethan Allen's CEO Farooq Kathwari has forecasted profitability in 2011, others are more skeptical. Sales plummeted in 2010 and even with heavy cost cutting the company was still losing money.[24]

C.F. Martin, manufacturer of guitars favored by Elvis Presley, Gene Autry, and Eric Clapton, sells its average price guitar around $2,000 to $3,000, with limited editions going for over $100,000. To avoid laying off skilled wood workers during the recent recession, Martin brought out a solid wood version of a 1930s model that lacks frills such as inlays. It is called the 1 Series model, so named for its simplicity, and sells for under $1,000. It would sell out its first year's output of 8,000 guitars without a problem.[25]

Pricing Products Too Low Sometimes managers price their products too low, thereby reducing company profits. This seems to happen for two reasons. First, managers attempt to buy market share through aggressive pricing. Usually, however, these price cuts are quickly met by competitors. Thus, any gain in market share is short-lived, and overall industry profits end up falling. Second, managers have a natural tendency to want to make decisions that can be justified objectively. The problem is that companies often lack hard data on the complex determinants of profitability, such as the relationship between price changes and sales volumes, the link between demand levels and costs, and the likely responses of competitors to price changes. In contrast, companies usually have rich, unambiguous information on costs, sales, market share, and competitors' prices. As a result, managers tend to make pricing decisions based on current costs, projected short-term share gains, or current competitor prices rather than on long-term profitability.

IKEA uses the low price of its furniture in this advertisement to encourage shoppers to buy as much seating as they need—all for a competitive price.

The problem of "underpricing" can be solved by linking information about price, cost, and demand within the same decision support system. The demand data can be developed via marketing research. This will enable managers to get the hard data they need to calculate the effects of pricing decisions on profitability.

GEOGRAPHIC PRICING

Because many sellers ship their wares to a nationwide or even a worldwide market, the cost of freight can greatly affect the total cost of a product. Sellers use several different geographic pricing tactics to moderate the impact of freight costs on distant customers. The following methods of geographic pricing are the most common:

→ **FOB origin pricing:** FOB origin pricing, also called *FOB factory* or *FOB shipping point,* is a price tactic that requires the buyer to absorb the freight costs from the shipping point ("free on board"). The farther buyers are from sellers, the more they pay, because transportation costs generally increase with the distance merchandise is shipped.

→ **Uniform delivered pricing:** If the marketing manager wants total costs, including freight, to be equal for all purchasers of identical products, the firm will adopt uniform delivered pricing, or "postage stamp" pricing. With uniform delivered pricing, the seller pays the actual freight charges and bills every purchaser an identical, flat freight charge. L.L. Bean uses uniform delivered pricing: If you purchase something from its catalog, you will be charged a flat freight rate.

→ **Zone pricing:** A marketing manager who wants to equalize total costs among buyers within large geographic areas—but not necessarily all of the seller's market area—may modify the base price with a zone-pricing tactic. Zone pricing is a modification of uniform delivered pricing. Rather than using a uniform freight rate for the entire United States (or its total market), the firm divides it into segments or zones and charges a flat freight rate to all customers in a given zone. The U.S. Postal Service's parcel post rate structure is probably the best-known zone-pricing system in the country.

→ **Freight absorption pricing:** In freight absorption pricing, the seller pays all or part of the actual freight charges and does not pass them on to the buyer. The manager might use this tactic in intensely competitive areas or as a way to break into new market areas.

→ **Basing-point pricing:** With basing-point pricing, the seller designates a location as a basing point and charges all buyers the freight cost from that point, regardless of the city from which the goods are shipped. Thanks to several adverse court rulings, basing-point pricing has waned in popularity. Freight fees charged when none were actually incurred, called *phantom freight,* have been declared illegal.

OTHER PRICING TACTICS

Unlike geographic pricing, other pricing tactics are unique and defy neat categorization. Thus, we simply call this group "other." Managers use these tactics for various reasons—for example, to stimulate demand for specific products, to increase store patronage, and to offer a wider variety of merchandise at a specific price point. "Other" pricing tactics include a single-price tactic, flexible pricing, professional services pricing, price lining, leader pricing, bait pricing, odd–even pricing, price bundling, and two-part pricing. A brief overview of each of these tactics follows, along with a manager's reasons for using that tactic or a combination of tactics to change the base price.

Single-Price Tactic A merchant using a **single-price tactic** offers all goods and services at the same price (or perhaps two or three prices). Retailers using this tactic include One Price Clothing Stores and Your $10 Store. One Price Clothing Stores, for example, tend to be small, about 3,000 square feet. Their goal is to offer merchandise that would sell for at least $15 to $18 in other stores. The stores carry pants, shirts, blouses, sweaters, and shorts for juniors, misses, and large-

Pricing objectives are profit oriented, sales oriented, or status quo. If a company's objective is to be the dominant sales leader in an industry, it will pursue a sales-oriented pricing goal. An organization attempting to just preserve its position in the marketplace usually pursues status quo goals. A company committed to maximum shareholder value is aggressive in pursuing profit-oriented pricing goals. Which goals do you think car dealers follow?

sized women. The stores do not feature any seconds or irregular items, and everything is sold for under $10.

Single-price selling removes price comparisons from the buyer's decision-making process. The consumer just looks for suitability and the highest perceived quality. The retailer enjoys the benefits of a simplified pricing system and minimal clerical errors. However, continually rising costs are a headache for retailers following this strategy. In times of inflation, they must frequently raise the selling price.

Sometimes using a single price tactic can open the door for competition. For years, UPS prided itself on charging one price to all its customers. But when FedEx Corp. entered the market, one reason for its swift success was its variable pricing, which recognized inherent value differences between customers, orders (parcels versus messages), and times of delivery (8 A.M. versus afternoon).[26]

Flexible Pricing **Flexible pricing** (or **variable pricing**) means that different customers pay different prices for essentially the same merchandise bought in equal quantities. This tactic is often found in the sale of shopping goods, specialty merchandise, and most industrial goods except supply items. Car dealers, many appliance retailers, and manufacturers of industrial installations, accessories, and component parts commonly follow the practice. It allows the seller to adjust for competition by meeting another seller's price. Thus, a marketing manager with a status quo pricing objective might readily adopt the tactic. Flexible pricing also enables the seller to close a sale with price-conscious consumers. If buyers show promise of becoming large-volume shoppers, flexible pricing can be used to lure their business.

The obvious disadvantages of flexible pricing are the lack of consistent profit margins, the potential ill will of high-paying purchasers, the tendency for

single-price tactic
A price tactic that offers all goods and services at the same price (or perhaps two or three prices).

flexible pricing (variable pricing)
A price tactic in which different customers pay different prices for essentially the same merchandise bought in equal quantities.

salespeople to automatically lower the price to make a sale, and the possibility of a price war among sellers.

Trade-Ins Flexible pricing and trade-ins often go hand-in-hand. About 57 percent of all new car sales involve a trade-in.[27] Trade-ins occur for other products as well, such as musical instruments, sporting goods, jewelry, and some appliances. If a trade-in is involved, the consumer must negotiate two prices, one for the new product and one for the existing product. The existence of a trade-in raises several questions for the purchaser. For example, will the new product's price differ depending on whether there is a trade-in? Are consumers better off trading in their used product toward the purchase of the new one from the same retailer, or should they keep the two transactions separate by dealing with different retailers? Several car buying guides, such as **Edmunds.com** and **AutoTrader.com** advise consumers to keep the two transactions separate.[28]

Recent research found that trade-in customers tend to care more about the trade-in value they receive than the price they pay for the new product. Thus, these buyers tend to pay more than purchasers without a trade-in. Analysis of data from the automobile market found that, on average, trade-in customers end up paying $452 more than customers who simply buy a new car from a dealer.[29]

Professional Services Pricing Professional services pricing is used by people with lengthy experience, training, and often certification by a licensing board— for example, lawyers, physicians, and family counselors. Professionals sometimes charge customers at an hourly rate, but sometimes fees are based on the solution of a problem or performance of an act (such as an eye examination) rather than on the actual time involved. A surgeon might perform a heart operation and charge a flat fee of $5,000. The operation itself requires only four hours, resulting in a hefty $1,250 hourly rate. The physician justifies the fee because of the lengthy education and internship required to learn the complex procedures of a heart operation. Lawyers also sometimes use flat-rate pricing, such as $500 for completing a divorce and $50 for handling a traffic ticket.

Those who use professional pricing have an ethical responsibility not to overcharge a customer. Because demand is sometimes highly inelastic, such as when a person requires heart surgery or a daily insulin shot to survive, there may be a temptation to charge "all the traffic will bear."

Price Lining When a seller establishes a series of prices for a type of merchandise, it creates a price line. **Price lining** is the practice of offering a product line with several items at specific price points. For example, HON, an office furniture manufacturer, might offer its four-drawer file cabinets at $125, $250, and $400. The Limited might offer women's dresses at $40, $70, and $100, with no merchandise marked at prices between those figures. Instead of a normal demand curve running from $40 to $100, The Limited has three demand points (prices). Theoretically, the "curve" exists only because people would buy goods at the in-between prices if it were possible to do so. For example, a number of dresses could be sold at $60, but no sales will occur at that price because $60 is not part of the price line.

Price lining reduces confusion for both the salesperson and the consumer. The buyer be offered a wider variety of merchandise at each established price. Price lines also enable a seller to reach several market segments. For buyers, the question of price might be quite simple: All they have to do is find a suitable product at the

price lining
The practice of offering a product line with several items at specific price points.

predetermined price. Moreover, price lining is a valuable tactic for the marketing manager, because the firm might be able to carry a smaller total inventory than it could without price lines. The results might include fewer markdowns, simplified purchasing, and lower inventory carrying charges.

Price lines also present drawbacks, especially if costs are continually rising. Sellers can offset rising costs in three ways. First, they can begin stocking lower-quality merchandise at each price point. Second, sellers can change the prices, although frequent price line changes confuse buyers. Third, sellers can accept lower profit margins and hold quality and prices constant. This third alternative has short-run benefits, but its long-run handicaps might drive sellers out of business.

AT&T has set up a two-tiered price line for its smartphone broadband users. Instead of being able to pay $30 for unlimited use, it now offers 200 megabytes for $15 a month or $25 for 2 gigabytes, with added charges if they exceed those ceilings. AT&T says that 98 percent of its customers consume less than 2 gigabytes a month.[30] Verizon has decided to follow AT&T's lead. To date, Sprint Nextel and T-Mobile are staying with a flat rate price in an attempt to win market share.[31]

Leader Pricing **Leader pricing** (or **loss-leader pricing**) is an attempt by the marketing manager to attract customers by selling a product near or even below cost in the hope that shoppers will buy other items once they are in the store. This type of pricing appears weekly in the newspaper advertising of supermarkets, specialty stores, and department stores. Leader pricing is normally used on well-known items that consumers can easily recognize as bargains at the special price. The goal is not necessarily to sell large quantities of leader items, but to try to appeal to customers who might shop elsewhere.

Leader pricing is not limited to products. Health clubs offer a one-month free trial as a loss leader. Lawyers give a free initial consultation. And restaurants distribute two-for-one coupons and "welcome to the neighborhood" free meal coupons.

Bait Pricing In contrast to leader pricing, which is a genuine attempt to give the consumer a reduced price, bait pricing is deceptive. **Bait pricing** tries to get the consumer into a store through false or misleading price advertising and then uses high-pressure selling to persuade the consumer to buy more expensive merchandise. You may have seen this ad or a similar one:

> REPOSSESSED: Singer slant-needle sewing machine . . . take over 8 payments of $5.10 per month . . . ABC Sewing Center.

This is bait. When a customer goes in to see the machine, a salesperson says that it has just been sold or else shows the prospective buyer a piece of junk no one would buy. Then the salesperson says, "But I've got a really good deal on this fine new model." This is the switch that might cause a susceptible consumer to walk out with a $400 machine. The Federal Trade Commission considers bait pricing a deceptive act and has banned its use in interstate commerce. Most states also ban bait pricing, but sometimes enforcement is lax.

Odd–Even Pricing **Odd–even pricing** (or **psychological pricing**) means pricing at odd-numbered prices to connote a bargain and pricing at even-numbered prices to imply quality. For years, many retailers have priced their products in odd numbers—for example, $99.95 or $49.95—to make consumers feel they are paying a lower price for the product.

leader pricing (loss-leader pricing)
A price tactic in which a product is sold near or even below cost in the hope that shoppers will buy other items once they are in the store.

bait pricing
A price tactic that tries to get consumers into a store through false or misleading price advertising and then uses high-pressure selling to persuade consumers to buy more expensive merchandise.

odd–even pricing (psychological pricing)
A price tactic that uses odd-numbered prices to connote bargains and even-numbered prices to imply quality.

Contrary to popular belief that the ".99" part of a price such as $19.99 makes the difference in purchasing behavior, new research finds that it's the left digits—the numbers that come before the .99—that determine whether consumers perceive a penny reduction as a bargain. Research participants were shown product prices that ended either in nine (e.g., $19.99 and $23.59) or in zero (e.g., $20.00 and $23.60). In half the cases, when the price ending changed from zero to nine, the left digit changed and the price became lower (e.g., $20.00 changed to $19.99). For the other half, the left digit stayed the same (e.g., $23.60 changed to $23.59). When the left digit changed, participants thought the price with the nine ending (e.g., $19.99) was much cheaper than the price with the zero ending (e.g., $20.00). When the left digit did not change, however, participants perceived the nine- and the zero-ending prices (e.g., $23.60 versus $23.59) as essentially the same. These results demonstrate that the "left-digit effect," changing the left digits to a lower number (20 to 19) rather than the right digits (.60 to .59), is what affected the participants' perception of the price.[32]

Even-numbered pricing is sometimes used to denote quality. Examples include a fine perfume at $100 a bottle, a good watch at $500, or a mink coat at $3,000.

This health club is trying to get new members in the door with a reduced membership fee. Which "other" pricing tactic do you think is represented here: single-price tactic, flexible pricing, professional services pricing, price lining, leader pricing, bait pricing, odd–even pricing, price bundling, or two-part pricing?

© Michael Newman/PhotoEdit, Inc.

The demand curve for such items would also be sawtoothed, except that the outside edges would represent even-numbered prices and, therefore, elastic demand.

Price Bundling Price bundling is marketing two or more products in a single package for a special price. Examples include the sale of maintenance contracts with computer hardware and other office equipment, packages of stereo equipment, packages of options on cars, weekend hotel packages that include a room and several meals, and airline vacation packages. Microsoft offers "suites" of software that bundle spreadsheets, word processing, graphics, e-mail, Internet access, and groupware for networks of microcomputers. Price bundling can stimulate demand for the bundled items if the target market perceives the price as a good value.

Services such as hotels sell a perishable commodity (hotel rooms and airline seats) with relatively constant fixed costs. Bundling can be an important income stream for these businesses because the variable cost tends to be low—for instance, the cost of cleaning a hotel room. Therefore, most of the revenue can help cover fixed costs and generate profits.

The automobile industry has a different motive for bundling. People buy cars only every three to five years. Thus, selling options is a somewhat rare opportunity for the car dealer. Price bundling can help the dealer sell a maximum number of options.

Bundling has also been used in the telecommunications industry. Companies offer local service, long distance, DSL Internet service, wireless, and even cable TV in various menus of bundling. Such bundling is not necessarily consumer focused. Telecom companies use bundling as a way to protect their market share and fight off competition by locking customers into a group of services. This makes

price bundling
Marketing two or more products in a single package for a special price.

comparison shopping difficult for consumers because they may not be able to determine how much they are really paying for each component of the bundle.

A related price tactic is **unbundling**, or reducing the bundle of services that comes with the basic product. Rather than raise the price of hotel rooms, some hotel chains have started charging registered guests for parking. To help hold the line on costs, some stores require customers to pay for gift wrapping. Airlines charge for food and checked baggage.

Clearly, price bundling—for example, a theater series pass or a vacation package that combines airfare, lodging, and meals—can influence consumers' purchase behavior. But what about the decision to consume a particular bundled product or service, such as eating the daily lunch buffet or attending a particular theater performance? Some research has focused on how people consume certain bundled products or services. According to this research, the key to consumption behavior is how closely consumers can link the costs and benefits of the exchange.[33] In a complex transaction such as a holiday package, it might be unclear which costs are paying for which benefits. In such cases, consumers tend to mentally downplay their up-front costs for the bundled product, so they might be more likely to forgo a benefit that's part of the bundle, such as a free dinner or a play.

Similarly, when people buy season tickets to a concert series, sporting event, or other activity, the sunk costs (price of the bundle) and the pending benefit (going to see an event) become decoupled. This reduces the likelihood of consumption of the event over time. For example, researchers found that theatergoers who purchased tickets to four plays were only 84 percent likely to use their first-play tickets and only 78 percent likely to use any given ticket across the four plays.[34] In contrast, theatergoers who purchased tickets to a single play were almost certain to use those tickets. This is consistent with the idea that in a one-to-one transaction (i.e., one payment, one benefit), the costs and benefits of that transaction are tightly coupled, resulting in strong sunk cost pressure to consume the pending benefit. In other words, "I bought this ticket, now I've got to use it."

In practice, these findings mean that a theater manager might expect a no-show rate of 20 percent when the percentage of season ticket holders is high, but a no-show rate of only 5 percent when the percentage of season ticket holders is low. With a high number of season ticket holders, a manager could oversell performances and maximize the revenue for the theater. Airlines routinely overbook in anticipation of a predictable percentage of no-shows.

The physical format of the transaction also figures in. A ski lift pass in the form of a booklet of tickets strengthens the cost-benefit link for consumers, whereas a single pass for multiple ski lifts weakens that link. Thus, the skier with a booklet of tickets is likely to use the ski lift more often than the skier who has just one pass, even though both paid the same amount at the outset.

Though price bundling of services can result in a lower rate of total consumption of that service, the same is not necessarily true for products. Consider the purchase of an expensive bottle of wine, which can be inventoried until needed. When the wine is purchased as a single unit, its cost and eventual benefit are tightly coupled. As a result, the cost of the wine will be quite important, and a person will likely reserve that wine for a special occasion. When purchased as part of a bundle (e.g., as part of a case of wine), however, the cost and benefit of that individual bottle of wine will likely become decoupled, reducing the impact of the cost on eventual consumption. As a result, a person will likely find the wine appropriate for many more (not-so-special) occasions. Thus, in contrast to the price bundling of services, the price bundling of physical goods could lead to an increase in product consumption.

unbundling
Reducing the bundle of services that comes with the basic product.

two-part pricing

A price tactic that charges two separate amounts to consume a single good or service.

Two-Part Pricing Two-part pricing means establishing two separate charges to consume a single good or service. Tennis clubs and health clubs charge a membership fee and a flat fee each time a person uses certain equipment or facilities. In other cases they charge a base rate for a certain level of usage, such as ten racquetball games per month, and a surcharge for anything over that amount.

Consumers sometimes prefer two-part pricing because they are uncertain about the number and the types of activities they might use at places like an amusement park. Also, the people who use a service most often pay a higher total price. Two-part pricing can increase a seller's revenue by attracting consumers who would not pay a high fee even for unlimited use. For example, a health club might be able to sell only 100 memberships at $700 annually with unlimited use of facilities, for total revenue of $70,000. However, perhaps it could sell 900 memberships at $200 with a guarantee of using the racquetball courts ten times a month. Every use over ten would require the member to pay a $5 fee. Thus, membership revenue would provide a base of $180,000, with some additional usage fees throughout the year.

Research has shown that when consumers are thinking of buying a good or service with two-part pricing they mentally process the base price, such as a membership fee, more thoroughly than the extra fee or surcharge (playing a game of tennis). Thus, they can underestimate the total price compared with when prices are not partitioned.[35] The researchers also found that low-perceived benefit components should be priced relatively low and vice versa. Consumers find a higher total price more acceptable when the high-benefit component is priced high than when the low benefit component is priced high. For example, assume John joins a health club and swims at the club four times a month. John really enjoys working out and views being a member of the club as part of a healthy life style (high value). He also swims after a workout once a week to unwind and relax. Swimming is not that important to John, but is enjoyable (low value). If the club charges $60 a month dues and $5 per swim, John perceives this as acceptable. According to the research, John would find it less attractive if the monthly dues were $40 and each swim was $10. Yet the total cost is the same!

Pay What You Want To many people, pay what you want or what you think something is worth is a very risky tactic.

Review

LO 3 Explain how discounts, geographic pricing, and other pricing tactics can be used to fine-tune the base price

© Cengage Learning 2013

Obviously, it wouldn't work for expensive durables such as automobiles. Imagine someone paying $1 for a new BMW! Yet this model has worked in varying degrees in restaurants and other service businesses. One of your authors has patronized a restaurant close to campus that uses "pay what you think it is worth." After several years, it is still in business. The owner said that the average lunch donation was around $8. Social pressures can come into play in a "pay what you want" environment because an individual doesn't want to appear poor or cheap to his or her peers.

Researchers recently conducted three separate pay what you want studies using a restaurant, movie tickets, and hot beverages. In the restaurant study and the hot drinks study, revenues were higher than baseline revenues. The researchers found that the money paid depended on an internal reference price (what they would normally pay), plus the notion of fairness, satisfaction with the experience, and income.[36]

Radiohead let buyers name their own price for the band's "In Rainbow" album. A café run by the Panera Bread chain in Clayton, Missouri, is trying the strategy by asking customers to "take what you need, leave your fair share" in wood and Plexiglas lockboxes. The producers and distributors of the movie *Freakonomics* did a one-night experiment using pay what you want. There was no choice for zero, nor an option for giving some of the money to charity. Movie goers could pay:

→ From $.01 to $5.00 at $.50 intervals

→ From $5.00 to $20.00 at $1.00 intervals

→ From $20.00 to $80.00 at $5.00 intervals

→ $90.00 and $100.00

While the full results have not been announced, out of 5,000 viewers, 18 paid a full $100.[37]

Another experiment was carried out at a rollercoaster ride at a large theme park. After each of the 113,047 participants rode the rollercoaster, they were given the option to buy a souvenir photo of themselves that had been taken during the ride. In one condition, the price of the photo was fixed at $15.95; in a separate condition, the buyers could pay whatever they wanted—including nothing at all—for the souvenir. Then, an extra dimension was added: half of the participants in each treatment were told that the company would donate half of the proceeds to charity. When the price was fixed at $15.95, just 0.50 percent (one half of one percent) of the participants bought the photo, and pledging to donate to charity barely raised the purchase rate, to 0.59 percent. Under the "pay what you want" condition, riders were far more likely to purchase the photos, although at a much-reduced price. When no charity offer was made, 8.39 percent of participants bought the photo for an average of 92¢, although the profit per rider was negligible. When half the proceeds went to charity, fewer riders—about 4.5 percent—made the purchase, but they paid an average of $5.33. Interestingly, riders who were able to dictate the price were less willing to buy the photo when part of their purchase price went to charity. The researchers hypothesize that stingy people that aren't willing to pay much

for the photo felt bad for donating so little to charity and didn't want to appear uncaring to others, so they refrained completely from buying.[38]

CONSUMER PENALTIES

More and more businesses are adopting **consumer penalties**—extra fees paid by consumers for violating the terms of a purchase agreement. (See Exhibit 20.2.)

Businesses impose consumer penalties for two reasons: They will allegedly (1) suffer an irrevocable revenue loss or (2) incur significant additional transaction costs should customers be unable or unwilling to complete their purchase obligations. For the company, these customer payments are part of doing business in a highly competitive marketplace. With profit margins in many companies increasingly coming under pressure, organizations are looking to stem losses resulting from customers not meeting their obligations. However, the perceived unfairness of a penalty may affect some consumers' willingness to patronize a business in the future.

Exhibit 20.2 Common Consumer Penalties

1. Airlines

- Some airlines charge a penalty of $100 or more for changing reservations on discount tickets; many airlines charge for overweight baggage or checking a bag.

2. Automobiles

- Penalties are imposed for early terminations of car leases. In some cases, deposits on canceled leases can be subject to penalties.
- Car owners in England pay penalties, administration fees, and commissions if they cancel an insurance policy early.

3. Banks

- Penalties are often associated with early withdrawal of certificates of deposit.
- Some banks charge penalties for too many withdrawals in a month.
- Some have monthly penalties of $5 to $10 if a client's balance falls below a minimum level.
- Banks can charge late fees, in addition to interest, for tardy payments.

4. Car Rentals

- Rental companies often have $25 to $100 penalties for no-shows for specialty vehicles. Budget, National, and Dollar/Thrifty are experimenting with no-show fees on all rentals.

5. Child Day Care

- Many day-care centers charge a penalty of up to $5 a minute when parents are late in picking up their children.

6. Cellular Phones

- Companies have cancellation penalties, often in the small print on the back of a contract, that can run as high as $525.

7. Credit and Debit Cards

- Some vendors now charge late fees (beyond normal interest). Lenders collect about $2 billion in late charges each year.

8. Cruises

- If a cruise is sailing, even though there are hurricane warnings, some cruise lines will assess penalties if a passenger cancels.
- Even trip cancellation insurance will not ensure a refund if the traveler has embarked on the trip.
- Britain is trying to crack down on excessive cancellation penalties on package holidays.
- The *Carnival Paradise* will disembark passengers found smoking.

9. Hotels

- Some hotels require 72 hours' cancellation notice, or the client must pay a penalty of one day's room cost.
- Most hotels have high charges for using in-room long-distance service.
- Hilton, Hyatt, and Westin have early departure fees.

10. Restaurants

- Some now charge up to $50 per person for no-show parties.

11. Retail Stores

- Circuit City and Best Buy are leading others in charging a 15 percent restocking fee on some returned items. A restocking fee is for putting a returned item back in inventory.

12. Trains

- Amtrak has a $20 penalty for a returned ticket and charges the same fee for changing a ticket.

13. Universities

- Some universities will give only a partial tuition refund if a student becomes ill after a course begins.

Source: Eugene Fram and Michael McCarthy, "The True Price of Penalties," *Marketing Management,* Fall 1999, 51.

LO 4
Product Line Pricing

Product line pricing is setting prices for an entire line of products. Compared to setting the right price on a single product, product line pricing encompasses broader concerns. In product line pricing, the marketing manager tries to achieve maximum profits or other goals for the entire line rather than for a single component of the line.

RELATIONSHIPS AMONG PRODUCTS

The manager must first determine the type of relationship that exists among the various products in the line:

→ If items are *complementary,* an increase in the sale of one good causes an increase in demand for the complementary product, and vice versa. For example, the sale of ski poles depends on the demand for skis, making these two items complementary.

→ Two products in a line can also be *substitutes* for each other. If buyers buy one item in the line, they are less likely to buy a second item in the line. For example, if someone goes to an automotive supply store and buys paste Turtle Wax for a car, it is very unlikely that he or she will buy liquid Turtle Wax in the near future.

→ A *neutral* relationship can also exist between two products. In other words, demand for one of the products is unrelated to demand for the other. For instance, Nestlé Purina sells chicken feed and Wheat Chex, but the sale of one of these products has no known impact on demand for the other.

JOINT COSTS

Joint costs are costs that are shared in the manufacturing and marketing of several products in a product line. These costs pose a unique problem in product pricing. In oil refining, for example, fuel oil, gasoline, kerosene, naphtha, paraffin, and lubricating oils are all derived from a common production process. Another example is the production of compact discs that combine photos and music.

Any assignment of joint costs must be somewhat subjective because costs are actually shared. Suppose a company produces two products, X and Y, in a common production process, with joint costs allocated on a weight basis. Product X weighs 1,000 pounds, and product Y weighs 500 pounds. Thus, costs are allocated on the basis of $2 for X for every $1 for Y. Gross margins (sales less the cost of goods sold) might then be as follows:

	Product X	Product Y	Total
Sales	$20,000	$6,000	$26,000
Less: cost of goods sold	$15,000	$7,500	$22,500
Gross margin	$ 5,000	($1,500)	$ 3,500

This statement reveals a loss of $1,500 on product Y. Is that important? Yes, any loss is important. However, the firm must realize that overall it earned a $3,500 profit on the two items in the line. Also, weight may not be the right way to allocate the joint costs. Instead, the firm might use other bases, including market value or quantity sold.

product line pricing
Setting prices for an entire line of products.

joint costs
Costs that are shared in the manufacturing and marketing of several products in a product line.

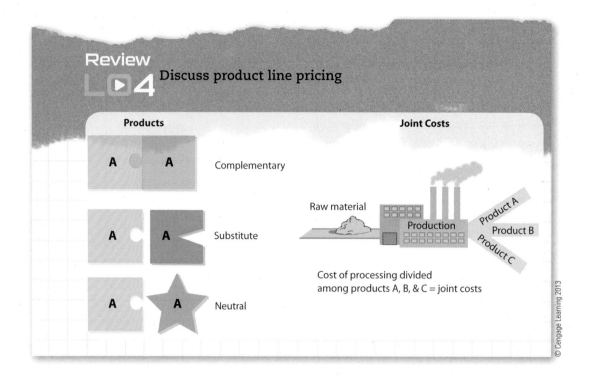

Products — Joint Costs

A A — Complementary

A A — Substitute

A A — Neutral

Raw material

Production

Product A
Product B
Product C

Cost of processing divided
among products A, B, & C = joint costs

© Cengage Learning 2013

LO5
Pricing during Difficult Economic Times

Pricing is always an important aspect of marketing, but it is especially crucial in times of inflation and recession. The firm that does not adjust to economic trends might lose ground that it can never make up.

INFLATION

When the economy is characterized by high inflation, special pricing tactics are often necessary. They can be subdivided into cost-oriented and demand-oriented tactics.

Cost-Oriented Tactics One popular cost-oriented tactic is *culling products with a low profit margin* from the product line. However, this tactic can backfire for three reasons:

→ A high volume of sales on an item with a low profit margin still makes the item highly profitable.

→ Eliminating a product from a product line reduces economies of scale, thereby lowering the margins on other items.

→ Eliminating the product affects the price-quality image of the entire line.

Another popular cost-oriented tactic is **delayed-quotation pricing**, which is used for industrial installations and many accessory items. Price is not set on the product until the item is either finished or delivered. Long production lead times force many firms to adopt this policy during periods of inflation. Builders of nuclear power plants, ships, airports, and office towers sometimes use delayed-quotation tactics.

delayed-quotation pricing
A price tactic used for industrial installations and many accessory items, in which a firm price is not set until the item is either finished or delivered.

Escalator pricing is similar to delayed-quotation pricing in that the final selling price reflects cost increases incurred between the time an order is placed and the time delivery is made. An escalator clause allows for price increases (usually across the board) based on the cost of living index or some other formula. As with any price increase, management's ability to implement such a policy is based on inelastic demand for the product. About a third of all industrial product manufacturers now use escalator clauses. Many companies do not apply the clause in every sale, however. Often it is used only for extremely complex products that take a long time to produce or with new customers.

Any cost-oriented pricing policy that tries to maintain a fixed gross margin under all conditions can lead to a vicious cycle. For example, a price increase will result in decreased demand, which in turn increases production costs (because of lost economies of scale). Increased production costs require a further price increase, leading to further diminished demand, and so on.

Demand-Oriented Tactics Demand-oriented pricing tactics use price to reflect changing patterns of demand caused by inflation or high interest rates. Cost changes are considered, of course, but mostly in the context of how increased prices will affect demand.

Price Shading **Price shading** is the use of discounts by salespeople to increase demand for one or more products in a line. Often shading becomes habitual and is done routinely without much forethought. Ducommun, a metals producer, is among the major companies that have succeeded in eliminating the practice. Ducommun has told its salespeople, "We want no deviation from book price" unless authorized by management.

To make the demand for a good or service more inelastic and to create buyer dependency, a company can use several strategies:

→ **Cultivate selected demand:** Marketing managers can target prosperous customers who will pay extra for convenience or service. Neiman Marcus, for example, stresses quality. As a result, the luxury retailer is more lenient with suppliers and their price increases than a dollar store might be. In cultivating close relationships with affluent organizational customers, marketing managers should avoid putting themselves at the mercy of a dominant firm. They can more easily raise prices when an account is readily replaceable. Finally, in companies where engineers exert more influence than purchasing departments do, performance is favored over price. Often a preferred vendor's pricing range expands if other suppliers prove technically unsatisfactory.

→ **Create unique offerings:** Marketing managers should study buyers'

---

escalator pricing
A price tactic in which the final selling price reflects cost increases incurred between the time the order is placed and the time delivery is made.

price shading
The use of discounts by salespeople to increase demand for one or more products in a line.

Cereal manufacturers have skirted around passing on costs by marketing unique value-added or multi-ingredient cereals, increasing the perceived quality of cereals and allowing companies to raise prices.

needs. If the seller can design distinctive goods or services uniquely fitting buyers' activities, equipment, and procedures, a mutually beneficial relationship will evolve. Buyers would incur high changeover costs in switching to another supplier. By satisfying targeted buyers in a superior way, marketing managers can make them dependent. Cereal manufacturers have skirted around passing on costs by marketing unique value-added or multi-ingredient cereals, increasing the perceived quality of cereals and allowing companies to raise prices. These cereals include General Mills' Basic 4, Clusters, and Oatmeal Crisp; Post's Banana Nut Crunch and Blueberry Morning; and Kellogg's Mueslix, Nutri-Grain, and Temptations.

→ *Change the package design:* Another way companies pass on higher costs is to shrink product sizes but keep prices the same. Scott Paper Company reduced the number of sheets in the smallest roll of Scott Clean paper towels from 96 to 60 and actually lowered the price by 10 cents a roll. The increases in costs for paper towels were tied to a 50 to 60 percent increase in the cost of pulp paper. The company also changed the names of the sizes to de-emphasize the magnitude of the rolls.

When Wrigley introduced its "Slim Pack" to replace its traditional packages of Juicy Fruit, Big Red, and other brands, it reduced the number of sticks per pack from 17 to 15, but left the $1.09 sticker intact. Unilever Foods' Country Crock shaved three ounces off its three-pound margarine tubs but did not take anything off the price. And Breyers and Edy's reduced their ice cream containers from 1.75 to 1.5 quarts but did not lower prices. Blue Bell ice cream countered with a promotional campaign that its containers are still a full half gallon.[39]

→ *Heighten buyer dependence:* Owens Corning supplies an integrated insulation service (from feasibility studies to installation) that includes commercial and scientific training for distributors and seminars for end users. This practice freezes out competition and supports higher prices.

→ *Make strong promotional claims and avoid discounting:* Recent research has found that strong product claims can create greater satisfaction and benefit for consumers. Consumers who were exposed to strong advertising claims about an energy drink's benefits could actually solve more puzzles. (The researchers used individuals' ability to solve puzzles to test the product's benefits.) Persons who bought the same energy drink, but at a discounted price, solved fewer puzzles. Thus, strong benefit promotions and paying full price might actually increase long run demand, according to this research.[40]

RECESSION

As discussed in Chapter 4, a recession is a period of reduced economic activity such as occurred recently in the United States. Reduced demand for goods and services, along with higher rates of unemployment, is a common trait of a recession. Yet astute marketers can often find opportunity during recessions. A recession is an excellent time to build market share because competitors are struggling to make ends meet.

Two effective pricing tactics to hold or build market share during a recession are value-based pricing and bundling. Value-based pricing, discussed earlier in the chapter, stresses to customers that they are getting a good value for their money. Charles of the Ritz, usually known for its pricey products, introduced the Express Bar during a recession. A collection of affordable cosmetics and skin treatment products, the Express Bar sold alongside regular Ritz products in department stores. Although lower-priced products offer lower profit margins, Ritz found that increases in volume can offset slimmer margins. For example, the company found that consumers will buy two or three Express Bar lipsticks at a time.

Sony has created a value-priced TV called the Bravia M series. It was created by Sony engineers in Mexico using mostly off-the-shelf parts. They are $200 cheaper than comparable Sony sets. In the service sector IWPR Group, an architecture marketing firm, slashed its monthly retainer from $20,000 to $5,000 opting instead for a percentage of sales it helps clients ring up.[41]

Bundling or *unbundling* can also stimulate demand during a recession. If features are added to a bundle, consumers may perceive the offering as having greater value. For example, suppose that Hyatt offers a "great escape" weekend for $119. The package includes two nights' lodging and a continental breakfast. Hyatt could add a massage and a dinner for two to create more value for this price. Conversely, companies can unbundle offerings and lower base prices to stimulate demand. A furniture store, for example, could start charging separately for design consultation, delivery, credit, setup, and hauling away old furniture.

Recessions are a good time for marketing managers to study the demand for individual items in a product line and the revenue they produce. Pruning unprofitable items can save resources to be better used elsewhere. Borden, for example, found that it made about 3,200 sizes, brands, types, and flavors of snacks—but got 95 percent of its revenues from just half of them.

Prices often fall during a recession as competitors try desperately to maintain demand for their wares. Even if demand remains constant, falling prices mean lower profits or no profits. Falling prices, therefore, are a natural incentive to lower costs. During the recent recession, companies implemented new technology to improve efficiency and then slashed payrolls. They also discovered that suppliers were an excellent source of cost savings; the cost of purchased materials accounts for slightly more than half of most U.S. manufacturers' expenses. General Electric's appliance division told 300 key suppliers that they had to reduce prices 10 percent or risk losing GE's business. Honeywell, Dow Chemical, and DuPont made similar demands of their suppliers. Specific strategies that companies use with suppliers include the following:

→ **Renegotiating contracts:** Sending suppliers letters demanding price cuts of 5 percent or more; putting out for rebid the contracts of those that refuse to cut costs.

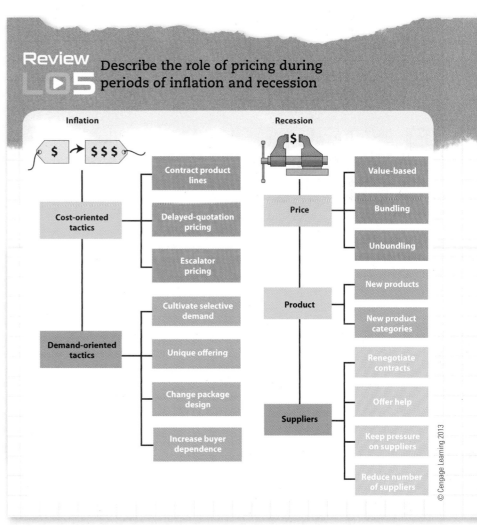

Review LO5 Describe the role of pricing during periods of inflation and recession

→ **Offering help:** Dispatching teams of experts to suppliers' plants to help reorganize and suggest other productivity-boosting changes; working with suppliers to make parts simpler and cheaper to produce.

→ **Keeping the pressure on:** To make sure that improvements continue, setting annual, across-the-board cost reduction targets, often of 5 percent or more a year.

→ **Paring down suppliers:** To improve economies of scale, slashing the overall number of suppliers, sometimes by up to 80 percent, and boosting purchases from those that remain.

Tough tactics like these help keep companies afloat during economic downturns.

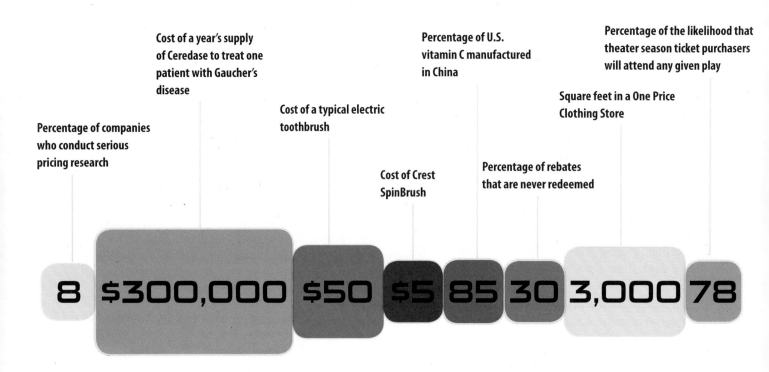

Percentage of companies who conduct serious pricing research — **8**

Cost of a year's supply of Ceredase to treat one patient with Gaucher's disease — **$300,000**

Cost of a typical electric toothbrush — **$50**

Cost of Crest SpinBrush — **$5**

Percentage of U.S. vitamin C manufactured in China — **85**

Percentage of rebates that are never redeemed — **30**

Square feet in a One Price Clothing Store — **3,000**

Percentage of the likelihood that theater season ticket purchasers will attend any given play — **78**

There would probably be little demand for a menu item that was out of the price/value range established by other items in McDonald's product line. For example, a $10 burger would be well out of the price range that McDonald's customers expect for that product class.

1 ...offers several related products.

2 ...sells related products individually and in combinations.

3 ...offers a line of products of various sizes, qualities, and prices.

4 ...presents a limited number of prices for all their product offerings.

What would you pay for a fast-food burger:

$1, $2, $3, $10, $12, $25, $32?

Review and Applications

 Describe the procedure for setting the right price. The process of setting the right price on a product involves four major steps: (1) establishing pricing goals; (2) estimating demand, costs, and profits; (3) choosing a price policy to help determine a base price; and (4) fine-tuning the base price with pricing tactics.

A price strategy establishes a long-term pricing framework for a good or service. The three main types of price policies are price skimming, penetration pricing, and status quo pricing. A price-skimming policy charges a high introductory price, often followed by a gradual reduction. Penetration pricing offers a low introductory price to capture a large market share and attain economies of scale. Finally, status quo pricing strives to match competitors' price.

1.1 A manufacturer of office furniture decides to produce antique-style rolltop desks reconfigured to accommodate personal computers. The desks will have built-in surge protectors, a platform for raising or lowering the monitor, and a number of other features. The high-quality, solid-oak desks will be priced far below comparable products. The marketing manager says, "We'll charge a low price and plan on a high volume to reduce our risks." Comment.

1.2 Janet Oliver, owner of a mid-priced dress shop, notes, "My pricing objectives are simple: I just charge what my competitors charge. I'm happy because I'm making money." React to Janet's statement.

1.3 What is the difference between a price policy and a price tactic? Give an example.

 Identify the legal and ethical constraints on pricing decisions. Government regulation helps monitor five major areas of pricing: unfair trade practices, price fixing, resales price maintenance, predatory pricing and predatory bidding, and price discrimination. Many states have enacted unfair trade practice acts that protect small businesses from large firms that operate efficiently on extremely thin profit margins; the acts prohibit charging below-cost prices. The Sherman Act and the Federal Trade Commission Act prohibit both price fixing, which is an agreement between two or more firms on a particular price, and predatory pricing, in which a firm undercuts its competitors with extremely low prices to drive them out of business. Finally, the Robinson-Patman Act makes it illegal for firms to discriminate between two or more buyers in terms of price.

2.1 What are the three basic defenses that a seller can use if accused under the Robinson-Patman Act?

 Explain how discounts, geographic pricing, and other pricing tactics can be used to fine-tune the base price. Several techniques enable marketing managers to adjust prices within a general range in response to changes in competition, government regulation, consumer demand, and promotional and positioning goals. Techniques for fine-tuning a price can be divided into three main categories: discounts, allowances, rebates, and value-based pricing; geographic pricing; and other pricing tactics.

The first type of tactic gives lower prices to those that pay promptly, order a large quantity, or perform some function for the manufacturer. Value-based pricing starts with the customer, considers the competition and costs, and then determines a price. Additional tactics in this category include seasonal discounts, promotion allowances, rebates (cash refunds), zero-percent financing, and markdown money.

Geographic pricing tactics—such as FOB origin pricing, uniform delivered pricing, zone pricing, freight absorption pricing, and basing-point pricing—are ways of moderating the impact of shipping costs on distant customers.

A variety of "other" pricing tactics stimulate demand for certain products, increase store patronage, and offer more merchandise at specific prices.

More and more customers are paying price penalties, which are extra fees for violating the terms of a purchase contract. The perceived fairness or unfairness of a penalty may affect some consumers' willingness to patronize a business in the future.

3.1 You are contemplating a price change for an established product sold by your firm. Write a memo analyzing the factors you need to consider in your decision.

writing

3.2 Columnist Dave Barry jokes that federal law requires this message under the sticker price of new cars: "Warning to stupid people: Do not pay this amount." Discuss why the sticker price is generally higher than the actual selling price of a car. Tell how you think car dealers set the actual prices of the cars they sell.

3.3 Divide into teams of four persons. Each team should choose one of the following topics: skimming, penetration pricing, status quo pricing, price fixing, geographic pricing, adopting a single-price tactic, flexible pricing, or professional services pricing. Each team should then pick a retailer that it feels most closely follows the team's chosen pricing strategy. Go to the store and write down examples of the strategy. Interview the store manager and get his or her views on the advantages and disadvantages of the strategy. Each team should then make an oral report in class.

team

3.4 The U.S. Postal Service regularly raises the price of a first-class stamp but continues to operate in the red year after year. Is uniform delivered pricing the best choice for first-class mail? Explain your reasoning.

3.5 How is the "information age" changing the nature of pricing?

3.6 Have you ever paid a price penalty? How did it affect your attitude toward that company?

3.7 Imagine that you are a marketing manager for a mid-sized amusement park. You have attended an industry-wide meeting where a colleague gave a talk about new pricing strategies for amusement parks. You were very motivated by the seminar. On your return to work, write a memo to your boss outlining the pros and cons of the new pricing strategy. End your memo with a recommendation either for or against à la carte pricing of attractions (pricing each attraction separately rather than charging a single high entrance fee).

writing

Discuss product line pricing. Product line pricing maximizes profits for an entire product line. When setting product line prices, marketing managers determine what type of relationship exists among the products in the line: complementary, substitute, or neutral. Managers also consider joint (shared) costs among products in the same line.

LO4

4.1 Develop a price line strategy for each of these firms:

a. a college bookstore

b. a restaurant

c. a video rental firm

Describe the role of pricing during periods of inflation and recession. Marketing managers employ cost-oriented and demand-oriented tactics during periods of economic inflation. Cost-oriented tactics include dropping products with a low profit margin, using delayed-quotation pricing and escalator pricing, and adding fees. Demand-oriented pricing methods include price shading and increasing demand through cultivating selected customers, creating unique offerings, changing the package size, and heightening buyer dependence.

LO5

To stimulate demand during a recession, marketers use value-based pricing, bundling, unbundling, and making strong promotional claims while avoiding discounting. Recessions are also a good time to prune unprofitable items from product lines. Managers strive to cut costs during recessions in order to maintain profits as revenues decline. Implementing new technology, cutting payrolls, and pressuring suppliers for reduced prices are common techniques used to cut costs. Companies also create new value-added products.

online

5.1 During a recession, what pricing strategies would you consider using to gain or maintain market share? Explain your answer.

5.2 After a decade of astounding growth and prosperity, Americans were challenged by the economic downturn of the early 2000s. As a result, pricing became an issue for many consumers looking to pinch pennies. This was also true in areas where penny-pinching isn't a common occurrence, like high-end retailers. Search *The Wall Street Journal* online archives (www.wsj.com) to find an article about pricing during a recession.

Key Terms

anchoring 732
bait pricing 747
base price 740
basing-point pricing 744
cash discount 741
consumer penalty 752
cumulative quantity
   discount 741
delayed-quotation pricing 754
escalator pricing 755
flexible pricing
   (variable pricing) 745
FOB origin pricing 744
freight absorption pricing 744
functional discount
   (trade discount) 741

joint costs 753
leader pricing (loss-leader
   pricing) 747
markdown money 742
noncumulative quantity
   discount 741
odd–even pricing (psychological
   pricing) 747
penetration pricing 732
predatory pricing 738
price bundling 748
price fixing 736
price lining 746
price shading 755
price skimming 731
price strategy 731

product line pricing 753
promotional allowance
   (trade allowance) 741
quantity discount 741
rebate 741
resale price maintenance 736
seasonal discount 741
single-price tactic 745
two-part pricing 750
unbundling 749
unfair trade practice acts 735
uniform delivered pricing 744
value-based pricing 742
zone pricing 744

Exercises

ETHICS EXERCISE

ethics

People feel better when they think they are getting a great bargain when they shop. Knowing this, some retailers mark up items above the traditional retail price and then offer a 60 percent discount. If they had simply discounted the normal retail price by 20 percent the resulting "sale price" would have been the same. One retailer says that he is just making shoppers happy that they got a great deal when he inflates the retail price before discounting.

Questions

1. What do you think?
2. Does the AMA Statement of Ethics address this issue? Go to www.marketingpower.com and review the statement. Then write a brief paragraph summarizing what the AMA Code of Ethics contains that relates to retail pricing.

MARKETING PLAN EXERCISE

For continued general assistance on business plans and marketing plans, visit **www.bplans. com** or **http://www.businessplans.org.** You can also refer to Appendix 1 of Chapter 2 for marketing plan checklist items related to pricing decisions. Once you've worked through this marketing plan exercise, you can complete the Part 6 Marketing Planning Worksheet on your companion Web site at www.cengagebrain.com. Continue the pricing stage of the strategic planning process for your chosen company with following exercises:

1. What price policy should your firm use? Are there any legal implications of this choice? Will there be differences in online versus off-line pricing policies? Are these differences related to your cost structure in the online environment? Why? Are these differences legal?

2. Note how easy it is to compare prices on the Internet. Check out price comparison sites such as **www.pricescan.com**, **www.mysimon.com,** and **www.bizrate.com**. Given how products and prices are displayed, how can your offering show a differential advantage if there is a price difference? As prices reach parity on the Internet, how else will you differentiate your products or services?

3. What kinds of price discounts can your company offer? Should discounted prices be offered to online buyers that off-line buyers do not receive? Why might you charge your online customers less than your off-line customers?

4. As you work on the Internet component of your marketing plan, you must decide how to set geographic pricing policies. Will you appear as a nongeographic specific Internet provider and offer the same shipping costs to all, or will you have to charge more for longer distances? Will you market your product or services locally, regionally, or nationally? Just because you are on the Internet, does that mean you have to try to serve all markets? Explain.

APPLICATION EXERCISE

You read in the chapter about the dangers of pricing products too low. It seems so obviously wrong, but do companies really price their products so low that they won't make any money? After all, companies are in business to make money, and if they don't, they're probably not in business for very long. Let's take a deeper look at the effects of pricing products too low or creating too deep discounts during sale periods.[42]

Activity

1. The average markup for a produce department is 28 percent on selling price. When sold at 28 percent markup on selling price, bananas usually account for 25 percent of department sales and 25 percent of department markup. This week, because bananas were on special sale at the retailer's cost, the department sold twice as many pounds of bananas as usual. However, they were sold at zero markup. If all other things remain the same, what is the average markup on selling price for the entire produce department this week?

HOW LOW CAN DRUG PRICES GO?

When Wal-Mart rolled out its new prescription-drug plan in 2006, lowering the prices on 331 commonly prescribed medications to a flat $4, Frank Ganci's doctor told him to check it out. He has no health insurance and his prescriptions were costing him $110 a month at his local pharmacy, so switching to Wal-Mart meant that he could get the same three medications for $12. Now he says he's a loyal Wal-Mart customer: "If they don't make up the money on prescriptions, they're going to make it up on my clothes and food purchases."

Industry analysts speculate that Wal-Mart is counting on customers like Ganci to spend the money they saved at the pharmacy on other products in the store. Wal-Mart insists that it can earn a profit on the $4 prescriptions alone, however, since more expensive medications are not discounted. "It can only be in our program if it is profitable," says Bill Simon, a Wal-Mart CEO.

It's true that pharmacies can buy some types of generics from manufacturers for less than $4. For example, a month's supply of fluoxetine, the generic version of Prozac, can be obtained for 75 cents. But store overhead and pharmacists' salaries bring the true cost closer to $15. It would be difficult for smaller pharmacies to match the $4 price point, which has some of Wal-Mart's competitors complaining that it violates predatory pricing laws. "You can't just sell something below your cost to drive out the small guy," says Rick Sain, co-owner of a drugstore in Tennessee. "You have to at least set a fair price. That's what all the states that have fair trade laws in place are looking into because you cannot dispense a prescription for $4. They are saying you can."

Wal-Mart later increased the price of certain generic drugs from $4 to $9 in order to bring the company into compliance with all "low-cost laws," according to a company statement. John Rector of the National Community Pharmacists Association says, "We don't know for certain whether it can make a profit on the $4 drugs so they don't violate these laws. But we strongly doubt it, and the fact is [raising some prices] gives us insight into what its business practices are."

Stores like Target and Kmart quickly lowered their own prices to match Wal-Mart's, but Walgreens and CVS both announced that their prices would remain the same. Tony Civello, CEO of Kerr Drug, insists, "We will not treat your prescription like T-shirts and blue jeans. Wal-Mart may choose to use some limited prescription drugs as a loss leader. But our patients' health care is not a loss leader. We will not compromise that."

Bill Vaughan, a policy analyst for Consumers Union, argues that the price slashing is actually step in the right direction. "It's the beginning of better competition in a sector where it's literally pennies per pill," he said. When a generic drug is introduced, pharmacies can charge as much as they like for it. One study found that markups were often as high as 4,000 percent. Few people compare drug prices from one pharmacy to the next, so pharmacies are able to mark up prices substantially.

Wal-Mart's prescription program seems to be raising consumer awareness as it demonstrates how low the prices of the drugs can go. The discounts are especially welcome among uninsured Americans and seniors living on fixed incomes. Legislators have listened to constituents who rely on the $4 plan and efforts are under way in states like Colorado and Minnesota to either repeal predatory-pricing laws or exempt prescription drugs from them.

The prescriptions in Wal-Mart's $4 program now make up more than 35 percent of all prescriptions they fill, and the company boasts that the program has saved consumers more than $340 million in drug costs already. Wal-Mart executive H. Lee Scott is enthusiastic about its future, saying, "The $4 prescription program is absolutely one of the coolest things that we have done in a long time."[43]

Questions

1. Do you believe Wal-Mart is engaging in predatory pricing with its $4 generic drug program? Why or why not?

2. Do you think that predatory pricing laws should be amended to exclude prescription drugs? Explain.

3. If you owned a pharmacy next door to a Wal-Mart store, what strategies could you try in order to compete? Would you match their prices if possible, or would you find other ways to add value? What could a small pharmacy like yours offer customers that Wal-Mart might not?

COMPANY CLIPS: Pricing Perspectives— Method, ReadyMade Magazine, Sephora, Vans, and Acid+All

Setting the right price is one of the most challenging aspects of a marketer's job. How high a price will the market bear? What kind of message does the price communicate? How flexible can our price be? The answer to those and a multitude of other questions relating to price vary by industry, by product categories within an industry, and even by brand and store.

This video shows you a wide range of pricing issues and concerns facing new brands, like method, *ReadyMade* Magazine, and Acid+All, and established brands, like Sephora and Vans. There are both similarities and differences in the tools each company uses to set and fine-tune its base price. One idea, however, unifies all of the companies: pricing is a considered strategy, not an afterthought.

Questions

1. Compare the pricing strategies of method, *ReadyMade* Magazine, and Acid+All. Do all of these relatively new brands use the same strategy? Explain.

2. In what ways is the pricing strategy of Sephora similar to that of Acid+All?

3. Does it make sense for method to use product line pricing? Why or why not?

4. What is Vans' primary strategy for setting prices on tickets to the Warped Tour it sponsors?

Notes

1. Kent Monroe and Jennifer Cox, "Pricing Practices That Endanger Profits," *Marketing Management*, September/October 2001, 42–46.
2. Walter L. Baker, Michael V. Mann, and Craig C. Zawada, "Building a Better Pricing Structure," *McKinsey Quarterly*, August 2010, www.mckinseyquarterly.com/Building_a_better_pricing_structure_2652.

3. David Kesmodell "Why the Price Is Rarely Right," *Bloomberg Businessweek*, February 18, 2010, 77–78.

4. *Ibid.*

5. Ellen Byron, "Gillette's Latest Innovation in Razors: The 11-Cent Blade," *Wall Street Journal*, October 1, 2010, B1.

6. Chris Anderson, "The Economics of Giving It Away," *Wall Street Journal*, February 1, 2009, W1, W2; and Vivian Pereira, "Brazilians Embracing New Free-Sample Outlets," *International Herald Tribune*, July 10–11, 2010, 14.

7. John R. Wilke, "China Defends Price Fixing by Vitamin Makers," *Wall Street Journal*, November 25, 2008, A1, A12.

8. Jeff Bennett and Peppi Kivinemi, "Car-Parts Makers Raided in Price Fixing Probe," *Wall Street Journal*, February 26, 2010, B1.

9. "Fresh Del Monte Settles Banana Price-Fixing Suits for More Than $3 Million," *Palm Beach Daily Business Review*, June 28, 2007.

10. Michael Orey, "Europe Incorporated Takes Aim at Price Fixers," *Bloomberg Businessweek*, November 2, 2009, 62.

11. Joseph Pereira, "Price-Fixing Makes Comeback After Supreme Court Ruling," *Wall Street Journal*, August 18, 2008, A1, A12.

12. *Ibid.*

13. *Ibid.*

14. Joseph Pereira, "State Law Targets Minimum Pricing," *Wall Street Journal*, April 28, 2009, D1, D5.

15. "Antitrust Trade and Practice; Predatory Bidding Mirrors Predatory Pricing," *New York Law Journal*, March 20, 2007, 3.

16. *Ibid.*; Alison Lo, John Lynch, and Richard Staelin, "How to Attract Consumers by Giving Them the Short End of the Stick," *Journal of Marketing Research*, February 2007, 128–141.

17. Marion Nestle, "Food Politics Abroad: The Plumpy'nut Furor," *The Atlantic*, September 7, 2010, www.theatlantic.com/life/archive/2010/09/food-politics-abroad-the-plumpynut-furor/62509/; Jonathan Banco, "Plumpy'nut and the Role of the Private Sector in International Development," The Inspired Economist, September 16, 2010, http://inspiredeconomist.com/2010/09/16/plumpy%E2%80%99nut-and-the-role-of-the-private-sector-in-international-development/; Andrew Rice, "A Product Too Crucial for Profit?" *New York Times*, September 4–5, 2010, 8–9; Alanna Shaikh, "The Plumpy'nut Dust Up: Nutriset's Side of the Story," AIDWATCH, May 6, 2010, aidwatchers.com/2010/05/the-plumpy%E2%80%99nut-dust-up-nutriset%E2%80%99s-side-of-the-story/; Christine Gorman, "Nutriset Sued over Plumpy'nut Patent," Global Health Report, April 9, 2010, http://globalhealthreport.blogspot.com/2010/04/nutriset-sued-over-plumpynut-patent.html.

18. Bruce Alford and Abhijit Biswas, "The Effects of Discount Level, Price Consciousness, and Sale Proneness on Consumers' Price Perception and Behavioral Intention," *Journal of Business Research*, September 2002, 775–783; V. Kuman, Vibhas Madan, and Srini Srinivasan, "Price Discounts or Coupon Promotions: Does It Matter?" *Journal of Business Research*, September 2004, 933–941; Cenk Kocas and Jonathan Bohlmann, "Segmented Switchers and Retailer Price Strategies," *Journal of Marketing*, May 2008, 124–142.

19. "Rebates Get What You Deserve," *Consumer Reports*, September 2009, 7.

20. *Ibid.*

21. "Probing Price Tags," *Wall Street Journal*, May 13, 2005, B1, B2.

22. Miguel Bustillo and Timothy W. Martin, "Wal-Mart Bets on Reduction in Prices," *Wall Street Journal*, April 9, 2010, B1, B3.

23. Paul Zioboro, "Safeway Takes Bullet in Grocery Price War," *Wall Street Journal*, October 16, 2009, B1, B5; "Safeway Says 2010 Profit Could Miss Expectations," *Reuters*, March 3, 2010, www.reuters.com/article/2010/03/03/safeway-idUSN0322988920100303.

24. "Ethan Allen Awaits the Payoff from Price Cut, Sales-Event Ban," *Wall Street Journal*, April 13, 2007, B3B; Carol Tice, "Ethan Allen's Profitability Forecast Seems Premature," BNET, June 23, 2010, www.bnet.com/blog/retail-stores/ethan-allen-8217s-profitability-forecast-seems-premature/710.

25. Timothy Aeppel, "Guitar Maker Revives No-Frills Act From '30's," *Wall Street Journal*, July 6, 2009, B1, B2; "How to Reach the New Customer," *Marketing News*, February 28, 2010, 19–22.

26. Frank V. Cespedes, Elliot B. Ross, and Benson P. Shapiro, "Seven Mistakes of Poor Pricers," *Wall Street Journal*, May 24, 2010, R8.

27. Rui (Juliet) Zhu, Xinlei (Jack) Chen, and Srabana Dasgupta, "Can Trade-Ins Hurt You? Exploring the Effect of a Trade-In on Consumers' Willingness to Pay for a Product," *Journal of Marketing Research*, April 2008, 159–170.

28. *Ibid.*

29. *Ibid.*

30. John Eggerton, "AT&T Adopts Tiered Wireless Broadband Pricing," B&C, June 2, 2010, www.broadcastingcable.com/article/453238-AT_T_Adopts_Tiered_Wireless_Broadband_Pricing.php.

31. Marguerite Reardon, "Sprint, T-Mobile Keep Prices Low on Wireless Broadband," *CNET* News, May 4, 2010, http://news.cnet.com/8301-30686_3-20004054-266.html.

32. Thomas Manoj and Vicki Morwitz, "Penny Wise and Pound Foolish: The Left Digit Effect in Price Cognition," *Journal of Consumer Research*, June 2005, 54–64; Manoj Thomas and Vicki Morwitz, "The Ease-of-Computation Effect: The Interplay of Metacognitive Experiences and Naïve Theories in Judgments of Price Differences," *Journal of Marketing Research*, February 2009, 81–91.

33. Dilip Soman and John Gourville, "Transaction Decoupling: The Effects of Price Bundling on the Decision to Consume," *MSI Report*, 2002, no. 98–131; Stefan Stremersch and Gerald J. Tellis, "Strategic Bundling of Products and Prices: A New Synthesis for Marketing," *Journal of Marketing*, January 2002, 55–71; "Forget Prices and Get People to Use the Stuff," *Wall Street Journal*, June 3, 2004, A2.

34. Dilip Soman and John Gourville, "Transaction Decoupling: How Price Bundling Affects the Decision to Consume," *Journal of Marketing Research*, February 2001, 30–44; "Does Price Bundling Really Work?" May 19, 2010, http://abranddayout.wordpress.com/2010/05/19/does-price-bundling-really-work/.

35. Rebecca Hamilton and Joydeep Srivastava, "When 2 + 2 Is Not the Same as 1 + 3: Variations in Price Sensitivity Across Components of Partitioned Prices," *Journal of Marketing Research*, August 2008, 450–461.

36. Ju-Young Kim, Martin Natter, and Martin Spann, "Pay What You Want: A New Participative Pricing Mechanism," *Journal of Marketing*, January 2009, 44–58.

37. "A Pay What You Want Experiment for the Freakonomics Movies," Freakonomics, September 22, 2010, http://freakonomics.blogs.nytimes.com.

marketing&you: Results.

© iStockphoto.com/ziggymaj

High scores on this poll indicate that you are very sensitive to prices and that your price consciousness affects how you shop. Conversely, a lower score suggests that you are not very price conscious.

38. Kate Shaw, "Pay What You Want Benefits Companies, Consumers, Charities," Ars Technica, July 19, 2010, http://arstechnica.com/science/news/2010/07/pay-what-you-want-benefits-companies-consumers-charities.ars.

39. Eric Newman, "As Inflation Resurfaces, So Does Package Shrink," *Brandweek*, June 9, 2008, 5.

40. Baba Shiv, Ziv Sarmon, and Dan Ariely, "Placebo Effects of Marketing Actions: Consumers May Get What They Pay for," *Journal of Marketing Research*, November 2005, 383–393.

41. Diana Ransom, "Smart Ways to Cut Prices," *Wall Street Journal*, April 23, 2009, R5.

42. This application exercise is based on the contribution of William H. Brannen (Creighton University) to *Great Ideas in Teaching Marketing*, a teaching supplement that accompanies McDaniel, Lamb, and Hair's *Introduction to Marketing*. Professor Brannen's entry titled "Can Your Marketing Students Solve the Banana Problem? Can You?" was a runner-up in the "Best of the Great Ideas in Teaching Marketing" contest held in conjunction with the publication of the eighth edition of *Marketing*.

43. Martin Sipkoff, "Wal-Mart, Other Discounters Facing Predatory-Pricing Concerns," *Drug Topics*, April 2, 2007; Sue Stock, "Wal-Mart Drug Plan in N.C.," *News & Observer*, Oct. 20, 2006; Jessie Male, "Generic Concern: Will Wal-Mart's $4 Prescriptions Do Much to Change Consumers' Pharmacy Habits?" *Grocery Headquarters*, Nov. 1, 2006; Pallavi Gogoi, "Drug Wars at the Big-Box Stores," *BusinessWeek*, May 24, 2007; Milt Freudenheim, "Side Effects at the Pharmacy," *The New York Times*, Nov. 30, 2006.

Marketing Miscue

6PM.COM'S $1.6 MILLION PRICING ERROR

Upon arrival at the 6pm.com Web site, customers are immediately congratulated for the smart-shopping skills that led them to the site. With brands such as Nike, Oakley, Nine West, Stride Rite, Columbia, and Diesel at discount prices, the Web site is a mecca for brandaholics seeking discounted merchandise. The online site offers products for all family members. The female shopper in the family is enticed with casual and contemporary fashion styles, as well as top-notch performance gear. The male shopper is presented with anywhere from performance to business casual to dress-for-success attire. Parents are encouraged to avoid the hassle of taking the kids to the store by shopping conveniently online. On 6pm.com, the promise is to have this wonderful brand-shopping experience at up to 75 percent off retail prices. This delivery promise was well-heeded when a pricing snafu led to everything on the site being priced at $49.95.

Zappos.com

Zappos.com started as an online shoe retailer. The idea was to create a Web site that offered the best shoe selection in terms of brands, styles, colors, sizes, and widths. Since the company's origination, the goal has broadened to one in which the company provides the best online service in many product categories. With fast and high-quality customer service as its mantra, ten years later the company is now comprised of ten separate companies under the Zappos Family umbrella:

Zappos.com, Inc. ("the management company")
Zappos IP, Inc. ("ZiP")
Zappos Development, Inc. ("Zappos.com" or "ZDev")
Zappos Merchandising, Inc. (:ZMerch")
Zappos Fulfillment Centers, Inc. ("ZFC")
Zappos CLT, Inc. ("ZCLT")
Zappos Insights, Inc. ("ZInsights")
Zappos Gift Cards, Inc. ("ZGift Cards")
Zappos Retail, Inc. ("ZRetail")
6pm.com, LLC ("6pm")

The rapidity at which the company has grown is attributed in no small part to its CEO Tony Hsieh (pronounced Shay). In 1999, Hsieh sold the company he co-founded to Microsoft for $265 million. Joining Zappos.com as an advisor and investor, Hsieh later became the company's CEO and helped grow the company to over $1 billion in gross merchandise sales annually. In November 2009, Zappos.com was acquired by Amazon.com in a deal valued at $1.2 billion. The passion for service was the common connection between Zappos.com and Amazon.com.

This passion for service is exemplified in the core values at Zappos.com:

→ Deliver WOW Through Service

→ Embrace and Drive Change

→ Create Fun and a Little Weirdness

→ Be Adventurous, Creative, and Open-Minded

→ Pursue Growth and Learning

- → Build Open and Honest Relationships with Communication
- → Build a Positive Team and Family Spirit
- → Do More with Less
- → Be Passionate and Determined
- → Be Humble

Delivering on These Values at a Very High Price!

In the wee hours of a May morning in 2010, the Zappos-owned 6pm.com e-commerce site had a major glitch in its pricing engine. Everything on the 6pm.com Web site was priced at $49.95 from midnight to 6 a.m. For example, a GPS system that normally sold for nearly $2,000 was sold for $49.95. A pair of Bruno Magli boots that usually sold on 6pm.com for $400 sold for $49.95. The pricing glitch affected products sold only on the 6pm.com site and not products available on both 6pm.com and Zappos.com.

The pricing mistake was attributed to an employee error in entering data into the pricing engine. Hsieh explained the pricing error on a company blog. He said that the current version of the pricing engine required near-programmer skills to manipulate and that a few symbols were missed in the coding of a new rule. Hsieh went on to say that, after this glitch, the internal pricing engine would be improved upon so that it would have a much easier to use interface with business owners. Additional checks and balances would also be added to further prevent the error from ever occurring again. Interestingly, the employee responsible for the programming error was not fired.

During the six hours of selling everything for $49.95, much of which was below cost, Zappos.com lost $1.6 million. While the terms and conditions on the company's Web site state that the company does not need to fulfill orders that are placed due to pricing mistakes, Hsieh felt as though it was the right thing for the company to do by honoring customers' orders at the noted price. Interestingly, Amazon.com, the parent company of Zappos.com, did not share this same policy when it experienced a similar pricing glitch a few months prior. In that instance, Amazon.com cancelled any orders that had not been fulfilled and gave customers a $25 gift card instead of the books that had been ordered at the wrong price.

Questions

1. What is the relationship between demand and price for products on the 6pm.com e-commerce site?

2. Should there be any legislation that requires companies to adhere to online prices even when posted in error?

Critical Thinking Case

WILL A NEW RESERVATION SYSTEM TRANSLATE TO HIGHER PRICES FOR TRAVELERS?

American Airlines, one of the top three airlines in the United States and a major international carrier via strategic alliances with leading carriers around the world, was founded in 1930 as American Airways. As an innovative leader in air travel, American Airlines started the frequent flyer program in 1981. Since then, every major airline in the world has adopted some form of a frequent flyer program. In late 2010, American Airlines once again took the lead in an airline initiative that could change the way consumers search for and ultimately purchase airline tickets.

© u99/u99/ZUMA Press/Newscom

In an effort to reduce distribution costs, gain greater control over the marketing of its airline tickets, and better meet customer expectations, American Airlines upgraded its reservation system. In making the upgrade, the company expected third party travel operators such as Expedia, Orbitz, and Priceline to follow suit.

The Reservation System

Consumers want low fares while also having the ability to customize their itineraries. Plus, they want to do this themselves and not have to go through a travel agent. Via an in-house reservation system called Direct Connect, American Airlines will be able to present a variety of individualized options to consumers, including prices, flight schedule, seat upgrades, lounge access, faster check-in, hotel reservations, and car rentals. Direct Connect constitutes a wholesale shakeup of the traditional reservation process that has relied historically on global distribution systems (GDS) such as Amadeus, Sabre, Worldspan, and Galileo. All of these global distribution systems were designed originally by airlines, but all are now operated by independent owners.

Middlemen such as Expedia and Orbitz conduct business via a GDS and do not want to upgrade their reservation systems to models such as Direct Connect. However, the Direct Connect technology will enable airlines to bypass the GDS and avoid paying the GDS fees. Airlines stopped paying commissions to travel agents in the 1990s, but the GDS model enables travel agents to sell tickets and collect fees from the sale of tickets via the GDS.

The Dispute

In December of 2010, American Airlines announced that it would no longer do business with Orbitz. By making this move, Orbitz could no longer sell American Airlines tickets on its online booking Web site. At the heart of the dispute was that American Airlines wanted Orbitz to use Direct Connect instead of GPS. Orbitz refused to switch reservation processes, so American Airlines withdrew its tickets. Beating American Airlines to the punch, Expedia announced on January 1, 2011 that American Airlines tickets were no longer an option on Expedia.com. Following suit, Sabre dropped American Airlines' ranking on its site thus making it difficult to find American Airlines fares on this GDS.

Some say that the bottom line is that American Airlines wants travelers to buy directly from its Web site, such as the process utilized by Southwest Airlines. From a pricing perspective, the middlemen such as Orbitz and Expedia say that this will allow American Airlines to raise ticket prices since customers will not have easy access to competitive pricing information. These distributors are charging that American Airlines' new Direct Connect model is anti-consumer and anti-choice. Conversely, American Airlines says that it will enable lower ticket prices since it will eliminate the cost of the middleman, contending that the GDS model used by online travel agencies prevents airlines from offering the lowest possible fares.

The chief financial officer at US Airways said that his company agreed in principle with what American Airlines was doing, citing the importance of lower airline distribution costs. Yet this competitive airline recently entered into an agreement with Expedia in which US Airways committed to offering all of the airline's content on Expedia through the GDS model. It could be that competitive rivals see this as an opportune time to appear more customer-friendly, in the hopes of gaining customer affinity while American Airlines battles it out with the middleman.

Questions

1. Identify each channel member's pricing objective.

2. What is American Airlines' pricing strategy?

7 Technology-Driven Marketing

chapter
21
Customer Relationship Management (CRM)

© iStockphoto.com/Juan Facundo Mora Soria; © Diego Cervo/Shutterstock.com

Learning Outcomes

1 Define customer relationship management

2 Explain how to identify customer relationships with the organization

3 Understand interactions with the current customer base

4 Outline the process of capturing customer data

5 Describe the use of technology to store and integrate customer data

6 Describe how to identify the best customers

7 Explain the process of leveraging customer information throughout the organization

LO1

What Is Customer Relationship Management?

Customer relationship management (CRM) focuses on understanding customers as individuals instead of as part of a group. To do so, marketers make their communications more customer-specific, such as the personalized marketing efforts used by Amazon.com. CRM was initially popularized as one-to-one marketing. But it has become a much broader approach to understanding and serving customer needs than one-to-one marketing.

Customer relationship management is a company-wide business strategy designed to optimize profitability, revenue, and customer satisfaction by focusing on precisely defined customer groups. This is accomplished by organizing the company around customer segments, establishing and tracking customer interactions with the company, fostering customer-satisfying behaviors, and linking all processes of the company from its customers through its suppliers. For example, Pandora targets consumers who listen to streaming audio. Then, by requiring users to log in, Pandora tracks their musical preferences and usage. The company can leverage this information to offer special promotions and make recommendations to specific target markets and individuals.

> ## CRM
> is a broad approach to understanding and serving customer needs

customer relationship management (CRM)
A company-wide business strategy designed to optimize profitability, revenue, and customer satisfaction by focusing on highly defined and precise customer groups.

marketing&you.

How do you feel about complaining? Enter your answers on the lines provided.

STRONGLY AGREE ‹ 1 2 3 4 5 6 › STRONGLY DISAGREE
AGREE   DISAGREE

_____ People are bound to end up with an unsatisfactory product once in a while, so they shouldn't complain to the store or the manufacturer about it.*

_____ It bothers me quite a bit if I don't complain about an unsatisfactory product.

_____ It sometimes feels good to get my dissatisfaction and frustration with a product off my chest by complaining.

_____ I often complain when I'm dissatisfied with a business or a product because I feel it is my duty to do so.

_____ I don't like people who complain to stores because usually their complaints are unreasonable.*

Source: Scale #264, *Marketing Scales Handbook*, G. Bruner, K. James, H. Hensel, eds., vol. III. © by American Marketing Association.

Now, total your score, reversing your answers for the items followed by an asterisk (for example, if you answered 3, enter 4). Find out what your score means after reading the chapter.

© iStockphoto.com/Juan Facundo Mora Soria

© iStockphoto.com/jhggymai

The difference between CRM and traditional mass marketing can be compared to shooting a rifle and a shotgun. If you have good aim, a rifle is the more efficient weapon to use. A shotgun, on the other hand, increases your odds of hitting the target when it is more difficult to focus. Instead of scattering messages far and wide across the spectrum of mass media (the shotgun approach), CRM marketers now are homing in on ways to effectively communicate with each individual customer (the rifle approach).

THE CUSTOMER RELATIONSHIP MANAGEMENT CYCLE

On the surface, CRM might appear to be a rather simplistic customer service strategy. But, while customer service is part of the CRM process, it is only a small part of a totally integrated approach to building customer relationships. CRM is often described as a closed-loop system that builds relationships with customers. Exhibit 21.1 illustrates this closed-loop system, one that is continuous and circular with no predefined starting or end point.[1]

To initiate the CRM cycle, a company must first *identify customer relationships with the organization.* This simply entails learning who the customers are or where they are located, or it might require more detailed information on the products and services they are using. Bridgestone/Firestone, a tire manufacturer and tire service company, uses a CRM system called OnDemand5.[2] OnDemand5 initially gathers information from a point-of-sale interaction. The types of information gathered include basic demographic information, how frequently consumers purchase goods, how much they purchase, and how far they drive.

Next, the company must *understand the interactions with current customers.* Companies accomplish this by collecting data on all types of communications a customer has with the company. Using its OnDemand5 system, Bridgestone/Firestone can add information based on additional interactions with the consumer, such as multiple visits to a physical store location and purchasing history. In this phase, companies build on the initial information collected and develop a more useful database.

Using this knowledge of its customers and their interactions, the company then *captures relevant customer data on interactions.* As an example, Bridgestone/Firestone can collect information such as the date of the last communication with a customer, how often the customer makes purchases, and whether the customer redeemed coupons sent through direct mail.

How can marketers realistically analyze and communicate with individual customers? How can huge corporations like FedEx and Williams-Sonoma manage relationships with each and every one of their millions of customers on a personal level? The answer lies in how information technology is used to implement the CRM system. Fundamentally, a CRM approach is no more than the relationship cultivated by a salesperson with the customer. A successful salesperson builds a relationship over time, constantly thinks about what the customer needs and wants, and is mindful of the trends and patterns in the customer's purchase history. A good salesperson often knows what the customer needs even before the customer knows. The salesperson might also inform, educate, and instruct the customer about new products, technology, or applications in anticipation of the customer's future needs or requirements.

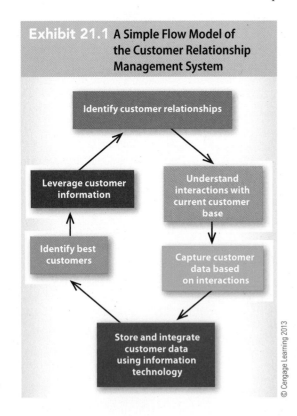

Exhibit 21.1 A Simple Flow Model of the Customer Relationship Management System

Identify customer relationships

Leverage customer information

Understand interactions with current customer base

Identify best customers

Capture customer data based on interactions

Store and integrate customer data using information technology

© Cengage Learning 2013

customer experience

Tracking Consumer Experiences with Google Analytics

Since the early days of the Internet, companies have known that a good Web presence is essential to brand image. But with the growing importance of an online presence, it also became clear that measuring the effectiveness of the Web site is crucial. Web analytics, and specifically Google Analytics, enables companies to measure online and offline marketing effectiveness in visitor attraction, conversion rate, user experiences, and an ROI for the Web site. As an online measurement tool, at a basic level, Google Analytics can show companies the number of daily visitors to the site, the average conversion rates on a variety of outcomes, the most visited pages, the average time spent on each page, the average visit depth, the geographic dispersion of visitors, the amount of revenue the site is producing, its top-selling products, and many other metrics. At a deeper level, Google Analytics can show companies the value of each customer, the value of the Web page, the difference in ROI between new and returning customers, variations of conversion rates, variations in bounce rate, the effectiveness of Internal search tools, and how many visits it takes a noncustomer to become a new customer. Using Google Analytics, a company can even use search engine optimization methods and Google AdWords to identify profitable key terms. And best of all, most of it is free. Here are some of the results:

- Global realtor RE/MAX gets more than two million visits a month. Google Analytics showed them that 90 percent came from search engines and used the search term "remax" and 70 percent of people searched for properties on their site. They also found that moving the property search function to the home page was important.

- The American Cancer Society needed to get the most bang for its fundraising buck. With Google Analytics, they were able to improve site design, functionality, and technology. For example, they were able to optimize their AdWords keywords around content so they could measure ROI on this tool. Google Analytics also helped them develop cancer education programs online by using search engine optimization for clinical trial information.

- Discount Tires found the Internet was one of its most successful distribution channels. Using Google Analytics and AdWords, online sales increased 14 percent in the first week. They also learned how to revise the wording on their Web site, which reduced their abandonment rate by 36 percent.

How can marketers utilize Google Analytics (think about building brand loyalty, e-mail campaigns, retaining customers, targeting the marketing message, etc.)? It's free; what's in this for Google?

Source: Joseph Hair, Robert Bush, and David Ortinau, *Marketing Research: Within a Changing Information Environment,* 4th ed. (Burr Ridge, IL: McGraw-Hill/Irwin, 2009).

This kind of thoughtful attention is the basis of successful CRM systems. Information technology is used not only to enhance the collection of customer data, but also to *store and integrate customer data* throughout the company and, ultimately, to "get to know" customers on a personal basis. Customer data are the firsthand responses that are obtained from customers through investigation or by asking direct questions. These initial data, which might include individual answers to questionnaires, responses on warranty cards, or purchases recorded by electronic cash registers, have not yet been analyzed or interpreted.

The value of customer data depends on the system that stores the data and the consistency and accuracy of the data captured. Obtaining high-quality, actionable data from various sources is a key element in any CRM system. Bridgestone/Firestone accomplishes this by managing all information in a central database accessible by marketers. Different kinds of database management software are available, from extremely high-tech, expensive, custom-designed databases to standardized programs. Oracle, the world's largest CRM software company, offers customized

© PSL Images/Alamy

software for any type of CRM application.[3] In contrast, Net.ERP software offers users database software in a standardized format that is available off-the-shelf at a much lower cost.

Every customer wants to be a company's main priority. Yet not all customers are equally important in the eyes of a business. Some customers are simply more profitable for the company than others. Consequently, the company must identify *its profitable and unprofitable customers*. Data mining is an analytical process that compiles actionable data about the purchase habits of a firm's current and potential customers. Essentially, data mining transforms customer data into customer information a company can use to make managerial decisions. The NetERP software enables managers to customize their "dashboard" to obtain real-time reports on top-selling items and gross sales over a given time period. Similarly, Bridgestone/Firestone uses OnDemand5 to analyze its data to determine which customers qualify for the MasterCare Select program. It also identifies customers who have not made a purchase in the past 8 to 12 months.

Once customer data are analyzed and transformed into usable information, the information must be *leveraged*. The CRM system sends the customer information to all areas of a business because the customer interacts with all aspects of the business (e.g., sales or marketing, operations, production, accounting). Essentially, the company is trying to enhance customer relationships by getting the right information to the right person in the right place at the right time.

Bridgestone/Firestone utilizes the information in its database to develop different marketing campaigns for each type of customer. For example, MasterCare Select customers receive free tire rotation, maps, roadside assistance, and lost-key service. Customers are also targeted by promotions aimed at increasing store visits, upgrades to higher-end tires, and purchases of additional services. Since the company customized its mailings to each type of customer, visits to stores have increased by more than 50 percent.[4]

IMPLEMENTING A CUSTOMER RELATIONSHIP MANAGEMENT SYSTEM

Our discussion of a CRM system has assumed two key points. First, customers take center stage in any organization. Second, the business must manage the customer relationship across all points of customer contact throughout the entire organization. The Seattle Mariners baseball team took proactive steps to increase customer attendance at games based on these two points. The team implemented a loyalty card program to help the Mariners "better understand the fans." By collecting information from every interaction a customer has with the Mariners, from visiting concession stands to purchasing tickets online and even frequenting retail stores that sell Mariner merchandise, marketers were able to track the number of games consumers were attending. They sent reminder e-mail messages if a fan was close to achieving "season-ticket holder" status and they also monitored complaints.

customer-centric
A philosophy under which the company customizes its product and service offering based on data generated through interactions between the customer and the company.

For example, when the CRM system identified a complaint from a fan about the smell of garlic fries, the organization moved the fan to an area where there were no frequent consumers of garlic fries.[5]

In the next sections, we examine how a CRM system is implemented and follow the progression depicted in Exhibit 21.1 as we explain each step in greater detail.

LO2
Identify Customer Relationships

Companies that have a CRM system follow a customer-centric focus or model. **Customer-centric** is an internal management philosophy similar to the marketing concept discussed in Chapter 1. Under this philosophy, the company customizes its product and service offering based on data generated through interactions between the customer and the company. This philosophy transcends all functional areas of the business (production, operations, accounting, etc.), producing an internal system where all of the company's decisions and actions are a direct result of customer information.

A customer-centric company builds long-lasting relationships by focusing on what satisfies and retains valuable customers. For example, Sony's Playstation Web site, **playstation.com**, focuses on learning, customer knowledge management, and **empowerment** to market its gaming computer entertainment system. The site is designed to create a community of users who can join PlayStation Underground where they will "feel like they belong to a subculture of intense gamers." To achieve this objective, the Web site offers online shopping, opportunities to try new games, customer support, and information on news, events, and promotions. The interactive features include online gaming and message boards.

The PlayStation is designed to support Sony's CRM system. When PlayStation users want to access amenities on the site, they are required to log in and supply information such as their name, e-mail address, and birth date. Users can opt to fill out a survey that asks questions about the types of computer entertainment systems they own, how many games are owned for each console, expected future game

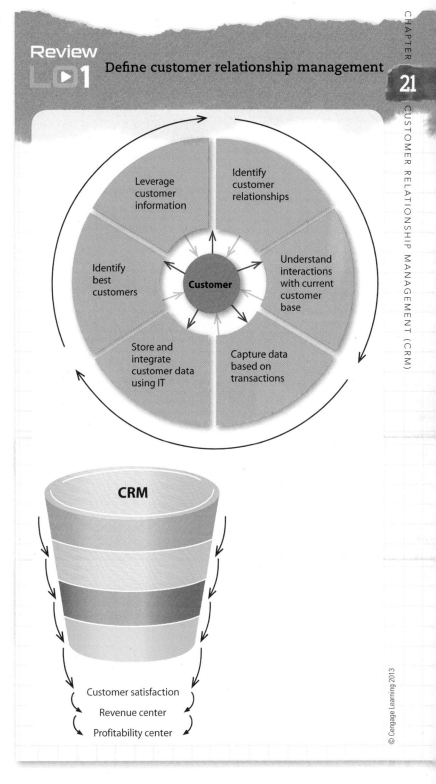

Review
LO1 Define customer relationship management

© Cengage Learning 2013

empowerment
Delegation of authority to solve customers' problems quickly—usually by the first person that the customer notifies regarding the problem.

© iStockphoto.com/Juan Facundo Mora Soria

learning
An informal process of collecting customer data through customer comments and feedback on product or service performance.

knowledge management
The process by which learned information from customers is centralized and shared in order to enhance the relationship between customers and the organization.

purchases, time spent playing games, types of games played, and level of Internet connectivity. Armed with this information, Sony marketers are then able to tailor the site, new games, and PlayStation hardware based on players' replies to the survey and use of the Web site.[6]

Customer-centric companies continually learn ways to enhance their product and service offerings. **Learning** in a CRM environment involves collecting customer information through comments and feedback on product and service performance. As just described, Sony uses its PlayStation Web site to gather information from surveys and message boards so that it can offer more customer-friendly products and services.

Each unit of a business typically has its own way of recording what it learns and perhaps even its own customer information system. The departments' different interests make it difficult to pull all of the customer information together in one place using a common format. To overcome this problem, companies using CRM rely on knowledge management. **Knowledge management** is a process by which customer information is centralized and shared in order to enhance the relationship between customers and the organization. Information collected includes experiential observations, comments, customer actions, and qualitative facts about the customer. For example, PlayStation marketers gather survey information and generate a computer file for each customer that is available to the call center as well as on the Web site. If a PlayStation user registers and purchases a yellow console but then wants to change to a silver console, he or she can call the customer service line, and the representative on the other end will change the order and indicate its availability.[7]

An **interaction** is a touch point at which a customer and a company representative exchange information and develop learning relationships. With CRM, the customer, not the organization, defines the terms of the interaction, often by stating his or her preferences. The organization responds by designing products and services around customers' desired experiences. For example, students can purchase the Student Advantage Discount Card for a nominal fee

Review
LO2 Explain how to identify customer relationships with the organization

Central Information System

Company

data
data
data
data
Customer
data
data
data

Marketers

Marketers can pull information from data whenever needed

● **Interaction, learning**

● **Knowledge management**

♦ **Marketer**

© Cengage Learning 2013

and use it to obtain discounts from affiliated retailers such as T-Mobile, Foot Locker, Target, Timberland, and Barnes & Noble. Student Advantage tracks the cardholders' spending patterns and behaviors to gain a better understanding of what the college customer wants. Student Advantage then communicates this information to the affiliated retailers, who can tailor their discounts to meet college students' needs. Ultimately, everyone benefits from this program: Cardholders get relevant discounts, and retailers enjoy increased sales.[8]

The success of CRM—building lasting and profitable relationships—can be directly measured by the effectiveness of the interaction between the customer and the organization. In fact, what further differentiates CRM from other strategic initiatives is the organization's ability to establish and manage interactions with its current customer base. The more latitude (empowerment) a company gives its representatives, the more likely the interaction will conclude in a way that satisfies the customer.

interaction
The point at which a customer and a company representative exchange information and develop learning relationships.

L❯3

Understand Interactions of the Current Customer Base

The *interaction* between the customer and the organization is the foundation on which a CRM system is built. Only through effective interactions can organizations learn about the expectations of their customers, generate and manage knowledge about them, negotiate mutually satisfying commitments, and build long-term relationships.

Exhibit 21.2 illustrates the customer-centric approach for managing customer interactions. Following a customer-centric approach, an interaction can occur through a formal or direct communication channel, such as a phone, the Internet, or a salesperson. Interactions also occur through a previous relationship a customer has had with the organization, such as a past purchase or a survey response, or through some current transaction or request by the customer, such as an actual product purchase, a request for repair service, or a response to a coupon offer. In short, any activity or touch point a customer has with an organization, either directly or indirectly, constitutes an interaction.

Best Buy, an electronic retail superstore, offers a Performance Service Plan (PSP) on products bought in-store or online. The PSP guarantees products against damage and malfunctioning. If customers need assistance, they can contact the company by mail, phone, in-store, or online. All initial purchase contact information is kept in the customer database, along with copies of the PSP. If a customer calls the Customer Care 1-800 number, the representative will have access to all of this information and can either help the customer

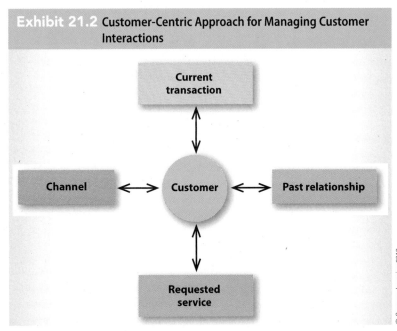

Exhibit 21.2 Customer-Centric Approach for Managing Customer Interactions

© Cengage Learning 2013

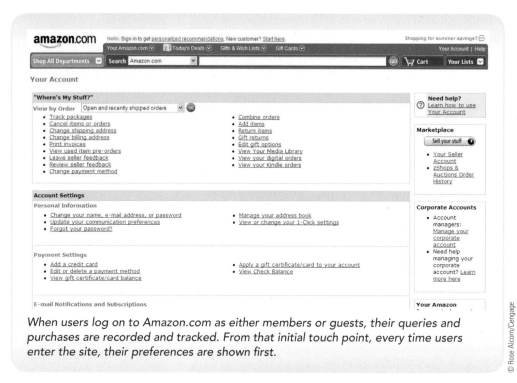

When users log on to Amazon.com as either members or guests, their queries and purchases are recorded and tracked. From that initial touch point, every time users enter the site, their preferences are shown first.

or refer him or her to another representative. Thus, any form of communication with Best Buy, whether initiated by the customer or by a company representative, qualifies as an interaction or touch point.[9]

Companies that effectively manage customer interactions recognize that customers provide data to the organization that affect a wide variety of touch points. In a CRM system, **touch points** are all areas of business where customers have contact with the company, either personally or virtually, and data can be collected. Touch points might include a customer registering for a particular service, a customer communicating with customer service for product information, a customer completing and returning the warranty information card for a product, or a customer talking with salespeople, delivery personnel, and product installers. In the Best Buy example, touch points include the initial customer-initiated purchase and the customer-initiated call to the Customer Care line. Data gathered at these touch points, once interpreted, provide information that affects touch points inside the company. For example, interpreted information might be redirected to marketing research, to develop profiles of extended warranty purchasers; to production, to analyze recurring problems and repair components; and to accounting, to establish cost-control models for repair service calls. With a CRM system, touch points become critical parts of the service delivery process.

Web-based interactions are an increasingly popular touch point for customers to communicate with companies on their own terms. Instead of wasting time with phone numbers and mail surveys, companies are publicizing their Web sites as the first touch point for customer interactions. Web users can evaluate and purchase products, make reservations, indicate preferential data, and provide customer feedback on services and products. Data from these Web-based interactions are then captured, compiled, and used to segment customers, refine marketing efforts, develop new products, and deliver a degree of individual customization to improve customer relationships.

With the popularity of social media, more companies have begun to use it for "social" CRM.[10] Essentially, social CRM takes the best of traditional CRM, such as behavioral targeting, and expands it to include ways to engage customers through social media. Part of this new paradigm includes new customer recommendation value, or the net promoter score, which measures how much a customer influences the behavior of other customers through recommendations on social media. Social CRM enables marketers to focus more on the relationship aspect of CRM. For example, online retailer Zappos is famous for its use of Twitter, Facebook, and blogs

touch points
All possible areas of a business where customers communicate with that business.

© Rose Alcorn/Cengage

to communicate with its customers. Comcast extends its customer service through Twitter. REI empowers customers to "carve your own adventure" through their YouTube channel. JetBlue uses Facebook and Twitter to provide advice and updates to travelers. To do this, companies must understand customers' digital ecosystem, such as what sites they use, whether they post opinions, and the major influencers in the category.

Additionally, when a user logs on to Amazon.com, for example, as a member or guest, that user's queries and purchases are recorded and tracked. From that initial touch point, every time that user enters the site, his or her preferences are shown first. If the user has purchased any books or music in the past, the site will recommend new books or CDs from either the same or a similar author or artist. Similarly, if customers request a book by a particular author without making a purchase, they will be informed on a subsequent visit about

Review LO3 Understand interactions with the current customer base

Interactions

Customer

- Web
- Point of Sale
- Kiosk
- Customer Service
- Delivery, Installation
- Survey
- Product Registration

© Cengage Learning 2013

new material that author has for sale. Recommendations are made and sent through e-mail for members that deepens the relationship between customer and company.[11]

Another touch point is through **point-of-sale interactions** in stores or at information kiosks. Many point-of-sale software programs enable customers to easily provide information about themselves without feeling their privacy has been violated. The information is then used for marketing and merchandising activities, and to accurately identify the store's best customers and the types of products they buy. Data collected at point-of-sale interactions is also used to increase customer satisfaction through the development of in-store services and customer recognition promotions. For example, Barnes & Noble offers a MasterCard that gives members five percent back on all Barnes & Noble purchases. Members also collect points for making purchases outside Barnes & Noble and redeem those points for gift cards. Barnes & Noble can then track purchases and identify the best customers.

LO4
Capture Customer Data

Vast amounts of data can be obtained from the interactions between an organization and its customers. Therefore, in a CRM system, the issue is not how much data can be obtained, but rather what types of data should be acquired and how the data can be used for relationship enhancement.

The traditional approach for acquiring data from customers is through channel interactions. Channel interactions include store visits, conversations with salespeople, interactions via the Web, traditional phone conversations, and wireless

point-of-sale interactions
Communications between customers and organizations that occur at the point of sale, normally in a store.

© Thinkstock Images/Jupiterimages

communications, such as cell phone conversations and satellite communications. In a CRM system, channel interactions are viewed as prime information sources based on the channel selected to initiate the interaction rather than on the data acquired. For example, if a consumer logs on to the Sony Web site to find out why a Sony device is not functioning properly and the answer is not available online, the consumer is then referred to a page where he or she can describe the problem. The Web site then e-mails the problem description to a company representative, who will research the problem and reply via e-mail. Furthermore, Sony will follow up with a brief satisfaction survey also sent via e-mail. Sony continues to use the e-mail mode of communication because the customer has established this as the preferred method of contact.[12] In some cases, companies use online chat to answer questions customers have about products they are looking for. For example, 24 Hour Fitness has an online chat window that opens when a potential customer visits the Web site and begins to review the site. If the customer remains on the site, the online chat window prompts them to indicate if they need help finding something specific.

Interactions between the company and the customer facilitate collection of large amounts of data. Companies can obtain not only simple contact information (name, address, phone number), but also data pertaining to the customer's current relationship with the organization—past purchase history, quantity and frequency of purchases, average amount spent on purchases, sensitivity to promotional activities, and so forth. GEICO, for example, at the time of policy renewal for its auto insurance customers, requests information pertaining to lifestyles (activities, interests, opinions, etc.), cultural factors (ethnicity, religion, etc.), and customer life stage (family composition, number and age of children, children living at home, etc.) for the purposes of pricing and customizing insurance packages for its customers. These data are also used for planning new product

Review

LO 4 Outline the process of capturing customer data

Collects customer information during every transaction, interaction.

Company

Information

Web
Point of sale
Kiosk
Customer service
Delivery, installation
Product use, consumption
Survey
Product registration

Customer

© Cengage Learning 2013

offerings such as vehicle maintenance insurance and gap insurance for lease customers along with cross-selling other GEICO services such as life insurance, home insurance, and marine insurance.[13]

In this manner, a lot of information can be captured from one individual customer across several touch points. Multiply this by the thousands of customers across all of the touch points with an organization, and the volume of data can rapidly become unmanageable for company personnel. The large volumes of data resulting from a CRM initiative can be managed effectively only through the use of technology. Furthermore, once customer data are collected, the question of who owns the data becomes extremely salient.

LO 5

Store and Integrate Customer Data

Customer data are only as valuable as the system in which the data are stored and the consistency and accuracy of the data captured. Gathering data is further complicated by the fact that data needed by one unit of the organization, such as sales and marketing, often are generated by another area of the business or even a third-party supplier, such as an independent marketing research firm. Thus, companies must use information technology to capture, store, and integrate strategically important customer information. This process of centralizing data in a CRM system is referred to as data warehousing.

A **data warehouse** is a central repository (*database*) of customer data collected by an organization. Essentially, it is a large computerized file of all information collected in the previous phase of the CRM process, for example, information collected in channel, transaction, and product/service touch points. The core of the data warehouse is the **database**, "a collection of data, especially one that can be accessed and manipulated by computer software."[14] The CRM database focuses on collecting vital statistics on consumers, their purchasing habits, transaction methods, and product usage in a centralized repository that is accessible by all functional areas of a company. Traditionally, this information was stored in separate computer systems throughout the company. By utilizing a data warehouse, however, marketing managers can quickly access vast amounts of information required to make decisions. For example, Continental Airlines used to store data in a variety of operational systems that could not be integrated. As a result, managers did not have the depth and breadth of information to facilitate decision making. Now the Continental data warehouse centralizes information from multiple sources. The warehouse is accessible by 35 departments and 1,300 employees. The database content includes everything from flight schedules, seat inventory, and customer profiles to employee and crew payroll. Even aircraft parts and maintenance are available in the system to aid in distribution decision making.[15]

When a company builds its database, the first step is to develop a list. A **response list** is based on customers and prospective customers who have indicated an interest in a product or service. They may have responded to a direct mail offer, an online advertisement, a print ad in a magazine or newspaper, or a TV commercial. Response lists tend to be especially valuable because past behavior is a strong predictor of future behavior and because consumers who have indicated interest in the product or service are more prone to purchase. Companies might

data warehouse
A central repository for data from various functional areas of the organization that are stored and inventoried on a centralized computer system so that the information can be shared across all functional departments of the business.

database
A collection of data, especially one that can be accessed and manipulated by computer software.

response list
A customer list that includes the names and addresses of individuals who have responded to an offer of some kind, such as by mail, telephone, direct-response television, product rebates, contests or sweepstakes, or billing inserts.

compiled list
A customer list that is developed by gathering names and addresses from telephone directories and membership rosters, usually enhanced with information from public records, such as census data, auto registrations, birth announcements, business start-ups, or bankruptcies.

find it valuable to enhance their customer records with information about the customers' or prospective customers' demographics and lifestyle characteristics. They can often accomplish this by augmenting with compiled lists. **Compiled lists** are created by an outside company that has collected names and contact information for potential consumers. This information is usually obtained from telephone directories and membership rosters of various groups. Many lists are available, ranging from those owned by large list companies, such as Dun & Bradstreet for business-to-business data and Donnelley and R. L. Polk for consumer lists, to small groups or associations that are willing to sell their membership lists. Indeed, many lists are compiled from people who have opted in to the list after they have purchased a related product. Data compiled by large data-gathering companies are usually very accurate.

In this phase companies typically are collecting channel, transaction, and product/service information such as store, salesperson, communication channel, contact information, relationship, and brands. For example, when Philips wanted to determine how to best sell its Cool Skin Shaver accessories, it used existing information to expand its database. By sending an e-mail message to registered users, Philips was able to collect information including whether or not consumers purchased online, and if so, the "landing page" on the Web site, the number of "unsubscribes" when sent an e-mail message, and the timeliness of response.[16]

A customer database becomes even more useful to marketing managers when it is enhanced to include more than simply a customer's or prospect's name, address, telephone number, and transaction history. Database enhancement involves purchasing information on customers or prospects to better describe their needs or determine how responsive they might be to marketing programs. Types of enhancement data typically include demographic, lifestyle, or behavioral information. Lands' End, for example, has enhanced its database to better understand purchasing patterns. The database not only pinpoints popular clothing items, but also attempts to explain why. In one instance, sales of raincoats increased sharply in the Northeast. Because the database is linked to regional weather information, analysts were able to explain the sudden boost in raincoat sales.[17]

Database enhancement can increase the effectiveness of marketing programs. By learning more about their best and most profitable customers, marketers can maximize the effectiveness of marketing communications and cross-selling. Database enhancement also helps a company find new prospects. Before opening a new store, H-E-B grocery company (**www.heb.com**) uses database enhancement and customer profiling to identify and learn as much as possible about potential customers. Each store is then designed to be unique and to offer the products those customers want.

©Mike Booth/Alamy

When the company opened one of its upscale Central Market stores in Fort Worth, Texas, customer profiles indicated that Fort Worth residents have a strong sense of Western heritage. The Fort Worth location, therefore, offers customers chipotle-smoked barbecue ribs, game birds, and briskets. The store has also adjusted the way it cuts and sells beef to meet local preferences, and it carries an expanded selection of peppers and fresh tortillas for its Hispanic customers. Once open, the stores continue to use databases to collect information about customer preferences and to adjust product offerings.

Multinational companies building worldwide databases often face difficult problems when pulling together internal data about their customers. Differences in language, computer systems, and data-collection methods can be huge obstacles to overcome. In spite of the challenges, many global companies are committed to building databases. Unilever is using the Internet not only to educate consumers about the brand but also to develop relationships with its customers by providing helpful information. Web site visitors can get information on removing stubborn stains and solving similar consumer problems. They also receive a discount on their next purchase in exchange for completing an online questionnaire. Unilever has collected information on more than 30 million loyal customers from numerous countries.[18]

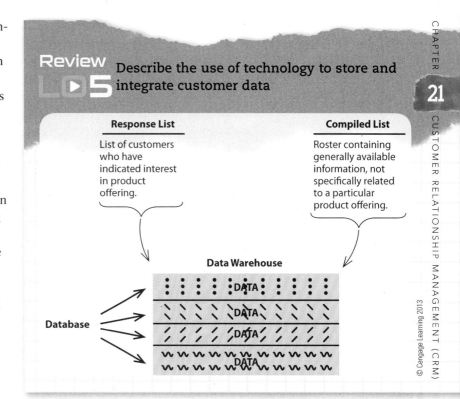

Review LO5 Describe the use of technology to store and integrate customer data

Response List
List of customers who have indicated interest in product offering.

Compiled List
Roster containing generally available information, not specifically related to a particular product offering.

Data Warehouse

Database

LO6
Identifying the Best Customers

CRM manages interactions between a company and its customers. To be successful, companies must identify customers who yield high profits or potential profits. To do so, significant amounts of data must be gathered from customers, stored and integrated in the data warehouse, and then analyzed and interpreted for common patterns that can identify homogeneous customers who are different from other customer segments. Because not all customers are the same, organizations need to develop interactions that target *individual* customer needs and wants. Likewise, not all customers generate the same revenue for a company. Recall, from Chapter 8, the 80/20 principle—80 percent of a company's revenue is generated by 20 percent of its customers. Therefore, the question becomes, how do we identify the 20 percent of our customer base that contributes 80 percent of our revenue? In a CRM system, the answer is data mining.

DATA MINING

Data mining is used to find hidden patterns and relationships in the customer data stored in the data warehouse. It is a data analysis approach that identifies patterns of characteristics that relate to particular customers or customer groups. Although businesses have been conducting such analyses for many years, the procedures typically were performed on small data sets containing as few as 300 to 400 customers. Today, companies analyze billions of customer shopping patterns stored in their data warehouses. Nokia, for example, examined over six billion pieces of data to develop its N-Series mobile phone. Walmart's data warehouse, believed to be second in size only to the Pentagon's, contains over a petabyte (trillions of characters) of customer and market data. Walmart uses its huge data warehouse to help each of its stores adapt its merchandising mix to local neighborhood preferences.

Using data mining, marketers can search the data warehouse, capture relevant data, categorize significant characteristics, and develop customer profiles. In the Philips razor example, marketers wanted to build a relationship with consumers through e-mail. By assessing response and nonresponse rates along with online purchases, they developed a profile of consumers likely to purchase Cool Skin accessories over the Internet. Moreover, once Philips was successful with Cool Skin accessories, it used this approach on other product lines.[19]

When using data mining, it is important to remember that the real value is in the company's ability to transform its data from operational bits and bytes into information marketers need for successful marketing strategies. Companies must go beyond merely creating a mailing list. They must analyze the data to identify and profile the best customers, calculate their lifetime value, and ultimately predict purchasing behavior through statistical modeling.

A wide range of companies have used data mining successfully. Albertsons Supermarkets uses data mining to identify commonly purchased items that should be placed together on shelves and to learn what soft drinks sell best in different parts of the country. Harrah's is one of the best examples of a company that uses data mining effectively. They identify their most profitable customers, design incentive systems, and then test the relative effectiveness of the marketing strategies. Using data mining, Camelot Music discovered that a large number of senior citizens were purchasing rap and alternative music. When managers investigated further, they discovered seniors were buying the music as gifts for their grandchildren. Finally, TheKnot.com, a company that helps plan weddings, asks users to register and provide basic information on its Web site. Its database stores information and creates an initial profile of a customer. From the initial contact, the Web site gathers data as the customer uses the site. For example, when a user adds a product to the registry, the database is updated to reflect that change. Thus, if a consumer adds a different brand or product to the list, the site will tailor product recommendations to reflect that change.[20]

Before the information is leveraged, several types of analyses are run on the data. These analyses include customer segmentation, recency-frequency-monetary (RFM) analysis, lifetime value (LTV) analysis, and predictive modeling.

Customer Segmentation Recall that *customer segmentation* is the process of breaking large groups of customers into smaller, more homogeneous groups. This type of analysis generates a "profile" or picture of the customers' similar demographic, geographic, and psychographic traits as well as their previous purchase behavior; it focuses particularly on the best customers. Profiles of the best customers can be compared and contrasted with other customer segments. For example, a bank could segment consumers on frequency of usage, credit, age, and turnover. Once a profile of the best customer is developed using these criteria, it can be used to screen other potential consumers. Similarly, customer profiles can be used to introduce customers selectively to specific marketing actions. For example, young customers with an open mind can be introduced to home banking, and older, well-established customers to investment opportunities.

Recency-Frequency-Monetary (RFM) Analysis Customers who have purchased recently and often and have spent considerable money are more likely to purchase again. Recency-frequency-monetary (RFM) analysis identifies those customers most likely to purchase again because they have bought recently, bought frequently, or spent a specified amount of money with the firm. Firms develop equations to identify the "best customers" (often the top 20 percent of the customer base) by assigning a score to customer records in the database on how often, how recently, and how much they have spent. Customers are then ranked to determine which ones move to the top of the list and which ones fall to the bottom. The ranking provides the basis for maximizing profits because it enables the firm to use the information in its customer database to select those persons who have proved to be good sources of revenue. Harrah's Entertainment used data mining and RFM to identify 90 market segments to target with its marketing programs. Using direct feedback from the slots as to whether its strategies are working, Harrah's continuously adjusts its marketing tactics to focus on the most profitable segments.[21]

Lifetime Value (LTV) Analysis Recency, frequency, and monetary data can also be used to create a lifetime value model on customers in the database. Whereas RFM looks at how valuable a customer currently is to a company, **lifetime value (LTV) analysis** projects the future value of the customer over a period of years. One of the basic assumptions in any lifetime value calculation is that marketing to repeat customers is more profitable than marketing to first-time buyers. That is, it costs more to find a new customer in terms of promotion and gaining trust than to sell more to a customer who is already loyal.

Customer lifetime value has a number of benefits. It shows marketers how much they can spend to *acquire* new customers, it tells them the level of spending to *retain* customers, and it facilitates targeting new customers who look as though they will be profitable customers. Cadillac has calculated the lifetime value of its top customers at $332,000. Similarly, Pizza Hut figures its best customers are worth $8,000 in bottom-line lifetime value.

Predictive Modeling The ability to reasonably predict future customer behavior gives marketers a significant competitive advantage. Through **predictive modeling**, marketers try to determine, based on some past set of occurrences, what the odds are that some other

lifetime value (LTV) analysis
A data manipulation technique that projects the future value of the customer over a period of years using the assumption that marketing to repeat customers is more profitable than marketing to first-time buyers.

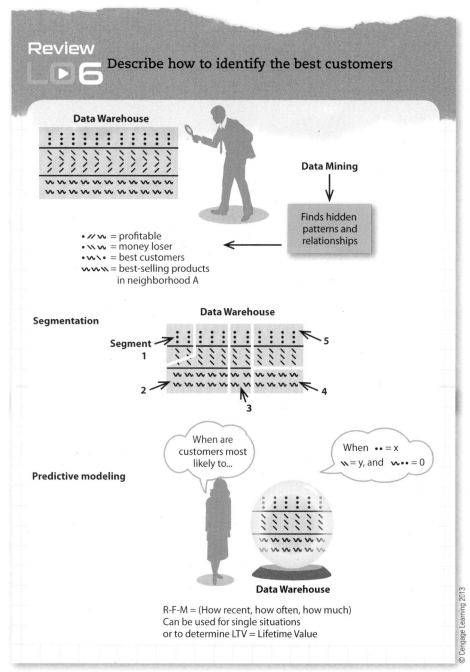

Review
LO6 Describe how to identify the best customers

Data Warehouse

Data Mining

Finds hidden patterns and relationships

• // ʍ = profitable
• \\ ʍ = money loser
• ʍ\ = best customers
ʍʍʍ = best-selling products in neighborhood A

Segmentation

Data Warehouse

Segment 1 · · · · · 5
2 · · · · 4
3

Predictive modeling

When are customers most likely to...

When •• = x
ʍ = y, and ʍ••• = 0

Data Warehouse

R-F-M = (How recent, how often, how much)
Can be used for single situations
or to determine LTV = Lifetime Value

predictive modeling
A data manipulation technique in which marketers try to determine, based on some past set of occurrences, what the odds are that some other occurrence, such as a response or purchase, will take place in the future.

campaign management
Developing product or service offerings customized for the appropriate customer segment and then pricing and communicating these offerings for the purpose of enhancing customer relationships.

occurrence, such as an Internet inquiry or purchase, will take place in the future. SPSS Predictive Marketing is one tool marketers can use to answer questions about their consumers. The software requires minimal knowledge of statistical analysis. Users operate from a prebuilt model, which generates profiles in three to four days. SPSS also has an online product that predicts Web site users' behavior. Harrah's uses predictive modeling to attract millions of customers. Its models include the ages, gender, zip codes, amount of time spent gambling, and how much individuals have won or lost. Analyses of the data enable Harrah's to target individuals with special offers, such as getaway weekends and gourmet restaurant meals, to attract them back to the casinos to gamble more. Predictive modeling enabled Harrah's to average 22 percent growth for the past five years while its stock price tripled.[22] Harrah's management uses predictive modeling to develop long-term, personalized, and profitable relationships with each of their customers.

L●7
Leverage Customer Information

Data mining identifies the most profitable customers and prospects. Managers can then design tailored marketing strategies to best appeal to the identified segments. In CRM this is commonly referred to as leveraging customer information to facilitate enhanced relationships with customers. Exhibit 21.3 shows some common CRM marketing database applications.

CAMPAIGN MANAGEMENT

Through campaign management, all areas of the company participate in the development of programs targeted to customers. **Campaign management** involves monitoring and leveraging customer interactions to sell a company's products and to increase customer service. Campaigns are based directly on data obtained from customers through various interactions. Campaign management includes monitoring the success of the communications based on customer reactions through sales, orders, callbacks to the company, and the like. If a campaign appears unsuccessful, it is evaluated and changed to better achieve the company's desired objective. Stave Puzzles, the "Rolls-Royce" of puzzles, produces handcrafted wood puzzles. Each puzzle is unique and can be customized as the customer desires. Steve Richardson, the company's cofounder, has narrowed his customer base to his "Hot Hundred" most valuable customers. To manage his customer base and ensure they are receiving optimal service, he tracks not only standard information such as contact data and orders, but also birthdays, anniversaries, relationships between customers, phone conversations, inquiries, and workshop visits.[23]

Campaign management involves developing customized product and service offerings for the appropriate customer

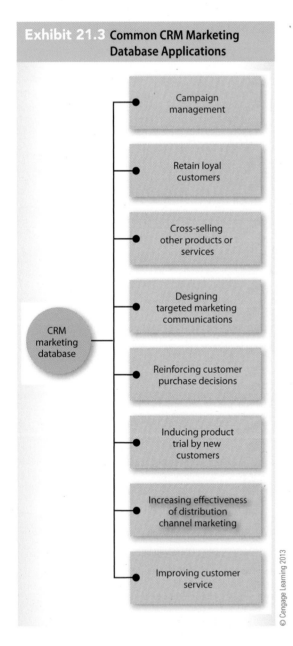

Exhibit 21.3 Common CRM Marketing Database Applications

- Campaign management
- Retain loyal customers
- Cross-selling other products or services
- Designing targeted marketing communications
- Reinforcing customer purchase decisions
- Inducing product trial by new customers
- Increasing effectiveness of distribution channel marketing
- Improving customer service

CRM marketing database

© Cengage Learning 2013

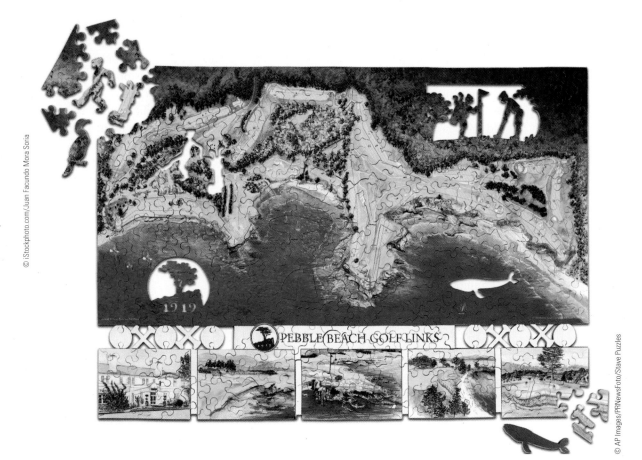

segment, pricing these offerings attractively, and communicating these offers in a manner that enhances customer relationships. Customizing product and service offerings requires managing multiple interactions with customers, as well as giving priority to those products and services that are viewed as most desirable for a specifically designated customer. Even within a highly defined market segment, individual customer differences will emerge. Therefore, interactions among customers must focus on individual experiences, expectations, and desires. Stave Puzzles customizes its marketing campaigns by tailoring mailings to eight different segments. For example, the monthly buyers and top 10 percent of the customers receive individual reminder notes about special occasions and previous purchases.

RETAINING LOYAL CUSTOMERS

If a company has identified its best customers, then it should make every effort to maintain and increase their loyalty. When a company retains an additional 5 percent of its customers each year, profits will increase by as much as 25 percent. What's more, improving customer retention by a mere 2 percent can decrease costs by as much as 10 percent.[24] For example, The Palace of Auburn Hills, a sporting venue, is home to the NBA Detroit Pistons and the WNBA Detroit Shock. To increase game attendance, the arena developed its MyPal rewards card, which enables fans to receive e-mail updates. As a result, game attendance has increased for all types of consumers.[25]

Loyalty programs reward loyal customers for making multiple purchases. The objective is to build long-term, mutually beneficial relationships between a company and its key customers. Marriott, Hilton, and Starwood Hotels, for instance, reward their best customers with special perks not available to customers who stay less frequently. Travelers who spend a specified number of nights per year receive reservation guarantees, upgrades to better rooms, welcome gifts like fruit baskets and wine in their rooms, free phone service, and access to concierge lounges. In addition to rewarding good customers, loyalty programs provide businesses with a wealth of information about their customers and shopping trends that can be used to make future business decisions. Drugstore chain CVS has an ExtraCare program that allows customers to register for a card that is swiped prior to each purchase and gives discounts and offers special in-store promotions. The coupons and discounts are based on purchase history, which enables the company to sell more products. The ExtraCare program helps CVS respond to what customers really want, based on information collected from card sales, and has attracted more than 50 million customers.[26]

CROSS-SELLING OTHER PRODUCTS AND SERVICES

CRM provides many opportunities to cross-sell related products. Marketers can use the database to match product profiles and consumer profiles so that they can cross-sell customers products that match their demographic, lifestyle, or behavioral characteristics. American Collegiate Marketing, a magazine subscription service targeted to students and educators (**www.magazineline.com**), uses past customer purchase information gleaned from its database of millions of magazine subscribers to feature new magazines that might interest the customer. Past purchase behavior can show that subscribers to *Sports Illustrated,* for instance, are also interested in general news magazines such as *Time* and *Newsweek*. Similarly, to increase purchasing across different departments and in different product lines, Wegmans Food Markets monitors sales using a frequent buyer card. Using data mining, it discovered that 80 percent of shoppers buying baby food also bought flowers. As a result, Wegmans was able to develop a more effective method for cross-selling products.[27]

Internet companies use product and customer profiling to reveal cross-selling opportunities while a customer is surfing their site. Past purchases on a particular Web site and the site a surfer comes from give online marketers clues about the surfer's interests and what items to cross-sell. Fry's Outpost electronics (**www.frys.com**), a computer-goods e-tailer, adjusts the pages visitors see depending on what they click on at the site or what they purchased in the past. For instance, if a surfer always goes to computer game pages or has purchased games in the past, Outpost will automatically place offers for other game titles on part of the screen. Depending on what a shopper puts in a shopping cart, Outpost will flash promotions for related items—a leather case for someone who is buying a PDA, for example. These days many organizations are using CRM technology. See the Global Box to learn how online charities use CRM.

DESIGNING TARGETED MARKETING COMMUNICATIONS

Using transaction and purchase data, a database enables marketers to track customers' relationships to the company's products and services and modify the marketing message accordingly. For example, Kraft Foods teamed with Wegmans

global perspectives

Online Charities Use CRM Tools

A new type of nonprofit organization has emerged recently that takes online technology to a completely new level. Based on theories of customer relationship management in the for-profit world, organizations such as Globalgiving.com and Kiva.org are enabling ordinary people to make extraordinary differences in the lives of people across the globe. For example, Globalgiving.com has a database of small international projects that donors can select to participate in by making a donation directly to the project. One of the most popular gifts is to send a child in India to school for a year—for a donation of $40. The organization uses database technology and the Internet to enable people to choose a project—based on cause type such as education or social issues, or location such as India or Brazil—and make a direct donation that has an immediate effect. Their Web site is an online marketplace that connects people with causes around the world. In addition, the donor gets regular updates, in some cases from the individual that was helped, about the progress of the project. Kiva.org, which is similar in its global mission, enables donors to make very low interest loans to aspiring business owners in developing countries. The organization combines the principles of microfinance and poverty reduction along with a strong database and Internet presence to create results. Indeed, the payback rate for donors to Kiva.org is about 90 percent. Most donors reinvest in another project. Kiva.org also maintains a strong connection to donors through messages and updates. Other similar organizations in the U.S. fund domestic projects as well. Donorschoose. org enables people to directly donate to school projects in low income areas. Modestneeds.org makes it possible for people to donate to individuals or families that need assistance due unforeseen circumstances. According to Keith Taylor, the founder of Modest Needs, "The e-commerce model has changed philanthropy. Donors expect the same level of interaction they get from Amazon. com."[28]

Food Markets to determine which advertising campaigns were most effective for frequent buyers of Kraft Macaroni & Cheese. Kraft used the results to better reach its frequent buyers in future campaigns.[29]

Customers can also be segmented into infrequent users, moderate users, and heavy users. A segmented communications strategy can then be developed based on which group the customer falls into. Communications to infrequent users might encourage repeat purchases through a direct incentive such as a limited-time price discount for ordering again. Communications to moderate users might use fewer incentives and more reinforcement of past purchase decisions. Communications to heavy users would be designed around loyalty and reinforcement of the purchase rather than price promotions. For example, Nike Store Toronto offers the Air Max Club (AMC), a loyalty club for customers. Club members can collect points and redeem them for gift certificates, movies, and books. Customers considered "most valuable" are identified when they swipe their card to collect points, thereby alerting the salesperson. A message on the salesperson's screen indicates the customer should receive a special thank-you and possibly a prize. The system also generates customized coupons based on purchase history. The company has found that club members spend about 50 percent more than the average customer.[30]

REINFORCING CUSTOMER PURCHASE DECISIONS

As you learned in the consumer behavior chapter, cognitive dissonance is the feeling consumers experience when they recognize an inconsistency between their values and opinions and their purchase behavior. In other words, they doubt the soundness of their purchase decision and often feel anxious. CRM offers marketers an excellent opportunity to reach out to customers to reinforce the purchase decision. By thanking customers for their purchases and telling them they are important, marketers can help cement a long-term, profitable relationship. Guests staying at the quaint Village Country Inn nestled in the Green Mountains of Vermont receive a handwritten thank-you note from the Inn's proprietors within a week of their stay. The note thanks the guests for visiting and encourages them to return in the future.

Updating customers periodically about the status of their order reinforces purchase decisions. Post-sale e-mail messages also afford the chance to provide more customer service or cross-sell other products. Minutes after customers order merchandise from Amazon's Web site, for example, they receive an e-mail message acknowledging their order. Every few days thereafter, customers receive updates that allow them to track the shipment of the order, from ship date to receipt. Similarly, Sumerset Houseboats builds customized, luxury houseboats priced at about $250,000 each. The company uses its Web site to monitor customer profiles, post company information, and communicate with customers. For example, it posts daily pictures of progress on houseboats being built. By reinforcing customers' decisions, Sumerset is able to offset the feeling of cognitive dissonance.[31]

Inducing Product Trial by New Customers

Although significant time and money are expended on encouraging repeat purchases by the best customers, a marketing database is also used to identify new customers. Because a firm using a marketing database already has a profile of its best customers, it can easily use the results of modeling to profile potential customers. EATEL, a regional telecommunications firm, uses modeling to identify prospective residential and commercial telephone customers and successfully attract their business.

Marketing managers generally use demographic and behavioral data overlaid on existing customer data to develop a detailed customer profile that is a powerful tool for evaluating lists of prospects. For instance, if a firm's best customers are 35 to 50 years of age, live in suburban areas, own luxury cars, like to eat at Thai restaurants, and enjoy mountain climbing, then the company can find prospects already in its database or customers who currently are identified as using a competitor's product that match this profile. Procter & Gamble uses its Web site to test customer interest in new products. Customers who visit the Web site are encouraged to sign up for free trial samples and then provide feedback. P&G also uses the demographic data and customer feedback to make product and promotion decisions. More recently, they have expanded their efforts to build relationships with customers into social media.

INCREASING EFFECTIVENESS OF DISTRIBUTION CHANNEL MARKETING

In Chapter 13 you learned that a marketing channel is a business structure of interdependent organizations, such as wholesalers and retailers, that move a product from the producer to the ultimate consumer. Most marketers rely on indirect channels to move their products to the end user. Thus, marketers often lose touch with the customer as an individual since the relationship is really between the re-tailer and the consumer. Marketers in this predicament often view their customers as aggregate statistics because specific customer information is difficult to gather.

With CRM databases, manufacturers now have a tool to gain insight into who is buying their products. Instead of simply unloading products into the distribution channel and leaving marketing and relationship building to dealers, auto manu-facturers today are using Web sites to keep in touch with customers and prospects, learn about their lifestyles and hobbies, understand their vehicle needs, and develop relationships hoping that these consumers will reward them with brand loyalty in the future. BMW and Mercedes-Benz USA, as well as other vehicle manufactur-ers, have databases with names of millions of consumers who have expressed an interest.

With many brick-and-mortar stores setting up shop online, companies are now challenged to monitor purchases of customers who shop both in-store and online. This concept is referred to as multichannel marketing. After Lands' End determined that multichannel customers are the most valuable, the company targeted market-ing campaigns toward retaining these customers and increased sales significantly. Talbots and Victoria's Secret have also developed successful campaigns to serve multichannel customers.

Companies are also using radio-frequency identification (RFID) technology to improve distribution. The technology uses a microchip with an antenna that tracks anything from a soda can to a car. A computer can locate the product anywhere. The main implication of this technology is that companies will enjoy a reduction in theft and loss of merchandise shipments and will always know where merchandise is in the distribution channel. Moreover, as this technology is further developed, marketers can gather information on product usage and consumption.[32]

IMPROVING CUSTOMER SERVICE

CRM marketing techniques increasingly are being used to improve customer service. The level of customer service provided by companies is influential in cus-tomer retention. *Customer retention* is the percentage of customers that repeatedly purchase products from a company. Amazon uses several Web site tools that get customers to return. For example, customers can build wish lists of items, much like a gift registry, so friends and family can make purchases for birthdays and other occasions. Amazon also offers recommendations for products based on past purchase and search behavior. These recommendations are listed when a registered customer logs on to the site. Last, Amazon stores all customer payment and ship-ping information so customers can make a purchase with one click and then track the shipment (**www.amazon.com**). Amazon makes the process of searching for and purchasing books and other products easy and efficient.

PRIVACY CONCERNS AND CRM

Before rushing out to invest in a CRM system and build a database, marketers should consider consumers' reactions to the growing use of databases. Many Amer-icans and customers abroad are concerned about databases because of the potential for invasion of privacy. The sheer volume of information in databases makes this information vulnerable to unauthorized access and use. A fundamental aspect of marketing using CRM databases is providing valuable services to customers based

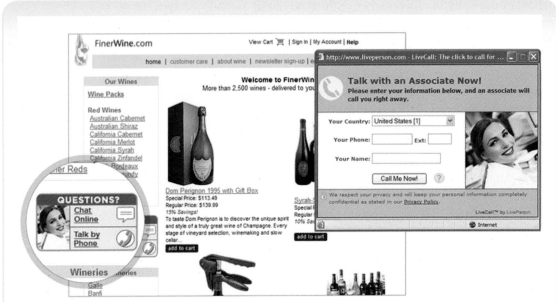

The Internet is quickly becoming the channel of choice for today's consumers—especially when it comes to customer service. Using a service such as LivePerson, a company can include a click-to-chat button on its Web site's "Contact Us" or FAQ pages for customers who want personalized information or care. The chat button is visible only when agents are available to chat, ensuring that help is offered only when it can be delivered quickly and efficiently.

on knowledge of what customers really value. It is critical, however, that marketers remember these relationships are built on trust. Although database technology enables marketers to compile ever-richer information about their customers that can be used to build and manage relationships, if customers feel their privacy is being violated, then the relationship becomes a liability.

Privacy Issues Must Be Resolved for CRM's Success CRM is a hot marketing topic and a popular business tool. But it also sparks hot debates regarding consumers' privacy. American businesses have collected consumer data for years. Policies and laws govern what businesses can do with that information once it is collected. Current laws cover several industries including finance, health care, retail, automotive and transportation, technology, and direct marketing. The Gramm-Leach-Bliley Act enforces privacy guidelines for financial information, the Health Insurance Portability and Accountability Act (HIPAA) regulates medical records, and the National Do-Not-Call list governs telemarketing. Most recently, the CAN-SPAM Act provided guidelines for e-mail.

Companies have taken initiatives, too. Many have developed independent privacy policies designed to govern how they collect, use, share, and protect the personal information of consumers and employees. According to the Benchmark Study of Corporate Privacy Practices Report, 98 percent of U.S. companies have a privacy policy in effect. Nevertheless, more than half of those companies believe their policy may be difficult to understand. One problem is that only 53 percent require mandatory training for policy enforcement. Consequently, consumer information is still vulnerable to unethical corporate practices.

Despite consumers' concerns, company executives realize customer information is very profitable. Companies can profit by sharing the information with a third party or by purchasing third-party information to build a more comprehensive database. As a result, companies are struggling to balance consumer trust and profitability. For example, the Walt Disney Company used to have a strict policy that did not allow it to share information collected on its Web site with third parties. Once executives realized the value of the information, however, they amended the privacy policy to enable third-party companies to send promotions to consumers. To ensure continued consumer trust, Disney allows consumers to opt in or opt out of third-party promotions. Additionally, Disney offers consumers updated privacy information on its Web site and sends e-mail messages to registered users explaining any privacy policy changes.[33]

How does a firm's privacy policy affect your purchasing decisions? Do you think it is ethical for a company to post a privacy policy but not have mandatory enforcement? What are the most important issues in establishing a privacy policy for a business?

The popularity of the Internet for e-commerce and customer data collection and as a repository for sensitive customer data has alarmed privacy-minded customers. Online users complain loudly about being "spammed," and Web surfers, including children, are routinely asked to divulge personal information to access certain screens or purchase goods or services. Internet users are disturbed by the amount of information businesses collect on them as they visit various sites in cyberspace. Indeed, many users are unaware of how personal information is collected, used, and distributed. The government actively sells huge amounts of personal information to list companies. State motor vehicle bureaus sell names and addresses of individuals who get driver's licenses. Hospitals sell the names of women who just gave birth on their premises. Consumer credit databases are often used by credit card marketers to prescreen targets for solicitations. Online and offline privacy concerns are growing and ultimately will have to be dealt with by businesses and regulators.

Privacy policies for companies in the United States are largely voluntary, and regulations on how personal data are collected and used are being developed. But collecting data on consumers outside the United States is a different matter. For database marketers venturing beyond U.S. borders, success requires careful navigation of foreign privacy laws. For example, under the European Union's European Data Protection Directive, any business that trades with a European organization must comply with the EU's rules for handling information about individuals or risk prosecution. More than 50 nations have, or are developing, privacy legislation. Europe has the strictest legislation regarding the collection and use of customer data, and other countries are reviewing that legislation in formulating their policies.

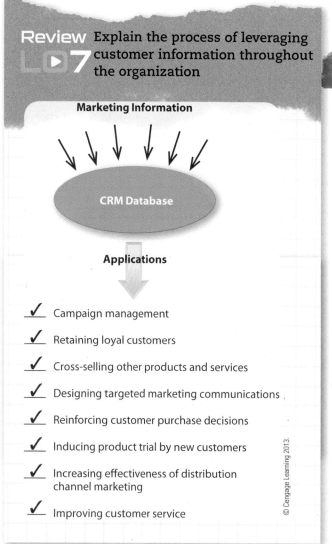

Review LO7 Explain the process of leveraging customer information throughout the organization

Marketing Information

CRM Database

Applications

✓ Campaign management

✓ Retaining loyal customers

✓ Cross-selling other products and services

✓ Designing targeted marketing communications

✓ Reinforcing customer purchase decisions

✓ Inducing product trial by new customers

✓ Increasing effectiveness of distribution channel marketing

✓ Improving customer service

© Cengage Learning 2013.

© iStockphoto.com/Juan Facundo Mora Soria

CHAPTER 21 CUSTOMER RELATIONSHIP MANAGEMENT (CRM)

CHAPTER 21 CUSTOMER RELATIONSHIP MANAGEMENT (CRM)

ANATOMY OF a Customer Relations Decision: Zane's Cycles

Zane's Cycles' best customers? The ones it keeps.

1 Gather data
Zane's offers its customers free bicycle maintenance in exchange for answering survey questions.

2 Leverage data
Zane's uses the data supplied by each customer to draw up a profile of each customer, which guides its one-to-one marketing efforts.

3 Analyze data
How much to acquire a new customer or retain one? Zane's calculates its Customer Lifetime Value as $12,500.

4 Capitalize on the data
Zane's best employees understand "CLV" and focus on long-term customer experience and relationships. The company has grown an average of 23.5 percent/year.

If a customer leaves disappointed or unhappy, Zane's Cycles doesn't just lose the profit from that single transaction, it risks $12,500.

Review and Applications

Define customer relationship management. Customer relationship management (CRM) is a company-wide business strategy designed to optimize profitability, revenue, and customer satisfaction by focusing on highly defined and precise customer groups. This is accomplished by organizing the company around customer segments, encouraging and tracking customer interaction with the company, fostering customer-satisfying behaviors, and linking all processes of a company from its customers through its suppliers.

1.1 Identify the six components of the CRM process.

1.2 Form a team and identify several local businesses that would benefit from a CRM strategy. Select one business and outline a plan for implementing a CRM strategy for that business. You might want to visit the company and interview managers about their current initiatives. When you have completed your CRM plan, share it with the class—and the company.

1.3 General Motors installs the "OnStar" system in many of its vehicles. OnStar is a location, information, and communication system available to drivers who wish to subscribe to the service. Go to the OnStar Web site, **www.onstar.com**, and read about some of the services that are offered to consumers. Based on what you learn, write a short report describing the various ways that OnStar can be used as a CRM tool, specifically in the context of creating interactions, gathering customer data, and customizing service offerings to customers.

Explain how to identify customer relationships with the organization. Companies that implement a CRM system adhere to a customer-centric focus or model. A customer-centric company focuses on learning the factors that build long-lasting relationships with valuable customers and then builds its system on what satisfies and retains those customers. Building relationships through CRM is a strategic process that focuses on learning, managing customer knowledge, and empowerment.

2.1 Briefly explain the concept of a customer-centric focus. Why is this so important in a CRM process?

2.2 What is meant by knowledge management? Why is it so important in a CRM system?

Understand interactions with the current customer base. The interaction between the customer and the organization is considered to be the foundation on which a CRM system is built. Only through effective interactions can organizations learn about the expectations of their customers, generate and manage knowledge about them, negotiate mutually satisfying commitments, and build long-term relationships. Effective management of customer interactions recognizes that customers provide information to organizations across a wide variety of touch points. Consumer-centric organizations are implementing new and unique approaches for establishing interactions specifically for this purpose. They include Web-based interactions, point-of-sale interactions, and transaction-based interactions.

3.1 Develop a plan for establishing and managing interactions with a business's customers. In this plan, identify the key touch points for customers, explain how the data warehouse would be designed, and indicate the main interaction methods that would be promoted to the customer.

Outline the process of capturing customer data. Based on the interaction between the organization and its customers, vast amounts of information can be obtained. In a CRM system, the issue is not how much data can be obtained, but rather what type of data should be acquired and how those data can be used effectively for relationship enhancement. The channel, transaction, and product or service consumed all constitute touch points between a customer and the organization. These touch points represent possible areas within a business where customer interactions can take place and, hence, the opportunity for acquiring data from the customer.

4.1 Assume you are the manager for a Hard Rock Cafe. Your boss has asked you to evaluate how the company is using its Web site to gather customer data. Go to the Web site for the Hard Rock Cafe (www.hardrock.com) and provide a detailed critique on how the site is used for capturing customer data. Comment on the types of customer data the Web site is designed to capture, and explain how those data would benefit your local Hard Rock operation.

LO5 Describe the use of technology to store and integrate customer data.

Customer data gathering is complicated because information needed by one unit of the organization (e.g., sales and marketing) is often generated by another area of the business or even a third-party supplier (e.g., an independent marketing research firm). Because of the lack of standard structure and interface, organizations rely on technology to capture, store, and integrate strategically important customer information. The process of centralizing data in a CRM system is referred to as data warehousing. A data warehouse is a central repository of customer information collected by an organization.

5.1 Briefly explain the concept of a data warehouse. In the context of a CRM framework, why is a data warehouse such an important tool?

5.2 What is being written about customer data in today's periodicals? Search your favorite database of articles using keywords such as "customer data" and "data warehousing." Are certain industries better represented in the citation list generated by your search? Are certain issues more prevalent? Read a selection of at least three to four articles and write a brief analysis of what is being discussed in the press regarding these CRM topics.

LO6 Describe how to identify the best customers.

Customer relationship management, as a process strategy, attempts to manage the interactions between a company and its customers. To be successful, organizations must identify customers who yield high profitability or high potential profitability. To accomplish this task, significant amounts of information must be gathered from customers, stored and integrated in the data warehouse, and then analyzed for commonalities that can produce segments that are highly similar, yet different from other customer segments. A useful approach to identifying the best customers is recency-frequency-monetary (RFM) analysis. Data mining uses RFM, predictive modeling, and other approaches to identify significant relationships among several customer dimensions within vast data warehouses. These significant relationships enable marketers to better define the most profitable customers and prospects.

6.1 Explain the concept of data mining. Provide five examples of companies that are currently using data mining and explain why each is using it.

LO7 Explain the process of leveraging customer information throughout the organization.

One of the benefits of a CRM system is the capacity to share information throughout the organization. This allows an organization to interact with all functional areas to develop programs targeted to its customers. This process is commonly referred to as campaign management. Campaign management involves developing customized product/service offerings for the appropriate customer segment and pricing and communicating these offerings for the purpose of enhancing customer relationships.

7.1 Campaign management is a benefit derived by an organization's ability to leverage and disseminate information throughout the company. Briefly define campaign management and explain how a business might apply it to its daily operations. In your answer, select a particular business as an example of effective campaign management.

7.2 What kind of product testing is currently going on at the Procter & Gamble Web site (**www.pg.com**)? Sign up to participate and find out how the company implements its one-to-one marketing plan through its Web site.

online

Key Terms

campaign management *788*

compiled list *784*

customer relationship
   management (CRM) *773*

customer-centric *777*

data warehouse *783*

database *783*

empowerment *777*

interaction *778*

knowledge management *778*

learning *778*

lifetime value (LTV) analysis *787*

point-of-sale interactions *781*

predictive modeling *787*

response list *783*

touch points *780*

Exercises

ETHICS EXERCISE

ethics

By combining several of its databases of parental purchasing behavior and the results of its market research, Maxwell, Inc., believes it has the tools to launch one-to-one marketing messages for the six- to nine-year-old fans of its JoyMax educational toy products without violating the law. In spite of potential parental backlash, Maxwell believes the approach will help it customize new children's products and increase the company's share of these profitable young customers.

Questions

1. What do you think? Should Maxwell use one-to-one marketing tools to communicate with children?

2. Does the AMA Statement of Ethics address marketing to children? Go to **www.market-ingpower.com** and review the statement. Then write a brief paragraph on how the AMA Statement of Ethics relates to Maxwell's dilemma.

MARKETING PLAN EXERCISE

Your final strategic marketing plan exercise is to identify the ways in which your company will leverage the capabilities of database technology for implementation, evaluation, and control. A strategic plan is effective only when it is acted upon, so implementation guidelines should list specific action plans and a recommended time frame. Evaluation is needed to see if actual marketing activities are resulting in expected objectives. If not, control measures will need to take place. Use the following exercises to guide you through the additional technology aspects of a strategic marketing plan and then complete the Part 7 Marketing Plan Worksheet, found by logging in to the companion Web site at **www.cengagebrain.com**:

1. Specify how you will tailor your marketing strategies to reach and serve your most profitable customers and prospects

   → Identify the best customers

   → Retain loyal customers

   → Cross-sell other products or services

   → Target marketing communications

© iStockphoto.com/Juan Facundo Mora Soria

→ Reinforce customer purchase decisions

→ Induce product trials

→ Increase effectiveness of channels

→ Improve customer service

2. Investigate the expansion of your marketing efforts to include a database marketing program. How will you collect data? How will you use it? What effect will the creation of the database have on your diverse marketing methods (mailings, catalogs, e-mailings, coupon distribution, product sample distribution, and so on)? How will this data be used? Write your online privacy policy.

3. Project management tools are the best way to set up your implementation, evaluation, and control program. Visit www.allpm.com to learn about project planning, alternative software tools, and free project information. For a free timeline utility tool, visit www. smartdraw.com. Decide whether the marketing or operations department will manage the implementation and control of the plan.

4. Make sure performance standards are set for each area of the marketing plan. Comparing performance against objectives is why objectives must be stated in numerical terms. What will your objectives be in terms of traffic (hits), sales, page views, visits per customer, and length of average visit (in minutes)? Which measurement is most important? Why?

APPLICATION EXERCISE

Understanding how companies use consumer information can be difficult if you have never had a job or internship that required you to use databases or customer profiles.[34]

Activities

1. Save all the direct-mail advertising that comes to your mailbox for at least a week. Ask your parents or friends to collect direct mail that they receive as well.

2. Once you have your stack of mail, organize it according to the household that received it. For example, if friends and family helped you collect mail, then keep mail sent to each address together. Make a list of all material in each group.

3. To what kind of customer is each piece of mail targeted? What leads you to that conclusion?

4. Based on the content of the mail pieces, determine what kind of information the various companies have about you, your friends, or your family in their databases. Are there indications on the mailers about what kind of interactions the recipient has had with the sender of the marketing piece?

5. Write out an aggregate profile for each address. If you were a direct marketer, what kind of products and services would you market to each? What kind of offers would you create?

CASE STUDY: Petco.Com

TURNING NEGATIVE REVIEWS INTO POSITIVE SALES

On Petco.com, you can buy a soft-sided travel carrier for your cat for only $19.99. You might think twice, though, after seeing that customers gave it only two "paws" out of five overall for pet satisfaction, appearance, and quality. The reviews reveal more serious reasons to hesitate before adding the product to your cart. A customer with the screen name "Disgruntled Bunny" reports: "The mesh on the sides was such poor quality that my cat was able to rip it to shreds and escape in a matter of seconds!" Another customer recommends buying a carrier with stronger sides, adding, "It costs more but is safer for your pet, so it's worth it."

Products have long been rated on sites such as Amazon.com and those that exist entirely for customer reviews, but Petco was one of the first mainstream retailers to create a forum on its own Web site for criticism. The risk was obvious: Customers could pan products and send buyers running. But Petco reports that business is booming, even with bad reviews like Disgruntled Bunny's.

New research is proving what Petco already learned: Peer reviews work. Shoppers are turning to everyday people for product advice. The 2007 Edelman Trust Barometer reports that over half of Americans said they trust "a person like me" for information about a company or product. David Brain, CEO of Edelman, urges companies to stop relying on "top-down communications delivered to an elite audience and move to peer-to-peer dialogue."

Making customer reviews public has an immediate impact on sales and brand loyalty. Data from ForeSee Results revealed that 40 percent of online shoppers said peer ratings on Web sites influenced their purchasing decisions. Furthermore, this group was 21 percent more satisfied with its purchases than other buyers and was 18 percent more likely to buy from the same site again.

According to Petco executive John Lazarchic, most users who search for products by customer ratings shop longer, buy more, and return less: "The savings in returns alone pays for all the technology involved in the review and ratings feature." And if one product gets too many bad reviews, it usually prompts customers to buy higher-rated, more expensive merchandise instead.

Other advantages? Reviews build camaraderie with an online community where shoppers can connect. They can boost a site's ratings on search sites. And they establish credibility. As long as the reviews aren't overwhelmingly negative, positive reviews have been shown to outweigh the negatives in shoppers' minds. For example, a four-paw review on Petco.com would outweigh one-paw ratings by seven to one.

Lazarchic insists that reviews provide valuable feedback. Critical comments are shared within the company and can instigate changes. In fact, they're finding that the risk is not in receiving too many negative comments on a product, but too few. When no one is responding, it looks like no one is buying it. Or, if they are, they don't care enough about it to talk about it. Petco had that problem at first. In the beginning, when the company posted a small link for users to click and write a review, the silence was deafening. So they added promotional banners to the site and advertised drawings in which lucky reviewers would receive cash prizes. Within a couple of weeks, they'd gotten 4,500 new comments.

Analysts warn that to maintain credibility, reviews shouldn't be edited unless necessary. Petco removes the names of rival brands, URLs, and personal information, but less than 10 percent of the reviews they receive are deleted. Now they're experimenting with the idea of using customer comments as marketing tools in print catalogs, offline ads, e-mail messages, and point-of-purchase displays. In print circulars, for example, Petco highlights its five-paw rated products.

Many of their customers' e-mail addresses are collected through a loyalty program in Petco stores, which means those shoppers might not have visited the Web site. By including customer comments in e-mail ads, it expands the reach of the review program and boosts sales of products those shoppers may not have considered in the store.

According to a Nielsen BuzzMetrics study, the customers most likely to write reviews on Web sites are empty nesters and "young transitionals" without children. Petco found that on their site, reviewers tend to be women with higher levels of education and income who are passionate about their pets. It is generally someone who wants to be helpful, share her opinion, and feel important—someone, perhaps, like Disgruntled Bunny, who wants to warn others of the dangers of defective travel carriers before another cat escapes.[35]

Courtesy, Petco, Inc.

1. A customer-centric company builds long-lasting relationships by focusing on what satisfies and retains valuable customers. Discuss how Petco follows this customer-centric philosophy.

2. Go to Petco.com and read some of the customer reviews for various types of products. Do the one- and two-paw ratings tend to outnumber those with four and five paws, or the other way around? Can you find a customer review that Petco could use to market a product in a company circular or e-mail ad?

3. Now that Petco has identified the type of customer most likely to write reviews of their products, discuss the kinds of promotions that might encourage continued loyalty and response online from them in the future. What could they do to appeal to these customers?

4. Many mainstream retailers are still hesitant to post customer reviews on their Web sites. If you were consulting with one of these companies, what arguments would you use to convince management to try them?

COMPANY CLIPS: Method—Spreading the News about Green Cleaning

© NKP MEDIA, INC./Cengage

It is not uncommon for companies to be a bit protective of their brands. As you read in Chapter 10, brand equity and perception are indicators of marketing success. But in today's fast-paced markets, much can be gained by turning ownership of the brand over to consumers. Method is a company that understands the benefits to this risky proposition. Founders Eric Ryan and Adam Lowry created a brand that its customers can take ownership of and have actually built a customer feedback channel that most businesses dream of achieving. Brand advocates, or method's most enthusiastic customers, are the company's most vocal proponents and take an almost evangelical approach to sharing the benefits of green cleaning with the market.

Questions

1. How has method identified customer relationships with the organization? What does the company do to nurture those relationships?

2. Identify the touch points mentioned in the video and list the types of information method could gather at each one.

3. What is the role of technology in method's CRM system?

Notes

1. Joseph Hair, Robert Bush, and David Ortinau, *Marketing Research: Within a Changing Information Environment*, 4th ed. (Burr Ridge, IL: McGraw-Hill/Irwin, 2009).
2. Mitchell1 CRM, "Customer Retention Marketing," www.m1products.net/bps/crm/index.html.
3. Oracle Web site, "About," www.oracle.com/us/corporate/mission-statement/index.html.

4. Richard Levey "Bridgestone/Firestone Minds the Gap," *Direct*, September 1, 2002, http://directmag.com/mag/marketing_bridgestonefirestone_minds_gap.

5. Jeff Sweat, "Keep 'Em Happy," *InformationWeek*, January 28, 2002, www.informationweek.com/news/6500459.

6. SAP Customer Success Story, "Playstation.com Chooses mySAP CRM," http://h20338.www2.hp.com/enterprise/downloads/playstation.pdf.

7. *Ibid.*

8. Student Advantage Web site, "About Our Company," www.studentadvantage.com/static/about.shtml.

9. Best Buy Web site, "Warranties and Performance Plan Basics," www.bestbuy.com/site/olspage.jsp?type=page&categoryId=cat10008&contentId=1043363604723&id=cat12098.

10. "CRM Moves from Elite to Everyman: Four Elements for Creating a Social CRM Strategy," *ORGANIC*, 2010, www.organic.com/Assets/whitepaper_social_crm_20100312123657.pdf.

11. Amazon.com Help, "Recommendations," www.amazon.com/gp/help/customer/display.html?ref=hp_rel_topic?ie=UTF8&nodeId=13316081.

12. Sony eSupport, "Contact Other Sony Divisions," http://support.sony.com/US/perl/contact-sales.pl?.

13. "Group 1 and iWay Software Parnet to Enhance Enterprise-Wide Data Quality and Customer Data Integration; Combination of Powerful Data Quality and Data Integration Technologies Provides Comprehensive Single Customer View," *PRNewswire*, January 15, 2002, http://tbutton.prnewswire.com/prn/11690X72534600.

14. "Database," *Merriam-Webster*, www.merriam-webster.com/dictionary/database.

15. "Continental Airlines Maximizes Database Availability," *TDWI*, www.tdwi.org/Publications/display.aspx?id=6442&t=y; "Continental Airlines Relies on Consolidation Strategy," www.snwonline.com/case_studies/continental_airlines_08-05-02.asp.

16. "The Key to Effective CRM: Building an Interactive Dialog," presentation in Utrecht, The Netherlands, December 4, 2003.

17. Rick Whiting, "The Data-Warehouse Advantage," *InformationWeek.com*, July 28, 2003, www.informationweek.com/news/12802974; John Courtmanche, "Continental Is Merging Databases, Testing Operational CRM," *1to1 Magazine*, May/June 2001.

18. Unilever Global Company Web site, http://unilever.com.

19. "The Key to Effective CRM: Building an Interactive Dialog."

20. "The Knot Ties in Consumers with Personalization," *Consumer-Centric Benchmarks* for 2001 & Beyond, www.risnews.com.

21. Jack Schofield, "Casino Rewards Total Loyalty," January 15, 2004, www.technology.guardian.co.uk/online/story/0,3605,1122850,00.html; Christina Binkley, "Lucky Numbers: A Casino Chain Finds a Lucrative Niche: The Small Spenders," *Wall Street Journal*, May 4, 2000, A1, A10; Darrell Dunn, "Personal Touch for VIPs: Client-Tracking System Helps Harrah's Tailor Sales Efforts for Frequent Visitors," *InformationWeek*, November 4, 2003, www.informationweek.com/news/16000115.

22. Stephen Baker, "Math Will Rock Your World," *BusinessWeek*, January 23, 2006, 54–62.

23. Jaimie Seaton, "Stave Solves the Relationship Puzzle," *1to1 Magazine*, August 4, 2003, www.1to1media.com/view.aspx?DocID=27434.

24. B. Weitz, S. Castleberry, and J. Tanner, *Selling* (Burr Ridge, IL: McGraw-Hill/Irwin, 2007), 196–197.

25. "The MyPal Rewards Program Scores Big with Fans," *1to1 Magazine*, April 2003.

26. "ExtraCare," CVS Caremark Web site, phx.corporate-ir.net/phoenix.zhtml?c=183405&p=irol-cvsextracare.

27. "The Importance of Customer Loyalty," Santella and Associates, www.santella.com/frequent.htm.

28. Ben Gose, "Give and Take: Direct Giving Websites Rely on Fees to Help Cover Costs," *Chronicle of Philanthropy*, August 7, 2008, http://philanthropy.com/article/GiveTake/61377/; Sue Hoye and Elizabeth Schwinn, "Competition for Donations Is Going Global, Fund Raiser Predicts," *Chronicle of Philanthropy*, August 7, 2008, http://philanthropy.com/article/Competition-for-Donations-Is/61384/; Rachel Emma Silverman "A New Generation Reinvents Philanthropy," *Wall Street Journal*, August 21, 2007, http://online.wsj.com/article/SB118765256378003494-email.html; Kiva Web site, "About Us," http://www.kiva.org/about; Globalgiving Web site, "About globalgiving," www.globalgiving.org/aboutus; DonorsChoose.org, "How It Works," www.donorschoose.org/about;. Modest Needs Web site, "The Modest Needs Mission," http://www.modestneeds.org/explore/mission.

29. "The Importance of Customer Loyalty."

30. www.nike.com/canada/siteInfo/loyalty.html.

31. www.sumerset.com; Christopher Caggiano, "Building Customer Loyalty, the Harley Way," *Inc.*, November 15 2000, www.inc.com/articles/2000/11/21166.html.

32. Kit Davis, "Track Star, RFID Is Racing to Market," *Consumer Goods Magazine*, June 1, 2003, http://consumergoods.edgl.com/magazine/June-2003/Track-Star52676.

33. Janis Mara, "Companies Alter Privacy Policies," *Internetnews.com*, January 2, 2004, www.internetnews.com; "Ponemon Institute, International Association of Privacy Professionals Release Results of Benchmark Privacy Practices Survey," June 4, 2003, www.privacyassociation.org/about_iapp/2003_06_04_ponemon_institute_iapp_release_results.

34. This application exercise is based on the contribution of Kenneth J. Radig (Medaille College) to *Great Ideas in Teaching Marketing*, a teaching supplement that accompanies McDaniel, Lamb, and Hair's *Introduction to Marketing*. Professor Radig's entry titled "Direct Mail Assignment" was a runner-up in the "Best of the Great Ideas in Teaching Marketing" contest held in conjunction with the publication of the eighth edition of *Marketing*.

35. Joan Voight, "Getting a Handle on Customer Reviews," *Adweek*, July 2, 2007, www.adweek.com/news/advertising/getting-handle-customer-reviews-89478; "Online Shoppers Give Thumbs Up to Customer Product Reviews," *Business Wire*, January 9, 2007, www.businesswire.com/news/home/20070109005702/en/Online-Shoppers-Give-Thumbs-Customer-Product-Reviews; Ken Magill, "Petco Tests Product Reviews," *Direct*, March 1, 2006, http://directmag.com/disciplines/email/marketing_petco_tests_product.

marketing&you:
Results.

A low score on this poll suggests that you think it is acceptable to complain, whereas a high score suggests you think it is inappropriate to complain, even when you receive a bad product or service. People who perceive complaining to be most acceptable also tend to be aggressive, and those who regard complaining as inappropriate tend to be unassertive and generally passive.

© iStockphoto.com/Juan Facundo Mora Soria

22 Social Media and Marketing

Learning Outcomes

1 Describe social media, how it is used, and its relation to integrated marketing communications.

2 Explain how to create a social media campaign

3 Evaluate the various methods of measurement for social media

4 Explain consumer behavior on social media

5 Describe the social media tools in a marketer's toolbox and how they are useful

6 Describe the impact of mobile technology on social media

LO1
What Is Social Media?

The most exciting thing to happen to marketing and promotion is the increasing use of online technology to promote brands, particularly using social media. Social media has changed the way that marketers can communicate with their brands—from mass messages to intimate conversations. As marketing moves into social media, marketers must remember that for most people, social media is meant to be a social experience, not a marketing experience. In fact, social media is many things to different people, though most people think of it as digital technology. Brian Solis, of FutureWorks, defines **social media** as "any tool or service that uses the Internet to facilitate conversations. . . ."[1] However, social media can also be defined

> ... for most people, **social** media is meant to be a social experience, not a marketing experience.

marketing&you.

How much are you influenced by other people's opinions?

STRONGLY DISAGREE 1 2 3 4 5 6 7 STRONGLY AGREE

_____ I rarely purchase the latest fashion or technology until I am sure others approve.

_____ It is important that others like the brands I buy.

_____ When buying products, I generally purchase those brands that I think others will approve of.

_____ If other people can see me using a product, I often purchase the brand they expect me to buy.

_____ I like to know what brands and products made good impressions on others.

_____ If I want to be like someone, I often try to buy the same brands they buy.

_____ I often identify with other people by purchasing the same products and brands they purchase.

_____ To make sure I buy the right product or brand, I monitor what others are buying and using online.

_____ If I have little experience with a product, I often ask my friends online about the product.

_____ I often consult other people through review sites to help choose the best alternative available from a product class.

Total your score and find out what it means at the end of the chapter.

Source: Scale #191, *Marketing Scales Handbook*, G. Bruner, K. James, H. Hensel, eds., Vol. III. © by American Marketing Association. Reprinted with permission.

social media
Any tool or service that uses the
Internet to facilitate conversations.

relative to traditional advertising such as television and magazines in that traditional marketing media offers a mass media method of interacting with consumers while social media offers more one-to-one ways to meet consumers.

There are several implications for marketers and they can interact with their customers. First, marketers must realize that they often do not control the content. Consumers are taking their thoughts, wishes, and experiences with brands online and sharing them with the world. Therefore, marketers must realize that it is not enough to have a great ad campaign. Now, more than ever, the product or service must be great. Second, the ability to share experiences amplifies the impact of word of mouth to whole new levels that can eventually affect the bottom line. As such, this has huge ramifications for customer service. For example, United Airlines suffered a loss of consumer confidence and market value when they failed to make good on damage to a musician's guitar. Dave Carroll complained that his guitar was damaged by baggage handlers on a 2008 flight. United refused to compensate him for it; Carroll became so enraged that he wrote a song and made a music video decrying the customer service of United Airlines. It was viewed by more than three million people and elicited 14,000 comments. United's stock price decreased 10 percent.[2] Was this the reason? It's hard to tell, but this example does show the potential power of an unhappy customer. Third, social media allows marketers to listen. Domino's Pizza listened to much of what was being posted about its product (and it was not nice) and then decided to take that information and change the product. Social media, along with traditional marketing research, allowed Domino's to gain the insight needed to completely reinvent the product. They then used the simple act of transparency to launch an award-winning promotional campaign. Fourth, social media also has more sophisticated methods of measuring how marketers meet and interact with consumers than traditional advertising. Currently, social media includes tools and platforms such as social networks, blogs, microblogs, and media sharing sites, which can be accessed through a growing number of devices, such as computers, laptops, smartphones, e-readers, tablets, and netbooks. This technology changes daily, offering consumers new ways to experience social media platforms, which must constantly innovate to keep up with consumer demands. Last, social media allows marketers to have much more direct and meaningful conversations with customers. It is no longer mass media but rather a form of relationship building that will ultimately bring the customer and brand closer.

At the basic level, social media consumers want to exchange information, collaborate with others, and have conversations. Social media has changed how and where conversations take place, making human interaction global through popular technology. Research shows that more than 73 percent of active online users have read a blog and more than half belong to at least one social network. John Haydon, a marketing consultant, said, "The real value of social media is that it exponentially leverages word-of-mouth."[3] Clearly, conversations are happening online; it is up to the marketer to decide if engaging in those conversations will be profitable and to find the most effective method of entering the conversation.

Marketers are so interested in online communications because it is wildly popular; brands, companies, individuals, and celebrities promote their messages online. Today, Lady Gaga reigns as the queen of social media: She holds the record for being the living person with the most Facebook Fans; on Twitter, she directly interacts with her millions of followers; the music video for the song "Bad Romance" holds the title of most viewed video ever on YouTube. Lady Gaga's celebrity is due in large part to being a highly effective brand—her messages resonate with audiences worldwide, and she makes her brand easily accessible through popular social media platforms. Her carefully crafted social media strategy has translated into real money; Lady Gaga recently debuted on the Forbes Celebrity 100 Power List for 2010 at number 4 for earning more than $62 million (including her corporate sponsorships and endorsements) in the 12 months prior to the article.[4] As far as brands go, very few marketers have leveraged social media to drive sales of core products better than Lady Gaga.[5]

HOW CONSUMERS USE SOCIAL MEDIA

Before beginning to understand how to leverage social media for brand building, it is important to understand what consumers are using and how they are using it. Hoping to replicate some of Lady Gaga's social media success, many marketers are looking to get their message on the fastest growing social media platform—Facebook. Facebook originated as a community for college students that opened to the general public as its popularity grew. There are hundreds of millions of users on Facebook. Facebook is so large that if it were a country, it would be the third largest in the world. The largest area of growth in new profiles is the baby boomer segment, who use it as a way to connect with old friends and keep up with family. Other social networks, such as MySpace and Bebo, offer alternative networks to other demographics. MySpace has a large music-oriented following, and many bands and musicians preview albums and music videos on MySpace pages. Videos are one of the most popular tools by which marketers reach consumers and YouTube is by far the largest online video repository—it has more content than any major television network. Due to its connection with Google, YouTube offers a powerful search tool as well.[6] Flickr is a popular photo sharing site, where millions of people upload new photos daily. Twitter boasts hundreds of millions of registered users who average billions of tweets daily. Technorati tracks hundreds of millions of blogs and indexes an estimated two million new blog posts per day.[7] More than half of Technorati's active users have uploaded photos, and almost a quarter have uploaded videos. The bottom line, according to Universal McCann's Comparative Study on Social Media Trends, is that "if you are online, you are using social media."[8]

Increased usage of alternative platforms such as smartphones and tablet computers has further contributed to the proliferation of social media usage. In the United States, 90 percent of 18- to 29-year-olds own a mobile phone. Among this group, 95 percent have sent a text message, 65 percent have accessed the Internet, and at least 23 percent have accessed a social networking site using their phones.[9] In April 2010, Apple released the much-anticipated iPad tablet computer. More than 8,500 native iPad apps (many of which connect to social networks) are available for download, and within the first two months of the tablet's release, 35 million downloads had already been recorded.[10] The overall impact of tablet computing on social media (and thus the discipline of marketing) is yet to be seen, but given the incredible impact that the smartphone has had in its short lifespan, tablets could prove to be game changing.

Social Commerce A new area of growth in social media is social commerce, which combines social media with the basics of e-commerce. **Social commerce** is a subset of e-commerce that involves the interaction and user contribution aspects of social online media to assist online buying and selling of products and services.[11] Basically, social commerce relies on user-generated content on Web sites to assist consumers with purchases. On the Web site **www.polyvore.com,** members create collages of photographs of clothing items that create a fashionable look.

social commerce
A subset of e-commerce that involves the interaction and user contribution aspects of social online media to assist online buying and selling of products and services.

Photographs come from various retailers and include accessories, clothes, shoes, and makeup. Once the look is complete, other members view the looks and can click on the individual items to see price and retailers. Social commerce sites often include ratings and recommendations (like Amazon) and social shopping tools (like Groupon). In fact, Groupon is one of the fastest growing social media tools out there and continues to revolutionize the way that consumers access deals. In general, social commerce sites are designed to help consumers make more informed decisions on purchases or services.

SOCIAL MEDIA AND INTEGRATED MARKETING COMMUNICATIONS

While marketers typically employ a social media strategy alongside traditional channels like print and broadcast, many budget pendulums are swinging toward social media. In the U.S. Interactive Marketing Forecast, 2009 to 2014, Forrester predicts that mobile marketing, social media, e-mail marketing, display advertising, and search marketing will grow from 13 percent of advertising spending in 2010 to more than 21 percent of spending by 2014. The bulk of this budget will still go to search marketing (almost doubling in 2014), but substantial investments will also be made in mobile marketing and social media.[12] Spending in digital and online media is expected to surpass the amount of spending on traditional print advertising.

A unique consequence of social media is the widespread shift from one-to-many communication to many-to-many communication. Instead of simply putting a brand advertisement on television with no means for feedback, social media allows marketers to have conversations with consumers, forge deeper relationships, and build brand loyalty. Social media also allows consumers to connect with each other, share opinions, and collaborate on new ideas according to their interests. In 2009, Grey Goose Vodka created an online community exclusively for bartenders. This community enabled mixologists to chat with each other and share ideas and anecdotes about their common trade. The Grey Goose online community was intended not so much to advertise the brand but to create a shared space and provide genuine value to bartenders. The brand advocacy then came naturally.[13] With social media, the audience is often in control of the message, the medium, the response, or all three. This distribution of control is often difficult for companies to adjust to, but the focus of social marketing is unavoidably on the audience, and the brand must adapt to succeed. The interaction between producer and consumer becomes less about entertaining (although some do), and more about listening, influencing, and engaging. One great example is Dorito's "Crash the Superbowl" campaign where the company allows consumers to make the television ads, post them, and then vote for their favorite ads. The winning ads run during the Superbowl broadcast (www.crashthesuperbowl.com).

In 2009, Hewlett-Packard used social media to avert a PR crisis after a video claiming that HP was racist garnered two million views on YouTube. Because it was aware of its customers' social dialogs, HP learned about the groundswell early on and was able to quell the story before

GREY GOOSE
World's Best Tasting Vodka

Image courtesy of The Advertising Archives

it gained too much momentum.[14] Mountain Dew's marketing team tested the limits of consumer control and the power of social media by moving the brand's advertising almost entirely online. The team tapped into the brand's core consumer demographic—18- to 39-year-old males with strong Facebook, MySpace, and YouTube presences—to build line extensions and help choose a marketing partner.

Using consumers to develop and market product is called **crowdsourcing**. Crowdsourcing describes how the input of many people can be leveraged to make decisions that used to be based on the input of only a few people.[15] Companies get feedback on marketing campaigns, new product ideas, and other marketing decisions by asking its customers to weigh in. After major retailer Gap launched a redesigned logo that received negative response, it opted to crowdsource a consumer-approved logo. Gap asked its customers to design an updated logo to replace the new, unpopular logo. After more than 1,000 people posted negative comments about the effort on its Facebook page, the Gap elected to revert back to the old logo.[16] Crowdsourcing offers a way for companies to engage heavy users of a brand and receive input, which in turn increases those users' brand advocacy and lessens the likelihood that a change will be disliked enough to drive away loyal customers. Marketers are even using crowdsourcing to find their new creative ideas and agencies are there to facilitate the process.

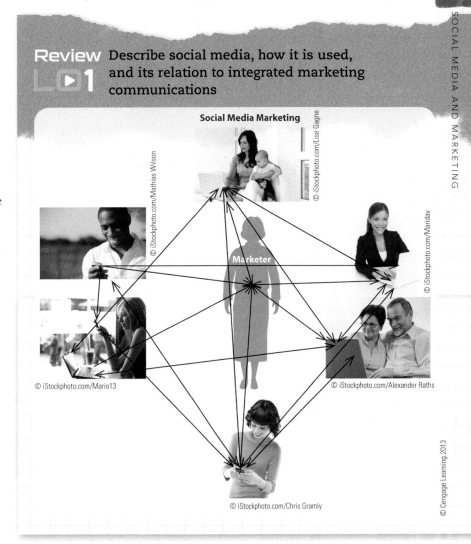

Review LO1 Describe social media, how it is used, and its relation to integrated marketing communications

Social Media Marketing

© iStockphoto.com/Mathias Wilson
© iStockphoto.com/Lise Gagne
© iStockphoto.com/Maridav
Marketer
© iStockphoto.com/Mario13
© iStockphoto.com/Alexander Raths
© iStockphoto.com/Chris Gramly
© Cengage Learning 2013

#

Creating and Leveraging a Social Media Campaign

Social media is an exciting new field, and its potential for expanding a brand's impact is enormous. Because its costs are often minimal and its learning curve is relatively low, some organizations are tempted to dive headfirst into social media. However, as with any marketing campaign, it is always important to start with a strategy. For most organizations, this means starting with a marketing or communications plan, as covered in Chapter 2. The basic areas of a situation analysis, objectives and evaluation, are still key. It is important to link communication objectives (for example, improving customer service) to the most effective social media tools

crowdsourcing
Using consumers to develop and market product.

A young woman tastes a glass of red wine during an online wine tasting. People from all parts of Germany regularly meet online to taste wine and exchange opinions via Twitter, generating earned media buzz for the winery whose wine they are drinking.

(for example, Twitter) and be able to measure it. It is also important to understand the various types of media involved.

The new communication paradigm created by a shift to social media marketing raises questions about categorization. In light of the convergence of traditional and digital media, researchers have explored different ways that interactive marketers can categorize media types. One such researcher, Sean Corcoran of Forrester Research, devised a distinction between owned, earned, and paid media. **Owned media** is online content that an organization creates and controls. Owned media include blogs, Web sites, Facebook pages, and other social media presences. The purpose of owned media is to develop deeper relationships with customers. **Earned media** is a public-relations term connoting free media such as mainstream media coverage. In an interactive space, media is earned through word of mouth or online buzz about something the brand is doing. Earned media include viral videos, retweets, comments on blogs, and other forms of customer feedback resulting from a social media presence. **Paid media** is content paid for by the company to be placed online. Paid media is similar to marketing efforts that utilize traditional media such as newspaper, magazine, and television advertisements. In an interactive space, paid media include display advertising, paid search words, and other types of direct online advertising.[17]

To leverage all three types of media, marketers must follow a few key guidelines. First, they must maximize owned media by reaching out beyond their existing Web sites to create portfolios of digital touch points. This is especially true for brands with tight budgets, as the organization might not be able to afford much paid media. Second, marketers must recognize that aptitude at public and media relations no longer translates into earned media. Instead, markets must learn how to listen and respond to stakeholders. This will stimulate word of mouth. Finally, marketers must understand that paid media is not dead, but should serve as a catalyst to drive customer engagement.[18] If balanced correctly, all three typed of media can be powerful tools for interactive marketers.

THE LISTENING SYSTEM

The first action a marketing team should take when initiating a social media campaign is simple—it should just listen. Customers are on social media and assume that the brand is there as well. They expect a new level of engagement with brands. Developing an effective listening system is necessary to both understanding and engaging an online audience. Marketers must not only hear what is being said about the brand, the industry, the competition, and the customer—they must also pay attention to who is saying what and ultimately act upon the information. The specific ways that customers and noncustomers rate, rank, critique, praise, deride, recommend, snub, and generally discuss brands are all

owned media
Online content that an organization creates and controls.

earned media
A public relations term connoting free media such as mainstream media coverage.

paid media
Content paid for by a company to be placed online.

important. Think of it as market research—these are customers telling marketers what they want and need (and don't want and need). Negative comments and complaints are of particular import, both because they can illuminate unknown brand flaws and because they are the comments that tend to go viral. Listening is important because consumers believe that if they are saying negative things about a brand and nothing changes, that the brand is insincere. Consumers will take their business elsewhere. Online tools such as Google Alerts, Google Blog Search, Twitter Search, SiteVolume, Social Mention, and Socialcast are extremely helpful in the development of efficient, effective listening. In Exhibit 22.1, social media strategist Jeremiah Owyang outlines eight stages of effective listening. Listening to customers communicate about one's own brand can be very revealing, but social media is also a great way to monitor competitors' online presences, fans, and followers. Paying attention to the ways that competing brands attract and engage with their customers can be particularly enlightening for both small businesses and global brands.

SOCIAL MEDIA OBJECTIVES

After establishing a listening platform, the organization should develop a list of objectives for its social media team to accomplish. These objectives must be developed with a clear understanding of how social media changes the communication dynamic with and for customers. Remember—attempting to reach a mass audience

Exhibit 22.1 Eight Stages of Effective Listening

Stage	Description	Resources Required	Purpose
Stage 1: Without objective	The organization has established a listening system but has no goals.	Social media notification tools (Google Alerts)	Keep up with brand and competitor information.
Stage 2: Tracking brand mentions	The organization tracks mentions in social space but has no guidance on next steps.	A listening platform with key word report capabilities (Radian6)	Track discussions, understand sentiment, and identify influencers to improve overall marketing strategy.
Stage 3: Identifying market risks and opportunities	The organization seeks discussions online that may result in identification of problems and opportunities.	A listening platform with a large staff dedicated to the client (Converseon)	Staff seeks out discussions and reports to other teams, such as product development and sales. These teams then engage the customers directly or conduct further research.
Stage 4: Improving campaign efficiency	The organization uses tools to get real time data on marketing efficiency.	Web analytics software (Google Analytics)	See a wealth of information about consumers' behavior on their Web site (and social media).
Stage 5: Measuring customer satisfaction	The organization collects information about satisfaction, including measures of sentiment.	Insight platforms that offer online focus group solutions	Measure impact of satisfaction or frustration during interaction.
Stage 6: Responding to customer inquiry	The organization identifies customers where they are (e.g. Twitter).	A customer service team is allowed to make real time responses.	Generate high sense of satisfaction for customer, but generates public complaints.
Stage 7: Better understanding customers	The organization adds social information to demographics and psychographics to gain a better profile.	Social CRM systems to sync data	Social CRM marries database and social media to create a powerful analytical tool. (See Chapter 21 for more on CRM.)
Stage 8: Being proactive and anticipating customer demands	The organization examines previous patterns of data and social behavior to anticipate needs.	Advanced customer database with predictive application (yet to be created)	Modify social media strategy to pre-empt consumer behavior modifications based on trends.

Source: Eight Stages of Effective Listening from Jeremiah Owyang, "Web Strategy Matrix: The Eight Stages of Listening," Web Strategy, November 10, 2009www.web-strategist.com/blog/2009/11/10/evolution-the-eight-stages-of-listening. Reprinted with permission.

with a static message will never be as successful as influencing people through conversation. Marketing managers must set objectives that reflect this reality. Here are some practical ideas that marketing managers should consider when setting social media objectives:

→ **Listen and learn.** Monitor what is being said about the brand and competitors, and glean insights about audiences. Use online tools and do research to implement the best social media practices. If you have established a listening strategy, this objective should already be accomplished.

→ **Build relationships and awareness.** Open dialogs with stakeholders by giving them compelling content across a variety of media. Engage in conversations and answer customers' questions candidly. This will both increase Web traffic and boost your search engine ranking. This is where crowdsourcing can be useful for product development and communication campaign feedback.

→ **Promote products and services.** The clearest path to increasing the bottom line using social media is to get customers talking about products and services, which ultimately translates into sales.

→ **Manage your reputation.** Develop and improve the brand's reputation by responding to comments and criticism that appear on blogs and forums. Additionally, organizations can position themselves as helpful and benevolent by participating in other forums and discussions. Social media makes it much easier to establish and communicate expertise.

→ **Improve customer service.** Customer comments about products and services will not always be positive. Use social media to find displeased customers and engage them directly to solve their service issues.

Review
LO2 Explain how to create a social media campaign

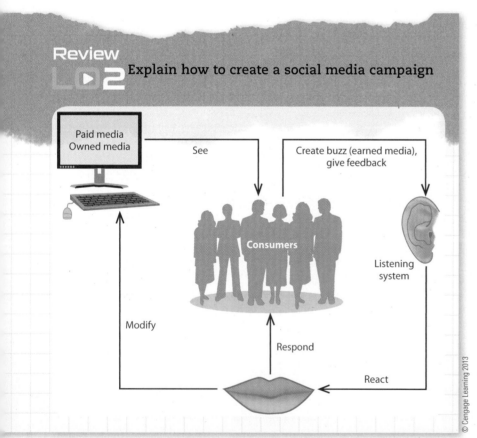

© Cengage Learning 2013

BUILDING TRUST ONLINE

Many people find it difficult to trust Wall Street, government, big business, and other institutions. As marketers, we know that trust is at the center of customer relationships. People are willing to pass judgment with or without good information.[19] In order to succeed with any marketing campaign, customers' trust must be earned. This is especially true for social media. If customers trust you, they'll happily engage with you, provide feedback, and promote your products. If they don't, they'll let their friends know why. What should a brand do to gain customer trust?

→ The most important thing is responsiveness. Because there are no other cues, people will judge trust according to how fast and how effective the response is from a post. Wait too long and your efforts become "unhelpful."

→ Online content must be up to date, easy to understand, and valuable. Be the translator for your customers as they wade through message after message.

→ Make sure that your Web site is easy to navigate and gives customers quick access to the information and media that they came for. Consider using various types of media such as video and audio that tend to increase the trust levels. For example, Domino's president Patrick Doyle used video to apologize for an employee prank as well as to pledge to make tastier pizza.[20]

→ Make your social space fun and interactive. Interactivity is all about forging relationships—giving something and receiving something of value. Treat customers like people, not data, and they will treat you as a credible resource, not junk mail.

→ Follow contemporary design trends. Your audience will inevitably judge your book by its cover.[21]

LO3
Evaluation and Measurement of Social Media

Social media has the potential to revolutionize the way organizations communicate with stakeholders. Given the relative ease and efficiency with which organizations can use social media, a positive return on investment is likely for many—if not most—organizations. A Forrester Research report found that 95 percent of marketers planned to increase or maintain their investments in social media. However, though they understand that it is a worthwhile investment, most marketers have not been able to figure out how to measure the benefits of social media. As social media evolves, so do the measurements and metrics that track it.[22] However, as with traditional advertising, marketers lack hard evidence as to the relative effectiveness of these tools. Some marketers accept this unknown variable and focus on the fact that social media is less about return on investment (ROI) than about deepening relationships with customers. However, others work tirelessly to better understand the measurement of social media's effectiveness. While literally hundreds of metrics have been developed to measure social media's value, these metrics are meaningless unless they are tied to key performance indicators.[23] For example, a local coffee shop manager might measure the success of her social media presence by the raw number of friends on Facebook and followers on Twitter

Facebook CEO Mark Zuckerberg introduces new features for Facebook during the keynote address at a one-day developer conference sponsored by Facebook. Behind him, you can see the myriad ways social networking sites could interact.

© iStockphoto.com/Juan Facundo Mora Soria

© Mike Kepka/San Francisco Chronicle/Corbis

she has accumulated. But these numbers depend entirely on context. The rate of accumulation, investment per fan and follower, and comparison to similarly sized coffee shops are all important variables to consider. Without context, measurements are meaningless.

There are three key areas of measurement:

→ **Social media measurement:** Ever-changing metrics that are used to determine the ROI of each tool. Social media measurement determines, for example, the conversion rate of a Facebook friend. Tools include Google Analytics, SocialMention, Twinfluence, Twitalyzer, and Klout, among others.[24]

→ **Public relations measurement:** Because many modern PR campaigns entail social media, public relations measurement exists to calculate the impact of social media on press coverage and other elements of PR. Tools include DIY Dashboard, Tealium, and Vocus, which quantizes information such as share of voice relative to competitors, stories by location, and a sentiment analysis for each press hit.

→ **Social media monitoring::** Used less for campaign metrics and more for customer service improvement, brand management, and prospecting. Tools include BlogPulse, Technorati, Trendrr, Google Trends, Tweetdeck, Visible Technologies, and Trackur. Google News Alerts, a free online tool, leverages Google's search technology to report relevant news stories and blog posts about any topic or organization.

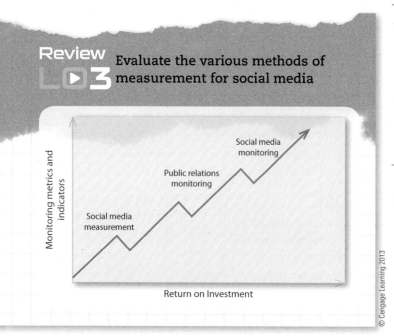

Review
LO 3 Evaluate the various methods of measurement for social media

LO 4
Social Behavior of Consumers

Social media has changed the way that people interact in everyday lives. Some say it has made people smarter by enabling people (especially children) access to so much information and interactivity. It allows people to stay in touch in ways never before experienced. Social media has reinvented politics and civic engagement (just see the 2008 presidential election and the 2010 Tea Party movement to see how it changed elections). Social media has drastically changed the advertising business from an industry based on mass media models (e.g., TV) to an industry based on relationships and conversations. This all has implications for how consumers use social media and the purposes for which they use it.[25]

So once objectives have been determined and measurement tools have been implemented, it is important to identify the consumer who the marketer is trying to reach. Who is using social media? What types of social media do they use? How do they use it? Are they just reading it or do they actually create it? Does Facebook attract younger users? Do Twitter users retweet viral videos? These types of questions must be considered because they determine not only which tools will be most effective, but also, more importantly, whether launching a social media campaign even makes sense for a particular organization.

Understanding an audience necessitates understanding how that audience uses social media. In *Groundswell*, Charlene Li and Josh Bernoff of Forrester Research identify six categories of social media users:

1. **Creators:** Those who produce and share online content such as blogs, Web sites, articles, and videos

2. **Critics:** Those who post comments, ratings, and reviews of products and services on blogs and forums

3. **Collectors:** Those who use RSS feeds to collect information and vote for Web sites online

4. **Joiners:** Those who maintain a social networking profile and visit other sites

5. **Spectators:** Those who read blogs, listen to podcasts, watch videos, and generally consume media

6. **Inactives:** Those who do none of these things[26]

A recent study determined that 24 percent of social media users functioned as creators, 37 percent functioned as critics, 21 percent functioned as collectors, 51 percent functioned as joiners, and 73 percent functioned as spectators. While participation in each of these categories trended upwards, inactives decreased from 44 percent in 2007 to only 18 percent in 2009.[27] However, recent Forrester research shows that the number of people who contribute content is slowing down. Participation in most categories fell slightly, prompting analysts to recommend that marketers re-examine how they are engaging with their customers online. Despite the apparent slow down, research also shows that more social networking "rookies" are classified as joiners. Another bright spot is a new category, "conversationalists," or people who post status updates on social-networking sites and microblogging services such as Twitter. Conversationalists represent 31 percent of users.[28] This gives marketers a general idea of who is using social media and how to engage them. It is similar to any type of market segmentation—especially the 80/20 rule. Consider that those who are creating content and active on social media could be those consumers most likely to actively engage with a brand as well as actively post negative comments on social media. The critics and collectors make up most of this group. However, it is important not to miss the joiners and spectators as they can be easily swayed by the comments of their fellow customers.

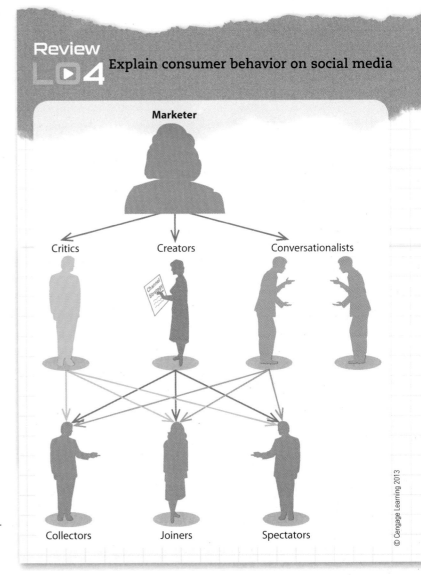

Review
LO4 Explain consumer behavior on social media

L◉5
Social Media Tools: Consumer and Corporate Generated Content

Given that it is important for marketers to engage with customers on social media for the reasons mentioned earlier, there are several tools and platforms that can be employed as part of an organization's social media strategy. Blogs, microblogs, social networks, media creation and sharing sites, social news sites, review sites, and virtual worlds all have their place in a company's social marketing plan. These are all tools in a marketing manager's toolbox, available when applicable to the marketing plan, but not necessarily to be used all at once. Because of the breakneck pace at which technology changes, this list of resources will surely look markedly different five years from now. More tools emerge every day, and branding strategies must keep up with the ever-changing world of technology. For now, the resources highlighted in this section remain a marketer's strongest set of platforms for conversing and strengthening relationships with customers.

Sean Combs, AKA P. Diddy, shows off his Twitter page. Combs uses Twitter as a blog to keep fans updated on his activities.

© Jared Milgrim/Corbis

BLOGS

Blogs have become staples in many social media strategies and are often a brand's social media centerpiece. A **blog** is a publicly accessible Web page that functions as an interactive journal, whereby readers can post comments on the author's entries. Some experts believe that every company should have a blog that speaks to current and potential customers not as consumers, but as people.[29] Blogs allows marketers to create content in the form of posts, which ideally build trust and a sense of authenticity in customers. Once posts are made, audience members can provide feedback through comments. Because it opens a dialog and gives customers a voice, the comments section of a blog post is one of the most important avenues of conversation between brands and consumers.

Blogs can be divided into two broad categories: corporate and professional blogs, and noncorporate blogs such as personal blogs. **Corporate blogs** are sponsored by a company or one of its brands and maintained by one or more of the company's employees. They disseminate marketing controlled information, and are effective platforms for developing thought leadership, fostering better relationships with stakeholders, maximizing search engine optimization, attracting new customers, endearing the organization with anecdotes and stories about brands, and providing an active forum for testing new ideas. Because blogs are designed to be updated daily, corporate blogs are dynamic and highly flexible, giving marketers the opportunity to adapt their messages more frequently than any other communication channel.

Several brands use blogs effectively. GM's Fastlane Blog is considered a corporate best. It is packed with audio, video, and photos, and is organized into categories that offer something for everyone. One of Fastlane Blog's biggest draws is its high-quality writing. Each reader comment is answered in a fun and pithy tone, encouraging participation and continued readership (http://fastlane.gmblogs.com). Southwest Airlines' "Nuts about Southwest" (www.blogsouthwest.com) and Dell (which has created a hub for several blogs) also produce successful corporate blogs.

In contrast, **noncorporate blogs** are independent and not associated with the marketing efforts of any particular company or brand. Because these blogs contain information not controlled by marketers, they are perceived to be more authentic than corporate blogs. Mommy bloggers, women who review children's products and discuss family-related topics on their personal blogs, use noncorporate blogs. The goal of mommy blogs is to share parenting tips, relate experiences, and become part of a community. Because of the popularity of these and other types of blog, many bloggers receive products and/or money from companies in exchange for a review. Many bloggers disclose where they received the product or if they were paid but an affiliation is not always clear. Because of this, bloggers must disclose any financial relationship with a company per FTC rules. It is important for marketing managers to understand the rules behind complimentary products to bloggers as well as the high potential for social buzz; four out of five noncorporate bloggers post brand or product reviews. Even if a company does not have a formal social media strategy, chances are that the brand is still out in the blogosphere, whether or not a marketing manager approached a blogger.

Microblogs **Microblogs** are blogs with strict post length limits. Twitter, the most popular microblogging platform, requires that posts are no more than 140 characters in length. However, there are several others including Jaiku, Tumblr, Plurk, Spoink, and of course Facebook's status updates. Originally designed as a short messaging system used for internal communication, Twitter has gained global popularity and is now used as a communication and research tool by individuals and brands around the world. A large part of Twitter's success stems from the fact that the platform is extremely versatile: posts and private messages can be sent and received via text messages, smartphone apps, desktop clients, external Web sites, tablet computers, and e-mail, among others. Twitter posts, commonly called tweets, can be amended with photos, videos, and external links. Recently Twitter has changed its interface to include visuals such as video and photos and has added new products to try to monetize the site. It has also developed promoted tweets, which are ads that appear in search results and user feeds both on Twitter.com and third-party clients that access the service, such as TweetDeck, twhirl, TwitterBerry, and Tweetie.

Despite its strict character limit, Twitter has proven effective for disseminating breaking news, promoting longer blog posts and campaigns, sharing links, announcing events, and promoting sales. By following, retweeting, responding to potential customers' tweets, and tweeting content that inspires customers to engage the brand, corporate Twitter users can lay a foundation for meaningful two-way conversation quickly and effectively. Research has found that when operated correctly, corporate Twitter accounts are well respected and well received. Twitter can be used to build communities, aid in customer service, gain prospects, increase awareness, and in the case of nonprofits, fundraise.

The ways that a business can use Twitter to successfully engage with customers are almost limitless. The Kogi Korean BBQ truck provides gourmet tacos to Los

noncorporate blogs
Independent blogs that are not associated with the marketing efforts of any particular company or brand.

microblogs
Blogs with strict post length limits.

Angeles residents throughout the night. Because traffic, construction, and other issues prevent the truck from parking at the same location every night, owner Mark Manguera uses Twitter to inform his late night customers of where the truck will be located each evening. Because its tweets are informative, useful, and relevant to the business, Kogi Korean BBQ has built a Twitter following of tens of thousands.[30]

Using Twitter for Business Although it might be tempting to be on Twitter, it might not be for every company. There are few things to consider before developing your Twitter presence:

1. Make sure that Twitter fits your social media strategy. If it does, make sure to cross promote with other platforms such as Facebook.

2. Make sure that your tweets are authentic and not blatant brand promotion. If they are not useful, they are ignored.

3. Engage in two-way conversation by following those who follow you, replying to tweets, and retweeting compelling messages. Retweeting builds goodwill and strengthens relationships. Research shows that Twitter users often are more likely to share opinions about companies and products at least once per week.[31]

4. Because following everyone can be overwhelming, use some of the thousands of tools built to help manage tweets (such as Tweetdeck).

5. Provide value in your tweets. Less is often more on Twitter.

6. Be outgoing, energetic, and informative. Retain a unique voice and post with personality.

SOCIAL NETWORKS

Social networking sites allow individuals to connect—or network—with friends, peers, and business associates. Connections are made around shared interests, shared environments, or personal relationships. Depending on the site, connected individuals might be able to send each other messages, track each other's activity, see each other's personal information, share multimedia, or comment on each other's blog and microblog posts. Depending on its goals, there are several social networks that a marketing team might engage as part of its social media strategy: Facebook is the largest and fastest growing network, Google+ is Google's newest entry into social media, LinkedIn is geared toward professionals and businesses who use it to recruit professionals, and niche networks such as Bebo, Last.fm, WeAreTeachers, BlackPlanet, and Match.com cater to specialized markets. There is a niche social network for just about every demographic and interest. Beyond those already established, an organization might decide to develop a brand-specific social network or community. Although all social networking sites are different, some marketing goals can be accomplished on any such site. Given the right strategy, increasing awareness, targeting audiences, promoting products, forging relationships, highlighting expertise and leadership, attracting event participants, performing research, and generating new business are attainable marketing goals on any social network.

Facebook is by far the largest social networking site, and it is popular with both individuals and groups. How an individual uses Facebook is a bit different from the way a group or company uses Facebook, as summed up in Exhibit 22.2. While individual Facebook users create profiles, brands, organizations, and nonprofit causes operate as pages. As opposed to individual profiles,

social networking sites
Web sites that allow individuals to connect—or network—with friends, peers, and business associates.

all pages are public, and are thus subject to search engine indexing. By maintaining a popular Facebook page, a brand not only increases its social media presence, it also helps to optimize search engine results. Pages often include photo and video albums, brand information, and links to external sites. The most useful page feature,

Exhibit 22.2 Facebook Lingo

Non-individual (usually corporate)	Individual
Page	Profile
Fan of a page, tells fan's friends that the user is a fan, creates mini-viral campaign	Friend a person, send private messages, write on their wall, see friend-only content
Public, searchable	Privacy options, not searchable unless user enabled

© Cengage Learning 2013

however, is the Wall. The Wall allows a brand to communicate directly with fans via status updates, which enables marketers to build databases of interested stakeholders. When an individual becomes a fan of your organization or posts on your Wall, that information is shared with the individual's friends, creating a mini viral marketing campaign. Other Facebook marketing tools include groups, applications, and ads. Facebook is an extremely important platform for social markers.

Facebook has proved to be fertile ground for new marketing ideas and campaigns. By creating a Facebook application called Real or Fake, Adobe used the social network's built in software platform to advertise student editions of the Photoshop photo editing software to college students. When users installed the Real or Fake application, they gained access to weekly images, which they were challenged to distinguish as authentic or digitally manipulated. After they took the challenge, users were directed to tutorials that demonstrated how the altered photos were manipulated using Photoshop. By the end of the campaign, Adobe had earned additional Facebook fans and had witnessed an increase in page views from 5,057 to 53,000 per week. More than 6 percent of Real or Fake users actually purchased the Photoshop software. Through this campaign, Adobe did not just establish a social media presence, but also created a novel way to engage its fans.[32] Coca-Cola's Facebook page, boasting five million fans, was developed by two individuals in California. Rather than assuming its management, Coke decided to work with fans to maintain the page. Again, to succeed in social media, organizations must learn to share control with the customer.

Understanding Facebook

Many businesses are finding that Facebook might be more useful than their original Web sites. But it is important to consider a few key issues before developing a Facebook strategy.

1. Before settling on Facebook, investigate other major social networks. A niche network might be a better fit for your brand.

These images were used as part of Adobe's Real or Fake game on Facebook. Can you tell which is real and which is fake? The chameleon is fake (those are goat's horns imposed on its head) and the road is real (it's in Morocco).

2. Marketers sometimes rush their brands onto Facebook without first developing a social media strategy. Instead of jumping in haphazardly, do the research, develop objectives, and plan your Facebook presence carefully.

3. Assess your brand's activity on blogs, microblogs, and other social networks. Integrate your online presences into a cohesive brand image. Typically, Facebook can be the hub for the brand's social media presence.

4. Provide valuable and interesting media and information and incentivize Facebook fans with exclusive content.

5. Follow your strategy and work toward your objectives. Learn from your mistakes.

LinkedIn features many of the same services as Facebook (profiles, status updates, private messages, company pages, and groups), but is oriented around business and professional connections. Unlike Facebook, LinkedIn features a question-and-answer forum whereby users can ask for advice and share expertise in specific fields, and a file hosting service, whereby users can upload intellectual property such as slides, presentations, and other shared documents.[33] LinkedIn is used primarily by professionals who wish to build their personal brands online and businesses who are recruiting employees and freelancers.

MEDIA SHARING SITES

Media sharing sites allow users to upload and distribute multimedia content such as videos and photos. Sites such as YouTube and Flickr are particularly useful to brands' social marketing strategies because they add a vibrant interactive channel on which to disseminate content. The distribution of user-generated content has changed markedly over the past few years. Today, organizations can tell compelling brand stories through videos, photos, and audio.

Photo sharing sites allow users to archive and share photos. Flickr, Picasa, TwitPic, Photobucket, Facebook, and Imgur all offer free photo hosting services that can be utilized by individuals and businesses alike. For example, to strengthen its image of transparency and its relationship with potential donors, the American Red Cross maintained hundreds of Hurricane Katrina disaster photos and tracked sentiments about the Red Cross' services on Flickr throughout the crisis.[34]

Video creation and distribution have also gained popularity among marketers because of video's rich ability to tell stories. YouTube, the highest-trafficked video-based Web site and the sixth highest-trafficked site overall, allows users to upload and stream their videos to an enthusiastic and active community.[35] YouTube is not only large (in terms of visitors), but it also attracts a diverse base of users: age and gender demographics are remarkably balanced.

Many entertainment companies and movie marketers have used YouTube as a showcase for new products, specials, and movie trailers. For example, Lions Gate Entertainment purchased ad space on the YouTube home page in 15 countries to promote the Avatar movie trailer. Some teen clothing brands such as Forever 21 and JCPenney build followings on YouTube by posting hauls—videos made by teens that focus on fashion. Clearly, user-generated content can be a powerful tool for brands that can use it effectively.

A podcast, another type of user-generated media, a digital audio or video file that is distributed serially for other people to listen to or watch. Podcasts can be streamed online, played on a computer, uploaded to a portable media player (such as an iPod), or downloaded onto a smartphone. Podcasts are like radio shows that

media sharing sites
Web sites that allow users to upload and distribute multimedia content such as videos and photos.

are distributed through various means and not linked to a scheduled time slot. Although they have not experienced the exponential growth rates of other digital platforms, podcasts have amassed a steadily growing number of loyal devotees. A good example of effective use of the medium is Fidelity Investments' Podcast Series, which offers clients and non-clients alike free information about stock market investment.[36]

SOCIAL NEWS SITES

Social news sites allow users to decide which content is promoted on a given Web site by voting that content up or down. Users post news stories and multimedia for the community to vote on crowdsourced communities such as Reddit, Digg, and Yahoo! Buzz. The more interest from readers, the higher the story or video is ranked. Marketers have found that these sites are useful for promoting campaigns, creating conversations around related issues, and building Web site traffic.[37] If it is voted up, discussed, and shared enough to be listed among the most popular topics of the day, content posted to a crowdsourced site can go viral across other sites, and eventually, the entire Web. Social bookmarking sites such as Del.ici.ous and StumbleUpon are similar to social news sites, but the objective of their users is to collect, save, and share interesting and valuable links. On these sites, users categorize links with short, descriptive tags. Users can search the site's database of links by specific tags, or add their own tags to others' links. In this way, tags serve as the foundation for information gathering and sharing on social bookmarking sites.[38]

LOCATION-BASED SOCIAL NETWORKING SITES

Considered by many to be the next big thing in social marketing, location sites like Gowalla and Loopt should be on every marketer's radar. Essentially, **location-based social networking sites** combine the fun of social networking with the utility of location-based GPS technology. Foursquare, one of the most popular location sites, treats location-based micronetworking as a game: Users earn badges and special statuses based on their number of visits to particular locations. Users can write and read short reviews and tips about businesses, organize meet ups, and see which Foursquare-using friends are nearby. Foursquare updates can also be posted to linked Twitter and Facebook accounts for followers and friends to see. Location sites such as Foursquare are particularly useful social marketing tools for local businesses, especially when combined with sales promotions such as coupons, special offers, contests, and events. Location sites can be harnessed to forge lasting relationships with and deeply engrained loyalty in customers.[39] For example, a local restaurant can allow consumers to check in on Foursquare using their smartphone and receive a coupon for that day's purchases. Because the location site technology is relatively new, many brands are still figuring out how best to utilize it. Facebook added the Places feature to capitalize on this location-based technology, which allows people to "check in" and share their location with their online friends. It will be interesting to see how use of this technology grows over time.

REVIEW SITES

Individuals tend to trust other people's opinions when it comes to purchasing. According to The Neilsen Company,

social news sites
Web sites that allow users to decide which content is promoted on a given Web site by voting that content up or down.

location-based social networking sites
Web sites that combine the fun of social networking with the utility of location-based GPS technology.

Just Checking In: Location-Based Social Networks[40]

The newest addition to the social media arsenal is location-based social networks such as Foursquare, Gowalla, and Facebook's Places (as well as many others). Essentially these tools encourage users to "check in" to their physical location. For example, a user can check in at the local pub for happy hour and this information is broadcast to his or her friends via social networks. Additionally, Foursquare uses check-ins to award consumers with badges and titles (such as Mayor) and Gowalla allows users to leave their tips and photos. The service is still the playground of early adopters with just 4 percent of U.S. Internet users using location-based services. However, eMarketer projects that checking in is moving into the mainstream. And having Facebook Places will increase the rate toward mass adoption.

This is interesting, but not that valuable to marketers in and of itself. The real value of these tools is to find out why users create and share information . . . in other words, what motivates people to share this information? This insight should then be the foundation for an effective location-based social network promotion.

The real key is to deliver a compelling offer to consumers when they are close to making the purchase decision. As such, companies are tying location-based social networks into other promotions or activities. For example you can walk into that same pub and check in and get a happy hour special specifically for users of that platform. The pub can simply scan your phone to track it and then tie it to other offers using other social networks like Facebook. This then provides value to the customer by linking it to a promotion. Proximity data will help guide marketing messaging at various stages of the purchase funnel.

Because location-based social networks are in their infancy, they continue to innovate to find their social media niche. Foursquare is planning to augment its service with a smarter algorithm that will be able to tailor recommendations to check-ins. "Every check-in should mean something," said CEO and co-founder Dennis Crowley at ad:tech. "Foursquare should get smarter every time that you continue to check in. We should be able to offer special deals that you may be interested in and we should be able to offer recommendations for the type of things you should do next." Based on the bars you have checked in to, Foursquare will be able to make recommendations of other bars you might like. The same goes for shoe stores, restaurants, or spas— really any place that sells a product or service. This will be increasingly valuable as consumers travel to other cities or states where they might not have a great deal of experience.

Even consuming media like television shows can be subject to the check-in. A variety of new services have created entertainment check-ins—the act of checking into the television show or movie you are watching right now. Even CBS has developed a service—called Tv.com Relay—that is a browser based mobile app for smartphones that allows users to check-in to television shows. It already has more than 100,000 users. Tunerfish is backed by Comcast and network partners like HBO which offers behavioral incentives like rewards. The entertainment version of check-in is a way for consumers to link content with the social experience of television and share this information with new audiences. Expect continuous innovation of location based social media networks.

---

more than 70 percent of consumers said that they trusted online consumer opinions. This percentage is much higher than that of consumers who trust traditional advertising. Based on the early work of Amazon and eBay to integrate user opinions into product and seller pages, countless Web sites allowing users to voice their opinions have sprung up across every segment of the Internet market. **Review sites** allow consumers to post, read, rate, and comment on opinions regarding all kinds of products and services. For example, Yelp, the most active local review directory on the Web, combines customer critiques of local businesses with business information and elements of social networking to create an engaging, informative experience. On Yelp, users scrutinize local restaurants, fitness centers, tattoo parlors, and other businesses, each of which has a detailed

review sites
Web sites that allow consumers to post, read, rate, and comment on opinions regarding all kinds of products and services.

© iStockphoto.com/Juan Facundo Mora Soria

profile page. Business owners and representatives can edit their organizations' pages and respond to Yelp reviews both privately and publicly.[41] By giving marketers the opportunity to respond to their customers directly and put their businesses in a positive light, review sites certainly serve as useful tools for local and national businesses.

VIRTUAL WORLDS AND ONLINE GAMING

Virtual worlds and online gaming present additional opportunities for marketers to engage with consumers. These include massive multiplayer online games (MMOG) such as World of Warcraft and The Sims Online as well as online communities (or virtual worlds) such as Second Life, Poptropica, and Habbo Hotel. Consultancy firm KZero Worldwide reported that almost 800 million people participated in some sort of virtual world experience, and the sector's annual revenue approached $1 billion. Much of this revenue has come from in-game advertising—virtual world environments are often fertile grounds for branded content. Several businesses, such as IBM and consultancy firm Crayon, have developed profitable trade presences in Second Life. IBM has used its Second Life space to hold virtual conferences with more than 200 participants, while Crayon has held a number of virtual networking events and meet-and-greets in the virtual world.[42] Other organizations, such as the Center for Disease Control and Prevention and the American Cancer Society, have held their own virtual events in Second Life. Although unfamiliar to and even intimidating for many traditional marketers, the field of virtual worlds is an important, viable, and growing consideration for social media marketing.

One area of growth is social gaming. Nearly one quarter of people play games within social networking sites such as Facebook or on mobile devices such as the iPhone. Interestingly, the typical player is a 43-year-old woman with a full-time job and college education. Women are most likely to play with real-world friends or relatives as opposed to strangers. Most play multiple times per week and almost two-thirds play daily. Facebook is by far the largest social network for gaming. The top five games on Facebook are Farmville, Bejeweled Blitz, Texas Hold 'Em Poker, Café World, and Mafia Wars. Many play on mobile devices (and the demographic usually skews younger). Angry Birds sucks in

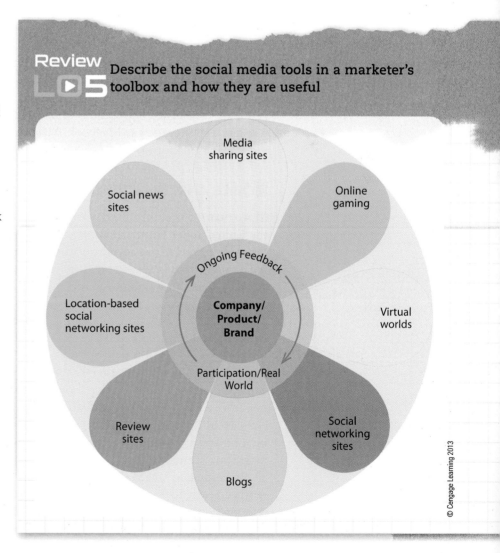

Review LO5 Describe the social media tools in a marketer's toolbox and how they are useful

users for 200 million minutes per day and Zynga's CityVille entices more than 100 million people a month. These are attractive because they are five-minute games and can be done while, for example, waiting for a train.[43] Because of the popularity of gaming with friends and relatives through these sites, marketers have to integrate their message based on the social network platforms and the demographic participating in social gaming.

Another popular type of online gaming targets a different group—MMOGs target the 18- to 34-year-old males. In these environments, thousands of people play simultaneously and the games have revenues of more than $400 billion annually. Regardless of the type of experience, brands must be creative in how the integrate into games. Social and real-world-like titles are the most appropriate for marketing and advertising (as opposed to fantasy games) and promotions typically include special events, competitions, and sweepstakes. In some games (such as the Sims), having ads increases the authenticity. For example, Nike offers shoes in Sims Online that allows the player to run faster.

L▶6
Social Media and Mobile Technology

While much of the excitement in social media has been based on Web sites and new technology uses, much of the growth lies in new platforms. These platforms include the multitude of smartphones such as iPhone and Blackberry as well as netbooks and iPads. The major implications of new platforms mean consumers can access popular Web sites such as Facebook, Mashable, Twitter, and Foursquare using from their various platforms.

MOBILE AND SMARTPHONE TECHNOLOGY

More than 25 percent of the world's population—and more than 75 percent of the United States population—owns a mobile phone.[44] It is no surprise then that the mobile platform is such an effective marketing tool—especially when targeting a younger audience. In the 2008 presidential campaign, Barack Obama's staff used text messaging to fundraise and organize support from college students, while grassroots organizations such as DoSomething.org used messaging to alert young people to volunteering opportunities. Smartphones up the ante by allowing individuals to do nearly everything they can do with a computer—from anywhere. With a smartphone in hand, reading a blog, writing an e-mail message, scheduling a meeting, posting to Facebook, playing a multiplayer game, watching a video, taking a picture, using GPS, and surfing the Internet might all occur during one ten-minute car ride. Smartphone technology, often considered the crowning achievement in digital convergence and social media integration, has opened the door to modern mobile advertising as a viable marketing strategy.

According to an eMarketer survey, United States mobile marketing spending reached nearly $593 million in 2010 and is expected to grow. There are several reasons for the recent popularity of mobile marketing. First, an effort to standardize mobile platforms has resulted in a low barrier to entry. Second, especially given younger audiences, there are more consumers than ever acclimating to once-worrisome privacy and pricing policies. Third, because most consumers carry their smartphones with them at all times, mobile marketing is uniquely effective at garnering consumer attention in real time. Fourth, mobile marketing is measurable: metrics and usage statistics make it an effective tool for gaining insight into consumer behavior. Finally, mobile marketing's response rate is higher than that of traditional media types such as print and broadcast advertisement. Some common mobile marketing tools include:

→ **SMS (short message service):** 160-character text messages sent to and from cell phones. SMS is typically integrated with other tools.

→ **MMS (multimedia messaging service):** Similar to SMS, but allows the attachment of images, videos, ringtones, and other multimedia to text messages.

→ **Mobile Web sites (MOBI and WAP Web sites):** Web sites designed specifically for viewing and navigation on mobile devices.

→ **Mobile ads:** Visual advertisements integrated into text messages, applications, and mobile Web sites. Mobile ads are often sold on a cost per click (CPM) basis.

→ **Bluetooth marketing:** A signal is sent to Bluetooth-enabled devices that allows marketers to send targeted messages to users based on their geographic locations.

→ **Smartphone applications (apps):** Software that is designed specifically for mobile and tablet devices.

Remy Martin, maker of high-end champagne cognac, used SMS, e-mail, and Web site promotions to advertise VIP events held concurrently in six United States cities. To ensure younger generations' interest in the events, Remy Martin also developed a WAP Web site called Remy's Chill Zone, whereby after opting in, users could gain additional information and engage with the brand on a deeper level. As a result, all six events sold out, and Remy Martin began dialogues with younger customers who had never before experienced its product. As this example illustrates, mobile is a great way to engage Generations X, Y, and the millennials.[45]

APPLICATIONS AND WIDGETS

Given the widespread adoption of Apple's iPhone, RIM's Blackberry line, Android-based phones, and other smartphones, it's no surprise that millions of applications have been developed for the mobile market. Dozens of new and unique apps that harness mobile technology are added to mobile marketplaces every day. While many apps perform platform-specific tasks, others convert existing content into a mobile-ready format. Whether offering new or existing content, when an app is well branded and integrated into a company's overall marketing strategy, it can create buzz and generate customer engagement.

One organization that used its smartphone applications effectively was when Volkswagen Group of America introduced the 2010 GTI sedan in an app called VW Real Racing GTI, which it promoted through Facebook, Twitter, YouTube, and other traditional channels. VW Real Racing GTI is a racing game that allows players to enjoy competitive racing on their mobile devices. VW Real Racing GTI connected with players—it is one of the most talked about apps from the Apple store, with nearly five million downloads.[46] Benjamin

Humanitarian Texting

In January 2010, a 7.0 earthquake struck Port au Prince, Haiti, and the surrounding areas. By the time the dust settled, 230,000 people had died, and 1.9 million more had been left homeless. Many organizations pledged countless hours of rescue and millions of dollars of aid, but the American Red Cross's text message–based donation campaign proved to be the crisis' true breakthrough story. By simply texting "HAITI" to 90999, individuals could make a $10 donation to the American Red Cross that was charged to the donator's monthly mobile phone bill. More than three million individuals raised more than $32 million for the American Red Cross's relief work throughout Haiti—simply by sending text messages.

A number of factors made the campaign successful. The major disaster inspired long-term news coverage, and the ease of texting a donation gave many people an easy way to help after being exposed to the tragedy. A televised public service announcement by First Lady Michelle Obama prompted a significant spike in donations, as did an NFL playoff game segment during which commentators discussed the Red Cross campaign.[47] In addition to the extensive coverage, the donation price point was not too high, but still significant enough to aid in the Red Cross' efforts.

An advertisement for the beauty store Sephora. The ad contains a QR, or two-dimensional barcode, that when scanned by a smartphone will connect to Sephora promotions.

Moore Paint focused on the fact that utility can be as effective a selling point as connectivity when it developed Color Capture, an app that allows iPhone users to match colors in photos to shades in the Benjamin Moore color collection. Users can also save their favorite colors and chip names for future use.[48] An increasingly popular smartphone marketing tool is the use of QR codes. QR codes are small, square bar codes that smartphones photograph and read in order to take the user to that product's Web site. Uses range from donating to a charity by photographing the code, to simply checking out that company's Web site for more information. It's convenient and drives Web traffic.

Web widgets, also known as gadgets and badges, are software applications that run entirely within existing online platforms. Essentially, a Web widget allows a developer to embed a simple application such as a weather forecast, horoscope, or stock market ticker into a Web site, even if the developer did not write (or does not understand) the application's source code. From a marketing perspective, widgets allow customers to display company information (such as current promotions, coupons, or news) on their own Web sites. Widgets are often cheaper than apps to develop, can extend your organization's reach beyond existing platforms, will broaden your listening system, and can make your organization easier to find.[49]

Allowing customers to promote up-to-date marketing material on their own blogs and Web sites is very appealing, but before investing in a marketing-oriented widget, you should consider a number of questions:

→ Does my organization regularly publish compelling content, such as news, daily specials, or coupons, on its Web site or blog?

→ Does my content engage individuals or appeal to their needs as customers?

Exhibit 22.3 Social Media Trends

Site	Change	Where Is It Now?
Facebook	Threaded commenting, up/down voting comments	
Twitter	Promoted Tweets	
Facebook/Bing	Linked searching in Bing. Search results include similar items liked by Facebook friends, people searches pull information from your profile to find the correct person.	
Foursquare/Facebook Places/ Location-based applications	Facebook Places is just introduced, Foursquare is gaining popularity away from major cities.	
Google+	Just released, claimed by some to be a Facebook killer because it allows users to stay connected across all of Google's pages.	
Key Ring, Cardstar, Google Wallet	Eliminates plastic loyalty cards and uses smartphones as a single digital repository for loyalty cards, credit cards, and other scannable or swipeable cards typically found in a wallet.	
Stickybits, Bakodo	Ability to use barcode scanner on a smartphone and QR code check-ins.	
Groupon, Livingsocial, Woot, and programs by Yelp, Zagat, and Open Table	Mainstream of the deal-a-day, social coupon trend.	

© iStockphoto.com/Juan Facundo Mora Soria

© Cengage Learning 2013

→ Is my content likely to inspire conversations with the company or with other customers? Will customers want to share my content with others?

If you can answer yes to these questions, a widget may be an effective tool for your organization.

THE CHANGING WORLD OF SOCIAL MEDIA

As you read through the chapter, some of the trends that we noted might already seem ancient to you. The rate of change in social media is astounding—usage statistics change daily for sites such as Facebook and Twitter. Some things that are only in the rumor mill as we write this might have exploded in popularity; others might have fizzled out without even appearing on your radar. In Exhibit 22.3 we've noted some of the items that seemed to be on the brink of exploding on to the social media scene. Take a moment to fill in the current state of each. Have you heard of it? Has it come and gone? Maybe it is still rumored, or maybe it is petered out. This exercise highlights not only the speed with which social media changes, but the importance of keeping tabs on rumors. Doing so may result in a competitive advantage by being able to understand and invest in the next big social media site.

Review
LO6 Describe the impact of mobile technology on social media

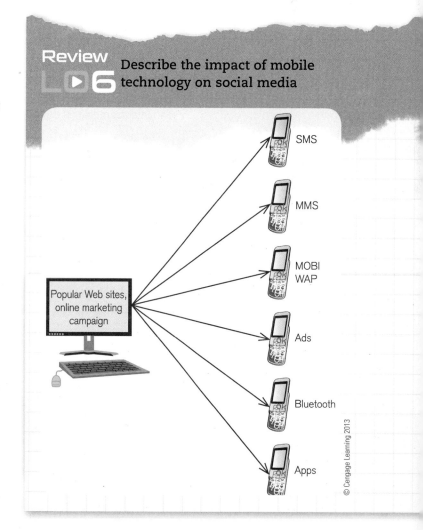

© Cengage Learning 2013

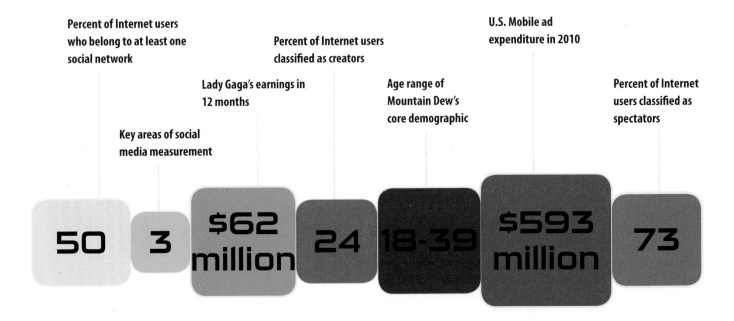

Percent of Internet users who belong to at least one social network

Key areas of social media measurement

Lady Gaga's earnings in 12 months

Percent of Internet users classified as creators

Age range of Mountain Dew's core demographic

U.S. Mobile ad expenditure in 2010

Percent of Internet users classified as spectators

50   3 $62 million   24   18-39 $593 million   73

Review and Applications

LO1 **Describe social media, how it is used, and its relation to integrated marketing communications.** Social media is any tool or service that uses the Internet as a basis to facilitate communication and conversation. At a basic level, consumers using social media want to exchange information, collaborate with others and have conversations with people (and brands). Social media has changed how and where conversation takes place, making human interaction global through popular technology

1.1 What are some ways that social media has changed your daily life? What can marketers take advantage of for their promotional purposes?

LO2 **Explain how to create a social media campaign.** It is important that marketers start with a strategy that is based on an overall marketing and promotions plan. The purpose of the social media strategy must be clear. It is also important to understand that social media has changed the types of media utilized. There are three primary types of media: owned media is where the organization creates and control content; earned media is coverage by others on the Web—essentially buzz; and paid media is content paid by the company to be placed online.

2.1 Why is having a social media campaign strategy important?

team **2.2** With a partner, choose a local business that is utilizing social media effectively. Analyze what they are doing by conducting your own social media monitoring. What tools can your team use? What are the company's objectives? What are they doing right?

LO3 **Evaluate the various methods of measurement for social media.** Measurement is an important area within social media. Three primary areas include social media measurement that determine the ROI of various tools; public relations measurement that attempts to quantify the impact of social media on traditional press coverage and other elements of PR; and social media monitoring which are tools used for customer service improvement, brand management and prospecting.

3.1 What are some tools businesses can use to measure social media? How effective are these tools?

3.2 What are some problems with measuring social media? (For example, what does a "like" really mean?)

Explain consumer behavior on social media. Social media usage is growing and has changed the way we do everything from communicate with family and friends to how brands provide service to its customers.

4.1 Go online to your favorite social media sites. What are brands that have garnered success there? What are some brands that have not been successful with social media? Provide some examples. Based on this comparison, what are the key ingredients to getting customers to engage with a brand?

online

Describe the social media tools in a marketer's toolbox and how they are useful. A number of tools and platforms can be employed as part of an organization's social media strategy. These include blogs, microblogs, social networks, media sharing sites, social news sites, location based social network sites, review sites, virtual worlds, and online gaming. Each has its own purpose within a social media plan.

5.1 Which tools do you think are the most useful for most businesses? Why?

5.2 Assume you are starting a new yogurt store on campus. Develop and write a brief profile of your likely target market. What social media tools do you think will be most effective at reaching that audience? Why?

writing

Describe the impact of mobile technology of social media Mobile technology (including devices like the iPad) have revolutionized the way people access information and stay connected. More than three-quarters of the United States owns a cell phone the growth of smartphones increase. Common tools include short message service (SMS), multimedia messaging service (MMS), mobile Web sites (MOBI), mobile ads, Bluetooth marketing, and apps.

6.1 What do you think is the future of mobile technology? How do you think mobile will change people's daily lives? How will mobile change marketing?

Key Terms

blog *816*
corporate blogs *816*
crowdsourcing *809*
earned media *810*
location-based social networking sites *821*

media sharing sites *820*
microblogs *817*
noncorporate blogs *817*
owned media *810*
paid media *810*
review sites *822*

social commerce *807*
social media *805*
social networking sites *818*
social news sites *821*

Exercises

ETHICS EXERCISE

ethics

As people become increasingly comfortable posting their lives online via social networks like Facebook or through microblogs like Twitter, some companies have begun to build web dossiers of consumers. They do this by mining the social web on Facebook, Twitter, blogs, and online forums. Then they sell it to other companies. And here is the deal . . . most consumers have no idea that this is being done.

While the use of customer data has been around for a few years (especially through companies like Amazon who use algorithms based on customer searches and purchases to make product recommendations), there are some privacy advocates who feel that mining and using data from the social Web crosses ethical lines. For their part, the companies that aggregate this information say that they are using this information to detect behavioral patterns in order for companies to provide better products and customer service.[50]

Questions

1. Do think that this practice violates privacy or is it acceptable since it uses information that a person has posted voluntarily?

2. What are some promising ways that companies can use this data?

3. What are some questionable ways that companies can use this data?

APPLICATION EXERCISE

One major issue regarding social media is the development of a company wide social media policy. In other words, a policy that states who can say what, when and where on social media platforms (e.g. Facebook, blogs, Twitter). Companies and nonprofit organizations alike are struggling with social media policies and we have seen an increase in the number of employees getting into trouble for things posted on their Facebook page. Take a look at Social Media Governance (http://socialmediagovernance.com/policies.php). Find a social media policy for a brand and one for a large nonprofit.

Questions

1. Why do you think social media policies are important?

2. What are some of the common elements you see in each of the examples of social media policies?

3. How do you think social media policies should extend to employees? Should what an employee posts on his or her Facebook be held against him or her regarding work life? Why or why not? Are there situations where firing an employee for private posting is fair?

CASE STUDY: Gatorade's Efforts at Integration

© Jin Lee/Bloomberg via Getty Images

Gatorade is one of the best known marketers in the world. As the producers of sports drinks and one of the first companies to make widespread use of athletes to endorse its products, Gatorade is best known for its creative television commercials. However, they also recognize the impact of social media on their brand and have done more than most brands to put that in the center of its marketing efforts.

Enter the Gatorade Mission Control Center in Chicago. This room sits literally in the middle of the marketing department and can be considered a war room for monitoring the brand's performance using real-time social media. The room features monitors that tap into services like Radian6 which turns data into visual meaning. For example, Gatorade's marketing team can use the data from Twitter to track sentiment about the brand, its competitors and its athlete partners. Gatorade can also monitor similar information found on blogs and social networks in order to portray a complete brand picture.

Senior Marketing Director, Consumer & Shopper Engagement Carla Hassan stated that Mission Control has been used to develop its "Gatorade has evolved" campaign. They also use this information for more conventional tactics—such as optimizing landing pages and increasing consumer engagement.[51]

Questions

1. Why do you think having the Mission Control central to the marketing department is important to Gatorade?

2. Why do you think social media is so important to Gatorade? Do you think it deserves this placement within the marketing mix?

3. Do you think that social media will be this important to most brands in the near future? Why or why not?

COMPANY CLIPS: Mobile Phone Marketing: Parents Beware

As more and more kids today are getting cell phones, concerns about marketing to children through mobile phones have increased. Children can easily subscribe to services that are then billed to the parents' phone bill without the parents' prior knowledge or consent. Although some mobile phone companies have taken measures to limit children's ability to make purchase decisions, it is largely up to the parents to monitor such activity. Pay-as-you-go services are ideal for kids' cell phones because the kids can only spend what their parents approve of and pay for ahead of time.

1. What type of marketing is often used in the types of games children purchase?

2. Describe the mobile marketing tools used by companies to influence children to purchase items on their phones.

3. Who is Kajeet targeting? Explain your reasoning.

Notes

1. Brian Solis, *Engage: The Complete Guide for Brands and Businesses to Build, Cultivate and Measure Success in the New Web* (Hoboken, NJ: John Wiley & Sons, 2010), 37.

2. Teressa Iezzi, *The Idea Writers* (Basingstroke, England: Palgrave McMillan, 2010).

3. "Social Media for Non Profits," *Primalmedia*, February 18, 2009, www.primalmedia.com/blog/social-media-non-profits.

4. Salma Jafri, "Lady Gaga's Social Media Success and Strategy," Suite101.com, July 5, 2010, www.suite101.com/content/lady-gagas-social-media-success-and-strategy-a257336; Dorothy Pomerantz, "Lady Gaga Leads List of Celeb 100 Newcomers," *Forbes*, June 28, 2010, http://www.forbes.com/2010/06/22/lady-gaga-kristin-stewart-business-entertainment-celeb-100-10-newcomers.html.

5. Andrew Hampp, "Gaga, Oooh La La: Why the Lady Is the Ultimate Social Climber," *Advertising Age*, February 22, 2010, http://adage.com/digitalalist10/article?article_id=142210.

6. Solis, *Engage*.

7. *Ibid*.

8. Universal McCann, "Power to the People–Wave3 Study on Social Media Trends," March 2008, www.slideshare.net/mickstravellin/universal-mccann-international-social-media-research-wave-3.

9. Aaron Smith, "Mobile Access 2010," Pew Internet & American Life Project, July 7, 2010, www.pewinternet.org/Reports/2010/Mobile-Access-2010.aspx.

10. Shane Snow, "iPad by the Numbers," *Mashable*, July 2010, http://mashable.com/2010/06/07/ipad-infographic-2.

11. Paul Marsden, "Simple Definition of Social Commerce," *Social Commerce Today*, June 2010, http://socialcommercetoday.com/social-commerce-definition-word-cloud-definitive-definition-list.

marketing&you: Results.

High scores suggest that you tend to be influenced by others opinions, whereas lower scores indicate less concern for what others think of a product or brand you use. Higher scores also suggest that you seek out others' opinions and are a more frequent user of review sites and social media focusing on popular brands and styles.

12. Shar VanBoskirk, "U.S. Interactive Marketing Forecast 2009 to 2014," *Forrester Research*, July 6, 2009, www.forrester.com/rb/Research/us_interactive_marketing_forecast,_2009_to_2014/q/id/47730/t/2.
13. "Digital Dozen: Step Up to the Bar," *Marketing News*, March 15, 2010, www.marketingpower.com/ResourceLibrary/Publications/MarketingNews/2010/3_15_10/Digital Dozen.pdf.
14. *Ibid.*
15. Jeff Howe, *Crowdsourcing: Why the Power of the Crowd Is Driving the Future of Business* (New York, NY: Three Rivers Press, 2009), 32.
16. Ryan Flinn, "Gap Scraps New Logo after Backlash, Revives Blue Box," *Bloomberg*, October 12, 2010, www.bloomberg.com/news/2010-10-12/gap-scraps-new-logo-after-online-backlash-will-return-to-blue-box-design.html.
17. Sean Corcoran, "Defining Earned, Owned and Paid Media," Forrester Blogs, December 16, 2009, http://blogs.forrester.com/interactive_marketing/2009/12/defining-earned-owned-and-paid-media.html; Brian Solis, "Why Brands Are Becoming Media," *Mashable*, February 11, 2010, http://mashable.com/2010/02/11/social-objects/
18. *Ibid.*
19. Greg Ferenstein, "The Science of Building Trust with Social Media," *Mashable*, February 24, 2010, http://mashable.com/2010/02/24/social-media-trust.
20. *Ibid.*
21. Jonathon Hensley, "How to Build Trust Online," *Marketing News*, March 15, 2010.
22. Erik Bratt, "Social Media ROI Success Stories," *MarketingProfs*, 2009, www.marketingprofs.com/store/product/27/social-media-roi-success-stories.
23. David Berkowitz, "100 Ways to Measure Social Media," *Inside the Marketers Studio*, November 17, 2009, www.marketersstudio.com/2009/11/100-ways-to-measure-social-media-.html.
24. Jim Sterne, *Social Media Metrics* (Hoboken, NJ: John Wiley & Sons, 2010).
25. Mike Laurie, "How Social Media Has Changed Us," *Mashable*, January 7, 2010, http://mashable.com/2010/01/07/social-media-changed-us/.
26. Charlene Li and Josh Bernoff, *"Groundswell": Winning in a World Transformed by Social Technologies* (Boston, MA: Harvard Business Press, 2009).
27. *North American Technographics Interactive Marketing Online Survey*, Forrester Research, June 2009, www.forrester.com/ER/Research/Survey/Excerpt/1,10198,726,00.html.
28. Juan Carlos Perez, "Forrester Notes Social Media Contributor Slowdown," *Computerworld*, September 28, 2010, www.computerworld.com/s/article/9188538/Forrester_notes_social_media_contributor_slowdown.
29. Dan Zarella, *The Social Media Marketing Book* (Beijing, China: O'Reilly, 2010).
30. Marketing Profs, "Building Community—Kogi Korean BBQ," *Twitter Success Stories*, 2009, www.marketingprofs.com/store/product/21/twitter-success-stories.
31. Niel Glassman, "Study Finds Users Welcome Brands to Their Social Networks," *Social Times*, Just 14, 2010, www.socialtimes.com/2010/06/study-finds-users-welcome-brands-to-their-social-networks.
32. Marketing Profs, "Adobe Systems," *Facebook Success Stories*, 2009, www.marketingprofs.com/store/product/35/facebook-success-stories.
33. Marketing Profs, *LinkedIn Success Stories*, 2009, www.marketingprofs.com/store/product/37/linkedin-success-stories.
34. Ramya Raghavan, "Using Video to Connect with Your Donors and Prospects," International Fundraising eConference, May 12–14, 2009.
35. Solis, *Engage*, 46.
36. Zarella, *The Social Media Marketing Book*.
37. Solis, *Engage*, 54.
38. Solis, *Engage*, 97.
39. Zarella, *The Social Media Marketing Book*.
40. Erica Swallow, "A Glimpse of the Future of Foursquare," *Mashable*, November 3, 2010, http://mashable.com/2010/11/03/future-of-foursquare; Yan-David Erlich, "Beyond the Checkin: Where Location-Based Social Networks Should Go Next," *Mashable*, July 1, 2010, http://mashable.com/2010/07/01/location-social-media; Jennifer Van Grove, "5 Huge Trends in Social Media Right Now," *Mashable*, August 20, 2010, http://mashable.com/2010/08/20/top-5-social-media-trends; "Why Location Is about More Than the Check-In," *eMarketer*, January 11, 2011, www.emarketer.com/Article.aspx?R=1008161&utm_source=IABSmartBrief&utm_medium=TextArticleMobileSocialUsers&utm_campaign=IAB0508&aff=IABSmartBrief.
41. Solis, *Engage*, 51.
42. "Social Gaming Integral to Social Networking," *Marketing Profs*, February 19, 2010, www.marketingprofs.com/charts/2010/3425/social-gaming-integral-tosocial-networking.
43. Irina Slutsky, "Nothing Casual about This Game Obsession," *Advertising Age*, January 10, 2011, 2.
44. Lon Safko and David K. Brake, *The Social Media Bible: Tactics, Tools & Strategies for Business Success* (Hoboken, NJ: John Wiley & Sons, 2009).
45. Marketing Profs, *Mobile Marketing Success Stories*, 2009, www.marketingprofs.com/store/product/36/mobile-marketing-success-stories.
46. "Real Racing GTI," Volkswagen Web site, www.vw.com/realracinggti/en/us (Accessed October 14, 2010).
47. Michael Bush, "Red Cross Delivers Real Mobile Results for a Real Emergency" *Advertising Age*, February 22, 2010, http://adage.com/digitalalist10/article?article_id=142204; Nicole Wallace and Ian Wilhelm, "Charities Text Messaging Success Shakes Up the Fundraising World," *Chronicle of Philanthropy*, February 11, 2010, 7.
48. *Marketing News* Staff, "Digital Dozen: Benjamin Moore Paints App Success," *Marketing News*, March 15, 2010, www.marketing-power.com/ResourceLibrary/Publications/MarketingNews/2010/3_15_10/Digital Dozen.pdf.
49. Beth Kanter, "Screencast: Using Widgets to Build Community on Blogs Featured on NTEN Blog," *Beth's Blog*, March 20, 2007, http://beth.typepad.com/beths_blog/2007/03/screncast_using.html.
50. Leah Betancourt, "How Companies Are Using Your Social Media Data," *Mashable*, March 2, 2010, http://mashable.com/2010/03/02/data-mining-social-media.
51. Adam Ostrow, "Inside Gatorade's Social Media Command Center," *Mashable*, June 15, 2010, http://mashable.com/2010/06/15/gatorade-social-media-mission-control.

Marketing Miscue

URBAN STORE FORMAT AT CVS: WHERE DID ALL THE CASHIERS GO?

Self-checkout has been implemented at various retailers. They can be found at most grocery stores and Home Depot even offers the option. But, grocery stores and Home Depot have kept their cashiers. A consumer can choose to go to a cashier line or to use one of two to four self checkout machines. At CVS, however, the new urban store format has resulted in consumers being forced to go through the self checkout. In the new urban stores, there may only be one cashier and that cashier is likely no longer found easily at the front of the store.

CVS CAREMARK

CVS Corporation and Caremark Rx Inc. merged in 2007 to form CVS Caremark, the largest pharmacy healthcare provider in the United States. Headquartered in Woonsocket, Rhode Island (USA), the company has more than $99 billion in annual revenue, filling more than one billion prescriptions annually. More than four million customers visit a CVS pharmacy store every day.

In 2010, CVS Caremark began converting about 300 CVS stores in large American cities to a more urban store concept. Research had shown that CVS customers in large cities were using the store more as a general, all-purpose store than just for pharmacy or over-the-counter healthcare products. As such, the company saw a need to stock a wider variety of products, including items such as grab-and-go sandwiches, fruit, refrigerated soft drinks and bottled water, and frozen food. As a part of this urban store concept, the company also revamped the stores with self-checkout machines. According to the company, the logic behind the self-checkout machines was the facilitation of quick and convenient shopping trips.

Self-checkout registers are intended to provide many benefits to CVS shoppers. The key benefit is the reduced checkout time since registers do not depend upon the number of clerks available to operate the registers. Additionally, some consumers, particularly in pharmacies, appreciate the privacy and anonymity of not having to deal with anyone who can see the items being purchased. However, the self-checkout does not come without disadvantages. In particular, an inexperienced customer can take an unreasonable amount of time in scanning their own items. As well, there are some over-the-counter healthcare products that require approval before the purchasing process can be validated. Thus, an employee of the store must assist in the purchasing process by inputting a validation code (e.g., after checking the person's identification). Another very common frustration at the self-checkout is the "unexpected item in bagging area" notification. These usually false alerts halt the checkout process and require a store attendant to assist with the continuance of the checkout process. From the retailer's point-of-view, a major benefit of self-checkout is reduced staffing requirements.

IMPLEMENTATION IS KEY

Self-checkout has to be implemented properly for benefits to accrue to both the customer and retailer. Unfortunately for CVS, concerns arose about the ability of the company to implement the self-checkout component of its urban store concept. Two major issues arose from the customer's perspective.

One, there was concern that CVS was implementing the self-checkout as a way to reduce headcount. This struck at the nerve of many customers who expressed concern about laying off workers during a recession. While CVS said that there would not be an impact on headcount, the company was vague when it came to the adjustment of workers' hours. Thus, while workers might not get laid off, they were likely to see fewer work hours per week.

Second, according to numerous consumer blogs, the machines at CVS were not working properly and/or conveniently. One customer likened the self-checkout registers at CVS to the first iteration of the Windows operating system—a good idea, but clunky, prone to errors, and not intuitive. The rampant need for assistance due to healthcare products requiring proof of age or identification was another point of concern in that the fewer number of available staff meant long waits for assistance, assuming assistance ever arrived. Finally, another customer who expressed a love for self-checkouts said that the registers at CVS were hands-down the worst ever experienced. Concerns such as this made some bloggers wonder if the automated checkouts at CVS were ready for prime time. Had CVS released the concept too soon or without a strong implementation plan?

Questions

1. Has the electronic checkout supplanted the need for good customer service?
2. How should CVS respond to customers' concerns?

Critical Thinking Case

LYON COLLEGE—TAKING CONTROL OF ITS SOCIAL MEDIA ECOSYSTEM

Lyon College is an independent, residential, co-educational, four-year undergraduate liberal arts college affiliated with the Presbyterian Church. Founded in 1872, it is the oldest independent college in Arkansas operating under its original charter. Situated on 136 acres in the scenic foothills of the Ozark Mountains, the college is located in Batesville, Arkansas. Batesville is approximately 90 miles northeast of Little Rock (the state capital) and about 110 miles northwest of Memphis, Tennessee. Nestled in the foothills of the Ozark Mountains and along the White River, the Batesville community of around 10,000 offers outdoor enthusiasts abundant opportunities for activities such as hiking, canoeing, camping, caving, rock climbing, water skiing, scenic photography, fishing, and hunting.

Conferring the Bachelor of Arts and Bachelor of Science degrees, Lyon College offers majors in accounting, art, biology, business administration, chemistry, early childhood, economics, English, history, mathematics, music, political science, psychology, religion and philosophy, Spanish, and theater. In the fall of 2010, the college enrolled 651 students from 28 states and eight countries. The middle 50 percent of entering freshmen scored between 23 and 28 on the ACT, and 53.5 percent ranked in the top quartile of their high school graduating class.

Lyon is ranked regularly among the nation's best liberal arts colleges in the *U.S. News & World Report*, *The Princeton Review*, the *Washington Monthly*, and forbes.com. Faculty members at the college are talented teachers and scholars. Over 90 percent of the full-time faculty holds a Ph.D. or other terminal degree appropriate to their field. The quality of the college's faculty is reflected in that fact that the Carnegie Foundation for the Advancement of Teaching and the Council for Advancement and Support of Education (CASE) has selected 14 Lyon faculty members in 22 years as Arkansas Professors of the Year. The U.S. Professors of the Year program salutes the most outstanding undergraduate instructors in the country—those who excel as teachers and influence the lives and careers of their students. It is recognized as one of the most prestigious awards honoring professors. Lyon's record of 14 Professor of the Year Awards is unmatched by any other liberal arts college in the country.

In late 2010, the college began an extensive planning initiative focused upon student recruitment and retention, alumni relations, and fundraising. Two specific student recruitment and retention objectives were identified: recruit 200+ new freshman students annually and 80 percent retention of students annually. A profile of the student market segments (potential and current students) revealed that the markets were comprised of Millennials and their parents who were likely to be baby boomers or Gen Xers. A dominant characteristic that applies across the board to this student-age group and their parent population is the use of technology. That is, these groups are generally marked by an increased use and familiarity with communications, media, and digital technologies. A 2008 marketing research study prepared for the college reported the following about current/potential college students and technology:

→ Their use of text messaging was up while their e-mail usage was down,

→ 69 percent had cell phones that were used largely to receive and deliver content, watch videos, play games, and surf the internet,

→ 93 percent of youth and 94 percent of parents were active online, and

→ 35 percent of all teen females blogged, while 20 percent of teen males blogged.

In sum, the marketing research firm suggested that today's college student is technologically savvy, with technology as familiar as a knife and fork to this college-age market segment.

Additionally, psychographic findings from the market research study suggested the following about today's college-age students:

→ They are increasingly cynical, fickle, and flighty,

→ They rely heavily on first impressions (e.g., very unlikely to go to a school their friends do not see as "cool"),

→ They are the most visually sophisticated of any generation, and

→ They are scanners, not readers.

Given the psychographic profile of the college-age population, in conjunction with the expectations regarding technological expertise, Lyon College recognized that it had to tell the Lyon College story in the social media ecosystem in which their current and future students exist. In an ecosystem comprised of social networks, blogs, wikis, event tools, photo and video sites, and chat rooms, the college needed an integrated marketing communication program that blended both digital and traditional media in an optimal mix. A truly optimal mix of digital and traditional media would enable the college to continually build and refine the relationship overtime—from prospect to matriculate to alumni to donor.

Questions

1. What social media platforms do you think are most critical for Lyon College to engage?

2. Pick one social media platform and explain how it might be used from prospect to matriculate to alumni to donor.

Appendix A Part 1: Marketing Plan Outline

I BUSINESS MISSION
II SITUATION ANALYSIS (SWOT ANALYSIS)
   A. Internal Strengths and Weaknesses
   B. External Opportunities and Threats
III OBJECTIVES
IV MARKETING STRATEGY
   A. Target Market Strategy
   B. Marketing Mix
      1. Product
      2. Place/Distribution
      3. Promotion
      4. Price
V IMPLEMENTATION, EVALUATION, AND CONTROL

As you read in Chapter 2, there is more than one correct format for a marketing plan. Many organizations have their own distinctive format or terminology for creating a marketing plan, and every marketing plan should be unique to the firm for which it was created. The format and order of presentation, therefore, must be flexible.

This appendix presents only one way to organize a marketing plan. The outline is meant to give you a more detailed look at what you need to include, topics you need to cover, and the types of questions you must answer in any marketing plan. But, depending on the product or service for which you are drafting a plan, this set of questions may only be the starting point for more industry-specific issues you need to address.

An actual marketing plan from E-motion Software follows this outline. The E-motion marketing plan includes annotations that tie each part of the plan to the material throughout the book. You'll see the correlation between chapter concepts and the elements of a professional marketing plan for a real company.

If you are assigned a marketing plan as a course requirement, this appendix can help you organize your work. In addition, worksheets that guide you through the process of marketing planning are available on your textbook's companion site. The worksheets can be completed electronically or printed out and filled in by hand.

I BUSINESS MISSION

→ What is the mission of the firm? What business is it in? How well is its mission understood throughout the organization? Five years from now, what business does it wish to be in?

→ Does the firm define its business in terms of benefits its customers want rather than in terms of goods and services?

II SITUATION ANALYSIS (SWOT ANALYSIS)

→ Has one or more competitive advantages been identified in the SWOT analysis?

→ Are these advantages sustainable against the competition?

A. Internal Strengths and Weaknesses

→ What is the history of the firm, including sales, profits, and organizational philosophies?

→ What is the nature of the firm and its current situation?

→ What are the firm's resources (financial, human, time, experience, asset, skill)?

→ What policies inhibit the achievement of the firm's objectives with respect to organization, resource allocation, operations, hiring, training, and so on?

B. External Opportunities and Threats

→ **Social:** What major social and lifestyle trends will have an impact on the firm? What action has the firm been taking in response to these trends?

→ **Demographics:** What impact will forecasted trends in the size, age, profile, and distribution of population have on the firm? How will the changing nature of the family, the increase in the proportion of women in the workforce, and changes in the ethnic composition of the population affect the firm? What action has the firm taken in response to these developments and trends? Has the firm reevaluated its traditional products and expanded the range of specialized offerings to respond to these changes?

→ **Economic:** What major trends in taxation and income sources will have an impact on the firm? What action has the firm taken in response to these trends?

→ **Political, Legal, and Financial:** What laws are now being proposed at international, federal, state, and local levels that could affect marketing strategy and tactics? What recent changes in regulations and court decisions affect the firm? What political changes are taking place at each government level? What action has the firm taken in response to these legal and political changes?

→ **Competition:** Which organizations are competing with the firm directly by offering a similar product? Which organizations are competing with the firm indirectly by securing its prime prospects' time, money, energy, or commitment? What new competitive trends seem likely to emerge? How effective is the competition? What benefits do competitors offer that the firm does not? Is it appropriate for the firm to compete?

→ **Technological:** What major technological changes are occurring that affect the firm?

→ **Ecological:** What is the outlook for the cost and availability of natural resources and energy needed by the firm? Are the firm's products, services, and operations environmentally friendly?

III OBJECTIVES

→ Is the firm's mission statement able to be translated into operational terms regarding the firm's objectives?

→ What are the stated objectives of the organization? Are they formally written down? Do they lead logically to clearly stated marketing objectives? Are objectives based on sales, profits, or customers?

→ Are the organization's marketing objectives stated in hierarchical order? Are they specific so that progress toward achievement can be measured? Are the objectives reasonable in light of the organization's resources? Are the objectives ambiguous? Do the objectives specify a time frame?

→ Is the firm's main objective to maximize customer satisfaction or to get as many customers as possible?

IV MARKETING STRATEGY
A. Target Market Strategy

→ Are the members of each market homogeneous or heterogeneous with respect to geographic, sociodemographic, and behavioral characteristics?

→ What are the size, growth rate, and national and regional trends in each of the organization's market segments?

→ Is the size of each market segment sufficiently large or important to warrant a unique marketing mix?

→ Are market segments measurable and accessible to distribution and communication efforts?

→ Which are the high- or low-opportunity segments?

→ What are the evolving needs and satisfactions being sought by target markets?

→ What benefits does the organization offer to each segment? How do these benefits compare with benefits offered by competitors?

→ Is the firm positioning itself with a unique product? Is the product needed?

→ How much of the firm's business is repeat versus new business? What percentage of the public can be classified as nonusers, light users, or heavy users?

→ How do current target markets rate the firm and its competitors with respect to reputation, quality, and price? What is the firm's image with the specific market segments it seeks to serve?

→ Does the firm try to direct its products only to specific groups of people or to everybody?

→ Who buys the firm's products? How does a potential customer find out about the organization? When and how does a person become a customer?

→ What are the major objections given by potential customers as to why they do not buy the firm's products?

→ How do customers find out about and decide to purchase the product? When and where?

→ Should the firm seek to expand, contract, or change the emphasis of its selected target markets? If so, in which target markets, and how vigorously?

- → Could the firm more usefully withdraw from some areas where there are alternative suppliers and use its resources to serve new, unserved customer groups?
- → What publics other than target markets (financial, media, government, citizen, local, general, and internal) represent opportunities or problems for the firm?

B. Marketing Mix

- → Does the firm seek to achieve its objective chiefly through coordinated use of marketing activities (product, place, promotion, and pricing) or only through intensive promotion?
- → Are the objectives and roles of each element of the marketing mix clearly specified?

1. Product

- → What are the major product/service offerings of the firm? Do they complement each other, or is there unnecessary duplication?
- → What are the features and benefits of each product offering?
- → Where are the firm and each major product in the life cycle?
- → What are the pressures among various target markets to increase or decrease the range and quality of products?
- → What are the major weaknesses in each product area? What are the major complaints? What goes wrong most often?
- → Is the product name easy to pronounce? Spell? Recall? Is it descriptive, and does it communicate the benefits the product offers? Does the name distinguish the firm or product from all others?
- → What warranties are offered with the product? Are there other ways to guarantee customer satisfaction?
- → Does the product offer good customer value?
- → How is customer service handled? How is service quality assessed?

2. Place/Distribution

- → Should the firm try to deliver its offerings directly to customers, or can it better deliver selected offerings by involving other organizations? What channel(s) should be used in distributing product offerings?
- → What physical distribution facilities should be used? Where should they be located? What should be their major characteristics?
- → Are members of the target market willing and able to travel some distance to buy the product?
- → How good is access to facilities? Can access be improved? Which facilities need priority attention in these areas?
- → How are facility locations chosen? Is the site accessible to the target markets? Is it visible to the target markets?
- → What are the location and atmosphere of retail establishments? Do these retailers satisfy customers?
- → When are products made available to users (season of year, day of week, time of day)? Are these times most appropriate?

3. Promotion

- → How does a typical customer find out about the firm's products?
- → Does the message the firm delivers gain the attention of the intended target audience? Does it address the wants and needs of the target market, and does it suggest benefits or a means for satisfying these wants? Is the message appropriately positioned?
- → Does the promotion effort effectively inform, persuade, educate, and remind customers about the firm's products?
- → Does the firm establish budgets and measure effectiveness of promotional efforts?

a. Advertising

- → Which media are currently being used? Has the firm chosen the types of media that will best reach its target markets?
- → Are the types of media used the most cost-effective, and do they contribute positively to the firm's image?
- → Are the dates and times the ads will appear the most

appropriate? Has the firm prepared several versions of its advertisements?

→ Does the organization use an outside advertising agency? What functions does the ad agency perform for the organization?

→ What system is used to handle consumer inquiries resulting from advertising and promotions? What follow-up is done?

b. **Public Relations**

→ Is there a well-conceived public relations and publicity program? Does the program have the ability to respond to bad publicity?

→ How are public relations normally handled by the firm? By whom? Have those responsible nurtured working relationships with media outlets?

→ Is the firm using all available public relations avenues? Is an effort made to understand each of the publicity outlet's needs and to provide each with story types that will appeal to its audience in readily usable forms?

→ What does the annual report say about the firm and its products? Who is being effectively reached by this vehicle? Does the benefit of the publication justify the cost?

c. **Personal Selling**

→ How much of a typical salesperson's time is spent soliciting new customers as compared to serving existing customers?

→ How does the sales force determine which prospect will be called on and by whom? How is the frequency of contacts determined?

→ How is the sales force compensated? Are there incentives for encouraging more business?

→ How is the sales force organized and managed?

→ Has the sales force prepared an approach tailored to each prospect?

→ Has the firm matched sales personnel with the target market characteristics?

→ Is there appropriate follow-up to the initial personal selling effort? Are customers made to feel appreciated?

→ Can database or direct marketing be used to replace or supplement the sales force?

d. **Sales Promotion**

→ What is the specific purpose of each sales promotion activity? Why is it offered? What does it try to achieve?

→ What categories of sales promotion are being used? Is sales promotion directed to the trade, the final consumer, or both?

→ Is the effort directed at all the firm's key publics or restricted to only potential customers?

4. **Price**

→ What levels of pricing and specific prices should be used?

→ What mechanisms does the firm have to ensure that the prices charged are acceptable to customers?

→ How price sensitive are customers?

→ If a price change is put into effect, how will the number of customers change? Will total revenue increase or decrease?

→ Which method is used for establishing a price: going rate, demand-oriented, or cost-based?

→ What discounts are offered, and with what rationale?

→ Has the firm considered the psychological dimensions of price?

→ Have price increases kept pace with cost increases, inflation, or competitive levels?

→ How are price promotions used?

→ Do interested prospects have opportunities to sample products at an introductory price?

→ What methods of payment are accepted? Is it in the firm's best interest to use these various payment methods?

V IMPLEMENTATION, EVALUATION, AND CONTROL

→ Is the marketing organization structured appropriately to implement the marketing plan?

→ What specific activities must take place? Who is responsible for these activities?

→ What is the implementation timetable?

→ What other marketing research is necessary?

→ What will be the financial impact of this plan on a one-year projected income statement? How does projected income compare with expected revenue if the plan is not implemented?

→ What are the performance standards?

→ What monitoring procedures (audits) will take place and when?

→ Does the firm seem to be trying to do too much or not enough?

→ Are the core marketing strategies for achieving objectives sound? Are the objectives being met, and are the objectives appropriate?

→ Are enough resources (or too many resources) budgeted to accomplish the marketing objectives?

I COMPANY DESCRIPTION

Scott Keohane and a partner founded E-motion Software in 2003 and established its worldwide headquarters in Austin, Texas. They envisioned software solutions that conformed to a particular business, not the other way around, with products designed to (1) improve operating efficiency, (2) empower users, (3) enhance security, (4) improve return on investment, and (5) streamline business processes. [Chapter 1: Market Orientation—focusing upon customer needs and integrating all activities to readily provide customer satisfaction, while achieving long-term company goals.] Ultimately, however, Keohane's partner did not want to remain with the company. Keohane converted the partner's shares into a note, according to the partnership agreement the two had in place.

The origins of the company were based in Keohane's ten years of entrepreneurial endeavors, with four years of this time spent as an independent consultant in the Oracle applications marketplace. Oracle is the world's largest enterprise software company. According to Oracle's Web site, the company's business is information—how to manage it, use it, share it, and protect it. Commercial enterprise information-management software systems, such as those offered by Oracle, promised seamless integration of all information flowing through a company.

In a global marketplace in which external company collaborations drive business efforts and internal cross-functional integration is critical for timely decision making, enterprise systems could help position companies in a highly competitive environment. [Chapter 7: Business Marketing—E-motion Software operates as a business marketer because it provides goods and services to organizations for purposes other than personal consumption.] Enterprise systems such as the Oracle E-Business Suite provided a simplified, unifying corporate technology platform. This type of platform enabled companies to utilize high-quality internal and external information both strategically and tactically. There were numerous product families in the E-Business Suite (e.g., advanced procurement, contracts, performance management, customer data/relationship management, financial, human resource management, logistics, manufacturing, marketing, order management, projects, sales, service, and supply chain management). [Chapter 10: E-Business is one product line in Oracle's product mix width. There are numerous product items in this product line.]

As an independent consultant, Keohane was continually asked to customize existing Oracle technology or create one-off applications to meet common requirements. The need for third-party products that would withstand upgrades to the underlying Oracle architecture was identified and E-motion Software was formed. The overall business concept was to utilize the Oracle E-Business Suite as the underlying framework for customization to fit a particular customer's needs. Soon after incorporation, E-motion Software became a member of the Oracle Partner Network. By joining the Oracle Partner Network, E-motion Software gained access to Oracle software licenses, technical training, marketing funds, and co-marketing opportunities. [Chapter 7: Strategic Partnership—E-motion Software partnered with Oracle so as to improve the offerings to its customers.]

II BUSINESS MISSION [Chapter 2: The foundation of any marketing plan is the firm's mission statement.]

Since its founding, E-motion Software has been committed to the Oracle E-Business Suite of Applications and to providing a level of support unmatched in the industry. The company's goals are to make Oracle applications more reliable, to enhance the applications' functionality, and to make the suite's use more efficient. [Chapter 2: What business is E-motion Software in?] The company's products offer an attractive alternative to in-house development and support. E-motion Software customers utilize functional products that are self-funding. That is, the savings achieved through a more efficient workforce and security enhances far exceed the cost of the company's products. The company's commitment extends from the methods used to build E-motion Software products to the company's simple installation procedures to the post-installation service. E-motion Software products run on multiple server platforms, require no customization, and are fully compatible with existing hardware and software warranties. [Chapter 2: E-motion Software is focused on markets served and benefits sought by its customers.]

III SITUATION ANALYSIS [Chapter 2: Marketers must understand the current and potential environment before defining marketing tactics.]

Industry Analysis [Chapter 2: Environmental scanning is the collection and interpretation of information about forces, events, and relationships in the external environment that may affect the future of the organization or the implementation of the marketing plan.]

Trends. The Enterprise Resource Planning (ERP) community has undergone a radical change since the turn of the century. Historically, applications were designed for the professional user or technology expert. Today's marketplace, however, has shifted from the professional user to employee users. That is, employees in all functional areas have access to and utilize information from the ERP application. Thus, ERP providers have shifted to developing applications intended for individual employee use instead of releasing bigger applications designed for the professional user. These self-service, employee-based applications have fundamentally changed the way ERP applications are sold, implemented, and administered.

Professional users are no longer the keepers of the data, manually entering and updating data from forms and memos. They have now become administrators in charge of ensuring data integrity. The promise of turning departments such as HR and benefits from manual intensive data entry shops to proactive reporting shops has shifted the marketplace to self-service suite applications. This trend has prompted the development of self-service applications that enable employees to utilize systems within their individual realms of expertise balanced with systems that are integrated across the firm.

Competitors. E-motion Software represents a new voice within the Oracle community. The company creates a niche in the marketplace and, as such, competition comes from a variety of sources. In 2003, there were no head-to-head competitors. Competition can be split into three very distinct groups: Oracle, consulting firms, and in-house development centers.

Apart from being the company that created the ERP industry, *Oracle* has resources that dwarf every other company in the ERP marketplace. The availability of capital and the size of the development group infer that Oracle can simply reallocate a small development team to work on competing products. Oracle has, however, repeatedly released products that were little more than advanced betas, resulting in weeks of downtime for companies implementing the new products. By building applications that require no customization to Oracle code, E-motion Software can confidently assure its customers that its products work.

Consulting firms could advise the client to include the cost of custom application development into the total cost of the consulting engagement. This is standard protocol for competing consultancies and would effectively stop E-motion Software from entering into a client site. Most consultancies, however, do not have a support and development center to handle ongoing system management. E-motion Software competes directly with consultancies by providing superior service at an affordable price.

The *in-house development center (IHDC)* poses a tricky problem for E-motion Software. If a company has an IHDC, it is usually a trusted source that knows the company, its standards, and its software. Additionally, the IHDC is usually considered a "no-cost" center because salaries are already included in the company's budget. Thus, program development and implementation is considered just another project with no additional cost. On the positive side, information technology (IT) budgets were slashed and IT departments scaled down over the past few years. While IT spending has begun to trend upward again, the creation of IHDC units has lagged this spending trend. E-motion Software capitalizes on this lag in IHDC unit development and upward spending trend.

Customer Profile. The marketplace has moved from professional users to employee users. Basically, professional users are now babysitters, ensuring that employees do not enter incorrect information into the system. This poses quite a quandary. Professional users must maintain the integrity of the system, while releasing control of it at the same time. This often forces the professional user to become a reactive unit, rushing to fix things when they break down. Employee users do not generally know the idiosyncrasies of the ERP system, of which there are many. Thus, to maintain system integrity and ensure data reliability, professional users are often double-checking employees' data entry and also answering help desk calls regarding how to use the system. This is not, however, what a self-service ERP solution is designed to deliver. E-motion Software has become part of the self-service arena by offering broad range of products designed to regain the efficiencies promised by self-service applications.

Technology. The costs of developing and maintaining an ERP solution require that the underlying technology be relevant for several years after product purchase and installation. The rapid emergence of Internet-based transactions (e.g., banking, loan applications, etc.) brought self-service applications to the forefront of business opportunity. Initially, Oracle attempted to use a mix of PL/SQL and DHTML code in the self-service offerings. This mix, however, did not provide the best-looking applications, had little functionality, and were difficult to implement. Oracle then switched to using Java Server Pages (JSP) as its self-service foundation, with PL/SQL and HTML as the accessory languages. Products with the JSP foundation were well received in the marketplace. E-motion Software adheres to Oracle's decision to use JSP, especially since JSP offers E-motion Software some key benefits: (1) JSP is robust and flexible, allowing all applications to use the same coding techniques, (2) JSP is recyclable, which means that E-motion Software can leverage existing code across new applications, (3) JSP is accessible because Java is one of the most well known programming languages, (4) JSP is portable, allowing E-motion Software to easily enter other ERP markets, and (5) the use of JSP means that E-motion Software will always comply with Oracle approved practices.

SWOT Analysis: The strengths, weaknesses, opportunities, and threats (SWOT) analysis provides a snapshot of E-motion Software's internal strengths and weaknesses and external opportunities and threats.

[Chapter 2: Performing a SWOT analysis allows firms to identify their competitive advantage.]

Strengths. [Chapter 2: Strengths are *internal* to the firm.]

→ Founder—Scott Keohane is not only extremely knowledgeable about the third-party marketplace, but he is also personally and financially dedicated to making the business a success.

→ Active and committed advisory council.

→ Reliable products and product support.

→ Member of Oracle Partner Network.

Weaknesses. [Chapter 2: Weaknesses are *internal* to the firm.]

→ A one-person company that has to supplement the company with independent consulting services.

→ Not enough time dedicated to company development.

→ While it has considerable anecdotal information, the company is lacking in marketing research.

→ Financial resources.

Opportunities. [Chapter 2: Opportunities are *external* to the firm.]

→ Changing marketplace that coincides with E-motion Software's product development

→ The move toward employee users instead of professional users

→ Growth market.

→ Technological changes.

→ Refocus on IT applications.

→ Persistent threat of security breaches.

→ Growing focus on cross-functional interactions in the business press.

→ New entries into the workforce (e.g., recent college graduates) are trained to use computers in decision making and thus expect companies to have data programs in place.

Threats. [Chapter 2: Threats are *external* to the firm.]

→ Competitors—all three groups of competitors likely have deeper pockets than E-motion Software.

→ Offerings can be duplicated by knowledgeable experts.

→ Limited market access across the United States.

→ Economies of scale in larger companies such as Oracle.

→ IT departments do not have unlimited budgets.

IV MARKETING OBJECTIVE

The marketing objective has been to establish the company as an expert in the third-party marketplace. [Chapter 2: The marketing objective statement provides a look at what the company seeks to accomplish. It is consistent with the priorities of the organization.] The third party product market for functions that are specifically designed for integration with Oracle applications is in its infancy. E-motion Software has to establish itself as a leader in this new marketplace. To accomplish this objective, customers must see that E-motion Software products are safe and secure and that they do not affect existing Oracle functionality or their Oracle warranty.

Objective Metric: Three major Oracle clients by the end of 2005 [Chapter 2: Stated objectives must be measurable and time specific.]

To accomplish this marketing objective, E-motion Software had to obtain three major Oracle clients by the end of 2005. These clients would serve as reference sites for the company. These clients would also enable E-motion Software to demonstrate the gains achieved by using E-motion Software products. As such, the clients needed to be vocal and create viral marketing within the industry.

Objective Metric: One client in each region of the United States by the end of 2006 [Chapter 2: Stated objectives must be measurable and time specific.]

Given the close-knit nature of Oracle clients through organizations such as the Oracle Application User's Group (OAUG), E-motion Software needed to gain clients within each of the major geographic areas in the United States: Northeast, Mid-Atlantic, Southeast, Midwest, Northwest, and West Coast.

V MARKETING STRATEGY

Target Market Strategy

E-motion Software's sales plan is based on the company's understanding of the marketplace and on how it will resolve inefficiencies with the use of the Oracle E-Business Suite of Applications. From his consulting experience in helping potential clients install and maintain their individualized suite of applications, Keohane has considerable understanding of users' needs. To obtain clients, E-motion Software relies on continuing relationships with prospective clients, maintaining relationships with other consulting firms, and reaching new clients via marketing and sales initiatives.

Geographically, E-motion Software directs its marketing and sales efforts within the contiguous United States. [Chapter 8: Geographic segmentation refers to segmenting markets by region of a country or the world, market size, market density, or climate.] Though global operations are potential clients, the current size of E-motion Software suggests that the U.S. marketplace is more viable at this time. [Chapter 8: Accessibility—the firm must be able to reach members of the targeted segment.] Within this marketplace, E-motion Software focuses upon companies that have between 500 and 10,000 employees. These are the small- to mid-size companies that utilize the Oracle E-Business Suite of Applications. Companies of this size are unlikely to have their own development staffs in place or have the desire to develop and/or support home-grown applications. [Chapter 8: Responsiveness—the targeted market must respond to the marketing mix offered by the company.] Within these small- to mid-size companies, the individual target customer varies by the product offering. For example, a database administrator is targeted for the company's system administrator products, and the IT director is targeted for the functional line of product offerings.

Marketing Mix [Chapter 2: Marketing mix (the four Ps) refers to the unique blend of product, place (distribution), promotion, and pricing strategies.]

Product. [Chapter 7: E-motion Software provides a business service to its customers.]

E-motion Software develops applications specifically for the Oracle E-Business Suite. For clients of Oracle applications who desire greater efficiency and an increase in ROI on their installed ERP systems, E-motion Software offers a line of products designed specifically to improve performance of the existing Oracle application installation. Clients that have in-house development staff will be able to lower the total cost of ownership of a product by having E-motion Software upgrade their Oracle installation. [Chapter 7: The buying center includes all persons in an organization who become involved in the purchase decision. In-house development staff will play a critical role in the buying process.] Clients without in-house staff, however, are more likely to benefit from E-motion Software installations because they would then be able to perform a greater number of tasks that were not offered by Oracle. [Chapter 7: In this instance, the members of the buying center are different from a company with an in-house development staff.]

As a product-based company, E-motion Software cannot ignore the importance of product marketing. The three product attributes that drive the business are level of service, usability, and clear return on purchase price. [Chapter 7: Quality, service, and price are important evaluative criteria in a purchase decision involving software products.] The reluctance of some customers to install relatively new third-party products into their ERP systems is an obstacle overcome via product marketing. [Chapter 7: This is often a new buy for the customer.] The company has to deliver on the promise of the products—that promise being that "E-motion Software products make the business process of our customers more efficient, while easily understanding the upgrades to the underlying Oracle Application." E-motion must remain focused on this promise during both the product development and the product delivery process. [Chapter 7: Keeping current customers satisfied is just as important as attracting new ones.]

E-motion Software's product line consists of functions that respond to inefficiencies identified from years of experience with Oracle ERP systems. Because the product portfolio is built expressly for the Oracle Applications E-Business Suite, the products are updated continually to maintain compatibility as well as to take advantage of new technologies and capabilities released by Oracle. [Chapter 10: Quality and functional modifications keep E-motion Software's products up-to-date with ongoing technological changes.] All products enjoy the following characteristics: tight integration with Oracle, intuitive design, compatible architecture, and streamlined interfaces. Product offerings are iPraise, Responsibility Management, Password Reset, and Global Directory. [Chapter 10: E-motion Software's product mix width is composed of one product—enterprise software. This product line is composed of four product items.]

iPraise. [Chapter 10: iPraise is an individual brand.] The employee appraisal system developed by E-motion Software is the most dynamic appraisal system available to Oracle customers. Combining E-motion Software's commitment to streamlined application interfaces with the vast functionality available to Oracle E-Business Suite customers, iPraise represents the next generation of appraisal systems. The system is flexible, allowing it to be configured to meet the specific needs of the organization. By using the appraisal configuration engine, the customer can choose to include or omit several aspects of the appraisal process and even determine in which order they are to be constructed. Thus, iPraise is a complete solution for Oracle customers. Customers can opt to integrate other modules of Oracle that have been configured previously with the E-Business Suite. Installing iPraise is fast and easy.

Responsibility Management. [Chapter 10: Responsibility Management is an individual brand.] Responsibility Management solves one of the most important questions faced by all Oracle system administrators:

"Who has access to which data?" Using Responsibility Management, a system administrator or database administrator can quickly, easily, and accurately identify who has access to which data in real-time. Responsibility Management can inform the administrator of the following:

→ Employees with particular responsibility

→ Employees without a single responsibility

→ User names that are not attached to any employee

→ User names that are attached to more than one employee

→ User accounts that are expiring in x number of days

→ User accounts created in x days prior

→ All users that have been given y responsibilities in x days prior

Results are displayed in a simple table that can be arranged and sorted. The table can also be exported to Excel for further investigation.

In addition to the query capabilities, Responsibility Management enables the system administrator to make changes to the user account, such as:

→ End-date a responsibility

→ User account expiration update for a particular responsibility

→ Bulk assignment of responsibilities (by organization, job, location, etc.)

→ Bulk end-dating of responsibilities (by organization, job, location, etc.)

Overall, Responsibility Management enables system administrators to enforce security policies by providing a simple, easy-to-use function to identify who has what responsibility. Each day that a person has access not identified with his or her position is unnecessary and insecure.

Password Reset. [Chapter 10: Password Reset is an individual brand.] Forgotten passwords are the single largest end-user issue. Every day, help desks are bombarded with calls from end-users who have forgotten their passwords. The standard Oracle log-in link does not provide a solution for this problem; thus, end-users are forced to call the help desk to reset the password. E-motion Software's Password Reset function is the solution.

Password Reset is modeled after the standard password reset functionality available on most Web sites. Even if the user is using Password Reset for the first time, all the components will seem familiar and the user will know where to go next without receiving complex instructions or training. Password Reset functions as a part of the Oracle applications. There are no outside Web sites to access or other applications to open. The user simply clicks on a link from the login page, enters the required information, and the password is reset. The user can then log in immediately with the new password. Password Reset validates a user's identity by going directly to the Oracle database and running queries against it. This tight integration ensures reliability.

Global Directory. [Chapter 10: Global Directory is an individual brand.] Most companies utilize a separate system for their corporate directory. This requires entering and maintaining all employee information in Oracle and then reentering that information into a separate system. Worse yet, they print the company directory from a separate system. Not only is this extremely inefficient, but there is a greater chance for error. In today's fast-changing world, employee information can change on a weekly basis. As a result, the "other" system is often neglected and its data are unreliable. Global Directory solves this issue by "going to source" and gathering data directly from the Oracle database; thus, Global Directory has up-to-the-minute validity. Global Directory allows users to query the database for a wide variety of information. The results can be customized to give your employees the depth of knowledge they require.

Global Directory functions as a part of the Oracle applications. There are no outside Web sites to access or other applications to open. Using the export function, users can transfer results into Excel, XML, or CSV, making it possible to utilize the information for items such as contact lists, distribution forms, and mailing labels.

Place/Distribution. E-motion Software is headquartered in Bedford, Massachusetts. However, home office location has little to do with the actual distribution of E-motion Software's products because the products are installed and implemented at the client company. E-motion Software will perform its own marketing channel functions (e.g., transactional, logistical, and facilitating) and does not foresee the need for any intermediaries in this process. [Chapter 13: Channel members facilitate the exchange between buyer and seller. E-motion Software is the only channel member engaged in getting its product to the customer. Thus, it uses a direct channel.] However, E-motion Software is a strong supporter of industry groups, such as the Oracle Applications User Group, and related industry events. Such support allows the company to become

recognized as a vendor among Oracle applications clients.

E-motion Software does offer a partner program for companies that wish to resell or refer E-motion Software products to Oracle ERP clients. The program is segmented into two separate categories. The Alliance Partner Referral Program is tailored for businesses that have customer relationships with companies in specific industries or with businesses or IT needs that E-motion Software programs can uniquely address. An Alliance Partner will identify E-motion Software customers and refer them to E-motion Software for a revenue share of the revenue from the referred account. As part of the program, Alliance Partner members receive all the training and materials needed to promote E-motion Software solutions to their client base. The Alliance Solution Provider Program is designed for qualified Oracle-focused consultancies with a strong track record for providing top-notch service to their clients. Partner program members are trained and certified by E-motion Software. Once certified, implementation partners can then configure and implement E-motion Software products with unparalleled service and support. [Chapter 13: This is a form of a strategic channel alliance for E-motion Software.]

Promotion [Chapter 16: E-motion software strives for integrated marketing communications.]

As a third party purveyor of products for Oracle, it is important for E-motion Software to convey, clearly and succinctly, its "reason for being." Company material has the heading: "E-motion Software: We keep the business of business moving." [Chapter 17: This is the company's unique selling proposition.] We emphasize the Oracle connection with the following statement on documents, as appropriate: "Oracle clients around the country are realizing true gains in productivity and efficiency by taking everyday tasks and putting them in *motion.*"

E-motion Software adheres to mainstream thinking regarding the promotion of third-party products for ERP solutions. [Chapter 16: As a complex buying decision, personal selling and strong print are effective methods for reaching potential customers.]

→ A cohesive, easy-to-maneuver, and user-friendly Web site (www.e-motionsoftware.com) [Chapter 16: Company Web sites can be used to introduce new products, promote existing products, obtain consumer feedback, post news releases, etc.]

→ Recorded demos on the company Web site (requires users to register for a demo user account) [Chapter 21: Registration is important for customer relationship management.]

Product Pricing Sheet

	License Price	Software Update & Support	Licensing Metric	Minimum
Application Infrastructure:				
Password Reset	$15,000	$2,700/year	Enterprise	N/A
Responsibility Management	$6	18%/year	User	2,000
User Application:				
iPraise	$10	18%/year	User	2,000
Corporate Information:				
Global Directory	$2	18%/year	User	2,000

→ Press releases as a member of the Certified Oracle Partner Network [Chapter 17: Public relations is an important element of the promotional mix. Press releases can place positive information in the news media to attract attention to E-motion Software.]

→ Demonstrations presented at trade shows and events [Chapter 18: Trade promotions push a product through the distribution channel and are popular among business marketers. Trade shows and events are an important aspect of sales promotions.]

→ Word-of-mouth and reference sites [Chapter 18: Referrals are a good source for leads in the personal selling process.]

→ The Internet via Google AdWords campaigns to drive potential clients to the company Web site [Chapter 22: The Internet has changed the advertising industry. Popular Internet sites sell advertising space to marketers, and search engine advertising is a popular approach.]

→ Product datasheets that provide pertinent product data, features, and benefits of installation (available on the company Web site or via hard copy) [Chapter 18: Product information is critical in the sales process.]

Importantly, E-motion Software is a company that relies heavily on direct selling to reach potential customers. [Chapter 18: Producers of most business goods rely more heavily on personal selling than advertising. Informative personal selling is common for installations such as those offered by E-motion Software.] This promotional method requires a large amount of cold calling. [Chapter 18: Personal selling is important when a product has high value and is technically complex. Relationship selling, or consultative selling, builds long-term relationships with clients.] E-motion Software purchases the names of potential customers from marketing services that collect such information from customers of Oracle ERP products. [Chapter 18: Generating leads is the first step in the selling process.]

Price. E-motion Software prices its products to sufficiently cover the costs associated with development, sales, and support and to provide cash flow for future growth and development. [Chapter 20: As a new company, E-motion Software is very concerned about covering its costs and having money left over for investment into the business. While not stated exactly, it appears that the company has a profit-oriented pricing objective.] The table above provides the company's standard price list. These list prices can vary, however, as there is a trickle-down effect in the industry. Essentially, pricing starts with Oracle, trickles through the consulting firm, and then down to E-motion products.

Prices are based on industry standards for classification. [Chapter 19: Status quo pricing is when a company meets the competition or going rate pricing. It appears that E-motion Software is using status quo logic in its price setting.] For example, Password Reset, as an enterprise system product, has a total purchase price of $15,000, with a $2,700 software update and support fee. [Chapter 20: Two-part pricing is when the company charges two separate amounts for the product. In this instance, the buyer pays the $15,000 for the enterprise system product and then pays another $2,700 for the update and fee.] Responsibility Management, iPraise, and Global Directory are priced on a per employee (user) basis with a minimum purchase per number of employees. For example, Global Directory is $2 per employee with a minimum purchase of 2,000 employees. Thus, the least amount a company could purchase this product for is $4,000. The 18 percent annual maintenance fee is the industry standard. [Chapter 20: This shows the two-part, status quo pricing.]

Five Years Financial Projection Plan

	2006	2007	2008	2009	2010
Revenues:					
iPraise	$50,000	$100,000	$600,000	$2,250,000	$5,500,000
Responsibility Mgt	$60,000	$80,000	$160,000	$420,000	$700,000
Password Reset	$225,000	$180,000	$180,000	$150,000	$75,000
Global Directory	$45,000	$75,000	$180,000	$300,000	$465,000
Cost of Goods Sold	0	0	0	0	0
General & Administrative	$350,000	$765,000	$1,600,000	$2,165,000	$2,600,000

VI IMPLEMENTATION, EVALUATION, AND CONTROL

Marketing Research

The company needs to keep abreast of two distinct segments in the marketplace: its client needs and Oracle's direction. E-motion Software needs to understand its clients and their ongoing needs. [Chapter 21: E-motion Software captures customer data, storing and integrating it into a customer database.] This includes meeting current needs and forecasting future needs as the Oracle Application Suite continues to evolve. E-motion Software must also maintain up-to-date and accurate intelligence on both current Oracle offerings and planned initiatives. [Chapter 9: Ongoing marketing research will help the company keep abreast of what is happening in the marketplace.] By doing this, it will be able to introduce products that complement new Oracle functions and will be less likely to offer products that compete for functions that are included at no charge in an Oracle license. Additionally, this will present opportunities to introduce products that complement new Oracle functionality.

Organizational Structure and Plan

As a start-up company, E-motion Software had only one member on its staff, Scott Keohane. As E-motion Software matured into a stable, profitable organization, the need for employees grew. The first employee need was in the area of sales. The plan was to hire a salesperson in early 2006 so Mr. Keohane could continue his consulting on a regular basis, while at the same time ensuring a steady supply of funds for continued development efforts. To obtain the financial flexibility it needed to manage its cash flow successfully, the company made contractors a significant component of its workforce. Contractors are used in the following areas: application development, database administration, and marketing. Current contractors have been associated with E-mo-

tion Software almost since the company's inception and are largely credited with its early successes.

To provide a management resource from which Keohane could receive regular advice and guidance, E-motion Software assembled a nonvoting, nonbinding advisory council to assist in decision making, overall strategy, and execution. The advisory council is composed of four outside members who have made a commitment to provide their expertise and experience, free of charge, to E-motion Software. Advisory members interact quarterly via teleconference.

Financial Projections

[Chapter 2: Evaluation and control are important mechanisms for monitoring the effectiveness of the marketing plan. Financial objectives are a common measure of success/failure.]

The financial objective is to be financially solvent within the first two years of operation.

Objective
Metric:
Sales of $250,000 by the end of 2005
Sales of $2 million by the end of 2007
Gross margin higher than 80 percent
Positive cash flow yearly

[Chapter 2: Stated objectives must be measurable and time-specific.]

The five-year financial projection plan (in U.S. dollars) for E-motion Software can be reviewed in the table above.

Implementation Timetable

[Chapter 2: Implementation is the process that turns a marketing plan into action assignments and ensures that these assignments are executed appropriately.]

2005

→ The company planned to have three major Oracle clients by the end of 2005.

→ The company planned to have secured at least one client in each region of the United States by the end of 2006. This means at least one customer in the Northeast, the Mid-Atlantic, the Southeast, the Midwest, the Northwest, and the West Coast.

→ Keohane planned to hire one full-time salesperson.

VII SUMMARY

E-motion Software continually monitors activities with current and potential clients. As a consultant in the industry, Keohane is always on the lookout for potential clients. He has set quarterly and yearly sales targets, and actual sales were compared to these quarterly plans. Additionally, Keohane continued in his efforts to enlist at least one client in each of the major geographic regions of the United States. However, it may take a qualified salesperson to devote the time necessary to acquire new customers. Additionally, by not being restricted to Keohane's current consultancies, a dedicated salesperson could more readily identify potential E-motion Software clients. Of major concern was the current financial strategy of supporting the new business by personal funds from consulting, which could have proven to be too onerous for Keohane.

Ultimately, the goal was to "make it big." The hope is that, over the next five years, the small products that E-motion Software developed would hopefully generate cash sufficient to build a larger module that one of the larger ERP companies (e.g., Oracle) would want to acquire.

Marketing Plan Appendix

The authors would like to thank E-motion Software for allowing us to include its marketing plan in the 12th edition of *Introduction to Marketing*. We greatly appreciate Mr. Keohane's contribution of a real plan used by his growing company, which demonstrates to students the level of detail and the elements required to build an effective plan.

Glossary

80/20 principle A principle holding that 20 percent of all customers generate 80 percent of the demand (Chapter 8).

A

ABC segmentation The supply-chain process whereby customers are placed into groups A, B, and C according to their overall long-term value to the firm and to the extent to which the firm can serve their desires (Chapter 14).

accessory equipment Goods, such as portable tools and office equipment, that are less expensive and shorter-lived than major equipment (Chapter 7).

activity-based costing (ABC) An accounting method used in measurement integration to assess the costs associated with each supply chain activity (Chapter 14).

adopter A consumer who was happy enough with his or her trial experience with a product to use it again (Chapter 11).

advergaming Placing advertising messages in Web-based or video games to advertise or promote a product, service, organization, or issue (Chapter 17).

advertising Impersonal, one-way mass communication about a product or organization that is paid for by a marketer (Chapter 17).

advertising appeal A reason for a person to buy a product (Chapter 17).

advertising campaign A series of related advertisements focusing on a common theme, slogan, and set of advertising appeals (Chapter 17).

advertising objective A specific communication task that a campaign should accomplish for a specified target audience during a specified period (Chapter 17).

advertising response function A phenomenon in which spending for advertising and sales promotion increases sales or market share up to a certain level but then produces diminishing returns (Chapter 17).

advocacy advertising A form of advertising in which an organization expresses its views on controversial issues or responds to media attacks (Chapter 17).

agents and brokers Wholesaling intermediaries who do not take title to a product but facilitate its sale from producer to end user by representing retailers, wholesalers, or manufacturers (Chapter 13).

agile supply chain management The supply chain strategy that focuses primarily on the ability of the firm to fulfill customer demand, even if this means somewhat higher costs (Chapter 14).

AIDA concept A model that outlines the process for achieving promotional goals in terms of stages of consumer involvement with the message; the acronym stands for attention, interest, desire, and action (Chapter 16).

anchoring Luxury retailers set a very high price on an item, which may never sell at that price, but makes all other offerings of the retailer seem cheap by comparison (Chapter 20).

applied research An attempt to develop new or improved products (Chapter 4).

arm's-length relationships A relationship between companies that is loose, characterized by low relational investment and trust, and usually taking the form of a series of discrete transactions with no/low expectation of future interaction or service (Chapter 13).

aspirational reference group A group that someone would like to join (Chapter 6).

assurance The knowledge and courtesy of employees and their ability to convey trust (Chapter 12).

atmosphere The overall impression conveyed by a store's physical layout, décor, and surroundings (Chapter 15).

attitude A learned tendency to respond consistently toward a given object (Chapter 6).

audience selectivity The ability of an advertising medium to reach a precisely defined market (Chapter 17).

automatic replenishment program An inventory management system that triggers shipments only once a good is sold to the customer; the program uses EDI linkage connected with bar code scanners at the point of purchase, so the supplier can view the inventory being held at the next tier of the supply chain in real time (Chapter 14).

automatic vending Using machines to offer goods for sale (Chapter 15).

average total cost (ATC) Total costs divided by quantity of output (Chapter 19).

average variable cost (AVC) Total variable costs divided by quantity of output (Chapter 19).

B

baby boomers People born between 1946 and 1964 (Chapter 4).

bait pricing A price tactic that tries to get consumers into a store through false or misleading price advertising and then uses high-pressure selling to persuade consumers to buy more expensive merchandise (Chapter 20).

Balanced Scorecard Approach A measurement system used to evaluate overall supply chain performance (Chapter 14).

base price The general price level at which the company expects to sell the good or service (Chapter 20).

basic research Pure research that aims to confirm an existing theory or to learn more about a concept or phenomenon (Chapter 4).

basing-point pricing A price tactic that charges freight from a given (basing) point, regardless of the city from which the goods are shipped (Chapter 20).

behavioral targeting (BT) A form of observation marketing research that uses data mining coupled with identifying Web surfers by their IP addresses (Chapter 9).

BehaviorScan A scanner-based research program that tracks the purchases of 3,000 households through store scanners in each research market (Chapter 9).

belief An organized pattern of knowledge that an individual holds as true about his or her world (Chapter 6).

benchmarks The standards set by measuring the best, quickest, and most efficient work practices (Chapter 14).

benefit segmentation The process of grouping customers into market segments according to the benefits they seek from the product (Chapter 8).

blog A publicly accessible Web page that functions as an interactive journal, whereby readers can post comments on the author's entries (Chapter 22).

brainstorming The process of getting a group to think of unlimited ways to vary a product or solve a problem (Chapter 11).

brand A name, term, symbol, design, or combination thereof that identifies a seller's products and differentiates them from competitors' products (Chapter 10).

brand equity The value of company and brand names (Chapter 10).

brand extensions A well-known and respected brand name from one product category is extended into other product categories (Chapter 6).

brand loyalty A consistent preference for one brand over all others (Chapter 10).

brand mark The elements of a brand that cannot be spoken (Chapter 10).

brand name That part of a brand that can be spoken, including letters, words, and numbers (Chapter 10).

break-even analysis A method of determining what sales volume must be reached before total revenue equals total costs (Chapter 19).

bullwhip effect A series of observed demand variation events that lead to amplified perceived demand and ordering, leading to a situation where actual supply and demand are misaligned (Chapter 14).

business analysis The second stage of the screening process where preliminary figures for demand, cost, sales, and profitability are calculated (Chapter 11).

business marketing (industrial marketing) The marketing of goods and services to individuals and organizations for purposes other than personal consumption (Chapter 7).

business processes Bundles of interconnected activities that stretch across firms in the supply chain (Chapter 14).

business product A product used to manufacture other goods or services, to facilitate an organization's operations, or to resell to other customers (Chapter 10).

business services Expense items that do not become part of a final product (Chapter 7).

business-to-business electronic commerce The use of the Internet to facilitate the exchange of goods, services, and information between organizations (Chapter 7).

buyer for export An intermediary in the global market that assumes all ownership risks and sells globally for its own account (Chapter 5).

buyer A department head who selects the merchandise for his or her department and may also be responsible for promotion and personnel (Chapter 15).

buying center All those persons in an organization who become involved in the purchase decision (Chapter 7).

C

campaign management Developing product or service offerings customized for the appropriate customer segment and then pricing and communicating these offerings for the purpose of enhancing customer relationships (Chapter 21).

cannibalization A situation that occurs when sales of a new product cut into sales of a firm's existing products (Chapter 8).

capital-intensive Using more capital than labor in the production process (Chapter 5).

captive brand A brand that carries no evidence of a retailer's affiliation, is manufactured by a third party, and is sold exclusively at the retailer (Chapter 10).

cash cow In the portfolio matrix, a business unit that usually generates more cash than it needs to maintain its market share (Chapter 2).

cash discount A price reduction offered to a consumer, an industrial user, or a marketing intermediary in return for prompt payment of a bill (Chapter 20).

casuist ethical theory A theory that compares a current ethical dilemma with examples of similar ethical dilemmas and their outcomes (Chapter 3).

category killers Specialty discount stores that heavily dominate a narrow merchandise segment (Chapter 15).

cause-related marketing The cooperative marketing efforts between a "for-profit" firm and a "nonprofit organization" (Chapter 3); A type of sponsorship involving the association of a for-profit company and a nonprofit organization; through the sponsorship, the company's product or service is promoted and money is raised for the nonprofit (Chapter 17).

Central America Free Trade Agreement (CAFTA) A trade agreement, instituted in 2005, that includes Costa Rica, the Dominican Republic, El Salvador, Guatemala, Honduras, Nicaragua, and the United States (Chapter 5).

central-location telephone (CLT) facility A specially designed phone room used to conduct telephone interviewing (Chapter 9).

chain stores Stores owned and operated as a group by a single organization (Chapter 15).

channel A medium of communication—such as a voice, radio, or newspaper—for transmitting a message (Chapter 16).

channel conflict A clash of goals and methods between distribution channel members (Chapter 13).

channel control A situation that occurs when one marketing channel member intentionally affects another member's behavior (Chapter 13).

channel leader (channel captain) A member of a marketing channel that exercises authority and power over the activities of other channel members (Chapter 13).

channel members All parties in the marketing channel that negotiate with one another, buy and sell products, and facilitate the change of ownership between buyer and seller in the course of moving the product from the manufacturer into the hands of the final consumer (Chapter 13).

channel partnering (channel cooperation) The joint effort of all channel members to create a channel that serves customers and creates a competitive advantage (Chapter 13).

channel power The capacity of a particular marketing channel member to control or influence the behavior of other channel members (Chapter 13).

closed-ended question An interview question that asks the respondent to make a selection from a limited list of responses (Chapter 9).

cobranding Placing two or more brand names on a product or its package (Chapter 10).

code of ethics A guideline to help marketing managers and other employees make better decisions (Chapter 3).

cognitive dissonance Inner tension that a consumer experiences after recognizing an inconsistency between behavior and values or opinions (Chapter 6).

commercialization The decision to market a product (Chapter 11).

communication The process by which we exchange or share meaning through a common set of symbols (Chapter 16).

comparative advertising A form of advertising that compares two or more specifically named or shown competing brands on one or more specific attributes (Chapter 17).

competitive advantage The set of unique features of a company and its products that is perceived by the target market as significant and superior to the competition (Chapter 2); One or more unique aspects of an organization that cause target consumers to patronize that firm rather than competitors (Chapter 16).

competitive advertising A form of advertising designed to influence demand for a specific brand (Chapter 17).

competitive intelligence (CI) An intelligence system that helps managers assess their competition and vendors in order to become more efficient and effective competitors (Chapter 9).

compiled list A customer list that is developed by gathering names and addresses from telephone directories and membership rosters, usually enhanced with information from public records, such as census data, auto registrations, birth announcements, business start-ups, or bankruptcies (Chapter 21).

component lifestyles The practice of choosing goods and services that meet one's diverse needs and interests rather than conforming to a single, traditional lifestyle (Chapter 4).

component parts Either finished items ready for assembly or products that need very little processing before becoming part of some other product (Chapter 7).

computer-assisted personal interviewing An interviewing method in which the interviewer reads the questions from a computer screen and enters the respondent's data directly into the computer (Chapter 9).

computer-assisted self-interviewing An interviewing method in which a mall interviewer intercepts and directs willing respondents to nearby computers where the respondent reads questions off a computer screen and directly keys his or her answers into a computer (Chapter 9).

concentrated targeting strategy A strategy used to select one segment of a market for targeting marketing efforts (Chapter 8).

concept test A test to evaluate a new-product idea, usually before any prototype has been created (Chapter 11).

consumer behavior Processes a consumer uses to make purchase decisions, as well as to use and dispose of purchased goods or services; also includes factors that influence purchase decisions and product use (Chapter 6).

consumer decision-making process A five-step process used by consumers when buying goods or services (Chapter 6).

consumer generated media (CGM) Media that consumers generate and share among themselves (Chapter 9).

consumer penalty An extra fee paid by the consumer for violating the terms of the purchase agreement (Chapter 20).

consumer product A product bought to satisfy an individual's personal wants (Chapter 10).

Consumer Product Safety Commission (CPSC) A federal agency established to protect the health and safety of consumers in and around their homes (Chapter 4).

consumer sales promotion Sales promotion activities targeting the ultimate consumer (Chapter 18).

continuous media schedule A media scheduling strategy in which advertising is run steadily throughout the advertising period; used for products in the latter stages of the product life cycle (Chapter 17).

contract manufacturing Private-label manufacturing by a foreign company (Chapter 5).

control Provides the mechanisms for evaluating marketing results in light of the plan's objectives and for correcting actions that do not help the organization reach those objectives within budget guidelines (Chapter 2).

convenience product A relatively inexpensive item that merits little shopping effort (Chapter 10).

convenience sample A form of nonprobability sample using respondents who are convenient or readily accessible to the researcher—for example, employees, friends, or relatives (Chapter 9).

convenience store A miniature supermarket that carries only a limited line of high-turnover convenience goods (Chapter 15).

cooperative advertising An arrangement in which the manufacturer and the retailer split the costs of advertising the manufacturer's brand (Chapter 17).

cooperative relationships A relationship between companies that takes the form of informal partnership with moderate levels of trust and information sharing as needed to further each company's goals (Chapter 13).

core service The most basic benefit the consumer is buying (Chapter 12).

corporate blogs Blogs that are sponsored by a company or one of its brands and maintained by one or more of the company's employees (Chapter 22).

corporate social responsibility Business's concern for society's welfare (Chapter 3).

cost competitive advantage Being the low-cost competitor in an industry while maintaining satisfactory profit margins (Chapter 2).

cost per click The cost associated with a consumer clicking on a display or banner ad (Chapter 17).

cost per contact The cost of reaching one member of the target market (Chapter 17).

cost per thousand (CPM) Allows marketers to compare the relative costs of specific media (Chapter 17).

countertrade A form of trade in which all or part of the payment for goods or services is in the form of other goods or services (Chapter 5).

coupon A certificate that entitles consumers to an immediate price reduction when they buy the product (Chapter 18).

credence quality A characteristic that consumers might have difficulty assessing even after purchase because they do not have the necessary knowledge or experience (Chapter 12).

crisis management A coordinated effort to handle all the effects of unfavorable publicity or of another unexpected unfavorable event (Chapter 17).

cross-docking A tactic where materials or goods are unloaded from an outbound carrier and transferred directly to an inbound carrier with little/no storage taking place in between (Chapter 14).

cross-tabulation A method of analyzing data that lets the analyst look at the responses to one question in relation to the responses to one or more other questions (Chapter 9).

crowdsourcing Using consumers to develop and market product (Chapter 22).

culture The set of values, norms, attitudes, and other meaningful symbols that shape human behavior, and the artifacts, or products, of that behavior as they are transmitted from one generation to the next (Chapter 6).

cumulative quantity discount A deduction from list price that applies to the buyer's total purchases made during a specific period (Chapter 20).

customer-centric A philosophy under which the company customizes its product and service offering based on data generated through interactions between the customer and the company (Chapter 21).

customer integration A competency that enables firms to offer long-lasting, distinctive, value-added offerings to those customers who represent the greatest value to the firm or supply chain (Chapter 14).

customer relationship management (CRM) A company-wide business strategy designed to optimize profitability, revenue, and customer satisfaction by focusing on highly defined and precise customer groups (Chapter 21).

customer relationship management process The prioritization of a firm's marketing focus on different customer groups according to each group's long-term value to the company or supply chain; designed to identify and build relationships with good customers (Chapter 14).

customer satisfaction Customers' evaluation of a good or service in terms of whether it has met their needs and expectations (Chapter 1).

customer service management process A multi-company, unified response system to the customer whenever complaints, concerns, questions, or comments are voiced; designed to ensure that customer relationships remain strong (Chapter 14).

customer value The relationship between benefits and the sacrifice necessary to obtain those benefits (Chapter 1).

D

data warehouse A central repository for data from various functional areas of the organization that are stored and inventoried on a centralized computer system so that the information can be shared across all functional departments of the business (Chapter 21).

database marketing The creation of a large computerized file of customers' and potential customers' profiles and purchase patterns (Chapter 9).

database A collection of data, especially one that can be accessed and manipulated by computer software (Chapter 21).

decision support system (DSS) An interactive, flexible computerized information system that enables managers to obtain and manipulate information as they are making decisions (Chapter 9).

decline stage The fourth stage of the product life cycle, characterized by a long-run drop in sales (Chapter 11).

decoding Interpretation of the language and symbols sent by the source through a channel (Chapter 16).

delayed-quotation pricing A price tactic used for industrial installations and many accessory items, in which a firm price is not set until the item is either finished or delivered (Chapter 20).

demand The quantity of a product that will be sold in the market at various prices for a specified period (Chapter 19).

demand management process The alignment of supply and demand throughout the supply chain to anticipate customer requirements at each level and create demand-related plans of action prior to actual customer purchasing behavior (Chapter 14).

demographic segmentation Segmenting markets by age, gender, income, ethnic background, and family life cycle (Chapter 8).

demography The study of people's vital statistics, such as their age, race and ethnicity, and location (Chapter 4).

deontological ethical theory A theory that states that people should adhere to their obligations and duties when analyzing an ethical dilemma (Chapter 3).

department store A store housing several departments under one roof (Chapter 15).

derived demand The demand for business products (Chapter 7).

destination stores Stores that consumers purposely plan to visit (Chapter 15).

development The stage in the product development process in which a prototype is developed and a marketing strategy is outlined (Chapter 11).

diffusion The process by which the adoption of an innovation spreads (Chapter 11).

direct channel A distribution channel in which producers sell directly to consumers (Chapter 13).

direct foreign investment Active ownership of a foreign company or of overseas manufacturing or marketing facilities (Chapter 5).

direct marketing (direct-response marketing) The techniques used to get consumers to make a purchase from a nonretail setting (Chapter 15).

direct retailing The selling of products by representatives who work door-to-door, office-to-office, or at home parties (Chapter 15).

discount store A retailer that competes on the basis of low prices, high turnover, and high volume (Chapter 15).

discrepancy of assortment The lack of all the items a customer needs to receive full satisfaction from a product or products (Chapter 13).

discrepancy of quantity The difference between the amount of product produced and the amount an end user wants to buy (Chapter 13).

disintermediation The elimination of intermediaries such as wholesalers or distributors from a marketing channel (Chapter 7).

distribution resource planning (DRP) An inventory control system that manages the replenishment of goods from the manufacturer to the final consumer (Chapter 14).

distributive justice Perceptions of fairness within channel interactions based on how resources are actually allocated among competing interests (Chapter 13).

diversification A strategy of increasing sales by introducing new products into new markets (Chapter 2).

dog In the portfolio matrix, a business unit that has low growth potential and a small market share (Chapter 2).

drugstore A retail store that stocks pharmacy-related products and services as its main draw (Chapter 15).

dual distribution (multiple distribution) The use of two (or more) channels to distribute the same product to target markets (Chapter 13).

dumping The sale of an exported product at a price lower than that charged for the same or a like product in the "home" market of the exporter (Chapter 5).

E

earned media A public relations term connoting free media such as mainstream media coverage (Chapter 22).

elastic demand A situation in which consumer demand is sensitive to changes in price (Chapter 19).

elasticity of demand Consumers' responsiveness or sensitivity to changes in price (Chapter 19).

electroencephalograph (EEG) A machine that measures electric pulses on the scalp and generates a record of electrical activity in the brain (Chapter 9).

electronic data interchange (EDI) Information technology that replaces the paper documents that usually accompany business transactions, such as purchase orders and invoices, with electronic transmission of the needed information to reduce inventory levels, improve cash flow, streamline operations, and increase the speed and accuracy of information transmission (Chapter 14).

electronic distribution A distribution technique that includes any kind of product or service that can be distributed electronically, whether over traditional forms such as fiber-optic cable or through satellite transmission of electronic signals (Chapter 14).

empathy Caring, individualized attention to customers (Chapter 12).

empowerment Delegation of authority to solve customers' problems quickly—usually by the first person that the customer notifies regarding a problem (Chapter 1, 21).

encoding The conversion of a sender's ideas and thoughts into a message, usually in the form of words or signs (Chapter 16).

environmental management When a company implements strategies that attempt to shape the external environment within which it operates (Chapter 4).

environmental scanning Collection and interpretation of information about forces, events, and relationships in the external environment that may affect the future of the organization or the implementation of the marketing plan (Chapter 2).

escalator pricing A price tactic in which the final selling price reflects cost increases incurred between the time the order is placed and the time delivery is made (Chapter 20).

ethics The moral principles or values that generally govern the conduct of an individual (Chapter 3).

ethnographic research The study of human behavior in its natural context; involves observation of behavior and physical setting (Chapter 9).

European Union (EU) A free trade zone encompassing 27 European countries (Chapter 5).

evaluation Gauging the extent to which the marketing objectives have been achieved during the specified time period (Chapter 2).

evoked set (consideration set) A group of brands, resulting from an information search, from which a buyer can choose (Chapter 6).

exchange People giving up something to receive something they would rather have (Chapter 1).

exchange rate The price of one country's currency in terms of another country's currency (Chapter 5).

exclusive distribution A form of distribution that establishes one or a few dealers within a given area (Chapter 13).

executive interviews A type of survey that involves interviewing businesspeople at their offices concerning industrial products or services (Chapter 9).

experience curves The curves represent data on a chart that show costs declining at a predictable rate as experience with a product increases (Chapter 2).

experience quality A characteristic that can be assessed only after use (Chapter 12).

experiment A method a researcher uses to gather primary data (Chapter 9).

export agent An intermediary who acts like a manufacturer's agent for the exporter. The export agent lives in the foreign market (Chapter 5).

export broker An intermediary who plays the traditional broker's role by bringing buyer and seller together (Chapter 5).

exporting Selling domestically produced products to buyers in another country (Chapter 5).

express warranty A written guarantee (Chapter 10).

extensive decision making The most complex type of consumer decision making, used when buying an unfamiliar, expensive product or an infrequently bought item; requires use of several criteria for evaluating options and much time for seeking information (Chapter 6).

external information search The process of seeking information in the outside environment (Chapter 6).

eye tracking Following and recording the movement of the eye as it looks at something (Chapter 9).

F

factory outlet An off-price retailer that is owned and operated by a manufacturer (Chapter 15).

family brand Marketing several different products under the same brand name (Chapter 10).

family life cycle (FLC) A series of stages determined by a combination of age, marital status, and the presence or absence of children (Chapter 8).

Federal Trade Commission (FTC) A federal agency empowered to prevent persons or corporations from using unfair methods of competition in commerce (Chapter 4).

feedback The receiver's response to a message (Chapter 16).

field service firm A firm that specializes in interviewing respondents on a subcontracted basis (Chapter 9).

fixed cost A cost that does not change as output is increased or decreased (Chapter 19).

flexible pricing (variable pricing) A price tactic in which different customers pay different prices for essentially the same merchandise bought in equal quantities (Chapter 20).

flighted media schedule A media scheduling strategy in which ads are run heavily every other month or every two weeks, to achieve a greater impact with an increased frequency and reach at those times (Chapter 17).

FOB origin pricing A price tactic that requires the buyer to absorb the freight costs from the shipping point ("free on board") (Chapter 20).

focus group Seven to ten people who participate in a group discussion led by a moderator (Chapter 9).

follow-up The final step of the selling process, in which the salesperson ensures that delivery schedules are met, that the goods or services perform as promised, and that the buyers' employees are properly trained to use the products (Chapter 18).

Food and Drug Administration (FDA) A federal agency charged with enforcing regulations against selling and distributing adulterated, misbranded, or hazardous food and drug products (Chapter 4).

Foreign Corrupt Practices Act A law that prohibits U.S. corporations from making illegal payments to public officials of foreign governments to obtain business rights or to enhance their business dealings in those countries (Chapter 3).

four Ps Product, place, promotion, and price, which together make up the marketing mix (Chapter 2).

frame error An error that occurs when a sample drawn from a population differs from the target population (Chapter 9).

franchisee An individual or business that is granted the right to sell another party's product (Chapter 15).

franchises The right to operate a business or to sell a product (Chapter 15).

franchisor The originator of a trade name, product, methods of operation, and so on, that grants operating rights to another party to sell its product (Chapter 15).

freight absorption pricing A price tactic in which the seller pays all or part of the actual freight charges and does not pass them on to the buyer (Chapter 20).

frequency The number of times an individual is exposed to a given message during a specific period (Chapter 17).

frequent buyer program A loyalty program in which loyal consumers are rewarded for making multiple purchases of a particular good or service (Chapter 18).

full-line discount stores A retailer that offers consumers very limited service and carries a broad assortment of well-known, nationally branded "hard goods" (Chapter 15).

functional discount (trade discount) A discount to wholesalers and retailers for performing channel functions (Chapter 20).

G

galvanic skin response (GSR) A change in the electric resistance of the skin associated with activation responses (Chapter 9).

gap model A model identifying five gaps that can cause problems in service delivery and influence customer evaluations of service quality (Chapter 12).

General Agreement on Tariffs and Trade (GATT) A trade agreement that contained loopholes that enabled countries to avoid trade-barrier reduction agreements (Chapter 5).

Generation X People born between 1965 and 1978 (Chapter 4).

Generation Y People born between 1979 and 1994 (Chapter 4).

generic product name Identifies a product by class or type and cannot be trademarked (Chapter 10).

geodemographic segmentation Segmenting potential customers into neighborhood lifestyle categories (Chapter 8).

geographic segmentation Segmenting markets by region of a country or the world, market size, market density, or climate (Chapter 8).

global brand A brand where at least one-third of the product is sold outside its home country or region (Chapter 10).

global marketing standardization Production of uniform products that can be sold the same way all over the world (Chapter 5).

global marketing Marketing that targets markets throughout the world (Chapter 5).

global vision Recognizing and reacting to international marketing opportunities, using effective global marketing strategies, and being aware of threats from foreign competitors in all markets (Chapter 5).

Greatest Generation Cohort before the baby boomers who grew up in the Great Depression and fought in World War II (Chapter 4).

green marketing the development and marketing of products designed to minimize negative effects on the physical environment or to improve the environment (Chapter 3).

green supply chain management The integration of environmentally conscious thinking into all phases of key supply chain management processes (Chapter 14).

gross domestic product (GDP) The total market value of all final goods and services produced in a country for a given time period (Chapter 5).

gross margin The amount of money the retailer makes as a percentage of sales after the cost of goods sold is subtracted (Chapter 15).

group dynamics Group interaction essential to the success of focus-group research (Chapter 9).

Group of Twenty (G-20) A forum for international economic development that promotes discussion between industrial and emerging-market countries on key issues related to global economic stability (Chapter 5).

growth stage The second stage of the product life cycle when sales typically grow at an increasing rate, many competitors enter the market, large companies might start acquiring small pioneering firms, and profits are healthy (Chapter 11).

H

heterogeneity The variability of the inputs and outputs of services, which causes services to tend to be less standardized and less uniform than goods (Chapter 12).

horizontal conflict A channel conflict that occurs among channel members on the same level (Chapter 13).

horizontal position One of three dimensions of supply chain network design; the position of a firm, relative to other firms, along the supply chain (Chapter 14).

horizontal structure One of three dimensions of supply chain network design; the number of tiers (columns) in the supply chain, representing the total number of levels through which goods and services must pass from the earliest to end stages of the chain (Chapter 14).

I

ideal self-image The way an individual would like to be (Chapter 6).

implementation The process that turns a marketing plan into action assignments and ensures that these assignments are executed in a way that accomplishes the plan's objectives (Chapter 2).

implied warranty An unwritten guarantee that the good or service is fit for the purpose for which it was sold (Chapter 10).

independent retailers Retailers owned by a single person or partnership and not operated as part of a larger retail institution (Chapter 15).

individual branding Using different brand names for different products (Chapter 10).

inelastic demand A situation in which an increase or a decrease in price will not significantly affect demand for the product (Chapter 19).

inflation A measure of the decrease in the value of money, expressed as the percentage reduction in value since the previous year (Chapter 4).

infomercial A 30-minute or longer advertisement that looks more like a TV talk show than a sales pitch (Chapter 17).

informational labeling A type of package labeling designed to help consumers make proper product selections and lower their cognitive dissonance after the purchase (Chapter 10).

InfoScan A scanner-based sales-tracking service for the consumer packaged-goods industry (Chapter 9).

innovation A product perceived as new by a potential adopter (Chapter 11).

inseparability The inability of the production and consumption of a service to be separated. Consumers must be present during the production (Chapter 12).

institutional advertising A form of advertising designed to enhance a company's image rather than promote a particular product (Chapter 17).

intangibility The inability of services to be touched, seen, tasted, heard, or felt in the same manner that goods can be sensed (Chapter 12).

integrated marketing communications (IMC) The careful coordination of all promotional messages for a product or a service to ensure the consistency of messages at every contact point at which a company meets the consumer (Chapter 16).

integrated relationships A relationship between companies that is tightly connected, with linked processes across and between firm boundaries, and high levels of trust and interfirm commitment (Chapter 13).

intensive distribution A form of distribution aimed at having a product available in every outlet where target customers might want to buy it (Chapter 13).

interaction The point at which a customer and a company representative exchange information and develop learning relationships (Chapter 21).

interactional justice Perceptions of fairness within channel interactions based on treatment in everyday interactions (Chapter 13).

internal information search The process of recalling past information stored in the memory (Chapter 6).

internal marketing Treating employees as customers and developing systems and benefits that satisfy their needs (Chapter 12).

internal operations integration Links internally performed work into a seamless process that stretches across departmental and/or functional boundaries, with the goal of satisfying customer requirements (Chapter 14).

International Monetary Fund (IMF) An international organization that acts as a lender of last resort, providing loans to troubled nations, and also works to promote trade through financial cooperation (Chapter 5).

interpersonal communication Direct, face-to-face communication between two or more people (Chapter 16).

introductory stage The first stage of the product life cycle in which the full-scale launch of a new product into the marketplace occurs (Chapter 11).

inventory control system A method of developing and maintaining an adequate assortment of materials or products to meet a manufacturer's or a customer's demand (Chapter 14).

involvement The amount of time and effort a buyer invests in the search, evaluation, and decision processes of consumer behavior (Chapter 6).

J

joint costs Costs that are shared in the manufacturing and marketing of several products in a product line (Chapter 20).

joint demand The demand for two or more items used together in a final product (Chapter 7).

joint venture When a domestic firm buys part of a foreign company or joins with a foreign company to create a new entity (Chapter 5).

K

keiretsu A network of interlocking corporate affiliates (Chapter 7).

keystoning The practice of marking up prices by 100 percent, or doubling the cost (Chapter 19).

knowledge management The process by which learned information from customers is centralized and shared in order to enhance the relationship between customers and the organization (Chapter 21).

L

lead generation (prospecting) Identification of those firms and people most likely to buy the seller's offerings (Chapter 18).

lead qualification Determination of a sales prospect's (1) recognized need, (2) buying power, and (3) receptivity and accessibility (Chapter 18).

leader pricing (loss-leader pricing) A price tactic in which a product is sold near or even below cost in the hope that shoppers will buy other items once they are in the store (Chapter 20).

Leagile supply chain strategy A supply chain management strategy that combines the best elements of the lean and agile strategies for a particular product/ market combination (Chapter 14).

lean supply chain management The strategy that focuses primarily on the removal of waste from the supply chain to achieve the lowest total cost to the members of the supply chain system (Chapter 14).

learning A process that creates changes in behavior, immediate or expected, through experience and practice (Chapter 6); An informal process of collecting customer data through customer comments and feedback on product or service performance (Chapter 21).

licensing The legal process whereby a licensor agrees to let another firm use its manufacturing process, trademarks, patents, trade secrets, or other proprietary knowledge (Chapter 5).

lifestyle A mode of living as identified by a person's activities, interests, and opinions (Chapter 6).

lifetime value (LTV) analysis A data manipulation technique that projects the future value of the customer over a period of years using the assumption that marketing to repeat customers is more profitable than marketing to first-time buyers (Chapter 21).

limited decision making The type of decision making that requires a moderate amount of time for gathering information and deliberating about an unfamiliar brand in a familiar product category (Chapter 6).

location-based social networking sites Web sites that combine the fun of social networking with the utility of location-based GPS technology (Chapter 22).

logistics The efficient and cost-effective forward and reverse flow as well as storage of goods, services, and related information into, through, and out of channel member companies. Logistics functions typically include transportation and storage of assets, as well as their sorting, accumulation, consolidation, and/ or allocation for the purpose of meeting customer requirements (Chapter 13).

logistics information system The link that connects all of the logistics components of the supply chain (Chapter 14).

loyalty marketing program A promotional program designed to build long-term, mutually beneficial relationships between a company and its key customers (Chapter 18).

M

major equipment (installations) Capital goods such as large or expensive machines, mainframe computers, blast furnaces, generators, airplanes, and buildings (Chapter 7).

mall intercept interview A survey research method that involves interviewing people in the common areas of shopping malls (Chapter 9).

management decision problem A broad-based problem that uses marketing research in order for managers to take proper actions (Chapter 9).

manufacturer's brand The brand name of a manufacturer (Chapter 10).

manufacturing flow management process A process that ensures that firms in the supply chain have the resources they need (Chapter 14).

marginal cost (MC) The change in total costs associated with a one-unit change in output (Chapter 19).

marginal revenue (MR) The extra revenue associated with selling an extra unit of output or the change in total revenue with a one-unit change in output (Chapter 19).

markdown money Money or discounts provided by vendors to department stores to help cover end-of-season discounts offered by department stores to clients (Chapter 20).

market People or organizations with needs or wants and the ability and willingness to buy (Chapter 8).

market development A marketing strategy that entails attracting new customers to existing products (Chapter 2).

market opportunity analysis (MOA) The description and estimation of the size and sales potential of market segments that are of interest to the firm and the assessment of key competitors in these market segments (Chapter 2).

market orientation A philosophy that assumes that a sale does not depend on an aggressive sales force but rather on a customer's decision to purchase a product. It is synonymous with the marketing concept (Chapter 1).

market penetration A marketing strategy that tries to increase market share among existing customers (Chapter 2).

market segment A subgroup of people or organizations sharing one or more characteristics that cause them to have similar product needs (Chapter 8).

market segmentation The process of dividing a market into meaningful, relatively similar, and identifiable segments or groups (Chapter 8).

market share A company's product sales as a percentage of total sales for that industry (Chapter 19).

marketing The activity, set of institutions, and processes for creating, communicating, delivering, and exchanging offerings that have value for customers, clients, partners, and society at large (Chapter 1).

marketing audit A thorough, systematic, periodic evaluation of the objectives, strategies, structure, and performance of the marketing organization (Chapter 2).

marketing channel (channel of distribution) A set of interdependent organizations that ease the transfer of ownership as products move from producer to business user or consumer (Chapter 13).

marketing concept The idea that the social and economic justification for an organization's existence is the satisfaction of customer wants and needs while meeting organizational objectives (Chapter 1).

marketing information Everyday information about developments in the marketing environment that managers use to prepare and adjust marketing plans (Chapter 9).

marketing mix A unique blend of product, place, promotion, and pricing strategies designed to produce mutually satisfying exchanges with a target market (Chapter 2).

marketing myopia Defining a business in terms of goods and services rather than in terms of the benefits that customers seek (Chapter 2).

marketing objective A statement of what is to be accomplished through marketing activities (Chapter 2).

marketing plan A written document that acts as a guidebook of marketing activities for the marketing manager (Chapter 2).

marketing planning Designing activities relating to marketing objectives and the changing marketing environment (Chapter 2).

marketing research The process of planning, collecting, and analyzing data relevant to a marketing decision (Chapter 9).

marketing research aggregator A company that acquires, catalogs, reformats, segments, and resells reports already published by marketing research firms (Chapter 9).

marketing research objective The specific information needed to solve a marketing research problem; the objective should be to provide insightful decision-making information (Chapter 9).

marketing research problem Determining what information is needed and how that information can be obtained efficiently and effectively (Chapter 9).

marketing strategy The activities of selecting and describing one or more target markets and developing and maintaining a marketing mix that will produce mutually satisfying exchanges with target markets (Chapter 2).

marketing-controlled information source A product information source that originates with marketers promoting the product (Chapter 6).

markup pricing The cost of buying the product from the producer plus amounts for profit and for expenses not otherwise accounted for (Chapter 19).

Maslow's hierarchy of needs A method of classifying human needs and motivations into five categories in ascending order of importance: physiological, safety, social, esteem, and self-actualization (Chapter 6).

mass communication The communication of a concept or message to large audiences (Chapter 16).

mass customization A strategy that uses technology to deliver customized services on a mass basis (Chapter 12).

mass merchandising A retailing strategy using moderate to low prices on large quantities of merchandise and lower service to stimulate high turnover of products (Chapter 15).

material and service supplier integration The strategic alignment between a firm and its supply chain materials and services providers that enables the firm to streamline work processes and provide smooth, high-quality customer experiences (Chapter 14).

materials requirement planning (MRP) (materials management) An inventory control system that manages the replenishment of raw materials, supplies, and components from the supplier to the manufacturer (Chapter 14).

materials-handling system A method of moving inventory into, within, and out of the warehouse (Chapter 14).

maturity stage The third stage of the product life cycle during which sales increase at a decreasing rate (Chapter 11).

measurement error An error that occurs when there is a difference between the information desired by the researcher and the information provided by the measurement process (Chapter 9).

measurement integration The performance assessment of the supply chain as a whole that also holds each individual firm or business unit accountable for meeting its own goals (Chapter 14).

media mix The combination of media to be used for a promotional campaign (Chapter 17).

media planning The series of decisions advertisers make regarding the selection and use of media, allowing the marketer to optimally and cost-effectively communicate the message to the target audience (Chapter 17).

media schedule Designation of the media, the specific publications or programs, and the insertion dates of advertising (Chapter 17).

media sharing sites Web sites that allow users to upload and distribute multimedia content such as videos and photos (Chapter 22).

medium The channel used to convey a message to a target market (Chapter 17).

merchant wholesaler An institution that buys goods from manufacturers and resells them to businesses, government agencies, and other wholesalers or retailers and that receives and takes title to goods, stores them in its own warehouses, and later ships them (Chapter 13).

Mercosur The largest Latin American trade agreement; includes Argentina, Bolivia, Brazil, Chile, Colombia, Ecuador, Paraguay, Peru, Uruguay, and Venezuela (Chapter 5).

metrics Standard measures that can be used repeatedly to assess performance on a supply chain-related process (Chapter 14).

microblogs Blogs with strict post length limits (Chapter 22).

mission statement A statement of the firm's business based on a careful analysis of benefits sought by present and potential customers and an analysis of existing and anticipated environmental conditions (Chapter 2).

modified rebuy A situation where the purchaser wants some change in the original good or service. (Chapter 7)

moral relativists Persons who believe that ethical truths depend on the individuals and groups holding them (Chapter 3).

morals The rules people develop as a result of cultural values and norms (Chapter 3).

motive A driving force that causes a person to take action to satisfy specific needs (Chapter 6).

multidomestic strategy When multinational firms enable individual subsidiaries to compete independently in domestic markets (Chapter 5).

multinational corporation A company that is heavily engaged in international trade, beyond exporting and importing (Chapter 5).

multiplier effect (accelerator principle) Phenomenon in which a small increase or decrease in consumer demand can produce a much larger change in demand for the facilities and equipment needed to make the consumer product (Chapter 7).

multisegment targeting strategy A strategy that chooses two or more well-defined market segments and develops a distinct marketing mix for each (Chapter 8).

mystery shoppers Researchers posing as customers who gather observational data about a store (Chapter 9).

N

need recognition Result of an imbalance between actual and desired states (Chapter 6).

needs assessment A determination of the customer's specific needs and wants, and the range of options the customer has for satisfying them (Chapter 18).

negotiation The process during which both the salesperson and the prospect offer special concessions in an attempt to arrive at a sales agreement (Chapter 18).

networking A process of finding out about potential clients from friends, business contacts, coworkers, acquaintances, and fellow members in professional and civic organizations (Chapter 18).

neuromarketing Studying microscopic changes in skin moisture, heart rate, brain waves, and other biometrics to see how consumers react to things such as package designs and ads (Chapter 9).

new buy A situation requiring the purchase of a product for the first time (Chapter 7).

new product A product new to the world, the market, the producer, the seller, or some combination of these (Chapter 11).

new-product strategy A plan that links the new-product development process with the objectives of the marketing department, the business unit, and the corporation (Chapter 11).

niche One segment of a market (Chapter 8).

niche competitive advantage The advantage achieved when a firm seeks to target and effectively serve a small segment of the market (Chapter 2).

noise Anything that interferes with, distorts, or slows down the transmission of information (Chapter 16).

nonaspirational reference group A group with which an individual does not want to associate (Chapter 6).

noncorporate blogs Independent blogs that are not associated with the marketing efforts of any particular company or brand (Chapter 22).

noncumulative quantity discount A deduction from list price that applies to a single order rather than to the total volume of orders placed during a certain period (Chapter 20).

nonmarketing-controlled information source A product information source that is not associated with advertising or promotion (Chapter 6).

nonprobability sample Any sample in which little or no attempt is made to get a representative cross section of the population (Chapter 9).

nonprofit organization An organization that exists to achieve some goal other than the usual business goals of profit, market share, or return on investment (Chapter 12).

nonprofit organization marketing The effort by nonprofit organizations to bring about mutually satisfying exchanges with target markets (Chapter 12).

nonstore retailing Selling to consumers through other means than by visiting a store (Chapter 15).

norm A value or attitude deemed acceptable by a group (Chapter 6).

North American Free Trade Agreement (NAFTA) An agreement between Canada, the United States, and Mexico that created the world's largest free trade zone (Chapter 5).

North American Industry Classification System (NAICS) A detailed numbering system developed by the United States, Canada, and Mexico to classify North American business establishments by their main production processes (Chapter 7).

O

observation research A research method that relies on four types of observation: people watching people, people watching an activity, machines watching people, and machines watching an activity (Chapter 9).

odd–even pricing (psychological pricing) A price tactic that uses odd-numbered prices to connote bargains and even-numbered prices to imply quality (Chapter 20).

off-price retailer A retailer that sells at prices 25 percent or more below traditional department store prices because it pays cash for its stock and usually doesn't ask for return privileges (Chapter 15).

one-to-one marketing An individualized marketing method that utilizes customer information to build long-term, personalized, and profitable relationships with each customer (Chapter 8).

online retailing A type of shopping available to consumers with access to the Internet (Chapter 15).

open-ended question An interview question that encourages an answer phrased in the respondent's own words (Chapter 9).

opinion leader An individual who influences the opinions of others (Chapter 6).

optimizers Business customers who consider numerous suppliers, both familiar and unfamiliar, solicit bids, and study all proposals carefully before selecting one (Chapter 8).

order fulfillment process A supply chain management process that involves generating, filling, delivering, and providing on-the-spot service for customer orders (Chapter 14).

order processing system A system whereby orders are entered into the supply chain and filled (Chapter 14).

order-to-cash cycle The amount of time between order placement, receipt of the customer's payment, and order shipment (Chapter 14).

original equipment manufacturers (OEMs) Individuals and organizations that buy business goods and incorporate them into the products that they produce for eventual sale to other producers or to consumers (Chapter 7).

outsourcing (contract logistics) A manufacturer's or supplier's use of an independent third party to manage an entire function of the logistics system, such as transportation, warehousing, or order processing (Chapter 14).

owned media Online content that an organization creates and controls (Chapter 22).

P

paid media Content paid for by a company to be placed online (Chapter 22).

penetration pricing A pricing policy whereby a firm charges a relatively low price for a product initially as a way to reach the mass market (Chapter 20).

perception The process by which people select, organize, and interpret stimuli into a meaningful and coherent picture (Chapter 6).

perceptual mapping A means of displaying or graphing, in two or more dimensions, the location of products, brands, or groups of products in customers' minds (Chapter 8).

perishability The inability of services to be stored, warehoused, or inventoried (Chapter 12).

personal selling A purchase situation involving a personal, paid-for communication between two people in an attempt to influence each other (Chapter 18).

personality A way of organizing and grouping the consistencies of an individual's reactions to situations (Chapter 6).

persuasive labeling A type of package labeling that focuses on a promotional theme or logo with consumer information being secondary (Chapter 10).

pioneering advertising A form of advertising designed to stimulate primary demand for a new product or product category (Chapter 17).

planned obsolescence The practice of modifying products so those that have already been sold become obsolete before they actually need replacement (Chapter 10).

planning The process of anticipating future events and determining strategies to achieve organizational objectives in the future (Chapter 2).

point-of-purchase (P-O-P) A promotional display set up at the retailer's location to build traffic, advertise the product, or induce impulse buying (Chapter 18).

point-of-sale interactions Communications between customers and organizations that occur at the point of sale, normally in a store (Chapter 21).

pop-up shops Temporary retail establishments that allow flexible locations without the long-term commitment of a more expensive retail lease (Chapter 15).

portfolio model A tool for allocating resources among products or strategic business units on the basis of relative market share and market growth rate (Chapter 2).

position The place a product, brand, or group of products occupies in consumers' minds relative to competing offerings (Chapter 8).

positioning Developing a specific marketing mix to influence potential customers' overall perception of a brand, product line, or organization in general (Chapter 8).

postponement The delay in final production in the Leagile supply chain management strategy that enables the company to take advantage of many of the benefits of lean supply chain management while still providing the agility that improves customer experiences (Chapter 14).

preapproach A process that describes the "homework" that must be done by a salesperson before he or she contacts a prospect (Chapter 18).

predatory pricing The practice of charging a very low price for a product with the intent of driving competitors out of business or out of a market (Chapter 20).

predictive modeling A data manipulation technique in which marketers try to determine, based on some past set of occurrences, what the odds are that some other occurrence, such as a response or purchase, will take place in the future (Chapter 21).

premium An extra item offered to the consumer, usually in exchange for some proof of purchase of the promoted product (Chapter 18).

prestige pricing Charging a high price to help promote a high-quality image (Chapter 19).

price That which is given up in an exchange to acquire a good or service (Chapter 19).

price bundling Marketing two or more products in a single package for a special price (Chapter 20).

price equilibrium The price at which demand and supply are equal (Chapter 19).

price fixing An agreement between two or more firms on the price they will charge for a product (Chapter 20).

price lining The practice of offering a product line with several items at specific price points (Chapter 20).

price shading The use of discounts by salespeople to increase demand for one or more products in a line (Chapter 20).

price skimming A pricing policy whereby a firm charges a high introductory price, often coupled with heavy promotion (Chapter 20).

price strategy A basic, long-term pricing framework, which establishes the initial price for a product and the intended direction for price movements over the product life cycle (Chapter 20).

primary data Information that is collected for the first time; used for solving the particular problem under investigation (Chapter 9).

primary membership group A reference group with which people interact regularly in an informal, face-to-face manner, such as family, friends, or fellow employees (Chapter 6).

private brand A brand name owned by a wholesaler or a retailer (Chapter 10).

probability sample A sample in which every element in the population has a known statistical likelihood of being selected (Chapter 9).

problem child (question mark) In the portfolio matrix, a business unit that shows rapid growth but poor profit margins (Chapter 2).

procedural justice Perceptions of fairness within channel interactions based on equal/just treatment by others during business processes that seek to resolve disputes or allocate resources (Chapter 13).

processed materials Products used directly in manufacturing other products (Chapter 7).

product Everything, both favorable and unfavorable, that a person receives in an exchange (Chapter 10).

product advertising A form of advertising that touts the benefits of a specific good or service (Chapter 17).

product category All brands that satisfy a particular type of need (Chapter 11).

product development A marketing strategy that entails the creation of new products for current customers (Chapter 2); the process of converting applications for new technologies into marketable products (Chapter 11).

product development and commercialization process The group of activities that facilitates the joint development and marketing of new offerings among a group of supply chain partner firms (Chapter 14).

product differentiation A positioning strategy that some firms use to distinguish their products from those of competitors (Chapter 8).

product item A specific version of a product that can be designated as a distinct offering among an organization's products (Chapter 10).

product life cycle (PLC) A biological metaphor that traces the stages of a product's acceptance, from its introduction (birth) to its decline (death) (Chapter 11).

product line A group of closely related product items (Chapter 10).

product line depth The number of product items in a product line (Chapter 10).

product line extension Adding additional products to an existing product line in order to compete more broadly in the industry (Chapter 10).

product line pricing Setting prices for an entire line of products (Chapter 20).

product mix All products that an organization sells (Chapter 10).

product mix width The number of product lines an organization offers (Chapter 10).

product modification Changing one or more of a product's characteristics (Chapter 10).

product offering The mix of products offered to the consumer by the retailer; also called the product assortment or merchandise mix (Chapter 15).

product placement A public relations strategy that involves getting a product, service, or company name to appear in a movie, television show, radio program, magazine, newspaper, video game, video or audio clip, book, or commercial for another product; on the Internet; or at special events (Chapter 17).

product/service differentiation competitive advantage The provision of something that is unique and valuable to buyers beyond simply offering a lower price than the competition's (Chapter 2).

production orientation A philosophy that focuses on the internal capabilities of the firm rather than on the desires and needs of the marketplace (Chapter 1).

profit Revenue minus expenses (Chapter 19).

profit maximization A method of setting prices that occurs when marginal revenue equals marginal cost (Chapter 19).

promotion Communication by marketers that informs, persuades, and reminds potential buyers of a product in order to influence an opinion or elicit a response (Chapter 16).

promotional allowance (trade allowance) A payment to a dealer for promoting the manufacturer's products (Chapter 20).

promotional mix The combination of promotional tools—including advertising, public relations, personal selling, and sales promotion—used to reach the target market and fulfill the organization's overall goals (Chapter 16).

promotional strategy A plan for the optimal use of the elements of promotion: advertising, public relations, personal selling, and sales promotion (Chapter 16).

psychographic segmentation Market segmentation on the basis of personality, motives, lifestyles, and geodemographics (Chapter 8).

public relations The marketing function that evaluates public attitudes, identifies areas within the organization the public may be interested in, and executes a program of action to earn public understanding and acceptance (Chapter 17).

public service advertisement (PSA) An announcement that promotes a program of a federal, state, or local government or of a nonprofit organization (Chapter 12).

publicity Public information about a company, product, service, or issue appearing in the mass media as a news item (Chapter 17).

pull strategy A marketing strategy that stimulates consumer demand to obtain product distribution (Chapter 16).

pulsing media schedule A media scheduling strategy that uses continuous scheduling throughout the year coupled with a flighted schedule during the best sales periods (Chapter 17).

purchasing power A comparison of income versus the relative cost of a set standard of goods and services in different geographic areas (Chapter 4).

push money Money offered to channel intermediaries to encourage them to "push" products—that is, to encourage other members of the channel to sell the products (Chapter 18).

push strategy A marketing strategy that uses aggressive personal selling and trade advertising to convince a wholesaler or a retailer to carry and sell particular merchandise (Chapter 16).

pyramid of corporate social responsibility A model that suggests corporate social responsibility is composed of economic, legal, ethical, and philanthropic responsibilities and that the firm's economic performance supports the entire structure (Chapter 3).

Q

quantity discount A price reduction offered to buyers buying in multiple units or above a specified dollar amount (Chapter 20).

quota A statement of the individual salesperson's sales objectives, usually based on sales volume alone but sometimes including key accounts (those with greatest potential), new accounts, repeat sales, and specific products (Chapter 18).

R

radio-frequency identification (RFID) An automatic identification method that uses radio signals that work with scanned bar codes to identify products; data is stored in and retrieved from the RFID tag, which is attached to a product (Chapter 14).

random error An error that occurs when the selected sample is an imperfect representation of the overall population (Chapter 9).

random sample A sample arranged in such a way that every element of the population has an equal chance of being selected as part of the sample (Chapter 9).

raw materials Unprocessed extractive or agricultural products, such as mineral ore, timber, wheat, corn, fruits, vegetables, and fish (Chapter 7).

reach The number of target consumers exposed to a commercial at least once during a specific period, usually four weeks (Chapter 17).

real self-image The way an individual actually perceives himself or herself (Chapter 6).

rebate A cash refund given for the purchase of a product during a specific period (Chapter 18, 20).

receiver The person who decodes a message (Chapter 16).

recession A period of economic activity characterized by negative growth, which reduces demand for goods and services (Chapter 4).

reciprocity The practice of business purchasers choosing to buy from their own customers (Chapter 7).

reference group A group in society that influences an individual's purchasing behavior (Chapter 6).

referral A recommendation to a salesperson from a customer or business associate (Chapter 18).

reintermediation The reintroduction of an intermediary between producers and users (Chapter 7).

relationship commitment A firm's belief that an ongoing relationship with another firm is so important that the relationship warrants maximum efforts at maintaining it indefinitely (Chapter 7).

relationship integration The ability of two or more companies to develop social connections that serve to guide their interactions when working together (Chapter 14).

relationship marketing A strategy that focuses on keeping and improving relationships with current customers (Chapter 1).

relationship selling (consultative selling) A sales practice that involves building, maintaining, and enhancing interactions with customers in order to develop long-term satisfaction through mutually beneficial partnerships (Chapter 18).

reliability The ability to perform a service dependably, accurately, and consistently (Chapter 12).

repositioning Changing consumers' perceptions of a brand in relation to competing brands (Chapter 8).

resale price maintenance Retailers must sell a manufacturer's product at or above a specific price (Chapter 20).

research design Specifies which research questions must be answered, how and when the data will be gathered, and how the data will be analyzed (Chapter 9).

response list A customer list that includes the names and addresses of individuals who have responded to an offer of some kind, such as by mail, telephone, direct-response television, product rebates, contests or sweepstakes, or billing inserts (Chapter 21).

responsiveness The ability to provide prompt service (Chapter 12).

retailer A channel intermediary that sells mainly to consumers (Chapter 13).

retailing All the activities directly related to the sale of goods and services to the ultimate consumer for personal, nonbusiness use (Chapter 15).

retailing mix A combination of the six Ps—product, place, promotion, price, presentation, and personnel—to sell goods and services to the ultimate consumer (Chapter 15).

return on investment (ROI) Net profit after taxes divided by total assets (Chapter 19).

returns management process A process that enables firms to manage volumes of returned product efficiently, while minimizing costs and maximizing the value of the returned assets to the firms in the supply chain (Chapter 14).

revenue The price charged to customers multiplied by the number of units sold (Chapter 19).

review sites Web sites that allow consumers to post, read, rate, and comment on opinions regarding all kinds of products and services (Chapter 22).

role specificity When each firm in a supply chain has clarity in terms of knowing which firm is the leader, which firms are the followers, and which responsibilities are assigned to each firm (Chapter 14).

routine response behavior The type of decision making exhibited by consumers buying frequently purchased, low-cost goods and services; requires little search and decision time (Chapter 6).

S

sales orientation The idea that people will buy more goods and services if aggressive sales techniques are used and that high sales result in high profits (Chapter 1).

sales presentation A formal meeting in which the salesperson presents a sales proposal to a prospective buyer (Chapter 18).

sales process (sales cycle) The set of steps a salesperson goes through in a particular organization to sell a particular product or service (Chapter 18).

sales promotion Marketing activities—other than personal selling, advertising, and public relations—that stimulate consumer buying and dealer effectiveness (Chapter 18).

sales proposal A formal written document or professional presentation that outlines how the salesperson's product or service will meet or exceed the prospect's needs (Chapter 18).

sample A subset from a larger population (Chapter 9).

sampling A promotional program that allows the consumer the opportunity to try a product or service for free (Chapter 18).

sampling error An error that occurs when a sample somehow does not represent the target population (Chapter 9).

satisficers Business customers who place an order with the first familiar supplier to satisfy product and delivery requirements (Chapter 8).

scaled-response question A closed-ended question designed to measure the intensity of a respondent's answer (Chapter 9).

scanner-based research A system for gathering information from a single group of respondents by continuously monitoring the advertising, promotion, and pricing they are exposed to and the things they buy (Chapter 9).

scrambled merchandising The tendency to offer a wide variety of nontraditional goods and services under one roof (Chapter 15).

screening The first filter in the product development process, which eliminates ideas that are inconsistent with the organization's new-product strategy or are obviously inappropriate for some other reason (Chapter 11).

search quality A characteristic that can be easily assessed before purchase (Chapter 12).

seasonal discount A price reduction for buying merchandise out of season (Chapter 20).

seasonal media schedule A media scheduling strategy that runs advertising only during times of the year when the product is most likely to be used (Chapter 17).

secondary data Data previously collected for any purpose other than the one at hand (Chapter 9).

secondary membership group A reference group with which people associate less consistently and more formally than a primary membership group, such as a club, professional group, or religious group (Chapter 6).

segmentation bases (variables) Characteristics of individuals, groups, or organizations (Chapter 8).

selective distortion A process whereby a consumer changes or distorts information that conflicts with his or her feelings or beliefs (Chapter 6).

selective distribution A form of distribution achieved by screening dealers to eliminate all but a few in any single area (Chapter 13).

selective exposure The process whereby a consumer notices certain stimuli and ignores others (Chapter 6).

selective retention A process whereby a consumer remembers only that information that supports his or her personal beliefs (Chapter 6).

self-concept How consumers perceive themselves in terms of attitudes, perceptions, beliefs, and self-evaluations (Chapter 6).

self-monitoring The extent to which consumers use their current situation to guide their social behavior (Chapter 6).

selling against the brand Stocking well-known branded items at high prices in order to sell store brands at discounted prices (Chapter 19).

sender The originator of the message in the communication process (Chapter 16).

service The result of applying human or mechanical efforts to people or objects (Chapter 12).

service mark A trademark for a service (Chapter 10).

shilling When bloggers do not disclose that they were paid to promote a product (Chapter 6).

shopping product A product that requires comparison shopping because it is usually more expensive than a convenience product and is found in fewer stores (Chapter 10).

simulated (laboratory) market testing The presentation of advertising and other promotion materials for several products, including a test product, to members of the product's target market (Chapter 11).

simultaneous product development A team-oriented approach to new-product development (Chapter 11).

single-price tactic A price tactic that offers all goods and services at the same price (or perhaps two or three prices) (Chapter 20).

social class A group of people in a society who are considered nearly equal in status or community esteem, who regularly socialize among themselves both formally and informally, and who share behavioral norms (Chapter 6).

social commerce A subset of e-commerce that involves the interaction and user contribution aspects of social online media to assist online buying and selling of products and services (Chapter 22).

social media Any tool or service that uses the Internet to facilitate conversations (Chapter 22).

social networking sites Web sites that allow individuals to connect—or network—with friends, peers, and business associates (Chapter 22).

social news sites Web sites that allow users to decide which content is promoted on a given Web site by voting that content up or down (Chapter 22).

socialization process How cultural values and norms are passed down to children (Chapter 6).

societal marketing orientation The idea that an organization exists not only to satisfy customer wants and needs and to meet organizational objectives, but also to preserve or enhance individuals' and society's long-term best interests (Chapter 1).

spatial discrepancy The difference between the location of a producer and the location of widely scattered markets (Chapter 13).

specialty discount store A retail store that offers a nearly complete selection of single-line merchandise and uses self-service, discount prices, high volume, and high turnover (Chapter 15).

specialty product A particular item for which consumers search extensively and are very reluctant to accept substitutes (Chapter 10).

specialty store A retail store specializing in a given type of merchandise (Chapter 15).

sponsored blog A blog in which a company pays a blogger to say things about a good or service (Chapter 6).

sponsorship A public relations strategy in which a company spends money to support an issue, cause, or event that is consistent with corporate objectives, such as improving brand awareness or enhancing corporate image (Chapter 17).

stakeholder theory A theory that holds that social responsibility is paying attention to the interest of every affected stakeholder in every aspect of a firm's operation (Chapter 3).

star In the portfolio matrix, a business unit that is a fast-growing market leader (Chapter 2).

status quo pricing A pricing objective that maintains existing prices or meets the competition's prices (Chapter 19).

stickiness A measure of a Web site's effectiveness; calculated by multiplying the frequency of visits times the duration of a visit times the number of pages viewed during each visit (site reach) (Chapter 7).

stimulus Any unit of input affecting one or more of the five senses: sight, smell, taste, touch, hearing (Chapter 6).

stimulus discrimination A learned ability to differentiate among similar products (Chapter 6).

stimulus generalization A form of learning that occurs when one response is extended to a second stimulus similar to the first (Chapter 6).

straight rebuy A situation in which the purchaser reorders the same goods or services without looking for new information or investigating other suppliers (Chapter 7).

strategic alliance (strategic partnership) A cooperative agreement between business firms (Chapter 7).

strategic business unit (SBU) A subgroup of a single business or a collection of related businesses within the larger organization (Chapter 2).

strategic channel alliance A cooperative agreement between business firms to use another business' already established distribution channel (Chapter 13).

strategic planning The managerial process of creating and maintaining a fit between the organization's objectives and resources and evolving market opportunities (Chapter 2).

subculture A homogeneous group of people who share elements of the overall culture as well as unique elements of their own group (Chapter 6).

supercenter A retailer that combines a full line of groceries and general merchandize with a wide range of services in one location (Chapter 15).

supermarket A large, departmentalized, self-service retailer that specializes in food and some nonfood items (Chapter 15).

supplementary services A group of services that support or enhance the core service (Chapter 12).

supplier relationship management process A supply chain management process that supports manufacturing flow by identifying and maintaining relationships with highly valued suppliers (Chapter 14).

supplies Consumable items that do not become part of the final product (Chapter 7).

supply The quantity of a product that will be offered to the market by a supplier at various prices for a specified period (Chapter 19).

supply chain The connected chain of all of the business entities, both internal and external to the company, that perform or support the logistics function (Chapter 14).

supply chain integration When multiple firms in a supply chain coordinate their activities and processes so that they are seamlessly linked to one another in an effort to satisfy the customer (Chapter 14).

supply chain management A management system that coordinates and integrates all of the activities performed by supply chain members into a seamless process, from the source to the point of consumption, resulting in enhanced customer and economic value (Chapter 14).

supply chain resilience The ability of a supply chain to bounce back from disruptions and continue operations in a timely and effective manner (Chapter 14).

supply chain sustainability A sustainable supply chain is one that employs renewable natural resources wherever possible (Chapter 14).

supply chain team An entire group of individuals who orchestrate the movement of goods, services, and information from the source to the consumer (Chapter 14).

survey research The most popular technique for gathering primary data, in which a researcher interacts with people to obtain facts, opinions, and attitudes (Chapter 9).

sustainability The idea that socially responsible companies will outperform their peers by focusing on the world's social problems and viewing them as opportunities to build profits and help the world at the same time (Chapter 3).

sustainable competitive advantage An advantage that cannot be copied by the competition (Chapter 2).

SWOT analysis Identifying internal strengths (S) and weaknesses (W) and also examining external opportunities (O) and threats (T) (Chapter 2).

systems approach A key principle of supply chain management—that multiple firms work together to perform tasks as a single, unified system, rather than as several individual companies acting in isolation (Chapter 14).

T

tangibles The physical evidence of a service, including the physical facilities, tools, and equipment used to provide the service (Chapter 12).

target market A defined group most likely to buy a firm's product (Chapter 4).

target market A group of people or organizations for which an organization designs, implements, and maintains a marketing mix intended to meet the needs of that group, resulting in mutually satisfying exchanges (Chapter 8).

teamwork Collaborative efforts of people to accomplish common objectives (Chapter 1).

technology and planning integration The creation and maintenance of information technology systems that connect managers across and through the firms in the supply chain (Chapter 14).

telemarketing The use of the telephone to sell directly to consumers (Chapter 15).

temporal discrepancy A situation that occurs when a product is produced but a customer is not ready to buy it (Chapter 13).

test marketing The limited introduction of a product and a marketing program to determine the reactions of potential customers in a market situation (Chapter 11).

third party logistics firm (3PL) A firm that is contracted to manage part or all of another firm's order fulfillment process (Chapter 14).

touch points All possible areas of a business where customers communicate with that business (Chapter 21).

trade allowance A price reduction offered by manufacturers to intermediaries, such as wholesalers and retailers (Chapter 18).

trade sales promotion Sales promotion activities targeting a channel member, such as a wholesaler or retailer (Chapter 18).

trademark The exclusive right to use a brand or part of a brand (Chapter 10).

trust The condition that exists when one party has confidence in an exchange partner's reliability and integrity (Chapter 7).

two-part pricing A price tactic that charges two separate amounts to consume a single good or service (Chapter 20).

U

unbundling Reducing the bundle of services that comes with the basic product (Chapter 20).

undifferentiated targeting strategy A marketing approach that views the market as one big market with no individual segments and thus uses a single marketing mix (Chapter 8).

unfair trade practice acts Laws that prohibit wholesalers and retailers from selling below cost (Chapter 20).

uniform delivered pricing A price tactic in which the seller pays the actual freight charges and bills every purchaser an identical, flat freight charge (Chapter 20).

unique selling proposition A desirable, exclusive, and believable advertising appeal selected as the theme for a campaign (Chapter 17).

unitary elasticity A situation in which total revenue remains the same when prices change (Chapter 19).

universal product code (UPC) A series of thick and thin vertical lines (bar codes), readable by computerized optical scanners, that represent numbers used to track products (Chapter 10).

universe The population from which a sample will be drawn (Chapter 9).

unsought product A product unknown to the potential buyer, or a known product that the buyer does not actively seek (Chapter 10).

Uruguay Round An agreement to dramatically lower trade barriers worldwide; created the World Trade Organization (Chapter 5).

usage-rate segmentation Dividing a market by the amount of product bought or consumed (Chapter 8).

utilitarian ethical theory A theory that holds that the choice that yields the greatest benefit to the most people is the choice that is ethically correct (Chapter 3).

V

value The enduring belief that a specific mode of conduct is personally or socially preferable to another mode of conduct (Chapter 6).

value-based pricing Setting the price at a level that seems to the customer to be a good price compared to the prices of other options (Chapter 20).

variable cost A cost that varies with changes in the level of output (Chapter 19).

vertical conflict A channel conflict that occurs between different levels in a marketing channel, most typically between the manufacturer and wholesaler or between the manufacturer and retailer (Chapter 13).

vertical structure One of three dimensions of supply chain network design; the number of suppliers or customers included within each individual tier (Chapter 14).

virtue A character trait valued as being good (Chapter 3).

W

want The way a consumer goes about addressing a need (Chapter 6).

warehouse membership clubs Limited-service merchant wholesalers that sell a limited selection of brand-name appliances, household items, and groceries on a cash-and-carry basis to members, usually small businesses and groups (Chapter 15).

warranty A confirmation of the quality or performance of a good or service (Chapter 10).

Web community A carefully selected group of consumers who agree to participate in an ongoing dialogue with a particular corporation (Chapter 9).

World Bank An international bank that offers low-interest loans, advice, and information to developing nations (Chapter 5).

World Trade Organization (WTO) A trade organization that replaced the old General Agreement on Tariffs and Trade (GATT) (Chapter 5).

Y

yield management systems (YMS) A technique for adjusting prices that uses complex mathematical software to profitably fill unused capacity by discounting early purchases, limiting early sales at these discounted prices, and overbooking capacity (Chapter 19).

Z

zone pricing A modification of uniform delivered pricing that divides the United States (or the total market) into segments or zones and charges a flat freight rate to all customers in a given zone (Chapter 20).

Organizational Index

Internet, 141
  and advertising media, 629–631
  for business, 818
  and communication, 585
  global marketing, impact of 170–171
  online retailing, 548–549
  pricing, 714–715
  privacy issues, 588
  public relations, 639
  sales promotion, 658, 660–661
  word-of-mouth communications, 403
interorganizational citizenship behaviors, 491
interpersonal communication, 581
introduction stage, product life cycle, 595–596
introductory stage, PLC, 405
inventory control system, 510–512
Italian market, 142

J

Japanese Americans, 108
jobs outsourcing, 135
joint costs, 753

K

keiretsu, 245
keystoning, 709
knockoff, 160
knowledge management, customers, 778
Korean Americans, 108
Kraft American, 109

L

labeling, 372–374
  persuasive, 372
labor
  costs, 34
  specialization/division of, 450
laboratory market testing, 396
laggards, new products, 401
language barriers, 167
late majority, 401
laws
  definition of, 55
leader
  channel, 468
  pricing, 747
lead generation, personal selling, 667–668
Leagile supply chain strategy, 505
lean supply chain management, 504
learning, customers, 778
legal factors
  environment, marketing, 115–121
  pricing, 735–740

level of service, retailing, 535
leveraging customer information, 788–795
  campaign management, 788–789
licensing, 158
life cycle
  products (See product life cycle (PLC))
life span, messages, 632
lifestyle center, 558
listening system, social media, 810–811
lobbying, 675
location
  retailing, 556–557
location-based social networking sites, 821, 822
logistics
  channels, 454, 455
  information system, 508
  order processing system, 509–510
  outsourcing, 520–521
  sourcing/procurement, 509
  in supply chain management, 508–514
low-income countries
  lower quality, 169
loyal, customer
  retention of, 789–790
loyalty marketing programs, 539, 657–658
  objective of, 657

M

machine-based research, 340–342
magazines, 626
mail
  direct, 546
  order, 546–547
management decision problem, 314
manufacturing flow management process, 500
mapping, supply chain management, 505–508
maquiladoras, 68
marginal revenue (MR), 709
markdown money, 742
market
  characteristics of, 273
  development, 27
  factors, in channels, 461
  share, advertising and, 612
marketers, 33
  consumer goods, 275
  customer value, 9
  employee training, role of, 12
  of products, 277
  segmentation bases, 274–283
  social class, 208
marketing, 3
  to African Americans, 105–107
  to Asian Americans, 107–109
  career in, 16
  cause-related, 77–79, 639

communication, promotional strategy and, 580–585
definition of, 2, 4, 17
  American Marketing Association's, 3
direct, 546–547
essence of, 11
ethics in, 261
ethnic markets, 103–109
everybody/average customer, 14
exchange, 3
external environment of, 90
federal legislation, 116–117
guerilla, 630–631
to Hispanic Americans, 103–105
important to business, 16
life, role in, 17
management philosophies, 4–7
managers, importance, 103
market orientation philosophy, 5–6
meaning of, 16
plan, one-page document, 20
production orientation philosophy, 4–5
promotion, role of, 15
relationship, 10
role in society, 16
sales orientation philosophy, 5
social media and (See social media)
societal marketing orientation philosophy, 6–7
marketing audit
  characteristics, 44
marketing career opportunities, 16
marketing channels, 449–483. See also channels
  defined, 449
  discrepancies, 451
  increasing effectiveness of distribution, 792–793
marketing concept, 5
marketing-controlled information source, 191–192
marketing decision support systems, 307
  decision support system (DSS), 307
  marketing information, 307
marketing management philosophies, 17
marketing managers, 195
  buying center
    implications of, 257–258
marketing metrics, 41, 287
  management decision, 189–190
  search engine optimization, 189
marketing miscues
  pricing, 768–769
marketing mix, 39–40, 115
  elements of, 42
  positioning, 295
  product P, 39
  services, 423–428
  target, 39
marketing myopia, 32

traditional mass marketing
   customer relationship management
      vs., 774
training
   sales force, 674
   as sales promotion tool,
      661–662
transactional functions, 454
transportation, supply chain management,
   513–514
trust, 9, 244
   and social media, 812–813
Twitter, and business, 818
two-part pricing, 750

U

unbundling, 749
   pricing, 757
underpricing, 744
unfair trade practice, 735–736
unfavorable publicity, 639–640
uniform delivered pricing, 744
unique selling proposition, 620
unitary elasticity, 699
Uruguay Round, 148
usage-rate segmentation, 283
utilitarian ethical theory, 59
utilitarianism, types of, 59

V

value-based pricing, 742–743
variables. *See also* segmentation bases
   cost, 706
   pricing, 745–746
VCRs, product life cycle, 409
vending, automatic, 545
vendors
   new product ideas, 390
vertical conflict, channel, 469–470
vertical structure, supply chain, 508
video game advertising, 630
Vietnamese Americans, 108
virtual shopping, 327
   environments, 328
virtual worlds, 823–824
virtue ethics, 60

W

wages, in China, 136
want, 186
warehouse membership clubs, 542
warehousing, 512–513
   data, 783
warranty, 375
   express, 375
   implied, 375
waste-disposal regulations, 68

waste management, 76
webinars, 665
web promoting, 339
Web sites, 113, 639
   mobile, 825
*Weyerhaeuser v. Ross-Simmons Hardwood
   Lumber Company*, 738–739
wholesale channels, 457
Why Do Americans Act Like That, 202–203
widgets, mobile, 825–827
width, products, 554
word-of-mouth communications,
   402–403
World Bank, 144, 146, 153
world economy
   multinational firms, impact of, 141
World Trade Organization (WTO), 148
world trading practices
   Uruguay Round, 148

Y

yield management systems (YMS), 705–706
YMS. *See* yield management systems (YMS)

Z

zero percent financing, 742
zone pricing, 744